Windows Vista® Resource Kit, Second Edition

*Mitch Tulloch, Tony Northrup, and Jerry Honeycutt
with the Windows Vista Team at Microsoft*

PUBLISHED BY
Microsoft Press
A Division of Microsoft Corporation
One Microsoft Way
Redmond, Washington 98052-6399

Library of Congress Control Number: 2008929779

Printed and bound in the United States of America.

1 2 3 4 5 6 7 8 9   QWT   3 2 1 0 9 8

Distributed in Canada by H.B. Fenn and Company Ltd.

A CIP catalogue record for this book is available from the British Library.

Microsoft Press books are available through booksellers and distributors worldwide. For further information about international editions, contact your local Microsoft Corporation office or contact Microsoft Press International directly at fax (425) 936-7329. Visit our Web site at www.microsoft.com/mspress. Send comments to rkinput@microsoft.com.

Microsoft, Microsoft Press, Active Directory, ActiveSync, ActiveX, Aero, Authenticode, BitLocker, ClearType, Direct3D, DirectX, ESP, Excel, Forefront, InfoPath, IntelliMirror, Internet Explorer, MSDN, MS-DOS, MSN, NetMeeting, OneCare, OneNote, Outlook, PowerPoint, ReadyBoost, ReadyDrive, SharePoint, SideShow, SQL Server, SuperFetch, Visio, Visual Basic, Visual SourceSafe, Visual Studio, Win32, Windows, Windows Live, Windows logo, Windows Media, Windows Mobile, Windows NT, Windows PowerShell, Windows Server, Windows Vista, WinFX, Xbox, and Xbox 360 are either registered trademarks or trademarks of the Microsoft group of companies. Other product and company names mentioned herein may be the trademarks of their respective owners.

The example companies, organizations, products, domain names, e-mail addresses, logos, people, places, and events depicted herein are fictitious. No association with any real company, organization, product, domain name, e-mail address, logo, person, place, or event is intended or should be inferred.

Acquisitions Editor: Martin DelRe
Project Editor: Maureen Zimmerman
Editorial Production: Custom Editorial Productions, Inc.
Technical Reviewer: Randall Galloway; Technical Review services provided by Content Master, a member of CM Group, Ltd.
Cover Design: Tom Draper Design
Cover Illustration: Todd Daman

Body Part No. X14-95076

Contents at a Glance

Table of Contents

What do you think of this book? We want to hear from you!

Microsoft is interested in hearing your feedback so we can continually improve our books and learning resources for you. To participate in a brief online survey, please visit:

www.microsoft.com/learning/booksurvey/

v

Part III   Desktop Management

Part VI Troubleshooting

30 Configuring Startup and Troubleshooting Startup Issues 1321

Appendices

What do you think of this book? We want to hear from you!

Microsoft is interested in hearing your feedback so we can continually improve our books and learning resources for you. To participate in a brief online survey, please visit:

www.microsoft.com/learning/booksurvey/

Foreword to the Second Edition

Welcome to the second edition of the *Windows Vista Resource Kit*!

This new edition updates the content of the previous edition to include the many improvements and new features introduced in Windows Vista Service Pack 1 (SP1). Whenever Windows Vista is referred to in this edition, you should assume that it means Windows Vista with Service Pack 1 applied to it unless otherwise indicated.

In addition to focusing on Windows Vista SP1 on the client side, this edition now gives primary focus to running Windows Server 2008 on the server side of a Windows Vista deployment. However, coverage of using Windows Server 2003 on the server side is still prominent wherever the differences between the two server platforms are significant.

Finally, the companion CD now also includes 25 sample Windows PowerShell scripts that you can use or customize to administer different aspects of Windows Vista clients in your environment.

We hope you find this second edition even more useful than the first!

–The Authors

Acknowledgments

The authors of the *Windows Vista Resource Kit* would like to thank the numerous Windows Vista product team members and other experts at Microsoft who contributed hundreds of hours of their valuable time toward this project by carefully reviewing chapter content for technical accuracy, writing Direct from the Source sidebars that provide valuable insights into the product, and tirelessly offering their advice, encouragement, and support as we worked on this project. We particularly would like to express our thanks to the following individuals (in alphabetical order) at Microsoft:

David Abzarian, Gabriel Aul, Ed Averett, Don Baker, Tim Ball, Deepak Bansal, Stephen Berard, Gloria Boyer, Jeff Braunstein, Steve Campbell, Matthew Carlson, Jim Cavalaris, Santosh Chandwani, Raymond Chen, Stella Chernyak, Tony Chor, Chris Corio, Joseph Dadzie, Joseph Davies, Doug Davis, Tom Edwards, Corina Feuerstein, Eric Fitzgerald, Purna Gathani, Max Georgiev, Scott Graham, Ian Hameroff, Dan Harman, Alex Heaton, Gary Henderson, Judith Herman, Tim Hines, Toby Hinshaw, Steve Hiskey, John Hrvatin, Michael Hunter, LaDeana Huyler, Matthew Kerner, Robert Kierzek, Kinshuman Kinshumann, Michael Krause, Eduaro Laureano, Judy Lavik, Mark Lawrence, Kukjin Lee, Mike Lewis, Jason Leznek, Alain Lissoir, Mike Loholt, Todd Manion, Craig Marl, Ken Maybee, Joe Melton, John Melton, Val Menn, Alan Morris, Elsie Nallipogu, Manu Namboodiri, Greg Nichols, Michael Niehaus, Frank Olivier, Kalpesh Patel, Parveen Patel, Annuska Perkins, Nelly Porter, David Power, David Pracht, Tim Rains, Anshul Rawat, Sterling Reasor, Mark Reynolds, Yong Rhee, Steve Riley, Mike Rosado, Mitsuru Saito, Hiroshi Sakakibara, David Satter, Chris Sfanos, Joe Sherman, Sreenivas Shetty, Robert Simpkins, Brian Singleton, Sampath Somasundaram, Doug Steen, Pat Stemen, Mike Stephens, Chittur Subbaraman, Michael Surkan, Quais Taraki, John Thekkethala, Scott Van Cleave, Winni Verhoef, Alex Wade, Rob Waggoner, Sarah Wahlert, James Walker, Bob Watson, Austin Wilson, Joey Wray, Kalven Wu, Eran Yariv, Xinyan Zan, and David Zipkin.

In addition to the names listed above, the following individuals also contributed their time and expertise to this second edition:

Omer Amin, Dmitry Anipko, Ed Averett, Varun Bahl, Kyle Beck, Avi Ben-Menahem, Stephen Berard, Gloria Boyer, Jeff Braunstein, Steve Campbell, Jim Cavalaris, Anjli Chaudhry, Gerardo Diaz Cuellar, Joseph Davies, Doug Davis, LeAnne Fossmeyer, Judith Herman, Ben Hunter, Samir Jain, Nick Judge, Kinshuman Kinshumann, Anton Kucer, Sharad Kylasam, Paul LeBlanc, Kukjin Lee, Mike Loholt, Mahesh Lotlikar, Dhananjay Mahajan, Aaron Margosis, Ken Maybee, Kapil Mehra, Craig Murphy, Manu Namboodiri, Ramesh Narayanan, Michael Niehaus, Frank Olivier, Greg Page, Joe Sherman, Richard Smith, Sampath Somasundaram, Pat Stemen, Mike Stephens, John Thekkethala, Abhishek Tiwari, Alex Wade, David Washington, Kalven Wu, and Ming Zhu.

If we've forgotten to include anyone in the above list, please forgive us!

Jerry Honeycutt would also like to express his thanks to Dave Field for the content he contributed to the deployment chapters.

Finally, we would also like to collectively thank our outstanding editorial team at Microsoft Press including Martin DelRe, Jenny Moss Benson, Maureen Zimmerman, and Maria Gargiulo for their unflagging energy and tireless commitment to working with us on this challenging project and making it a success. Thanks also to Jean Findley at Custom Editorial Productions (CEP), who handled the production aspects of this book, and to Becka McKay, our copy editor, who showed wonderful attention to detail. And thanks also to Randall Galloway, our technical reviewer for this second edition of the *Windows Vista Resource Kit*.

Thanks everybody!

–*The Authors*

Introduction

Welcome to the *Windows Vista Resource Kit, Second Edition*!

The Windows Vista Resource Kit is a comprehensive technical resource for deploying, maintaining, and troubleshooting Windows Vista. The target audience for this Resource Kit is experienced IT professionals who work in medium- and large-sized organizations, but anyone who wants to learn how to deploy, configure, support, and troubleshoot for Windows Vista in Active Directory environments will find this Resource Kit invaluable.

Within this Resource Kit, you'll find in-depth information and task-based guidance on managing all aspects of Windows Vista, including automated deployment, desktop management, sharing and collaboration, search and organization, patch management, client protection, networking, remote access, and systematic troubleshooting techniques. You'll also find numerous sidebars contributed by members of the Windows Vista product team that provide deep insight into how Windows Vista works, best practices for managing the platform, and invaluable troubleshooting tips. Finally, the companion CD includes additional documentation plus almost 150 sample scripts that you can customize and use to help you automate various aspects of managing Windows Vista clients in enterprise environments.

Overview of Book

The six parts of this book cover the following topics:

- **Part I Overview** Provides an introduction to the features of Windows Vista and an overview of security enhancements for the platform.

- **Part II Deployment** Provides in-depth information and guidance on deploying Windows Vista in enterprise environments, with particular focus on using the Microsoft Deployment Toolkit (MDT).

- **Part III Desktop Management** Describes how to use Group Policy to manage the desktop environment for users of Windows Vista computers and how to manage specific features such as disks and file systems, devices and services, sharing and collaboration, printing, search, and Internet Explorer.

- **Part IV Desktop Maintenance** Describes how to maintain the health of Windows Vista computers by using the eventing infrastructure, monitoring performance, managing software updates, managing client protection, and using Remote Assistance.

- **Part V Networking** Provides in-depth information on networking enhancements in Windows Vista including core networking improvements, wireless networking, Windows Firewall and IPsec enhancements, remote connectivity using virtual private networking (VPN) and Remote Desktop, and deploying IPv6.

- **Part VI Troubleshooting** Describes how to troubleshoot startup, hardware, and networking issues as well as how to interpret Stop messages.

Document Conventions

The following conventions are used in this book to highlight special features or usage:

Reader Aids

The following reader aids are used throughout this book to point out useful details:

Reader Aid	Meaning
Note	Underscores the importance of a specific concept or highlights a special case that might not apply to every situation.
Important	Calls attention to essential information that should not be disregarded.
Caution	Warns you that failure to take or avoid a specified action can cause serious problems for users, systems, data integrity, and so on.
On the CD	Calls attention to a related script, tool, template, or job aid on the Companion CD that helps you perform a task described in the text.

Sidebars

The following sidebars are used throughout this book to provide added insight, tips, and advice concerning different Windows Vista features:

Sidebar	Meaning
Direct from the Source	Contributed by experts at Microsoft to provide "from-the-source" insight into how Windows Vista works, best practices for managing Windows Vista clients, and troubleshooting tips.
How It Works	Provides unique glimpses of Windows Vista features and how they work.

Command-Line Examples

The following style conventions are used in documenting command-line examples throughout this book:

Style	Meaning
Bold font	Used to indicate user input (characters that you type exactly as shown).
Italic font	Used to indicate variables for which you need to supply a specific value (for example, *file_name* can refer to any valid filename).
Monospace font	Used for code samples and command-line output.
%SystemRoot%	Used for environment variables.

Companion CD

The Companion CD is a valuable addition to this book and includes the following:

- **Scripts, Tools, and Resources** Over 120 sample scripts written in Visual Basic Scripting Edition (VBScript) plus an additional 25 sample Windows PowerShell scripts are included for administering different aspects of Windows Vista from the command line. These scripts can be used as-is or can be customized to meet the needs of your environment. Also included are sample deployment scripts, troubleshooting tools, and links to supported tools and documentation referred to in the text. All of these resources are organized in subfolders named by chapter number, and the sample VBScript scripts and PowerShell scripts are also provided as separate .zip files in their own folders for easy access.

- **Additional Reading** A complete electronic version of the book *Introducing Windows Server 2008* is included, plus selected chapters from several other Microsoft Press titles.

- **Links to Additional Resources** Links to each author's website and to need-to-know online resources for Windows Vista are provided from the Links option on the opening screen for the CD.

- **eBook** An electronic version of the entire *Windows Vista Resource Kit* is included on the CD.

Full documentation of the contents and structure of the Companion CD can be found in the Readme.txt file on the CD.

Find Additional Content Online As new or updated material becomes available that complements your book, it will be posted online on the Microsoft Press Online Windows Server and Client website. Based on the final build of Windows Server 2008, the type of material you might find there includes updates to book content, articles, links to companion content, errata, sample chapters, and more. This website will be available soon at *www.microsoft.com/learning/books/online/serverclient* and will be updated periodically.

Digital Content for Digital Book Readers: If you bought a digital-only edition of this book, you can enjoy select content from the print edition's companion CD.
Visit http://go.microsoft.com/fwlink/?LinkId=120594 to get your downloadable content. This content is always up-to-date and available to all readers.

Using the VBScript Scripts

The VBScript scripts on the Companion CD must be run using Cscript.exe as the script host. You can do this in several ways:

- Type **cscript script_name.vbs <parameters>** at a command prompt. For a list of available parameters, type **cscript script_name.vbs /?** at a command prompt or open the script using Notepad and read the comments in the script.

- Configure the default script host on the local computer to Cscript.exe so that you can run scripts by typing **script_name.vbs <parameters>** at a command prompt. To set the default script host to Cscript.exe, type **cscript //h:cscript //nologo //s** at a command prompt.

- Use Group Policy to change the default script host on targeted computers to Cscript.exe by running the following batch file as a startup script:

  ```
  @echo off
  cscript //h:cscript //s
  ```

  For an example of how to do this, see the section titled "Creating and Managing Shares by Using Scripts" in Chapter 17, "Managing Sharing."

To function as intended, most VBScript scripts on the Companion CD must also be run using elevated privileges. To open an admin-level command prompt in Windows Vista, click Start and select All Programs. Then select Accessories, right-click Command Prompt, and select Run As Administrator. (As an alternative, create a shortcut to an elevated command prompt and save the shortcut on your Quick Launch toolbar.)

Many of these VBScript scripts can be run against remote computers by using the /c option, and alternative credentials can usually be specified by using the /u and /p options—type **cscript script_name.vbs /?** for more information concerning these methods. Note that alternative credentials can be supplied only for remote connections, and that the Remote Administration exception in Windows Firewall must first be opened to run these scripts against remote computers. You can configure Windows Firewall on remote computers by using Group Policy; see the section titled "Managing Windows Firewall Using Group Policy" in Chapter 27, "Configuring Windows Firewall and IPsec," for more information. Finally, note that some of these VBScript scripts might have reduced functionality when run against a remote computer.

Using the Windows PowerShell Scripts

To use the PowerShell scripts on the Companion CD, you must install Windows PowerShell on the Windows Vista computer where you will be running these scripts. See Microsoft Knowledge Base article KB 928439, "Windows PowerShell 1.0 Installation Package for Windows Vista," at *http://support.microsoft.com/kb/928439*, for information about how to obtain and install PowerShell onto a system running Windows Vista.

After you have installed PowerShell on your system, you then need to understand how the PowerShell execution policy on a system controls how scripts are run on that system before you can use the PowerShell scripts found on the Companion CD. To view the current script execution policy, open a Windows PowerShell command prompt and type **Get-ExecutionPolicy**.

PowerShell can have four possible values for the script execution policy on a system:

- **Restricted**   This is the default setting. No scripts will be allowed to run.
- **AllSigned**   This setting means that scripts need a digital signature before they can be run.
- **RemoteSigned**   This setting means that only scripts run from file shares, downloaded using Internet Explorer, or received as mail attachments must be signed.
- **Unrestricted**   This setting means that all scripts can be run.

The current execution policy for your system can be changed by running **Set-ExecutionPolicy** *<value>* from the PowerShell window, where *<value>* is one of the four values listed previously. Microsoft recommends that PowerShell scripts always be signed and that the execution policy be configured as AllSigned within a production environment. The PowerShell scripts on the Companion CD are therefore provided to you in two forms: as .ps1 files that have been digitally signed by Microsoft and that can be used in environments where the execution policy is configured as AllSigned, and as .txt files that you can use to customize these scripts for the particular needs of your own environment. After you have customized these scripts, you then need to either code-sign them or lower the execution policy on your systems. Note that Microsoft recommends the former, but if you do decide to use unsigned scripts in your environment, you should understand the risks involved in doing so and take suitable steps to mitigate these risks. For information on how to sign PowerShell scripts, see *http://technet.microsoft.com/en-us/library/bb978642.aspx*. You can also type **Get-Help about-signing** at the PowerShell command prompt for further information about signing scripts.

Note that Windows PowerShell version 1.0 does not remote. However, this does not mean that the scripts included on the Companion CD work only locally. PowerShell scripts that use Windows Management Instrumentation (WMI) can in fact operate against remote computers, and the same is true for scripts that use Active Directory Services Interface (ADSI) technology. If an individual PowerShell script does support remoting, this is mentioned in the help information for that script, which is available by using the *–help* switch.

Disclaimer Concerning Scripts

Note that the VBScript and PowerShell scripts included on the Companion CD are samples only and are not finished tools. These scripts are provided as proof-of-concept examples of how to administer Windows Vista clients using VBScript and PowerShell. Although the authors and reviewers have made every effort to test these scripts to ensure they work properly, these scripts are provided to you "as-is" with no warranty or guarantee concerning their functionality. You should therefore become thoroughly familiar with using these scripts in a test environment before trying to use them in a production environment.

Because these scripts are provided as proof-of-concept samples only, you may need to customize them if you intend to use them in your production environment. For example, the scripts as provided include only minimal error handling and assume that the clients they are being run against exist and are configured appropriately. The authors therefore encourage readers to customize these scripts to meet the needs of administering their networking environment.

Resource Kit Support Policy

Every effort has been made to ensure the accuracy of this book and the Companion CD content. Microsoft Press provides corrections to this book through the Internet at the following location:

http://www.microsoft.com/learning/support/search.aspx

If you have comments, questions, or ideas regarding the book or Companion CD content, or if you have questions that are not answered by querying the Knowledge Base, please send them to Microsoft Press by using either of the following methods:

E-mail:

rkinput@microsoft.com

Postal Mail:

Microsoft Press

Attn: Microsoft Vista Resource Kit

One Microsoft Way

Redmond, WA 98052-6399

Please note that product support is not offered through the preceding mail addresses. For product support information, please visit the Microsoft Product Support website at the following address:

http://support.microsoft.com

Part I
Overview

Chapter 1

Overview of Windows Vista Improvements

Windows Vista is a complex operating system with thousands of features. Understanding it thoroughly can require years of study. Fortunately, most IT professionals have experience with the earlier versions of Windows that Windows Vista is based upon, such as Windows XP. This chapter, which assumes that you are familiar with Windows XP, describes the architecture of Windows Vista (and Windows Vista with Service Pack 1), the most significant non-security-related improvements that are not discussed elsewhere in this book, the different editions of Windows Vista, and the hardware requirements for Windows Vista.

Note This high-level chapter is designed to quickly give IT professionals a broad view of changes in Windows Vista. However, it is also suitable for less-technical executive staff who need to understand the new technologies.

For an overview of Windows Vista security improvements, read Chapter 2, "Security in Windows Vista."

What's New

Windows Vista has hundreds of improvements over earlier Windows client operating systems. This chapter provides a very high-level overview of those features, focusing on features that are not discussed in depth elsewhere in this Resource Kit. Table 1-1 lists significant improvements to Windows Vista and the chapters in this book that provide detailed information about each improvement.

Table 1-1   Windows Vista Improvements

Improvement	Chapter
Security improvements	2
Deployment improvements	3 through 12
Application compatibility	4
Roaming profiles	14
Folder redirection	14
Offline Files	14
BitLocker	15
EFS	15
Windows Backup and Restore	15
Driver and service improvements	16
Power management	16
File and Media Sharing	17
Windows Meeting Space	18
Printing	19
Search	20
Internet Explorer	21
Reliability Monitor	22
Performance Monitor	22
WinSAT	22
Windows Error Reporting	22
Task Scheduler	22
Event Logging	22
Diagnostics	22, 31, 32
Remote Assistance improvements	23
Windows Update	24
BITS	24
User Access Control	25
Windows Defender	25
Networking improvements	26
Wireless security	26
Network Access Protection	26
Windows Firewall	27
IPsec	27
Windows Service Hardening	27
Remote access improvements	28
IPv6	29
Startup Repair	30
BCD and Startup changes	30

Note   The most significant changes to Windows Vista were designed to increase security. The changes are so numerous that this Resource Kit dedicates a separate chapter (Chapter 2) to describing them.

The sections that follow provide an overview of these features. For those features that are not discussed in detail in this book, this chapter provides Group Policy management information. This book does not cover features that are primarily used in home environments, such as parental controls, games, Windows Media Player, Windows Media Center, and Windows Movie Maker.

User Interactions

For users, the most important improvements to Windows Vista will be the visible changes to the user interface. This section discusses how the Windows Vista user interface has changed. As you read this section, consider which changes will require end-user training or changes to your desktop management settings prior to deployment.

Start Menu

The Windows Vista Start menu has been optimized to significantly reduce the time users spend searching for applications and files. Now, users can click Start and then type a few letters of an application's name to quickly find the application on the Start menu. To find a file, users can click the Start button, type part of the file's name or its contents, and then press Enter to open a Search window with the results. Figure 1-1 shows the improved Start menu.

The All Programs menu still exists, but takes up much less space, because folder contents appear within the Start menu itself. Menus and submenus will open much faster than they did in earlier versions of Windows.

To configure the Start menu, use the Group Policy settings located in User Configuration\ Policies\Administrative Templates\Start Menu And Taskbar.

Figure 1-1   With the Windows Vista Start menu, users can find applications much more easily.

New Explorers

The new Windows Vista Explorer windows, such as Documents, Pictures, and Music, help users browse and find files much more easily. Key elements of the Windows Vista Explorers include:

■ **Instant Search**   Perhaps the single most useful improvement is the Search box in the upper-right corner of all Explorer windows, as shown in Figure 1-2. Users can type a word or phrase in the Search box to quickly find a file anywhere on their computers. For more information about Search, read Chapter 20, "Managing Search."

■ **Navigation Pane**   Located along the left side of Explorer windows, this pane contains frequently used links to different Explorer windows.

■ **Command Bar**   This toolbar displays different tasks based on the folder's contents.

■ **Live Icons**   Displays a thumbnail of the file contents, including Microsoft Office files. Thumbnails can be scaled to larger sizes to show more detail, or to smaller sizes to show more files at once.

Figure 1-2   The Search box in the new Explorer windows finds files almost instantly.

- **Details Pane**   Displays file metadata, such as the resolution of pictures, the length of videos, and the author of Office documents. Viewing the Details pane is quicker than viewing a file's Properties dialog box.

- **Preview Pane**   Previews a file's contents for applications that have this feature enabled, such as Microsoft Office documents.

- **Address Bar**   A more powerful address bar features drop-down menus for each folder level, making it easier to quickly switch folders, especially on Tablet PCs.

ClearType

ClearType makes text appear clearer by manipulating pixel subcomponents to smooth fonts. In Windows Vista, ClearType is enabled by default and optimized for LCD displays, which are now the most common type of display. Additionally, Windows Vista includes six new fonts designed specifically to take advantage of ClearType: Calibri, Cambria, Candara, Consolas, Constantia, and Corbel. Studies have shown that improving type clarity can improve user productivity; ClearType can have a positive impact on your organization.

User Interfaces

Windows Vista offers several levels of user interface, including user interfaces that closely resemble earlier versions of Windows. Any computer, including computers running Windows Vista Starter, can support the Basic and Classic user interfaces. Figure 1-3 shows the Windows Vista Basic user interface; Figure 1-4 shows the Windows Vista Classic user interface.

Figure 1-3   The Windows Vista Basic user interface.

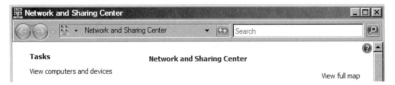

Figure 1-4   The Windows Vista Classic user interface.

Computers with graphics hardware that supports Windows Driver Display Model (WDDM) can use the Standard user interface (Figure 1-5) or the Aero user interface (Figure 1-6). When Aero is enabled, the user interface is significantly richer, with a transparent glass design and subtle effects such as dynamic reflections and smooth animations. Standard is available on all editions of Windows Vista except Windows Vista Starter; Aero is available only on the Home Premium, Business, Enterprise, and Ultimate editions of Windows Vista.

Figure 1-5   The Windows Vista Standard user interface.

Figure 1-6   The Windows Vista Aero user interface.

Note that Aero includes many subtle features that are impossible to highlight in a screenshot, such as partially transparent frames and shadows behind windows. Aero also includes many subtle improvements to usability, including:

- **Windows Flip**   Windows Flip is an update to the feature known as Alt+Tab in previous versions of Windows. Windows Flip displays thumbnails of each window, as shown in Figure 1-7. The desktop acts as one of your windows, so that you can quickly select it to minimize all open windows instantly.

Figure 1-7   Alt+Tab now displays thumbnail pictures of each window.

- **Windows Flip 3D**   In addition to using Alt+Tab, you can hold down the Windows key and press Tab to flip through three-dimensional views of all windows, as shown in Figure 1-8. Flip 3D can even show live processes such as playing video. You can also use the arrow keys or the scroll wheel on your mouse to browse through the open windows and select the window you need.

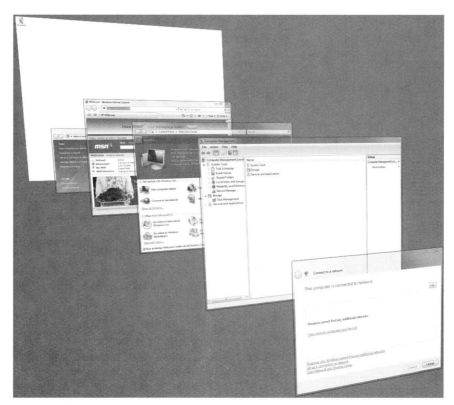

Figure 1-8   Windows Flip 3D acts like Alt+Tab but displays three-dimensional windows.

- **Live taskbar thumbnails**   With Windows Aero, when you hover your mouse over a tile on the taskbar, you see the "live" contents of the corresponding window without having to bring that window to the foreground, as shown in Figure 1-9.

Figure 1-9   Live taskbar thumbnails make it easier for users to find a specific window.

- **High dots per inch (DPI) support**   The user interface now scales better for high-resolution and high-DPI displays, such as those included with many new laptops. As a result, users can take advantage of high-DPI displays without being forced to read small text and work with tiny user interface elements.

To support Windows Aero, a computer must meet Windows Premium Ready requirements. A Windows Vista Premium Ready PC includes at least:

- 1-GHz, 32-bit (x86) or 64-bit (x64) processor
- 1 GB of system memory
- Support for DirectX 9 graphics with a Windows Display Driver Model (WDDM) driver, 128 MB of graphics memory (minimum, though this can be shared memory), Pixel Shader 2.0, and 32 bits per pixel
- 40 GB of hard-drive capacity with 15 GB free space
- DVD-ROM drive
- Audio output capability
- Internet access capability

For more information about hardware requirements, read the section titled "Choosing Hardware" later in this chapter.

Windows Sidebar and Gadgets

The Windows Sidebar is a pane on the side of the Windows Vista desktop that displays *gadgets*. Gadgets are mini-applications that can do almost anything, such as show news updates, display a picture slideshow, or show weather reports. Windows Vista includes several gadgets, you can download other gadgets, and developers can create custom gadgets (including internal gadgets that display information about your organization, such as the number of callers in a queue or the number of open tickets). The Sidebar helps to take advantage of the extra horizontal space provided by widescreen monitors.

Figure 1-10 shows administrative gadgets that enable you to quickly connect to a computer with Remote Desktop and monitor network latency, memory usage, processor utilization, disk free space, and currently assigned IP addresses. Windows Vista includes several gadgets, and you can download others from *http://gallery.live.com/default.aspx?pl=1*.

Figure 1-10   Gadgets show information on the side of the desktop.

To configure or disable the Windows Sidebar, use the Group Policy settings at the following location within either User Configuration or Computer Configuration:

Policies\Administrative Templates\Windows Components\Windows Sidebar

Internet Explorer

Windows Vista includes Internet Explorer 7. While Internet Explorer 7 can be installed on Windows XP, it includes an important security improvement only possible on Windows Vista: Protected Mode. Protected Mode runs Internet Explorer with minimal privileges, helping to prevent malicious websites from making permanent changes to a computer's configuration. For more information about Internet Explorer, read Chapter 21, "Managing Internet Explorer."

Speech Recognition

Windows Speech Recognition provides users with an alternative to traditional keyboard and mouse input. With Speech Recognition, users can speak into a microphone, and their spoken words will be input into the current application. Users can also use verbal commands to start and switch between applications, control the operating system, and fill out forms in Microsoft Internet Explorer.

Help and Support

Traditionally, Help and Support in Windows has described how features work. With Windows Vista, Help and Support focuses on the tasks instead, as shown in Figure 1-11, which helps users get work done. Microsoft can also provide regular updates and improvements to Windows Vista Help.

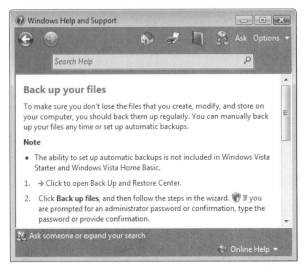

Figure 1-11   Help and Support is very task-oriented.

Media Sharing

Primarily a consumer feature, Media Sharing lets users share music, video, and pictures across the network. For security reasons, Media Sharing is disabled by default. For more information about Media Sharing, read Chapter 17, "Managing Sharing."

XPS

Windows Vista includes built-in support for the new XML Paper Specification (XPS). XPS is a document format that can be created from any printable document and then easily shared with almost any platform. For more information about XPS, read Chapter 19, "Managing Printing."

Performance

Although some features of Windows Vista, such as Aero, require high-performance hardware, Windows Vista is designed to perform similarly to earlier versions of Windows when run on the same hardware. The following sections describe technologies designed to improve Windows Vista performance.

ReadyBoost

Windows ReadyBoost uses a USB flash drive or a secure digital (SD) memory card to cache data that would otherwise need to be read from the much slower hard disk. Windows Vista uses SuperFetch technology to automatically determine which data to cache.

After you insert a USB flash drive or SD card greater than 256 MB in size, Windows Vista checks the performance to determine if the device is fast enough to work with ReadyBoost. (Flash devices designed for ReadyBoost display the phrase "Enhanced for Windows Ready-Boost" on the package, but other devices will also work.) If the device is fast enough, Windows Vista gives the user the option to enable ReadyBoost. Alternatively, users can manually enable ReadyBoost on compatible devices by viewing the drive's properties, as shown in Figure 1-12.

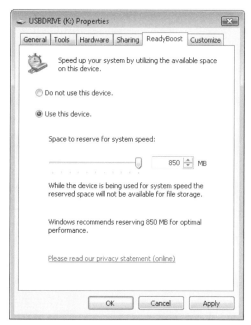

Figure 1-12   ReadyBoost uses flash memory to cache disk data.

If you remove the flash memory, ReadyBoost will be disabled, but the computer's stability will not be affected because the files stored on the flash memory are only temporary copies. Data on the flash memory is encrypted to protect privacy. For more information about ReadyBoost, see Chapter 15, "Managing Disks and File Systems."

ReadyDrive

While ReadyBoost works with external flash memory, Windows ReadyDrive uses specially designed hard disks that have built-in flash memory. By using the flash buffer on the hybrid hard disk to cache disk reads and writes, ReadyDrive can actually read and write from the hard disk without needing to spin the disk. This means that ReadyDrive can turn off the physical disk more often, thereby saving battery power and reducing wear on the disk. Ready-Drive can also improve startup and hibernate resume time because the information that is needed early in the startup and resume process is written to the flash memory.

Networking

Windows Vista networking components include improvements that will improve performance under specific circumstances. Most significantly, bandwidth utilization is increased over high-bandwidth, high-latency networks such as satellite or WAN connections. Networking in Windows Vista includes many other improvements that will have a positive impact on your network performance, stability, and security, especially over wireless networks. For more information, read Chapter 26, "Configuring Windows Networking."

SuperFetch

In the past, user applications were often unresponsive when the user had been away from the computer, because background processes such as search indexing or virus scans had consumed physical memory and forced Windows to move the user application's memory to the paging file. Windows Vista includes a memory-management technology called Windows SuperFetch that automatically restores application memory from the paging file to physical RAM when background processes complete their work. As a result, applications are more responsive when the user returns to the computer.

SuperFetch also helps improve responsiveness by tracking application usage and preloading the most frequently used applications into memory. This makes the system more responsive at startup or when a different user logs on. SuperFetch can even differentiate between weekends and weekdays and preload the applications that are most likely to be needed at any given time.

Automatic Disk Defragmentation

Files on a disk can become fragmented, which means that the file is spread out over different portions of the disk, rather than in an orderly sequence. When a disk drive must jump between different portions of a disk, performance is significantly slower. Although earlier versions of Windows include disk defragmentation tools, Windows Vista includes a new disk defragmenter that runs in the background and automatically defragments the hard disk as the need arises. The disk defragmenter runs when the computer is idle and takes advantage of low priority I/O to minimize the performance impact.

In Windows Vista, you should never think about fragmentation—Windows Vista keeps it under control without requiring the user or administrator to do anything. However, you can manually initiate disk defragmentation from the Computer Management console (as you can in Windows XP) or by using the defrag.exe command-line tool from an administrative command prompt. For more information about disk fragmentation, see Chapter 15.

Windows Experience Index

Many home users have a difficult time understanding a computer's performance. The Windows Experience Index (WEI) provides a single number that summarizes a computer's capabilities. Consumers can then reference this number to easily determine if software will run well on their computers. Figure 1-13 shows the WEI, which you can access from the computer's properties.

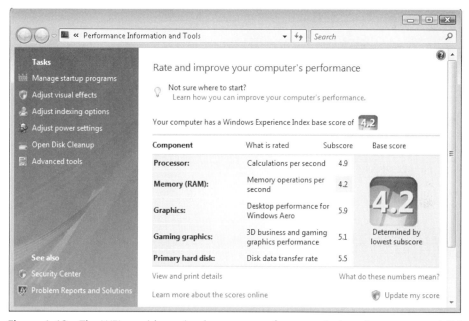

Figure 1-13   The WEI provides a simple summary of a computer's performance capabilities.

Each test results in a capability score between 1 and 5.9 for each of the following components: processor, memory, graphics, gaming graphics, and hard disk. Because a PC's performance is limited by the lowest performing component, the overall test result, or "base score," for the computer is determined by the lowest of the five scores.

WEI is a useful way to get a snapshot of a computer's performance. Although computers with a higher WEI will generally perform better than computers with a lower WEI, it is only a summary of the computer's performance capabilities. Performance can vary, especially when highly specialized tasks are taken into account. For more information about WEI, read Chapter 22, "Maintaining Desktop Health."

Low-Priority I/O

If multiple applications need simultaneous access to a resource, performance can suffer. For example, if a user is encrypting a file on the local hard disk and a virus scanner in the background is attempting to scan a different portion of the disk, Windows will divide time between the two processes, causing the hard disk to jump back and forth between different sectors. Thus, the background process can significantly reduce the performance of the user process.

Applications written to take advantage of low-priority I/O in Windows Vista can run at the same time as a user application without slowing down the application. Existing applications will not automatically use low-priority I/O; virus scanners, indexing services, and computer maintenance applications will need to be written specifically for Windows Vista to benefit from the performance improvements. In Windows Vista, a number of services are written to use low-priority I/O, including search indexing, automatic disk defragmentation, and Windows Defender's daily system scan.

Mobility

More and more new computers are laptops or Tablet PCs, which are used very differently from desktop computers. Mobile PCs must manage their power effectively, and the user should be able to easily monitor power usage and battery levels. Mobile PCs are also often used in meetings, which requires them to be able to easily connect to wireless networks and then find and use network resources.

The following sections provide a high-level overview of Windows Vista mobility improvements.

Windows Mobility Center

Windows Mobility Center, shown in Figure 1-14, provides a single tool to configure common mobile settings, including display brightness, volume, power plan, wireless network, external display (such as a network projector or additional monitor), and synchronization. Users with Tablet PCs can also rotate the display. Windows Mobility Center is available only on mobile PCs.

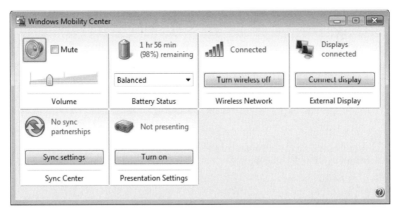

Figure 1-14   The Windows Mobility Center provides centralized control over mobile features.

To disable Windows Mobility Center, enable the following Group Policy setting within either Computer Configuration or User Configuration: Policies\Administrative Templates\ Windows Components\Windows Mobility Center\Turn Off Windows Mobility Center.

For more information about wireless networking enhancements in Windows Vista, read Chapter 26.

Sleep

Sleep is a new power state that combines the quick resume time of Standby (by keeping memory active in the computer) with the data-protection benefits of Hibernate (by storing a copy of memory to the hard disk in case power is lost).

When entering Sleep, Windows Vista initially behaves exactly like Standby–it minimizes power usage by turning off most of the computer's components, but keeps memory active so that the user can immediately resume working in open applications. If the battery power runs low, Windows Vista copies active memory to the hard disk, where it will be protected if power is lost, just as it would for Hibernate. Users can always use Sleep without needing to understand the differences between Standby and Hibernate.

For more information about Sleep, read Chapter 16, "Managing Devices and Services."

Improved Battery Meter

Mobile PC users need to constantly keep an eye on power levels. Windows Vista includes a battery meter in the system tray, similar to Windows XP. If you hover your mouse over the battery meter, as shown in Figure 1-15, you'll see the amount of time remaining that you can use the computer on your current battery. Click the battery meter to see the details of each battery, change the current power plan, and view a link to open the Windows Mobility center. Windows Vista will also notify you if your battery life reaches low and critical levels.

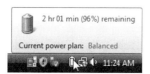

Figure 1-15   The new battery meter provides easy access to power information.

To remove the battery meter, enable the following Group Policy setting: User Configuration\ Policies\Administrative Templates\Start Menu And Taskbar\Remove The Battery Meter.

Presentation Settings

Many meetings include presentations driven by a Windows computer and an application such as Microsoft Office PowerPoint. Most often, the user has a mobile computer and con-nects the external video connector to a projector. To avoid problems during the presentation, such as a screensaver appearing, users can turn on presentation settings from the Windows Mobility Center.

When presentation settings are enabled, Windows Vista disables the screensaver by default. Additionally, you can adjust the volume (for example, you can mute the volume so that incoming instant messages don't play a sound) or set a different desktop background. Changing the background is a good way to hide any personal background pictures and to set a solid color to improve performance for presentations given over a network.

Presentation settings automatically turn off when you disconnect your mobile PC from a network projector or additional monitor, and also when you shut down or log off your mobile PC.

Network Projection

Network projectors are projectors that connect to computers across a network, rather than using a video connection. Network projectors are becoming common because users can easily display presentations from their mobile computers across networks without needing to connect the computers directly to the projectors.

Windows Vista includes native support for network projectors. To start the process, click Connect To A Network Projector from the Accessories folder on the Start menu. The Connect To A Network Projector Wizard can then search for a projector on the network, or you can enter the projector's address to connect to it directly. Projectors can be password-protected to reduce the risk of abuse. When you use the wizard, your desktop will be mirrored and presentation settings automatically optimized for network performance.

You can also use this feature in Windows Meeting Space so that you can simultaneously stream content to a projector and to a Windows Meeting Space session. For more information about Windows Meeting Space, see Chapter 18, "Managing Windows Meeting Space."

Sync Center

The Windows Vista Sync Center provides a single tool to manage data synchronization between two computers (such as when using Folder Redirection and Offline Files), and between a Windows Vista computer and devices such as personal digital assistants and mobile phones. With the Sync Center, users can initiate a manual sync, stop an in-progress sync, view the status of all current sync activities, and receive notifications to resolve conflicts. Third-party synchronization tools can still perform the actual data transfer while allowing the Sync Center to initiate or cancel the transfer. Additionally, Sync Center will open up third-party tools to configure options for synchronization tools not included with Windows Vista.

For more information about Sync Center, folder redirection, and Offline Files, read Chapter 14, "Managing Users and User Data."

Windows SideShow

Windows SideShow is a new technology designed to help users access information and applications without opening their mobile PCs. SideShow can take the form of a small, external display on a mobile PC (like those commonly found on mobile phones) or an external device that resembles a PDA.

SideShow uses gadgets, or add-in programs, to extend information from your computer onto the device or display. Gadgets run on a Windows SideShow–compatible device and update the device with information from your computer, such as e-mail messages and media files. Using a gadget, you can view information from your computer whether your mobile PC is on, off, or sleeping. You can also use gadgets to control programs remotely, such as Windows Media Player or Office PowerPoint.

Windows Vista comes with gadgets for Windows Mail and Windows Media Player 11; third-party software developers can create custom gadgets.

To configure or disable Windows SideShow, use the Group Policy settings located within both Computer Configuration and User Configuration at Policies\Administrative Templates\Windows Components\Windows Sideshow.

Offline Files

Windows Vista improves Offline Files, a Windows feature since Windows 2000 that synchronizes files stored on a file server with the local computer so that users can access the files while offline. Windows Vista includes many improvements to Offline Files, including:

- Files are always read from the local copy, improving network performance. All updates are performed directly to the server copy when the client computer is connected to the server.

- Delta Sync can reduce the bytes transferred when synchronizing updated files from a server.

- Ghosting displays a grayed icon for files in a folder that aren't synchronized.

- Windows Vista also includes support for synchronizing large files such as Microsoft Outlook PST files.

- Synchronized files can be searched using the features built into Windows Vista. For more information on new Search and Organization features in Windows Vista, see Chapter 20.

- The new Sync Center simplifies managing Offline Files and other synchronization relationships.

For more information about Offline Files, read Chapter 14.

Tablet PC

Tablet PCs are portable computers that enable input using a pen. With the special pen, users can write (or draw) directly on the Tablet PC's display. Previously, Microsoft provided Tablet PC features only with Windows XP Tablet PC Edition. With Windows Vista, Tablet PC features are included with Windows Vista Home Premium, Windows Vista Business, Windows Vista Enterprise, and Windows Vista Ultimate.

The following sections describe how Windows Vista improves upon the capabilities of Windows XP Tablet PC Edition.

To configure or disable Tablet PC features, use the Group Policy settings located within both Computer Configuration and User Configuration at Policies\Administrative Templates\Windows Components\Tablet PC.

Pen Improvements

Windows Vista includes the following significant pen improvements for Tablet PC computers:

- **Visual feedback**   Windows Vista provides visual pen feedback for single-tap, double-tap, and right-clicking, giving users confirmation that they've selected an item properly. You can disable this feature by using Pen And Input Devices in Control Panel.

- **Explorer check boxes**   Selecting multiple files in Explorer can be difficult with a Tablet PC, where Shift+clicking and Ctrl+clicking might not be available. In Windows Vista, when a user hovers over any set of files with a tablet pen, a small check box appears next to each file. The user can use the check boxes to select one or more files and then move, copy, or delete them as a group.

- **Pen flicks**   *Pen flicks* are gestures that Tablet PC users can make with a pen to quickly navigate and perform shortcuts. Navigational pen flicks include drag up, drag down, move back, and move forward. For example, instead of dragging the scroll bar down to read a web page, Tablet PC users can simply flick the pen and the window will scroll down. Editing functions that you can perform with pen flicks include copy, paste, delete, and undo. Users can also customize pen flicks to perform other functions.

- **Panning hand in Internet Explorer**   With *panning hand*, Tablet PC users can grab the page with the pen and move it directly. Users can click a hand icon on the Internet Explorer toolbar to toggle between panning and text selection modes.

- **New touch screen support**   In the past, users had to use a pen to interact with a Tablet PC—touching the screen with a finger had no effect. Windows Vista now supports touch input. With compatible hardware, users can use a finger to do many of the things that they would normally do with a mouse or a tablet pen. Tablet PC computers can therefore be used more quickly, without requiring the user to first pick up the pen.

- **Snipping Tool**   Tablet PC users can use Snipping Tool to capture a screenshot of any object on the screen by simply drawing a circle (or any other shape) around the object they want to capture. Users can then add handwritten comments to the snip and save it or send it in an e-mail message. If the image is captured from a web page, Snipping Tool attaches the URL automatically. Because Snipping Tool is an accessory in Windows Vista, desktop computer and non-Tablet PC users can also take advantage of this feature with the mouse.

Improvements to Tablet PC Input Panel

When running on a Tablet PC, Windows includes Tablet PC Input Panel, which helps users enter text with an on-screen keyboard or by reading their handwriting. Windows Vista includes the following improvements to Tablet PC Input Panel:

- **AutoComplete**   AutoComplete in Tablet PC Input Panel functions just like AutoComplete in programs such as Microsoft Internet Explorer and Microsoft Office Outlook. As Tablet PC users write a letter or series of letters, AutoComplete lists possible matches in Input Panel based on text that the user has entered before.

- **Enhanced ink erasing**   In Windows XP Tablet PC Edition 2005, users have to draw a Z-shaped scratch-out gesture to erase words or characters. Windows Vista allows for several new, more forgiving scratch-out gestures, including strikethrough, vertical scratch-out in the pattern of an M or W, circular scratch-out, and angled scratch-out. Some tablet pens include an eraser that users can use like a pencil eraser to delete writing.

- **Tablet PC Input Panel tab**   When Input Panel is closed, the Tablet PC Input Panel tab appears on the left edge of the screen by default. Users can quickly open Input Panel by tapping the tab.

Handwriting Recognition Improvements

Many Tablet PC users take advantage of handwriting recognition to input text. Windows Vista includes handwriting recognition improvements to make this type of input more efficient. First, the users can access the handwriting recognition personalization tool to manually train the handwriting recognizer to improve recognition accuracy.

Second, the new automatic learning feature causes the handwriting recognizer to learn the user's handwriting style or vocabulary during normal usage. Automatic learning collects data about the words users write most often and how they write them. For English, automatic learning creates a unique dictionary from a user's sent e-mail messages. It adds new words and terms to the dictionary, such as acronyms, industry jargon, and e-mail addresses. The recognizer prioritizes the words by their frequency to further improve handwriting recognition results. For East Asian languages, Windows Vista offers special recognition help for converting handwriting in Chinese (Traditional), Chinese (Simplified), Japanese, and Korean into text by remembering the corrections that you make to characters. As you make corrections, Windows Vista learns to distinguish more precisely between different characters so that you see better results the more you use your Tablet PC.

Deployment

For years, many IT departments have used imaging, a deployment technique that installs an operating system and applications as a single unit. However, earlier versions of Windows did not include direct support for imaging, so IT departments had to rely on third-party tools. All Windows Vista deployments use imaging, even standalone installations from DVD. Imaging deployment is extremely straightforward.

Following are some of the most significant features of image-based deployment:

- You can completely automate deployment, especially when used with Windows Deployment Services (WDS) and the Microsoft Deployment Solution Accelerator.

- You can inject custom drivers into images so that setup can detect all of your hardware.

- You can add applications to your images so that you do not have to deploy applications separately.

- You can add operating system updates to your images so that new computers are immediately up to date.

- Images can support multiple languages and hardware configurations, requiring you to maintain fewer images.

For more information about deployment changes, see Part II, "Deployment."

Note   For consumers, small offices, and one-off upgrades, Windows Easy Transfer provides a simple way for home users to transfer files and settings from a Windows XP computer to a new Windows Vista computer. As with Windows XP and earlier versions of Windows, users need to reinstall applications on the new computer. To connect the old and new computers, users can transfer information across a network, the USB-based Easy Transfer Cable, or removable media.

Reliability and Supportability

Although end users tend to focus on changes to the user interface, IT professionals benefit most from improvements to reliability and supportability. These types of improvements can significantly reduce the number of support center calls and improve the efficiency of IT departments. Additionally, Windows Vista can improve end users' satisfaction with their IT departments by reducing time spent solving computer problems.

The following sections describe important reliability and supportability improvements to Windows Vista.

Backups

Although large organizations might still choose an enterprise backup solution, Windows Vista includes robust tools for managing client computers that are perfect for small businesses and mobile users in enterprise environments.

For the first time ever, Windows Vista includes an image-based backup solution called Complete PC Backup. When the user creates a Complete PC Backup, Windows Vista copies the local disk to a VHD disk image file. If Windows is corrupted or the hard disk needs to be replaced, a user can quickly restore the Complete PC Backup by starting from the Windows Vista setup DVD and connecting the backup media—restoration typically takes less than an hour. Because it's a disk image, no applications need to be reinstalled.

Windows Vista also includes a traditional file-based backup system. However, the Windows Vista file backup offers significant improvements over Windows Backup included with earlier versions of Windows:

- It can be scheduled to run automatically.

- It stores backups in a ZIP-based structure that can be easily restored from any operating system.

- It manages the backup files for the user, and only backs up changed files.

- With sufficient disk space, it will keep multiple copies of a file that regularly changes to allow the user to restore to multiple versions of a file, in order to recover data that was lost days or weeks ago.

Restoring files can be simple enough for users to do without calling the support center. Users simply need to view a file's properties and then click the Previous Versions tab. Windows Vista shows them a list of available backups of the files. Backups might have been made through a scheduled backup, a restore point, or a volume shadow copy.

For more information about disk partitioning, read Chapter 15.

Disk Partitioning

Occasionally, administrators need to change the structure of disk partitions on a computer that already has an operating system installed. In earlier versions of Windows, this requires deleting existing partitions or installing a third-party tool. With Windows Vista, you can use the standard Disk Management user interface to dynamically change partition sizes, without affecting the data on that partition.

For more information about backups, read Chapter 15.

Reduced Restarts

Restarting a computer is a major inconvenience, because it requires users to save their work, close their applications, wait several minutes while the computer restarts, and then reopen all their applications to resume their work. Usually, users have to restart their computers after installing updates so that the installer can replace a file that is currently in use.

To reduce the need to restart after installing an update, Windows Vista applications that support side-by-side compliant dynamic-link libraries (DLLs) can install the new version of a file on the disk even if the old one is in use. The user can keep the application open, and the update will take effect automatically the next time the application is restarted. You will need to create updates specifically to take advantage of this feature; applications written before the release of Windows Vista cannot take advantage of side-by-side compliant DLLs.

Windows Vista also includes Microsoft Windows Installer (MSI) 4.0, which takes advantage of Windows Vista platform improvements to avoid the need to restart the computer after adding or removing applications packaged as MSIs. MSI 4.0 will not be available for earlier versions of Windows. However, packages created for MSI 4.0 are backward-compatible with earlier versions of Windows; developers can take advantage of MSI 4.0 features, and administrators can still use a single package to deploy applications to both Windows Vista and earlier versions of Windows.

If the computer must be restarted, applications that support Smart Relaunch can make it easier for users to continue working where they left off before the restart. With Smart Relaunch, applications such as key 2007 Microsoft Office system applications can automatically save documents and then restore application state after restarting the computer. Restart Manager, MSI 4.0, and Smart Relaunch do not require any administrative effort.

Improved Driver Reliability

Drivers perform more reliably in Windows Vista than in previous versions of Windows. With support for canceling synchronous input/output (I/O) operations in Windows Vista, drivers recover gracefully if they become blocked when attempting to perform I/O. Windows Vista also has new application programming interfaces (APIs) that allow applications to cancel pending I/O requests when a resource takes too long to become available. To help Microsoft and its partners identify and fix drivers that do not complete I/O in a timely fashion and that have not yet implemented the cancellation APIs, new instrumentation called Kernel Hang Reporting collects information to support triage and diagnosis. Although drivers designed for Windows Vista offer the best reliability, Windows Vista also supports many drivers created for Windows XP to offer the broadest hardware compatibility.

As a systems administrator, you do not need to understand the details of how these improvements are implemented; only developers do. However, you will benefit from the improved reliability.

For more information about drivers and devices, read Chapter 16.

System File and Registry Protection

Any code that runs in Kernel Mode, including most drivers, can potentially corrupt kernel data in ways that surface later. Diagnosing and fixing these bugs can be difficult and time consuming. Corruption of the registry tends to have a disproportionate impact on overall reliability, because this corruption can persist across system restarts.

Windows Vista prevents poorly written drivers from corrupting the registry and protects system settings from corruption or inadvertent changes that can cause the system to be unreliable or fail completely. Windows Resource Protection (WRP) protects critical system settings, files, and folders from changes by any source except a trusted installer. This prevents users from changing critical system settings and preventing Windows from starting. It also prevents installers from overwriting a system file that has been updated by Microsoft with an older version.

For more information about WRP, see Chapter 16.

Supportability

Many Windows Vista improvements will never be noticed by users because they are designed to benefit IT departments. Windows Vista is designed to be very easy to manage centrally, especially in Active Directory environments. Using the following Group Policy settings, you can centrally configure desktop settings, distribute updates, and aggregate events from anywhere in your enterprise:

- **Configuration management**   User Account Control (UAC) makes it much easier to keep users out of the Administrators group. With UAC, users will still be able to run their applications, but they won't be able to make changes that might negatively affect their computers, such as changing system settings or installing new applications. The control that UAC provides administrators will keep client computers much more stable. For more information about UAC, read Chapter 25, "Managing Client Protection."

- **Windows Resource Protection**   If a potentially dangerous change to the system does occur, Windows Resource Protection (WRP) can still prevent the problem from becoming serious. WRP protects system registry settings from accidental changes made by the user as well as changes made by unauthorized software, and it protects system files and settings from changes initiated by any process other than the Windows trusted installer.

- **Group Policy improvements**   Most enterprises already rely on Group Policy settings to centrally configure and manage their Windows computers. In Windows Vista, almost every aspect of the client computer is configurable using Group Policy settings. Wireless networking, removable storage devices, Internet Explorer, printers, and power management each have additional settings. For computers not in an Active Directory environment, you can use support for multiple local GPOs to specify different policies for different users on a single Windows Vista computer. The updated Network Location Awareness service in Windows Vista is used by Group Policy to more reliably apply policy updates. The new XML-based format for administrative templates provides multilingual custom group policy and new support for a central store improves domain replication performance. For more information, read Chapter 13, "Managing the Desktop Environment."

- **Built-in diagnostics**   Windows Vista is designed to detect many common types of problems, including network connectivity problems, intermittent hardware failures, and performance problems. After Windows Vista detects the problem, it walks the user through the process of troubleshooting using a simple user interface. These diagnostics won't solve all problems, but they can reduce the number of calls for support. Diagnostics also records a great deal of detailed information to the Event Log so that when you do have to troubleshoot a problem, you have the information you need to properly diagnose the issue. In some troubleshooting scenarios, such as when diagnosing wireless network problems, you can enable tracing to view an intensely detailed log of internal Windows Vista events. For more information, see Chapter 22, and Part VI of this book, "Troubleshooting."

- **Improved eventing**   The Windows Vista Event Log is improved to make it easier to find important events and filter insignificant events. You can create automated tools to respond to events and then launch those tools when specific events occur on client computers. Additionally, you can centrally collect significant events using event forwarding, without requiring a separate management infrastructure such as Microsoft System Center Operations Manager (SCOM). For more information, see Chapter 22.

- **Task Scheduler**   As with Windows XP, you can use Task Scheduler to run scripts or other tools at specific times. Windows Vista adds the ability to run tasks when specific events occur, which you can configure to either automatically fix the problem (for example, by cleaning up temporary files if disk space is low) or to notify the support center. You can also run tasks when a user locks or unlocks a session or when the computer is idle. If you need to run multiple tasks automatically on a computer, you can configure Task Scheduler to control the sequence and prevent the tasks from running simultaneously. For more information, see Chapter 22.

- **User Assistance**   You can add custom content to Windows Vista Help files to provide answers to questions about custom applications and internal network resources. You can also customize User Assistance to link users directly to an internal support center.

- **Remote Assistance**   Windows XP also includes Remote Assistance, but with Windows Vista it is faster, uses less bandwidth, and can function through Network Address Translation (NAT). In Windows Vista, you can configure many aspects of Remote Assistance via Group Policy as well. For more information, see Chapter 23, "Supporting Users Using Remote Assistance."

- **Drivers**   The new Driver Store is a cache of device drivers for millions of hardware devices, ready for installation when needed. Any user can install drivers that administrators have added to the Driver Store, enabling Standard users to install drivers that the IT department determines are safe. You can also grant Standard users the privilege to install devices based on class ID or device ID. For example, you might use this to grant users access to install printer drivers but not install network adapter drivers. For security reasons, you can block devices by class ID or device ID as well. To simplify maintenance of updated drivers, you can down distribute updated drivers by using Windows Update. For more information about drivers, see Chapter 16. For more information about Windows Update, see Chapter 24, "Managing Software Updates."

Roaming Profiles and Folder Redirection

Roaming Profiles is a feature that enables a user's profile to be stored in a shared folder so that the user can have the same desktop experience no matter which computer she logs on to (as long as that computer is part of the same domain). Folder Redirection is a related technology that stores users folders, such as Documents or Pictures, on a shared folder rather than the local computer.

Windows Vista makes improvements to both of these technologies. Most important, logging on with a roaming profile can be much faster because almost all of the user's data can be accessed using folder redirection, which reduces the amount of data that needs to be copied when the user logs on. Administrators also have better flexibility for determining how user data is stored, because many different profile folders can be redirected, including Desktop, Start Menu, Documents, and AppData. As an administrator, you can therefore store some data locally while keeping other data on the network—especially useful if you only need to store user data in shared folders to simplify backups.

For more information about Roaming Profiles and Folder Redirection, read Chapter 14.

Troubleshooting

Built-in diagnostics and failure-recovery mechanisms in Windows Vista minimize user impact when problems occur, reducing support costs and improving productivity for end users and support professionals. The following sections describe improvements to Windows Vista that will make it easier for end users to solve their own problems and for IT departments to troubleshoot the more challenging problems that still require IT support.

Repairing Unbootable Computers

Startup problems are among the most difficult to troubleshoot because you cannot start the operating system and use built-in troubleshooting tools. Often, administrators choose to reinstall the operating system rather than attempt to solve the problem—even though the solution might be as simple as replacing a single file.

With Windows Vista, you can start the Startup Repair tool (which replaces Recovery Console in Windows XP) either from the Windows Vista installation DVD or from a special startup menu preinstalled by your hardware manufacturer. When it has been started, the Startup Repair tool can address 80 percent of the known causes for unbootable systems. In many cases, Startup Repair can diagnose and automatically resolve the problem with no input required from the user. For more information, see Chapter 30, "Configuring Startup and Troubleshooting Startup Issues."

Built-in Diagnostics

Windows Vista contains built-in diagnostics—collections of instrumentation, troubleshooting, and resolution logic—to resolve external problems that affect the way Windows behaves. The framework that supports these diagnostics, called the Windows Diagnostic Infrastructure (WDI), is a new feature in Windows Vista. A number of diagnostic scenarios are implemented using WDI, addressing some of the most common and costly problems facing PC users. Built-in diagnostic scenarios in Windows Vista include:

■ **Hardware failures**   Disk failure and defective memory diagnostics. Disk Diagnostics can detect impending disk failures and notify the user or support center so that data can be backed up, the disk can be replaced, and the data can be restored before hardware failure occurs. Memory Diagnostics works with Microsoft Online Crash Analysis to detect crashes that might be caused by failing memory, provide guided support, and prompt the user to schedule a memory test the next time the computer is restarted. Administrators can launch Memory Diagnostics from the Startup Repair tool. For more information, see Chapter 31, "Troubleshooting Hardware, Driver, and Disk Issues."

- **Networking problems**   Network diagnostics for wireless and wired clients. For more information, see Chapter 32, "Troubleshooting Network Issues."

- **Client performance degradation**   Performance diagnostics, including slow startup, slow shutdown, and poor responsiveness.

- **Resource exhaustion**   Occasionally, when a user is running a large number of applications, the computer will simply run out of system resources, leading to hangs, crashes, and data loss. Resource Exhaustion Prevention warns users when critical resources are low—before a hang or crash occurs. It also identifies which applications a user should close to reclaim the resource and then helps the user close them. When Windows Vista issues a resource exhaustion warning, it logs events in the Event Log that include detailed data useful for subsequent analysis.

- **Power transition problems**   Power transition diagnostics to help troubleshooting problems going into or recovering from Standby, Sleep, or Hibernate.

- **Program Compatibility Assistant**   Identifies application installation failures that may be attributable to incompatibility with Windows Vista and offers possible fixes.

All of these built-in diagnostics scenarios take advantage of the new WDI framework in Windows Vista, and all of them are designed to improve reliability and reduce support costs. In enterprise environments, you manage built-in diagnostics through Group Policy. Administrators can choose to disable any diagnostic scenario or keep the diagnostic component in place and disable the resolution component for any diagnostic scenario. All built-in diagnostic scenarios raise events to Event Log. These events provide a record of which problems the built-in diagnostics have automatically repaired and also provide information to IT professionals to help solve problems that can't be resolved automatically.

Recovering from Service Crashes

In Windows Vista, most noncritical system services have a recovery policy that automatically restarts them if they fail, allowing the user to continue working after the service has crashed. The implicit and explicit dependencies between services are understood, and all appropriate services are restarted in the correct order when one of them crashes. This will help reduce application problems caused by failed services, which can be difficult for users to troubleshoot.

For more information about services, read Chapter 16.

Reliability Analysis Component

The Reliability Analysis Component (RAC) aggregates, analyzes, and correlates application, operating system, and hardware problems. The RAC calculates a stability index over time and tracks changes that are likely to affect stability, such as Windows updates, driver installations, and application installations.

Users can view RAC data via Reliability Monitor, which displays data collected from RAC in a stability chart and correlates the computer's stability index with important events that are likely to affect stability, such as driver failures and software installation. RAC data will also be available to health monitoring applications such as System Center Operations Manager. For more information about RAC and Reliability Monitor, see Chapter 22 and Chapter 31.

Architecture Improvements

The Windows Vista architecture closely resembles the Windows XP architecture, with some key changes. As with earlier versions of Windows, core components, such as the Windows Vista kernel and drivers, run in *Kernel Mode*. Kernel Mode provides the best performance, but code runs without security restrictions. Therefore, Kernel Mode processes can take almost any action on your computer, including reading the memory of other applications and over-writing files on your disk. Because of these security risks, Windows Vista allows only the most highly trusted code to run in Kernel Mode.

Applications and most services run in *User Mode*. User Mode applications can interact with hardware and other applications, but only indirectly. For example, if a User Mode application needs to send a packet across the network, it uses a Windows application programming inter-face (API) to run Windows code. While the process is running Windows code, it is tempo-rarily moved to Kernel Mode so that it can communicate with the network adapter. After the API call has completed, it is moved back to User Mode to continue running the application code.

In this way, only Windows code called using a Windows API is run in Kernel Mode, even though the application's process runs temporarily in Kernel Mode. Because User Mode components do not have direct access to hardware and must request access through Kernel Mode components that can verify the process's privileges, the security risks of User Mode processes are much less than those of Kernel Mode processes. Security features such as file permissions, user rights, and User Access Control (UAC) all work within User Mode to further control access.

> **Note**   The separation between User Mode and Kernel Mode is implemented at the hardware level, within the processor. Kernel Mode processes use Ring 0, while User Mode processes use Ring 3. Because the processor won't allow Ring 3 processes to access Ring 0 resources (including Kernel Mode memory), it is very difficult for malicious processes to directly bypass the security. To gain access to Kernel Mode resources without using Windows APIs, a User Mode process must identify a vulnerability in a Kernel Mode API and exploit it.

Figure 1-16 illustrates these relationships.

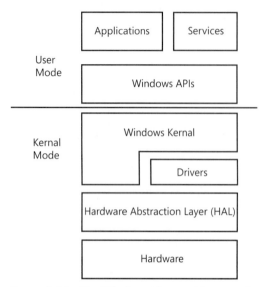

Figure 1-16 The Windows Vista architecture closely resembles earlier versions of Windows.

To understand the importance of running applications in User Mode, consider how Windows Vista handles errors for different types of processes: If an error (also known as an *unhandled exception*) occurs in User Mode, Windows catches the error and processes it with Windows Error Reporting. The failure of any single User Mode process doesn't affect the stability of the system. However, if an unhandled exception occurs in a Kernel Mode process, the stability of the operating system might be compromised. To protect the operating system, Windows Vista displays a *Stop* error (also known as a blue screen). Therefore, an error in a User Mode application doesn't directly impact the system or other applications, but an error in a Kernel Mode process causes the entire operating system to halt. For more information about Windows Error Reporting, see Chapter 22. For more information about Stop errors, see Chapter 33, "Troubleshooting Stop Messages," on the companion CD.

Microsoft creates most Kernel Mode components, and Microsoft makes a strong effort to test the security, reliability, and integrity of these components. Third-party hardware manufacturers are often responsible for developing the drivers, however. Because any vulnerability in a driver can provide malicious software with unrestricted Kernel Mode access to all aspects of your computer, you should be very careful about installing drivers. Whenever possible, use only drivers that have been signed by Microsoft, which proves that Microsoft has tested the driver. In 64-bit versions of Windows Vista, you don't have the option of using unsigned drivers. For more information about drivers, see Chapter 16.

Note *Microsoft Windows Internals, Fourth Edition* (Microsoft Press, 2004), by Mark Russinovich and David Solomon, provides detailed information about the Microsoft Windows architecture.

Many aspects of the Windows Vista kernel have been improved compared to earlier versions of Windows. For example, some video driver components can now run in User Mode, rather than Kernel Mode, to improve operating system stability. This allows Windows Vista to recover from a failed user-mode driver, as shown in Figure 1-17.

Figure 1-17   Windows Vista can automatically recover after some drivers fail.

These kernel changes improve the security and reliability of Windows Vista; however, they do not require administrators to configure or manage them. For detailed information about these changes, see "Kernel Enhancements for Windows Vista and Windows Server 2008" at *http://www.microsoft.com/whdc/system/vista/kernel-en.mspx.*

Windows Vista Service Pack 1 Improvements

In the first quarter of 2008, Microsoft released Windows Vista Service Pack 1, a major update to Windows Vista. Most of the updates resolve performance and reliability problems. As a result, you should deploy Service Pack 1 to your Windows Vista computers as quickly as possible after thoroughly testing all applications and hardware with the update.

The major improvements are:

- Usability improvements
    - The number of UAC (User Account Control) prompts is reduced from 4 to 1 when creating or renaming a folder at a protected location.
    - 32-bit operating systems must reserve part of the total 4 GB theoretical address space for video memory, bus address space, and other system resources. Therefore, even if a computer has 4 GB of physical memory installed, the operating system cannot address all of it. Prior to Service Pack 1, Windows Vista reported the amount of memory the operating system could address. With Service Pack 1 installed, Windows Vista will report the amount of physical system memory installed rather than report the amount of system memory available to the operating system.
    - When scanning, Windows Vista with Service Pack 1 will open Explorer instead of Windows Photo Gallery.
    - A Standard user is able to invoke the CompletePC Backup application, provided that the user can supply administrator credentials. Previously, only administrators could launch the application.

- ❑ The Remote Desktop client in Windows Vista provides user interface improvements for user and server authentication by streamlining the multiple steps users must follow to provide their credentials to Windows Server 2003 (or earlier) Terminal Servers, and simplifies the management of previously saved credentials.

- ❑ Users can rename or delete folders while working offline with redirected folders. This functionality is important to users who use Folder Redirection and work in offline mode for extended periods of time. This functionality is disabled by default, but you can enable it by enabling a registry setting.

- ■ New features

  - ❑ Adds support for new UEFI (Unified Extensible Firmware Interface) firmware for 64-bit systems, which allows Windows Vista SP1 to install to GPT format disks.

  - ❑ Adds support for x64 EFI network boot.

  - ❑ Adds support for Direct3D 10.1.

  - ❑ Adds support for exFAT, a new file system supporting larger overall capacity and larger files, which will be used in Flash memory storage and consumer devices.

  - ❑ Adds support for SD Advanced DMA (ADMA) on compliant SD standard host controllers. This new transfer mechanism, which is expected to be supported in SD controllers soon, will improve transfer performance and decrease CPU utilization.

  - ❑ Adds support to enable new types of Windows Media Center Extenders, such as digital televisions and networked DVD players, to connect to Windows Media Center.

  - ❑ Adds support for temporarily resizing the desktop to accommodate custom projector resolutions when connecting to Windows Network Projectors.

  - ❑ Adds support for backing up EFS encrypted files.

  - ❑ Adds an improved SRT (Startup Repair Tool). For more information, read Chapter 30.

- ■ Reliability improvements

  - ❑ Numerous improvements based on Windows Error Reporting feedback to Windows Calendar, Windows Media Player, drivers, and other Windows components to improve reliability have been added.

  - ❑ Improves reliability by preventing data loss while ejecting NTFS-formatted removable media.

  - ❑ Improves reliability of IPsec connections over IPv6 by ensuring that all Neighbor Discovery RFC traffic is IPsec exempted.

  - ❑ Improves wireless ad hoc connection (computer-to-computer wireless connections) success rate.

❑ Improves the success of peer-to-peer connections, such as Windows Meeting Space or Remote Assistance applications, when both computers are behind symmetric firewalls.

❑ Service Pack 1 incorporates numerous previously released hotfixes. For a detailed list, visit *http://support.microsoft.com/kb/936332.*

■ Performance improvements

❑ Improves file copy performance by 25 percent when copying files locally on the same disk on the same machine, is 45 percent faster when copying files from a remote non–Windows Vista system to a SP1 system, and is 50 percent faster when copying files from a remote SP1 system to a local SP1 system.

❑ Improves the copy progress estimation when copying files within Windows Explorer to about two seconds.

❑ Improves the speed of adding and extracting files to and from a compressed folder.

❑ Significantly improves the speed of moving a directory with many files underneath.

❑ Improves performance while copying files using BITS (Background Intelligent Transfer Service).

❑ Improves the time to read large images by approximately 50 percent.

❑ Improves ReadyBoost, SuperFetch, and interoperability with some USB hubs to reduce the time to resume from Standby and Hibernate.

❑ Improves the logic for selecting which network interface to use when multiple connections are available (such as wired and wireless connections).

❑ Improves overall media performance by reducing many glitches.

❑ Includes a new Remote Desktop compression algorithm to reduce network bandwidth required to send bitmaps or images via RDP. The compression, which you can configure with Group Policy settings, reduces the size of the RDP stream by as much as 25 to 60 percent.

❑ Improves the performance of browsing network file shares by consuming less bandwidth.

❑ Improves power consumption and battery life. For example, in certain circumstances, power consumption has been improved by addressing an issue that causes a hard disk to continue spinning when it should spin down.

❑ Improves power consumption when the display is not changing by allowing the processor to remain in its Sleep state, which consumes less energy.

❑ Addresses the problem of the Video chipset (VSync interrupt) not allowing the system to stay asleep.

- Security improvements

    - Improves BitLocker Drive Encryption by offering an additional multifactor authentication method that combines a key protected by the Trusted Platform Module (TPM) with a Startup Key stored on a USB storage device and a user-generated personal identification number (PIN). Additionally, BitLocker can now encrypt nonbootable volumes. For more information about BitLocker, see Chapter 15.

    - Enables single sign-on (SSO) for authenticated wired networks.

    - Allows only authenticated security applications to update Windows Security Center (WSC), reducing the risk of malware changing the status.

    - Allows RDP files to be signed. Administrators now have the control to differentiate the user experience based on the publisher's identity.

    - The cryptographic random number generation is improved to gather seed entropy from more sources, including a TPM when available, and replaces the general purpose pseudo-random number generator (PRNG) with an AES-256 counter mode PRNG for both user and Kernel Mode. Effective random number generation is important when generating encryption keys.

    - Adds a new PIN channel to securely collect smart card PINs via a computer. This new capability mitigates a number of attacks that today require using an external PIN reader to prevent.

    - Supports smart cards that use biometric authentication.

    - Improves security over Teredo interface by blocking unsolicited traffic by default.

    - Improves the OCSP (Online Certificate Status Protocol) implementation so that it can be configured to work with OCSP responses that are signed by trusted OCSP signers, separate from the issuer of the certificate being validated.

    - SP1 includes APIs by which third-party security applications can work alongside Kernel Patch Protection on 64-bit versions of Windows Vista. Before SP1, these tools needed to disable or weaken the protection offered by Kernel Patch Protection.

    - SP1 includes APIs to allow applications to control their own Data Execution Protection (DEP) policy. This provides developers with finer control on a process's DEP settings for security, testability, compatibility, and reliability. For more information about DEP, read Chapter 2.

- Support for new technologies

    - Adds full support for the latest IEEE draft of 802.11n wireless networking.

    - Adds support for Secure Sockets Tunnel Protocol (SSTP), a remote access VPN tunneling protocol supported by Windows Server 2008 VPN servers. SSTP provides a VPN connection using HTTPS, allowing connections to work through NAT, web proxies, and firewalls.

❑ Adds support for new strong cryptographic algorithms used in IPsec: SHA-256, AES-GCM, and AES-GMAC for ESP and AH; ECDSA, SHA-256, and SHA-384 for IKE and AuthIP.

❑ Adds the NIST SP 800-90 Elliptical Curve Cryptography (ECC) pseudo-random number generator (PRNG) to the list of available PRNGs.

❑ Adds support in the Wireless Client for a new FIPS (Federal Information Processing) compliant mode. This mode is FIPS 140-2 compliant because it moves the cryptographic processing from the wireless network card to an existing FIPS-approved cryptographic library.

❑ Enhances Windows Firewall and IPsec to use the new cryptographic algorithms that are Suite B–compliant.

❑ Enhances TCP Chimney network card support so that a TCP Chimney network card can also support Compound TCP.

❑ Adds support for Windows Smartcard Framework to enable compliance with the EU Digital Signature Directive and National ID / eID.

■ Desktop management

❑ The Group Policy Management Console (GPMC) is uninstalled with Service Pack 1, and the GPEdit tool will default to Local Group Policy Editing. However, Service Pack 1 users can download an updated version of the GPMC from *http://www.microsoft.com*, which will include new Group Policy capabilities including adding comments to GPOs or individual settings and searching for specific Group Policy settings.

❑ Allows users and administrators to control which volumes the disk defragmenter runs on.

❑ Adds file sharing troubleshooting to Network Diagnostics. For more information, read Chapter 32.

❑ Allows applications to prompt for elevation without using the secure desktop. This allows a remote helper to enter administrative credentials during a Remote Assistance session.

❑ Allows administrators to add a WSD (Web Services for Devices) Print Device to remote Windows Vista or Windows Server 2008 computers. This can be accomplished by using the Print Management Console.

❑ Improves printing to local printers from within a Terminal Server session.

❑ Adds a WMI interface as a replacement for the MoveUser.exe tool that was removed from Windows Vista. This allows customers to remap an existing workgroup or domain user account profile to a new domain user account profile.

❑ Allows an administrator to configure properties of a network, such as the name, and deploy it network-wide via a Group Policy snap-in.

❑ Allows KMS (Key Management Service) to run within a Virtual Machine environment.

■ Network Access Protection (NAP)

❑ Allows administrators to configure NAP Clients to receive updates from Windows Update or Microsoft Update, in addition to WSUS (Windows Server Update Services).

❑ Allows administrators to configure NAP Clients to define the time a client has to retrieve and submit Statements of Health. This allows the NAP client to respond in time when a particular connection has a time-out requirement.

❑ NAP clients can now use DNS server records to discover health registration authority (HRA) servers when there are no HRAs configured through local configuration or Group Policy.

❑ Allows healthy clients (typically in use by help desk personell) to establish IPsec connections to unhealthy computers to help resolve problems. This improves the supportability of NAP by allowing specific compliant computers to establish connections to non-compliant computers. For more information about NAP, refer to *Windows Server 2008 Networking and Network Access Protection (NAP)* (Microsoft Press, 2008).

■ Deployment improvements

❑ Enables support for hotpatching, a reboot-reduction servicing technology designed to maximize uptime. It works by allowing Windows components to be updated while they are still in use by a running process. Hotpatch-enabled update packages are installed via the same methods as traditional update packages and will not trigger a system reboot.

❑ Improves migration and upgrade scenarios relating to the component that allows alternate text input modalities such as speech, handwriting, and multibyte character input editors in applications that were not written specifically to support them.

❑ Improves deployment by enabling 64-bit versions of Windows Vista to be installed from a 32-bit operating system, allowing administrators to maintain just a single WinPE image.

❑ Improves update reliability and performance using several different improvements, including retrying failed updates in cases in which multiple updates are pending, and the failure of one update causes other updates to fail as well.

❑ Users are now required to enter a password hint during the initial setup of Windows Vista. A password hint helps prevent users from forgetting their passwords in workgroup environments.

❑ For customers upgrading from Windows XP to Windows Vista with SP1, the MSRT (Malicious Software Removal Tool) will not run as part of the upgrade as it does when installing Windows Vista without SP1.

■ Server improvements

❑ File sharing improvements made to support scalability in Windows Server 2008 are also added to Windows Vista, even though Windows Vista allows only 10 concurrent inbound connections.

❑ IIS also offers improved performance as a result of Windows Server 2008 development. These changes do not affect most Windows Vista users, however, because Windows Vista and Windows Server 2008 are aligned. These changes are included in Windows Vista SP1.

For more information about Windows Vista Service Pack 1, read the guides in "Windows Vista SP1 Guides for IT Professionals" at *http://www.microsoft.com/downloads/ details.aspx?FamilyID=e71f0083-1013-4f9c-a3f9-c56e7120a5e9.*

Windows Vista Editions

As with earlier versions of Windows, Microsoft has released several different versions (also known as Stock Keeping Units, or SKUs) of Windows Vista to meet the needs of different types of customers, as detailed in Table 1-2.

Table 1-2   Windows Vista Offerings by Customer Segment

For Consumers	For Small Businesses	For Medium to Large Businesses	For Emerging Markets
Windows Vista Ultimate	Windows Vista Ultimate	Windows Vista Enterprise	Windows Vista Starter
Windows Vista Home Premium	Windows Vista Business	Windows Vista Business	
Windows Vista Home Basic		Microsoft Desktop Optimization Package for Software Assurance	

Note   There are two other editions of Windows Vista Home Basic N and Business N. These editions are exactly like their counterparts except they do not include Windows Media Player.

Although several different editions of Windows Vista are available, the Windows Vista setup DVD contains every version. The specific edition installed is determined by the product key used to install the software. Users have the option of upgrading to a higher edition using Windows Anytime Upgrade. For example, if a Windows Vista Home Basic user decides she wants Media Center capabilities, she can use Windows Anytime Upgrade to upgrade to Windows Vista Home Premium or Windows Vista Ultimate editions.

In many ways, choosing Windows Vista editions is easier than it is for Windows XP. Each edition includes both 32- and 64-bit versions. Additionally, Media Center and Tablet PC capabilities are included with several Windows Vista editions instead of requiring their own versions of Windows.

Table 1-3 summarizes the differences among the versions of Windows Vista (excluding Windows Vista Starter Edition, which is discussed later in this section). The following sections describe each edition in more detail.

Table 1-3   Windows Vista Editions Features

Feature	Home Basic	Home Premium	Business	Enterprise	Ultimate
Scheduled backups		X	X	X	X
Complete PC Backup			X	X	X
Aero user interface		X	X	X	X
Support for dual processors (not counting individual processor cores)			X	X	X
Years of product support	5	5	10	10	5
Windows Media Center		X			X
Windows Movie Maker HD		X			X
Windows DVD Maker		X			X
Parental controls	X	X			X
Windows Fax And Scan			X	X	X
Network And Sharing Center			X	X	X
Wireless network provisioning			X	X	X
Incoming file and printer sharing connections	5	10	10	10	10
Tablet PC		X	X	X	X
Encrypting File System			X	X	X
Desktop deployment tools			X	X	X
Policy-based quality of service for networking			X	X	X
Control over driver installations			X	X	X
Network Access Protection Client			X	X	X
BitLocker Drive Encryption				X	X
Simultaneous installation of multiple user interface languages				X	X
Subsystem for UNIX-based applications				X	X

Windows Vista Starter

Created for use only in emerging technology countries, this version of Windows Vista provides a basic feature set. Users can take advantage of improvements to security, search, and organization. However, the Windows Vista Aero interface is not available, and Windows Vista Starter is available only in 32-bit versions; it is not available in a 64-bit version.

Windows Vista Home Basic

Like Windows XP Home Edition, this edition of Windows is designed to meet the needs of home users seeking a lower-cost operating system. Windows Vista Home Edition is sufficient for users who use their computers primarily for e-mail, instant messaging, and browsing the web. Features include:

- Instant Search
- Internet Explorer 7
- Windows Defender
- Windows Photo Gallery
- Windows Easy Transfer

Like Windows Vista Starter, Windows Vista Home Basic does not include the Aero user interface.

Windows Vista Home Premium

This edition of Windows includes all of the features of Windows Vista Home Basic, plus:

- Aero user interface
- Windows Media Center
- Tablet PC support
- Windows DVD Maker
- Scheduled Backup
- Next Generation Gaming support
- Windows SideShow support

Windows Vista Business

This edition of Windows Vista will suit the needs of most business users, including small- and medium-sized businesses and enterprises. Windows Vista Business includes all the features included with Windows Vista Home Basic, plus:

- Aero user interface
- Tablet PC support

- Backup and restore capabilities (including Complete PC Backup, Automatic File backup, and ShadowCopy Backup)

- Core business features including joining domains, Group Policy support, and Encrypting File System (EFS)

- Fax And Scan

- Small Business resources

Windows Vista Business is available through volume licensing.

Windows Vista Enterprise

This edition builds on the Windows Vista Business feature set, adding:

- **Windows BitLocker Drive Encryption**   This encrypts all the files on your system disk to help protect you from data theft if an attacker gains physical access to your hard disk.

- **All worldwide interface languages**   This makes deployment easier in enterprises with offices in different countries and cultures.

- **Licensing rights to four virtual operating systems**   This makes it possible to run multiple versions of Windows within virtual machines—perfect for testing software or for running applications that require earlier versions of Windows.

- **The Subsystem for UNIX-based Applications (SUA)**   This can be used to compile and run POSIX applications in Windows.

Windows Vista Enterprise is available through Software Assurance and Enterprise Advantage.

Windows Vista Ultimate

Windows Vista Ultimate includes every feature provided with all other versions of Windows, including both Windows Vista Home Premium and Windows Vista Enterprise. Users who might use their computers both for work and personal use should choose Windows Vista Ultimate. Similarly, users who never want to find themselves missing a Windows feature in the future should choose Windows Vista Ultimate.

Business customers who choose Windows Vista Ultimate will encounter several drawbacks:

- **Deployment**   Volume licensing keys are not available for Windows Vista Ultimate. Its deployment and manageability in an enterprise scenario are not efficient for IT professionals to carry out, because each install requires manual and single-handled implementation. Furthermore, if customers acquire Windows Vista Ultimate through

OEMs, they won't have access to reimaging rights, which allow customers to install a standard corporate image instead of using the OEM's preinstalled operating system.

- **Manageability** Windows Vista Ultimate contains consumer features, such as Windows Media Center, that cannot be easily managed via Group Policy.

- **Support** Windows Vista Ultimate is not covered under Premier support: Companies that have installed Windows Vista Ultimate will need to get their support directly from their hardware manufacturers. In addition, the servicing policy for a consumer operating system such as Ultimate is limited to 5 years, rather than the 10 years for a business servicing policy, as is applicable to Windows Vista Enterprise.

Despite these drawbacks, Windows Vista Ultimate is available through Software Assurance at no additional charge. Business customers should choose Windows Vista Enterprise for most computers and install Windows Vista Ultimate only on specific computers that require media or home features.

Choosing Hardware

Windows Vista is designed to work with computer hardware that supports Windows XP and can even outperform Windows XP on the same hardware. Windows Vista is also designed to take advantage of modern hardware capabilities. The following sections describe the different Windows Vista logos and hardware requirements, which can help you choose hardware capable of providing the Windows Vista features you need.

Windows Vista Logos

Microsoft provides Windows Vista logos for hardware and software vendors to show that the product has been tested to work with Windows Vista. Two tiers of the logo, basic and premium, now help simplify purchasing decisions. The basic logo indicates a product has baseline functionality; the premium logo indicates a product will deliver advanced features such as Aero, Windows Media Center, Windows Movie Maker HD, and Meeting Space. Table 1-4 shows the different logos.

Table 1-4   Windows Vista Family of Logos

Logo Tier	On Computers	On Software and Devices	On Games
Premium logo	 Windows Vista™	CERTIFIED FOR Windows Vista™	 Games for Windows
Basic logo	Windows Vista™ BASIC	Works with Windows Vista™	

Software and hardware without the logo will probably work with your Windows Vista computers. However, setup might be more difficult, you might need to manually locate drivers, and applications might have compatibility problems.

Hardware Requirements

For the Windows Vista basic experience, a computer requires:

- A modern processor (at least 800 MHz)
- 512 MB of system memory
- A graphics processor that is DirectX 9–capable

For the Windows Vista premium experience, a computer requires:

- 1 GHz 32-bit (x86) or 64-bit (x64) processor
- 1 GB of system memory
- Support for DirectX 9 graphics with a Windows Display Driver Model (WDDM) driver, 128 MB of graphics memory (minimum), Pixel Shader 2.0, and 32 bits-per-pixel

- 40 GB of hard drive capacity with 15 GB free space
- DVD-ROM drive
- Audio output capability
- Internet access capability

Summary

Windows Vista includes many significant improvements from previous versions of Windows. Users will immediately notice the improved user interface, which is designed specifically to enhance user productivity. Performance improvements will help reduce annoying delays and make the most of legacy computer hardware. Mobile users will find it much easier to manage power and wireless networking capabilities, and users with Tablet PCs will benefit from the improved pen behavior and handwriting recognition.

Most Windows Vista improvements are designed to improve the efficiency of IT departments, however. Windows Vista deployment offers the efficiency of image-based deployment without requiring the use of third-party tools. Improved reliability, supportability, and troubleshooting capabilities can reduce the number of support center calls and allow IT professionals to resolve problems that must still be escalated more quickly.

Windows Vista is available in several different editions; however, most IT professionals will choose Windows Vista Business or Windows Vista Enterprise. You can probably deploy Windows Vista using your existing computer hardware. If you do need to purchase additional computers, you must understand the varying hardware requirements for different Windows Vista features.

This chapter provides only an overview of significant improvements. The remainder of this Resource Kit discusses improvements in depth and provides detailed information about how to manage Windows Vista in enterprise environments.

Additional Resources

These resources contain additional information and tools related to this chapter.

Related Information

- Chapter 2, "Security in Windows Vista," includes an overview of security improvements.
- Chapter 3, "Deployment Platform," explains Windows Vista deployment.
- Chapter 15, "Managing Disks and File Systems," includes more information about ReadyBoost, ReadyDrive, BitLocker Drive Encryption, and Encrypting File System.
- Chapter 16, "Managing Devices and Services," includes detailed information about improvements to managing drivers.

- Chapter 18, "Managing Windows Meeting Space," includes more information about Meeting Space.

- Chapter 22, "Maintaining Desktop Health," includes more information about Windows Resource Protection.

- Chapter 24, "Managing Software Updates," includes information about Automatic Updates and driver updates from Microsoft.

- Chapter 30, "Configuring Startup and Troubleshooting Startup Issues," includes information about the Startup Repair tool.

- Chapter 31, "Troubleshooting Hardware, Driver, and Disk Issues," includes information about improved hardware diagnostics.

- Chapter 32, "Troubleshooting Network Issues," includes information about Windows Vista network diagnostics.

On the Companion CD

- A link to where you can download the latest version of the whitepaper "Kernel Enhancements for Windows Vista and Windows Server 2008"

- GetWindowsVersion.vbs

- GetWindowsInstallation.vbs

- VistaUpgradeReadiness.vbs

- GetProcessorArchetecture.vbs

Chapter 2
Security in Windows Vista

To create Windows Vista, Microsoft examined every operating system component to find ways to improve the security. This examination resulted in thousands of minor security improvements throughout the Windows operating system code. Although these improvements are too numerous to mention individually, a number of significant security improvements are important enough for you to understand how they will impact your networks.

This chapter provides an overview of the most important Windows Vista security improvements, explains how they can improve common security scenarios, and offers information about how you can use these security improvements to meet your organization's security requirements. In most cases, you will find more detailed information about each security feature in other chapters of this Resource Kit. This chapter cross-references the more detailed chapters.

Addressing Specific Security Concerns with Windows Vista

Windows Vista includes many new and improved security technologies. Although understanding security technologies often requires more detailed knowledge, the security scenarios that these technologies serve are practical and straightforward. The sections that follow describe how Windows Vista security features work together to improve the security in regard to three major, common concerns: wireless networks, spyware and other kinds of malware, and network worms.

Each security technology is discussed in more detail later in this chapter and elsewhere in this Resource Kit.

Wireless Networks

Wireless networks have improved user productivity by allowing people to connect to the Internet and to their internal networks from almost anywhere—meeting rooms, airports, hotels, coffee shops, and thousands of other wireless hotspots. However, public wireless networks are almost never encrypted, and even private wireless networks might fail to meet your organization's security requirements. Note that a *wired* public Internet connection carries the same risk. Public connections of any kind must be clear-text at Layer 2 because you don't have the opportunity to exchange security keys. For this reason, it's imperative that you use a virtual private network (VPN) to encrypt your data when connecting to your internal network over a public network.

Wireless networking was built into Windows XP, and it is also built into Windows Vista. However, Windows Vista provides significant improvements to the manageability, and thus the security, of wireless networking. With Windows Vista, you can configure wireless security settings for mobile clients in your organization using Active Directory Group Policy or automated scripts. You can also configure Windows Firewall to block all incoming requests from public wireless networks (the default), while allowing specific incoming requests when connected to your internal network.

Windows Vista also makes connecting to private wireless networks more secure. *Wireless Single Sign-On* can connect to a wireless network before the user authenticates to the Active Directory domain. Windows Vista also supports the latest wireless security, including *Wi-Fi Protected Access 2 (WPA2)*. For more information about wireless networking improvements in Windows Vista, see Chapter 26, "Configuring Windows Networking."

Help Desk Calls Related to Malware

Security threats have constantly changed to adapt to each new generation of operating system. In the past several years, the prevalence of *malware* (a broad term that encompasses viruses, worms, Trojan horses, and rootkits, as well as spyware and other potentially unwanted software) has soared.

> **Note**   Microsoft uses the term *spyware and potentially unwanted software* to refer to software that is unwanted but is not unambiguously harmful. In this book, the definition of malware includes both clearly malicious viruses and worms and the more ambiguous spyware and potentially unwanted software.

Viruses, worms, and Trojan horses can spread from computer to computer by exploiting software vulnerabilities or tricking users with *social engineering* techniques. Spyware and potentially unwanted software spread via these techniques and also by legitimate installations initiated by users. Users will install an application, unaware of the undesired functionality of the program or of a program that is bundled with the application.

Because of the challenges in identifying malware, it might be impossible to eliminate the threat completely. However, Windows Vista has many new security features to protect computers from malware. Most significantly, User Account Control (UAC) limits the ability of malware to install by enabling IT professionals to deploy users as Standard users, rather than administrators. This helps prevent users from making potentially dangerous changes to their computers without limiting their ability to control other aspects on their computers, such as time zone or power settings. For anyone who does log on as an administrator, UAC makes it more difficult for malware to have a computer-wide impact.

Similarly, the Protected Mode of Internet Explorer runs Internet Explorer without the necessary privileges to install software (or even write files outside of the Temporary Internet Files directory), thereby reducing the risk that Internet Explorer can be abused to install malware without the user's consent. Windows Defender detects many types of spyware and other potentially unwanted software and prompts the user before applications can make potentially malicious changes. Windows Service Hardening limits the damage attackers can do in the event that they are able to successfully compromise a service, thereby reducing the risk of attackers making permanent changes to the operating system or attacking other computers on the network. Although Windows Vista cannot eliminate malware, these new technologies can significantly reduce malware-associated costs.

Windows Vista is designed to block many types of common malware installation techniques. The sections that follow describe how Windows Vista protects against malware that attempts to install without the user's knowledge through bundling and social engineering, browser exploits, and network worms.

> **Note**   Although rootkits can be very difficult to detect because they operate below the operating system level, Microsoft offers a free tool named RootkitRevealer that can help with the detection process. To download RootkitRevealer, visit *http://technet.microsoft.com/en-us/ sysinternals/bb897445.aspx*.

Protecting Against Bundling and Social Engineering

Two of the most common ways malware becomes installed on a computer are bundling and social engineering. With bundling, malware is packaged with useful software. Often the user is not aware of the negative aspects of the bundled software. With social engineering, the user is tricked into installing the software. Typically, the user receives a misleading e-mail containing instructions to open an attachment or visit a website.

Windows Vista offers significantly improved protection against both bundling and social engineering. With the default settings of Windows Vista, malware that attempts to install via bundling or social engineering must circumvent two levels of protection: UAC and Windows Defender.

UAC either prompts the user to confirm the installation of the software (if the user is logged on with an administrative account) or prompts the user for administrative credentials (if the user is logged on with a Standard account). This feature makes users aware that a process is trying to make significant changes and allows them to stop the process. Standard users are required to contact an administrator to continue the installation. For more information, see the section titled "User Account Control" later in this chapter.

Windows Defender real-time protection blocks applications that are identified as malicious. Windows Defender also detects and stops changes the malware might attempt to make, such as configuring the malware to run automatically upon a reboot. Windows Defender notifies the user that an application has attempted to make a change and gives the user the opportunity to block or proceed with the installation. For more information, see the section titled "Windows Defender" later in this chapter.

Note   Windows Defender adds events to the System Event Log. Combined with event subscriptions or a tool such as Microsoft Systems Center Operations Manager (SCOM), you can easily aggregate and analyze Windows Defender events for your organization.

These levels of protection are illustrated in Figure 2-1.

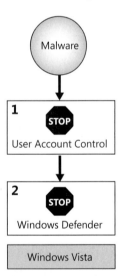

Figure 2-1   Windows Vista uses defense-in-depth to protect against bundling and social engineering malware attacks.

With Windows XP and earlier versions of Windows, bundling and social engineering malware installations were likely to succeed, because none of these protections was included with the operating system or service packs.

Defense-in-Depth

Defense-in-depth is a proven technique of layered protection that reduces the exposure of vulnerabilities. For example, you might design a network with three layers of packet filtering: a packet-filtering router, a hardware firewall, and software firewalls on each of the hosts (such as Internet Connection Firewall). If an attacker manages to bypass one or two of the layers of protection, the hosts are still protected.

The real benefit of defense-in-depth is its ability to protect against human error. Whereas a single layer of defense is sufficient to protect you under normal circumstances, an administrator who disables the defense during troubleshooting, an accidental misconfiguration, or a newly discovered vulnerability can disable that single layer of defense. Defense-in-depth provides protection even when a single vulnerability exists.

Although most new Windows Vista security features are preventative countermeasures that focus on directly mitigating risk by blocking vulnerabilities from being exploited, your defense-in-depth strategy should also include detective and reactive countermeasures. Auditing and third-party intrusion-detection systems can help to analyze an attack after the fact, enabling administrators to block future attacks and possibly identify the attacker. Backups and a disaster recovery plan enable you to react to an attack and limit the potential data lost.

Protecting Against Browser Exploit Malware Installations

Historically, many malware installations have occurred because the user visited a malicious website, and the website exploited a vulnerability in the web browser to install the malware. In some cases, users received no warning that software was being installed. In other cases, users were prompted to confirm the installation, but the prompt might have been misleading or incomplete.

Windows Vista provides four layers of protection against this type of malware installation:

- Automatic Updates, enabled by default, helps keep Internet Explorer and the rest of the operating system up to date with security updates that can fix many security vulnerabilities. Automatic Updates can obtain security updates from either Microsoft.com or from an internal Windows Server Update Services server. For more information, read Chapter 24, "Managing Software Updates."

- Internet Explorer Protected Mode provides only extremely limited rights to processes launched by Internet Explorer, even if the user is logged on as an administrator. Any process launched from Internet Explorer has access only to the temporary Internet files directory. Any file written to that directory cannot be executed.

- For administrators, UAC prompts the user to confirm before computer-wide configuration changes are made. For Standard users, the limited privileges block most permanent per-computer changes unless the user can provide administrative credentials.

- Windows Defender notifies the user if malware attempts to install itself as a browser helper object, start itself automatically after a reboot, or modify another monitored aspect of the operating system.

These levels of protection are illustrated in Figure 2-2.

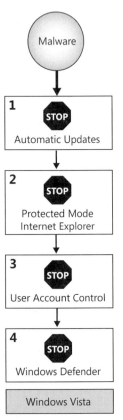

Figure 2-2   Windows Vista uses defense-in-depth to protect against browser exploit malware installations.

Protecting Against Network Worms

Bundling, social engineering, and browser exploits all rely on the user to initiate a connection to a site that hosts malware, but worms can infect a computer without any interaction from the user. Network worms spread by sending network communications across a network to exploit a vulnerability in remote computers and install the worm. After it is installed, the worm continues looking for new computers to infect.

If the worm attacks a Windows Vista computer, Windows Vista offers four levels of protection:

- Windows Firewall blocks all incoming traffic that has not been explicitly permitted (plus a few exceptions for core networking functionality in the domain and private profiles). This feature blocks the majority of all current worm attacks.

- If the worm attacks an updated vulnerability in a Microsoft component, Automatic Updates—which is enabled by default—might have already addressed the security vulnerability.

- If the worm exploits a vulnerability in a service that uses Windows Service Hardening and attempts to take an action that the service profile does not allow (such as saving a file or adding the worm to the startup group), Windows Vista will block the worm.

- If the worm exploits a vulnerability in a user application, limited privileges enabled by UAC block system-wide configuration changes.

These levels of protection are illustrated in Figure 2-3.

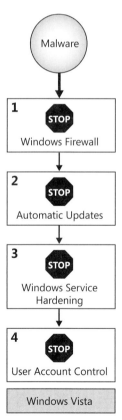

Figure 2-3   Windows Vista uses defense-in-depth to protect against network worms.

The original release of Windows XP lacked all of these levels of protections. With Windows XP Service Pack 2, Windows Firewall and Automatic Updates are enabled, but the other levels of protection offered by Windows Vista are unavailable.

Data Theft

As mobile computers, network connectivity, and removable media have become more common, so has data theft. Many businesses and government organizations store extremely valuable data on their computers, and the cost of having the data fall into the wrong hands could be devastating.

Today, many organizations mitigate the risk of data theft by limiting access to data. For example, applications might not allow confidential files to be stored on mobile computers. Or, users simply might not be allowed to remove computers from the office. These limitations do successfully reduce the risk, but they also reduce employee productivity by not allowing the staff to benefit from mobile computing.

Windows Vista provides data protection technologies designed to meet stricter security requirements while still allowing users to work with confidential data in a variety of locations. Consider the following common data theft scenarios, and how Windows Vista mitigates the risks of each.

Physical Theft of a Mobile Computer or a Hard Disk, or Recovering Data from a Recycled or Discarded Hard Disk

Operating systems can provide active protection for the data stored on your hard disk only while the operating system is running. In other words, file access control lists (such as that provided by NTFS) cannot protect data if an attacker can physically access a computer or hard disk. In recent years, there have been many cases of stolen mobile computers whose confidential data was extracted from the hard disk. Data is often recovered from computers that are recycled (by assigning an existing computer to a new user) or discarded (at the end of a computer's life), even if the hard disk had been formatted.

Windows Vista reduces the risk of this type of data theft by allowing administrators to encrypt files stored on the disk. As with Windows XP, Windows Vista supports *Encrypting File System (EFS)*. EFS enables administrators and users to selectively encrypt files or to mark an entire folder to encrypt all files it contains. In addition to the capabilities offered by Windows XP, Windows Vista enables you to configure EFS using Group Policy settings so that you can centrally protect an entire domain without requiring users to understand encryption.

EFS cannot protect Windows system files, however. Protecting Windows from offline attack (booting from removable media to access the file system directly or moving the hard disk to a different computer) helps ensure the integrity of the operating system even if a computer is stolen. BitLocker Drive Encryption, new to Windows Vista, provides encryption for the entire system volume—thus protecting not only the operating system but also any data stored on the same volume (drive letter). BitLocker can work transparently with supported hardware, or it can require multifactor authentication by requiring users to enter a password before allowing the volume to be decrypted. Depending on your security requirements, you can use BitLocker with existing computer hardware by storing the decryption keys on removable media or even having users type in a decryption key before Windows boots.

Copying Confidential Files to Removable Media

Organizations with strict security requirements often limit access to confidential data to computers on the local network, and then do not allow those computers to be removed from the facility. Historically, these organizations would remove floppy drives from the computers to prevent users from saving confidential files. Recently, however, there has been a huge increase in the types of removable media available. Specifically, mobile phones, PDAs, portable audio players, and USB drives often have several gigabytes of storage capacity. Because they are small and extremely common, they might be overlooked even if a facility has security staff available to search employees entering or leaving a building.

Windows Vista enables you to use Group Policy settings to limit the risk of removable media. Using the Group Policy settings in Computer Configuration\Policies\Administrative Templates\System\Device Installation\Device Installation Restrictions, administrators can:

- Allow installation of entire classes of devices (such as printers) using the Allow Installation Of Devices Using Drivers That Match These Device Setup Classes setting.

- Disallow all unsupported or unauthorized devices using the Prevent Installation Of Devices That Match Any Of These Device IDs setting.

- Disallow any kind of removable storage device using the Prevent Installation Of Removable Devices setting.

- Override these policies if necessary for troubleshooting or management purposes using the Allow Administrators To Override Device Installation Policy setting.

For more information on managing devices, see Chapter 16, "Managing Devices and Services." For more information on using Group Policy to manage Windows Vista computers, see Chapter 13, "Managing the Desktop Environment."

Accidentally Printing, Copying, or Forwarding Confidential Documents

Often, users need to share confidential documents to collaborate efficiently. For example, a user might e-mail a document to another user for review. However, when the document is copied from your protected shared folder or intranet, you lose control of the document. Users might accidentally copy, forward, or print the document, where it can be found by a user who shouldn't have access.

There's no perfect solution to protect electronic documents from copying. However, the *Rights Management Services (RMS)* client, built into Windows Vista, enables Windows Vista computers to open RMS-encrypted documents and enforce the restrictions applied to the document. With an RMS infrastructure and an application that supports RMS, such as Microsoft Office, you can:

- Allow a user to view a document, but not save a copy of it, print it, or forward it.

- Restrict users from copying and pasting text within a document.

- Make it very difficult to open the document using a client that does not enforce RMS protection.

To use RMS, you need an RMS infrastructure and supported applications in addition to Windows Vista. However, Windows Vista is a key part of RMS. For more information about RMS, see the section titled "Rights Management Services (RMS)" later in this chapter.

New and Improved Windows Vista Security Features

This section describes the most visible and tangible Windows Vista security improvements, which are listed in Table 2-1. Architectural and internal improvements—as well as improvements that require additional applications or infrastructure—are described later in this chapter.

Table 2-1 Windows Vista Security Improvements

Improvement	Description
User Account Control	Reduces the risk of malware using user privileges to make unwanted changes.
Windows Defender	Attempts to detect and block unwanted software.
Windows Firewall	Filters incoming and outgoing network traffic. New improvements provide greater flexibility and manageability.
Internet Explorer Protected Mode	Reduces risks associated with visiting websites, such as installing malware or visiting fraudulent sites.
BitLocker	Encrypts the entire system volume.
Encrypting File System	Encrypts files and folders other than system files. Improvements provide greater flexibility and manageability.
Auditing enhancements	Provide more granular control over which events are audited.
Smart card improvements	Simplify deployment and management of smart cards.
Credential Manager enhancements	Enable users to perform common credential management security tasks, such as resetting PINs.

The sections that follow describe these features in more detail. For detailed recommendations on how to configure Windows Vista security settings, refer to the Windows Vista Security Guide, available at *http://www.microsoft.com/downloads/details.aspx?FamilyID=a3d1bbed-7f35-4e72-bfb5-b84a526c1565*. For an interesting description of how Windows Vista security changes have led to real-world improvements, read "Windows Vista Security One Year Later" at *http://blogs.msdn.com/windowsvistasecurity/archive/2008/01/23/windows-vista-security-one-year-later.aspx*.

User Account Control (UAC)

Over the years, the most common security threats have changed from viruses, to worms, and most recently, to spyware and Trojan horses. To help protect users from these types of malicious software, Microsoft recommends using accounts with limited privileges (known as Standard user accounts in Windows Vista, or Limited user accounts in Windows XP). Standard user accounts help prevent malware from making system-wide changes such as installing software that affects multiple users—if a user lacks permission to install a new application to a shared location such as %SystemRoot%\Program Files, any malware the user accidentally runs is also prevented from making those changes. In other words, malware run in the context of the user account has the same security restrictions as the user.

Although Standard user accounts do improve security, using Standard user accounts with Windows XP and earlier versions of Windows results in two major problems:

- Users cannot install software, change the system time or time zone, install printers, change power settings, add a WEP key for wireless settings, or perform other common tasks that require elevated privileges.

- Many poorly written applications require administrative privileges and do not run correctly with limited privileges.

Although logging on to your computer as a Standard user offers better protection from malware, working with this type of account has been so difficult in the past that many organizations choose to give users administrative privileges on their computers. Windows Vista UAC is a set of features that offers the benefits of Standard user accounts without the unnecessary limitations. First, all users (including administrators) run with limited privileges by default. Second, Windows Vista allows Standard user accounts to change the time zone (but not the time) and perform other common tasks without providing administrative credentials, which enables organizations to configure more users with Standard accounts. Third, UAC enables most applications—even those that require administrative privileges on Windows XP—to run correctly in Standard user accounts.

Direct from the Source: How Users Are Prompted When Permission Is Denied

Many enterprises are starting to lock down their users even on Windows XP in an attempt to improve security and to comply with various regulations. Windows Vista allows you to lock down these users even more by giving the users an "Access Denied by Policy" message box when they attempt to do something that would require elevated privileges. You can configure this by defining the User Account Control: Behavior Of The Elevation Prompt For Standard Users Group Policy setting as No Prompt.

Steve Hiskey

Lead Program Manager, Windows Security Core

Admin Approval Mode

With Windows XP and earlier versions of Windows, any process started by a user logged on as an administrator would be run with administrative privileges. This situation was troublesome, because malware could make system-wide changes, such as installing software, without confirmation from the user. In Windows Vista, members of the Administrators group run in *Admin Approval Mode*, which (by default) prompts administrators to confirm actions that require more than Standard privileges. For example, even though a user might log on as an administrator, Windows Messenger and Windows Mail will run only with Standard user privileges.

To do this, Admin Approval Mode creates two access tokens when a member of the Administrators local group logs on: one token with full permissions and a second, restricted token that mimics the token of a Standard user. The lower-privilege token is used for nonadministrative tasks, and the privileged token is used only after the user's explicit consent. As shown in Figure 2-4, Windows Vista prompts the user for consent before completing an action that requires administrative privileges.

Figure 2-4   UAC prompts Administrators to confirm administrative actions.

Many organizations will use the benefits of UAC to create Standard, rather than Administrator, user accounts. Admin Approval Mode offers some protection for those users who need administrator privileges—such as developers—by requiring confirmation before an application makes any potentially malicious changes. Like most Windows Vista security improvements, the consent prompt is enabled by default but can be disabled using Group Policy settings. Additionally, the consent prompt can require the user to type an administrative password or, for Standard users, simply inform them that access is not permitted.

Direct from the Source: Developers Should Run as Standard Users

One of my favorite aspects of Windows Vista is the trend toward reducing the privilege that applications run with by default. This protects users from damaging their computers unknowingly and further allows for trust in the fidelity of the operating system. Unfortunately, many developers make a common mistake that prevents their code from running well in a lesser-privileged environment: They run as administrators! If you are

---

writing a new application for Windows Vista, you should be designing and running your application as a Standard user. This is the easiest way for you as a developer to understand the impact of User Account Control and the other technologies that will affect your code.

Chris Corio

Program Manager, Windows Security

Enabling Non-Administrators to Make Configuration Changes

Standard user accounts in Windows Vista can make configuration changes that don't compromise the computer's security. For example, Standard user accounts in Windows Vista have the right to change the time zone on their computers, an important setting for users who travel. In Windows XP, ordinary user accounts do not have this right by default, an inconvenience that causes many IT professionals to deploy accounts for mobile users as administrators and sacrifice the security benefits of using ordinary user accounts. Additionally, Standard users can now connect to encrypted wireless networks and add VPN connections—two tasks commonly required by enterprises.

However, Standard user accounts in Windows Vista do not have the right to change the system time, because many applications and services rely on an accurate system clock. As shown in Figure 2-5, a user who attempts to change the time is prompted for administrative credentials.

Figure 2-5   UAC prompts Standard users for Administrator credentials.

Some applications do not run in Windows XP without administrative privileges, because these applications attempt to make changes to file and registry locations that affect the entire computer (for example, C:\Program Files, C:\Windows; HKEY_LOCAL_MACHINE), and Standard user accounts lack the necessary privileges. Registry and file virtualization in Windows Vista redirects many of these per-machine file and registry writes to per-user locations. This feature enables applications to be run by a Standard user, whereas on previous operating systems, these applications would have failed as Standard user. Ultimately, this will enable more organizations to use Standard user accounts because applications that would otherwise require administrative privileges can run successfully without any changes to the application.

Note   Do not confuse file and registry virtualization with operating system virtualization products such as Microsoft Virtual PC or Microsoft Virtual Server. File and registry virtualization virtualizes just those operating system components, not the computer's hardware.

For more information about UAC, see Chapter 25, "Managing Client Protection."

How It Works: File Virtualization

Windows Vista includes a filter driver extension to the file system that intercepts access-denied errors before the file operation can be returned to the application. If the file location that generated the access-denied error is in a place where the operating system is configured to virtualize data, a new file path is generated and retried without the application knowing that this has occurred.

Steve Hiskey

Lead Program Manager, Windows Security Core

Windows Defender

Windows Defender is a feature of Windows Vista that provides protection from spyware and other potentially unwanted software. Windows Defender is signature-based, using descriptions that uniquely identify spyware and other potentially unwanted software to detect and remove known applications. Windows Defender regularly retrieves new signatures from Microsoft so that it can identify and remove newly created spyware and other potentially unwanted software. Microsoft does not charge for signature updates.

Additionally, Windows Defender real-time protection monitors critical touchpoints in the operating system for changes usually made by spyware. Real-time protection scans every file as it is opened and also monitors the Startup folder, Run keys in the registry, Windows add-ons, and other areas of the operating system for changes. If an application attempts to make a change to one of the protected areas of the operating system, Windows Defender prompts the user to take appropriate action.

As shown in Figure 2-6, Windows Defender can also run a scan on-demand to detect and remove known spyware. By default, Windows Defender will scan Windows Vista computers daily at 2:00 A.M. for malware infections; however, you can configure this behavior. Although Windows Defender real-time protection attempts to prevent most infections, nightly scanning allows Windows Defender to detect and remove newly discovered malware that might have circumvented the defenses of real-time protection.

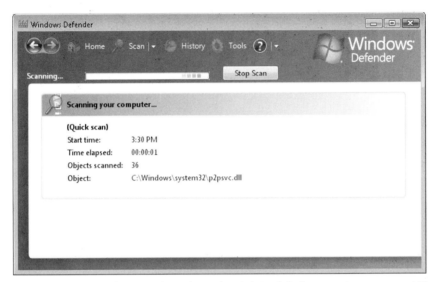

Figure 2-6   Users who suspect malware has infected their computer can run a Windows Defender scan on-demand.

The Microsoft SpyNet Community enables Windows Defender to communicate discoveries about new applications and whether users identify applications as malware or legitimate. Depending on how you configure Windows Defender, it can provide feedback to the SpyNet community about new applications and whether or not users choose to allow the application to be installed. Feedback from the SpyNet Community helps Microsoft and users distinguish malware from legitimate software, enabling Windows Defender to more accurately identify malware and reduce the number of false alarms. Providing private feedback to the SpyNet Community is optional; however, all users can benefit from the information gathered by the community.

In addition to these features, Windows Defender includes Software Explorer. Software Explorer provides users with control over many different types of applications, including applications that install themselves into the browser and into applications that start automatically. Software Explorer is primarily intended for users who manage their own computers. In enterprise environments, IT departments will typically handle software removal.

Windows Defender can also be installed on Windows XP with Service Pack 2. For more information about Windows Defender, see Chapter 25.

Windows Firewall

Windows Vista has an enhanced version of the Windows Firewall that was first included in Windows XP Service Pack 2. The Windows Firewall combines the functionality of a bidirectional host firewall and Internet Protocol security (IPsec) into a single, unified utility with a consistent user interface. Unlike a perimeter firewall, the Windows Firewall runs on each computer running Windows Vista and provides local protection from network attacks that might pass through your perimeter network or originate inside your organization. It also provides computer-to-computer connection security (IPsec) that allows you to require authentication and data protection for all communications.

The Windows Firewall is a stateful firewall, so it inspects and filters all TCP/IP version 4 (IPv4) and TCP/IP version 6 (IPv6) traffic. Unsolicited incoming traffic is dropped unless it is a response to a request by the host (solicited traffic) or it is specifically allowed (that is, it has been added to the exceptions list or permitted by an inbound rule). Outgoing traffic from interactive applications is allowed by default, but outgoing traffic from services is limited by the firewall to that which is required according to each service's profile in Windows Service Hardening. You can specify traffic to be added to the exceptions list and create inbound and outbound rules according to application name, service name, port number, destination network, domain membership, or other criteria by configuring Windows Firewall with Advanced Security settings.

For traffic that is allowed, the Windows Firewall also allows you to request or require that computers authenticate each other before communicating and to use data integrity and data encryption while exchanging traffic.

In Windows Vista, the Windows Firewall has many new features, including:

- **Management integration with IPsec**   Windows XP and earlier operating systems used two separate interfaces, even though the Windows Firewall and IPsec had a significant amount of feature overlap. Now, as Figure 2-7 shows, you can manage both using a single interface.

- **New user and command-line interfaces**   Improved interfaces simplify management and enable automated, scripted control over firewall settings.

- **Full IPv6 support**   If your organization uses IPv6, you can now take advantage of Windows Firewall.

- **Outbound filtering**   You can filter traffic being sent from a client computer as well as traffic being received by the computer. This enables you to restrict which applications can send traffic and where they can send it. For example, you might filter management alerts so that they can be sent only to your internal network. The outbound filtering feature in the Windows Firewall is not intended to prevent an infected computer from communicating, which is generally not possible (the malware might simply disable the firewall). Rather, outbound filtering allows administrators to assign policies to machines to prohibit known behavior, such as preventing unauthorized peer-to-peer software from communicating.

Figure 2-7   You can use a single tool to manage both Windows Firewall and IPsec.

- **Windows Service Hardening**   This feature limits the actions a service can take and also limits how the service communicates on the network, reducing the damage caused during a security compromise.

- **Full Group Policy integration**   This enables you to centrally configure the Windows Firewall on all computers in your Active Directory domain.

- **Filtering traffic by new properties**   The Windows Firewall can filter traffic by:

    - Active Directory groups (authorized users and authorized computers)

    - Internet Control Message Protocol (ICMP) extensions

    - IP address lists

    - Port lists

    - Service names

    - Authenticated by IPsec

❑   Encrypted by IPsec

❑   Interface type

■ **IP address authentication**   The Windows Firewall supports IP address authentication with the ability to have two rounds of authentication with different credentials in each, including user credentials if desired.

■ **Application-based IPsec policies**   The Windows Firewall now supports application-based IPsec policies.

■ **Simplified IPsec policy**   This type of policy makes it much easier to deploy Server and Domain Isolation. When configured with a simplified policy, client computers make two connections to a destination: one in clear-text and one with IPsec. The client computer will drop whichever connection does not receive a reply. With a single rule, then, client computers can adapt themselves to communicate with IPsec or in clear-text, whichever the destination supports.

For detailed information about the Windows Firewall, see Chapter 27, "Configuring Windows Firewall and IPsec."

Note   One of the biggest challenges of protecting computers is that security settings can degrade over time. For example, support desk personnel might change a security setting while troubleshooting a problem and forget to correct it. Even if you enable Automatic Updates, a mobile computer might fail to download updates while disconnected from the network. To help you detect security vulnerabilities, use Microsoft Baseline Security Analyzer (MBSA), available at *http://www.microsoft.com/technet/security/tools/mbsahome.mspx*. MBSA can audit security settings on multiple computers on your network. MBSA is also a great way to verify security settings on new computers before deploying them.

Internet Explorer Security Features

Microsoft Internet Explorer 7 Plus features a focus on the core security architecture changes that offer dynamic protection against data theft, fraudulent websites, and malicious and hidden software, as well as improvements to the platform for web developers. Microsoft has made architectural enhancements to Internet Explorer 7 that make it less of a target for attackers and other malicious people, which will help users browse with better peace of mind. However, as security is tightened, compatibility and extensibility tend to suffer. With Internet Explorer 7, Microsoft is working hard to ensure that this balance is met effectively so that users can have the safest and best possible browsing experience.

Note   The "Plus" in the name indicates the version of Internet Explorer 7 included in Windows Vista, which includes capabilities that do not exist in Internet Explorer 7 for Windows XP.

Internet Explorer 7 includes the following security features:

- **Internet Explorer Protected Mode**   In Protected Mode, Internet Explorer 7 runs with reduced permissions to help prevent user or system files or settings from changing without the user's explicit permission. The new browser architecture also introduces a "broker" process that helps to enable existing applications to elevate out of Protected Mode in a more secure way. This additional defense helps verify that scripted actions or automatic processes are prevented from downloading data outside of the low-rights directories such as the Temporary Internet Files folder. Protected Mode is available only when using Internet Explorer 7 with Windows Vista when UAC is enabled. Protected Mode is not available in the version of Internet Explorer 7 for Windows XP.

- **URL handling protections**   Internet Explorer 7 has a single function to process URL data, significantly reducing the internal attack surface. This new data handler ensures greater reliability while providing more features and increased flexibility to address the changing nature of the Internet as well as the globalization of URLs, international character sets, and domain names.

- **ActiveX Opt-In**   ActiveX Opt-In automatically disables all controls that the developer has not explicitly identified for use on the Internet. This mitigates the potential misuse of preinstalled controls. In Windows Vista, users are prompted by the Information Bar before they can access a previously installed ActiveX Control that has not yet been used on the Internet but has been designed to be used on the Internet. This notification mechanism enables the user to permit or deny access on a control-by-control basis, further reducing available surface area for attacks. Web sites that attempt automated attacks can no longer secretly attempt to exploit ActiveX Controls that were never intended to be used on the Internet.

- **Protection against cross-domain scripting attacks**   New cross-domain script barriers help protect users from cross-domain attacks, which attempt to transfer cookies and other information to domains that should not have access to them. This adds further protection against malware by limiting the ability of malicious websites to manipulate vulnerabilities in other sites and initiate the download of undesired content to a user's computer.

- **Fix My Settings**   Most users install and operate applications using the default configuration, so Internet Explorer 7 ships with security settings that provide the maximum level of usability while maintaining controlled security. In rare instances, a custom application might legitimately require a user to lower security settings from the default, but it is critical that the user reverse those changes when the custom settings are no longer needed. The Fix My Settings feature warns users with an Information Bar when current security settings might put them at risk. Clicking the Fix My Settings option in the Information Bar instantly resets Internet Explorer 7 security settings to the Medium-High default level. In Active Directory environments, you can configure the required permissions for internal applications, so security restrictions do not need to be a concern.

- **Phishing filters and window restrictions**   Phishing websites attempt to use social engineering techniques to trick users into providing private information. For example, a website might impersonate an intranet site to trick the user into typing his or her user name and password. The Phishing filter works by analyzing site content for known characteristics of phishing techniques, and by using a global network of data sources to assess whether a site should be trusted. Additionally, all windows display the address bar, and scripts can no longer conceal the address bar. This makes it easier for users to identify the source of a website and makes it obvious that a window is in fact from a site and not from the operating system, thus mitigating certain social engineering attempts to steal a user's password by mimicking a logon dialog box. Additionally, scripts can be restricted from opening, resizing, or repositioning windows.

- **Security Status Bar**   The new Security Status Bar in Internet Explorer 7 helps users quickly differentiate authentic websites from suspicious or malicious ones by enhancing access to digital certificate information that helps validate the trustworthiness of e-commerce sites. The new Security Status Bar also provides users with clearer, more prominent visual cues indicating the safety and trustworthiness of a site, and it supports information about High Assurance certificates for stronger identification of secure sites (such as banking sites).

Additionally, each of these features is configurable by using Group Policy, enabling centralized control over Internet Explorer security. For more information about Internet Explorer, refer to Chapter 21, "Managing Internet Explorer."

BitLocker

Using BitLocker Drive Encryption, organizations can reduce the risk of confidential data being lost when a user's mobile PC is stolen. Its full-volume encryption seals the symmetric encryption key in a Trusted Platform Module (TPM) 1.2 chip (available in some newer computers) or a USB flash drive. BitLocker has two TPM modes:

- **TPM only**   This is transparent to the user, and the user logon experience is unchanged. However, if the TPM is missing or changed, BitLocker will enter recovery mode, and you will need a recovery key or PIN to regain access to the data. This provides protection from hard-disk theft with no user training necessary.

- **TPM with startup key**   The user will also need a startup key to log on to the computer. A startup key can be either physical (a USB flash drive with a computer-readable key written to it) or personal (a password set by the user). This provides protection from both hard-disk theft and stolen computers (assuming the computer was shut down or locked); however, it requires some effort from the user.

 Note   To manage TPM chips, Windows Vista includes the TPM Management snap-in.

BitLocker works by storing "measurements" of various parts of the computer and operating system in the TPM chip. In its default configuration, BitLocker instructs the TPM to measure the master boot record, the active boot partition, the boot sector, the Windows Boot Manager, and the BitLocker storage root key. Each time the computer is booted, the TPM computes the SHA-1 hash of the measured code and compares this to the hash stored in the TPM from the previous boot. If the hashes match, the boot process continues; if the hashes do not match, the boot process halts. At the conclusion of a successful boot process, the TPM releases the storage root key to BitLocker; BitLocker decrypts data as Windows reads it from the protected volume.

BitLocker protects Windows from offline attacks. An offline attack is a scenario in which an attacker starts an alternate operating system to gain control of the computer. The TPM releases the storage root key only when instructed to by BitLocker running within the instance of Windows Vista that initially created the key. Because no other operating system can do this (even an alternate instance of Windows Vista), the TPM never releases the key, and therefore the volume remains a useless encrypted blob. Any attempts to modify the protected volume will render it unbootable.

Note   Prior to SP1, BitLocker Drive Encryption could protect only the Windows partition. To protect other partitions, before SP1, users could use EFS. After installing SP1, you can use BitLocker Drive Encryption to encrypt any partition. However, you should still use EFS to protect data when multiple users use the same computer.

As shown in Figure 2-8, individual users can enable BitLocker from the Control Panel. Most enterprises should use Active Directory to manage keys, however.

Figure 2-8   You can enable BitLocker from the Control Panel.

Key management and data recovery requirements are the primary reason BitLocker is targeted towards enterprises. As with any type of encryption, if you lose the key, you also lose access to your data. Just as if you were a malicious attacker, the entire Windows partition will be inaccessible without the key. The most effective way to manage keys is to leverage an enterprise's existing Active Directory Domain Services infrastructure to remotely escrow recovery keys. BitLocker also has a disaster recovery console integrated into the early boot components to provide for "in the field" data retrieval. Individual users can use the BitLocker key-management tools to create a recovery key or an additional startup key and store the key on removable media (or any location besides the encrypted volume). Administrators can create scripts to automate key creation and recovery.

BitLocker provides an important layer of protection, but it is only one part of Windows Vista data protection. BitLocker:

- DOES make it very difficult for an attacker to gain access to your data from a stolen computer or hard disk.

- DOES encrypt the entire Windows volume, including the hibernation file, the page file, and temporary files (unless they are moved to some other volume).

- DOES allow you to easily recycle or reuse drives by simply deleting the encryption keys.

- DOES NOT protect data from network attacks.

- DOES NOT protect data while Windows is running.

- DOES NOT protect data on volumes other than the Windows partition. Use EFS to encrypt data on other volumes.

Other security technologies, such as EFS, Windows Firewall, and NTFS file permissions, provide data protection while Windows is running. For more information about BitLocker, see Chapter 15, "Managing Disks and File Systems."

The Three Pillars of Information Security

The three pillars of information security are known as the *CIA triad*:

- **Confidentiality**   Let people who should see your data access it, but nobody else.

- **Integrity**   Know who has created, viewed, and modified your data, and prevent unauthorized changes and impersonations of legitimate users.

- **Availability**   Allow users to access data when they need it, even when attacks and natural disasters occur.

BitLocker provides confidentiality by encrypting data and making it more difficult for an attacker who has physical access to a hard drive to access that data. BitLocker can also provide integrity by detecting changes to critical system files. It does not improve availability, however. In fact, if you don't plan to quickly recover systems with lost keys, BitLocker might reduce availability.

> **Direct from the Source: Trustworthy Administrators**
>
> Do you trust your administrators? It's a serious question, and it deserves serious thought. I asked this question in a packed seminar room of nearly 1,000 attendees listening to my presentation on security policies and, astonishingly, no one raised a hand. That frightened me and even left me speechless for a few moments—and those who know me will admit this is an uncommon occurrence! If we can't trust the very people we hire to build and manage the mission-critical networks upon which our business successes depend, we might as well unplug it all and revert to the days of stone knives and bearskins.
>
> Administrators have nearly or absolutely unfettered access to everything in your network. That's a lot of power concentrated in a few people—power that can be used for good or abused for bad. What are you doing to help ensure that the people you entrust with such power will use it only for good?
>
> To put it boldly: You must trust your administrators. You need a process for interviewing, investigating, hiring, monitoring, and terminating these employees. I know that many of you reading this book are administrators, and might be getting a bit incensed at what I'm writing. You're probably thinking, "Who is he to assume I'm malicious?" But recall my TechEd experiment: In an audience composed of (presumably) mostly administrators, zero percent said they trusted other administrators. That's got to mean something. Technical measures can make it more difficult for malicious administrators to carry out their ill will, but sufficiently motivated people will find ways around the protection. Administrators who can't be trusted really must be replaced; there's no other alternative.
>
> *Steve Riley*
>
> *Senior Security Strategist*

Encrypting File System (EFS)

EFS is a file encryption technology (supported only on NTFS volumes) that protects files from offline attacks such as hard-disk theft. EFS is entirely transparent to end users, because encrypted files behave exactly like unencrypted files. However, if a user does not have the correct decryption key, the file is impossible to open, even if an attacker bypasses the operating system security.

EFS is especially useful for securing sensitive data on mobile PCs or on computers that several users share. Both kinds of systems are susceptible to attack by techniques that circumvent the restrictions of access control lists (ACLs). An attacker can steal a computer, remove the hard disk drives, place the drives in another system, and gain access to the stored files. Files encrypted by EFS, however, appear as unintelligible characters when the attacker does not have the decryption key.

Windows Vista includes the following new features for EFS:

- Storing both user and recovery keys on smart cards. If smart cards are used for logon, EFS operates in a Single Sign-On mode, where it uses the logon smart card for file encryption without further prompting for the PIN. New wizards guide users through the process of creating and selecting smart card keys, as well as the process of migrating their encryption keys from an old smart card to a new one. The command-line utilities for smart cards have also been enhanced to include these features. Storing encryption keys on smart cards provides especially strong protection for mobile and shared computer scenarios.

- Encrypting the system page file.

For more information about EFS, see Chapter 15.

Auditing Enhancements

Windows Vista auditing is very granular, allowing you to enable auditing for very specific events. This reduces the number of irrelevant events, potentially reducing the "noise" generated by false-positive auditing events. This, in turn, can enable operations staff to more easily detect significant events. Combined with the new Windows Event Collector service, you can build a system to aggregate only the most important security events in your organization.

To view the new categories, run the following command from an administrative command prompt:

```
Auditpol /get /category:*
System audit policy
Category/Subcategory                      Setting
System
  Security System Extension               No Auditing
  System Integrity                        Success and Failure
  IPsec Driver                            No Auditing
  Other System Events                     Success and Failure
  Security State Change                   Success
Logon/Logoff
  Logon                                   Success
  Logoff                                  Success
  Account Lockout                         Success
  IPsec Main Mode                         No Auditing
  IPsec Quick Mode                        No Auditing
  IPsec Extended Mode                     No Auditing
  Special Logon                           Success
  Other Logon/Logoff Events               No Auditing
Object Access
  File System                             No Auditing
  Registry                                No Auditing
  Kernel Object                           No Auditing
  SAM                                     No Auditing
  Certification Services                  No Auditing
```

```
   Application Generated              No Auditing
   Handle Manipulation                No Auditing
   File Share                         No Auditing
   Filtering Platform Packet Drop     No Auditing
   Filtering Platform Connection      No Auditing
   Other Object Access Events         No Auditing
Privilege Use
   Sensitive Privilege Use            No Auditing
   Non Sensitive Privilege Use        No Auditing
   Other Privilege Use Events         No Auditing
Detailed Tracking
   Process Termination                No Auditing
   DPAPI Activity                     No Auditing
   RPC Events                         No Auditing
   Process Creation                   No Auditing
Policy Change
   Audit Policy Change                Success
   Authentication Policy Change       Success
   Authorization Policy Change        No Auditing
   MPSSVC Rule-Level Policy Change     No Auditing
   Filtering Platform Policy Change   No Auditing
   Other Policy Change Events         No Auditing
Account Management
   User Account Management            Success
   Computer Account Management        No Auditing
   Security Group Management          Success
   Distribution Group Management      No Auditing
   Application Group Management       No Auditing
   Other Account Management Events    No Auditing
DS Access
   Directory Service Changes          No Auditing
   Directory Service Replication      No Auditing
   Detailed Directory Service Replication  No Auditing
   Directory Service Access           No Auditing
Account Logon
   Kerberos Ticket Events             No Auditing
   Other Account Logon Events         No Auditing
   Credential Validation              No Auditing
```

Similarly, you can use the *Auditpol /set* command to enable granular auditing. For information about how to configure auditing in Active Directory environments using Group Policy settings, read Microsoft Knowledge Base article 921469, "How to use Group Policy to configure detailed security auditing settings for Windows Vista–based and Windows Server 2008–based computers in a Windows Server 2008 domain, in a Windows Server 2003 domain, or in a Windows 2000 domain," at *http://support.microsoft.com/kb/921469*. For more information about Windows event logs and event log collection, see Chapter 22, "Maintaining Desktop Health."

Smart Card Improvements

For many organizations, the risk that a password will be stolen or guessed is not acceptable. To supplement password security, organizations implement multifactor authentication that requires both a password and a second form of identification. Often, that second form of identification is a smart card, which contains a digital certificate that uniquely identifies the card holder and a private key for use in authentication.

Both Windows 2000 and Windows XP support authentication via smart cards. However, previous versions of Windows required administrators to deploy and maintain additional components to support their smart card infrastructure, such as cryptography modules and communications support for card readers. Smart card improvements in Windows Vista both simplify and improve smart card management.

To simplify development of smart card software tools (which is typically done by the smart card provider), a common *cryptographic service provider (CSP)* implements all the standard back-end cryptographic functions that hardware and software developers need. In addition, integrated third-party Card Modules make it easier to rapidly deploy a smart card solution and enable protected, predictable communications between the CSP and other components of the smart card infrastructure. Microsoft is also working with smart card providers to improve the technology by certifying smart card modules and making module updates available with Windows Update.

Additionally, smart card users will need to enter their PINs less frequently because of Kerberos improvements, and users will be able to reset their PINs without calling the support desk.

Credential Manager Enhancements

Windows Vista includes new tools to enable administrators to better support credential management for roaming users, including the new Digital Identity Management Services (DIMS) and a new certificate enrollment process. Among other improvements, users can now reset their own smart card personal identification numbers (PINs) without calling the support center. Additionally, users can now back up and restore credentials stored in the Stored User Names And Passwords key ring.

To improve the security of Task Scheduler, Windows Vista can use Service-for-User (S4U) Kerberos extensions to store credentials for scheduled tasks, instead of storing the credentials locally where they might be compromised. This has the added benefit of preventing scheduled tasks from being impacted by password expiration policies.

Architectural and Internal Windows Vista Security Improvements

Whenever possible, Windows Vista security features have been designed to be transparent to end users and to require no administration time. Nonetheless, administrators and developers can benefit from understanding the architectural improvements. This section describes these architectural and internal improvements, as well as improvements that require additional applications or infrastructure. Table 2-2 describes these features.

Table 2-2   Architectural and Internal Windows Vista Security Improvements

Improvement	Description
Code Integrity	Detects malicious modifications to kernel files at startup.
Windows Resource Protection	Prevents potentially dangerous changes to system resources.
Kernel Patch Protection	Blocks potentially malicious changes that might compromise the integrity of the kernel on 64-bit systems.
Required Driver Signing	Requires drivers to be signed, which improves reliability and makes it more difficult to add malicious drivers. Mandatory on 64-bit systems.
Windows Service Hardening	Allows system services to access only those resources they normally need to access, reducing the impact of a compromised service.
Authorization Manager	Provides administrators with a tool for configuring that users are allowed to access features of supported .NET Framework applications.
Network Access Protection Client	When used together with Windows Server 2008, helps to protect your network from clients who do not meet your security requirements.
Web Services for Management	Reduces risks associated with remote management by supporting encryption and authentication.
Crypto Next Generation services	Allows the addition of custom cryptographic algorithms to meet government requirements.
Data Execution Prevention	Reduces the risk of buffer overflow attacks by marking data sections of memory as nonexecutable.
Address Space Layout Randomization	Reduces the risk of buffer overflow attacks by assigning executable code to random memory locations.
New Logon Architecture	Simplifies development of custom logon mechanisms.
Rights Management Services client	Provides support for opening Rights Management Services protected documents when the proper applications are installed and the necessary infrastructure is in place.
Multiple local Group Policy objects	Allows administrators to apply multiple local Group Policy objects to a single computer, simplifying security configuration management for workgroup computers.

The sections that follow describe these features in more detail.

Code Integrity (CI)

When Windows starts up, Code Integrity (CI) verifies that system files haven't been maliciously modified and ensures that there are no unsigned drivers running in Kernel Mode. The boot loader checks the integrity of the kernel, the Hardware Abstraction Layer (HAL), and the boot-start drivers. After those files are verified, CI verifies the digital signatures of any binaries that are loaded into the kernel's memory space. Additionally, CI verifies binaries loaded into protected processes and the cryptography dynamic-link libraries (DLLs).

CI works automatically and does not require management.

> **Note**   CI is an example of a detective countermeasure, because it can identify that the computer was compromised after the fact. Although it is always preferable to prevent attacks, detective countermeasures such as CI enable you to limit the damage caused by the attack by detecting the compromise so that you can repair the computer. You should also have a response plan in place to enable you to quickly repair a system that has had critical files compromised.

Windows Resource Protection (WRP)

Any code that runs in kernel mode, including many types of drivers, can potentially corrupt kernel data in ways that surface later. Diagnosing and fixing these bugs can be difficult and time-consuming. Corruption of the registry tends to have a disproportionate impact on overall reliability, because this corruption can persist across reboots.

Windows Vista protects system settings from corruption or inadvertent changes that can cause the system to run incorrectly or to not run at all. Windows Resource Protection (WRP), the follow-on to the Windows File Protection (WFP) feature found in previous Windows platforms, sets tight ACLs on critical system settings, files, and folders to protect them from changes by any source (including administrators) except a trusted installer. This prevents users from changing critical system settings that can render systems inoperable.

Windows Vista also prevents poorly written drivers from corrupting the registry. This protection enables the memory-management component to achieve protection the vast majority of the time, with low overhead. Protected resources include:

- Executable files, libraries, and other critical files installed by Windows
- Critical folders
- Essential registry keys installed by Windows Vista

WRP will not allow you to modify protected resources, even if you provide administrative credentials. As demonstrated in Figure 2-9, access will always be denied.

Figure 2-9   WRP protects critical resources—even if you have administrative credentials—to reduce the risk of software making dangerous changes.

How It Works: Mandatory Integrity Control

One of my favorite new security features in Windows Vista is *Mandatory Integrity Control (MIC)*. It's a classical computer science concept from the 1970s that's finally getting its first commercial implementation—and of this I'm quite proud.

Although *discretionary access control lists (DACLs)* are useful, they have some limitations. They do little to safeguard system stability, and they can't stop malicious software from tricking users into executing it. MIC adds the notion of trustworthiness evaluation into the operating system. Subjects with low degrees of trustworthiness can't change data of higher degrees; subjects with high degrees of trustworthiness can't be forced to rely on data of lower degrees. MIC implements an information flow policy and provides the enforcement mechanism.

When a user logs on, Windows Vista assigns an integrity token to the user. The token includes an integrity label that determines the level of access the token—and therefore the user—can achieve. Securable objects (files, folders, pipes, processes, threads, window stations, registry keys, services, printers, shares, interprocess objects, jobs, and directory objects) also receive an integrity security identifier (SID), which is stored in the *system access control list (SACL)* of the object's security descriptor. The label in the SID specifies the integrity level of the object.

During an access check, before checking the user's access through the DACL, Windows Vista checks the integrity level of the user and compares it to the integrity level of the requested object. If the user's level dominates (that is, is equal to or greater than) the object's level, the user will be allowed to write to the object, subject to the DACL, of course. If the user's level doesn't dominate the object's, the user can't write to the object regardless of what the DACL says. Integrity control, therefore, trumps access lists.

Windows Vista defines four integrity levels: low, medium, high, and system. Standard users receive medium; elevated users receive high. Processes that you start and objects that you create receive your integrity level (medium or high), or they receive low if the executable file's level is low; system services receive system integrity. Objects that lack an integrity label are treated as medium by the operating system—this prevents low integrity code from modifying unlabeled objects.

Consider this scenario: You receive an attachment in an e-mail. When you save the attachment, it's written with low integrity because it came from the Internet—an untrusted source. When you execute the attachment, its process runs at low integrity because the file object is labeled low; therefore, your data (labeled medium or high) is protected from malicious writes by the attachment (although it will be able to read your data).

Internet Explorer Protected Mode is built around mandatory integrity control. Internet Explorer process and extensions run at low integrity and therefore have write access only to the Temporary Internet Files\Low folder, History, Cookies, Favorites, and the HKEY_CURRENT_USER\Software\LowRegistry key. MIC prevents Internet Explorer from writing anywhere else in the file system or registry—so no more silent installs of keystroke loggers into your Startup folder. And because the desktop runs at medium integrity, Internet Explorer can't send messages to it—thwarting shatter-style attacks. Because these new restrictions might break some applications, a compatibility mode virtualizes access to medium integrity resources (such as the Documents folder and the HKEY_CURRENT_USER hive) by redirecting writes to low integrity locations.

Although it's completely invisible, MIC is an important advance in maintaining the security and stability of Windows Vista. I hope you'll come to appreciate it as much as I do.

Steve Riley

Senior Security Strategist

Kernel Patch Protection

64-bit versions of Windows Vista, like the 64-bit versions of Windows XP and Windows Server 2003, support *Kernel Patch Protection* technology. Kernel Patch Protection prevents unauthorized programs from patching the Windows kernel, giving you greater control over core aspects of the system that can affect overall performance, security, and reliability. Kernel Patch Protection detects changes to critical portions of kernel memory. If a change is made in an unsupported way (for example, a user-mode application does not call the proper operating system functions), Kernel Patch Protection creates a Stop error to halt the operating system. This prevents kernel-mode drivers from extending or replacing other kernel services and preventing third-party software from updating any part of the kernel.

Specifically, to prevent Kernel Patch Protection from generating a Stop error, 64-bit drivers must avoid the following practices:

■ Modifying system service tables

■ Modifying the interrupt descriptor table (IDT)

- Modifying the global descriptor table (GDT)
- Using kernel stacks that are not allocated by the kernel
- Updating any part of the kernel on AMD64-based systems

In practice, these factors are primarily significant to driver developers. No 64-bit driver should ever be released that would cause problems with Kernel Patch Protection, so administrators should never need to manage or troubleshoot Kernel Patch Protection. For detailed information, read "An Introduction to Kernel Patch Protection" at *http://blogs.msdn.com/windowsvistasecurity/archive/2006/08/11/695993.aspx.*

Note   Kernel Patch Protection, hardware-based Data Execution Prevention (DEP), and required driver signing are the primary reasons 64-bit systems can be more secure than 32-bit systems.

Required Driver Signing

Drivers typically run as part of the kernel, which gives them almost unprotected access to system resources. As a result, drivers that have bugs or are poorly written, or malware drivers specifically written to abuse these privileges, can significantly impact a computer's reliability and security.

To help reduce the impact of drivers, Microsoft introduced driver signing beginning with Windows 2000. Signed drivers have a digital signature that indicates they have been approved by Microsoft and are likely to be free from major weaknesses that might impact system reliability. Administrators can configure Windows 2000 and later operating systems to block all unsigned drivers, which can dramatically decrease the risk of driver-related problems.

However, the large number of unsigned 32-bit drivers has made blocking unsigned drivers impractical for most organizations. As a result, most existing Windows computers allow unsigned drivers to be installed.

With 64-bit versions of Windows Vista, all kernel-mode drivers must be digitally signed. A kernel module that is corrupt or has been subject to tampering will not load. Any driver that is not properly signed cannot enter the kernel space and will fail to load. Although a signed driver is not a guarantee of security, it does help identify and prevent many malicious attacks, while allowing Microsoft to help developers improve the overall quality of drivers and reduce the number of driver-related crashes.

Mandatory driver signing also helps improve the reliability of Windows Vista, because many system crashes result from vulnerabilities in kernel-mode drivers. Requiring the authors of these drivers to identify themselves makes it easier for Microsoft to determine the cause of system crashes and work with the responsible vendor to resolve the issue. System administrators also benefit from digitally signed and identified drivers because they get additional visibility into software inventory and install state on client computers. From a compatibility perspective, existing Windows Hardware Quality Labs–certified x64 kernel drivers are considered validly signed in Windows Vista.

Windows Service Hardening

Historically, many Windows network compromises (especially worms) resulted from attackers exploiting vulnerabilities in Windows services. Because many Windows services listen for incoming connections, and often had system-level privileges, a vulnerability could allow an attacker to perform administrative tasks on a remote computer.

Windows Service Hardening, a new feature in Windows Vista, restricts all Windows services from performing abnormal activities in the file system, registry, network, or other resources that could be used to allow malware to install itself or attack other computers. For example, the Remote Procedure Call (RPC) service is restricted to performing network communications on defined ports only, eliminating the possibility of abusing it to, for instance, replace system files or modify the registry (which is what the Blaster worm did). Essentially, Windows Service Hardening enforces the security concept of least privilege on services, granting them only enough permission to perform their required tasks.

> **Note**   Windows Service Hardening provides an additional layer of protection for services based on the security principle of defense in depth. Windows Service Hardening cannot prevent a vulnerable service from being compromised—a task Windows Firewall and Automatic Updates supports. Instead, Windows Service Hardening limits how much damage an attacker can do in the event the attacker is able to identify and exploit a vulnerable service.

Windows Service Hardening reduces the damage potential of a compromised service by:

■ Introducing a per-service security identifier (SID) to uniquely identify services, which subsequently enables access control partitioning through the existing Windows access control model covering all objects and resource managers that use ACLs. Services can now apply explicit ACLs to resources that are private to the service, which prevents other services, as well as the user, from accessing the resource.

■ Moving services from LocalSystem to a lesser-privileged account, such as LocalService or NetworkService, to reduce the privilege level of the service.

■ Stripping unnecessary Windows privileges on a per-service basis—for example, the ability to perform debugging.

■ Applying a write-restricted token to services that access a limited set of files and other resources, so that the service cannot update other aspects of the system.

■ Assigning services a network firewall policy to prevent network access outside the normal bounds of the service program. The firewall policy is linked directly to the per-service SID and cannot be overridden or relaxed by user- or administrator-defined exceptions or rules.

A specific goal of Windows Service Hardening was to avoid introducing management complexity for users and system administrators. Every service included in Windows Vista has been through a rigorous process to define its Windows Service Hardening profile, which is applied automatically during Windows Vista installation and requires no ongoing administration, maintenance, or interaction from the end user. For these reasons, there is no administrative interface for managing Windows Service Hardening. For more information about Windows Service Hardening, see Chapter 27.

> **Note**   Third-party software developers can also take advantage of the Windows Service Hardening security benefits by providing profiles for custom services.

Authorization Manager

Authorization Manager (AzMan.msc) is now included with Windows Vista. Windows Authorization Manager (AzMan) is an application Role-Based Access Control (RBAC) framework for applications that integrate the AzMan framework. AzMan provides a Role-based MMC user interface and development interfaces. AzMan has the following benefits for application administrators and developers:

- **Common RBAC Administration**   An easy-to-use, common, role-based administrative experience; administrators learn fewer authorization models and require less training.

- **Natural Role-based Development Model**   Easy to integrate with native or managed applications; provides broad RBAC management and enforcement functionality.

- **Flexible Authorization Rules**   Offers the ability to define membership through dynamic Lightweight Directory Access Protocol (LDAP) queries or custom rules.

- **Centralized Administration**   Multiple applications can be managed centrally and leverage common application groups.

- **Flexible Storage Options**   Policy can be stored in Active Directory, XML files, or SQL Server.

- **Platform Integration and Alignment**   Offers support for platform features such as Active Directory groups and attributes and Windows security auditing, as well as assurance of proper integration of system access control objects such as the NT access token and better alignment for future Windows access control features and products.

- **Reduced Software Development and Maintenance Costs**   Developers avoid the expense or tradeoffs of custom access control. AzMan does the expensive work of a full-featured authorization solution, including a complete RBAC model, policy storage (within Active Directory, SQL, or XML), an MMC user interface, built-in application group support, rule and query support, integrated system auditing, and performance optimizations.

■ **Enhanced Security**   Platform technologies are rigorously tested, broadly used, and continually refined. A common RBAC model takes advantage of administrators' existing knowledge, resulting in fewer access control mistakes.

Previously, developers had to create a custom user interface for enabling administrators to control security features of an application. Alternatively, organizations had to rely on developers to make changes to the code to enforce authorization restrictions. AzMan provides abstractions that allow developers to integrate low-level application operations and preserve the ability of application administrators to define roles and tasks without requiring code changes.

Authorization Manager is also included with Windows Server 2003 and can be installed on Windows XP computers. For more information about Authorization Manager, refer to the Windows Server 2003 Help and Support.

Network Access Protection Client

Most networks have perimeter firewalls to help protect the internal network from worms, viruses, and other attackers. However, attackers can penetrate your network through remote access connections (such as a VPN) or by infecting a mobile PC and then spreading to other internal computers after the mobile PC connects to your local area network (LAN).

Windows Vista, when connecting to a Windows Server 2008 infrastructure, supports Network Access Protection (NAP) to reduce the risk of attackers entering through remote access and LAN connections using Windows Vista's built-in NAP client software. If a Windows Vista computer lacks current security updates, virus signatures, or otherwise fails to meet your requirements for a healthy computer, NAP can block the computer from reaching your internal network.

However, if a computer fails to meet the requirements to join your network, the user doesn't have to be left frustrated. Client computers can be directed to an isolated quarantine network to download updates, antivirus signatures, or configuration settings required to comply with your health requirements policy. Within minutes, a potentially vulnerable computer can be protected and once again allowed to connect to your network.

NAP is an extensible platform that provides an infrastructure and API for health-policy enforcement. Independent hardware and software vendors can plug their security solutions into NAP so that IT administrators can choose the security solutions that meet their unique needs. NAP helps to ensure that every machine on the network makes full use of those custom solutions.

Microsoft will also release NAP client support for Windows XP SP2. For more information about Network Access Protection, see *http://www.microsoft.com/technet/itsolutions/network/nap/default.mspx*.

Web Services for Management

Web Services for Management (WS-Management) makes Windows Vista easier to manage remotely. An industry-standard web services protocol for protected remote management of hardware and software components, WS-Management—along with the proper software tools— allows administrators to run scripts and perform other management tasks remotely. In Windows Vista, communications can be both encrypted and authenticated, limiting security risks. Microsoft management tools such as Systems Center Configuration Manager 2007 use WS-Management to provide safe and secure management of both hardware and software.

Crypto Next Generation (CNG) Services

Cryptography is a critical component of Windows authentication and authorization services, which use cryptography for encryption, hashing, and digital signatures. Windows Vista delivers Crypto Next Generation (CNG) services, which was requested by many governments and organizations. CNG allows new algorithms to be added to Windows for use in Secure Sockets Layer/Transport Layer Security (SSL/TLS) and Internet Protocol security (IPsec). Windows Vista also includes a new security processor to enable trust decisions for services such as rights management.

For organizations that are required to use specific cryptography algorithms and approved libraries, CNG is an absolute requirement.

Data Execution Prevention (DEP)

One of the most commonly used techniques for exploiting vulnerabilities in software is the buffer overflow attack. A buffer overflow occurs when an application attempts to store too much data in a buffer, and memory not allocated to the buffer is overwritten. An attacker might be able to intentionally induce a buffer overflow by entering more data than the application expects. A particularly crafty attacker can even enter data that instructs the operating system to run the attacker's malicious code with the application's privileges.

Perhaps the most well-known buffer overflow exploit in recent years is the CodeRed worm, which exploited a vulnerability in an Index Server Internet Server Application Programming Interface (ISAPI) application shipped as part of an earlier version of Microsoft Internet Information Server (IIS) to run malicious software. The impact of the CodeRed worm was tremendous, and it could have been prevented by the presence of Data Execution Prevention (DEP).

DEP marks sections of memory as containing either data or application code. The operating system will not run code contained in memory marked for data. User input—and data received across a network—should always be stored as data, and would therefore not be eligible to run as an application.

32-bit versions of Windows Vista include a software implementation of DEP that can prevent memory not marked for execution from running. 64-bit versions of Windows Vista work with the 64-bit processor's built-in DEP capabilities to enforce this security at the hardware layer, where it would be very difficult for an attacker to circumvent it.

Note   DEP provides an important layer of security for protection from malicious software. However, it must be used alongside other technologies, such as Windows Defender, to provide sufficient protection to meet business requirements.

As Figure 2-10 shows, DEP is enabled by default in both 32- and 64-bit versions of Windows Vista. By default, DEP protects only essential Windows programs and services to provide optimal compatibility. For additional security, you can protect all programs and services.

Figure 2-10   You can enable or disable DEP from the Performance Options dialog box or from Group Policy settings.

Address Space Layout Randomization (ASLR)

Address Space Layout Randomization (ASLR) is another defense capability in Windows Vista that makes it harder for malicious code to exploit a system function. Whenever a Windows Vista computer is rebooted, ASLR randomly assigns executable images (.dll and .exe files) included as part of the operating system to one of 256 possible locations in memory. This makes it harder for exploit code to locate and therefore take advantage of functionality inside the executables.

Windows Vista also introduces improvements in heap buffer overrun detection that are even more rigorous than those introduced in Windows XP SP2. When signs of heap buffer tampering are detected, the operating system can immediately terminate the affected program, limiting damage that might result from the tampering. This protection technology is enabled for operating system components, including built-in system services, and can also be leveraged by ISVs through a single API call.

New Logon Architecture

Logging onto Windows provides access to local resources (including EFS-encrypted files) and, in Active Directory environments, protected network resources. Many organizations require more than a user name and password to authenticate users. For example, they might require multifactor authentication using both a password and biometric identification or a one-time password token.

In Windows XP and earlier versions of Windows, implementing custom authentication methods required developers to completely rewrite the Graphical Identification and Authentication (GINA) interface. Often, the effort required did not justify the benefits provided by strong authentication, and the project was abandoned. Additionally, Windows XP supported only a single GINA.

With Windows Vista, developers can now provide custom authentication methods by creating a new Credential Provider. This requires significantly less development effort, meaning more organizations will offer custom authentication methods for Windows Vista.

The new architecture also enables Credential Providers to be event-driven and integrated throughout the user experience. For example, the same code used to implement a fingerprint authentication scheme at the Windows logon screen can be used to prompt the user for a fingerprint when accessing a particular corporate resource. The same prompt also can be used by applications that use the new credential user interface API.

Additionally, the Windows logon user interface can use multiple Credential Providers simultaneously, providing greater flexibility for environments that might have different authentication requirements for different users.

Rights Management Services (RMS)

Microsoft Windows Rights Management Services (RMS) is an information-protection technology that works with RMS-enabled applications to help safeguard digital information from unauthorized use both inside and outside your private network. RMS provides persistent usage policies (also known as usage rights and conditions) that remain with a file no matter where it goes. RMS persistently protects any binary format of data, so the usage rights remain with the information—even in transport—rather than merely residing on an organization's network.

RMS works by encrypting documents and then providing decryption keys only to authorized users with an approved RMS client. To be approved, the RMS client must enforce the usage rights assigned to a document. For example, if the document owner has specified that the contents of the document should not be copied, forwarded, or printed, the RMS client will not allow the user to take these actions.

In Windows Vista, RMS is now integrated with the new XML Paper Specification (XPS) format. XPS is an open, cross-platform document format that helps customers effortlessly create, share, print, archive, and protect rich digital documents. With a new print driver that outputs XPS, any application can produce XPS documents that can be protected with RMS. This basic functionality will significantly broaden the range of information that can be protected by RMS.

The 2007 Microsoft Office system provides even deeper integration with RMS through new developments in Microsoft SharePoint. SharePoint administrators can set access policies for the SharePoint document libraries on a per-user basis that will be inherited by RMS policies. This means that users who have "view-only" rights to access the content will have that "view-only" access (no print, copy, or paste) enforced by RMS, even when the document has been removed from the SharePoint site. Enterprise customers can set usage policies that are enforced not only when the document is at rest, but also when the information is outside the direct control of the enterprise.

Although the Rights Management Services components are built into Windows Vista, they can be used only with a rights management infrastructure and an application that supports RMS, such as Microsoft Office. The RMS client can also be installed on Windows 2000 and later operating systems. For more information about how to use RMS, visit *http://www.microsoft.com/rms*.

Multiple Local Group Policy Objects

As an administrator, you can now apply multiple Local Group Policy objects to a single computer. This simplifies configuration management, because you can create separate Group Policy objects for different roles and apply them individually, just as you can with Active Directory Group Policy objects. For example, you might have a Group Policy object for computers that are members of the Marketing group, and a separate Group Policy object for mobile computers. If you need to configure a mobile computer for a member of the Marketing group, you can simply apply both local Group Policy objects, rather than creating a single local Group Policy object that combines all of the settings.

Summary

Windows Vista security improvements touch almost every aspect of the operating system. The details of the security features are discussed throughout this Resource Kit, but this chapter has provided an overview of key security improvements to enable you to create a comprehensive security plan and better understand how Windows Vista will impact the security of your organization.

Windows Vista security improvements align with several different security principles:

- **Secure by default**   Computers should be at their most secure when initially configured, because many organizations accept the default settings. Windows Vista provides a highly secure environment when initially deployed, requiring little or no additional hardening to meet most organizations' security requirements.

- **Reduce the attack surface**   Any application, service, or operating system component might contain vulnerabilities. The more services and applications that are enabled by default in an operating system, the greater the risk of a vulnerability being exploited. Windows Vista minimizes the attack surface by enabling only essential operating system services and components. For those services that must be enabled, components such as Windows Firewall allow only essential network communications.

- **Assign least privilege**   Users, applications, and services should have only the minimum privileges they absolutely need. For example, users should not have administrator permissions on their desktop computer because a virus or Trojan horse could misuse those permissions. UAC, Internet Explorer Protected Mode, and Windows Service Hardening enforce least privilege for users, Internet Explorer, and system services.

- **Update software**   Systems change, and new bugs and insecure practices are discovered all the time. Software must be updated regularly, but the update process can also expose you to attack. In Windows Vista, Automatic Updates and WSUS provide controlled but automated distribution of software updates. Kernel Patch Protection and driver signing provide a level of protection from unreliable or malicious updates. Network Access Protection helps ensure that clients connected to your internal network have the required level of security updates.

- **Protect data in storage and transit**   Although you might consider computer files and communications safe within a physically secure facility, the increase in mobile communications means that your data requires additional protection. BitLocker, EFS, and RMS provide data encryption that protects your files from even offline attacks, and you can use improved CNG services to use your own encryption techniques. Windows Firewall's IPsec capabilities and improvements to Web Services for Management can protect your communications in transit. Smart card improvements, Credential Manager enhancements, and a new logon architecture give you more confidence when authenticating users.

Combined with features such as CI, WRP, ASLR, and AzMan, these improvements offer multiple layers of protection that you can use to limit your organization's security risks.

Additional Resources

These resources contain additional information and tools related to this chapter.

Related Information

- Chapter 15, "Managing Disks and File Systems," includes more information about BitLocker and Encrypting File System.

- Chapter 21, "Managing Internet Explorer," includes more information about protecting Internet Explorer.

- Chapter 25, "Managing Client Protection," includes more information about User Account Control and Windows Defender.

- Chapter 26, "Configuring Windows Networking," includes more information about protecting wireless networks.

- Chapter 27, "Configuring Windows Firewall and IPsec," includes more information about Windows Service Hardening.

- Download the latest version of the Windows Vista Security Guide, at *http://www.microsoft.com/downloads/details.aspx?FamilyID=a3d1bbed-7f35-4e72-bfb5-b84a526c1565&DisplayLang=en*. It provides detailed information about how to best configure Windows Vista security for your organization.

- "Microsoft Windows Vista: An Inflection Point for Kernel Security and 64-Bit Computing," at *http://www.microsoft.com/downloads/details.aspx?FamilyID=802e48a3-c79a-4530-b41b-808c43f806e6&DisplayLang=en*, offers information about Kernel Patch Protection in Windows Vista.

- "Kernel Enhancements for Windows Vista and Windows Server 2008" at *http://www.microsoft.com/whdc/system/vista/kernel-en.mspx*.

On the Companion CD

- A link where you can download the latest version of the Windows Vista Security Guide

- Chapters from *Microsoft Security Resource Kit, Second Edition*:
  - ❏ Chapter 1, "Key Principles of Security"
  - ❏ Chapter 2, "Understanding Your Enemy"
  - ❏ Chapter 28, "Assessing the Security of a Network"

Part II
Deployment

Chapter 3
Deployment Platform

Windows Vista deployment technology has evolved significantly since Windows XP Professional. For example, it supports file-based disk imaging to make high-volume deployments quicker, more efficient, and more cost effective. Windows Vista also provides more robust deployment tools through the Windows Automated Installation Kit (Windows AIK), including Windows System Image Manager and Windows Preinstallation Environment.

This chapter helps you get started with the new Windows Vista deployment platform by introducing these tools, describing how they relate to each other, and providing you with a basic understanding of why and when to use each tool. The remaining chapters in Part II, "Deployment," describe in detail the tools introduced in this chapter. The *Windows Automated Installation Kit User's Guide* in the Windows Automated Installation Kit also details each tool described in this chapter. You can download the Windows Automated Installation Kit from the Microsoft Download Center at *http://www.microsoft.com/downloads.*

Tools Introduction

Windows Vista introduces numerous changes to the technology you use for deployment. The new Windows AIK includes most of these tools. Others are built in to the operating system. The Windows AIK fully documents all of the tools described in this chapter, including command-line options for using them, how they work on a detailed level, and so on.

> **Note**   The Windows AIK is not included in the Windows Vista media. (By comparison, Windows XP has a file called Deploy.cab that includes its deployment tools.) Instead, you can download the Windows AIK from the Microsoft Download Center at *http://www.microsoft.com/download*.

The following features are new for Windows Vista deployment:

- **Windows System Image Manager**   Windows System Image Manager (Windows SIM) is a tool for creating your distribution shares and editing answer files. It exposes all configurable settings in Windows Vista; you can use it to save customizations in Unattend.xml. The Windows AIK includes the Windows SIM.

- **Windows Setup**   Setup for Windows Vista installs the Windows image (.wim) file and uses the new Unattend.xml answer file to automate installation. Unattend.xml replaces the set of answer files used in earlier versions of Windows (Unattend.txt, Sysprep.inf, and so on). Because image-based Setup is faster, you can use it in high-volume deployments and for automating image maintenance. Microsoft made numerous improvements to Windows Vista Setup (now called Setup.exe instead of Winnt.exe or Winnt32.exe), such as a completely graphical user interface, use of a single answer file (Unattend.xml) for configuration, and support for configuration passes (phases).

- **Sysprep**   The System Preparation (Sysprep) tool prepares an installation of Windows Vista for imaging, auditing, and deployment. You use imaging to capture a customized Windows Vista image that you can deploy throughout your organization. You use audit mode to add additional device drivers and applications to a Windows Vista installation and test the integrity of the installation before handing off the computer to the end user. You can also use Sysprep to prepare an image for deployment. When the end user starts Windows Vista, Windows Welcome starts. Unlike earlier versions of Windows, Windows Vista includes Sysprep natively—you no longer have to download the current version.

- **Windows Preinstallation Environment**   Windows Preinstallation Environment 2.0 (Windows PE 2.0) provides operating system features for installing, troubleshooting, and recovering Windows Vista. Windows PE 2.0 is the latest release of Windows PE based on Windows Vista. With Windows PE, you can start a computer from a network or removable media. Windows PE provides the network and other resources necessary to install and troubleshoot Windows Vista. Windows Vista Setup, Windows Deployment Services (Windows DS), SMS 2003 Operating System Deployment (OSD) Feature Pack, System Center Configuration Manager 2007, and Microsoft Deployment Toolkit (MDT) 2008 all use Windows PE to start computers. The Windows AIK includes Windows PE.

- **Package Manager**   You use Package Manager to apply language packs and other updates provided by Microsoft. Previous versions of Windows use Update.exe, and an update installer was made available for each update. Package Manager is a native part of

Windows Vista. You can use it to apply updates to Windows Vista *online* (running on a computer) and *offline* (stored in an image file).

■ **New command-line configuration tools**   Windows Vista and the Windows AIK include numerous new and improved command-line tools for customizing and configuring the operating system. Examples include Diskpart.exe, Drvload.exe, Peimage.exe, and so on.

■ **ImageX**   ImageX is a new command-line tool that you can use to capture, modify, and apply file-based disk images for deployment. Windows Vista Setup, Windows Deployment Services (Windows DS), Systems Management Server (SMS) 2003 OSD, System Center Configuration Manager 2007, and MDT 2008 all use ImageX to capture, edit, and deploy Windows Vista images. The Windows AIK includes ImageX.

■ **Windows Imaging**   Microsoft delivers Windows Vista on product media as a highly compressed Windows Imaging (.wim) file. You can install Windows Vista directly from the Windows Vista media or customize the image for deployment. Windows Vista images are file-based, allowing you to edit them nondestructively. You can also store multiple operating system images in a single .wim file.

Windows Vista Service Pack 1

Windows Vista Service Pack 1 (SP1) doesn't introduce new deployment tools or technologies. However, Windows Vista SP1 makes several changes that address identified issues and improve the Windows Vista deployment experience. For example, Windows Vista SP1:

■ Adds support for hotpatching, a restart-reduction servicing technology that maximizes uptime. (Hotpatching works by allowing Windows components to be updated while they are still in use by a running process. Update packages that support hotpatching are installed through the same methods as traditional update packages but will not trigger a restart.)

■ Improves update deployment by retrying failed updates when multiple updates are pending and also when the failure of one update causes other updates to also fail.

■ Improves robustness during update installation by improving resilience to transient errors (for example, sharing violations and access violations) and unexpected interruptions (for example, power failure).

■ Improves the uninstallation experience for updates by improving the uninstallation routines in custom operating system installation code.

■ Enables more reliable operating system installation by optimizing operating system installers so that they are run only as required during update installation. (Fewer installers running results in fewer points of failure, leading to a more robust and reliable installation.)

- Improves using Windows Preinstallation Environment (Windows PE) as a deployment platform for Windows Vista.

- Improves Windows Vista deployment by enabling customers to install 64-bit versions of Windows Vista from a 32-bit operating system. (This allows IT pros to maintain a single Windows PE image.)

- Improves deployment by supporting the installation of offline boot-critical storage drivers. (With SP1, Windows PE automatically looks to a hidden partition for drivers. It will search that partition recursively, and if boot-critical drivers are present, Windows PE will load them.)

Windows Vista Deployment Terminology

The following terms are unique to Windows Vista deployment and MDT 2008. Understanding this terminology will help you better understand the deployment content in this book and the resources it refers to:

- **Answer file**   A file that scripts the answers for a series of dialog boxes during installation. The answer file for Windows Setup is often called Unattend.xml. You can use Windows SIM to create and modify this answer file. MDT 2008 builds answer files automatically, which you can customize if necessary.

- **Catalog file**   A binary file that contains the state of all of the settings and packages in a Windows Vista image. When you use Windows SIM to create a catalog file, that file queries the Windows Vista image for a list of all settings in that image. Because the contents of a Windows Vista image can change over time, it is important that you re-create the catalog file whenever you update an image.

- **Component**   A part of the Windows Vista operating system that specifies the files, resources, and settings for a specific Windows Vista feature or part of a Windows Vista feature. Some components include unattended installation settings, which you can customize by using Windows SIM.

- **Configuration pass**   A phase of Windows Vista installation. Different parts of the Windows Vista operating system are installed and configured in different configuration passes. You can specify Windows Vista unattended installation settings to be applied in one or more configuration pass. For more information about configuration passes, see the *Windows Automated Installation Kit User's Guide*.

- **Configuration set**   A file and folder structure that contains files that control the preinstallation process and define customizations for the Windows Vista installation.

- **Deployment point**   In MDT 2008, a deployment point contains the collection of source files necessary to install operating systems and provides a mechanism for installing them from the deployment point (Windows PE boot images).

- **Destination computer**   The computer on which you install Windows Vista during deployment. You can either run Windows Setup on the destination computer or copy a master installation onto a destination computer. The term *target computer* is also commonly used.

- **Distribution share**   A folder that contains the source files for Windows products that you install. It may also contain additional device drivers and application files. You can create this folder manually or by using Windows SIM. In MDT 2008, the distribution share contains operating system, device driver, application, and other source files that you configure by creating builds and distributing through deployment points.

- **Image-based setup**   A setup process based on applying a disk image of an operating system to the computer.

- **Master computer**   A fully assembled computer containing a master installation of Windows Vista. The term *source computer* is also commonly used.

- **Master image**   A collection of files and folders (usually compressed into one file) captured from a master installation. This image contains the base operating system as well as additional configurations and files.

- **Master installation**   A Windows Vista installation on a master computer to be captured as a master image. You create the master installation using automation to ensure a consistent and repeatable configuration each time.

- **Package**   A group of files that Microsoft provides to modify Windows Vista features. Package types include service packs, security updates, language packs, and hotfixes.

- **Task sequence**   A sequence of tasks to run on a destination computer to install Windows Vista and applications and then configure the destination computer. In MDT 2008, task sequences drive the installation routine, and the component responsible for executing the task sequence is the Task Sequencer.

- **Task Sequencer**   The MDT 2008 component that runs the task sequence when installing a build.

- **Technician computer**   The computer on which you install MDT 2008 or Windows SIM. This computer is typically located in a lab environment, separate from the production network. In MDT 2008, this computer is usually called the *build server*.

- **Unattend.xml**   The generic name for the Windows Vista answer file. Unattend.xml replaces all of the answer files in earlier versions of Windows, including Unattend.txt, Winbom.ini, and others.

- **.wim**   A filename extension that identifies Windows image files created by ImageX.

- **Windows Vista feature**   An optional feature of Windows Vista that you can enable or disable.

- **Windows image file**   A single compressed file containing a collection of files and folders that duplicate a Windows installation on a disk volume.

Platform Components

Understanding the new deployment tools and how they interconnect is the first step in beginning a Windows Vista deployment project. Figure 3-1 illustrates the Windows Vista deployment platform. At the lowest tier are Windows Imaging (.wim) files, which are highly compressed, file-based operating system images.

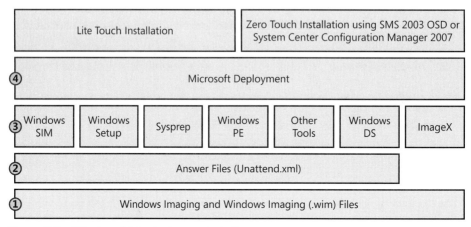

Figure 3-1   Windows Vista deployment platform components.

At the second tier are answer files. Earlier versions of Windows had numerous answer files, including Unattend.txt and Sysprep.inf, to drive the deployment process. Windows Vista uses a single XML-based answer file, Unattend.xml, to drive all of its *configuration passes*. (A configuration pass is an installation phase.) This improvement makes configuration more consistent and simplifies engineering.

At the third tier are the various deployment tools for Windows Vista. The Windows Vista distribution media includes some of these tools, including Sysprep and other command-line tools. The Windows AIK includes the bigger tools, such as Windows SIM, Windows PE, Windows DS, and ImageX. These are the basic tools necessary to create, customize, and deploy Windows Vista images. They are standalone tools that don't provide a deployment framework or add business intelligence and best practice to the process.

The fourth tier, MDT 2008, provides the missing framework, business intelligence, and best practices. MDT 2008 is a process and technology framework that uses all of the tools in the third tier, potentially saving your organization hundreds of hours of planning, developing, testing, and deployment. MDT 2008 is based on best practices developed by Microsoft, its customers, and its partners. It includes time-proven management and technology guidance as well as thousands of lines of thoroughly tested script code that you can use as is or customize to suit your organization's requirements.

Using MDT 2008, you can perform both Lite Touch Installation (LTI) and Zero Touch Installation (ZTI) deployment. LTI requires very little infrastructure and is suitable for most small and medium businesses. ZTI requires an SMS 2003 or System Center Configuration Manager 2007 infrastructure and is suitable for organizations that already have either infrastructure in place.

The following sections provide more information about the components shown in Figure 3-1. For more information about the deployment process using the components in the first three tiers, see the section titled "Basic Deployment Process" later in this chapter. For more information about the deployment process using MDT 2008, see the section titled "Microsoft Deployment Toolkit Process" later in this chapter.

Windows Imaging

Windows Vista is distributed in .wim files, which use the new image-file format. This format has the following advantages:

- Windows Imaging files are a file-based image format that lets you store multiple images in one file. You can perform partial volume captures by excluding files, such as paging files, you don't want to deploy using the image.

- This format reduces file sizes significantly by using a compressed file format and single-instance storage techniques: The image file contains one physical copy of a file for each instance of it in the image file, which significantly reduces the size of image files that contain multiple images.

- You can service the image contained in the .wim file—adding and deleting packages, software updates, and device drivers, for example—without re-creating a new image by applying it, customizing it again, and recapturing it.

- You can mount .wim files as folders, making it easier to update files in images they contain.

- Windows Imaging files allow you to apply an image nondestructively to the destination computer's hard disk. You can also apply an image to different-sized destination drives because .wim files don't require the destination hard disk to be the same size or larger than the source hard disk.

- Windows Imaging files can span media so that you can use CD-ROMs to distribute large .wim files.

- Windows PE .wim files are bootable. For example, you can start Windows PE from a .wim file. In fact, Windows Setup and Windows DS start Windows PE from the .wim file Boot.wim, which you can customize by adding items such as device drivers and scripts.

 Note ImageX is the tool you use to manage .wim files. For more information about ImageX, see the section titled "ImageX" later in this chapter and Chapter 6, "Developing Disk Images."

Answer Files

An answer file is an XML-based file that contains settings to use during a Windows Vista installation. An answer file can fully automate all or part of the installation process. In an answer file, you provide settings such as how to partition disks, the location of the Windows Vista image to install, and the product key to apply. You can also customize the Windows Vista installation, including adding user accounts, changing display settings, and updating Microsoft Internet Explorer favorites. Windows Vista answer files are commonly called Unattend.xml.

You use Windows SIM (see the section titled "Windows SIM" later in this chapter) to create an answer file and associate it with a particular Windows Vista image. This association allows you to validate the settings in the answer file against the settings available in the Windows Vista image. However, because you can use any answer file to install any Windows Vista image, settings in the answer file for components that do not exist in the Windows image are ignored.

The components section of an answer file contains all the component settings that are applied during Windows Setup. Components are organized into different configuration passes: windowsPE, offlineServicing, generalize, specialize, auditSystem, auditUser, and oobeSystem. (See the section titled "How It Works: Configuration Passes" later in this chapter.) Each configuration pass represents a different installation phase. You can apply settings during one or more passes. If a setting is available in more than one configuration pass, you can choose the pass in which to apply the setting.

> **Note**   The *Windows Automated Installation Kit User's Guide* in the Windows AIK fully documents the components you can configure using Windows SIM and the settings available for each component.

Microsoft uses packages to distribute software updates, service packs, and language packs. Packages can also contain Windows features. By using Windows SIM, you can add packages to a Windows Vista image, remove them from a Windows Vista image, or change the settings for features within a package.

The Windows Foundation Package, included in all Windows Vista images, includes all core Windows Vista features such as Media Player, Games, and Backup. Features are either enabled or disabled in Windows Vista. If a Windows Vista feature is enabled, the resources, executable files, and settings for that feature are available to users on the system. If a Windows Vista feature is disabled, the package resources are not available, but the resources are not removed from the system.

Windows SIM

Windows SIM is the tool you use to create and configure Windows Vista answer files. You can configure components, packages, and answer file settings. Windows Setup uses Unattend.xml to configure and customize the default Windows Vista installation for all configuration passes. For instance, you can customize Internet Explorer, configure Windows Firewall, and specify the hard drive configuration. You can use Windows SIM to customize Windows Vista in the following ways and more:

- Install third-party applications during installation.

- Customize Windows Vista by creating answer files (Unattend.xml).

- Apply language packs, service packs, and updates to an image during installation.

- Add device drivers to an image during installation.

With earlier versions of Windows, you have to edit answer file settings manually using a text editor, even after initially creating an answer file by using Windows Setup Manager. The Windows Vista answer file (Unattend.xml) is based on XML and far too complex to edit manually, however. So you must use Windows SIM to edit Windows Vista answer files. Figure 3-2 shows Windows SIM.

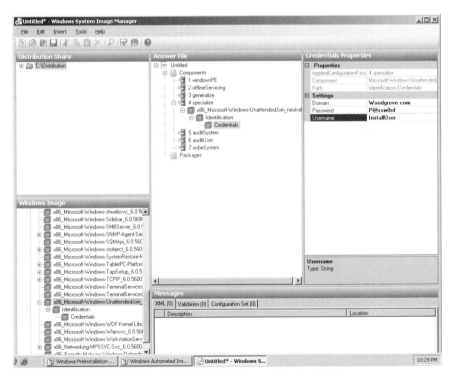

Figure 3-2   Windows SIM.

Windows Setup

Windows Setup (Setup.exe) is the program that installs Windows Vista. It uses image-based setup (IBS) to provide a single, unified process with which all customers can install Windows. IBS performs clean installations and upgrades of Windows. Windows Setup and IBS allow you to deploy Windows Vista in your organization easily and cost effectively.

Windows Setup includes several new features that facilitate faster and more consistent installations:

- **Improved image management**   Windows Vista images are stored in a single .wim file. A .wim file can store multiple instances of the operating system in a single, highly compressed file. The install file, Install.wim, is located in the Sources folder on the Windows Vista media.

- **Streamlined installation**   Windows Setup is optimized to enable the deployment scenarios used by most organizations. Installation takes less time and provides a more consistent configuration and deployment process, resulting in lower deployment costs.

- **Faster installations and upgrades**   Because Windows Setup is now image-based, installing and upgrading Windows Vista is faster and easier. You can perform clean installations of Windows Vista by deploying the Windows image to destination computers; you perform upgrades by installing a new image onto an existing installation of Windows. Windows Setup protects the previous Windows settings during the installation.

Sysprep

You use Sysprep to prepare a master installation for imaging and deployment. Sysprep does the following:

- **Removes computer-specific data from Windows Vista**   Sysprep can remove all computer-specific information from an installed Windows Vista image, including the computer security identifier (SID). You can then capture and install the Windows installation throughout your organization.

- **Configures Windows Vista to boot in audit mode**   You can use audit mode to install third-party applications and device drivers, as well as to test the functionality of the computer, before delivering the computer to the end user.

- **Configures Windows Vista to boot to Windows Welcome**   Sysprep configures a Windows Vista installation to boot to Windows Welcome the next time the computer starts. Generally, you configure a system to boot to Windows Welcome as a final step before delivering the computer to the end user.

- **Resets Windows Product Activation**   Sysprep can reset Windows Product Activation up to three times.

Sysprep.exe is located in the %WinDir%\system32\sysprep directory on all Windows Vista installations. (You do not have to install Sysprep separately, as in earlier versions of Windows, because it's a native part of the installation.) You must always run Sysprep from the %WinDir%\system32\sysprep directory on the version of Windows Vista with which it was installed.

For more information about Sysprep, see the *Windows Automated Installation Kit User's Guide* in the Windows AIK.

Windows PE

Prior to Windows PE, organizations often had to use MS-DOS boot floppies to start destination computers and then start Windows Setup from a network share or other distribution media. MS-DOS boot floppies had numerous limitations, however, including no support for the NTFS file system, no native networking support, and a requirement to locate 16-bit device drivers that worked in MS-DOS.

Now Windows PE 2.0 provides a minimal Win32 operating system with limited services—built on the Windows Vista kernel—that you use to prepare a computer for Windows Vista installation, copy disk images to and from a network file server, and start Windows Setup. Windows PE 2.0 is designed solely as a standalone preinstallation environment and as an integral component of other setup and recovery technologies, such as Windows Setup, Windows DS, the SMS 2003 OSD, System Center Configuration Manager 2007, and MDT 2008. Unlike earlier versions of Windows PE, which were only available as a Software Assurance (SA) benefit, Windows PE 2.0 is now publicly available in the Windows AIK.

Windows PE provides the following features and capabilities:

- Native support for NTFS 5.x file system, including dynamic volume creation and management

- Native support for TCP/IP networking and file sharing (client only)

- Native support for 32-bit (or 64-bit) Windows device drivers

- Native support for a subset of the Win32 Application Programming Interface (API); optional support for Windows Management Instrumentation (WMI) and Windows Script Host (WSH)

- Can be started from multiple media, including CD, DVD, USB Flash Drive (UFD), and Windows DS

Windows PE runs every time you install Windows Vista, whether you install the operating system by booting the computer with the Windows Vista DVD or deploy Windows Vista from Windows DS. The graphical tools that collect configuration information during the setup phase run within Windows PE. In addition, you can customize and extend Windows PE to meet specific deployment needs. For example, MDT 2008 customizes Windows PE for LTI by adding device drivers, deployment scripts, and so on.

For more information about Windows PE, see Chapter 9, "Preparing Windows PE."

> **Note**   Because Windows PE is only a subset of Windows Vista, it has limitations. For example, Windows PE automatically stops running the shell and reboots after 72 hours of continuous use to prevent piracy. You cannot configure Windows PE as a file or Terminal Server. Moreover, mapped driver letters and changes to the registry are not persistent between sessions. For more information about the limitations of Windows PE, see the *Windows Preinstallation Environment User's Guide* in the Windows AIK.

Other Tools

Windows Vista also provides various command-line tools that are useful during deployment:

- **BCDEdit**   Boot Configuration Data (BCD) files provide a store to describe boot applications and boot application settings. The objects and elements in the store effectively replace Boot.ini. BCDEdit is a command-line tool for managing BCD stores. You can use BCDEdit for a variety of purposes, including creating new stores, modifying existing stores, and adding boot menu options. BCDEdit serves essentially the same purpose that Bootcfg.exe served in earlier versions of Windows.

- **Bootsect**   Bootsect.exe updates the master boot code for hard-disk partitions to switch between BOOTMGR and NTLDR. You can use this tool to restore the boot sector on your computer. This tool replaces FixFAT and FixNTFS.

- **DiskPart**   DiskPart is a text-mode command interpreter in Windows Vista. You can use DiskPart to manage objects (disks, partitions, or volumes) by using scripts or direct input at a command prompt.

- **Drvload**   The Drvload tool adds out-of-box drivers to a booted Windows PE image. It takes one or more driver .inf files as inputs. To add a driver to an offline Windows PE image, use the Peimg tool. If the driver .inf file requires a reboot, Windows PE will ignore the request. If the driver .sys file requires a reboot, you cannot add the driver with Drvload.

- **Expand**   Expand.exe expands one or more compressed update files. Expand.exe supports opening updates for Windows Vista as well as previous versions of Windows. By using Expand, you can open and examine updates for Windows Vista on a Windows XP or Windows Server 2003 operating system.

- **Intlcfg**   Use the International Settings Configuration Tool (Intlcfg.exe) to change the language, locale, fonts, and input settings to a Windows Vista image. Typically, you run intlcfg.exe after applying one or more language packs to your Windows image. You can run the intlcfg command on an offline Windows image or on a running Windows operating system.

- **Lpksetup**   You can use Lpksetup to perform unattended or silent-mode language pack operations. Lpksetup runs only on an online Windows Vista operating system.

- **Oscdimg**   Oscdimg is a command-line tool for creating an image (.iso) file of a customized 32-bit or 64-bit version of Windows PE. You can then burn an .iso file to a CD-ROM or DVD-ROM.

- **Peimg**   Peimg.exe is a command-line tool for creating and modifying Windows PE 2.0 images offline.

- **Powercfg**   You can use the Powercfg tool to control power settings and configure computers to default to Hibernate or Standby modes.

- **Winpeshl**   Winpeshl.ini controls whether a custom shell is loaded in Windows PE instead of the default Command Prompt window.

- **Wpeinit**   Wpeinit is a command-line tool that initializes Windows PE each time it boots. When Windows PE starts, Winpeshl.exe executes Startnet.cmd, which launches Wpeinit.exe. Wpeinit.exe specifically installs PnP devices, processes Unattend.xml settings, and loads network resources. Wpeinit replaces the initialization function previously supported using the Factory.exe –winpe command. Wpeinit outputs log messages to C:\Windows\system32\wpeinit.log.

- **Wpeutil**   The Windows PE utility (Wpeutil) is a command-line tool that you can use to run various commands in a Windows PE session. For example, you can shut down or reboot Windows PE, enable or disable Windows Firewall, set language settings, and initialize a network.

Windows DS

Windows Deployment Services is the updated and redesigned version of Remote Installation Services (RIS) in Windows Server 2008, and a Windows DS update is also available for Windows Server 2003. This update is in the Windows AIK. Windows DS helps organizations rapidly deploy Windows operating systems, particularly Windows Vista. Using Windows DS, you can deploy Windows operating systems over a network without having to be physically present at the destination computer and without using the media.

Windows DS delivers a better in-box deployment solution than RIS. It provides platform components that enable you to use custom solutions, including remote boot capabilities; a plug-in model for PXE server extensibility; and a client-server communication protocol for diagnostics, logging, and image enumeration. Also, Windows DS unifies on a single image format (.wim) and provides a greatly improved management experience through the Microsoft Management Console (MMC) and scriptable command-line tools.

For organizations that already have RIS deployed, Windows DS maintains parity with RIS by providing both coexistence and migration paths for RIS. Windows DS will continue to support RIS images in legacy or mixed mode. Windows DS also provides tools to migrate RIS images to the new .wim image file format.

Windows DS was initially released as an update for Windows Server 2003, and Windows Server 2008 introduces new features. Windows DS uses the Trivial File Transfer Protocol (TFTP) to download network boot programs and images. In Windows Server 2008, TFTP uses a configurable windowing mechanism that reduces the number of packets network boot clients send, improving performance. Also, Windows DS now logs detailed information about clients to the Windows Server 2008 logging component (Crimson). You can export and process these logs by using Microsoft Office InfoPath or other data mining tools. The most significant new feature, and possibly the most anticipated, is multicast. Multicast deployment allows you to deploy Windows Vista to many computers simultaneously, conserving network bandwidth.

For more information about Windows DS, see Chapter 10, "Configuring Windows DS."

ImageX

ImageX is the Windows Vista tool that you use to work with .wim image files. ImageX is an easy-to-use command-line utility. You use ImageX to create and manage .wim image files. With ImageX, you can capture images and apply them to destination computers' hard drives. You can mount .wim image files as folders and thereby edit images offline. ImageX addresses the challenges that organizations faced when using sector-based imaging formats or the MS-DOS XCopy command to copy an installation of Windows onto new hardware. For example, sector-based imaging:

- Requires that the destination computer use the same Hardware Abstraction Layer (HAL) as the master computer.

- Requires that the destination computer boot from the same type of mass-storage controller as the master computer.

- Destroys the existing contents of the destination computer's hard drive, complicating migration scenarios.

- Duplicates the hard drive exactly; therefore, the image can deploy only to partitions that are the same type and at least as large as the source partition on the master computer.

- Does not allow for direct modification of image-file contents.

The limitations of sector-based imaging led Microsoft to develop ImageX and the accompanying .wim image file format. You can use ImageX to create an image, modify the image without going through the extraction and re-creation process, and deploy the image to your environment— all using the same tool.

Because ImageX works at the file level, it provides numerous benefits. It provides more flexibility and control over your images. For example, you can mount an image on to a folder and then add files to, copy files from, and delete files from the image using a file-management tool such as Windows Explorer. ImageX allows for quicker deployment of images and more rapid installations. With the file-based image format, you can also deploy images nondestructively so that ImageX does not erase the destination computer's hard drive.

ImageX also supports highly compressed images. First, .wim files support single instancing: File data is stored separately from path information so that .wim files can store duplicate files that exist in multiple paths one time. Second, .wim files support two compression algorithms—fast and maximum—which give you control over the size of your images and the time required to capture and deploy them.

Deployment Scenarios

In general, you will perform automated Windows Vista deployments in three scenarios: Upgrade Computer (in-place upgrade), New Computer (wipe-and-load), and Replace Computer. The following sections provide an overview of each scenario.

Upgrade Computer Scenario

You can upgrade from Windows XP to Windows Vista in-place. Windows Vista editions can upgrade some previous editions of Windows XP, as shown in Table 3-1. Some restrictions exist, depending on which edition of Windows XP you are upgrading. This scenario is called Upgrade Computer.

Although upgrading might be the simplest way to deploy Windows Vista, you run the risk of preserving misconfigurations and unauthorized software or settings. In many cases, the existing system configuration is difficult to assess and change-control processes are more difficult to implement. Upgrading from Windows XP computers in an unknown state to Windows Vista does not change the computer's status—its state is still unknown. A better scenario for managed environments is to use the New Computer scenario with user state migration to preserve settings selectively.

Table 3-1   Windows Vista Edition Upgrade Matrix

Previous Windows Edition	Home Basic	Home Premium	Business	Ultimate
Windows XP Professional	○	○	●	●
Windows XP Home	●	●	●	●
Windows XP Media Center Edition	○	●	○	●
Windows XP Tablet PC Edition	○	○	●	●
Windows XP Professional x64	○	○	○	○
Windows 2000 Professional	○	○	○	○

● In-place upgrade possible
○ Requires clean installation

Note   If you are currently using Windows 2000 Professional or Windows XP Professional x64, you are eligible for an upgrade to a corresponding or higher edition of Windows Vista, but a clean install is required. For versions of Windows earlier than Windows 2000, upgrades are not available. These earlier versions of Windows require a full installation of Windows Vista. If the edition of Windows Vista that you choose to install will result in a loss of functionality over your current edition of Windows, you must do a clean installation, or you must complete the installation on a new partition on your computer.

New Computer Scenario

In the New Computer scenario, shown in Figure 3-3, you install a clean copy of Windows Vista on a clean (freshly partitioned and formatted) hard drive. This scenario has the most consistent results, creating a configuration in a known state. Installing a known configuration on a clean computer is the foundation of good configuration management. You can use established change-control processes to closely manage any subsequent changes.

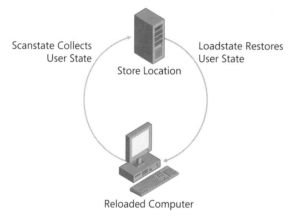

Figure 3-3   Wipe-and-load installation.

Note   You can use migration technologies such as the User State Migration Tool (USMT) to migrate user profile and application data from the previous version of Windows to Windows Vista. This helps ensure that no data is lost while still establishing the best possible system configuration. For more information about using USMT, see Chapter 7, "Migrating User State Data."

Replace Computer Scenario

Windows migration technologies such as the Windows Easy Transfer tool and USMT allow for side-by-side data migration between an old computer running Windows 2000, Windows XP, or Windows Vista and a new computer running Windows Vista. This scenario, which is called Replace Computer, allows you to perform a clean installation on the new computer and simply migrate data and settings from the old one. Figure 3-4 shows an overview of this upgrade method.

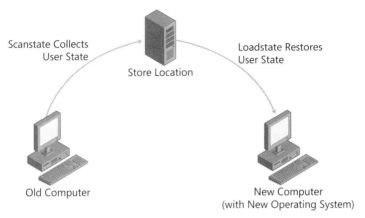

Figure 3-4   Side-by-side upgrades begin with a clean, new system.

Understanding Setup

To automate Windows Setup, you must first understand the installation process. Knowing the underlying process will help you understand the decisions you must make when developing Windows Vista for deployment.

The Windows Vista installation process is simple. All editions of Windows Vista use the same installation image (Install.wim in the Sources folder of the installation media). The product key determines which edition of Windows Vista installs. This simplifies the installation process and allows the use of one basic image to install all systems. The installation process is divided into three phases: Windows Preinstallation Environment (Windows PE), Online Configuration, and Windows Welcome.

Windows Setup runs in *phases*, which the following sections describe. These phases— Preinstallation Phase, Online Configuration Phase, and Windows Welcome Phase—occur in order and simply designate a point in the installation process. Windows Setup also has configuration *passes*. Each configuration pass performs a specific function and applies related settings from the Unattend.xml answer file.

On the Disc   The *Windows Automated Installation Kit User's Guide* (Waik.chm), which is in the Windows AIK, fully describes the command-line options for running Windows Setup (Setup.exe).

You can customize the setup process at many phases through the use of answer files. The following list describes the answer files you use to customize the Windows Vista installation experience:

- **Unattend.xml**   The generic name given to an answer file that controls most unattended installation actions and settings for most phases. When named Autounattend.xml and placed in the appropriate folder, this file can fully automate installations from the original Windows Vista media.

- **SetupComplete.cmd**   Although it is not actually an answer file, this file controls installation activity at the end of the online configuration phase. You can use it to copy files and settings or to install applications.

- **Oobe.xml**   Oobe.xml is a content file you use to customize the out-of-box experience: Windows Welcome, Welcome Center, and ISP Signup.

Preinstallation Phase

During the preinstallation phase, Windows Setup loads and prepares the target system for installation. Figure 3-5 illustrates where this phase fits in the installation process.

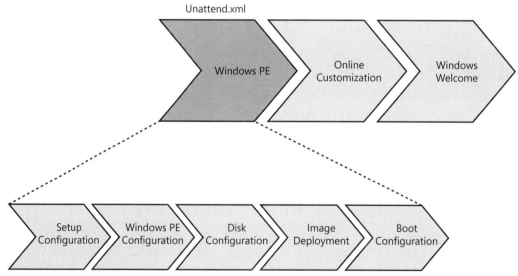

Figure 3-5   Windows PE phase.

Tasks performed during the preinstallation phase include:

- **Windows Setup configuration**   Setup is configured by using either the Windows Setup dialog boxes (interactive) or an answer file (unattended). Windows Setup configurations include adding a product key and configuring a disk.

- **Windows PE configuration**   Answer files settings are applied during the Windows PE configuration pass.

- **Disk configuration**   The hard disk is prepared for image deployment. This might include partitioning and formatting the disk.

- **Windows image file copy**   The Windows Vista image is copied to the disk from the distribution media or a network share. By default, the image is contained in Sources\Install.wim on the product media or distribution share.

- **Prepare boot information**   The Windows Vista boot configuration is finalized. This includes configuring single- or multiboot configuration settings.

- **Process answer file settings in the offlineServicing configuration pass**   Updates are applied to the Windows Vista image, and packages are applied to it, including software fixes, language packs, and other security updates.

 Note   Windows Setup produces numerous log files that are useful for troubleshooting installation. For more information about these log files, see "Windows Vista setup log file locations" at *http://support.microsoft.com/default.aspx/kb/927521*.

Online Configuration Phase

During this phase, Windows Vista performs customization tasks related to the computer's identity. Figure 3-6 shows where this phase fits into the overall process.

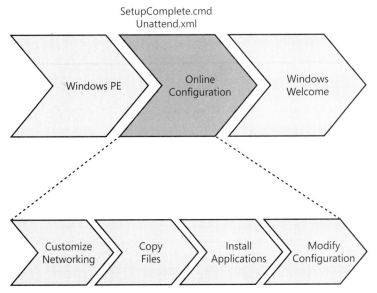

Figure 3-6   Online Configuration phase.

The Specialize pass, which runs during this phase, creates and applies computer-specific information. For example, you can use an unattended setup answer file (Unattend.xml) to configure network settings, international settings, and domain information, as well as run installation programs. You can also copy files, install applications, and modify system configuration by supplying a custom SetupComplete.cmd file to be run during this phase.

During the Online Configuration Phase, you can use scripts to install applications and configure the destination computer. However, a task sequencer, which enables you to filter tasks based on conditions, such as whether a particular device is installed, is better suited to this purpose. A task sequencer also provides advanced features such as the ability to wait until a certain condition arises before continuing, and grouping tasks into folders and then filtering the entire group.

On the Disc   The companion CD includes a script-based task sequencer, Taskseq.wsf, that provides all these advanced features and more. It reads tasks sequences from .xml files and then executes them. The file Sample_Task_Sequences.zip includes sample task sequences that demonstrate how to build .xml files for Taskseq.wsf. Do not run these sample task sequences on production computers. Read the documentation included in the source code for more information about using Taskseq.wsf.

Windows Welcome Phase

In this phase, shown in Figure 3-7, the installation is finalized and any first-use customizations you want to apply are presented. You can customize the Windows Welcome screens and messages and store these customizations in an Oobe.xml file.

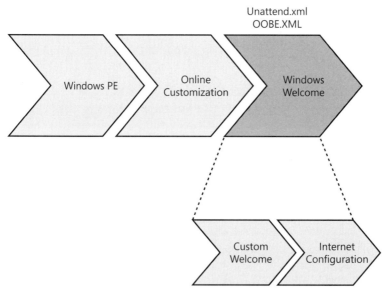

Figure 3-7   Windows Welcome phase.

Direct from the Source: Text Mode Setup Is Gone

The basic process used to install Windows XP has been unchanged since the earliest days of Microsoft Windows NT. This time-consuming procedure involved an initial text-mode installation step in which every operating system file was decompressed and installed, all registry entries were created, and all security was applied. Now with Windows Vista, this text-mode installation phase is completely gone. Instead, a new setup program performs the installation, applying a Windows Vista image to a computer.

After this image is applied, it needs to be customized for the computer. This customization takes the place of what was called mini-setup in Windows XP and Windows 2000. The purpose is the same: the operating system picks the necessary settings and configuration for the specific computer to which it was deployed.

The image preparation process has also changed. With Windows XP, you would Sysprep a computer to prepare the reference operating system for deployment. With Windows Vista, you'll still run Sysprep.exe (installed by default in C:\Windows \System32\Sysprep), which will generalize the computer for duplication.

Windows Vista is provided on the DVD as an already-installed, generalized (Sysprepped) image, ready to deploy to any computer. Some customers may choose to deploy this image as-is (possibly injecting fixes or drivers using the servicing capabilities provided by the deployment tools).

Michael Niehaus

Lead Developer for Microsoft Deployment Toolkit Solution Accelerators

---

Basic Deployment Process

Figure 3-8 illustrates the basic deployment process using only the Windows Vista deployment tools to build images for high-volume deployments. Although this is useful background information, direct use of these tools isn't recommended. Using a framework like MDT 2008 is the best way to deploy Windows Vista.

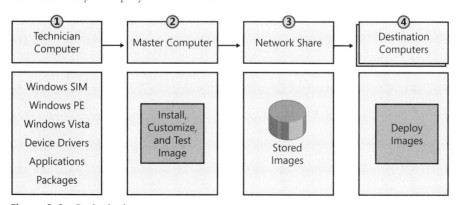

Figure 3-8   Basic deployment process.

- **Technician Computer**   You build a distribution share on a technician computer. The distribution share includes the Windows Vista source files, applications, device drivers, and packages. You use Windows SIM to configure the distribution share by adding source files to it. You also use Windows SIM to create and customize the Windows Vista answer file to use for installation.

- **Master Computer**   On a master computer, you create a master installation by running Windows Setup from the distribution share, using an answer file you created with Windows SIM. The installation should be fully automated to ensure a consistent, repeatable process from one build to the next. After creating the master installation, run Sysprep to prepare it for duplication. In low-volume deployments, you can skip this step and deploy directly from the Windows Vista image that Microsoft provides and then customize the installation during deployment.

- **Network Share**   You use ImageX to capture an image of the master installation from the master computer. Then you store the image on a network share accessible to the destination computers to which you're deploying the image. Alternatives to deploying from a network share include deploying the image from a DVD or deploying the image from Windows DS.

- **Destination Computers**   On the destination computers, run Windows Setup to install Windows Vista. Windows Setup accepts the image file and answer file to use as command-line options. Using Windows Setup to apply an image to destination computers is preferable to using ImageX to apply the image. Windows Setup includes logic that ImageX does not include, such as properly preparing the BCD.

How It Works: Configuration Passes

Like earlier versions of Windows, Windows Vista Setup runs in phases. These phases are called configuration passes. The following list describes each configuration pass that Windows Setup runs:

- **windowsPE**   Configures Windows PE options as well as basic Windows Setup options. These options can include setting the product key and configuring a disk.

- **offlineServicing**   Applies updates to a Windows Vista image. Also applies packages, including software fixes, language packs, and other security updates.

- **generalize**   The generalize pass runs only if you run sysprep /generalize. In this pass, you can minimally configure Windows Vista, as well as configure other settings that must persist on your master image. The sysprep /generalize command removes system-specific information. For example, the unique SID and other hardware-specific settings are removed from the image.

- **specialize**   Creates and applies system-specific information. For example, you can configure network settings, international settings, and domain information.

- **auditSystem** Processes unattended Setup settings while Windows Vista is running in system context, before a user logs on to the computer in audit mode. The auditSystem pass runs only if you boot in audit mode.

- **auditUser** Processes unattended Setup settings after a user logs onto the computer in audit mode. The auditUser pass runs only if you boot in audit mode.

- **oobeSystem** Applies settings to Windows Vista before Windows Welcome starts.

Microsoft Deployment Toolkit Process

MDT 2008 is a holistic approach to desktop deployment, bringing together the people, processes, and technology required to perform highly successful, repeatable, and consistent deployment projects. Because of its strong focus on methodology and best practices, MDT 2008 is much more valuable than the sum of its parts. Not only does it have the benefit of decreasing the time required to develop a desktop-deployment project, but it also reduces errors and helps you create a higher-quality desktop-deployment project.

Microsoft recommends that you use MDT 2008 to deploy Windows Vista instead of using the basic deployment tools directly. All of the deployment tools in Windows Vista and the Windows AIK are huge improvements over the deployment tools for earlier versions of Windows. However, they are simply tools without a framework and without any business logic. They have no "glue" to bind them into an end-to-end process. MDT 2008 provides this glue in the form of a complete technology framework. Internally, MDT 2008 is an extremely complex solution. It provides solutions for the problems facing most customers during deployment, including preinstallation phases (disk partitioning, formatting, and so on), installation (disk imaging), and postinstallation phases (user state migration, application installation, customization, and so on). Even though MDT 2008 is complex internally, the solution makes building, customizing, and deploying Windows Vista images easier by masking the details.

Direct from the Source: MDT 2008

Microsoft has invested a lot to provide innovative technologies that help customers deploy desktops effectively, especially the new capabilities around file-based imaging, component-based architectures, hardware independence, and so on. These have significant benefits in reducing image count, costs, and complexity.

However, where we have heard a lot of feedback from our customers and partners is around the best practices and methodology to use these tools most effectively. We also hear from industry analysts that most of the migration challenges customers face are around building teams, schedules, project plans, business cases, and building the right set of images as well as process and methodology. Technology, in itself, plays a smaller role than we would think in successful deployments.

The challenges our customers face are the following:

- No standard set of deployment guidelines—this results in widely varying results and costs for desktop deployments.

- Focus has been more on technology and less on methodology—this has caused varying types of solutions and, therefore, varying results.

- Customer perception of cost/complexity—because of the lack of repeatable and consistent process around the technology.

- Unclear guidance on which of our many new tools to use and when.

This realization is the reason, with Windows Vista and the Microsoft 2007 Office System, that we have been extremely focused on enhancing our guidance around deployments. The result is the significantly improved MDT 2008 methodology for desktop deployment. We are working with industry experts, system integrators, and deployment/management software providers to enhance this guidance so that it captures best practices from throughout the industry.

Manu Namboodiri

Windows Vista Product Management

Figure 3-9 describes the typical process for using MDT 2008 to deploy Windows Vista. The process is the same whether you're capturing an image in the lab or deploying images in a production environment. Additionally, MDT 2008 provides a user interface to configure all of its processes. Behind the scenes, thousands of lines of code work to implement your choices during deployment.

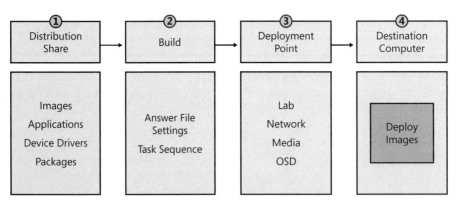

Figure 3-9   Microsoft Deployment Toolkit process.

The following list describes each part of the MDT 2008 process. (See Chapter 6 and Chapter 12, "Using Microsoft Deployment," for more information.)

■ **Distribution share**   After installing MDT 2008 on a build server in a lab environment, you first use the Deployment Workbench to stock the distribution share with source files. Source files include Windows Vista images, applications, device drivers, and packages. The Deployment Workbench provides a user interface for adding all source files to the distribution share. The user interface also provides intelligence, such as error checking and building a device driver database for device driver injection during deployment.

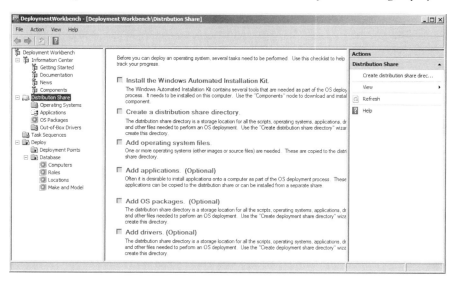

■ **Task sequence**   After the distribution share is fully stocked, you use the Deployment Workbench to create a *task sequence*. A task sequence associates source files from the distribution share with a list of steps to take during installation. The task sequence specifies when to take each step and when to skip it (filtering). The task sequence supports reboots during installation, and data collected during the task sequencer persists between reboots. The task sequence represents one of the primary customization points for MDT 2008.

■ **Deployment point**   After creating a task sequence, you create *deployment points* for installing it. A deployment point is a subset of the MDT 2008 distribution share in much the same way that configuration sets are subsets of Windows SIM distribution shares.

A deployment point specifies which source files and task sequences from the distribution share to distribute and how to distribute them. Deployment points also provide a way to connect to the deployment point and begin installation. For example, a network deployment point copies a subset of the distribution share to another network location and generates a Windows PE boot image that automatically connects to the distribution share and begins installation. An OSD deployment point creates a subset of the distribution share that you can deploy by using an OSD deployment program. A special deployment point, called a Lab deployment point, always points to the full distribution share on the build server.

Deployment points are customizable. The primary customization points for deployment points are rules, which are stored in a file called CustomSettings.ini. This file contains rules for installing Windows Vista on destination computers and configuring it. You can configure the Windows Deployment Wizard user interface, for example, by hiding certain screens and automating others. You can also target specific Windows Vista settings at different groups of computers based on MAC address, location, and so on.

■ **Destination computer**   With a fully stocked distribution share, a defined task sequence, and a defined deployment point, you can use MDT 2008 to deploy Windows Vista to destination computers. You can use LTI to deploy Windows Vista. To use LTI, you start the destination computer using the deployment point's Windows PE boot image. You can put the boot image on removable media (DVD, UFD, and so on) or add it to a Windows DS server. Either way, you start the destination computer using the Windows PE boot image provided by the deployment point to begin the Windows Deployment Wizard. The wizard displays several pages to collect data from you (computer name, domain membership, applications to install, and so on), and then installs the operating system without any further interaction.

You can also use ZTI to deploy Windows Vista. To deploy Windows Vista using ZTI, you can create an OSD deployment point and then create the program in SMS 2003. MDT 2008 integrates directly in System Center Configuration Manager 2007, so the process is easier. For more information about using ZTI, see Chapter 12.

Note that Figure 3-9 makes no reference to creating a master installation and capturing an image. In MDT 2008, creating and capturing an image is an LTI process. You can configure any deployment point to automatically capture an image of an installation and store the image in the distribution share. After you make this choice, the imaging process is fully automated. You don't have to run Sysprep. You don't have to run ImageX. The Windows Deployment Wizard automatically runs Sysprep and then runs ImageX to capture the image and store it in the distribution share. Then you can simply add the image to the distribution share using Deployment Workbench.

The process for OSD images for SMS 2003 is just a bit more complicated, however. The Windows Deployment Wizard will fully prepare the computer for imaging, but you must use the OSD Image Capture Wizard to capture the image and store it in the MDT 2008 distribution share. For more information about this process, see Chapter 6.

 Note   You can download MDT 2008 from *http://technet.microsoft.com/en-us/desktopdeployment/default.aspx.*

> ### New Features for MDT 2008
>
> MDT 2008 is the fourth generation and retitled version of Microsoft Business Desktop Deployment (BDD) 2007. It focuses on tight integration with new deployment features in System Center Configuration Manager 2007 as well as features and guidance to support server deployment.
>
> MDT 2008, combined with System Center Configuration Manager 2007, allows you to dynamically install packages, automatically determine user state store locations, back up computers and database settings, install to computers unknown to the System Center Configuration Manager 2007 database, perform offline updates, install language packs offline and online, and monitor deployments using an updated Microsoft Operations Manager (MOM) 2007 Management Pack.
>
> In addition to the new integration with System Center Configuration Manager 2007, MDT 2008 also enhances LTI for desktop and server computers. This release allows LTI to configure disk and network interface cards (NICs), including static TCP/IP configuration; migrate from LTI to System Center Configuration Manager 2007; create custom task sequences or modify task sequences based on new client, server, and replace templates; invoke web service calls from rules; and deploy operating system images using the new multicast feature in Windows Server 2008 Windows DS.

Summary

The new Windows Vista deployment platform and tools will make deploying the operating system in your organization easier than deploying earlier versions of Windows. The new .wim file format makes it possible to deploy highly compressed image files. Windows Vista helps reduce image count by removing hardware dependencies from the image. Modularization in Windows Vista makes servicing images easier than legacy methods so that you no longer have to apply, customize, and recapture an image to update it. The new answer file format, Unattend.xml, provides a more flexible and consistent configuration. Finally, the new deployment tools, ImageX and Windows SIM, provide a robust way to create, customize, and manage Windows Vista images.

Although the Windows AIK provides the basic tools for customizing and deploying Windows Vista, MDT 2008 provides a more flexible framework for deploying Windows Vista in organizations. With MDT 2008, you can create and customize multiple image builds. The framework includes automation common to most organizations and is highly extensible to suit any requirements.

Additional Resources

The following resources contain additional information and tools related to this chapter.

Related Information

- *Windows Automated Installation Kit User's Guide* in the Windows AIK includes detailed information about each of the tools described in this chapter.

- Chapter 6, "Developing Disk Images," includes more information about using MDT 2008 to create distribution shares, create builds, and capture disk images.

- Chapter 9, "Preparing Windows PE," includes more information about customizing Windows PE for Windows Vista deployment.

- Chapter 10, "Configuring Windows DS," includes more information about installing, configuring, and using Windows DS to deploy Windows Vista.

- Chapter 12, "Using Microsoft Deployment," includes more information about using Microsoft Deployment to deploy Windows Vista images.

- *http://www.microsoft.com/technet/desktopdeploy/* contains the latest information about using Microsoft Deployment to deploy Windows Vista.

- Deployment Forum at *http://www.deploymentforum.com/* is a member-driven community for IT professionals deploying Windows Vista.

- Download the latest version of Microsoft Deployment Toolkit (MDT).

On the Companion CD

- Taskseq.wsf
- Sample_Task_Sequences.zip
- A link from where you can download the latest version of the Microsoft Deployment Toolkit

Chapter 4
Planning Deployment

This chapter helps you plan Windows Vista deployment in your organization. Deploying an operating system requires careful planning. Application compatibility, user state migration, automation, and other issues complicate the process—making deployment more than just installing a new operating system on a handful of desktop computers. This chapter helps you use the best planning tools available and discover issues that require planning so that you can make informed decisions early in the process.

Microsoft Deployment Toolkit (MDT) 2008 provides the ultimate deployment planning information for Windows Vista deployment. The solution includes end-to-end guidance for initiating, planning, developing, and deploying a new project. It also includes job aids that provide convenient document templates for recording your decisions. The scope of the MDT 2008 planning guidance is broad. This chapter guides you through the process of using MDT 2008 to plan large-scale deployment projects. For more information about MDT 2008 and how it relates to the other Windows Vista deployment tools, see Chapter 3, "Deployment Platform."

Using Microsoft Deployment Toolkit for Planning

MDT 2008 is Microsoft's best offering for high-volume Windows Vista deployment projects. It reduces complexity and increases standardization by allowing you to deploy a hardware and software baseline to all users and computers. With standard baselines, you can more easily manage the computing environment and spend less time managing and deploying computers and more time on mission-critical tasks.

MDT 2008 provides automation tools and guidance that help reduce labor and increase reliability by producing standardized configurations. It provides fully developed processes for you to do the following:

■ Document the project's business case.

■ Take an inventory of the existing production computers to determine the installed application base and the types of hardware currently deployed.

■ Determine which applications can be redeployed on new systems and start a process for packaging or scripting those applications so that you can reinstall them quickly and consistently without user intervention.

■ Define a strategy for addressing applications that cannot be supported on the new platform.

■ Determine which types of hardware will be reused as part of the new computer deployment and which types might need to be retired.

■ Create an imaging process to produce a standard enterprise image of Windows Vista to aid in configuration management and to speed deployments.

■ Establish a process for capturing user state from existing computers and for restoring user state on the newly deployed computers.

■ Provide a method for backing up the current computer before deploying Windows Vista.

■ Establish a network map of the client computers, servers, and other networking equipment to assist in planning for deployment.

■ Provide an end-to-end process for the actual deployment of the new computers. The guidance includes Lite Touch and Zero Touch installations.

■ Create a plan for training users to use Windows Vista.

Although you can certainly undertake a high-volume deployment project without MDT 2008, that approach is discouraged. This is because without MDT 2008, you must develop your own planning, development, and deployment processes. You also must define your own best practices and develop your own automation. By using MDT 2008 as your deployment framework, you save potentially hundreds of hours that you would otherwise spend writing scripts, writing answer files, developing images, and so on. MDT 2008 handles most scenarios intrinsically, and you can easily extend MDT 2008 for additional scenarios. You can even use MDT 2008 with most third-party deployment technologies. In fact, many third-party deployment vendors will be extending MDT 2008 in their own product lineups. This chapter assumes you'll be using MDT 2008.

MDT 2008 has four major components: the *Planning Guide*; the technical feature team guides; the job aids; and the solution framework. The following sections describe these components in more detail.

> **Note** Install MDT 2008 to browse the planning documentation it contains. To learn how to install MDT 2008, see the section titled "Installing Microsoft Deployment Toolkit" later in this chapter.

Direct from the Source: Planning with Microsoft Deployment Toolkit

Microsoft intends MDT 2008 to provide the best planning tools possible for deploying Windows Vista. Many IT professionals think of MDT 2008 as code that they can use to kick-start their own development effort—nothing more. Nothing is further from the truth, however. MDT 2008 is not technology driven—it is business driven and provides planning guidance based on deployment best practices.

Planning a complex desktop deployment project is difficult without help. And errors in planning can cost significant time and money down the road. MDT 2008 planning guidance is based on input from Microsoft consultants, deployment partners, and customers and the hard experience from millions of desktops deployed. It leads you through all of the planning steps from beginning to end. To save you even more time and prevent much confusion, MDT 2008 also includes planning templates called job aids. These templates help you more quickly gather the information necessary to make good decisions and correctly execute the plans when developing and deploying the project.

MDT 2008 is Microsoft's recommended methodology for deploying Windows, using either Zero Touch Installation (ZTI) or Lite Touch Installation (LTI). The best practice–driven planning guidance in combination with the deployment framework the solution provides helps you get started in the right direction.

Manu Namboodiri

Windows Vista Product Management

Planning Guide

The *Planning Guide* describes how to plan, manage, and complete the desktop-deployment project. It includes guidance for project planning, developing schedules, building teams, and so on. Everyone participating in the project should read this guide for a better understanding of the project as a whole. Your management team should use its guidance to manage the daily activities of the project, however.

As illustrated in Figure 4-1, the *Planning Guide* divides deployment projects in to five phases: Envisioning, Planning, Developing, Stabilizing, and Deployment. It provides a scheduling template that includes the five phases. You can use this template to build your own schedule and estimate the required resources and time.

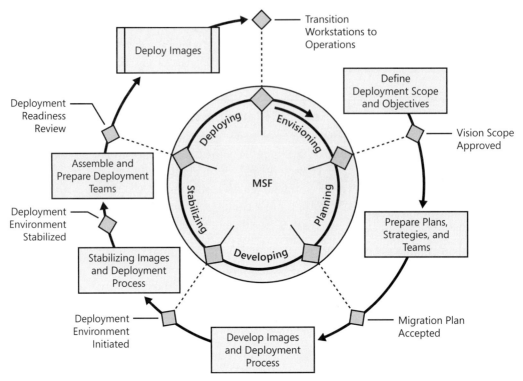

Figure 4-1   Deployment phases for deploying Windows Vista using MDT 2008.

Each feature team guide in MDT 2008 also acknowledges the five deployment phases. Each guide contains a top-level section for each phase that describes the tasks and deliverables that each team must complete for that phase. Performing the technical work around the five deployment phases ensures that the work each feature team performs remains synchronized. The following sections describe each phase.

Envisioning

The initial phase of the planning process involves envisioning the deployment project and determining goals and expected outcomes. The Envisioning Phase is largely a management exercise; the technical feature teams aren't assembled until this phase is complete. The Envisioning Phase includes several key steps, for which MDT 2008 provides job aids to help complete:

- **Set up teams**   The initial task is to define the teams that will plan, design, and perform the deployment. The section titled "Feature Team Guides" later in this chapter lists the MDT 2008 feature teams.

- **Perform a current assessment**   This step includes identifying existing systems and applications, determining existing operating systems, and identifying deficiencies in the current environment that the Windows Vista deployment will address.

- **Define business goals**   Concrete, quantifiable business goals should drive your need for the deployment. Rather than simply planning to deploy the latest technology for technology's sake, identify key deficiencies in the existing system that Windows Vista will address as well as process and productivity gains that the deployment will make possible.

- **Create vision statement and define scope**   Create a vision statement that defines how planned technology changes (including the Windows Vista deployment) will meet the defined business goals. The scope determines the extent of the vision that can be accomplished through the Windows Vista deployment.

- **Create user profiles**   Develop an accurate and complete picture of users' functions, needs, and wants. Refine these into user profiles that accurately identify the types of users in the organization. Understanding the users and what they need is the first step in determining how to structure the deployment to benefit the most users.

- **Develop a solution concept**   Create this high-level document to define how the team will meet the requirements of the project.

- **Create risk-assessment documents**   In this step, evaluate the overall deployment with the intent to anticipate, address, mitigate, and prevent risks associated with the deployment. Documentation of risk assessment is an ongoing task throughout the project.

- **Write a project structure**   This document describes how the team manages and supports the project and describes the administrative structure for the project team. This document should define standards that the team will use, including methods of communication, documentation standards, and change-control standards.

- **Approve milestones**   When you complete the initial planning and documentation, identify and schedule key milestones for the deployment.

Planning

The Envisioning Phase creates the framework for the Windows Vista deployment. The Planning Phase serves as a transition between vision and implementation, laying the groundwork for the actual deployment. The Planning Phase uses the documents and processes created in the Envisioning Phase to add structure and content to the deployment plan. Key steps in this phase include the following tasks. MDT 2008 provides job aids to address many of these tasks.

- **Create the development and testing environment**   Build a testing lab that adequately embodies the target deployment environment, using virtualization to reduce the cost of lab creation. In addition to resources such as servers and sample target systems used to develop and test the deployment, the lab should also include the resources that the Deployment feature team will use to prepare and accomplish the final deployment.

- **Develop the solution design**   This document builds on the solution concept, project structure, and other documents created during the Envisioning Phase to define the conceptual, logical, and physical solution designs for the planned deployment. This document serves as a roadmap for the Deployment feature team to begin building the deployment.

■ **Create the functional specification**   This document defines the requirements of all stakeholders targeted by the deployment and serves as a contract between the customer and the project team. It should clearly define the goals, scope, and outcomes of the deployment.

■ **Develop the project plan**   This document is a collection of plans that address the tasks the Deployment feature team will perform to carry out the project as defined by the functional specification. Each plan in this document covers a particular area, such as facilities and hardware, testing, training, and communication.

■ **Create the project schedule**   This schedule compiles individual schedules created by team members for the purpose of planning deployment activities.

■ **Complete a computer inventory**   During the Planning Phase, a complete computer inventory must be made to identify existing systems and applications that the deployment will affect. In addition, the server resources to be used for deployment must also be identified and evaluated for suitability.

■ **Perform network analysis**   Diagram network topology and identify and inventory network devices.

Developing

The Developing Phase is the period during which the team builds and unit-tests the solution. The Developing Phase includes six key tasks:

■ **Start the development cycle**   In this initial step, the team creates a lab server for development work and begins the process of creating images, installation scripts, and application packages. The team should also create an issue-tracking system so that team members can communicate about and coordinate solutions to issues.

■ **Prepare the computing environment**   In this key task, the teams build a deployment environment with facilities such as servers, networking, system backup, and data repositories (such as Microsoft Visual SourceSafe) with separate workspaces (computers and network shares) for each feature team. This environment provides the infrastructure for teams to work both independently and jointly as necessary to complete their development tasks.

■ **Develop the solution scripts**   In this step, the teams begin the process of packaging applications, creating computer images, and developing remediation steps for application-compatibility issues. The teams also plan how and what user data will be retained and migrated during the deployment and validate that network infrastructure (shares, credentials, and other components) are in place and functioning properly prior to deployment.

■ **Develop deployment procedures**   Using the documents, processes, and other resources created to this point, begin creating the documents that the teams will use to accomplish the deployment and post-deployment tasks. These documents include training materials for users, administrators, and others who will maintain systems and applications after deployment; a plan for communicating with users about the upcoming changes; and site-deployment procedures to simplify and standardize the deployment of solutions across sites.

■ **Develop operations procedures**   This document describes the operations procedures to support, maintain, and operate the solution following deployment. Key processes to describe include maintenance, disaster recovery, new-site installation, performance and fault monitoring, and support and troubleshooting.

■ **Test the solution**   Perform test deployments and remedy any issues that arise, using the issue-tracking framework created during the Planning Phase to monitor and address these issues.

Stabilizing

The Stabilizing Phase addresses the testing of a solution that is feature-complete. This phase is usually when pilots are conducted, with an emphasis on real-world testing and with the goal of identifying, prioritizing, and fixing bugs. Key tasks in this phase include:

■ **Conducting the pilot**   At this stage, the teams use a small pilot deployment to test the deployment and identify any remaining issues. Procedures, resources, and personnel should be in place to assist in addressing any user issues that arise during the pilot deployment. This key task should also include obtaining user feedback as well as review and remediation of issues identified during the pilot.

■ **Operational-readiness review**   All teams at this stage perform a complete operational-readiness review to determine that the deployment plan is ready to move forward to full-scale deployment. The solution is frozen at this stage, and any remaining issues are addressed.

■ **Final release**   This task incorporates all fixes and issue resolutions to create the final release of the solution, which should now be ready for full deployment.

Deploying

During the Deploying Phase, the team deploys the solution and ensures that it is stable and usable. The key tasks involved in the Deploying Phase include:

■ **Deploying core technology**   Based on the plans and procedures developed in the Planning Phase, install, configure, and test deployment servers at each site. Also, train administration staff in preparation for deployment.

■ **Deploying sites**   Teams perform the deployment of Windows Vista at each site using the procedures and resources developed during the Planning and Building Phases.

Team members remain on site to stabilize each site deployment, ensuring that users can move forward with reliable systems and applications and that the goals of the deployment plan for the site have been met.

- **Stabilizing the deployment**   At this key step, the Deployment feature team ensures stabilization across all sites and addresses any remaining deployment issues.

- **Completing the deployment**   This step marks the transition from deployment to operations and support. Ongoing operations are transitioned from the Deployment feature team to permanent staff. Reporting systems are activated and support processes are fully operational.

Feature Team Guides

In an MDT 2008 project, a *feature team* is a cross-organizational team that focuses on solving a particular problem, such as security. Feature teams divide the work into discrete parts that are easier for you to manage. Figure 4-2 illustrates the relationship between feature teams in MDT 2008. These teams help you to apply specialized expertise to necessary areas. Most important, feature teams foster ownership of specific problem spaces by empowering the team to complete the work and holding the team accountable. The solution provides a feature team guide for each feature team that MDT 2008 defines.

The feature team guides provide information about specific technical areas, such as application management or computer imaging. By separating the technical content from the planning content, you can focus on the documents that are most appropriate for your role. Feature team guides lead you through planning, building, and deploying specific tasks within a larger deployment project. For example, the *Image Engineering Feature Team Guide* is specific to using MDT 2008 to build disk images, although the project includes many other technical areas.

Each feature team guide contains checkpoints that refer to milestones in the *Planning Guide*. These checkpoints ensure that activities occurring among different teams remain synchronized. The feature team guides also separate step-by-step processes from conceptual content. This separation helps you to jump straight to the technical content, assuming that you're already familiar with the concepts and processes contained in the body of the guide.

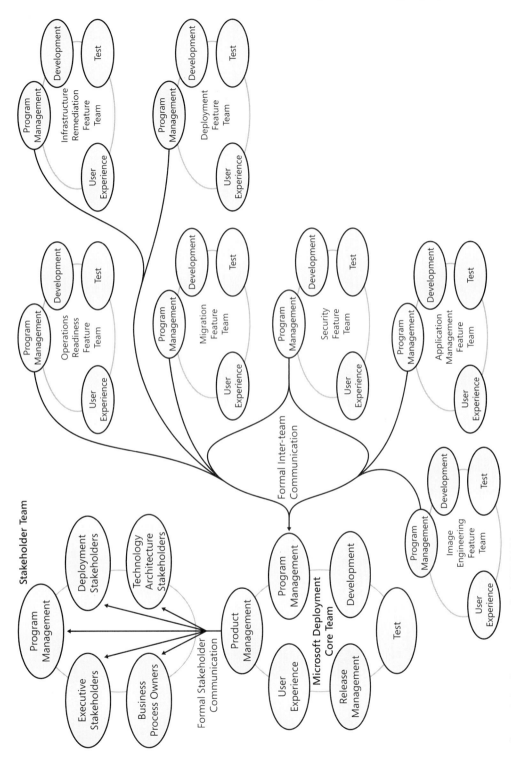

Figure 4-2   Feature teams in MDT 2008.

MDT 2008 provides the following feature team guides:

- **Application Management Feature Team Guide** This guide targets the team responsible for assisting in the planning, deployment, and migration of applications. It includes three technical subguides: the *Office Deployment Guide*, which describes how to deploy the 2007 Office system as part of a large Windows Vista deployment initiative; the *Application Compatibility Guide*, which describes how to discover and mitigate application compatibility issues; and the *Application Packaging Guide*, which describes how to package applications for automated deployment.

- **Image Engineering Feature Team Guide** This guide focuses on creating computer images of Windows Vista. It includes comprehensive guidance on how to implement, customize, and operate the automated imaging process included in the MDT 2008 solution. It includes three technical subguides: the *Image Customization Guide*, *Workbench Imaging Guide*, and *SCCM Imaging Guide*.

- **Deployment Feature Team Guide** This guide targets the team responsible for executing computer deployments. It provides information on server placement and capacity planning as well as specific information on deployment tools and processes. It includes five technical subguides: *Deployment Customization Desktop Samples*, *Deployment Customization Guide*, *Preparing for LTI Tools*, *Preparing for SCCM*, and *Preparing for SMS 2003*.

- **Infrastructure Remediation Feature Team Guide** This guide describes how to assess the current computer hardware to determine hardware upgrade requirements and how to analyze the network for any limitations or constraints that may affect the deployment.

- **Operations Readiness Feature Team Guide** This guide targets the people who manage the IT operations environment. It provides guidance for integrating the IT operations requirements into the overall deployment process.

- **Security Feature Team Guide** This guide focuses on how to assess computer security requirements. It provides guidance for integrating security requirements into the imaging and deployment process.

- **Test Feature Team Guide** This guide describes how to test the solution and set up a test lab for it.

- **Migration Feature Team Guide** This guide describes how to identify users' state data, save it, and restore it after deploying Windows Vista. It includes the technical subguide *User State Migration Guide*.

Solution Framework

You use the solution framework (technology files) to set up the imaging and deployment servers. This framework helps you create standard desktop configurations. It includes tools to build and deploy custom Windows Vista images with a variety of special needs, such as backing up the destination computer prior to deployment, capturing and restoring user state, enabling BitLocker Drive Encryption, and so on. By using the solution framework as your starting point, you can take advantage of the deployment best practices that Microsoft and its customers have developed over several years, most of which are manifested in the framework's script code.

> **Note**   The solution framework does not contain copies of Windows Vista or the 2007 Office system. To use MDT 2008, you must acquire licensed copies of this software and other hardware-specific software such as DVD-player software and CD-creation software. Each feature team guide in MDT 2008 describes requirements for using the guidance as well as the tools.

Job Aids

MDT 2008 provides job aids (document templates) as starting points for project deliverables. For example, where the *Planning Guide* indicates the need for a functional specification, the solution includes a job aid that shows what type of content to include in the functional specification. You can customize the job aids to fit your specific needs. The following list describes each job aid in MDT 2008:

- **Application Knowledge Sheet**   Provides a template for recording application information.
- **Assessment Template**   Provides a template for recording infrastructure information.
- **Client Build Requirements**   Provides a template for recording the required client configuration, including operating system and core applications settings.
- **Communications Plan**   Describes how to communicate project status and information within the organization and outside the organization.
- **Current State Assessment Template**   Describes and assesses the current infrastructure.
- **Deployment Plan**   Describes how to perform deployment and migration.
- **Functional Specification**   Provides an overview of the project's requirements.
- **Inventory Template**   Provides a template for recording software and hardware inventory.
- **Network and Workstation Hardware Upgrades List**   Provides a template for recording the necessary network and computer hardware upgrades.
- **Pilot Plan**   Describes how to pilot-test the project in the organization.
- **Risk Template Tool**   Describes and assesses the top risks to the project.
- **Test Cases Workbook**   Provides a template for recording the results of test cases.
- **Test Plan**   Describes the methodologies and tools to use for testing.
- **Test Specification**   Describes how to test the project.
- **Training Plan**   Describes how, when, and what types of training will be provided.
- **Vision Scope**   Outlines the overall project objectives and responsibilities.

Planning Low-Volume Deployment

In low-volume deployment projects, such as in a small or medium-sized business, the planning guidance in MDT 2008 can be overwhelming. The MDT 2008 technology framework is well-suited to low-volume deployment projects. In fact, a small business can prepare MDT 2008 to deploy Windows Vista in as little as a few hours. Medium-sized businesses can accomplish the same in a few days. Even though you can use the MDT 2008 technology framework without using its planning guidance, you should still put some effort into planning your deployment. This section describes some of the planning steps you should take in this scaled-down scenario.

The first step in the deployment process is to assess your business needs so that you can define the project scope and objectives. Next, decide how best to use Windows Vista to meet those needs. Then assess your current network and desktop configurations, determine whether you need to upgrade your hardware or software, and choose the tools for your deployment. Having made these decisions, you are ready to plan your deployment. An effective plan typically includes the following:

- A schedule for the deployment.

- All the details for customizing Windows Vista to suit your requirements.

- An assessment of your current configuration, including information about users, organizational structure, network infrastructure, and hardware and software. Create a test environment in which you can deploy Windows Vista by using the features and options in your plan. Have your test environment mirror your production network as closely as possible, including hardware, network architecture, and business applications.

- Test and pilot plans. When you're satisfied with the results in your test environment, roll out your deployment to a specific group of users to test the results in a controlled production environment. This is your pilot test.

- A rollout plan. Finally, roll out Windows Vista to your entire organization.

Creating the deployment plan is a cyclical process. As you move through each phase, modify the plan based on your experiences.

Note   Even if you choose not to use the deployment guidance in MDT 2008, you can still use the job aids it includes, which provide templates for planning a Windows Vista deployment more quickly and more thoroughly.

Scope and Objectives

The scope is the baseline for creating a specification for your deployment project. The scope of your deployment project is defined largely by your answers to the following questions:

- What business needs do you want to address with Windows Vista?

■   What are the long-term goals for the deployment project?

■   How will your Windows Vista client computers interact with your IT infrastructure?

The scope is simply a statement of what you're trying to accomplish and how you plan to accomplish it. Your statement of scope need only be a few paragraphs long and should not be longer than a page.

Current Environment

Document your existing computing environment, looking at your organization's structure and how it supports users. Use this assessment to determine your readiness for desktop deployment of Windows Vista. The three major areas of your computing environment to assess include your hardware, software, and network.

■   **Hardware**   Do your desktop and laptop computers meet the minimum hardware requirements for Windows Vista? In addition to meeting these requirements, all hardware must be compatible with Windows Vista. For more information, see Chapter 1, "Overview of Windows Vista Improvements."

■   **Software**   Are your applications compatible with Windows Vista? Make sure that all your applications, including custom-designed software, work with computers running Windows Vista. For more information about application compatibility, see Chapter 8, "Deploying Applications."

■   **Network**   Document your network architecture, including topology, size, and traffic patterns. Also, determine which users need access to various applications and data, and describe how they obtain access.

Where appropriate, create diagrams to include in your project plan. Diagrams convey more information than words alone. A good tool for creating these diagrams is Microsoft Office Visio 2007. See *http://www.microsoft.com/office* for information.

Configuration Plan

Determine which features to include in your configuration and how to implement these features to simplify the management of users and computers in your organization. An important means of simplification is standardization. Standardizing desktop configurations makes it easier to install, update, manage, support, and replace computers that run Windows Vista. Standardizing users' configuration settings, software, hardware, and preferences simplifies deploying operating system and application upgrades, and configuration changes can be guaranteed to work on all computers.

When users install their own operating system upgrades, applications, device drivers, settings, preferences, and hardware devices, a simple problem can become complex. Establishing standards for desktop configurations prevents many problems and makes it easier for you to identify and resolve problems. Having a standard configuration that you can install on any computer minimizes downtime by ensuring that user settings, applications, drivers, and preferences are the same as before the problem occurred. The following list provides an overview of some of the features that you must plan for:

- **Management**   Desktop management features allow you to reduce the total cost of ownership in your organization by making it easier to install, configure, and manage clients. For more information about Windows Vista management features, see Part III of this book, "Desktop Management."

- **Networking**   You can configure computers that run Windows Vista to participate in a variety of network environments. For more information about Windows Vista networking features, see Part V of this book, "Networking."

- **Security**   Windows Vista includes features to help you secure your network and computers by controlling authentication and access to resources and by encrypting data stored on computers. These features include BitLocker Drive Encryption, Windows Firewall with Advanced Security, and so on. For more information about Windows Vista security features, see Chapter 2, "Security in Windows Vista."

Testing and Piloting

Before rolling out your deployment project, you need to test it for functionality in a controlled environment. Before you begin testing your deployment project, create a test plan that describes the tests you will run, who will run each test, a schedule for performing tests, and the expected results. The test plan must specify the criteria and priority for each test. Prioritizing your tests can help you avoid slowing down your deployment because of minor failures that you can easily correct later; it can also help you identify larger problems that might require redesigning your plan.

The testing phase is essential because a single error can be replicated to all computers in your environment if it is not corrected before you deploy the image. Create a test lab that is not connected to your network but mirrors your organization's network and hardware configurations as closely as possible. Set up your hardware, software, and network services as they are in your production environment. Perform comprehensive testing on each hardware platform, testing both application installation and operation. These steps can greatly increase the confidence of the project teams and the business-decision makers, resulting in a higher-quality deployment.

Microsoft recommends that you pilot the project (roll out the deployment) to a small group of users after you test the project. Piloting the installation allows you to assess the success of the deployment project in a production environment before rolling it out to all users. The primary purpose of pilot projects is not to test Windows Vista, but to get user feedback. This feedback will help to determine the features that you must enable or disable in Windows Vista. For pilots, you might choose a user population that represents a cross-section of your business in terms of job function and computer proficiency. Install pilot systems by using the same method that you plan to use for the final rollout.

The pilot process provides a small-scale test of the eventual full-scale rollout: You can use the results of the pilot, including any problems encountered, to finalize your rollout plan. Compile the pilot results and use the data to estimate upgrade times, the number of concurrent upgrades you can sustain, and peak loads on the user-support functions.

Rolling Out

After you thoroughly test your deployment plan, pilot the deployment to smaller groups of users, and are satisfied with the results, begin rolling out Windows Vista to the rest of your organization. To finalize the rollout plan, you need to determine the following:

- The number of computers to include in each phase of the rollout

- The time needed to upgrade or perform a clean installation for each computer that you include

- The personnel and other resources needed to complete the rollout

- The time frame during which you plan to roll out the installations to different groups

- Training needed for users throughout the organization

Throughout the rollout, gather feedback from users and modify the deployment plan as appropriate.

Windows Vista Requirements

To plan deployment, you must understand the deployment requirements for Windows Vista. The following sections describe the minimum hardware requirements and the migration paths for Windows Vista. For more information about Windows Vista hardware requirements and editions, see Chapter 1.

Hardware Requirements

Table 4-1 describes the minimum hardware requirements for installing Windows Vista. Part of the deployment Planning Phase is collecting a hardware inventory. Compare the hardware requirements in Table 4-1 to your hardware inventory to identify any computers that require upgrades or replacements.

Table 4-1   Minimum Hardware Requirements

Hardware	Minimum Requirement
Processor	800 MHz 32-bit or 64-bit processor
Memory	512 MB
Graphics Processor	SVGA (800 × 600)
Hard Disk Drive	20 GB
Free Hard Disk Drive Space	15 GB
Optical Drive	CD-ROM Drive

Note   You cannot upgrade Windows XP x64 to Windows Vista x64.

Upgrade Paths

Table 4-2 describes the Windows Vista upgrade and migration paths. As shown in the table, performing an in-place upgrade from Windows XP with Service Pack 2 (SP2) or later to Windows Vista is supported. Using Windows Easy Transfer to migrate user state data from Windows 2000 with SP4 or later to Windows Vista is also supported. However, upgrading or migrating user state data from Microsoft Windows 98 to Windows Vista is not supported.

Table 4-2   Windows Vista Migration Paths

From	Upgrade to Windows Vista	Migrate to Windows Vista Using Windows Easy Transfer	Migrate to Windows Vista Using USMT
Windows 95	No	No	No
Windows 98	No	No	No
Windows 98 Second Edition (SE)	No	No	No
Windows NT 4.0	No	No	No
Windows 2000 with SP4 or later	No	Yes	Yes
Windows XP with SP2 or later	Yes	Yes	Yes
Windows Vista	Yes (higher SKU)	Yes	Yes

Note   To assess the readiness of client computers for Windows Vista, you can use the Microsoft Assessment and Planning Solution Accelerator, a centralized and agentless tool that can remotely inventory computers, identify their supported Windows Vista experience, and recommend specific hardware upgrades where appropriate. For more information on this tool, see "Windows Vista Hardware Assessment 2.1" found at *http://www.microsoft.com/downloads/ details.aspx?FamilyId=67240B76-3148-4E49-943D-4D9EA7F77730&displaylang=en.*

Preparing for Development

Whether your organization uses MDT 2008 or not, it will likely require multiple feature teams to develop high-volume deployment projects. Most feature teams need a lab environment. Although each feature team can construct a separate lab, most organizations create a single lab that shares facilities such as servers, networks, system backup, and source control with separate workspaces (computers and network shares) for each feature team. With this environment, feature teams can work separately when necessary and jointly when appropriate. It also helps minimize the number of computers and servers required.

The remaining chapters in Part II of this book, "Deployment," describe specific lab require-ments for each feature team working on a high-volume deployment project. The Planning Phase is the best time to begin preparing the development environment, however. The process includes installing MDT 2008, stocking the lab environment with the files necessary to perform each feature team's job, locating application media, and so on. The following sections describe steps to complete during the Planning Phase to expedite the development process.

Application Management

The Application Management feature team is responsible for repackaging applications or automating their installation and configuration. Organizations can have hundreds or thousands of applications. Often, users install each application differently on each computer, leading to inconsistency across computers and resulting in support and management issues.

Repackaging or automating an application's installation has many benefits. Most obviously, it allows applications to install without user intervention, which is especially desirable when deploying applications as part of a disk image or during disk image deployment. In addition, repackaging or automating leads to consistency that lowers deployment and ownership costs by reducing support issues and enhancing management. Chapter 8 describes a process for repackaging and automating application installations.

Before migrating from your current version of Windows to Windows Vista, the application compatibility feature test must also test applications to ensure that they are compatible with Windows Vista. You might have several thousand applications installed across distributed networks. Compatibility problems with one or many of these applications can disrupt productivity and damage the user experience and satisfaction with the project. Testing applications and solving compatibility problems saves time and money for the organization. It also prevents roadblocks to future deployment projects based on perceived pain.

Although most applications developed for earlier versions of Windows will probably perform well on Windows Vista, some applications might behave differently because of new technologies within the new operating system. Test the following applications to ensure compatibility:

- Custom tools, such as logon scripts
- Core applications that are part of the standard desktop configurations, such as office productivity suites
- Line-of-business (LOB) applications, such as Enterprise Resource Planning (ERP) suites
- Administrative tools, such as antivirus, compression, backup, and remote-control applications

Chapter 5, "Testing Application Compatibility," describes how to build an application compatibility test lab and how application compatibility integrates into the overall deployment process. The following list describes steps you can take during the Planning Phase to begin building the lab environment for application packaging and compatibility testing:

- **Installation media**   For each application you test, repackage, and automate, you must have a copy of the application's installation media, any configuration documentation, and product keys. If your IT department doesn't have the media or other information, check with the subject matter expert (SME) for each application.

■ **Destination computers**   Within the lab, the Application Management feature team requires destination computers that resemble computers found in the production environment. Each destination computer should have Windows Vista installed on it to test applications' compatibility with the operating system and application installation.

■ **Application Compatibility Toolkit**   For more information on the Application Compatibility Toolkit (ACT), see Chapter 5. MDT 2008 provides a user interface for downloading the most recent version of the ACT.

■ **SQL Server**   Install Microsoft SQL Server in the lab environment. The ACT stores the application inventory using SQL Server, which is available on volume-licensed media.

■ **Host computer with network shares**   You must have a computer on which to host the application installations. Shares on this computer hold the original installation sources and completed packages. You can install the ACT and SQL Server on the host computer.

■ **Application packaging software**   The Application Management feature team needs software with which to repackage applications. Chapter 8 describes this software. The application packaging software will be installed on each team member's development computer.

■ **Deployment mechanism**   The Application Management feature team requires a mechanism for deploying ACT and application packages. This can be through logon scripts, a local website, or another deployment mechanism.

Image Engineering

You're probably already familiar with disk imaging tools, such as Symantec Ghost or ImageX (the Windows Vista imaging tool). Using imaging tools effectively is a significant challenge, however, and this challenge is the reason that Microsoft developed MDT 2008. With MDT 2008, you do not have to engineer the entire imaging process; the framework provides most of the code for you already. All that's left is for you to customize it to suit your organization's requirements. Using MDT 2008 to build Windows Vista images involves the following steps:

■ **Create a build server**   The build server is the host for MDT 2008 and its distribution share.

■ **Configure a distribution share**   The distribution share contains the source files (Windows Vista, applications, device drivers, and so on) from which you build operating system images.

■ **Create and customize task sequences**   After stocking the distribution share, you create task sequences. Task sequences associate source files from the distribution share with the steps necessary to install and configure them. For more information about answer files and task sequences, refer to Chapter 3.

- **Create deployment points**   Deployment points are copies of the distribution share that are ready to deploy. For each deployment point, MDT 2008 provides a Windows PE boot image that you can use to connect to the deployment point and install builds from it.

- **Build initial operating system images**   With MDT 2008, building a custom Windows Vista image is as simple as installing the operating system from a deployment point by using the Windows Deployment Wizard. This is a Lite Touch Installation process that requires minimal user interaction and automatically captures a Windows Vista image and stores it back in the distribution share.

Chapter 6, "Developing Disk Images," describes how to use MDT 2008 to build custom Windows Vista images. In preparation for the development process, you can begin building the lab during the Planning Phase, as the following list describes:

- **Windows Vista media**   You will need media and volume license keys for Windows Vista.

- **Destination computers**   You will need computers on which to create, install, and test Windows Vista images.

- **Build computer for MDT 2008**   You must have a computer on which to host MDT 2008 and the distribution share. The lab server should have a DVD-RW drive and should be networked with the destination computers. You can install MDT 2008 on a desktop or server computer.

- **Windows Deployment Services**   The lab environment should contain a server running Windows Deployment Services (Windows DS). Using Windows DS to boot destination computers is much faster than burning DVDs and starting computers with them.

- **Additional source files**   Early in the Planning Phase, the Image Engineering feature team can begin assembling the source files required to stock the distribution share. Source files include device drivers and hardware-specific applications for each computer in the production environment. Additionally, the team should begin assembling any security updates and operating system packages that must be added to the distribution share.

> **Note**   The Planning Phase is the best time to install MDT 2008 in the lab environment and begin familiarizing yourself with it. The section titled "Installing Microsoft Deployment Toolkit" later in this chapter describes the requirements for installing MDT 2008 and how to install MDT 2008 in the lab environment.

Deployment

Deployment is an intense, time-consuming process during any high-volume deployment. MDT 2008 provides planning guidance and tools that help streamline the following processes:

- Planning server placement
- Evaluating server and network capacity

- Installing the distribution shares and tools
- Deploying the client computers

Chapter 12, "Using Microsoft Deployment," describes how to use MDT 2008 to deploy Windows Vista using LTI and ZTI processes. During the Planning Phase, the Deployment feature team should begin preparing the lab environment as described in the following list:

- **Production replica**   The Deployment feature team needs a replica of the production environment to unit-test the combined efforts of all the other feature teams. Destination computers should be running the versions of Windows found in the production environment with user data loaded. These computers are used for the unit-test deployment, including user state migration.

- **Network shares on a host computer**   Two types of network shares are required: one for the MDT 2008 distribution share and a second for the data server share. These shares could be all on the same physical server or on separate servers. Also, it's useful to store images of the production computers on the host computer to restore them quickly and easily after each test pass.

- **Windows Deployment Services**   The lab environment should contain a server running Windows Deployment Services (Windows DS). Using Windows DS to boot destination computers is much faster than burning DVDs and starting computers with them. The Deployment feature team can use the same Windows DS server as the Image Engineering feature team.

Infrastructure Remediation

Understanding the network environment is critical with any project that introduces changes. To plan and prepare to incorporate these changes, first understand the current status of the organization's environment, identify other sources of change that may affect this project, perform a risk-mitigation approach to the changes, and then incorporate the proposed changes. Organizations can solve and possibly avoid most networking problems by creating and maintaining adequate network documentation. Using a networking tool, the team can:

- Gather information necessary to help understand a network as it exists today.
- Plan for growth.
- Diagnose problems when they occur.
- Update the information with network changes—either in real time or scheduled.
- Work with the information to manage network assets. (Often, an apparently simple configuration change can result in an unexpected outage.)
- Present information visually so that the network structure appears in as much detail as necessary for each task.

The Infrastructure Remediation feature team must have access to SQL Server. The team uses SQL Server to create hardware inventory reports against the application-compatibility database. This could be the same installation that the Application Management feature team uses. The team must also have access to current network topology diagrams and network device inventory information.

Operations Readiness

The Operations Readiness feature team is responsible for a smooth and successful handoff of the deployed solution to the Operations staff. This aspect of the overall project is important because the success of the handoff directly reflects the success of the deployment project. To ensure success, the activities of the feature teams must be integrated with the ongoing management and operating functions of the Operations staff. The Operations Readiness feature team can facilitate deployment by completing the following tasks:

- Confirm that the workstation roles identified in the functional specification are valid.
- Analyze and evaluate the management tools currently in use.
- Assess the maturity of the operations environment in key operational areas.
- Establish effective management processes and tools in deficient key areas.
- Develop a training program for operations and support staff.
- Prepare the operations staff for the pilot.

The Operations Readiness feature team does not initially have any additional lab requirements.

Security

The Security feature team has an important role in the overall success of the deployment project. Security is a primary concern in all organizations, and the goal of the Security feature team is to secure the organization's data. Inadequate security in an organization can result in lost or corrupted data, network downtime, lost productivity, frustrated employees, over-worked IT employees, and possibly stolen proprietary information that results in lost revenue. To ensure that adequate security measures are in place, the Security feature team should:

- Analyze and determine the existing security level of the organization.
- Identify vulnerabilities caused by software upgrades and update network security specifications accordingly.
- Ensure that security measures are current.

The Security feature team does not initially have any additional lab requirements. For more information about Windows Vista security features, see Chapter 2.

Migration

One of the most tedious and time-consuming tasks during deployment is identifying data files and settings on users' current computers (known as *user state*), saving them, and then restoring them. Users spend significant time restoring items such as wallpaper, screen savers, and other customizable features. And most users don't remember how to restore these settings. Migrating user state can increase user productivity and satisfaction. In MDT 2008, the Migration feature team performs the following tasks:

- Inventory existing production client computer applications.

- Identify applications with data or preference migration requirements.

- Prioritize the application list to be addressed.

- Identify SMEs for each application.

- Identify data file requirements for each application.

The Migration feature team completes these tasks in cooperation with the Application Management feature team. Therefore, the Migration feature team can and should share a lab environment with the other two teams.

- **Installation media**   For each application containing settings to migrate, you must have a copy of the application's installation media, any configuration documentation, and product keys. If your IT department doesn't have the media or other information, check with the subject matter expert (SME) for each application.

- **Destination computers**   The Migration feature team requires computers in the lab on which to test user state migration solutions. Destination computers should be running the versions of Windows found in the production environment with applications and user data loaded. These computers are used for the unit-test user state migration.

- **Host computer**   You must have a computer on which to host application source files and migration solutions. It's useful to store images of the destination computers on the host computer to restore them quickly and easily after each test pass.

- **Data store**   The data store is a network share on which you can put user state data during testing. You can create the data store on the host computer, or you can optionally create the data store on each destination computer.

- **User State Migration Tool**   MDT 2008 uses the User State Migration Tool (USMT) to migrate user state. The functionality is already built in to the MDT 2008 framework. The team must download and prepare the distribution share with the USMT executables, however. Chapter 7, "Migrating User State Data," describes where to place these files.

Installing Microsoft Deployment Toolkit

If you're installing MDT 2008 on Windows XP Professional or Windows Server 2003 with Service Pack 1, you must install additional prerequisite software. This additional software is already installed in Windows Vista and Windows Server 2008. The following list describes software that you must install before installing and using MDT 2008 on Windows XP Professional or Windows Server 2003 with Service Pack 1:

- **Offline Servicing Kernel Update**   Download the offline servicing kernel update from *http://support.microsoft.com/kb/926044/*.

- **Microsoft Windows Installer 3.1**   Download Windows Installer 3.1 from *http://www.microsoft.com/downloads/details.aspx?FamilyID=889482fc-5f56-4a38-b838-de776fd4138c&DisplayLang=en*.

- **Microsoft .NET Framework 2.0**   The Windows AIK distribution media includes the Microsoft .NET Framework 2.0 installation file. Alternatively, download the .NET Framework 2.0 from the following addresses:

  - ❏ x86: *http://www.microsoft.com/downloads/details.aspx?FamilyID=0856eacb-4362-4b0d-8edd-aab15c5e04f5&DisplayLang=en*

  - ❏ x64: *http://www.microsoft.com/downloads/details.aspx?FamilyID=b44a0000-acf8-4fa1-affb-40e78d788b00&DisplayLang=en*

- **Microsoft Management Console (MMC) 3.0**   Download MMC 3.0 from the following addresses:

  - ❏ **Windows Server 2003 x86**   *http://www.microsoft.com/downloads/info.aspx?na=22&p=1&SrcDisplayLang=en&SrcCategoryId=&SrcFamilyId=&u=%2fdownloads%2fdetails.aspx%3fFamilyID%3d4c84f80b-908d-4b5d-8aa8-27b962566d9f%26DisplayLang%3den*

  - ❏ **Windows Server 2003 x64 Edition**   *http://www.microsoft.com/downloads/info.aspx?na=22&p=3&SrcDisplayLang=en&SrcCategoryId=&SrcFamilyId=&u=%2fdownloads%2fdetails.aspx%3fFamilyID%3db65b9b17-5c6d-427c-90aa-7f814e48373b%26DisplayLang%3den*

  - ❏ **Windows XP Professional x86**   *http://www.microsoft.com/downloads/info.aspx?na=22&p=2&SrcDisplayLang=en&SrcCategoryId=&SrcFamilyId=&u=%2fdownloads%2fdetails.aspx%3fFamilyID%3d61fc1c66-06f2-463c-82a2-cf20902ffae0%26DisplayLang%3den*

  - ❏ **Windows XP Professional x64 Edition**   *http://www.microsoft.com/downloads/info.aspx?na=22&p=4&SrcDisplayLang=en&SrcCategoryId=&SrcFamilyId=&u=%2fdownloads%2fdetails.aspx%3fFamilyID%3d1391d79c-9699-487a-bbc5-f5471fae7169%26DisplayLang%3den*

■ **Windows Script Host (WSH) 5.6**   Download WSH 5.6 from *http://www.microsoft.com/ downloads/details.aspx?FamilyID=c717d943-7e4b-4622-86eb-95a22b832caa&Display-Lang=en.*

> **Note**   If you choose to install only the MDT 2008 documentation, the only software requirements are Microsoft .NET Framework 2.0 and MMC 3.0. The remaining software in the previous list is not required to view the documentation.

To install MDT 2008

1. Right-click MicrosoftDeploymentToolkit_*platform*.msi, where *platform* is either x86 or x64, and then click Install.

2. Click Next to skip the welcome page.

3. On the End-User License Agreement page, review the license agreement, click I Accept The Terms In The License Agreement, and then click Next.

4. On the Custom Setup page, choose the features to install and then click Next. To change a feature's state, click the feature and then choose a state (Will Be Installed On Local Hard Drive, Entire Feature Will Be Unavailable, and so on). The following list describes each feature:

   ❏ **Documents**   This feature installs the solution's guidance and job aids. By default, this feature is installed in C:\Program Files\Microsoft Deployment Toolkit\ Documentation.

   ❏ **Tools and templates**   This feature installs the solution's wizards and template deployment files, such as Unattend.xml. By default, this feature is installed in C:\Program Files\Microsoft Deployment Toolkit.

5. Click Install to install the solution.

6. Click Finish to complete the installation and close the installer.

> **Note**   Earlier versions of MDT 2008, including Business Desktop Deployment 2007 Solution Accelerator, included a feature to create a distribution share. MDT 2008 does not create a distribution share during installation, however. Instead, you create a distribution share or upgrade an existing distribution share by using Deployment Workbench.

The following list describes the subfolders in the MDT 2008 program folder (C:\Program Files\Microsoft Deployment Toolkit) after installing the solution:

■ **Bin**   Contains the MMC Deployment Workbench add-in and supporting files.

■ **Documentation**   Contains the MDT 2008 documentation and job aids.

■ **Downloads**   Provides storage for components that MDT 2008 downloads.

> **Note**   The hard drive containing the program folders must have at least 1 gigabyte of free space available. MDT 2008 downloads components, including the Windows AIK, to the Downloads folder.

■ **ManagementPack**   Contains the MDT 2008 management pack files.

■ **Samples**   Contains sample task sequence scripts.

■ **SCCM**   Contains files that support Microsoft System Center Configuration Manager 2007 integration.

■ **Scripts**   Contains scripts that the Deployment Workbench uses.

■ **Templates**   Contains template files that the Deployment Workbench uses.

Starting Deployment Workbench

Deployment Workbench is the MDT 2008 tool that you use to stock distribution shares, create task sequences, and create deployment points. See Chapter 6 for more information about using Deployment Workbench to stock a distribution share and create custom Windows Vista images. To start Deployment Workbench, click Start, point to All Programs, point to Microsoft Deployment Toolkit, and then click Deployment Workbench. The console tree shows the following items:

■ **Information Center**   This item provides access to the documentation, breaking news about MDT 2008, and the components required for using Deployment Workbench. The Documentation item helps you quickly navigate the solution's guidance. Click a process in the diagram to see a description of that process and related documents.

■ **Distribution Share**   Under this item are the operating systems, applications, operating system packages, and out-of-box drivers that the distribution share contains. Click any item below Distribution Share and then view its contents in the details pane. This item includes a checklist that indicates required and optional preparation steps and whether or not you've performed them.

■ **Task Sequences**   Click Task Sequences in the console tree to see a list of task sequences in the details pane.

■ **Deploy**   The Deploy item contains two items below it: Deployment Points and Database. Click Deployment Points in the console tree to see a list of deployment points in the details pane. Click Database to edit the MDT 2008 database. For more information about the database, see Chapter 12.

> **Note**   For the Deployment Workbench MMC, the default view includes the Action pane.
> To remove the Action pane, author the management console. To author the console, run
> C:\Program Files\Microsoft Deployment Toolkit\Bin\DeploymentWorkbench.msc /a. Click
> View, click Customize, clear the Action Pane check box, and then click OK. To save changes,
> from the File menu, click Save. When prompted to choose whether or not to display a single
> window interface, click Yes.

Updating Microsoft Deployment Toolkit Components

After installing MDT 2008 and becoming familiar with Deployment Workbench, download
and install the additional components that MDT 2008 requires. The following components
are mandatory in MDT 2008:

- **Windows Automated Installation Kit**   You can install the Windows Automated
  Installation Kit (Windows AIK) manually by downloading it from the Microsoft
  Download Center at *http://www.microsoft.com/downloads* or use Deployment
  Workbench to download and install it automatically.

- **MSXML Services 6.0**   You can preinstall MSXML Services 6.0 or use Deployment Workbench to download and install it. The Windows AIK distribution media includes the
  MSXML Services 6.0 installation file. You can also download MSXML Services 6.0 from
  http://www.microsoft.com/downloads/details.aspx?FamilyID=993c0bcf-3bcf-4009-be21-
  27e85e1857b1&DisplayLang=en. Download both x86 and x64 versions at this URL.
  Windows Server 2008 already includes this component.

To download components using Deployment Workbench

1. In Deployment Workbench, under Information Center, click Components.

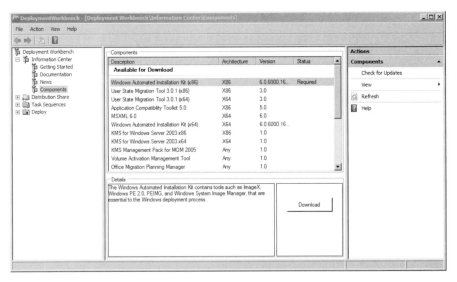

2. In the Available For Download section of the Components list, click a component. In the bottom pane, click Download. Deployment Workbench displays the download status in the Components list. When it finishes downloading the component, it moves the component to the Downloaded section in the right pane.

3. In the Downloaded section of the Components list, click a downloaded component. In the bottom pane, click Install to install the component or Browse to open the folder containing the component in Windows Explorer. MDT 2008 cannot install some components automatically. To install them, click Browse to open the folder containing the component and then manually install the component.

> **Note**   Check the Internet for updated components frequently. On the Deployment Workbench main menu, from the Action menu, click Check For Updates. On the Check For Updates page of the Check For Updates Wizard, select the Check The Internet check box and then click Check.

Summary

Early planning is important to a successful Windows Vista deployment project. MDT 2008 provides the most comprehensive deployment planning guidance from Microsoft. It includes time-proven best practices from Microsoft's own experience, its partners, and its customers.

Planning to deploy Windows Vista is a far larger initiative than just figuring out how to install the operating system. Key planning topics include compatibility testing, application packaging, image engineering, user state migration, security, and deployment. This Resource Kit and MDT 2008 help you plan and develop solutions for each of these topics.

Additional Resources

The following resources contain additional information and tools related to this chapter.

Related Information

■ Chapter 6, "Developing Disk Images," explains how to plan and engineer Windows Vista disk images by using MDT 2008.

■ Chapter 7, "Migrating User State Data," explains how to plan and design a user state migration solution by using USMT.

■ Chapter 8, "Deploying Applications," includes more information about packaging and automating application installations. This chapter also discusses application-compatibility remediation.

- Chapter 11, "Using Volume Activation," explains how to account for Windows Vista volume activation in large-scale deployment projects.

- Chapter 12, "Using Microsoft Deployment," explains how to use MDT 2008 to deploy Windows Vista by using LTI and ZTI.

- The *Planning Guide* in MDT 2008 includes planning and management guidance based on Microsoft Solution Framework.

- Deployment Forum at *http://www.deploymentforum.com/* is a member-driven community where you can ask and answer deployment planning questions.

Chapter 5

Testing Application Compatibility

Application compatibility is often a deployment-blocking issue. It's also the issue that most deployment projects focus on the least—until things begin to fall apart. By focusing on application compatibility early, you can better ensure a successful deployment project.

Three common reasons that application compatibility blocks operating-system deployment are fear, uncertainty, and doubt. Companies simply don't know what applications are in their environments, whether or not the applications are compatible with Windows Vista, and what risks each application poses if it fails after deployment.

To help overcome these issues, this chapter describes the Microsoft tools that are available for discovering the applications in your environment, evaluating their compatibility with Windows Vista, and then developing fixes for any issues. The primary tool is the Microsoft Application Compatibility Toolkit (ACT) 5.0.

Understanding Compatibility

Application compatibility is often a deployment-blocking issue. Since the arrival of Microsoft Windows as a ubiquitous application platform, independent software vendors (ISVs) and internal developers have created thousands of applications for it. Many are mission-critical applications—some of which aren't compatible with the latest version of Windows. Types of applications that might not be compatible include the following:

- Line-of-business (LOB) applications such as enterprise resource-planning suites
- Core applications that are part of standard desktop configurations
- Administrative tools, such as antivirus, compression, and remote-control applications
- Custom tools, such as logon scripts

What Compatibility Means

Applications designed for earlier versions of Windows have been carried forward for a number of reasons. Maybe the application is a necessary tool that is used daily to accomplish some otherwise tedious task. Maybe users have learned the application and are reticent to move to another, similar application. Maybe the application has no replacement, because the original creator either is no longer in business or has left the company. All these issues make application compatibility a critical issue that you must consider when deploying a new operating system such as Windows Vista. In this chapter, you learn the many issues that affect application compatibility, how to discover the applications on which the organization depends, and what you can do to assure that mission-critical applications work with Windows Vista.

An application is compatible with Windows Vista if it runs as designed in Windows Vista— that is, the application should install and remove correctly. Users should be able to create, delete, open, and save any data files that are native to the application. Common operations such as printing should work as expected. A compatible application runs on Windows Vista out of the box without any special assistance. If an application is not compatible, you might find that a newer, compatible version of the application is available, or that using one of the tools that Microsoft provides to remediate the compatibility problem is all you need. You might also find that an application will require a combination of fixes to run properly. This chapter discusses all of these scenarios.

Why Applications Fail

The following list describes common compatibility issues for Windows Vista, particularly when using an application originally designed for Windows XP:

- **User Account Control (UAC)**   In Windows Vista, all interactive users, including members of the administrators group, run as standard users. UAC is the mechanism through which users can elevate applications to full administrator privileges. Because of UAC, applications that require administrator rights or check for administrator privileges behave differently in Windows Vista, even when run by a user as administrator.

■ **Windows Resource Protection (WRP)**   WRP is designed to protect the system in a read-only state to increase system stability, predictability, and reliability. This will affect specific files, folders, and registry keys. Updates to protected resources are restricted to the operating-system trusted installers, such as Windows Servicing. This helps to protect components and applications that ship with the operating system from any impact of other applications and administrators. This can be an issue for custom installations not detected as setup by Windows Vista when they try to replace WRP files and registry settings and check for specific versions and values.

■ **Internet Explorer Protected Mode (IEPM)**   In Windows Vista, Internet Explorer 7 processes run in IEPM with greatly restricted privileges to help protect users from attack. IEPM significantly reduces the ability of an attack to write, alter, or destroy data on the user's computer, or to install malicious code. This could impact ActiveX controls and other script code that try to modify higher integrity level objects.

■ **Operating System and Internet Explorer Versioning**   Many applications check the version of the operating system and behave differently or fail to run when an unexpected version number is detected. You can resolve this issue by setting appropriate compatibility modes or applying versioning shims (application-compatibility fixes).

■ **New Folder Locations**   User folders, My Documents folders, and folders with localization have changed in Windows Vista. Applications with hard-coded paths may fail. You can mitigate this using directory junctions or by replacing hard-coded paths with appropriate API calls to get folder locations.

■ **Session 0 Isolation**   Running services and user applications together in Session 0 poses a security risk because services run at elevated privilege and therefore are targets for malicious agents looking for a means to elevate their own privilege level. In earlier versions of the Windows operating system, services and applications run in the same session as the first user who logs on to the console (Session 0). To help protect against malicious agents in Windows Vista, Session 0 has been isolated from other sessions. This could impact services that communicate with applications using window messages.

Choosing the Best Tool

You can use four primary tools to mitigate application-compatibility issues: Program Compatibility Assistant, Program Compatibility Wizard, ACT, and application virtualization. The following sections describe each tool and when using it is appropriate versus using other tools or technologies.

The first two tools provide approaches for users and one-off support issues but are not for use in a large-scale deployment. The remainder of this chapter focuses on using ACT to inventory, analyze, and mitigate compatibility issues, because this is the tool that organizations primarily use in large-scale deployment.

Program Compatibility Assistant

If you have an individual application that needs Windows Vista compatibility remediation, one mitigation tool that might be effective is the built-in Program Compatibility Assistant. To run the Program Compatibility Assistant, right-click the application's .exe file, click Properties, and then click the Compatibility tab to view the application's compatibility settings, as shown in Figure 5-1. If the program is used by multiple users on the same computer, click Show Settings For All Users to change the settings selected here to affect all users.

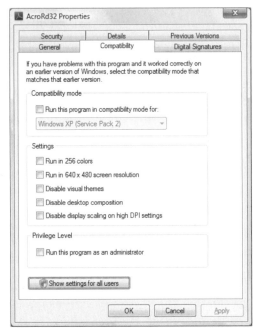

Figure 5-1   Compatibility settings.

Program Compatibility Wizard

The Program Compatibility Wizard can help resolve many application issues. Using the wizard, you can test various compatibility options on various programs to find the setting that allows the programs to run under Windows Vista. To start the Program Compatibility Wizard, click the Start button, click Control Panel, click Programs, and then click Use An Older Program With This Version Of Windows. The Program Compatibility Wizard starts as shown in Figure 5-2. To begin the application compatibility diagnostic process, click Next.

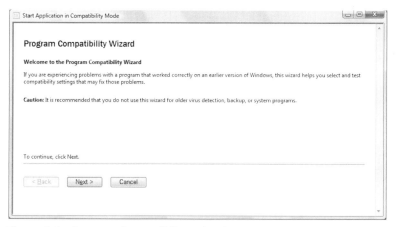

Figure 5-2 Program Compatibility Wizard.

> **Tip** To get the most accurate results with this wizard, log on to the computer with a user account that has Standard user rights, not administrator rights.

Application Compatibility Toolkit

Use the ACT for anything more than a few one-off, simple mitigations. It helps you create an inventory of the applications in your organization. It also helps identify which applications are compatible with Windows Vista and which applications require further testing. The following are some of the major components of the ACT solution:

- **Application Compatibility Manager** A tool that enables you to collect and analyze your data so that you can identify any issues prior to deploying a new operating system, updating to a new version of Internet Explorer, or deploying a Windows update in your organization. You use this program heavily during the initial phases of an application migration project. Consider this tool as the primary user interface for ACT.

- **Application Compatibility Toolkit Data Collector** The Application Compatibility Toolkit Data Collector is distributed to each computer and scans by using compatibility evaluators. Data is collected and stored in the central compatibility database.

- **Setup Analysis Tool (SAT)** Automates the running of application installations while monitoring the actions taken by each application's installer.

- **Standard User Analyzer (SUA)** Determines the possible issues for applications running as a Standard user in Windows Vista.

ACT is indispensable for testing a wide variety of applications across a variety of computers and operating systems within your organization, using solutions based on a common pool of application fixes provided by vendors and end users. You can use the ACT tools separately or together, based on your organization's needs. Some tools, such as the Setup Analysis Tool and

Standard User Analyzer, are intended for developers to enable application remediation and are not necessarily used in the scanning and mitigation process.

Application Virtualization

In some instances, such as when standard application mitigation strategies fail, virtualization technologies might be appropriate. For example, you can use Microsoft Virtual PC 2007 as a safety net for applications that aren't compatible with Windows Vista. In fact, Windows Vista Enterprise Edition includes licensing to operate up to four instances of earlier versions of Windows concurrently.

Using Virtual PC 2007, users can run multiple operating systems on a single computer that is running the Windows Vista operating system. This way, you can proceed with your Windows Vista deployment rather than delay because of application incompatibility. Your organization can take full advantage of the new features and capabilities in Windows Vista and still provide end users access to run earlier versions of mission-critical applications. And the organization can realize a return on the investment of upgrading to Windows Vista faster than they would by implementing other short-term application compatibility solutions.

Virtual PC 2007 provides a time-saving and cost-saving solution anywhere users must run multiple operating systems (x86 operating systems only) and is an excellent short-term solution for mitigating application compatibility issues; it allows you to continue with Windows Vista deployment. However, you should consider selecting a longer-term solution.

Very often, even if an application does work with Windows Vista, it will still create conflicts with other applications running in the same environment because they are competing for system resources. Application virtualization plays a key role in mitigating those concerns.

Microsoft SoftGrid Application Virtualization transforms applications into virtualized, network-available services, resulting in dynamic delivery of software that is never installed, never conflicts, and minimizes costly application-to-application regression testing. By using this technology, users and their application environments are no longer computer-specific, and the computers themselves are no longer user-specific. Although SoftGrid typically provisions applications to run independently of each other in isolated environments, SoftGrid does permit some application interaction. You should carefully examine any dependencies that applications might have on one another and sequence applications together if they rely on interacting with each other.

This allows IT administrators to be flexible and responsive to business needs and significantly reduces the cost of computer management, including enabling application and operating system migrations, by separating the application deployment from the core operating-system image. SoftGrid is an integral tool in the Microsoft Desktop Optimization Pack for Software Assurance solution, a dynamic desktop solution available to Software Assurance customers that helps reduce application deployment costs, enable delivery of applications as services, and better manage and control enterprise desktop environments. See the "Windows Vista for the Enterprise Web" site at *http://www.microsoft.com/windows/products/windowsvista/ enterprise/default.mspx.*

Understanding the ACT

Figure 5-3 illustrates the architecture of ACT. The following list describes each component of this architecture:

- **Application Compatibility Manager (ACM)**   A tool that enables you to configure, collect, and analyze your data so that you can fix any issues prior to deploying a new operating system, updating your version of Internet Explorer, or deploying a Windows update in your organization.

- **Data Collection Package (DCP)**   An .msi file created by the ACM for deploying to each of your client computers. Each DCP can include one or more compatibility evaluators, depending on what you are trying to evaluate.

- **ACT Log Processing Service**   A service used to process the ACT log files uploaded from your client computers. It adds the information to your ACT database.

- **ACT Log Processing Share**   A file share, accessed by the ACT Log Processing Service, to store the log files that will be processed and added to the ACT database.

- **ACT Database**   A Microsoft SQL Server database that stores the collected application, computer, device, and compatibility data. You can view the information stored in the ACT database as reports from the ACM.

- **Microsoft Compatibility Exchange**   A web service that propagates application compatibility issues from the server to the client and enables the client computers to connect to Microsoft via the Internet to check for updated compatibility information.

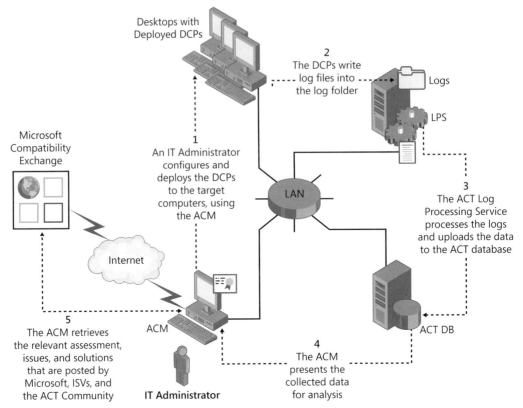

Figure 5-3   ACT architecture.

Support Topologies

Figure 5-4 shows the topologies that ACT supports in the order that Microsoft recommends them. For example, Microsoft most highly recommends using the distributed ACT Log Processing Service, ACT Log Processing share, and ACT Database topology, and least recommends using a Consolidated Server. If you choose to employ a topology based on distributed logging with a rollup to your central share, you must move the files to the ACT Log Processing share before actual processing can occur. You can move the files manually or use a technology such as Distributed File System Replication (DFSR) or any other similar technology already employed in your organization.

Distributed ACT Log Processing Service (LPS), ACT Log Processing Share (LPS Share), and ACT Database

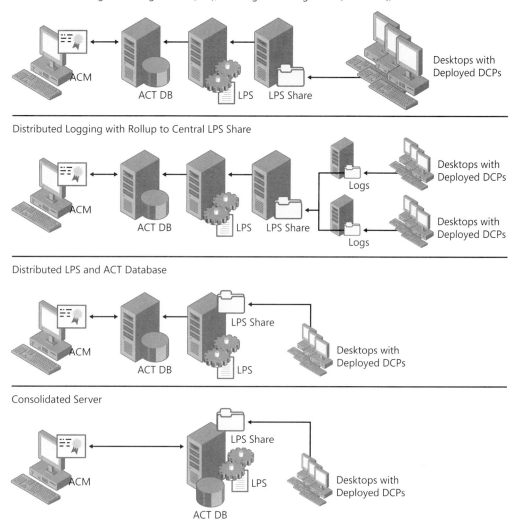

Figure 5-4   Supported topologies.

Compatibility Evaluators

In addition to collecting application and hardware inventory, ACT includes compatibility evaluators. Compatibility evaluators are run-time detection tools specifically designed to log behaviors as they occur on the user's computer and locate potential compatibility issues. ACT includes the following compatibility evaluators:

- **Inventory Collector**   Examines each of your organization's computers, identifying the installed applications and system information.

- **Internet Explorer Compatibility Evaluator (IECE)**   Identifies potential website and web application issues resulting from the release of a new operating system.

- **User Account Control Compatibility Evaluator (UACCE)**   Identifies potential compatibility issues because of an application running under a Protected Administrator (PA) or Standard User (SU) account on the Windows Vista operating system. When running, UACCE monitors your running applications to verify interactions with the operating system and identify potentially incompatible activities.

- **Update Compatibility Evaluator (UCE)**   Identifies the potential impact of a new Windows update. Using the collected update impact data, you can prioritize your testing and reduce the uncertainty in deploying updates.

- **Windows Vista Compatibility Evaluator (WVCE)**   Identifies potential compatibility issues resulting from deprecated components in the new operating system, Graphical Identification and Authentication (GINA) DLLs, and the isolation required by Session 0 applications.

A DCP can include one or more compatibility evaluators, depending on what you are trying to evaluate. The Application Compatibility Manager groups the evaluators based on tasks as described in the following sections.

Planning for ACT

ACT provides a way for you to create an inventory for your organization, including your installed applications, computers, and devices. It also enables you to collect compatibility data, to determine the impact of that data in your organization, and, finally, to create mitigation packages to fix the compatibility issues, when possible. The following list describes the three phases for effectively using ACT in your organization:

- **Collecting Data**   Before you can analyze your potential compatibility issues, you must first collect your organization's inventory and the associated compatibility issues.

- **Analyzing Issues**   After collecting your inventory and associated compatibility data, you can organize and analyze your issues. This includes categorizing, prioritizing, setting your deployment status, and setting your application assessment to create customized reports.

- **Testing and Mitigating Issues**   After analyzing your compatibility issue reports, you can test your applications to determine whether or not the specified compatibility issues are actually problems within your organization. If you determine that the issues are valid, you can create mitigation packages to fix the issues by using the Compatibility Administrator. You can also use the other developer tools provided with ACT—including the Internet Explorer Compatibility Tool, the Setup Analysis Tool, and the Standard User Analyzer tool—to determine additional issues and possible mitigation strategies.

Targeting Deployment

For greater control over your collected data, you should deploy DCPs to a small subset of computers based on specific groupings, such as location and department—for example, a DCP for users in the Human Resources department. This enables better categorization and analysis of an application throughout the organization.

If your organization already has a hardware asset inventory list, it is recommended that you sample each unique hardware configuration so that you can synchronize with the Microsoft Compatibility Exchange and obtain the relevant driver compatibility issues. If you do not have a comprehensive inventory, Microsoft recommends that you distribute the DCPs based on the factors described in Table 5-1.

Table 5-1   DCP Deployment Considerations

Consideration	Description
Do you have a managed, unmanaged, or mixed environment?	You categorize your organization as a managed environment, an unmanaged environment, or a mixed management environment through the following criteria:
	■ **Managed environment** IT administrators strictly control and manage the application installation and usage based on need and the various divisions in the organization. In this situation, an IT administrator can deploy a DCP on a limited subset of computers for each department, based on known needs and requirements.
	■ **Unmanaged environment** Users typically have administrator privileges on their computers and can install applications at their own discretion. Because users in an unmanaged environment can install any software they choose, you would need to deploy your DCPs to more computers than you would if you were in a managed environment.
	■ **Mixed environment** Your organization uses both managed and unmanaged environments, depending on an individual group's needs and administrative privileges.
How do you use specific applications in your organization?	It is very important that you provide coverage for all applications required by users in your organization, but it's even more important that you provide coverage for your LOB applications. For the most complete coverage of application usage, you must do the following:
	■ Consult with your local administrators, support engineers, and department heads to ensure that all applications are in use during the data collection process.
	■ Ensure that "seasonal" applications are covered. For example, fiscal year accounting applications might be used only once a year.
	■ Attempt to perform the data collection when few employee vacations are scheduled or at the beginning of the week to avoid weekends. Otherwise, you might have limited or incomplete results because of the decreased application usage.
Do you use role-based applications?	Your organization may use role-based applications, which are applications that relate to job function and the role that a user performs within your organization. A common example is accountants (a financial role) and their finance-related applications. Reviewing application usage in conjunction with job function and roles enables better application coverage in your organization.

Table 5-1   DCP Deployment Considerations

Consideration	Description
How do you distribute your applications in your organization?	You can distribute applications in many ways within an organization—for example, by using Group Policy, IntelliMirror, Microsoft System Management Server (SMS), or a custom distribution method. Reviewing your software distribution system policies in conjunction with your application inventory enables better application coverage and narrows the deployment of your DCPs.
What is the geographic breakdown of your organization?	You must consider the geographic distribution of your organization when planning for your DCP deployment (for example, if you have branches in North America, Asia, and Europe). You must then consider the application usage patterns across each geographic region. You must account for divisional applications, localized versions of applications, and applications specific to the geographic location and export restrictions. We recommend that you consult with technical and business leaders from each region to understand these differences.
What types of computers do you have in your organization and how are they used?	Computer types and usage patterns can play an important role in your DCP deployment. The following sections describe some of the most common computer types and usage patterns:

- **Mobile and laptop computers**   Mobile users frequently work offline, occasionally synchronizing with the corporate network through either a LAN or VPN connection. Because of the high possibility of a user going offline for long periods of time, you must consider the odds of the user being online for the DCP to be downloaded and installed, and then online again for the logged data to be uploaded.

- **Multiuser computers**   Multiuser computers are typically located in university computer labs, libraries, and organizations that enable job sharing. These computers are highly secure and include a core set of applications that are always available, as well as many applications that can be installed and removed as necessary. Because these computers typically have a basic set of applications assigned to users or computers, you can narrow the application coverage and usage to identify only a subset of client computers to receive the DCP.

- **AppStations/TaskStations**   AppStations running vertical applications are typically used for marketing, claims and loan processing, and customer service. TaskStations are typically dedicated to running a single application, such as on a manufacturing floor as an entry terminal or in a call center. Because both of these types of computers do not commonly allow users to add or to remove applications and might be designated for specific users and job roles, the application coverage and usage can be narrowed to identify a subset of client computers to receive the DCP.

- **Kiosks**   Kiosks are generally in public areas. These computers run unattended and are highly secure, generally running a single program by using a single-use account and automatic logon. Because these computers typically run a single application, the application coverage and usage can be narrowed to identify a subset of computers to receive the DCP.

Choosing a Deployment Method

Microsoft recommends that you base your method for deploying the DCP on your existing infrastructure. You can choose one of several ways to distribute a DCP to your identified client computers, including the following (listed in order of preference):

- **System Center Configuration Manager 2007**   After performing an inventory of your applications, you can use the software deployment feature in System Center Configuration Manager 2007 to deploy the DCPs to the client computers.

- **Group Policy Software Installation**   Create an .msi package for each DCP, and then use the Group Policy Software Installation feature of Active Directory in Windows Server 2008, Windows Server 2003, and Windows Server 2000 for deployment. All client computers to which you will deploy the DCP must be part of the Active Directory forest.

- **Logon scripts**   While logged on to a domain from the client computers, you can initiate the installation of DCPs using logon scripts in Windows Server 2008, Windows Server 2003, and Windows Server 2000.

- **Non-Microsoft deployment software**   If your organization has a non-Microsoft software deployment infrastructure, use that method to deploy the DCPs. For information about the requirements of the non-Microsoft deployment software, consult the software vendor.

- **Manual distribution**   For computers that are not connected to the network or that have slow connections, such as small branch offices, manual distribution methods are available. These methods include distributing the collection packages through e-mail or on physical media such as a USB flash device (UFD) or CD.

> **Important**   If you create a DCP on a computer running Windows Vista, you will be unable to run the package on a computer running Windows 2000. You will also be unable to run a DCP package created on a computer running Windows 2000 on a computer running Windows Vista. Because of this, Microsoft recommends that you create the DCP on a computer that is running either the Windows XP (SP2) or Windows Server 2003 (SP1) operating system.

Choosing a Log File Location

When you are creating a DCP in the Application Compatibility Manager, you can select an output location for your log files. The following configuration options are available:

- **Select a default ACT Log Processing share location**   If you use this option, the DCP automatically writes the log files to the ACT Log Processing share. If the ACT Log Processing share is unavailable when the specified upload time interval is reached, the DCP will make two more attempts. If the problem persists, the DCP will store the log file in the location defined in the next bullet. All files are then retried during the next upload interval.

- **Select the Local (%ACTAppData%\DataCollector\Output) location**   If you use this option, the DCP creates the log files on the local system and the computer Administrator must manually copy the files to the ACT Log Processing share location. This is a good option for mobile users that are not always connected to the network. If you select this option, Microsoft recommends that you either notify your end users to copy the collected data to the ACT Log Processing share or employ an alternate method to collect the data from the client computers and copy the information into the ACT Log Processing share.

■ **Type an alternate network share location**   If you use this option, you must verify that the DCP service can write to the location. This is a good option for companies that are geographically diverse (for example, if you have branches in North America and Europe). An IT Administrator can create DCPs and file shares individually for North America and Europe, which further enables administrators at a central location to roll up all of the collection log files to a central location. These log files are then mapped to the ACT Log Processing share for final processing and entry into the ACT database.

Preparing for the ACT

Before configuring and running ACT, you must verify that you are using supported software, that you meet the minimum hardware requirements, and that you have configured the required permissions and infrastructure. Table 5-2 lists the software required by ACT. Table 5-3 lists the hardware requirements for using ACT.

You must provide special system requirements before you can successfully use the Update Compatibility Evaluator (UCE), the Setup Analysis Tool (SAT), or the Compatibility Administrator. For more information, see the ACT 5.0 documentation.

Table 5-2 Software Requirements for ACT

Software	Supported Versions
Operating systems	■ Windows Vista
	■ Windows XP with Service Pack 2
	■ Windows Server 2003 with Service Pack 1
	■ Windows Server 2008
	Note: The Application Compatibility Manager, the Internet Explorer Compatibility Test Tool, and the Compatibility Administrator are not supported on Windows 2000. However, you can run DCPs and the Setup Analysis Tool (SAT) on computers running Windows 2000 Update Rollup 1 for Service Pack 4 (SP4).
Proxy server	ACT supports only the Internet Security and Acceleration (ISA) Server 2004 proxy server.
Database	After ACT has been installed, it requires one of the following database components: Microsoft SQL Server 2005, SQL Server 2005 Express Edition, or SQL Server 2000.
	Note: ACT does not support the Microsoft Database Engine (MSDE).
.NET Framework	ACT requires .NET Framework 2.0. It does not run on .NET Framework 3.0. However, client computers running the deployed DCPs do not require the .NET Framework.

Table 5-3   Hardware Requirements for ACT

ACT Component	Minimum Requirement	Recommended Requirement
Application Compatibility Manager client and ACT Log Processing Service servers	550-megahertz (MHz) processor with 256 megabytes (MB) of RAM	2.8-gigahertz (GHz) processor with 2 gigabytes (GB) of RAM
ACT client databases	1-GHz processor with 512 MB of RAM	2.8-GHz processor with 2 GB of RAM

Sharing the Log Processing Folder

If your DCPs write to a network ACT Log Processing share, you must verify that you have the correct permissions at both the share and the folder levels:

- **Share-Level Permissions**   Verify that the Everyone group has Change and Read permissions for the ACT Log Processing share folder.

- **Folder-Level Permissions (NTFS Only)**   Verify that the Everyone group has Write access and that the ACT Log Processing Service account has List Folder Contents, Read, and Write permissions. If the ACT Log Processing Service is running as Local System, this must be the *domain\computer$* account. If the ACT Log Processing Service is running with a user account, this is the user account information.

Preparing for Microsoft Compatibility Exchange

Configure your organization's infrastructure to support the Microsoft Compatibility Exchange while also protecting your intranet security and stability. The recommended method of configuration requires you to allow the appropriate users, on designated computers, to access the Microsoft Compatibility Exchange through your security and network infrastructure. To configure the infrastructure to support the Microsoft Compatibility Exchange, follow these steps:

1. Configure your firewalls and URL scanners to allow access to the Microsoft Compatibility Exchange by setting the following conditions:

2. Allow outbound access for the standard Secure Sockets Layer (SSL) TCP port 443, on any computer running the Application Compatibility Manager.

3. Restrict outbound access to the Microsoft Compatibility Exchange, allowing access only from designated computers and designated users within your organizations.

4. Enable access to the Microsoft Compatibility Exchange (*https://appinfo.microsoft.com/ AppProfile50/ActWebService.asmx*), which is only necessary if passing through a firewall.

5. Grant the db_datareader, db_datawriter, and db_owner database roles to any user account that will log on to the computer running the ACT Log Processing Service.

6. Grant the db_datareader and db_datawriter database roles to any user account that will log on to the computer running the Application Compatibility Manager.

Installing the ACT 5.0

You can download the ACT from the Microsoft Download Center at *http://www.microsoft.com/ downloads/details.aspx?FamilyID=24da89e9-b581-47b0-b45e-492dd6da2971&DisplayLang=en.* Before you install the ACT, ensure that the computer on which you're installing it meets the requirements described earlier, in the section titled "Preparing for the ACT."

To install the ACT

1. Right-click Application Compatibility Toolkit.msi and then click Install.

2. On the License Agreement page, click I Accept The Terms In The License Agreement and then click Next.

3. On the Installation Folder page, optionally click Change to change the installation folder and then click Next.

4. Click Install.

5. Click Finish.

Configuring the ACM

Before you can use the ACM to collect and to analyze your compatibility data, you must configure the tool. This includes configuring the following: your SQL Server instance and database, your ACT Log Processing Service account, and your ACT Log Processing share.

The ACT Configuration Wizard enables you to configure the ACT database, the ACT Log Processing share, and the ACT Log Processing Service account. Before running the wizard, you must verify the following:

- You are an Administrator on the computer, and you have read and write permissions to the database.

- Your domain computer has write permissions to the ACT Log Processing Service share.

- The ACT Log Processing Service account has read and write permissions to the ACT database for the *domain\computer$* account.

- The ACT client is installed on any computer that acts as an ACT Log Processing Server.

To configure the ACM

1. Click Start, point to All Programs, point to Microsoft Application Compatibility Toolkit 5.0, and then click Application Compatibility Manager to start the ACT Configuration Wizard.

2. Review the information on the page and then click Next.

3. On the Select The Configuration Option page, click Enterprise Configuration and then click Next.

4. On the Configure Your ACT Database Settings page, type the name of the SQL Server instance that will contain the ACT database in the SQL Server box and then click Connect. In the Database box, type a unique name for your new database, such as **ACT_Database**, and then click Create. Click Next.

5. On the Configure Your Log File Location page, type the path of the folder in which to store the ACT log files in the Path box or click Browse to choose an existing folder or create a new folder. In the ShareAs box, type a name for the share and then click Next.

6. On the Configure Your ACT Log Processing Service Account page, click Local System to use your local system account credentials to start the ACT Log Processing Service and then click Next. You also have the option to click User Account. If you choose this option, ACT will use the local computer user account to start the ACT Log Processing Service. Additionally, for this option, you must enter your User Name, Password, and Domain, and provide Log On As A Service user rights.

7. Click Finish.

You have the option to change any of your ACT configuration settings after completing the configuration wizard. On the Tools menu, click Settings and then make your changes in the Settings dialog box (Figure 5-5).

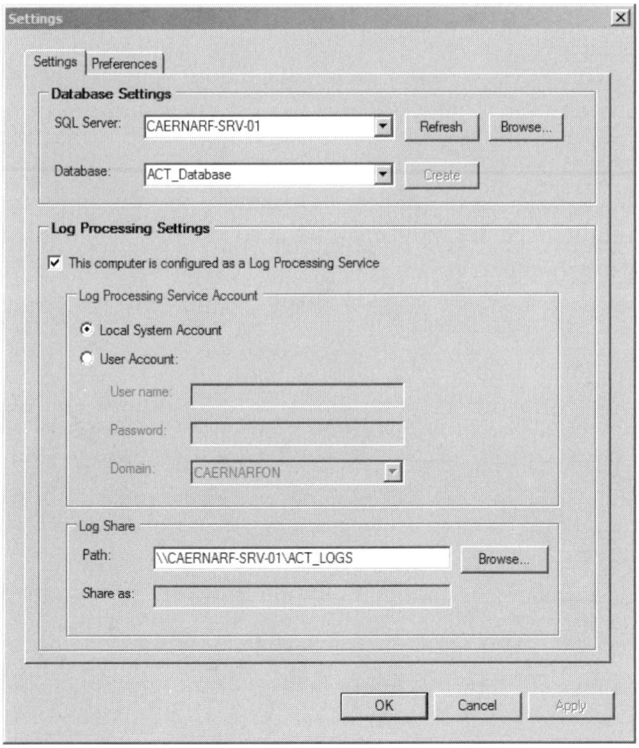

Figure 5-5   ACT settings.

Collecting Compatibility Data

ACT enables you to collect an inventory of all installed software, hardware, and devices within your organization. Additionally, ACT provides compatibility evaluators, which you will use in your data collection packages (DCPs) for deployment to your client computers. Compatibility evaluators are run-time detection tools designed to log behaviors as they occur on the user's computer and locate potential compatibility issues.

The ACT collects data according to the following workflow:

1. You create a new data collection package (DCP) by using the Application Compatibility Manager. Each data collection package can contain one or more compatibility evaluators, including the Inventory Collector.

2. You deploy the DCPs to your identified subset of client computers using System Center Configuration Manager 2007, Group Policy, or any other software distribution technology. The evaluators run for the length of time that you specified when creating the DCP and then the data (.cab) file is uploaded to your ACT Log Processing share.

3. The ACT Log Processing Service, running on a server, accesses the data from the ACT Log Processing share, processes the data, and then uploads the information to your ACT database.

4. The Application Compatibility Manager reads the data from your ACT database to determine how many computers have uploaded data and the status of the collection process. The Application Compatibility Manager also uses the data from the ACT database to enable reporting and viewing of the collected data.

By using the ACM, you can create DCPs to gather your installed software, hardware, and device information, in addition to determining any associated compatibility issues based on applications, websites, or Windows updates for your selected client computers. ACT includes the compatibility evaluators described in the section titled "Compatibility Evaluators" earlier in this chapter.

After creating a DCP, deploy it using the method chosen from the list in the section titled "Choosing a Deployment Method" earlier in this chapter. Because a DCP is an .msi file that installs silently, deploying it is just like deploying any other application. For more information about deploying applications, see Chapter 8, "Deploying Applications."

To create a DCP for deploying Windows Vista

1. In the ACM, click File and then click New.

2. The New_Package dialog box appears. In the Package Name box, type a unique name for your DCP, such as **Vista_Deployment**.

3. In the Evaluate Ccompatibility When area, click Deploying A New Operating System Or Service Pack. This evaluator option includes the Inventory Collector, the UACCE, and

the WVCE by default. You can optionally click Advanced to choose the specific evaluators to include in the package.

4. In the When To Monitor Application Usage area, configure the starting time, duration, and upload interval.

5. In the Output Location box, keep your default value, previously specified in the Configuration Wizard.

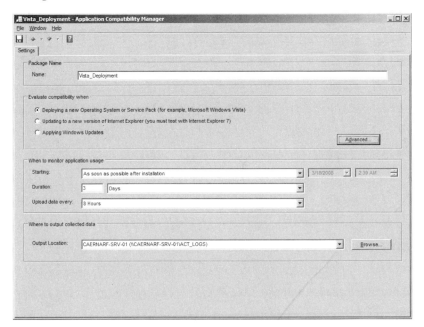

6. On the File menu, click Save And Create Package, saving the compiled DCP as an .msi file in an accessible location, such as a network share.

To view the status of a DCP

1. In ACM, click Collect in the left pane.

2. Click By Status in the Current View section of the Collect screen. The Collect screen changes to show you the deployed DCPs and their status, including whether they are in progress or complete.

Analyzing Compatibility Data

ACT enables you to organize and to analyze your data by using categorization, prioritization, organizational assessments, issue and solution management, report management, and filtering. You can access and view all your compatibility data by using the Quick Reports area of the ACM, shown in Figure 5-6.

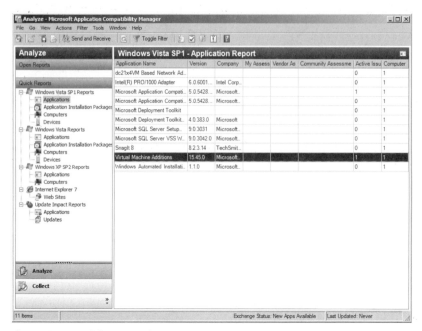

Figure 5-6   Quick Reports in ACM.

Creating and Assigning Categories

You can create, modify, and assign categories to all your applications, computers, devices, websites, and updates for a more customized ACT compatibility report and for filtering purposes. After priority, the second most commonly used analysis tool is assigning arbitrary categories to each piece of software:

- Software vendor can be a useful category because you might have varying relationships with each of your vendors. Generating reports and groupings by software vendor can be useful when you have discussions with that vendor and evaluate the vendor's performance with regard to your compatibility needs.

- Test complexity can be useful for planning and assigning resources. Applications with higher complexity might require additional resources or help to make support decisions. For example, you might assign additional resources to a Business Critical application with an elevated test complexity but remove a Nice To Have application with an elevated test complexity from the supported software list.

- Unit of deployment is another commonly used set of categories, such as Division and Region. Your organization might choose a different naming convention for this information, but typically, this category enables you to track the software needs of one unit of deployment so that as the necessary software is tested and approved, that deployment unit can proceed.

Because the category option is a completely extensible multiple-selection string value, you can potentially use it for just about anything. Some creative uses include creating a category for signoff from multiple owners so that only when all categories have been selected (indicating that each group has signed off) can the software be authorized. You can brainstorm other ideas about how to use categories and how your group perceives the organization of its software ecosystem.

> **Note**   By default, the Master Category List dialog box has two categories: Software Vendor and Test Complexity. These are the only default subcategories. For more information about creating and assigning categories and subcategories, see "Categorizing Your Data" in the ACT documentation.

To create new categories and subcategories

1. In the ACM, click Analyze.

2. On the Analyze screen, in the Quick Reports pane, click Applications in the Windows Vista SP1 Reports section.

3. On the Actions menu, click Categories.

4. In the Assign Categories dialog box, click Master Category List.

5. In the Categories area of the Master Category List dialog box, click Add, type the name of the new category, and then press Enter.

6. In the Subcategories area of the Master Category List dialog box, click Add, type the name of a new subcategory, and then press Enter. Repeat this step for each subcategory that you want to add to the category.

7. Click OK to close the Master Category List dialog box.

8. Click OK to close the Assign Categories dialog box.

To assign a category or subcategory

1. In the ACM, click Analyze.

2. On the Analyze screen, in the Quick Reports pane, click Applications in the Windows Vista SP1 Reports section.

3. In the Windows Vista SP1 – Application Report, right-click an application and then click Categories.

4. In the Assign Categories dialog box, select the check box next to each category and subcategory to which you want to assign the application.

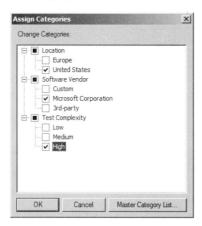

5. Click OK to close the Assign Categories dialog box.

Prioritizing Compatibility Data

You can prioritize any of your collected compatibility data, except for your setup installation packages, based on your organization's requirements. Prioritizing your data enables you to organize your data better, for both a more customized ACT compatibility report and filtering purposes. The following priority levels are available:

- **Priority 1 – Business Critical**   Includes any item that is so important to your organization that, unless you can certify it, you will not continue with your deployment.

- **Priority 2 – Important**   Includes any item that your organization regularly uses but can continue to function without. It is your choice whether or not to continue your deployment without certification.

- **Priority 3 – Nice To Have**   Includes any item that does not fall into the previous two categories, but that should appear in your ACT compatibility reports. These items will not prevent you from continuing with your deployment.

- **Priority 4 – Unimportant**   Includes any item that is irrelevant to your organization's daily operations. You can use this priority level to filter the unimportant items from your reports.

- **Unspecified**   The default priority level, which is automatically assigned to any item. Your organization can use this priority level to denote applications that have not yet been reviewed.

To prioritize your compatibility data

1. In the ACM left pane, click Analyze.

2. In the Quick Reports pane, click Applications in the Windows Vista SP1 Reports section.

3. Right-click an application in the Windows Vista SP1 – Application Report and then click Priority.

4. In the Assign Priority dialog box, click a priority and then click OK.

Assessing Application Compatibility

You can set your organization's assessment rating for each application, application installation report, and website. Setting your assessment rating enables you to specify which applications might be problematic while going through your organization's testing process. Additionally, setting your assessment enables you to organize your data better, for both a more customized ACT compatibility report and for filtering purposes.

> **Note**   Microsoft, the application vendor, and the ACT Community also can add assessment ratings. You can view high-level assessment summaries and specific application assessment details in the applicable report screen or report detail screen. For more information about how to view the assessment details, see the ACT documentation.

Your assessment choices include the following:

■ **Works**   Indicates that during your organization's testing process, you did not experience any issues.

■ **Works with minor issues or has solutions**   Indicates that during your organization's testing process, you experienced minor issues (severity 3), such as showing a typographical error, or an issue that already had a known solution.

■ **Does not work**   Indicates that during your organization's testing process, you experienced a severity 1 or severity 2 issue.

■ **No data**   Neither your organization, Microsoft Corporation, the vendor of the application or website, nor the ACT Community has provided any data.

To assess your compatibility data

1. In the ACM left pane, click Analyze.

2. In the Quick Reports pane, click Applications in the Windows Vista SP1 Reports section.

3. Right-click an application in the Windows Vista SP1 – Application Report and then click Assessment.

4. In the Set Assessment dialog box, click an assessment and then click OK.

Setting the Deployment Status

You can set your organization's deployment status for each application, application installation report, website, and Windows update. Setting your deployment status enables you to determine where each item is in your testing process. Additionally, setting your deployment status enables you to organize your data better, for both a more customized ACT compatibility report and for filtering purposes. Your deployment status choices include the following:

■ **Not Reviewed**   Your organization has not yet reviewed this item to determine its impact, testing requirements, or deployment options.

- **Testing**   Your organization is in the process of locating compatibility issues.

- **Mitigating**   Your organization is in the process of creating and applying solutions for your compatibility issues.

- **Ready To Deploy**   Your organization has completed its testing and mitigation processes and has determined that you can deploy the item in your organization.

- **Will Not Deploy**   Your organization has decided that you will not deploy the item in your organization.

To assess your deployment status

1. In the ACM left pane, click Analyze.

2. In the Quick Reports pane, click Applications in the Windows Vista SP1 Reports section.

3. Right-click an application in the Windows Vista SP1 – Application Report and then click Deployment Status.

4. In the Set Deployment Status dialog box, click a deployment status and then click OK.

Managing Compatibility Issues

Although the compatibility evaluators, the Microsoft Compatibility Exchange, and the ACT Community all provide information about application compatibility issues, you could still uncover an undocumented issue. After you add your compatibility issue, you can use the Microsoft Compatibility Exchange to upload and to share your issue information with both Microsoft and the ACT Community, if you are a member. You can also add compatibility solutions to any compatibility issue in your ACT database, regardless of whether or not you entered the issue.

You also can resolve any active compatibility issue in your ACT database, regardless of whether or not you entered the issue. Resolving an issue means that you are satisfied with the state of the issue and are closing it from further edits. However, you can still add solutions or reactivate the issue if you discover that you resolved it in error. Marking an issue as resolved also changes the issue status from a red X to a green check mark in your compatibility reports, report detail screens, and for the overall group score in the ACT Community data.

To add a compatibility issue

1. In the ACM left pane, click Analyze.

2. In the Quick Reports pane, click Applications in the Windows Vista SP1 Reports section.

3. In the Windows Vista SP1 – Application Report, right-click an application and then click Open.

4. On the Actions menu, click Add Issue to open the New Issue dialog box.

5. In the Title box, type a title for the issue.

6. In the Priority list, click a priority.

7. In the Severity list, click a severity level.

8. In the Symptom list, click a symptom.

9. In the Cause list, click a cause for the issue.

10. In the Affected Operating Systems dialog box, select the check boxes next to each operating system on which this issue appears.

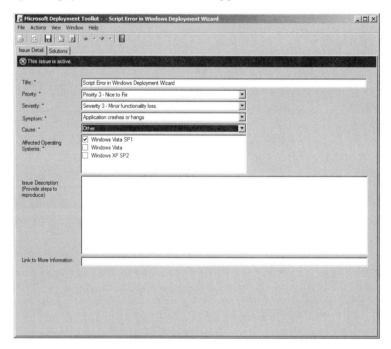

11. In the Issue Description box, type a description of the issue.

12. On the File menu, click Save.

To add a compatibility solution

1. In the ACM left pane, click Analyze.

2. In the Quick Reports pane, click Applications in the Windows Vista SP1 Reports section.

3. In the Windows Vista SP1 – Application Report, right-click an application and then click Open.

4. On the Issues tab, double-click the issue for which you want to add a solution.

5. Click the issue's Solutions tab.

6. On the Actions menu, click Add Solution.

7. In the Title box, type a title for the solution.

8. In the Solution Type box, click a solution type.

9. In the Solution Details box, type a description of the solution.

10. Click Save.

To resolve a compatibility issue

1. In the ACM left pane, click Analyze.

2. In the Quick Reports pane, click Applications in the Windows Vista SP1 Reports section.

3. In the Windows Vista SP1 – Application Report, right-click an application and then click Open.

4. On the Issues tab, double-click the issue that you want to resolve.

5. On the Actions menu, click Resolve. A note appears in the Issues tab that says the issue is resolved and a green check mark appears in the Status column of the Issues tab.

Filtering Compatibility Data

You can filter your organization's compatibility issue data by selecting specific restriction criteria in context, based on the report that you are viewing. For example, you can filter your applications by category, your websites by priority, or a Windows update by deployment status.

To create a filter

1. In the ACM, click Analyze.

2. On the Analyze screen, in the Quick Reports pane, click Applications in the Windows Vista SP1 Reports section.

3. Click Filter, Toggle Filter to turn on the filter.

4. In the Filter pane, choose a field, an operator, and a value on which to filter. For example, to display only applications with a company name containing *Microsoft*, click Company in the Field column, click Contains in the Operator column, and type **Microsoft** in the value column. After adding a clause (row), the ACM automatically adds a new, empty clause.

5. Add additional clauses as necessary. You can specify if all clauses must be true or if any one of the clauses must be true by choosing And or Or in the And/Or column for each individual clause.

6. Click View, Refresh to display the compatibility database based on your filter.

You can further edit your filter by clicking the Filter menu and then clicking Cut, Copy, Paste, Insert Clause, Delete Clause, or Clear.

To save a filter

1. On the File menu, click Save As.

2. In the Save As dialog box, type the path and filename of the ACM Report File (.adq) to save and then click Save.

To export a report

1. On the File menu, click Export Report.

2. In the Export Report Data dialog box, choose from one of the following report types in the Save As Type list:

   ❑ Microsoft Excel Files (*.xls)

   ❑ SV (Comma Delimited) (*.csv)

   ❑ XML Document (*.xml)

3. In the File Name box, type the path and filename of the report and then click Save.

Synchronizing with the Compatibility Exchange Service

ACT enables you to synchronize your ACT database with Microsoft and the ACT Community through the Microsoft Compatibility Exchange Web service. This web service downloads new information from authoritative sources, such as Microsoft and independent software vendors, and it uploads your compatibility issues to Microsoft.

To synchronize with the Microsoft Compatibility Exchange

1. In ACM, click Actions and then click Send/Receive.

2. In the Confirm dialog box, optionally click View The Specific Applications To Be Shared With The ACT Community to view a list of the applications for which you are sending your compatibility data. You can clear the check box next to any application you don't want to share with the community.

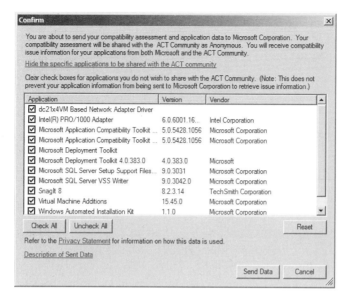

3.   Click Send Data.

4.   Review the updated issue data for your applications in the ACM.

Rationalizing an Application Inventory

After you have finished organizing and analyzing your data, Microsoft recommends that you create an application portfolio for your organization. The application portfolio is a list of all the applications in your organization, including their specific details and compatibility status.

To create an application portfolio

1.   Collect your application inventory and compatibility data by using ACT.

2.   Organize your data based on your organization's requirements and then analyze the information.

3.   Identify any applications that are missing from the inventory.

4.   Select specific versions of your inventoried applications to be included in your deployment.

Identifying the Missing Applications

You must identify any applications that were not located during the automated inventory collection process. These applications might be located on portable computers or high-security systems that cannot be accessed for inventory. In this situation, you must document the application manually.

To identify missing applications

1. Distribute the application portfolio in your organization; specifically, distribute it to those who have knowledge of the required applications currently in use.

2. Request that the group specified in step 1 review the portfolio for errors.

3. Review the feedback provided from step 2 to analyze the errors in the existing portfolio.

4. Make the appropriate changes to the portfolio based on the review.

5. Publish the revised application portfolio and obtain stakeholder approval of the list and application compatibility status.

Selecting Specific Application Versions

To help reduce the long-term total cost of ownership (TCO), you must reduce the number of supported applications in your organization. For each supported application, you must allocate time, training, tools, and resources to plan, deploy, and support the application. Standardizing your list of supported applications can help to reduce the amount of effort required to support your deployed computer configurations.

If you determine that multiple applications are performing the same task in your organization, Microsoft recommends that you select a single application and include it in your standard portfolio, with an emphasis on the following criteria:

- The application is part of a suite of applications. Applications that are part of a suite (for example, Microsoft Office Word 2007 in the Microsoft 2007 Office System) are more difficult to eliminate from your portfolio because you typically must eliminate the entire suite.

- The vendor supports the application on the new operating system. Identifying support options early can reduce your costs later.

- The application adheres to the Designed for Windows logo program. Applications that display the current compatibility logo have met stringent guidelines for compatibility with the current version of Windows.

- The application provides an .msi package for deployment. If the application provides an .msi package, you will spend less time preparing the application for deployment.

- The application is Active Directory–aware. You can manage Active Directory–aware applications through Group Policy.

- The application is the latest version available in your inventory. Deploying a later version helps ensure the long-term support of the application because of obsolescence policies.

- The application provides multilingual support. Multilingual support within the application, when coupled with multilingual support in the operating system (such as the multilingual support in Windows Vista), enables your organization to eliminate localized versions of the application.

- The application provides a greater number of features. Applications that support a greater number of features are more likely to address the business needs of a larger number of your users.

To select the appropriate version of an application

1. Identify the latest version of the application currently installed in your organization.

2. Determine if a later version of the application is currently available. If so, Microsoft recommends that you include the later version of the application in your analysis.

3. Verify that you have vendor support for each version of the application.

4. Identify the license availability and cost for each application and version.

5. Select from all the versions available one version that is supported on all your client computers.

6. Validate the selected version in your test environment, verifying that it is compatible with your new operating system, Windows update, or Internet Explorer version.

Testing and Mitigating Issues

After you analyze your issues in the ACM, you can continue to explore your compatibility issues by using several development tools provided with the ACT. The development tools enable you to test for a variety of compatibility issues, including website and web application issues, issues related to running as a Standard user in Windows Vista, and issues that might arise because of actions taken by an application's installer program. Additionally, ACT provides a tool that can help you resolve many of your compatibility issues: the Compatibility Administrator. To successfully resolve your compatibility problems, you must follow these steps:

- **Identify your most critical applications**   Create an inventory of your organization's applications and then verify certification status of the included applications to see if they require testing.

- **Identify any application compatibility problems**   Test each application, determining any compatibility issues if necessary.

- **Resolve any application compatibility issues**   Identify and create application compatibility solutions by using the ACT tools, which include the Internet Explorer Compatibility Test Tool, either the standalone version or the virtual version of the Setup Analysis Tool (SAT), the Standard User Analyzer (SUA), and the Compatibility Administrator.

- **Deploy or distribute your test and certified applications and solutions**   Use a deployment and distribution tool, such as System Center Configuration Manager 2007, to deploy your certified applications and compatibility issue solution packages to your client desktops.

When testing an application in a new operating system, Microsoft recommends that you retain the default security feature selections. Microsoft also recommends that you thoroughly test the applications, replicating as many of the usage scenarios from within your organization as possible. Finally, Microsoft recommends that you enter your issues and solutions into the ACM so that you can track the data from a central location.

When testing a website or a web application, Microsoft recommends that you include both intranet and extranet sites, prioritizing the list based on how critical the site or the application is to your organization. Microsoft also recommends that you thoroughly test the websites and web applications, replicating as many of the usage scenarios from within your organization as possible. Finally, Microsoft recommends that you enter your issues into the ACM so that you can share that data with both Microsoft and the ACT Community to receive potential solutions for your issues.

Building a Test Lab

Your test environment should be a long-term investment in the overall deployment process. Retain the test environment after the deployment to assist in future deployment projects. To create the test environment, you must determine how to model the production environment in the test environment and configure the test environment to support automated testing of the mitigation strategies.

Microsoft recommends that you establish a dedicated and isolated lab environment for use in developing and testing the application compatibility mitigation. The lab should mirror your production environment as closely as possible. In some cases, you might find that it is better to open the test network up to existing production services, instead of replicating your production environment in detail. For example, you might want to permit your Dynamic Host Configuration Protocol (DHCP) packets to pass through routers into the test network. Some operations can be safely conducted in the production environment, such as the application inventory collection process. At a minimum, your lab environment should include:

- DHCP services
- Domain Name System (DNS) services
- Microsoft SQL Server 2000, Microsoft SQL Server 2005, or Microsoft SQL Server 2005 Express Edition
- Lab test user accounts, with both normal user and administrative privileges
- Network hardware to provide Internet access (for downloading updates, files, and so on)
- Test computers that accurately reflect production computers in both software and hardware configuration
- A software library representing all the applications to be tested

- Microsoft Virtual Server 2005 (optional)
- Windows Internet Naming Service (WINS) services (optional)

In most instances, you must test the mitigation strategies more than once and be able to revert reliably to a previous test state. Automating your testing process enables you to ensure reproducibility and consistency in your testing process. Using test automation tools enables you to run your test cases in a standardized, reproducible manner. Using disk-imaging software for physical images of the servers and using software virtualization features for reversing changes to virtualized hard disks enables you to restore your test environment back to a previous state.

Modeling the Production Environment

The goal of the test environment is to model your production environment. The more accurate the production environment, the greater the validity of the testing performed in that test environment. Microsoft recommends the following best practices in creating your test environment:

- Use virtual or physical images of production computers to create their test environment counterparts. Virtual or physical images can help ensure that the test environment configuration accurately reflects the production environment. In addition, the images contain live information (such as users, user profiles, and file permissions) to use in testing.

- Physically separate your test environment from your production environment. A physically separate test environment enables you to use an identical IP configuration and helps ensure that tests conducted in the test environment do not affect the production environment. Using the identical IP address, subnets, and other network configuration information helps to ensure the fidelity of the test environment. However, duplicating IP addresses might not always be the best option when applications do not rely on a hard-coded IP address. You might also pass some network traffic through the router from the production environment to reduce the need for replicating network services. For example, opening the ports for DHCP to pass through eliminates the need for a separate DHCP server in the test lab.

- Ensure that your test environment is at the same service pack and update level as your production environment. Before performing application mitigation testing, update your lab environment by applying service packs and updates or by refreshing the virtual or physical images of your production counterparts. Consider adding the test environment to the change-management process to simplify tracking the updates.

- Ensure that you perform all of your application mitigation tests by using accounts that have similar permissions as the accounts in your production environment. For example, if your organization does not allow users to run as Administrators on their local computers, ensure that similar permissions are granted to users in the test environment. This process ensures that you can determine potential security issues.

Using the Standard User Analyzer

The Standard User Analyzer (SUA) tool enables you to test your applications and monitor API calls to detect potential compatibility issues resulting from the new User Account Control (UAC) feature in Windows Vista. UAC requires that all users (including members of the Administrator group) run as Standard users until the application is deliberately elevated. However, not all applications can run properly as a Standard user because of access violations. For more information about SUA, see the Standard User Analyzer Usage document (SUAnalyzer.rtf), in the \Microsoft Application Compatibility Toolkit 5\Standard User Analyzer folder, where Microsoft Application Compatibility Toolkit 5 is the folder in which you installed the toolkit.

To test an application by using SUA

1. Click Start, click All Programs, click Microsoft Application Compatibility Toolkit 5.0, click Developer And Tester Tools, and then click Standard User Analyzer.

2. In the Target Application box, type the path and filename of the application that you want to test by using the SUA.

3. In the Parameters box, type any command-line options for the application.

4. In the Symbols Path box, type **C:\Windows\Symbols**.

5. Click Launch. Exercise each of the application's features and then close the application.

6. Click through each of the SUA tabs, reviewing the detected issues.

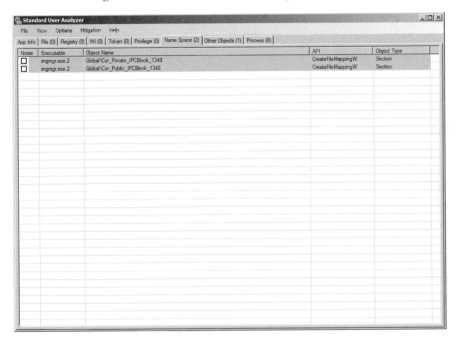

Using the Compatibility Administrator

The Compatibility Administrator tool can help you to resolve many of your compatibility issues by enabling the creation and the installation of application mitigation packages (shims), which can include individual compatibility fixes, compatibility modes, and AppHelp messages. The flowchart in Figure 5-7 illustrates the steps required while using the Compatibility Administrator to create your compatibility fixes, compatibility modes, and AppHelp messages.

Figure 5-7   Using the Compatibility Administrator.

The following terminology is used throughout the Compatibility Administrator:

- **Application fix**   A small piece of code that intercepts API calls from applications, transforming them so that Windows Vista will provide the same product support for the application as previous versions of the operating system. This can mean anything from disabling a new feature in Windows Vista to emulating a particular behavior of a previous version of the Win32 API set.

- **Compatibility mode**   A group of compatibility fixes that work together and are saved and deployed as a single unit.

- **AppHelp message**   A blocking or nonblocking message that appears when a user starts an application that you know has major functionality issues with Windows XP or Windows Vista.

- **Application mitigation package**   The custom database (.sdb) file, which includes any compatibility fixes, compatibility modes, and AppHelp messages that you plan on deploying together as a group.

The Compatibility Administrator is the primary tool that most IT professionals will use when testing and with mitigation application compatibility issues. To start the Compatibility Administrator, click Start, click All Programs, click Microsoft Application Compatibility Toolkit 5.0, and then click Compatibility Administrator.

Creating a Custom Compatibility Database

You must apply compatibility fixes, compatibility modes, and AppHelp messages to an application and then store them in a custom database. After creating and applying the fixes, you can deploy the custom databases to your local computers to fix the known issues.

To create a custom database

1. On the Compatibility Administrator toolbar, click New.

2. The New Database(*n*) [Untitled_*n*] entry appears under the Custom Databases item in the left pane.

To save a custom database

1. On the Compatibility Administrator toolbar, click File, Save.

2. In the Database Name dialog box, type a name for the compatibility database and then click OK.

3. In the Save Database dialog box, type the path and filename of the new compatibility database and then click Save.

Creating a Compatibility Fix

The Compatibility Administrator provides several compatibility fixes found to resolve many common application compatibility issues. You might find that a compatibility fix is not properly associated with an application because it was not found during previous testing by Microsoft or the ISV (independent software vendor). If this is the case, you can use the Compatibility Administrator to associate the compatibility fix with the application. Compatibility fixes apply to a single application only. Therefore, you must create multiple fixes if you need to fix the same issue in multiple applications.

To create a new compatibility fix

1. In the left pane of the Compatibility Administrator, click the custom database to which you will apply the compatibility fix.

2. On the Database menu, click Create New and then click Application Fix.

3. Type the name of the application to which this compatibility fix applies, type the name of the application vendor, browse to the location of the application file (.exe) on your computer, and then click Next.

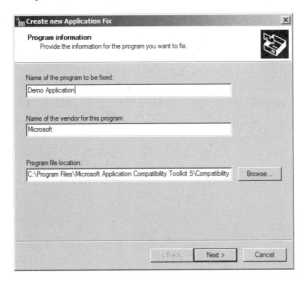

4. Select an operating system to emulate, click any applicable compatibility modes to apply
    to your compatibility fix, and then click Next. If you know that an application worked
    properly with a previous operating system version, such as Window XP, you can apply
    the existing compatibility mode and then test the application to ensure that it works on
    Windows Vista.

5. Select any additional compatibility fixes to apply to your compatibility fix. Click Test
    Run to verify that your choices enable the application to work properly. When you are
    satisfied that the application works, click Next.

6. Click Auto-Generate to automatically select the files that the Compatibility Administrator
    recommends to represent your application and then click Finish. The Compatibility
    Administrator adds your compatibility modes, fixes, and matching information to your
    custom database, and the information appears in the right pane.

Creating a Compatibility Mode

The Compatibility Administrator provides several compatibility modes, groups of
compatibility fixes found to resolve many common application compatibility issues. You can
create custom compatibility modes that contain multiple fixes and then apply these compatibility
modes to applications.

To create a compatibility mode

1. In the left pane of the Compatibility Administrator, click the custom database to which
    you will apply the compatibility mode.

2. On the Database menu, click Create New and then click Compatibility Mode.

3. Type the name of your custom compatibility mode in the Name Of The Compatibility
    Mode text box.

4. Select each of the available compatibility fixes to include in your custom compatibility mode and then click >. If you are unsure which compatibility modes to add, you can click Copy Mode to copy an existing compatibility mode.

5. Click OK after adding all of the applicable compatibility modes.

Creating AppHelp Messages

The Compatibility Administrator enables you to create the following blocking or nonblocking AppHelp messages, which appear when a user starts an application that you know has functionality issues with Windows Vista:

- **Blocking AppHelp message (also called a HARDBLOCK)**   Prevents the application from starting. Instead, it provides an error message dialog box that explains why the application did not start. In this situation, you can also define a specific URL where the user can download an updated driver or other fix to resolve the issue. When using a blocking AppHelp message, you must also define the file-matching information to identify the problematic version of the application and allow the corrected version to continue.

- **Non-blocking AppHelp message (also called a NOBLOCK)**   Allows the application to start but also provides an error message dialog box to the user. The dialog box includes information about security issues, updates to the application, or changes to the location of network resources.

To create an AppHelp message

1. In the left pane of the Compatibility Administrator, click the custom database to which you will apply the AppHelp message.

2. On the Database menu, click Create New and then click AppHelp Message.

3. Type the name of the application to which this AppHelp message applies, type the name of the application vendor, browse to the location of the application file (.exe) on your computer, and then click Next.

4. Click Auto-Generate to automatically select the files the Compatibility Administrator recommends to represent your application and then click Next.

5. Select one of the following options for your AppHelp message:

    ❑ **Non-blocking**   Display a message and allow this program to run.

    ❑ **Blocking**   Display a message but also do not allow this program to run.

6. Click Next. Type the URL and message text to appear when the user starts the application and then click Finish.

Deploying Application Mitigation Packages

Distribution of the custom compatibility databases (.sdb files) can be facilitated using a variety of methods such as logon scripts, System Center Configuration Manager 2007, injection into disk images, and so on. After the file is on the target system, the actual installation of the custom databases is done using a tool that ships with the operating system, called Sdbinst.exe. After the file exists on the target computer, the custom database file must be installed (registered) before the operating system will identify the fixes present when launching the affected applications. (For example, the command line might be sdbinst c:\Windows\ AppPatch\myapp.sdb.) After the database file is registered on a computer, the compatibility information will be used any time the application is launched. Table 5-4 describes the command-line options for sdbinst.exe, which has the following syntax:

sdbinst [-?] [-q] filename.sdb [-u] [-g {guid}] [-n name]

Table 5-4   Sdbinst.exe Command-Line Options

Option	Description
-?	Displays help text
-q	Runs quietly with no message boxes
filename.sdb	Specifies the filename of the database to install
-u	Uninstalls the database
-g {guid}	Specifies the GUID of the database to uninstall
-n name	Specifies the name of the database to uninstall

The Sdbinst.exe command can be written into a logon script to automatically install the custom database from a share network location when the users log on to their computers. This process could even be accomplished as part of a custom job to be pushed out to the desktops via System Center Configuration Manager 2007 or another third-party management application. One of the best methods of distribution of these custom databases is to include them in your disk image. Installing them as part of the original image before adding the application that needs the fixes assures that the application will run from the first time the user needs it.

Summary

For many companies, issues with application compatibility prevent them from fully taking advantage of technology that they are already paying for, such as Windows Vista. Many of the issues are related to the fear, uncertainty, and doubt about whether or not the applications in their environment are compatible with Windows Vista, however, and you can help overcome these concerns by creating an application inventory and then rationalizing it. In the case of application compatibility, knowledge helps companies overcome challenges.

This chapter described the primary tool that Microsoft provides for gaining this understanding and then putting it to use by helping to create a rationalized application portfolio and testing and mitigation compatibility issues. That tool is the Application Compatibility Toolkit, and it is available as a free download from the Microsoft Download Center.

Additional Resources

You can use the resources in this section to learn more about application compatibility.

Related Information

- Chapter 7, "Migrating User State Data," describes how to migrate users' documents and settings as part of a Windows Vista deployment.

- Chapter 8, "Deploying Applications," describes how to deploy applications as part of a Windows Vista deployment.

- Windows Vista TechCenter at *http://technet.microsoft.com/en-us/windowsvista/ aa905066.aspx* contains a wealth of resources for application compatibility.

- Microsoft Application Compatibility Toolkit 5.0 at *http://technet.microsoft.com/en-us/ appcompat/aa905102.aspx* describes the ACT.

- Microsoft Application Compatibility Toolkit 5.0 at *http://www.microsoft.com/ downloads/details.aspx?FamilyId=24DA89E9-B581-47B0-B45E-492DD6DA2971& displaylang=en* contains the ACT download.

Chapter 6
Developing Disk Images

Windows Vista natively supports image-based deployment. Image-based deployment is the most efficient method in high-volume deployment projects. Two factors make image-based deployment superior to other methods: time and cost. Creating a single image that you deploy to each computer is significantly faster than installing the operating system on each computer manually or using unattended installation. Image-based deployment significantly reduces costs by allowing you to better manage the computing environment: You're starting each computer with a known, standardized configuration. It also reduces deployment errors and support costs by using a standardized, stable, and repeatable process to develop and deploy operating systems.

Although the process of building and deploying images is not new, Windows Vista specifically addresses the challenges of the process. First, Windows Vista makes servicing images (adding device drivers, security updates, and so on) easier. You don't have to rebuild and recapture an image every time you need to service it. Second, you can use Windows Vista to build hardware- and language-independent images. For example, Windows Vista images are not dependent on the hardware abstraction layer (HAL), so you can build and maintain fewer images.

The Windows Automated Installation Kit (Windows AIK) provides essential tools for building Windows Vista images. These tools include Windows System Image Manager (SIM) for customizing Windows Vista, Windows Preinstallation Environment 2.0 for starting computers, and ImageX for capturing images. The Windows AIK also includes extensive documentation about using these tools. You can download the Windows AIK, including the *Windows Automated Installation Kit User's Guide*, from *http://www.microsoft.com/downloads*.

Although the Windows AIK provides essential imaging tools, Microsoft Deployment Toolkit (MDT) 2008 is a complete deployment framework that provides end-to-end guidance for planning, building, and deploying Windows Vista images. MDT 2008 takes full advantage of the Windows AIK as well as other tools such as the User State Migration Tool 3.0, Application Compatibility Toolkit 5.0, Microsoft System Center Configuration Manager 2007, and so on. Microsoft recommends that you use MDT 2008 to develop and deploy Windows Vista images, so this chapter focuses primarily on MDT 2008. For readers who prefer to use the Windows AIK directly, *Windows Automated Installation Kit User's Guide* provides complete information about using the Windows AIK tools.

Getting Started

A typical cause of difficult deployment efforts is the number of images that you must manage. In heterogeneous environments with diverse requirements, you often build numerous images. Adding new hardware, language packs, security updates, and drivers usually requires re-creating each disk image. Updating multiple images with a critical security update and testing each of them requires a lot of effort from you. Therefore, one of Microsoft's major design goals in Windows Vista is to significantly reduce the number of images you must maintain and help you maintain those images more easily.

A key way that Windows Vista helps you reduce the number of images you must build and maintain is by reducing dependencies on components that typically differ from one image to the next. These include languages, HALs, and device drivers. For example, unlike earlier versions of Windows, Windows Vista images are no longer tied to a HAL type. (Windows Vista supports only ACPI-based computers.) The operating system can redetect the HAL when you apply it to each destination computer. Windows Vista is also language neutral, which means that all languages are operating system components, and adding or removing language packages is very easy. In addition to reducing dependencies, Microsoft modularized Windows Vista to make customization and deployment easier, based the installation of Windows Vista on the file-based disk imaging format called Windows Imaging (WIM), and made other significant deployment features to the core operating system. (See Chapter 3, "Deployment Platform.")

MDT 2008 is a framework for these tools and features. Rather than using each tool and feature individually and using scripts to cobble them together, this chapter recommends that you develop and deploy Windows Vista images by using MDT 2008. To learn how to install MDT 2008, see Chapter 4, "Planning Deployment."

Prerequisite Skills

To build Windows Vista images—with or without MDT 2008—you should be familiar with the following tools and concepts:

- Unattended setup answer files (Unattend.xml)
- Windows AIK, including the following tools:
    - Windows SIM
    - ImageX
- Hardware device drivers and hardware-specific applications
- Microsoft Visual Basic Scripting Edition (VBScript)
- Disk imaging technologies and concepts, including Sysprep
- Windows Preinstallation Environment

Lab Requirements

While developing and testing Windows Vista images, you will copy large volumes of files between the build server and destination computers. Because of these high-volume data transfers, you should establish a lab that is physically separate from the production network. Configure the development lab to represent the production environment as much as possible.

Lab Hardware

Ensure that the following hardware is available in the lab environment:

- **Network switches and cabling**   100 megabits per second (Mbps) or faster is recommended to accommodate the high volumes of data.
- **Keyboard Video Mouse (KVM) switches**   It's useful to have the client computers connected to a KVM switch to minimize the floor space required to host the computers.
- **CD and DVD burner**   A system should be available in the lab for creating CD-ROMs or DVD-ROMs.
- **Client computers**   In the lab, duplicate any unique type of computer configuration found in the production environment to allow for testing each hardware configuration.
- **Build server**   This computer (running Windows XP with Service Pack 2, Microsoft Windows Server 2003 with Service Pack 1, or a newer version of Windows) can be a client- or server-class computer. The computer should have at least 50 gigabytes (GB) of disk space and backup equipment, such as a tape drive or a storage area network (SAN). Using Windows Server 2008 is recommended, because it already includes the MDT 2008 prerequisites.

Network Services

Make sure that the following network services are available in the lab environment:

- **A Windows domain for the computers to join and to host user accounts**   This domain could be a Microsoft Windows 2000, Windows Server 2003, or Windows Server 2008 domain.

- **Dynamic Host Configuration Protocol (DHCP) services**   DHCP provides TCP/IP addresses to client computers.

- **Domain Name System (DNS) services**   DNS provides TCP/IP host name resolution to client and server computers.

- **Windows Internet Naming Service (WINS)**   WINS provides NetBIOS name resolution to client and server computers. This service is optional but recommended.

- **Microsoft Windows Deployment Services (Windows DS)**   Windows DS delivers Windows PE to computers that do not yet have an operating system. Windows DS servers require a Windows Server 2003 or later domain. For more information about Windows DS, see Chapter 10, "Configuring Windows DS."

- **Internet access**   The lab (or a portion of the lab) should have access to the Internet for downloading software updates.

Caution   Windows protects users against malicious programs by warning them when they try to run a program that they have downloaded from the Internet. Users must acknowledge the warning to continue. This warning, however, prevents MDT 2008 from installing applications automatically during the build process. After verifying that the file is safe, disable the warning by right-clicking the file, clicking Properties, and then clicking Unblock. Windows does not display this warning when files are downloaded from sites listed in the Trusted Sites security zone, and Windows Server 2003 with Service Pack 1 or later does not allow program downloads from untrusted sites.

Installation Media

- Windows media (x86 and x64 editions) and product keys. Windows Vista is available on the volume-licensed media. MDT 2008 also supports retail media.

Note   Earlier versions of Windows, such as Windows XP, supported slipstreaming. This process allowed you to integrate a service pack into the operating system source files. For example, you could integrate Service Pack 1 with the original release of Windows XP to create Windows XP with Service Pack 1 media. Microsoft does not support slipstreaming service packs into Windows Vista. Instead, you can download fully integrated media from the volume licensing website, TechNet, or MSDN.

■ Any additional application media you plan to include in the images, such as the 2007 Microsoft Office system. The 2007 Office system is available on the volume-licensed media and MDT 2008 supports retail media.

■ Any hardware-specific software, such as device drivers, CD-ROM burner software, and DVD-viewing software. Downloading all of the known device drivers and hardware-specific applications early in the process saves time when developing and building Windows Vista images.

Direct from the Source: Deployment Tools

You will use the following tools to deploy Windows Vista:

■ **Sysprep**   This is the updated version, modified for Windows Vista.

■ **Setup**   A new installation tool for Windows Vista that replaces WINNT and WINNT32.

■ **ImageX**   The new command-line tool for creating WIM images.

■ **Windows SIM**   A tool for creating and modifying Unattend.xml files.

■ **Peimg**   The tool for customizing Windows PE 2.0 images.

■ **Windows DS**   The new version of RIS, which adds the ability to deploy Windows Vista images as well as Windows PE 2.0 boot images.

■ **Pnputil**   This is the new tool for adding and removing drivers from the Windows Vista driver store.

■ **Pkgmgr**   Use this new Windows Vista tool for servicing the operating system.

■ **Ocsetup**   Replaces Sysocmgr and is used for installing Windows components.

■ **Bcdedit**   A new Windows Vista tool for editing boot configuration data.

■ **Application Compatibility Toolkit 5.0**   Use this updated tool to assess whether or not your applications are compatible with Windows Vista.

■ **User State Migration Tool 3.0**   An updated tool for capturing and restoring user state.

■ **BitLocker**   The full-volume drive-encryption capability included in Windows Vista Enterprise and Ultimate editions.

You can forget about using these tools:

■ **Remote Installation Services (RIS)**   RIS has been replaced by Windows DS, but Windows DS still offers legacy support on Windows Server 2003.

■ **Setup Manager and Notepad**   Use Windows SIM instead for editing unattended setup configuration files.

■ **Winnt.exe and Winnt32.exe**   Use Setup instead.

- **Sysocmgr** Replaced by Ocsetup and Pkgmgr.
- **MS-DOS Boot Floppies** Forget them. Use Windows PE.

Michael Niehaus, Lead Developer for Microsoft Deployment Toolkit

Management and Infrastructure Solutions

Capturing Images with Microsoft Deployment Toolkit

In MDT 2008, creating an image is essentially a Lite Touch Installation (LTI) process (containing applications, language packs, and various customizations), which ends by capturing an image of the destination computer in the lab. However, the process is much different for System Center Configuration Manager than it is for other methods, because MDT 2008 integrates fully into System Center Configuration Manager. The following list outlines the overall process (illustrated in Figure 6-1) for using Deployment Workbench to create and capture operating system images by using MDT 2008:

- **Prepare the distribution share** Prepare the distribution share by storing operating system source files, applications, out-of-box device drivers, and packages in it. The section titled "Configuring the Distribution Share" later in this chapter describes this step in detail.

- **Create and configure a task sequence** A *task sequence* associates an operating system with an unattended-setup answer file (Unattend.xml) and a sequence of tasks to run during installation. The section titled "Creating Task Sequences" later in this chapter describes this step in detail.

- **Create and configure a lab deployment point** A *deployment point* provides the information necessary to connect to the distribution share and install a build from it. Some deployment points are copies of the distribution share that you can distribute to other locations. Lab deployment points always connect to the distribution share directly, however. Deployment points also provide the Windows PE boot images necessary to start destination computers and connect to the deployment point. The section titled "Creating the Lab Deployment Point" later in this chapter describes this step in detail.

- **Run the Windows Deployment Wizard on the lab computer** Start the destination lab computer using the Windows PE image that the lab deployment point provides and then install a build from the distribution share. During the initial interview, the Windows Deployment Wizard will prompt you to specify whether or not you want to create a custom image after LTI is complete. The section titled "Capturing a Disk Image for LTI" later in this chapter describes this step in detail.

- **Add the custom image as an operating system source** After capturing the custom image, you add it to the distribution share as an operating system source. You can then deploy this custom image by using LTI or ZTI (Zero Touch Installation) with SMS 2003, as described in Chapter 12, "Using Microsoft Deployment."

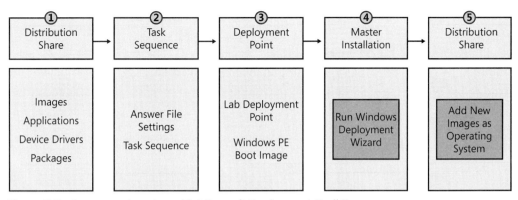

Figure 6-1   Image engineering with Microsoft Deployment Toolkit.

Navigating Deployment Workbench

To start Deployment Workbench, click Start, point to All Programs, point to Microsoft Deployment Toolkit, and then click Deployment Workbench. The console tree shows the following items:

- **Information Center**   This item provides access to the documentation, breaking news about MDT 2008, and the components required for using Deployment Workbench. Chapter 4 describes this item in detail.

- **Distribution Share**   Under this item are the operating systems, applications, operating system packages, and out-of-box drivers that the distribution share contains. Files you add to the distribution share are simply source files that MDT 2008 uses to create builds. Figure 6-2 shows Deployment Workbench with all items expanded and the Distribution Share item selected.

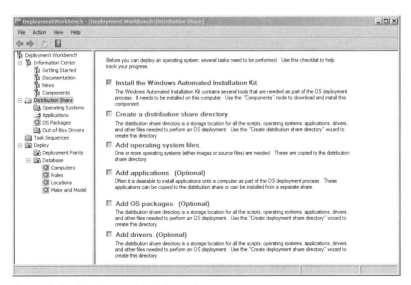

Figure 6-2   Deployment Workbench.

- **Task Sequences**   You see a list of task sequences in the Task Sequences pane. Task Sequences associate source files from the distribution share, particularly operating systems, with the series of steps required to install and configure them.

- **Deploy**   The Deploy item contains two items below it: Deployment Points and Database. In Deployment Points, you see a list of deployment points in the details pane. Deployment points contain the settings and files necessary to install builds from the distribution share or copies of the distribution share. In Database, you see the MDT 2008 database. For more information about the database, see Chapter 12.

Note   The default view in Deployment Workbench includes the action pane. The action pane often gets in the way of viewing the entire details pane. You can remove the action pane by authoring the management console. To author the console, run C:\Program Files\Microsoft Deployment Toolkit\Bin\DeploymentWorkbench.msc /a. Click View, click Customize, clear the Action Pane check box, and then click OK. Save your changes by clicking File, and then clicking Save on the main menu. When prompted if you want to display a single window interface, click Yes.

Creating a Distribution Share

Unlike the previous version of MDT 2008 (the Solution Accelerator for Business Desktop Deployment [BDD] 2007), you must now create a distribution share. You can create a new distribution share. You can also upgrade a BDD 2007 distribution share to MDT 2008.

Note   Microsoft strongly recommends that you select the Backup Existing Scripts And Configuration Files check box on the Specify Directory page. By selecting this option, you are able to easily recover your previous distribution share if the upgrade process goes awry.

To create a new distribution share

1. In the Deployment Workbench console tree, right-click Distribution Share and then click Create Distribution Share Directory.

2. On the Specify Directory page, click Create A New Distribution Share, type the path of the share in the Path For New Distribution Share Directory box, and then click Finish.

To upgrade a BDD 2007 distribution share for MDT 2008

1. In the Deployment Workbench console tree, right-click Distribution Share and then click Create Distribution Share Directory.

2. On the Specify Directory page, click Upgrade An Existing Distribution Share, type the path of the share in the Path To Existing Distribution Share Directory box, select the Backup Existing Scripts And Configuration Files check box, and then click Finish.

Configuring the Distribution Share

Using Deployment Workbench, you configure the distribution share in the following ways (at a minimum, you must add Windows Vista):

- Add, remove, and configure operating systems.

- Add, remove, and configure applications.

- Add, remove, and configure operating system packages, including updates and language packs.

- Add, remove, and configure out-of-box device drivers.

When you add operating systems, applications, operating system packages, and out-of-box device drivers to the distribution share, Deployment Workbench stores the source files in the distribution share folder specified when you create the distribution share (see the section titled "Creating a Distribution Share" earlier in this chapter). The default is *D*:\Distribution, where *D* is the volume with the most available space. You associate source files in the distribution share with task sequences later in the development process. In the distribution share's Control folder, Deployment Workbench stores metadata about operating systems, applications, operating system packages, and out-of-box device drivers in the following files:

- **Applications.xml**   Contains metadata about applications in the distribution share.

- **Drivers.xml**   Contains metadata about device drivers in the distribution share.

- **OperatingSystems.xml**   Contains metadata about operating systems in the distribution share.

- **Packages.xml**   Contains metadata about operating system packages in the distribution share.

Adding Windows Vista

All Windows Vista editions are in a single image file, Install.wim, which is in the Sources folder on the distribution media. For more information about the Windows Vista distribution media and Install.wim, see the Windows AIK. To build images based on Windows Vista, you must add the Windows Vista media to the MDT 2008 distribution share. Distribution shares must contain at a minimum the Windows Vista source files.

In addition to adding Windows Vista media to the distribution share, you can add Windows Vista images that already exist in Windows DS. MDT 2008 will not copy these files to the distribution share. Instead, MDT 2008 uses the files from their original location during deployment. There is a requirement for doing this. You must copy the following files from the

\Sources directory on the Windows Vista with Service Pack 1 media to C:\Program Files\Microsoft Deployment\bin:

- Wdsclientapi.dll

- Wdscsl.dll

- Wdsimage.dll

To add Windows Vista to a distribution share

1. In the Deployment Workbench console tree, right-click Operating Systems under Distribution Share and click New to start the New OS Wizard.

2. On the OS Type page, select Full Set Of Source Files and then click Next. This option copies the entire set of operating system source files from the distribution media or folder containing the distribution media. Optionally, you can add operating system images from a specific Windows DS server by selecting Windows Deployment Services Images. You can also click Custom Image File to add a custom image, created by using the Windows Deployment Wizard. For more information about creating a custom image, see the section titled "Capturing a Disk Image for LTI" later in this chapter.

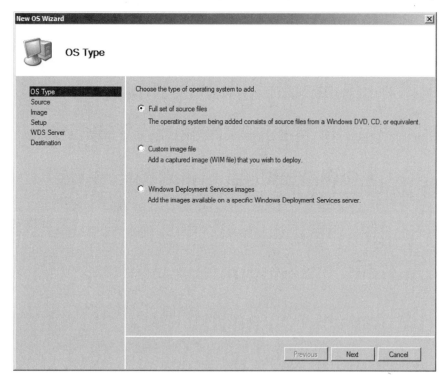

3. On the Source page, type the path containing the operating system source files you're adding to the distribution share, or click Browse to select the path, and then click Next. If you've staged (precopied the source files to the local computer) the operating system

files on the local hard disk, you can select Move The Files To The Distribution Share Instead Of Copying Them to speed the process.

4. On the Destination page, type the name of the operating system folder to create in the distribution share and then click Finish. You can accept the default name, which Deployment Workbench derives from the source files, or use a name that describes the operating system version and edition. For example, you can use Windows Vista Enterprise and Windows Vista Business to distinguish between the different editions of Windows Vista. Deployment Workbench uses the default name to create a folder for the operating system in the distribution share's Operating Systems folder.

The copy process can take several minutes to complete; the move process takes only seconds. After you add an operating system to the distribution share, it appears in the details pane of Operating Systems. Also, the operating system appears in the distribution share in Operating Systems*subfolder* (shown in Figure 6-3), where *subfolder* is the destination specified when adding the operating system.

Figure 6-3   Operating Systems in the distribution share.

To remove Windows Vista from the distribution share

1. In the Deployment Workbench console tree, click Operating Systems.

2. In the details pane, right-click the operating system you want to remove and then click Delete.

> **Note**   When an operating system is deleted from Deployment Workbench, Deployment Workbench also removes it from the Operating Systems folder in the distribution share. In other words, removing an operating system from Deployment Workbench also removes it from the file system.

Adding Applications

You must add each application to the distribution share that you intend to deploy by using MDT 2008. Deployment Workbench gives you the option to copy the application source files directly into the distribution share or to just add a reference to the application source files to the distribution share and leave them in their original location. Generally, if the network location containing the application source files will not be available during deployment, you should copy the application source files to the distribution share.

In addition to specifying how to add application source files to the distribution share, you can specify the command line for installing the application, dependencies between applications, and other settings for each application. After adding an application to the distribution share, you can install it at one of two points in the process:

- **During the Windows Deployment Wizard**   During the interview, the Windows Deployment Wizard prompts the user with a list of applications that are available for installation. The user can then choose which applications to install. You can configure the applications that the Windows Deployment Wizard installs by using the MDT 2008 database and then skip the application installation pages of the wizard—automating application installation without requiring user intervention. For more information about using the MDT 2008 database, see Chapter 12.

- **During the task sequence**   Application installations added to the task sequence—the sequence of tasks that occur during installation to prepare, install, and configure the build on the destination computer—occur when the Windows Deployment Wizard executes the task sequence on the destination computer. This is fully automated.

Chapter 8, "Deploying Applications," describes how to plan for and develop automated application installation. Chapter 8 describes differences between core applications, which are common to every desktop in the organization, and supplemental applications, which are not. You deploy each type of application differently, depending on the strategy you choose for application deployment. The strategies are as follows:

- **Thick image**   Install applications to the build that you're using to create disk images. You can install applications by using the Windows Deployment Wizard or by adding applications to the task sequence.

- **Thin image**   Application deployment usually occurs outside of operating system deployment, probably using a systems-management infrastructure such as System Center Configuration Manager 2007.

■ **Hybrid image**   You install applications to the build you're deploying to destination computers (most likely a custom image) and possibly install additional applications using a systems-management infrastructure. You can install the applications by using the Windows Deployment Wizard or by adding them to the task sequence.

> **Caution**   Do not allow an application to restart the computer. The Windows Deployment Wizard must control reboots or the task sequence will fail. See the section titled "Installation Reboots" later in this chapter for more information about configuring reboots.

To add an application to the distribution share

1. In the Deployment Workbench console tree, right-click Applications and then click New to start the New Application Wizard. Applications is located under Distribution Share.

2. On the Application Type page, do one of the following and then click Next:

   ❑ Select Application With Source Files to copy the application source files to the distribution share. During deployment, the Windows Deployment Wizard installs the application from the distribution share.

   ❑ Select Application Without Source Files Or Elsewhere On The Network. Choosing this option does not copy the application source files to the distribution share. During deployment, the Windows Deployment Wizard installs the application from another location on the network. You also choose this option to run a command that requires no application source files.

   ❑ Select Application Bundle. Choosing this option does not add an application to the distribution share. Instead, it creates a placeholder to which you can associate dependencies. Then, by installing the placeholder application (the bundle), you also install its dependencies.

3. On the Details page, provide the information described in Table 6-1 and then click Next.

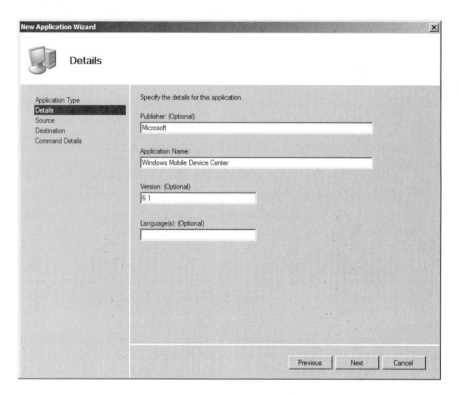

Table 6-1   The Specify The Details For This Application Page

In This Location	Provide This Information
Publisher box	Name of the application's publisher
Application Name box	Name of the application
Version box	Version label for the application
Languages box	Languages that the application supports

4. On the Source page, type the path of the folder containing the application to be added or click Browse to open it and then click Next. If you choose to copy the application source files to the distribution share, Deployment Workbench copies everything in this folder to the distribution share; otherwise, it adds this path to the application's metadata as the application's installation path. If the application source files are staged on the local hard disk, you can optionally select Move The Files To The Distribution Share Instead Of Copying Them to move them quickly to the distribution share instead of copying them.

5. On the Destination page, type the name of the folder to create for the application within the distribution share's Applications folder and then click Next. The default value is the publisher, application name, and version label concatenated.

> **Caution**   Make sure that the destination specified on the Specify The Destination page is unique. Otherwise, during an LTI deployment, the Windows Deployment Wizard will display multiple applications having the same name but installing different applications. If necessary, change the name on the Destination page to ensure that it is unique.

6. On the Command Details page, type the command to use to install the application silently, and then click Finish. For example, type **msiexec /qb /i program.msi**. The command is relative to the working directory specified in the Working Directory box. For help finding the appropriate command to automate the installation of various applications, see Chapter 8.

After you add an application to the distribution share, it appears in the Applications details pane. It also appears in the distribution share in Applications*subfolder*, where *subfolder* is the destination specified when adding the application.

To edit an application in the distribution share

1. In the Deployment Workbench console tree, click Applications.

2. In the details pane, right-click the application and then click Properties.

3. On the General and Details tabs, edit the application information and then click OK.

To provide an uninstall registry key name

1. In the Deployment Workbench console tree, click Applications.

2. In the details pane, right-click the application and then click Properties.

3. On the Details tab, type the uninstall registry key name in the Uninstall Registry Key Name box and then click OK.

The Windows Deployment Wizard uses the uninstall registry key name to determine if an application is already installed on the destination computer. This is a subkey of HKLM\\ Software\\Microsoft\\Windows\\CurrentVersion\\Uninstall. If the Windows Deployment Wizard detects the presence of this key, it assumes that the application is already installed and skips the installation of that application and any dependencies. In the Uninstall Registry Key Name box, type the name of the subkey—not the entire path.

To disable an application

1. In the Deployment Workbench console tree, click Applications.

2. In the details pane, right-click the application you want to disable and then click Properties.

3. Click the General tab, clear the Enable This Application check box, and then click OK.

If you add an application that you intend to install during the task sequence, disable the application by clearing the Enable This Application check box. The application will still install during the task sequence, but the user will not see it in the applications list.

To remove an application from the distribution share

1. In the Deployment Workbench console tree, click Applications.

2. In the details pane, right-click the application you want to remove and then click Delete.

When you delete an application from Deployment Workbench, it is also removed from the Applications folder in the distribution share. In other words, removing an application from Deployment Workbench also removes it from the file system.

Specifying Application Dependencies

Using Deployment Workbench, you can specify dependencies between applications. For example, if application A is dependent on application B, Deployment Workbench will ensure that application B is installed before installing application A.

To create a dependency between two applications

1. In the Deployment Workbench console tree, click Applications.

2. In the details pane, right-click the application that has a dependency and then click Properties.

3. Click the Dependencies tab, do any of the following, and then click OK:

   ❏ To add an application to the Dependencies list, click Add, and then select an application. Deployment Workbench displays only those applications that have already been added to the distribution share.

   ❏ To remove an application from the Dependencies list, select an application from the list, and then click Remove.

   ❏ To reorder the applications in the Dependencies list, select an application in the list and then click Up or Down. The Windows Deployment Wizard installs the dependent applications in the order specified in the Dependencies list.

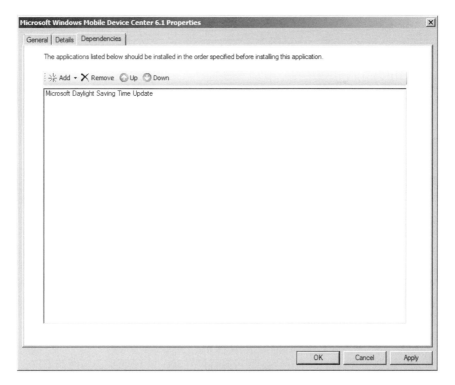

Installation Reboots

Do not allow an application to restart the computer. The Windows Deployment Wizard must control reboots, or the task sequence will fail. For example, you can use REBOOT=REALLYSUPPRESS to prevent some Windows Installer–based applications from restarting. You can cause the Windows Deployment Wizard to restart the computer after installing an application by selecting the Reboot The Computer After Installing This Application check box on the Details tab of the *Application* Properties dialog box of Deployment Workbench, where *Application* is the name of the application.

Direct from the Source: Reboots in MDT 2008

When a user first logs on to the computer, he can run commands in different ways. One way is to add *RunSynchronous* to the <Microsoft-Windows-Setup> child element *FirstLogonCommands* during the oobeSystem pass.

MDT 2008 doesn't use *RunSynchronous*, because it needs to support more complex installation scenarios. For example, an MDT 2008 installation needs to support reboots between application installations, and *RunSynchronous* doesn't support reboot-and-pick-up-where-it-left-off. Instead, MDT 2008 adds a command to *RunSynchronous* to initially start the task sequence. Then, if the task sequence needs to restart the

---

> computer, it adds a shortcut to the StartUp group, which continues the task sequence after the computer restarts.
>
> *Michael Niehaus, Lead Developer for Microsoft Deployment Toolkit*
>
> *Management and Infrastructure Solutions*

To restart the computer after installing an application

1. In the Deployment Workbench console tree, click Applications.

2. In the details pane, right-click the application for which the Windows Deployment Wizard must restart the computer after installation and then click Properties.

3. Click the Details tab, select the Reboot The Computer After Installing This Application check box, and then click OK. Selecting this check box causes the Windows Deployment Wizard to restart the computer after installing the application and then continue with the next step in the task sequence.

Adding Packages

Packages include operating system updates and language packs. The Windows Deployment Wizard automatically installs operating system updates during deployment. Users can choose which language packages to install during LTI deployment. You can configure language pack installation for ZTI, as described in Chapter 12. The following sections include more information about updates and languages.

To add a package to the distribution share

1. In Deployment Workbench, right-click OS Packages and then click New to start the New Package Wizard. OS Packages is located under Distribution Share.

2. On the Specify Directory page, type the path containing the package files you want to add to the distribution share, or click Browse to open it, and then click Finish. Deployment Workbench adds all the packages it finds in the folder and all its subfolders.

After Distribution Workbench adds packages to the distribution share, they appear in the OS Packages details pane. The packages also appear in the distribution share in the Packages folder.

To disable a package and prevent its installation

1. In the Deployment Workbench console tree, click OS Packages.

2. In the details pane, right-click the package you want to disable and then click Properties.

3. Click the General tab, clear the Enable (Approve) This Package check box to disable the package, and then click OK.

To remove a package from the distribution share

1. In the Deployment Workbench console tree, click OS Packages.

2. In the details pane, right-click the package you want to remove and then click Delete.

When a package is deleted from Deployment Workbench, it is also removed from the Packages folder in the distribution share. In other words, removing a package from Deployment Workbench also removes it from the file system.

Adding Updates

When you are developing an image, take care to ensure that all critical security updates are included in the image so that computers deployed with the image are as up to date as possible. Table 6-2 describes different approaches to performing these updates. (When you use MDT 2008, the first method is recommended.)

Table 6-2   Updating Windows Vista Images

Method	Benefits	Drawbacks
Download the security updates from the Microsoft website and then install them as part of the image-build process. You can look for updates in the Knowledge Base and in the Download Center.	The process is very easy to perform; you can install updates simply by adding them to the distribution share.	The image is vulnerable before the updates are installed and the computer is restarted, providing an opportunity for exploitation; the application process can also be time-consuming. However, building images in a closed lab environment mitigates this risk.
Use Microsoft Windows Server Update Services (WSUS) or System Center Configuration Manager 2007 to install the security update post-deployment.	The process is easy to perform and picks up new updates as soon as they are approved.	The image is vulnerable before the updates are installed and the computer is restarted, providing an opportunity for exploitation; the application process can also be time-consuming.
		Depending on the System Center Configuration Manager 2007 server configuration, it may take an hour or more before all updates are applied; having the System Center Configuration Manager 2007 client included in the image and communicating with a specific site may result in all computers built from the image communicating with only that site.

Table 6-2   Updating Windows Vista Images

Method	Benefits	Drawbacks
Download the security updates from the Microsoft website and then integrate them into the Windows installation source before beginning the unattended build process.	The image is protected at all times from known security exploits, and the image-build process completes faster because all security updates are installed before building the image.	Integrating the security updates takes some effort. It may not be obvious which updates you can integrate; you will need to install some as part of the unattended build process.

> **Note**   Download the required Windows security updates from the Microsoft Knowledge Base or Download Center. In the future, you will be able to download updates from the Microsoft Update Catalog, too.

Adding Language Packs

Language packs make possible a multilingual Windows environment. Windows Vista is language neutral, and all language and locale resources are added to Windows Vista through language packs (Lp.cab files). By adding one or more language packs to Windows Vista, you can enable those languages when installing the operating system. As a result, you can deploy the same Windows Vista image to regions with different language and locale settings, reducing development and deployment time.

The following resources provide additional information about language packs in Windows Vista:

- Chapter 12 includes instructions on installing language packs during deployment.
- The *Toolkit Reference* in MDT 2008 lists the properties you can configure to install language packs automatically.
- The topic "Manage Language Packs for Windows" in the *Windows Automated Installation Kit User's Guide* includes more information about Windows Vista language packs.

Adding Out-of-Box Drivers

Depending on the type of computer in the environment and the hardware it contains, you require software from the hardware vendors to make computers in the production environment fully functional. Some of this software is provided on a CD-ROM or DVD-ROM by the hardware manufacturer, but you must download other software from the Internet.

Deployment Workbench makes adding device drivers to the distribution share an easy process. You simply specify a folder containing one or more device drivers, and Deployment Workbench copies them to the distribution share and organizes them into folders as appropriate. However, you must make sure that you've extracted device drivers from any compressed files containing them. In other words, Deployment Workbench looks for each device driver's .inf file and any related files.

With MDT 2008, you can group device drivers. When you add a device driver by using Deployment Workbench, you can create groups and associate the device driver with any of those groups. Then, you can associate a device driver group with each task sequence you create in the distribution share. You can also specify device driver groups during deployment, as described in Chapter 12. The most common reason to group device drivers is to group them by computer model. By doing so, you can prevent scenarios that cause MDT 2008 to install device drivers on computers for which they are not intended.

> **Note**   No device drivers are required to run Windows Vista in a Microsoft Virtual PC 2007 virtual machine, but installing the latest version of the Microsoft Virtual PC Additions improves performance.

To add device drivers to the distribution share

1. In Deployment Workbench, right-click Out-Of-Box Drivers and then click New to start the New Driver Wizard. Out-Of-Box Drivers is located under Distribution Share.

2. On the Specify Directory page, type the path containing the device drivers you want to add to the distribution share or click Browse to open it.

3. In the These Drivers Can Be Assigned To One Or More Groups As They Are Being Imported list, choose the device driver groups to which you want to assign the drivers you are importing.

4. Optionally, select the Import Drivers Even If They Are Duplicates Of An Existing Driver check box. Choosing this option allows Deployment Workbench to import duplicate drivers, if they exist, but Microsoft recommends against this.

5. Click Finish. Deployment Workbench adds all the device drivers it finds in the folder and its subfolders.

After Deployment Workbench adds device drivers to the distribution share, they appear in the Out-Of-Box Drivers details pane. Also, the device drivers appear in the distribution share in the Out-Of-Box Drivers folder.

To disable a device driver

1. In the Deployment Workbench console tree, click Out-Of-Box Drivers.

2. In the details pane, right-click the device driver you want to disable and then click Properties.

3. Click the General tab, clear the Enable This Driver check box, and then click OK.

To remove a device driver from the distribution share

1. In the Deployment Workbench console tree, click Out-Of-Box Drivers.

2. In the details pane, right-click the device driver you want to remove and then click Delete.

When a device driver is deleted from Deployment Workbench, it is also removed from the Out-Of-Box Drivers folder in the distribution share. In other words, removing a device driver from Deployment Workbench also removes it from the file system.

To assign a device driver to a group

1. In the Deployment Workbench console tree, click Out-Of-Box Drivers.

2. In the details pane, right-click the device driver you want to edit and then click Properties.

3. On the Groups tab, select the device drivers group to include the device driver and then click OK. You can optionally create new device driver groups by clicking Add.

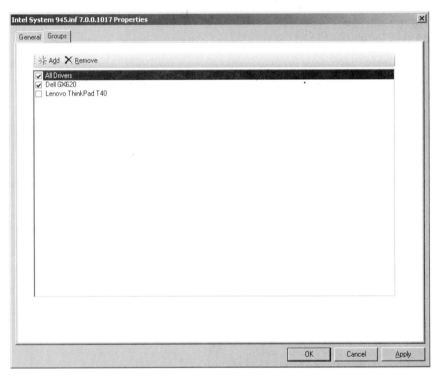

Creating Task Sequences

A task sequence binds operating system source files with the steps necessary to install them. A task sequence is associated with the following:

- **Operating system**   Choose an operating system image to use for the build.

■ **Unattended setup answer file (Unattend.xml)**   Create an answer file that describes how to install and configure the operating system on the destination computer. For example, the answer file can contain a product key, organization name, and information necessary to join the computer to a domain. Generally, allow MDT 2008 to control the settings in Unattend.xml and use the MDT 2008 database to configure destination computers.

> **Note**   This chapter assumes that you are configuring task sequences and deployment points for the purpose of capturing custom images. The settings you configure by using the instructions in this chapter are different than the settings you will configure when deploying images to production computers. For more information about those settings, see Chapter 12.

To create a task sequence for image capture

1. In the Deployment Workbench console tree, right-click Task Sequences and then click New to start the New Task Sequence Wizard.

2. On the General Settings page, provide the information described in Table 6-3 and then click Next.

Table 6-3   The General Settings Page

In This Location	Provide This Information
Task Sequence ID box	Unique ID for the task sequence. You cannot change this ID later, so decide on a naming scheme for task sequence IDs in advance. Because you're creating task sequences for image capture in a lab, one possible naming convention is Lab*NN*.
Task Sequence Name box	Descriptive name for the task sequence. Users see this name during LTI.
Task Sequence Comments box	Additional information about the task sequence. Users see this description during LTI. Describe the build and what it installs in the image.

3. On the Select Template page, choose a template task sequence to use as a starting point and then click Next. You can customize the template later. For the purpose of building images, choose the Standard Client Task Sequence template.

4. On the Select OS page, choose an operating system image to install with this task sequence and then click Next. Only the operating system images added to Operating Systems earlier are visible.

5. On the Specify Product Key page, perform one of the following tasks and then click Next:

    ❑ Select Specify The Product Key For This Operating System and then type the product key in the Product Key box.

    ❑ Select Do Not Specify A Product Key At This Time.

For more information about volume activation and product keys in MDT 2008, see Chapter 11, "Using Volume Activation." Chapter 11 describes when a product key is necessary. Generally, volume license customers deploying Windows Vista to 25 or more computers should select the Do Not Use A Product Key When Installing option. Customers using Windows Vista Multiple Activation Keys (MAKs) should select the Use The Specified Product Key option and then type a product key in the Product Key box.

6.   On the OS Settings page, provide the information described in Table 6-4 and then click OK. The values you provide on this page are irrelevant, as you are creating a build for image capture, and you will change these values during production deployment.

Table 6-4   The OS Settings Page

In This Location	Provide This Information
Full Name box	Owner name
Organization box	Name of the organization
Internet Explorer Home Page box	URL of the default Internet Explorer home page, such as the URL of the organization's intranet home page

7.   On the Admin Password page, select Do Not Specify An Administrator Password At This Time and then click Finish. Do not specify a local Administrator password for image task sequences so that you can specialize the password during deployment.

After you add a task sequence to the distribution share, it appears in the Task Sequences details pane. It also in appears the distribution share in Control*subfolder*, where *subfolder* is the task sequence ID. Deployment Workbench stores metadata about each build in Task-Sequences.xml, which is also located in the distribution share's Control folder.

To disable a task sequence

1.   In the Deployment Workbench console tree, click Task Sequences.

2.   In the details pane, right-click the task sequence you want to disable and then click Properties.

3.   On the General tab, clear the Enable This Task Sequence check box and then click OK. Alternatively, you can hide the task sequence by selecting the Hide This Task Sequence In The Deployment Wizard check box.

Note   Disabling a build prevents the Windows Deployment Wizard from displaying it in the list of builds the user can choose from during an LTI deployment.

To remove a task sequence

1.   In the Deployment Workbench console tree, click Task Sequences.

2.   In the details pane, right-click the task sequence you want to remove and then click Delete.

To edit the task sequence's answer file (Unattend.xml)

1. In the Deployment Workbench console tree, click Task Sequences.

2. In the details pane, right-click the task sequence containing the answer file you want to edit, and then click Properties.

3. On the OS Info tab, click Edit Unattend.xml to open the build's answer file in Windows SIM.

For more information about using Windows SIM to edit Unattend.xml, see the topic "Windows System Image Manager Technical Reference" in the Windows AIK.

Direct from the Source: Reducing Image Count

We put the 2007 Office system and a virus scanner on every image. That way, the customer can be productive regardless of the method we use to deploy other applications. Also, a lot of things just make sense to put in the image so that the user doesn't have to download them later; I can't think of a single customer who doesn't have Adobe Acrobat Reader.

The VPN and dialer installation programs are in the image, but we don't install them. When we deploy the image, the task sequence checks WMI to see if it's a mobile device. If it's a mobile device, we then install the VPN and dialer software; otherwise, we delete the installation programs.

We also never use a product key. Instead, we use the Key Management Service to simplify our images and reduce key loss. Chapter 11 describes the Key Management Service.

Having a single image to deploy is very handy and works well. We encourage people to change an image only when they need new software. Whenever a new update or device driver is required, we just replicate that information and then inject it into the image, rather than making a new image every month and replicating the image. If this is the approach you plan to take, image versioning is very important to track.

Doug Davis, Lead Architect

Management Operations & Deployment, Microsoft Consulting Services

---

Editing a Task Sequence

In MDT 2008, the task sequence is a list of tasks to run during deployment. However, it's not a linear list of tasks like a batch script. The task sequence is organized into groups and specifies conditions, or filters, that can prevent tasks and entire groups from running in certain situations.

MDT 2008 uses a *task sequencer* to run the task sequence. The task sequencer runs the task sequence from top to bottom in the order specified. Each task in the sequence is a step, and steps can be organized into groups and subgroups. When you create a task sequence in Deployment Workbench, you can choose a task sequence template. A key feature of the task sequence is that it stores state data, or variables, on the destination computer. These variables persist, even across reboots. The task sequencer can then use these variables to test conditions and possibly filter tasks or groups. The task sequencer also can restart the computer and gracefully continue the task sequence where it left off. These are important characteristics when driving a deployment process from beginning to end.

Task sequences contain the following types of items:

- **Tasks**   Within a task sequence, tasks do the actual work. Tasks are commands that the task sequencer runs during the sequence, such as partitioning the disk, capturing user state, and installing the operating system. In the task sequence templates provided by MDT 2008, most tasks are commands that run scripts.

- **Groups**   The task sequence can be organized into groups, which are folders that can contain subgroups and tasks. Groups can be nested as necessary. For example, the default task sequence puts tasks in groups by phase and deployment type.

You can filter both tasks and groups, including the groups and tasks they contain, based on conditions that you specify. Groups are especially useful for filtering, because you can run an entire collection of tasks based on a condition such as the deployment phase or type of deployment.

On the Disc   The companion CD includes sample scripts (.reg files, .vbs, and .cmd files) that you can use to customize Windows Vista during deployment. Use the instructions in this section to add one of these customization scripts to your task sequence. For example, ShowDefender.cmd is a script that configures Windows Defender so that the user always sees the icon, whereas MenuSort.reg restores the sort order of the Start and Favorites menus.

Writing Scripts for MDT 2008

To customize the task sequence, you'll usually write a script. Most scripts that run during the task sequence must interact with the task sequencer's environment.

The sample script VRKDisplayOSDVar.vbs on this book's companion CD shows how to read values from the task sequencer's environment. To test this script, run it during deployment. The Windows Deployment Wizard opens a second Command Prompt window that you can use for debugging purposes. In this window, type **VRKDisplayOSD-Var *variable***, where *variable* is the name of a variable you want to display. For example, try **VRKDisplayOSDVar DeploymentType** or **VRKDisplayOSDVar Phase**.

Another sample script on this book's companion CD, VRKFolderExists.vbs, shows how to write values to the task sequencer's environment. To test this script, run it during deployment in the second Command Prompt window. In this window, type **VRKFolder-Exists MININTEXISTS C:\Minint**. This script will set the variable MININTEXISTS to true if the folder C:\Minint exists on the disk. You can then test this variable in the task sequence, as described in the section titled "Configuring the Options Tab" later in this chapter. You'll also find a similar script, VRKFileExists.vbs, on this book's companion CD. Use the scripts as starting points for writing your own scripts to customize the task sequence.

To edit a task sequence

1. In the Deployment Workbench console tree, click Task Sequences.

2. In the details pane, right-click the task sequence you want to edit and then click Properties.

3. Click the Task Sequence tab, edit the task sequence as described in Table 6-5, and then click OK. For more information about settings on the Properties and Options tabs, see the sections titled "Configuring Group and Task Properties" and "Configuring the Options Tab" later in this chapter.

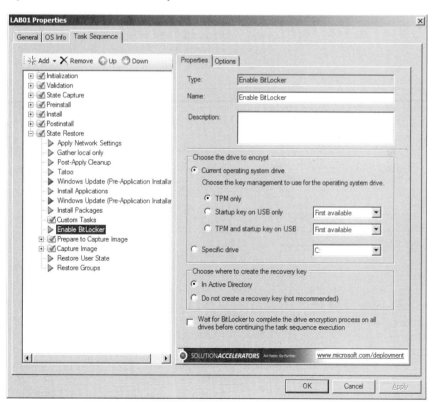

Table 6-5   Editing a Task Sequence

To	Use These Steps
Add a group	In the task sequence, select the item beneath which you want to create a new group, click Add, and then click New Group. Deployment Workbench creates and selects a new group called New Group.
Add a task	In the task sequence, select the item beneath which you want to create a new task, click Add, and then choose the type of task you want to create by clicking General and then choosing one of the following (MDT 2008 supports more tasks than those listed here, but they are already in the task sequence or are primarily for server deployment): ■ Run Command Line ■ Set Task Sequence Variable ■ Run Command Line As Deployment Workbench creates and selects a new task with a name relating to the type of task you're creating.
Add a reboot	In the task sequence, select the item beneath which you want to add a reboot, click Add, click General, and then click Restart Computer. Deployment Workbench creates and selects a new task that restarts the destination computer.
Add an application	In the task sequence, select the item beneath which you want to add an application installation, click Add, click General, and then click Install Application. Then select the Install Application step you just added, and on the Properties tab, click Install A Single Application. Choose the application you want to install from the Application To Install list.

Caution   If you install antivirus software as part of the task sequence, be sure to carefully test how the antivirus software interacts with the deployment process before moving to a production environment. Antivirus software can prevent MDT 2008 from successfully deploying Windows Vista and applications. If necessary, you can always disable the antivirus software and then re-enable it at the end of the task sequence.

To edit an item in a task sequence

In the task sequence, select the item to edit and then edit the settings in the right pane.

Note   MDT 2008 includes a variety of special tasks, such as the Enable BitLocker task or Install Operating System task, that you can configure. You change settings for these tasks by selecting the step in the left pane and then configuring the task on the Properties tab. In general, the most interesting tasks to configure are Validate (under Validation and under Preinstall\New Computer Only), Format and Partition Disk (under Preinstall\New Computer Only), Install Operating System (under Install), Apply Network Settings (under State Restore), and Enable BitLocker (under State Restore).

To remove an item in a task sequence

In the task sequence, select the item to remove and then click Remove. If a group is removed, Deployment Workbench removes the group and everything it contains, including subgroups and tasks.

To reorder an item in a task sequence

In the task sequence, select the item you want to reorder and then click Up or Down to change its position within the task sequence. During deployment, the Windows Deployment Wizard runs the tasks from top to bottom in the order specified.

Configuring Group and Task Properties

In the task sequence, every group and task has a Properties tab. Each group and task has a name and description that you can edit on the Properties tab. Run Command Line and Run Command Line As tasks also have a command line and a starting folder location that you can edit. Other tasks have additional properties, depending on the type of task. The following list describes what you see on the Properties tab:

- **Type**   The Type box indicates the type of task. You cannot change the type.
- **Name**   In the Name box, type a short, descriptive name for the group or task. During deployment, this name appears in the task sequencer's status window.
- **Description**   In the Description box, type a description of the group or task.
- **Command Line (Run Command Line and Run Command Line As tasks only)**   In the Command Line box, type the command to run at this step in the task sequence. Include any command-line arguments. Environment variables are also permitted in command lines.
- **Start In (tasks only)**   In the Start In box, type the path in which to start the command. This path specifies the current working directory for the command. If you do not provide a path in this box, the paths in the Command Line box must be fully qualified or the command must be in the path.

Configuring the Options Tab

Groups and tasks have the following settings on the Options tab (shown in Figure 6-4):

- **Disable This Step**   Select the Disable This Step check box to disable the task or group, including all groups and tasks it contains.
- **Success Codes (tasks only)**   List the return codes that indicate successful completion. The Windows Deployment Wizard determines whether or not a task completed successfully by comparing its return code to each code in the Success Codes box. If it finds a match, the task completed successfully. A success code of 0 usually represents successful completion. A success code of 3010 usually represents a successful completion with a reboot required. Thus, most of the tasks in the templates that MDT 2008 provides list the success codes as *0 3010*.

■ **Continue On Error**   If an error occurs in the current task, select the Continue On Error check box to continue with the next step in the task sequence. If you clear this check box, the Windows Deployment Wizard stops processing and displays an error message if the task or group did not complete successfully.

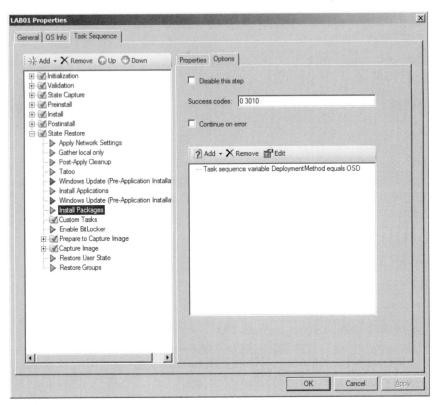

Figure 6-4   The Options tab.

Additionally, on the Options tab, you can filter the group or tasks based on conditions specified in the Conditions list. If the condition evaluates to true, the group or task runs. If the condition evaluates to false, the group (and all of the groups and tasks that group contains) or task does not run. See the following sections for more information about conditions you can add to the Conditions list.

Task Sequence Variables

Task sequence variables allow you to compare a variable to a static value using a variety of conditions, such as equal, greater than, and less than. The task sequencer maintains numerous variables that you can use in these tests. For example, the task sequencer defines a variable called DeploymentMethod that indicates the method of deployment. One possible value of DeploymentMethod is OSD. For a complete list of variables that the task sequencer maintains, see the *Toolkit Reference* in MDT 2008.

To add a variable to an item's Conditions list

1. On the Options tab, click Add and then click Task Sequence Variable to display the Task Sequence Variable Condition dialog box.

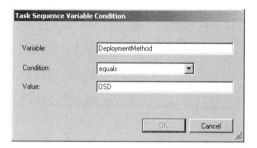

2. In the Variable box, type the name of the variable you want to test. For a full list of variables that you can test, see the *Toolkit Reference* in MDT 2008.

3. From the Condition list, choose one of the following conditions:

   - ❑ exists

   - ❑ equals

   - ❑ not equals

   - ❑ greater than

   - ❑ greater than or equals

   - ❑ less than

   - ❑ less than or equals

4. In the Value box, type the static value you want to compare to the variable using the condition specified in the previous step.

If Statements

Use If statements to combine variables into bigger expressions. For example, create an If statement that evaluates to true only if all the conditions it contains are true. (This is the same as a logical AND.) Create an If statement that evaluates to true if any of the conditions it contains are true. (This is the same as a logical OR.)

To add an If statement to an item's Conditions list

1. On the Options tab, click Add and then click If Statement to display the If Statement Properties dialog box.

2.   In the If Statement Properties dialog box, choose one of the following options and then click OK:

   ❑   All conditions (and)

   ❑   Any conditions (or)

   ❑   None

3.   From the Conditions list, select the If statement added in the previous step and then add task sequence variables to it as described in the previous section.

If you chose All Conditions, all variables added must evaluate to true for the group or task to run. If you chose Any Conditions, the group or task will run if any one of the variables added evaluates to true.

> **Note**   You can nest If statements to create complex logic. If you are familiar with Boolean logic, represent Boolean expressions as If statements in the Conditions list.

Operating System Versions

The task sequencer allows you to filter tasks and groups based on the computer's current operating system. For example, you can choose to run a preinstallation task only if the destination computer is currently running Windows XP Professional SP2.

To add an operating system filter to an item's Conditions list

1.   On the Options tab, click Add, and then click Operating System Version to display the Task Sequence OS Condition dialog box.

2.   From the Architecture list, click either X86 or X64.

3.   From the Operating system list, choose an operating system version and a service pack level.

4.   From the Condition list, choose one of the following conditions:

   ❑   equals

   ❑   not equals

- ❏ greater than

- ❏ greater than or equals

- ❏ less than

- ❏ less than or equals

WMI Queries

The task sequencer allows you to filter tasks and groups based on WMI queries. The WMI query must return a collection. If the collection is empty, the result evaluates to false. If the collection is not empty, the result evaluates to true. The following are some sample WMI queries you could use to filter tasks in the task sequence:

- ■ SELECT * FROM Win32_ComputerSystem WHERE Manufacturer = 'Dell Computer Corporation'. This is true only if WMI reports the computer's manufacturer as *Dell Computer Corporation.*

- ■ SELECT * FROM Win32_OperatingSystem WHERE OSLanguage = '1033'. This is true only if WMI reports the operating-system language as 1033.

- ■ SELECT * FROM Win32_Service WHERE Name = 'WinMgmt'. This is true only if the WinMgmt service is available.

- ■ SELECT * FROM Win32_Processor WHERE DeviceID = 'CPU0' AND Architecture = '0'. This is true only if the processor architecture is x86.

- ■ SELECT * FROM Win32_Directory WHERE Name = 'D:\Somefolder'. This is true only if D:\Somefolder exists on the computer.

To add a WMI query to an item's Conditions list

1. On the Options tab, click Add and then click Query WMI to display the Task Sequence WMI Condition dialog box.

2. In the WMI Namespace box, type the WMI namespace in which to run the query. The default namespace is *root\cimv2*.

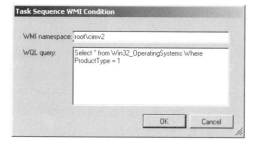

3. In the WQL Query box, type the WMI query.

Creating the Lab Deployment Point

Whereas a *distribution share* contains the files necessary to install and configure a build on a destination computer, a *deployment point* defines a subset of those files and how to connect to them. For example, the distribution share might contain multiple operating systems and hundreds of applications. A deployment point defines which of those files to distribute and how to access them through a network connection or removable media.

> **Note**   Environments using System Center Configuration Manager 2007 to deploy Windows Vista do not use Deployment Workbench to create or deploy images. In this scenario, you use Deployment Workbench only to edit the MDT 2008 database, because MDT 2008 fully integrates into SCCM System Center Configuration Manager 2007. For more information about using System Center Configuration Manager 2007 to deploy and optionally capture a Windows Vista image, see Chapter 12.

MDT 2008 supports four types of deployment points:

- **Lab**   This is a basic, single-server deployment point. This deployment point references all the content in the distribution share. When building custom images, you will usually use a lab deployment point.

- **Network**   This is a subset of the distribution share that you can replicate to many servers based on your organization's requirements. You can choose the builds, images, device drivers, updates, and applications that are replicated to a network deployment point.

- **Media**   This is a subset of the distribution share that you can put on a DVD, USB flash disk, and so on to perform standalone, potentially network-disconnected deployments.

- **OSD**   This is a copy of all the scripts, tools, and other files necessary to properly configure custom actions in the SMS 2003 OSD for performing a ZTI deployment. The images, applications, and device drivers are part of this replica.

For each deployment point, you can create .wim and .iso Windows PE boot image files that automatically connect to the deployment point and begin the installation. During the LTI process, the Windows Deployment Wizard allows the user to choose which build to install from the deployment point.

To create a lab deployment point for image capture

1. In the Deployment Workbench console tree, right-click Deployment Points under Deploy and click New to start the New Deployment Point Wizard.

2. On the Choose Type page, select Lab Or Single-Server Deployment and then click Next.

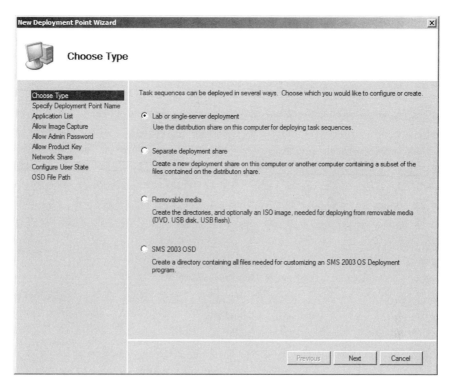

3. On the Specify Deployment Point Name page, type a name for the deployment point and then click Next. For the lab deployment point, *Lab* is a good name.

4. On the Application List page, verify that the Allow Users To Select Additional Applications On Upgrade check box is selected if you want to select applications to install when the Windows Deployment Wizard begins. Click Next.

5. On the Allow Image Capture page, verify that the Ask If An Image Should Be Captured check box is selected and then click Next. During the deployment interview, the Windows Deployment Wizard will ask whether or not to create an image of the destination computer after it installs the build on it.

6. On the Allow Admin Password page, verify that the Ask User To Set The Local Administrator Password check box is cleared to prevent the Windows Deployment Wizard from prompting for a local Administrator password. Click Next.

7. On the Allow Product Key page, verify that the Ask User For A Product Key check box is cleared to prevent the Windows Deployment Wizard from prompting for a product key during installation and then click Next—if you specified a product key when you created the build, as described earlier in this chapter.

8. On the Network Share page, type a name for the share and then click Next. The default share name is *folder*$, where *folder* is the name of the folder containing the distribution share. The dollar sign ($) hides the share in the network browser list.

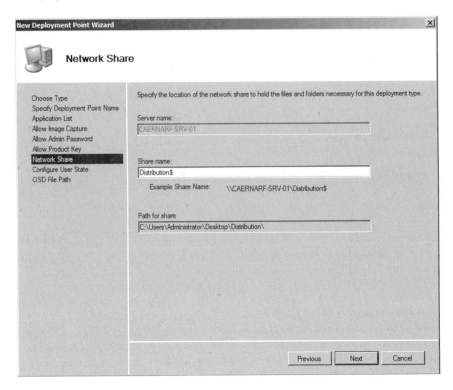

9. On the Configure User State page, click the Do Not Save Data And Settings option and then click Finish. Imaging is by its nature a New Computer scenario (see Chapter 4), so you have no reason to capture and restore user state.

To remove a deployment point

1. In the Deployment Workbench console tree, click Deployment Points. Deployment Points is located under Deploy.

2. In the details pane, right-click the deployment point you want to remove and then click Delete.

Note   Removing a deployment point from Deployment Workbench does not remove the share from the computer. You must manually remove any shares you created.

Configuring the Deployment Point

The Windows AIK comes with Windows PE. No additional files are necessary to create Windows PE boot images for MDT 2008. Deployment Workbench automatically customizes Windows PE .wim files when a deployment point is updated. Optionally, you can configure the deployment point to generate the following Windows PE images:

- LTI bootable RAM disk ISO image

- Generic bootable RAM disk ISO image

You don't need to manually customize Windows PE to add network interface card (NIC) device drivers to it. Deployment Workbench automatically adds the NIC device drivers that you add to the distribution share to the Windows PE boot images. You have the additional option of automatically adding video and system device drivers from the distribution share to the Windows PE boot images.

Updating a deployment point causes Deployment Workbench to update its configuration files, source files, and Windows PE images. Deployment Workbench updates the deployment point's files and generates the Windows PE boot images when you update the deployment point, not when you create it. Deployment Workbench stores these boot images in the distribution share's Boot folder. After you have updated the deployment point and generated Windows PE images, you can add the .wim image file to Windows DS. Optionally, you can burn the Windows PE .iso images to DVDs by using most commercial CD-burning software. Windows DS is the best way to start the Windows PE boot images on lab computers. Updating the boot images is faster than burning new DVDs, and booting destination computers is quicker. For more information, see Chapter 10.

> **Note**   You must use the same platform edition of Windows PE to start computers for installing each platform edition of Windows. In other words, you must start destination computers using the x86 edition of Windows PE to install the x86 edition of Windows Vista. Likewise, you must use the x64 edition of Windows PE to install the x64 edition of Windows Vista. If you use mismatched editions, you might see errors indicating that the image is for a different type of computer. Deployment Workbench automatically chooses the correct platform edition of Windows PE to match the operating system you're deploying.

To learn more about customizing Windows PE, see the *Windows Preinstallation Environment User's Guide* in the Windows AIK.

To configure a deployment point for imaging in the lab

1. In the Deployment Workbench console tree, click Deployment Points under Deploy.

2. In the details pane, right-click the deployment point you want to configure and then click Properties.

3. Click the General tab and then choose the platforms that the deployment point supports. To indicate that the deployment point supports the x86 platform, select the x86 check box. To indicate that the deployment point supports the x64 platform, select the x64 check box. This option determines the platforms for which Deployment Workbench generates Windows PE boot images.

4. Click the Rules tab and then edit the deployment point's settings. These settings are located in CustomSettings.ini, which is located in the deployment point's Control folder. For more information about the settings that you can configure on this tab, see the *Toolkit Reference* in MDT 2008.

5. Click the Windows PE tab, edit the settings described in Table 6-6, and then click OK.

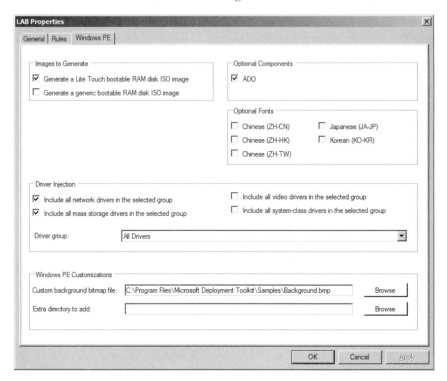

Table 6-6   Windows PE Settings

Area	Settings
Images to Generate	**Generate A Lite Touch Bootable RAM Disk ISO Image**. Select this option to generate ISO images that start from RAM disk. **Generate A Generic Bootable RAM Disk ISO Image**. Select this option to generate a generic Windows PE bootable image that starts from RAM disk and does not contain MDT 2008.

Table 6-6   Windows PE Settings

Area	Settings
Driver Injection	**Include All Network Drivers in the Selected Group**. Select this option to inject all network drivers found in the distribution share into the Windows PE boot images.
	Include All Mass Storage Drivers in the Selected Group. Select this option to inject all mass storage drivers found in the distribution share into the Windows PE boot images.
	Include All Video Drivers in the Selected Group. Select this option to inject all video drivers found in the distribution share into the Windows PE boot images.
	Include All System-Class Drivers in the Selected Group. Select this option to inject all system drivers (such as motherboard drivers) in the distribution share into the Windows PE boot images.
	You can limit the device drivers that Deployment Workbench includes in the Windows PE image by selecting a driver group from the Driver Group list.
Optional Components	**ADO**. Select this option to add the Microsoft ActiveX Data Objects (ADO) optional component to the Windows PE bootable images.
Optional Fonts	Select the font support to add to the Windows PE boot images that Deployment Workbench generates. You must add these fonts when performing a Lite Touch deployment of Windows Vista images when the setup files are Japanese, Korean, or Chinese. The Optional Fonts area provides the following options: ■ Chinese (ZH-CN) ■ Chinese (ZH-HK) ■ Chinese (ZH-TW) ■ Japanese (JA-JP) ■ Korean (KO-KR) Adding additional fonts to Windows PE boot images increases the size of the images. Add additional fonts only if necessary.
Windows PE Customizations	**Custom Background Bitmap File**. Type the path and filename of a bitmap file to use as the Windows PE background.
	Extra Directory To Add. Type the path of a folder containing extra files and subfolders to add to the Windows PE bootable images.

Deployment Workbench always generates .wim image files, which you can use to start destination computers using Windows DS. Choose to generate only the Windows PE bootable ISO images that are actually required. If you limit the number of images generated, the updating process is faster.

Updating the Deployment Point

After creating and configuring a deployment point in Deployment Workbench, update it to create it on the file system. Updating a deployment point creates the folder structure, shares the folder structure, configures settings, and generates Windows PE boot images.

Note   You must update the deployment point if you make any changes to the General, Rules, or Windows PE tabs. The Windows PE boot images will not contain your updated settings until you update the deployment point.

To update the lab deployment point, in the Deployment Points details pane, right-click the deployment point to update and then click Update.

Capturing a Disk Image for LTI

In MDT 2008, installing a build and capturing an image is essentially an LTI deployment that ends with the Windows Deployment Wizard capturing an image of the destination computer. When you create a deployment point, Deployment Workbench provides the option of prompting to capture an image (the Ask If An Image Should Be Captured check box). You must enable this option, as described in the section titled "Configuring the Deployment Point" earlier in this chapter.

Then, when you install the build on the destination lab computer, the Windows Deployment Wizard asks if you want to capture an image after installation is complete. The wizard also allows you to specify a destination for the image. The default destination is the Captures folder in the distribution share, and the default filename is *task sequence*.wim, where *task sequence* is the ID of the task sequence you installed.

To capture an image, start a lab computer using the Windows PE boot image generated by updating the deployment point. Start the Windows PE boot image in either of two ways. One way is to burn the .iso images to a DVD. This process is slow and tedious. These ISO image files reside in the \Boot folder of the distribution share. The other way is to add the LiteTouchPE_x86.wim or LiteTouchPE_x64.wim image files to the Boot Images item of a Windows DS server. The .wim image files are in the \Boot folder of the distribution share. For more information about installing and configuring Windows DS, see Chapter 10.

To capture an image using the Windows Deployment Wizard

1. Start the lab computer using the Windows PE boot image you created in the section titled "Updating the Deployment Point" earlier in this chapter. You can start this boot image by burning it to a DVD or by adding it to Windows DS. For more information about Windows DS, see Chapter 10.

2. In the Welcome To Windows Deployment dialog box, click Run The Deployment Wizard and then click Next.

3. In the User Credentials dialog box, type the credentials necessary to connect to the distribution share (user name, domain, and password) and then click OK. The Windows Deployment Wizard starts automatically. You must use an account that has Read and Write access to the distribution share, such as an account that is a member of the local Administrators group on the computer that contains the distribution share.

4. On the Select A Task Sequence To Execute On This Computer page, choose a task sequence to run from the list of available task sequences and then click Next.

5. On the Configure The Computer Name page, type a computer name or accept the default and then click Next. The default, randomly generated computer name is reasonable, since the computer name will change during deployment to the production environment.

6. On the Join The Computer To A Domain Or Workgroup page, click Join A Workgroup. In the Workgroup box, type a workgroup name or accept the default and then click Next. If you join the computer to a domain, the Windows Deployment Wizard does not prompt you to capture an image.

7. On the Specify Whether To Restore User Data page, select Do Not Restore User Data And Settings and then click Next.

8. On the Locale Selection page, choose your locale and keyboard layout and then click Next. Your choice here is irrelevant, because the Windows Deployment Wizard will configure the locale and keyboard layouts during deployment to the production environment.

9. On the Select The Time Zone page, select a time zone and then click Next. Your choice here is irrelevant, because the Windows Deployment Wizard will configure the time zone during deployment to the production environment.

10. On the Select One Or More Applications To Install page, select the check box next to each application that you want to install on the image and then click Next.

11. In the Specify Whether To Capture An Image page, select Capture An Image Of This Reference Computer. In the Location box, type the UNC path of the folder in which to store the image. In the File Name box, type the filename of the image and then click Next. The default UNC path is the Captures folder of the distribution share; the default image filename is the ID of the task sequence being installed.

12. On the Ready To Begin page, click Begin.

After you click Begin, the task sequencer begins running the build's task sequence. By default, it begins by partitioning and formatting the hard disk. Then it installs and configures the operating system, runs Sysprep to prepare the computer for imaging, and restarts the computer in Windows PE to capture the image. The Windows Deployment Wizard stores the captured image in the folder specified on the Specify Whether To Capture An Image page, which is the distribution share's Captures folder by default. After capturing the image, you can add it to the distribution share as a custom image by using the steps described in the section titled "Configuring the Distribution Share" earlier in this chapter. For more information about deploying your custom Windows Vista image, see Chapter 12.

Capturing a Disk Image for ZTI

Capturing a disk image for deployment by ZTI is similar to the process of capturing an image for LTI, with minor differences. This section describes how to capture an image for ZTI by using the SMS 2003 Image Capture Wizard. Before proceeding, you must have a working SMS 2003 infrastructure, and you must have OSD installed.

Creating an Image Capture CD

Rather than using the Windows Deployment Wizard to actually capture the image, you use the SMS 2003 Image Capture Wizard.

To create an Image Capture CD using OSD

1. In the SMS Administrator Console, right-click the Image Packages item, click All Tasks, and then click Create Operating System Image Capture CD.

2. On the Operating System Image Capture CD Wizard welcome page, click Next.

3. On the Windows PE Settings page, do the following and then click Next:

   a. Select the Include Additional Network Drivers From This Location check box and then type the path to any additional network drivers required in the environment.

   b. Select the Include Additional Storage Drivers From This Location check box and then type the path to any additional storage drivers required in the environment.

4. On the Create CD Image page, type the path and filename of the .iso file you want to create and then click Next.

Preparing the Image for Capture

To prepare an image for the SMS 2003 Image Capture Wizard, start a lab computer using the Windows PE boot image generated by updating the lab deployment point. This process is the same as that described in the section titled "Capturing a Disk Image for LTI" earlier in this chapter. Then use the SMS 2003 Image Capture Wizard to capture the image. The Windows Deployment Wizard must prepare the computer for the SMS 2003 Image Capture Wizard; it provides an option during the interview process for doing this.

1. Start the lab computer using the Windows PE boot image you created in the section titled "Updating the Deployment Point" earlier in this chapter. You can start this boot

image by burning it to a DVD or by adding it to Windows DS. For more information about Windows DS, see Chapter 10.

2. In the Welcome To Windows Deployment dialog box, click Run The Deployment Wizard and then click Next.

3. In the User Credentials dialog box, type the credentials necessary to connect to the distribution share (user name, domain, and password) and then click OK. The Windows Deployment Wizard starts automatically.

4. On the Select A Task Sequence To Execute On This Computer page, choose a task sequence to run from the list of available task sequences and then click Next.

5. On the Configure The Computer Name page, type a computer name or accept the default and then click Next. The default, randomly generated computer name is reasonable, since the computer name will change during deployment to the production environment.

6. On the Join The Computer To A Domain Or Workgroup page, click Join A Workgroup. In the Workgroup box, type a workgroup name or accept the default and then click Next. If you do not select Join A Workgroup, the Windows Deployment Wizard does not prompt you to capture an image.

7. On the Specify Whether To Restore User Data page, select Do Not Restore User Data And Settings and then click Next.

8. On the Locale Selection page, choose your locale and keyboard layouts and then click Next. Your choice here is irrelevant, because the Windows Deployment Wizard will configure the locale and keyboard layouts during deployment to the production environment.

9. On the Select The Time Zone page, select a time zone and then click Next. Your choice here is irrelevant, because the Windows Deployment Wizard will configure time zone during deployment to the production environment.

10. On the Select One Or More Applications To Install page, select the check box next to each application that you want to install on the image and then click Next.

11. In the Specify Whether To Capture An Image page, select Prepare To Capture The Machine and then click Next. This causes the Windows Deployment Wizard to copy Sysprep and its related files to the destination computer without actually running Sysprep. The SMS 2003 Image Capture Wizard will run Sysprep.

12. On the Ready To Begin page, click Begin.

After clicking Begin, the task sequencer begins running the build's task sequence. By default, it begins by partitioning and formatting the hard disk and then it installs and configures the build. The task sequence does not run Sysprep, however, and it does not capture an image file.

Capturing the Image

Before you use the SMS 2003 Image Capture Wizard to prepare and capture an image of the lab computer, be sure that the computer is configured to boot from the CD drive.

To capture an image using the Image Capture CD

1. On the lab computer containing the installed build, insert the Image Capture CD created as described earlier in the chapter, in the section titled "Creating an Image Capture CD."

2. On the Welcome page of the SMS 2003 Image Capture Wizard, click Next.

3. On the Image Destination page, do the following and then click Next:

    a. In the Image File Name box, type the name of the .wim file you want to create.

    b. In the Network Location box, type the UNC path where you want to store the image file. For MDT 2008, type *server*\Distribution$\Captures, where *server* is the name of the server containing the distribution share.

    c. In the Account Name box, type the name of an account that has write permission to the network location. Specify the account using the format *Domain\User*.

    d. In the Password box, type the password for the account.

4. On the Sysprep information page, do the following and then click Next:

    a. In the Local Administrator's Password box, type the password for the local Administrator account.

    b. In the Confirm Password box, confirm the password for the local Administrator account.

    c. In the Sysprep Parameters box, edit the Sysprep command-line options, if necessary.

5. In the Image Properties dialog box, provide any comments, version information, and developer information necessary and then click Next.

6. Click Finish. The SMS 2003 Image Capture Wizard runs Sysprep and then shuts down the computer.

7. Turn the computer on and start the computer using the Image Capture CD. If prompted to press a key to boot from the CD, press any key. The SMS 2003 Image Capture Wizard captures an image of the lab computer with no interaction.

Manually Preparing Images

The distribution share and answer files describes to Windows Setup how to install and configure Windows Vista. It includes the settings (answer file) as well as device drivers and packages that you want to add to the operating system. It might also contain applications that you want to install.

A common way to deliver operating systems to users is to create an image of the configuration. This is particularly true when the distribution includes other files, such as applications. Creating an image that you install on each destination computer is quicker and more efficient than installing the uncustomized Windows Vista image and then installing applications on each destination computer.

Sysprep prepares a Windows Vista installation for imaging or delivery to end users. Sysprep removes all user-specific information from a system and resets any system-specific security identifiers (SIDs) to allow the system to be duplicated. Once duplicated, systems using the duplicated image will register their own SIDs with the domain in which they are deployed. Sysprep has several command-line options to control its behavior. Table 6-7 lists the command options.

Table 6-7   Sysprep Command-Line Options

Option	Description
/audit	Restarts the computer into audit mode. In audit mode, you can add additional drivers or applications to Windows Vista. You can also test an installation of Windows Vista before it is sent to an end user. If you specify an unattended Windows Vista setup file, the audit mode of Windows Setup runs the auditSystem and auditUser configuration passes.
/generalize	Prepares the Windows installation to be imaged. If you specify this option, all unique system information is removed from the Windows installation. The system's SID is reset, any system restore points are cleared, and event logs are deleted. The next time the computer starts, the specialize configuration pass runs. A new SID is created, and the clock for Windows activation resets (if the clock has not already been reset three times).
/oobe	Restarts the computer into Windows Welcome mode. Windows Welcome allows end users to customize the Windows operating system, create user accounts, name the computer, and complete other tasks. Any settings in the oobeSystem configuration pass in an answer file are processed immediately before Windows Welcome starts.
/reboot	Restarts the computer. Use this option to audit the computer and to verify that the first-run experience operates correctly.
/shutdown	Shuts down the computer after Sysprep completes.
/quiet	Runs Sysprep without displaying on-screen confirmation messages. Use this option if you automate Sysprep.
/quit	Closes Sysprep after running the specified commands.
/unattend: *answerfile*	Applies settings in an answer file to Windows during unattended installation. You can create this answer file in Windows SIM.
answerfile	Specifies the path and filename of the answer file to use.

When you've created a Windows Vista installation that you plan to image, you then use Sysprep to generalize the system. The following command generalizes the system and prepares it to run the Windows Welcome Wizard on the next restart:

```
sysprep /oobe /generalize
```

You can also use Sysprep to create build-to-order systems. The following command lets you place a system into audit mode on the next restart, wherein you can install additional applications and modify configurations:

```
sysprep /audit /generalize /reboot
```

The following command completes the customization and prepares the system to run the Windows Welcome on the next boot:

```
sysprep /oobe
```

When all system preparations have been made, the system is ready for imaging. You can load the image onto a DVD, copy it to a network share or distribution point, or leave it on the system for use on the next system start.

Customizing Microsoft Deployment Toolkit

You can brand some components in MDT 2008. You can customize Deployment Workbench and the Windows Deployment Wizard. For example, you can customize Workbench.xml in C:\Program Files\Microsoft Deployment\Bin to change the text displayed in the Deployment Workbench title bar and for each item in the console tree. Although it's generally safe to customize the *<Name>* tag in Workbench.xml, you should avoid changing other tags.

The LTI process is driven by .xml files called *definition files*. You can brand the entire LTI process by customizing the following files, which are in *D*:\Distribution\Scripts, where *D* is the drive containing the distribution share:

- **BDD_Welcome_ENU.xml**   Customize this file to change the text displayed on the Windows Deployment Wizard's Welcome page.

- **Credentials_ENU.xml**   Customize this file to change the text displayed in the User Credentials dialog box.

- **DeployWiz_Definition_ENU.xml**   Customize this file to change the text for each page displayed by the Windows Deployment Wizard.

- **Summary_Definition_ENU.xml**   Customize this file to change the text in the Deployment Summary dialog box, which displays at the end of the LTI process.

Summary

The new Windows Vista installation architecture and tools make deploying the operating system in your organization easier than deploying earlier versions of Windows. The new .wim file format makes it possible to deploy highly compressed image files. Windows Vista helps reduce image count by removing hardware and other dependencies from the image. Modularization in Windows Vista makes servicing images easier than with legacy methods, so you no longer have to apply, customize, and recapture an image to update it. The new answer file format, Unattend.xml, provides a more flexible and consistent configuration. Finally, the new deployment tools, ImageX and Windows SIM, provide a robust way to create, customize, and manage Windows Vista images.

Although the Windows AIK provides the basic tools for customizing and deploying Windows Vista, MDT 2008 provides a more flexible framework for deploying Windows Vista in businesses. MDT 2008 enables you to create and customize multiple image builds. The framework includes automation common to most businesses and is highly extensible to suit any requirements. For example, by using MDT 2008 to deploy Windows Vista, you can include custom actions that run during deployment.

Additional Resources

The following resources contain additional information and tools related to this chapter.

Related Information

- Chapter 3, "Deployment Platform," includes information about the Windows Vista installation architecture, its key components and technologies, and it describes how the various components interact.

- Chapter 4, "Planning Deployment," includes information about installing and preparing MDT 2008 for use. This chapter also describes how to use the MDT 2008 guidance.

- Chapter 10, "Configuring Windows DS," explains how to install and configure Windows DS and how to add images to and deploy images from Windows DS.

- Chapter 11, "Using Volume Activation," includes more information about Windows Vista product keys and volume activation.

- Chapter 12, "Using Microsoft Deployment," includes more information about using MDT 2008 to deploy Windows Vista images in the production environment.

- *Toolkit Reference* in MDT 2008 lists the properties you can configure in a deployment point.

- *Windows Automated Installation Kit User's Guide* contains detailed information about the tools and technologies included in the Windows AIK. This guide is in the file Waik.chm in the Windows AIK.

On the Companion CD

- VRKDisplayOSDVar.wsf
- VRKFileExists.wsf
- VRKFolderExists.wsf
- WIMChangeSample.vbs
- ConfigSamples.zip

Chapter 7
Migrating User State Data

Operating system deployment always involves *user state migration*—the process of migrating users' documents and settings from one operating system to another. Even when you don't migrate user state during deployment, users will spend countless hours trying to restore their preferences (desktop backgrounds, screensavers, and themes). Because this manual process reduces user productivity and usually increases support calls, organizations often choose to migrate some portion of user state to new operating systems as they are deployed.

User satisfaction is another reason to elevate the importance of user state migration in your project. Users are simply more satisfied and feel less overwhelmed when they sit down in front of a new operating system and they don't have to recover their preferences. The fact is that unsatisfied users can lead to poor post-implementation reviews and can have negative consequences for future deployment projects. For example, user dissatisfaction with previous projects can stall a deployment project that you know will benefit the company in the long term. Keep the users happy.

This chapter helps you decide which user state migration tools best suit your environment. It then explores the User State Migration Tool 3.0.1 (USMT), including customizing and automating the user state migration process. You'll learn how to identify user state data, how to plan the user state migration project, and how to execute the user state migration using tools such as Windows scripting and Microsoft Deployment Toolkit (MDT) 2008.

Evaluating Migration Technologies

Whether you decide to migrate user state individually, as part of a high-volume deployment project, or not at all, you should evaluate the available options to ensure that you make the best choices for your environment. The size and scope of the migration project factor into your choice, as will the type and amount of user state data you choose to migrate.

The following sections describe the different options that Microsoft provides. A variety of third-party products are also available for migrating user state. If you're using MDT 2008 as your deployment framework, Microsoft recommends that you use USMT to migrate user state to Windows Vista. USMT handles most common scenarios out of the box and exceptional cases are easy to configure. Additionally, MDT 2008 already includes the pre-deployment and post-deployment logic for saving and restoring user state.

Windows Easy Transfer

Windows Easy Transfer is the Windows Vista equivalent of the Microsoft Windows XP Files And Settings Transfer Wizard. This tool leads the user through a series of pages to determine how much data to migrate and which migration method to use (disc or removable media, USB cable connection, or network). Using Windows Easy Transfer is not appropriate in high-volume deployment projects because it is a completely manual process. However, in bench deployments, Windows Easy Transfer can be a viable tool for migrating user state on individual computers.

Note   Windows Easy Transfer can transfer user state data using a special USB cable available from most cable vendors. The Easy Transfer Cable includes circuitry that links two computers using their USB ports and can transfer data at 25 Mb/sec.

User State Migration Tool

Use USMT to migrate user state in high-volume deployment projects. It can execute complex, repeatable migrations of user state data between operating systems. You can script USMT; you can execute it as part of an MDT 2008 Lite Touch Installation (LTI) or Zero Touch Installation (ZTI); or you can execute it directly at the command prompt.

In addition to document and settings migration, USMT can migrate application preferences for Microsoft Office applications between versions of Office. For example, USMT can migrate Office XP or later settings to newer versions of Office, including the Microsoft 2007 Office system.

This chapter mostly describes USMT because of its power and flexibility in large-scale migrations. Later in this chapter you will learn how to plan, develop, and deploy a custom migration project by using USMT.

Microsoft IntelliMirror

Microsoft introduced IntelliMirror with Microsoft Windows 2000 so that users' data and settings could follow them from computer to computer on the network. For more information about IntelliMirror, see Chapter 14, "Managing Users and User Data." The following two IntelliMirror features in particular minimize the need to migrate user state when deploying Windows Vista, because these features store user state on the network.

- **Roaming user profiles**   Roaming user profiles ensure that users' data and settings follow them on the network. This feature copies users' data and settings to a network server when they log off their computers and then restores their data and settings when they log on to another computer, anywhere on the network. This feature provides a transparent way to back up users' data and settings to a network server.

- **Folder redirection**   Folder redirection allows IT professionals to redirect certain folders (My Documents, Application Data, and so on) from the user's computer to a server. This feature protects users' data by storing it on a network server, thereby providing centralized storage and administrator-managed backups. When used with roaming user profiles, folder redirection speeds the logon process by removing documents and other large files from the user profile.

> **Note**   Windows Vista stores user profiles using a different folder hierarchy than Windows XP. Therefore, carefully review Chapter 14 before you rely on IntelliMirror in any migration project.

Using Windows Easy Transfer

Although USMT will generally be used in most enterprise environments, some businesses may find Windows Easy Transfer a simple and useful alternative to using USMT. This section briefly describes the basic functionality of Windows Easy Transfer, which can be particularly useful in bench deployments. Before you use Windows Easy Transfer, check for the following prerequisites:

- The destination computer must be running Windows Vista. Windows Vista can create a Windows Easy Transfer data collection disk to execute the data collection portion of the migration on previous versions of Windows, but the destination computer must be running Windows Vista.

- The source computer can be running any of the following operating systems:
  - ❑ Windows 2000 SP4 (files only)
  - ❑ Windows XP SP2
  - ❑ Windows Vista

- You must decide which user state data to migrate. Windows Easy Transfer does not offer the same level of granularity as USMT, but you can choose from the following:

    ❑ All user accounts, files, and settings

    ❑ My user account, files, and settings only

    ❑ Advanced options, which allows you to choose specific files to migrate

Windows Easy Transfer, shown in Figure 7-1, steps the user through a series of pages to define and execute the user state migration. Whether you are refreshing computers or replacing computers, Windows Easy Transfer can move user accounts, files and folders, program settings, Internet settings and favorites, and e-mail settings from a computer running earlier versions of Windows to Windows Vista.

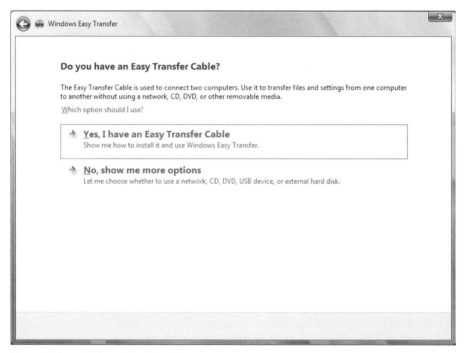

Figure 7-1 Windows Easy Transfer.

Before using Windows Easy Transfer, though, you must prepare it for use by copying it to media that you can use to run it on earlier versions of Windows. To do this, follow these steps:

1. Start Windows Easy Transfer: Click Start, click All Programs, click Accessories, click System Tools, and then click Windows Easy Transfer.

2. On the Welcome screen, click Next to continue.

3. If you have any programs open, Windows Easy Transfer will prompt you to close them. You can close them yourself, or you can click Close All in Windows Easy Transfer, and it

will close them for you. Then click Next to continue. If you don't see the Windows Vista taskbar, press the Windows key.

4. Click Start A New Transfer.

5. Click My New Computer.

6. Click No, Show Me More Options.

7. Click No, I Need To Install It Now.

8. Choose the destination for the Windows Easy Transfer files. If you want to use a USB flash disk (UFD) or portable USB hard drive, make sure it's plugged into the computer. If you want to put the files on a network share, make sure the computer is on the network. In any case, any computer on which you want to run Windows Easy Transfer using these files must also have access to the same hard disk or network share. This chapter does not recommend creating a Windows Easy Transfer CD or DVD, because using removable media or a network share is quicker and more convenient.

9. Type the path of the folder in which to put the Windows Easy Transfer files and then click Next.

10. Click No, I Need To Use A CD, DVD, Or Other Removable Media.

11. Click Close.

After preparing the Windows Easy Transfer files, you will have a removable drive or network share that contains program files you run on the source computer—the computer from which you are moving the user's documents and settings. Use the instructions in the following sections, depending on the scenario: Refresh Computer or Replace Computer.

Refresh Computer

This section describes how to use Windows Easy Transfer with the Refresh Computer scenario. Recall that in this scenario, you are not replacing the computer. Instead, you are formatting the hard drive and then installing Windows Vista on it. As a result, you must save user documents and settings in a temporary location. To do this, follow these steps:

1. On the user's computer, run Windows Easy Transfer. To start Windows Easy Transfer, open the path that contains the Windows Easy Transfer files (on a UFD, removable USB drive, or network share) and then double-click Migwiz.exe.

2. Click Use A CD, DVD, Or Other Removable Media.

3. Connect the portable USB drive or network share and then click External Hard Disk Or To A Network Location. This chapter does not recommend using CDs or a UFD. CDs are slow and inconvenient, and UFDs are unlikely to hold all of an average user's documents and settings.

4. In Network Location, type the path of the file in which you want to store the migration data. This is not a folder path; it's the path and name of the file you want Windows Easy Transfer to create. The location can be on a network share or it can be on a portable drive. Microsoft recommends that you create a password to protect the information. Click Next.

5. Click All User Accounts, Files, And Settings to transfer documents and settings for users who share the computer. You can also limit the files that Windows Easy Transfer moves by clicking My User Account, Files, And Settings Only, or by clicking Advanced Options.

6. Review the list of files and settings that Windows Easy Transfer will transfer. If you want to customize the list, click Customize. When you are ready, click Transfer to begin the process.

7. After Windows Easy Transfer finishes, click Close.

8. With the computer's user documents and settings safely stored in temporary storage, you can now install Windows Vista on the computer. Continue with the remainder of these steps after successfully installing Windows Vista.

9. After installing Windows Vista, connect the computer to the portable drive or network share on which you stored the migration data. In Windows Explorer, open the folder containing the migration data and then double-click the migration (.mig) file. This starts Windows Easy Transfer.

10. Type the path and name of the migration file you want to restore, type the password you created to protect the file, and then click Next.

11. For each account from the earlier version of Windows listed, choose an account in Windows Vista to which you want to transfer the documents and settings. You can create a new account by simply typing its name in the text box. Click Next.

12. Click Transfer to begin transferring the documents and settings from the migration file to the computer.

13. Click Close when Windows Easy Transfer finishes and then log off the computer. You must log off the computer for the changes to take effect.

Replace Computer

This section describes how to use Windows Easy Transfer with the Replace Computer scenario. In this scenario, you are replacing a computer running an earlier version of Windows with a new computer running Windows Vista. In this case, you can certainly use the steps described in the previous section to transfer documents and settings from the old computer to temporary storage, replace the computer, and then restore documents and settings to the new computer. However, transferring documents and settings from the old computer to the new computer through the network is a simpler solution, which you can do by following these steps:

1. Make sure both computers, the old computer and the new computer, are on the network.

2. On the new computer, complete the following steps:

    a. Run Windows Easy Transfer. To start Windows Easy Transfer, open the path that contains the Windows Easy Transfer files (on a UFD, removable USB drive, or network share) and then double-click Migwiz.exe. Do not open the file from the Start menu.

    b. Click Transfer Directly, Using A Network Connection.

    c. Click Use A Network Connection.

    d. If Windows Easy Transfer prompts you to unblock it in Windows Firewall, click Yes.

    e. Click No, I Need A Key and then write down the eight-character key that Windows Easy Transfer gives you. Windows Easy Transfer uses this key to encrypt the data it transfers over the network.

3. On the old computer, complete the following steps:

    a. Run Windows Easy Transfer. To start Windows Easy Transfer, open the path that contains the Windows Easy Transfer files (on a UFD, removable USB drive, or network share) and then double-click Migwiz.exe. Do not open the file from the Start menu.

    b. Click Transfer Directly, Using A Network Connection.

    c. Click Use A Network Connection.

    d. If Windows Easy Transfer prompts you to unblock it in Windows Firewall, click Yes.

    e. Click Yes, I Have A Key and then type the eight-character key that Windows Easy Transfer gave you in the previous step. Windows Easy Transfer will then connect to the other computer.

    f. Click Next and then confirm that Windows Easy Transfer is connected on both computers.

4. Click All User Accounts, Files, And Settings to transfer documents and settings for users who share the computer. You can also limit the files that Windows Easy Transfer moves by clicking My User Account, Files, And Settings Only, or by clicking Advanced Options.

5. For each account from the earlier version of Windows listed, choose an account in Windows Vista to which you want to transfer the documents and settings. You can create a new account by simply typing its name in the text box. Click Next.

6. Click Transfer to begin transferring the documents and settings from the migration file to the computer.

7. Click Close when Windows Easy Transfer finishes and then log off the computer. You must log off the computer for the changes to take effect.

Planning User State Migration Using USMT

Thoughtful planning is a critical factor in the success of any user state migration project. By identifying the scope of the migration, you can plan storage space requirements, labor, and development time required to successfully implement the migration solution. This section describes user state migration planning topics such as using subject matter experts (SMEs), identifying and prioritizing user state data, storing user state data, and testing the effort.

 Note   The team responsible for planning and developing user state migration must work hand-in-hand with the team responsible for application deployment. Both teams will share a lab environment, application portfolio, SMEs, and so on. For more information, see Chapter 8, "Deploying Applications." In some cases, the same IT professionals responsible for application deployment are also responsible for user state migration.

Direct from the Source: Planning

The main thing I have found about user state migration is that very few companies actually know which files they need to migrate. Even fewer have an idea about settings. The largest concern is, of course, lost data—the settings matter less.

Customers who use IntelliMirror features such as folder redirection and offline folders are the easiest to deal with; however, these customers are the minority. There are really only two ways to get user data and files. Asking the client which files they use never works and just drags out the process. You're left with another way that drives user feedback: to do full backups on your proof-of-concept and pilot groups and run standard USMT without any custom settings. When users ask for files to be recovered from the backup, you add them to the custom settings to be retained.

The second way takes a little bit longer and is what I call *intern-ware*: If you have an intern, you can give him or her this busy work. Figure out which applications are critical to you, search the registry for "open with," and cross-reference the file extensions to the program.

Doug Davis, Lead Architect

Management Operations & Deployment, Microsoft Consulting Services

Choosing Subject Matter Experts

Although IT professionals in small organizations probably know each application and the settings used in the computing environment, this is highly unlikely to be the case in large organizations that potentially have thousands of applications. In large organizations, you should use SMEs to help in the planning, development, and stabilizing processes. SMEs, though not necessarily experts, are the users who are most familiar with the applications and data to migrate, and they're usually stakeholders in seeing that the process is properly performed.

Use SMEs to assist with several key tasks:

- Locating application source media, such as CDs or DVDs

- Identifying document storage locations for each application

- Identifying application configuration data and settings to migrate

- Selecting the operating system preferences to migrate

- Consulting on file relocations that will be performed as part of the migration

Identifying User State Data

User state data can consist of many elements: settings that customize the user experience, application data created by the user, e-mail and messaging settings and data, and even personal data. The following sections describe examples of user state data.

Operating System Settings

The following list describes many of the operating system files and settings that you will want to migrate. (USMT migrates most of these by default.)

- **Appearance settings**   Examples include wallpaper, colors, sounds, and screensaver settings.

- **User interface settings**   Examples include mouse pointers, whether double-clicking a folder opens it in a new window or in the same window, and whether users must click or double-click an item to open it.

- **Internet Explorer settings**   Examples include home pages, favorites, cookies, security settings, and proxy settings.

- **Mail settings**   Examples include mail server settings, signature files, and contact lists.

Application Data and Settings

You will find application data in a number of locations. As you inventory the applications in your environment, consider the following potential locations for application settings and data storage:

- **The Program Files folder**   Many applications still store settings and data directly in the applications folder within Program Files. As you plan the migration, consider whether or not you can safely redirect the application data to a different location. This will assist with future attempts to allow use of the application by Standard (nonadministrator) users.

- **A specific folder on the local disk**   Many applications define a data storage location on the local disk for storage of application settings and data. This location is often the root of the system drive.

- **The user's profile folder**   Many applications store data in user profile folders. Search the Documents and Settings folder (Windows XP) or the Users folder (Windows Vista) for application settings and data files.

Users' Documents

Users will store data in a variety of locations. The following strategies will help you locate users' documents:

- **Search user profile folders**   The Desktop and My Documents folders are only two of many locations where you will find user data in the user profile folders. Ideally, however, these two folders are the primary location of users' documents.

- **Interview users and SMEs**   Survey users and interview SMEs to determine common storage locations for documents. An intranet website, possibly based on Microsoft Windows SharePoint Services, is an ideal data-collection tool.

- **Scan a sample of disks**   Search the local disks for common document file extensions such as .doc and .xls. Although you can't scan every disk in the organization, you can scan a representative sample to give you an idea of where you'll find documents.

- **Search Recent Documents**   Scan the Recent folder in users' profiles to determine the locations most frequently used to store data. This can expose some of the less intuitive storage locations. Search a representative sample of users in the organization.

Direct from the Source: USMT and ACT

Application Compatibility Toolkit 4.0 (ACT 4.0) always grabbed the registered file extensions in the log files but never posted them to the database. In my review of the functional specification of version ACT 5.0, I asked to have that log data posted to the database even if it wasn't exposed in the GUI.

> With a little SQL work, you should be able to use ACT to find out which applications you are migrating and then sort the file extensions you need for USMT in a more logical fashion. For example, you can extract the file extensions that are a high priority from the ACT database for applications in the portfolio and then focus on migrating those applications first.
>
> *Doug Davis, Lead Architect*
>
> *Management Operations & Deployment, Microsoft Consulting Services*

Prioritizing Migration Tasks

As you compile your user state migration requirements, prioritize them according to their impact on the organization. It's important to the success of this project to concentrate first on mission-critical data and later on preferences such as desktop wallpaper or screensaver settings. Prioritizing requirements helps the development personnel to prioritize their work. SMEs are a valuable source of input when prioritizing the migration requirements.

Choosing a Data Store Location

USMT stores user state in a data store. USMT can create the data store in a variety of locations and media during migration. By default, USMT creates a store file that contains compressed user data. It can also encrypt the data store to protect the data during the transition to the new operating system. As you prepare for user state migration, you must determine the best location for the USMT data store.

Consider the following when locating the USMT data store:

- **USMT cannot store multiple operations in the same file**   USMT operations can collect data from more than one user but cannot store more than one operation in a single store file. In a high-volume migration, you can either locate the data store locally (which is only possible because the Windows Vista imaging process is nondestructive) or locate each data store on the network (possibly organized by computer name). Note that MDT 2008 handles the data store location automatically and provides choices for customizing it.

- **User state data can use significant space**   When creating your migration plan, you can run the Scanstate component of USMT with the /p command-line option to create a size estimate. The file Usmtsize.txt will be stored in the store folder location. If you're locating the data store on a server, rather than locally, run this command on a representative sample of computers in the environment to calculate the storage required.

- **The USMT data store must be accessible to both the source and target systems**   When writing to or reading from the data store, USMT must have access to that data store. Locate the file somewhere that will be available to both computers. MDT 2008 handles this issue somewhat transparently. If you're locating the data store locally, access is not an issue.

Local Data Stores

You can locate the USMT data store on the local disk in the Upgrade Computer or Refresh Computer scenarios. (See Chapter 4, "Planning Deployment," for a description of deployment scenarios.) ImageX and Windows Vista Setup are *nondestructive*, which means that they can install the operating system without destroying the data on the disk. This optimizes the speed of the migration process, because network speeds and removable media speeds are factored out of the process. MDT 2008 provides the option to use local data stores.

Networked Data Stores

In the Replace Computer (side-by-side) and New Computer scenarios, you can put the USMT data store on a network server. In these scenarios, putting the data store on the network is necessary because the local data store will not be available in the post-installation phase.

Removable Storage

You can also store USMT store files on removable media during the migration process. You can use flash disks and portable hard disks to simplify this process. Because this step adds interaction to the process, using portable storage is not recommended except in bench deployments.

Automating USMT

The full power of the USMT is realized when you automate migration. Through the use of scripting techniques—or tools such as MDT 2008 and Microsoft System Center Configuration Manager 2007—you can automate the migration of large numbers of systems. The following list describes each option:

- **Scripting**   You can execute USMT with a variety of scripting tools, including VBScript and Batch script files. By including the appropriate command-line options, you can automate the migration process to collect and restore user state data. End users can then execute these scripts to migrate their own data.

- **Microsoft Deployment Toolkit**   MDT 2008 fully enables user state migration as part of the LTI and ZTI deployment processes. MDT 2008 can download the USMT components and add them to the appropriate locations in the distribution share. You can customize the location of the data stores and customize the migration .xml files to include or exclude user state as defined by your requirements. Using the default migration .xml files with MDT 2008 is an extremely simple, straightforward process. Thus, the only real effort is in creating custom migration .xml files for USMT.

■ **System Center Configuration Manager 2007**   System Center Configuration Manager 2007 can be used as-is or in concert with MDT 2008 to automate user state migration as part of operating system deployment. For more information about using USMT with System Center Configuration Manager 2007 alone, see the System Center Configuration Manager 2007 documentation.

Testing User State Migration

After you set up the USMT migration .xml files and infrastructure, you should conduct a test pass to ensure that the solution works as planned. Test modularly: start with migration files first, followed by command-line options and automation. As you create the project plan, define testable criteria. With a test plan already established, you will be prepared to begin testing as soon as the development is complete.

Creating a Lab Environment

Establish a test lab with equipment and settings similar to systems in production in your organization. The goal is to test each scenario you will see in the production environment. Duplicate your production environment in as much detail as possible. Set up migration servers and data stores, configure source and target client systems, and prepare and place control files in the appropriate locations. Finally, execute the test and measure the results. The team responsible for user state migration should share a lab environment with the team responsible for application deployment. (For more information, see Chapter 8.)

Choosing Sample Data

If possible, conduct the migration tests on actual production data. You can copy this data from production systems as you prepare for the testing. For example, you can create images of SME computers for testing purposes. Testing on production data helps ensure that you expose the migration infrastructure to all scenarios that will be seen in the production environment.

Be sure to choose the following types of production data:

■ **Operating system settings**   You should test desktop and appearance settings. Users can nominate elements for testing, or you can select a sample based the results of user surveys. Test user profile settings and user preference settings to ensure that they are properly migrated. Identify a set of user settings that you can test.

■ **Application data and settings**   Include application data such as configuration files and data files in your test plan. Test application registry settings and initialization files to ensure that they are properly migrated. Work with developers and SMEs to identify a representative sample of these configuration settings to test.

■ **Users' documents**   Choose a representative sample of user data. Include sources such as My Documents and any custom data folders found in your environment.

Running the Test

Run the USMT test using the migration .xml files and procedures you have developed for the production environment. The goal is to simulate the production migration with as much detail as possible. Be sure to use any scripts and processes designed to automate the USMT process.

Validating the Test Results

Following the migration test, verify all user state elements that have been defined for testing. View each setting and test each migrated application. Open the e-mail client and operate applications to ensure that user customizations still exist in the new system. Identify any errors and list any items that failed to migrate. Investigate these elements to ensure that you properly configured the control files for the migration. If necessary, retest to verify that problems have been resolved.

Installing USMT

You can install USMT directly on each client computer or stage it on a network share. If you're using MDT 2008, it can download USMT for you and install it in the distribution share automatically. MDT 2008 already contains logic for installing USMT on each computer and using it to save and restore user state data.

USMT supports both the x86 and x64 platforms. The installation file is InstallUSMT301_ *Platform*.msi, where *Platform* is either x86 or x64. Download the USMT installation file for each platform from *http://www.microsoft.com/downloads/details.aspx?FamilyID=799ab28c-691b-4b36-b7ad-6c604be4c595&DisplayLang=en*.

You can install USMT in a number of ways to support use in your organization: locally, on a network share, on a MDT 2008 distribution share, or with System Center Configuration Manager 2007. The last two options enable migration during LTI and ZTI deployment projects. The following sections describe each option in more detail.

Manually Packaging USMT Installation Files

MDT 2008 is unable to silently install USMT 3.0 on computers during deployment. This issue is resolved by using USMT 3.0.1. If you're still using USMT 3.0, use the following steps for the x86 and x64 versions of USMT 3.0 to repackage their files into cabinet files from which MDT 2008 can extract USMT 3.0:

1.   Manually install the x86 or x64 version of USMT 3.0 on a computer running Windows XP or Windows Vista, depending on which version you're packaging.

---

2. Copy C:\Program Files\Microsoft Deployment Toolkit\Samples\USMT30_
    platform.ddf, where *platform* is either x86 or x64, from a computer on which MDT
    2008 is installed. If USMT 3.0 is installed in a location other than the default
    (C:\Program Files\USMT30), edit USMT30_*platform*.ddf to indicate its path.

3. Run the command **makecab /F USMT30_*platform*.ddf** and then, copy the .cab
    file it creates to \Tools*platform* folder in the MDT 2008 distribution share.

Local Installation

The USMT installation file installs the USMT tools to the Program Files folder on the
computer and creates any applicable registry entries. Manually installing USMT locally is
not recommended for high-volume deployment projects.

Network Staging

Installing USMT 3.0.1 to a network share requires an additional step. After installing USMT
on a local computer, you can copy the contents of the C:\Program Files\USMT301 to a
network share. After the scripts are on the network, they can run the USMT components.

Microsoft Deployment Toolkit

Installing USMT in MDT 2008 is not the same as installing USMT on the local computer. To
install USMT in MDT 2008, you simply copy the x86 installation file to the distribution
share's Tools\x86 folder or copy the x64 installation file to the distribution share's Tools\
x64 folder. MDT 2008 will automatically install and run USMT on each computer during LTI
and ZTI deployments.

In MDT 2008, the Deployment Workbench can even download the USMT components for
you and automatically store them in the distribution share. For more information about
installing MDT 2008 and downloading components using Deployment Workbench, see
Chapter 4.

System Center Configuration Manager 2007

You can use USMT with System Center Configuration Manager 2007 to manage user state
migrations during operating system deployment. For more information, see the System
Center Configuration Manager 2007 documentation.

Understanding USMT Components

After installing USMT 3.0.1, USMT is located in C:\Program Files\USMT301 on the local computer. The installer copies many files into this folder, including .dll files, component manifests, and other application initialization files. (See Figure 7-2.) Most of the files support the two main executables: Scanstate.exe and Loadstate.exe.

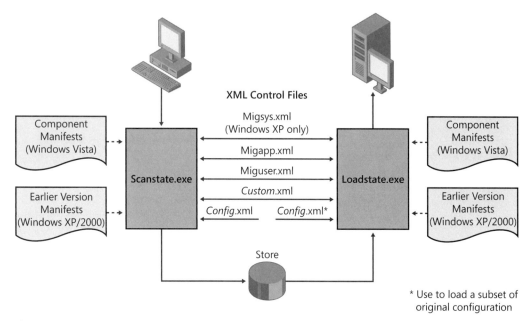

Figure 7-2 USMT components.

In addition to Scanstate and Loadstate, USMT uses three migration .xml files—MigSys.xml, MigApp.xml, and MigUser.xml—to perform basic file and settings migrations based on default criteria. You can customize these files, along with custom .xml files, to migrate additional files and settings or to exclude some of the default files and settings. For more information about migration .xml files, see the section titled "Developing Migration Files" later in this chapter.

Scanstate and Loadstate save and restore user state data, respectively. You can run them directly from a command prompt. They provide several command-line options that control their behavior.

Scanstate.exe

You use Scanstate to save user state data. By default, this program places user state data into the data store location as defined by the three migration .xml files. The following describes an abbreviated syntax of Scanstate, and Table 7-1 describes each command-line option:

```
Scanstate.exe [Store][/i:[path\]filename] [/config:[path\]file] [/o] [/p]
```

Table 7-1   Scanstate.exe Command-Line Options

Option	Description
Store	Specifies a path to the data store.
/i:[*path*\]*filename*	Identifies a migration .xml to use when saving state data. You can use this option multiple times.
/config:[path\]*file*	Specifies a Config.xml file. (See the section titled "Developing Migration Files" later in this chapter.)
/o	Overwrites existing data in the data store.
/p	Creates a size estimate file (USMTsize.txt) in the location specified by *Store*.

Note   Scanstate supports many other command-line options. For a complete list of these options, see *http://technet2.microsoft.com/WindowsVista/en/library/91f62fc4-621f-4537-b311-1307df0105611033.mspx?mfr=true* and the USMT.chm help file in USMT.

Loadstate.exe

You use Loadstate to restore user state from the data store. By default, this program restores user state to the location from which Scanstate originally saved it—unless one of the migration .xml files redirects it. (Loadstate can use different migration .xml files than Scanstate.) The following describes an abbreviated syntax of Loadstate, and Table 7-2 describes each command-line option:

```
Loadstate.exe [Store][/i:[path\]filename]
```

Table 7-2   Loadstate.exe Command-Line Options

Option	Description
Store	Specifies a path to the data store.
/i:[*path*\]*filename*	Identifies a migration .xml to use when restoring state data. You can use this option multiple times.
/config:[path\]*file*	Specifies a Config.xml file. (See the section titled "Developing Migration Files" later in this chapter.)

Note   Loadstate supports many other command-line options. For a complete list of these options, see *http://technet2.microsoft.com/WindowsVista/en/library/91f62fc4-621f-4537-b311-1307df0105611033.mspx?mfr=true* and the USMT.chm help file in USMT.

XML Migration Files

Both Scanstate and Loadstate use three migration .xml files to control migrations. In addition to these three files, you can specify one or more custom .xml files to migrate custom applications or customize the standard migrations. The following section, "Developing Migration Files," describes the .xml files that come with USMT and how to build custom migration files.

Developing Migration Files

USMT ships with three standard migration .xml files. You can customize these files to control the behavior of USMT during migration. In addition to the three standard files, you can develop custom .xml files to migrate special application settings and files. The three migration .xml files included with USMT are:

- **MigSys.xml**   When migrating to a computer running Windows XP, this file controls which operating system and browser settings to migrate. You can customize this file for specific needs. This file is not used when migrating to Windows Vista, because USMT uses manifests to migrate these settings.

- **MigApp.xml**   This file controls which application settings to migrate to both Windows XP and Windows Vista. You can customize this file for specific needs.

- **MigUser.XML**   This file controls which user folders, files, and file types to migrate to both Windows XP and Windows Vista. You can customize this file for specific needs.

Customizing USMT

You manage USMT through command-line options and the migration .xml files. You can modify the default files to control some aspects of the migration and create custom .xml files to migrate specific application settings and data. The following list describes customization points for USMT:

- **Command-Line Control**   You can use command-line options, such as /ui and /ue, to include and exclude specific users during the migration process. You can also specify custom .xml files and manage encryption and compression options.

- **Customizing the Migration XML Files**   You can modify the migration .xml files to exclude portions of a standard migration or to redirect data and settings during the migration process. This capability is especially helpful for scenarios in which you want to consolidate migrated data.

- **Generating Config.xml**   You can generate a Config.xml file to exclude an entire component from the migration. For example, you can exclude the entire Documents folder or exclude all of the settings for a specific application. Using this file to exclude components is easier than modifying the migration .xml files because you don't have to understand the migration rules or syntax. Using this file is also the only way to exclude operating system settings when migrating to Windows Vista; USMT does not use MigSys.xml when migrating to Windows Vista. For more information about Config.xml, see the USMT.chm help file in USMT.

Control File Syntax

The default migration .xml files use XML elements to control migration behavior. These files cover the most common applications, documents, and settings. If you want to migrate settings and application data that the default migration .xml files don't cover, you should create a custom .xml file. The full XML reference for USMT is available at *http://go.microsoft.com/ fwlink/?LinkId=73855*. The USMT.chm help file in USMT also describes how to create migration .xml files.

This book's companion CD contains sample custom .xml files for WinZip 11 (WinZip11.xml) and Nero AG Nero Burning ROM 7 (Nero7.xml). You can use these files as starting points for developing your own custom .xml files. When reviewing these files, match each line to the XML reference. Also, each file contains comments that document their constructions. You'll find additional examples at *http://go.microsoft.com/fwlink/?LinkId=74496*.

Note   The best practice is to create custom migration .xml files instead of adding application data and settings to the default migration .xml files. Doing so makes maintaining those settings easier over time and prevents confusion.

Deploying Migration Files

By default, Scanstate and Loadstate look for the migration .xml files in the same folder that the programs start from (C:\Program Files\USMT301). You can copy your customized versions of these files into the program folder, or you can store them centrally and use command-line options to specify the location of these files. The following list describes how to deploy custom migration .xml files for standalone use, with MDT 2008, and with System Center Configuration Manager 2007:

- **Standalone use**   You can store the migration .xml files in the USMT program folder or place them in a central location. If you store them in the USMT program folder, you don't need to specify a path on the command line. If you store them centrally, you must specify the full path (scanstate *server**share**computer* /i:*server**share*\custom.xml).

- **Microsoft Deployment Toolkit**   MDT 2008 has a specific organization for distribution shares. You must store custom migration .xml files in the Tools*platform* folder of the distribution share, where *platform* is either x86 or x64.

- **System Center Configuration Manager 2007**   System Center Configuration Manager 2007 uses USMT to migrate user state data during operating system deployments. You can specify the location of migration .xml files and data stores during the configuration of System Center Configuration Manager 2007. See the System Center Configuration Manager 2007 documentation for more information.

Using USMT in Microsoft Deployment Toolkit

User state migrations can be launched and controlled in a number of ways. Among these are direct command-line execution, scripting, MDT 2008, and System Center Configuration Manager 2007. The section titled "Understanding USMT Components" earlier in this chapter describes the command-line options for running USMT directly or driving it by using scripts. This section describes how to enable USMT in MDT 2008 as well as how to add custom migration .xml files to MDT 2008.

How It Works: State Migration in MDT 2008

Chapter 6, "Developing Disk Images," describes the task sequence and Task Sequencer that MDT 2008 uses for deploying Windows Vista. The default task sequence separates the process into two phases. One of the pre-installation phases is State Capture; one of the post-installation phases is State Restore. The entire state migration work is tucked into these two phases.

In the State Capture phase, the Capture User State step runs ZTIUserState.wsf /capture to capture user state. It uses settings from the deployment point's CustomSettings.ini file or the MDT 2008 database. In the State Restore phase, the Restore User State step runs ZTIUserState.wsf /restore to restore the state data captured in the Capture User Step.

The first step in ZTIUserState.wsf is to install USMT 3.0.1 on the computer–if USMT 3.0.1 is not already installed–whether the script is capturing user state or restoring it. (ZTIUserState.wsf will also install and use USMT 3.0 if USMT 3.0.1 is not available, but you must package it as described in the sidebar titled "Manually Packaging USMT Installation Files.") ZTIUserState.wsf installs the correct platform version of USMT. For the /capture command-line option, ZTIUserState.wsf reads its settings (UDDShare, UDDir, and so on) from the environment and then chooses the best place to create the data store based upon UserDataLocation. In the final step, the script executes ScanState with the command-line arguments that it assembled from the data in the environment. For the /restore command-line option, ZTIUserState.wsf retrieves information about the data store it created from the environment and then runs LoadState using the command line that it assembled from that information.

Downloading USMT Components

MDT 2008 can automatically download USMT components and place them in the correct folders. The advantage of allowing MDT 2008 to download the components is that MDT 2008 always downloads the most recent version of the files. You can also manually install USMT components by downloading and copying them to the Tools*platform* folder in the MDT 2008 distribution share. Use the locations specified in Table 7-3 to locate the destination for each file.

Table 7-3   USMT File Locations

File	Copy to
InstallUSMT301_x86.msi	\Tools\x86
InstallUSMT301_x64.msi	\Tools\x64

To download and install the USMT files using Deployment Workbench

1. In the Deployment Workbench, click the Components item in the console tree. (See Figure 7-3.)

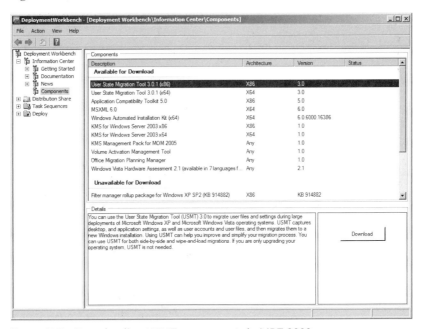

Figure 7-3   Downloading USMT components in MDT 2008.

2. Click State Migration Tool 3.0.1 (*platform*), where *platform* is either x86 or x64, in the Available For Download section of the details pane, and then click Download. Deployment Workbench will download the most current version of the USMT components and add them to the appropriate folders of the distribution share (Tools\x86 and Tools\x64). After downloading USMT, Deployment Workbench moves it to the Downloaded section.

3. In the Downloaded section, click User State Migration Tool 3.0.1 (*platform*), where *platform* is either x86 or x64, and then click Browse to open the folder in which Deployment Workbench copied the files in Explorer.

Specifying the Data Store Location

The data stores can be within the MDT 2008 distribution share. However, creating a share for the data stores on a separate server is better than putting the data stores in the distribution share, as it spreads the load and allows you to more easily dedicate resources to user state migration.

After creating the share for the data stores, you configure the data store location by customizing properties in each deployment point's CustomSettings.ini file, as shown in Figure 7-4. To configure CustomSettings.ini, right-click a deployment point in Deployment Workbench and click Properties; then configure CustomSettings.ini on the Rules tab. You can also customize these properties in the MDT 2008 database. For more information about CustomSettings.ini and the MDT 2008 database, see Chapter 12, "Using Microsoft Deployment." Table 7-4 describes these properties.

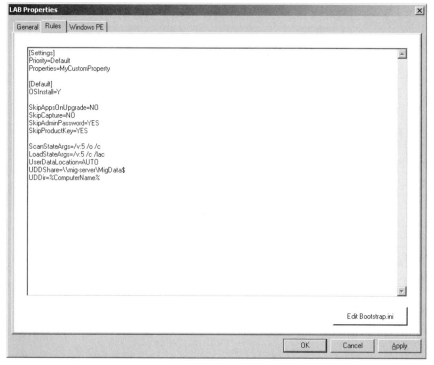

Figure 7-4   Configuring USMT settings in CustomSettings.ini.

Table 7-4   **USMT Properties in MDT 2008**

Property	Controls
LoadStateArgs=*arguments*	The arguments passed to LoadState. MDT 2008 inserts the appropriate logging, progress, and data store parameters. If this value is not included in the settings file, state restore process is skipped. For example, LoadStateArgs=/v:5 /c /lac.
ScanStateArgs=*arguments*	The arguments passed to ScanState. MDT 2008 inserts the appropriate logging, progress, and data store parameters. If this value is not included in the settings file, the user state backup process is skipped. For example, ScanStateArgs=/v:5 /o /c. Use the property USMTMigFiles to specify the .xml files to be used by ScanState.exe instead of using the /i parameter in the ScanStateArgs property. This prevents the ZTIUserState script from potentially duplicating the same list of .xml files.
UDDShare=*Path*	The network share in which to create data stores. For example, UDDShare=\\server\MigData$.
UDDir=*Folder*	The folder where the user state migration data is stored. This folder exists beneath the network shared folder specified in UDDShare. For example, UDDir=%ComputerName%.
UserDataLocation=[*blank* | AUTO | NETWORK | NONE]	The location in which user state migration data is stored: ■ **BLANK** For LTI, the Windows Deployment Wizard prompts for the storage location. For ZTI, this is the same as setting the property to NONE. ■ **AUTO** MDT 2008 creates the data store on a local hard disk, if space is available. Otherwise, it creates the data store on the network location specified in the UDShare and UDDir properties. ■ **NETWORK** MDT 2008 creates the data store in the location designated by the UDShare and UDDir properties.
UDProfiles=*Profile1, Profile2, ProfileN*	A list of user profiles to save during the MDT 2008 State Capture phase by ScanState.exe. For example, UDProfiles=Administrator, Patrice, Dave.

> **Note**   You can also use removable media and local data stores during a user state migration by not setting the UserDataLocation value. The Windows Deployment Wizard will prompt you for the user data location. See the *Toolkit Reference* in MDT 2008 for more details about these properties.

Adding Custom Migration Files

MDT 2008 will use only the default migration .xml files unless you indicate the path to your custom .xml files. As with other properties in MDT 2008, you can configure them in each deployment point's CustomSettings.ini file or add them to the MDT 2008 database.

Set the property USMTMigFiles to the name of each custom migration .xml file. If you don't configure this property, MDT 2008 uses the default migration files: MigApp.xml, MigUser.xml, and MigSys.xml. If you do configure this option, MDT 2008 uses only the files specified in the property. Therefore, if you configure this property, it must also include the default migration .xml files. For example, the following line in CustomSettings.ini adds Custom.xml to the default .xml files:

```
USMTMigFiles1=MigApp.xml
USMTMigFiles2=MigUser.xml
USMTMigFiles3=MigSys.xml
USMTMigFiles4=Custom.xml
```

Note   Do not try to customize the script that drives the USMT process (ZTIUserState.wsf) to add migration .xml files by adding the /i command-line option. This can potentially cause the script to work improperly and makes upgrading to future versions of MDT 2008 problematic. Add custom migration .xml files only by customizing the USMTMigFiles property.

Summary

Migrating user state is an important aspect of desktop deployment because it minimizes lost productivity and increases user satisfaction. User state migration requires thorough planning and a good understanding of user, application, and system settings, as well as knowledge of the location of data files in your environment. SMEs can assist with the identification of files and settings for migration, and you should test all migration projects extensively to ensure that they will function properly in your production environment.

USMT offers the most powerful migration options for high-volume deployment projects. As a user state migration engine, USMT has support built in to MDT 2008. In fact, you can provide support for migration most common data and settings with not much more effort than clicking a button in Deployment Workbench to download the USMT components and customizing each deployment point's CustomSettings.ini. By creating custom migration .xml files, you can add support for corner cases and custom applications that your organization uses.

Additional Resources

You can use the resources in this section to learn more about user state migration tools and their use.

Related Information

- "Migrating to Windows Vista Through the User State Migration Tool" at *http://www.microsoft.com/technet/windowsvista/deploy/migusmt.mspx* includes details on using USMT with Windows Vista.

- "Getting Started With User State Migration Tool 3.0" at *http://www.microsoft.com/technet/WindowsVista/library/usmt/91f62fc4-621f-4537-b311-1307df010561.mspx?mfr=true* contains USMT 3.0–specific guidance.

- "Windows Vista Migration Step-by-Step Guide" at *http://www.microsoft.com/technet/windowsvista/library/1a3fbe72-9de8-4b94-b254-586a61843a04.mspx#BKMK_M1* includes guidance on using Windows Easy Transfer.

- "Transferring files and settings: frequently asked questions" at *http://windowshelp.microsoft.com/Windows/en-US/Help/96d5d811-6d52-4dff-b39b-76c64a131dfe1033.mspx* has a list of commonly asked questions about user state migration.

- Chapter 12, "Using Microsoft Deployment," includes more information on using MDT 2008 to migrate users.

- Chapter 14, "Managing Users and User Data," includes details on roaming user profiles and Folder Redirection.

- USMT.chm, the USMT Help file, includes detailed information on creating XML control files.

On the Companion CD

- WinZip11.xml, a sample custom migration .xml file for WinZip 11
- Nero7.xml, a sample custom migration .xml file for Nero AG Nero Burning ROM 7

Chapter 8

Deploying Applications

Deploying applications is an important aspect of desktop deployment, and how you choose to deploy applications affects choices you make when deploying the operating system. For example, will you include applications in the operating system image or deploy them later? Including applications in the operating system image provides good performance but low flexibility; deploying them later provides poorer performance but higher flexibility.

During the planning stages of your deployment project, you must identify each application used in the environment. Then you prioritize the application inventory so that you can focus on the most important applications first and possibly eliminate applications that are duplicates or no longer in use.

After creating a prioritized application inventory, you must find and mitigate compatibility issues (a process described in Chapter 5, "Testing Application Compatibility"). Then you determine how to deploy the applications. This chapter helps you make these decisions and use the tools that Microsoft provides for deploying applications, including Microsoft Deployment Toolkit (MDT) 2008. See Chapter 5 to learn how to create an application inventory, test applications for compatibility with Windows Vista, and resolve the compatibility issues you find.

Preparing the Lab

Planning application deployment requires a lab environment for application repackaging. Within an organization, different teams that work on deployment (image engineering, application packaging, and so on) can and often should share a single lab environment. Sharing a lab enables teams to more easily share deliverables and integration-test their work with other components. In a shared lab environment, however, each team must have its own workspace on the file server and dedicated computers on which to work.

Although the lab must have access to the Internet, it should be separate from the production network. However, if you don't install any server components like Dynamic Host Configuration Protocol, separating the lab from the production network is not a rigid requirement. Application repackaging does not require that the lab mirror the production network. The lab must provide storage space for application source files and repackaged applications.

The following list describes the recommended requirements for a lab used to repackage applications:

- Lab server configured as follows:

  ❑ Windows Server 2008

  ❑ A Microsoft Active Directory directory service domain

  ❑ Dynamic Host Configuration Protocol (DHCP) services

  ❑ Domain Name System (DNS) services

  ❑ Windows Internet Naming Service (WINS) services (optional)

  ❑ Microsoft SQL Server 2000 or Microsoft SQL Server 2005

  ❑ Microsoft Virtual Server 2005 (or Microsoft Virtual PC 2007)

- Lab test accounts (restricted users and administrator)
- Network hardware to provide connectivity
- Internet access (for downloading updates, files, and so on)
- Test computers that accurately reflect production computers
- Source files for all applications to be tested and repackaged
- Software repackaging tools

On the Disc   MDT 2008 provides prescriptive guidance for building and using a deployment lab. For more information, see the *Infrastructure Remediation Feature Team Guide*, *Test Feature Team Guide*, and *Preparing the Lab* in MDT 2008.

Planning Deployment

Creating an application inventory is the key task you must complete when planning application deployment. You use the inventory to prioritize applications—determining which are not compatible with Windows Vista, which you must repackage for automatic installation, and so on. ACT provides tools for collecting an application inventory based on the production network. For more information about using ACT to inventory applications, see Chapter 5.

After creating an application inventory, you must take the following planning steps for each application in the list:

- **Priorities**   Prioritize the application inventory so that you can focus on the most important applications first. While you are prioritizing the inventory, you might discover duplicate applications (different versions of the same application or different applications fulfilling the same purpose) that you can eliminate. You may also discover many applications that were used for a short-term project and are no longer required.

- **Categories**   Categorize each application in the inventory as a *core application* or a *supplemental application*. A core application is common to most computers (virus scanners, management agents, and so on), whereas a supplemental application is not. Chapter 5 recommends additional ways in which you can categorize applications, such as by department, geography, cost center, worker type, and so on.

- **Installation Method**   Determine how to install the application automatically. Whether the application is a core or supplemental application, you achieve the best results by completely automating the installation. You cannot automate the installation of some legacy applications; you must repackage them. If so, the best time to choose a repackaging technology is while planning deployment. For more information about repackaging technologies, see the section titled "Repackaging Legacy Applications" later in this chapter.

- **Subject Matter Experts**   You will not have the in-depth understanding of all applications in the organization that you will need to repackage them all. Therefore, for each application, identify a *subject matter expert* (SME) who can help you make important decisions. A good SME is not necessarily a highly technical person. A good SME is the person most familiar with an application, its history in the organization, how the organization uses it, where to find the media, and so on.

- **Configuration**   Based on feedback from each application's SME, document the desired configuration of each application. You can capture the desired configuration in transforms that you create for Windows Installer–based applications or within packages you create when repackaging legacy applications. Configuring legacy applications is usually as easy as importing Registration Entries (.reg) files on the destination computer after deployment.

MDT 2008 includes templates for documenting and prioritizing the application inventory. These are in %ProgramFiles%\Microsoft Deployment Toolkit\Documentation\Job Aids after installing MDT 2008. The file Inventory Template.xls helps you record and prioritize the application inventory. The file Assessment Template provides a template for recording the planned configuration and installation method of each application.

ACT 5.0 provides data organization features that supersede the application inventory templates in MDT 2008, however. With ACT 5.0, you can categorize applications a number of ways: by priority, risk, department, type, vendor, complexity, and so on. You can also create your own categories for organizing the application inventory. For more information, see Chapter 5.

Priorities

After creating an application inventory, the next step is to prioritize the list. Prioritizing the application inventory is not a task that you perform unilaterally. Instead, you will want to involve other team members, management, and user representatives in the review of priorities.

The priority levels you choose to use might include the following:

- **High** High-priority applications are most likely mission-critical or core applications. These are applications that are pervasive in the organization or are complex and must be addressed first. Examples of high-priority applications include virus scanners, management agents, Microsoft Office, and so on.

- **Medium** Medium-priority applications are nice to have but not essential. These are applications that are not as pervasive or complex as high-priority applications. For example, a custom mailing-list program might be a medium-priority application, because you can replicate the functionality in another application. To test if an application is indeed a medium priority, answer this question: What's the worst that would happen if all the high-priority applications are deployed, but not this application? If you foresee no major consequences, the application is a medium priority.

- **Low** Low-priority applications are applications that deserve no attention in the process. Examples of low-priority applications are duplicate applications, applications that users have brought from home and installed themselves, and applications that are no longer in use. When prioritizing an application as low, record the reason for that status in case you must defend the decision later.

Prioritizing the application list helps you focus on the applications in an orderly fashion. Within each priority, you can also rank applications by order of importance. Ranking applications in an organization using thousands of applications is a foreboding task, however. Instead, you might want to rank only the high-priority applications or repeat the prioritization process with only the high-priority applications.

Categories

After prioritizing the application list, you must categorize each high- and medium-priority application. You can drop the low-priority applications from the list, as you have no intention of addressing them. The following categories help you determine the best way to deploy an application:

- **Core Application** A core application is an application common to most of the computers in the organization, or one that must be available the first time you start a computer after installing the operating system. For example, virus scanners and security software are usually core applications, because they must run the first time you start the computer. Mail clients are core applications, because they are common to all users and computers. The following list contains specific examples of what most organizations might consider core applications:

❏ Adobe Acrobat Reader

❏ Corporate screen savers

❏ Database drivers and connectivity software

❏ Macromedia Flash Player

❏ Macromedia Shockwave

❏ Microsoft Office

❏ Network and client management software, such as OpenManage clients

❏ Terminal emulation applications, such as TN3270

❏ Various antivirus packages

❏ Various Microsoft Internet Explorer plug-ins

❏ Various Microsoft Office Outlook plug-ins

■ **Supplemental Applications**   Supplemental applications are applications that aren't core applications. These are applications that are not common to most computers in the organization (department-specific applications) and aren't required when you first start the computer after installing a new operating system image. Examples of supplemental applications include applications that are department-specific, such as accounting software, or role-specific, such as dictation software. The following list contains what most organizations consider supplemental applications:

❏ Microsoft Data Analyzer 3.5

❏ Microsoft SQL Server 2005 Client Tools

❏ Microsoft Visual Studio 2005/2008

❏ Various CAD applications

❏ Various Enterprise Resource Planning (ERP) systems

Installation Methods

For each high- and medium-priority application, you must determine the best way to install it. For each, consider the following:

■ **Automatic Installation**   Most applications provide a way to install automatically. For example, if the application is a Windows Installer package file (with the .msi file extension), you can install the application automatically. Later in this chapter, the section titled "Automating Installation" describes how to automatically install applications packaged with common technologies. In this case, you don't need to repackage the application unless you want to deploy a configuration that isn't possible otherwise.

- **Repackaged Application**   If an application does not provide a way to install automatically, you can repackage it to automate and customize installation by using one of the packaging technologies described in the section titled "Repackaging Legacy Applications" later in this chapter. Repackaging applications is a complex process and is quite often the most costly and tedious part of any deployment project. Make the decision to repackage applications only after exhausting other possibilities. Doing so requires technical experience with repackaging applications or using third-party companies to repackage the application for you.

- **Screen Scraping**   You can automate most applications with interactive installers by using a tool that simulates keystrokes, such as Windows Script Host. (See the section titled "Windows Script Host" later in this chapter.) Understand that this method is more of a hack than a polished solution, but sometimes you're left with no other choice. Occasionally, the installation procedure may require the user to use the mouse or otherwise perform some complex task that cannot be automated easily. In these circumstances, automating the installation process may not be feasible.

For each application, record the installation method. Does the application already support automated installation? If so, record the command required to install the application. Are you required to repackage the application? If so, record the packaging technology you'll use and the command required to install the application. If you will use screen scraping to install the application, indicate that decision in the application inventory.

Subject Matter Experts

In a small organization with a few applications, you might know them all very well. In a large organization with thousands of applications, you will know very few of them well enough to make good decisions about repackaging applications. Therefore, for each application you must identify a subject matter expert (SME). This SME does not necessarily have to be an expert with the application, despite the name, but the SME should have the most experience with it. In other words, each application's SME will have insight into how the organization installs, configures, and uses that application. The SME will know the application's history and where to find the application's source media. Record the name of each application's SME in the application inventory.

Configurations

During planning, with the SME's help, you should review each application and record the following:

- The location of the installation media. Often, the SME is the best source of information about the location of the source media, such as CDs, disks, and so on.

- Settings that differ from the application's default settings that are required to deploy the application in a desired configuration.

- External connections. For example, does the application require a connection to a database, mainframe, website, or other application server?

- Constraints associated with the application.

Choosing a Deployment Strategy

Most companies share a common goal: create a corporate-standard desktop configuration based on a common image for each operating system version. They want to apply a common image to any desktop in any region at any time, and then customize that image quickly to provide services to users.

In reality, most organizations build and maintain many images—sometimes even hundreds of images. By making technical and support compromises and disciplined hardware purchases, and by using advanced scripting techniques, some organizations have reduced the number of images they maintain to between one and three. These organizations tend to have the sophisticated software distribution infrastructures necessary to deploy applications—often before first use—and keep them updated.

Business requirements usually drive the need to reduce the number of images that an organization maintains. Of course, the primary business requirement is to reduce ownership costs. The following list describes costs associated with building, maintaining, and deploying disk images:

- **Development costs**   Development costs include creating a well-engineered image to lower future support costs and improve security and reliability. They also include creating a predictable work environment for maximum productivity balanced with flexibility. Higher levels of automation lower development costs.

- **Test costs**   Test costs include testing time and labor costs for the standard image, the applications that might reside inside it, and those applications applied after deployment. Test costs also include the development time required to stabilize disk images.

- **Storage costs**   Storage costs include storage of the distribution points, disk images, migration data, and backup images. Storage costs can be significant, depending on the number of disk images, number of computers in each deployment run, and so on.

- **Network costs**   Network costs include moving disk images to distribution points and to desktops.

As the size of image files increases, costs increase. Large images have more updating, testing, distribution, network, and storage costs associated with them. Even though you update only a small portion of the image, you must distribute the entire file.

Thick Images

Thick images are monolithic images that contain core applications and other files. Part of the image-development process is installing core applications prior to capturing the disk image, as shown in Figure 8-1. To date, most organizations that use disk imaging to deploy operating systems are building thick images.

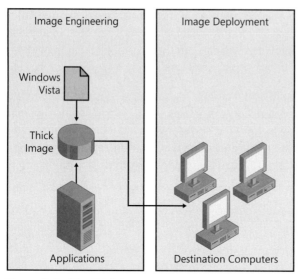

Figure 8-1   The thick image process.

The advantage of thick images is simplicity. You create a disk image that contains core applications and thus have only a single step to deploy the disk image and core applications to the destination computer. Thick images also can be less costly to develop, as advanced scripting techniques are not often required to build them. In fact, you can build thick images by using MDT 2008 with little or no scripting work. Finally, in thick images, core applications are available on first start.

The disadvantages of thick images are maintenance, storage, and network costs, which rise with thick images. For example, updating a thick image with a new version of an application requires you to rebuild, retest, and redistribute the image. Thick images require more storage and use more network resources in a short span of time to transfer.

If you choose to build thick images that include applications, you will want to install the applications during the disk-imaging process. In this case, see the following sections of this chapter:

■ See "Automating Installation" to learn how to install applications silently.

■ See "Injecting in a Disk Image" to learn how to add applications to the distribution points you create by using MDT 2008 and capturing them in a disk image.

Thin Images

The key to reducing image count, size, and cost is compromise. The more you put in an image, the less common and bigger it becomes. Big images are less attractive to deploy over a network, more difficult to update regularly, more difficult to test, and more expensive to store. By compromising on what you include in images, you reduce the number you maintain and you reduce their size. Ideally, you build and maintain a single, worldwide image that you customize post-deployment. A key compromise is when you choose to build *thin images*.

Thin images contain few if any core applications. You install applications separately from the disk image, as shown in Figure 8-2. Installing the applications separately from the image usually takes more time at the desktop and possibly more total bytes transferred over the network, but spread out over a longer period of time than a single large image transfer. You can mitigate the network transfer by using trickle-down technology that many software distribution infrastructures provide, such as Background Intelligent Transfer Service (BITS).

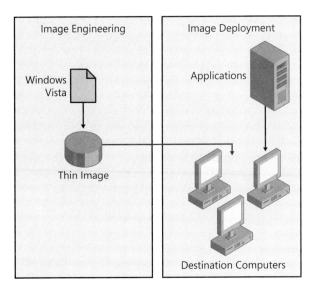

Figure 8-2   The thin image process.

Thin images have many advantages. First, they cost less to build, maintain, and test. Second, network and storage costs associated with the disk image are lower, because the image file is physically smaller. The primary disadvantage of thin images is that post-installation configuration can be more complex to develop initially, but this is offset by the reduction in costs to build successive images. Deploying applications outside of the disk image often requires scripting and usually requires a software distribution infrastructure. Another disadvantage of thin images is that core applications aren't available on first start, which might be necessary in high-security scenarios.

If you choose to build thin images that do not include applications, you should have a systems-management infrastructure, such as System Center Configuration Manager 2007, in place to deploy applications. To use a thin image strategy, you will use this infrastructure to deploy applications after installing the thin image. You can also use this infrastructure for other post-installation configuration tasks, such as customizing operating system settings.

Hybrid Images

Hybrid images mix thin and thick image strategies. In a hybrid image, you configure the disk image to install applications on first run, giving the illusion of a thick image but installing the applications from a network source. Hybrid images have most of the advantages of thin images. However, they aren't as complex to develop and do not require a software distribution infrastructure. They do require longer installation times, however, which can raise initial deployment costs.

An alternative is to build one-off thick images from a thin image. In this case, you build a reference thin image. After the thin image is complete, you add core applications and then capture, test, and distribute a thick image. Testing is minimized because creating the thick images from the thin image is essentially the same as a regular deployment. Be wary of applications that are not compatible with the disk-imaging process, however.

If you choose to build hybrid images, you will store applications on the network but include the commands to install them when you deploy the disk image. This is different than installing the applications in the disk image. You are deferring application installs that would normally occur during the disk-imaging process to the image-deployment process. They become a post-installation task. Also, if you have a systems-management infrastructure in place, you will likely use it to install supplemental applications post-deployment. In this scenario, see the following sections of this chapter:

- See "Automating Installation" to learn how to install applications silently.
- See "Injecting in a Disk Image" to learn how to add applications to distribution points you create by using MDT 2008 and install them during deployment.

Automating Installation

To achieve a fully automated deployment process, the packages you install must support unattended installation. Many setup programs support /s or /q command-line options for silent or quiet installations; others don't.

Often you can find out if the package supports unattended installation by typing **setup /?** at the command prompt, where *setup* is the filename of the setup program. If the setup program doesn't provide clues, you need to know which vendor's product was used to create the package. You can usually tell by running the setup program and looking for logos, for example, or checking the file properties. Armed with that information, read the following sections to learn how to install packages created by different packaging software automatically. Table 8-1 summarizes the necessary commands.

Table 8-1   Unattended Package Installation

Package Type	Command for Unattended Installation
Windows Installer	msiexec.exe /i *package*.msi /qn ALLUSERS=2
InstallShield Windows Installer	*setup*.exe /s /v"/qn"
	Optionally, you can extract the Windows Installer database from the compressed file and use the command msiexec.exe /i *setup*.msi ISSETUPDRIVEN=1 /qn to install it.
Legacy InstallShield	*setup*.exe /s /sms
	To create the Setup.iss file necessary to run setup silently, type **setup**.**exe** **/r** to create a Setup.iss from your responses to the setup program's dialog boxes and then copy Setup.iss from %SystemRoot% to the folder containing the package.
Legacy InstallShield PackageForTheWeb	*setup*.exe /a /s /sms
	To create the Setup.iss file necessary to run setup silently, type **setup**.**exe** **/a /r** to create the Setup.iss based on your responses and then copy Setup.iss from %SystemRoot% to the folder containing the package.
Legacy Wise Installation System	*setup*.exe /s

GSB Useful Deployment Websites

The following websites are outstanding resources for automating the installation of applications, as well as other deployment topics:

- AppDeploy.com at *http://www.appdeploy.com*

  This website provides comprehensive information about deploying applications that are packaged using a variety of technologies.

- SourceForge at *http://unattended.sourceforge.net*

  This visually nondescript website contains a wealth of information, including information about automating the installation of many legacy installers.

- Real Men Don't Click at *http://isg.ee.ethz.ch/tools/realmen*

  Don't let the name or odd URL detract from this website's usefulness. It describes how to automate a variety of processes, including software installation.

- InstallShield at *http://www.installshield.com/microsite/packaging%5ebook1/*

  This web page contains the e-book "The Administrator Shortcut Guide to Software Packaging for Desktop Migrations." This guide is an excellent resource to learn about packaging applications for deployment.

Windows Installer

Windows Installer is an installation and configuration service that helps reduce ownership costs by providing a component-based application-installation architecture. Installation is consistent across all applications packaged for Windows Installer. Packages are easily customizable, installations are protected from errors, and a rollback mechanism provides for recovery in case of failure. Windows Installer supports application and feature advertising. Windows Installer provides many other benefits, and most ISVs are now using it to package their applications. Windows Vista includes Windows Installer 4.0. For more information about its new features, see *http://msdn2.microsoft.com/en-us/library/aa372808.aspx*.

Windows Installer 4.0 is compatible with User Account Control (UAC) in Windows Vista. By using elevated installation, an administrator can authorize Windows Installer to install applications or security updates on behalf of users who aren't members of the Administrators group. For more information about UAC, see Chapter 25, "Managing Client Protection."

Windows Installer packages provide the following to enable flexible application deployment:

- **Command-line options**   You use command-line options to specify options, filenames, and path names—as well as control the action of the installation at run time.

- **Properties (variables) on the command line**   Properties are variables that Windows Installer uses during an installation. You can set a subset of these, called public properties, on the command line.

- **Transforms**   A transform is a collection of changes you can apply to a base Windows Installer package (.msi) file. You can customize applications by using Windows Installer transform (.mst) files. You configure transforms to modify a Windows Installer package to dynamically affect installation behavior according to your requirements. You associate transforms with a Windows Installer package at deployment time. Transforms for Windows Installer package files are similar to answer files that you might have used to automate the installation of an operating system such as Windows Vista.

The number of applications packaged as Windows Installer databases is multiplying rapidly. Nearly all software vendors are packaging their applications using this technology. And what often looks like a self-contained, self-extracting setup program with a filename such as Setup.exe is often a file that decompresses to a Windows Installer database. You can usually extract the database by using a tool such as WinZip (from WinZip Computing at *http://www.winzip.com*) or by running the setup program and looking in the %UserProfile%\Local Settings\Temp for the package file. Windows Installer databases have the .msi file extension.

To install Windows Installer databases unattended using Msiexec.exe, use the /qb command-line option for a basic user interface or the /qn command-line option for no user interface. Also, to ensure that the package installs for all users, add the *ALLUSERS*=2 property. For example, the command

```
msiexec.exe /i program.msi /qn ALLUSERS=2
```

installs the package file *program*.msi with no user interaction and for use by all users who share the computer.

> **Note**   You can learn more about Windows Installer at *http://msdn2.microsoft.com/en-us/library/aa372866.aspx*. For a list of command-line options, see *http://technet2.microsoft.com/WindowsServer/en/library/9361d377-9011-4e21-8011-db371fa220ba1033.mspx?mfr=true*.

InstallShield

Some Windows Installer databases that Macrovision InstallShield (*http://www.macrovision.com/products/installation/installshield.htm*) creates require that you install them by running Setup.exe. Trying to install the .msi file using Msiexec.exe results in a message that you must run Setup.exe to start the installation. When the developer uses InstallShield Script, this requirement is enforced to ensure that the needed version of the InstallShield Script Engine (ISScript.msi) is installed on the computer before proceeding. If it is not detected, the required version of InstallShield Script Engine is installed automatically before starting Windows Installer. You can automate this installation a couple of ways:

- Use InstallShield's command-line support that Setup.exe offers. Not only does Setup.exe provide command-line option support, but you may also pass options to the Windows Installer setup database by using the /v command-line option. Following /v, you may specify any options you want to pass to the Windows Installer setup database within double quotation marks. For example, the following command installs the application silently and passes the /qn option:

  ```
  setup.exe /s /v"/qn"
  ```

- Deploy the InstallShield Script Engine separately as part of your core applications before any setup files that require it. You may then safely bypass running Setup.exe by installing the Windows Installer setup database with Msiexec and including the *ISSETUPDRIVEN* public property. You can extract the embedded Windows Installer setup database by looking in the %Temp% folder after the welcome message for the installation wizard is displayed. Then, use the following command to install it:

  ```
  msiexec.exe /i setup.msi ISSETUPDRIVEN=1 /qn
  ```

Legacy InstallShield

Packages created using legacy InstallShield technologies usually have the filename Setup.exe. To create an unattended installation for a legacy InstallShield package, you need to create an InstallShield script, which has the .iss file extension. Many applications come with such a file, but they're easy to create otherwise.

To create an InstallShield response file

1. Run the setup program using the /r command-line option. This creates a Setup.iss file based on how you configure the installation as you step through the setup program. The result is the file Setup.iss in %SystemRoot%.

2. Copy Setup.iss from %SystemRoot% to the folder containing the package.

3. Run the setup program using the /s command-line option. The setup program runs silently using the responses provided by the Setup.iss file.

> **Important**   Packages created by InstallShield will spawn a separate process and then return immediately to the calling program. This means that the setup program runs asynchronously, even if you start the setup program using start /wait. You can add the /sms command-line option to force the setup program to pause until installation is finished, however, making the process synchronous.

Legacy InstallShield PackageForTheWeb

PackageForTheWeb is an InstallShield-packaged application contained in a self-contained, self-extracting file. You create a Setup.iss file and use it in almost the same way as described in the previous section. The difference is that you must use the /a command-line option to pass the command-line options to the setup program after the file extracts its contents. For example, a file that you downloaded called Prog.exe will expand its contents into the temporary folder and then run Setup.exe when finished. To pass command-line options to Setup.exe, you must use the /a command-line option. The following procedure demonstrates how this extra option changes the steps.

To create an InstallShield PackageForTheWeb response file

1. Run the setup program using the /a /r command-line options: Type **setup.exe** **/a** **/r**. This creates a Setup.iss file based on the way you configure the installation as you step through the setup program. The Setup.iss file is in %SystemRoot%.

2. Copy Setup.iss from %SystemRoot% to the folder containing the package.

3. Run the setup program using the /a /s command-line options: Type **setup.exe** **/a** **/s**. The setup program runs silently using the responses in the Setup.iss file.

Legacy Wise Installation System

Packages created using Wise Installation System (*http://www.wise.com*) recognize the /s command-line option for unattended installation. No tool is available to script the installation, however.

Windows Script Host

Some applications cannot be automated with command-line options. These applications might provide a wizard-based setup routine but require the user to click buttons or press keys on the keyboard to install the application. If a user can complete the installation by using only the keyboard, you can automate the installation by creating a script (a series of text commands) that simulates keystrokes. This technique is called *screen scraping*.

You can screen scrape by using Windows Script Host. Specifically, you use the *SendKeys()* method to send keystrokes to an application. For more information about the *SendKeys()* method and an example that you can use to quickly create your own screen-scraping scripts, see *http://windowssdk.msdn.microsoft.com/en-us/library/8c6yea83.aspx.*

 On the Disc   The companion CD contains the sample script Sendkeys.vbs, which provides a shell for using the *SendKeys()* method without having to write your own script. It accepts two command-line options: sendkeys.vbs *program textfile*, where *program* is the path and filename of the program you want to drive, and *textfile* is the path and filename of the text file containing the keystrokes, one keystroke per line, to send to the program. See *http://windowssdk.msdn .microsoft.com/en-us/library/8c6yea83.aspx* for a list of key codes. If you need to pause before sending more keystrokes, add a line to the file that contains *sleep*. Each line that contains *sleep* will pause for one second. The file Sendkeys.txt is a sample *textfile* you can use with Sendkeys.vbs; for example, type **sendkeys.vbs notepad.exe sendkeys.txt** and watch what happens.

Repackaging Legacy Applications

Some legacy installers don't support silent installations, and some that do support silent installations don't provide a way to script settings. No legacy installers provide the management capabilities that Windows Installer provides.

If you have an application that is not designed for Windows Installer and does not support another automated installation technique, you can repackage it into the Windows Installer setup database so that you can use the features of Windows Installer to distribute and manage the application. A repackaged application combines the entire feature set of the application into a single feature. After repackaging an application, you use Windows Installer to install it. However, repackaged applications lack the flexibility to customize the application installation efficiently.

 Caution   Do not repackage Microsoft Office. The Office package files include logic that customizes the installation for the destination computer and user. Repackaging the package file loses this logic, potentially preventing the package from installing correctly in some configurations.

The Repackaging Process

Windows Installer provides no functionality for repackaging applications. However, numerous vendors sell repackaging products for Windows Installer. See the next section, "Repackaging Tools," for a list of vendors.

Repackaging is not new. Organizations have historically repackaged applications to customize their installation and configuration. However, Windows Installer transforms eliminate the need to repackage Windows Installer–based applications just to customize them. In fact, repackaging applications that already install from a Windows Installer setup database is bad practice and is not supported.

Repackaging an application is a process that compares snapshots to determine the contents of the new package. The following steps provide an overview of the repackaging process:

1. Take a snapshot of the computer's current configuration.

2. Install the application.

3. Take a second snapshot of the computer's new configuration.

4. Create a package that contains the differences between the two snapshots. The repackaging tool detects all differences between the two snapshots, including all changes to the registry and file system. Since numerous processes are running in Windows Vista at any time, the package file will likely contain settings and files related to processes outside of the application.

5. Clean the package to remove noise (unnecessary files and settings).

> **Caution**   Don't let the simplicity of these five steps trick you into believing that repackaging is easy. Application repackaging is very often the most expensive part of any deployment project. When you undertake the repackaging of an organization's applications, you can count on a labor- and resource-intensive effort, particularly in organizations with thousands of applications, many of which the organization must repackage. Budget, plan, and schedule accordingly.

Repackaging Tools

You must use tools not included with Windows Installer to create Windows Installer packages. The following list includes some of the variety of tools available:

■ **AdminStudio**   Available in multiple versions, including a free download, AdminStudio is a powerful and flexible repackaging tool. The following versions are available:

❑ **AdminStudio Configuration Manager Edition**   This free download from Microsoft integrates with System Center Configuration Manager 2007 to simplify repackaging. AdminStudio Configuration Manager Edition prepares legacy Setup.exe packages for deployment by converting them to Windows Installer .msi packages. To download AdminStudio Configuration Manager Edition, see *http://technet.microsoft.com/en-us/configmgr/bb932316.aspx.*

❑ **AdminStudio Professional Edition**   This full version of AdminStudio is a complete solution for packaging, customizing, testing, and distributing applications. The full version includes all of the features included with AdminStudio Configuration Manager Edition, plus additional features. To download a trial of AdminStudio, see the AdminStudio software overview page at *http://www.macrovision.com/products/installation/adminstudio.htm.*

■ **Wise Package Studio**   Wise offers products for repackaging, testing, and configuring the deployment of applications. See *http://www.wise.com/Products/Packaging.aspx* for more information.

Injecting in a Disk Image

This section describes how to add applications to distribution points you build with MDT 2008, and then inject those applications into disk images or install them when deploying the disk image. If you're not using MDT 2008 to build and deploy Windows Vista, see Chapter 4, "Planning Deployment," to learn why using MDT 2008 is a better way to deploy Windows Vista than using the Microsoft Windows Automated Installation Kit alone.

When planning application deployment, you choose between three deployment strategies: thick image, thin image, and hybrid image, as we described earlier in this chapter. If you're using a thin image strategy, you won't be injecting applications into disk images. Instead, you'll use a systems-management infrastructure such as SMS to deploy applications after installing the thin disk image. If you're using a thick image strategy, you will install applications when you create the disk image. In other words, you will add the application installations to the MDT 2008 task sequence that you use to create the disk image. If you're using a hybrid image strategy, you will install applications during deployment. In this case, you will add the application installations to the MDT 2008 task sequence that you're deploying to destination computers.

> **Note**   This chapter does not describe how to start or use Deployment Workbench. For more information about using Deployment Workbench, see Chapter 6, "Developing Disk Images."

Direct from the Source: Infrastructure

One question I hear repeatedly around the deployment space concerns the amount of infrastructure required. Even with a moderately large (thick) image, customers still need to deploy additional applications. I typically suggest dynamic application distribution—applications that the user had before are dynamically reinstalled on the new configuration before the user logs on to the computer.

However, this requires a stable infrastructure. On average, three applications will need to be added for each computer—three applications not already included in the thick image. On average, 4,805 files per computer will be migrated by using User State Migration Tool (USMT), and 900 megabytes will be transferred. Therefore, a 1,000-computer deployment would require the following infrastructure:

- Computers: 1,000
- Applications: 2,952
- Files: 4,805,594
- Gigabytes: 977.60

Doug Davis, Lead Architect

Management Operations & Deployment, Microsoft Consulting Services

Adding Applications

When you add an application to a distribution share, you're simply describing for MDT 2008 how to install the application by using the command line and optionally copying the application source files to the distribution share. If you don't copy the application source files to the distribution share, MDT 2008 installs the application from the source location you specify, such as a network share.

To add an application to a distribution share

1. In the Deployment Workbench console tree, right-click Applications and then click New to begin the New Application Wizard. Applications is under Distribution Share. In MDT 2008, you must create a distribution share before adding applications to it. For more information about creating distribution shares, see Chapter 6.

2. On the Application Type page, do one of the following and then click Next:

   ❑ Click the Application With Source Files option. Choosing this option copies the application source files to the distribution share. During deployment, MDT 2008 installs the application from source files it copied to the distribution share.

❑ Click the Application Without Source Files Or Elsewhere On The Network option. Choosing this option does not copy the application source files to the distribution share. During deployment, MDT 2008 installs the application from another location on the network. You also choose this option to run a command that requires no application source files.

❑ Application bundle. This option creates essentially a dummy application with which you can associate other applications (dependencies). If you select the application bundle during deployment, MDT 2008 will install all of its dependencies. For more information about dependencies, see the section titled "Creating Dependencies."

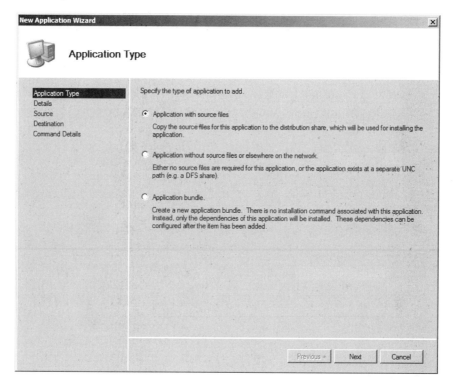

3. On the Details page, provide the following information about the application and then click Next:

   a. In the Publisher box, type the name of the application's publisher (optional).

   b. In the Application Name box, type the name of the application.

   c. In the Version box, type a version label for the application (optional).

   d. In the Languages box, type the languages supported by the application (optional).

4. On the Source page, type the path of the folder containing the application you want to add and then click Next. If you've chosen to copy the application source files to the distribution share, Deployment Workbench copies everything in this folder to the distribution share; otherwise, it adds this path to the application's metadata as the application's installation path.

> **Note**   If you select the Move The Files To The Distribution Share Instead Of Copying Them check box, the New Application Wizard will move the source files instead of copying them. Use this option if you want to stage applications on the local hard disk before moving them into the distribution share.

5. On the Destination page, type the name of the folder to create for the application within the distribution share and then click Next. The default value is the publisher, application name, and version label concatenated.

6. On the Command Details page, type the command to use to install the application silently, and then click Add. For example, type **msiexec /qb /i** *program***.msi**. The command is relative to the working directory specified in the Working Directory box.

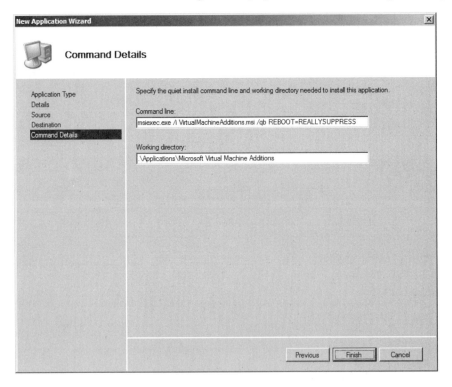

After adding an application to the distribution share, you see it in the Applications details pane. You also see it in the distribution share in Applications*subfolder*, where *subfolder* is the destination you specified when adding the application.

Creating Dependencies

Often, an application has dependencies. For example, application A is dependent on application B if you must install application B before installing application A. MDT 2008 allows you to specify application dependencies for each application you add to the distribution point. You can make an application dependent only on other applications that you've added to the distribution share.

To add dependencies to an application

1. In the Deployment Workbench console tree, click Applications.

2. In the details pane, right-click the application that has a dependency on another application and then click Properties.

3. On the Dependencies tab, do the following:

   ❑ To add an application to the dependencies list, click Add and then select an application. Deployment Workbench only displays applications in this list that you've already added to the distribution share.

   ❑ To remove an application from the dependencies list, select an application in the dependencies list and then click Remove.

   ❑ To reorder the applications in the dependencies list, select an application in the dependencies list and then click Up or click Down. MDT 2008 installs the dependent applications in the order specified by the dependencies list.

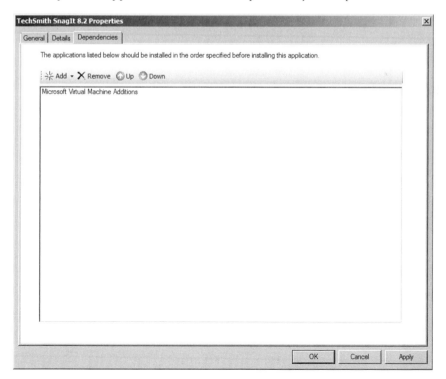

Installing Applications

In MDT 2008, the task sequence specifies the tasks that run during deployment and their order. You can install applications during the imaging process by adding a step to the task sequence that installs the application at the appropriate time. For more information about customizing the task sequence, see Chapter 6. Although this approach is useful for injecting applications in to a disk image, using the MDT 2008 database or CustomSettings.ini is more appropriate during deployment in production. For more information, see Chapter 12, "Using Microsoft Deployment."

Without creating additional groups in the task sequence, the best place to add application installs is to the Custom Tasks group, which MDT 2008 creates in each task sequence's default task sequence. The instructions in this section show you how to install an application as a step under this group.

> **Note**   If you add an application to the distribution share without installing it via the task sequence, the Windows Deployment Wizard will allow the user to install the application optionally during deployment. Also, you can choose applications to install automatically during a zero touch deployment by configuring the deployment point to install the application automatically. For more information about zero touch deployment, see Chapter 12.

To add an application installation to a task sequence

1. In the Deployment Workbench console tree, click Task Sequences.

2. In the details pane, right-click the task sequence in which you want to install an application and then click Properties.

3. On the Task Sequence tab, click Custom Tasks in the task sequence and then click Add, click General, and then click Application.

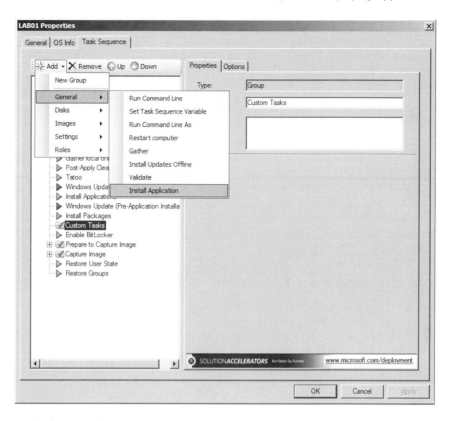

4. Click the Install Application task that you just added to the task sequence, select the Install A Single Application option, and then choose an application in the Application To Install list.

Note   In MDT 2008, the task sequence is very flexible. For example, you can install applications at almost any point during the State Restore phase. You can filter application installation tasks on a variety of variables. For more information about editing task sequences in MDT 2008, see Chapter 6.

Summary

Careful planning is the most important task you must undertake when deploying applications with Windows Vista. The first step is building an application inventory. Then you must prioritize, categorize, and document the installation of each application. MDT 2008 and ACT provide tools that help with this step.

Another key planning step is determining the right type of deployment strategy for your organization. Thick images are monolithic images that contain core applications and other files. They are large and costly to maintain and deploy. Thin images are bare images. You install applications post-deployment using a systems-management infrastructure, such as System Center Configuration Manager 2007. Hybrid images use a combination of both strategies. The deployment strategy you choose determines how you build images.

After careful planning, you repackage the applications that don't provide an automated installation and document the installation commands for those that do. Then add applications to your MDT 2008 distribution share and add steps to the task sequence that installs the application when you build the disk image (thick image) or when you deploy the disk image (hybrid image).

> **Note**   If you're not using MDT 2008 to deploy Windows Vista, see Chapter 4 to learn why using MDT 2008 is a better way to deploy Windows Vista than using the Microsoft Windows Automated Installation Kit alone. If you're not using MDT 2008, see *Windows Automated Installation Kit User's Guide* to learn how to install applications by using an answer file.

Additional Resources

The following resources contain additional information and tools related to this chapter.

Related Information

- Chapter 2, "Security in Windows Vista," includes more information about how Windows Vista security features affect applications.

- Chapter 5, "Testing Application Compatibility," describes how to use ACT 5.0 to create an application inventory, analyze it, and then mitigate compatibility issues.

- Chapter 6, "Developing Disk Images," includes more information about building custom Windows Vista disk images that include applications.

- Chapter 7, "Migrating User State Data," includes more information about migrating application settings from earlier versions of Windows to Windows Vista.

- "Repackaging Applications to Support the Microsoft Windows Installer Service," found at *http://technet.microsoft.com/en-us/library/bb742606.aspx*, includes more information about repackaging applications.

- "Windows Server 2003 Deployment Guide," found at *http://www.microsoft.com/ technet/prodtechnol/windowsserver2003/library/DepKit/c283b699-6124-4c3a-87ef-865443d7ea4b.mspx*, includes additional deployment best practices and planning guidelines.

- The Office Resource Kit, found at *http://technet.microsoft.com/en-us/library/ cc303401.aspx*, includes more information about customizing and deploying Office.

- "SendKeys Method," found at *http://windowssdk.msdn.microsoft.com/en-us/library/ 8c6yea83.aspx*, includes more information about using Windows Script Host as a screen-scraping tool to automate application installations.

■ "Application Compatibility," found at *http://technet.microsoft.com/en-us/windowsvista/aa905066.aspx*, includes more information about downloading and using ACT to resolve compatibility issues.

On the Companion CD

■ Sendkeys.vbs

■ Sendkeys.txt

Chapter 9

Preparing Windows PE

Half the job of installing Windows Vista or building disk images is starting the computer and preparing for installation. You use Microsoft Windows Preinstallation Environment (Windows PE) 2.1 to start computers, which is similar to using MS-DOS in the old days. Windows PE allows you to fully automate the preparation and installation process. This chapter describes how to use, customize, and automate Windows PE for the purpose of installing Windows Vista in enterprise environments.

Earlier versions of Windows PE, including Windows PE 2004 and Windows PE 2005, were available only to Software Assurance (SA) customers. Windows Vista installation is entirely based on Windows PE and disk imaging by using ImageX; therefore, Windows PE is freely available as part of the Windows Automated Installation Kit (Windows AIK). Windows PE is highly customizable, and you can use the documentation included in the Windows AIK to accomplish most tasks. This chapter describes the most common ways to customize Windows PE, however, as well as how to start it in various scenarios.

In most circumstances, you should use Microsoft Deployment Toolkit (MDT) 2008 to deploy Windows Vista. In this case, you can use Deployment Workbench to customize Windows Vista and automatically generate images that you can use to start Windows PE with a variety of media. Although the information in this chapter does describe how to customize Windows PE manually, Microsoft recommends that you use MDT 2008 to generate Windows PE images in most cases.

Exploring Windows PE

Windows PE, which is supplied with Windows Vista and in the Windows AIK, is the installation engine for Windows Vista. It is directly bootable from CD, DVD, and USB Flash Drives (UFDs). You can also start Windows PE by using Windows Deployment Services (Windows DS) and the Preboot Execution Environment (PXE) extensions to DHCP (if supported by the network adapters of your computers).

Windows PE is a minimal Windows operating system that provides limited services based on the Windows Vista kernel. It also provides the minimal set of features required to run Windows Vista Setup, install Windows Vista from networks, script basic repetitive tasks, and validate hardware. For example, with Windows PE, you can use powerful batch scripts, Windows Script Host (WSH) scripts, and HTML Applications (HTAs) to fully automate computer preparation and Windows Vista installation, rather than the limited batch commands in MS-DOS. Examples of what you can do with Windows PE include:

- Create and format disk partitions, including NTFS file-system partitions, without rebooting the computer before installing Windows Vista on them. Formatting disks with NTFS by using an MS-DOS–bootable disk required third-party utilities. Windows PE replaces the MS-DOS–bootable disk in this scenario, allowing you to format disks with NTFS without using third-party utilities. Also, the file-system utilities that Windows PE provides are scriptable, so you can completely automate the setup-preparation process.

- Access network shares to run preparation tools or install Windows Vista. Windows PE provides network access comparable to Windows Vista. In fact, Windows PE provides the same network drivers that come with Windows Vista, allowing you to access the network quickly and easily. Customizing MS-DOS–bootable disks to access network shares was time-consuming and tedious.

- Use all the mass-storage devices that rely on Windows Vista device drivers. Windows PE includes the same mass-storage device drivers that Windows Vista provides, so you no longer have to customize MS-DOS–bootable disks for use with specialized mass-storage devices. Once again, Windows PE allows you to focus on important jobs rather than on maintaining MS-DOS–bootable disks.

- Customize Windows PE by using techniques and technologies that are already familiar to you. Windows PE is based on Windows Vista, so you are already familiar with the techniques and tools used to customize Windows PE. You can customize it in a variety of scenarios:

    - Addition of hardware-specific device drivers

    - Automation through use of Unattend.xml answer files

    - Execution of scripts (batch, WSH, and HTA) to perform specific actions

The following sections provide more detail about the features and limitations of Windows PE. They focus specifically on using Windows PE in high-volume deployment scenarios, rather than in manufacturing environments.

Direct from the Source: Windows PE 2.1

Windows PE 2.1, the new version that will be released with Windows Vista, is a key part of the deployment process. Even the standard DVD-based installation of Windows Vista uses Windows PE 2.1, and most organizations will be using it (often customized for the organization's specific needs) as part of their deployment processes.

Compared to MS-DOS–based deployment, Windows PE 2.1 brings numerous benefits, including less time spent trying to find 16-bit real-mode drivers. (It's not even possible to find these any more for some newer network cards and mass storage adapters.) Better performance from 32-bit and 64-bit networking stacks and tools, as well as large memory support, are also advantages. And don't forget support for tools such as Windows Scripting Host, VBScript, and hypertext applications.

Windows PE has been available for a few years (the latest version, Windows PE 2005, was released at the same time as Windows XP SP2 and Windows Server 2003 SP1), but not all organizations could use it; it required that you have Software Assurance on your Windows desktop operating system licenses. With Windows PE 2.1, that's no longer the case. All organizations will be able to download Windows PE 2.1 from *www.microsoft.com* and use it freely for the purposes of deploying licensed copies of Windows Vista.

Like Windows Vista itself, Windows PE 2.1 is provided as an image that is componentized and can be serviced both online and off. As with Windows PE 2005, several optional components can be added, although Windows PE 2.1 includes some new ones: MSXML 3.0, Windows Recovery Environment, language packs, font packs, and so on. New tools like Peimg.exe are provided for servicing Windows PE 2.1. You can also use Peimg.exe for adding drivers, including mass storage devices, which no longer require any special handling.

Michael Niehaus, Lead Developer for Microsoft Deployment Toolkit

Management and Infrastructure Solutions

Capabilities

Windows PE is a bootable image that you can start by using removable media (CD, DVD, or UFD). You can also use Windows DS to start Windows PE. Because the Windows Vista deployment tools do not work in 16-bit environments, Windows PE replaces the MS-DOS– bootable disk in *all* deployment scenarios. It's a lightweight 32-bit or 64-bit environment that supports the same set of networking and mass-storage device drivers that Windows Vista supports, and it provides access to similar features, including NTFS and standalone distributed file system (DFS). Windows PE includes the following features:

- **Hardware independence**   Windows PE is a hardware-independent Windows environment for both x86 and x64 architectures. You can use the same preinstallation environment on all the desktop computers and servers without creating and maintaining different bootable disks for different hardware configurations.

- **APIs and scripting capabilities**   Windows PE contains a subset of the Win32 APIs; a command interpreter capable of running batch scripts; and support for adding WSH, HTA, and Microsoft ActiveX Data Objects (ADO) to create custom tools or scripts. The scripting capabilities in Windows PE far exceed the capabilities of MS-DOS–bootable disks. For example, the command interpreter in Windows PE supports a more robust batch-scripting language than does MS-DOS, allowing you to use more advanced scripts.

- **Network access**   Windows PE uses Transmission Control Protocol/Internet Protocol (TCP/IP) to provide network access and supports standard network drivers for running Windows Vista Setup and installing images from the network to the computer. You can easily add or remove network drivers from a customized version of Windows PE. In contrast, customizing MS-DOS–bootable disks to access network shares is frustrating, mostly because you need to build and maintain numerous disks. Windows PE alleviates this frustration by supporting the network drivers that Windows Vista supports, and Windows PE is easier to customize with additional network drivers.

- **Mass-storage devices**   Windows PE includes support for all mass-storage devices that Windows Vista supports. As new devices become available, you can easily add or remove drivers into a customized version of Windows PE. Customizing an MS-DOS–bootable disk to access atypical mass-storage devices requires tracking down and installing the 16-bit device drivers. However, Windows PE supports many of these mass-storage devices out of the box. And customizing Windows PE to support additional mass-storage devices is easier because it uses standard, readily available Windows device drivers.

- **Disk management**   Windows PE includes native support for creating, deleting, formatting, and managing NTFS partitions. Also, Windows PE provides full, unrestricted access to NTFS file systems. With Windows PE, you don't have to restart the computer after formatting a disk.

- **Support for the PXE protocol**   If the computer supports PXE, you can start it automatically from a Windows PE image located on a Windows DS server—and Windows DS doesn't install the Windows PE image on the computer's hard disk. Starting Windows PE from the network makes it a convenient tool to use in all deployment scenarios. Also, you can customize a Windows PE image for recovery and troubleshooting purposes, and adding it to Windows DS makes it a convenient tool to use in production.

> **Note**   You must build a custom Windows PE image from the Windows PE source files, as described in the section titled "Customizing Windows PE" later in this chapter.

You manage and deploy Windows PE by using the Windows PE Kit included with the Windows AIK. This tool kit includes the Windows PE User Guide, the Windows Imaging Interface Reference, and Windows PE tools such as:

- **Bootsect**   A tool for managing boot sectors on hard disks and flash drives
- **DiskPart**   A command-line disk-partitioning tool
- **Drvload**   A command-line tool for device-driver management
- **Oscdimg.exe**   A tool for creating CD and DVD ISO image files
- **Peimg.exe**   A tool for customizing Windows PE images
- **ImageX**   The Windows Vista image-capture and maintenance tool, which you use to customize Windows PE image files, capture operating-system images, and apply images to destination computers

> **Note**   The *Windows Preinstallation Environment User's Guide* (Winpe.chm) provides complete, portable documentation of the command-line options for all of the tools discussed in this chapter. This help file is located in the Windows AIK, which you can download from the Microsoft download center at *http://www.microsoft.com/downloads*.

Limitations

Windows PE has the following limitations:

- To reduce its size, Windows PE includes only a subset of the available Win32 APIs: I/O (disk and network) and core Win32 APIs.
- Windows PE doesn't fit on floppy disks, but you can write a custom Windows PE image to a bootable CD or DVD.
- Windows PE supports TCP/IP and NetBIOS over TCP/IP for network connectivity, but it doesn't support other protocols, such as Internetwork Packet Exchange/Sequenced Packet Exchange (IPX/SPX).
- The Windows on Windows 32 (WOW32) subsystem allows 16-bit applications to run on the 32-bit Windows platform. The WOW32 subsystem isn't available in Windows PE, so 16-bit applications won't run in 32-bit versions of Windows PE. Similarly, in the x64 version of Windows PE, the WOW64 subsystem is not available, so applications must be fully 64-bit compliant.

- To install 64-bit Windows Vista, you must use 64-bit Windows PE. Likewise, installing 32-bit Windows Vista requires 32-bit Windows PE.

- Drive letter assignments aren't persistent between sessions. After you restart Windows PE, the drive letter assignments will be in the default order.

- Changes to the registry aren't persistent between sessions. To make permanent changes to the registry, you must edit the registry offline by mounting the image with ImageX and then loading hive files into Registry Editor.

- Windows PE supports distributed file system (DFS) name resolution to standalone DFS roots only.

- You can't access files or folders on a computer running Windows PE from another computer. Likewise, Windows PE can't act as a Terminal Server, so you can't connect to it by using Remote Desktop.

- Windows PE requires a VESA-compatible display device and will use the highest screen resolution it can determine is supported. If the operating system can't detect video settings, it uses a resolution of 640 by 480 pixels.

- Windows PE doesn't support the Microsoft .NET Framework or the Common Language Runtime (CLR).

- Windows PE does not support the installation of Windows Installer package (.msi) files.

- Windows PE does not support 802.1x.

- To prevent its use as a pirated operating system, Windows PE automatically reboots after 72 hours.

New Features

Windows PE 2.1 contains several new features over earlier versions of Windows PE:

- **Security Updates**   Windows PE now includes support for Secure Socket Layer (SSL).

- **Tools for .wim file management**   You can customize and boot Windows Imaging (.wim) files with the ImageX command-line tool and the Windows Imaging File System Filter (WIM FS Filter) driver.

- **New boot support**   You can boot Windows PE from the .wim file on the Windows OPK DVD, the Windows AIK DVD, or from the ImageX command-line tool with the /boot option.

- **72-hour reboot support**   The Windows PE reboot clock is extended from 24 hours to 72 hours.

- **Plug and Play (PnP) support**   Hardware devices can be detected and installed while Windows PE is running. This supports any in-box PnP device, including removable media and mass-storage devices. This feature is enabled by default.

- **Drvload tool**   Use this new command-line tool to add out-of-box drivers to Windows PE when booted. Drvload installs drivers by taking driver .inf files as input.

- **Peimg tool**   Use this new command-line tool to customize a Windows PE image offline. With Peimg, you can add and remove drivers, Windows PE components, and language packs.

- **Boot Configuration Data (BCD)**   Use this new boot configuration file to customize boot options. This file replaces Boot.ini.

- **Boot Sector tool (bootsect)**   Use this tool for deploying to earlier versions of Windows by changing the previous version of Windows boot code to support the boot manager (Bootmgr) for Windows Vista. This tool replaces FixFAT and FixNTFS.

- **Automatic writable RAM drive**   When booting from read-only media, Windows PE automatically creates a writable RAM disk (drive X) and allocates 32 megabytes (MB) of the RAM disk for general-purpose storage. By using compressed NTFS, the 32 MB is addressable up to 60 MB.

- **[LaunchApps] section in Winpeshl.ini**   This section is expanded to enable command-line options.

Setting up the Environment

You will need to build an environment for customizing Windows PE images before deployment. Having everything in the appropriate location will simplify the task of creating builds and will help you establish repeatable methods for creating and updating builds.

Create this environment on a technician or lab computer. If you're using MDT 2008 to deploy Windows Vista, configure the Windows PE customization environment on the build server. In fact, installing and configuring MDT 2008 installs all of the requirements for building custom Windows PE images.

Installing the Windows AIK

Windows PE ships with the Windows AIK, which is available from the Microsoft Download Center at *http://www.microsoft.com/downloads*. Install the Windows AIK on your Windows PE build system from the installation DVD. (Microsoft provides the Windows AIK as a downloadable DVD image.) Installing the Windows AIK is a requirement for installing and using MDT 2008. Therefore, a build server containing MDT 2008 already has the files necessary to build and customize Windows PE images. For more information about installing MDT 2008 and the Windows AIK, see Chapter 4, "Planning Deployment."

Before installing Windows AIK, you need to prepare your build system for the Windows AIK installation. In addition to certain system requirements, installing the Windows AIK also has software prerequisites. These requirements are similar to the requirements for installing and

using MDT 2008 (Windows Server 2008 already contains all of the prerequisites for the
Windows AIK):

- MSXML Parser 6.0

- .NET Framework 2.0

- An x86 or x64 computer running Windows XP Professional Service Pack 2, Windows
  Server 2003 Service Pack 1 with KB926044, Windows Vista, or Windows Server 2008

- Approximately 1.1 gigabytes (GB) of free disk space, plus additional space for images
  and Windows PE builds

Note   You can download the Windows AIK from the Microsoft Download Center at
*http://www.microsoft.com/downloads/details.aspx?FamilyID=94bb6e34-d890-4932-81a5-
5b50c657de08&DisplayLang=en*. After downloading the Windows AIK, burn it to a DVD or
mount it using virtual DVD software, such as Ahead Nero ImageDrive.

To install the Windows AIK

1. From the Windows AIK media or a folder containing the Windows AIK, run waik-
   platform.msi, where *platform* is either x86 or amd64.

2. Accept the EULA and choose the default location for the installation files. You must use
   the default installation location if you're using MDT 2008. The examples in this chapter
   are based on a default Windows AIK installation.

3. Complete the installation wizard to install Windows AIK.

Note   The Windows Installer file Waik*platform*.msi includes the Windows AIK tools. The file
Winpe.cab actually includes the Windows PE source files. To install Windows PE, Winpe.cab
must be in the same folder as the .msi file.

Configuring the Build Environment

Windows AIK will install the Windows PE build and imaging tools to the following folders:

- **C:\Program Files\Windows AIK\Tools**   Contains Windows AIK program files

- **C:\Program Files\Windows AIK\Tools*platform***   Contains ImageX program files for
  different processor architectures

- **C:\Program Files\Windows AIK\Tools\PETools**   Contains Window PE source files

- **C:\Program Files\Windows AIK\Tools\Servicing**   Contains servicing files

Windows AIK also provides a command prompt that opens on the Windows AIK tools folders
(Figure 9-1). You can use commands within this command prompt interface to create your
Windows PE build environment. The build environment is a copy of the build scripts and

Windows PE source files that you customize and then use to create a new Windows PE image file. The Copype.cmd script is designed to create the build environment. Use the following syntax to create the Windows PE environment, where *platform* is either x86 or amd64 and *destination* is the folder to which you want to copy the files:

```
copype.cmd platform destination
```

Figure 9-1   Use the Windows PE Tools Command Prompt to work with Windows PE.

> **Note**   To follow the examples in this chapter, run the command **copype x86 c:\winpe_x86**. You can use an alternative location for your build environment, but you will need to make the appropriate modifications to the examples provided with this chapter.

Removing the Build Environment

When the Peimg utility installs components, it modifies the access control lists (ACLs) of the Windows PE build files and folders, making it difficult to remove them in the future. You can work around this by using the Windows Server 2008 tool Takeown.exe to take ownership of the affected resources.

To remove the Windows PE build environment

1. Take ownership of the folder structure using the Takeown command:

    ```
    takedown /F c:\winpe_x86\* /R
    ```

2. Use the Change ACLs (cacls) command to give yourself permission to remove the folders (*user* is your user account):

    ```
    cacls  c:\winpe_x86\* /T /G user:F
    ```

3. Remove the folder:

    ```
    rd /s /q c:\winpe_x86\
    ```

Working with Windows PE

Most Windows PE tasks have just a few basic steps. Applications and customizations might vary the process somewhat, but the basic process is the same. This section gives you an overview of the Windows PE build process. In later sections, you learn how to customize Windows PE in greater depth.

On the Disc   This book's companion CD includes a sample batch script called Makeimg.cmd that automates most of the process this section describes. Use this batch script as a starting point for automating your own Windows PE customizations. By automating these customizations, you create a repeatable, testable process for building Windows PE images that you can be sure is more reliable than a manual process.

Applying Windows PE

After you create the Windows PE build environment, the first step in creating a new Windows PE build is to apply the Windows PE base image to the build. This process essentially copies the Windows PE source files from the .wim image file to the build folder. Use ImageX to apply the Windows PE base image. See "What Is ImageX" in the *Windows Automated Installation Kit User's Guide* for more information about ImageX and .wim image files. An example of the command to apply the base image is shown here (where 1 is the image number within Winpe.wim to be applied and *c:\winpe_x86\base* is the path in which to copy the image contents):

imagex /apply .\x86\winpe.wim 1 c:\winpe_x86\base

Note   .\x86\winpe.wim specifies the location of the .wim file for the x86 platform within the PETools folder. You must create the base subfolder in the C:\winpe_x86 folder before running this command.

Adding Optional Components

This Windows PE base image includes a number of pre-staged application support components; you can add more if they are available. To import an additional component or language pack to the base Windows PE build image, use the Peimg.exe command.

Before you can install a component or language pack, you must first import it. This process makes the component or language pack part of the base build image's *component store*. If you don't install the component, it will be removed from the final image when it is captured. After you have imported all required components, you must install them to make them part of the final Windows PE build.

To import a component into the component store

1. List the components, or packages, in the component store to see whether or not the component is already present by running the following command (see the sidebar titled "Pre-Staged Components" for descriptions of these components):

```
peimg /list c:\winpe_x86\base
```

   This command displays a list of packages in the current image. A plus sign (+) in the INS column indicates installed packages, and a minus sign (–) indicates packages that are not installed. For more information about Peimg.exe, see "PEImg Command-Line Options" in the *Windows Automated Installation Kit User's Guide*.

2. Use the Peimg.exe command to import the component. The following command imports the French Base Language Pack for Windows PE from the Windows AIK DVD (D: in this instance):

```
peimg /import=D:\winpe_langpacks\x86\fr-fr\lp.cab c:\winpe_x86\base
```

> **Note**   Many components that you can import also include their own language packs. For instance, the base components included with Windows PE have language packs on the Windows AIK DVD. Be sure to import the applicable accompanying language packs so that you can use the components in the language you require.

To install a component that is already in the component store

1. List the components in the component store to get the full name of the component to be installed. You can also use the component names described in the sidebar titled "How It Works: Pre-Staged Components."

2. Use the Peimg command to install the component that you imported. The following example installs language packs into the build:

```
peimg /install=Microsoft-Windows-WinPE-LanguagePack-Package c:\winpe_x86\base
```

> **Note**   You can use wildcards in the install command. For example, using the string *install=*LanguagePack** in the preceding example would install all imported language packs.

How It Works: Pre-Staged Components

The base Windows PE image in the Windows AIK build includes a number of pre-staged components. These components have been imported into the base component store, but are not actually installed into the image. When you prepare and capture the image, these components will be removed if not installed using the peimage /install command. Components included with (but not installed into) the base image include:

- **WinPE-HTA-Package**   HTML Application support

- **WinPE-MDAC-Package**   Microsoft Data Access Component support

- **WinPE-Scripting-Package**   Windows Script Host support

- **WinPE-SRT-Package**   Windows Recovery Environment component

- **WinPE-XML-Package**   Microsoft XML (MSMXL) Parser support

You can apply additional components, language packs, and device drivers to the image as well.

Copying Applications

You can also copy applications into the Windows PE image build so that you can use them during the Windows Vista implementation process.

To copy an application into a base build

1. Use operating system copy commands to copy the application to the appropriate location:

```
xcopy /chery myapp.exe "c:\winpe_x86\base\program files\myapp\myapp.exe"
```

Adding Device Drivers

Windows PE can make use of Windows Vista device drivers to provide hardware support for Windows Vista installation processes. Use the Peimg command to add device drivers to the base Windows PE build (offline), where *path* is the path containing the device driver .inf files:

```
peimg /inf=path c:\winpe_x86\base
```

Windows PE can also add device drivers dynamically when running (online). Use the drvload.exe command to load device drivers while operating:

```
drvload.exe path[,path]
```

Installing Updates

You install updates to Windows PE using the same process by which you add components: You import them into the component store and then you install them.

To install a Windows PE update to the build

1. Import the update using the Peimg tool, where *update.cab* is the name of the file containing the update:

    ```
    peimg /import=update.cab c:\winpe_x86\base
    ```

2. List components to get the full name of the update:

    ```
    peimg /list c:\winpe_x86\base
    ```

3. Install the update, where *full_name_of_update* is the name of the update you found in step 2:

    ```
    peimg /install=full_name_of_update c:\winpe_x86\base
    ```

Prepping the Image

After you have added all required components, applications, and updates to the image, you can prepare it for capture. The preparation process removes all components that you have not installed and prepares the image for capture.

> **Note**   After you have prepared an image, you can no longer service that image, which is why you work from a copy of the Windows PE image that you apply from the .wim image file, rather than preparing a mounted .wim image file.

To prepare an image for capture

1. Ensure that all required components have been installed. You can do this by listing the components in the component store and verifying that a plus sign (+) is next to the component's name:

    ```
    peimg /list c:\winpe_x86\base
    ```

2. Use the Peimg command to prep the Windows PE image:

    ```
    peimg /prep c:\winpe_x86\base
    ```

    Peimg confirms your intent to prepare the image.

3. Enter **yes** to confirm the /prep command. You can prevent the prompt by using the /f command-line option.

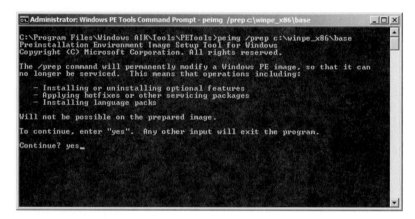

Capturing the Image

When you have prepared the image, it is ready for capture. Use ImageX to capture the image into a Windows Imaging (.wim) file.

To capture the Windows PE image

1. Use ImageX to capture an image of your Windows PE build folders:

    ```
    imagex /boot /capture c:\winpe_x86\base c:\winpe_x86\ISO\sources\boot.wim "Windows PE"
    ```

> **Note**   The /boot option marks the image as a bootable image. The /capture option instructs ImageX to capture the contents of C:\winpe_x86\base in the image file c:\winpe_x86\ISO\sources\boot.wim and name it *Windows PE*. For an explanation of all ImageX commands, see the "Deployment Tools Technical Reference" topic in the *Windows Automated Installation Kit User's Guide* (WAIK.chm).

Creating Bootable Media

Using the /boot flag during capture marks the Boot.wim file that you created in the previous section as a bootable image file. By placing this file on bootable media and preparing that media for booting, you can create a bootable image of Windows PE.

Many Windows maintenance and troubleshooting utilities can make use of Windows PE, including utilities created for managing disks and recovering systems. Windows Recovery Environment (Windows RE) is one example of a recovery tool that uses Windows PE. Many other utilities created by third-party manufacturers also use Windows PE.

This section covers the creation of bootable Windows PE media based on CDs, DVDs, UFDs, and hard disks. You can use all of these technologies for Windows Vista deployment, creating an array of possible solutions for corporate deployments.

Staging a Boot Image

The Windows PE boot image needs supporting files to be made bootable. If you copy your boot.wim file into the ISO\Sources folder of the build directory, you can create your bootable Windows PE by using the entire ISO folder hierarchy. A completed ISO folder hierarchy looks similar to Figure 9-2.

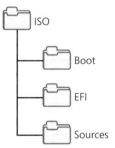

ISO

Boot

EFI

Sources

Figure 9-2   Windows PE ISO folder hierarchy.

To stage a captured Windows PE boot image   If the Boot.wim file is not in the build environment's Sources folder, because you captured it to a different path than recommended in the previous section, copy it to the Sources folder of the Windows PE build directory (*path* is the path containing the Boot.wim file you captured by using ImageX):

```
xcopy /chery c:\path\boot.wim
c:\winpe_x86\ISO\Sources\boot.wim
```

Creating Bootable CD/DVD Media

After the boot image is properly staged, you can create a bootable CD or DVD that uses your Windows PE image.

To create a bootable Windows PE CD or DVD

1. Use the Oscdimg.exe command to create an .iso image that can be burned onto a CD or DVD:

   ```
   oscdimg -n -bc:\winpe_x86\etfsboot.com c:\winpe_x86\ISO c:\winpe_x86\winpe_x86.iso
   ```

2. Using a CD/DVD burning application, burn the .iso image to a CD or DVD.

Creating Bootable UFD Media

USB Flash Drives are available that have the capacity to hold an entire custom Windows Vista deployment. The first step, however, is to make your bootable Windows PE media. After you've accomplished this, you can copy any custom images and Unattend.xml files you have made onto the UFD for deployment.

> **On the Disc** This book's companion CD includes a sample batch script named Makeufd.cmd that prepares a UFD and copies the Windows PE boot files to it. Do not use this script as is. It is a sample that will repartition and format the target drive before copying Windows PE to it. You must customize this batch script for your own requirements.

To create bootable Windows PE UFD media

1. Insert your bootable UFD device into an available USB port on your system.

2. Use the DiskPart utility to prepare the device for loading Windows PE. To run DiskPart, type **diskpart** at the command prompt and then press Enter.

3. Run the commands shown in Table 9-1 to prepare the UFD.

Table 9-1   Preparing a UFD for Windows PE

Command	Description
list disk	Lists available disks.
select disk *n*	Where *n* is the UFD you are preparing.
	Be sure to select the correct disk when using DiskPart. DiskPart will clean your primary hard disk as easily as it will clean your UFD device.
clean	Removes the current partition structures.
create partition primary size=*size*	*size* is the size of the disk as shown in the list. If you omit *size*, DiskPart will use all of the available space for the partition.
select partition 1	Selects the partition you created in the previous command.
active	Marks the new partition as active.
format fs=FAT32	Formats the UFD partition with the FAT32 file system.
assign	Assigns the next available drive letter to your UFD.
exit	Quits DiskPart.

4. Use the Bootsect.exe command to write a new boot sector to the UFD, where *e:* is the drive letter assigned to the UFD device:

```
Bootsect /nt60 e: /force
```

5. Copy the contents of the ISO folder to your UFD, where *e:* is the drive letter assigned to the UFD device:

```
xcopy /chery c:\winpe_x86\ISO\*.* e:\
```

6. Safely remove your UFD.

> **Note** Some UFD devices do not support this preparation process. If necessary, use the UFD device manufacturer's processes and utilities to make the disk bootable. After you've done this, proceed from step 4 to prepare the device.

Making Your UFD Bootable

Creating a bootable UFD requires careful work. Many UFDs are not bootable and need to be converted before use. They are shipped with a flag value set to cause Windows to detect them as removable media devices rather than USB disk devices.

To make your UFD bootable, consult with the device manufacturer to obtain directions or utilities that will convert the device. Many manufacturers make these instructions available through their product support systems. Ask specifically how to switch the removable media flag. This action will cause Windows to detect the device as a USB hard disk drive and will allow you to proceed with the preparations for creating a bootable UFD.

Booting from a Hard Disk Drive

Although it might seem strange to be booting Windows PE from a hard disk drive, you can do this to perform refresh installations of Windows Vista. By loading Windows PE onto the hard disk and booting it to RAM, you can repartition your systems disks and install the new Windows Vista image. You can also use Windows PE as the basis for the Windows RE to recover unbootable systems.

To boot Windows PE from a hard disk drive

1. Boot your computer from prepared Windows PE media.

2. Using DiskPart, prepare the computer's hard disk for installation of Windows PE. Use the DiskPart commands shown in Table 9-2.

Table 9-2   **Preparing a Hard Drive for Windows PE**

Command	Description
select disk 0	0 is the primary hard disk drive.
clean	Removes the current partition structures.
create partition primary size=*size*	*size* is a partition size large enough to hold the Windows PE source files.
select partition 1	Selects the partition created by the previous command.
active	Marks the new partition as active.
format	Formats the new partition.
exit	Quits DiskPart.

3. Make your hard disk bootable:

    ```
    bootsect /nt60 c:
    ```

4. Copy the Windows PE files from your Windows PE media to your hard disk:

    ```
    xcopy /chery x:\*.* c:\
    ```

Customizing Windows PE

Most Windows PE customization tasks will involve the processes described in the previous section. You will import and install additional components, add applications, import and install updates, and prepare and capture the resulting image.

Other tasks you might see when customizing your Windows PE implementation include adding hardware-specific device drivers and customizing the actual settings used by Windows PE when it runs. This section covers the installation of device drivers and details changes that you can make to base Windows PE configuration settings. Additional information on automating Windows PE is covered in the section titled "Automating Windows PE" later in this chapter.

Windows PE supports four configuration files to control startup and operation. These files can be configured to launch custom shell environments or execute specified actions:

- **BCD**   The Boot Configuration Data (BCD) file stores the boot settings for Windows PE. This file is edited with the Windows Vista command-line tool, BCDEdit.

- **Winpeshl.ini**   During startup, you can start custom shell environments using the Winpeshl.ini file. This file is located in the %SystemRoot%\System32 folder of the Windows PE image. You can configure this file with the path and the executable name of the custom shell application.

- **Startnet.cmd**   Windows PE uses the Startnet.cmd file to configure network startup activities. By default, the Wpeinit command is called to initialize Plug and Play devices and start the network connection. You can also add other commands to this script to customize activities during startup.

■ **Unattend.xml**   Windows PE operates in the windowsPE setup configuration pass of a Windows Vista installation. In this pass, Windows PE uses the appropriate sections of the Unattend.xml file to control its actions. Windows PE looks in the root of the boot device for this file. You can also specify its location by using the Startnet.cmd script or by using Wpeutil.exe with the appropriate command-line options.

Your final environment can run custom application shells (Figure 9-3).

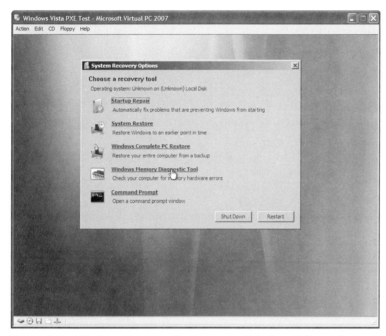

Figure 9-3   Windows Recovery Environment (Windows RE) running on Windows PE.

Automating Windows PE

Most Windows PE automation is done by customizing Unattend.xml, the Windows Vista unattended answer file. Use the Windows System Image Manager (Windows SIM) to create and edit this file. Unattend.xml allows you to control automation tasks in all the major installation passes. You can put it in the root of your Windows PE media to automate the installation process.

Automating with Unattend.xml

Windows SIM is the primary tool for creating and modifying Unattend.xml. It is designed to validate each automation step against the actual files in an image to ensure that you use proper syntax to build the automation. This provides an extra measure of assurance that unattended installations will work as planned.

When beginning the process of creating an answer file, be sure to create a catalog file if necessary to allow Windows SIM to validate your choices against the image file. Add answer file options to the answer file by right-clicking a component and choosing Add Setting To Pass 1 WindowsPE. The setting will then appear in the answer file pane, where you can configure it. When you complete answer file customization, you can validate the answer file by clicking Tools and then choosing Validate Answer File. Any settings that are not configured or that use invalid configuration settings will be listed in the Messages pane. When you are satisfied with the answer file, save it to the root folder of your Windows PE media. When you boot a system using this media, the answer file is automatically detected and will control the operation of Windows PE.

> **Note**   For more detailed information on using Windows SIM to create automation files, see the *Windows Automated Installation Kit User's Guide*.

Adding Images to Windows DS

When you have completed building a Windows PE image, you can use Windows DS to deploy it to clients. This allows you to use the PXE boot automation services of Windows DS to replace portable media as the primary method of initiating Windows Vista installations.

To add a Windows PE boot image to Windows DS

1. In the Windows DS Administration Console, expand your Windows DS server and right-click Boot Images.

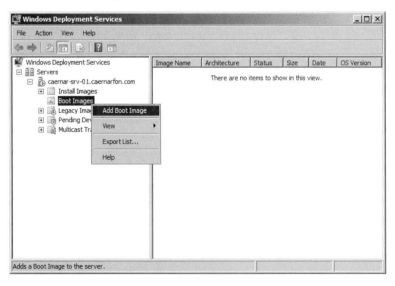

2. Click Add Boot Image to launch the Add Image Wizard.

3. Follow the instructions in the wizard to select and import your custom Windows PE image.

 Note   For more information on the configuration and operation of Windows DS, see Chapter 10, "Configuring Windows DS."

Using Windows PE with Microsoft Deployment Toolkit

MDT 2008 provides an infrastructure solution for automating the deployment of Windows Vista. Part of the infrastructure is the support for automatically customizing and building Windows PE images. You manage the actual process of building the Windows PE image files by using wizards and scripting, greatly simplifying the process of adding device drivers and packages, automating settings, and prepping and capturing the deployment image.

You use Deployment Workbench to manage most operations regarding the creation and deployment of Windows Vista images and applications. This scripted environment is able to dynamically update Windows PE as updates are made to the Windows Vista distribution.

Chapter 6, "Developing Disk Images," describes how to use Deployment Workbench to create distribution shares, task sequences, and deployment points. Deployment points (other than Microsoft Systems Management Server 2003 Operating System Deployment Feature Pack deployment points) automatically generate Windows PE images when you update them. As shown in Figure 9-4, you can customize a deployment point's Windows PE image and choose which types of Windows PE images the deployment point generates when you update it. Table 9-3 describes Windows PE settings that you can customize for each deployment point.

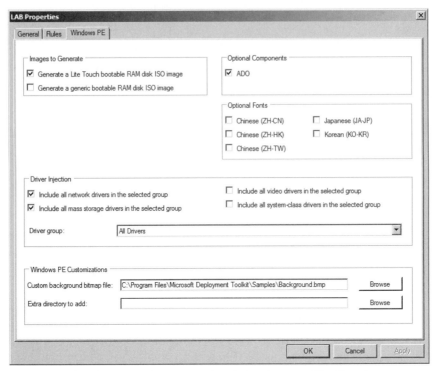

Figure 9-4   Configure Windows PE Settings in Deployment Workbench.

Table 9-3   Windows PE Settings in a Deployment Point

Area	Settings
Images to Generate	■ **Generate A Lite Touch Bootable RAM Disk ISO** **Image** Select this option to generate ISO images that start from RAM disk. ■ **Generate A Generic Bootable RAM Disk ISO** **Image** Select this option to generate a generic Windows PE bootable image that starts from RAM disk and does not contain MDT 2008.

Table 9-3   **Windows PE Settings in a Deployment Point**

Area	Settings
Driver Injection	■ **Include All Network Drivers In The Selected Group** Select this option to inject all network drivers found in the distribution share into the Windows PE boot images.
	■ **Include All Mass Storage Drivers In The Selected Group** Select this option to inject all mass storage drivers found in the distribution share into the Windows PE boot images.
	■ **Include All Video Drivers In The Selected Group** Select this option to inject all video drivers found in the distribution share into the Windows PE boot images.
	■ **Include All System-Class Drivers In The Selected Group** Select this option to inject all system drivers (such as motherboard drivers) in the distribution share into the Windows PE boot images.
	You can limit the device drivers that Deployment Workbench includes in the Windows PE image by selecting a driver group from the Driver Group list.
Optional Components	■ **ADO** Select this option to add the ADO optional component to the Windows PE bootable images.
Optional Fonts	■ Select the font support to add to the Windows PE boot images that Deployment Workbench generates. You must add these fonts when performing a lite touch deployment of Windows Vista images when the setup files are Japanese, Korean, or Chinese. The Optional Fonts area provides the following options:
	❑ Chinese (ZH-CN)
	❑ Chinese (ZH-HK)
	❑ Chinese (ZH-TW)
	❑ Japanese (JA-JP)
	❑ Korean (KO-KR)
	Adding additional fonts to Windows PE boot images increases the size of the images. Add additional fonts only if necessary.
Windows PE Customizations	■ **Custom Background Bitmap File** Type the path and filename of a bitmap file to use as the Windows PE background.
	■ **Extra Directory To Add** Type the path of a folder containing extra files and subfolders to add to the Windows PE bootable images.

Summary

Unlike earlier versions of Windows, Windows PE 2.1 is the only preinstallation platform for installing Windows Vista. Windows PE is publicly available in the Windows AIK.

You can approach using Windows PE in two ways. You can customize it through MDT 2008, which is the most appropriate approach if you're using MDT 2008 to deploy Windows Vista. Alternatively, you can customize Windows PE manually by using the tools available in the Windows AIK. You can customize Windows PE to fit almost any deployment scenario by adding device drivers and components, adding scripts and HTAs, and so on.

You can also start Windows PE in multiple ways. First, you can burn your custom Windows PE image to a CD or DVD and then start the computer using the disk. Second, you can put the Windows PE image on a bootable UFD and then use the UFD to start the computer. Last (and the most convenient option), you can add the custom Windows PE boot image to a Windows DS server and then start computers remotely.

Additional Resources

The following resources contain additional information and tools related to this chapter.

Related Information

- *Windows Automated Installation Kit User's Guide* (WAIK.chm)
- *Windows Preinstallation Environment User's Guide* (WinPE.chm)
- *Image Engineering Feature Team Guide* in MDT 2008
- Chapter 6, "Developing Disk Images"
- Chapter 10, "Configuring Windows DS"

On the Companion CD

- Makeimg.cmd
- Makeufd.cmd

Chapter 10

Configuring Windows DS

Windows Deployment Services (Windows DS) is the updated and redesigned version of Remote Installation Service (RIS) in Windows Server 2008, and a Windows DS update is also available for Windows Server 2003. You can use Windows DS to rapidly deploy Windows Vista by using Pre-Boot Execution Environment (PXE). Using Windows DS, you can deploy Windows Vista over a network. You can also use Windows DS to start remote computers using Windows Preinstallation Environment (Windows PE) boot images and then install Windows Vista using customized, scripted deployment solutions, such as Microsoft Deployment Toolkit (MDT) 2008.

Windows DS delivers a better in-box deployment solution than RIS. It provides platform components that allow for custom solutions, including remote boot capabilities; a plug-in model for PXE server extensibility; and a client-server communication protocol for diagnostics, logging, and image enumeration. Also, Windows DS uses a single image format (.wim) and provides a greatly improved management experience through the Microsoft Management Console (MMC) and scriptable command-line tools. For organizations that already have a RIS implementation deployed, Windows DS maintains parity with RIS by providing both coexistence and migration paths for RIS. First, Windows DS continues to support RIS images in legacy or mixed mode. Second, Windows DS provides tools to migrate RIS images to the new Windows Imaging (.wim) file format.

This chapter describes the architecture of Windows DS and the requirements for using it. It also describes the key features of Windows DS and how to use them in specific scenarios, primarily how MDT 2008 uses Windows DS to start destination computers and install operating systems.

Introducing Windows DS

Windows DS supports remote, on-demand deployment of Windows Vista and Windows Preinstallation Environment (Windows PE) images located in a central image store. It is available as an add-on to Windows Server 2003 systems running RIS and is the native remote installation technology provided with Windows Server 2008.

Windows DS images are collected from client master systems and stored in single instance storage (SIS) on the server. Clients can be booted from PXE-compliant network adapters or by using remote client boot disks. The Windows DS client boots into a customized Windows PE image, and the user can select the installation image from a list of images stored on the server. Windows DS installations can also be scripted for unattended installation support and to support Lite Touch Installation (LTI) and Zero Touch Installation (ZTI) scenarios.

This chapter covers the setup and configuration of Windows DS to support Windows Vista client deployment and helps you learn how to prepare and collect the Windows Vista client image for centralized deployment. It also briefly covers how to integrate Windows DS with automation environments such as MDT 2008.

Service Architecture

The Windows DS architecture has three major categories of components:

- **Management components** Management components are a set of tools that you use to manage the server, operating system images, and client computer accounts. The Windows DS MMC snap-in is a management component, and the command-line interface is another.

- **Server components** Server components include a PXE server for network booting a client to load and install an operating system. Server components also include a shared folder and image repository that contains boot images, installation images, and files that you need specifically for network boot.

- **Client components** Client components include a graphical user interface (GUI) that runs within Windows PE and communicates with the server components to select and install an operating system image.

Figure 10-1 illustrates the various components of Windows DS. The following sections describe the image store, PXE server, management, and client components in more detail.

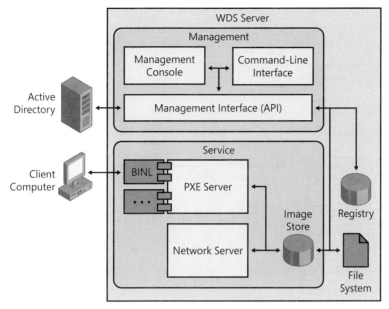

Figure 10-1   Windows DS architecture.

Image Store

Figure 10-2 describes how Windows DS organizes the image store.

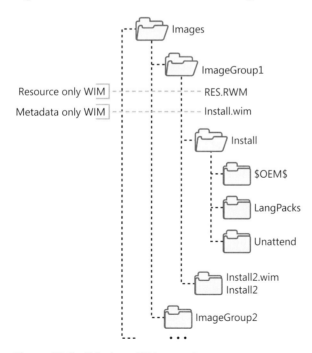

Figure 10-2   Windows DS image store.

Organizing images into groups, as shown in Figure 10-2, provides two benefits. First, image groups allow you to better manage and organize images. For example, you can manage the security of an entire image group, rather than managing the security of individual images. Second, image groups provide units of single instancing. This means that all of the images within an image group use SIS to significantly compress their contents. The file Res.rwm contains all of the file resources for the image group, and this file uses SIS. Each image file (Install.wim and Install2.wim in Figure 10-2) contains only metadata that describes the image file contents based on the contents of Res.rwm.

Windows DS references images by their group name and image filename. For example, the image ImageGroup1\Install2.wim refers to the image file Install2.wim in the group ImageGroup1.

PXE Services

The Windows DS PXE server is built on a unified and scalable architecture. As shown in Figure 10-3, it uses plug-ins to provide access to the data store. The PXE server supports one or more plug-ins, and each plug-in can use any data store. Windows DS provides a default BINL plug-in, as shown earlier in Figure 10-1.

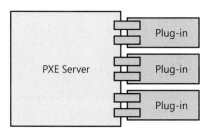

Figure 10-3   Windows DS PXE server.

Developers can use published APIs to create PXE server plug-ins. You can find these APIs in the Windows Vista SDK. The SDK also includes samples that developers can use to create their own plug-ins. For example, a developer can create a PXE server plug-in that works without requiring Active Directory and reads settings from a Microsoft SQL Server database.

Management

Windows DS provides two management tools that significantly simplify management tasks. The first tool is an MMC console that provides a graphical user interface for common management tasks. After installing Windows DS, you start this console by clicking Windows Deployment Services in the Administrative Tools folder of the Start menu. Examples of common tasks include adding images and configuring server settings. The second tool is Wdsutil. Wdsutil provides all of the management features that the console provides and more. It has a command-line interface that you can use to script management tasks. Both tools use the management API that Windows DS provides, and both tools enable remote administration.

Other management utilities include:

- **Capture utility**   The Windows DS capture utility captures images to the .wim file format. It includes a light version of the ImageX /*capture* functionality and provides a GUI for it. You can use this to add the resulting .wim file to the image store.

- **Active Directory Users And Computers extension**   You can use this extension to administer legacy RIS functionality and configure settings on the Remote Install tab of computer accounts.

- **Risetup and Riprep**   Windows DS provides updated versions of Risetup and Riprep for upgrade scenarios (available for Windows Server 2003 only).

The Windows DS management console (Figure 10-4) provides significant administrative control. You can add and remove servers. You can configure a variety of options, including computer naming rules, DHCP settings, PXE response settings, and so on. Of course, you can add and remove installation and boot images. You can also organize images into image groups. The Windows DS management console gives you full control over the image groups and images you add to it. You can configure permissions for each image group and for individual images, too. You can also associate an answer file with each individual image. The Windows DS management console helps you better manage images for different platforms. For example, you can associate different boot programs and boot images with the x86, x64, and ia64 platforms. You can also associate a global answer file with each platform.

Figure 10-4   Windows DS management console.

Client

The Windows DS client is a special version of Windows Setup that runs only within Windows PE. In other words, when you deploy Windows Vista to the destination computer using Windows DS, the Windows DS client runs within Windows PE on the client computer. This approach allows deployment of Windows Vista as well as images for previous versions of Microsoft Windows.

The Windows DS client drives the setup experience as follows:

- **Language selection**   For Windows Vista, the client prompts the user to choose a language. This choice applies to the setup user interface and the operating system installation. The user can also install additional language packs (Windows Vista Enterprise, Windows Vista Business, and Windows Vista Ultimate editions only).

- **Credentials gathering**   The client prompts the user for required credentials.

- **Image selection**   The client displays a list of images available to the user and then allows the user to choose an image to install on the destination computer.

- **Disk configuration**   The client allows the user to partition and format the destination computer's hard disks. The client provides the same options as Windows Setup.

However, you can automate all of the settings that the client prompts for. To automate these settings, you use Microsoft Windows System Image Manager (Windows SIM) to create an Unattend.xml file. For more information about creating answer files, see the *Windows Automated Installation Kit User's Guide*.

Operating Modes

To provide a clear path between legacy RIS functionality and the new Windows DS functionality, Windows DS supports three modes (Legacy and Mixed modes are available only in Windows Server 2003):

- **Legacy mode**   This mode uses OSChooser and Riprep (sector-based) images. This mode is compatible with RIS. Moving from RIS-only functionality to legacy mode happens when you install the Windows DS update on a server running RIS.

- **Mixed mode**   This mode supports both OSChooser and Windows PE for boot environments and Riprep and ImageX imaging. Moving from legacy mode to mixed mode happens when you configure Windows DS and add .wim image files to it.

- **Native mode**   This mode supports only the Windows PE boot environment and ImageX image files. The final move to native mode occurs after you have converted all legacy images to the .wim image file format and have disabled the OSChooser functionality.

Your choice of operating mode will depend on which client operating systems you are deploying and what your investment has been into legacy Riprep images. You don't need to abandon your current deployment images; operating in mixed mode allows you to continue to deploy legacy RIS images from OSChooser. It also allows you to deploy new .wim images of Windows Vista using Windows PE.

The mode used by Windows DS is not a simple selection in a dialog box. Each mode is activated in a specific way. The following sections describe each mode in more detail and how to configure each mode.

Legacy Mode

In Windows DS, legacy mode is functionally equivalent to that of RIS (Windows DS binaries with RIS functionality). In legacy mode, only the Client Installation Wizard (OSChooser) will be present as the boot operating system. Therefore, only Risetup and Riprep images are supported. You will not be using the new Windows DS management tools; rather, legacy RIS utilities will be the only way to manage the server. Legacy mode is available only on Windows Server 2003.

You configure legacy mode by first installing RIS on Windows Server 2003 and optionally adding legacy images to it. Then, you install the Windows DS update, as described in the section titled "Installing Windows DS" later in this chapter. You do not configure Windows DS by using Wdsutil or the Windows DS management console.

To configure Windows DS in legacy mode in Windows Server 2003

1. Install the RIS optional component on Windows Server 2003 with SP1 and then configure it by running Risetup. Optionally, you can add images to it.

2. Install the Windows DS update. (Windows Server 2003 SP2 installs the update by default.) The Windows Automated Installation Kit (Windows AIK) includes the Windows DS update for Windows Server 2003.

Mixed Mode

Mixed mode describes a server state in which both OSChooser and Windows PE boot images are available. In mixed mode, access to the old Risetup and Riprep images is possible through OSChooser. Additionally, you can access the new .wim image files via a Windows PE boot image. A boot menu allows users to choose RIS or Windows PE. You will use legacy management tools to manage Risetup and Riprep images and the new Windows DS management tools to manage all facets of the server, including the .wim image files. WDS mixed mode is available only on Windows Server 2003.

You configure mixed mode by first installing RIS on Windows Server 2003 and adding legacy images to it. Then, you install the Windows DS update, as described in the section titled "Installing Windows DS" later in this chapter. Last, you run Wdsutil or use the Windows DS management console to configure Windows DS and then optionally add .wim images to the image store.

To configure Windows DS in mixed mode in Windows Server 2003

1. Install the RIS optional component on Windows Server 2003 with SP1 and then configure it by running Risetup. Optionally, you can add images to it.

2. Install the Windows DS update. (Windows Server 2003 SP2 installs the hotfix by default.) The Windows AIK includes the Windows DS update.

3. Run **wdsutil /initialize-server** or configure the server in the Windows DS management console.

Native Mode

Native mode describes a Windows DS server with only Windows PE boot images. In this mode, OSChooser is not available, and Windows DS deploys only .wim image files to client computers. You use the Windows DS management console or Wdsutil to manage Windows DS in native mode. Native mode is available on both Windows Server 2003 and Windows Server 2008. Native mode is the only mode that Windows Server 2008 supports.

To configure Windows DS in native mode in Windows Server 2003

1. Install the RIS optional component on Windows Server 2003 with SP1. Do not configure the RIS service or add images to it.

2. Install the Windows DS update. (Windows Server 2003 SP2 installs the update by default.) The Windows DS update is available in the Windows AIK.

3. Run **wdsutil /initialize-server** or configure the server in the Windows DS management console.

> **Note**   The Windows DS server may be forced to native mode from any other mode. This is a one-way operation and is accomplished by using Wdsutil management utility. The command **wdsutil /Set-Server /ForceNative** changes the Windows DS server to native mode.

Planning for Windows DS

Windows DS doesn't have significant requirements for the system on which you install it, but you need to put some thought into which services and applications must exist in your environment to support Windows DS, including the actual server requirements, client computer requirements, and network requirements.

Windows DS supports booting computers directly from a boot image over the network. This image boots using the PXE boot specification and needs to be able to receive broadcast messages from PXE clients. This will require some planning to make sure clients will be able to find and communicate with the Windows DS server. As a result, you must consider the Windows DS requirements for DHCP and routing. This section discusses requirements you need to consider for Windows DS.

Server Requirements

The hardware requirements for running Windows Server 2003 or Windows Server 2008 are sufficient to support most Windows DS installations. If you are supporting a large number of images or if you are expecting greater than normal client load, investigate adding additional memory for performance and additional hard drive space for image storage.

The following list describes the software and service requirements for installing and using Windows DS:

■ **Active Directory**   A Windows DS server must be either a member of an Active Directory domain or a domain controller (DC) for an Active Directory domain. Active Directory is used by Windows DS to track Windows DS clients and Windows DS servers. In addition, systems can be preconfigured in Active Directory, instructing Windows DS on how to image them.

■ **Dynamic Host Configuration Protocol (DHCP)**   You must have a working DHCP server with an active scope on the network because Windows DS uses PXE, which in turn uses DHCP. The DHCP server does not have to be on the Windows DS server. The type of DHCP server is not critical for Windows DS to function properly. To operate Windows DS and DCHP on the same server, see the section titled "DHCP Requirements" later in this chapter.

■ **Domain Name System (DNS)**   A working DNS server on the network is required to run Windows DS. The DNS server does not have to be running on the Windows DS server. DNS is used to locate Active Directory domain controllers and Windows DS servers.

■ **Installation media**   Windows Vista media or a network location that contains the contents of the media is required to install Windows DS.

■ **An NTFS partition on the Windows DS server**   The server running Windows DS requires an NTFS partition for the image store. You should not create the image store on the partition containing the operating system files, so an additional partition is necessary.

■ **Service Pack 1 and RIS installed (Windows Server 2003 only)**   If you're installing Windows DS on a server running Windows Server 2003, you must install RIS for the Windows DS update package to be run. Windows DS also requires at least Service Pack 1.

> **Note**   Installing and administering Windows DS requires the administrator to be a member of the local Administrators group on the Windows DS server.

Client Requirements

The client requirements to support installation using Windows DS will vary based on how you intend to use Windows DS. The following list outlines the requirements for PXE booting to Windows DS and installing images:

■ **Hardware requirements**   The Windows DS client must meet the minimum hardware requirements of the operating system you're installing. The Windows DS client must also have enough memory to run Windows PE, because Windows DS uses Windows PE to start the client computer.

- **PXE DHCP-based boot ROM version .99 or later network adapter**   To boot directly from the Windows DS server, the computer's network adapter must contain a PXE boot ROM. If this is not the case, the client can be booted using a DVD boot disk, a Windows PE boot image copied to the computer's hard disk, or a USB Flash Drive (UFD). See the section titled "Preparing Discover Images" later in this chapter.

  All computers meeting the NetPC or PC 98 specifications should have the ability to boot from the network adapter. Investigate the BIOS settings of the destination computer to determine if you can enable a Boot From Network option. When the option is enabled, the computer should briefly display an option to press F12 to boot from the network during each startup.

- **Network access to the Windows DS server**   The client must have broadcast access to the Windows DS server to enable PXE booting. Windows PE boot disks can allow you to boot to Windows PE using Windows DS as an image store without broadcast access.

> **Note**   The account performing the installation must be a member of the Domain Users Active Directory security group. Domain Users have permission to join computers to the domain.

DHCP Requirements

Windows DS will configure accessible DHCP servers during installation, adding required scope options to the DHCP scopes. It may be necessary under some circumstances to modify DHCP servers manually to support advanced Windows DS scenarios. The following list describes how to manage DHCP scope modifications:

- **Microsoft DHCP and Windows DS on the same server**   When Windows DS is installed on the same physical server as the DHCP service, the Windows DS PXE server and the DHCP server will both attempt to listen on port 67 for DHCP requests. To prevent this, the Windows DS PXE server must be configured to not listen on this port. (See Figure 10-5.) You must add DHCP option tag 60, set to the string "PXEClient" to all active DHCP scopes. This allows booting PXE clients to learn about the presence of the Windows DS PXE Server from the DHCP response generated by the DHCP server.

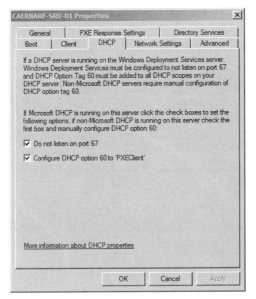

Figure 10-5   Configuring DHCP options in Windows DS.

- **Microsoft DHCP and Windows DS on separate servers**   When Windows DS and Microsoft DHCP exist on different servers, no additional settings are required. Both servers respond to DHCP requests: The DHCP server responds with an IP address offer; the Windows DS PXE server responds with the PXE boot information.

- **Third-party DHCP and Windows DS**   No additional action should be required for Windows DS to coexist with third-party DHCP servers. The Windows DS PXE server will respond with boot file location information only, allowing DHCP to service the IP address request.

> **Note**   RIS required the RIS server to be activated as a DHCP server in Active Directory. This is not required to operate Windows DS.

Routing Requirements

When DHCP and Windows DS are located on different subnets, or if clients are located on a different subnet than the Windows DS server, IP Helpers must be configured on network routers to enable forwarding of DHCP and PXE boot requests to the appropriate servers. (See Figure 10-6.)

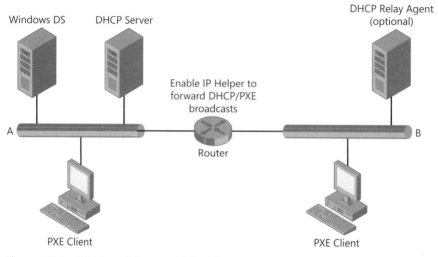

Figure 10-6   Windows DS on multiple subnets.

Note   An alternative to enabling IP Helpers on your routers is to install a DHCP relay agent on the remote network, configuring appropriate scope options to allow the remote clients to locate the Windows DS server.

Capacity Requirements

Windows DS servers can generate a lot of network traffic when servicing multiple, simultaneous client requests. Plan for this network load by designing your deployment network for sufficient capacity. You can deploy multiple Windows DS servers or use multicast (Windows Server 2008 only) in environments that experience significant installation activity. You can allocate access to Windows DS services by using DHCP scopes and IP subnetting. You can also configure IP Helper tables to direct clients to one or another Windows DS server based on client network ID.

Installing Windows DS

Windows DS is installed as an update to Windows Server 2003 or added as a role in Windows Server 2008. The following procedures outline the basic installation steps for Windows DS. Refer to the appropriate guidance (listed in the "Additional Resources" section at the end of this chapter) for complete instructions and planning advice.

Windows Server 2003

To completely install Windows DS on a Windows Server 2003 computer, you must first install RIS. After RIS is installed, you install the Windows DS update or Windows Server 2003 SP2 (which contains the update). The Windows AIK also includes the Windows DS update, which you can install on any server after extracting the file from the Windows AIK media.

To install RIS on Windows Server 2003

1. In the Add Or Remove Programs utility in Control Panel, click Add/Remove Windows Components.

2. Select the check box next to Remote Installation Services and then click Next.

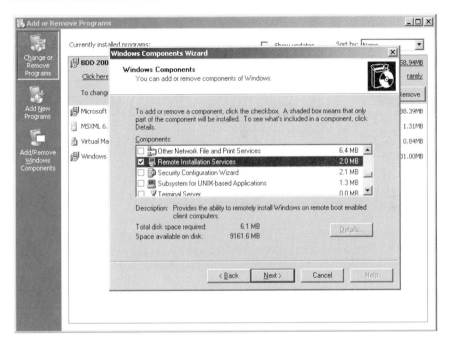

To install the Windows DS update

1. Run the Windows DS update from the Windows AIK. The file is windows-deployment-service-update-*platform*.exe, where *platform* is either x86 or x64, and is found in the WDS folder on the Windows AIK DVD. (If you have already installed Service Pack 2 for Windows Server 2003, you do not need to perform this task.)

2. On the Windows Deployment Services Setup Wizard welcome page, click Next.

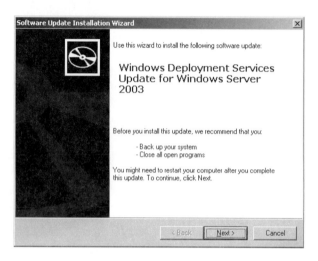

3. On the Microsoft Software License Terms page, click I Accept The Terms In The License Agreement. Click Next.

4. The Updating Your System page displays installation progress.

5. On the Completion page, click Finish to restart the computer.

> **Note**   Unless you plan to use Riprep legacy images, you can proceed with the configuration of Windows DS at this point. To enable Windows DS mixed mode, ensure that you do not install this update until at least one Riprep image is installed on the RIS server. For more information on the installation and configuration of RIS, see "Designing RIS Installations" in the *Windows Server 2003 Resource Kit*.

Windows Server 2008

You can install Windows DS by using the Add Roles Wizard, located in Server Manager.

To add the Windows DS server role

1. Start the Add Roles Wizard from Server Manager.

2. Click Next to skip the Before You Begin screen.

3. Select the Windows Deployment Services role and click Next.

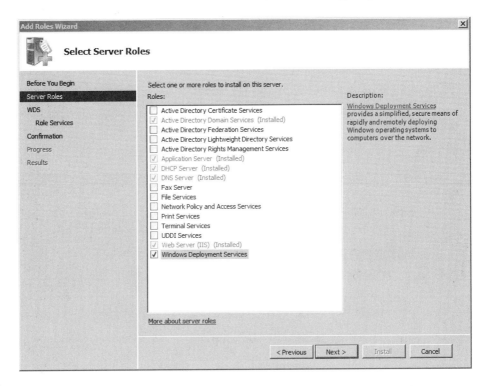

4. Additional information on installing and using Windows DS is displayed.

5. Click Next when you are ready to proceed.

6. On the Select Role Services page, click Next to install both the Deployment Server and the Transport Server role services. The Deployment Server role service contains all of the core Windows DS functionality. The Transport Server role service contains the core networking components.

7. On the Confirm Installation Selections page, click Install.

8. Windows DS is installed.

9. Click Close to complete the Add Roles Wizard.

Configuring Windows DS

After Windows DS is installed, you will need to add the server to the management console and then configure it. Windows DS automatically adds the local computer to the console. If you want to add a remote server, you must add it.

To add a server to Windows DS

1. Open the Windows DS management console by selecting Windows Deployment Services from Administrative Tools.

2. Right-click Servers in the Windows DS console tree and then click Add Server.

3. In the Add Server dialog box, choose a computer to add to the console. The server will be added and will now need to be configured.

To initially prepare the Windows DS server

1. In the Windows DS console tree, right-click the server and click Configure Server.

2. On the Windows Deployment Services Configuration Wizard welcome page, make sure that your environment meets the requirements, and then click Next.

3. Enter a path for the image store and then click Next. The folder should be on a partition other than the partition containing the system files. If you choose to create the image store on the system drive, a warning message will appear. Click Yes to continue or click No to choose a new installation location (recommended).

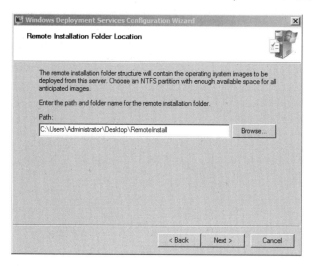

4. Configure DHCP Option 60 settings and then click Next. See the section titled "DHCP Requirements" earlier in this chapter for information on how to properly configure these settings.

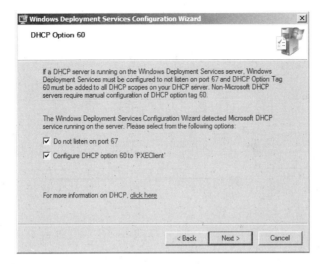

5. Set a PXE Server initial settings policy and then click Finish to complete configuration. See the section titled "DHCP Requirements" earlier in this chapter for information on how to properly configure these settings.

6. On the Configuration Complete page, you can add images to the server (default) or clear the Add Images To The Windows Deployment Services Server Now check box if you want to add images at another time. To add images to your server, see the section titled "Importing Images" later in this chapter.

Preparing Discover Images

For client computers that do not support PXE booting, you can create boot disks using a DVD, a hard disk, or a UFD. You can create these disks by using the Windows DS administration tools or the Windows PE administration tools from the Windows AIK. The process begins by creating a Windows PE boot image using the Windows DS console or Wdsutil. After this image is created, a bootable disk is made using Oscdimg from the Windows AIK.

To create a discover image using the management console

1. In the Windows DS management console, click Boot Images. Boot Images is under Servers, *server name*, where *server name* is the name of the Windows DS server.

2. Right-click a boot image that you previously added to Windows DS to use as a discover image and then click Create Discover Boot Image.

3. On the Discover Image Metadata page, type a name and description for the discover image. Then choose the location in which to create the image and the Windows DS server to respond to it. Click Next.

4.   Click Finish.

To create a discover image using Wdsutil

1.   Run the following command using elevated credentials:

```
Wdsutil /new-discoverimage /image:boot_image/architecture:architecture
/destinationimage /filepath:discover_image
```

Boot_image is the name of the boot image you want to use to create the discover image (not the filename), and *discover_image* is the file path and filename of the new Windows PE boot image. *Architecture* is either x86 or x64.

To create a bootable DVD using the discover image

1.   To create a Windows PE build environment, open a command prompt and run the following commands:

```
md c:\Winpe\Boot
md c:\Winpe\Sources
```

2.   Copy the discover image created in the previous procedures to the Sources folder of the build environment:

```
copy d:\sources\boot.wim c:\Winpe\Sources
```

3.   Copy boot files from the Windows AIK, where *architecture* is the processor architecture for the computer being used (either x86 or x64):

```
xcopy c:\Program Files\Windows AIK\tools\architecture\boot c:\WinPE\boot
```

4.   Run the following command in the folder C:\Program files\Windows AIK\tools\ *architecture*, where *architecture* is x86 or x64:

```
oscdimg -n -bc:\winpe\boot\etfsboot.com c:\winpe c:\winpe.iso
```

5. Burn the .iso file winpe.iso to a DVD by using a third-party DVD mastering program.

Note For more information on creating bootable media, see Chapter 9, "Preparing Windows PE."

Importing Images

After you have installed and configured the Windows DS service, you can add additional Windows PE boot images (boot.wim) and Windows Vista install images (install.wim). This process is straightforward: Files Boot.wim and Install.wim from the Windows Vista media are used for this purpose. For example, you can add the boot image that MDT 2008 creates to Windows DS, allowing you to connect to deployment points and run MDT 2008 task sequences across the network.

Note For more information on creating custom boot and install images that you can use with Windows DS, see Chapter 9, and Chapter 6, "Developing Disk Images."

Importing Boot Images

To prepare to service client computers, you must import a Windows PE boot image. Although Windows DS includes the boot loader code, it does not include the actual Windows PE boot image. You can import boot images directly from the Windows Vista or Windows Server 2008 source files. You can also customize boot images with hooks into services such as MDT 2008. For example, MDT 2008 builds custom Windows PE boot images that connect to MDT 2008 deployment points to install operating system builds. You can add these custom Windows PE boot images to Windows DS to streamline the LTI deployment process.

To add a boot image using the Windows DS management console

1. Insert a Windows Vista DVD into the server's DVD-ROM drive or make an installation source available to the server over the network.

2. Right-click the Boot Images folder and then click Add Boot Image. Boot Images is located under Servers, *server name*, where *server name* is the name of the Windows DS server to which you're adding the boot image.

3. On the Image File page, click Browse to select the boot image and then click Open. For example, you can select the default boot image Source\boot.wim on the Windows Vista media.

4. On the Image File page, click Next.

5. On the Image Metadata page, type a name and description of the image and then click Next. The default name and description is derived from the contents of the boot image file.

6. On the Summary page, click Next to add the image to Windows DS.

7. When the import task is completed, click Finish.

Importing Install Images

Windows Vista includes an installation image on the media. The installation image (Install.wim) can include multiple editions of Windows Vista. You can import one or more of these editions into Windows DS for deployment over the network.

> **On the Disc**   This book's companion CD includes a sample script, VRKAddInstallImage.vbs, that demonstrates how to script the addition of installation images to Windows DS. A similar script, VRKListImages.vbs, demonstrates how to write a script that iterates install images. These scripts are samples only and should be customized to meet the specific needs of your deployment environment.

To import a Windows Vista Install image

1. Insert a Windows Vista DVD into the server's DVD-ROM drive or make an installation source available to the server over the network.

2. Right-click the Install Images folder in the Windows DS management console and then click Add Image Group. Install Images is under Servers, *server name*, where *server name* is the name of the Windows DS server to which you're adding the installation image.

3. Name the Image Group and then click OK. This prepares a single instance store location for image import. It also allows you to group similar images together for optimal use of disk space and security.

4. Right-click Install Images and then click Add Install Image.

5. Choose the Image Group you created in the previous steps and then click Next.

6. In the Image File page, click Browse, choose the Install.wim file you're adding to the server, and then click Open. This file is located in the Sources folder of the Windows Vista DVD. Click Next to continue.

7. Choose the image(s) you want to import from the selections presented on the List Of Available Images page. Click Next.

8. Click Next on the Summary page to begin the import process. The process can take several minutes to finish.

9. When the import task is completed, click Finish.

> **Note**   Copying the source files to the local hard drive and then importing the image in to Windows from the local source files is faster than importing the image from the DVD.

Managing Image Security

It is important to properly secure boot and installation images to prevent their unauthorized use. A fully configured image might include corporate applications and data, proprietary configurations, and even codes and keys required to activate line of business (LOB) applications.

One way to prevent unauthorized installations is by controlling the clients that are allowed to receive images. You can accomplish this through pre-staging, where clients are registered with Active Directory through the use of a globally unique identification number (GUID). Another way is to enable administrative approval for client installations.

To configure an image file's access control list

1.   Right-click the image and then click Properties.

2.   On the Security tab, configure the access control list (ACL) and then click OK. The image's ACL must give a user Read and Execute permissions for the user to be able to install the image. In the following figure, members of the Installations group can install the image secured by this ACL.

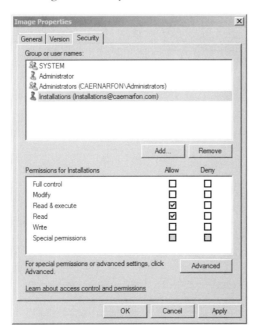

> **Note**   In addition to securing individual images, you can secure image groups. Right-click an image group, click Security, and then configure the group's ACL on the Security tab. By default, images in an image group inherit the group's permissions.

Pre-staging Client Computers

Pre-staging client computer accounts allows you to restrict Windows DS to respond only to known clients. You can also cause specific Windows DS servers to respond to the pre-staged client, assign specific install images, and control client provisioning automatically. You configured these settings when you installed Windows DS, as described in the section titled "Installing Windows DS" earlier in this chapter.

To pre-stage a system, you will need to know the system's GUID. You can find this value in the system's BIOS, in the documentation delivered with the system, or on a tag affixed to the system's case. This value is entered into the Active Directory computer account details for the system to pre-assign its membership in the Active Directory infrastructure.

To pre-stage a client system

1. In Active Directory Users And Computers, find the organizational unit (OU) where the computer will be staged.

2. Right-click the OU, click New, and then click Computer.

3. Type a name for the computer and then click Next. Optionally, click Change to choose the user or group with permission to join this computer to the domain.

4. On the Managed page, select the check box next to This Is A Managed Computer. Type the computer's GUID and then click Next.

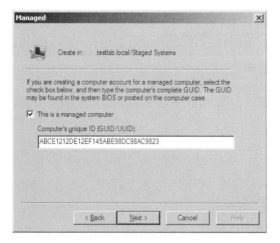

5. On the Host Server page, choose Any Available Remote Installation Server or select the Windows DS server that will serve this client. Click Next.

6. Click Finish to complete the wizard.

Configuring Administrator Approval

An alternative to pre-staging computers or allowing unrestricted access to Windows DS images is to require administrator approval before allowing installation. You accomplish this on the PXE Response Settings tab of each server. You configured these settings when you installed Windows DS, as described in the section titled "Installing Windows DS" earlier in this chapter.

To require administrative approval for unknown computers

1. In the Windows DS management console, right-click the server and then click Properties.

2. On the PXE Response Settings tab, click Respond To All (Known And Unknown) Client Computers and then select the For Unknown Clients, Notify Administrator And Respond After Approval check box.

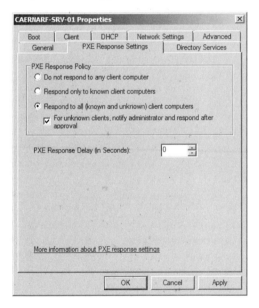

Systems booted to Windows PE will enter a pending state until an administrator approves their installation. Find systems in this state in the Pending Devices item of the Windows DS management console.

Installing Windows Vista

Destination computers must support booting from the network. Windows DS uses PXE technology to boot from the network and start the Windows DS client. You must also ensure that the computer's BIOS is configured to boot from the network.

To install Windows Vista from Windows DS

1. Start or reboot the destination computer.

2. When the destination computer starts and the Windows DS boot loader prompts you to press F12, press F12 to download and start the Windows DS client. Make sure you've enabled network boot in the computer's BIOS.

3. On the Windows Deployment Services page, choose a locale and keyboard layout and then click Next.

4. When prompted to connect to the Windows DS server, type the account and password to use for the connection and then click OK.

5. On the Select The Operating System You Want To Install page, choose an operating system image and then click Next.

6. On the Where Do You Want To Install Windows page, choose a partition on which to install Windows Vista and then click Next. To repartition the disk using advanced options, click Drive Options (Advanced).

7. Windows Setup will install Windows Vista, prompting for required settings that are not specified in an unattended-setup answer file.

Capturing Custom Images

Windows DS can deploy more than just default images from the Windows Vista media. You can create custom boot images and install images and then import them into Windows DS for automated distribution. Chapter 9 describes how to create custom Windows PE boot images. After creating a custom image, you can import it using the instructions in the section titled "Importing Images" earlier in this chapter.

To create a custom installation image for Windows DS, you must first install an existing image on a destination computer, customize it, and then capture the destination computer. Image capture is a two-step process. First, you must create a Windows PE capture image to support for the image-capture process. Then you capture an image from a system that has been prepared for imaging using the Sysprep utility.

To create an image-capture image

1. Click the Boot Images item in the Windows DS console tree.

2. Right-click the image to use as a capture image and then click Create Capture Boot Image.

3. On the Capture Image Metadata page, type a name and description for the capture image and then specify the location and filename of the image file to create. Click Next to create the capture image.

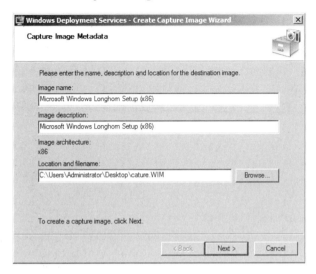

4. Click Finish.

5. Import the custom capture boot image by using the instructions in the section titled "Importing Images" earlier in this chapter.

To create a custom Windows Vista install image

1. Create a master installation by installing a Windows Vista image and then customizing the installation to meet your requirements. You can install Windows Vista on your master computer either from media or using Windows DS. To learn how to install Windows Vista using Windows DS, see the section titled "Installing Windows Vista" earlier in this chapter.

2. From a command prompt on the master computer, change directories to \Windows\System32\Sysprep and run the following command:

```
sysprep /oobe /generalize /reboot
```

3. When the reference computer reboots and the Windows DS boot loader prompts you to press F12, press F12 to download and start the Windows DS client. Make sure you've enabled network boot in the computer's BIOS.

4. In Windows Boot Manager, select the capture boot image.

5. On the Windows Deployment Wizard Image Capture Wizard, click Next.

6. On the Image Capture Source page, choose the volume to capture from the Volume To Capture list and then provide a name and description for the image. Click Next to continue.

7. On the Image Capture Destination page, click Browse to choose the location where you want to store the captured image. In the File Name text box, type a name for the image using the .wim filename extension, and then click Save. Click Upload Image To WDS Server and then type the name of the WDS server and click Connect. If prompted for credentials, provide a user name and password for an account with sufficient privileges to connect to the WDS server. Choose the image group in which to store the image from the Image Group list.

8. Click Finish.

Creating Multicast Transmissions

Multicasting enables you to deploy an image to numerous client computers at the same time without overburdening the network. By using multicast, you transmit image data only once, drastically reducing the amount of network bandwidth that is used to deploy images from Windows DS.

Consider implementing multicasting if your organization:

■ Has network routers that support multicasting.

■ Is a large company that requires many concurrent client installations. If your organization deploys images to only a small number of computers at the same time, multicasting might not be the right choice.

■ Wants to use network bandwidth efficiently. This is because with this feature, images are sent over the network only once, and you can specify limitations (for example, to only use 10 percent of your bandwidth). If your organization does not have bandwidth overload issues, multicasting might not be worth the effort.

■ Has enough disk space on client computers for the image to be downloaded. When multicasting, Windows DS downloads the image to the client computer instead of installing it from the server.

■ Meets the requirements listed in the following section.

Note You create and manage multicast transmissions by using the Multicast Transmission item in Windows Deployment Services. For step-by-step guidance on creating multicast transmissions, see "Step-by-Step Guide for Windows Deployment Services in Windows Server 2008" at *http://technet2.microsoft.com/windowsserver2008/en/library/e95677cc-0094-429d-9bd7-315bd663d6c21033.mspx?mfr=true*.

Multicast Prerequisites

To use multicast in your organization, you must have all of the following:

- Routers that support multicasting. In particular, your network infrastructure needs to support the Internet Group Management Protocol (IGMP) to properly forward multicast traffic. Without the IGMP, multicast packets are treated as broadcast packets, which can lead to network flooding.

- At least one install image that you want to transmit on the server.

- The Boot.wim file from the Windows Server 2008 media (located in the \Sources folder). Do not use the Boot.wim from the Window Vista media unless your version of Windows Vista has SP1 integrated into the DVD. If you use the Windows Vista without Service Pack 1 Boot.wim file for multicast transmissions, you will be able to create the transmission, but people who boot into it will not be able to join it.

- Internet Group Membership Protocol (IGMP) snooping should be enabled on all devices. This will cause your network hardware to forward multicast packets only to those devices that are requesting data. If IGMP snooping is turned off, multicast packets are treated as broadcast packets and will be sent to every device in the subnet.

Transmission Types

There are two types of multicast transmissions:

- Auto-Cast. This option indicates that as soon as an applicable client requests an install image, a multicast transmission of the selected image begins. Then, as other clients request the same image, they are also joined to the transmission that is already started.

- Scheduled-Cast. This option sets the start criteria for the transmission based on the number of clients that are requesting an image and/or a specific day and time. If you do not select either of these check boxes, the transmission will not start until you manually start it. Note that in addition to these criteria, you can start a transmission manually at any time by right-clicking it and then clicking Start.

Using Windows DS with Microsoft Deployment Toolkit

For LTI, MDT 2008 generates Windows PE boot images that connect to the deployment point and starts the Windows Deployment Wizard. The Windows Deployment Wizard allows the user to select an operating build to configure, applications to install, and so on.

MDT 2008 generates boot images when you update deployment points. MDT 2008 generates .iso image files that you can burn to DVD. You then use the DVD to start destination computers. MDT 2008 also generates Windows PE .wim boot images that you can add to Windows DS. Starting the MDT 2008 Windows PE boot images by using Windows DS is more convenient and quicker than using DVDs. You find these boot images in the MDT 2008 distribution share under the Boot folder. The filename is LiteTouchPE_*platform*.wim, where *platform* is x86 or x64. Import this boot image into Windows DS using the instructions in the section titled "Importing Images" earlier in this chapter.

> **On the Disc**   This book's companion CD includes a sample script, VRKAddBootImage.vbs, that adds boot images to Windows DS. You can use this script to quickly add MDT 2008 boot images. These scripts are samples only and should be customized to meet the specific needs of your deployment environment.

MDT 2008 can also use Windows Vista installation images from Windows DS. By doing so, you can use installation sources that already exist in a Windows DS server without duplicating the files in a MDT 2008 distribution share. This requires that you copy Wdsclientapi.dll, Wdscsl.dll, and Wdsimage.dll from the Sources folder of the Windows Vista media to the folder C:\Program Files\Microsoft Deployment\bin. It also requires that at least one Windows Vista source exists within the distribution share and that you create and update a lab deployment point. MDT 2008 uses the setup program files from distribution share to install the Windows Vista image from the Windows DS server.

To add images from Windows DS to a MDT 2008 distribution share

1. Add a full set of Windows Vista source files to the MDT 2008 distribution share. See Chapter 6 for more information.

2. Copy the following files from the Sources folder of the Windows Vista media to the folder C:\Program Files\Microsoft Deployment\bin:

    ❑ Wdsclientapi.dll

    ❑ Wdscsl.dll

    ❑ Wdsimage.dll

3. In the MDT 2008 Deployment Workbench console tree, right-click Operating Systems under Distribution Share and then click New to start the New OS Wizard.

4. On the OS Type page, select Windows Deployment Services Images and then click Next to add an image from a Windows DS server to the distribution share.

5. On the WDS Server page, type the name of the Windows DS server from which to add the operating system images and then click Finish.

6. Deployment Workbench adds all of the installation images it finds in Windows DS to Operating Systems.

Summary

Windows DS provides a solution for the network-based installation of Windows Vista. It's built on standard Windows Vista setup technologies, including Windows PE, .wim image files, and image-based setup. Using Windows DS can help reduce cost and complexity of Windows Vista deployments.

In Windows Server 2008, Windows DS replaces RIS. It's also available as an update for Windows Server 2003, and it provides a clear migration path from RIS for customers using legacy RIS images.

Although Windows DS provides the technology necessary to capture and remotely deploy custom operating system images, it does not provide end-to-end technology or guidance for high-volume deployment projects. It also does not provide tools or guidance for customizing the custom images you deploy with settings, applications, device drivers, and so on. MDT 2008 builds on Windows DS by adding both end-to-end guidance and tools for building and customizing images and then deploying them by using Windows DS.

Additional Resources

The following resources contain additional information and tools related to this chapter.

Related Information

- Microsoft Windows Deployment Services website, at *http://technet2.microsoft.com/ windowsserver2008/en/library/e95677cc-0094-429d-9bd7-315bd663d6c-21033.mspx?mfr=true*, includes more information about Windows DS.

- Infrastructure Planning and Design guide "Windows Deployment Services" at *http://technet.microsoft.com/en-us/library/cc265612.aspx.*

- "TechNet Webcast: Windows Deployment Services: Setup and Deployment," at *http://msevents.microsoft.com/CUI/WebCastEventDetails.aspx?EventID=1032309096& EventCategory=4&culture=en-US&CountryCode=US*, includes more information about setting up Windows DS.

- "Step-by-Step Guide for Windows Deployment Services in Windows Server 2008," at *http://technet2.microsoft.com/windowsserver2008/en/library/e95677cc-0094-429d-9bd7-315bd663d6c21033.mspx?mfr=true*, includes step-by-step instructions for using Windows DS.

- Chapter 6, "Developing Disk Images," includes more information about building custom Windows Vista images that you can deploy using Windows DS.

- Chapter 9, "Preparing Windows PE," includes more information about creating custom Windows PE images that you can use with Windows DS.

- Chapter 12, "Using Microsoft Deployment," includes more information about using Windows DS to deploy Windows Vista with MDT 2008 and Windows DS.

On the Companion CD

- VRKAddBootImage.vbs

- VRKAddInstallImage.vbs

- VRKListImages.vbs

Chapter 11
Using Volume Activation

Casual copying of volume-licensed operating systems and applications is a problem for both Microsoft and its customers. Microsoft intellectual property is improperly used, and customers are not able to enjoy full access to features and accessory applications designed for genuine Microsoft Windows operating systems and genuine Microsoft Office programs. This chapter explains how the new volume activation features in Windows Vista address these challenges.

A complete understanding of Microsoft's new volume activation technology helps organizations protect their software investments and allows for more effective control and management of Windows and Microsoft Office licensing. You will learn how to use product keys in your environment and how to decide which volume activation technology is best for your organization.

Introduction

Traditional volume-licensed media ship with a *product key* designed to activate an unlimited number of computers. This approach is effective for organizations that maintain large numbers of systems, enabling them to build deployment images using volume-licensed product keys and to deploy them to hundreds or thousands of computers. Unfortunately, this distribution method also creates media that can be copied and shared with an unlimited number of users, with few repercussions for the party making the copies.

Microsoft does not support users of copied operating systems; when those users have a support issue, they are often surprised to discover that the application they purchased was, in fact, stolen. In addition to the obvious embarrassment this discovery causes, the customer must then purchase a supported version of the application to gain access to product support— an expense the customer might not be prepared to bear. Also, users of copied software cannot access tools and applications made available under the *Windows Genuine Advantage* (WGA) and Microsoft Genuine Software initiatives. These initiatives verify the product key of properly licensed systems before allowing downloads of free tools and applications.

Volume Activation

Microsoft has designed a means by which Windows operating systems and Microsoft Office programs can be activated, ensuring that both Microsoft and the customer are protected from casual copying. Through the creation of limited-use product keys (called *Multiple Activation Keys*, or MAKs) or by requiring systems to periodically renew their activation using a *Key Management Service* (KMS) infrastructure, Microsoft has given enterprises a solution that protects their license investments. This solution has several benefits, in addition to solving the problems of intellectual property theft and customers' loss of product support:

- **Simpler activation of licensed systems**   The new KMS infrastructure is simple to operate, requiring little time for proper configuration and activation. Systems imaged for this environment automatically maintain their activation with no additional effort on the part of information technology (IT) administrators. No product key ever has to be entered on individual computers.

- **Better software asset management**   Administrators will be able to generate reports on software activation using a provided reporting tool, System Center Operations Manager 2007, or a non-Microsoft license auditing tool. By knowing the number of activated products in their environment, administrators can monitor *volume license* usage and know when to budget for additional licenses. Microsoft's online license management portals allow administrators to request additional keys to activate the computers purchased to replace stolen systems or to reactivate systems that have gone out of tolerance (OOT) or have been re-imaged.

- **Better license management tools**   You can prepare reference systems for image capture. Windows can be activated using scripts after systems are imaged, providing automation of activation and reducing administrative effort. These new capabilities allow much tighter control of activation keys. You can now ensure that activation keys are used only to activate your organization's computers without extensive custody control processes.

Note   Microsoft recommends using a repeatable build process to prepare systems for imaging. This approach ensures that these system images have never been activated before. Microsoft Deployment Toolkit 2008 (MDT 2008) provides a framework for a repeatable build process.

Activation Options

This section describes each activation method and provides information to help you decide which method best suits your requirements. Table 11-1 provides an overview of the major attributes of each activation method.

> **Note**   Retail editions of Windows Vista are activated with individual activation keys.

Table 11-1   Volume Activation Options

	OEM Activation	MAK Activation	KMS Activation
Advantages of Each Option			
Permanent activation	●	● This advantage does not hold true if hardware falls out of tolerance.	○
Automation	●	●	●
Reporting	○	●	●
Tolerates hardware changes	●	○	● Replacing the system drive causes KMS-activated computers to fall out of tolerance.
Disadvantages of Each Option			
Requires key management	○	●	○
Requires KMS infrastructure	○	○	●
Requires external communications	○	●	● Microsoft must activate the computer running KMS before KMS client computers can activate themselves.

Original Equipment Manufacturer

Microsoft *original equipment manufacturer* (OEM) partners use a hardware security module (HSM), software, and an ID parameter chosen by the OEM to generate a public key, which Microsoft uses to create a unique OEM signing certificate. The certificate–along with special BIOS tables and product keys specific to the OEM and its particular product–is used to activate an installed version of the Windows Vista operating system and tie it to an OEM's specific hardware.

Advantages of OEM activation include permanent activation, activation without connecting to any activation provider, and the ability for OEMs to use custom media images. (The recovery media is also activated.) Drawbacks for the customer are the need to maintain recovery media specific to each OEM system configuration versus having a generic image to use across all hardware.

Organizations can also provide system images created from volume license media for OEM imaging; however, these systems must be activated using KMS or MAK.

Multiple Activation Key

MAK activation uses a technology similar to that used with MSDN and TechNet Plus subscriptions. Each product key can activate a specific number of systems. If the use of volume-licensed media is not controlled, excessive activations result in a depletion of the activation pool. MAKs are activation keys; they are not used to install Windows but rather to activate it after installation. You can use MAKs to activate any volume edition of the Windows Vista operating system.

The MAK is obtained from the Microsoft Licensing website (*http://www.microsoft.com/ licensing/resources/vol/default.mspx*) and is used to activate each system under MAK management. As each system contacts Microsoft's activation servers, the activation pool is reduced. You can perform activation online over the Internet or by telephone. Check the number of remaining activations online and request additional activations to make up for re-imaged or stolen systems.

Advantages of MAK activation include the ability to automate key assignment and activation, availability of online reports regarding key utilization, and no requirement to periodically renew activation. Drawbacks include the need to request additional keys when the number of activations passes the preset limit, the need to manage the installation of MAKs (automated by Microsoft Deployment Toolkit 2008), the requirement for reactivation when significant hardware changes occur, and the potential need to manually activate systems using a telephone when no Internet connection is available.

Key Management Service

The KMS can be the least labor-intensive activation option available. With the initial setup of one or more KMS computers, the KMS activation infrastructure is self-maintaining and relatively problem-free. You can install KMS computers on Windows Vista systems or on systems with servers running Windows Server 2008. KMS can scale to hundreds of thousands of KMS clients per server. Most organizations can operate just two redundant KMS computers for their entire infrastructure.

Note   To support organizations not yet using Windows Server 2008, Microsoft enables KMS to run on Microsoft Windows Server 2003 SP1. To download KMS for Windows Server 2003, see *http://www.microsoft.com/downloads/details.aspx?FamilyId=81D1CB89-13BD-4250-B624-2F8C57A1AE7B&displaylang=en.*

KMS computers can automatically advertise their presence through the use of Domain Name System (DNS) service (SRV) resource records. Organizations using dynamic DNS have the benefit of automatic registration and resolution of KMS computers with no administrative intervention. Microsoft DNS and Berkeley Internet Name Domain (BIND) version 8.x and later support dynamic DNS and SRV resource records. In organizations with nonstandard dynamic DNS server permissions, the DNS administrator may have to modify server permissions to allow automatic registration of the KMS SRV resource records in DNS. This requirement should be familiar to these organizations because similar accommodations must be made for Microsoft Active Directory directory service SRV resource publishing.

KMS usage is targeted to managed environments where at least 25 physical computers regularly connect to the organization's network. Windows Vista computers activate themselves only after verifying that the required threshold of computers has been met. A KMS requires a minimum of 25 Windows Vista physical computers or 5 Windows Server 2008 physical servers before each operating system type can activate itself after contacting the KMS.

Note   Systems operating in virtual machine (VM) environments can be activated using KMS but do not contribute to the count of activated systems.

Advantages of KMS activation include automatic activation with little or no IT intervention, use of a single product key to activate and reactivate all systems, no Internet connection requirement (after the KMS computer has been activated), low network bandwidth use, and reporting through use of System Center Operations Manager 2007. Drawbacks include the requirement to set up the KMS infrastructure and the potential manual effort that may be required if dynamic DNS is not available.

If dynamic DNS is not available (because of server limitations or DNS security settings), you must manually create the SRV, A, and AAAA resource records for the KMS in DNS as appropriate. If the organization's DNS does not support SRV records, administrators must register the host name or address of the KMS computer (or computers) on the Windows Vista reference systems prior to imaging. This requirement can make maintenance more difficult when KMS locations change, requiring changes to the reference image and to active systems.

> **Note** Some efficiency can still be achieved by using a single host name for manual KMS registration and then by using the round-robin capabilities of DNS to load-balance two or more KMS computers from the same host name.

How It Works: Activation Timeline

Systems activated with KMS periodically renew their activations with the KMS computer by following these steps:

- After installation, during a 30-day grace period, Windows Vista attempts to activate every two hours.

- After activation, Windows Vista attempts to renew activation every 7 days on a sliding 180-day window. (Every renewal starts the 180 days again.)

- If Windows Vista cannot renew activation for 180 days, it enters a 30-day grace period. During the 30-day grace period, Windows Vista attempts to activate every two hours.

- If at the end of the 30-day grace period Windows Vista cannot activate, the operating system will persistently notify the user that he or she is not using a genuine copy of Windows Vista.

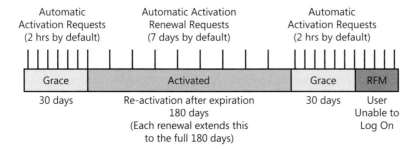

> **Note** The behavior is different for Windows Vista without Service Pack 1 (SP1) than Windows Vista with SP1 for computers that are not activated within the grace period. Without SP1, Windows Vista enters Reduced Functionality Mode (RFM). For more information about Reduced Functionality Mode in Windows Vista, see Microsoft Knowledge Base article 925582 "The behavior of reduced functionality mode in Windows Vista" found at *http://support.microsoft.com/default.aspx/kb/925582*. With SP1, Windows Vista persistently notifies the user that activation is required, without reducing the functionality of the operating system.

> ### Direct from the Source: KMS in Practice
>
> Where KMS is up and running, it has been very successful—even though customers tend to be confused and are expecting something very different. It works very simply (so simply that you turn it on from a command prompt), so the lack of an MMC or anything difficult is often anticlimactic after all the planning it requires up front. My point is that you must do your planning, but the actual implementation takes seconds. For example, KMS should be redundant (installed on two computers). And System Center Operations Manager 2007 should monitor it. This chapter covers these and other planning steps.
>
> *Doug Davis, Lead Architect*
>
> *Management Operations & Deployment, Microsoft Consulting Services*

Activation Terminology

This chapter uses terms specific to volume-license activation. To promote a more complete understanding of this topic, the following list describes some of the terms:

- **Activation**   The process of validating software with the manufacturer.
- **Confirmation Identifier (CID)**   A digitally signed value returned by a Microsoft clearinghouse to activate a system.
- **Installation Identifier (IID)**   A code generated by combining a system's hardware ID (created by scanning the system hardware) and the product ID (derived from the Windows installation). This code is transmitted to a Microsoft activation clearinghouse during system activation.
- **Office Genuine Advantage (OGA)**   An initiative that tracks the product keys from licensed versions of Microsoft Office programs to ensure that they are not reused on other computers. Users who validate their copies of Microsoft Office products gain access to add-ins and updates to those products.
- **Product key**   A code used to validate installation media, such as CDs, during installation. Product keys, also known as CD keys, do not prove licensing for a product, but they do discourage casual copying of software. All Windows product keys use five groups of five characters, with the format XXXXX-XXXXX-XXXXX-XXXXX-XXXXX.
- **Software Asset Management (SAM)**   An initiative promoted by Microsoft as a way to maintain accurate inventories of installed and licensed software. This practice helps organizations maintain legally licensed versions of all the software they need.
- **Volume license**   A license, purchased from Microsoft or another software vendor, to use multiple copies of an operating system or program.

- **Windows Anytime Upgrade (WAU)**   An upgrade service, primarily intended for home users, to allow upgrades from one edition of Windows Vista to a more advanced edition. WAU is available in Windows Vista Business as a way to upgrade to Windows Vista Ultimate (also a business-compatible product). This feature can be disabled by administrators. For more information about WAU, see *http://www.microsoft.com/windows/products/windowsvista/buyorupgrade/windowsanytimeupgrade/overview.mspx*.

- **Windows Genuine Advantage (WGA)**   A Microsoft initiative to ensure that users of copied Windows operating systems become aware of their counterfeit versions. By recording the product key and a signature from the computer's basic input/output system (BIOS), Microsoft can effectively determine when retail versions of Windows have been copied and when volume-activated versions of Windows have been excessively distributed.

- **Windows Product Activation (WPA)**   A way to ensure that customers are using genuine Windows operating systems purchased from Microsoft resellers. This tool, which was first part of Windows XP, defeated casual copying of Windows XP by ensuring that other systems had not recently been activated with the same product key.

Planning an Activation Infrastructure

You can use this section to help plan the activation infrastructure. Using the knowledge of how each activation method works and knowing the limitations of each are important parts of the planning process. The next step is to understand how you can apply volume activation to the environment.

Analyzing Activation Options

Certain activation options make more sense than others do when the patterns of network connectivity and system usage are analyzed. Computers that are out of the office for months at a time will not be able to use KMS activation, and MAK activation may be unnecessarily complex for environments in which 400 static desktops could be activated using a single KMS computer.

Network Connectivity

Evaluate the following questions regarding network connectivity:

- Does the target system have access to the network where a KMS structure is to be deployed?

- How many computers will be activated?

- Will systems be activated over a slow wide area network (WAN) link? Repetitive KMS activations, even though they are small, can cumulatively impact network performance.

- Do the organization's DNS servers support SRV resource records and dynamic DNS updates?

- If MAK is being considered, do all computers have individual Internet connectivity to contact the Microsoft clearinghouse?

If the environment can support the connectivity requirements, KMS is the simplest option to configure and manage. But it may not serve all purposes and can be supplemented by MAK or even retail or OEM activations where required.

Computer Connection Patterns

Keep the following questions in mind while evaluating computer usage patterns:

- How often will client computers connect to the activation infrastructure? KMS clients must renew their activations at least every 180 days.

- Do clients have limited access to the Internet? KMS or MAK proxy activation may be required to activate computers in these environments.

- Are systems on a high-security, isolated (air gap) network? To activate systems with no access to the IT infrastructure, use manual MAK proxy activation or use retail or OEM activation.

Other Activation Questions

In addition to the preceding questions, you should consider the following points to help you determine which solution to use:

- Are computers KMS-eligible? You cannot use KMS to activate computers that don't have the correct ACPI_SLIC BIOS marker. These systems must use OEM or MAK activation.

- Are the systems in the environment using OEM activation? If systems are already activated by the OEM, activation is not required at this time. If the organization uses volume licensing, however, consider establishing the KMS infrastructure to support re-imaging over time using volume-licensed media.

Mapping Computers to Activation Options

After the earlier questions have been answered, you can map systems in certain groups to the appropriate activation option. Create a worksheet similar to Table 11-2. List each activation option applicable to the environment and count the number of systems that will use each option. The total number of systems listed should equal the total number known to exist in the environment. This step allows you to better visualize the activation infrastructure.

Table 11-2 Mapping Computers to Activation Options

Criteria	Type of Activation	Number of Computers
Total number of computers to be activated		100,000
Number of computers that will not connect at least once every 180 days	MAK	–3,000
Number of computers in target environments that have fewer than 25 computers	MAK	–1,000
Number of computers that will regularly connect to the network	KMS	–95,000
Number of computers in disconnected environments, where number of computers is greater than 25 and there is no Internet connectivity	KMS	–250
Number of computers in disconnected environments, where number of computers is fewer than 25 and there is no Internet connectivity	MAK	–750
Remaining computer count should be zero		0

Implementing OEM Activation

OEM activation uses the resources of the Microsoft OEM partner or system builder to activate each operating system as it is installed. OEMs can install images based on both OEM and volume-licensed media during the installation process. Most systems that OEMs sell include a standard build of Windows Vista preactivated by the manufacturer. Additional scenarios present themselves for large companies that negotiate system imaging with the OEM. This guide presents these scenarios for completeness, but they have no bearing on deployment using Microsoft Deployment Toolkit 2008 (MDT 2008), which is designed to use volume-licensed media and applications.

Drawbacks of OEM activations include reliance on the OEM for system-imaging support and activation. Organizations that buy unloaded systems or that re-image systems on site will not benefit from OEM activation.

Installing Volume-Licensed Images on OEM Systems

For KMS activation to work, computers obtained through the OEM channels that have an ACPI_SLIC table in the system BIOS are required to have a valid Windows marker in the same ACPI_SLIC table. The appearance of the Windows marker is important for volume-license customers who are planning to use Windows Vista volume-licensed media to re-image or upgrade OEM through the re-imaging rights provided in their volume-license agreement. Not having the appropriate BIOS marker results in the following error on these systems and prevents them from activating using a KMS:

```
Error: Invalid Volume License Key
In order to activate, you need to change your product key to a valid Multiple Activation
Key (MAK) or Retail key.
You must have a qualifying operating system license AND a Volume license Windows Vista
upgrade license, or a full license for Windows Vista from a retail source.
ANY OTHER INSTALLATION OF THIS SOFTWARE IS IN VIOLATION OF YOUR AGREEMENT AND APPLICABLE
COPYRIGHT LAW.
Error Code:
0xC004F059
Description:
The Software Licensing Service reported that a license in the computer BIOS is invalid.
```

The options to resolve the preceding error include the following:

- Use a MAK to activate the computer.

- Contact your OEM for a replacement motherboard that contains a valid Windows marker in the ACPI_SLIC table.

- Purchase new systems with Microsoft Windows preinstalled to ensure that a valid BIOS is installed in the system.

 Note   Volume-licensed versions of Microsoft Windows require upgrading from a qualifying operating system according to the terms of the volume-licensing agreement.

OEM Imaging of Volume Editions

Organizations can choose to build a reference system using volume-licensed media. These images can be applied to target systems by the OEM; however, these systems require activation using either KMS or MAK methods.

Implementing MAK Activation

Organizations that have fewer than 25 active Windows Vista systems or that have small, remote offices or traveling staff will want to use MAK activation for at least some of their Windows Vista systems. Systems activated with MAKs are permanently activated unless significant modifications are made to system components.

Obtaining MAKs

Organizations that participate in one of Microsoft's volume license plans can obtain MAKs. Websites such as eOpen at *https://eopen.microsoft.com/EN/default.asp*, Microsoft Volume Licensing Services (MVLS) at *https://licensing.microsoft.com/eLicense/L1033/Default.asp*, MSDN at *http://msdn2.microsoft.com/en-us/subscriptions/default.aspx*, and TechNet at *http://technet.microsoft.com/en-us/subscriptions/default.aspx* can be used to register new licenses and obtain product keys. These keys can then be used to complete system installations. MAKs can be automatically applied to systems after installation, before imaging, or after imaging. Windows Vista includes scripts that you can use to manage MAK installation and activation. You cannot specify a MAK during setup or add it through an offline process; you must install it from within the operating system.

> **Note** It is important to remember that entering the MAK does not activate Windows Vista automatically. By default, a computer attempts to activate automatically online after installing a MAK. If the computer does not have a consistent Internet connection, the system must be manually activated by making an online connection to Microsoft's activation system or by telephone.

Managing MAKs

Administrators can view MAKs in the appropriate online portal (MVLS, eOpen, MSDN, or TechNet). Administrators can view the number of activations against each key and get a report of the number of activated systems under management. This number rises as systems are re-imaged and should be monitored to ensure that adequate activations remain to support the organization.

Obtaining Additional MAK Activations

As the number of available activations becomes depleted, you can request additional activations through the appropriate online licensing portal or by telephone.

Assigning MAKs to Windows Vista Systems

MAKs are essentially multiple-use product activation keys. Each system on which a MAK is used contacts Microsoft activation servers on the Internet and uses the key to obtain activation. Assign MAKs after installation of the operating system, either manually or through scripting.

> **Note** Microsoft is developing the Volume Activation Management Tool to enable centralized MAK deployment activation. For more information about this tool, see the section titled "Volume Activation Management Tool" later in this chapter.

Manually Assigning MAKs

One way to assign a MAK to a Windows Vista system is through the System Properties property sheet.

To manually enter a MAK using the System Properties property sheet

1. Click Start, right-click Computer, and then click Properties.

2. In the System Properties property sheet, click Change Product Key to open the Windows Activation dialog box.

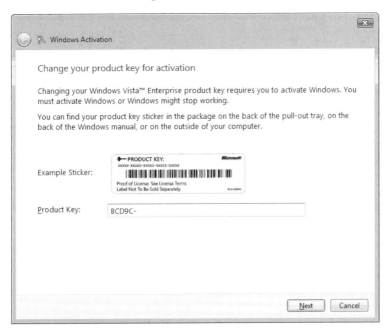

> **Note**   If necessary, click Continue at the Windows Security prompt to display the Windows Activation dialog box.

3. In the Product Key box, type the product key and then click Next to store and activate the MAK.

Automating MAK Assignment

You can also assign MAKs by using the Slmgr.vbs script included with Windows Vista. This script supports several options and is used for everything from adding, changing, and removing product keys to activating a KMS computer. For more information about using this script, see the section titled "Configuring KMS Activation" later in this chapter.

To install a MAK using Slmgr.vbs

1. Execute Slmgr.vbs with the *-ipk* option using the following command, where *MAK* is the Multiple Activation Key:

```
cscript %systemroot%\System32\Slmgr.vbs -ipk MAK
```

2. To force immediate activation of Windows on a computer with Internet connectivity using the new MAK, issue the following command:

```
cscript %systemroot%\System32\Slmgr.vbs -ato
```

Note   Other Slmgr.vbs options let users obtain the IID and install the CID used with telephone activation. See the section titled "Configuring KMS Activation" later in this chapter for a description of this script's options.

MAK Integration with the Deployment Workbench

In MDT 2008, the Windows Deployment Wizard runs the Windows Installation Wizard to apply MAKs during client setup. You can prepare the reference image for KMS activation and activate it using a MAK if it will not be used within the KMS infrastructure. The automated MAK application is executed after computer imaging. For more information on automating volume activation using MDT 2008, see the section titled "Activation in Microsoft Deployment Toolkit 2008" later in this chapter.

Direct from the Source: MAK in Enterprises

Some companies aren't yet in a position to use KMS activation. Currently, Windows Vista is the only shipping operating system that supports KMS activation. Companies that have a policy preventing them from putting desktop computers in their data centers and who haven't deployed Windows Server 2008 must use MAK activation until Microsoft releases an update for Windows Server 2003 or they deploy Windows Server 2008.

Within an enterprise, each organization can have its own MAK key. So, it's possible for a very large, multiple-division enterprise to have a single MAK key for the enterprise or multiple MAK keys with one for each division. For this, you must understand Microsoft licensing and how each company is licensed.

Doug Davis, Lead Architect

Management Operations & Deployment,

Microsoft Consulting Services

Volume Activation Management Tool

The Volume Activation Management Tool (VAMT) makes it easier for IT professionals to distribute MAKs from a centralized console and to activate multiple target computers. For more information, see *http://technet.microsoft.com/en-us/windowsvista/bb892849.aspx*. You can download the tool from *http://www.microsoft.com/downloads/details.aspx? familyid=12044DD8-1B2C-4DA4-A530-80F26F0F9A99&displaylang=en*. VAMT supports MAK activation in two ways:

- **MAK independent activation**   Many environments maintain a single system image for deployment across the enterprise. With MAK independent activation, an IT professional can distribute a MAK key to one or more connected computers within a network and, optionally, instruct those computers to activate over the Internet immediately.

- **MAK proxy activation**   This activation method is designed for environments that preclude direct access to the Internet—such as financial and government networks in which the only current method of activation is phone activation. With MAK proxy activation, customers can acquire and send a list of system IIDs to the Microsoft clearinghouse. The proxy retrieves the corresponding CIDs from the Microsoft clearinghouse and distributes them to the client computers. This method even allows activation in cases where the IID and CID lists must be transported by disk or other medium to an Internet-enabled system.

In Figure 11-1, a VAMT infrastructure has been installed to manage MAK activation. Computers in each location are activated as follows:

- **Headquarters**   Dedicated VAMTs at Headquarters discover clients and configure them with MAKs. Headquarters clients then use MAK independent activation to contact the Microsoft clearinghouse to activate.

- **Site A**   A desktop computer running the VAMT discovers and distributes MAKs to clients on this remote network. The clients then use MAK independent activation to activate.

- **Site B**   Desktop computers in sites connected to Headquarters can use the resources of the Headquarters VAMT computers. If those computers do not have connectivity to the Microsoft clearinghouse, the VAMTs can use MAK proxy activation to relay the activation to the clearinghouse.

- **Site C**   Isolated sites can use a local VAMT to collect activation requests, forwarding them on removable media to an Internet-connected VAMT computer. Activation responses can then be transported back to the isolated site and relayed to the client systems.

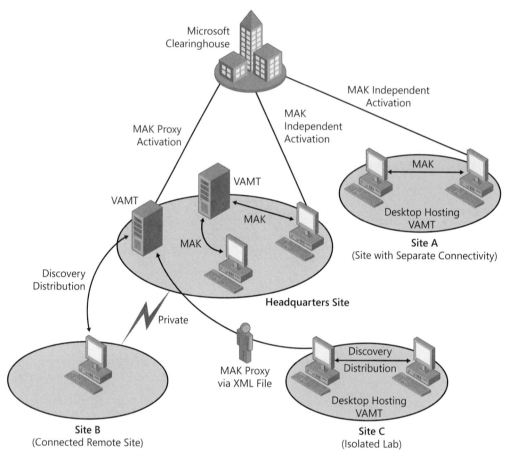

Figure 11-1   The VAMT infrastructure.

Implementing KMS Activation

KMS activation relies primarily on the proper setup and operation of one or more computers running KMS. KMS computers, running either Windows Vista or Windows Server 2008, must be installed with the customer-specific volume license key. Properly configured Windows Vista volume clients, by default, seek a KMS computer by using DNS queries unless they are preconfigured with the address of one or more KMS computers. Systems activated by a KMS computer renew their activation keys at 7-day intervals under normal operation, operating up to 180 days (or 210 days when the 30-day grace period is taken into account) without renewal when they are unable to contact a KMS computer. This approach allows traveling systems to remain in full operation for up to seven months without requiring contact with a KMS computer.

Installing a KMS Computer

All the tools required for KMS computer operation are already included in Windows Vista and Windows Server 2008. Installation of an enterprise volume-license key enables the KMS computer to activate its service with Microsoft. By default, the KMS computer attempts to register its SRV resource information with the primary DNS of the system's primary DNS domain.

To activate KMS on a computer that will run the KMS

1. Install an enterprise volume-license key by running the following command in an elevated Command Prompt window, where *Key* is the enterprise volume license key:

```
cscript %systemroot%\System32\Slmgr.vbs -ipk Key
```

> **Note**   You can use the key provided for KMS computer activation on only two systems, up to 10 times for each system. If you are using this key in a test lab, you should be sure to request an extension to support activation of the production KMS computers.

2. Activate the KMS computer using the Internet by running this script:

```
cscript %systemroot%\System32\Slmgr.vbs -ato
```

3. To activate the KMS using a telephone, start the Windows Activation Wizard by running this command:

```
slui.exe 4
```

4. Ensure that the KMS port (default is 1688/TCP) is allowed through all firewalls between the KMS computer and KMS client computers.

> **Important**   You must not provide unsecured access to your KMS hosts over an uncontrolled network such as the Internet. Doing so can lead to exposure to penetration attempts and unauthorized activation by computers outside the organization.

5. Make any configuration changes required for the environment. See the section titled "Configuring KMS Activation" later in this chapter for details on KMS configuration settings.

By using the Slmgr.vbs script and editing the KMS computer's registry, you can change the configuration of KMS. Configure KMS to register SRV resource records on multiple DNS domains, not to register with DNS at all, to use nonstandard ports, and even to control client-renewal intervals. For these changes to take effect, restart the Software Licensing Service. Details on these settings and how to configure them are included in the section titled "Configuring KMS Activation."

Required Resources

KMS computers require no additional resources beyond those required by volume-licensed editions of Windows Vista or Windows Server 2008. For co-hosted scenarios, configure the KMS to run as a low priority, sparing processor cycles for other applications. KMS has been tested to provide as many as 20,000 activations per hour on a single system. Two KMS computers can provide more than 400,000 activations in a 10-hour day, satisfying the needs of even the largest enterprises. KMS can be co-hosted with other services, such as Active Directory domain controller roles or file and print services, and it is supported in VM configurations.

Note   Computers running beta versions of KMS do not support activation of Windows Vista RTM clients.

KMS Infrastructure

KMS uses the Software Licensing Service built into Windows Vista and Windows Server 2008. Activating with an enterprise volume-license key converts the Software Licensing Service to the KMS computer role, allowing KMS clients to use the KMS computer in their activation process.

Figure 11-2 shows an enterprise network supporting clients in three branch offices. Site A, which has more than 25 client computers (but no secure TCP connectivity to Headquarters), can support its own KMS. Site B must use MAK activation, because KMS does not support sites with fewer than 25 client computers, and the site is not connected by a private WAN. Site C can use KMS, because it is connected to Headquarters using a private WAN.

Clients making KMS activation requests must be able to communicate with the KMS computer. For this reason, at least one KMS computer should be installed for any network site separated from other sites by a public network.

Note   KMS requires activation requests from 25 or more client computers before it begins activating computers. For this reason, KMS is not effective for small, remote offices (fewer than 25 client computers). These offices can activate across a WAN or can be activated using MAKs if KMS performance across the WAN is inadequate.

KMS requests and responses use just a bit more than 200 bytes of network bandwidth. This load should not adversely affect the resources of most local area networks (LANs) and can even support KMS activation across uncongested WANs.

Caution   KMS can be used over secure WANs but should not be used over public networks. Doing so exposes the KMS computer to penetration attempts and enables unidentified KMS clients to receive activations, a violation of volume-licensing agreements.

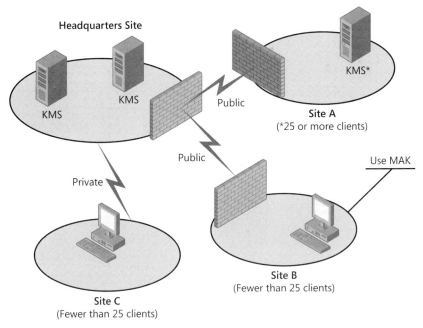

Figure 11-2   Enterprise activation infrastructure example.

DNS Registration (KMS Autodiscovery)

For KMS autodiscovery to work properly, DNS servers must support both dynamic DNS registrations and SRV resource records. Versions of Microsoft DNS included with Microsoft Windows 2000 Server, Windows Server 2003, Windows Server 2008, and BIND DNS versions 8 through 9.4.0 support this functionality.

KMS automatically attempts to register SRV resource records with the DNS server for the system's primary DNS suffix. KMS can contact additional DNS servers as well. If needed, administrators can create a registry entry (HKLM\SOFTWARE\Microsoft\Windows NT\CurrentVersion\SL\DnsDomainPublishList) where the key contains a list of DNS domains with which KMS will attempt to register resource records. The system running KMS requires permission to register resource records in each domain. Each DNS server administrator might need to modify DNS permissions to make this possible.

> **Note**   If dynamic DNS registration does not work for any reason, the DNS server administrator must enter SRV records manually. The records should be named _VLMCS._TCP.*DNSDomain-Name*, where *DNSDomainName* is the name of a DNS domain. Time to Live (TTL) for these records should be 60 minutes. The KMS computer address and port (default 1688/TCP) should also be included in each record. KMS clients do not use the priority or weight fields when selecting a KMS computer. Instead, they randomly select a KMS computer from the complete list of KMS computers that DNS returns for their domain.

Installing KMS Client Computers

You need to do very little to client systems to enable KMS activation. Systems installed using volume-licensed media automatically seek out KMS computers by default. If a KMS computer is found, no further action is necessary. A client first checks the DNS domain specified by its primary DNS suffix for a KMS SRV record. If an SRV record is not found, domain-joined computers check the DNS domain corresponding to their Active Directory DNS domain. Workgroup client computers check the DNS domain that the Dynamic Host Configuration Protocol (DHCP) specifies (option 15 per Request for Comments [RFC] 2132).

Computer Imaging

Systems being prepared for imaging can be prepared normally. The reference computer should be imaged before activation. If the system was activated during preparation, use the System Preparation Tool (Sysprep) to reset the activation timers.

To reset a volume-licensed system to allow KMS activation

1. Execute Slmgr.vbs with the *-ipk* option, installing the generic product setup key as shown in the following example, where *product key* is the generic setup key for that version of Windows Vista:

```
cscript C:\Windows\System32\Slmgr.vbs -ipk <product key>
```

> **Note**   The generic setup key can be found in \sources\pid.txt on the installation media.

2. Run **sysprep /generalize** to reset activation timers and prepare the image for capture.

KMS Client Activation

KMS clients retry activation every two hours by default, but you can force KMS client activation manually for systems that will be disconnected for travel.

To manually activate a KMS client system

1. Click Start, right-click Computer, and then click Properties.

2. In the System Properties property sheet, click Click Here To Activate Windows Now to launch Windows Activation.

3. If necessary, click Continue to enable Windows Activation.

4. Windows Vista then contacts a KMS computer and attempts to activate.

Enabling Standard User Activation

By default, activation requires administrative privileges. However, in scenarios in which users do not have local administrator access and autoactivation cannot be completed during the initial 30-day grace period, you may elect to make these operations available to Standard users. You can set a registry entry, HKLM\SOFTWARE\Microsoft\Windows NT\Current-Version \SL\UserOperations (REG_DWORD), to 1 to enable Standard users to install product keys, activate, and rearm computers. With this registry setting enabled, all product key installation, activation, and rearm requests must be done using the built-in Slmgr.vbs script.

KMS Integration with the Deployment Workbench

In MDT 2008, the Windows Deployment Wizard configures KMS client settings during desktop computer image preparation. This option does not insert an activation key. Instead, the KMS client seeks a computer running KMS after computer imaging. For more information on automating volume activation using MDT 2008, see the section titled "Activation in Microsoft Deployment Toolkit 2008" later in this chapter.

KMS Reporting

You can collect and report on KMS statistics in several ways. You can use the Slmgr.vbs script to display a limited amount of information about KMS, such as the status of the current volume license. More detailed information is available in the KMS application event logs, which can be collected and tabulated by System Center Operations Manager 2007. Likewise, you can use outside vendor tools that can monitor or tabulate event logs to create KMS-related reports and alerts.

KMS Event Log Entries

The licensing service logs events to the Application Event Log. The KMS computer logs 12290 events to a separate log. Both the KMS client and the KMS computer log each activation request. The KMS response to these events can be tabulated to approximate the number of activated systems supported by the KMS computer. Totaling the results for all computers running KMS yields a global activation picture for the organization. Problems are also recorded in the event logs and can be traced by date and time to help discover the cause of activation issues. An explanation of KMS event log entries is in the section titled "KMS Event Log Entries" later in this chapter.

MOM Pack for KMS Activation

Organizations that have standardized on System Center Operations Manager 2007 can use it for event monitoring and activation reporting. It can alert administrators to problems and provide input into SAM systems to let organizations track activated software.

Configuring KMS Activation

You can activate and maintain KMS computers in several ways. In addition to the simple options provided with Slmgr.vbs, you can use registry entries and Windows Management Instrumentation (WMI) calls for more sophisticated configuration settings.

Using Slmgr.vbs to Configure KMS

Slmgr.vbs has capabilities that you can use to activate and configure both KMS service computers and KMS client computers. This section describes the available options and how they are used.

KMS Computer Configuration

Table 11-3 describes the options used to configure and report on KMS computers. Slmgr.vbs provides additional options that Table 11-3 doesn't describe. To see them, view Slmgr.vbs in a text editor to read the comments.

Table 11-3   Slmgr.vbs Service Command-Line Options

Option	Purpose
-ipk Product Key	Install enterprise license key (where Product Key represents the actual key) to enable KMS computer functionality
-dli	Display license information
-ato	Attempt immediate activation
-sprt port	Set KMS computer listening port (where port is the port ID)
-sdns	Enable dynamic DNS publishing (default)
-cdns	Disable dynamic DNS publishing
-cpri	Set KMS processor priority to low
-spri	Set KMS processor priority to normal (default)
-rearm	Reset activation timer and initialization (used for imaging)
-xpr	Display the date when the current KMS-based activation will expire

KMS Client Configuration

Table 11-4 describes the options used to configure and report on KMS client computers.

Table 11-4   Client Command-Line Options

Option	Purpose
-ipk	Install product key (used to replace MAK)
-dli	Display license information
-ato	Attempt immediate activation
-skms KMS Server[:port] | :port	Set name and port of KMS computer to be used (where KMS Server is the name of the computer running KMS and port is the port ID)

Table 11-4   Client Command-Line Options

Option	Purpose
-ckms	Clear name of KMS computer used
-rearm	Reset activation timer and initialization (used for imaging)

Using Registry Entries to Configure KMS

You can manage some KMS configuration settings directly in the registry. This section outlines these registry entries and provides typical values where appropriate.

KMS Computer Configuration

The registry entries shown in Table 11-5 can be used to configure the KMS or can contain information about KMS configuration.

Table 11-5   KMS Registry Entries and What They Control

Registry Entry	Description
Found under HKLM\SOFTWARE\Microsoft\Windows NT\CurrentVersion\SL	
DisableDnsPublishing (REG_DWORD)	Setting to nonzero value disables dynamic DNS
EnableKmsLowPriority (REG_DWORD)	Setting to nonzero value sets low priority
KeyManagementServiceListeningPort (REG_SZ)	Sets the KMS computer port
DnsDomainPublishList (REG_MULTI_SZ)	Sets a list of DNS domains to publish KMS
VLActivationInterval (REG_DWORD)	Sets interval for activation attempts (minutes)
VLRenewalInterval (REG_DWORD)	Sets client renewal interval (minutes)
KeyManagementServiceVersion (REG_SZ)	Used for MOM interface
Found under HKU\S-1-5-20\SOFTWARE\Microsoft\Windows NT\CurrentVersion\SL	
KeyManagementServiceRegisteredDomainName (REG_SZ)	Stores cached domain name when KMS is enabled—is populated during name and domain changes
KeyManagementServiceRegisteredHostName (REG_SZ)	Stores cached host name when KMS is enabled—is populated during name and domain changes
KeyManagementServiceRegisteredPortNumber (REG_SZ)	Stores cached port number when KMS is enabled—is populated during name and domain changes

KMS Client Configuration

The registry entries shown in Table 11-6 can be used to configure the KMS client or can contain information about KMS activation status.

Table 11-6   KMS Client Registry Entries and What They Control

Registry Entry	Description
Found under HKLM\SOFTWARE\Microsoft\Windows NT\CurrentVersion\SL	
KeyManagementServiceName (REG_SZ)	Used to force a specific KMS service computer
KeyManagementServicePort (REG_SZ)	Used to force a specific KMS port
UserOperations (REG_DWORD)	Used to enable Standard User product activation

Using WMI to Configure KMS

This section contains the KMS-specific WMI methods that Windows Vista supports. WMI calls can be issued through scripting tools and custom applications to manage Windows Vista settings.

KMS Computer Configuration

Table 11-7 lists WMI methods that are specific to KMS computer operation.

Table 11-7   KMS Computer WMI Methods

Class	Name	Description
SoftwareLicensingService	*IsKeyManagementServiceMachine*	Is KMS enabled? 1=True, 0=False
	VLActivationInterval	Interval for activation attempts (minutes)
	VLRenewalInterval	Interval for activation renewals (minutes)
	KeyManagementServiceCurrentCount	Count of currently active volume clients: -1=non-KMS system
SoftwareLicensingProduct	*LicenseStatus*	0=Unlicensed, 1=Licensed, 2=OOBGrace, 3=OOTGrace (OOBGrace represents the out-of-box grace period.) (OOTGrace represents the OOT grace period.)
	GracePeriodRemaining	Remaining time before activation is required

KMS Client Configuration

Table 11-8 lists WMI methods that apply to KMS client computer operation.

Table 11-8   KMS Client WMI Methods

Class	Name	Description
SoftwareLicensingService	*KeyManagementServiceMachine*	Registered KMS computer name; null if not manually set
	VLActivationInterval	Interval for activation attempts (minutes)
	VLRenewalInterval	Interval for activation renewals (minutes)
	KeyManagementServiceCurrentCount	Count of currently active volume clients: −1=non-KMS system
	KeyManagementServiceProductKeyID	Cached product ID
	ClientMachineID	The unique identifier for this volume client computer
	AcquireGenuineTicket	Acquire a Windows Genuine Ticket online
SoftwareLicensingProduct	*LicenseStatus*	0=Unlicensed, 1=Licensed, 2=OOB-Grace, 3=OOTGrace, 4 =NonGenuineGrace
	GracePeriodRemaining	Remaining time before reactivation is required

Activation in Microsoft Deployment Toolkit 2008

In MDT 2008, you automate the application of enterprise license keys and MAKs through the Deployment Workbench and Windows Deployment Wizard. You can further automate the process through modifications to the CustomSettings.ini file located in Control in the MDT 2008 distribution folder.

This section gives an overview of this process, which is covered in more detail in Chapter 12, "Using Microsoft Deployment." During LTI preparation, the Windows Deployment Wizard asks for Windows Vista activation keys, as shown in Figure 11-3. The wizard inserts these keys during the LTI deployment process to automate the application of these keys during deployment.

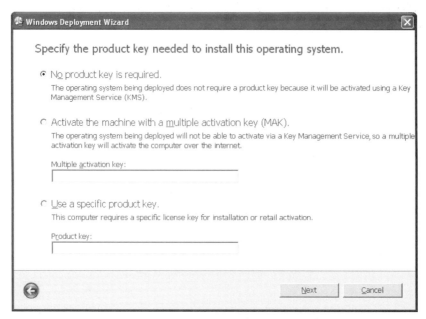

Figure 11-3   Windows Deployment Wizard product key page.

Using the Windows Deployment Wizard

The wizard presents the following options at this stage:

- The No Product Key Is Required option is used to configure a KMS client computer.

- The Activate The Computer With A Multiple Activation Key option lets you type a MAK, which is used with Slmgr.vbs to launch activation of the system.

- Use the Use A Specific Product Key option to enter a retail product key for retail editions of Windows Vista. (These systems require Internet or telephone activation following installation.)

Note   For the product key pages to be displayed, the value *SkipProductKey* in CustomSettings.ini must be set to *No*. CustomSettings.ini can be found in the Control folder within the Distribution share on the MDT 2008 server.

How It Works: Automating Activation in MDT 2008

In MDT 2008, you can automate product activation by configuring three values in CustomSettings.ini. Each deployment point has its own CustomSettings.ini, which you can edit by using Deployment Workbench or by locating it in the Control folder of the distribution share.

The three values are *ProductKey*, *OverrideProductKey*, and *SkipProductKey*. The value specified for *ProductKey* is injected into Unattend.xml. During the actual deployment process, the ZTIConfigure.wsf script will insert the product key into the Unattend.xml. The value of *OverrideProductKey* is used to run the Slmgr.vbs script to set a MAK key. The key will be applied by ZTILicensing.wsf during the state restore phase. The values assigned should be in the XXXXX-XXXXX-XXXXX-XXXXX-XXXXX format. Set *SkipProductKey* to *YES* to prevent the Windows Deployment Wizard from prompting for a product key. (See Figure 11-3.)

If you want to hard-code the values in the CustomSettings.ini (not secure, since these are clear text), here is an example:

[Default]

OverrideProductKey=XXXXX-XXXXX-XXXXX-XXXXX-XXXXX

For KMS activation, do not specify a value for *ProductKey* or *OverrideProductKey*. Client computers will automatically discover the KMS computer via DNS and activate with it.

Automating the Windows Deployment Wizard

In MDT 2008, information entered during the operating system build process is stored in the CustomSettings.ini file and in .xml files within the Control folder of the Distribution share. This information is used to answer certain questions normally asked by the Windows Deployment Wizard. Chapter 12 describes how to automate the build process.

Troubleshooting Volume Activation

Several issues can arise with volume activation; you can deal with some common issues quickly.

Common Problems

This section lists common issues that can arise with volume activation:

- **MAK depletion**   MAKs can become depleted through system maintenance that requires reactivation or through system replacements. You can request additional activations through the volume license portal through which the MAK was originally acquired, by telephone, or by contacting a Microsoft licensing partner.

- **MAK activation failure**   Loss of Internet connectivity is the most common cause of activation failure. Open Microsoft Internet Explorer and then test Internet connectivity. If Internet connectivity cannot be established or if MAK activation still fails, use an alternate method of activation, such as by telephone.

- **KMS count too low** If the number of computers that connect with KMS falls below 25, KMS client computers will not be activated, and activated KMS clients are in danger of letting their activation expire. Check the current count for the KMS computer by using the Slmgr.vbs with the *-dli* option. System Center Operations Manager 2007 also includes a rule to generate an alert if the KMS count falls below a configurable threshold.

- **KMS computer outage** KMS computer installations should be documented to decrease the chances of inadvertently removing an active KMS computer from the environment. If a KMS computer cannot be contacted, check the service computer itself to ensure that it is receiving requests from client computers. (Check for KMS 12290 event log entries.) Check server DNS entries and network connectivity between the client and the server.

- **KMS connectivity issues** Network routers, Windows Firewall with Advanced Security, and firewalls not from Microsoft can prevent access to KMS. Ensure that the KMS computer listening port (by default, port 1688/TCP) is open on the computer's firewall.

- **KMS computer event log wraps, overwriting events** During normal operation, the KMS computer generates a large number of 12290 events. Ensure that the KMS event log is configured with sufficient space to manage these events. If used, System Center Operations Manager 2007 automatically collects these events on a configurable, scheduled basis so that log wrapping is not an issue.

- **Activation behind a proxy server** Microsoft Knowledge Base article 921471, "Activation fails when you try to activate Windows Vista or Windows Server 2008 over the Internet," at *http://support.microsoft.com/kb/921471/en-us*, describes a situation in which the client attempting activation is behind a proxy server configured to use Basic authentication. Although this is not a default configuration for Microsoft Internet Security and Acceleration (ISA) Server, it is a valid configuration for many proxied networks.

If you must use Basic authentication, type the following URLs in the proxy's exception list:

- *http://go.microsoft.com/**
- *https://sls.microsoft.com/**
- *https://sls.microsoft.com:443*
- *http://crl.microsoft.com/pki/crl/products/MicrosoftRootAuthority.crl*
- *http://crl.microsoft.com/pki/crl/products/MicrosoftProductSecureCommunications.crl*
- *http://www.microsoft.com/pki/crl/products/MicrosoftProductSecureCommunications.crl*
- *http://crl.microsoft.com/pki/crl/products/MicrosoftProductSecureServer.crl*
- *http://www.microsoft.com/pki/crl/products/MicrosoftProductSecureServer.crl*

Note You can find more information about troubleshooting volume activation in the *Volume Activation 2.0 User Guide* at *http://technet.microsoft.com/en-us/windowsvista/bb892849.aspx*.

Event Log Entries

The entries shown in Table 11-9 appear in event logs on KMS clients and on KMS computers. Checking logs on both computers can lead to the discovery of causes of KMS activation failure.

All events are logged in the Windows Application Event Log except for event 12290, which is in its own event log under Applications And Services/Key Management Service.

Table 11-9   Event Log Entries for Volume Activation

EventID	Logged by	Description	Message
12288	Client	Remote procedure call (RPC) submit or submit failure	The client has sent an activation request to the KMS computer.
12289	Client	KMS response validation	The client has processed an activation response from the KMS computer.
12290	KMS	KMS service computer-side log for each request	An activation request has been processed.
12291	KMS	KMS initialization failure	KMS failed to start.
12292	KMS	Renewal timer initialization failure	KMS failed to initialize the renewal timer.
12293	KMS	DNS resource record publishing failure	Publishing the KMS to DNS failed.
12294	KMS	DNS resource record publishing success	Publishing the KMS to DNS is successful.

Resolving Activation Issues

If a computer running Windows Vista with SP1 configured for KMS activation fails to find a KMS in the initial 30-day grace period or fails to renew its activation within 210 days after activation, it persistently notifies the user (Windows Vista without SP1 enters RFM), and the desktop background changes to black. After the system is activated, it restores the desktop background and stops notifying the user.

Activating Non-Genuine Systems

When a system has exceeded its grace period, take one of the following actions to restore normal functionality:

- **Use KMS**   Reconnect a KMS-activated computer to the network that houses the KMS computer. The computer automatically contacts the KMS computer to renew its activation.

- **Enter a MAK**   If a KMS computer cannot be returned to its home network but is able to access the Internet, it can be restored using a MAK. If the computer is unable to connect to the Internet, you can also use telephone activation. Changing to the MAK does not provide an additional grace period. The computer continues to notify the user until it is activated—either by the Internet or by telephone. You can also supply the MAK through scripting by using the Slmgr.vbs script with the *-ipk* option. (See the section titled "Configuring KMS Activation" earlier in this chapter for details.) If a computer has exceeded its grace period, the Windows Activation dialog box seen in Figure 11-4 appears.

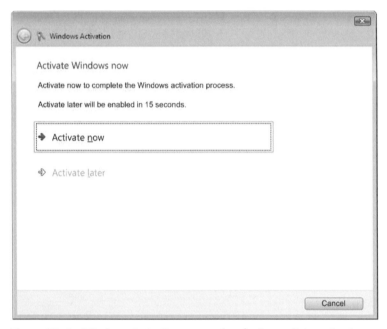

Figure 11-4   Windows Activation prompting for immediate activation.

Resetting the Activation Grace Period

The following list describes how to reset the activation grace period:

- **Sysprep /generalize**   Using the Sysprep command-line image preparation tool with the /generalize option resets the grace period for activation, providing an additional 30 days to activate the system. Because this is Sysprep, you will also be resetting the system state and creating a clean slate as when imaging the computer.

- **Slmgr.vbs –rearm**   You can return a computer to its initial activation state for the current license by using the Slmgr.vbs script with the -rearm option. This option resets the computer's activation timer and reinitializes some activation parameters, including a KMS client's unique machine ID (also known as client machine ID, or CMID). The number of times you can repeat this is limited and depends on how many times sysprep /generalize has been run to create the distribution media. The maximum number of rearms possible from shipped media is three.

Note   Using *-rearm* requires administrator privileges.

Allowing Standard Users to Activate Windows Vista

Typically, system functions such as Windows Activation require administrator privileges and are protected by Windows Vista User Access Control (UAC). An administrator can allow users to access this feature through the use of a special web page, as shown in Figure 11-5. The Standard User Product Activation Web Page includes Microsoft ActiveX controls to execute required scripts to apply a new key and activate. The page (productactivation.htm and windows-vista.png, contained in StandardUserProductActivation.zip) can be customized by an administrator and placed in the %SystemRoot%\System32\SLUI folder.

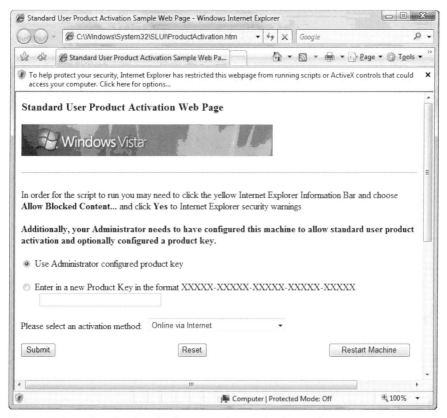

Figure 11-5   Using the Standard User Product Activation Web Page.

When a user starts a non-genuine computer, the Windows Activation dialog box opens and offers the user a chance to activate Windows Vista. When logged on, the user can open the Standard User Product Activation Web Page and choose the appropriate option to activate the computer.

To deploy the Standard User Product Activation Web Page for users

1. On the reference computer, install the web page (productactivation.htm and windowsvista.png, found in StandardUserProductActivation.zip) into a folder accessible by standard users, such as %SystemRoot%\System32\SLUI.

> **Note**   You can also use ImageX to insert these files into an existing image.

2. Customize the web page for the organization to include support information such as telephone numbers and contact information.

3. Optionally, configure an administrator-specified product key in a file named Pid.txt. The web page is designed to look for this file in the %SystemRoot%\System32\SLUI folder. The format of the product key is the standard five-by-five product key format used with Windows Vista (XXXXX-XXXXX-XXXXX-XXXXX-XXXXX).

4. Deploy this web page as a Microsoft Internet Explorer favorite to users by using one of the following methods:

    ■ Install as part of a reference image.

    ■ Use the Microsoft Internet Explorer Administration Kit (IEAK).

    ■ Use Group Policy in Active Directory environments.

    ■ Configure the FavoritesList option in the component Microsoft-Windows-IE-InternetExplorer in an unattended setup file.

Summary

Through volume activation, Windows Vista protects organizations' investments by preventing unauthorized use of their product keys. Three volume activation options are available to accommodate your organization's specific requirements.

OEM activation enables OEMs to pre-activate Windows Vista on their customers' computers. MAK activation is a straightforward approach to using a single product key to activate multiple computers. Use this option for computers that don't have regular access to the corporate network, such as lab computers, mobile computers, and so on. KMS activation is the easiest option, as it requires little effort to configure the KMS infrastructure and eliminates the burden of configuring product keys during the deployment process.

This chapter described the three options in detail. It described when to use each option and how to combine them as necessary. It also described in detail how to configure KMS activation by using the script Slmgr.vbs, the registry, and WMI.

Additional Resources

The following resources contain additional information and tools related to this chapter.

Related Information

- Microsoft eOpen at *https://eopen.microsoft.com/EN/default.asp*.

- Microsoft Volume Licensing Services (MLVS) at *https://licensing.microsoft.com/ eLicense/L1033/Default.asp*.

- MSDN at *http://msdn2.microsoft.com/en-us/subscriptions/default.aspx*.

- TechNet at *http://technet.microsoft.com/en-us/subscriptions/default.aspx*.

- The MOM pack for volume activation at *http://go.microsoft.com/fwlink/?LinkId=76333*.

- KMS for Windows Server 2008 at *http://www.microsoft.com/downloads/ details.aspx?FamilyID=bbf2eb61-2b30-4f2d-bccd-df53e220b8e9&DisplayLang=en*.

- Microsoft Knowledge Base article 921471, "Activation fails when you try to activate Windows Vista or Windows Server 2008 over the Internet," at *http://support.microsoft.com/ kb/921471/en-us*.

- Volume Activation 2.0 User Guide at *http://technet.microsoft.com/en-us/windowsvista/ bb892849.aspx*.

- Volume Activation Management Tool at *http://www.microsoft.com/downloads/ details.aspx?familyid=12044DD8-1B2C-4DA4-A530-80F26F0F9A99&displaylang=en*.

- Microsoft Knowledge Base article 925582, "The behavior of reduced functionality mode in Windows Vista," at *http://support.microsoft.com/kb/925582*.

- Microsoft Knowledge Base article 925616, "Error message when you start Windows Vista: 'Your activation period has expired,'" at *http://support.microsoft.com/kb/925616*.

Chapter 12
Deploying with Microsoft Deployment Toolkit

Windows Vista and the Windows Automated Installation Kit (Windows AIK) include the low-level tools necessary to deploy the operating system. However, they don't provide a framework for managing and automating high-volume Windows Vista deployments or business logic for managing complex projects. Microsoft Deployment Toolkit 2008 (MDT 2008) provides this framework and business logic, making it Microsoft's primary tool for deploying Windows Vista.

This chapter describes how to use MDT 2008 to deploy Windows Vista. It assumes that you've already created a distribution share in a lab and populated it with applications, device drivers, and packages. It also assumes that you've already designed and built custom Windows Vista disk images, as described in Chapter 6, "Developing Disk Images." This chapter helps you configure and customize MDT 2008 for Lite Touch Installation (LTI) and Zero Touch Installation (ZTI) deployment. ZTI includes using Microsoft Systems Management Server (SMS) 2003 and Microsoft System Center Configuration Manager 2007.

Introducing MDT 2008

The following sections introduce key concepts for using MDT 2008 to deploy Windows Vista. Specifically, the section titled "Deployment Scenarios" describes the scenarios that MDT 2008 supports, and the section titled "Comparing LTI and ZTI" describes each deployment method that MDT 2008 supports.

This chapter describes how to do both LTI and ZTI deployments. In MDT 2008, LTI and ZTI have a common base of code and functionality that blurs the distinction between the two methods. LTI relies entirely on MDT 2008, the Windows AIK, and potentially Windows Deployment Services (Windows DS). However, MDT 2008 supports two ZTI scenarios:

- **ZTI with SMS 2003**   When using MDT 2008 with SMS 2003, you use the Deployment Workbench to build disk images, as Chapter 6 describes. Then, you deploy those images by using the Operating System Deployment (OSD) Feature Pack.

- **ZTI with System Center Configuration Manager 2007**   When using MDT 2008 with System Center Configuration Manager 2007, you don't use the Deployment Workbench to build disk images. In fact, you don't use Deployment Workbench for anything other than editing the deployment database. That's because MDT 2008 integrates fully into System Center Configuration Manager 2007.

Deployment Scenarios

The following list describes the scenarios supported by MDT 2008:

- **New Computer**   A new installation of Windows is deployed to a new computer. This scenario assumes that there is no user data or profile to preserve.

- **Upgrade Computer**   The current Windows operating system on the target computer is upgraded to the target operating system. The existing user state migration data, user profile, and applications are retained (as supported by the target operating system).

- **Refresh Computer**   A computer currently running a supported Windows operating system is refreshed. This scenario includes computers that must be re-imaged for image standardization or to address a problem. This scenario assumes that you're preserving the existing user state data on the computer.

- **Replace Computer**   A computer currently running a supported Windows operating system is replaced with another computer. The existing user state migration data is saved from the original computer. Then, a new installation of Windows is deployed to a new computer. Finally, the user state data is restored to the new computer.

Based on your existing environment, you can select any combination of these scenarios in the deployment. For example, if you are upgrading only existing computers, only the Refresh Computer scenario or the Upgrade Computer scenario is necessary. If you're deploying new computers for some users and upgrading the remaining computers, use the Upgrade Computer, Replace Computer, and Refresh Computer scenarios as appropriate.

Comparing LTI and ZTI

In many instances, you will use a combination of LTI and ZTI to deploy the target operating systems to the destination computers. In MDT 2008, LTI and ZTI use the same common set of scripts and configuration files (such as CustomSettings.ini) for deploying the target operating system. However, in some instances one method of deployment may be more advantageous than the other.

The following list compares deploying operating systems using LTI versus ZTI (with SMS 2003 and System Center Configuration Manager 2007):

- **Using LTI with Deployment Workbench**   LTI requires minimal infrastructure to operate. You can deploy target operating systems over the network by using a shared folder or locally by using a removable storage device (CD, DVD, USB hard drive, and so on). You can initiate the deployment process automatically (by using Windows DS) or manually. You initially configure LTI by using Deployment Workbench and then further customize CustomSettings.ini for your environment. In LTI deployment, you provide configuration settings for groups of computers. The configuration settings for each individual computer are usually provided manually during the deployment process or through the deployment database. As a result, customizing LTI usually takes less effort than customizing ZTI.

- **Using ZTI with SMS 2003 and Deployment Workbench**   This scenario requires SMS 2003, SMS 2003 SP2, and the SMS 2003 OSD Feature Pack. You deploy target operating systems from SMS 2003 distribution points. You can initiate the installation process by SMS 2003 or by Windows DS. The ZTI deployment process is always initiated automatically. As with LTI, you initially configure ZTI with SMS 2003 by using Deployment Workbench and then further customize CustomSettings.ini for your environment. In ZTI with SMS 2003 deployment, you must provide all configuration settings for each target computer being deployed. By definition, there is no manual configuration in ZTI. As a result, customizing ZTI usually takes more effort than customizing LTI.

- **Using ZTI with System Center Configuration Manager 2007**   This scenario requires System Center Configuration Manager 2007. You deploy target operating systems from System Center Configuration Manager 2007 distribution points. As when using SMS 2003, you can start the process by using System Center Configuration Manager 2007 or Windows DS. Unlike when using SMS 2003, you don't use Deployment Workbench to build or customize images. Instead, MDT 2008 fully integrates into System Center Configuration Manager 2007 so that you perform almost all work within System Center Configuration Manager 2007. The only reason for using Deployment Workbench in this scenario is to edit the deployment database.

Deployment Points

Whereas a *distribution share* contains the files necessary to install and configure a build on a destination computer, a *deployment point* replicates a subset of those files and defines how to connect to them. For example, the distribution share might contain multiple operating systems and hundreds of applications. A deployment point defines which of those files to distribute and how to access them through a network connection or removable media.

You create deployment points by using the New Deployment Point Wizard in Deployment Workbench. The New Deployment Point Wizard allows management of the following types of deployment points. (See Chapter 6 for more information about deployment points.)

- **Lab or single-server deployment (LAB)**   A lab deployment point connects to the primary distribution share. You typically use a lab deployment point when building disk images in a lab environment. For example, Chapter 6 shows you how to use a lab deployment point to build images for LTI and images for ZTI with SMS 2003. A distribution share can have only one lab deployment point.

- **Separate deployment share (Network)**   Network deployment points are copies of the primary distribution share. Create the network deployment point on the same computer on which Deployment Workbench is running or on another computer. MDT 2008 replicates the chosen parts of the distribution share to the new network deployment point.

- **Removable media (Media)**   Media deployment points are folders containing a subset of the primary distribution share that you can copy to DVDs, external hard disks, or USB storage devices. You can use media deployment points to deploy to remote offices, home offices, mobile users, and so on.

- **SMS 2003 OSD (OSD)**   OSD deployment points are shared folders that you can use to create SMS OSD Feature Pack–managed images. Use this option only for ZTI-based deployments when using SMS 2003. You don't use OSD deployment points for System Center Configuration Manager 2007.

Resource Access

Before starting the deployment, create additional shared folders in which to store the user state migration data and the deployment logs. You can create these shared folders on any server that is accessible to destination computers. Refer to your deployment plan to guide you on server placement. The following list describes the shared folders you should create:

- **MigData**   Stores the user state migration data during the deployment process
- **Logs**   Stores the deployment logs during the deployment process

> **Note**   MigData and Logs are recommended shared folder names. You can use any name for these shared folders. However, the remainder of this chapter refers to these shared folders by these names.

During deployment to destination computers, the MDT 2008 deployment scripts connect to the deployment point shares and shared folders. Create accounts for use by these scripts when accessing these resources.

After creating the additional shared folders, configure the appropriate shared folder permissions. Ensure that unauthorized users are unable to access user state migration information and the deployment logs. Only the destination computer creating the user state migration information and the deployment logs should have access to these folders.

For each shared folder, disable inheritance and remove existing permissions. Then give the Domain Computers group the Create Folder/Append Data permission for each folder only. Repeat for the Domain Users group. Also, add the CREATOR OWNER group to each shared folder, giving it the Full Control permission for subfolders and files only. Also give each group that will have administrator access to migration data and log files the same permissions.

The permissions that you set in these steps allow a target computer to connect to the appropriate share and create a new folder in which to store user state information or logs. The folder permissions prevent other users or computers from accessing the data stored in the folder.

Using LTI with MDT 2008

Prior to deploying Windows Vista by using the LTI scenario with MDT 2008, be sure to perform the following steps, as described in Chapter 6:

- Add the appropriate resources to the distribution share. To add applications to the distribution share, see Chapter 8, "Deploying Applications."

- Create and customize task sequences that install Windows Vista as required.

- Create the lab deployment point in Deployment Workbench.

Creating Deployment Points

For LTI, you need to create separate deployment share or removable media deployment points to replicate the contents of the lab distribution share, specifically:

- Create a network deployment point when you want to create a deployment point in another location or across WAN links to reduce network traffic.

- Create a media deployment point when you need to deploy to computers that are unable to connect to network resources.

To create a network or media deployment point for LTI

1. In Deployment Workbench, right-click Deployment Points and then click New. Deployment Points is located under Deploy in the left pane.

2. On the Choose Type page of the New Deployment Point Wizard, click one of the following, and then click Next:

    ❑ **Separate Deployment Share**   Creates a new deployment share on the same computer on which Deployment Workbench is running, or on another computer. Choose this option when creating a deployment point for LTI on the network.

❑   **Removable Media**   Creates folders to deploy images by using removable media. Choose this option when creating a deployment point for LTI that you will distribute to users who can't connect to a network deployment point.

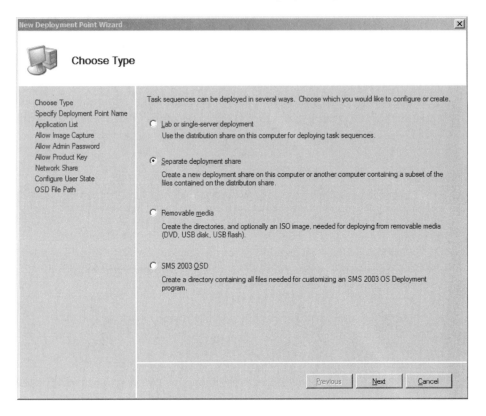

3. On the Specify Deployment Point Name page, in the Deployment Point Name text box, type a name for the deployment point and then click Next.

4. On the Application List page, clear or select the Allow Users To Select Additional Applications On Upgrade check box and then click Next. Enabling this option displays the page in the Windows Deployment Wizard that prompts users to select additional applications to be installed at the same time they are upgrading. The wizard page is displayed in Windows Deployment Wizard when performing an Upgrade scenario.

5. On the Allow Admin Password page, select the Ask User To Set The Local Administrator Password check box if you want to prompt the user for the local Administrator password during installation and then click Next.

6. On the Allow Product Key page, select the Ask User For A Product Key check box if you want to prompt the user for a product key during installation and then click Next.

7. On the Network Share page, provide the following information and then click Next. (The account in which you're running MDT 2008 must have permission to create the folder and share on the destination computer.)

   ❑ **Server Name**   The name of the computer that will host the shared folder

   ❑ **Share Name**   The share to be created on the computer that will host the shared folder

   ❑ **Path For Share**   The fully qualified path folder to share on the computer that will host the shared folder

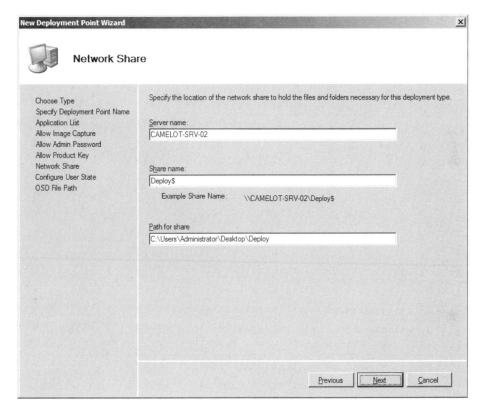

8. On the Configure User State page, select one of the following options, and then click Finish:

   ❑ **Automatically Determine The Location On The Network**   Allows the MDT 2008 deployment scripts and process rules to automatically determine the best location on the network.

   ❑ **Automatically Determine The Location On The Local System**   Allows the MDT 2008 deployment scripts and process rules to automatically determine the best location based on local available disk space on the target computer.

❑   **Specify A Location**   Saves the user state migration data to a specific location. In the Location text box, type the fully qualified path to the location for storing the user state migration data.

❑   **Do Not Save Data And Settings**   Discards any existing user state migration data. Choose this option if you're deploying a new computer with no existing data.

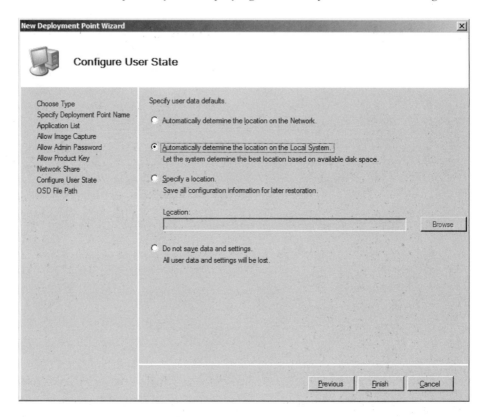

Note   MDT 2008 doesn't create the deployment point or any image files (.iso and .wim files) associated with it until you configure and then update it. To update a deployment point, right-click it and click Update. MDT 2008 creates the boot images for the deployment point in the deployment point's Boot folder. For more information about updating a deployment point, see Chapter 6.

Preparing Windows DS

In the deployment process, Windows DS servers are responsible for starting Windows PE on destination computers to prepare the computers for image installation. After you install and initially configure Windows DS (see Chapter 10, "Configuring Windows DS"), ensure that Windows PE images created by updating deployment points in Deployment Workbench have the appropriate flat-file image structures and add them to the Windows DS server.

For more information about setting up and configuring the Windows DS server, see the following resources:

- Chapter 10
- *Windows Deployment Services Update, Step-by-Step Guide*, which ships with Windows DS
- *Windows Deployment Services* Update help file (wds.chm), supplied with Windows DS

Windows DS is responsible for initiating the deployment process for Pre-boot eXecution Environment (PXE) boot-enabled destination computers. With MDT 2008, the LTI process is compatible with Windows DS only in mixed or native mode. If you're using both LTI and ZTI with SMS 2003 scenarios, you must use Windows DS in mixed mode.

Configuring Resources

In addition to the shared folders that the section titled "Resource Access" describes, the MDT 2008 scripts may require access to other resources, including application or database servers, such as Microsoft SQL Server 2005. The resources that the installation requires access to depend on the applications you've added to the distribution and the customizations you've made to MDT 2008 and the task sequence.

For LTI, you need to grant access to the deployment point to the credentials specified in one the following ways:

- UserID, UserPassword, and UserDomain properties in the CustomSettings.ini file. MDT 2008 uses these credentials to connect to the deployment point and other network resources. Make sure the credentials used in these properties have Read and Execute permission on the deployment point. By providing these credentials in CustomSettings.ini, you can fully automate the LTI installation process.
- Windows Deployment Wizard. If you don't provide the credentials in CustomSettings.ini, you provide the credentials necessary to connect to the deployment point when you start the Windows Deployment Wizard on the destination computer. Make sure that the credentials used to start the Windows Deployment Wizard have at least Read and Execute permission on the deployment point.

Make sure that the credentials used for LTI (defined in CustomSettings.ini or used to start the Windows Deployment Wizard) have read and execute access to the following resources:

- **Deployment point**   Configure access to the deployment point created in Deployment Workbench.
- **Any resources accessed by using the ZTIConnect.wsf script**   Configure access to resources that are referenced by using the ZTIConnect.wsf script.
- **Any resources on application or database servers**   Configure access to applications or databases that are accessed through the SQLServer, SQLShare, and Database properties.

> **Note** Other connections to the same servers, such as Named Pipes and Remote Procedure
> Call (RPC), use the same credentials listed here. Use the ZTIConnect.wsf script to establish
> these connections. For more information about the ZTIConnect.wsf script, see "Connecting to
> Network Resources" in the *Deployment Customization Desktop Samples* in MDT 2008.

Configuring CustomSettings.ini

CustomSettings.ini is the primary customization file for MDT 2008, particularly for LTI. The
customizations you perform are specific to your organization. The names of the servers,
default gateways for each subnet, MAC addresses, and other details are unique to your organization, of course. The customization that you perform configures the deployment processes to
run properly in your network environment. The examples in this section are provided as
guides to help you in your customization. For more information on other configuration
scenarios, see *Deployment Customization Desktop Samples* in MDT 2008.

The following listing shows a customized version of the CustomSettings.ini file after
completing the New Deployment Point Wizard in Deployment Workbench. The initial
contents of CustomSettings.ini depend on the answers given to the New Deployment Point
Wizard, of course. The section titled "Customizing CustomSettings.ini" later in this chapter
describes in more detail how to customize these settings for different computers.

CustomSettings.ini Modified by Deployment Workbench

```
[Settings]
Priority=Default
Properties=MyCustomProperty

[Default]
OSInstall=Y
ScanStateArgs=/v:5 /o /c
LoadStateArgs=/v:5 /c /lac
DeployRoot=\\NYC-AM-FIL-01\Distribution$
UserDataLocation=NONE
SkipAppsOnUpgrade=NO
SkipCapture=NO
SkipAdminPassword=YES
SkipProductKey=YES
```

The CustomSettings.ini file in the listing contains the property values for all the target
computers to be deployed using this version of the file. This version of the file contains no
values that are unique to a specific target computer, because all of the settings are defined
in the [Default] section. In this case, the target computer–specific configuration values are
manually provided during the installation process by using the Windows Deployment
Wizard. Table 12-1 explains the properties and corresponding values used in the listing.

> **Note**   In MDT 2008, the document *Toolkit Reference* defines these and dozens of other settings that you can define in CustomSettings.ini. Of all the guides in MDT 2008, the *Toolkit Reference* is the most useful, particularly for IT professionals already familiar with the MDT 2008 basic concepts.

Table 12-1   **Explanation of CustomSettings.ini Properties for LTI**

Line in CustomSettings.ini	Purpose
[Settings]	Indicates the start of the *[Settings]* section.
Priority=Default	Establishes the sequence in which the process parses subsections to locate values for the variables. In this example, the *[Default]* section is the only subsection that is parsed for variables.
Properties=MyCustomProperty	Indicates any additional properties to locate. The properties listed here are in addition to the properties listed in ZTIGather.xml. ZTIGather.wsf parses ZTIGather.xml to obtain a list of the properties. The property names defined here are added to them.
[Default]	Indicates the start of the *[Default]* section. The settings defined in this section apply to all computers.
OSInstall=Y	Indicates that the computer is supposed to perform an operating system deployment.
ScanStateArgs=/v:5 /o /c	Parameters passed to the ScanState.exe tool in the User State Migration Tool (USMT). These parameters are passed to ScanState.exe during state capture.
LoadStateArgs=/v:5 /c /lac	Parameters passed to the LoadState.exe tool in USMT. These parameters are passed to LoadState.exe during state restore.
UserDataLocation=NONE	Indicates where the user state migration data should be saved. The value *NONE* indicates that the user state migration data should not be saved.
SkipAppsOnUpgrade=YES	Indicates if the Windows Deployment Wizard prompts the user to install applications during an upgrade. If the property is set to *YES*, the wizard page is skipped and not displayed.
SkipCapture=YES	Indicates if the Windows Deployment Wizard prompts to capture an image. If the property is set to *YES*, the wizard page is skipped and not displayed.
SkipAdminPassword=YES	Indicates if the Windows Deployment Wizard prompts to set the local Administrator password. If the property is set to *YES*, the wizard page is skipped and not displayed.
SkipProductKey=YES	Indicates if the Windows Deployment Wizard prompts for a product key. If the property is set to *YES*, the wizard page is skipped and not displayed.

Automating the LTI Process

You can use LTI to automate much of the deployment process. ZTI provides full deployment automation using the MDT 2008 scripts, SMS 2003 or System Center Configuration Manager 2007, and Windows DS. However, LTI is designed to work with fewer infrastructure requirements.

You can reduce (or eliminate) the wizard pages that are displayed in the Windows Deployment Wizard during the LTI deployment process. You can also skip the entire Windows Deployment Wizard by specifying the SkipWizard property in CustomSettings.ini. To skip individual wizard pages, use the following properties (see the *Toolkit Reference* in MDT 2008 for a description of each property):

- SkipAdminPassword
- SkipApplications
- SkipAppsOnUpgrade
- SkipBDDWelcome
- SkipBitLocker
- SkipBitLockerDetails
- SkipBuild
- SkipCapture
- SkipComputerBackup
- SkipComputerName
- SkipDeploymentType
- SkipDomainMembership
- SkipFinalSummary
- SkipLocaleSelection
- SkipPackageDisplay
- SkipProductKey
- SkipSummary
- SkipTimeZone
- SkipUserData

> **Note**   Automating LTI by using CustomSettings.ini alone is not realistic. Defining custom settings for each computer by using CustomSettings.ini is difficult. The ideal tool to use for fully automating LTI is the MDT 2008 database, which enables you to easily associate settings with individual computers and define settings that apply to groups of computers. For more information about using the MDT 2008 database, see the section titled "Using the MDT 2008 Database" later in the chapter.

For each wizard page that you skip, provide the values for the corresponding properties that are normally collected through the wizard page in the CustomSettings.ini and BootStrap.ini files (or by using the MDT 2008 database). For more information on the properties that you need to configure in the CustomSettings.ini and BootStrap.ini files, see "Providing Properties for Skipped Windows Deployment Wizard Pages" in the *Toolkit Reference* in MDT 2008.

The following listing illustrates a CustomSettings.ini file used for a Refresh Computer scenario to skip all Windows Deployment Wizard pages. In this sample, the properties to provide when skipping the wizard page are immediately beneath the property that skips the wizard page.

CustomSettings.ini File for a Refresh Computer Scenario

```
[Settings]
Priority=Default
Properties=MyCustomProperty

[Default]
OSInstall=Y
ScanStateArgs=/v:5 /o /c
LoadStateArgs=/v:5 /c /lac /lae
SkipAppsOnUpgrade=Yes
SkipCapture=Yes
SkipAdminPassword=YES
SkipProductKey=YES

SkipDeploymentType=Yes
DeploymentType=REFRESH

SkipDomainMembership=Yes
JoinDomain=Americas
DomainAdmin=Administrator
DomainAdminDomain=Americas
DomainAdminPassword=

SkipUserData=yes
UserDataLocation=AUTO
UDShare=\\nyc-am-dep-01\Dellimage\OSDUsmt
UDDir=%ComputerName%

SkipComputerBackup=yes
ComputerBackuplocation=AUTO
BackupShare=\\nyc-am-dep-01\Dellimage\OSDBackup
BackupDir=%ComputerName%
```

```
SkipBuild=Yes
BuildiD=Enterprise

SkipComputerName=Yes
ComputerName=%ComputerName%

SkipPackageDisplay=Yes
LanguagePacks1={3af4e3ce-8122-41a2-9cf9-892145521660}
LanguagePacks2={84fc70d4-db4b-40dc-a660-d546a50bf226}

SkipLocaleSelection=Yes
UILanguage=en-US
UserLocale=en-CA
KeyboardLocale=0409:00000409

SkipTimeZone=Yes
TimeZoneName=China Standard Time

SkipApplications=Yes
Applications1={a26c6358-8db9-4615-90ff-d4511dc2feff}
Applications2={7e9d10a0-42ef-4a0a-9ee2-90eb2f4e4b98}
UserID=Administrator
UserDomain=Americas
UserPassword=P@ssw0rd

SkipBitLocker=Yes
SkipSummary=Yes
Powerusers1=Americas\JoinRis
```

Performing LTI Deployments

To deploy a computer using LTI, start the destination computer by running LiteTouch.vbs from the deployment point or by using the Windows PE boot image generated by updating the deployment point. Start the Windows PE boot image in either of two ways. One way is to burn the .iso images to a DVD. This process is slow and tedious. These ISO image files reside in the \Boot folder of the deployment point. The other way is to add the LiteTouchPE_x86.wim or LiteTouchPE_x64.wim image files to the Boot Images item of a Windows DS server. The .wim image files are in the \Boot folder of the deployment point. For more information about installing and configuring Windows DS, see Chapter 10.

Before beginning installation, verify that the folders in the following list no longer exist on the target computer:

- **%SystemDrive%\MININT**   This folder is preserved through the deployment process and contains deployment state information (such as user state migration information and log files).

- **%SystemDrive%_SMSTaskSequence**   This folder contains state information specific to Task Sequencer.

The Windows Deployment Wizard creates and uses these folders (on the drive where the operating system is installed) during the deployment process. If a previous deployment terminates abnormally, these folders may still exist on the target computer, and if you don't manually remove them, the process will continue from the point where the process abnormally terminated instead of starting from the beginning. Be sure to remove these folders, if they exist, before initiating deployment.

To start an LTI deployment using Windows Deployment Wizard

1. Start the Windows Deployment Wizard using one of the following methods:

   ❏ Start the wizard manually by connecting to the appropriate deployment point (for example, *servername*\Distribution$\Scripts) and typing **cscript litetouch.vbs**.

   ❏ Start the Lite Touch Windows PE image by using Windows DS. Any images created by Deployment Workbench automatically start the Windows Deployment Wizard. See Chapter 10 to learn how to add these boot images to Windows DS.

2. If prompted by the Welcome To Windows Deployment dialog box, click Run The Deployment Wizard and then click Next.

3. If prompted by the User Credentials dialog box, type the credentials necessary to connect to the deployment point (user name, domain, and password) and then click OK. The Windows Deployment Wizard starts automatically. You must use an account that has read and write access to the deployment point, such as an account that is a member of the local Administrators group on the computer that contains the deployment point.

4. On the Select A Task Sequence To Execute On This Computer page, choose a task sequence to run from the list of available task sequences and then click Next.

5. On the Specify The Product Key Needed To Install This Operating System page, select one of the following options and then click Next:

   ❏ **No Product Key Is Required**   Assign product keys to target computers by using a KMS.

   ❏ **Activate The Machine With A Multiple Activation Key (MAK)**   Assign a MAK to the target computer and activate the computer over the Internet. In the Multiple Activation Key text box, type the MAK to be assigned to the target computer.

   ❏ **Use A Specific Product Key**   Assign a specific license key for installation or retail activation. In the Product Key text box, type the product key to be assigned to the target computer.

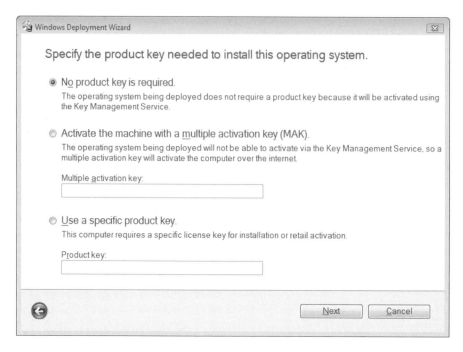

6. On the Choose A Migration Type page, select one of the following options, and then click Next:

    ❑ **Refresh This Computer**   Optionally, save the existing user state migration data. Deploy the desktop standard environment, including operating system and applications. Restore user state migration data on the same computer.

    ❑ **Upgrade This Computer**   Upgrade the existing computer by using the upgrade features supported by the target operating system. The upgrade process will fail on target computers that have users who logged on by using Remote Desktop sessions. Ensure that no users are connected to the target computer by Remote Desktop before initiating the Windows Deployment Wizard.

> **Note**   Replace This Computer isn't a choice on this page, because MDT 2008 provides a template task sequence specifically for the Replace Computer scenario.

7. On the Configure The Computer Name page, in the Computer Name text box, type the computer name to assign to the target computer and then click Next.

8. On the Join The Computer To A Domain Or Workgroup page, select one of the following options and then click Next:

    ❑ **Join A Domain**   Select this option to join an existing Active Directory domain. In the Domain text box, type the name of the domain to be joined. In the User Name text box, type the name of a user account that has sufficient permissions to create the computer account in the domain. In the Domain text box, type the name of the domain where the user account specified in the User Name text box is located. In the Password text box, type the password for the user account specified in the User Name text box. In the Organizational Unit text box, type the name of the organizational unit (OU) in Active Directory where the computer account will be created.

❏ **Join A Workgroup**   Select this option to join a Windows workgroup. In the Work-group text box, type the name of the workgroup to join.

9. On the Specify Where To Save Your Data And Settings page, select one of the following options and then click Next:

❏ **Automatically Determine The Location**   Allow the MDT 2008 deployment scripts and process rules to automatically determine the best location based on local available disk space on the target computer. Optionally, select the Allow Data And Settings To Be Stored Locally When Possible check box to give preference to storing the data locally.

❏ **Specify A Location**   Save the user state migration data to a specific location. In the Location text box, type the fully qualified path to the locations for storing the user state migration data.

❏ **Do Not Save Data And Settings**   Discard any existing user state migration data or deploy a new computer with no existing data.

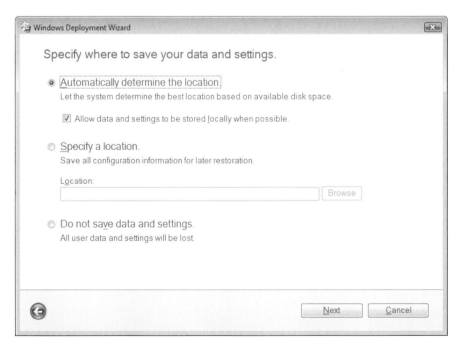

10. On the Specify Where To Save A Complete Computer Backup page, select one of the following options and then click Next:

   ❑ **Automatically Determine The Location**   Allow the MDT 2008 deployment scripts and process rules to automatically determine the best location based on local available disk space on the target computer. Optionally, select the Allow Data And Settings To Be Stored Locally When Possible check box to give preference to storing the data locally.

   ❑ **Specify A Location**   Save the computer image backup to a specific location. In the Location text box, type the fully qualified path to the locations for storing the computer backup.

   ❑ **Do Not Back Up The Existing Computer**   Discard any existing data on the target computer or deploy a new computer with no existing data.

> **Note**   Windows Complete PC Backup is a feature of Windows Vista only. MDT 2008 uses the ImageX utility during migration, because it works on all platforms that MDT 2008 supports. Use the Windows Complete PC Backup for enhanced disaster-recovery protection after migration is complete.

11. On the Locale Selection page, select one of the options from the What Is Your Locale list and then click Next. Also choose a keyboard locale from the Keyboard list. When upgrading a computer from a previous version of Windows, Deployment Workbench prevents selecting a locale. During an upgrade, Windows Vista upgrades the existing version of Windows with the same language that is currently installed.

12. On the Set The Time Zone page, select the time zone where the target computer is to be deployed.

13. On the Select One Or More Applications To Install page, select the appropriate applications to deploy and then click Next.

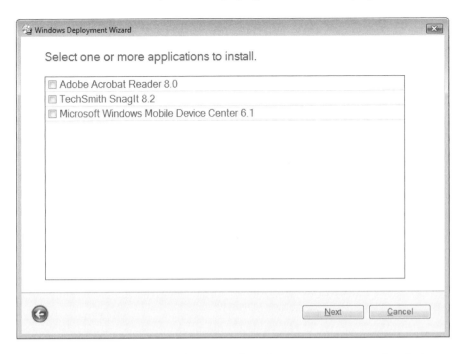

14. On the Administrator Password page, in the Administrator Password and Please Confirm Administrator Password text boxes, type the password for the local built-in Administrator account on the target computer and then click Next.

15. On the Specify The BitLocker Configuration page, select one of the following options, and then click Next:

- ❏ **Do Not Enable BitLocker For This Computer**   Deploy the target operating system without enabling BitLocker Drive Encryption.

- ❏ **Enable BitLocker Using TPM**   Enable BitLocker Drive Encryption and use Trusted Platform Module (TPM), a startup key, or both. You can also choose whether or not to create a recovery key in Active Directory.

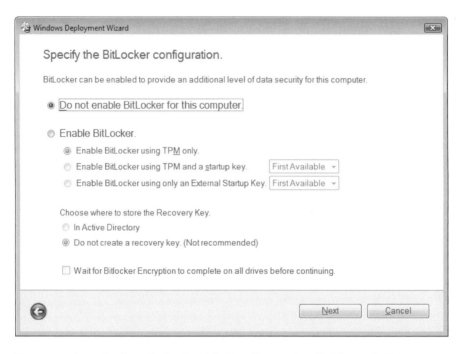

16. If prompted on the Specify Credentials For Connecting To Network Shares page, provide the following information and then click Next:

   ❑ **User Name**   The user name of the account that has appropriate permissions on the network shared folders used by the deployment scripts

   ❑ **Domain**   The domain where the user account, specified in the User Name box, is located

   ❑ **Password**   The password for the user account specified in the User Name box

17. Review the information on the Ready To Begin page and then click Begin. The Windows Deployment Wizard finishes and the deployment of the target operating system begins.

Using ZTI with SMS 2003

Prior to deploying Windows Vista by using the ZTI scenario with SMS 2003, be sure to perform the following steps, as described in Chapter 6:

■ Add the appropriate resources to the distribution share. To find out how to add applications to the distribution share, see Chapter 8, "Deploying Applications."

■ Create and customize task sequences that install Windows Vista as required.

■ Create the lab deployment point in Deployment Workbench.

■ Capture and add an operating system image to the distribution share that's prepared for SMS 2003 OSD. For step-by-step instructions, see Chapter 6.

Creating an OSD Deployment Point

For ZTI, you need to create an OSD deployment point. An OSD deployment point is a folder that contains the files necessary to deploy by using the SMS 2003 OSD Feature Pack.

To create an OSD deployment for SMS 2003

1. In Deployment Workbench, right-click Deployment Points and then click New. Deployment Points is located under Deploy in the left pane.

2. On the Choose Type page of the New Deployment Point Wizard, click SMS 2003 OSD and then click Next.

3. On the Specify Deployment Point Name page, in the Deployment Point Name text box, type a name for the deployment point and then click Next.

4. On the Network Share page, provide the following information and then click Next. (The account in which you're running MDT 2008 must have permission to create the folder and share on the destination computer.)

   ❑ **Server Name**   The name of the computer that will host the shared folder

   ❑ **Share Name**   The share to be created on the computer that will host the shared folder

   ❑ **Path For Share**   The fully qualified path folder to share on the computer that will host the shared folder

5. On the Configure User State page, select one of the following options and then click Next:

   ❑ **Automatically Determine The Location On The Network**   Allows the MDT 2008 deployment scripts and process rules to automatically determine the best location on the network.

   ❑ **Automatically Determine The Location On The Local System**   Allows the MDT 2008 deployment scripts and process rules to automatically determine the best location based on local available disk space on the target computer.

   ❑ **Specify A Location**   Saves the user state migration data to a specific location. In the Location text box, type the fully qualified path to the location for storing the user state migration data.

   ❑ **Do Not Save Data And Settings**   Discards any existing user state migration data. Also choose this option if you're deploying a new computer with no existing data.

6. On the OSD File Path page, type the path to the SMS 2003 OSD installation directory. Then click Create. MDT 2008 copies required files from the OSD installation to the deployment point.

> **Note**   MDT 2008 doesn't create the deployment point or any image files associated with it until you configure and then update it. For more information about updating a deployment point, see the section titled "Updating the Deployment Point" later in this chapter.

Preparing Windows PE for SMS 2003

To use ZTI with SMS 2003, you must create customized Windows PE images for use by the SMS 2003 OSD Feature Pack. You use Deployment Workbench to create the Windows PE images.

Although you can create the Windows PE images manually as described in Chapter 9, "Preparing Windows PE," Microsoft recommends that you use Deployment Workbench. You can also create a Windows PE image file by using the SMS 2003 OSD Feature Pack. However, you cannot customize the version that the SMS OSD Feature Pack creates, and it does not include Windows Management Instrumentation (WMI). Deployment Workbench automatically customizes Windows PE and adds WMI as an optional component.

Preparing the Windows PE images requires the following steps, each of which is described in further detail in this chapter:

1. Customize Windows PE by using Deployment Workbench.

2. Provide access to the contents of the .iso file created in the previous step.

3. Import the customized version of Windows PE into SMS 2003 OSD.

4. Create the SMS 2003 OSD Image Installation CD based on the customized Windows PE image.

Customizing Windows PE

You use Deployment Workbench to customize the version of Windows PE to use for ZTI deployment. You can also manually configure Windows PE in situations in which you want to provide more customization than provided by Deployment Workbench. Deployment Workbench provides enough customization to fully automate the Windows PE portion of the deployment process.

With MDT 2008, you use Windows PE 2004 or Windows PE 2005 for ZTI with SMS 2003 deployment. It doesn't support Windows PE 2.0 for ZTI. When customizing Windows PE, you will need the appropriate operating system source files to provide the files to build a bootable version of Windows PE. Table 12-2 lists the versions of Windows PE and the operating system source files required to build the corresponding version of Windows PE.

Table 12-2 Windows PE and Operating System Source Files

Windows PE Version	Required Operating System Source Files
Windows PE 2004	Windows XP SP2
Windows PE 2005	Windows Server 2003 SP1

Use Deployment Workbench to prepare a Windows PE .iso file. Burn the .iso file onto a CD and then create an SMS 2003 OSD Feature Pack image from the CD. You then create an SMS 2003 OSD Feature Pack package based on the SMS 2003 image. Transfer the SMS 2003 OSD Feature Pack image to a Windows DS server as a legacy image.

To use Deployment Workbench to prepare the Windows PE, follow these high-level steps, which the following sections describe in detail:

1. Add the appropriate operating systems to the distribution share.

2. Configure the Windows PE 2004/2005 tab.

3. Update the deployment point.

4. Burn a CD from the Windows PE .iso file that Deployment Workbench created.

> **Note** You can also manually customize Windows PE 2004 or Windows PE 2005 for use by ZTI with SMS 2003. You can use this process when you want to perform further customization of the Windows PE images. For more information on manually customizing Windows PE, see "Customizing Windows PE Manually" in *Preparing for SMS 2003* in MDT 2008.

Adding Required Operating Systems   Building Windows PE images for ZTI requires the Windows PE source files and the operating system source files matching them. Table 12-2 lists the operating system source files required for each version of Windows PE. You must add both sets of source files to the distribution share by using Deployment Workbench. Then, Deployment Workbench can automatically create the Windows PE images for you.

Add the Windows PE 2004 or Windows PE 2005 operating system source files to the distribution share before you prepare the Windows PE images. These become the Windows PE source for MDT 2008 with SMS 2003 deployments and are eventually deployed to the target computers. Chapter 6 describes how to add operating system source files to the distribution share by using Deployment Workbench.

You also need to add a version of Windows XP with Service Pack 2 or Windows Server 2003 with Service Pack 1 to the distribution share by using Deployment Workbench. Customizing Windows PE 2004 or Windows PE 2005 for use by ZTI with SMS 2003 requires certain files from these operating systems, as described earlier in this chapter. Chapter 6 describes how to add operating system images to a distribution share.

Configuring the Windows PE 2004/2005 Tab   In Deployment Workbench, configure the Windows PE 2004/2005 tab in the properties of an OSD deployment point before you create the .iso file that contains a customized version of Windows PE. Configuring the Windows PE 2004/2005 tab provides Deployment Workbench with the necessary information for automatically customizing Windows PE.

To configure the Windows PE 2004/2005 tab

1. In the Deployment Workbench console tree, click Deployment Points under Deploy.

2. If you haven't already created an OSD deployment point, create one by using the instructions in the section titled "Creating an OSD Deployment Point" earlier in this chapter.

3. In the details pane, right-click the deployment point that you want to use to prepare Windows PE and then click Properties.

> **Note**   Only OSD deployment points support ZTI with SMS 2003 and Windows PE 2004 or Windows PE 2005.

4. In the deployment point's Properties dialog box, click the Windows PE 2004/2005 tab.

5. In the Windows PE Source list, select the source for Windows PE created by the New OS Wizard in the Operating Systems item in the distribution share.

6. In the Windows Source list, select the source for Windows XP Service Pack 2 for Windows PE 2004 (or Window Server 2003 Service Pack 1 for Windows PE 2005) created by the New OS Wizard in the Operating Systems item in the distribution share.

7. In the Driver Injection section, in the Driver Group box, select the driver group in the Out-of-Box Drivers item in the distribution share.

8. In the Driver Injection section, select the Include All Network Drivers In The Selected Group check box if you want to include all network drivers.

9. In the Windows PE Customizations section, in the Custom Background Bitmap File box, type the path and filename of the background image to display when Windows PE is running.

10. In the Windows PE Customizations section, in the Extra Directory To Add text box, optionally type the path of a folder to include in the Windows PE image if you want to copy additional files and folders on to the image.

11. Click OK.

Updating the Deployment Point   Update the deployment point to create the .iso file that contains the customized version of Windows PE. Updating the deployment point causes Deployment Workbench to create a customized version of Windows PE by using the Windows PE source files, Windows XP Service Pack 2 or Windows Server 2003 Service Pack 2 source files, and the configuration settings on the Windows PE 2004/2005 tab.

To update the deployment point

1. In Deployment Workbench, click Deployment Points under Deploy.

2. In the details pane, right-click the OSD deployment point that contains the Windows PE image that you want to update and then click Update.

When the update completes, the Generic_OSD_x86.iso file appears in the OSD deployment point's Boot folder (not in the distribution share). The filename is Generic_OSD_x64.iso for 64-bit systems.

Providing Access to Windows PE Image

To import your customized Windows PE .iso file into SMS 2003 OSD, you need to provide access to the contents of the .iso file (Generic_OSD_x86.iso or Generic_OSD_x64.iso). The Update Windows PE Wizard in SMS 203 OSD needs to copy the contents of the .iso file to create a .wim file that can be used by SMS 2003 OSD. To provide the Update Windows PE Wizard access to the contents of the Windows PE .iso file, do one of the following:

■ Burn the contents of the .iso file to a CD. The .iso file that you created contains the customized version of Windows PE. The CD that you burn will be a copy of that image.

■ Load the .iso file on the computer running SMS 2003 (with a site server role) by using Microsoft Virtual CD-ROM Control Panel. You would install Microsoft Virtual CD-ROM Control Panel on the computer with the SMS site server role that has the SMS 2003 OSD Feature Pack installed.

For more information on either of these methods, see "How to customize Windows PE by using the source files that are included with the Microsoft SMS 2003 Operating System Deployment (OSD) Feature Pack" at *http://support.microsoft.com/kb/916902*.

Importing Windows PE into SMS 2003 OSD

After burning the Windows PE .iso image to a DVD, you must import it into the SMS 2003 OSD Feature Pack. To do that, use the SMS Administrator Console.

To import the Windows PE image into the SMS OSD Feature Pack

1. Start the SMS Administrator Console on the computer with the SMS site server role on which SMS 2003 OSD is installed.

2. In the SMS Administrator Console, right-click Image Packages, point to All Tasks, and then click Update Windows PE.

3. On the Welcome To The Update Windows PE Wizard page, click Next.

4. On the Windows PE Settings page, in the Source Folder text box, type the path to the Windows PE image file contents and then click Next.

5. On the Window PE Update Complete page, click Finish.

6. Close the SMS Administrator Console.

Creating the SMS 2003 OSD Image Installation CD

After you have imported your customized version of Windows PE into the SMS 2003 OSD Feature Pack, you are ready to create the .iso file that contains the SMS 2003 OSD Feature Pack operating system installation CD. The SMS 2003 OSD Feature Pack operating installation CD is used to initiate the deployment process when you are unable to initiate the process by using the SMS Client or Windows Deployment Services (Windows DS).

You start the target computer with the SMS 2003 OSD Feature Pack operating system installation CD to initiate the deployment process. After the process is initiated, the rest of the ZTI deployment process occurs without user interaction.

To create the SMS 2003 OSD operating system image installation CD

1. In the SMS Administrator Console, open the Image Packages item.

2. Right-click the Image Packages item, point to All Tasks, and then click Create Operating System Image Installation CD.

3. On the Welcome To The Operating System Image Installation CD Wizard page, click Next.

4. On the Installation Settings page, select the Automatically Choose The OS Package To Install By Running A Custom Program Or A Script check box and then click Next.

5. On the Install From SMS Distribution Points page, ensure that the central site server is specified in the list of servers, click Select All, and then click Next.

6. On the Automatically Select Operating System Package page, in the File Name box, type ***servername*\ZTI$\ZeroTouchInstallation.vbs**, where *servername* is the name of the server hosting the shared folder.

> **Note**   The ZeroTouchInstallation.vbs file must reside on the same server as the distribution point on which the image packages reside, because you cannot provide a second set of credentials to connect to a different server.

> **Note**   In the lab environment, add the */debug:true* option to the end of the command to provide additional debugging and troubleshooting information by using pop-ups displayed in Windows PE.

7. In the User Name box, type the name of the client account. Then, in the Password text box and the Confirm Password text box, type the password of the client account. The account credentials are stored on the installation CD in an encrypted format. Click Next.

8. On the Windows PE Settings page, if additional network drivers are required, select the Include Additional Network Drivers From This Location check box and then type the fully qualified path to any additional network drivers required in the environment.

9. If additional storage drivers are required, select the Include Additional Storage Drivers From This Location check box and then type the fully qualified path to any additional storage drivers required in the environment. Click Next.

10. On the Create CD Image page, in the Name text box, type the name of the CD image.

11. In the File Name text box, type the filename for the CD image.

12. On the Wizard Complete page, click Finish.

Preparing Windows DS

In the deployment process, Windows DS servers are responsible for starting Windows PE on destination computers in New Computer scenarios. For more information about setting up and configuring the Windows DS server, see the following resources:

■ Chapter 10

■ *Windows Deployment Services Update, Step-by-Step Guide*, which ships with Windows DS

■ *Windows Deployment Services* Update help file (wds.chm), supplied with Windows DS

Windows DS is responsible for initiating the deployment process for Pre-boot eXecution Environment (PXE) boot-enabled destination computers in New Computer scenarios. With MDT 2008, the ZTI with SMS 2003 process is compatible with Windows DS only in legacy or mixed mode. If you're using both LTI and ZTI with SMS 2003 scenarios, you must use Windows DS in mixed mode.

Configuring Resources

In addition to the shared folders described in the section titled "Resource Access" earlier in this chapter, the MDT 2008 scripts may require access to other resources, including application or database servers, such as Microsoft SQL Server 2005. The resources that the installation requires access to depends on the applications you've added to the distribution and the customizations you've made to MDT 2008 and the task sequence.

For ZTI, you must provide access to MDT 2008 resources to the SMS 2003 Advanced Client Network Access Account as well as the account specified in the CustomSettings.ini file using the UserID, UserPassword, and UserDomain properties. Make sure both accounts have appropriate access to the following resources:

■ **MDT 2008 deployment point**   Configure access to the deployment point created in Deployment Workbench.

- **Any resources accessed by using the Connect to UNC action**   Supply credentials when configuring a Connect to UNC action. In addition to a connection to shared folders, use the credentials supplied in the Connect To UNC action to authenticate to application or database servers.

- **Any resources on application or database servers**   Configure access to applications or databases that are accessed through the SQLServer, SQLShare, and Database properties. To authenticate on these application or database servers, use the Connect To UNC action to connect to any share on that server. Other connections, such as Named Pipes or Remote Procedure Call (RPC), will use the same credentials supplied in the Connect to UNC action.

Configuring ZTI Package Selection

Table 12-3 describes the phases of deployment of the operating system packages to the target computer. These phases occur during different steps in the deployment process.

Table 12-3   Deployment Phases and the Credentials Required

Shared Folder	Credentials Available
Validation	Any credentials.
State Capture	Any credentials.
Package Selection	Credentials in Ripinfo.ini that provide access to the distribution point. Credentials in Ripinfo.ini that provide access to the shared folder specified in the *[UserCommand]* section.
Preinstall	Any credentials.
Postinstall	Any credentials.
State Restore	Any credentials.

When Windows PE is used to prepare the target computer for installation, the SMS 2003 OSD Feature Pack uses the information in the Ripinfo.ini file to locate and run the command in the *[UserCommand]* section. (The command is ZeroTouchInstallation.vbs.) The SMS 2003 OSD Feature Pack ignores the *[ImageInfo]* section and passes control to ZeroTouchInstallation.vbs.

When you initiate the installation of Windows PE from a CD, the CD-based method ignores the *[UserCommand]* section and uses the information in the *[ImageInfo]* section. The CD-based method is not automated and requires manual selection of the image to install. This phase exists only when you are installing a new operating system installation (New Computer and Replace Computer scenarios).

During the Package Selection Phase, only a limited number of credentials are available. These credentials are stored in the Ripinfo.ini file and are used by OSD to provide access to the resources. The credentials supplied in Ripinfo.ini include credentials as specified in the following sections:

- *[RIPInfo]*   The credentials in *[RIPInfo]* are used to authenticate access for the shared folder on the distribution point where the package image is stored.

- **[UserCommand]**   The credentials in the *[UserCommand]* section are used to authenticate access to the shared folder where the command-line program is stored (which may also be on the same distribution point). The following listing is a sample Ripinfo.ini file:

Sample Ripinfo.ini

```
[RIPInfo]
Images=1
LocalImage=Yes
WizTitle=XPSP2
AllowMachineName=No
SiteCode=SMS
ManagementPoint=SERVER1:80
Reserved1=5EDBD289503F9DA5B84F6BA5320EACCB250DA92CA96A46E265F7732A4071BF0BD196976C659D66
Reserved2=E35E5E17C5AD023A280D3DBC9D5C0DF0042E583113F3A183CE7A9DDE0E15640B29D4AFC6BE517A
Reserved3=66AEA099AE219FD2A1AB1C4E97D1D3E9C67E58F60B

[UserCommand]
CommandLine=""\\Server1\SMSPKGE$\SMS00001\ZeroTouchInstallation.vbs" /phase:NewComputer"
/scriptlog
NetworkShare=\\Server1\SMSPKGE$\SMS00001
Reserved1=2BDEF2AE706BC58AEA1B1DF04F0BD8CF5C0AAB5DDB1F43E25F2D6967E794E2F62416DCD3736A27
Reserved2=965B5E10C5D97A355AA70B0082C94BADE1A90C403969116AF008F0618690CDAFB7A374FD7E7E56
Reserved3=C3ABADA631DDDC0686C3C3CFF748EB6F0E5FCE89AD
```

You can only connect to the following two servers during the Package Selection Phase:

- The distribution point specified in the *[RIPInfo]* section
- The server hosting the network share specified in the *[UserCommand]* section

> **Note**   If both of these sections point to the distribution point, you can access resources only on the distribution point.

Configuring SMS 2003

The following sections describe how to configure SMS 2003 for MDT 2008, including configuring the operating system package and the user state migration package.

Configuring the Operating System Image

Configure a particular operating system to use the ZTI scripts by using the SMS Administrator Console. The SMS 2003 OSD Feature Pack defines phases that occur during the deployment of the SMS 2003 OSD Feature Pack image to the target computer. Table 12-4 lists these phases. Configure each phase with the appropriate ZTI script settings to fully automate the Windows Vista deployment.

Prior to configuring the image, first create an SMS 2003 OSD Feature Pack package and program. For more information on how to perform these tasks, see the SMS 2003 OSD Feature Pack help.

Table 12-4   SMS 2003 OSD Phases

Phase	Custom Action Name	Phase Description
Validation	Zero Touch Installation—Validation	Performs validation checks to make sure that the operating system installation can proceed; specifically blocks installation on server operating systems
State Capture	Zero Touch Installation—State Capture	Gathers information from the configuration file, databases, and the local computer to determine how the image installation process should proceed, including whether or not enough space is available for a local USMT state backup; invokes USMT Scanstate as appropriate
Preinstall	Zero Touch Installation—Preinstall	Confirms that the necessary information has been gathered (or, in the New Computer or Replace Computer scenarios, gathers it)
Postinstall	Zero Touch Installation—Postinstall	Updates the Sysprep.inf file with information gathered in the previous custom actions
State Restore	Zero Touch Installation—State Restore	Invokes USMT Loadstate to restore the user state that was previously backed up

Before continuing, create an SMS 2003 OSD Feature Pack package and program for the target operating system. For more information on performing these tasks, see *Microsoft Systems Management Server 2003 Operating System Deployment Feature Pack Users Guide*.

To configure the Validation Phase actions

1. In the SMS Administrator Console, expand Image Packages, expand *Package*, and then click Programs (where *Package* is the name of the package to be configured).

2. In the details pane, double-click *Program* (where *Program* is the name of the program to be configured).

3. In the *Program* Properties dialog box (where *Program* is the name of the program to be configured), click the Advanced tab.

4. From the Phase list, select Validation and then click Add. The Add Action: Validation dialog box appears.

5. From the list of action types, select Custom and then click OK.

6. Complete the custom actions by using the information listed in Table 12-5, where *servername* is the name of the server hosting the distribution point shared folder.

Table 12-5   Validation Phase Actions

Field	Value
Name	Zero Touch Installation—Validation
Command line	ZeroTouchInstallation.vbs
Files	*servername*\ZTI$\BuildFolder*.*

To configure the State Capture Phase actions

1. In the SMS Administrator Console, expand Image Packages, expand *Package* (where *Package* is the name of the package to be configured), and then click Programs.

2. In the details pane, double-click *Program* (where *Program* is the name of the program to be configured).

3. In the *Program* Properties dialog box (where *Program* is the name of the program to be configured), click the Advanced tab.

4. From the Phase list, select State Capture and then click Add. The Add Action: State Capture dialog box appears.

5. From the list of action types, select Custom and then click OK.

6. Complete the custom actions by using the information listed in Table 12-6, where *servername* is the name of the server hosting the distribution point shared folder.

Table 12-6   State Capture Phase Actions

Field	Value
Name	Zero Touch Installation—State Capture
Command line	ZeroTouchInstallation.vbs
Files	*servername*\ZTI$\BuildFolder*.*

To configure the Preinstall Phase actions

1. In the SMS Administrator Console, expand Image Packages, expand *Package* (where *Package* is the name of the package to be configured), and then click Programs.

2. In the details pane, double-click *Program* (where *Program* is the name of the program to be configured).

3. In the *Program* Properties dialog box (where *Program* is the name of the program to be configured), click the Advanced tab.

4. From the Phase list, select Preinstall and then click Add. The Add Action: Preinstall dialog box appears.

5. From the list of action types, select Custom and then click OK.

6. Complete the custom actions by using the information listed in Table 12-7, where *servername* is the name of the server hosting the distribution point shared folder.

Table 12-7   Preinstall Phase Actions

Field	Value Name
Name	Zero Touch Installation—Preinstall
Command line	ZeroTouchInstallation.vbs
Files	*servername*\ZTI$\BuildFolder*.*

To configure the Postinstall Phase actions

1. In the SMS Administrator Console, expand Image Packages, expand *Package* (where *Package* is the name of the package to be configured), and then click Programs.

2. In the details pane, double-click *Program* (where *Program* is the name of the program to be configured).

3. In the *Program* Properties dialog box (where *Program* is the name of the program to be configured), click the Advanced tab.

4. From the Phase list, select Postinstall and then click Add. The Add Action: Postinstall dialog box appears.

5. From the list of action types, select Custom and then click OK.

6. Complete the custom actions by using the information listed in Table 12-8, where *servername* is the name of the server hosting the distribution point shared folder.

Table 12-8   Postinstall Phase Actions

Field	Value
Name	Zero Touch Installation—Postinstall
Command line	ZeroTouchInstallation.vbs
Files	*servername*\ZTI$\BuildFolder*.*

To configure the State Restore Phase actions

1. In the SMS Administrator Console, expand Image Packages, expand *Package* (where *Package* is the name of the package to be configured), and then click Programs.

2. In the details pane, double-click *Program* (where *Program* is the name of the program to be configured).

3. In the *Program* Properties dialog box (where *Program* is the name of the program to be configured), click the Advanced tab.

4. From the Phase list, select State Restore and then click Add. The Add Action: State Restore dialog box appears.

5. From the list of action types, select Custom and then click OK.

6. Complete the custom actions by using the information listed in Table 12-9, where *servername* is the name of the server hosting the distribution point shared folder.

Table 12-9   State Restore Phase Actions

Field	Value
Name	Zero Touch Installation—State Restore
Command line	ZeroTouchInstallation.vbs
Files	*servername*\ZTI$\BuildFolder*.*

Creating a ZTI User State Migration Package

When replacing an existing computer, you need to capture user state from the existing
computer so that you can restore the user state information to the new target computer. In
this scenario, you will not deploy an operating system to the existing computer. Instead, you
will create an SMS 2003 package and program to capture the user state information. This is a
standard SMS 2003 package and program, not an SMS 2003 OSD package and program. After
you create the SMS 2003 package and program, you advertise the package and program to the
existing computers (the computers being replaced).

Deployment Workbench automatically creates the source files required to create the SMS
package and program to perform user state capture. The files are stored in the OldComputer
folder immediately beneath the folder that is the root for the deployment point. For example,
if the root of the deployment point is C:\ZTI, the path to the source files for creating the SMS
package is C:\ZTI\OldComputer.

To create the SMS package and program to perform user state capture

1. On a computer that has the SMS administration tools installed, start the SMS
    Administrator Console.

2. In the console tree, open the Packages item.

3. In the console tree, right-click Packages, click New, and then click Package.

4. On the General tab, in the Name box, type **package_name**, where *package_name* is an
    appropriate name for the package. (For example, type **MDT 2008 Old Computer Package**.)

5. On the Data Source tab, click This Package Contains Source Files and then click Set. In
    the Set Source Directory dialog box, in Source Directory, type **unc_path**, where *unc_path*
    is the UNC path to the OldComputer folder on the distribution point. (For example,
    type **\\nyc-fs-01\ZTI$\OldComputer**.) Click OK.

6. In the console tree, expand Packages, expand *package_name* (where *package_name* is the
    name of the package you created in the previous step), right-click Programs, click New,
    and then click Program.

7. On the General tab, in the Name box, type **program_name**, where *program_name* is an
    appropriate name for the program. (For example, type **Old Computer State Capture**.)
    In the Command Line text box, type **ZeroTouchInstallation.vbs /debug:true**.

8. On the Environment tab, in the Program Can Run dialog box, select Whether Or Not A
    User Is Logged On.

9. In the console tree, open Advertisements, right-click Advertisements, click All Tasks, and then click Distribute Software.

10. On the Welcome To The Distribute Software Wizard page, click Next.

11. On the Package page, click Select An Existing Package.

12. In the Packages dialog box, select the package you created earlier and then click Next.

13. On the Distribution Points page, select the appropriate distribution points for your environment and then click Next.

14. On the Advertise A Program page, click Next.

15. On the Select A Program To Advertise page, in the Programs dialog box, select the program you created earlier and then click Next.

16. On the Advertisement Target page, select or create a collection that contains the computers to be replaced (the old computers). Click Next.

17. On the Advertisement Name page, in the Name text box, type ***advertisement_name*** (where *advertisement_name* is the name for the advertisement) and then click Next.

18. On the Advertise To Subcollections page, select to advertise to subcollections as appropriate for the collection you selected.

19. On the Advertisement Schedule page, select the appropriate schedule for your environment.

20. On the Assign Program page, select whether or not the program is mandatory after a period of time based on your environment.

21. On the Completing The Distribute Software Wizard page, review the information in the Details dialog box and then click Finish.

Configuring CustomSettings.ini

The file CustomSettings.ini is the primary file you use to customize MDT 2008 deployment. The customizations you perform are specific to your organization. For example, the names of the servers, default gateways for each subnet, MAC addresses, and other details are unique to your organization, of course. The customization that you perform configures the deployment processes to run properly in your network environment. The examples in this section are provided as guides to help you in your customization. For more information on other configuration scenarios, see *Toolkit Reference* in MDT 2008.

For ZTI, you must customize the configuration of MDT 2008 to provide full automation of the ZTI deployment process. The target computer–specific configuration values are added manually after you run the New Deployment Point Wizard and before the installation process begins. The following list shows a version of the CustomSettings.ini file after further customization to include target computer–specified settings. Table 12-10 explains the properties and corresponding values used in the listing.

CustomSettings.ini file Customized for Target Computer Settings

```
[Settings]
Priority=Default, MACAddress
Properties=MyCustomProperty

[Default]
OSInstall=Y
ScanStateArgs=/v:5 /o /c
LoadStateArgs=/v:5 /c /lac
UserDataLocation=NONE
OSDINSTALLSILENT=1

[00:0F:20:35:DE:AC]
OSDNEWMACHINENAME=HPD530-1
OSDINSTALLPACKAGE=DAL00342
OSDINSTALLPROGRAM=CustomVista

[00:03:FF:FE:FF:FF]
OSDNEWMACHINENAME=BVMXP
OSDINSTALLPACKAGE=NYC00002
OSDINSTALLPROGRAM=SpecialVista
```

Table 12-10   Explanation of CustomSettings.ini Properties for ZTI

Line in CustomSettings.ini	Purpose
[Settings]	Indicates the start of the *[Settings]* section.
Priority=Default, MACAddress	Establishes the sequence in which the process parses subsections to locate values for the variables. In this example, the *[Default]* section is parsed first and then the section that corresponds to the media access control (MAC) address of the target computer (MACAddress).
	The sections for the target computers (*[00:0F:20:35:DE:AC]* and *[00:03:FF:FE:FF:FF]*) contain computer-specific settings.
Properties=MyCustomProperty	Indicates any additional properties to locate. The properties listed here are in addition to the properties listed in ZTIGather.xml. ZTIGather.wsf parses ZTIGather.xml to obtain a list of the properties.
[Default]	Indicates the start of the *[Default]* section.
OSInstall=Y	Indicator of whether or not the target computer is authorized to have the target operating system installed.
ScanStateArgs=/v:5 /o /c	Parameters passed to the ScanState.exe tool in the USMT. These parameters are passed to ScanState.exe during the State Capture Phase.
LoadStateArgs=/v:5 /c /lac	Parameters passed to the LoadState.exe tool in USMT. These parameters are passed to LoadState.exe during the State Restore Phase.
UserDataLocation=NONE	Indicates where the user state migration data should be saved. The value *NONE* indicates that the user state migration data should not be saved.

Table 12-10   Explanation of CustomSettings.ini Properties for ZTI

Line in CustomSettings.ini	Purpose
OSDINSTALLSILENT=1	Controls the display of Microsoft Systems Management Server (SMS) 2003 Operating System Deployment (OSD) Feature pack (OSD_wizards). When the property is set to a value of 1, no wizard pages are displayed.
[00:0F:20:35:DE:AC]	Section that contains all the properties and settings that are specific to the target computer with the matching MAC address. In this sample, the target computer has a MAC address of [00:0F:20:35:DE:AC].
[00:03:FF:FE:FF:FF]	Section that contains all the properties and settings that are specific to the target computer with the matching MAC address. In this sample, the target computer has a MAC address of [00:03:FF:FE:FF:FF].
OSDNEWMACHINENAME=HPD530-1 OSDNEWMACHINENAME=BVMXP	Specifies the new computer name to be assigned to the target computer by the SMS OSD Feature Pack. In this sample, the computers names HPD530-1 and BVMXP are assigned to each respective target computer.
OSDINSTALLPACKAGE=DAL00342 OSDINSTALLPACKAGE=NYC00002	Specifies the SMS OSD Feature Pack package to install on the target computer. In this sample, the package names DAL00342 and NYC00002 are assigned to each respective target computer.
OSDINSTALLPROGRAM=CustomVista OSDINSTALLPROGRAM=SpecialVista	Specifies the name of the SMS OSD Feature Pack program to run for the specified package (OSDInstall-Package). In this sample, the package names Custom-Vista and SpecialVista are assigned to each respective target computer.

Performing ZTI Deployments

After an SMS 2003 OSD package is prepared for deployment, you use the SMS Administrator Console to begin deployment. This section describes how to initiate deployment. For more information about how to run the Deployment Wizard, see *Microsoft Systems Management Server 2003 Operating System Deployment Feature Pack Users Guide*.

Before beginning installation, verify that the folders in the following list no longer exist on the target computer:

- **%SystemDrive%\MININT**   This folder is preserved through the deployment process and contains deployment state information (such as user state migration information and log files).

- **%SystemDrive%_SMSTaskSequence**   This folder contains state information specific to Task Sequencer.

The Windows Deployment Wizard creates and uses these folders (on the drive where the operating system is installed) during the deployment process. If a previous deployment terminates abnormally, these folders may still exist on the target computer, and if you don't manually remove them, the process will continue from the point where the process abnormally terminated instead of starting from the beginning. Remove these folders, if they exist, before initiating deployment.

To start a deployment in the SMS Administrator Console

1. In the Refresh Computer scenario, ensure that the SMS package for user state migration has been deployed and completed for each target computer. For more information on creating the SMS package for user state migration, see the section titled "Creating a ZTI User State Migration Package" earlier in this chapter.

2. In the SMS Administrator Console, open the SMS OSD Feature Pack operating system image to be deployed.

3. Select the appropriate distribution points.

4. Select the applications to advertise.

5. Select the target collection for the image.

> **Note**   The images distributed to the distribution points are very large. For environments in which low-speed links connect sites, the images may not be available on the distribution points within the site for long periods of time (possibly 24 hours or longer).

Using ZTI with System Center Configuration Manager 2007

Using MDT 2008 with System Center Configuration Manager 2007 is far different than using MDT 2008 with SMS 2003. When using MDT 2008 with SMS 2003, you still use the Deployment Workbench to stock the distribution share, build and capture images, and so on. When using MDT 2008 with System Center Configuration Manager 2007, however, you don't use the Deployment Workbench for these tasks. Instead, MDT 2008 integrates directly into System Center Configuration Manager 2007. You only ever use Deployment Workbench to edit the MDT 2008 database. You'll also notice that for customers who already have a System Center Configuration Manager 2007 infrastructure in place, using MDT 2008 with System Center Configuration Manager 2007 is more streamlined than using it with SMS 2003. The integration of MDT 2008 with System Center Configuration Manager 2007 is clearly a positive thing for most customers.

Before using System Center Configuration Manager 2007 to deploy images to target computers, ensure that the deployment environment is properly configured to run ZTI with System Center Configuration Manager 2007:

1. Install System Center Configuration Manager 2007. For more information about installing and configuring System Center Configuration Manager 2007, see *http://technet.microsoft.com/en-us/library/bb693836.aspx*.

2. Upgrade the Solution Accelerator for Business Desktop Deployment (BDD) 2007 to MDT 2008 or install MDT 2008. An upgrade path exists from BDD 2007 to MDT 2008. For additional information on this capability, see the *Getting Started Guide* in MDT 2008. For more information about installing MDT 2008, see Chapter 4, "Planning Deployment."

> **Note**   For integrated System Center Configuration Manager 2007 support with Deployment Workbench, install Microsoft Deployment on each computer running the Configuration Manager console. This allows you to use MDT 2008 and System Center Configuration Manager 2007 integration on each server running System Center Configuration Manager 2007.

3. Enable Microsoft Deployment integration with the System Center Configuration Manager 2007. The following section, "Enabling System Center Configuration Manager 2007 Console Integration," provides more information.

Enabling System Center Configuration Manager 2007 Console Integration

Before you can use the System Center Configuration Manager 2007 integration features of MDT 2008, run the System Center Configuration Manager 2007 integration script. The script copies the appropriate integration files to the folder in which System Center Configuration Manager 2007 is installed. It also adds Windows Management Instrumentation (WMI) classes for the new MDT 2008 custom actions. The classes are added by compiling a new Managed Object Format (MOF) file that contains the new class definitions.

To run the System Center Configuration Manager 2007 Integration script

1. Close the System Center Configuration Manager 2007 console.

2. Click Start, click All Programs, click Microsoft Deployment Toolkit, and then click Configure ConfigMgr Integration. The integration script starts.

3. On the Options tab, click Install The ConfigMgr Extensions.

4. In the Site Server Name box, type the name of the System Center Configuration Manager 2007 server on which to install MDT 2008 integration.

5. In the Site Code box, type the System Center Configuration Manager 2007 site code to install MDT 2008 integration.

6. Click Finish.

Configuring Resource Access

During deployment to target computers, the System Center Configuration Manager 2007 client connects to the distribution point shares and shared folders. Create accounts within System Center Configuration Manager 2007 for the client to use when accessing these resources. (The following sections provide more details about each step required.)

To configure the appropriate resource access

1. Configure the System Center Configuration Manager 2007 Network Access account.

2. Create additional shared folders.

Configure the Network Access Account

The System Center Configuration Manager 2007 client needs an account to provide credentials when accessing the System Center Configuration Manager 2007 distribution points, MDT 2008 deployment points, and shared folders. This account is called the Network Access account.

To configure the Network Access account

1. Create the user account and password in an Active Directory domain.

2. On a computer that has the System Center Configuration Manager 2007 administration tools installed, start the Configuration Manager console.

3. In the Configuration Manager console, in the console tree, click Client Agents. Client Agents is located under Site Database, Site Management, *site*, Site Settings.

4. In the details pane, right-click Computer Client Agent and then click Properties.

5. In the Computer Client Agent Properties dialog box, click the General tab. In Network Access Account, in Account (Domain\User), click Set.

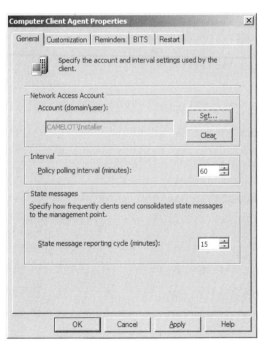

6. In the Windows User Account dialog box, type the name and password of the account to use. Then, confirm the password in the Confirm Password box.

Create Additional Shared Folders

After configuring the Network Access account, create an additional shared folder in which to store deployment logs. System Center Configuration Manager 2007 uses a state migration point to store migration data, so migration data is not needed. See the section titled "Resource Access" earlier in this chapter for more information about the logs share.

The shared permissions on the logs folder should include the Advanced Client account. The default permissions set on the System Center Configuration Manager 2007 distribution point shares should provide the appropriate resource access. The permissions set allow a target computer to connect to the appropriate share and create deployment logs. The folder permissions should prevent other users or computers from accessing the data stored in the folder.

For System Center Configuration Manager 2007 to capture and restore user data, it must be configured as a user state migration point. For additional information about setting up System Center Configuration Manager 2007 for this role, see the Configuration Manager Documentation Library at *http://technet.microsoft.com/en-us/library/bb680651.aspx*.

Configuring System Center Configuration Manager 2007 to Respond to PXE Boot Requests

You can configure System Center Configuration Manager 2007 to respond to Pre-Boot Execution Environment (PXE) boot requests using Windows DS. This integration allows System Center Configuration Manager 2007 to directly service PXE boot requests received by Windows DS as a PXE service point, which in turn allows target computers to boot images that System Center Configuration Manager 2007 manages using PXE.

Configure a computer running System Center Configuration Manager 2007 with the PXE service point role. The PXE service point responds to PXE boot requests made by computers defined in System Center Configuration Manager 2007 and then interacts with System Center Configuration Manager 2007 infrastructure to determine the appropriate deployment actions to take. In addition to the methods described in this chapter, you can use the traditional Windows DS methods for responding to PXE boot requests. For more information, see Chapter 10.

To configure System Center Configuration Manager 2007 to respond to PXE boot requests

1. Ensure that the required infrastructure exists to support integration (especially Active Directory, DHCP, and Windows DS). For more information on ensuring that the required infrastructure exists, see Chapter 10.

2. Configure a computer running System Center Configuration Manager 2007 with the PXE service point role. For more information on configuring the PXE service point role in System Center Configuration Manager 2007, see "How to Configure the PXE Service Point" in the Configuration Manager Documentation Library included with System Center Configuration Manager.

3. Import target computer information and assign the computer to a System Center Configuration Manager 2007 collection. For more information about importing target computer information, see "How to Add a New Computer to the Configuration Manager 2007 Database" in the Configuration Manager Documentation Library included with System Center Configuration Manager and the section titled "Defining Computers in System Center Configuration Manager 2007" in this chapter.

4. Create and advertise the PXE operating system deployment task sequence to the target collection or device (imported in the previous step).

See the following resources for more information:

- Creating task sequences: "How to Manage Task Sequences" in the Configuration Manager Documentation Library included with System Center Configuration Manager

- Advertising task sequences: "How to Advertise Task Sequences" in the Configuration Manager Documentation Library included with System Center Configuration Manager

Note   The task sequence must be advertised with the Make This Task Sequence Available To Boot Media And PXE check box enabled. If this box is not selected, the task sequence will not be available for PXE deployments.

Defining Computers in System Center Configuration Manager 2007

System Center Configuration Manager 2007 does not support running task sequences on computers that have not been defined to the System Center Configuration Manager 2007 database. To work around this limitation, MDT 2008 offers two scenarios: boot media and PXE boot.

Boot Media

MDT 2008 provides an operating system media pre-execution hook. This hook is executed before System Center Configuration Manager 2007 checks to determine if the computer is defined within the System Center Configuration Manager 2007 database. This hook allows the executed command to take steps to add the computer to the System Center Configuration Manager 2007 database. It also adds the computer to a collection so that the computer receives at least one task sequence.

On the New Boot Image page, the Import Microsoft Deployment Task Sequence Wizard has a check box named Add Media Hook Files For Unknown Computer Support With Boot Media. If you select this check box, the script files needed to run a new wizard as part of the pre-execution hook are added to the boot image being created. A URL for a Web service can verify whether or not the computer is defined to System Center Configuration Manager 2007. The Web service must be deployed to a Web server, and you must add the computer to the System Center Configuration Manager 2007 console and to a collection. For more information about the operating system media pre-execution hook, see "Operating System Media Pre-Execution Hook" at *http://technet.microsoft.com/en-us/library/bb694075.aspx.*

To set up a Web service to use with the operating system media pre-execution hook

1. Verify a System Center Configuration Manager 2007 server configured with the Server Locator Point (SLP) exists in the environment. This would normally be the central site server, because it needs to know the boundaries of all System Center Configuration Manager 2007 sites in the hierarchy. The Microsoft Deployment Web service will contact the SLP to determine the System Center Configuration Manager 2007 site code in which a computer is assigned.

2. Verify MDT 2008 is installed on a server running Internet Information Services (IIS). This does not have to be the same computer used for other MDT 2008 functions, although it typically would exist on that server. The server must have the Microsoft .NET Framework 2.0 installed. If .NET 2.0 was installed after IIS, you must run Aspnet_regiis.exe to add ASP.NET support to IIS. See *http://msdn2.microsoft.com/en-us/library/k6h9cz8h(VS.80).aspx* for more information.

3. In the IIS Manager Microsoft Management Console (MMC), right-click the default website (or any other appropriate website) and then click Add Application. Provide an alias, such as Microsoft Deployment, and then the path. For example, %ProgramFiles%\Microsoft Deployment Toolkit.

4. Edit the Web.config file in the installation directory (%ProgramFiles%\Microsoft Deployment Toolkit\web.config) to specify the name of the System Center Configuration Manager 2007 server running the SLP, in addition to the name of the server running the central site System Center Configuration Manager 2007 provider. Usually, both of these will be set to the same server name. The Web service will normally run as the NETWORK SERVICE account. If System Center Configuration Manager 2007 is running on the same computer, NT AUTHORITY\NETWORK SERVICE would need permissions to System Center Configuration Manager 2007. If System Center Configuration Manager 2007 is running on a different computer, the computer account (such as DOMAIN\COMPUTER$) would need permissions. In either case, you can edit the web.config to specify an account to be used, done through uncommenting the <identity> entry. Whatever account you specify needs to have permissions to import computer entries, check site boundaries, and modify collections.

5. Test the Web service using a Web browser. Specify a URL using the server name and the application created in the previous step. For example, open *http://*servername/ *MicrosoftDeployment/UnknownComputer.asmx.* You should see a Web page that says the following operations are supported:

   ❏ AddComputer

   ❏ GetADSite

   ❏ GetAssignedSite

   ❏ IsComputerKnown

6. Click the GetADSite link and then click Invoke on the resulting page to test the GetAD-Site Web service. This Web service returns the Active Directory site name for the TCP/IP address the client used to connect to the Web service. This might not return a valid name if the Web service is executed from a web browser on the same host, because the loopback address of 127.0.0.1 is not a member of an Active Directory site.

7. On the original page that lists the supported operations, click the GetAssignedSite link. Specify the IP address and subnet address of a client that should be within the boundaries of one of the System Center Configuration Manager 2007 sites in the hierarchy, and then click Invoke. The subnet address is the IP address with the mask applied. If the client's IP address is 10.1.1.1 with a subnet mask of 255.255.255.0, the subnet address would be 10.1.1.0. Verify that the returned site code is correct. If no site code is returned, verify the SLP server name configured and make sure the site boundaries are configured correctly.

8. On the original page that lists the supported operations, click the IsComputerKnown link. Specify either a media access control (MAC) address or a system management basic input/output system (SMBIOS) globally unique identifier (GUID), or both, for a computer already known to a ConfigMgr site, and the site code for that site and then click Invoke. Verify the results.

9. On the original page that lists the supported operations, click the AddComputer link. Specify a site code to which the computer should be added, the computer name to be assigned (this can be a temporary name, to be overridden when the computer becomes a System Center Configuration Manager 2007 client), at least one of the MAC address and SMBIOS GUID properties, and optionally, a collection to which the computer should be added. This collection must be owned by the specified site. Typically this would be a collection associated with an operating system deployment task sequence.

10. When all of the Web services have been validated, use the Import Microsoft Deployment Task Sequence Wizard to create a new boot image. As part of that boot image creation process, specify that you want to include a media hook and specify the Web service URL that was created in this section.

PXE Boot

System Center Configuration Manager 2007 integrates with Windows DS to support PXE boot to known computers. If the computer is not known to the local System Center Configuration Manager 2007 site, it will not respond to the PXE request. To work around this problem, MDT 2008 offers a PXE filter, which hooks into Windows DS and adds new computers to the System Center Configuration Manager 2007 database before the console sees the request. By doing so, System Center Configuration Manager 2007 can respond to the request.

A wizard provides the means to install the new PXE filter. To execute the wizard, click Start, click All Programs, click Microsoft Deployment, and then click Configure WDS PXE Filter. This action requires that Microsoft Deployment be installed on the Windows DS server and that Windows DS be running the Systems Management Server 2003 PXE role.

The PXE filter calls PXEFilter.vbs, a Microsoft Visual Basic Scripting Edition (VBScript) file located in the %ProgramFiles%\Microsoft Deployment Toolkit\Scripts folder, which determines whether or not to add the computer to the System Center Configuration Manager 2007 database. You must edit the script for each installation to specify the name of the System Center Configuration Manager 2007 server, the site code of the server, the collection ID to which new computers are added, and (optionally) the credentials required for a connection to the Systems Management Server 2003 provider remotely. Credentials are required only when the PXE server is not on the same computer as System Center Configuration Manager 2007.

Making these changes to the scripts will result in System Center Configuration Manager 2007 responding to PXE requests from all unknown computers. Ensure that operating systems are not deployed to computers they were not intended for. It might be necessary to edit the scripts to filter the requests using the IP address of the request or handle only requests received from computers on dedicated staging subnets and ignore requests without adding the computers to the System Center Configuration Manager 2007 database.

To make the unknown computer support option work correctly

1. Add the PXE server computer account to the Systems Management Server 2003 Admins security group.

2. Add the following rights within System Center Configuration Manager:

   ❑ Sites Class: Administer

   ❑ Collections Class: Create, Modify, Modify Resource, Read, Read Resource

Required Packages and Templates

Table 12-11 describes the packages and images that are required by the task sequence templates that MDT 2008 integrates into System Center Configuration Manager 2007. These packages and images must exist (or be created) for the task sequences to run correctly.

Table 12-11   Required Packages and Templates

Package or Image	Contains
Boot image package	Boot image used to initiate the ZTI deployment process.
Microsoft Deployment Files package	Contents of the Microsoft Deployment distribution share directory. The files used from the distribution share directory are the scripts and control files.
Operating stem image	Image of the operating system to be deployed to the target computer.
Client package	System Center Configuration Manager 2007 client installation files.
USMT package	USMT files used to capture and restore user state.
Custom Settings package	Unattended files and CustomSettings.ini.
Sysprep files package	The specific System Preparation Tool (Sysprep) files defined for a package.

In addition to the packages and images required by the task sequence templates, consider creating and including the following elements in the task sequences to provide similar functionality in Deployment Workbench:

- **Application packages**   This package includes any applications that you want to install as part of the operating system deployment (similar to the Applications node in Deployment Workbench). These packages are created as packages and programs in System Center Configuration Manager 2007. For more information on how to create these packages, see "Tasks for Software Distribution" in the Configuration Manager Documentation Library included with System Center Configuration Manager.

- **Windows package file packages**   These packages include any Windows package files (such as language packs, security updates, and service packs) that you want to install as part of the operating system deployment (similar to the OS Packages node in Deployment Workbench). These packages are created as packages in System Center Configuration Manager 2007. For more information on how to create these packages, see "Tasks for Software Distribution" in the Configuration Manager Documentation Library, included with System Center Configuration Manager.

- **Device driver package**   System Center Configuration Manager 2007 uses driver packages to control the distribution of drivers to distribution points. System Center Configuration Manager 2007 always considers all available drivers when deciding what is needed for a particular computer. For more information about how to include device drivers in the operating system image, see "How to Install Drivers on a Configuration Manager Client Using a Task Sequence" in the Configuration Manager Documentation Library included with System Center Configuration Manager.

Advertising a Task Sequence

You initiate the ZTI deployment process by advertising the task sequences created in System Center Configuration Manager 2007. If you configure System Center Configuration Manager 2007 to respond to PXE boot requests, advertising the task sequence automatically configures the boot image referenced in the task sequence for PXE boot.

Advertise task sequences to collections using the New Advertisement Wizard. Before running the New Advertisement Wizard, you must know what target collections and desired run-time behavior they want for the advertisement they are creating. Read access to the task sequence is required to advertise the task sequence, and the task sequence must exist prior to creating the advertisement. For more information on advertising task sequences, see "How to Advertise Task Sequences" in the Configuration Manager Documentation Library included with System Center Configuration Manager.

Customizing MDT 2008

MDT 2008 customization provides the necessary configuration settings for the destination computers. The configuration settings include the values that you would normally provide if you were manually deploying the operating system. You accomplish this customization by using one or more of these options:

- Configure the CustomSettings.ini file.
- Configure the BootStrap.ini file.
- Retrieve information from the MDT 2008 database.

For LTI-based deployments, any configuration settings that you don't specify in the Custom-Settings.ini file, the BootStrap.ini file, or the database must be provided when running the Windows Deployment Wizard. This gives you the flexibility to fully automate the LTI process or have the majority of configuration settings provided when running the Windows Deployment Wizard.

For ZTI-based deployments, you must provide all of the configuration settings in the Custom-Settings.ini file, the BootStrap.ini file, or the MDT 2008 database.

For more information, see the following resources:

- For the syntax and structure of the CustomSettings.ini file, see "Identify the Custom-Settings.ini Syntax" in *Deployment Customization Guide* in MDT 2008.
- For the syntax and structure of the BootStrap.ini file, see "Identify the BootStrap.ini Syntax" in *Deployment Customization Guide* in MDT 2008.

Configuring Multiple Computers

Whenever possible, apply configuration settings to multiple computers. You can define groups of computers and then apply configuration settings to the groups you define. Group-based configuration settings allow you to apply the same settings to a group of client computers. After you apply group-based settings, you can apply computer-specific configuration settings through computer-based settings.

Selecting a Grouping Method

You can use different methods to group client computers. After you determine how you want to group computers, select the appropriate properties.

Using the processing rules in MDT 2008, you can group computers based on any property that might be applied to a group of computers (such as Make, Model, DefaultGateway, and so on). Table 12-12 lists methods of grouping computers, descriptions of the methods, and the properties that you can use to group the computers.

Table 12-12   Grouping Methods

Grouping Method	Description	Properties
Geographically	Group configuration settings based on resources located within a geographic region (such as a shared folder on a computer within a geographic region).	DefaultGateway
Target computer hardware attributes	Group configuration settings based on hardware attributes (such as the make of the computer or processor architecture of the target computer).	Architecture CapableArchitecture Make Model HALName
Target computer software attributes	Group configuration settings based on software attributes (such as the operating system version of the target computer).	OSVersion
Default attributes	Apply configuration settings to all target computers when the properties are not located in other sections.	Default

In most instances, you can nest computer groupings. For example, you can use the Default-Gateway property to designate the IP subnets on which a computer resides within a geographic location. You can define locations by using the user-defined properties in the *[DefaultGateway]* section, as shown in the following listing. When grouping computers by hardware configuration, you can use a variety of methods, and the script searches for the substituted value. For instance, if you specify *Priority=Make*, the script substitutes the value for *Make* that it determines through a Windows Management Instrumentation (WMI) call and looks for the corresponding section, such as *[Dell Computer Corporation]*.

Grouping with [DefaultGateway]

```
[DefaultGateway]
172.16.0.3=NYC
172.16.1.3=NYC
172.16.2.3=NYC
172.16.111.3=DALLAS
172.16.112.3=DALLAS
172.16.116.3=WASHINGTON
172.16.117.3=WASHINGTON

[NYC]
UDShare=\\NYC-AM-FIL-01\MigData
SLShare=\\NYC-AM-FIL-01\Logs
Packages1=NYC00010-Install
Packages2=NYC00011-Install
Administrator1=WOODGROVEBANK\NYC Help Desk Staff

[DALLAS]
UDShare=\\DAL-AM-FIL-01\MigData
SLShare=\\DAL-AM-FIL-01\Logs
Administrator1=WOODGROVEBANK\DAL Help Desk Staff
```

You can find the complete source to the CustomSettings.ini file used in these examples in "Basic CustomSettings.ini File for ZTI" in the *Deployment Customization Samples Guide* in MDT 2008.

Applying the Properties to the Groups

After you identify the ways you want to group configuration settings, determine which properties and corresponding configuration settings you will apply to each group. Properties that you can group are properties that you can apply to multiple computers. Properties that you can apply to groups of computers include:

- BackupDir
- BackupShare
- CaptureGroups
- ComputerBackupLocation
- Packagesx
- SLShare
- UDDir
- UDShare
- UDProfiles

You should not apply properties that are specific to individual computers to groups of computers. These properties include:

- AssetTag
- HostName

- IPAddress

- OSDNewMachineName

- SerialNumber

 Note   MDT 2008 supports dozens of properties in CustomSettings.ini. The document *Toolkit Reference* in MDT 2008 contains a complete reference of all the settings it supports.

Configuring Individual Computers

For LTI, configuration settings that you apply to a group of computers may be sufficient. You can supply the remainder of the computer-specific settings interactively in the Windows Deployment Wizard.

For ZTI (or if you want to fully automate your LTI-based deployment), you need to provide computer-specific configuration settings in addition to the settings that apply to groups of computers. You can use the configuration settings for individual computers to override or augment settings for groups of computers based on the priority. For more information about determining the priority of processing rules, see "Priority Reserved Property" in the *Deployment Customization Guide* in MDT 2008.

Selecting an Identification Method

More than one method is available for identifying individual computers (just as when identifying groups of computers). After you select the method for identifying an individual target computer, you can select the appropriate properties.

The processing rules in MDT 2008 allow you to identify individual computers based on any property that might be applied to only one computer (such as AssetTag, MACAddress, UUID, and so on). Table 12-13 lists the methods of identifying individual computers, descriptions of the methods, and properties that you can use to identify the individual computers.

Table 12-13   Identifying Individual Computers

Identification Method	Description	Properties
Target computer hardware attributes	Identify the target computer by using the hardware configuration.	MACAddress
Target computer software attributes	Identify the target computer by using the software or firmware configuration.	Product (in conjunction with Make and Model)
		UUID
Target computer user-defined attributes	Identify the target computer by using attributes that are assigned to the computer but are not a part of the hardware or software configuration.	AssetTag SerialNumber

Applying the Properties to the Individual Computers

After you select the methods for identifying individual computers, determine which properties and corresponding configuration settings you will apply to each destination computer. These configuration settings typically apply to only one computer, because the configuration settings are unique to that computer. In instances in which a configuration setting is being applied to several computers, use group-based processing rules.

Properties that are typically applied to individual computers include:

- AssetTag

- HostName

- IPAddress

- OSDNewMachineName

- SerialNumber

If a group-based setting has a higher priority and the configuration setting is found in that group, the same configuration setting for an individual computer is ignored. For more information about deployment processing rule priority, see "Priority Reserved Property" in the *Deployment Customization Guide* in MDT 2008.

Customizing CustomSettings.ini

The CustomSettings.ini file is the primary configuration file for MDT 2008. All configuration settings are specified either directly or indirectly:

- Directly in the CustomSettings.ini file

- Indirectly in the MDT 2008 database that is referenced in the CustomSettings.ini file

The CustomSettings.ini file syntax is very similar to many .ini files. The CustomSettings.ini file in the following listing illustrates a CustomSettings.ini file customized for a ZTI-based deployment. For further explanation of the CustomSettings.ini file in the listing, see "Basic CustomSettings.ini File for ZTI" in *Deployment Customization Guide* in MDT 2008.

CustomSettings.ini for ZTI

```
[Settings]
Priority=Default, MACAddress
Properties=CustomProperty

[Default]
OSInstall=Y
ScanStateArgs=/v:5 /o /c
LoadStateArgs=/v:5 /c /lac
UserDataLocation=NONE
CustomProperty=TRUE
OSDINSTALLSILENT=1
```

```
[00:0F:20:35:DE:AC]
OSDNEWMACHINENAME=HPD530-1
OSDINSTALLPACKAGE=DAL00342
OSDINSTALLPROGRAM=CustomVista

[00:03:FF:FE:FF:FF]
OSDNEWMACHINENAME=BVMXP
OSDINSTALLPACKAGE=NYC00002
OSDINSTALLPROGRAM=SpecialVista
```

A CustomSettings.ini file includes:

- **Sections**   Sections are identified by brackets that surround the section name (for example, *[Settings]*). In the previous listing, the sections include *[Settings]*, *[Default]*, *[00:0F:20:35:DE:AC]*, and *[00:03:FF:FE:FF:FF]*. CustomSettings.ini has the following types of sections:

  - ❏ **Required sections**   Only the *[Settings]* section is required. All other sections are optional. The MDT 2008 scripts require the *[Settings]* section in CustomSettings.ini to locate the reserved properties (Priority and Properties).

  - ❏ **Optional sections**   The optional sections in the CustomSettings.ini file are used to assign a group of configuration settings to groups of computers or to individual computers. In the previous listing, the configuration settings in the *[Default]* section are applied to more than one computer, and the configuration settings in the *[00:0F:20:35:DE:AC]* and *[00:03:FF:FE:FF:FF]* sections are applied to the corresponding computers.

- **Properties**   Properties are variables that need to have values assigned. Properties are followed by an equal sign (=). The scripts scan the CustomSettings.ini file to locate the properties.

- **Values**   Values are the configuration settings assigned to the properties. Values are preceded by an equal sign. The scripts scan the CustomSettings.ini file to locate the values. In the previous listing, the value assigned to the *LoadStateArgs* property is */v:5 /c /lac*.

For more information on the syntax of the CustomSettings.ini file, see "Identify the Custom-Settings.ini Syntax" in the *Deployment Customization Guide* in MDT 2008.

Customizing BootStrap.ini

Configure the BootStrap.ini file to specify property settings prior to accessing the Custom-Settings.ini file. In other words, the BootStrap.ini file describes how to connect to the deployment point, which contains the CustomSettings.ini file. Configure the BootStrap.ini file to help the MDT 2008 scripts locate the following:

- The appropriate MDT 2008 deployment point
- The appropriate SMS 2003 OSD Feature Pack package and program

For example, in the New Computer scenario for ZTI with SMS 2003, you specify the SMS 2003 OSD Feature Pack properties in BootStrap.ini so that the MDT 2008 scripts know which SMS 2003 OSD Feature Pack package to use (because CustomSettings.ini is in the package).

The syntax of the BootStrap.ini file is identical to the CustomSettings.ini file. The BootStrap.ini file contains a subset of the properties that are used in the CustomSettings.ini file. Table 12-14 lists the common properties that are configured in BootStrap.ini.

Table 12-14   Common Properties Configured in BootStrap.ini

Property Name	LTI	ZTI
DeployRoot	✓	
SkipBDDWelcome	✓	
UserDomain	✓	
UserID	✓	
UserPassword	✓	
KeyboardLocale	✓	
OSDInstallSilent		✓
OSDInstallPackage		✓
OSDInstallProgram		✓

Deployment Workbench creates the BootStrap.ini file when a deployment point is created. After the initial creation, make all further customizations manually. For more information on configuring the BootStrap.ini file syntax, see "Identify the BootStrap.ini Syntax" in *Deployment Customization Guide* in MDT 2008.

Using the MDT 2008 Database

You can configure the rules for LTI and ZTI deployments in the MDT 2008 database by using Deployment Workbench. For ZTI with System Center Configuration Manager 2007, editing the database is in fact the only reason to use the workbench. The benefits of using the database include:

- **A more generic version of CustomSettings.ini**   Storing the configuration settings in the MDT 2008 database removes most of the detail from CustomSettings.ini. This change helps make the CustomSettings.ini file more generic so that you can use the same file in multiple deployment points.

- **A centralized repository for all property configuration settings**   Centralizing the configuration for all property settings ensures consistency across all deployment points.

To configure the rules in the configuration database

1. Create the database by using Deployment Workbench. The following section, "Creating the MDT 2008 Database," describes this step.

2. Configure the property values in the MDT 2008 database by using the Database item in Deployment Workbench. The section titled "Configuring the MDT 2008 Database" later in this chapter describes this step in more detail.

3.   Configure CustomSettings.ini to include the appropriate database queries for returning the property values stored in the MDT 2008 database. The section titled "Configuring the Database Access" later in this chapter describes this step in more detail.

Creating the MDT 2008 Database

Before configuring the database, you must create it in SQL Server. Deployment Workbench creates this database automatically by using the New DB Wizard. Of course, this section assumes that SQL Server is already installed and configured locally or remotely in your environment and that you have permission to create databases.

To create the MDT 2008 database in SQL Server

1.   In Deployment Workbench, right-click Database and then click New. Database is located under Deploy in the console tree.

2.   On the SQL Server Details page, in the SQL Server Name box, type the name of the server hosting SQL Server and click Next. Optionally, provide an instance and port and specify the network library to use for the connection.

3.   On the Database page, choose Create A New Database, type the name of the database in the Database text box, and then click Next. You can also choose to repair or connect to an existing database.

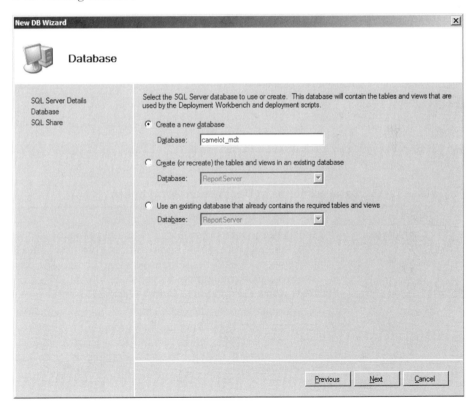

4.   On the SQL Share page, optionally type the name of any share on the server running
     SQL Server and then click Finish. MDT 2008 uses this share only if necessary to
     create a secure connection to the computer running SQL Server when using integrated
     security. Specify this share only if the Windows Deployment Wizard is not able to
     connect to SQL Server during deployment. The wizard will attempt to connect to this
     share using the connection credentials specified as described in the section titled
     "Configuring Resource Access" earlier in this chapter.

Configuring the MDT 2008 Database

MDT 208 organizes the property values in the database by the method for applying them
to destination computers. An item beneath the Database item in Deployment Workbench
represents each method, as shown in Figure 12-1 and as listed in Table 12-15.

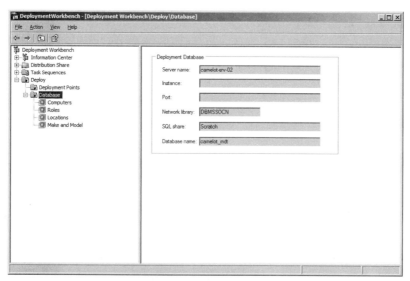

Figure 12-1   Database organization in Deployment Workbench.

Table 12-15   Database Items in Deployment Workbench

Node	Use This Node to Define
Computers	Specific target computers based on the AssetTag, UUID, SerialNumber, and MACAddress properties. You can associate property settings, applications, packages, roles, and administrative-level accounts with a computer. For more information on configuring this node, see "Create a New Computers Item" in *Deployment Customization Guide* in MDT 2008.
Roles	A group of computers based on the tasks performed by the users of the target computers (by using the Role property). You can associate property settings, applications, packages, and administrative-level accounts with a role. For more information on configuring this node, see "Create a New Roles Item" in *Deployment Customization Guide* in MDT 2008.

Table 12-15   Database Items in Deployment Workbench

Node	Use This Node to Define
Locations	A group of computers using the DefaultGateway property of the target computers to identify a geographic location. You can associate property settings, applications, packages, roles, and administrative-level accounts with a location. For more information on configuring this node, see "Create a New Locations Item" in *Deployment Customization Guide* in MDT 2008.
Make And Model	A group of computers using the Make And Model properties of the target computers. You can associate property settings, applications, packages, roles, and administrative-level accounts with target computers that are of the same make and model. For more information on configuring this node, see "Create a New Make and Model Item" in *Deployment Customization Guide* in MDT 2008.

Note   Create the items in the Roles node before you create the other items beneath other nodes (Computers, Locations, and Make and Model), because the other nodes can be associated with roles.

Configuring the Database Access

After you have configured the property values in the MDT 2008 database, you need to configure CustomSettings.ini to perform the appropriate database queries. You can easily do this by using the Configure DB Wizard in Deployment Workbench. Run the Configure DB Wizard for each deployment point defined in Deployment Workbench with which you want to use the database.

To configure CustomSettings.ini for database queries

1. In the Deployment Workbench console tree, expand Deploy and then click Deployment Points.

2. In the details pane, right-click the name of the deployment point for which you want to configure database access and then click Configure DB.

3. On the Computer Options page, choose from the following options and then click Next:

    ❑ **Query For Computer-Specific Settings**   Queries the settings configured on the Details tab of the Properties dialog box of the computer item.

    ❑ **Query For Roles Assigned To This Computer**   Queries the roles associated with the computer on the Roles tab of the Properties dialog box of the computer item.

    ❑ **Query For Applications To Be Installed On This Computer**   Queries the applications to be installed on the computer, as configured on the Applications tab of the Properties dialog box of the computer item.

❑ **Query For SMS Packages To Be Installed On This Computer**   Queries the packages to be installed on the computer, as configured on the Packages tab of the Properties dialog box of the computer item.

❑ **Query For Administrators To Be Assigned To This Computer**   Queries the accounts that will be made members of the local Administrators group on the target computer, as configured on the Administrators tab of the Properties dialog box of the computer item.

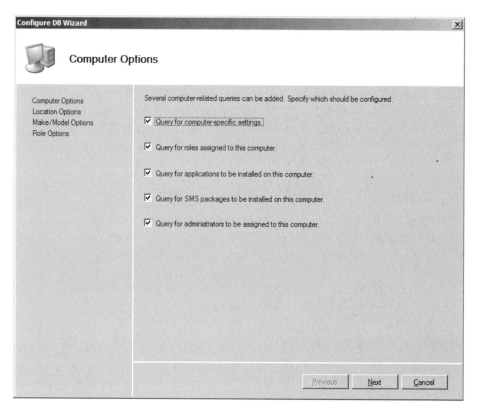

4.   On the Location Options page, choose from the following options, and then click Next:

❑ **Query For Location Names Based On Default Gateways**   Queries for location names based on the IP addresses of the default gateways configured on the Identity tab of the Properties dialog box of the location item.

❑ **Query For Location Specific Settings**   Queries the settings configured on the Details tab of the Properties dialog box of the location item.

❑ **Query For Roles Assigned For This Location**   Queries the roles associated with the location on the Roles tab of the Properties dialog box of the location item.

❑ **Query For Applications To Be Installed For This Location**   Queries the applications to be installed on the target computers within the location configured on the Applications tab of the Properties dialog box of the location item.

❑ **Query For SMS Packages To Be Installed For This Location**   Queries the packages to be installed on the target computers within the location configured on the Packages tab of the Properties dialog box of the location item.

❑ **Query For Administrators To Be Assigned For This Location**   Queries the accounts that will be made members of the local Administrators group on the target computers within the location configured on the Administrators tab of the Properties dialog box of the location item.

5.   On the Select Make And Model Query Options page, choose from the following options and then click Next:

❑ **Query For Model Specific Settings**   Queries the settings configured on the Details tab of the Properties dialog box of the make and model item.

❑ **Query For Roles Assigned To Computers With This Make And Model**   Queries the roles associated with the make and model on the Roles tab of the Properties dialog box of the make and model item.

❑ **Query For Applications To Be Installed On Computers With This Make And Model**   Queries the applications to be installed on the target computers with the make and model configured on the Applications tab of the Properties dialog box of the make and model item.

❑ **Query For SMS Packages To Be Installed On Computers With This Make And Model**   Queries the packages to be installed on the target computers with the make and model configured on the Packages tab of the Properties dialog box of the make and model item.

❑ **Query For Administrators To Be Assigned To Machines With This Make And Model**   Queries the accounts that will be made members of the local Administrators group on the target computer with the make and model configured on the Administrators tab of the Properties dialog box of the make and model item.

6.   On the Select Role Query Options page, choose from the following options and then click Finish:

❑ **Query For Role Specific Settings**   Queries the settings configured on the Details tab of the Properties dialog box of the role item.

❑ **Query For Applications To Be Installed For This Role**   Queries the applications to be installed on computers that perform this role, as configured on the Applications tab of the Properties dialog box of the role item.

❑ **Query For SMS Packages To Be Installed For This Role**   Queries the packages to be installed on computers that perform this role, as configured on the Packages tab of the Properties dialog box of the role item.

❑ **Query For Administrators To Be Assigned For This Role**   Queries the accounts that will be made members of the local Administrators group on computers that perform this role, as configured on the Administrators tab of the Properties dialog box of the role item.

After you complete the Configure DB Wizard, the CustomSettings.ini file is configured to perform the selected queries. For more information, see the following resources in MDT 2008:

- "Automating Deployment to a Specific Computer" in *Deployment Customization Desktop Samples.*

- "Automating Deployment by Role" in *Deployment Customization Desktop Samples.*

- "Automating Deployment by Location" in *Deployment Customization Desktop Samples.*

- "Automating Deployment by Computer Make and Model" in *Deployment Customization Desktop Samples.*

- See the corresponding section for each property under "Property Reference" in *Toolkit Reference.*

- See the corresponding section for each table and view in the configuration database under "Tables and Views in the Deployment Workbench Database" in *Toolkit Reference.*

Summary

This chapter provided step-by-step instructions for configuring MDT 2008 to deploy Windows Vista by using LTI or ZTI. LTI is a simple way to deploy Windows Vista in small- and medium-sized businesses. It requires no infrastructure and is very easy to set up and customize. ZTI requires SMS 2003 OSD or System Center Configuration Manager 2007 and a considerable amount of customization to be used effectively. It's appropriate in large organizations that already have an SMS 2003 or System Center Configuration Manager 2007 infrastructure in place. In contrast to SMS 2003, which requires you to build images by using the Deployment Workbench, MDT 2008 integrates completely into System Center Configuration Manager 2007.

Additional Resources

The following resources contain additional information and tools related to this chapter.

Related Information

- Chapter 3, "Deployment Platform," includes information about the Windows Vista installation architecture and its key components and technologies. This chapter describes how the various components interact.

- Chapter 4, "Planning Deployment," includes information about installing and preparing MDT 2008 for use. This chapter also describes how to use the MDT 2008 guidance.

- Chapter 6, "Developing Disk Images," explains how to design and develop custom Windows Vista disk images for use with MDT 2008 LTI and ZTI with SMS 2003.

- Chapter 10, "Configuring Windows DS," explains how to install and configure Windows DS and how to use it with MDT 2008.

- Chapter 11, "Using Volume Activation," includes more information about Windows Vista product keys and volume activation.

- *Toolkit Reference* in MDT 2008 lists the properties you can configure in a deployment point.

- *Windows Automated Installation Kit User's Guide* includes detailed information about the tools and technologies included in the Windows AIK. This guide is in the file Waik.chm in the Windows AIK.

Part III
Desktop Management

Chapter 13

Managing the Desktop Environment

Group Policy is a powerful tool for managing the computer and user configuration of client computers in many mid-market and enterprise environments. Using Group Policy, administrators can configure and lock down different aspects of desktop and mobile PCs and the experience of users on these computers. Windows Vista Service Pack 1 with Remote Server Administration Tools (RSAT) includes several new features and enhancements to Group Policy, including new, XML-based administrative template files (and a domain-wide central store for maintaining these files), multiple local Group Policy Objects, Starter Group Policy Objects (Starter GPOs), Administrative Template and Group Policy Object commenting, Administrative Template filtering, Group Policy preferences, and hundreds of new policy settings for managing different aspects of Windows Vista computers and their users. This chapter describes these new features and enhancements and how to implement them in Active Directory environments running Windows Server 2008 and Windows Server 2003.

Understanding Group Policy in Windows Vista Service Pack 1

Windows Vista Service Pack 1 with RSAT provides new and enhanced features in the area of Group Policy management, processing, and settings. These features and enhancements make Group Policy easier to manage, more reliable, better-performing, and easier to troubleshoot in enterprise environments where Active Directory is deployed.

Group Policy Issues on Earlier Versions of Windows

The way that Group Policy is implemented in earlier versions of Windows resulted in a number of issues and limitations on platforms such as Windows XP, Windows Server 2003, and Windows 2000 Server. These issues and limitations included:

■   Administrative Template (ADM) files used a proprietary syntax that made it complicated for administrators to create their own custom ADM template files to extend Group Policy management functionality by extending or introducing new registry-based policy settings for Windows, other Microsoft software products, third-party applications from Independent Software Vendors (ISVs), and custom internal applications. In addition, the syntax for ADM template files made it difficult for administrators to develop local-ized versions that they could use to view registry-based Administrative Template policy settings in their own languages. (Using multiple languages with ADM files resulted in a mixture of languages in the user interface—the ADM file with the latest date/timestamp overwrote the other ADM files.) All these limitations made it difficult for administrators to create their own custom Group Policy solutions for managing registry-based settings, especially in global enterprises with multilingual environments.

■   Whenever you used the Group Policy Object Editor on an administrative workstation to create a new domain-based Group Policy Object (GPO), the entire set of default ADM template files was automatically copied from the %SystemRoot%\inf folder on the computer where the GPO was being edited to the Group Policy Template (GPT)—the physical portion of the GPO stored on the domain controllers for your domain. For each GPO that you create, the GPT is created at %SystemRoot%\SYSVOL\domain \Policies\ *GPO_GUID* and also appears in the SYSVOL share at *domain_controller_name*\ SYSVOL*domain_name*\Policies*GPO_GUID*, where *GPO_GUID* is a folder named after the globally unique identifier (GUID) of the GPO. (The other, logical portion of each GPO is stored in the Group Policy Container or GPC, found in the CN=Policies, CN=System container in Active Directory.) The File Replication Service (FRS) replicates the contents of each GPT folder within the SYSVOL share to all domain controllers in the domain, and the storage cost of having copies of all the default ADM template files stored in each GPT is at least 4 megabytes (MB) per GPO. The result of these conditions in large enterprise environments—where dozens or even hundreds of GPOs are deployed—was SYSVOL bloat, a condition that caused excessive replication traffic whenever a change was made to the settings in a GPO. For domain controllers at different sites linked by slow WAN links, such excessive replication traffic could at times affect the availability and performance of network applications relying on other forms of traffic. This issue was exacerbated when events occurred that caused all GPOs to change simultaneously, such as when permissions on GPOs were modified when upgrading a domain from Windows 2000 to Windows Server 2003.

■   To help reduce Group Policy traffic over slow WAN links, a feature called slow-link detection was used on earlier versions of Windows. Slow-link detection used exchanges of ICMP packets to detect increased network latency and reduced responsiveness. When a slow link was detected, which by default corresponded to a latency of more than 10 milliseconds, the client pinged the domain controller three times using 2-kilobyte Echo Response packets, then used the returned Echo Response packets to determine the effective bandwidth for the network link to the domain controller. If the effective bandwidth was determined to be fewer than 400 kilobits per second, the client identified the network link as a slow link and informed the domain controller. If the link was identified as a slow link, Group Policy processed only security settings and administrative template settings during background policy refresh. Because slow-link detection used ICMP for determining effective network bandwidth, problems arose if host or perimeter firewalls blocked ICMP traffic. In addition, being unable to block ICMP traffic increased the attack surface of computers.

- Group Policy processing took place only during startup (processing of machine settings), logon (processing of user settings), and at scheduled background policy refresh intervals, which by default for client computers and member servers was every 90 minutes plus a random offset of up to 30 minutes. For domain controllers, the interval was every five minutes. However, Group Policy was implemented on earlier versions of Windows in such a way that Group Policy processing would not take place during the following types of events: when a client computer recovered from hibernation or standby; when a mobile computer was docked with its docking station; when a computer established a virtual private network (VPN) connection with a remote computer or network; and when a client computer successfully exited network quarantine. As a result of these limitations and circumstances, earlier versions of Windows might not have the latest Group Policy settings for the domain applied to them. If updates to the Group Policy settings mitigated security vulnerabilities, this could result in temporary security vulnerabilities until the next round of background policy refresh occurred. In addition, if a domain controller temporarily became unavailable when scheduled background policy refresh was to occur, no mechanism was available to alert the client computer that policy should be refreshed when the domain controller became available again. Instead, the client computer would log an error event in the Event Log and attempt policy refresh at the next scheduled refresh time.

- Configuring the Local Computer Policy (also called the Local Group Policy Object or LGPO) on standalone computers resulted in settings that applied to all users (including administrators) on the computer. This limitation made it difficult to lock down and administer shared computers for kiosk use in environments such as libraries and other public places, as well as for Windows computers used in other non–Active Directory environments, since all configured settings applied not just to ordinary users but also to local administrators on the computer.

- Troubleshooting Group Policy currently requires enabling logging on the core Group Policy engine Userenv.dll. Log files generated by Userenv.dll are stored in the %Windir%\Debug\Usernmode folder and contain Group Policy function trace statements conflated with roaming profile load and unload function statements, making these log files hard to interpret when trying to diagnose Group Policy failure.

■   Although Windows XP Service Pack 2 and Windows Server 2003 Service Pack 1 and later support more than 1,800 different policy settings covering a wide variety of areas, you can't use Group Policy to manage many of these features on earlier versions of Windows. For example, you have no native way to use Group Policy to control power management, to block the installation and use of removable drives such as USB key drives, or to deploy printers to users based on the location of their computers. (Third-party solutions do exist, however, for adding some of these functionalities to Group Policy on these platforms.)

New Group Policy Features in Windows Vista SP1 with Remote Server Administration Tools (RSAT)

To address these Group Policy issues and limitations on earlier versions of Windows, Windows Vista Service Pack 1 with RSAT includes the following new features and enhancements:

■   New XML-based administrative template (ADMX) files that use standard XML syntax are now included in Windows Vista instead of the proprietary syntax used in ADM template files in previous versions of Windows. Language-specific resources are stored in separate Architecture Description Markup Language (ADML) files so that administrators can display Group Policy settings in their own localized languages. For more information, see the section titled "Understanding ADMX Template Files" later in this chapter.

■   ADMX template files can be stored in a central store in the SYSVOL share on domain controllers instead of within each GPT. In addition, when you configure a central store for ADMX files, the Group Policy Management Console included in RSAT will not copy or read ADMX files in an individual GPO. These enhancements considerably reduce SYSVOL bloat, which reduces replication traffic and makes Group Policy processing more efficient. Placing ADMX template files in a central store also makes them easier to manage and update across a domain. For more information, see the section titled "Configuring the Central Store" later in this chapter.

■   Instead of using ICMP, Windows Vista now uses Network Location Awareness version 2.0 (NLA v2.0) to allow Group Policy to detect the current state of network connectivity for the computer. With NLA, Windows Vista computers can determine when domain controllers become available or unavailable to the client. NLA also allows Windows Vista computers to refresh Group Policy in the background after they wake up from Sleep, when they establish a VPN connection, when they dock with a docking station, and when they successfully exit network quarantine. And with NLA, Group Policy can detect slow links without using ICMP and can process Group Policy on the client even when a firewall blocks all ICMP traffic.

■ Support for Multiple Local Group Policy Objects (MLGPOs) is now available in Windows Vista. Using MLGPOs provides increased flexibility for configuring standalone computers for shared use, and you can even configure MLGPOs in domain environments if required. For more information, see the section titled "Understanding Multiple Local Group Policy" later in this chapter.

■ Windows Vista now includes a new method to enable trace logging for troubleshooting issues with Group Policy Processing. This method separates Group Policy function trace statements from those created by other operating system activities so that log files are easier to interpret when you are trying to diagnose Group Policy failure.

■ Windows Vista now supports more than 2,500 different policy settings, compared to the 1,800 settings supported on previous platforms. These settings include several new policy categories, such as power management, blocking device installation, printer deployment based on location, and more. For a summary of these new policy setting categories, see the section titled "New Group Policy Settings in Windows Vista" later in this chapter. For detailed information concerning the policy settings for a particular category, see the chapter in this Resource Kit that deals with this topic area. For example, for more information about using Group Policy to assign printers based on location, see Chapter 19, "Managing Printing."

■ Group Policy Management Console (GPMC) is now included as part of the Remote Server Administration Tools (RSAT), which is provided both as a built-in feature of Windows Server 2008 and as a separate download for Windows Vista Service Pack 1. (Note that you cannot install the downloadable RSAT on Windows Vista RTM computers; you can install it only on Windows Vista SP1 or later.) RSAT provides tools for managing Windows Server 2008 roles and services, and the downloadable RSAT for Windows Vista SP1 has the same version of GPMC that is included with the built-in RSAT feature of Windows Server 2008 and is available in both 32-bit and 64-bit platforms. The new version of GPMC that is included as part of RSAT provides access to the following features:

❏ **Starter Group Policy Objects**   These provide a foundation for creating Group Policy Objects with preconfigured Administrative Template policy settings. A new Group Policy Object created from a Starter Group Policy Object contains all the policy settings included in the Starter GPO. Windows Vista Service Pack 1 supports two types of Starter GPOs: Custom Starter GPOs, which allow user-created Starter GPOs; and System Starter GPOs, which are read-only Starter GPOs used to distribute predefined configurations. Like Group Policy Objects, Starter GPOs can be backed up and restored. Also, you can import and export Starter GPOs from .cab files, which makes them very portable.

❏ **Administrative Template policy setting filtering**   This new feature lets you apply inclusive filters against the Admininstrative Templates All Settings node. This new filtering allows you to filter Administrative Template policy settings to include

Managed/Unmanaged and Configured/Not Configured policy settings. Also, you can use keywords searches for searching within the policy title, explain text, or comments of Administrative Template policy settings. Last, you can filter on the application or platform requirements, such as for all policy settings that meet "At least Windows Server 2008."

❑ **Comments tab**   Each Administrative Template policy setting and Group Policy Object now has an additional property tab named Comments. This provides a location that allows administrators to add descriptive comments to the policy setting or Group Policy Object. Also, the new filtering features support filtering on the contents of the comments field.

❑ **Group Policy Preferences**   This new feature extends the functionality of existing Group Policy by allowing Administrators to perform functions that previously required scripting knowledge. Group Policy preferences allows managing drive mappings, registry settings, Local Users And Groups, files, folders, and shortcuts to client computers. Group Policy preferences can be managed from Windows Vista SP1 with RSAT or Windows Server 2008. Preference client side extensions are included in Windows Server 2008, whereas downloadable versions of the preferences client side extensions are available for Windows Vista RTM and later, Windows XP Service Pack 2 or later, and Windows Server 2003 Service Pack 1 or later from the Microsoft Download Center.

> **Note**   Unless otherwise indicated, for the remainder of this chapter any reference to Windows Vista should be understood as referring to Windows Vista SP1 or later.

New Group Policy Settings in Windows Vista

Group Policy in Windows Vista includes several new policy areas that administrators can use to configure and lock down various aspects of client computers and the experience of users who use them. In addition, some existing policy areas have been enhanced with new settings that provide new functionality. Table 13-1 summarizes many of these new and enhanced policy categories and indicates their location within Group Policy Object Editor. This table also indicates where you can find additional information on these policy settings within this Resource Kit. Table 13-2 summarizes some of the new and enhanced policy categories that include settings for locking down the desktop experience for users in enterprise environments.

Direct from the Source: Windows Vista Group Policy Settings Stick Better Than Glue

Windows Vista Group Policy significantly improves control and use of removable storage devices such as "memory sticks," also known as USB drives. These policy settings would have been helpful in preventing security incidents and administrator overreaction (involving epoxy adhesive) recently reported on the Internet and through organizations including National Public Radio (NPR) and CBS News.

In one such situation, the computer administration staff at the Los Alamos Nuclear Laboratory in New Mexico used glue to seal the USB ports on computer workstations after determining that a contract employee had transferred documents onto her personal USB drive, ostensibly to complete some work at home. These were classified documents, and this was not the first incident of data being removed without authorization.

Sadly, had computers at Los Alamos Nuclear Laboratory used the Windows Vista operating system, new policy settings controlling Write access for removable storage devices could easily have prevented copying any files onto USB drives—no glue necessary! You can apply these new policy settings to Active Directory domain–based GPOs or to a new Multiple Local Group Policy Object (MLGPO) on the local workstation, preventing users without administrator access on the local computer from copying files (but allowing approved administrators to have read/write capability).

An alternative approach to managing USB drive access is to use the policy setting that allows only a specific DEVICE ID (such as an approved USB drive) to have Read access at the workstation. You can accomplish this by creating a GPO that uses the policy setting Allow Installation Of Devices That Match Any Of These Device Ids and then listing the approved DEVICE ID, and by using the setting Prevent Installation Of Devices Not Described By Other Policy Settings. This approach is better than glue, and you won't be "stuck" if you need to open access later to more devices.

References

CBS News: *http://www.cbsnews.com/stories/2006/10/24/national/main2122004.shtml?source=RSSattr=HOME_2122004*

ComputerWorld Online: *http://www.computerworld.com/action/article.do?command=viewArticleBasic&articleId=9004517*

NPR News (audio source of the glue-in-the-ports anecdote): *http://www.npr.org/templates/story/story.php?storyId=6479586*

Mark Lawrence, Senior Program Manager

Windows Enterprise Management Division (WEMD)

Table 13-1   New and Enhanced Group Policy Areas in Windows Vista

Category	Description	Location	More Info
Attachment Manager	Configures behavior for evaluating high-risk attachments	User Configuration\Policies\Administrative Templates\Windows Components\ Attachment Manager	Not covered
BitLocker Drive Encryption	Configures behavior of BitLocker Drive Encryption	Computer Configuration\Policies\ Administrative Templates\Windows Components\BitLocker Drive Encryption	Chapter 15
Deployed Printers	Deploys a printer connection to a computer	Computer Configuration\Policies\ Windows Settings\Deployed Printers User Configuration\Windows Settings\ Deployed Printers	Chapter 19
Device Installation	Permits or restricts device installation based on device class or ID	Computer Configuration\Policies\ Administrative Templates\System\Device Installation	Chapter 16
Disk Diagnostic	Configures level of information displayed by disk-failure diagnostics	Computer Configuration\Policies\ Administrative Templates\System\ Troubleshooting And Diagnostics\Disk Diagnostic	Chapter 31
Disk NV Cache	Configures hybrid hard-disk properties	Computer Configuration\Policies\ Administrative Templates\System\Disk NV Cache	Chapter 16
Event Log Service	Configures behavior for event logs	Computer Configuration\Policies\ Administrative Templates\Windows Components\Event Log Service	Chapter 22
Internet Explorer	Configures Microsoft Internet Explorer	Computer Configuration\Policies\ Administrative Templates\Windows Components\Internet Explorer User Configuration\Policies\Administrative Templates\Windows Components\Internet Explorer	Chapter 21
Network Sharing	Prevents users from sharing from within their profile paths	User Configuration\Policies\Administrative Templates\Windows Components\Network Sharing	Chapter 17
Offline Files	Configures slow-link mode for offline files	Computer Configuration\Policies\ Windows Settings\Network\Offline Files	Chapter 14

Table 13-1   New and Enhanced Group Policy Areas in Windows Vista

Category	Description	Location	More Info
Online Assistance	Configures whether or not users can access untrusted Help content and other Help-related settings	Computer Configuration\Policies\ Administrative Templates\Online Assistance User Configuration\ Administrative Templates\Online Assistance	Not covered
Performance Control Panel	Disables access to performance tool	Computer Configuration\Policies\ Administrative Templates\System\ Performance Control Panel	Chapter 22
		User Configuration\Policies\Administrative Templates\System\Performance Control Panel	
Power Management	Configures power management options, notifications, behavior of power button, sleep behavior, hard-disk settings, and video settings	Computer Configuration\Policies\ Administrative Templates\System\Power Management	Chapter 16
Regional and Language Options	Restricts access to Regional and Language Options	Computer Configuration\Policies\ Administrative Templates\Control Panel\Regional And Language Options	Not covered
		User Configuration\Policies\Administrative Templates\Control Panel\Regional And Language Options	
Remote Assistance	Configures behavior of remote assistance	Computer Configuration\Policies\ Administrative Templates\System\Remote Assistance	Chapter 23
Removable Storage	Controls reading data from and writing data to removable storage devices	Computer Configuration\Policies\ Administrative Templates\System\ Removable Storage Access	Chapter 16
		User Configuration\Policies\Administrative Templates\System\Removable Storage Access	
Search	Prevents indexing files in offline files cache	Computer Configuration\Policies\ Administrative Templates\Windows Components\Search	Chapter 20
Terminal Services	Configures Remote Desktop client behavior	Computer Configuration\Policies\ Administrative Templates\Windows Components\Terminal Services	Chapter 28
		User Configuration\Policies\Administrative Templates\Windows Components\ Terminal Services	

Table 13-1 New and Enhanced Group Policy Areas in Windows Vista

Category	Description	Location	More Info
Trouble-shooting and Diagnostics	Controls the behavior of built-in diagnostics	Computer Configuration\Policies\ Administrative Templates\System\ Troubleshooting And Diagnostics	Chapter 31
User Account Protection	Configures elevation-prompt behavior and related settings	Computer Configuration\Policies\ Windows Settings\Security Settings\Local Policies\Security Options	Chapter 25
Windows Customer Experience Improvement Program	Configures Customer Experience Improvement Program behavior	Computer Configuration\Policies\ Administrative Templates\Windows Components\Windows Customer Experience Improvement Program	Chapter 22
Windows Defender	Configures Windows Defender behavior	Computer Configuration\Policies\ Administrative Templates\Windows Components\Windows Defender	Chapter 25
Windows Error Reporting	Configures Windows Error Reporting behavior, including advanced settings and consent behavior	Computer Configuration\Policies\ Administrative Templates\Windows Components\Windows Error Reporting User Configuration\Policies\Windows Components\Administrative Templates\Windows Error Reporting	Chapter 22
Windows Firewall with Advance Security	Configures Windows Firewall and IPsec settings	Computer Configuration\Policies\ Windows Settings\Security Settings\ Windows Firewall With Advance Security	Chapter 27
Windows Logon Options	Displays message when logging on with cached credentials and configures behavior when logon hours expire	Computer Configuration\Policies\ Administrative Templates\Windows Components\Windows Logon Options User Configuration\Policies\Administrative Templates\Windows Components\ Windows Logon Options	Chapter 14
Windows Update	Enables Windows Update Power Management to automatically wake the system to install scheduled updates	Computer Configuration\Policies\ Administrative Templates\Windows Components\Windows Update	Chapter 22

Table 13-2   New and Enhanced Group Policy Categories for Locking Down User Desktops

Category	Description	Location	More info
Desktop	Configures desktop wallpaper	User Configuration\Policies\Administrative Templates\Desktop	Not covered
Desktop Windows Manager	Configures Desktop Windows Manager (DWM) behavior	User Configuration\Policies\Administrative Templates\Windows Components\Desktop Windows Manager	Not covered
Folder Redirection	Enables localization of redirected subfolders of Start menu and Documents	Computer Configuration\Policies\Administrative Templates\System\Folder Redirection User Configuration\Policies\Administrative Templates\System\ Folder Redirection	Chapter 14
Logon	Removes entry point for Fast User Switching	Computer Configuration\Policies\ Administrative Templates\System\Logon	Not covered
Programs	Hides programs in Control Panel	User Configuration\Policies\Administrative Templates\Control Panel\Programs	Not covered
Start Menu And Taskbar	Locks down behavior of Start menu and taskbar	User Configuration\Policies\Administrative Templates\Start Menu And Taskbar	Not covered
User Profiles	Configures behavior of roaming and locally cached profiles	Computer Configuration\Policies\ Administrative Templates\System\User Profiles User Configuration\Policies\Administrative Templates\System\User Profiles	Chapter 14
Windows Explorer	Configures behavior of Explorers and Previous Versions	User Configuration\Policies\Administrative Templates\Windows Components\Windows Explorer	Not covered

Tables 13-1 and 13-2 are not meant to be an exhaustive list of all new and enhanced categories of policy settings in Windows Vista. For a complete list of all Group Policy settings in Windows Vista Service Pack 1, see the Group Policy Settings Reference spreadsheet available from the Microsoft Download Center at *http://www.microsoft.com/downloads/details.aspx? familyid=2043B94E-66CD-4B91-9E0F-68363245C495&displaylang=en.* In addition to the usual list of details concerning each policy setting (name, explain text, registry key, and so on), the Windows Vista Service Pack 1 version of the Group Policy Settings Reference spreadsheet includes three new columns:

■ **Reboot Required**   "Yes" in this column means that Windows requires a restart before the described policy setting is applied.

- **Logoff Required**   "Yes" in this column means that Windows requires the user to log off and log on again before the described policy setting is applied.

- **Active Directory Schema or Domain Requirements**   "Yes" in this column means that you must extend your Active Directory Schema before deploying this policy setting.

The Windows Vista Service Pack 1 version of the Group Policy Settings Reference spreadsheet also includes security policy settings and registry-based Administrative Template policy settings.

Understanding ADMX Template Files

In previous versions of Microsoft Windows, administrative template (.adm) files are used to surface the registry-based policy settings found under Computer Configuration\Administrative Templates and User Configuration\Administrative Templates in the Group Policy Object Editor. These ADM template files use a complex, text-based syntax that makes it difficult to provide a localized view of Administrative Template settings. Windows XP and Windows Server 2003 come with five default ADM template files: Conf.adm, Inetres.adm, System.adm, Wmplayer.adm, and Wuau.adm. Most Administrative Templates settings are described in Inetres.adm and System.adm. These default ADM template files are located in the %Windir%\inf folder, and when a GPO is created, the ADM template files on the administrative workstation are copied to the GPO in the SYSVOL share and replicated to other domain controllers in the domain.

In Windows Vista, however, ADMX template files have replaced ADM template files. ADMX template files use an XML-based syntax instead of the proprietary syntax used by ADM template files. ADMX template files provide the following benefits over ADM template files:

- SYSVOL bloat is avoided because ADMX template files are not stored within GPO folders on SYSVOL.

- You can now store ADMX template files in a single, central store for the whole domain, making them easier to maintain.

- With ADMX template files, Local Group Policy Editor can display policy settings in the local language for the user without affecting any other user's view of the policy settings.

- ADMX template files support strong versioning, which simplifies their creation and management.

Types of ADMX Template Files

There are two types of ADMX template files:

- **ADMX language-neutral files**   These files have the extension .admx and surface the actual registry-based policy settings that you can configure using the Local Group Policy Editor user interface. Windows Vista has more than one hundred different .admx files—generally one for each category of Group Policy settings. For example, the

RemovableStorage.admx file contains the registry-based settings that surface in the Local Group Policy Editor under Computer Configuration\Policies\Administrative Templates\System\Removable Storage Access and User Configuration\Policies\ Administrative Templates\System\Removable Storage Access.

■ **ADML language-specific files**   These files have the extension .adml and comply with the Architecture Description Markup Language (ADML) syntax. For each .admx file, there can be multiple .adml files, one for each installed language. These .adml files provide the localized display text for Administrative Templates settings in the Local Group Policy Editor using the currently installed language of the user.

For example, consider an administrator of a global enterprise who resides in the United States. This administrator creates a GPO from his administrative workstation running Windows Vista Service Pack 1 with RSAT that is configured to use U.S. English as its default language. If an administrator in Germany then browses the same domain and uses the Group Policy Management Console to edit this GPO, the policy settings will be displayed in German in the Group Policy Object Editor, because this administrator's workstation is configured to use German as its default language. This multilingual Group Policy behavior will occur as long as .adml files for both English and German are found in the central store so that administrators in different geographical locations can access them.

How It Works: "Supported on" and "Requirements" Text

Group Policy is an enterprise configuration management system. ADMX files are always supersets of previous operating systems' registry-based policy settings. This allows for an administrator to support management of multiple operating systems from a single platform. The Group Policy Object Editor registry-based policy settings display values for the "Requirements:" (in extended view) or "Supported on:" (in the properties page) context of an administrative template policy setting to allow an administrator to determine which systems will be affected by different ADMX policy settings. The policy setting will apply to a specific operating system or component version based on the "Supported on:" text information. Note: If the policy setting is not applicable to a client workstation operating system, it will not have any effect.

Judith Herman, Group Policy Programming Writer

Windows Enterprise Management Division UA

Local Storage of ADMX Template Files

ADMX template files are stored locally on Windows Vista computers in the following locations:

■ **ADMX language-neutral (.admx) files**   Found under the %SystemRoot%\Policy-Definitions folder.

■ **ADML language-specific (.adml) files**   Found under the %SystemRoot% \Policy-Definitions*MUI_culture* folders, where *MUI_culture* is the name of the installed language and culture. For example, .adml files for U.S. English are found under the %SystemRoot%\PolicyDefinitions\en-US folder.

Domain Storage of ADMX Template Files

You can copy ADMX template files to a central store in Active Directory environments running Windows Server 2003 or Windows Server 2008. This makes it easier to maintain a single master set of ADMX template files for all Windows Vista and Windows Server 2008 computers in the domain. In addition, the GPMC in RSAT will automatically look for this central store, and when the GPMC finds it, it will use the ADMX template files stored in this location instead of the ADMX template files stored on the local computer. Copying an ADMX template file from a Windows Vista computer to the central store makes this ADMX template file available to Group Policy administrators anywhere in the domain and makes Group Policy settings display properly regardless of the administrator's locally installed language.

In a domain environment where the central store has been created and configured, ADMX template files are stored in the following locations on your domain controllers:

■ **ADMX language-neutral (.admx) files**   Found under the %SystemRoot% \sysvol\domain\policies\PolicyDefinitions folder.

■ **ADML language-specific (.adml) files**   Found under the %SystemRoot% \sysvol\domain\policies\PolicyDefinitions*MUI_culture* folders, where *MUI_culture* is the name of the installed language. For example, .adml files for U.S. English are found under the %SystemRoot%\sysvol\domain\policies\PolicyDefinitions\en-US folder.

Note   You must manually create and populate the central store with ADMX template files if you want to use this feature. For more information, see the section titled "Configuring the Central Store" later in this chapter.

How It Works: ADMX Central Store on Microsoft Windows 2000 and Microsoft Windows 2003 Server Domains

A central store can be created in a Microsoft Windows 2000 or Microsoft Windows 2003 server domain. The ADMX central store is simply a set of specifically named folders on the SYSVOL of the domain to contain the ADMX files. The Group Policy Object Editor will be able to access the ADMX central store no matter which version of domain exists, as long as an administrator is using the Group Policy Object Editor on a Windows Vista workstation.

Judith Herman, Group Policy Programming Writer

Windows Enterprise Management Division UA

Considerations When Working with ADMX Template Files

The following considerations apply when working with ADMX template files:

- Windows Vista includes only ADMX template files and does not include any of the default ADM template files used in downlevel Windows platforms. The default ADMX template files in Windows Vista have superseded the default ADM template files used in earlier platforms.

- If you add the default ADM files to a GPO, Windows Vista's version of Group Policy Object Editor will not read them. For example, if you have customized the System.adm file from a previous version of Windows, and this ADM file is in the GPO, you will not see your customized settings when you open this GPO in the Group Policy Object Editor of a Windows Vista computer.

- If ADMX template files exist on both the local Windows Vista computer and in a central store on domain controllers, the ADMX template files in the central store are used for surfacing policy settings when Group Policy Object Editor is used on domain computers.

- Policy settings in ADMX template files that have Supported On text that says "At least Windows Vista Service Pack 1" are available only to computers running Windows Vista Service Pack 1 or Windows Server 2008. These settings are not available to computers running earlier versions of Microsoft Windows and have no effect on the registry of these computers when they are targeted by the GPO. In addition, domain-based policy settings that exist only in ADMX template files can be managed only from computers running Windows Vista Service Pack 1 with RSAT or Windows Server 2008 because they are not exposed in the versions of Group Policy Object Editor available on earlier versions of Windows.

- You can import an ADM template file into the %Windir%\inf folder on a Windows Vista computer in the usual way by right-clicking the appropriate (computer or user) Administrative Templates node in Group Policy Object Editor and selecting Add/ Remove Templates. Windows Vista has no interface for importing ADMX template files into %SystemRoot%\PolicyDefinitions, however.

- Administrators who have developed custom ADM template files can migrate these files to the new ADMX format by using ADMX Migrator. For more information, see the section titled "Using ADMX Migrator" later in this chapter.

- The Group Policy Object Editor included with Windows Vista can read and display both ADMX template files and custom-developed ADM files, but not the default ADM template files used with earlier versions of Windows. (Note that this does not cause any issues, because the ADMX files of Windows Vista contain a superset of the policy settings found in the ADM files of earlier versions of Windows.) If a Windows Vista computer includes a custom (nondefault) ADM template file stored in the %Windir%\inf folder on the local computer, the policy settings defined in this file will be displayed in a separate node called Classic Administrative Templates (ADM) found under Computer Configuration\Administrative Templates or User Configuration\Administrative Templates, depending on where the ADM template file was imported to (see Figure 13-1). If ADM template files are stored in a GPO in SYSVOL, the same behavior occurs when you use Group Policy Object Editor on a Windows Vista computer to open the GPO.

■ If you use the GPMC to create a new GPO from a Windows Vista Service Pack 1 computer running RSAT, and this GPO is never edited using the Group Policy Object Editor on earlier version of Windows, the GPO folder will not contain either ADM or ADMX template files. This approach helps reduce the size of each GPO folder by about 4 MB over previous platforms and thus helps reduce SYSVOL bloat on your domain controllers. However, if you create a new GPO from a Windows Vista computer by using the GPMC and then edit the GPO using the Group Policy Object Editor from an earlier version of Windows, the ADM template files found in %Windir%\inf on the earlier version of Windows are automatically copied to the GPO folder and replicated to all domain controllers in the domain.

Important   It is a best practice that after you edit Group Policy Objects using the GPMC included in Windows Server 2008 or the GPMC included with RSAT for Vista SP1, you do *not* use earlier versions of either the GPMC or the Group Policy Object Editor.

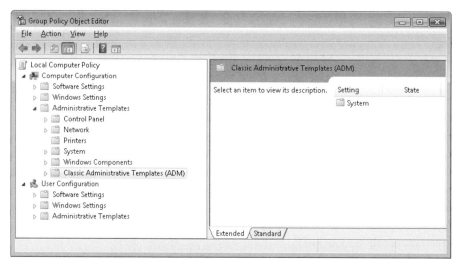

Figure 13-1   In the Classic Administrative Templates (ADM) node, policy settings surfaced by ADM template files are displayed in Group Policy Object Editor.

Caution   Just as with earlier versions of Windows, Microsoft does not recommend that you customize the default ADMX files used in Windows Vista Service Pack 1. If you customize the default ADMX or ADM files, your customization settings may be lost when Microsoft releases updated versions of these files.

> ## Direct from the Source: Fixing the SYSVOL Bloat Issue
>
> SYSVOL bloat is caused by the operation of the Group Policy Object Editor automatically populating each GPO with the default set of ADM files during the editing session. This causes approximately 4 MB to be copied to SYSVOL for every GPO created and edited. This happens whether or not you are setting registry-based policy settings. A large organization can easily have 1,000 or more GPOs for the organization. This adds up to quite a large amount of disk space being used for storing ADM files in each GPO.
>
> ADMX files are not copied into individual GPOs when created or edited using a Windows Vista workstation. Using Windows Vista workstations to create and edit GPOs, you can fix the SYSVOL space bloat issue. A word of caution here: You will see a SYSVOL space savings only if all Group Policy administrators are using Windows Vista workstations to create and edit GPOs. The existing GPOs or GPOs edited by previous operating systems may contain ADM files on SYSVOL, even if the GPO was created using a Windows Vista version of Gpedit.msc.
>
> Note that the GPMC is no longer installed as part of the operating system for Windows Vista SP1. To edit domain-based GPOs using a Windows Vista SP1 workstation, you will first have to download and install the Remote Server Administration Tools (RSAT).
>
> *Judith Herman, Group Policy Programming Writer*
>
> *Windows Enterprise Management Division UA*

Understanding Multiple Local Group Policy

Another new feature of Windows Vista is support for Multiple Local Group Policy Objects (MLGPOs). MLGPOs simplify the task of locking down shared-use computers, such as kiosk computers in libraries. Although MLGPOs are primarily intended for use on standalone computers, they can also be used on domain-joined computers (though you're better off creating multiple domain GPOs whenever possible).

Types of MLGPOs

Earlier versions of Windows support only a single Local Group Policy Object (LGPO) per computer—also known as Local Computer Policy. With these Windows platforms, you could only manage standalone computers with Group Policy by configuring their LGPO; you could manage domain-joined computers with Group Policy both by configuring their LGPO and also by using one or more domain-based GPOs to target the Active Directory container (domain, organizational unit, or site) to which the computer or user belongs.

Although you cannot manage LGPOs on earlier versions of Windows using GPMC, you can open them in Group Policy Object Editor and configure them on the local computer. An earlier version of Windows that had been clean-installed had no LGPO until created when an administrator first used the Local Group Policy Editor. The newly created LGPO is stored in the hidden directory, %Windir%\System32\GroupPolicy, and has a file structure similar to the Group Policy Template (GPT) for a domain-based GPO. Not all domain-based policy settings are included in the local GPO.

Windows Vista computers, however, have three levels of LGPO (which is why they are called MLGPOs):

- **Local Computer Policy**   This is the default LGPO. It will affect all users on the computer and also contains the only available local computer policy. This level consists of a single MLGPO whose policy settings apply to all users on the computer, including local administrators. Local Group Policy contains both computer and user settings, and its behavior in Windows Vista is the same as on earlier versions of Windows. Because this is the only MLGPO that contains computer settings, however, you usually use this MLGPO to apply a set of policy settings uniformly to all users of the computer.

- **Administrators and Non-Administrators Local Group Policy**   Users on a Windows Vista computer are either members of the local Administrators group or not members of this group. Users that are members of Administrators have full administrative privileges on the computer (though elevation may be required to realize these privileges); those who are not members of this group have limited privileges. This level has two MLGPOs: one for users who belong to the Administrators group and one for those who don't. These MLGPOs have only user settings and do not contain any machine settings. You can use these MLGPOs to apply different policy settings to administrators and standard users. These settings apply only to user-based policy and do not affect the computer side.

- **User-Specific Local Group Policy**   This level consists of one or more MLGPOs—one per local user account you create on the computer. These MLGPOs have only user settings and do not contain any machine settings, and they allow you to apply a different set of policy settings to each local user on the computer if necessary. These settings apply only to user-based policy and do not affect the computer side.

Note   Windows Vista does not support using ad hoc local groups for configuring Local Group Policy for groups of users on the computer, nor can you use any built-in groups other than Administrators (and Non-Administrators) to configure Local Group Policy for groups of users on the computer. For example, you cannot create a MLGPO for users who belong to the Backup Operators built-in group on the computer.

MLGPOs and Group Policy Processing

On earlier versions of Windows, Group Policy processing is applied in the following order:

1. Local Computer Policy

2. Site GPOs

3. Domain GPOs

4. Organizational unit GPOs

Policy is applied so that the policy setting closest to the user or computer takes precedence unless the ordering is changed using GPMC capabilities (override, block from above, disable GPO or computer/user portions of the GPO). For example, if a certain policy is configured as Enabled at the domain level but Disabled at the OU level, and the computer and/or user objects are also contained at this OU level, the last value (Disabled) wins and is the effective value for the policy.

Windows Vista uses the same Group Policy processing order, as well as the "last writer wins" method. However, because Windows Vista includes three levels of local policy, processing this policy requires additional steps:

1. Local Computer Policy

2. Administrators and Non-Administrators Local Group Policy (user-based policy only)

3. User-Specific Local Group Policy (user-based policy only)

For information on how to configure MLGPOs, see the section titled "Editing Multiple Local Group Policy" later in this chapter. For information on how to disable processing of Multiple Local Group Policy in a domain environment, see the section titled "Configuring Group Policy Processing" later in this chapter.

Managing Windows Vista Computers Using Group Policy

Managing Group Policy for the Windows Vista platform involves the following tasks:

- Configuring the central store
- Adding ADMX template files to the store
- Creating and editing domain-based GPOs
- Editing Multiple Local Group Policy
- Migrating ADM template files to ADMX format
- Configuring Group Policy processing

The following sections explain how to perform these tasks and more.

Configuring the Central Store

You must manually create and configure the central store for ADMX template files in Active Directory domains running Windows Server 2008 and Windows Server 2003. To create and configure the central store, follow these steps:

1. Log on to the domain controller hosting the PDC Emulator flexible single master operations (FSMO) role using a user account that is a member of the Domain Admins built-in group.

2. Open Windows Explorer and select the following folder from the left folder tree: %SystemRoot%\sysvol\domain\policies

3. Create a subfolder named PolicyDefinitions within this folder.

4. Select the newly created PolicyDefinitions folder from the left folder tree and create a subfolder for each language that your Group Policy administrators will use. You must name these subfolders using the appropriate ISO language identifiers. For example, U.S. administrators should create a subfolder named EN-US under the PolicyDefinitions folder, as shown in Figure 13-2.

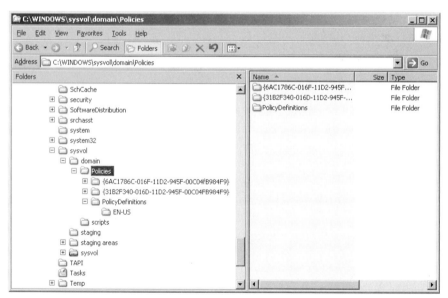

Figure 13-2 The folder structure for the central store where ADMX template files are stored for the domain.

After you create this folder structure for the central store on the PDC Emulator, the File Replication Service (FRS) will replicate this structure to all domain controllers in the domain. You choose the PDC Emulator as the domain controller on which to manually create this folder structure, because the PDC Emulator is the default choice for the focus of the Group Policy Management Console.

> **Note**   For a list of ISO language identifiers, see *http://msdn2.microsoft.com/en-us/library / ms693062.aspx.*

Adding ADMX Template Files to the Central Store

After you have configured the central store, you must populate it using ADMX template files. You can copy these ADMX template files from a Windows Vista computer by following these steps:

1. Log on to an administrative workstation running Windows Vista using a user account that is a member of the Domain Admins built-in group.

2. Open a command prompt and type the following command:

```
xcopy %SystemRoot%\PolicyDefinitions\* %LogonServer%\sysvol\%UserDNSDomain%\policies\
PolicyDefinitions /s /y
```

3. Repeat this process from any administrator workstations running Windows Vista that have different languages installed.

After you have copied the ADMX template files to the central store, the central store will be replicated to all domain controllers in the domain as the contents of the SYSVOL share are replicated by the File Replication Service (FRS). Whenever you want to update the files or copy a custom ADMX file, you must do this manually.

Direct from the Source: Create and Populate the ADMX Central Store in a Single Step

As long as the ADMX central store directory exists, the Group Policy Object Editor will ignore the local versions of the ADMX files. It is recommended that as soon as the central store is created, the ADMX (and associated ADML files) are used to populate the central store. If there is an empty central store directory when the Vista Group Policy Object Editor is started, the administrative template nodes will not display any policy settings. This is because the Group Policy Object Editor only reads administrative template policy settings display information from the empty central store.

Judith Herman, Group Policy Programming Writer

Windows Enterprise Management Division UA

Creating and Editing GPOs

After you have configured the central store and have copied ADMX template files to it, administrators can create and edit domain-based GPOs that use the templates in this store and apply these GPOs to computers running Windows Vista and Windows Server 2008.

Creating the central store is not a requirement for using Group Policy to manage Windows Vista computers. For example, in the absence of a central store, an administrator can use the GPMC running on a Windows Vista Service Pack 1 with RSAT administrative workstation to create GPOs and then use the GPMC to configure these GPOs. The advantage of configuring a central store is that all GPOs created and edited after the store is configured have access to all the ADMX files within the store, which makes the central store useful for deploying any custom ADMX files you want to share with other administrators in your domain. To use the updated Group Policy Management Console (GPMC) included in the Remote Server Administration Tools (RSAT), you must do the following:

1. Obtain the appropriate RSAT package (x86 or x64) for your Windows Vista Service Pack 1 or later computer from the Microsoft Download Center at *http://support.microsoft.com/kb/941314/en-us* and install the RSAT .msu package on your computer.

2. Open Programs And Features from Control Panel and select Turn Windows Features On Or Off.

3. In the Windows Features dialog box, expand Remote Server Administration Tools followed by Feature Administration Tools.

4. Select the check box next to Group Policy Management Tools and click OK.

Alternatively, instead of managing Group Policy by installing RSAT on a Windows Vista SP1 computer, you could manage it directly from a Windows Server 2008 computer by installing the Remote Server Administration Tools feature using the Add Features Wizard in Server Manager.

To create and configure a GPO, follow these steps:

1. Log on to an administrative workstation running Windows Vista Service Pack 1 with RSAT using a user account that is a member of the Domain Admins built-in group.

2. Right-click Start and then click Properties. On the Start Menu tab, click Customize. Then in the Customize Start Menu dialog box, scroll down to System Administrative Tools, select Display On The All Programs Menu And The Start Menu, and click OK.

3. Click Start, then Administrative Tools, and then Group Policy Management. (Alternatively, you can type **gpmc.msc** in the Start Search box and then click gpmc.msc when it appears under Programs in your search results.)

4. Respond to the UAC prompt by clicking Continue.

5. Expand the console tree to select the domain or OU to which you will link the new GPO when you create it.

6. Right-click this domain or OU and select Create A GPO In This Domain And Link It Here.

7. Type a descriptive name for your new GPO and then click OK.

8. Expand the domain or OU to display the GPO link for your new GPO beneath it.

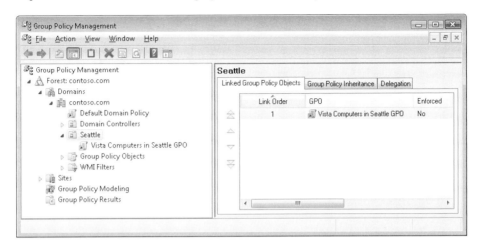

9. Right-click the GPO link and then select Edit to open the GPO.

10. Configure policy settings as desired for the computers targeted by the GPO.

Note   If a domain controller is unavailable when a Windows Vista computers tries to log on to the network, the computer will log on using cached credentials and will use the local copies of the ADMX template files to surface Administrative Templates policy settings in the Local Group Policy Editor. Also, if an administrator uses a Windows Vista Service Pack 1 with RSAT computer to launch GPMC or the Local Group Policy Editor, and no central store is found, local copies of the ADMX template files will be used to surface Administrative Templates policy settings in the Local Group Policy Editor.

Editing Multiple Local Group Policy

To edit different MLGPOs on a Windows Vista computer, follow these steps:

1. Log on to an administrative workstation running Windows Vista using a user account that is a member of the local Administrators built-in group.

2. Type **mmc** in the Start menu and then click mmc.exe when it appears under Programs in your search results.

3. Respond to the UAC prompt by clicking Continue.

4. Select File and then select Add/Remove Snap-in.

5. Select Group Policy Object Editor from the list of available snap-ins and then click Add.

6. Do one of the following:

    ❏   To create a custom MMC console for editing the Local Computer Policy, click Finish.

❑ To create a custom MMC console for editing the Administrators Local Group Policy, click Browse, click the Users tab, select Administrators, click OK, and then click Finish.

❑ To create a custom MMC console for editing the Non-Administrators Local Group Policy, click Browse, click the Users tab, select Non-Administrators, click OK, and then click Finish.

❑ To create a custom MMC console for editing the Local Group Policy for a specific local user account, click Browse, click the Users tab, select that user account, click OK, and then click Finish.

7. Alternatively, instead of creating multiple different custom MMC consoles, you can add multiple instances of the Group Policy Object Editor snap-in to a single custom MMC console with each snap-in having a different MLGPO as its focus, as shown in Figure 13-3.

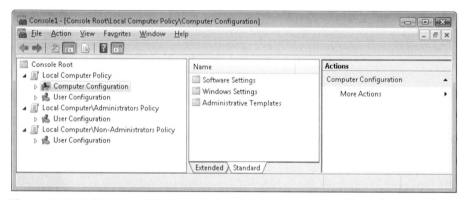

Figure 13-3 Editing Local Computer Policy, Administrators Local Group Policy, and Non-Administrators Local Group Policy all from a single MMC console.

MLGPOs do not exist until you actually configure their settings using the Local Group Policy Editor. You can delete MLGPOs that you no longer need by following these steps:

1. Log on to an administrative workstation running Windows Vista Service Pack 1 using a user account that is a member of the local Administrators built-in group.

2. Type **mmc** in the Start menu and then click mmc.exe when it appears under Programs in your search results.

3. Respond to the UAC prompt by clicking Continue.

4. Select File and then select Add/Remove Snap-in.

5. Select Group Policy Object Editor from the list of available snap-ins and then click Add.

6. Click Browse and then click the Users tab.

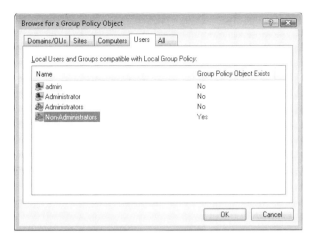

7. Right-click the user or group (Administrators or Non-Administrators) for which you want to delete the associated MLGPO, select Remove Group Policy Object, click Yes, and then click OK.

> **Note** You can also temporarily disable a MLGPO by right-clicking its associated user or group, selecting Properties, and then selecting the check boxes to disable the user and machine (if available) portions of the MLGPO.

You can also choose to edit only the Local Computer Policy on a Windows Vista computer (similar to the way you would do this in earlier versions of Windows) by following these steps:

1. Log on to an administrative workstation running Windows Vista using a user account that is a member of the Administrators built-in group.

2. Type **gpedit.msc** in the Start menu and then click gpedit.msc when it appears under Programs in your search results.

3. Respond to the UAC prompt by clicking Continue.

4. Configure policy settings as desired.

Using ADMX Migrator

ADMX Migrator is an MMC snap-in developed by FullArmor that simplifies the task of converting existing Group Policy ADM template files to ADMX template files so that your enterprise can take advantage of the additional capabilities of this new format. ADMX Migrator is available from *http://www.microsoft.com/downloads/details.aspx?FamilyId=0F1EEC3D-10C4-4B5F-9625-97C2F731090C* on the Microsoft Download Center and can be installed on Windows Vista, Windows Server 2008, Windows Server 2003 Service Pack 1 or later, and Windows XP Service Pack 2 or later provided that MMC 3.0 and the .NET Framework 2.0 are installed.

With ADMX Migrator, administrators can:

- Use a graphical user interface called ADMX Editor to convert ADM files to ADMX format and to create and edit custom ADMX template files.

- Use a command-line tool called ADMX Migrator Command Window to granularly control template migration settings.

- Choose multiple ADM template files for conversion to ADMX format.

- Detect collisions resulting from duplicate names.

During the conversion process, any items that cannot be validated against the ADMX schema are preserved in an Unsupported section instead of being deleted.

 Note Annotations within ADM template files are removed during the conversion process.

Converting ADM Template Files to ADMX Format

To convert a custom ADM file into ADMX format, install FullArmor ADMX Migrator and then follow these steps:

1. Click Start, click All Programs, click FullArmor, expand FullArmor ADMX Migrator, and then click ADMX Editor.

2. Respond to the UAC prompt as required to open FullArmor ADMX Migrator.

3. Right-click the root node in the console tree and then select Generate ADMX From ADM.

4. Browse to locate and select your custom ADM file and then click Open.

5. Click Yes when the message appears saying that the ADM file was successfully converted to ADMX format. This will load the new ADMX file into the ADMX Migrator.

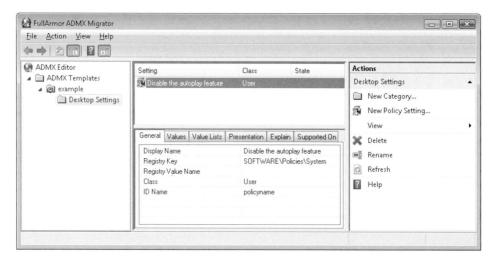

The converted ADMX template file is saved in the %UserProfile%\AppData\Local\Temp folder using the same name as the .adm file but with the .admx extension. Copy this .admx file to the central store for your domain and you'll be able to configure the policy settings defined by it when you create and edit domain-based GPOs.

Creating and Editing Custom ADMX Template Files

You can create new ADMX template files and modify existing ones by using FullArmor ADMX Migrator:

1. Click Start, click All Programs, click FullArmor, expand FullArmor ADMX Migrator, and then click ADMX Editor.

2. Respond to the UAC prompt as required to open FullArmor ADMX Migrator.

3. Right-click the ADMX Templates node under the root node and select one of the following:

   ❑ Select New Template to create a new ADMX template file. After you create this file, you can right-click this template and select New Category to add categories of policy settings. After you add categories, you can right-click these categories and select New Policy Setting to define new registry-based policy settings: Type a descriptive name, a full path to the registry key, and a default value (optional) for the key.

   ❑ Select Load Template to open an existing ADMX template file for editing. After you open the file, you can add or delete categories and policy settings as desired.

Caution   Do not modify the default ADMX template files included with Windows Vista.

Configuring Group Policy Processing

Windows Vista includes two new policy settings that affect how Group Policy processing is performed:

■ **Turn Off Local Group Policy Objects Processing**   This policy setting is found under Computer Configuration\Policies\Administrative Templates\System\Group Policy. Enabling this policy setting prevents Local GPOs (LGPOs) from being applied when Group Policy is processed on the computer.

Caution   Do not enable this policy setting within LGPOs on a standalone computer; the Group Policy service does not honor this policy setting from a Local GPO when in a workgroup. Enable this policy only on domain-based GPOs if you want to completely disable application of LGPOs during Group Policy processing.

■ **Startup Policy Processing Wait Time** This policy setting is found under Computer Configuration\Policies\Administrative Templates\System\Group Policy. Enabling and configuring this policy setting determines how long Group Policy must wait for network availability notifications during startup policy processing. The default value for this policy setting when it is enabled is 120 seconds and configuring this policy setting overrides any system-determined wait times. (The default wait time for Windows Vista computers is 30 seconds.) If you are using synchronous startup policy processing, the computer is blocked until the network becomes available or the configured wait time is reached. If you are using asynchronous startup policy processing, the computer is not blocked and policy processing takes place in the background. In either case, configuring this policy setting overrides any system-computed wait times.

Using Advanced Group Policy Management

Microsoft Advanced Group Policy Management (AGPM) is part of the Microsoft Desktop Optimization Pack (MDOP) 2008, a dynamic desktop solution available to Software Assurance (SA) customers that helps application deployment costs, supports delivery of applications as services, and allows for easier management and control of enterprise desktop environments. AGPM is based on GPOVault Enterprise Edition, a software solution developed by Desktop-Standard and acquired by Microsoft. AGPM integrates seamlessly with the GPMC and provides the following benefits relating to Group Policy management in enterprise environments:

■ More granular administrative control through role-based administration, a robust delegation model, and change-request approval

■ Reduced risk of Group Policy failures by supporting offline editing of GPOs, recovery of deleted GPOs, repair of live GPOs, difference reporting, and audit logging

■ More effective Group Policy change management through the creation of GPO template libraries, version tracking, history capture, quick rollback of deployed changes, and subscription to policy change e-mail notifications

Note that AGPM 2.5 is supported only on Windows Vista RTM and Windows Server 2003. AGPM 3.0, which is scheduled for release in mid 2008, will be compatible only with Windows Server 2008 and Windows Vista SP1.

For more information about AGPM and other MDOP components, see *http://www.microsoft.com/windows/products/windowsvista/enterprise/default.mspx.*

Troubleshooting Group Policy

The Group Policy engine in Windows Vista Service Pack 1 no longer records information in the Userenv.log. Instead, you can find detailed logging of information concerning Group Policy issues by using the following methods:

■ Use Event Viewer to view events in the Group Policy operational log for resolving issues relating to Group Policy processing on the computer.

■ Enable debug logging for the Group Policy Object Editor to generate a GpEdit.log for resolving issues relating to malformed ADMX files.

> **Note**   For additional information on how to troubleshoot Group Policy application issues for Windows Vista Service Pack 1, see "Troubleshooting Group Policy Using Event Logs" at *http://technet2.microsoft.com/WindowsVista/en/library/7e940882-33b7-43db-b097-f3752c84f67f1033.mspx?mfr=true.*

Using Event Viewer

The operational log for Group Policy processing on the computer can be found in Event Viewer under Applications and Service Logs\Microsoft\Windows\Group Policy\ Operational, as shown in Figure 13-4.

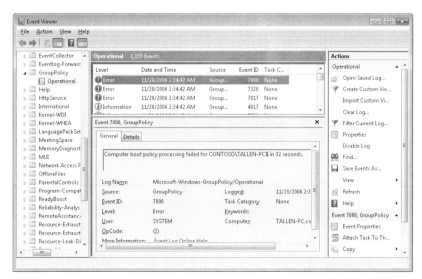

Figure 13-4   Operational log for Group Policy in Event Viewer.

> **Note**   For more information on using Event Viewer in Windows Vista, see Chapter 22, "Maintaining Desktop Health."

This Group Policy Application channel within Event Viewer records each of the step-by-step policy-processing events that occur as Group Policy is applied on the client. This logging channel is an administrator-friendly replacement for the Userenv.log used on previous versions of Windows for troubleshooting Group Policy processing. (The Userenv.log was challenging to parse on those platforms for Group Policy events because several other types of events could be recorded in the same log.) These Group Policy operational events can provide valuable troubleshooting information such as user name, GPO list, and policy-processing metrics such as total processing time and individual extension processing time. In addition, a unique activity ID allows for the grouping of events that occur during each Group Policy processing cycle.

> **Note**   Only the Group Policy engine logs events in the System Event Log; Group Policy extension DLLs do not log events in this channel—they log their events in the Group Policy Operational Event Log.

Table 13-3 summarizes the different ranges of event IDs in the Group Policy Application channel and their meaning.

Table 13-3   Event ID Ranges for Group Policy Operational Log

Range	Meaning
4000–4299	Scenario Start Events
5000–5299	Corresponding success scenario End Events (Scenario Start Event + 1000)
5300–5999	Informational Events
6000–6299	Corresponding warning scenario End Events (Scenario Start Event + 2000)
6300–6999	Warning Events (Corresponding Informational Event +1000)
7000–7299	Corresponding error scenario End Events (Scenario Start Event + 3000)
7300–7999	Error Events (Corresponding Informational Event +2000)
8000–8999	Policy Scenario Success Events

> **Note**   Administrative events relating to Group Policy are still logged in the System Event Log, as on legacy Windows platforms, except that the event source for these events is now Group Policy instead of USERENV. Another advantage in Windows Vista, however, is that Group Policy script-processing errors (the scripts deployed through the Group Policy script extension) are now logged through the same mechanism as the rest of the Group Policy errors.

Enabling Debug Logging

Windows Vista provides optional debug logging for the Group Policy Editor that provides much more detailed logging than is available from within Event Viewer. You can enable debug logging by creating and configuring the following REG_DWORD registry value:

HKLM\Software\Microsoft\Windows NT\CurrentVersion\Winlogon\GPEditDebugLevel

The value normally used for troubleshooting purposes is 0x10002. Configuring this registry value will create a GpEdit.log in the %SystemRoot%\debug\usermode folder. The following sample output for this log file indicates malformed .ADMX files named test.admx and test.adml.

```
GPEDIT(b6c.10c8) 12:10:03:713 PDX parser: Parsing file 'C:\Windows\PolicyDefinitions
\FolderRedirection.admx'.
GPEDIT(b6c.10c8) 12:10:03:716 PDX parser: Obtained appropriate PDX resource file 'C:\Windows
\PolicyDefinitions\en-US\FolderRedirection.adml' for language 'en-US'.
GPEDIT(b6c.10c8) 12:10:03:717 PDX parser: Parsing resource file 'C:\Windows\PolicyDefinitions\
en-US\FolderRedirection.adml'.
GPEDIT(b6c.10c8) 12:10:03:719 PDX parser: Parsing resource file completed successfully.
GPEDIT(b6c.10c8) 12:10:03:720 PDX parser: Successfully parsed file.
GPEDIT(b6c.10c8) 12:10:03:720 PDX parser: Parsing file 'C:\Windows\PolicyDefinitions
\test.admx'.
GPEDIT(b6c.10c8) 12:10:03:721 CSAXErrorHandlerImpl::fatalError: Parsing error, hr = 0xc00cee
2d, message = 'Incorrect document syntax.
GPEDIT(b6c.10c8) 12:10:11:223 CSAXParser::ParseURL: parseURL for C:\Windows
\PolicyDefinitions\test.admx failed with 0xc00cee2d.
GPEDIT(b6c.10c8) 12:10:11:223 PDX parser: Failed to parse C:\Windows\PolicyDefinitions
\test.admx with 0xc00cee2d.
```

Using GPLogView

GPLogView.exe is a command-line troubleshooting tool that you can use to dump Group Policy–related events logged in the System Event Log channel and the Group Policy Operational Event Log channel. GPLogView.exe works only on Windows Vista; it is not included with Windows Vista but is available as a separate download from *http://go.microsoft.com/fwlink/ ?LinkId=75004*. The command-line options for this tool are:

- **-?**   Shows this usage message.
- **-o [output file name]**   Output filename required for text, xml, or html; not valid if -m is specified.
- **-n**   Do not output the activity ID.
- **-p**   Dump the process ID and thread ID associated with each event.
- **-a [activity id guid]**   Shows only events matching the given activity ID.
- **-m**   Runs the tool in monitor mode displaying events in real time.
- **-x**   Dumps the event in XML; the only other options allowed with this option are -m and -a but not both together.
- **-h**   Dumps the events in HTML format; -m or -x option not allowed, and -a and -n are allowed, but not both together. Also must specify -o option.
- **-q [Query file name]**   Uses the query specified by query file.
- **-l [Publisher name]**   If -q is specified, the publisher name must be specified.

The following examples illustrate the use of this tool:

- GPLogView.exe -o GPEvents.txt
- GPLogView.exe -n -o GPEvents.txt

- GPLogView.exe -a ea276341-d646-43e0-866c-e7cc35aecc0a -o GPEvents.txt

- GPLogView.exe -p -o GPEvents.txt

- GPLogView.exe -x -o GPEvents.xml

- GPLogView.exe -x -m

- GPLogView.exe -x -a ea276341-d646-43e0-866c-e7cc35aecc0a -o GPEvents.xml

- GPLogView.exe -h -o GPEvents.html

- GPLogView.exe -h -a ea276341-d646-43e0-866c-e7cc35aecc0a -o GPEvents.html

- GPLogView.exe -h -q somequeryFile.txt -l Microsoft-Windows-GroupPolicy -oGPEvents.html

Using GPResult

GPResult.exe is a command-line tool built into Windows Vista and Windows Server 2008 that can be used for displaying Group Policy settings and Resultant Set of Policy (RSoP) for a specified user or a computer. The version of GPResult.exe included with Windows Vista Service Pack 1 and Windows Server 2008 has two new command-line switches:

- **/x *filename***   Saves the report in XML format at the location and with the filename specified by the *filename* parameter.

- **/h *filename***   Saves the report in HTML format at the location and with the filename specified by the *filename* parameter.

In addition, GPResult now requires command-line parameters when it is run. For more information concerning GPResult.exe syntax and usage, see *http://technet2.microsoft.com/ windowsserver2008/en/library/dfaa3adf-2c83-486c-86d6-23f93c5c883c1033.mspx?mfr=true*. For additional information, see this post on the Ask The Directory Services Team blog: *http://blogs.technet.com/askds/archive/2007/12/04/an-old-new-way-to-get-group-policy-results.aspx*.

Direct from the Source: An Ordered Approach to Troubleshooting Group Policy

To successfully troubleshoot Group Policy issues on Windows Vista, we recommend the following sequence of steps:

1. Start with Administrative Events under Custom Views in Event Viewer. Identify any policy failures that occurred and then examine their descriptions, the Details tab, and the More Information link for these events.

2. Open the Group Policy Operational log and obtain the *activity ID* from a failure event. Then use GPLogView.exe with the -a option to filter events for this activity ID and export the results as either HTML or XML for analysis and archiving.

> **3.** Analyze the GPLogView.exe output to review step-by-step policy-processing scenario events to identify any failure point and error codes for possible future troubleshooting.
>
> *Mark Lawrence, Senior Program Manager*
>
> *Windows Enterprise Management Division (WEMD), with the help of information provided by Dilip Radhakrishnan of the Group Policy Program Managers team*

Summary

Best practices for using Group Policy to manage Windows Vista computers include:

- Begin by migrating your administrative workstations to Windows Vista Service Pack 1, which will allow you to start managing Group Policy for Windows Vista computers immediately.

- After you edit Group Policy Objects using the GPMC included in Windows Server 2008 or the GPMC included with RSAT for Vista Service Pack 1, do not use earlier versions of either the GPMC or the Group Policy Object Editor.

- Create a central store on domain controllers running Windows Server 2008 or Windows Server 2003 and copy the ADMX files from your Windows Vista Service Pack 1 computers to this store.

- Migrate your custom ADM files to ADMX format using ADMX Migrator. Do not migrate the default ADM files found on previous versions of Windows; Windows Vista does not need them.

- If you are a Software Assurance (SA) customer, obtain the Desktop Optimization Pack for Software Assurance (DOPSA) so that you can use the enhanced functionality of the Advanced Group Policy Management (AGPM) component of this package.

Additional Resources

The following resources contain additional information and tools related to this chapter.

Related Information

- The Windows Server Group Policy TechCenter at *http://technet.microsoft.com/en-us/ windowsserver/grouppolicy/default.aspx*

- "What's New in Group Policy in Windows Vista" at *http://www.microsoft.com/technet/ windowsvista/library/gpol/a8366c42-6373-48cd-9d11-2510580e4817.mspx?mfr=true*

- "Group Policy Frequently Asked Questions (FAQ)" at *http://technet2.microsoft.com/windowsserver/en/technologies/featured/gp/faq.mspx*

- "Group Policy Preferences Frequently Asked Questions (FAQ)" at *http://technet2.microsoft.com/windowsserver/en/technologies/featured/gp/preferencesfaq.mspx*

- The white paper "Group Policy Preferences Overview," available at *http://www.microsoft.com/downloads/details.aspx?FamilyID=42e30e3f-6f01-4610-9d6e-f6e0fb7a0790&DisplayLang=en*

- The white paper "Planning and Deploying Group Policy," available at *http://www.microsoft.com/downloads/details.aspx?FamilyID=73d96068-0aea-450a-861b-e2c5413b0485&DisplayLang=en*

- The white paper "Advanced Group Policy Management Overview," available at *http://www.microsoft.com/downloads/details.aspx?FamilyID=993a34d0-c274-4b46-b9fc-568426b81c5e&DisplayLang=en*

- ADMX Migrator, available at *http://www.microsoft.com/downloads/details.aspx?FamilyID=0f1eec3d-10c4-4b5f-9625-97c2f731090c&DisplayLang=en*

- Group Policy Log View (GPLogView), available at *http://www.microsoft.com/downloads/details.aspx?FamilyID=bcfb1955-ca1d-4f00-9cff-6f541bad4563&DisplayLang=en*

- "Group Policy Settings Reference for Windows Server 2008 and Windows Vista SP1," available at *http://www.microsoft.com/downloads/details.aspx?familyid=2043b94e-66cd-4b91-9e0f-68363245c495&displaylang=en&tm*

- "Overview Series: Advanced Group Policy Management" at *http://technet2.microsoft.com/WindowsVista/en/library/e73f25da-42fc-4ca5-a969-6e8bc7e64d761033.mspx?mfr=true*

- "Step-by-Step Guide to Managing Multiple Local Group Policy Objects" at *http://technet2.microsoft.com/WindowsVista/en/library/9c7ecc7d-8784-4b8d-ba1f-ba1882ba83741033.mspx?mfr=true*

- "Managing Group Policy ADMX Files Step-by-Step Guide" at *http://technet2.microsoft.com/WindowsVista/en/library/02633470-396c-4e34-971a-0c5b090dc4fd1033.mspx?mfr=true*

- "Deploying Group Policy Using Windows Vista" at *http://technet2.microsoft.com/WindowsVista/en/library/5ae8da2a-878e-48db-a3c1-4be6ac7cf7631033.mspx?mfr=true*

- "Troubleshooting Group Policy Using Event Logs" at *http://technet2.microsoft.com/WindowsVista/en/library/7e940882-33b7-43db-b097-f3752c84f67f1033.mspx?mfr=true*

- The *Windows Group Policy Resource Kit: Windows Server 2008 and Windows Vista* (Microsoft Press, 2008)

- ADMX Schema on MSDN: *http://msdn2.microsoft.com/en-us/library/aa373476.aspx*

- Group Policy Team Blog at *http://blogs.technet.com/grouppolicy/*

- KB article 929841, "How to create a Central Store for Group Policy Administrative Templates in Window Vista," at *http://support.microsoft.com/kb/929841*

- KB article 937887, "All the check boxes are selected when you enable a Group Policy setting in Windows Vista," at *http://support.microsoft.com/kb/937887*

- KB article 921468, "Security auditing settings are not applied to Windows Vista–based and Window Server 2008–based computers when you deploy a domain-based policy" at *http://support.microsoft.com/kb/921468*

- KB article 921469, "How to use Group Policy to configure detailed security auditing settings for Windows Vista–based and Windows Server 2008–based computers in a Windows Server 2008 domain, in a Windows Server 2003 domain, or in a Windows 2000 domain" at *http://support.microsoft.com/kb/921469*

- KB article 948030, "Internet Explorer Maintenance–related Group Policy results are not displayed correctly in Group Policy Management Console on a Windows Vista–based computer," at *http://support.microsoft.com/kb/948030*

- KB article 940668, "Some services do not start, and you receive an error message after you join a Windows Vista–based computer to a Windows 2000–based domain: "1279, a privilege that the service requires to function properly does not exist"," at *http://support.microsoft.com/kb/940668*

- KB article 940452, "The Welcome screen may be displayed for 30 seconds, and the logon script interacts with you when you try to log on to a computer that is running Windows Vista or Windows Server 2008," at *http://support.microsoft.com/kb/940452*

- KB article 810869, "The Recycle Bin does not appear on the desktop," at *http://support.microsoft.com/kb/810869*

On the Companion CD

- A link to where you can download the latest version of "Group Policy Settings Reference for Windows Server 2008 and Windows Vista SP1," a Microsoft Office Excel spreadsheet detailing Group Policy settings available in Windows Vista Service Pack 1 and Windows Server 2008.

- ListGroupPolicyComputer.vbs

- ListGroupPolicyUser.vbs

- ListGroupPolicyUserOrComputer.vbs

- ListHotFixes.vbs

- ListNICconfiguration.vbs

- ListTimeZone.vbs

- ReportSecureScreenSaver.vbs

Chapter 14
Managing Users and User Data

Large enterprises need secure, reliable, and highly available methods of managing user data and settings. These methods must also work in a variety of networking scenarios ranging from mobile users to shared computer environments to connections over slow and unreliable wide area network (WAN) links. Windows Vista has enhancements to three technologies available on earlier versions of Windows: Roaming User Profiles (RUP), Folder Redirection (FR), and Offline Files. These enhancements make managing user data and settings for Windows Vista computers easier and provide users with a more consistent and reliable experience as they share computers, work from remote sites, or travel.

Understanding User Profiles in Windows Vista

User profiles are implemented in Windows Vista in a significantly different way than they are implemented with earlier versions of Windows. Deploying roaming user profiles for Windows Vista computers therefore requires an understanding of how user profiles are implemented in Windows Vista and how this implementation is different from Windows XP Professional and Windows 2000 Professional. Understanding these differences is particularly important for organizations that have mixed environments containing both Windows Vista and earlier versions of Windows, which is typically the case during a gradual desktop migration scenario.

Types of User Profiles

A user profile is a collection of folders and registry data that describes a user's environment when the user logs on to a client computer. Specifically, user profiles contain:

■ A folder hierarchy that stores desktop icons, shortcut links, startup applications, and other data and settings. The structure of this folder hierarchy is discussed further in the section titled "User Profile Namespace in Windows Vista" later in this chapter.

- A registry hive that stores user-defined desktop settings, application settings, persistent network connections, printer connections, and so on. The registry hive for a user profile, which is the Ntuser.dat file in the root of the user's profile folder, is mapped to the HKEY_CURRENT_USER portion of the registry when the user logs on. Ntuser.dat (a system file located in the root of the user's profile folder) maintains the user environment preferences when the user is logged on to the computer.

Windows clients support two kinds of user profiles:

- **Local user profiles**   Local user profiles are stored on the client computer. When a user logs on to a Windows computer for the first time, a local user profile is created for the user and stored by default on %SystemDrive% inside the \Users\user_name folder on Windows Vista and in the \Documents And Settings*user_name* folder on previous versions of Windows. Whenever the user logs on to the computer, the user's local user profile is loaded and the user's desktop environment is configured according to the data and settings stored in this profile. When the user logs off the computer, any configuration changes made to the user's desktop environment are saved in the user's profile when the profile unloads.

  All Windows computers support local user profiles by default, and the advantage of local user profiles is that they maintain the unique desktop environment of each user who logs on to the computer. Local user profiles thus enable several users to share the same computer while keeping their own user settings and data. The disadvantage of local user profiles is that they are local to the computer. This means that when the user logs on to a different computer, the user's data and settings do not follow her. This makes it difficult for users to roam, or use any available computer, in an enterprise environment.

- **Roaming user profiles**   Roaming user profiles are stored in a central location on the network, which is generally a shared folder on a file server. When the user logs on to a client computer, the roaming user profile is downloaded from the network location and loaded onto the client computer to configure the user's desktop environment. When the user logs off the computer, any configuration changes made to the user's desktop are saved to the network share. In addition to maintaining a copy of the roaming profile on the network share, Windows also keeps a locally cached copy of the roaming profile on each computer the user logs on to.

  Roaming user profiles are supported only in Active Directory environments and must be deployed and configured appropriately. An advantage of roaming user profiles is that they allow a user to log on to any available computer on the network, download her profile, load the profile, and experience her unique desktop environment. Another advantage of roaming profiles is that they can be assigned to individual users or to groups of users, which provides flexibility in how desktop environments are deployed. The Windows XP implementation of roaming profiles has several disadvantages that have been improved upon in Windows Vista; the section titled "Understanding

Roaming User Profiles and Folder Redirection" later in this chapter discusses these disadvantages and enhancements.

Mandatory user profiles and *super mandatory* user profiles are two variations of roaming user profiles. Mandatory user profiles are read-only versions of roaming user profiles that have been preconfigured to provide a consistent desktop environment that the user cannot modify. When a user account is configured to use a mandatory user profile, the user downloads the profile from the network share during logon. When the user logs off, any changes made to the user's desktop environment are not uploaded to the profile stored on a network location, and the changes made are overwritten during the next logon when the roaming profile is downloaded from the server. Super mandatory user profiles have this same characteristic of mandatory user profiles: They are read-only and not copied back to the network upon logoff. What makes them different, however, is that super mandatory profiles are required for the user to log on. Any condition that prevents the super mandatory user profile from loading also prevents the user from logging on to the computer. Therefore, super mandatory user profiles should be used only in environments where the network infrastructure is very reliable and the presence of the user profile is critical.

User Profiles for Service Accounts

In Windows Vista, special identities that are used for service accounts—such as Local System, Local Service, and Network Service—also have user profiles. The profiles for these accounts are located as follows:

- **Local System**   %WinDir%\System32\config\systemprofile
- **Local Service**   %WinDir%\ServiceProfiles\LocalService
- **Network Service**   %WinDir%\ServiceProfiles\NetworkService

---

User Profile Namespace

The hierarchy of folders within a user's profile folder is called the *user profile namespace*. In Windows Vista, this namespace is organized in a significantly different manner than in earlier versions of Windows, including Windows XP and Windows 2000. Understanding these differences is essential for understanding how roaming profiles work in mixed environments that include both Windows Vista and earlier versions of Windows.

User Profile Namespace in Windows XP

In Windows XP and Windows 2000, the user profile namespace is characterized as follows:

- Local user profiles are stored within the root folder %SystemDrive%\Documents And Settings.

- Each user who has logged on at least once to the computer has a user profile folder named after his user account. For example, user Tony Allen (tallen@contoso.com) has the user profile folder %SystemDrive%\Documents And Settings\tallen; the local Administrator account has the user profile folder %SystemDrive%\Documents And Settings\Administrator; and so on.

- A special profile folder, %SystemDrive%\Documents And Settings\All Users, contains common program items such as Start Menu shortcuts and desktop items that are accessible to all users who log on to the computer. By customizing the contents of the All Users profile, you can provide all users who log on to the computer with access to programs and shortcuts they need in addition to those items within their own personal Start Menu and Desktop folders. The All Users profile does not contain a registry hive because Windows does not load this profile. Instead, Windows writes all shared settings to the HKEY_LOCAL_MACHINE hive of the registry on the computer.

- A special hidden profile folder, %SystemDrive%\Documents And Settings\Default User, is used as a template for all new local user profiles created on the computer. When a user logs on to the computer for the first time, and no Default Domain User profile is stored in the NETLOGON share on domain controllers (and no roaming profile is already stored in a network location for users with a roaming user profile configured), the Default User profile is loaded and copied to %SystemDrive%\Documents And Settings*user_name* as the user's local profile. If a Default User profile is stored in the NETLOGON share, this profile (instead of SystemDrive%\Documents And Settings\Default User) is copied to %SystemDrive%\Documents And Settings*user_name* as the user's local profile.

- %SystemDrive%\Documents And Settings\LocalService and %SystemDrive%\Documents And Settings\NetworkService are two special, super-hidden profile folders automatically created for the LocalService and NetworkService built-in accounts used by the Service Control Manager to host services that don't need to run as LocalSystem. Windows requires these special profiles; you should not modify them.

The hierarchy of folders (the namespace) within a user folder on Windows XP consists of a mix of application settings folders and user data folders, many of which are hidden. Some of the important folders in this namespace include:

- **Application Data**   Contains application-specific data, such as custom dictionaries or vendor-specific data. The directories inside Application Data are roamed between computers.

- **Cookies**   Contains Microsoft Internet Explorer cookies.

- **Desktop**   Contains desktop items including files and shortcuts.

- **Favorites**   Contains Internet Explorer favorites.

- **Local Settings**   Contains application settings and data that are either computer-specific or are too large to roam effectively with the profile. (The directories inside Local Settings are not roamed between computers.) Subfolders of this folder include Application Data, History, Temp, and Temporary Internet Files.

- **My Documents**   This folder is the default location for any documents the user creates. Subfolders of this folder include My Pictures, My Music, and other application-specific folders.

- **NetHood**   Contains shortcuts to My Network Places items.

- **PrintHood**   Contains shortcuts to printer folder items.

- **Recent**   Contains shortcuts to documents used most recently.

- **SendTo**   Contains shortcuts to document storage locations and applications.

- **Start Menu**   Contains shortcuts to program items.

- **Templates**   Contains shortcuts to template items.

The implementation of the user profile namespace in Windows XP has several disadvantages:

- A user profile consists of a mixture of application and user data folders stored at the root of the profile. This means that the user profile provides no clean separation of user data from application data. For example, the %SystemDrive%\Documents And Settings *user_name*\Local Settings\Application Data folder contains either computer-specific data and settings that cannot (or should not) roam with the user's profile, or it contains data and settings that are too large to roam effectively. (They would delay the logon experience if they were roamed.) On the other hand, the %SystemDrive%\Documents And Settings*user_name*\Application Data folder contains data and settings that should roam when roaming user profiles are implemented. This confusion of having roaming and non-roaming data and settings stored in two similarly named folders sometimes leads to third-party vendors creating applications that store their data and settings in the wrong folder, affecting the ability of these applications to roam along with the user who uses them.

- My Pictures, My Music, and My Videos are subfolders of My Documents even though they are designed to contain media files rather than conventional documents. This makes configuring Folder Redirection unnecessarily complex and sometimes leads to nondocument, user-managed data being unnecessarily redirected.

- No guidelines or restrictions exist for how third-party applications should store their per-user settings and data within the user's profile. For example, third-party applications might create new subfolders of the user profile root folder for storing per-user information instead of storing it within existing folders in the namespace. Third-party applications also sometimes combine computer-specific and per-user settings within the Application Data folder, which can make it difficult for certain applications to roam when roaming user profiles are configured.

- Users have no simple and intuitive way of securely sharing portions of their user profiles and the data they contain for other users to access over the network. This makes it difficult, for example, for inexperienced users to share specific documents within their My Documents folders.

User Profile Namespace in Windows Vista

To address concerns with the user profile namespace in earlier versions of Windows, the following changes have been implemented for user profiles in Windows Vista:

- The root of the user profile namespace has been moved from %SystemDrive%\ Documents And Settings to %SystemDrive%\Users. This means, for example, that the user profile folder for user Tony Allen (tallen@contoso.com) is now found at %SystemDrive%\Users\tallen instead of %SystemDrive%\Documents And Settings\tallen.

- The *My* prefix has been dropped from folders storing user-managed data files to simplify their appearance. For example, documents are now stored in Documents instead of in My Documents.

- The Windows Vista versions of My Music, My Pictures, and My Videos (and possibly other folders, such as My Virtual Machines if you install Microsoft Virtual PC) are no longer subfolders of My Documents. Instead, the Music, Pictures, Videos, and similar user-managed data folders are now stored under the root profile folder and are peers of the Documents folder. The user profile namespace has been flattened in this way to help provide better separation between user-managed data and application settings and to simplify how Folder Redirection works in Windows Vista.

- New subfolders have been added under the root profile folder to help better organize user-managed data and settings and to help prevent "profile pollution," when users or applications save data files in the root profile folder or in subfolders not intended for that particular purpose. Specifically, the following new profile subfolders have been added in Windows Vista:
  - ❑ **Contacts**   The default location for storing the user's contacts
  - ❑ **Downloads**   The default location for saving all downloaded content
  - ❑ **Searches**   The default location for storing saved searches
  - ❑ **Links**   The default location for storing Explorer Favorite Links
  - ❑ **Saved Games**   The default location for storing saved games

None of these profile subfolders exists within Windows XP user profiles.

- A new, hidden folder named AppData located under the profile root is used as a central location for storing all per-user application settings and binaries. In addition, the following three subfolders under AppData better separate state information and help applications roam:

- ❏ **Local**   This folder stores computer-specific application data and settings that cannot (or should not) roam, as well as user-managed data or settings too large to support roaming effectively. The AppData\Local folder within a Windows Vista user profile is essentially the same as the Local Settings\Application Data under the root folder of a Windows XP user profile.

- ❏ **Roaming**   This folder stores user-specific application data and settings that should (or must) roam along with the user when roaming user profiles are implemented. The AppData\Roaming folder within a Windows Vista user profile is essentially the same as the Application Data folder under the root folder of a Windows XP user profile.

- ❏ **LocalLow**   This folder allows low-integrity processes to have Write access to it. Low-integrity processes perform tasks that could potentially compromise the operating system. For example, applications started by the protected mode of Internet Explorer must use this profile folder for storing application data and settings. The LocalLow profile folder has no counterpart in Windows XP.

- ■ The All Users profile has been renamed Public to better describe its purpose. (Anything stored in this folder is publicly available to all users on the computer.) The contents of certain subfolders within this profile, such as Desktop, merge with the user's own profile when the user logs on to the computer, just as the All Users profile does in Windows XP. As with All Users in Windows XP, the Public profile in Windows Vista has no per-user registry hive because the operating system never loads the profile. In addition, application data stored in the All Users profile in Windows XP is now stored in the hidden %SystemDrive%\ProgramData folder in Windows Vista.

- ■ Users can now easily and securely share individual files from within their user profile folders and subfolders. For more information on how to do this, see Chapter 17, "Managing Sharing."

- ■ The Default User profile has been renamed Default. As with Default User in Windows XP, the Default profile in Windows Vista is never loaded and is copied only when creating new profiles. The Default profile thus acts as a template for creating each user's profile when he or she logs on for the first time.

 Note   Only the local default user folder has changed from Default User to Default. The default roaming user profile located on the NETLOGON share on domain controllers is now called Default User.v2.

Table 14-1 compares the user profile namespace for Windows Vista with that of Windows XP. The folders in the first column are subfolders (or special files) of the root profile folder %SystemDrive%\Users*user_name*; the folders in the second column are rooted at %System-Drive%\Documents And Settings*user_name*. Many of these folders are hidden.

Table 14-1   User Profile Namespace in Windows Vista and Windows XP

Windows Vista	Windows XP
N/A	Local Settings
AppData	N/A
AppData\Local	Local Settings\Application Data
AppData\Local\Microsoft\Windows\History	Local Settings\History
AppData\Local\Temp	Local Settings\Temp
AppData\Local\Microsoft\Windows\Temporary Internet Files	Local Settings\Temporary Internet Files
AppData\LocalLow	N/A
AppData\Roaming	Application Data
AppData\Roaming\Microsoft \Windows\Cookies	Cookies
AppData\Roaming\Microsoft\Windows\Network Shortcuts	NetHood
AppData\Roaming\Microsoft\Windows\Printer Shortcuts	PrintHood
AppData\Roaming\Microsoft\Windows\Recent	Recent
AppData\Roaming\Microsoft\Windows\Send To	SendTo
AppData\Roaming\Microsoft\Windows\Start Menu	Start Menu
AppData\Roaming\Microsoft\Windows\Templates	Templates
Contacts	N/A
Desktop	Desktop
Documents	My Documents
Downloads	N/A
Favorites	Favorites
Links	N/A
Music	My Documents\My Music
Pictures	My Documents\My Pictures
Searches	N/A
Saved Games	N/A
Videos	My Documents\My Videos

Note   Windows Vista allows users to use the Encrypting File System (EFS) to encrypt all files and folders within their user profiles except for Ntuser.dat and the AppData\Roaming\ Microsoft\Credentials subfolder, which is essentially the same behavior as user profile encryption in Windows XP. To encrypt files that EFS cannot encrypt, use BitLocker. For more information, read Chapter 15, "Managing Disks and File Systems."

How It Works: Moving User Profiles

In previous versions of Windows, the moveuser utility (part of the Windows Server 2003 Resource Kit Tools) can be used to map an existing local user account profile to a new domain profile when a computer in a workgroup is being joined to a domain. The moveuser utility can also be used to map an existing domain account profile to a new domain account profile. In Windows Vista, however, moveuser will not work and has been replaced by a downloadable User Profile WMI provider. For more information on obtaining this WMI provider, see KB article 930955, "Moveuser.exe is incompatible with Windows Vista and is replaced by the new Win32_UserProfile WMI functionality," at *http://support.microsoft.com/kb/930955.*

Application Compatibility Issues

Because of the significant changes to the user profile namespace in Windows Vista, particularly the new root profile folder %SystemDrive%\Users and the flattening of the profile folder hierarchy, some application compatibility issues may arise with legacy, third-party, and in-house developed applications. For example, if a legacy application developed for Windows XP has %SystemDrive%\Documents And Settings*user_name*\My Documents hard-coded as the location for storing user data files created with the application, the application could fail because this path does not exist in Windows Vista.

To resolve these compatibility issues, Windows Vista has a number of directory junction points created within user profile folders. These junction points automatically cause applications trying to access legacy profile paths to traverse the junction and be redirected to the new profile paths used in Windows Vista. For example, a junction under %SystemDrive% named Documents And Settings points to %SystemDrive%\Users so that any legacy application that tries to access the nonexistent %SystemDrive%\Documents And Settings folder in Windows Vista will be redirected automatically to %SystemDrive%\Users.

Junction points are super-hidden (the *system* and *hidden* attributes are set) and can be displayed by using the dir /AL command at the command prompt, where the L option displays all reparse points (junction points or symbolic links) within the current directory. For example, running this command from within the root profile folder for user Tony Allen displays 10 junction points:

```
C:\Users\tallen>dir /AL
 Volume in drive C has no label.
 Volume Serial Number is 70E7-7600

 Directory of C:\Users\tallen

11/17/2006  10:36 AM    <JUNCTION>      Application Data [C:\Users\tallen\AppData\Roaming]
11/17/2006  10:36 AM    <JUNCTION>      Cookies [C:\Users\tallen\AppData\Roaming\Microsoft\
windows\Cookies]
```

```
11/17/2006  10:36 AM    <JUNCTION>      Local Settings [C:\Users\tallen\AppData\Local]
11/17/2006  10:36 AM    <JUNCTION>      My Documents [C:\Users\tallen\Documents]
11/17/
2006  10:36 AM    <JUNCTION>      NetHood [C:\Users\tallen\AppData\Roaming\Microsoft\Windows
\Network Shortcuts]
11/17/2006  10:36 AM    <JUNCTION>      PrintHood [C:\Users\tallen\AppData\Roaming\Microsoft
\Windows\Printer Shortcuts]
11/17/
2006  10:36 AM    <JUNCTION>      Recent [C:\Users\tallen\AppData\Roaming\Microsoft\Windows
\Recent]
11/17/
2006  10:36 AM    <JUNCTION>      SendTo [C:\Users\tallen\AppData\Roaming\Microsoft\Windows
\SendTo]
11/17/2006  10:36 AM    <JUNCTION>      Start Menu [C:\Users\tallen\AppData\Roaming\Microsoft
\Windows\Start Menu]
11/17/2006  10:36 AM    <JUNCTION>      Templates [C:\Users\tallen\AppData\Roaming\Microsoft
\Windows\Templates]
               0 File(s)              0 bytes
              10 Dir(s)  35,494,162,432 bytes free
```

Direct from the Source: Working with Directory Junction Points

It's important to mention that directory junction points (DJs) are not designed for enumeration. This means you can't do dir <DJ> to list the contents under the folder that the junction points to, because this would result in an infinite loop. For example, "%UserProfile%\AppData\Local\Application Data" actually points to "%UserProfile%\AppData\Local" itself. To prevent this from happening, there is a Deny Read ACE on these DJs. Instead of enumeration, applications can access only files directly using a path that contains the DJ. For example, you can't do dir "%UserName%\My Documents" but if you have a Foo.txt file in your Documents directory, you *can* do notepad "%UserProfile%\My Documents\Foo.txt" to directly open the file.

One impact of this change is that you cannot use the traditional xcopy command to copy user profiles anymore, because it doesn't handle DJs correctly. Instead, you should use the new robocopy command (which is now included in Windows Vista), because it has an /XJD option to ignore all directory junctions during the copy.

Ming Zhu, Software Design Engineer

Microsoft Windows Shell Team

Windows Vista actually uses two types of junction points:

■ **Per-user junctions**   Per-user junctions are created inside user profiles to provide compatibility for legacy applications. The junction from %SystemDrive%\Users\ *user_name*\My Documents to C:\Users*user_name*\Documents is an example of a per-user junction created by the Profile service when the user profile is created.

■ **System Junctions**   System junctions include any other junctions created on the system that are not located within the user profile namespace for a user that has logged on to the system. The junction from %SystemDrive%\Documents And Settings to %System-Drive%\Users is an example of a system junction created when Windows Vista is installed on the system. In addition, any junctions found in the All Users, Public, and Default User profiles are also system junctions, because these profiles are never loaded.

Tables 14-2 through 14-5 show the various junction points implemented in Windows Vista to provide compatibility with legacy applications developed for Windows XP or Windows 2000.

Table 14-2   Junctions Within User Profiles

Junction Creation Location	Junction Destination
Junction for Parent Folder	
Documents And Settings	Users
Junctions for User Data Legacy Folders	
Documents And Settings\ user_name\My Documents	Users\user_name\Documents
Documents And Settings\ user_name\My Documents\ My Music	Users\user_name\Music
Documents And Settings\ user_name\My Documents\My Pictures	Users\user_name\Pictures
Documents And Settings\ user_name\My Documents\ My Videos	Users\user_name\Videos
Junctions for Per-User Application Data Legacy Folders	
Documents And Settings\ user_name\Local Settings	Users\user_name\AppData\Local
Documents And Settings\ user_name\Local Settings\ Application Data	Users\user_name\AppData\Local
Documents And Settings\ user_name\Local Settings\ Temporary Internet Files	Users\user_name\AppData\Local\Microsoft\Windows\ Temporary Internet Files
Documents And Settings\ user_name\Local Settings\History	Users\user_name\AppData\Local\Microsoft\Windows\History
Documents And Settings\ user_name\Application Data	Users\user_name\AppData\Roaming
Junctions for Per-User Operating System Settings Legacy Folders	
Documents And Settings\ user_name\Cookies	Users\user_name\AppData\Roaming\Microsoft\Windows\ Cookies
Documents And Settings\user_name\Recent	Users\user_name\AppData\Roaming\Microsoft\Windows\ Recent Items

Table 14-2   Junctions Within User Profiles

Junction Creation Location	Junction Destination
Documents And Settings*user_name*\Nethood	Users*user_name*\AppData\Roaming\Microsoft\Windows\Network Shortcuts
Documents And Settings*user_name*\Printhood	Users*user_name*\AppData\Roaming\Microsoft\Windows\Printer Shortcuts
Documents And Settings*user_name*\SendTo	Users*user_name*\AppData\Roaming\Microsoft\Windows\Send To
Documents And Settings*user_name*\StartMenu	Users*user_name*\AppData\Roaming\Microsoft\Windows\Start Menu
Documents And Settings*user_name*\Templates	Users*user_name*\AppData\Roaming\Microsoft\Windows\Templates

Table 14-3   Junctions for Default User Legacy Profiles

Junction Creation Location	Junction Destination
Documents And Settings\Default User	Users\Default
Documents And Settings\Default User\Desktop	Users\Default\Desktop
Documents And Settings\Default User\My Documents	Users\Default\Documents
Documents And Settings\Default User\Favorites	Users\Default\Favorites
Documents And Settings\Default User\My Documents\My Music	Users\Default\Music
Documents And Settings\Default User\My Documents\My Pictures	Users\Default\Pictures
Documents And Settings\Default User\My Documents\My Videos	Users\Default\Videos
Documents And Settings\Default User\Application Data	Users\Default\AppData\Roaming
Documents And Settings\Default User\Start Menu	Users\Default\AppData\Roaming\Microsoft\Windows\Start Menu
Documents And Settings\Default User\Templates	Users\Default\AppData\Roaming\Microsoft\Windows\Templates
Program Files (Localized name)	Program Files
Program Files\Common Files (Localized Name)	Program Files\Local Files

Table 14-4   Junctions for All Users Legacy Folders

Junction Creation Location	Junction Destination
Users\All Users	ProgramData
ProgramData\Public Desktop	Users\Public\Public Desktop
ProgramData\Public Documents	Users\Public\Public Documents
ProgramData\Favorites	Users\Public\Favorites
Users\Public\Public Documents\ Public Music	Users\Public\Public Music
Users\Public\Public Documents\ Public Pictures	Users\Public\Public Pictures
Users\Public\Public Documents\ Public Videos	Users\Public\Public Videos
ProgramData\Application Data	ProgramData
ProgramData\Start Menu	ProgramData\Microsoft\Windows\Start Menu
ProgramData\Templates	ProgramData\Microsoft\Windows\Templates

Table 14-5   Legacy Profile Folders Where Junctions Are Not Required

Legacy Location	Reason
Documents And Settings*user_name*\Desktop	Handled by junction at Documents And Settings
Documents And Settings*user_name*\Favorites	Handled by junction at Documents And Settings
Documents And Settings*user_name*\Local Settings\Temp	Handled by junction for Local Settings folder to Local

Note   The junction from Users\All Users to ProgramData shown in Table 14-4 is actually a symbolic link and not a junction point. Symbolic links (*symlinks*) are new to Windows Vista and are not supported on previous versions of Windows. You can create symlinks, junction points, and hard links using the mklink command. For more information on new NTFS features in Windows Vista, see Chapter 15.

Implementing Corporate Roaming

Roaming user profiles and Folder Redirection are two technologies that provide enterprises with the ability for users to roam between computers and access their unique, personal, desktop environments together with their personal data and settings. Corporate roaming also provides enterprises with flexibility in seating arrangements: Users are not (or need not be) guaranteed the same computer each time they work, such as in a call center where users have no assigned desk or seating and must therefore share computers with other users at different times or on different days. Corporate roaming has the additional benefit of simplifying per-user backup by providing administrators with a centralized location for storing all user data and settings, namely the file server where roaming user profiles are stored.

Understanding Roaming User Profiles and Folder Redirection

Roaming user profiles is a technology that has been available on Windows platforms since Microsoft Windows NT 4.0. Roaming profiles works by storing user profiles in a centralized location, typically within a shared folder on a network file server called the profile server. Because roaming profiles stores the entire profile for a user (except for the Local Settings profile subfolder), all of a user's data and application settings can roam. When roaming profiles are enabled, a user can log on to any computer on the corporate network and access his desktop, applications, and data in exactly the same way as on any other computer.

Roaming user profiles has some drawbacks as a corporate roaming technology, particularly on earlier versions of Windows:

■ User profiles can grow very large over time. For example, the Documents folder for a user might contain numerous spreadsheets, Microsoft Office Word documents, and other user-managed data files. Because the entire profile for the user is downloaded from the profile server during logon and uploaded again during logoff, the logon/logoff experience for the user can become very slow during profile synchronization, particularly over slow WAN links or over dial-up connections for mobile users.

■ Roaming profiles are saved only at logoff. This means that although administrators can easily back up profiles stored on the central profile server, the contents of these profiles (including user data within them) may not be up to date. Roaming profiles therefore present challenges in terms of providing real-time access to user-managed data and ensuring the integrity of this data.

■ Roaming profiles cause all settings for a user to be roamed, even for applications that do not have roaming capabilities and even for data and settings that have not been changed. And if a user has a shortcut on his desktop to an application installed on one computer and then roams to a second computer where that application has not been installed, the shortcut will be roamed but it will not work on the second computer, which can cause frustration for users.

■ Roaming profiles do not support multiple simultaneous logons by a user across several computers. For example, if a user is simultaneously logged on to two computers and modifies the desktop background differently on each computer, the conflict will be resolved on a last-writer-wins basis.

■ Finally, roaming profiles take some effort to configure and manage on the part of administrators. Specifically, a profile file server must be deployed, roaming profiles must be created and stored on the server, and user accounts must be configured to use these roaming profiles. You can also use Group Policy to manage different aspects of roaming profiles.

Because of the limitations of roaming profiles, a second corporate roaming technology called Folder Redirection was first introduced in Windows 2000. Folder Redirection works by providing the ability to change the target location of special folders within a user's profile from a default location within the user's local profile to a different location either on the local computer or on a network share. For example, an administrator can use Group Policy to change the target location of a user's My Documents folder from the user's local profile to a network share on a file server. Folder Redirection thus allows users to work with data files on a network server as if the files were stored locally on their computers.

Folder Redirection provides several advantages as a corporate roaming technology:

■ You can implement Folder Redirection together with roaming user profiles to reduce the size of roaming user profiles. This means that not all of the data in a user's profile needs to be transferred every time the user logs on or off of the network—a portion of the user's data and settings is transferred instead using Folder Redirection. This can considerably speed up logon and logoff times for users compared with using roaming profiles alone.

■ You can also implement Folder Redirection without roaming user profiles to provide users with access to their data regardless of which computer they use to log on to the network. Folder Redirection thus provides full corporate roaming capabilities for any folders that are redirected. On Windows XP, these include the My Documents (which can optionally include My Pictures), Application Data, Desktop, and Start Menu folders within a user's profile.

Folder Redirection as implemented on earlier versions of Windows has some drawbacks, however:

■ Folder Redirection is hard-coded to redirect only a limited number of user profile folders. Some key folders such as Favorites and Cookies are not redirected, which limits the usefulness of this technology for corporate roaming purposes unless combined with roaming user profiles.

■ Folder Redirection by itself does not roam an application's registry settings, limiting its usefulness as a corporate roaming technology. For an optimum roaming experience, implement Folder Redirection together with roaming user profiles.

Because of the limitations of the way roaming user profiles and Folder Redirection are implemented in earlier versions of Windows, these two corporate roaming technologies have been enhanced in Windows Vista in several ways:

- When you implement roaming user profiles together with Folder Redirection, Windows Vista copies the user's profile and redirects folders to their respective network locations. The net result is an enhanced logon experience that brings up the user's desktop much faster than when you implement these two technologies on earlier versions of Windows. Specifically, when all user data folders are redirected and roaming user profiles are deployed, the only thing slowing logon is the time it takes to download Ntuser.dat (usually a relatively small file) from the profile server. (A small part of the App-Data\Roaming\Microsoft directory is also roamed, even when the AppData\Roaming folder has been redirected. This folder contains some encryption certificates.)

- The changes made to the user profile space (described in the section titled "User Profile Namespace In Windows Vista" earlier in this chapter) separate user data from application data, making it easier to roam some data and settings using roaming profiles and to roam others using Folder Redirection.

- The number of folders that can be redirected using Group Policy has been considerably increased, providing greater flexibility for administrators in choosing which user data and settings to redirect. The list of folders that can be redirected in Windows Vista (called *knownfolders*) now includes AppData, Desktop, Start Menu, Documents, Pictures, Music, Videos, Favorites, Contacts, Downloads, Links, Searches, and Saved Games.

- Offline Files, which can be used in conjunction with Folder Redirection, has also been in enhanced in a number of ways in Windows Vista. For more information concerning this, see the section titled "Working with Offline Files" later in this chapter.

Note Roaming user profiles is the only way of roaming user settings (the HKCU registry hive); Folder Redirection is the primary way of roaming user folders.

How It Works: Roaming User Profiles and Terminal Services

There are actually four different ways to configure roaming profiles for users. Windows Vista reads these roaming profile configuration settings in the following order and uses the first configured setting that it finds:

1. Terminal Services roaming profile path as specified by Terminal Services policy setting

2. Terminal Services roaming profile path as specified on the Terminal Services Profile tab of the properties sheet for the user account in Active Directory Users And Computers

3. Per-computer roaming profile path as specified using the policy setting Computer Configuration\Policies\Administrative Templates\System\User Profiles\ Set Roaming Profile Path For All Users Logging Onto This Computer

4.   Per-user roaming profile path as specified on the Profile tab of the properties sheet for the user account in Active Directory Users And Computers

Note that Remote Desktop to a Windows Vista computer does not support the Terminal Server profile path or Group Policy settings regarding Terminal Services. Even though both use RDP, Terminal Services policies do not apply to Windows Vista Remote Desktop.

Implementing Folder Redirection

You can use Group Policy to implement Folder Redirection in enterprise environments. The policy settings for configuring Folder Redirection of knownfolders is found under User Configuration\Policies\Windows Settings\Folder Redirection (Figure 14-1).

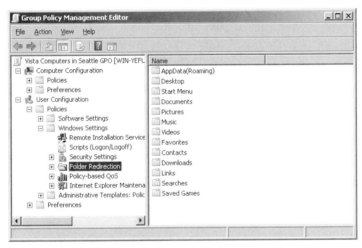

Figure 14-1   Folder Redirection policies in Group Policy.

To implement Folder Redirection in an Active Directory environment, follow these steps:

1.   Create a share on the file server where you will be storing redirected folders and assign suitable permissions to this share. (See the sidebar titled "Direct from the Source: Securing Redirected Folders" later in this chapter for information on the permissions needed for this share.)

2.   Create a Folder Redirection GPO (or use an existing GPO) and link it to the organizational unit that contains the users whose folders you want to redirect.

3.   Open the Folder Redirection GPO in the Group Policy Object Editor and navigate to User Configuration\Policies\Windows Settings\Folder Redirection. Configure each Folder Redirection policy as desired.

> **Note**   Group Policy may take up to two processing cycles to successfully apply Group Policy objects that contain Folder Redirection settings. This is because Windows Vista (and XP) has Fast Logon Optimization, which basically applies Group Policy in the background asynchronously. Some parts of Group Policy, such as Software Installation and Folder Redirection, require Group Policy to apply synchronously, however. This means that on first policy application, Folder Redirection policy is recognized, but because it is applied asynchronously, it cannot be processed immediately. Therefore, Group Policy flags synchronous application to occur on the next logon.

Direct from the Source: Securing Redirected Folders

The following recommendations for secure Folder Redirection permissions are based on Microsoft Knowledge Base article 274443.

When using Basic Redirection, follow these steps to make sure that only the user and the domain administrators have permissions to open a particular redirected folder:

1. Select a central location in your environment where you would like to store Folder Redirection, and then share this folder. This example uses FLDREDIR.

2. Set Share Permissions for the Authenticated Users group to Full Control.

3. Use the following settings for NTFS Permissions:

    ❑ CREATOR OWNER – Full Control (Apply to: Subfolders and Files Only)

    ❑ System – Full Control (Apply to: This Folder, Subfolders, and Files)

    ❑ Domain Admins – Full Control (Apply to: This Folder, Subfolders, and Files) (This is optional and is needed only if you require that admins have full control.)

    ❑ Authenticated Users – Create Folder/Append Data (Apply to: This Folder Only)

    ❑ Authenticated Users – List Folder/Read Data (Apply to: This Folder Only)

    ❑ Authenticated Users – Read Attributes (Apply to: This Folder Only)

    ❑ Authenticated Users – Traverse Folder/Execute File (Apply to: This Folder Only)

4. Use the option Create A Folder For Each User under the redirection path or the option Redirect To The Following Location and use a path similar to \\server\FLDREDIR\%*username*% to create a folder under the shared folder, FLDREDIR.

When using Advanced Redirection, follow these steps:

1. Select a central location in your environment where you would like to store Folder Redirection, and then share this folder. This example uses FLDREDIR.

2. Set Share Permissions for the Authenticated Users group to Full Control.

3. Use the following settings for NTFS Permissions:

    ❑ CREATOR OWNER – Full Control (Apply to: Subfolders and Files Only)

    ❑ System – Full Control (Apply to: This Folder, Subfolders, and Files)

    ❑ Domain Admins – Full Control (Apply to: This Folder, Subfolders, and Files) (This option is required only if you want administrators to have full control.)

    ❑ <each group listed in policy> – Create Folder/Append Data (Apply to: This Folder Only)

    ❑ <each group listed in policy> – List Folder/Read Data (Apply to: This Folder Only)

    ❑ <each group listed in policy> – Read Attributes (Apply to: This Folder Only)

    ❑ <each group listed in policy> – Traverse Folder/Execute File (Apply to: This Folder Only)

4. Use the option Create A Folder For Each User under the redirection path or use the option Redirect To The Following Location and use a path similar to \\server\FLDREDIR\%*username*% to create a folder under the shared folder, FLDREDIR.

When using advanced FR policies, you must complete the last four bullet steps in the preceding list for each group listed in the policy. Most likely, the user will belong to only one of these groups, but for the user folder to create properly, the ACLs on the resource must account for all of the groups listed in the FR settings. Additionally, one hopes that the administrator will use Group Policy filtering to ensure that only the users listed in the FR policy settings actually apply the policy. Otherwise, it's just a waste of time, because the user will try to apply the policy but FR will fail because the user is not a member of any of the groups within the policy. This creates a false error condition in the Event Log, but it's actually a configuration issue.

Mike Stephens

Technical Writer for Group Policy

Configuring Redirection Method

You can configure the redirection method for redirecting folders on the Target tab of the properties for each policy setting. Three redirection methods are possible, plus a fourth option for certain folders:

■ **Not Configured**   Choosing this option returns the Folder Redirection policy to its default state. This means that folders that have previously been redirected stay redirected and folders that are local to the computer remain so. To return a redirected folder to its original target location, see the section titled "Configuring Policy-Removal Options" later in this chapter.

- **Basic Redirection**   Administrators should choose this option if they plan to store redirected folders for all their users targeted by the GPO on the same network share (Figure 14-2).

- **Advanced Redirection**   Administrators should choose this option if they want to store redirected folders for different groups of users on different network shares. For example, the Documents folders for users in the Human Resources group could be redirected to \\DOCSRV\HRDOCS, the Documents folders for users in the Managers group could be redirected to \\DOCSRV\MGMTDOCS, and so on.

  If a user belongs to more than one security group listed for a redirected folder, the first security group listed that matches the group membership of the user will be used to determine the target location for the user's redirected folder.

- **Follow The Documents Folder**   This option is available only for the Music, Pictures, and Videos folders. Choosing this option redirects these folders as subfolders of the redirected Documents folder and causes these subfolders to inherit their remaining Folder Redirection settings from the Folder Redirection settings for the Documents folder.

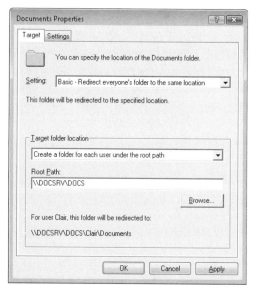

Figure 14-2   Choosing a redirection method and target folder location on the Target tab of a Folder Redirection policy.

Configuring Target Folder Location

If you select either the Basic Redirection or Advanced Redirection option on the Target tab, you have three possible target folder locations to choose from, plus a fourth location for the Documents folder:

- **Create A Folder For Each User Under The Root Path**   This is the default setting for the target folder location option. Choosing this option lets you specify a root path for redirecting the selected folder for all users targeted by the GPO. You must specify this path as a UNC path. For example, if you select this option for the Documents policy setting and the root path \\DOCSRV\DOCS is specified, any users targeted by this GPO will have a folder named \\DOCSRV\DOCS*user_name*\Documents created on the file server the next time they start up their computers, where *user_name* is a folder named after the user name of each user targeted by the GPO.

- **Redirect To The Following Location**   Choose this option if you want to redirect several users to the same redirected folder using the specified UNC path. For example, if you redirect the Desktop folder to \\DOCSRV\DESKTOP and select this option, all users targeted by the GPO will load the same desktop environment when they log on to their computers.

  Another use for this option would be to redirect the Start Menu folder to ensure that all targeted users have the same Start menu. If you do this, be sure to configure suitable permissions on the redirected folder to allow all users to access it.

- **Redirect To The Local UserProfile Location**   Choose this option if you want to redirect a previously redirected folder back to its local user profile location. For example, selecting this option for the Documents policy setting redirects the Documents folder back to %SystemDrive%\Users*user_name*\Documents.

- **Redirect To The User's Home Directory**   This option is available only for the Documents folder. Choosing this option redirects the Documents folder to the user's home folder. (The user's home folder is configured on the Profile tab of the properties sheet for the user's account in Active Directory Users And Computers.) If you also want the Pictures, Music, and Videos folders to follow the Documents folder to the user's home folder, select the Also Apply Redirection Policy To Windows 2000, Windows 2000 Server, Windows XP And Windows Server 2003 Operating Systems option on the Settings tab of the policy setting.

> **Note**   You can specify only a UNC path for the root path for redirecting folders to a network share. You cannot specify a mapped drive for this path. This is because network drives are mapped only after all Group Policy extensions have been processed on the client computer.

> **Note**   You can use any of the following environment variables within the UNC path you specify for a target folder location in a Folder Redirection policy: %USERNAME%, %USERPRO-FILE%, %HOMESHARE%, and %HOMEPATH%. You cannot use any other environment variables for UNC paths specified in Folder Redirection policies. This is because other environment variables are not defined when the Group Policy service loads the Folder Redirection extension (Fdeploy.dll) during the logon process.

Configuring Redirection Options

You can configure three redirection options for each Folder Redirection policy (but only two for certain policy settings). These redirection options are specified on the Settings tab of the policy setting. (See Figure 14-3.)

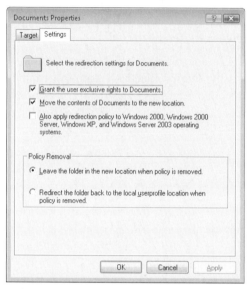

Figure 14-3   Choosing additional redirection options and policy removal options on the Settings tab of a Folder Redirection policy.

The three redirection options available on the Settings tab are:

- **Grant The User Exclusive Rights To** *folder_name*   This option is selected by default and provides Full Control NTFS permissions on the redirected folder to the user to whom the policy is applied. For example, user Tony Allen (tallen@contoso.com) would have Full Control permissions on the folder \\DOCSRV\DOCS\tallen\Documents. In addition, the LocalSystem account has Full Control so that Windows can sync the contents of the local cache with the target folder. Changing this option after the policy has been applied to some users will only affect any new users who receive the policy, and the option will only apply to newly created folders. (If the folder already exists, ownership is the only item checked.)

   Clear this option if you want Folder Redirection to check the ownership of the folder. Also clear this option if you want to allow members of the Administrators group access to each user's redirected folder. (This requires that administrators have appropriate NTFS permissions assigned to the root folder.)

- **Move The Contents Of** *folder_name* **To The New Location**   This option is selected by default and causes any files the user has in the local folder to move to the target folder on the network share. Clear this option if you only want to use the Folder Redirection policy to create the target folders on the file server for users targeted by the GPO but you want to leave users' documents on their local computers.

■ **Also Apply Redirection Policy To Windows 2000, Windows 2000 Server, Windows XP And Windows Server 2003 Operating Systems**   This option is not selected by default and is available only for knownfolders that could be redirected on earlier versions of Windows, which include Documents, Pictures, Desktop, Start Menu, and Application Data. If you choose to redirect one of these folders and leave this option cleared, and then try to apply the policy, a dialog box will appear indicating that Windows Vista wants to write this redirection policy in a format that only Windows Vista computers can understand. If you select this option and apply the policy setting, the policy will be written in a format that these earlier versions of Windows can understand.

Configuring Policy-Removal Options

In several scenarios, a Folder Redirection policy can become out of scope for a specific user:

■ The Folder Redirection GPO becomes unlinked from the OU to which it was previously linked.

■ The Folder Redirection GPO is deleted.

■ The user's account is moved to a different organizational unit and the Folder Redirection GPO is not linked to that OU.

■ The user becomes a member of a security group to which security filtering has been applied to prevent the Folder Redirection GPO from applying to the group.

In any of these scenarios, the configured policy-removal option determines the behavior of the Folder Redirection policy. The two policy-removal options for Folder Redirection policies are as follows:

■ **Leave The Folder In New Location When Policy Is Removed**   This is the default option and leaves the redirected folder in its present state when the policy goes out of scope. For example, if a GPO redirects the Documents folder to \\DOCSRV\DOCS*user_name* \Documents, and this GPO goes out of scope for the users to which it applies, the users' Documents folders will remain on the file server and will not be returned to the users' local profiles on their computers.

■ **Redirect The Folder Back To The Local UserProfile Location When Policy Is Removed**   Choosing this option causes the redirected folder to be returned to the user's local profile when the GPO goes out of scope.

Folder Redirection and Sync Center

When Folder Redirection policy is first processed by a Windows Vista computer, a message appears above the notification area indicating that a sync partnership is being established to keep the local and network copies of the redirected folders synchronized. Clicking this notification opens Sync Center, where the user can view additional details. For more information about Sync Center, see the section titled "Managing Offline Files Using Sync Center" later in this chapter.

Direct from the Source: Folder Redirection Server Path and Folder Name Concerns

When specifying a path for a user's redirected folder, the recommended technique is to put the folder under the user's name so as to have a similar folder hierarchy as the local profile. For example, put the Documents folder under \\Server\Share*UserName*\ Documents and the Pictures folder under \\Server\Share*UserName*\Pictures.

Sometimes administrators may want to redirect different folders into different shares. In this case, you can use %UserName% as the target folder, for example by redirecting the Documents folder to \\Server\Docs*username* and the Pictures folder to \\Server\Pics*username*. This is not recommended, however, and here's why: In Windows Vista, names of special folders such as Documents and Pictures are MUI-enabled, which means that all of the localized names of the folder are actually stored in a file named desktop.ini. The desktop.ini file has an entry like this: Localized-ResourceName=@%SystemRoot%\system32\shell32.dll,-21770. This means that when displaying the folder in Explorer, Explorer actually goes into shell32.dll, fetches the resource ID 21770, and then uses that resource to display the folder's name. The result is called the *display name* of the folder. Different users can choose different UI languages—the resources of these different languages will be different, so the same folder will show different names for different users.

Applying this to a user's profile means that each folder under a user's profile has a display name, and this display name will not change as long as the same desktop.ini file is there, even if the underlying file system folder name is changed. So if you redirect the Documents folder to \\Server\Docs*username*, the display name will still be Documents. Similiarly, if you redirect the Pictures folder to \\Server\Pics*username*, the folder will still show Pictures as the display name. The user won't see any difference on his Windows Vista client computer. So far, so good—at least as far as the user is concerned. The bad news, however, is for the administrator: If the administrator examines the \\Server\Docs folder, she will see a huge number of Documents folders and not the *username* folder as expected.

Therefore, you should specify the redirected folder path to match the local folder if possible. If you have to choose the %UserName% pattern, one solution to this problem is to select the Give Exclusive Access option for the redirected folder so that administrators won't be able to access the desktop.ini file, which means Explorer will then fall back to showing the real file system folder name. If that is not an option, you'll need to use a script to modify each of the permissions of each user's desktop.ini file to remove Allow Read access for administrators. This might be your only choice if you select the Redirect

To Home Directory option for the Documents folder, because a home directory usually uses the user name as the folder name, and Give Exclusive Access does not work with home directories, either.

Ming Zhu, Software Design Engineer

Microsoft Windows Shell Team

Considerations for Mixed Environments

The following considerations apply when you implement Folder Redirection in mixed environments that consist of both Windows Vista and Windows XP or Windows 2000 client computers:

■ If you configure a Folder Redirection policy on a computer running an earlier version of Windows and apply it to Windows Vista computers, the Windows Vista computers will apply this policy as if they were running the earlier version of Windows. For example, suppose that you create a Folder Redirection policy on Windows Server 2003 that redirects the My Documents folder belonging to users targeted by this GPO to \\DOCSRV\DOCS*user_name*\My Documents. When you apply this policy to Windows Vista computers, it will redirect users' Documents folders to \\DOCSRV\ DOCS*user_name*\My Documents and not to \\DOCSRV\DOCS*user_name*\ Documents. The policy will also automatically cause Music, Videos, and Pictures to follow Documents. (Pictures will follow only if the policy for the Pictures folder hasn't been configured separately, however.)

■ If you configure a Folder Redirection policy on a Windows Vista or Windows Server 2008 computer and apply it to both Windows Vista computers and computers running an earlier version of Windows, best practice is to configure the policy only for knownfolders that can be redirected on computers running earlier versions of Windows. (You can also use Folder Redirection policies configured from Windows Vista or Windows Server 2008 computers to manage Folder Redirection for earlier versions of Windows, but only for shell folders that can be redirected on those earlier versions of Windows.) For example, you can configure redirection of the Documents folder, which will redirect both the Documents folder on Windows Vista computers and the My Documents folder on Windows XP or Windows 2000 computers. If you configure redirection of the Favorites folder, however, this policy will redirect the Favorites folder on Windows Vista computers, but the policy will be ignored by earlier versions of Windows targeted by this policy. In environments in which users are undergoing gradual or staged transition from earlier Windows versions to Windows Vista, following this approach will minimize confusion for users. In a pure Windows Vista environment, however, you can redirect any of the knownfolders supported by Folder Redirection policy on Windows Vista or Windows Server 2008.

- When you create a Folder Redirection policy from a computer running an earlier version of Windows, the policy settings for Folder Redirection are stored in a hidden configuration file named fdeploy.ini, which is stored in SYSVOL in the Group Policy Template (GPT) under *GPO_GUID*\Users\Documents And Settings\fdeploy.ini. This file contains a FolderStatus section that lists the different folders that are being redirected by this policy, a flag for each folder indicating its redirection settings, and a list of UNC paths to which the folder should be redirected for users belonging to different security groups represented by the SIDs of these groups. If the Folder Redirection policy is then modified from a Windows Vista or Windows Server 2008 computer, a second file named fdeploy1.ini is created in the same location as fdeploy.ini, and only Windows Vista and later computers can recognize and apply the Folder Redirection policy settings contained in this file. The presence or absence of these two files and their configuration indicates to Windows Vista computers targeted by this GPO whether they are in pure Windows Vista environments or mixed environments containing earlier versions of Windows. Thus if you configure a Folder Redirection policy on a Windows Vista or Windows Server 2008 computer and select the Also Apply Redirection Policy To Windows 2000, Windows 2000 Server, Windows XP And Windows Server 2003 Operating Systems option described earlier, no fdeploy1.ini file is created in the GPO. (If such a file was already present, it is deleted.) Instead, when the policy is applied, the fdeploy.ini file is configured so that the policy can also be applied to earlier versions of Windows.

- Adding a Windows Vista knownfolder to an existing Folder Redirection policy previously created from an earlier version of Windows will remove the ability to save Folder Redirection settings from an earlier version of Windows. This is due to the way that the Folder Redirection snap-in works in Windows Vista. Specifically, if you add any Windows Vista knownfolder to an existing policy setting that was compatible with earlier versions of Windows, the Windows Vista version of the Folder Redirection snap-in writes both files (fdeploy.ini and fdeploy1.ini). However, the snap-in marks the fdeploy.ini file as read-only. This prevents earlier versions of the Folder Redirection snap-in from changing the Folder Redirection settings. The administrator then gets an Access Denied error message because the Folder Redirection settings must now be managed from Windows Vista. (Windows Vista keeps both policy files synchronized.)

- In mixed environments in which a Folder Redirection policy is configured on a Windows Vista or Windows Server 2008 computer and applied to both Windows Vista computers and computers running an earlier version of Windows, be sure to choose Follow The Documents Folder as the redirection method for the Music and Videos folders. If you try to redirect the Music and Videos folders to a location other than under the Documents folder, compatibility with earlier versions of Windows will be broken. You can, however, redirect the Pictures folder to a location other than under Documents. (This option is available in earlier versions of Windows.)

■   In mixed environments, administrators can even configure folders such as Favorites—which cannot be roamed on earlier versions of Windows—so that they roam between Windows Vista and computers running an earlier version of Windows. To do this, simply redirect the %SystemDrive%\Users*user_name*\Favorites folder in Windows Vista to \\profile_server\Profiles*user_name*\Favorites within the roaming profile of the earlier version of Windows. Unfortunately, this method adds data into the user profile to enable having user data in both versions of Windows. This additional data can slow down logons and logoffs when logging on clients running previous versions of Windows.

How It Works: FR and/or RUP in Mixed Environments

One of the major benefits of Folder Redirection (FR) is to expedite logons by removing information from the profile. However, Folder Redirection in mixed environments works only with Roaming User Profiles (RUP), which involves adding data back into the Windows XP profile. The net result is the following in different mixed environment scenarios:

■   **Mixed environment with Folder Redirection only**   This can't be done—to redirect folders such as Favorites, you have to implement RUP. Adding RUP in this scenario has the potential to cause slow logons because users would then be required to wait for the profile to download. Is implementing RUP so that you can roam user data worth the tradeoff here?

■   **Mixed environment with RUP only**   You can do this by implementing FR for Windows Vista clients but not for XP clients. Windows Vista FR redirects special folders such as Favorites back into the Windows XP user profile. The Good: Windows Vista user data is copied to the server using FR. The Bad: Windows XP profiles can become larger and subsequently cause longer logons and logoffs. Additionally, user data is available immediately on Windows Vista; user data is only as current as the last logon on Windows XP.

■   **Mixed with both FR and RUP**   Current FR policy should redirect the five folders (the ones prior to Windows Vista) outside the user profile. The Good: This choice speeds up logons and logoffs (especially for My Documents). The Bad: New FR policy for Windows Vista clients is required to redirect special folders such as Favorites back into the user profile, and this adds more data back into the Windows XP user profiles, which can again slow down logons and logoffs. But when users no longer use Windows XP, you can change the FR policy to redirect all of the knownfolder data out of the user profile, thereby speeding up logons.

Mike Stephens

Technical Writer for Group Policy

Additional Group Policy Settings for Folder Redirection

You can configure additional behavior for Folder Redirection by using the following Group Policy settings:

- **Use Localized Subfolder Names When Redirecting Start And My Documents**   You can find this setting under Computer Configuration\Policies\Administrative Templates\ System \Folder Redirection and User Configuration\Policies\Administrative Templates\ System\Folder Redirection; it applies only to computers running Windows Vista or later. Administrators can use this setting to specify if Folder Redirection should use localized names for the All Programs, Startup, My Music, My Pictures, and My Videos subfolders when redirecting the parent Start menu and legacy My Documents folder respectively. Enabling this policy setting causes Windows Vista to use localized folder names for these subfolders in the file system when redirecting the Start menu or legacy My Documents folder. Disabling this policy setting or leaving it Not Configured causes Windows Vista to use the standard English names for these subfolders when redirecting the Start menu or legacy My Documents folder. (This policy is valid only when Windows Vista processes a legacy redirection policy already deployed for these folders in an existing localized environment.)

- **Do Not Automatically Make Redirected Folders Available Offline**   You can find this user setting under User Configuration\Policies\Administrative Templates\System\Folder Redirection; it applies to computers running Windows XP or later. By default, all redirected shell folders are available for offline use. This setting lets you change this behavior so that redirected shell folders are not automatically available for offline use. (Users can still choose to make files and folders available offline, however.) Enabling this setting forces users to select the files manually if they want to make them available offline. Disabling this setting or leaving it Not Configured automatically makes redirected folders available offline (including subfolders within these redirected folders). Enabling this setting, however, does not prevent files from being automatically cached if the network share is configured for Automatic Caching, nor does it affect the availability of the Make Available Offline menu option in the user interface. (Do not enable this setting unless you are sure that users will not need access to their redirected files if the network share becomes unavailable.)

Note   Some policy settings for managing Offline Files can also affect Folder Redirection behavior, because Folder Redirection subscribes to Offline Files. You can find these policy settings under Computer Configuration\Policies\Administrative Templates\Network\Offline Files and User Configuration\Policies\Administrative Templates\Network\Offline Files. Before you configure any of these Offline Files policy settings, be sure to investigate what impact (if any) they may have on Folder Redirection if you have implemented it in your environment. For more information concerning Group Policy settings for Offline Files, see the section titled "Managing Offline Files Using Group Policy" later in this chapter.

Troubleshooting Folder Redirection

A common issue with Folder Redirection occurs when administrators pre-create target folders instead of allowing Folder Redirection policies to create these folders automatically. Typically, the problems that arise result from one of three causes:

- The target folder does not exist.

- The target folder has incorrect NTFS permissions.

- The user is not the owner of the target folder.

The Folder Redirection extension (fdeploy.dll) logs events in the Application log, so be sure to check this log if you experience problems with Folder Redirection. In addition, you can enable diagnostic logging of the Folder Redirection extension by configuring the Fdeploy-DebugLevel registry value found under the following registry key:

HKLM\Software\Microsoft\Windows NT\CurrentVersion\Diagnostics Set

FdeployDebugLevel is a DWORD value that you should set to 0x0F to enable Folder Redirection debugging. In earlier versions of Windows, the resulting log file is saved under %WinDir%\Debug\UserMode\fdeploy.log. In Windows Vista, however, adding this registry key simply means that more detailed information on Folder Redirection activity is logged in the event logs.

 Note   Failure of Folder Redirection policies affects the Folder Redirection extension (fdeploy.dll) only on a per-folder basis.

Implementing Roaming User Profiles

To implement roaming user profiles for users of Windows Vista computers in an Active Directory environment, follow these steps:

1. Prepare the file server where you want to store roaming user profiles for users by creating a shared folder on the server. (This server is sometimes called the *profile server*; a typical sharename for this shared folder is Profiles.)

2. Assign the permissions shown in Tables 14-6 and 14-7 to the underlying folder being shared and to the share itself. Also confirm that the permissions in Table 14-8 are automatically applied to each roaming user profile folder.

3. Create a default network profile for users and copy it to the NETLOGON share on a domain controller. Let it replicate to other domain controllers in the domain. (This step is optional and is typically necessary only if you want to preconfigure a roaming user profile for your users so that they will all have the same desktop experience when they first log on. If you do not create a default network profile, Windows Vista will use the local %SystemRoot%\Users\Default profile instead.)

4. Open Active Directory Users And Computers and configure the profile path on the Profile tab for each user who will roam.

Additional, optional steps include configuring roaming profiles as mandatory profiles or as super mandatory profiles if desired.

Table 14-6   NTFS Permissions for Roaming Profile Parent Folder

User Account	Minimum Permissions Required
Creator/Owner	Full Control – Subfolders And Files Only
Administrator	None
Security group of users needing to put data on share	List Folder/Read Data, Create Folders/Append Data – This Folder Only
Everyone	No Permissions
Local System	Full Control – This Folder, Subfolders And Files

Table 14-7   Share-Level (SMB) Permissions for Roaming Profile Share

User Account	Default Permissions	Minimum Permissions Required
Everyone	Full Control	No Permissions
Security group of users needing to put data on share	N/A	Full Control

Table 14-8   NTFS Permissions for Each User's Roaming Profile Folder

User Account	Default Permissions	Minimum Permissions Required
%UserName%	Full Control, Owner Of Folder	Full Control, Owner Of Folder
Local System	Full Control	Full Control
Administrators	No Permissions*	No Permissions
Everyone	No Permissions	No Permissions

*This is true unless you set the Add The Administrator Security Group To The Roaming User Profile Share policy, in which case the Administrators group has Full Control (requires Windows 2000 Service Pack 2 or later).

Creating a Default Network Profile

As explained earlier in this chapter, when a user logs on to a Windows Vista computer for the first time, Windows Vista tries to find a profile named Default User.v2 in the NETLOGON share on the domain controller authenticating the user. If Windows Vista finds a profile named Default User.v2 in the NETLOGON share, this profile is copied to the user's computer to form the user's local profile on the computer. If Windows Vista does not find a profile named Default User.v2 in NETLOGON, the Default profile under %SystemDrive%\Users on the user's computer is copied instead as the user's local profile.

To create a default network profile, follow these steps:

1. Log on to any computer running Windows Vista using any domain user account.

2. Configure the desktop settings, Start menu, and other aspects of your computer's environment as you want users who log on to Windows for the first time to experience them.

3. Log off and then log on using an account that belongs to the Domain Admins group.

4. Click Start, right-click Computer, and then select Properties.

5. Click Advanced System Settings. In the System Properties dialog box, click the Advanced Settings tab and then click Settings under User Profiles. The User Profiles dialog box opens.

6. Select the user profile you previously configured in step 2 and click Copy To. The Copy To dialog box opens.

7. Type *domain_controller*\NETLOGON\Default User.v2 in the Copy To dialog box.

8. Click Change, type **Everyone**, and then click OK twice to copy the local user profile you previously configured to the NETLOGON share as the default network profile Default User v.2.

9. Type *domain_controller*\NETLOGON in the Quick Search box and press Enter to open the NETLOGON share on your domain controller in a Windows Explorer window. Verify that the profile has been copied.

> **Note**   You may already have a Default User profile in NETLOGON that you created previously as a default network profile for users of computers running earlier versions of Windows. This network profile is not compatible with Windows Vista. See the section titled "Considerations for Mixed Environments" earlier in this chapter for more information.

Configuring a User Account to Use a Roaming Profile

After you have created a PROFILES share and configured it with suitable permissions on a file server, you can configure new user accounts to use roaming user profiles. To do this, follow these steps:

1. Log on to a domain controller as a member of the Domain Admins group (or any administrator workstation running an earlier version of Windows on which adminpak.msi has been installed).

2. Open Active Directory Users And Computers and select the organizational unit containing the new user accounts for which you want to enable roaming.

3. Select each user account in the OU that you want to configure. For each account, right-click it and select Properties.

4. Click the Profile tab, select the check box labeled Profile Path, type *profile_server* **Profiles\\%username%** in the Profile Path text box, and then click OK.

The selected new user accounts are now ready to use roaming profiles. To complete this procedure, have each user log on to a Windows Vista computer using his or her user credentials. When the user logs on to Windows Vista for the first time, the Default User.v2 profile is copied from NETLOGON to the user's local profile and then copied as *user_name*.v2 to the PROFILES share on the profile server. For example, a user named Jacky Chen (jchen@contoso.com) who logs on to a Windows Vista computer for the first time will receive the roaming user profile *profile_server*\Profiles\jchen.v2. The .v2 suffix identifies this profile as compatible only with Windows Vista or later.

Implementing Mandatory Profiles

The procedure for implementing mandatory user profiles is similar to the procedure for implementing roaming user profiles described earlier in the chapter, with the following differences:

- Instead of assigning the Authenticated Users built-in group Full Control of the Profiles folder on the profile server, assign this group Read permission and the Administrators group Full Control instead.

- Follow the steps in the section titled "Creating a Default Network Profile," but instead of copying the domain user profile you configured to *domain_controller*\NETL-OGON\Default User.v2, copy the profile to *profile_server*\Profiles\Mandatory.v2.

- Browse to locate the super-hidden *profile_server*\Profiles\Mandatory.v2\Ntuser.dat file and change its name to ntuser.man. (Super-hidden files have the *hidden* and *system* attributes set.)

- Follow the steps in the section titled "Configuring a User Account to Use a Roaming Profile," but instead of typing **profile_server\Profiles\%username%** in the Profile Path text box, type **profile_server\Profiles\Mandatory**.

Any user who now logs on with this mandatory user profile will be able to configure the desktop environment while logged on to the network, but when the user logs off, any changes made to the environment will not be saved.

> **Caution**   Do not add .v2 to the profile path of the user object in Active Directory Users And Computers. Doing so may prevent Windows Vista from locating the roaming or mandatory profile. You should apply the .v2 suffix only to the name of the user folder on the central file server.

> **Caution**   It is acceptable to use the existing server and file share where you store your current roaming user profiles. If you do so, however, each user will have two roaming profile folders: one for Windows Vista and one for Windows XP. The added folder also means additional storage requirements for the server. Ensure that the server hosting the share has adequate free disk space and adjust any disk-quota policies accordingly.

Implementing Super Mandatory Profiles

The procedure for implementing super mandatory profiles is similar to the procedure for implementing mandatory user profiles described earlier, with the following differences:

- Instead of copying the domain user profile you configured to *domain_controller*\ NETLOGON\Default User.v2, copy the profile to *profile_server*\Profiles\ Mandatory.man.v2.

- Instead of typing ***profile_server*\Profiles\%*username*%** in the Profile Path text box, type ***profile_server*\Profiles\Mandatory.man**.

After you have implemented these profiles, users will be able to configure their desktop environments while logged on to the network, but when they log off, any changes they made to their environments will not be saved. In addition, if the profile server is unavailable when the user tries to log on to the network (or if the super mandatory profile does not load for any other reason), Windows Vista will not allow the user to log on to the computer.

Using Roaming User Profiles Together with Folder Redirection

If you configure both Folder Redirection and roaming user profiles, do not store redirected folders within the user's roaming profiles, but instead store them on the network share where Folder Redirection is targeted. This reduces the size of a user's roaming profile, speeds up its download time, and improves the user's logon experience.

In general, best practice is to configure Folder Redirection first, make sure it applies success- fully, and then deploy roaming user profiles. Also, users should log off all computers and follow these steps on one computer first (with all their main data).

Considerations for Mixed Environments

The following considerations apply when implementing roaming user profiles in mixed environments that consist of both Windows Vista and Windows XP or Windows 2000 client computers:

- Default network profiles created for computers running an earlier version of Windows are not compatible with default network profiles created for Windows Vista computers because the profile namespace of Windows Vista is incompatible with the profile namespace of Windows XP. Because of this incompatibility, users who log on to a computer running an earlier version of Windows cannot roam their profiles to Windows

Vista computers and vice versa. If users must use both Windows Vista computers and earlier versions of Windows, they will need separate roaming profiles for each computer and must manage the profiles separately. If Folder Redirection is implemented, however, part of the user profiles (the redirected folders) can be shared between the two desktop environments.

- If users need to roam across both Windows Vista computers and computers running earlier versions of Windows, you will need twice the usual space to store their roaming profiles. For example, if user Jacky Chen roams across both Windows Vista and computers running an earlier version of Windows, he will have two roaming profiles on the profile server:

  - *profile_server*\Profiles\jchen, which is his roaming profile on earlier versions of Windows

  - *profile_server*\Profiles\jchen.v2, which is his roaming profile on Windows Vista computers

  These two user profiles are incompatible and will not share any data unless you have also implemented Folder Redirection for the user. Specifically, if you implement all available Folder Redirection policies for this user (including those that apply to earlier versions of Windows), only the HKCU settings will be unavailable between platforms.

In Windows Vista, disk quotas configured on roaming profiles no longer prevent users from logging off as disk quotas do on earlier versions of Windows. However, disk quotas will prevent roaming profiles from being uploaded to the profile server when the user logs off. No user data is lost, however, because the data still remains in the user's local user profile on the computer. Data could be lost, however, if profiles are set to be deleted after the user logs off—for example, in a Terminal Services scenario. In this case, any changes the user made during his current session would be gone, but the server copy of his profile would still be intact.

> **Note**   For information about how to migrate user profiles for previous versions of Windows to environments running Windows Vista and Windows Server 2008, see KB 947025 "Support guidelines for migrating roaming user profiles data to Windows Vista or to Windows Server 2008" found at *http://support.microsoft.com/kb/947025*.

Managing User Profiles Using Group Policy

You can manage the behavior of user profiles (especially roaming user profiles) in Active Directory environments by using Group Policy settings found under Computer Configuration\Policies\Administrative Templates\System\User Profiles and User Configuration\Policies\Administrative Templates\System\User Profiles. You do not need to reboot or log off for these settings to take effect after you have configured them.

Tables 14-9 and 14-10 describe the per-computer and per-user policy settings for user profiles new to Windows Vista.

Table 14-9   New Per-Computer Group Policy Settings for Managing User Profiles in Windows Vista

Policy Setting	Notes
Delete User Profiles Older Than A Specified Number Of Days On System Restart	Allows administrators to delete user profiles automatically on system restart if the profiles have not been used within a specified number of days.
	Enabling this policy setting causes the User Profile Service to automatically delete all user profiles on the computer upon reboot that have not been used within the specified number of days on the next system restart.
Do Not Forcefully Unload The Users Registry At User Logoff	Allows administrators to prevent Windows Vista from forcefully unloading the user's registry at user logoff. (By default, Windows Vista will always unload the user's registry even if there are open handles to per-user registry keys during user logoff.)
	Enabling this policy setting causes Windows Vista not to forcefully unload the user's registry during logoff, but instead unload the registry when all open handles to per-user registry keys have been closed.
	Disabling this policy setting or leaving it Not Configured causes Windows Vista to always unload the user's registry at logoff even if there are open handles to per-user registry keys during user logoff.
	Do not enable this policy by default, because it may prevent users from getting updated versions of their roaming user profiles. Instead, only enable this policy when you are experiencing application compatibility issues related to unloading the user's registry.

Table 14-9   New Per-Computer Group Policy Settings for Managing User Profiles in Windows Vista

Policy Setting	Notes
Set Maximum Wait Time For The Network If A User Has A Roaming User Profile Or Remote Home Directory	Allows administrators to specify how long Windows Vista should wait for the network to become available if the user has a roaming user profile or remote home directory and the network is currently unavailable. (By default, when the user has a roaming user profile or a remote home directory, Windows Vista waits 30 seconds for the network to become available when the user logs on to the computer.) If the network is still unavailable after the maximum wait time has expired, Windows Vista continues the logon for the user without a network connection, but the user's roaming profile will not synchronize with the server, nor will the remote home directory be used for the logon session. However, if the network does become available before the maximum wait time has expired, Windows Vista proceeds immediately with the user logon. (Windows Vista will not wait if the physical network connection is unavailable on the computer—for example, if the media is disconnected.)
	Enabling this policy setting causes Windows Vista to wait for the network to become available up to the maximum wait time specified in this policy setting. (Specifying a value to zero will cause Windows Vista to proceed without waiting for the network.)
	Disabling this policy setting or leaving it Not Configured causes Windows Vista to wait for the network for a maximum of 30 seconds.
	You should enable this policy setting in scenarios in which the network takes longer to initialize than is typical—for example, when using a wireless network.
Set Roaming Profile Path For All Users Logging Onto This Computer	Allows administrators to specify if Windows Vista should use the specified network path (usually *Computername**Sharename*\%UserName%) as the roaming user profile path for all users logging on to the computer. (If %UserName% is not specified, all users logging on to the computer will use the same roaming profile folder specified in the policy.)
	Enabling this policy setting causes all users logging on to the computer to use the specified roaming profile path.
	Disabling this policy setting or leaving it Not Configured causes users logging on to the computer to use their local profile or standard roaming user profile.

Table 14-10   New Per-User Group Policy Setting for Managing User Profiles in Windows Vista

Policy Setting	Notes
Network Directories To Sync At Logon/Logoff Time Only	Allows administrators to specify which network directories should be synchronized only at logon and logoff using Offline Files.
	Use this policy setting in conjunction with Folder Redirection to help resolve issues with applications that do not function well with Offline Files while the user is online. (See the section titled "Implementing Folder Redirection" earlier in this chapter for more information.)
	Enabling this policy setting causes the network paths specified in this policy setting to be synchronized only by Offline Files during user logon and logoff and to be taken offline while the user is logged on.
	Disabling this policy setting or leaving it Not Configured causes the network paths specified in this policy setting to behave like any other cached data using Offline Files and to continue to remain online while the user is logged on (provided that the network paths are accessible).
	Do not use this policy setting to suspend root redirected folders such as AppData\Roaming, Start Menu, or Documents. You should suspend only subfolders of these parent folders.

The following user profile policy settings are no longer supported in Windows Vista:

■   Connect Home Directory To Root Of The Share

■   Maximum Retries To Unload And Update The User Profile

■   Timeout For Dialog Boxes

In addition, the behavior of two user profile policy settings has changed in Windows Vista:

■   **Limit Profile Size**   Instead of preventing the user from logging off, the roaming user profile will not be copied to the server upon logoff. Disabling this setting or leaving it Not Configured means that the system does not limit the size of user profiles. When you enable this setting, you can:

    ❑   Set a maximum permitted user profile size.

    ❑   Determine if the registry files are included in the calculation of the profile size.

    ❑   Determine if users are notified when the profile exceeds the permitted maximum size.

❑ Specify a customized message notifying users of the oversized profile.

❑ Determine how often the customized message is displayed.

This setting affects both local and roaming profiles.

■ **Prompt User When A Slow Network Connection Is Detected**   Provides users with the ability to download their roaming profiles even when a slow network connection with the profile server is detected. Enabling this policy setting allows users to specify if they want their roaming profiles to be downloaded when a slow link with the profile server is detected. In earlier versions of Windows, a dialog box is displayed to the user during logon if a slow network connection is detected. The user can then choose whether or not to download the remote copy of the user profile. In Windows Vista, a check box appears on the logon screen instead and the user must choose whether or not to download the remote user profile before Windows Vista detects the network connection speed.

Disabling this policy setting or leaving it Not Configured means that the system uses the local copy of the user profile and does not consult the user. If you have also enabled the Wait For Remote User Profile policy setting, the system downloads the remote copy of the user profile without consulting the user. In Windows Vista, the system will ignore the user choice made on the logon screen.

If you enable the Do Not Detect Slow Network Connections policy setting, this policy setting is ignored. If you enable the Delete Cached Copies Of Roaming Profiles policy setting, no local copy of the roaming profile is available to load when the system detects a slow connection.

Note   For additional information on policy settings for user profiles, see the Group Policy Settings Reference Windows Vista available from the Microsoft Download Center at *http://go.microsoft.com/fwlink/?LinkId=54020*. This reference is also found in the Chapter 13 folder on the companion CD included with this Resource Kit.

Working with Offline Files

Offline Files is a feature of Windows Vista Business, Enterprise, and Ultimate editions that allows users to access files stored in shared folders on network file servers even when those shared folders are unavailable, such as when a network problem occurs or when a file server is offline. Offline Files has been around since Windows 2000 and provides several advantages for corporate networks:

■ Users can continue working with files stored on network shares even when those file servers become unavailable because of network interruption or some other problem.

■ Users in branch offices can continue working with files stored on file servers at corporate headquarters when the WAN link between the branch office and headquarters fails, becomes unreliable, or becomes congested.

■ Mobile users can continue working with files stored on network shares when they are traveling and unable to connect to the remote corporate network.

Enhancements to Offline Files in Windows Vista

Offline Files functionality has been completely redesigned for Windows Vista to improve performance, reliability, flexibility, manageability, and ease of use. The following list summarizes the enhancements and changes to Offline Files in Windows Vista compared with Windows XP:

■ The user experience with Offline Files is now more seamless and less disruptive when a transition occurs between online and offline mode. Synchronization occurs automatically when configured, and users are notified concerning sync conflicts by the appearance of the Sync icon in the notification area of the taskbar. By clicking or right-clicking this icon, users can choose from various options provided to resolve conflicts, including opening the new Sync Center utility in Control Panel, which is described later in this chapter in the section titled "Managing Offline Files Using Sync Center." Synchronization of other files where no conflict occurs then continues in the background while the user decides how to resolve each conflict.

■ The user also has a more consistent user interface experience (compared with Windows XP) when files have been transitioned to offline mode. For example, if a network folder on Windows XP contains five files, and two of them are made available for offline use, only those two files will be visible when the user has the folder open in Windows Explorer while the server is unavailable. In the same scenario in Windows Vista, however, all five files will be visible in Explorer, and the unavailable files will be displayed with ghosted placeholders (see Figure 14-4). This change causes less confusion for users by providing a consistent view of the namespace on the file server regardless of whether or not any files are available offline. In addition, if you configure caching on the network folder so that all files that users open from the share will automatically be made available offline, Offline Files will automatically create placeholders for all the files within the folder.

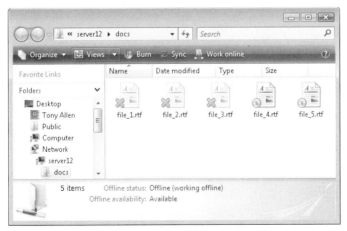

Figure 14-4   Working offline with a network folder that contains five files, two of which have been made available for offline use.

- The synchronization process has been streamlined and made more efficient by the use of a new sync algorithm known as Bitmap Differential Transfer (BDT). BDT keeps track of which blocks of a file in the local cache (also called client-side cache, or CSC) are being modified when you are working offline. Then, when a sync action occurs, BDT sends only those blocks that have changed to the server. This provides a definite performance improvement over Windows XP, where the entire file is copied from the local cache to the server even if only a small portion of the file has been modified. In addition, because of the performance improvement brought about by BDT, any file type can now be marked for offline use in Windows Vista. This is another improvement over Windows XP, where certain file types such as .pst and .mdb files are excluded by default from being made available offline, either because of their large size or because of the frequency of modification. Note that BDT is used only when syncing from the client to the server, and not the other way around. Also, it works only for files that are modified in place and hence does not work for certain applications like Word, PowerPoint, and so on.

- Mobile users and users at branch offices where network latency is high now benefit from an improved slow-link mode of operation. When Windows Vista determines that the network throughput between the local computer and the remote server has dropped below a specified level, Offline Files automatically transitions to the new slow-link mode of operation. When Offline Files is running in slow-link mode, all read and write requests are satisfied from the local cache, and any sync operations must be initiated manually by the user. Offline Files will continue running in slow-link mode until the user attempts to transition back to online mode by clicking Work Online on the command bar of Windows Explorer. When online mode is operational again, Windows Vista will test network throughput and packet latency every two minutes by default to determine whether to remain online or transition back to slow-link mode again.

> **Note**   Slow-link mode is not enabled by default and must be enabled using Group Policy. For more information, see the section titled "Managing Offline Files Using Group Policy" later in this chapter. For information about the different modes of operation of offline files in Windows Vista, see the section titled "How Offline Files Works" later in this chapter.

- Offline Files in Windows Vista now lets you configure a limit for the total amount of disk space used for your local cache, which includes both automatically and manually cached files. In addition, you can also configure a second limit within this total local cache size limit to specify the total disk space that can be used for automatically cached files. By contrast, in Windows XP you can specify a limit only for the total amount of disk space to be used for automatically cached files; you have no way to limit the amount of disk space used in XP for manually cached files.

- Limits for total cached files and automatically cached files can be configured using Group Policy. Note that when the limit for automatically cached files has been reached, the files that have been least-used recently drop out of the cache to make room for newer ones. By contrast, manually cached files are never removed from the cache unless you specifically delete them.

- Offline Files modes of operations now apply to individual SMB shared folders and DFS scopes. By contrast, Offline Files modes in Windows XP apply only to an entire network file server or domain-based DFS namespace. This means that in Windows Vista, for example, when a network error is detected when trying to connect to a file or folder within a DFS namespace, only the DFS link that includes that file or folder will be transitioned from online mode to offline. When the same scenario occurs with Windows XP, the entire DFS namespace is taken offline.

- Offline Files in Windows Vista now allows each file within the local cache to be encrypted using the EFS certificate of the user doing the encryption. By contrast, in Windows XP you can encrypt the entire local cache only by using the Local System account. This change improves privacy of information by preventing access to cached files by other users of the computer. When the local cache is encrypted, the first user who makes a particular file available offline will be the only user who will be able to access that file when working offline; other users will be able to access that file only when working online. Encryption of the Offline Files cache can be configured using Group Policy; see the section titled "How Offline Files Works" later in this chapter for more information. Note that you cannot encrypt files that are currently in use. Also, when an encrypted file is made available offline, the file is automatically encrypted in the client-side cache.

- Offline Files in Windows Vista can also be programmatically managed using either the WMI provider or Win32/COM interfaces. For more information, see *http://msdn2.microsoft.com/en-us/library/cc296092(VS.85).aspx*.

Note   All changes to Offline Files in Windows Vista, including Bitmap Differential Transfer, are compatible with any Windows Server operating system that fully supports the SMB protocol, including Windows Server 2000, Windows Server 2003, Windows Server 2003 R2, and Windows Server 2008. For more information about new features and enhancements for Offline Files in Windows Vista, see "What's New in Offline Files for Windows Vista," found at *http://technet2.microsoft.com/WindowsVista/en/library/bb819260-0fdc-4003-bc23-04beac2108bd1033.mspx?mfr=true*.

> ## How It Works: Improvements to Slow-Link Mode in Windows Vista SP1
>
> Slow-link mode for Offline Files has been modified in Windows Vista SP1 in order to enhance user experience. There are two main modifications.
>
> First, in Windows Vista RTM only the outbound network characteristics were checked to determine if a path should be in slow-link mode or not. In Windows Vista SP1, however, both the inbound and outbound characteristic are now checked, with the smaller of the two values being used to determine if the scope should be transitioned to slow-link mode.
>
> Second, in Windows Vista RTM, Offline Files would check every two minutes to determine if the network was slow when in online mode. This meant that when a scope came online, for example after establishing VPN connection, the client computer could be online for up to two minutes before transitioning to slow-link mode, and this resulted in a poor user experience. In Windows Vista SP1 however, Offline Files now determines if the network is slow as soon as the scope comes online, so that the scope can be immediately transitioned to slow-link mode.

How Offline Files Works

When a user chooses to make a particular file available for offline use, Windows automatically creates a copy of that file within the local cache on the user's local computer. When the network becomes unavailable (for example, when a mobile user disconnects from the network) the user can then work with the local copy of the file by opening it and editing it using the appropriate application. Later, when the network becomes available again (for example, when the mobile user reconnects to the network), Windows will synchronize (sync) the local and remote copies of the file. In addition, users can also manually sync their locally cached versions of files with the remote copies whenever they choose.

When a file that has been made available for offline use is modified, the local and remote copies become different. What happens now when a sync operation occurs depends on which copy of the file has been modified:

- If the local copy of the file stored in the local cache on the user's computer has been modified but the remote copy is unchanged, the sync operation will typically overwrite the remote copy with the local version, because the local copy is the more recent version of the file.

- If the local copy is unchanged but the remote copy has been modified, the sync operation will typically overwrite the local copy with the remote version, because the remote copy is the more recent version of the file.

- If both the local and remote copies of the file have been modified, a sync conflict will occur and Windows will prompt the user to resolve the conflict in one of three ways:

❑ By deciding which copy (local or remote) of the file should be considered the master copy and which copy should be updated.

❑ By deciding to keep both copies of the file as is, in which case one copy of the file is renamed and both versions are then copied and stored in both locations (local and remote).

❑ By ignoring the conflict, in which case the conflict will usually occur again the next time you try to sync the file.

Sync operations also have an effect when offline files are added or deleted. For example, when the local copy of a file is deleted, the remote copy will also be deleted during the next sync operation. And when a file is added to one location (local or remote) but not the other, it will be copied to the other location when sync next occurs.

Understanding Modes of Operation

Offline Files in Windows Vista has four modes of operation:

■ **Online mode**   This is the default mode of operation and provides the user with normal access to files and folders stored on network shares and DFS scopes. In online mode, any changes made to files or folders are applied first to the network server and then to the local cache. Reads, however, are satisfied from the cache, thus improving the end-user experience.

■ **Auto offline mode**   If Offline Files detects a network error during a file operation with an SMB shared folder or DFS scope, Offline Files automatically transitions the network share to auto offline mode. In this mode, file operations are performed against the local cache. Certain file operations cannot be performed in auto offline mode, however, such as accessing previous versions of files. When Offline Files is in auto offline mode, by default it automatically tries to reconnect to the network share every two minutes. If the reconnection is successful, Offline Files transitions back to online mode. Note that users also cannot initiate a manual sync when in auto offline mode.

■ **Manual offline mode**   When a user has a particular network share open in Windows Explorer, the user can force a transition from online mode to manual offline mode for that share by clicking Work Offline on the command bar of Windows Explorer. Available file operations in manual offline mode are the same as when in auto offline mode. Manual offline mode persists across restarting the computer, and the user has the options of manually syncing an offline item by clicking Sync on the command bar of Windows Explorer and of forcing a transition to online mode by clicking Work Online on the command bar of Windows Explorer. If the user forces synchronization of an offline item, the item remains offline.

■ **Slow-link mode**   If the Configure Slow-Link Mode policy setting has been enabled and applied to the user's computer using Group Policy, a network share will automatically transition to slow-link mode when Offline Files is in online mode but network performance degrades below the specified threshold. For more information, see the section titled "Managing Offline Files Using Group Policy" later in this chapter.

> **Note**   In Windows Vista SP1, you can now rename and delete offline files when in offline mode. However, this feature must first be enabled in the registry. See *http://support.microsoft.com/kb/942845* for more information.

Figure 14-5 summarizes the conditions under which transitions occur between different modes.

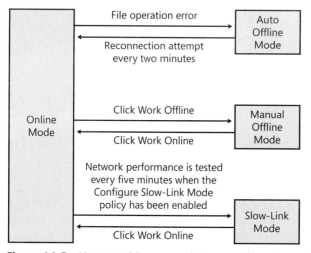

Figure 14-5   How transitions occur between different modes.

Table 14-11 summarizes where various file operations are satisfied (on the local cache or network server) for each mode.

Table 14-11   Where File Operations Are Satisfied for Each Mode

Mode	Open/Create File	Read from File	Write to File	Browse Folder
Online	Server	Cache (if in sync with server)	Server then cache	Server
Auto offline	Cache	Cache	Cache	Cache
Manual offline	Cache	Cache	Cache	Cache
Slow-link	Cache	Cache	Cache	Cache

Table 14-12 summarizes the availability of synchronization (manual or automatic) for each mode.

Table 14-12   Availability of Synchronization for Each Mode

Mode	Automatic Synchronization	Manual Synchronization
Online	Available	Available
Auto offline	Not available	Not available
Manual offline	Not available	Available
Slow-link	Not available	Available

Managing Offline Files

Windows Vista and Windows Server 2008 provide several tools for managing Offline Files:

- Windows Explorer
- Offline Files in Control Panel
- Sync Center in Control Panel
- Offline Settings on the server
- Group Policy

Note   The Client-Side Caching Command-Line Options (CSCCMD) command-line tool (Csc-cmd.exe) used for managing Offline Files in previous versions of Windows is no longer sup-ported in Windows Vista.

Managing Offline Files Using Windows Explorer

As shown earlier in Figure 14-4, items (files or folders) that are available offline are displayed in Windows Explorer with a Sync icon overlay, whereas items that are unavailable offline are displayed in ghosted form as placeholders with an X icon overlay. To make an item in a network share available offline, right-click the file and then select Always Available Offline (you must be online to perform this action). You can also make an item available offline using the Offline Files tab of the item's Properties sheet (see Figure 14-6).

Figure 14-6   The Offline tab on a file's Properties sheet.

You can also configure the Details view of Windows Explorer to show the offline status and offline availability of items in network shares (see Figure 14-7). The offline availability of an item can be either of the following:

- **Available**   The item has been made available for offline use.
- **Not available**   The item has not been made available for offline use.

The offline status of an item can be:

- **Online**   Offline Files is in online mode so that both the network version and the locally cached version of the item are available. (Reads are satisfied from cache; writes, opens, and creates go to the server.)
- **Offline (not connected)**   Offline Files is in auto offline mode so that only the locally cached version of the item is available.
- **Offline (working offline)**   Offline Files is in manual offline mode so that only the locally cached version of the item is available.
- **Offline (slow connection)**   Same behavior as Offline (not connected) mentioned earlier.
- **Offline**   Neither version of the item is available, because the item has not been made available for offline use.

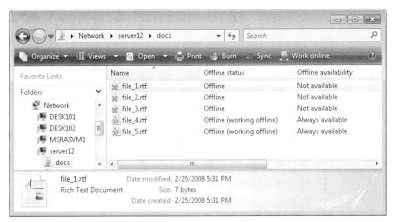

Figure 14-7   Two additional columns are available for Offline Files in the Details view of Windows Explorer.

To synchronize a particular offline item in Windows Explorer, right-click the file and select Sync. To synchronize all offline items in a network share manually, click Sync on the command bar. If an offline item is online, you can also synchronize it by clicking Sync Now on the Offline Files tab of the item's Properties sheet. Other ways of synchronizing offline items are described in the section titled "Managing Offline Files Using Sync Center" later in this chapter.

Managing Offline Files Using the Offline Files Control Panel

Users of unmanaged computers can configure their Offline Files settings using the Offline Files Control Panel tool (see Figure 14-8). On managed networks where Group Policy is being used to manage Offine Files settings for users' computers, configuration settings in the Offline Files Control Panel on users' computers will appear dimmed (unavailable). For more information on Group Policy settings for managing Offline Files, see the section titled "Managing Offline Files Using Group Policy" later in this chapter.

Figure 14-8   The General tab of the Offline Files Control Panel tool.

The Offline Files Control Panel includes the following four tabs:

- **General**   Lets you enable or disable Offline Files on the computer, open Sync Center, and view all offline files on your computer including files in SMB shared folders, DFS scopes, and mapped network drives. Note that Offline Files is enabled by default on Windows Vista.

- **Disk Usage**   Lets you view and configure the total disk space used by Offline Files on your computer and the space available for temporary offline files. You also can use this tab to delete all temporary offline files on your computer. Note that All Offline Files refers to both automatically cached and manually cached offline files, whereas Temporary Offline Files refers to automatically cached files only.

- **Encryption**   Lets you encrypt or unencrypt the local cache on your computer using EFS. Note that you can encrypt only the locally cached versions of these files, not their network versions.

- **Network**   Lets you see if Offline Files slow-link mode has been enabled for your computer and how often your computer checks the connection speed after you manually transition to online mode. Note that the user cannot directly configure the settings on this tab; slow-link settings can be configured only by using Group Policy.

Note   Windows Vista indexes offline files by default. Indexing of offline files can be toggled on and off by using the Indexing Options Control Panel. For more information, see Chapter 20, "Managing Search."

Managing Offline Files Using Sync Center

Sync Center is a new feature of Windows Vista that lets you synchronize versions of offline files between a Windows Vista computer and a network server. You can also use Sync Center to synchronize content between a Windows Vista computer and mobile devices such as portable music players, digital cameras, and mobile phones, either by plugging these devices into your computer using a USB connection or over a wireless networking connection. You can use Sync Center for the following tasks:

- Set up sync partnerships between your computer and the remote server or mobile device.

- Initiate or stop synchronization between members of a sync partnership.

- Schedule synchronization to occur for a partnership at a scheduled time or when an action or event occurs.

- Resolve sync conflicts when the same file is modified in different locations.

- View the status of sync partnerships and identify sync errors and warnings (see Figure 14-9).

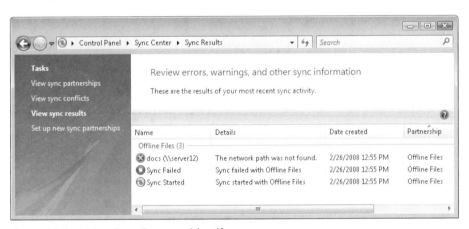

Figure 14-9   Using Sync Center to identify sync errors.

You can also open Sync Center by clicking the Sync icon in the Notification Area of the taskbar. You can also right-click this icon and initiate or terminate synchronization, view sync conflicts, or view synchronization results.

Configuring Offline Files on the Server

When you create a shared folder on a Windows Server 2008 file server, you also have the option of configuring Offline Files settings for items located within that folder. Configure Offline Files settings for a shared folder by clicking Caching on the Advanced Sharing properties for the folder (see Figure 14-10).

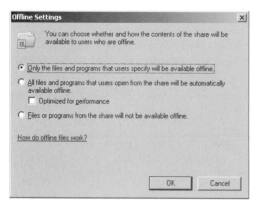

Figure 14-10   Offline Files settings for a shared folder on a network server.

Three caching options are available for shared folders:

- **Only The Files And Programs That Users Specify Will Be Available Offline**   This is the default setting and is used to configure manual caching of items in the folder. This means that if the user wants an item to be available offline, the user must manually select it to be made available offline using one of the methods described earlier in this chapter.

- **All Files And Programs That Users Open From The Share Will Be Automatically Available Offline**   This setting is used to configure automatic caching of items, which means that every time a user accesses an item in the shared folder, the item will be made temporarily available offline on his computer. If you also select the Optimized For Performance option, all programs are automatically cached so that they can run locally. (This option is particularly useful for file servers that host applications, because it reduces network traffic and improves server scalability.)

- **Files Or Programs From This Share Will Not be Available Offline**   With this setting, no caching is performed. (Items in the shared folder cannot be made available offline.)

Note   You can also select specific files to be cached automatically using Group Policy by enabling and configuring the Administratively Assigned Offline Files policy setting. For more information, see the next section of this chapter.

Direct from the Source: CSC Server Settings for RUP/FR

When setting up an RUP or FR server, one thing to consider is how to set the CSC settings on the share. RUP/FR behaves quite differently when used together with CSC: RUP uses its own synchronization algorithm to keep the local copy in sync with the server, so it does not rely on CSC. As a best practice, Microsoft always recommends that you configure the RUP server to disable CSC (with the setting Files Or Programs From This Share Will Not Be Available Offline). FR, in the other hand, depends heavily on

CSC to provide synchronization between the client cache and the server. So the typical setting on FR share is manual caching (Only The Files Or Programs The Users Specify Will Be Available Offline). You don't need to set it to auto caching (All Files And Programs That The Users Open From This Share Will Be Automatically Available Offline), because the FR client side will automatically pin the folder so that it will always be available offline.

However, the preceding recommendation has an exception. Because Windows Vista and Windows XP have separate profiles in the server (the Windows Vista profile has a .v2 suffix), if you have both Windows XP and Windows Vista clients in your organization and have RUP deployed on both platforms, you can't share data between them. To share a specific folder between them, you can deploy a special folder redirection policy for Windows Vista client computers to redirect only a certain folder (such as Favorites) to the Windows XP RUP share. In this configuration, you cannot disable CSC entirely on the RUP share. Instead, you need to set up manual caching to let CSC work against this share for Windows Vista. Don't worry about RUP in Windows XP, though—RUP tries to keep the CSC out of the picture by bypassing CSC to talk directly to the server.

Ming Zhu, Software Design Engineer

Microsoft Windows Shell Team

Managing Offline Files Using Group Policy

Group Policy settings for managing Offline Files have been enhanced in Windows Vista with three new policy settings:

- **Configure Slow-Link Mode**   This policy setting allows you to enable and configure the slow-link mode of Offline Files (see Figure 14-11). When Offline Files is operating in slow-link mode, all file requests are satisfied from the Offline Files cache, just as when the user is working offline. However, the user can manually initiate synchronization on demand. When the synchronization completes, the system continues to operate in the slow-link mode until the user transitions the share to online mode.

   If you enable this policy setting, Offline Files will operate in slow-link mode if the end-to-end network throughput between the client and the server is below the throughput threshold parameter, or if the network latency is above the latency threshold parameter.

   You can configure slow-link mode by specifying thresholds for Throughput (bits per second) and Latency (in milliseconds) for specific UNC paths. You can specify one or both threshold parameters.

   When a share is transitioned to slow-link mode, the user can force the share to transition to online mode. However, the system periodically checks to see whether or not a connection to a server is slow. If the connection is slow, the share will again be transitioned to slow-link mode.

> **Note**   You can use wildcards (*) for specifying UNC paths.

If you disable or do not configuring this policy setting, Offline Files will not transition to slow-link mode.

> **Note**   The Configure Slow-Link Mode policy setting replaces the Configure Slow Link Speed policy setting used by earlier versions of Windows.

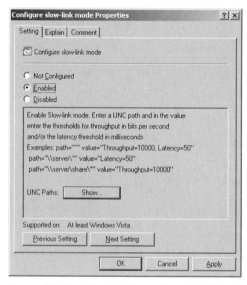

Figure 14-11   The Configure Slow-Link Mode policy setting.

- **Limit disk space used by offline files**   This policy limits the amount of the computer's disk space that can be used to store offline files (see Figure 14-12). Using this setting, you can configure how much total disk space (in megabytes) is used for storing offline files. This includes the space used by automatically cached files and files that are specifically made available offline. Files can be automatically cached if the user accesses a file on an automatic caching network share. This setting also disables the ability to adjust, through the Offline Files Control Panel item, the disk space limits on the Offline Files cache. This prevents users from trying to change the option while a policy setting controls it.

  If you enable this policy setting, you can specify the disk space limit for offline files and also specify how much of that disk space can be used by automatically cached files.

  If you disable this policy setting, the system limits the space that offline files occupy to 25 percent of the total space on the drive where the Offline Files cache is located. The limit for automatically cached files is 100 percent of the total disk space limit.

If you do not configure this policy setting, the system limits the space that offline files occupy to 25 percent of the total space on the drive where the Offline Files cache is located. The limit for automatically cached files is 100 percent of the total disk space limit. However, the users can change these values using the Offline Files control applet.

If you enable this setting and specify a total size limit greater than the size of the drive hosting the Offline Files cache, and that drive is the system drive, the total size limit is automatically adjusted downward to 75 percent of the size of the drive. If the cache is located on a drive other than the system drive, the limit is automatically adjusted downward to 100 percent of the size of the drive.

If you enable this setting and specify a total size limit less than the amount of space currently used by the Offline Files cache, the total size limit is automatically adjusted upward to the amount of space currently used by offline files. The cache is then considered full.

If you enable this setting and specify an auto-cached space limit greater than the total size limit, the auto-cached limit is automatically adjusted downward to equal the total size limit.

> **Note**   The Limit Disk Space Used By Offline Files policy setting replaces the Default Cache Size policy setting used by earlier versions of Windows.

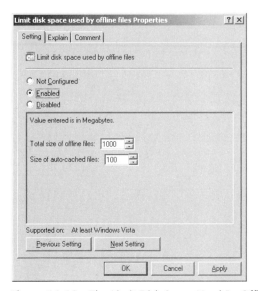

Figure 14-12   The Limit Disk Space Used By Offline Files Policy setting.

■ **Turn On Economical Application Of Administratively Assigned Offline Files**   This policy setting allows you to turn on economical application of administratively assigned Offline Files.

If you enable this policy setting, only new files and folders in administratively assigned folders are synchronized at logon. Files and folders that are already available offline are skipped and are synchronized later.

If you disable or do not configure this policy setting, all administratively assigned folders are synchronized at logon.

In addition to these three new policy settings, many policy settings for Offline Files used by earlier versions of Windows no longer apply to Windows Vista. Table 14-13 summarizes which Offline Files policy settings now apply to Windows Vista. These policy settings are located in one of two locations:

■ Per-machine policy settings for Offline Files are found under Computer Configuration\Policies\Administrative Templates\Network\Offline Files.

■ Per-user policy settings for Offline Files are found under User Configuration\Policies\Administrative Templates\Network\Offline Files.

Table 14-13   Offline Files Policy Settings for Windows Vista

Name of Policy Setting	Per-Machine	Per-User	Applies to Windows Vista
Action On Server Disconnect	✓	✓	
Administratively Assigned Offline Files	✓	✓	✓
Allow Or Disallow Use Of The Offline Files Feature	✓		✓
At Logoff, Delete Local Copy Of User's Offline Files	✓		
Configure Slow-Link Speed	✓		
Configure Slow-Link Mode	✓		✓ (New—replaces Configure Slow-Link Speed policy)
Default Cache Size	✓		
Encrypt The Offline Files Cache	✓		✓
Event Logging Level	✓	✓	
Files Not Cached	✓		
Initial Reminder Balloon Lifetime	✓	✓	
Limit Disk Space Used By Offline Files	✓		✓ (New—replaces Default Cache Size policy)
Non-Default Server Disconnect Actions	✓	✓	
Prevent Use Of Offline Files Folder	✓	✓	
Prohibit 'Make Available Offline' For These Files And Folders	✓	✓	
Prohibit User Configuration Of Offline Files	✓	✓	

Table 14-13 Offline Files Policy Settings for Windows Vista

Name of Policy Setting	Per-Machine	Per-User	Applies to Windows Vista
Reminder Balloon Frequency	✓	✓	
Reminder Balloon Lifetime	✓	✓	
Remove 'Make Available Offline'	✓	✓	✓
Subfolders Always Available Offline	✓		
Synchronize All Offline Files Before Logging Off	✓	✓	
Synchronize All Offline Files When Logging On	✓	✓	
Synchronize Offline Files Before Suspend	✓	✓	
Turn Off Reminder Balloons	✓	✓	
Turn On Economical Application Of Administratively Assigned Offline Files	✓		✓ (New to Windows Vista)

Direct from the Source: Troubleshooting Common User Profile, Folder Redirection, and Client-Side Caching Issues in Windows Vista

The following lists describe some common support issues with FR, RUP, and CSC in Windows Vista:

User Profile Issue Troubleshooting

Symptom: Loading temporary profile error during user logon: "Windows cannot find the local profile and is logging you on with a temporary profile. Changes you make to this profile will be lost when you log off"

Possible Cause #1: SID in ProfileList structure deleted.

Explanation: Microsoft does not recommend that you delete User Profiles using anything other than the Control Panel item (Computer Properties\Advanced System Settings\User Profiles\Settings). When the folder structure for a User Profile has been deleted using Explorer or the command prompt, the corresponding registry entries under the ProfileList registry key are left behind.

Resolution: Remove the corresponding SID entry under the ProfileList registry key: HKEY_LOCAL_MACHINE\Software\Microsoft\Windows NT\CurrentVersion\ ProfileList.

Possible Cause #2: User in Guests group

Explanation: During logon, the interactive user is checked for membership in the local Guests group and the domain Guest group, if the user is the member of a domain.

Resolution: If appropriate, remove the affected user from the local Guests/Domain Guest membership (see *http://support.microsoft.com/kb/940453*).

Possible Cause #3: Insufficient permissions (roaming profile)

Explanation: If permissions have been altered on a working roaming profile, the user may encounter this error.

Resolution: Correct the permissions so that the user has Full Control over her Roaming User Profile folders. If a locked-down user profile is required, use a mandatory user profile.

Folder Redirection Troubleshooting

Symptom: Duplicate folders in user profile

Possible Cause #1: Partial sync

Explanation: Users in Windows Vista can select various folders within their user profiles to redirect to a local or remote drive. If only some of the contents of a folder are moved, the user may see multiple folders under a user profile, such as two folders named Documents or Music.

Resolution: Allow the session to complete data transfer before logoff.

Possible Cause #2: Local and remote copy of files kept

Explanation: When a user's folder is being redirected the user will be asked if he wants to move all current content. If the user chooses not to move the contents, but only to copy, duplicate folders will appear under the user profile—one local, one remote.

Resolution: This is by design.

Possible Cause #3: Program creating folder locally (application compatibility)

Explanation: After a user has redirected a User Profile folder or folders successfully, upon running an application, a local instance of the User Profile folder(s) may be created. This behavior is due to the application using only local resources or having a fixed path for resources and not using the environment variables. This is an application-specific issue.

Resolution: Update the application or do not redirect the affected User Profile folder(s).

Client-Side Caching Troubleshooting

Symptom: Files/folders not seen while offline

Possible Cause #1: Sync has not completed (because it occurs during background).

Explanation: This is a fundamental change from Windows XP: Windows Vista Offline Files will synchronize in the background as user activity allows; this means that users will not have to wait for files to synchronize before completing a logoff. However, this also means that, depending on the volume and type of data that is to be synchronized, synchronization may need further logon sessions to complete.

Resolution: Allow longer logon sessions for larger amounts of data to be synchronized.

Possible Cause #2: Sync has not completed.

Explanation: Another possible root cause of incomplete synchronization is the same as in Windows XP—namely, if a file is in use, open file handles will prevent the file from synchronizing.

Resolution: This is an unchanged behavior and is by design.

Possible Cause #3: Offline files respond slowly over a VPN connection.

Explanation: On a Windows Vista–based computer, you experience slow performance after you establish a VPN connection. Additionally, it may take several minutes to open a redirected shell folder. This problem occurs if the following conditions are true:

- Offline files are enabled on the computer.
- Some offline files are cached on the local computer.
- You logged on to the computer when you were offline.
- The VPN connection is based on a slow connection.

This problem usually lasts several minutes and then disappears.

Resolution: See *http://support.microsoft.com/kb/934202*. (This issue has been fixed in Service Pack 1.)

Possible Cause #4: Changes to an offline file are not saved to the server when files are synchronized.

Explanation: When you modify an offline file in Windows Vista, the changes are not saved to the server when files are synchronized. When this problem occurs, you receive the following error message: "Access Denied". Additionally, a .tmp file that corresponds to the file appears on the server. You may experience this symptom even when you have Change permissions to the shared resource.

Resolution: See *http://support.microsoft.com/kb/935663*. (This issue has been fixed in Service Pack 1.)

Paul D. LeBlanc

Supportability Program Manager

Summary

Folder Redirection, Offline Files, and Roaming User Profiles are IntelliMirror technologies that have been enhanced in Windows Vista in numerous ways to provide better support for corporate roaming scenarios and high availability for file server scenarios. You can implement these features using the procedures outlined in this chapter; you can manage various aspects of their behavior using Group Policy and from the user interface.

Additional Resources

The following resources contain additional information and tools related to this chapter.

Related Information

- Chapter 13, "Managing the Desktop Environment," for more information about Group Policy in Windows Vista.

- "Managing Roaming User Data Deployment Guide," found at *http://technet2.microsoft.com/WindowsVista/en/library/fb3681b2-da39-4944-93ad-dd3b6e8ca4dc1033.mspx?mfr=true.*

- "What's New in Offline Files for Windows Vista" at *http://technet2.microsoft.com/WindowsVista/en/library/bb819260-0fdc-4003-bc23-04beac2108bd1033.mspx?mfr=true.*

- TechNet Webcast: Offline Files and Folder Redirection in Windows Vista (Level 300) at *http://msevents.microsoft.com/cui/WebCastEventDetails.aspx?culture=en-US&EventID =1032352489&CountryCode=US.*

- TechNet Webcast: New Backup and Offline Files Features in Windows Vista (Level 300) at *http://msevents.microsoft.com/cui/WebCastEventDetails.aspx?EventID =1032306238&EventCategory=3&culture=en-US&CountryCode=US.*

- TechNet Webcast: Windows Server 2008 and Windows Vista Better Together Technologies (Level 200) at *http://msevents.microsoft.com/cui/WebCastEvent Details.aspx?EventID=1032366189&EventCategory=4&culture=en-US&CountryCode=US.*

- KB 927387 "Common file and registry virtualization issues in Windows Vista" at *http://support.microsoft.com/default.aspx/kb/927387.*

- KB 930128 "Error message when you try to access the My Documents, My Music, My Pictures, and My Videos folders in Windows Vista: 'Access is Denied'" at *http://support.microsoft.com/kb/930128.*

- KB 929831 "A description of known issues with the FolderLocation settings in the Windows Vista Unattend.xml file" at *http://support.microsoft.com/kb/929831.*

- KB 940017 "User profiles may be deleted after you restart a computer that is running Windows Vista or Windows Server 2008" at *http://support.microsoft.com/kb/940017*.

- KB 947242 "A temporary profile is loaded after you log on to a Windows Vista–based system" at *http://support.microsoft.com/kb/947242.*

- KB 940453 "A temporary user profile is created every time that you log on to a Windows Vista–based computer that is connected to a domain" at *http://support.microsoft.com/ kb/940453.*

- KB 947215 "Error message when you log on to a Windows Vista–based computer by using a temporary profile: 'The User Profile Service failed the logon. User profile cannot be loaded'" at *http://support.microsoft.com/kb/947215.*

- KB 947025 "Support guidelines for migrating roaming user profiles data to Windows Vista or to Windows Server 2008" at *http://support.microsoft.com/kb/947025.*

- KB 947222 "When you redirect the Documents folder on a Windows Vista–based computer to a network share, the folder name unexpectedly changes back to Documents" at *http://support.microsoft.com/kb/947222.*

- KB 920727 "Folders cannot perform Group Policy redirection or manual redirection on a Windows Vista–based computer" at *http://support.microsoft.com/kb/920727.*

- KB 926193 "When you log on to Windows Vista on a new computer, you do not see the expected files in the My Documents folder" at *http://support.microsoft.com/kb/926193.*

- KB 926167 "How to customize the Favorites Links list in common file dialog boxes in Windows Explorer in Windows Vista" at *http://support.microsoft.com/kb/926167.*

- KB 262845 "Support for DFS-based shares for Offline Files" at *http://support.microsoft.com/kb/262845.*

- KB 942960 "How to move the client-side caching (CSC) folder to a new location in Windows Vista" at *http://support.microsoft.com/kb/942960.*

- KB 937475 "How to change the location of the CSC folder by configuring the Cache-Location registry value in Windows Vista" at *http://support.microsoft.com/kb/937475.*

- KB 942974 "On a Windows Vista–based client computer, you can still access offline files even though the file server is removed from the network" at *http://support.microsoft.com/kb/942974.*

- KB 939390 "Error messages occur on a Windows Vista–based computer when you work offline in a redirected Internet Explorer 7 Favorites folder" at *http://support.microsoft.com/kb/939390.*

- KB 942845 "You cannot delete or rename the Offline Files when you work offline on a Windows Vista–based computer" at *http://support.microsoft.com/kb/942845.*

On the Companion CD

- AddLocalUserToLocalGroup.vbs
- ChangeLocalUserPassword.vbs
- CreateLocalGroup.vbs
- CreateLocalUsers.vbs
- RemoveLocalUserFromLocalGroup.vbs
- ReportGroupMembers.vbs
- ReportLocalDisabledAccounts.vbs
- ReportLocalGroupNames.vbs
- ReportLocalUserNames.vbs
- ReportLockedOutLocalUsers.vbs

Chapter 15

Managing Disks and File Systems

The most important aspect of a computer is the user data. Businesses depend on the privacy of their intellectual property to stay competitive, and government organizations depend on confidentiality for national security. Thus, it's critical that Windows protects the availability, integrity, and privacy of the user data on client computers. Windows Vista provides several important improvements to disk and file management.

Administrators will appreciate the ability to dynamically resize partitions. As an administrator, you might use this capability if you need to create multiple, smaller partitions from a single partition (which is required when enabling BitLocker Drive Encryption), or if you need to grow a partition to provide more space for users.

Windows Vista also includes several improvements that both users and administrators will appreciate. Most notable is that Windows Vista now includes scheduled backups and gives users the ability to restore backed-up files without calling IT support. If you choose to take advantage of scheduled backups and Previous Versions, your users will be able to restore corrupted or deleted files from the file's Properties dialog box. You can also back up and restore a complete computer image using Complete PC backup, greatly reducing the time required to restore a computer after a hard disk failure or system corruption.

Windows Vista includes a new feature called ReadyBoost to improve disk I/O performance, especially on computers with slower disk drives. With ReadyBoost, Windows Vista can take advantage of the high random-read speed for flash memory cards by storing a disk cache on suitable removable media, such as a USB Flash drive. Users can enable ReadyBoost without IT support.

With previous versions of Windows, disk defragmentation has caused disk I/O performance to decrease gradually over time. By default, Windows Vista is scheduled to automatically defragment the disk weekly. This should prevent fragmentation from significantly affecting disk performance under most conditions.

To improve data security, you can use BitLocker Drive Encryption to encrypt an entire volume, protecting the data on the disk even if the disk is physically removed from the computer. BitLocker works alongside EFS: BitLocker can encrypt system files and the page file, along with any other files on the volume, whereas EFS is intended primarily to encrypt user files.

This chapter describes these features in more detail.

Overview of Partitioning Disks

Before you can format disks into volumes that applications can access, you must partition them. Windows Vista provides flexible partitioning that you can change even after you have formatted a volume. However, it's still important to plan partitions ahead for features such as BitLocker Drive Encryption, which has very specific partitioning requirements.

Note   If Windows discovers a problem with a volume, it might schedule ChkDsk to run the next time the computer starts. Large volumes, especially volumes bigger than a terabyte, can take a very long time to check—more than an hour. During this time, the computer will be offline. Therefore, when you plan the size of your partitions, consider the time required for Windows to perform a ChkDsk operation at startup.

The sections that follow describe how to partition disks in Windows Vista.

How to Choose Between MBR or GPT

Master Boot Record (MBR) and Globally Unique Identifier Partition Table (GPT) are two different disk partitioning systems. MBR is the most common system and is supported by every version of Windows, including Windows Vista. GPT is an updated and improved partitioning system and is supported on Windows Vista, Windows Server 2008, and 64-bit versions of Windows XP and Windows Server 2003.

GPT offers several advantages over MBR:

- In Windows, GPT can support up to 128 partitions. MBR supports only four partitions.

- GPT accurately describes physical disk geometry, allowing Windows to create partitions and logical drives on cylinder boundaries. Although Windows attempts to do this for MBR, the geometry that MBR reports has no relationship to a modern drive's physical geometry, because it has been altered to enable larger capacities. Different disk vendors have created vendor-specific workarounds for this problem that are difficult to manage. Therefore, partitioning is more reliable when using GPT.

- GPT can support larger partition sizes. In theory, a GPT disk can be up to 18 exabytes in size (about 18,000,000 terabytes).

- GPT uses primary and backup partition tables for redundancy and CRC32 fields for improved partition data structure integrity. MBR does not have redundant partition tables.

> **Note**   All GPT disks start with a protective MBR partition to prevent previously released MBR disk tools, such as Microsoft MS-DOS FDISK or Microsoft Windows NT Disk Administrator, from damaging the GPT partition because they don't recognize the partition type. If you mount an MBR disk in a 32-bit version of Windows XP, it will see only the protective MBR partition.

To boot from a GPT disk, a Windows Vista or Windows Server 2008 computer must support EFI. BIOS-based systems must boot from an MBR disk, though they can use a second GPT disk as a data disk. All removable media must use MBR.

For more information about GPT, read the Windows and GPT FAQ at *http://www.microsoft.com/ whdc/device/storage/GPT_FAQ.mspx.*

Converting from MBR to GPT Disks

You can convert disks only from MBR to GPT, or vice versa, if the disk contains no partitions or volumes. You can convert a disk in two ways:

- In the Disk Management snap-in, right-click the MBR drive you want to convert to GPT and then click Convert To GPT Disk. If the drive is not empty or contains partitions, this option is unavailable.

- In the DiskPart command-line tool, select the drive you want to convert and run the command **convert gpt**. Similarly, to convert from GPT to MBR, run the command **convert mbr**.

> **Note**   When a dynamic disk is converted between MBR and GPT types, it must first be converted to a basic disk, then converted to MBR or GPT as appropriate, and then converted back to a dynamic disk. When you use the Disk Management snap-in, the conversion to a basic disk and then back to a dynamic disk happens automatically in the background. If you're using the command-line DiskPart tool, you must explicitly make the conversions.

GPT Partitions

For EFI computers that boot from a GPT disk, the boot disk must contain at least the following partitions:

- **EFI System Partition (ESP)**   On EFI computers, the ESP is about 100 megabytes (MB) and contains the Windows Boot Manager files. For more information about startup files, read Chapter 30, "Configuring Startup and Troubleshooting Startup Issues." The ESP has the following partition GUID:

   ```
   DEFINE_GUID (PARTITION_SYSTEM_GUID, 0xC12A7328L, 0xF81F, 0x11D2, 0xBA, 0x4B, 0x00,
   0xA0, 0xC9, 0x3E, 0xC9, 0x3B)
   ```

- **Microsoft Reserved Partition (MSR)**   The Microsoft Reserved Partition (MSR) reserves space on each disk drive for subsequent use by operating system software. On drives smaller than 16 gigabytes (GB), the MSR is 32 MB. On drives 16 GB or larger, the MSR is 128 MB. GPT disks do not allow hidden sectors. Software components that formerly used hidden sectors now allocate portions of the MSR for component-specific partitions. For example, converting a basic disk to a dynamic disk causes the MSR on that disk to be reduced in size, and a newly created partition holds the dynamic disk database. The MSR has the following partition GUID:

   ```
   DEFINE_GUID (PARTITION_MSFT_RESERVED_GUID, 0xE3C9E316L, 0x0B5C, 0x4DB8, 0x81, 0x7D,
   0xF9, 0x2D, 0xF0, 0x02, 0x15, 0xAE)
   ```

- **Data partition**   This partition stores Windows Vista system files and user files. The data partition has the following partition type GUID:

   ```
   DEFINE_GUID (PARTITION_BASIC_DATA_GUID, 0xEBD0A0A2L, 0xB9E5, 0x4433, 0x87, 0xC0, 0x68,
   0xB6, 0xB7, 0x26, 0x99, 0xC7);
   ```

Additionally, dynamic disks can use two different GPT partitions:

- A data container partition corresponding to the MBR partition 0x42, with the following GUID:

   ```
   DEFINE_GUID (PARTITION_LDM_DATA_GUID, 0xAF9B60A0L, 0x1431, 0x4F62, 0xBC, 0x68, 0x33,
   0x11, 0x71, 0x4A, 0x69, 0xAD);
   ```

- A partition to contain the dynamic configuration database, with the following GUID:

   ```
   DEFINE_GUID(PARTITION_LDM_METADATA_GUID, 0x5808C8AAL, 0x7E8F, 0x42E0, 0x85, 0xD2, 0xE1,
   0xE9, 0x04, 0x34, 0xCF, 0xB3);
   ```

Data disks (non-boot disks) must have an MSR and a data partition. Standard users will typically see only the data partitions; however, the other partitions will be visible to administrators using the Disk Management snap-in or the DiskPart tool.

Choosing Basic or Dynamic Disks

Traditional hard disks are called basic disks in Windows Vista, and they have the same functionality that basic disks have always had, plus a few extras. You can create new partitions (called *simple volumes* in Windows Vista), delete partitions, and extend or shrink the existing partitions. The ability to extend or shrink an existing partition is an important new feature in Windows Vista.

Dynamic disks, first introduced in Windows 2000, provide all the functionality of the basic disk, plus the ability to span a volume across multiple dynamic disks or stripe multiple dynamic disks to create a larger (and faster) volume. Dynamic disks present difficulties, however, because they are not accessible from operating systems other than the operating system instance that converted the disk to dynamic. This makes dynamic disks inaccessible in multiboot environments, and makes recovering data more difficult in the event of partial hard disk failure. You should always use basic disks unless you have a specific requirement that can be met only by dynamic disks.

Working with Volumes

In earlier versions of Windows, your choices for resizing volumes and partitions after they had been created are limited. If you need to add space to a volume, your only choice is to make the disk a dynamic disk and then create a spanned volume. If you want to expand or contract a partition, your only choice is to use third-party tools. In Windows Vista, however, you can now expand and contract volumes without data loss and without requiring a reboot.

How to Create a Simple Volume

In Windows Vista, the term *simple volume* has been expanded to include both partitions on basic disks and simple volumes on dynamic disks. If your only need is a simple volume, your best choice is a basic disk, because a simple volume doesn't use the advanced features of a dynamic disk.

To create a simple volume, open the Disk Management snap-in and follow these steps:

1. Right-click an unallocated space on one of the disks and then click New Simple Volume. The New Simple Volume Wizard appears.

2. Click Next. On the Specify Volume Size page, enter the size of volume you want to create in MB. The default is the maximum space available on the disk. Click Next.

3. On the Assign Drive Letter Or Path page, assign a drive letter or mount point. Click Next.

4.   On the Format Partition page, choose the formatting options for the volume and then click Next.

5.   Click Finish on the summary page of the wizard and the volume will be created and formatted according to your selections.

> **Note**   The Disk Management snap-in always creates simple volumes on dynamic disks or primary partitions on basic GPT disks. For basic MBR disks, the first three volumes created will be primary partitions. The fourth simple volume on a basic MBR disk is created as an extended partition and a logical drive. Further simple volumes on the basic MBR disk are logical drives.

Creating simple volumes using the command line or a script requires that you know whether the disk you're creating the volume on is a dynamic or basic disk. The DiskPart tool is not as flexible as the Disk Management snap-in, which automatically adjusts to create either a volume or a partition, depending on the disk type. With DiskPart, you must create a partition on a basic disk and a volume on a dynamic disk.

How to Create a Spanned Volume

A spanned volume uses the free space on more than one physical hard disk to create a bigger volume. The portions of disk used to create the volume do not need to be the same size and can actually include more than one free space on a disk. A spanned volume provides no additional speed benefits and increases the risk of catastrophic failure leading to data loss. The failure of any disk involved in the spanned volume will make the entire volume unavailable.

> **Note**   To achieve a speed benefit with multiple disks, you must use striping, such as that provided by RAID 1 or RAID 5. With striping, every file on a volume is evenly distributed between multiple physical disks. With striping, files can be read from or written to multiple disks simultaneously, increasing throughput. Spanning simply appends one disk to the next, so any given file is probably stored only on a single disk. The best way to add striping is to use a computer or add-on card that supports hardware RAID.

If you still want to create a spanned volume, follow these steps:

1.   Open the Disk Management snap-in.

2.   Right-click a free-space segment that you want to include in the spanned volume and then select New Spanned Volume from the shortcut menu. The New Spanned Volume Wizard appears.

3.   Click Next. On the Select Disks page, select from the available disks and then click Add to add the disks to the spanned volume. Select each disk in the Selected column and set the amount of space to use on that disk for the spanned volume. Click Next.

4. On the Assign Drive Letter Or Path page, the default is to assign the next available drive letter to the new volume. You can also mount the volume on an empty NTFS folder on an existing volume. Click Next.

5. On the Format Volume page, choose the formatting options for the new volume. Windows Vista supports only NTFS formatting from the Disk Management snap-in. To format with FAT or FAT32, you need to use the command line. Click Next.

6. Click Finish on the summary page to create the volume.

Creating a spanned volume using DiskPart is a somewhat more complicated process than creating a simple volume. You can't just create the spanned volume in one step; you need to first make sure that the disks to be used are converted to dynamic. Then you create a simple volume on the first disk of the spanned volume, extend the volume to the second disk, and then add any additional disks involved in the span. Finally, you must assign the volume to a drive letter or mount point.

How to Create a Striped Volume

A striped volume uses the free space on more than one physical hard disk to create a bigger volume. Unlike a spanned volume, however, a striped volume writes across all volumes in the stripe in small blocks, distributing the load across the disks in the volume. The portions of disk used to create the volume need to be the same size; the size of the smallest free space included in the striped volume will be the determinant.

A striped volume is faster than a simple volume, because reads and writes happen across multiple disks at the same time. However, this additional speed comes with an increased risk of catastrophic failure leading to data loss when compared to a volume residing on a single physical disk, because the failure of any disk involved in the spanned volume will make the entire volume unavailable.

To create a striped volume, follow these steps:

1. Open the Disk Management snap-in.

2. Right-click a free-space segment that you want to include in the striped volume and then click New Striped Volume. The New Striped Volume Wizard appears.

3. Click Next. On the Select Disks page, select from the available disks and then click Add to add the disks to the striped volume. Set the amount of space to use on the disks for the striped volume. Click Next.

4. On the Assign Drive Letter Or Path page, the default is to assign the next available drive letter to the new volume. You can also mount the volume on an empty NTFS folder on an existing volume. Click Next.

5. On the Format Volume page of the New Striped Volume Wizard, choose the formatting options for the new volume. Windows Vista supports only NTFS formatting from the Disk Management snap-in. To format with FAT or FAT32, you need to use the command line. Click Next.

6. Click Finish on the summary page to create the volume. If the disks are basic disks, you'll be warned that this operation will convert them to dynamic disks. Click Yes to convert the disks and create the striped volume.

How to Resize a Volume

New to Windows Vista is the ability to expand and contract simple volumes without a third-party tool. You can also expand and contract spanned volumes, but striped volumes are fixed in size. To change the size of a striped volume, you need to delete and re-create it.

> **Note**   Third-party products offer additional flexibility in resizing partitions, allowing the resizing of partitions with no available unallocated space immediately adjacent to the partition that you want to extend, and also allowing you to control the placement of the unallocated space after shrinking the partition.

To shrink a volume, follow these steps:

1. Open the Disk Management snap-in.

2. Right-click the volume you want to shrink and then click Shrink Volume.

3. The Shrink dialog box opens and shows the maximum amount you can shrink the volume by in megabytes. If desired, decrease the amount to shrink the volume and then click Shrink. The shrink process will proceed without further prompting.

You can also use DiskPart interactively from an elevated command line, using exactly the same steps as you would use with a script. The interactive steps for shrinking a volume as much as possible are:

DiskPart

```
Microsoft DiskPart version 6.0.6000
Copyright (C) 1999-2007 Microsoft Corporation.
On computer: VISTA
```

```
DISKPART> list volume
```

```
Volume ###   Ltr  Label         Fs     Type        Size    Status      Info
----------   ---  -----------   -----  ----------  -------  ---------   --------
Volume 0     F    New Volume    NTFS   Simple       20 GB   Healthy
Volume 1     E    New Volume    NTFS   Simple       40 GB   Healthy
Volume 2     R                         DVD-ROM       0 B    No Media
Volume 3     C                  NTFS   Partition    75 GB   Healthy     System
Volume 4     D    New Volume    NTFS   Partition    52 GB   Healthy
```

DISKPART> **select volume 4**

  Volume 4 is the selected volume.

DISKPART> **shrink querymax**

  The maximum number of reclaimable bytes is: 26 GB

DISKPART> **shrink**

  DiskPart successfully shrunk the volume by: 26 GB

> **Note**   In the code list, the command shrink querymax queries the volume to determine the maximum amount of shrinkage that the volume will support. The actual number will depend on the amount of free space on the volume, the fragmentation level, and where critical files are located on the volume.

To extend a volume, the steps are similar:

1. Open the Disk Management snap-in.

2. Right-click the volume you want to extend and then click Extend Volume. The Extend Volume Wizard appears.

3. Click Next. The Select Disks page appears.

4. Select the disks and set the amount of space from each disk to include in the extended volume. If you are extending a volume on a basic disk, and you choose noncontiguous unallocated space or space on a second disk, the extension will also convert any disks involved to dynamic disks as part of the extension. Click Next.

5. On the Completing The Extend Volume Wizard page, click Finish. If the extension requires conversion to a dynamic disk, you'll see a warning.

How to Delete a Volume

You can delete a volume from either the Disk Management snap-in or the command line. Deleting a volume permanently erases the data stored on the volume.

From the Disk Management snap-in, simply right-click the volume and then click Delete Volume. From the DiskPart command-line tool at an elevated command prompt, select the volume and then use the delete volume command, as the following commands demonstrate:

```
C:\temp>DiskPart
```

```
Microsoft DiskPart version 6.0.6000
Copyright (C) 1999-2007 Microsoft Corporation.
On computer: VISTA
DISKPART> list volume
  Volume ###  Ltr  Label       Fs      Type        Size   Status      Info
  ----------  ---  ----------  -----   ----------  ------- ----------  --------
  Volume 0    F    New Volume  NTFS    Simple       20 GB  Healthy
  Volume 1    E    New Volume  NTFS    Simple       40 GB  Healthy
  Volume 2    R                        DVD-ROM       0 B   No Media
  Volume 3    C                NTFS    Partition    75 GB  Healthy     System
  Volume 4    D    New Volume  NTFS    Partition    52 GB  Healthy
DISKPART> select volume 0
Volume 0 is the selected volume.
DISKPART> delete volume
DiskPart successfully deleted the volume.
```

File System Fragmentation

As files are created, deleted, and modified over time, their size and physical location on the hard disk will change. If a file size needs to increase, and the hard disk doesn't have room directly adjacent to the existing file, the file system automatically places the new portion of the file where it can find the room and then marks the necessary structures so that the file system can find the entire file when an application needs it. The file is now in two (or more) fragments.

Fragmentation is normal behavior and is completely transparent to both applications and users. The problem is that over time, more and more files become fragmented and even highly fragmented, increasing the amount of time that it takes for the hard disk controller to locate all the fragments. Not only does this slow down file access, but it also places additional stress on the hard disk itself.

By default, Windows Vista will defragment the hard drive at 1:00 A.M. every Wednesday. If the computer is off at this time, defragmentation will start shortly after the computer boots next. Ideally, defragmentation will run when the computer is not in use, minimizing the performance impact. However, the user impact is minimal, because the defragmenter uses both low CPU priority and low-priority I/O.

How It Works: Defragmentation Algorithm Improvements

Many systems administrators have been captivated by the graphical defragmentation displays in previous versions of Windows. You'll notice the graphics are gone in Windows Vista. Unfortunately, displaying the layout of files and highlighting files that had even one fragmentation made many performance-focused administrators obsessed with eliminating every single fragmented file.

Fragmentation does reduce disk performance, but having a couple of fragments in a large file doesn't make a difference—even years of reading and writing a large file with a single fragment would never add up to a significant amount of time. For this reason, Microsoft tweaked the Windows Vista defragmentation algorithm so that it does not defragment a file if a segment is longer than 64 MB. In those circumstances, the relatively significant effort required to rearrange files just to combine two 64 MB fragments isn't worth the effort, so Windows Vista doesn't bother.

If you run a different defragmentation tool (including the defragmenter in Windows XP), those fragments will show up, and they'll probably look significant because the fragmented file is so large. (Typically, the entire file appears red if it has even a single fragment.) Trust the algorithm, though—a few fragments don't matter.

To manually defragment a file system or configure the automatic disk defragmentation schedule, follow these steps:

1. Click Start and then click Computer.

2. Right-click the drive and then click Properties.

3. Click the Tools tab and then click Defragment Now. The Disk Defragmenter appears, as shown in Figure 15-1.

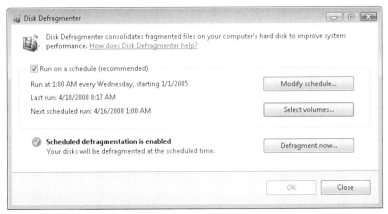

Figure 15-1   The Windows Vista Disk Defragmenter interface has been greatly simplified.

4. In the Disk Defragmenter dialog box, click Defragment Now to begin defragmentation. If you have Windows Vista Service Pack 1 installed, you can also click Select Volumes to choose which volumes are automatically defragmented. However, the default setting of Select All Disks is recommended.

You can continue to use the computer while defragmentation takes place, but it might be a little slower. You can also adjust the defragmentation schedule for a single computer from this interface.

For more complete control of defragmentation, you can use the command-line defragmentation tool, Defrag.exe, from an elevated command prompt. Defrag.exe has the following syntax:

```
Defrag <volume> -a [-v]
Defrag <volume> [{-r | -w}] [-f] [-v]
Defrag -c [{-r | -w}] [-f] [-v]
```

The options for defrag are:

- **<volume>**   The drive letter or mount point of the volume to defragment.

- **-c**   Defragment all local volumes on the computer.

- **-a**   Display a fragmentation analysis report for the specified volume without defragmenting it. Analysis reports resemble the following:

```
Analysis report for volume C:

    Volume size                    = 68.56 GB
    Free space                     = 58.78 GB
    Largest free space extent      = 31.64 GB
    Percent file fragmentation     = 10 %
```

- **-r**   Partial defragmentation. Don't attempt to defragment segments larger than 64 MB in size. This setting is enabled by default.

- **-w**   Full defragmentation. Attempt to defragment all segments, regardless of size.

- **-f**   Force defragmentation. Use when available disk space is low. Defragmentation isn't as efficient when little free-disk space is available, but you can still make improvements.

- **-v**   Verbose mode. Provides additional detail and statistics.

On this book's companion CD, you'll find two scripts that you can use to analyze and defragment files:

- **DefragAnalysis.vbs**   Analyzes all the local volumes on the computer to provide statistics on files and fragmentation.

- **DefragAllDrives.vbs**   Defragments all local volumes on the computer. This is similar to running defrag –c.

Backup and Restore

Windows Vista includes the all-new Backup And Restore Center, shown in Figure 15-2. The Backup And Restore Center uses Shadow Copy to take a snapshot of your files, allowing the backup to completely back up even open files without problems.

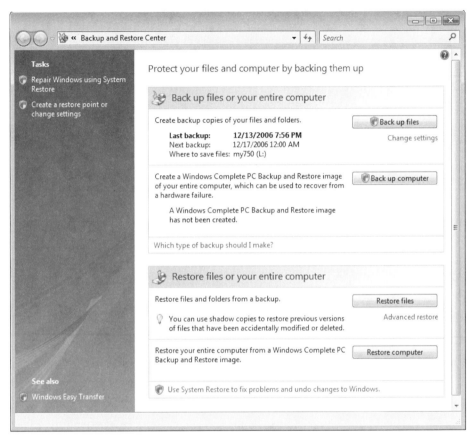

Figure 15-2   The Backup And Restore Center for Windows Vista Ultimate Edition.

The Backup And Restore Center supports two kinds of backup:

- **Complete PC**   Backs up an entire volume to a .vhd disk-image file (compacted to remove empty space), allowing you to quickly restore a computer and all running applications. However, backups take up much more space and are more time-consuming. Complete PC backups typically need to be done only once after a computer is initially configured. Complete PC backups can be stored only on local media such as a DVD or a removable hard disk.

- **Files and folders**   Stores user files and documents to compressed (.zip) files. File backups are incremental by default, and thus are very quick. Additionally, file backups do not back up system files, program files, EFS-encrypted files, temporary files, files in the

Recycle Bin, or user profile settings. File backups can back up to either local media or a shared folder on the network.

> **Note**   File backups are faster because they don't back up system or application files. However, Complete PC backups are surprisingly fast. Because Complete PC backups read the disk block by block, the read performance is faster than reading the disk file by file, which requires the disk to jump between different files.

The Backup and Restore Center supports backing up data files to CD, DVD, hard disk (fixed or removable), or a network share. (Windows Vista Home Basic doesn't support backing up to a network share.) When doing a Windows Complete PC Backup And Restore image, you can back up only to CD, DVD, or hard disk, and you can't include the drive to which you are backing up in the backup.

> **Note**   You cannot save backups to a USB Flash drive, but you can use an external USB hard drive or CF or SD memory cards.

All editions of Windows Vista except for Starter Edition support file backups. Only Business, Enterprise, and Ultimate Editions of Windows Vista support Complete PC backup.

How File Backups Work

The Backup And Restore Center provides graphical tools for manually initiating backup and restore sessions, and for scheduling automatic backups. All client computers that store important data should have automatic backup scheduled. For more information, read the section titled "Best Practices for Computer Backups" later in this chapter.

After you first configure automatic file backup using the Backup And Restore Center, Windows Vista will regularly back up all files. The first time a backup is performed, a full backup is done, including all important user documents. Subsequent backups are incremental, backing up only changed files. Older backups are discarded when the disk begins to run out of space.

For example, if you configure a nightly scheduled backup and change a file every day, a copy of that file will be stored in each day's Backup Files folder (described later). By storing multiple versions of a single file, Windows Vista gives users the opportunity to choose from several older copies of a file when using the Previous Versions tool (also described later). When you restore files, you only need to restore from a single backup, because Windows Vista automatically locates the most recent version of each file. In previous versions of Windows, you need to first restore from the last full backup and then restore any updates from incremental or differential backups.

Windows Vista uses Shadow Copy to back up the last saved version of a file. Therefore, if a file is open during the backup (such as the storage file for local e-mail or an open document), the file will be backed up. However, any changes the user makes since last saving the file are not backed up.

Only administrators can configure scheduled backups or manually initiate a backup. However, once configured, scheduled backups do not require a user to provide administrative credentials. Restoring files does not require administrative privileges unless a user attempts to restore another user's file.

If you perform a file backup to a shared folder, the credentials used to run the backup must have Full Control share and NTFS permissions for the destination folder (known as Co-owner permissions in the Windows Vista Setup Wizard). To reduce security risks, set up a user account to be used only by the backup application, and configure share and NTFS permissions to grant access only to the backup user. The backup account requires administrative privileges to the computer being backed up, but it needs permissions only to the share and folder on the target computer. You cannot back up a computer running Windows Vista Home Edition because it does not support shared folder permissions or authenticating as a specific user account.

File and Folder Backup Structure

The Backup tool in Windows XP creates a single file with a .bkf extension when you perform a backup. Backups in Windows Vista provide a more flexible and reliable file structure.

When a user chooses to perform a backup to an external hard disk, Windows Vista automatically creates a folder in the root of the hard disk using the computer name. Within that folder, backups are saved in this format: Backup Set <*year-month-day*> <*time*>. For example, if your computer name is Computer, your backup location is E, and you backed up on January 22, 2007 at 16:32:00, that backup would be located in E:\Computer\Backup Set 2007-01-22 163200.

The folder structure is created when the user first performs a backup. Automatic incremental backups that occur afterward store additional copies of changed files within subfolders. However, the name of the Backup Set folder is never updated, so the date indicated by the folder name will be older than the dates of the files contained within the folder. A new Backup Set folder is created only when the user performs a full backup.

Within each Backup Set folder, Backup creates a series of Backup Files folders that are named using the date on which the incremental backup was performed. Additionally, Backup creates a Catalogs folder within the root Backup Set folder. Figure 15-3 shows a backup folder structure for a computer named D820 that is configured to save backups to the L drive. File permissions on all folders and files are restricted to administrators, who have full control, and to the user who configured the backup, who has read-only permissions by default.

Figure 15-3   The backup folder structure includes separate folders for each computer, backup set, backup session, and catalog.

Note   When restoring files, Windows Vista looks for a folder with the current computer's name in the root of the backup media. If you need to restore files created on a different Windows Vista computer, you can either rename the folder to the current computer's name or perform an Advanced Restore and select the Files From A Backup Made On A Different Computer option on the What Do You Want To Restore page of the Restore Files (Advanced) Wizard.

Within each of the backup folders is a series of compressed (.zip) files named "Backup files *xxx*.zip", where *xxx* is an incremental number to make each filename unique. For example, a backup folder might contain the following files:

- Backup files 1.zip

- Backup files 2.zip

- Backup files 138.zip

Note   Because the .zip files used for backups are compressed and stored in fewer files, they take up less space on the backup media. Overall, backups take about half the space of the original files. Compression levels vary widely, though. Text and XML files are typically compressed to less than one-tenth the original space. Backups of video, music, and picture files take up the same space as the original files, because the files are already compressed.

These are standard ZIP files that you can open by using the ZIP decompression capabilities in Windows or by using other ZIP file tools. Because Windows can search .zip files, you can quickly find a backup of a specific file by searching the backup folders and then extracting that file from the compressed folder without directly accessing the Backup And Restore Center. This makes restoring files possible even if you need to use a different operating system.

The Catalogs folder contains a file named GlobalCatalog.wbcat. This file uses a proprietary format and contains an index of the individual files that have been backed up and the ZIP file the backup is contained within, which Windows Vista uses to locate a file quickly for restoration. The Catalogs folder also contains a list of file permissions for each backed-up file. Therefore, permissions will be intact if you restore files using the Backup And Restore Center. However, if you restore a file from the compressed folder directly, the file will inherit the permissions of the parent folder rather than keeping the file permissions of the original file.

How Complete PC Backups Work

Complete PC backups make a block-by-block backup of your system volume to a virtual hard disk (.vhd) file, which must be stored on local storage such as a second hard disk. Like file backups, subsequent backups to the same media automatically perform only an incremental backup. In other words, only the portions of the hard disk that have changed are copied to the existing Complete PC backup. Unlike file backups, only a single version of the Complete PC backup is kept—multiple versions are not stored.

The Backup And Restore Center does not provide a graphical tool for scheduling automatic Complete PC backups. Instead, you should rely on automatic file backups and manually create a Complete PC backup only after you have made significant changes to a computer's configuration. Alternatively, you can use the WBAdmin command-line tool to schedule a Complete PC backup, as described in the next section.

How to Start a Complete PC Backup from the Command Line

The simplest way to initiate a Complete PC backup is to follow the prompts in the Backup And Restore Center. If you want to automate or schedule Complete PC backups, however, you can use the WBAdmin.exe command-line tool.

For example, to initiate a Complete PC backup of the C drive to the L drive, you would run the following command line from an elevated command prompt:

```
wbadmin start backup –backupTarget:L: -include:C: -quiet
```

```
wbadmin 1.0 - Backup command-line tool
(C) Copyright 2004 Microsoft Corp.

Retrieving volume information...

This would backup volume Local Disk(C:) to L:.

Backup to L: is starting.

Running shadow copy of volumes requested for backup.
Running backup of volume Local Disk(C:), copied (0%).
Running backup of volume Local Disk(C:), copied (18%).
Running backup of volume Local Disk(C:), copied (40%).
Running backup of volume Local Disk(C:), copied (77%).
Running backup of volume Local Disk(C:), copied (98%).
```

```
Backup of volume Local Disk(C:) completed successfully.
Backup completed successfully.

Summary of backup:
------------------

Backup of volume Local Disk(C:) completed successfully.
```

The behavior is identical to the Complete PC backups initiated from the graphical Backup And Restore Center. The first time you initiate a Complete PC backup, it backs up every block on the system volume. Each subsequent time, it simply updates the previous backup.

You can use the same command to schedule a task from the command line. If you use Task Scheduler, you must configure the task to run with administrative privileges. You can do this by providing an administrative user account and selecting the Run With Highest Privileges check box on the General tab of the task's Properties dialog box.

How to Restore a Complete PC Backup

Because Complete PC backups must rewrite the entire contents of the disk, you can restore Complete PC backups only by booting from the Windows Vista DVD and loading System Recovery tools. Restoring a Complete PC backup from System Recovery tools allows you to quickly get a computer running after replacing a failed hard disk, or when the previous operating system installation has been corrupted (for example, by an irreparable malware installation).

To restore a Complete PC backup, follow these steps:

1.   Connect the backup media to your computer. For example, if the Complete PC backup was performed to an external USB hard drive, connect that drive to your computer.

2.   Insert the Windows Vista DVD in your computer. Ensure that the computer is configured to boot from the DVD.

3.   Restart your computer. When prompted to boot from the DVD, press a key. If you are not prompted to boot from the DVD, you may have to configure your computer's startup sequence.

4.   Windows Vista setup loads. When prompted, select your regional preferences and then click Next.

5.   Click Repair Your Computer to launch RecEnv.exe.

6.   Select your keyboard layout and then click Next.

7. System Recovery scans your hard disks for Windows Vista installations. If the standard Windows Vista drivers do not detect a hard disk because it requires drivers that were not included with Windows Vista, click Load Drivers to load the driver. Select an operating system to repair and then click Next.

8. Let the Startup Repair Wizard run if you think it might be able to recover the Windows Vista installation without requiring a full backup. Otherwise, click Cancel to stop Startup Repair from searching for problems. If Startup Repair begins automatic repairs, you might not be able to cancel them.

9. If prompted by Startup Repair to run System Restore, click Cancel. If you allow the Startup Repair Wizard to finish without solving your problem, click the View Advanced Options For System Recovery And Support link.

10. In the System Recovery Options dialog box, click Windows Complete PC Restore, as shown in Figure 15-4. If the backup was saved to a DVD, insert the DVD now. The Windows Complete PC Restore Wizard appears.

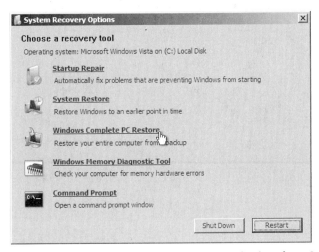

Figure 15-4   You can restore a Complete PC backup from System Recovery.

On the Restore Your Entire Computer From A Backup page, the most recent backup will be automatically selected. If this is the correct backup to restore, click Next, as shown in Figure 15-5. Otherwise, click Restore A Different Backup, click Next, and then select the correct backup.

11. On the final page, select the Format And Repartition Disks check box only if the disk is not formatted. Be sure that you are prepared to overwrite all the data on your current disk and then click Finish, as shown in Figure 15-6.

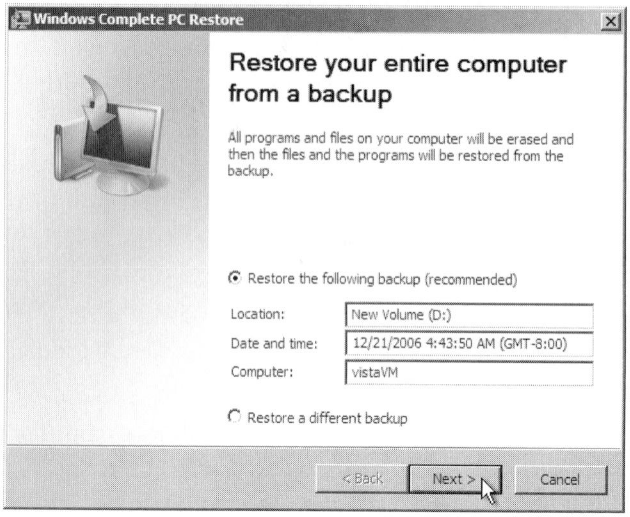

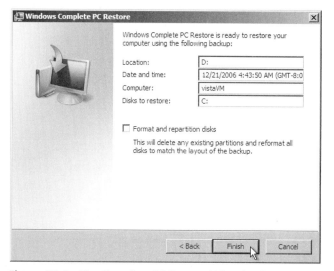

Figure 15-5   Select the correct Complete PC backup to restore.

Figure 15-6   The Complete PC Restore Wizard writes an entire disk image, including system files and user documents.

12.   When prompted, select the I Confirm check box and then click OK.

Windows Complete PC Restore reads the data from the backup and overwrites existing files. Typically, the restore will take 30 to 60 seconds per gigabyte. You can restore to a different-sized hard disk, as long as the hard disk is large enough to store the backup. After the restore is complete, the computer will restart using the restored files.

Complete PC Backup Structure

Complete PC backups use a similar folder structure to file backups. When you create a Complete PC backup, Windows creates a WindowsImageBackup folder in the root of the backup media. Within that folder, it creates a folder with the current computer's name. It then creates a Catalog folder containing the GlobalCatalog and BackupGlobalCatalog files, and a "Backup *<year>-<month>-<date> <time>*" folder containing the disk image file. Figure 15-7 illustrates this folder structure for a computer named D820 that stores backups on the external L drive.

```
▲ 🖳 Computer
  ▷ 🖴 Local Disk (C:)
  ▲ 💾 my750 (L:)
    ▷ 📁 WindowsImageBackup
    ▲ 📁 d820
        📁 Backup 2006-12-28 204742
        📁 Catalog
```

Figure 15-7   The Complete PC folder structure includes separate folders for each computer, backup session, and catalog.

To back up an entire volume, Complete PC creates a .vhd disk image file. This is the same file format used by Microsoft Virtual PC and Microsoft Virtual Server. In fact, you can mount the .vhd files as secondary disks in either Virtual PC or Virtual Server, granting you quick access to individual files contained within the backup from a virtual computer. You cannot easily boot from a Complete PC .vhd file, however.

> **Note**   Microsoft Virtual Server 2005 R2 SP1 includes VhdMount, a command-line tool for mounting .vhd files so that you can browse their contents. This is an excellent way to extract files from a Complete PC backup.

Complete PC backups also create several other files:

- A MediaId file in the *<ComputerName>* folder to identify the disk image
- GlobalCatalog and BackupGlobalCatalog files in the Catalog folder to track the Complete PC backup image versions
- Numerous XML files in the Backup folder that contain configuration settings for the backup file

Best Practices for Computer Backups

The backup and restore tools built into Windows Vista are intended for home users and small businesses. Typically, enterprises will need a third-party backup-management tool to manage the large number of client computers.

However, Windows Vista backup can be very useful in many common scenarios:

- **Mobile users**   Mobile users often travel with their computers, preventing network backups from succeeding. For these users, you should provide external storage that they can use to back up their computers while they are away from the office. Typically, this would be an external USB hard drive. Mobile users can also back up to writable DVDs (if the computer is equipped with a DVD burner) or a large-capacity portable audio player that can act as an external hard disk.

- **Users who work from home**   Users who work from home may not have sufficient bandwidth to participate in network backups. Additionally, their connectivity may not always be stable enough to allow them to store important files on your internal servers. To reduce the risk of these workers losing important data, equip users with external storage and configure automatic backups.

- **Small or branch offices**   To back up computers in small or branch offices with a 100-Mbps or faster local area network (LAN), configure a server with sufficient disk storage for backups from each computer. Then schedule automatic backups to store files to a shared folder on the server. Alternatively, you can use network attached storage (NAS).

Keeping an external hard disk attached to a computer with automatic updates enabled is the most convenient and reliable way to back up a computer. However, because the backup media is physically close to the computer, this configuration does not protect against common data recovery scenarios such as theft, fire, or electrical surges. To protect against these threats, users should perform weekly full backups to a second external storage device and then store that storage device securely at a different location. For the best protection, users should have two off-site storage devices and alternate between them, so that one device is always off-site, even when a backup is being performed.

How to Manage Backup Using Group Policy Settings

You can use Group Policy to manage Windows Backup options in an enterprise environment. The policy settings for Windows Backup are both user and computer settings. The user-specific settings are client-only settings and are found in the following location:

User Configuration\Administrative Templates\Windows Components\Backup\Client

The computer settings are for both the client and the server and are found in the following locations:

Computer Configuration\Administrative Templates\Windows Components\Backup\Client

Computer Configuration\Administrative Templates\Windows Components\Backup\Server

Table 15-1 lists the available policy settings for Windows Backup. Client settings are available for both User and Computer scopes, but Server settings are available only in the Computer scope. These settings are written to the registry on targeted computers under the following registry key:

HKLM\Software\Policies\Microsoft\Windows\Backup

Table 15-1   Group Policy Settings for Windows Backup

Policy	Client or Server	Description
Prevent The User From Running The Backup Status And Configuration Program	Client	Enabling this policy prevents the user from running the Backup Status and Configuration program. The user will be unable to configure, initiate, or restore a backup.
Prevent Backing Up To Local Disks	Client	Enabling this policy prevents the user from choosing a local disk (internal or external) as a backup target.
Prevent Backing Up To Network Shared Folder	Client	Enabling this policy prevents the user from choosing a network share as a backup target.
Prevent Backing Up To Optical Media (CD/DVD)	Client	Enabling this policy prevents the user from choosing a CD or DVD as a backup target.
Turn Off Backup Configuration	Client	Enabling this policy prevents the user from running the file backup application. The restore functionality is still available, as is Windows Complete PC Backup.
Turn Off Restore Functionality	Client	Enabling this policy prevents the user from using restore. File backups and Windows Complete PC Backup are still available.
Turn Off Complete PC Backup Functionality	Client	Enabling this policy prevents the user from using Windows Complete PC Backup. File backups and restore are still available.
Allow Only System Backup	Server	Enabling this policy prevents the user from backing up nonsystem volumes.
Disallow Locally Attached Storage As Backup Target	Server	Enabling this policy prevents the user from backing up to locally attached storage devices.
Disallow Network As Backup Target	Server	Enabling this policy prevents the user from backing up to a network share.
Disallow Optical Media As Backup Target	Server	Enabling this policy prevents the user from backing up to CD or DVD drives.
Disallow Run-Once Backups	Server	Enabling this policy prevents the user from running on-demand backups.

Previous Versions and Shadow Copies

Windows Vista can also restore earlier versions of files so that users can quickly recover a file that has been accidentally modified, corrupted, or deleted. Depending on the type of file or folder, users can open, save to a different location, or restore a previous version. Previous Versions is available in Windows Vista Business, Enterprise, and Ultimate Editions.

The sections that follow describe the Volume Shadow Copy technology and the Previous Versions user interface.

How Volume Shadow Copy Works

To provide backups for files that are in use, Windows Vista uses the Volume Shadow Copy service, which was first introduced with Windows XP. Volume Shadow Copy mitigates file access between applications and the backup process. In other words, if a backup tool needs to access a file currently in use, Volume Shadow Copy creates a shadow copy of that file and then provides the backup process access to the shadow copy. Figure 15-8 illustrates the relationship between Volume Shadow Copy components.

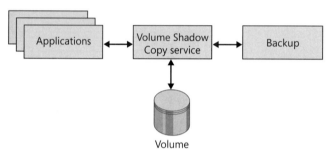

Figure 15-8   Volume Shadow Copy allows you to back up open files.

Volume Shadow Copy works with any application. Some applications, however, can communicate directly with the Volume Shadow Copy service to ensure that backed-up files are consistent. If an application keeps several files in use at the same time, they might become inconsistent if two files must be synchronized, and one of those files is updated after another is backed up in an earlier state.

> **Note**   Application developers can build Volume Shadow Copy integration into their applications using the Volume Shadow Copy Service SDK. For more information, go to *http://www.microsoft.com/downloads/details.aspx?FamilyID=0b4f56e4-0ccc-4626-826a-ed2c4c95c871.*

To provide backup access to a file that is open and being updated, Volume Shadow Copy needs to be able to make two versions of the file accessible: one that is currently in use by the application, and a second that is a snapshot of the file when backup first requested access to a volume shadow copy. Volume Shadow Copy handles this transparently by storing copies of changed files in Volume Shadow Copy storage. Volume Shadow Copy stores a copy of the original state of any modified portion of a file, which allows the original file to be updated without interrupting the backup process. In other words, if a user modifies a file after the backup starts, the file will be in the state it was in when the backup began.

How to Manage Shadow Copies

You can manage the Volume Shadow Copy service using the Vssadmin command-line tool from an elevated command prompt. You can use this tool to run the following commands:

- **Vssadmin List Providers**   Lists registered Volume Shadow Copy providers. Windows Vista includes "MS Software Shadow Copy Provider 1.0."

- **Vssadmin List Shadows**   Lists existing volume shadow copies, the time the shadow copy was created, and its location. The following sample output shows two shadow copies:

```
vssadmin 1.1 - Volume Shadow Copy Service administrative command-line tool
(C) Copyright 2001-2005 Microsoft Corp.

Contents of shadow copy set ID: {79f6e5e8-0211-43bf-9480-c65e51b4b40d}
   Contained 1 shadow copies at creation time: 12/20/2006 1:05:08 PM
      Shadow Copy ID: {26fc6f1c-9610-4c0c-b10b-7e9f6fab042c}
         Original Volume: (C:)\\?\Volume{3e59796e-cf1b-11da-af4b-806d6172696f}\
         Shadow Copy Volume: \\?\GLOBALROOT\Device\HarddiskVolumeShadowCopy1
         Originating Machine: VISTA
         Service Machine: VISTA
         Provider: 'MS Software Shadow Copy provider 1.0'
         Type: ClientAccessibleWriters
         Attributes: Persistent, Client-
accessible, No auto release, Differential, Auto recovered

Contents of shadow copy set ID: {d14c728d-ff85-4be1-b048-24f3aced48a9}
   Contained 1 shadow copies at creation time: 12/20/2006 4:42:12 PM
      Shadow Copy ID: {271752a4-e886-4c92-9671-10624ca36cd4}
         Original Volume: (C:)\\?\Volume{3e59796e-cf1b-11da-af4b-806d6172696f}\
         Shadow Copy Volume: \\?\GLOBALROOT\Device\HarddiskVolumeShadowCopy2
         Originating Machine: VISTA
         Service Machine: VISTA
         Provider: 'MS Software Shadow Copy provider 1.0'
         Type: ClientAccessibleWriters
         Attributes: Persistent, Client-
accessible, No auto release, Differential, Auto recovered
```

- **Vssadmin List ShadowStorage**   Lists the volume shadow storage space currently in use, the space that is reserved for future use (labeled as allocated), and the maximum space that might be dedicated. This space is used to store changes while a shadow copy is active. The following sample output was generated using a computer that currently had about 3 GB of files stored in a shadow copy, but that might allocate as much as 6.4 GB:

```
vssadmin 1.1 - Volume Shadow Copy Service administrative command-line tool
(C) Copyright 2001-2005 Microsoft Corp.

Shadow Copy Storage association
   For volume: (C:)\\?\Volume{3e59796e-cf1b-11da-af4b-806d6172696f}\
   Shadow Copy Storage volume: (C:)\\?\Volume{3e59796e-cf1b-11da-af4b-806d6172696f}\
   Used Shadow Copy Storage space: 2.985 GB
   Allocated Shadow Copy Storage space: 3.249 GB
   Maximum Shadow Copy Storage space: 6.436 GB
```

- **Vssadmin List Volumes** Lists volumes that are eligible for shadow copies.

- **Vssadmin List Writers** Lists shadow copy writers, which support communicating with the Volume Shadow Copy service to ensure that files are captured in a consistent state. By default, subscribed writers include an operating system writer, a registry writer, a WMI writer, and a search service writer, among others. SQL Server also provides a Volume Shadow Copy writer.

- **Vssadmin Resize ShadowStorage** Resizes Volume Shadow Copy storage. You can use this command to increase the maximum space that might be used by Volume Shadow Copy. Typically, this is unnecessary. However, if you discover that backups are failing on a computer because of an extremely high volume of changes during a backup, and Vssadmin List ShadowStorage reveals that the used Shadow Copy Storage space is at the maximum, you might be able to resolve the problem by manually increasing the maximum size.

> **Note** Vssadmin in Windows Vista does not provide all of the commands that Windows Server 2003 provides. This is because the ability to manually create and manage shadow copies typically is unnecessary on client computers.

How to Restore a File with Previous Versions

With Previous Versions, users can quickly restore a file to an earlier state that was established either when a shadow copy or a file backup was made. Previous Versions cannot restore a file from a Complete PC backup, even though you might be able to extract the file manually from the Complete PC disk image. However, Complete PC backups do initiate a Volume Shadow Copy, and a version of a file might be available from the shadow copy.

To restore an earlier version of a file, follow these steps:

1. Right-click the file and then click Restore Previous Versions. The Previous Versions tab appears, as shown in Figure 15-9.

> **Note** If you have deleted the file, but you remember the filename, create a file with the exact same filename in the same folder, and follow these steps using that file. The file can be empty; as long as the filename matches, you'll be able to restore an earlier version. Otherwise, you can view the Previous Versions tab in the Properties dialog box for the parent folder and restore just the file you need. You can also browse for the file manually using the Backup And Restore Center.

2. If an earlier version of the file is available, click it and then click Restore if the button is available. For system files, you can click Open or Copy. The Copy File dialog box appears, as shown in Figure 15-10.

Figure 15-9   Previous Versions allows users to restore an earlier version of the file without calling the support center.

Figure 15-10   When restoring a file, you can overwrite the existing file or save it with a different name.

3. You can choose to overwrite the existing file or save the recovered file with a different name.

4. Click Finish.

To allow users to take advantage of previous versions, provide them with an online backup solution using the Backup And Restore Center. Most often, backups for computers connected to your internal network are saved to a shared folder on a server. For mobile users, backups can be saved to external hard disks.

How to Configure Previous Versions with Group Policy Settings

You can configure Previous Versions with six Group Policy settings, located in Administrative Templates\Windows Components\Windows Explorer\Previous Versions (under both Computer Configuration and User Configuration):

- **Prevent Restoring Previous Versions From Backups**   When you enable this setting, the Restore button is disabled on the Previous Versions tab. Users will still be able to see whether or not previous versions are available (unless you enable the following setting), but the versions will be inaccessible. This setting is disabled by default.

- **Prevent Restoring Local Previous Versions**   When you enable this setting, the Restore button on the Previous Versions tab is disabled when the file to be restored is a local file. This setting is disabled by default.

- **Prevent Restoring Remote Previous Versions**   When you enable this setting, the Restore button on the Previous Versions tab is disabled when the file to be restored is on a remote computer. This setting is disabled by default.

- **Hide Previous Versions List For Local Files**   When you enable this setting, the Previous Versions tab is removed from the file Properties dialog box, and the Restore Previous Versions menu item is removed from the file shortcut menu. This setting is disabled by default.

- **Hide Previous Versions List For Remote Files**   When you enable this setting, the behavior is the same as with the previous setting, but it affects files on remote computers instead of local files. This setting is disabled by default.

- **Hide Previous Versions Of Files On Backup Location**   When you enable this setting, previous versions that were created with a backup are hidden. Previous versions created by shadow copies will still be available. This setting is disabled by default.

Windows ReadyBoost

Windows Vista supports Windows ReadyBoost, which uses external USB Flash drives as a hard disk cache, thus improving disk read performance in some circumstances. Supported external storage types include USB thumb drives, as shown in Figure 15-11; SD cards; and CF cards.

Figure 15-11   ReadyBoost uses flash storage to improve disk read performance.

External storage must meet the following requirements:

- Capacity between 256 MB and 4 GB, with at least 64 KB of free space
- At least a 2.5 MB/sec throughput for 4 KB random reads
- At least a 1.75 MB/sec throughput for 512 KB random writes

Unfortunately, most flash storage provides only raw throughput performance statistics measured under ideal conditions, not the very specific 4 KB random reads required by ReadyBoost. Therefore, the most effective way to determine if a specific flash drive meets ReadyBoost requirements is simply to test it. Windows Vista automatically tests removable storage when attached. If a storage device fails the test, Windows Vista will automatically retest the storage on a regular basis.

Some devices will show the phrase "Enhanced for Windows ReadyBoost" on the packaging, which means Microsoft has tested the device specifically for this feature. If you connect a flash drive that meets these requirements, AutoPlay will provide ReadyBoost as an option, as shown in Figure 15-12.

Figure 15-12   AutoPlay will prompt the user to use a compatible device with ReadyBoost.

Alternatively, you can configure ReadyBoost by right-clicking the device in Explorer, clicking Properties, and then clicking the ReadyBoost tab. As shown in Figure 15-13, the only configuration option is to configure the space reserved for the cache. You must reserve at least 256 MB. Larger caches can improve performance.

Figure 15-13   The ReadyBoost cache must be at least 256 MB.

Windows Vista uses the SuperFetch algorithm (the successor to Windows Prefetcher) to determine which files should be stored in the cache. SuperFetch monitors files that users access (including system files, application files, and documents) and preloads those files into the ReadyBoost cache. All files in the cache are encrypted using 128-bit AES. Because the Ready-Boost cache stores a copy of the files, the flash drive can be removed at any point without affecting the computer—Windows Vista will simply read the original files from the disk.

ReadyBoost provides the most significant performance improvement under the following circumstances:

- The computer has a slow hard disk drive. Computers with a primary hard disk Windows Experience Index subscore of lower than 4.0 will see the most significant improvements.

- The flash storage provides fast random, nonsequential reads. Sequential read speed is less important.

- The flash storage is connected by a fast bus. Typically, USB memory card readers are not sufficiently fast. However, connecting flash memory to an internal memory card reader might provide sufficient performance.

Computers with fast hard disks (such as 7,200- or 10,000-RPM disks) might realize minimal performance gains, because of the already high disk I/O. ReadyBoost will read files from the cache only when doing so will improve performance. Hard disks outperform flash drives during sequential reads, but flash drives are faster during nonsequential reads (because of the latency caused when the drive head must move to a different disk sector). Therefore, ReadyBoost reads from the cache only for nonsequential reads.

 Note   In the author's informal experiments, enabling ReadyBoost on a 1-GB flash drive on a laptop computer with a WEI disk subcomponent rating of 3.7 decreased Windows startup times by more than 30 percent. Gains on computers with a WEI disk subcomponent rating of more than 5 were minimal.

ReadyBoost creates a disk cache file named ReadyBoost.sfcache in the root of the flash drive. The file is immediately created for the full size of the specified cache; however, Windows Vista will gradually fill the space with cached content. Windows Vista does not provide tools to monitor ReadyBoost performance or examine the encrypted cache. However, you can casually monitor usage if you choose a flash drive that includes a usage light. Additionally, timing everyday tasks with and without the cache can reveal performance gains.

BitLocker Drive Encryption

Microsoft BitLocker Drive Encryption is a new Windows Vista feature that improves data integrity and confidentiality. Without Service Pack 1, BitLocker encrypts only system volumes. After installing Service Pack 1, BitLocker can encrypt any volume. BitLocker can use Trusted Platform Module (TPM) security hardware to wrap and seal keys used to encrypt the volumes, helping to protect the volumes from offline attacks. Alternatively, BitLocker can use a USB Flash drive to store the Startup Key used to encrypt the volumes. BitLocker is available in the Enterprise and Ultimate Editions of Windows Vista.

BitLocker is designed primarily for use with TPM, which is a hardware module included in many new laptops available today, as well as some desktops. TPM modules must be version 1.2 for use with BitLocker. The TPM module is a permanent part of the motherboard.

If a TPM 1.2 module is not available, computers can still take advantage of BitLocker encryption technology as long as the computer's BIOS supports reading from a USB Flash device before the operating system is loaded. However, you cannot use BitLocker's integrity verification capabilities without a TPM 1.2 module.

Unlike EFS, BitLocker can encrypt entire volumes, including the page file, hibernation file, registry, and temporary files, which might hold confidential information. EFS can encrypt only user files. Additionally, when used with TPM hardware, BitLocker can help protect your system integrity by ensuring that critical Windows startup files have not been modified (which might occur if a rootkit or other malware was installed). Additionally, if the hard disk was moved to a different computer (a common method for extracting data from a stolen hard disk), the user will be forced to enter a recovery password before gaining access to the protected volumes.

How BitLocker Encrypts Data

BitLocker encrypts entire volumes. The contents of the volumes can be decrypted only by someone with access to the decryption key, known as the Full Volume Encryption Key (FVEK). Windows Vista actually stores the FVEK in the volume metadata; this is not a problem because the FVEK itself is encrypted using the Volume Master Key (VMK).

Both the FVEK and the VMK are 256 bits. The FVEK always uses AES encryption to protect the volume. By editing the Computer Configuration\Administrative Templates\Windows Components\BitLocker Drive Encryption\Configure Encryption Method Group Policy setting, you can set the specific AES encryption strength to one of four values:

- AES 128 bit with Diffuser (this is the default setting)
- AES 256 bit with Diffuser (this is the strongest setting, but using it may negatively affect performance)
- AES 128 bit
- AES 256 bit

> **Note**   For more information about the encryption algorithms used, and the use of diffusers, read "AES-CBC + Elephant Diffuser: A Disk Encryption Algorithm for Windows Vista" at *http://download.microsoft.com/download/0/2/3/0238acaf-d3bf-4a6d-b3d6-0a0be4bbb36e/ BitLockerCipher200608.pdf.*

Windows Vista encrypts and decrypts disk sectors on the fly as data is read and written (as long as it has access to the FVEK) using the FVE Filter Driver (fvevol.sys). As shown in Figure 15-14, the FVE Filter Driver, like all filter drivers, resides between the file system (which expects to receive the unencrypted contents of files) and the volume manager (which provides access to the volume). Therefore, applications and users are not aware of encryption when everything is functioning normally.

Encrypting and decrypting data does affect performance. While reading from and writing to a BitLocker-encrypted volume, some processor time will be consumed by the cryptographic operations performed by BitLocker. The actual impact depends on several factors, including caching mechanisms, hard drive speed, and processor performance. However, Microsoft has put great effort into implementing an efficient AES engine so that the performance impact on modern computers is minimal.

How BitLocker Protects Data

Before BitLocker grants access to the FVEK and the encrypted volume, it needs to obtain a key from the authorized user and/or the computer. If the computer has a TPM chip, authentication can happen in several different ways. If the computer doesn't have a TPM chip, you can use only a USB key. The sections that follow describe the different authentication techniques.

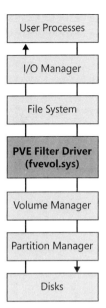

Figure 15-14   The FVE Filter Driver transparently encrypts and decrypts disk contents.

TPM (Use BitLocker Without Additional Keys)

BitLocker uses the TPM to unlock the VMK. The Windows startup process uses the TPM to verify that the hard disk is attached to the correct computer (and thus, the hard disk has not been removed) and that important system files are intact (preventing access to the hard drive if malware or a rootkit has compromised system integrity). When the computer is validated, TPM unlocks the VMK, and Windows Vista can start without prompting the user, as illustrated in Figure 15-15. This validation technique provides some level of protection without affecting the user at all.

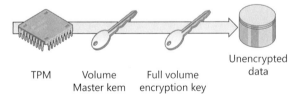

Figure 15-15   TPM-only authentication validates computer integrity without prompting the user.

TPM with External Key (Require Startup USB Key At Every Startup)

In addition to the protection described in the previous paragraph, the TPM requires an external key provided by the user (see Figure 15-16). This requires the user to insert a USB Flash drive (or any other BIOS-enumerable storage device) containing the key, effectively authenticating both the user and the integrity of the computer. This can protect the data in the event the computer is stolen while the computer was shut down or in hibernation—resuming from standby does not require BitLocker protection. For this authentication technique to be effective, the user must store the external key separately from the computer to reduce the risk that they will be stolen simultaneously.

> **Note** An excellent way to prevent yourself from losing your startup key and to avoid leaving it connected to your computer is to connect your USB startup key to your key ring. If you leave the USB key connected, it is more likely to be stolen with the computer, and malicious software might be able to copy the key.

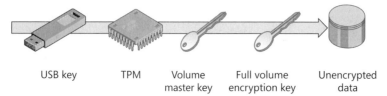

| USB key | TPM | Volume master key | Full volume encryption key | Unencrypted data |

Figure 15-16 For better security, require users to insert a USB Flash drive to authenticate them to TPM.

TPM with PIN (Require PIN At Every Startup)

This requirement prevents the computer from starting until the user types a personal identification number (PIN), as illustrated in Figure 15-17. This helps to protect the data in the event the computer is stolen while shut down. You should never use PINs to protect computers that need to start automatically without a human present, such as computers that are configured to start up for maintenance or backup purposes, or computers that act as servers.

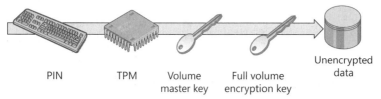

| PIN | TPM | Volume master key | Full volume encryption key | Unencrypted data |

Figure 15-17 For better security, require users to type a PIN to authenticate them to TPM.

> **Note** Be sure to change your PIN frequently. Though TCG-compliant TPMs offer protection from password-guessing attacks by forcing the user to wait between attempts, laptop keys show wear. This is especially true if you enter the PIN using your rarely used function keys (on most keyboards, you can use the standard number keys as well). If you use the same PIN for years, the keys in your PIN may show more wear than other keys, allowing a sophisticated attacker to guess the characters in your PIN, thus reducing the number of keys the attacker needs to guess. To further minimize this risk, use a long PIN and use the same key multiple times in your PIN.

When requiring a PIN, the computer's TPM hardware forces a non-resettable delay between PIN entry attempts (the exact delay varies between TPM vendors). Because of this delay, a four-digit PIN might take an entire year to crack. Without this delay, a random four-digit PIN could be cracked in less than a day. Because of this password-guessing weakness when a delay is not enforced by TPM, BitLocker does not allow PIN authentication on computers that do not have TPM hardware.

How It Works: PIN Authentication

In this authentication scenario, the administrator sets up a PIN when BitLocker is turned on. BitLocker hashes the PIN using SHA-256. The resulting nonreversible hash is used as authorization data sent to the TPM to seal the VMK. The VMK is now protected by both the TPM and the PIN. To unseal the VMK, the user enters the PIN when the computer starts, the PIN is hashed, and the result is submitted to the TPM. If the submitted hash (and other PCRs) is correct (proving that the user entered the same PIN), the TPM unseals the VMK.

The following authentication techniques are available regardless of whether or not the computer has a TPM.

TPM with PIN and External Key

After you install Windows Vista Service Pack 1, you have an additional option for BitLocker security on computers with a TPM: requiring the user to type a PIN and insert a USB key. This provides the highest level of BitLocker protection by requiring something the user knows (the PIN) and something the user has (the external key). For an attacker to successfully access data on a BitLocker-protected partition, the attacker would need to acquire the computer with the hard disk, to have the USB key, and to work with the computer's owner to acquire the PIN.

External Key (Require Startup USB Key At Every Startup)

The user provides the VMK on a USB Flash drive or similar external storage so that BitLocker can decrypt the FVEK and the volume without requiring TPM hardware. The external key can be either the standard key or a recovery key created to replace a lost external key.

Using a startup key without TPM does allow you to encrypt a volume without upgrading your hardware. However, it does not provide boot integrity, and it will not detect if the hard disk has been moved to a different computer.

Recovery Password

The user enters a 48-character recovery password, which decrypts the VMK, granting access to the FVEK and the volume. The recovery password is designed with checksums so that IT support can read the password to a user over the phone and easily detect if a user has mistyped a character. For more information, read the section titled "How to Recover Data Protected by BitLocker" later in this chapter.

Clear Key

No authentication occurs. BitLocker does not check the integrity of the computer or operating system, and the VMK is freely accessible, encrypted with a symmetric key stored in the clear on the hard disk. However, the volume remains, in fact, encrypted. This is used only when BitLocker is disabled (to upgrade the computer's BIOS, for example). When BitLocker is re-enabled, the clear key is removed and the VMK is rekeyed and re-encrypted. For more information, read the section titled "How to Disable or Remove BitLocker Drive Encryption" later in this chapter.

BitLocker Phases

The stages of BitLocker startup are:

- **System integrity verification (if a TPM is present)**   Components of the computer and the Windows Boot Manager write values to the platform configuration registers (PCR) of the TPM as the boot process proceeds, including a measurement of the master boot record (MBR) executable code.

- **User authentication (optional)**   If user authentication is configured, the Windows Boot Manager collects a key from USB storage or a PIN from the user.

- **VMK retrieval**   The Windows Boot Manager requests that the TPM decrypt the VMK. If the hashes of the measurements written to the PCR match those taken when BitLocker was set up, the TPM will supply the VMK. If any measurement does not match the recorded value, the TPM does not supply the decryption key, and the BitLocker gives the user the option to enter the recovery key.

- **Operating system startup**   At this point, the Windows Boot Manager has validated the system integrity and now has access to the VMK. The VMK must be passed to the operating system loader; however, the Windows Boot Manager must avoid passing it to a potentially malicious operating system loader and thus compromising the security of the VMK. To ensure that the operating system loader is valid, the Windows Boot Manager verifies that operating system loader executables match a set of requirements. The Windows Boot Manager also verifies that the boot configuration data (BCD) settings have not been modified. It does so by comparing them to a previously generated digital signature known as a message authenticity check (MAC). The BCD MAC is generated using the VMK, ensuring that it cannot be easily rewritten.

  After the operating system loader is started, Windows can use the VMK to decrypt the FVEK and then use the FVEK to decrypt the BitLocker-encrypted volume. With access to the unencrypted data on the volume, Windows loads normally.

Direct from the Source: BitLocker Volumes

Prior to transitioning to the operating system, the OS Loader ensures that it will hand off at most one key (VMK) to the OS. Prior to handing off the key to the OS, the following conditions must apply:

- All components up to and including BOOTMGR must be correct. If they were not correct, the VMK would not be available.

- VMK must be correct to validate the MAC of the metadata. BOOTMGR verifies this MAC.

- OS Loader must be the loader approved by metadata associated with VMK. Verified by BOOTMGR.

- BCD settings must be the settings approved by metadata associated with VMK. Verified by BOOTMGR.

- VMK must correctly decrypt the FVEK stored in the validated metadata. Verified by BOOTMGR.

- The FVEK must successfully decrypt data stored on the volume. An incorrect FVEK will result in invalid executable code or invalid data. In some cases, this is caught by code integrity.

  - MFT must be encrypted by the correct FVEK to access all files.

  - Phase 0 drivers, including fvevol.sys, must be encrypted by the correct FVEK.

  - Registry must be encrypted by the correct FVEK.

  - Kernel and HAL must be encrypted by the correct FVEK.

  - Phase 1 components must be encrypted by the FVEK, as fvevol.sys (encrypted by the FVEK) will only decrypt using the same FVEK.

  - Phase 2 components must also be encrypted by the FVEK, etc.

The last point is particularly important, and it is only true if the data on the volume is entirely encrypted; in other words, a volume where encryption was paused halfway through is not secure.

Jamie Hunter, Lead Software Development Engineer

Many-Core Strategies and Incubation

BitLocker Requirements

To enable BitLocker on a Windows Vista computer, the computer must meet the following requirements:

- Unless you plan to rely solely on a USB startup key, the computer must have a TPM v1.2 (revision 85 or later), and it must be enabled. (TPM chips may be disabled by default and can be turned on using the computer's BIOS.) The TPM provides boot-process integrity measurement and reporting.

- The computer must have v1.21 (revision 0.24 or later) TCG-compliant (Trusted Computing Group) BIOS with support for TCG specified Static Root Trust Measurement (SRTM) to establish a chain of trust prior to starting Windows.

- If you plan to use a USB startup key, the BIOS must support the USB Mass Storage Device Class2, including both reading and writing small files on a USB flash drive in the preoperating system environment.

- The computer must have at least two volumes to operate, and they must be in place before Windows Vista is installed:

  - The boot volume is the volume that contains the Windows operating system and its support files; it must be formatted with NTFS. Data on this volume is protected by BitLocker.

  - The system volume is the volume that contains the hardware-specific files needed to load Windows Vista computers after the BIOS has booted the platform. For BitLocker to work, the system volume must not be encrypted, must differ from the operating system volume, and must be formatted with NTFS. Your system volume should be at least 1.5 GB. Data written to this volume—including additional user data—is not protected by BitLocker.

You can have multiple instances of Windows Vista installed on a computer with a BitLocker-encrypted volume, and they will all be able to access the volume if you enter the recovery password every time you need to access the volume from a different partition. You can also install earlier versions of Windows on volumes not encrypted with BitLocker. However, earlier versions of Windows will not be able to access the BitLocker-encrypted volume.

How to Configure BitLocker Partitions

BitLocker requires at least two partitions, both with NTFS enabled. Ideally, you should configure these partitions prior to deploying a Windows Vista computer. If you need to configure partitions for BitLocker after installing a Windows Vista Ultimate Edition computer, you can use the BitLocker Drive Preparation Tool.

The BitLocker Drive Preparation Tool is available only as a Windows Ultimate Extra. Therefore, you cannot use it with a Windows Vista Enterprise Edition computer. To install the BitLocker Drive Preparation Tool, follow these steps:

1. Click Start, click All Programs, and then click Windows Update.

2. Click Check For Updates.

3. Under There Are Windows Ultimate Extras Available For Download, click View Available Extras. If this link does not appear, the BitLocker Drive Preparation Tool might already be installed.

4. On the Choose The Updates You Want To Install page, under Windows Ultimate Extras, select BitLocker And EFS Enhancements. Click Install.

After installing the BitLocker Drive Preparation Tool, follow these steps to configure your computer's partitions for BitLocker:

1. Click Start, click All Programs, click Accessories, click System Tools, click BitLocker, and then click BitLocker Drive Preparation Tool.

2. Click I Accept.

3. On the Preparing Drive For BitLocker page, click Continue.

4. The BitLocker Drive Preparation Tool shrinks your C drive and then creates a new S partition, marks it as active, and copies the necessary files to the new S partition.

5. Click Finish.

6. Click Restart Now to restart your computer.

Now the computer has a small boot partition–separate from the system partition–that meets the disk partitioning requirements for BitLocker.

How to Enable the Use of BitLocker on Computers Without TPM

BitLocker can store decryption keys on a USB Flash drive instead of using a built-in TPM module. This allows you to use BitLocker on computers that do not have the TPM hardware. Using BitLocker in this configuration can be risky, however, because if the user loses the USB Flash drive, the encrypted volume will no longer be accessible and the computer will not be able to start without the recovery key. Windows Vista does not make this option available by default.

To use BitLocker encryption on a computer without a compatible TPM, you will need to change a computer Group Policy setting by following these steps:

1. Open the Group Policy editor by clicking Start, typing **gpedit.msc**, and then pressing Enter.

2. Navigate to Computer Configuration\Administrative Templates\Windows Components\BitLocker Drive Encryption.

3. Enable the Control Panel Setup: Enable Advanced Startup Options setting and then select the Allow BitLocker Without A Compatible TPM check box.

How to Enable BitLocker Encryption

To enable BitLocker, follow these steps:

1. Perform a full backup of the computer. Then, run a check of the integrity of the BitLocker partition using ChkDsk. For more information about using ChkDsk, read Chapter 31, "Troubleshooting Hardware, Driver, and Disk Issues."

2. Open Control Panel. Click Security. Under BitLocker Drive Encryption, click Protect Your Computer By Encrypting Data On Your Disk.

3. On the BitLocker Drive Encryption page, click Turn On BitLocker (see Figure 15-18).

Figure 15-18   If your partitions are properly configured and your computer has a TPM (or the TPM requirement has been disabled), you can enable BitLocker.

4. If available (the choice can be blocked by a Group Policy setting), in the Set BitLocker Startup Preferences dialog box, select your authentication choice.

5. If you chose to use a USB key, the Save Your Startup Key dialog box appears, as shown in Figure 15-19. Select the startup key and then click Save.

6. On the Save The Recovery Password page, shown in Figure 15-20, choose the destination to save your recovery password. The recovery password is a small text file containing brief instructions, a drive label and password ID, and the 48-digit recovery password. The choices are to store it on a USB drive, save it to a local or remote folder, or print the password. Be sure to save the password and the recovery key on separate devices. You can repeat this step to save the password to multiple locations. Keep the recovery passwords safe—anyone with access to the recovery password can bypass BitLocker security. Click Next.

Figure 15-19   You can save the startup key to a USB Flash drive.

Figure 15-20   Save the recovery password to regain access to BitLocker-encrypted volumes if you lose the key.

> **Note**   It is strongly recommended that you save your recovery password to more than one location or device to ensure that you can recover it in the event that the BitLocker drive becomes locked. Keep the recovery keys safe and separate from the protected computer. Additionally, ensure that BitLocker-protected volumes are regularly backed up.

7. On the Encrypt The Volume page, select the Run BitLocker System Check check box and click Continue if you are ready to begin encryption. Click Restart Now. Upon rebooting, BitLocker will ensure that the computer is fully compatible and ready to be encrypted.

8. BitLocker displays a special screen confirming that the key material was loaded. Now that this has been confirmed, BitLocker will begin encrypting the C drive after Windows Vista starts, and BitLocker will be enabled.

Encryption occurs in the background; the user can work on the computer (though free disk space and processor time will be partially consumed by BitLocker). If BitLocker encounters a disk-related problem, it will pause encryption and schedule a ChkDsk to run the next time you restart your computer. After the problem has been fixed, encryption will continue.

A notification message is displayed in the system tray during encryption. An administrator can click the BitLocker system tray icon and then choose to pause the encryption process if the computer's performance is impacted, although the computer will not be protected until encryption is completed.

How to Manage BitLocker Keys on a Local Computer

To manage keys on a local computer, follow these steps:

1. Open Control Panel and click Security. Under BitLocker Drive Encryption, click Manage BitLocker Keys.

2. In the BitLocker Drive Encryption window, click Manage BitLocker Keys.

Using this tool, you can perform the following actions (which vary depending on the authentication type chosen):

- **Duplicate the Recovery Password**   Provides the following options:
    - ❑ Save The Password On A USB Drive
    - ❑ Save The Password In A Folder
    - ❑ Print The Password
- **Duplicate the Startup Key**   When you use a USB startup key for authentication, this action allows you to create a second USB startup key with an identical key.
- **Reset the PIN**   When you use a PIN for authentication, this action allows you to change the PIN.

If you are using Windows Vista Ultimate Edition and have installed the BitLocker And EFS Enhancements as described in the section titled "How to Configure BitLocker Partitions" earlier in this chapter, you can also use the Secure Online Key Backup tool to store the recovery password on the Microsoft digital locker website. This tool is primarily intended for consumers and small businesses, because enterprises should manage BitLocker recovery keys internally.

To use the Secure Online Key Backup tool, follow these steps:

1. Open Control Panel and click Security. Click Secure Online Key Backup. If the option does not appear, you need to install the BitLocker And EFS Enhancements, as described in the section titled "How to Configure BitLocker Partitions" earlier in this chapter.

2. In the Secure Online Key Backup window, click Save Your BitLocker Recovery Password.

3. In the Store Your Recovery Password On The Digital Locker Website window, type your Windows Live ID e-mail address and password. If you do not yet have a Windows Live ID, click Sign Up For Windows Live and follow the prompts that appear. Click Submit.

After the Secure Online Key Backup tool stores your recovery password, you can choose to print the password. Store the printed recovery password separately from your computer to prevent an attacker from acquiring both your computer and the recovery password. Later, you can return to the Secure Online Key Backup tool to restore the recovery password after authenticating with your Windows Live ID. For more information about the Microsoft digital locker, visit *http://windowsmarketplace.com/content.aspx?ctId=302*.

How to Manage BitLocker from the Command Line

To manage BitLocker from an elevated command prompt or from a remote computer, use the Manage-bde.wsf script (included with Windows Vista in the System32 folder). Use Cscript.exe to run Manage-bde.wsf, as the following example demonstrates:

```
C:\Windows\system32>cscript manage-bde.wsf -status
```

```
Microsoft (R) Windows Script Host Version 5.7
Copyright (C) Microsoft Corporation. All rights reserved.

Disk volumes that can be protected with
BitLocker Drive Encryption:
Volume C: []
[OS Volume]

    Size:                  698.64 GB
    Conversion Status:     Fully Decrypted
    Percentage Encrypted:  0%
    Encryption Method:     None
    Protection Status:     Protection Off
    Lock Status:           Unlocked
    Automatic Unlock:      Disabled
    Key Protectors:        None Found
```

Run the following command to enable BDE on the C drive, store the startup key on the F drive, and generate a random recovery password:

```
C:\Windows\System32>cscript manage-bde.wsf -on C: -StartupKey F: -RecoveryPassword
```

```
Microsoft (R) Windows Script Host Version 5.7
Copyright (C) Microsoft Corporation. All rights reserved.

Volume C:
[OS Volume]
Key Protectors Added:

    Recovery Key:
      ID: {9EFCCD77-16E4-40C2-929C-82F4B218B5DF}
      External Key File Name:
        9EFCCD77-16E4-40C2-929C-82F4B218B5DF.BEK

    Saved to directory F:

    Numerical Password:
      ID: {150B1305-F98B-4677-9A70-80BD3431BADF}
      Password:
        496342-325028-168718-226798-029007-470206-189211-604197

ACTIONS REQUIRED:


    1. Save this numerical recovery password in a secure location away from
    your computer:

    496342-325028-168718-226798-029007-470206-189211-604197

    To prevent data loss, save this password immediately. This password helps
    ensure that you can unlock the encrypted volume.

    2. Insert a USB flash drive with an external key file into the computer.

    3. Restart the computer to run a hardware test.
    (Type "shutdown /?" for command line instructions.)

    4. Type "manage-bde -status" to check if the hardware test succeeded.

NOTE: Encryption will begin after the hardware test succeeds.
```

After you run the command, restart the computer with the recovery key connected to complete the hardware test. After the computer restarts, BDE will begin encrypting the disk.

You can also use the Manage-bde.wsf script to specify a startup key and a recovery key, which could allow a single key to be used on multiple computers. This is useful if a single user has multiple computers, such as a user with both a Tablet PC computer and a desktop computer. It can also be useful in lab environments, where several users might share several different computers. Note, however, that a single compromised startup key or recovery key will require all computers with the same key to be rekeyed.

For detailed information about using Manage-bde.wsf, run **Cscript manage-bde.wsf -?** from a command prompt.

How to Recover Data Protected by BitLocker

When you use BitLocker, the encrypted volumes will be locked if the encryption key is not available, causing BitLocker to enter recovery mode. Likely causes of the encryption key not being available include:

- Modification of one of the boot files.
- BIOS is modified and the TPM disabled.
- TPM is cleared.
- An attempt is made to boot without the TPM, PIN, or USB key being available.
- The BitLocker-encrypted disk is moved to a new computer.

After the drive is locked, you can boot only to recovery mode, as shown in Figure 15-21. In recovery mode, you enter the recovery password using the function keys on your keyboard (just as you do when entering the PIN), pressing F1 for the digit 1, F2 for the digit 2, and so forth, with F10 being the digit 0. You must use function keys, because localized keyboard support is not yet available at this phase of startup.

If you have the recovery key on a USB Flash drive, you can insert the recovery key and press Esc to restart the computer. The recovery key will be read automatically during startup.

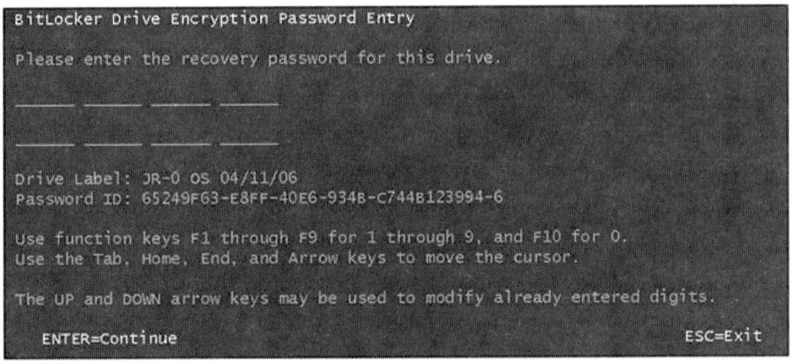

```
BitLocker Drive Encryption Password Entry

Please enter the recovery password for this drive.

____  ____  ____

____  ____  ____

Drive Label: JR-0 OS 04/11/06
Password ID: 65249F63-E8FF-40E6-9348-C744B123994-6

Use function keys F1 through F9 for 1 through 9, and F10 for 0.
Use the Tab, Home, End, and Arrow keys to move the cursor.

The UP and DOWN arrow keys may be used to modify already entered digits.

   ENTER=Continue                                      ESC=Exit
```

Figure 15-21   Recovery mode prompts you for a 48-character recovery password.

If you cancel recovery, the Windows Boot Manager will provide instructions for using Startup Repair to fix a startup problem automatically. Do not follow these instructions; Startup Repair cannot access the encrypted volume. Instead, restart the computer and enter the recovery key.

Additionally, you can use the BitLocker Repair Tool to help recover data from an encrypted volume. For more information, see *http://support.microsoft.com/kb/928201*.

How to Disable or Remove BitLocker Drive Encryption

Because BitLocker intercepts the boot process and looks for changes to any of the early boot files, it can cause problems in the following nonattack scenarios:

- Upgrading or replacing the motherboard or TPM
- Installing a new operating system that changes the master boot record or the boot manager
- Moving a BitLocker-encrypted disk to another TPM-enabled computer
- Repartitioning the hard disk
- Updating the BIOS
- Installing a third-party update outside the operating system (such as hardware firmware updates)

To avoid entering BitLocker recovery mode, you can temporarily disable BitLocker, which allows you to change the TPM and upgrade the operating system. When you re-enable BitLocker, the same keys will be used. You can also choose to decrypt the BitLocker-protected volume, which will completely remove BitLocker protection. You can only re-enable BitLocker by repeating the process to create new keys and re-encrypt the volume. To disable or decrypt BitLocker, follow these steps:

1. Log on to the computer as Administrator.

2. From Control Panel, open BitLocker Drive Encryption.

3. Click Turn Off BitLocker for the volume that has BitLocker enabled.

4. Choose Disable BitLocker Drive Encryption to use a clear key (Figure 15-22). To completely remove BitLocker, choose Decrypt The Volume.

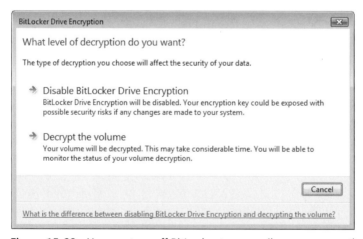

Figure 15-22   You can turn off BitLocker temporarily or permanently.

How to Permanently Decommission a BitLocker Drive

Compromises in confidentiality can occur when computers or hard disks are decommissioned. For example, a computer that reaches the end of its usefulness at an organization might be discarded, sold, or donated to charity. The person who receives the computer might extract confidential files from the computer's hard disk. Even if the disk has been formatted, data can often be extracted.

BitLocker reduces the risks of decommissioning drives. For example, if you use a startup key or startup PIN, the contents of the volume are inaccessible without this additional information or the drive's saved recovery information.

You can more securely decommission a drive by removing all key blobs from the disk. By deleting the BitLocker keys from the volume, an attacker would need to crack the encryption— a task that is extremely unlikely to be accomplished within anyone's lifetime. As a cleanup task, you should also discard all saved recovery information such as recovery information saved to Active Directory Domain Services.

To remove all key blobs on a secondary drive (data volume), you can format that drive from Windows Vista or the Windows Vista Recovery Environment. Note that this format operation will not work on a drive that is currently in use. For example, you cannot use it to more securely decommission the drive used to run Windows.

To remove all key blobs on a running drive, you can create a script that performs the following tasks:

1. Calls the *Win32_EncryptableVolume.GetKeyProtectors* method to retrieve all key protectors (*KeyProtectorType 0*).

2. Creates a not-to-be-used recovery password BLOB (discarding the actual recovery password) by using *Win32_EncryptableVolume.ProtectKeyWithNumericalPassword* and a randomly generated password sequence. This is required because *Win32_EncryptableVolume.DeleteKeyProtector* will not remove all key protectors.

3. Uses *Win32_EncryptableVolume.DeleteKeyProtector* to remove all the usable key protectors associated with the identifiers mentioned previously.

4. Clears the TPM by calling the *Win32_TPM.Clear* method.

For more information about developing a script or application to perform secure decommissioning on a BitLocker-encrypted drive, refer to the *Win32_EncryptableVolume* WMI provider class documentation at *http://msdn2.microsoft.com/en-us/library/aa376483.aspx* and the *Win32_TPM* WMI provider class documentation at *http://msdn2.microsoft.com/en-us/library/aa376484.aspx*.

How to Prepare Active Directory for BitLocker

BitLocker is also integrated into Active Directory. In fact, although you can use BitLocker without Active Directory, enterprises really shouldn't—key recovery is an extremely important part of using BitLocker, and Active Directory is a reliable and efficient way to store recovery keys so that you can restore encrypted data if a key is lost. For detailed instructions on how to configure Active Directory to backup BitLocker and TPM recovery information, read "Configuring Active Directory to Back up Windows BitLocker Drive Encryption and Trusted Platform Module Recovery Information" at *http://go.microsoft.com/fwlink/?LinkId=78953*. For information about retrieving recovery passwords from Active Directory, read "How to use the BitLocker Recovery Password Viewer for Active Directory Users and Computers tool to view recovery passwords for Windows Vista" at *http://support.microsoft.com/?kbid=928202*.

How to Manage BitLocker with Group Policy

BitLocker has several Group Policy settings located in Computer Configuration\Administrative Templates\Windows Components\BitLocker Drive Encryption that you can use to manage the available features. Table 15-2 lists these policies, which are written to the registry on targeted computers under the following registry key:

HKLM\Software\Policies\Microsoft\FVE

Table 15-2   Group Policy Settings for BitLocker Drive Encryption

Policy	Description
Turn On BitLocker Backup To Active Directory Domain Services	Enabling this policy silently backs up BitLocker recovery information to Active Directory.
Control Panel Setup: Configure Recovery Folder	Enabling this policy and configuring a default path for it sets the default folder to display when the user is saving recovery information for BitLocker. The user will have the ability to override the default.
Control Panel: Configure Recovery Options	Enabling this policy allows you to control which recovery mechanisms the user can choose. Disabling the recovery password will disable saving to a folder or printing the key, because these actions require the 48-digit recovery password. Disabling the 256-bit recovery key will disable saving to a USB key. If you disable both options, you must enable Active Directory Domain Services backup or a policy error will occur.
Control Panel: Enable Advanced Startup Options	Enabling this policy allows configuring additional startup options and allows enabling of BitLocker on a non-TPM–compatible computer. On TPM-compatible computers, a secondary authentication can be required at startup—either a USB key or a startup PIN, but not both.
Configure Encryption Method	Enabling this policy allows configuration of the encryption method used by BitLocker Drive Encryption. The default if this key is not enabled is 128-bit AES with Diffuser. Other choices that can be configured are 256-bit AES with Diffuser, 128-bit AES, and 256-bit AES.

Table 15-2   Group Policy Settings for BitLocker Drive Encryption

Policy	Description
Prevent Memory Overwrite On Restart	Enabling this policy prevents Windows from overwriting memory on restarts. This potentially exposes BitLocker secrets but can improve restart performance.
Configure TPM Platform Validation Profile	Enabling this policy allows detailed configuration of the Platform Configuration Register (PCR) indices. Each index aligns with Windows components that run during startup.

The Costs of BitLocker

Most security features require a tradeoff. The benefit to any security feature is that it reduces risk and thus reduces the cost associated with a security compromise. Most security features also have a cost—purchase price, increased maintenance, or decreased user productivity.

The benefit of using BitLocker is reduced risk of loss of data confidentiality in the event of a stolen hard disk. Like most security features, BitLocker has costs (aside from any software or hardware costs):

- If a PIN or external key is required, the startup experience is not transparent to the user. If the user loses his PIN or startup key, he will need to wait for a support center representative to read him the password so that he can start his computer.

- In the event of hard disk failure or data corruption, recovering data from the disk can be more difficult.

You should implement BitLocker in your organization only if the reduced security risks outweigh these costs. For more information about cost/benefit analysis, read the Security Risk Management Guide at *http://www.microsoft.com/technet/security/guidance/ complianceandpolicies/secrisk/default.mspx.*

Encrypting File System

BitLocker is not a replacement for the Encrypting File System (EFS) introduced in Windows 2000, but it is a supplement to the EFS that ensures that the operating system itself is protected from attack. Best practices for protecting sensitive computers and data will combine the two features to provide a high level of assurance of the data integrity on the system.

EFS continues to be an important data-integrity tool in Windows Vista. EFS allows the encryption of entire volumes or individual folders and files and can support multiple users using the same computer, each with protected data. Additionally, EFS allows multiple users to have secure access to sensitive data while protecting the data against unauthorized viewing or modification. EFS cannot be used to encrypt system files, however, and it should be combined with BitLocker to encrypt the system drive where sensitive data must be protected. EFS is susceptible to offline attack using the SYSKEY, but when you combine EFS with BitLocker to encrypt the system volume, this attack vector is protected.

EFS uses symmetric key encryption along with public key technology to protect files and folders. Each user of EFS is issued a digital certificate with a public and private key pair. EFS uses the keys to transparently encrypt and decrypt the files for the logged-on user. Authorized users work with encrypted files and folders just as they do with unencrypted files and folders. Unauthorized users receive an Access Denied message in response to any attempt to open, copy, move, or rename the encrypted file or folder.

Files are encrypted with a single symmetrical key and then the symmetrical key is encrypted twice: once with the user's EFS public key to allow transparent decryption, and once with the recovery agent's key to allow data recovery.

The sections that follow describe how to manage EFS keys. For general information about EFS, read "Encrypting File System in Windows XP and Windows Server 2003" at *http://technet.microsoft.com/en-us/library/bb457065.aspx.*

How to Export Personal Certificates

To prevent being unable to access an encrypted file, you can export your personal certificate. When you export your certificate, you can then copy or move the encrypted file to another computer and still access it by importing the certificate you exported.

To export your personal certificate, follow these steps:

1. Open Windows Explorer and select a file that you have encrypted.

2. Right-click the file and then select Properties.

3. Click Advanced on the General tab.

4. Click Details on the Advanced Attributes tab to open the User Access dialog box.

5. Select your user name and then click Back Up Keys to open the Certificate Export Wizard.

6. Click Next to select the file format to use.

7. Click Next and enter a password to protect the key. Repeat the entry and then click Next.

8. Enter a path and filename to save the file to, or browse for a path. Click Next.

9. Click Finish to export the certificate and then click OK to confirm that it was saved successfully.

If you are using Windows Vista Ultimate Edition and have installed the BitLocker And EFS Enhancements as described in the section titled "How to Configure BitLocker Partitions" earlier in this chapter, you can also use the Secure Online Key Backup tool to store the EFS recovery certificate on the Microsoft digital locker website. This tool is primarily intended for consumers and small businesses, because enterprises should manage EFS recovery certificates internally.

To use the Secure Online Key Backup tool, follow these steps:

1. Open Control Panel, click Security, and then click Secure Online Key Backup. If the option does not appear, you need to install the BitLocker And EFS Enhancements, as described in the section titled "How to Configure BitLocker Partitions" earlier in this chapter.

2. In the Secure Online Key Backup window, click Save Your EFS Recovery Certificate.

3. In the Store Your EFS Certificate On The Digital Locker Website window, type your Windows Live ID e-mail address and password. If you do not yet have a Windows Live ID, click Sign Up For Windows Live and follow the prompts that appear. Click Submit.

After the Secure Online Key Backup tool stores your EFS recovery certificate, you can return to the Secure Online Key Backup tool to restore it after authenticating with your Windows Live ID. For more information about the Microsoft digital locker, visit *http://windowsmarketplace.com/content.aspx?ctId=302.*

How to Import Personal Certificates

You can share encrypted files with other users if you have the certificate for the other user. To allow another user to use a file that you have encrypted, you need to import her certificate onto your computer and add her user name to the list of users who are permitted access to the file.

To import a user certificate, follow these steps:

1. Click Start, type **mmc**, and then press Enter to open a blank Microsoft Management Console.

2. Click File and then click Add/Remove Snap-in.

3. Select Certificates and click Add. Select My User Account and click Finish. Click OK to close the Add Or Remove Snap-in dialog box.

4. Click Certificates and then double-click Trusted People.

5. Under Trusted People, right-click Certificates. On the All Tasks menu, click Import to open the Certificate Import Wizard.

6. Click Next and then browse to the location of the certificate you want to import.

7. Select the certificate and then click Next.

8. Type the password for the certificate and then click Next.

9. Click Next to place the certificate in the Trusted People store.

10. Click Finish to complete the import.

11. Click OK to acknowledge the successful import and then exit the MMC.

How to Grant Users Access to an Encrypted File

When you have a user's certificate, you can add that user to the list of users who have access to a file. A user's certificate will automatically be on a computer if the user has previously logged on to the computer.

To add a user whose certificate you have imported to the users who can access a file, follow these steps:

1. Open Windows Explorer and highlight the file you want to give access to.

2. Right-click the file and then select Properties.

3. Click Advanced on the General tab.

4. Click Details on the Advanced Attributes tab to open the User Access dialog box.

5. Click Add to open the Encrypting File System dialog box and then select the user you want to permit to use the encrypted file.

6. Click OK to add the user to the list of users who have access to the file.

7. Click OK until you've exited out of the dialog boxes.

You do not need to grant EFS access to allow users to access files across the network—EFS does not affect shared folders.

Symbolic Links

Windows Vista includes *symbolic links*. Symbolic links act like shortcuts, but they provide a transparent link to the target file at the file-system level, rather than within Explorer. Therefore, although a user can double-click a shortcut from Explorer to open the original file, a symbolic link will actually trick applications into thinking they are directly accessing the target file.

As an administrator, you might need to use symbolic links for backward compatibility. For example, if an application expects to find a file in the root of the C drive, but you need to move the file to a different location on the local disk, you can create a symbolic link in the root of the C drive to the file's new location, allowing the application to continue to access the file in the root of the C drive. Windows Vista uses symbolic links for backward compatibility with user profiles in earlier versions of Windows. For more information, read Chapter 14, "Managing Users and User Data."

How It Works: Symbolic Links, Hard Links, Junction Points, and Shortcuts

Windows Vista supports four different types of links, each providing a slightly different function:

- **Shortcuts**   Shortcuts are files with a .lnk extension. If you double-click them within the Windows Shell, Windows will open the target file. However, the file system treats .lnk files just like any other files. For example, opening a .lnk file from a command prompt does not open the target file.

- **Hard links**   Hard links create a new directory entry for an existing file, so a single file can appear in multiple folders (or in a single folder using multiple filenames). Hard links must all be on a single volume.

- **Junction points**   Also known as soft links, junction points reference a folder using an absolute path. Windows automatically redirects requests for a junction point to the target folder. Junction points do not have to be on the same volume.

- **Symbolic links**   A pointer to a file or folder. Link junction points, symbolic links are almost always transparent to users. (Occasionally, a program might use an outdated API that does not respect a symbolic link.) Symbolic links use relative paths, rather than absolute paths.

How to Create Symbolic Links

By default, only administrators can create symbolic links. However, you can grant other uses access using the Computer Configuration\Windows Settings\Security Settings\Local Policies\User Rights Assignment\Create Symbolic Links setting.

To create a symbolic link, open a command prompt with administrative privileges and use the Mklink command. For example, the following command creates a symbolic link from C:\myapp.exe to Notepad in the system directory:

```
C:\>mklink myapp.exe %windir%\system32\notepad.exe
```

```
symbolic link created for myapp.exe <<===>> C:\Windows\system32\notepad.exe
```

 Note   Developers can call the *CreateSymbolicLink* function to create symbolic links. For more information, go to *http://msdn2.microsoft.com/en-us/library/aa363866.aspx*.

After you create this symbolic link, the Myapp.exe link behaves exactly like a copy of the Notepad.exe file. Explorer displays symbolic links using the standard shortcut symbol. However, shortcuts always have a .lnk extension, whereas symbolic links can have any extension. At a command prompt, the Dir command uses the <SYMLINK> identifier to distinguish symbolic links and displays the path to the target file:

```
C:\>dir
```

```
    Volume in drive C has no label.
    Volume Serial Number is BC33-D7AC

    Directory of C:\

09/18/2006  04:43 PM                     24 AUTOEXEC.BAT
09/18/2006  04:43 PM                     10 config.sys
12/27/2006  12:16 PM    <SYMLINK>           myapp.exe [C:\Windows\system32\notepad.exe]
12/23/2006  04:47 PM    <DIR>               Program Files
11/29/2006  03:31 PM    <DIR>               Users
12/27/2006  08:39 AM    <DIR>               Windows
```

Because a symbolic link is only a link, any changes made to the link actually impact the target file and vice versa. If you create a symbolic link and then delete the target file, the symbolic link will remain, but any attempts to access it will return a File Not Found error, because Windows Vista will automatically attempt to access the link target. If you delete a target file and later replace it with a file of the same name, that new file will become the link target. Deleting a link does not affect the link target.

Attribute changes to the symbolic link, such as marking a file hidden or as a system file, are applied to both the symbolic link and the target file.

How to Create Relative or Absolute Symbolic Links

Relative symbolic links identify the location of the target based on their own folder. For example, a relative symbolic link to a target file in the same folder will always attempt to access a target with the specified filename in the same folder, even if the symbolic link is moved. You can create relative or absolute symbolic links, but all symbolic links are relative by default. For example, consider the following commands, which attempt to create a symbolic link named link.txt to a file named target.txt and then attempt to access the symbolic link before and after moving the target file:

```
C:\>mklink link.txt target.txt
C:\>type link.txt
```

```
    Hello, world.
```

```
C:\>REM Move link.txt to a different folder
C:\>move link.txt C:\links


        1 file(s) moved.


C:\>cd links
C:\links>type link.txt


  The system cannot find the file specified.


C:\links>move \target.txt C:\links
C:\links>type link.txt


  Hello, world.
```

In the previous example, moving the symbolic link to a different folder caused Windows Vista to be unable to locate the target, because the symbolic link was a relative link pointing to a file named target.txt in the same folder. When both the link and the target were moved to the same folder, the symbolic link worked again.

Now consider the same example using an absolute symbolic link, created by specifying the full path to the target file:

```
C:\>mklink link.txt C:\target.txt
C:\>type link.txt


  Hello, world.


C:\>REM Move link.txt to a different folder
C:\>move link.txt C:\links


        1 file(s) moved.


C:\>cd links
C:\links>type link.txt


  Hello, world.


C:\links>move C:\target.txt C:\links\
C:\links>type link.txt


  The system cannot find the file specified.
```

In the last example, specifying the full path to the target file created an absolute symbolic link that referenced the full path to the target file. Therefore, the symbolic link still worked after it was moved to a different folder. However, moving the target file made it inaccessible.

How to Create Symbolic Links to Shared Folders

You can create symbolic links on the local file system to files stored on other local drives or shared folders. However, when you use the Mklink command, you must always specify the absolute path to the remote target file, because the Mklink command by default assumes that the location is relative. For example, suppose you want to create a symbolic link named C:\link.txt that targets a file on a shared folder at Z:\target.txt. If you run the following commands, you will successfully create a symbolic link at C:\link.txt:

```
C:\>Z:
Z:\>mklink C:\link.txt target.txt
```

However, that file will link to C:\target.txt, and not the intended Z:\target.txt. To create a link to the Z:\target.txt file, you need to run the following command:

```
C:\>mklink C:\link.txt Z:\target.txt
```

The Mklink command also allows you to create a symbolic link targeting a UNC path. For example, if you run the following command, Windows Vista will create a symbolic link file called link.txt that opens the target.txt file:

```
Mklink link.txt \\server\folder\target.txt
```

If you enable remote symbolic links (discussed later in this section), they can be used to store symbolic links on shared folders and automatically redirect multiple Windows Vista network clients to a different file on the network.

By default, you can use symbolic links only on local volumes. If you attempt to access a symbolic link located on a shared folder (regardless of the location of the target), or copy a symbolic link to a shared folder, you will receive an error. You can change this behavior by configuring the following Group Policy setting:

Computer Configuration\Administrative Templates\System\NTFS File System\Selectively Allow The Evaluation Of A SymbolicLlink

When you enable this policy setting, you can select from four settings:

- **Local Link To Local Target**   Enabled by default, this allows local symbolic links to targets on the local file system.

- **Local Link To Remote Target**   Enabled by default, this allows local symbolic links to targets on shared folders.

- **Remote Link To Remote Target**   Disabled by default, this allows remote symbolic links to remote targets on shared folders.

■ **Remote Link To Local Target**   Disabled by default, this allows remote symbolic links to remote targets on shared folders.

Enabling remote links can introduce security vulnerabilities. For example, a malicious user could create a symbolic link on a shared folder that references an absolute path on the local computer. When a user attempts to access the symbolic link, he will actually be accessing a different file that might contain confidential information. In this way, a sophisticated attacker might be able to trick a user into compromising the confidentiality of a file on his local computer.

How to Use Hard Links

Hard links create a second directory entry for a single file, whereas symbolic links create a new file that references an existing file. This subtle difference yields significantly different behavior.

You can create hard links by adding the /H parameter to the Mklink command. For example, the following command creates a hard link from link.txt to target.txt:

```
C:\>mklink /H link.txt target.txt
```

```
Hardlink created for link.txt <<===>> target.txt
```

As with symbolic links, any changes made to the hard link are automatically made to the target (including attribute changes) and vice versa, because the file itself is stored only once on the volume. However, hard links have several key differences:

■ Hard links must refer to files on the same volume; symbolic links can refer to files or folders on different volumes or shared folders.

■ Hard links can refer only to files; symbolic links can refer to either files or folders.

■ Windows Vista maintains hard links, so the link and the target remain accessible even if you move one of them to a different folder.

■ Hard links survive deleting the target file. A target file is deleted only if the target file and all hard links are deleted.

■ If you delete a symbolic link target and then create a new file with the same name as the target, the symbolic link will open the new target. Hard links will continue to reference the original target file, even if you replace the target.

■ Hard links do not show up as symbolic links in Dir command-line output, and Explorer does not show a shortcut symbol for them. Hard links are indistinguishable from the original file.

■ Changes made to file permissions on a hard link apply to the target file and vice versa. With symbolic links, you can configure separate permissions on the symbolic link, but the permissions are ignored.

Windows XP supports hard links by using the "fsutil hardlink" command. Windows Vista hard links are compatible with Windows XP hard links, and the "fsutil hardlink" command continues to function in Windows Vista.

Disk Quotas

Administrators can configure disk quotas to control how much of a volume a single user can fill with files. This is most useful when implemented on a server that hosts shared folders. However, you might also need to implement disk quotas on client computers in environments where multiple users access a single computer, because they can help prevent a single user from completely filling a volume and thereby preventing other users from saving files. Disk quotas have not changed significantly since Windows XP.

Before enabling disk quotas, consider if they are worthwhile. Managing disk quotas requires administrators to monitor disk quota events, such as a user exceeding a disk storage threshold. Administrators must then work with users to either increase the quota or identify files that can be removed. Often, it is less expensive to simply add more disk storage, even if the users do not closely manage their disk usage.

How to Configure Disk Quotas on a Single Computer

To configure disk quotas on a single computer, follow these steps:

1. Click Start and then click Computer.

2. In the right pane, right-click the drive on which you want to configure the quotas and then click Properties.

3. Click the Quota tab and then click Show Quota Settings. The Quota Settings dialog box appears.

4. Select the Enable Quota Management check box, as shown in Figure 15-23.

From this dialog box, you can configure the following disk quota options:

- **Enable Quota Management**   Quota management is disabled by default. Select this check box to enable quota management.

- **Deny Disk Space To Users Exceeding Quota Limit**   By default, users are warned only if they exceed their quota limits. Selecting this check box causes Windows to block disk access after the quota has been exceeded. Typically, warning users is sufficient, provided that you also log the events and follow up with users who do not clean up their disk space. Denying disk access will cause applications to fail when they attempt to write more data to the disk and can cause users to lose unsaved work.

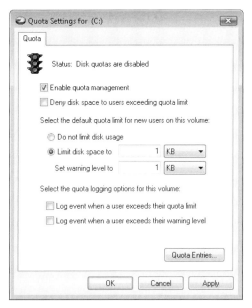

Figure 15-23   Disk quotas control how much of a disk users can fill.

> **Note**   To determine quota limitations for users, developers can call the *Management-ObjectSearcher.Get* WMI method to retrieve a *ManagementObjectCollection* object and then access the collection's *QuotaVolume* item.

- **Do Not Limit Disk Usage**   Does not configure disk quotas for new users by default. You can still use the Quota Entries window to configure disk quotas for users.

- **Limit Disk Space To and Set Warning Level To**   Creates a disk quota by default for new users. The value in the Set Warning Level To box should be lower than that in the Limit Disk Space To box so that the user receives a warning before running out of available disk space.

- **Log Event When A User Exceeds Their Quota Limit and Log Event When A User Exceeds Their Warning Level**   Configures Windows Vista to add an event when the user exceeds her quota. You should typically select this check box and then monitor the events so that IT support can communicate directly with the user to keep the user within her quotas (or increase the quotas as needed).

Additionally, you can click Quota Entries to configure quota settings for existing users and groups.

How to Configure Disk Quotas from a Command Prompt

To view and manage disk quotas from scripts or from the command line, use the Fsutil administrative command-line utility. Useful Fsutil commands include:

- **fsutil quota query C:**   Displays quota information about the C volume, as the following example shows:

```
C:\>fsutil quota query C:
```

```
FileSystemControlFlags = 0x00000301
    Quotas are tracked on this volume
    Logging for quota events is not enabled
    The quota values are incomplete

Default Quota Threshold = 0xffffffffffffffff
Default Quota Limit     = 0xffffffffffffffff

SID Name        = BUILTIN\Administrators (Alias)
Change time     = Tuesday, April 11, 2006    7:54:59 AM
Quota Used      = 0
Quota Threshold = 18446744073709551615
Quota Limit     = 18446744073709551615
```

- **fsutil quota track C:**   Enables disk quotas on the C volume.

- **fsutil quota disable C:**   Disables disk quotas on the C volume.

- **fsutil quota enforce C:**   Enables disk quota enforcement on the C volume, which causes Windows Vista to deny disk access if a quota is exceeded.

- **fsutil quota modify C: 3000000000 5000000000 Contoso\User**   Creates a disk quota entry for the user Contoso\User. The first number (3,000,000,000 in the preceding example) enables a warning threshold at about 3 GB, and the second number (5,000,000,000 in the preceding example) enables an absolute limit of about 5 GB.

For complete usage information, run **Fsutil** /? from a command prompt.

How to Configure Disk Quotas by Using Group Policy Settings

To configure disk quotas in an enterprise, use the Active Directory Group Policy settings located at Computer Configuration\Administrative Templates\System\Disk Quotas. The following settings are available:

- Enable Disk Quotas

- Enforce Disk Quota Limit

- Default Quota Limit And Warning Level

- Log Event When Quota Limit Exceeded
- Log Event When Quota Warning Level Exceeded
- Apply Policy To Removable Media

Each of these settings relates directly to a local computer setting described earlier, except for Apply Policy To Removable Media. If you enable this setting, quotas also apply to NTFS-formatted removable media. Quotas never apply to fixed or removable media unless they are formatted with NTFS.

Disk Tools

Microsoft provides several free tools that are very useful for managing disks and file systems, as the sections that follow describe. For information about tools used for troubleshooting disk problems, refer to Chapter 31.

Disk Usage

Perhaps the biggest challenge of managing file systems is managing disk usage. Quotas can help, but often, you will still need to manually identify folders and files that are consuming large amounts of disk space.

The free Disk Usage (Du) tool, available for download from *http://technet.microsoft.com/en-us/sysinternals/bb896651.aspx*, can identify the mount of disk space a folder and its subfolders consume. Run **Du.exe** with the folder you want to analyze. For example:

```
du C:\users\
```

```
Du v1.31 - report directory disk usage
Copyright (C) 2005-2006 Mark Russinovich
Sysinternals - www.sysinternals.com

Files:        96459
Directories:  19696
Size:         51,641,352,816 bytes
Size on disk: 47,647,077,498 bytes
```

EFSDump

Users can share EFS-encrypted files by adding other user certificates to a file. However, auditing the users who have rights to files would be very time-consuming using the Windows Explorer graphical interface. To more easily list users who have access to encrypted files, use EFSDump, available for download from *http://www.microsoft.com/technet/sysinternals/FileAndDisk/efsdump.mspx*.

For example, to list the users who have access to files in the encrypted subfolder, run the following command:

```
efsdump -s encrypted
```

```
EFS Information Dumper v1.02
Copyright (C) 1999 Mark Russinovich
Systems Internals - http://www.sysinternals.com

C:\Users\User1\Documents\Encrypted\MyFile.txt:
DDF Entry:
    COMPUTER\User1:
        User1(User1@COMPUTER)
DDF Entry:
    COMPUTER\User2:
        User2(User2@COMPUTER)
DRF Entry:
```

SDelete

When you delete a file, Windows removes the index for the file and prevents the operating system from accessing the file's contents. However, an attacker with direct access to the disk can still recover the file's contents until it has been overwritten by another file—which might never happen. Similarly, files that have been EFS-encrypted leave behind the unencrypted contents of the file on the disk.

With the SDelete tool, available for download from *http://www.microsoft.com/technet/ sysinternals/Security/SDelete.mspx*, you can overwrite the contents of free space on your disk to prevent deleted or encrypted files from being recovered.

To use SDelete to overwrite deleted files on the C drive, run the following command:

```
sdelete -z C:
```

```
SDelete - Secure Delete v1.51
Copyright (C) 1999-2005 Mark Russinovich
Sysinternals - www.sysinternals.com

SDelete is set for 1 pass.
Free space cleaned on C:
```

Streams

NTFS files can contain multiple streams of data. Each stream resembles a separate file but is listed within a single filename. Streams are accessed using the syntax "*file:stream*", and by default, the main stream is unnamed (and hence is accessed when you simply specify the filename).

For example, you can use the Echo command to create a file or a specific stream. To create a stream named Data for the file named Text.txt, run the following command:

```
echo Hello, world > text.txt:data
```

Directory listings will show the text.txt file is zero bytes long, and opening the file in a text editor will show nothing. However, it does contain data in the Data stream, which you can demonstrate by running the following command:

```
more < text.txt:data
```

```
  Hello, world
```

Legitimate programs often use streams. However, malicious software also uses streams to hide data. You can use the Streams program, available at *http://www.microsoft.com/technet/sysinternals/FileAndDisk/Streams.mspx*, to list streams. For example, to list all files with streams within the Windows directory, run the following command:

```
streams -s %windir%
```

```
  Streams v1.56 - Enumerate alternate NTFS data streams
  Copyright (C) 1999-2007 Mark Russinovich
  Sysinternals - www.sysinternals.com

  C:\Windows\Thumbs.db:
      :encryptable:$DATA 0
  C:\Windows\PLA\System\LAN Diagnostics.xml:
      :Ov1ieca3Feahez0jAwxjjk5uRh:$DATA    2524
      :{4c8cc155-6c1e-11d1-8e41-00c04fb9386d}:$DATA         0
  C:\Windows\PLA\System\System Diagnostics.xml:
      :Ov1ieca3Feahez0jAwxjjk5uRh:$DATA    5384
      :{4c8cc155-6c1e-11d1-8e41-00c04fb9386d}:$DATA         0
  C:\Windows\PLA\System\System Performance.xml:
      :Ov1ieca3Feahez0jAwxjjk5uRh:$DATA    500
      :{4c8cc155-6c1e-11d1-8e41-00c04fb9386d}:$DATA         0
  C:\Windows\PLA\System\Wireless Diagnostics.xml:
      :Ov1ieca3Feahez0jAwxjjk5uRh:$DATA    3240
      :{4c8cc155-6c1e-11d1-8e41-00c04fb9386d}:$DATA         0
  C:\Windows\ShellNew\Thumbs.db:
      :encryptable:$DATA 0
  C:\Windows\System32\Thumbs.db:
      :encryptable:$DATA 0
```

As you can see from this output, several files in subdirectories within the C:\Windows\ directory have a stream named $DATA.

Sync

In some cases, Windows might cache data before writing it to the disk. When a computer is shut down normally, all cached data is written to the disk. If you plan to shut a computer down forcibly (by initiating a Stop error or disconnecting the power), you can run the Sync command to flush all file system data to the disk. Sync is also useful to ensure that all data is written to removable disks.

You can download Sync from *http://www.microsoft.com/technet/sysinternals/FileAndDisk/Sync.mspx*. The simplest way to use Sync is to run it with no parameters, which flushes data for all disks:

sync

```
Sync 2.2: Disk Flusher for Windows 9x/Me/NT/2K/XP
Copyright (C) 1997-2004 Mark Russinovich
Sysinternals - www.sysinternals.com

Flushing: C
```

To flush data for the F drive removable disk and then eject it, run the following command:

sync -r -e F:

```
Sync 2.2: Disk Flusher for Windows 9x/Me/NT/2K/XP
Copyright (C) 1997-2004 Mark Russinovich
Sysinternals - www.sysinternals.com

Flushing: F
```

MoveFile and PendMoves

Files can't be moved when they're in use by the operating system or an application. If a file is constantly in use, you can schedule Windows to move the file during startup using the MoveFile tool, available for download from *http://www.microsoft.com/technet/sysinternals/FileAndDisk/pendmoves.mspx*.

Use MoveFile exactly like you would use the Move command. For example:

movefile file.txt test\file.txt

```
Movefile v1.0 - copies over an in-use file at boot time
Move successfully scheduled.
```

The file will not be moved immediately. However, the next time the computer is restarted, Windows will move the file. If you want to delete a file that is constantly in use (a common requirement for removing malicious software), provide "" as the destination. For example:

```
movefile file2.txt ""
```

```
Movefile v1.0 - copies over an in-use file at boot time
Move successfully scheduled.
```

The same download that includes MoveFile includes the PendMoves command, which displays moves and deletions that have been scheduled. You can simply run the command without parameters, as the following example demonstrates:

```
pendmoves
```

```
PendMove v1.1
Copyright (C) 2004 Mark Russinovich
Sysinternals - wwww.sysinternals.com

Source: C:\Users\User1\Documents\file.txt
Target: C:\Users\User1\Documents\dest\file.txt

Source: C:\Users\User1\Documents\file2.txt
Target: DELETE

Time of last update to pending moves key: 2/27/2008 10:08 AM
```

Summary

Windows Vista uses local storage, which is typically based on hard disks, to store critical operating system files. Users rely on the same storage for confidential files. Because the integrity of the operating system and the security of your organization depend on the disks and file systems stored within each Windows Vista computer, you must carefully consider your client-storage management requirements.

Fortunately, Windows Vista provides simple disk and volume management using either graphical or command-line tools. Windows Vista improves on Windows XP by allowing partitions to be dynamically resized and thereby allowing administrators to reconfigure partitions without reformatting a disk or using third-party tools.

Windows Vista provides several features for managing disks and file systems. To provide data recovery in the event of a failed hard disk, corrupted files, or accidentally deleted data,

Windows Vista provides both manual and scheduled backups. If backups are available online, users can use Previous Versions to recover a file without contacting the support center. Complete PC backup and restore enables you to replace a hard disk and get a computer up and running within minutes without needing to reinstall user applications.

To improve random access disk performance, ReadyBoost can use removable flash storage to cache disk contents. ReadyBoost will automatically prompt the user when compatible media is attached, unless an administrator has disabled the feature. ReadyBoost offers the biggest performance gains on computers with slow disk access.

As with earlier versions of Windows, Windows Vista supports EFS to encrypt user files. To encrypt the system volume, including the hibernation and paging file, Windows Vista also supports BitLocker Drive Encryption. BitLocker requires a decryption key before Windows can start. The key can be provided by a hardware TPM chip, a USB key, a combination of the two, or a combination of a TPM chip and a PIN.

Additional Resources

These resources contain additional information and tools related to this chapter.

Related Information

- Chapter 30, "Configuring Startup and Troubleshooting Startup Issues," includes more information about startup files and Startup Repair.

- Chapter 31, "Troubleshooting Hardware, Driver, and Disk Issues," includes more information about ChkDsk.

- "Windows and GPT FAQ" at *http://www.microsoft.com/whdc/device/storage/ GPT_FAQ.mspx* includes detailed information about GPT.

- "BitLocker Drive Encryption: Technical Overview" at *http://technet2.microsoft.com/ WindowsVista/en/library/ba1a3800-ce29-4f09-89ef-65bce923cdb51033.mspx* includes detailed information about BitLocker.

- "Security Risk Management Guide" at *http://www.microsoft.com/technet/security/ guidance/complianceandpolicies/secrisk/default.mspx* includes more information about cost/benefit analysis.

- "BitLocker Drive Encryption Team Blog" at *http://blogs.technet.com/bitlocker/* provides the latest BitLocker news direct from the Microsoft BitLocker team.

On the Companion CD

- DefragAllDrives.vbs

- DefragAnalysis.vbs

- DiskDriveInventory.vbs

- DisksAndVolumes.vbs

- ListFreeSpace.vbs

- ModifyPageFileSetting.vbs

- ReportPageFileSize.vbs

- SetVolumeLabel.vbs

- VolumeDirty.vbs

Chapter 16
Managing Devices and Services

Windows Vista includes numerous enhancements in the area of supporting devices, including a new driver store, driver staging, a new driver-ranking algorithm, and more. From the end user's perspective, the effect of these enhancements is seamless installation of Plug and Play devices as well as helpful diagnostics and error reporting when device problems arise. Windows Vista also now supports the use of Group Policy to block installation of removable storage devices. This improvement helps enterprises protect business-sensitive information by preventing users from connecting USB drives and other removable storage devices to their computers. Power management has also been enhanced in Windows Vista: Enterprises can reduce costs by using Group Policy to control power-down settings for monitors, automatic sleep behavior, and other aspects both of desktop and mobile computers. Finally, Windows Vista includes enhancements to the Windows services model to provide faster startup and a more secure service environment.

Managing Devices

Managing devices and device drivers is an important aspect of overall desktop management for enterprises. Windows Vista includes enhancements to improve how you install, configure, and manage devices. Understanding these changes is essential for administrators who deploy, maintain, and troubleshoot Windows Vista computers.

Changes to Device Management in Windows Vista

Table 16-1 summarizes many of the changes that have been implemented in Windows Vista for the installation, configuration, and management of devices. Many of these changes are significant for IT professionals who manage Windows Vista computers in enterprise environments. The sections that follow detail how many of these enhancements work.

Table 16-1 Changes to Device Support and Management in Windows Vista

Description	Significance
Driver Store	Provides a central and authoritative point from which device driver files are copied to their final location when devices are installed.
Windows Resource Protection (WRP)	Replaces Windows File Protection (WFP) and protects the integrity of system files and system registry settings, including device drivers and device settings. Drivers are added to the list of WRP-protected files on the system only if they have been specifically flagged for protection by WRP when being staged to the Driver Store.
Inbox drivers	Windows Vista ships with more than 19,500 inbox drivers (compared to only 10,000 in Windows XP) to provide enhanced support for both new and existing types of devices. More than 11,000 additional drivers were made available for download on Windows Update when Windows Vista was released (compared to only 2,000 when Windows XP was released).
New standards for driver development	The Windows Logo Program Requirements Version 3.0 details new guidelines for vendors developing drivers to ensure that devices can be installed silently under nonprivileged Standard user accounts without the need for reboots or local administrative privileges on the system.
Driver staging	Speeds up device installation and provides driver verification to prevent Plug and Play detection of devices from causing a hang or crash during device installation as a result of poorly written or corrupt drivers.
Driver packaging	Keeps all files needed for device installation in a single location during staging.
New tools for managing driver packages	Administrators can use PnPutil.exe, DrvLoad.exe, and other tools to add or remove driver packages from the driver store using either online or offline staging.
Mandatory driver signing	Requires all device drivers developed for 64-bit versions of Windows Vista to be digitally signed.
Internal and third-party driver signing	Provides enterprises with guidelines and tools for signing in-house and third-party (out-of-box) developed drivers.
INF changes	Changes to INF file syntax to verify Windows Vista compatibility and ensure that only verified drivers are added to the store.
New driver-ranking algorithm	A new algorithm for how Windows Vista determines which version of a driver is the most stable version for a particular device.
Recursive searching for driver paths	During driver installation, driver paths—including the specified directory and all its subdirectories—are now searched recursively to find suitable drivers with fewer end-user prompts. In addition, Windows Vista automatically searches multiple paths, including the local Driver Store, removable media, network shares, and even Windows Update to locate and install the most suitable driver for a newly detected device.
New diagnostic logging	When enabled, driver diagnostic logging now writes information to the event logs instead of a separate log file.
Windows Error Reporting	When a device driver or device install fails for any reason, the user is prompted to send information to Microsoft using Windows Error Reporting (WER). Microsoft and Independent Software Vendors (ISVs) can then analyze the information and provide updated drivers if needed.

Table 16-1   Changes to Device Support and Management in Windows Vista

Description	Significance
Windows Update / Microsoft Update	Microsoft and ISVs can provide updated drivers that can be silently and transparently downloaded and installed on users' computers when they become available.
Windows Display Driver Model	A new video device driver model called Windows Display Driver Model (WDDM) replaces the XP Device Driver Model (XDDM) and provides enhanced functionality, including full Advanced Configuration and Power Interface (ACPI) support for video output devices, support for Aero Glass, and improved video driver stability.
Windows System Assessment	Windows Vista has a new tool, Windows System Assessment (WinSAT), for benchmarking system performance and determining Aero Glass compatibility and the level of Aero Glass that can be used on the system. You can also use WinSAT to troubleshoot device driver issues during system startup.
New Group Policy settings for managing device installation and error reporting	Provides enhanced ways for using WER to control device installation and report driver failures. Blocking installation of devices by device manufacturer, device class, or specific device ID using Group Policy is also supported, and users can receive customized feedback when installation of a device is blocked.
New Group Policy settings for blocking installation and use of removable storage devices	Helps to protect enterprises against accidental or malicious information leakage using portable storage devices such as USB flash drives and portable media players. Policies can be configured to either block installation of removable media entirely or allow users only to read from such media but not write to them.
New Group Policy settings for Power Management	Provides enterprises with a way of configuring and enforcing power policy across computers in the enterprise.
Removal of support for Standard HALs	Standard (non-ACPI) Hardware Abstraction Layers (HALs) are no longer supported in Windows Vista.
Removal of support for IEEE 1394 (FireWire)	Support for IEEE 1394 network has been removed from Windows Vista.

Understanding Device Installation in Windows Vista

Deploying, managing, and troubleshooting devices and device drivers in Windows Vista requires knowledge of how device installation works, including the following concepts:

- The new Driver Store
- Driver packaging
- Driver staging vs. installation
- Driver ranking
- Driver signing
- Tools for managing the Driver Store

Note   64-bit versions of Windows Vista do not support 32-bit device drivers or 16-bit applications. For more information, see KB 946765, "A description of the differences between 32-bit versions of Windows Vista and 64-bit versions of Windows Vista," found at *http://support.microsoft.com/kb/946765*.

Driver Store and Driver Packaging

The Driver Store is a new, central location in Windows Vista where all driver files are stored before they are copied to their final destinations during device installation. The location of the Driver Store on a Windows Vista system is the following:

%SystemRoot%\System32\DriverStore

Driver files are stored in folders called driver packages, which are located within the File-Repository subfolder under the preceding path. For example, the driver package developed by Microsoft that contains core mouse support files is contained in the following folder:

%SystemRoot%\System32\DriverStore\FileRepository\msmouse.inf_3dfa3917

Within this folder are the driver (.sys) files, driver setup (.inf) files, Precompiled INF (.pnf) files, and an XML manifest (.man) file that contains the manifest of all the files within the driver package. Together, all of these different files add up to the driver package, which contains all the files needed to install the device. To protect these driver files, the NTFS permissions on the Driver Store and all its subfolders and files is Full Control for the LocalSystem account and Read & Execute for the Everyone built-in identity.

This central store and driver package architecture is different from Windows XP, where driver source files needed for installing devices are typically found in several locations, including:

- %SystemRoot%\Driver Cache\I386\drivers.cab
- %SystemRoot%\Driver Cache\I386\service_pack.cab (for example, sp2.cab)
- .inf files under %Windir%\inf
- .sys files under %SystemRoot%\System32\Drivers
- Support DLLs under %SystemRoot%\System32
- Third-party co-installers in various locations

The following benefits result from maintaining a single, central store as an authoritative point from which to install driver files when new Plug and Play devices are detected:

- Allows for potentially faster device installations, more reliable driver rollback, and a single standard for uninstalling drivers
- Allows you to protect drivers by using Windows Resource Protection (WRP), the successor to Windows File Protection (WFP) in earlier versions of Windows

■ Uses index files to minimize the performance impact on installing devices when the Driver Store grows in size as a result of the addition of new packages

Driver Staging vs. Installation

When the Plug and Play service detects a new device in Windows XP, the driver files are extracted from .cab files found under %SystemRoot%\Driver Cache\I386, from .cab files on vendor-supplied media, or directly from Windows Update. The files are then copied to different locations as required to install the drivers and enable the device. Installing a device on Windows XP works like this: you connect the device, the Plug and Play service detects it, and then Windows searches the driver search path for a suitable driver and installs the device. In Windows XP, therefore, the device has to be present on (or connected to) the system for device driver installation to occur.

In Windows Vista, however, device installation takes place in two distinct steps:

1. **Staging** The process of adding driver packages to the Driver Store

2. **Installation** The process of installing drivers from the Driver Store when the Plug and Play service detects a device

Driver staging is performed under the LocalSystem security context. Adding driver packages to the Driver Store requires administrative privileges on the system. During driver staging, driver files are verified, copied to the store, and indexed for quick retrieval—but they are not installed on the system. The staging process verifies the driver packages against the following criteria to ensure that the drivers will not destabilize the system when they are installed later:

■ The driver package must be complete and contain all files needed to install the device. This means that the INF file for the device must specify all the files needed during driver installation and all of those files must also be present.

■ When drivers are installed, they cannot display any interactive user-mode prompts or require any software-first installation facilities. This is because Windows Vista requires all device drivers to be installed under the noninteractive LocalSystem security context.

■ Plug and Play device driver components must be able to be installed in their entirety under the noninteractive LocalSystem security context. If the driver installation routine attempts to display any interactive user-interface elements, installation will hang, timing out after five minutes. The user will be prompted to specify the location of new drivers for the device. (You can use Group Policy to modify the default device installation time-out value—see the section titled "Managing Device Installation Behavior" later in this chapter for more information.)

■ The INF files and other driver files must not have been tampered with or modified. The integrity of the driver files is verified by the Plug and Play service.

■ The driver must not be listed on the known bad drivers list, which is maintained within a DLL on the system and cannot be modified.

If the driver package fails any of these criteria, staging of the package to the Driver Store will fail (except in the case of the third bullet item in the preceding list). This prevents Windows Vista from being destabilized and possibly crashing when the user attempts to install the device requiring the package. Staging failure, however, has no impact on the system—it simply means that the package is not added to the store.

The device does not need to be present on (or connected to) the system when its driver package is being staged. Driver packages can be staged from media (CD, DVD, and so on) or from network locations. Windows Vista comes with numerous inbox drivers that are staged during Setup so that they can be available for device installs when the user first logs on to the system.

Third-party driver packages can be staged in two ways:

- When the device is connected, by using vendor-supplied media and the Add New Hardware Wizard. (The Add New Hardware Wizard is for legacy devices not recognized by Plug and Play.)

- When the device is disconnected, by using staging tools such as PnPutil.exe or DrvLoad.exe. In addition, many device vendors are likely to provide .exe files that will stage drivers to the driver store.

You can also stage driver packages by using the Microsoft Deployment Toolkit 2008 (MDT 2008). Using MDT 2008, an administrator can stage new drivers by simple drag-and-drop operations. In addition, you can group drivers so that they can be targeted to specific makes and models of computers that require them. For more information on MDT 2008, see Part II, "Deployment."

Finally, you can stage driver packages by using Windows Automated Installation Kit (Windows AIK) to embed them in deployment images. See the documentation for the Windows AIK included on this book's companion CD for more information.

Note   There is no hard-coded limit on the size to which the Driver Store can grow as new driver packages are staged. The Driver Store uses index files that are updated during stages to minimize the performance impact on installation time as the Driver Store grows in size.

Driver Staging and Installation Process   The driver staging and installation process alternates between user mode and kernel mode as follows:

1. The driver package is copied to a temporary secure location within the user profile as Configuration Management Interface (CMI) objects. The Driver Store then validates trust for the driver package under the LocalSystem context.

2. If verification succeeds, the driver package is copied from the temporary location to the Driver Store under LocalSystem context. After the driver package has been added to the store, its INF file is parsed to determine the names and locations of the required driver files. This information is added to the index files for the store. The driver package in the temporary location is then deleted.

In addition, during the staging process, a system restore point is created to allow for quick rollback to an earlier state in case installing the driver destabilizes the system. (You can use Group Policy to disable the creation of automatic restore points when drivers are updated or installed. See the section titled "Managing Device Installation Behavior" later in this chapter for more information.)

3. If the driver package needs updating later (for example, if a new version of the driver is released on Windows Update), this is initiated under the User context but takes place under the System context. (This step is optional.)

4. When the Plug and Play service detects the presence of the device, the driver is installed from the Drive Store under LocalSystem context. Installation takes place silently and transparently from the user's perspective, because no additional prompts for files are needed.

    Note that a Found New Hardware message balloon may appear above the notification area as the device is being installed, and a second balloon notifies the user after the device is installed. However, you can use Group Policy to disable these notifications. See the section titled "Managing Device Installation Behavior" later in this chapter for more information.

5. If the vendor-supplied driver requires the installation of support software (for example, a control center for a display driver) in addition to the core device driver, a Finish Install page is displayed and runs under the User context (requires local Administrator privileges or elevation) to allow the user to install the required support software for the device. (This step is optional.)

For more information about driver staging, see the section titled "Managing Driver Packages" later in this chapter.

Detailed Installation Process   The following steps offer a detailed description of the device installation process:

1. Windows Vista detects that a new device is present.

2. The Plug and Play service queries the device for identifiers.

3. Windows Vista checks the three Driver Store index files—infpub.dat, infstore.dat, and drvindex.dat—found under %SystemRoot%\inf to determine if an inbox or previously staged driver package is available for the device. If the driver has previously been staged, Windows Vista can install the driver without requiring the user to provide administrative credentials. In other words, standard users can install devices that have drivers staged in the Driver Store.

4. If no driver package for the device is found within the Driver Store, Windows Vista recursively searches for a driver package for the device within the configured driver search locations. (The steps from here on take place in the Found New Hardware Wizard, and only after the user elevates.) If a suitable driver package is found, Windows

Vista confirms that the user has the permissions needed to install the device and verifies that the package has a trusted and valid digital signature. If the driver package satisfies these conditions, the package is then copied (staged) to the Driver Store. If no inbox driver is found for the device, Windows Vista can search Windows Update for a suitable driver, and if no driver is found, there Windows will prompt the user to supply the driver media if available.

5. The Plug and Play service copies the driver files from the Driver Store to their final locations on the system.

6. The Plug and Play service configures the registry so that Windows Vista can use the new driver.

7. The Plug and Play service starts the driver and the device becomes functional.

Managing Driver Packages

Managing driver package involves adding and removing packages from the Driver Store. Drivers can be staged in two ways:

- **Online staging** This involves adding driver packages to the Driver Store while Windows Vista is running on the system. You can perform online staging of driver packages by using tools such as PnPutil.exe or DrvLoad.exe, as discussed later in this section.

> **Note** For developers creating custom tools for driver staging, Microsoft provides DevCon, a sample application that demonstrates how to list, stage, install, and remove device drivers programmatically. DevCon and its source code are included with the Windows Driver Kit (WDK). For more information, see WDK Releases at *http://www.microsoft.com/whdc/devtools/wdk/betawdk.mspx.*

- **Offline staging** This involves adding driver packages to images for purposes of deploying Windows Vista with prestaged drivers needed by the targeted computer systems. You can perform offline staging of driver packages by using tools such as Package Manager and PEimg.exe, or by using drag-and-drop operations with BDD to add driver packages to the Out-Of-Box Drivers folder under a Distribution Share in Deployment Workbench.

> **Note** You can use the Out-Of-Box Drivers under a Distribution Share in BDD Deployment Workbench folder only to deploy core device drivers. If you also need to deploy a supporting application (Setup.exe file) for a third-party driver, you need to package it and deploy it as an application in BDD. For more information on using BDD to deploy Windows Vista, see Part II, "Deployment."

Using PnPutil.exe   PnPutil.exe is the tool of choice for online staging of driver packages to running Windows Vista systems. PnPutil.exe supersedes the DevCon.exe tool available for managing device drivers on earlier versions of Windows. You can run PnPutil.exe from a Command Prompt window or script it for batch operations.

The following examples use PnPutil.exe to perform various actions against the Driver Store. For the full syntax of this command, type **pnputil /?** at an elevated command prompt.

- **pnputil –a a:\usbcam.inf**   Adds the package specified by Usbcam.inf into the Driver Store. This command requires you to run PnPutil.exe with administrator credentials but does not require that the device be connected to the computer.

- **pnputil –a *path_to_INF_files**.inf**   Stages multiple drivers using a single command or script. You must first place all driver packages into the central directory referenced in the command.

- **pnputil –e**   Enumerates all packages that have been published (staged) in the Driver Store. If no third-party drivers are published, this will return the error "No published driver packages were found on the system."

- **pnputil.exe –d *INF_name***   Deletes the specified package from the Driver Store, provided that no currently installed device is using the driver. This command also purges the index of any reference to the driver package being removed. Note that this *INF_name* is the "published" name of a third-party package in the Driver Store, as returned by the pnputil –e command. This command requires you to run pnputil.exe with administrator credentials.

- **pnputil.exe –f –d *INF_name***   Forcibly deletes the specified driver package. (You can use this if necessary to remove a package associated with a device that is physically installed in the system, or when using –d alone returns an error accessing the package. However, this is not recommended as doing this causes problems for the device[s] that are left still referencing the driver package that was forcibly removed.) Note that this *INF_name* is the "published" name of a third-party package in the Driver Store, as returned by the pnputil –e command. This command requires you to run pnputil.exe with administrator credentials.

Sample output from enumerating staged drivers on a Windows Vista computer might look like this:

```
C:\Users\tallen>pnputil -e
Microsoft PnP Utility

Published name : oem1.inf
Driver package provider : Realtek Semiconductor Corp.
Class : Sound, video and game controllers
Driver version and date : 01/10/2006 5.10.00.6000
Signer name : microsoft windows hardware compatibility publisher
```

Note that when using pnputil –a to stage multiple drivers using a single command or script, the command or script can sometimes halt before finishing. This can occur if either of the following conditions are true:

- The driver package is incomplete or damaged.

- The driver paths in the INF span multiple media.

If this occurs, troubleshoot the issue by stepping through the command or script to identify the problem driver and replacing it with an updated driver designed for Windows Vista.

Other Staging Tools   Other tools that you can use for staging driver packages include:

- **DrvLoad.exe**   Use this to add drivers to a running instance of Windows Preinstallation Environment (Windows PE).

- **PEimg.exe and Package Manager**   See the Windows AIK documentation on this book's companion CD for more information on how to use these tools for offline staging.

- **BDD**   See Part II, "Deployment," for more information on using the BDD to deploy Windows Vista.

Driver Signing

Using the Windows Driver Kit (WDK), enterprise administrators can sign custom-developed drivers using Authenticode and then stage these drivers to Windows Vista systems or images. Windows Vista provides the ability to digitally sign drivers using an organization's own digital certificate, such as one generated by an enterprise certification authority (CA). An organization can use its digital certificate to sign unsigned drivers or to replace the driver vendor's signature with its own. The administrator can then use Group Policy settings to distribute the digital certificate to client computers and configure them to install only those drivers that the organization has signed. For information on how to do this, see "Step by Step Guide to Device Driver Signing and Staging" found at *http://technet2.microsoft.com/windowsserver2008/en/ library/4bbbeaa0-f7d6-4816-8a3a-43242d71d5361033.mspx?mfr=true*. For information on the WDK, see *http://www.microsoft.com/whdc/DevTools/WDK/*.

> **Note**   Although you can use unsigned drivers with 32-bit versions of Windows Vista, 64-bit versions of Windows Vista require all device drivers to be digitally signed by the developer. For more information, see KB 946765, "A description of the differences between 32-bit versions of Windows Vista and 64-bit versions of Windows Vista," found at *http://support.microsoft.com/kb/946765*.

Driver Ranking

Windows XP uses the following algorithm to arbitrate between several possible drivers when installing a device:

1.   Inbox drivers are given first preference.

2. Windows Hardware Quality Labs (WHQL)–signed drivers are given next preference, with the most recent driver preferred.

3. Unsigned drivers are given lowest preference, with the most recent driver preferred.

Windows Vista supports the following eight levels of digital signature, listed in order of decreasing preference:

1. Microsoft-signed WHQL Certified drivers

2. Microsoft-signed inbox drivers (NT Build Lab Certified)

3. Microsoft-signed WinSE Certified drivers

4. Drivers that have been signed using Authenticode (Enterprise CA)

5. Drivers that have been signed using Authenticode (Class 3 CA Certified)

6. Drivers that have been signed using Authenticode (MAKECERT.EXE Certified)

7. Microsoft-signed WHQL Certified drivers for a previous version of the Windows operating system

8. Unsigned drivers

Note   For the purposes of calculating rank, WHQL, DQS, INBOX, STANDARD, and PREMIUM are all equal for both Windows XP and Windows Vista.

In addition to if (and how) drivers are signed, Windows Vista uses the following criteria to determine which version of a driver should be installed for a particular device:

■ The value of the feature score specified in the driver INF file if one is provided

■ How closely the PNPID of the device matches the PNPID of the driver

■ How recent the driver is compared to other suitable drivers

■ The driver version

Note   Date and version are considered only if every other aspect of the driver rank is equal—such as both signed/unsigned, same hardware ID match, and so on.

For WDDM display drivers, the driver arbitration algorithm is more complex:

1. WHQL or inbox driver

2. WHQL Certified or Authenticode-signed driver for a downlevel Windows operating system

3. Unsigned driver

4. WDDM driver preferred over any other technology

5. Device ID

6. Driver date

7. Driver version

> **Note**   Driver arbitration for audio devices and printers follows a similar algorithm to that used for WDDM display drivers.

Although the default driver-ranking process favors Microsoft-signed drivers over Authenticode-signed drivers, you can modify this behavior by configuring the following Group Policy setting:

Computer Configuration\Policies\Administrative Templates\System\Device Installation\Treat All Digitally Signed Drivers Equally In The Driver Ranking And Selection Process

For more information, see the section titled "Managing Device Installation Behavior" later in this chapter.

Managing Devices Using Group Policy

Group Policy is the recommended method for managing device installation behavior across an enterprise network where Active Directory is deployed. Windows Vista includes four types of policy settings for controlling device installation behavior:

- **Device Installation policies**   Used to manage device installation behavior

- **Driver Installation policies**   Used to manage driver installation behavior relating to driver signing and driver search paths

- **Driver Installation policy for Standard users**   Used to specify which drivers Standard users (non-Administrators) are allowed to install

- **Device Installation Restrictions policies**   Used to block the installation and use of devices such as removable storage devices

Managing Device Installation Behavior

Policy settings for controlling device installation behavior are found under the following node in Group Policy Object Editor:

Computer Configuration\Policies\Administrative Templates\System\Device Installation

Policies controlling device installation behavior, described in Table 16-2, are per-computer policies only. All of these policies apply only to Windows Vista or later, so if a GPO with these policies configured is linked to an organizational unit where computer accounts for earlier versions of Windows are present, these policy settings will have no effect on the clients running earlier versions of Windows. Although the configured policy settings will be available for use on the computer without a reboot, they will take effect for only device installations initiated after the policy settings have been applied. In other words, the policy settings are not retroactive, and they will not affect the state of any devices that were installed previously.

Table 16-2   Policies for Managing Device Installation Behavior in Windows Vista

Policy Name	Description
Treat All Digitally Signed Drivers Equally In The Driver Ranking And Selection Process	When selecting which driver to install, do not distinguish between drivers signed by a Microsoft Windows Publisher certificate and drivers signed by others.
	If you enable this setting, all valid Authenticode signatures are treated equally for the purpose of selecting a device driver to install. Selection is based on other criteria (such as matching hardware/compatible IDs) rather than whether the driver was signed by a Microsoft Windows Publisher certificate or by another Authenticode certificate. A signed driver is still preferred over an unsigned driver. However, drivers signed by Microsoft Windows Publisher certificates are not preferred over drivers signed by other Authenticode certificates.
	If you disable or do not configure this setting, drivers signed by a Microsoft Windows Publisher certificate are selected for installation over drivers signed by other Authenticode certificates.
Turn Off "Found New Hardware" Balloons During Device Installation	Do not display "Found New Hardware" balloons during device installation.
	If you enable this setting, "Found New Hardware" balloons will not appear while a device is being installed.
	If you disable or do not configure this setting, "Found New Hardware" balloons will appear while a device is being installed, unless the driver for the device has suppressed the balloons.
Configure Device Installation Timeout	Specifies the number of seconds the system will wait for a device installation task to complete. If the task is not completed within the specified number of seconds, the system will terminate the installation.
	If you enable this setting, the system will wait for the number of seconds specified before forcibly terminating the installation.
	If you disable or do not configure this setting, the system will wait 300 seconds (5 minutes) for any device installation task to complete before terminating installation.
Do Not Create System Restore Point When New Device Driver Installed	Specifies whether or not a system restore point is created when a new device driver is installed on your computer.
	If you enable this setting, system restore points will not be created when a new device driver is installed or updated.
	If you disable or do not configure this setting, a system restore point will be created whenever a new driver is installed or an existing device driver is updated.

Table 16-2 Policies for Managing Device Installation Behavior in Windows Vista

Policy Name	Description
Allow Remote Access To The PnP Interface	Specifies whether remote access to the Plug and Play interface is allowed.
	If you enable this setting, remote connections to the Plug and Play interface will be allowed.
	If you disable or do not configure this setting, the Plug and Play interface will not be available remotely.
	Note that this policy should be enabled only if the administrator of the system requires the ability to retrieve information about devices on this system from another remote computer, such as using Device Manager to connect to this system from a remote computer.
Do Not Send A Windows Error Report When A Generic Driver Is Installed On A Device	Specifies whether or not to send a Windows Error Report when a generic driver is installed on a device.
	If you enable this setting, a Windows Error Report will not be sent when a generic driver is installed.
	If you disable or do not configure this setting, a Windows Error Report will be sent when a generic driver is installed.

Best practices for configuring these policy settings include:

- Disable the Do Not Create System Restore Point When New Device Driver Installed policy setting or leave it Not Configured. System restore points are automatically created as a protection in case installing a new driver or updating an existing driver destabilizes the system and causes it to crash or hang.

- If you enable the Configure Device Installation Timeout policy setting, you cannot specify a time shorter than the default value of 300 seconds. Some devices, such as RAID controllers and other boot-critical devices, can take a long time to initialize, and the default value for this setting was chosen to accommodate Plug and Play installation of such devices to prevent boot failure. The reason an installation timeout value is specified at all is that improperly written driver installation prackages can hang during installation, causing the system itself to hang. This was a problem in earlier versions of Windows because an improperly written driver could cause an interactive prompt to be displayed in the background where it couldn't be accessed. In Windows Vista, however, device installation has been moved out of Newdev.dll into the Plug and Play service (DrvInst.exe), and the PnP service launches a separate, new process instance for each device installation. These architectural changes to how device installation works in Windows Vista make it much harder for an improperly written driver to hang the Plug and Play service. If the installation process instance does hang, however, the timeout value set here kills the process and displays the Add New Hardware Wizard, allowing the user to specify a different driver to install. However, the reason for allowing administrators to be able to configure this policy setting is that if the administrator knows that the installation of some driver package(s) on some device(s) will take longer than the default timeout period (but not actually be critically hung from UI), they can allow the system to wait for a longer period of time for the installation to complete.

Managing Driver Installation Behavior

Policy settings for controlling driver installation behavior including driver signing and driver search are found under either or both Computer Configuration\Policies\Administrative Templates\System\Driver Installation and User Configuration\Policies\Administrative Templates\System\Driver Installation. Table 16-3 describes these policies; they apply to Windows Vista and also to certain earlier Windows clients as indicated. Configured policy settings will be applied during the next background refresh of Group Policy. In other words, these policies do not require a reboot or logon/logoff to take effect after you configure them.

Table 16-3   Policies for Managing Driver Installation Behavior in Windows Vista

Policy Name	Description
Configure Driver Search Locations	Configures the location that Windows Vista searches for drivers when it finds a new piece of hardware. By default, Windows Vista searches the following places for drivers: local installation, floppy drives, CD-ROM drives, and Windows Update. Using this setting, you may remove the floppy and CD-ROM drives from the search algorithm, which can speed up the process of searching for drivers and give you more control over which drivers are installed.
	If you enable this setting, you can remove the locations by selecting the associated check box next to the location name.
	If you disable or do not configure this setting, Windows Vista searches the installation location, floppy drives, and CD-ROM drives.
	Note: To prevent searching Windows Update for drivers, also see Turn Off Windows Update Device Driver Searching in Computer Configuration\Policies\Administrative Templates\System\Internet Communication Management\Internet Communication Settings.
	This policy is per-user, is named Turn Off Windows Update Device Driver Search Prompt, and is found under User Configuration\Policies\Administrative Templates\System\Driver Installation. This policy applies to systems running at least Microsoft Windows XP Professional or the Windows Server 2003 family.
Turn Off Windows Update Device Driver Search Prompt	Specifies whether or not the administrator will be prompted about going to Windows Update to search for device drivers using the Internet. This setting has an effect only if Turn Off Windows Update Device Driver Searching in Computer Configuration\Policies\Administrative Templates\System/Internet Communication Management\Internet Communication Settings is disabled or not configured.
	If you enable this setting, administrators will not be prompted to search Windows Update.
	If you disable or do not configure this setting, and Turn Off Windows Update Device Driver Searching is disabled or not configured, the administrator will be prompted for consent before going to Windows Update to search for device drivers.
	This policy is both per-computer and per-user and is found under both Computer Configuration\Policies\Administrative Templates\System\Driver Installation and User Configuration\Policies\Administrative Templates\System\Driver Installation. This policy applies to systems running at least Windows XP Professional with SP2.

Table 16-3   Policies for Managing Driver Installation Behavior in Windows Vista

Policy Name	Description
Code Signing For Device Drivers	Determines how the system responds when a user tries to install device driver files that are not digitally signed. This setting establishes the least secure response permitted on the systems of users in the group. Users can use System in Control Panel to select a more secure setting, but when this setting is enabled, the system does not implement any less secure setting.
	When you enable this setting, use the drop-down box to specify the desired response:
	"Ignore" directs the system to proceed with the installation even if it includes unsigned files.
	"Warn" notifies the user that files are not digitally signed and lets the user decide whether to stop or to proceed with the installation and whether or not to permit unsigned files to be installed. "Warn" is the default.
	"Block" directs the system to refuse to install unsigned files. As a result, the installation stops, and none of the files in the driver package are installed.
	To change driver file security without specifying a setting, use System in Control Panel. Right-click My Computer, click Properties, click the Hardware tab, and then click the Driver Signing button.
	This policy is per-user and is found under User Configuration\Policies\Administrative Templates\System\Driver Installation. This policy applies to systems running at least Windows 2000. However, this policy no longer applies to Windows Vista, and it exists in the policy template only for an administrator to configure it for systems running earlier versions of Windows.

If you want to completely prevent users from searching Windows Update for drivers when installing devices, enable the policy setting Computer Configuration\Policies\Administrative Templates\System\Internet Communication Management\Internet Communication Settings\Turn Off Windows Update Device Driver Searching. Enabling this policy has the same effect as following these steps on the local computer:

1. Open System in Control Panel.

2. Click Advanced System Settings and then click the Hardware tab.

3. Click the Windows Update Driver Settings button.

4. Select the option Never Check For Drivers When I Connect A Device.

Managing Driver Installation Behavior for Standard Users

You can use the following policy setting for controlling driver installation behavior for Standard users:

Computer Configuration\Policies\Administrative Templates\System\Driver Installation\Allow Non-Administrators To Install Drivers For These Device Setup Classes

This policy applies only to Windows Vista or later and can be used to specify a list of device setup class globally unique identifiers (GUIDs) describing device drivers that Standard users can install on the system. Enabling this setting allows these users to install new drivers for the specified device setup classes. (The drivers must be signed according to Windows Driver Signing Policy or be signed by publishers already in the TrustedPublisher store.) Disabling this policy setting or leaving it Not Configured means that only members of the local Administrators built-in group can install new device drivers on the system.

To configure this policy, follow these steps:

1. Open the GPO linked to the OU where your target users have their computer accounts using Group Policy Object Editor on a Windows Vista computer.

2. Navigate to the policy setting and double-click it to open it.

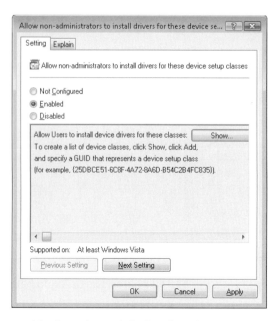

3. Enable the policy. Click the Show button and then click Add.

4. Type the GUID for the device setup class for the device type you want to allow Standard users to be able to install on computers targeted by the GPO. For example, to allow users to install imaging devices such as digital cameras and scanners, type **{6bdd1fc6-810f-11d0-bec7-08002be2092f}** in the Add Item text box. Continue by adding other GUIDs as needed.

See the next section for more information concerning this policy setting.

More Info   For a list of device setup classes and their GUIDs, see *http://msdn2.microsoft.com/en-US/library/ms791134.aspx*.

Blocking Installation of Removable Devices

Policy settings for blocking device installation are found under the following node in the Group Policy Object Editor:

Computer Configuration\Policies\Administrative Templates\System\Device Installation\Device Installation Restrictions

Policies for blocking device installation, described in Table 16-4, are per-computer policies only. All of these policies apply only to Windows Vista or later, so if a GPO with these policies configured is linked to an organizational unit where computer accounts for earlier versions of Windows are present, these policy settings will have no effect on the clients running earlier versions of Windows. Configured policy settings will be applied during the next background refresh of Group Policy. In other words, these policies do not require a reboot or logon/logoff to take effect after you configure them.

Table 16-4   Computer Policies for Blocking Device Installation in Windows Vista

Policy Name	Description
Allow Administrators To Override Device Installation Restriction Policies	Allows members of the Administrators group to install and update the drivers for any device, regardless of other policy settings.
	If you enable this setting, administrators can use Add Hardware Wizard or Update Driver Wizard to install and update the drivers for any device.
	If you disable or do not configure this setting, administrators are subject to all policies that restrict device installation.
	If this computer is a Terminal Server, enabling this policy also affects redirection of the specified devices from a Terminal Services Client to this computer.
Allow Installation Of Devices Using Drivers That Match These Device Setup Classes	Specifies a list of device setup class GUIDs describing devices that can be installed. This setting is intended for use only when the Prevent Installation Of Devices Not Described By Other Policy Settings setting is enabled and does not have precedence over any setting that would prevent a device from being installed.
	If you enable this setting, any device with a hardware ID or compatible ID that matches one of the IDs in this list can be installed or updated, if that installation has not been specifically prevented by any of the following policy settings: Prevent Installation Of Devices That Match These Device IDs, Prevent Installation Of Devices For These Device Classes, or Prevent Installation Of Removable Devices. If another policy setting prevents a device from being installed, the device cannot be installed even if it is also described by a value in this setting.
	If you disable or do not configure this setting and no other policy describes the device, the setting Prevent Installation Of Devices Not Described By Other Policy Settings determines whether or not the device can be installed.
	If this computer is a Terminal Server, enabling this policy also affects redirection of the specified devices from a Terminal Services Client to this computer.
Prevent Installation Of Devices Using Drivers That Match These Device Setup Classes	Specifies a list of Plug and Play device setup class GUIDs for devices that cannot be installed.
	If you enable this setting, new devices cannot be installed and existing devices cannot be updated if they use drivers that belong to any of the listed device setup classes.
	If you disable or do not configure this setting, new devices can be installed and existing devices can be updated as permitted by other policy settings for device installation.
	Note: This policy setting takes precedence over any other policy settings that allow a device to be installed. If this policy setting prevents a device from being installed, the device cannot be installed or updated, even if it matches another policy setting that would allow installation of that device.
	If this computer is a Terminal Server, enabling this policy also affects redirection of the specified devices from a Terminal Services Client to this computer.

Table 16-4   Computer Policies for Blocking Device Installation in Windows Vista

Policy Name	Description
Allow Installation Of Devices That Match Any Of These Device IDs	Specifies a list of Plug and Play hardware IDs and compatible IDs that describe devices that can be installed. This setting is intended for use only when the setting Prevent Installation Of Devices Not Described By Other Policy Settings is enabled and does not take precedence over any policy setting that would prevent a device from being installed.
	If you enable this setting, any device with a hardware ID or compatible ID that matches an ID in this list can be installed or updated, if that installation has not been specifically prevented by any of the following policy settings: Prevent Installation Of Devices That Match These Device IDs, Prevent Installation Of Devices For These Device Classes, or Prevent Installation Of Removable Devices. If another policy setting prevents a device from being installed, the device cannot be installed even if it is also described by a value in this policy setting.
	If you disable or do not configure this setting and no other policy describes the device, the setting Prevent Installation Of Devices Not Described By Other Policy Settings determines whether or not the device can be installed.
	If this computer is a Terminal Server, enabling this policy also affects redirection of the specified devices from a Terminal Services Client to this computer.
Prevent Installation Of Devices That Match Any Of These Device IDs	Specifies a list of Plug and Play hardware IDs and compatible IDs for devices that cannot be installed.
	If you enable this setting, a device cannot be installed or updated if its hardware ID or compatible ID matches one in this list.
	If you disable or do not configure this setting, new devices can be installed and existing devices can be updated, as permitted by other policy settings for device installation.
	Note: This policy setting takes precedence over any other policy settings that allow a device to be installed. If this policy setting prevents a device from being installed, the device cannot be installed or updated, even if it matches another policy setting that would allow installation of that device.
	If this computer is a Terminal Server, enabling this policy also affects redirection of the specified devices from a Terminal Services Client to this computer.
Prevent Installation Of Removable Devices	Prevents removable devices from being installed.
	If you enable this setting, removable devices may not be installed, and existing removable devices cannot have their drivers updated.
	If you disable or do not configure this setting, removable devices can be installed and existing removable devices can be updated as permitted by other policy settings for device installation.
	Note: This policy setting takes precedence over any other policy settings that allow a device to be installed. If this policy setting prevents a device from being installed, the device cannot be installed or updated, even if it matches another policy setting that would allow installation of that device.
	For this policy, a device is considered removable when the drivers for the device to which it is connected indicate that the device is removable. For example, a Universal Serial Bus (USB) device is reported to be removable by the drivers for the USB hub to which the device is connected.
	If this computer is a Terminal Server, enabling this policy also affects redirection of the specified devices from a Terminal Services Client to this computer.

Table 16-4   Computer Policies for Blocking Device Installation in Windows Vista

Policy Name	Description
Prevent Installation Of Devices Not Described By Other Policy Settings	This setting controls the installation policy for devices that are not specifically described by any other policy.
	If you enable this setting, any device that is not described by either Allow Installation Of Devices That Match These Device IDs or Allow Installation Of Devices For These Device Classes cannot be installed or have its driver updated.
	If you disable or do not configure this setting, any device that is not described by the Prevent Installation Of Devices That Match These Device IDs, Prevent Installation Of Devices For These Device Classes, or Deny Installation Of Removable Devices policies can be installed and have its driver updated.
	If this computer is a Terminal Server, enabling this policy also affects redirection of the specified devices from a Terminal Services Client to this computer.
Display A Custom Message When Installation Is Prevented By Policy (Balloon Title)	Specifies a custom message that is displayed to the user in the title of the notification balloon when policy prevents the installation of a device.
	If you enable this setting, this text is displayed as the title text of the message displayed by Windows Vista whenever device installation is prevented by policy.
	If you disable or do not configure this setting, Windows Vista displays a default title whenever device installation is prevented by policy.
Display A Custom Message When Installation Is Prevented By Policy (Balloon Text)	Specifies a custom message that is displayed to the user in the text of the notification balloon when policy prevents the installation of a device.
	If you enable this setting, this text is displayed as the main body text of the message displayed by Windows Vista whenever device installation is prevented by policy.
	If you disable or do not configure this setting, Windows Vista displays a default message whenever device installation is prevented by policy.

More Info   For information on how to identify device IDs for Plug and Play devices, see *http://msdn2.microsoft.com/en-us/library/ms791083.aspx*.

Windows Resource Protection and Device Drivers

Microsoft recommends that ISVs who develop third-party drivers for Windows Vista include the following setting in the [Version] section of their INF files:

PnPLockDown=1

Including this setting, called the lockdown flag, causes Windows Resource Protection (WRP) to prevent users with administrative privileges from deleting or modifying the driver files referenced in the INF file. However, this is a recommendation only, and ISVs are not required to include this setting in case compatibility issues should arise.

Troubleshooting Device Installation

The following sections outline specific troubleshooting steps with regard to device installation. For general guidance on troubleshooting hardware problems in Windows Vista, see Chapter 31, "Troubleshooting Hardware, Driver, and Disk Issues."

Using Event Logs

Windows event logs can be useful for troubleshooting device installation problems and driver issues. In addition to checking the System event log, you should check the Operational logs under Applications And Services Logs\Microsoft\Windows\DriverFrameworks-UserMode when experiencing problems installing devices and device drivers. For more information on using Event Viewer, see Chapter 22, "Maintaining Desktop Health."

Using WinSAT

Windows System Assessment Tool (WinSAT) is a tool included in Windows Vista that provides a benchmark of system performance based on ratings of the following components:

- Processor
- Physical memory (RAM)
- Hard disk (%SystemDrive% only)
- Graphics and gaming graphics

WinSAT runs before first user logon on a Windows Vista system, and the results are saved in both the registry and in an XML file saved in the %SystemRoot%\Performance\WinSAT\ Datastore directory. You can also run WinSAT on demand by opening System in Control Panel, clicking Windows Experience Index, and then clicking Update My Score. WinSAT stores a history of up to 100 system assessments and discards the oldest assessment when the limit is reached. WinSAT never deletes the initial assessment produced during the Machine Out Of Box Experience (MOOBE).

WinSAT can also be useful to determine which drivers are slowing down the boot process or blocking a system from sleep mode. Problem drivers will be flagged under Performance Issues with messages such as "Drivers are causing Windows to start slowly" or "Drivers are interfering with Windows entering sleep mode." The solution to these situations is usually to update the problem drivers. However, these messages might also be reported as a result of configuration issues with devices.

More Info   WinSAT use can also be scripted. See "Scripting in Windows Vista: The System Assessment Tool" at *http://www.microsoft.com/technet/scriptcenter/topics/vista/winsat.mspx* for more information. The script MeasureWinSat.vbs in the Chapter 22 folder on the companion CD shows an example of using VBScript to obtain a system's last reported WinSAT ratings.

Using Windows Error Reporting

When a device driver or device install fails for any reason, the user is prompted to send information to Microsoft using Windows Error Reporting (WER), where Microsoft, Independent Software Vendors (ISVs), and Independent Hardware Vendors (IHVs) can analyze the information and provide updated drivers if needed. When a user makes a report, an entry is created on the WER site, logging the problem. Data is collected for the following types of device installation failures:

- **Device errors**   Errors with distinct Device Manager codes.
- **Import errors**   Problems staging device drivers.
- **Install errors**   Errors when a driver has been successfully staged but fails to install when the device is connected to the system.
- **Driver not found**   Matching driver package cannot be located.
- **Driver protection errors**   WRP processing errors: driver is flagged as protected but fails to meet criteria.
- **Generic driver found**   Reported when a specific driver for a device is not available and Windows Vista installs a generic driver.
- **Windows Update errors**   When a user encounters one of these errors and elects to report it, additional data is collected. The data gathered depends on the nature of the problem.

In each case, WER tracks the following information:

- Number of users (hits) who have seen the same problem in the last 30 days
- Number of hits per locale (English, German, French, and so on)
- Number of hits by operating system version
- Total number of hits
- Bugs filed on this problem

Developers use the information gathered to track high-profile driver requests and petition manufacturers to provide drivers through either Windows Update or the WER interface itself. Both internal Microsoft employees and manufacturers have access to WER data and the WinQual Site found at *https://winqual.microsoft.com*. If a driver becomes available, it can be added to the response portion of the WER interface. After users elect to report the data, they are prompted to fill out a survey. (Note that if the IHV or ISV creates a response for given error, the user can see the response without filling out a survey.) This response may be edited to provide a link to the driver on the third-party website, which should decrease the number of support calls requesting drivers for devices.

> **Note**   By default, Windows Vista sends a Windows Error Report when a generic driver is installed on a device. You can use Group Policy to modify this behavior. See the section titled "Managing Device Installation Behavior" earlier in this chapter for more information.

Using the SetupAPI Log File

In Windows XP, the SetupAPI.log found under %Windir% is a plain text log file that you can use to troubleshoot issues with installing devices. In Windows Vista, this log is now moved to %Windir%\inf and consists of two separate log files: SetupAPI.app.log and SetupAPI.dev.log. Each log file is made up of distinct sections, with each section representing one device install:

```
<Log Header>
>>>   Section header
      Device Driver install section 1
<<<   End Section
>>>   Section header
      Device Driver install section 2
<<<   End Section
>>>   Section header
      Device Driver install section 3
<<<   End Section
...
```

The INF file for the device driver controls device installation, and the SetupAPI logs record a series of entries corresponding to each instruction in the INF file, along with whether the action succeeded or failed. When parsing these logs to troubleshoot device installation issues, a good place to start is looking for problem descriptions such as "device did not install" or "wrong driver installed."

The following example illustrates a device installation problem reported in the SetupAPI logs:

```
>>>   [Device Install (Hardware initiated) - USB\VID_045E&PID_00BD\{0D51C6EB-7E08-D342-9E60-
177B6A619B96}]
>>>   Section start 2006/08/17 13:40:16.348
      ump: Creating Install Process: DrvInst.exe 13:40:16.348
      ndv: Retrieving device info...
      ndv: Setting device parameters...
      ndv: Building driver list...
      dvi: {Build Driver List} 13:40:16.645
      dvi:      Searching for hardware ID(s):
      dvi:          usb\vid_045e&pid_00bd&rev_0100
      dvi:          usb\vid_045e&pid_00bd
      dvi:      Searching for compatible ID(s):
      dvi:          usb\class_ff&subclass_ff&prot_ff
      dvi:          usb\class_ff&subclass_ff
      dvi:          usb\class_ff
      dvi:      Enumerating INFs from path list 'C:\Windows\INF'
      inf:      Searched 0 potential matches in published INF directory
```

```
        inf:      Searched 34 INFs in directory: 'C:\Windows\INF'
        dvi: {Build Driver List - exit(0x00000000)} 13:40:16.818
        ndv: Selecting best match...
        dvi: {DIF_SELECTBESTCOMPATDRV} 13:40:16.819
        dvi:      No class installer for 'Microsoft® Fingerprint Reader'
        dvi:      No CoInstallers found
        dvi:      Default installer: Enter 13:40:16.821
        dvi:          {Select Best Driver}
!!!     dvi:              Selecting driver failed(0xe0000228)
        dvi:          {Select Best Driver - exit(0xe0000228)}
!!!     dvi:      Default installer: failed!
!!!     dvi:      Error 0xe0000228: There are no compatible drivers for this device.
        dvi: {DIF_SELECTBESTCOMPATDRV - exit(0xe0000228)} 13:40:16.824
        ndv: {Core Device Install}
        ndv:      Device install status=0xe0000203
        ndv:      Performing device install final cleanup...
        ndv:      Queueing up error report since device installation failed...
        ndv: {Core Device Install - exit(0xe0000203)}
        ump: Server install process exited with code 0xe0000203 13:40:16.832
<<<  Section end 2006/08/17 13:40:16.837
<<<  [Exit status: FAILURE(0xe0000203)]
```

The problem reported is failure to install the Microsoft Fingerprint Reader, and the cause of the problem is reported in the error message "There are no compatible drivers for this device."

By default, Windows Vista logs device behavior in the SetupAPI logs at a more verbose level than in previous versions of Windows. You can use the following DWORD registry value to configure the verbosity level for these logs:

HKLM\Software\Microsoft\Windows\CurrentVersion\Setup\LogLevel

The default setting for this value is 0x2000ffff. For information on how to configure logging levels for the SetupAPI logs, see the white paper "Debugging Device Installation in Windows Vista" found at *http://www.microsoft.com/whdc/driver/install/diagnose.mspx.*

Using Driver INF Files

Windows Resource Protection (WRP) protects the integrity of system files and system registry settings, including device drivers and device settings. Drivers are added to the list of WRP-protected files on the system only if they have been specifically flagged for protection by WRP when being staged to the Driver Store.

When a driver package that has been specifically flagged for WRP protection, and that driver package is staged to the Driver Store, an event is logged to the event logs to indicate this. To verify that a third-party driver you plan to install will be protected using WRP, open the INF file for the driver and look for Pnplockdown=1 in the [Version] section.

Resolving Driver Installation Issues

If a device on your system has a driver that was not designed for Windows Vista, or it has a file-based installation program that won't run successfully, you may be able to work around the issue in one of three ways:

- By running the driver installation program in Windows XP Service Pack 2 compatibility mode

- By using administrative credentials to run the driver installation program

- By locating the INF file for your driver and manually installing the driver

For more information concerning these workarounds, see KB 927524, "You cannot install a device driver by using its installation program in Windows Vista," found at *http://support.microsoft.com/kb/927524*.

Using Device Manager Error Codes

Device Manager error codes are the codes that accompany icons displayed with exclamation points (*bangs*) in the Device Manager console (devmgmt.msc). To view these error codes, open the properties of the problem device in Device Manager and look under Device Status on the General tab. You can view the hardware ID of the problem device by selecting Hardware Ids from the Property list box on the Details tab. When you parse SetupAPI logs, this ID can be useful for gaining further understanding of why the device did not install or is not working properly.

Windows Vista reports the same Device Manager error codes as previous versions of Microsoft Windows. Microsoft Knowledge Base article 245386, found at *http://support.microsoft.com/kb/245386*, documents these codes, explaining the meaning of each and the kinds of scenarios that can cause them to be reported.

Note   During a device installation, if a user is prompted to install the device in the future and responds by choosing No, a driver must still be installed. Otherwise, the Plug and Play service will continue to redetect the driver and prompt for installation. In this scenario, the Null driver (which actually means that the device is configured to use no driver) is installed and Device Manager displays error code 28. If the user later wants to install the device, the user must select the Update Driver option in Device Manager, because the device previously was assigned an error code because it could not be installed with any driver.

Device Manager error codes are reported only during device installation; they are never reported during driver staging. This means that if a Device Manager error code is reported, the problem occurred during device installation and not driver staging. A good place to start troubleshooting is looking at how physical installation of the device occurred and whether or not it was done properly. Device Manager error codes are also reported in the SetupAPI.dev.log file. See the section titled "Using the SetupAPI Log File" earlier in this chapter for more information.

> **Note**   If a Windows XP computer that has the Null driver installed for a device is upgraded to Windows Vista, the Null driver is not upgraded. This allows the device to be redetected after the upgrade so that an updated driver can be installed.

Using Driver Verifier

Another device driver troubleshooting tool is Driver Verifier, which can monitor kernel-mode drivers and graphics drivers and detect illegal function calls or other actions that could corrupt the system. Driver Verifier can subject drivers to a variety of stresses to uncover improper driver behavior. The Driver Verifier Manager tool (verifier.exe) is located in the %WinDir%\system32 and can be run either graphically (press Windows Logo Key+R, type **verifier**, and press Enter) or from an elevated command prompt using various parameters (type **verifier /?** to learn more about these parameters).

For more information about using Driver Verifier, see *http://msdn2.microsoft.com/en-us/library/ms792872.aspx*.

Repairing Driver Store Corruption

If the Driver Store becomes corrupt, new drivers cannot be added to it and Windows Vista may not be able to copy driver files from it. The inability to add new drivers or install new devices could therefore indicate problems with the Driver Store. Possible causes of Driver Store corruption can include:

- Interrupted write operations from sudden power loss.
- Damaged clusters on %SystemDrive%. (Use chkdsk.exe to resolve.)
- Bad memory being accessed during memory-mapped I/O.
- Malware or possibly even misbehaving anti-malware software.

If you suspect that Driver Store corruption is the problem, contact Microsoft Product Support Services (PSS) for troubleshooting.

> **Note**   With Windows Vista SP1, the index files will automatically detect corruption and rebuild the Driver Store. Therefore, users are no longer likely to notice these kinds of problems.

Repairing Index File Corruption

If the files used to index the Driver Store are missing or corrupt, new drivers cannot be added to the Driver Store. The inability to add new drivers or install new devices could therefore indicate problems with these index files. Possible causes of index file corruption are similar to causes of Driver Store corruption.

If index files become corrupt, restore them from your most recent system backup. The three index files for the Driver Store are Infpub.dat, Infstore.dat, and Drvindex.dat, and they are found under %SystemRoot%\inf. You can also use System Restore to restore index files because these files are added to protection points, but this approach is generally not recommended because reverting to a previous restore point can affect other aspects of the system and its installed software. Restoring from backup is therefore preferred.

Direct from the Source: Troubleshooting Driver Signing Issues

If you see a Windows Security dialog box with a check box that says Windows Can't Verify The Publisher Of This Driver Software, you should verify the validity of the driver signature by checking the following:

1. See if the INF file contains the "CatalogFile=*FileName*" entry and if the *FileName* matches the CAT file in the same directory.

2. If the preceding step is successful, double-click the catalog file, view the signature, view the certificate, and check the Certification Path tab. Verify that the entire chain of certificates is trusted. If not, add them all to the trusted root certification authority (CA) store on the local computer. The last one should be added to the trusted publisher store.

If you see a Windows security dialog box with a check box that says Always Trust Software From *Some_name*, install the certificate in the trusted publisher store on the local computer. Alternatively, you can select the check box and click Install, and the system will add the certificate automatically to the trusted publisher store. Note that you must use mmc.exe to install the certificate, not the certmgr.exe UI, because certmgr.exe installs the certificate in the current user's store only.

If the package is signed but an unsigned dialog box still shows, determine if any older unsigned versions of the driver are in the driver store. To do this, open a command prompt and type **pnputil.exe −e**. To remove a driver from the driver store, type **pnptuil −d** *OEMfilename.inf*, where *OEMFilename.inf* is the OEM filename listed by pnputil −e for the driver package.

To check if the catalog file actually contains the driver files, use the signtool.exe utility from the WDK/Platform SDK and type **signtool verify /c** *catalogfilename filename*.

Finally, to determine why your new latest fresh signed driver is losing to inbox drivers, do the following:

- Select the option to treat all signing as equal.

- Compare the date of your driver with that of the inbox driver.

- Check the version also to see if the dates are equal.

Sampath Somasundaram

SDET, DMI Team, Windows

Troubleshooting Device Issues

The following sections describe some solutions and workarounds for common device problems in Windows Vista—actual device problems as well as apparent ones (in other words, those that seem to be issues but are actually "by design"). Before you try any of the troubleshooting steps outlined here, however, first ensure that the following are true:

- You have obtained from your system's manufacturer the latest BIOS revision update and have applied it to your system's firmware.

- You have obtained from the manufacturers of your system's devices the latest device drivers and have installed them on your system.

Also be sure to first review the general troubleshooting tools and procedures outlined in Chapter 31 before proceeding with any of the troubleshooting steps described here.

Note   You will find contact information for hardware and software vendors in the following three Microsoft Knowledge Base articles: KB 65416 (*http://support.microsoft.com/kb/65416/EN-US/*), KB 60781 (*http://support.microsoft.com/kb/60781/EN-US/*) and KB 60782 (*http://support.microsoft.com/kb/60782/EN-US/*).

Troubleshooting Input Device Issues

Problem: Computer hangs when you try to resume from sleep by pressing the keyboard or clicking the mouse.

Workaround: Your USB mouse may not work with Windows Vista; for more information and a workaround, see KB 930091, "A Windows Vista–based computer does not resume from sleep mode if you move or click a USB mouse as the computer is entering sleep mode," at *http://support.microsoft.com/kb/930091*.

Problem: You can disable most USB devices, but not your USB keyboard.

Explanation: This issue is by design; for more information, see KB 937650, "The disable button on the driver tab of the parent USB host controller is not available in device manager after you connect a USB keyboard to a Windows Vista–based computer," at *http://support .microsoft.com/kb/937650.*

Problem: After you upgrade to Windows Vista, you can't use your fingerprint reader or other biometric device to log on.

Explanation and Workaround: This can happen because Windows Vista doesn't support the Graphical Identification and Authentication (GINA) components that legacy biometric devices require. Contact your hardware vendor for updated drivers or obtain a newer fingerprint reader that is compatible with Windows Vista. For more information, see "You Cannot Use a Fingerprint Reader or Another Biometric Device to Log On After You Upgrade to Windows Vista," at *http://support.microsoft.com/kb/926673.*

Troubleshooting Display and Monitor Issues

Problem: You encounter display issues when using multiple monitors.

Workaround: Try clearing the multiple monitor configuration of your computer by editing the registry setting as described in KB 934552, "How to clear the multiple monitor configuration of a computer that is running Windows Vista," found at *http://support.microsoft.com/kb/ 934552.*

Problem: Your display turns off immediately when you put your computer into hybrid sleep, and the LED light stops blinking.

Explanation: This issue is by design; for more information see KB 935264, "The display is turned off and you do not receive notification when a Windows Vista–based computer goes into hybrid sleep," found at *http://support.microsoft.com/kb/935264.*

Problem: Your display changes brightness when it resumes from sleep.

Workaround: You can configure Power Options to prevent this from happening. For more information, see KB 929249, "The display brightness may change after the computer resumes from a low-power sleep state on a Windows Vista–based computer," found at *http://support.microsoft.com/kb/929249.*

Troubleshooting USB Device Issues

Problem: You can't get a notification that it is safe to remove your USB device.

Workaround: Shut down your computer and then remove the device. For more information, see KB 927826, "A connected USB storage device does not appear when you click the 'Safely Remove Hardware' icon in the notification area in Windows Vista," found at *http://support.microsoft.com/kb/927826.*

Problem: When you remove your USB keyboard or mouse from your sleeping computer, it wakes from sleep.

Workaround: Configure Power Options as described in KB 935267, "The computer wakes when you remove a device from a computer that is running Windows Vista," found at *http://support.microsoft.com/kb/935267*.

Problem: Configuring the setting Allow The Computer To Turn Off This Device To Save Power does not persist across reboot.

Workaround: See KB 930312, "The 'Allow the computer to turn off this device to save power' power management option for a USB Root Hub does not remain selected after you restart Windows Vista," found at *http://support.microsoft.com/kb/930312*.

Problem: USB devices stop working when you use an external USB 2.0 hub.

Workaround: Disconnect and reconnect the hub. For more information, see KB 945360, "A USB 2.0 device that is attached to a USB 2.0 Hub may stop working correctly in Windows Vista," found at *http://support.microsoft.com/kb/945360*.

Troubleshooting IEEE 1394a Device Issues

Problem: Windows Vista does not enumerate an IEEE 1394a device after you connect it.

Explanation and Workaround: Windows Vista only enumerates a device that sets its link status to request enumeration. For more information, see KB 927827, "Windows Vista does not enumerate an IEEE 1394a device that you connect to the computer," found at *http://support.microsoft.com/kb/927827*.

Troubleshooting Memory Issues

Problem: You have 4 gigabytes (GB) of RAM in your computer, but the System utility in Control Panel displays less than this.

Explanation: This is an address space issue on x86 hardware. For more information, see KB 929580, "Windows Vista or Windows Server 2003 may report less memory than you expect," found at *http://support.microsoft.com/kb/929580*. See also KB 929605, "The system memory that is reported in the system information dialog box in Windows Vista is less than you expect if 4 GB of RAM is installed," found at *http://support.microsoft.com/kb/929605*.

Troubleshooting Processor Issues

Problem: You've replaced the processor on your computer, but the old processor settings are still being displayed in Device Manager.

Explanation and Workaround: For more information, see KB 930861, "Device Manager does not show updated processor information on a Windows Vista–based computer," found at *http://support.microsoft.com/kb/930861*.

Troubleshooting Networking Issues

Problem: You're experiencing dropped connections or poor performance for your wireless networking connection when your computer is running on battery power.

Explanation and Possible Workaround: This could be a power management issue. For more information, see KB 928152, "You may experience connectivity issues or performance issues when you connect a mobile PC that is running Windows Vista to a wireless access point," found at *http://support.microsoft.com/kb/928152*.

Problem: Your computer has a network adapter that supports Wake On LAN (WoL), but this isn't working.

Possible Workarounds: Uninstall the sample PassThru driver that is included in the Windows Driver Kit (WDK) or contact your antivirus software vendor.

Troubleshooting Power Management Issues

Problem: Changes made to the active power plan are not reflected in the Power Options utility in Control Panel.

Explanation and Workaround: This issue is by design. For more information, see KB 935799, "When you configure power options for the active power plan in Windows Vista, the changes are not reflected in the Power Options item in Control Panel," found at *http://support.microsoft.com/kb/935799*.

Troubleshooting Sleep and Hibernation Issues

Problem: You can't shut down, hibernate, or put your computer into sleep mode; or you can't resume from sleep or hibernation; or when you resume, your system is unstable or devices don't work properly.

Workarounds: Update your BIOS to the latest version, verify your BIOS settings, and check if you have any third-party power management applications on your system. For more information, see KB 927393, "You may experience power management–related symptoms on a computer that is running Windows Vista," found at *http://support.microsoft.com/kb/927393*.

Problem: The hibernation option is not available on your computer.

Explanation and Workaround: Provided that your system's hardware supports hibernation, you can use the powercfg command-line utility to enable hibernation, as described in KB 929658, "The Hibernate option is not available in Windows Vista," found at *http://support .microsoft.com/kb/929658*.

Problem: You can't use hibernation after using Disk Cleanup.

Explanation and Workaround: Disk Cleanup might have disabled your hibernation file. For more information, see KB 928897, "The hybrid sleep feature and the hibernation feature in Windows Vista may become unavailable after you use the Disk Cleanup Tool," found at *http://support.microsoft.com/kb/928897*.

Problem: Modifying the Put The Computer To Sleep setting can affect the Turn Off The Display Setting.

Explanation: This issue is by design. For more information, see KB 934550, "The 'Turn off the display' setting may change unexpectedly when you configure the 'Put the computer to sleep' setting in Windows Vista," found at *http://support.microsoft.com/kb/934550*.

Problem: Your computer wakes up unexpectedly when connected to the network.

Workaround: Configure your computer to wake only in response to magic packets. For more information, see KB 941145, "Unwanted wake-up events may occur when you enable the Wake On LAN feature in Windows Vista," found at *http://support.microsoft.com/kb/941145*.

Problem: When you remove your sleeping laptop from its docking station, it unexpectedly resumes from sleep.

Explanation and Workaround: This can be caused by USB issues. For more information, see KB 923943, "A Windows Vista–based portable computer unexpectedly resumes from a sleep state when you disconnect the computer from a docking station," found at *http://support .microsoft.com/kb/923943*.

Problem: When you try to put your computer into sleep mode, it appears to sleep and then immediately awakes.

Explanation and Workaround: This can be a USB issue. For more information, see KB 927821, "A computer that is running Windows Vista appears to sleep and then immediately wake," found at *http://support.microsoft.com/kb/927821*.

Additional Troubleshooting Tips

The following Microsoft Knowledge Base articles may also be helpful when troubleshooting hardware and device problems on computers running Windows Vista:

- KB 942462, "Device drivers in Windows Vista," found at *http://support.microsoft.com/ kb/942462*.

- KB 925518, "Programs that try to send a message to Session 0 may stop responding in Windows Vista," found at *http://support.microsoft.com/kb/925518*.

- KB 827218, "How to determine whether your computer is running a 32-bit version or a 64-bit version of the Windows operating system," found at *http://support.microsoft.com/ kb/827218*.

- KB 927525, "After you install a device or update a driver for a device, Windows Vista may not start," found at *http://support.microsoft.com/kb/927525*.

Understanding Power Management

The goal of power management in Microsoft Windows is to maximize energy efficiency. This is accomplished by minimizing the amount of power used while automatically providing required performance on demand. Previous versions of Windows delivered improvements in the area of power management, such as hibernation, standby, and the ability to power off monitors and hard drives. Windows Vista builds on these advances with new power-management capabilities, including:

- Improved support for Advanced Configuration and Power Interface (ACPI) 2.0. In addition, Windows Vista also provides support for selected features of ACPI 3.0.

- Standard (non-ACPI) Hardware Abstraction Layers (HALs) are no longer supported in Windows Vista; only the ACPI Programmable Interrupt Controller (PIC) HAL and ACPI Advanced Programmable Interrupt Controller (APIC) HAL are supported now in Windows Vista.

- Simplified power plan model, including three default power plans:
  - **Balanced**   Automatically balances system performance with energy consumption—for example, by speeding up the processor when performing CPU-intensive activities, such as playing a 3D game, and slowing the processor down when performing activities that require little CPU, such as editing a document in Microsoft Office Word. Balanced is the default power plan in Windows Vista.
  - **Power Saver**   Saves power at the expense of maximum performance. On mobile systems, this helps to maximize battery life. On desktop and server platforms, it works to reduce energy consumption.
  - **High Performance**   Maximizes system performance at the expense of power savings.

- Mobile users can easily switch between power plans using the enhanced battery meter in the notification area or the battery tile in Windows Mobility Center. Desktop and server users can switch power plans in Power Options in Control Panel.

- OEMs can customize the default power plans or create their own and install them as the system default. In addition, users can easily create their own custom power plans and manage them.

- A new Sleep mode called Hybrid Sleep is available. It combines the benefits of Standby and Hibernation. When the system transitions to Hybrid Sleep, a hibernation file is generated, and the system transitions to Sleep (ACPI S3 state). Sleep and resume time are improved, because in most cases, the system is resuming from memory (ACPI S3). In the event of a power failure, system state is still preserved and the computer will resume from the hibernation file.

- Sleep reliability improvements. Windows Vista does not query applications or services before transitioning to any of the sleep states. This is a departure from how Windows XP behaves. Applications may no longer prevent the system from going to sleep when a user clicks the Sleep button or closes the lid on a mobile PC. This helps prevent the system from accidentally remaining powered on when in a laptop bag or other closed environment.

- Resume performance improvements. Waking from Sleep mode is much faster, and improved power transition diagnostics help ensure consistent and predictable power transitions.

- Support for managing power settings using Group Policy. This allows businesses to easily configure the policies for powering off monitors and computers after a period of inactivity, saving money in utility expenses.

- Extensible power settings. Third-party drivers and applications can add new power settings to the system, and custom power settings can be managed in the same manner as system power settings.

- Standard (non-Admin) users can now modify most power settings on their computers. Administrators can use standard security descriptors to control access to settings on an individual power setting basis.

Note   Sleep will not function if any driver or application interferes with Sleep mode. For Hybrid Sleep to function, the video driver must support WDDM, and the system must be capable of sleeping. In Windows Vista, applications can no longer veto requests for sleep. (An override for Windows XP behavior is available, but not enabled by default.)

Direct from the Source: ACPI Sleep States

The Advanced Configuration and Power Interface Specification (ACPI) defines system power states using the Sx abbreviation (where x is the state number). For example, the S3 state refers to Sleep in Windows, when the system is in a low-power mode and the memory contents are preserved. The following table describes the other ACPI Sx states.

ACPI State Name	Windows State Name	Description
S0	[On]	In the S0 state, the computer is on and running applications. The processor is executing instructions and the user can interact with the system.
S1	[Sleep]	The S1 state is also referred to as Sleep in Windows, but it is rarely used on modern computers. The S1 state leaves all system devices on, but the processor is halted, and the processor is not executing instructions.

ACPI State Name	Windows State Name	Description
S2	[Sleep]	S2 is a lower-power version of S1. Very few systems support the S2 state.
S3	Sleep	S3 is the common Windows Sleep state. In the S3 state, the processor and most system devices are turned off. Main memory (RAM) is powered to preserve the user's open applications and documents. Only devices needed to wake the system from sleep (such as LAN Adapters and USB mice/keyboards) remain powered on.
S4	Hibernate	S4 is the Windows Hibernate state. In Hibernate, memory contents are written to a file on the disk. This file is called the hibernation file. All devices are powered off, and the processor is powered off as well. No instructions are executed on the processor.
S5	Shutdown	In Shutdown, no memory contents are preserved, and all system devices are powered off.

Pat Stemen, Senior Program Manager

Windows Kernel Team

Configuring Power Management Settings

Administrators can now use Group Policy to configure power management settings on Windows Vista computers in enterprise environments. In addition, the Power Options CPL has been enhanced to expose more advanced settings, and the powercfg.exe command provides full support for managing all power-configuration options from the command line.

Using the Power Options CPL

The Power Options tool in Control Panel (Figure 16-1) provides a central location where users can configure how their computer balances power consumption against performance, create and manage power plans, configure the behavior of the power buttons on the computer, and configure other advanced settings.

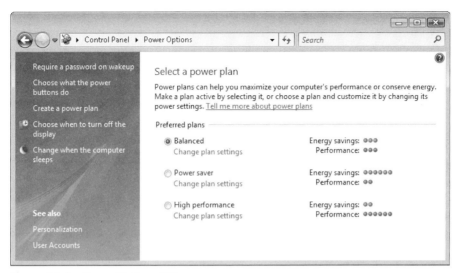

Figure 16-1   Power Options CPL.

Clicking either of the top two links on the left opens a screen where the user can configure the behavior of the power buttons on the computer and require that a password be specified when returning from Sleep (Figure 16-2).

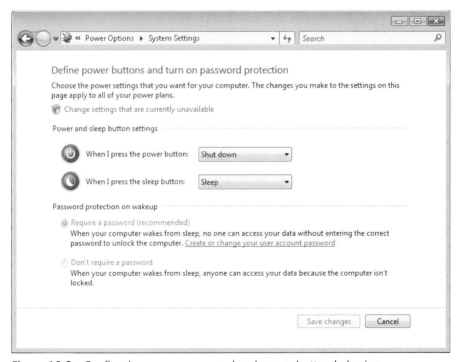

Figure 16-2   Configuring resume password and power button behavior.

In Windows Vista, Standard (non-Administrator) users can manage almost all power management settings on their computers. In earlier versions of Windows, users had to be local administrators to manage power settings on their computers. In addition, in Windows Vista there is a single set of power plans for the computer. All users have access to the same power settings across the computer. This is a departure from XP, where part of the power policy was specified on a per-user and other part on a per-computer basis. On Windows Vista, power plans and settings have been greatly simplified and are always on a per-computer basis. The helps to avoid situations in which power policy changes based on which user, if any, is currently logged on.

To manage advanced power options, click either of the lower two links on the upper left of the main Power Options screen and then click Change Advanced Power Settings to open the Advanced Settings tab for Power Options (Figure 16-3).

Figure 16-3   Configuring advanced power settings.

Advanced power settings provide more granular control over power consumption and the ability to change some settings not displayed elsewhere in Power Options. Additional settings include the power saving mode for wireless adapters, USB selective suspend, PCI Express Active-State Power Management, and Search and Indexing activity on the system.

Note that some systems will have additional power settings in Advanced power settings. For example, third-party drivers and applications may now add new power settings. Common third-party settings include power management options for video adapters.

> **Note**   When you click Change Settings That Are Currently Unavailable and respond to the UAC prompt, no new items will appear in the list, which can seem confusing. However, when you do this, some options that could not be edited before can now be edited.

How It Works: Power-Saving Modes for Wireless Network Adapters

On the Advanced Settings tab for Power Options, four different power-saving modes are displayed under Wireless Network Adapter (the On Battery settings are relevant only on mobile systems and computers with batteries):

- Maximum Performance
- Low Power Saving
- Medium Power Saving
- Maximum Power Saving

If Maximum Performance is chosen, the wireless adapter will not use any power management features but will communicate with the wireless access point at the maximum speed. However, if Maximum Power Saving is chosen, the wireless adapter will conserve energy by communicating with the wireless access point at a lower speed. This reduces wireless performance but conserves power and helps extend battery life on mobile PCs. The Low Power Saving and Medium Power Saving settings balance power savings and performance.

Note   You can configure additional advanced power settings by using the powercfg.exe command. See the section titled "Using the Powercfg Utility" later in the chapter for more information.

Using Group Policy

Power Management policy settings in Windows Vista are per-computer settings that apply only to computers running Windows Vista or later. Each Power Management policy setting may be configured independently for when the computer is plugged in or running on battery power. Table 16-5 lists many of the Power Management policy settings, which are found under Computer Management/Administrative Templates/System/Power Management and under the following subnodes beneath this node:

- **Button Settings**   Used to configure behavior of pressing power and sleep buttons, the Start menu power button, and lid switch on laptops.
- **Hard Disk Settings**   Used to specify the period of inactivity after which the hard drive will power down.
- **Notification Settings**   Used to specify low and critical battery levels and behaviors.
- **Sleep Settings**   Used to specify Sleep and Hibernation timeouts and behaviors.

■ **Video and Display Settings** Used to configure the display timeout. The display timeout controls the length of the period of inactivity before the display is automatically turned off.

> **Note** Table 16-5 includes Power Management policy settings that apply to both mobile and desktop/server computers. Except for the battery action and thresholds, each policy has a setting for when the computer is on battery power and when the computer is on AC/utility power.

Table 16-5 Selected Power Management Policy Settings for Windows Vista

Policy Name	Description
Critical Battery Notification Action	Specifies the action that Windows takes when battery capacity reaches the critical battery notification level. Possible actions include: ■ Take No Action ■ Sleep ■ Hibernate ■ Shut Down If you enable this policy setting, you must select the desired action. If you disable this policy setting or do not configure it, users can see and change this setting.
Low Battery Notification Action	Specifies the action that Windows takes when battery capacity reaches the low-battery notification level. Possible actions include: ■ Take No Action ■ Sleep ■ Hibernate ■ Shut Down If you enable this policy setting, you must select the desired action. If you disable this policy setting or do not configure it, users can see and change this setting.
Critical Battery Notification Level	Specifies the percentage of battery capacity remaining that triggers the critical-battery notification action. If you enable this policy, you must enter a numeric value (percentage) to set the battery level that triggers the critical notification. To set the action that is triggered, see the Critical Battery Notification Action policy setting. If you disable this policy setting or do not configure it, users can see and change this setting.
Low Battery Notification Level	Specifies the percentage of battery capacity remaining that triggers the low-battery notification action. If you enable this policy, you must enter a numeric value (percentage) that triggers the low-battery notification. To set the action that is triggered, see the Low Battery Notification Action policy setting. If you disable this policy setting or do not configure it, users can see and change this setting.

Table 16-5   Selected Power Management Policy Settings for Windows Vista

Policy Name	Description
Turn Off Low Battery User Notification	Disables a user notification when the battery capacity remaining equals the low-battery notification level. If you enable this policy, Windows will not show a notification when the battery capacity remaining equals the low-battery notification level. To configure the low-battery notification level, see the Low Battery Notification Level policy setting. The notification will be shown only if you configure the Low Battery Notification Action policy setting to No Action. If you do not configure this policy setting, users can see and change this setting.
Select The Power Button Action (On Battery)	Specifies the action that Windows Vista takes when a user presses the power button. Possible actions include: ■ Take No Action ■ Sleep ■ Hibernate ■ Shut Down If you enable this policy setting, you must select the desired action. If you disable this policy setting or do not configure it, users can see and change this setting.
Select The Sleep Button Action (On Battery)	Specifies the action that Windows Vista takes when a user presses the sleep button. Possible actions include: ■ Take No Action ■ Sleep ■ Hibernate ■ Shut Down If you enable this policy setting, you must select the desired action. If you disable this policy setting or do not configure it, users can see and change this setting.
Select The Lid Switch Action (On Battery)	Specifies the action that Windows Vista takes when a user closes the lid on a mobile PC. Possible actions include: ■ Take No Action ■ Sleep ■ Hibernate ■ Shut Down If you enable this policy setting, you must select the desired action. If you disable this policy setting or do not configure it, users can see and change this setting.

Table 16-5   Selected Power Management Policy Settings for Windows Vista

Policy Name	Description
Select The Start Menu Power Button Action (On Battery)	Specifies the action that Windows takes when a user presses the user interface sleep button. Possible actions include: ■ Take No Action ■ Sleep ■ Hibernate ■ Shut Down If you enable this policy setting, you must select the desired action. If you disable this policy setting or do not configure it, users can see and change this setting.
Turn Off The Hard Disk (On Battery)	Specifies the period of inactivity before Windows Vista turns off the hard disk. If you enable this policy, you must provide a value, in seconds, indicating how much idle time should elapse before Windows turns off the hard disk. If you disable this policy or do not configure it, users can see and change this setting. Note that this is a general setting that is not specific to mobile computers.
Specify A Custom Active Power Plan	Specifies a custom active power plan when you enter a power plan's GUID. Retrieve the custom power plan GUID by using powercfg, the power configuration command-line tool. Enter the GUID using the following format: XXXXXXXX-XXXX-XXXX-XXXX-XXXXXXXXXXXX. (For example, enter **103eea6e-9fcd-4544-a713-c282d8e50083**.) To specify a plan for the list of default Windows power plans, use the Active Power Plan policy setting. If you disable this policy or do not configure it, users can see and change this setting. Note that this is a general setting that is not specific to mobile computers. Also, a plan corresponding to the GUID-specified power plan must exist on the target computer.
Select An Active Power Plan	Specifies the active power plan from a list of default Windows Vista power plans. To specify a custom power plan, use the Custom Active Power Plan setting. To enable this setting, select Enabled and choose a power plan from the Active Power Plan list. If you disable this policy or do not configure it, users can see and change this setting.

Table 16-5 Selected Power Management Policy Settings for Windows Vista

Policy Name	Description
Specify The System Hibernate Time-out (On Battery)	Specifies the period of inactivity before Windows transitions the system to Hibernate.
	If you enable this policy setting, you must provide a value, in seconds, indicating how much idle time should elapse before Windows Vista transitions to Hibernate.
	If you disable this policy setting or do not configure it, users can see and change this setting.
Require A Password When A Computer Wakes (On Battery)	Specifies whether or not the user is prompted for a password when the system resumes from Sleep.
	If you enable this policy or if this policy is not configured, the user is prompted for a password when the system resumes from Sleep.
	If you disable this policy, the user is not prompted for a password when the system resumes from sleep.
Specify The System Sleep Timeout (On Battery)	Specifies the period of inactivity before Windows Vista transitions the system to Sleep.
	If you enable this policy setting, you must provide a value, in seconds, indicating how much idle time should elapse before Windows Vista transitions to Sleep.
	If you disable this policy setting or do not configure it, users can see and change this setting.
Turn Off Hybrid Sleep (On Battery)	Disables Hybrid Sleep, which refers to Sleep's usage of hibernation to store the contents of the computer's memory.
	If you enable this policy setting, a hibernation file (hiberfile.sys) is not generated when the system transitions to Sleep (Stand By).
	If you do not configure this policy setting, users can see and change this setting.
Turn Off Adaptive Display Timeout (On Battery)	Manages how Windows Vista controls the setting that specifies how long a computer must be inactive before Windows Vista turns off the computer's display.
	If you enable this policy, Windows Vista automatically adjusts the setting based on what the user does with the keyboard or mouse to keep the display on.
	If you disable this policy, Windows Vista uses the same setting regardless of the user's keyboard or mouse behavior.
	If you don't configure this setting, users can see and change this setting.
Turn Off the Display (On Battery)	Specifies the period of inactivity before Windows Vista turns off the display.
	If you enable this policy, you must provide a value, in seconds, indicating how much idle time should elapse before Windows Vista turns off the display.
	If you disable this policy or do not configure it, users can see and change this setting.

> ## Direct from the Source: Problems with Automatic Sleep
>
> Although a manually requested sleep (initiated, for example, by closing your laptop's lid or pushing the power button) cannot be prevented by software in Windows Vista, you can still prevent automatic sleep (idling-to-sleep) in several ways:
>
> - **API calls**   Applications, services, or drivers may call an API (*SetThreadExecutionState, PoRegisterSystemState*) to prevent automatic sleep because they are performing an important task that should not be interrupted. Common examples include burning a DVD, copying a large network file, and performing a system scan.
>
> - **Consistent processor (CPU) utilization greater than 20%**   The power manager checks processor utilization in an attempt to prevent automatic sleep when an application may be busy. Windows Vista has a power setting that adjusts the amount of processor activity that prevents automatic sleep. Administrators may change the setting value to 0% to disable the processor utilization check by using the batch file *PreventCpuActivityFromIdlingToSleep.bat* found on the companion CD (the GUIDs used in this batch file are documented in "Power Policy Configuration and Deployment in Windows Vista," found at *http://www.microsoft.com/ whdc/system/pnppwr/powermgmt/PMpolicy_Vista.mspx*).
>
> - **Network file sharing**   If, for example, a computer has shared files or printers that are currently opened by a remote computer, automatic sleep will be prevented on both computers.
>
> - **Media sharing**   Media sharing prevents automatic sleep because not all remote computers or media devices are capable of waking the computer from sleep over the network. This behavior may be configured in Advanced Settings in Power Options. The When Sharing Media setting under multimedia settings configures this behavior.
>
> *Nick Judge, Senior Development Lead*
>
> *Windows Kernel Development*

Using the Powercfg Utility

Powercfg is a command-line utility for configuring Windows power management policy. Powercfg.exe exposes all Power Management settings, including those that are not available in the user interface or from Group Policy. Power Management settings are now represented by GUIDs in Windows Vista, so using powercfg generally requires that you know the GUIDs for the settings you want to modify. However, powercfg.exe also supports aliases for most common GUIDs, and you can type **powercfg –aliases** to display a list of supported aliases. For example, this allows you to type **powercfg -setactive SCHEME_BALANCED** instead of having to specify the GUID for the Balanced power plan. The examples that follow illustrate the use of powercfg.exe on Windows Vista systems. You can run most of these commands while logged on as a Standard user, but a few, such as **–export** (for exporting power plans) and **-h** (for enabling or disabling hibernation support), must be run from an admin-level (elevated) command prompt.

To list the available power plans (called *power schemes* in powercfg.exe):

```
C:\>powercfg -L

Existing Power Schemes (* Active)
-----------------------------------
Power Scheme GUID: 381b4222-f694-41f0-9685-ff5bb260df2e  (Balanced)
Power Scheme GUID: 8c5e7fda-e8bf-4a96-9a85-a6e23a8c635c  (High performance) *
Power Scheme GUID: a1841308-3541-4fab-bc81-f71556f20b4a  (Power saver)
```

Listing power schemes lets you determine the GUID for each scheme. The asterisk beside the High performance scheme indicates that it is the active power plan. You can also quickly determine the active power scheme as follows:

```
C:\>powercfg -getactivescheme
Power Scheme GUID: 8c5e7fda-e8bf-4a96-9a85-a6e23a8c635c  (High performance)
```

To display detailed information (truncated in the following example) concerning the High performance power scheme in the preceding example:

```
C:\>powercfg -q 8c5e7fda-e8bf-4a96-9a85-a6e23a8c635c
Power Scheme GUID: 8c5e7fda-e8bf-4a96-9a85-a6e23a8c635c  (High performance)
  Subgroup GUID: fea3413e-7e05-4911-9a71-700331f1c294  (Settings belonging to no subgroup)
    Power Setting GUID: 0e796bdb-100d-47d6-a2d5-
f7d2daa51f51  (Require a password on wakeup)
      Possible Setting Index: 000
      Possible Setting Friendly Name: No
      Possible Setting Index: 001
      Possible Setting Friendly Name: Yes
    Current AC Power Setting Index: 0x00000001
    Current DC Power Setting Index: 0x00000001

  Subgroup GUID: 0012ee47-9041-4b5d-9b77-535fba8b1442  (Hard disk)
    Power Setting GUID: 6738e2c4-e8a5-4a42-b16a-e040e769756e  (Turn off hard disk after)
      Minimum Possible Setting: 0x00000000
      Maximum Possible Setting: 0xffffffff
      Possible Settings increment: 0x00000001
      Possible Settings units: Seconds
    Current AC Power Setting Index: 0x000004b0
    Current DC Power Setting Index: 0x000004b0

  Subgroup GUID: 19cbb8fa-5279-450e-9fac-8a3d5fedd0c1  (Wireless Adapter Settings)
    Power Setting GUID: 12bbebe6-58d6-4636-95bb-3217ef867c1a  (Power Saving Mode)
      Possible Setting Index: 000
      Possible Setting Friendly Name: Maximum Performance
      Possible Setting Index: 001
      Possible Setting Friendly Name: Low Power Saving
      Possible Setting Index: 002
```

```
      Possible Setting Friendly Name: Medium Power Saving
      Possible Setting Index: 003
      Possible Setting Friendly Name: Maximum Power Saving
   Current AC Power Setting Index: 0x00000000
   Current DC Power Setting Index: 0x00000000

 Subgroup GUID: 238c9fa8-0aad-41ed-83f4-97be242c8f20  (Sleep)
   Power Setting GUID: 29f6c1db-86da-48c5-9fdb-f2b67b1f44da  (Sleep after)
     Minimum Possible Setting: 0x00000000
     Maximum Possible Setting: 0xffffffff
     Possible Settings increment: 0x00000001
     Possible Settings units: Seconds
   Current AC Power Setting Index: 0x00000000
   Current DC Power Setting Index: 0x00000e10
...
```

To change the active power scheme to Balanced in the preceding example:

```
C:\>powercfg –setactive SCHEME_BALANCED
```

Verify the result:

```
C:\>powercfg -L

Existing Power Schemes (* Active)
-----------------------------------
Power Scheme GUID: 381b4222-f694-41f0-9685-ff5bb260df2e  (Balanced) *
Power Scheme GUID: 8c5e7fda-e8bf-4a96-9a85-a6e23a8c635c  (High performance)
Power Scheme GUID: a1841308-3541-4fab-bc81-f71556f20b4a  (Power saver)
```

To determine the available Sleep states supported by the system:

```
C:\>powercfg -a
The following sleep states are available on this system: Standby ( S1 S3 ) Hibernate Hybrid
Sleep
The following sleep states are not available on this system:
Standby (S2)
        The system firmware does not support this standby state.
```

For information concerning the differences between these different Sleep states, see *http://msdn2.microsoft.com/en-gb/library/ms798270.aspx.*

To display the source that has awakened the system from sleep:

```
C:\>powercfg -lastwake
Wake History Count - 1
Wake History [0]
  Wake Source Count - 1
  Wake Source [0]
    Type: Device
    Instance Path: ACPI\PNP0C0C\2&daba3ff&1
    Friendly Name:
    Description: ACPI Power Button
    Manufacturer: (Standard system devices)
```

To change the monitor timeout when running on AC power for the active power scheme to 30 minutes:

```
C:\>powercfg -setacvalueindex SCHEME_CURRENT SUB_VIDEO VIDEOIDLE 1800
C:\>powercfg -setactive SCHEME_CURRENT
```

To export a power scheme to a .pow file (proprietary binary format):

```
C:\>powercfg -export C:\newscheme.pow 8c5e7fda-e8bf-4a96-9a85-a6e23a8c635c
```

Use the *–import* switch to import a .pow file.

To disable hibernation on the computer:

```
C:\>powercfg -h off
```

To display detailed help for powercfg.exe:

```
C:\>powercfg /?
```

Understanding Services

Windows Vista services are long-running applications that run in the background and typically start up on boot and run independently of users logging on. Services handle low-level tasks that manage authentication, networking, and other tasks that need little or no user interaction to function. Third-party services such as firewalls and antivirus software can also run on Windows Vista.

Windows services are implemented using the Services API and are managed by the Service Control Manager (SCM). The SCM maintains a database of information concerning the services installed on the system and exposes these services to management using both user interface and command-line tools. Using these tools, administrators can:

- Configure a service to start automatically on system startup, to start the service manually on demand, or to disable the service.
- Start, stop, pause, and resume a service (depending on whether it is currently running).
- Specify a security context under which the service runs—typically one of the following: LocalSystem; a lower-privileged identity such as LocalService or NetworkService; or a custom user account created specifically for the service.
- Specify recovery actions to be taken when the service fails.
- View the dependencies of a service on other services.

Changes to Services in Windows Vista

Windows Vista has a number of changes to the implementation and management of services. These changes are designed to enhance the security, reliability, and performance of services as they run on the system. Table 16-6 summarizes the changes and enhancements to the services model in Windows Vista.

Table 16-6   Changes to the Windows Services Model in Windows Vista

Description	Significance
Running with least privileges	Enhances security by removing unnecessary privileges from the process token under which the service runs. For standalone services, SCM does this by checking the list of required privileges against the process token and removing any unnecessary privileges.
	A service can be configured with *required privileges*. This is typically a service designer action as opposed to an administrator action, since the list of required privileges is tied to the service design. When this is done, the SCM strips unnecessary privileges present in the service's account before starting up the service process. If the service process hosts multiple services, the SCM computes the union of the required privileges of all hosted services and strips unnecessary privileges. By default, no privilege stripping is performed, thus pre–Windows Vista services running on Windows Vista are not affected by this feature.
Service isolation	Uses restricted SIDs to enhance security by allowing services to run with fewer privileges while still maintaining access to objects such as registry keys that are configured to allow access only to administrators.
	In earlier versions of Windows, many services are configured to run under the powerful LocalSystem account because the resources they need access to are ACLed for LocalSystem access (because it is worrisome to allow access to any less-privileged process). Running under the LocalSystem account causes security vulnerabilities in the service code to have a huge impact, however. In Windows Vista (similar to earlier versions of Windows), services can be configured to run under less-privileged accounts. However, only in Windows Vista can the service designer configure the service to have a unique SID added to the process token (called the *service SID*) and ACL the resources used by the service (registry keys, for example) to allow full access by the service SID alone. This keeps the service account in lower privilege yet allows only the service process access to the resources as opposed to any process running the service account accessing the resources. This feature is called the *service SID feature*.
Service isolation	An enhancement to the service SID feature is also present in Windows Vista, and this is called the *restricted service SID feature*. If the service designer chooses this option, the service SID is added to the process token at service process startup as in the service SID case. (The SID is in a disabled state until the service starts up in the case of a shared process.) In addition, the process token is marked Write Restricted. What this means is that the service process code can write only to those resources explicitly ACLed for the service SID. For example, consider a registry key that allows full access to LocalService account. A restricted service process would not get write access to that key even if it were running under the LocalService account. The restricted service would get access only if the key were ACLed to allow write for the service SID. This feature is intended to mitigate the damage that a service can do to the system if it is exploited. Typically, these features are implemented by the service designer, not the administrator.

Table 16-6   Changes to the Windows Services Model in Windows Vista

Description	Significance
Restricted network access	Uses Windows Service Hardening (WSH) and per-service SIDs to enhance security by restricting access by a service to network resources such as ports and protocols.
Session 0 isolation	Enhances security by isolating services from user applications by running all services in Session 0 while user applications are required to run in Session 1 or higher. This means that a service that is marked as Interactive in earlier versions of Windows and can show a UI will no longer be able to show a UI in Windows Vista. Note that such services are already broken in previous versions of Windows with the introduction of Fast User Switching (FUS). Such services are expected to run a UI process in the user's session, which can throw the UI and communicate with the service using COM or RPC.
Delayed Auto-Start	Enhances performance immediately after startup by allowing startup of less-critical services to be delayed until after the system has booted. This enables Windows and applications to be usable sooner after startup.
Service state change notifications	Enhances performance by enabling the SCM to detect when a service has been created or deleted, or it has changed its status without having to poll the status of the service. The SCM can then notify the client of the change of status of the service. This feature works for local as well as remote clients.
Preshutdown notifications	Enhances reliability by allowing the SCM to notify services in advance of shutdown so that they have more time to clean up and shut down gracefully.
	In earlier versions of Windows and in Windows Vista as well, the computer shutdown has a fixed time limit by default for services to shut down. Although most services are unaffected by this, some services can have a dirty shutdown, which can cause long delays in starting up during the next boot (for example, a database recovery after a dirty shutdown might be quite time-consuming). In Windows Vista, such services can subscribe to preshutdown notifications. The system will send this notification after all users are logged off and before the computer shutdown is initiated. The services can take up as much time as they want before they stop. However, this can negatively impact shutdown time and has to be considered by the service designer. Again, this is a feature for the service designer to implement—it cannot be configured by the admin.
Shutdown ordering	Enhances reliability by allowing service owners to specify dependencies between services in a global dependency list to control the shutdown order for services.
	This is applicable only for services that subscribe to preshutdown notifications. In this case, such services can experience either an ordered or unordered shutdown. If they add themselves to the ordered list in the registry, the SCM will wait for the service to stop before proceeding to shut down the next service in the list. After ordered preshutdown is complete, unordered preshutdown begins. Note that the computer shutdown ordering of services is arbitrary, as before.

Table 16-6   Changes to the Windows Services Model in Windows Vista

Description	Significance
Detection of and recovery from nonfatal errors	Enhances reliability by allowing the SCM to detect nonfatal errors with services, such as memory leaks, and initiate specified recovery actions.
	In earlier versions of Windows, only allowed services can be configured with recovery actions (restart, run a script, and so on) when the process crashed. In Windows Vista, in addition, services can be configured to have recovery actions initiated if they stop with an error as opposed to crashing. Memory leaks and other issues therefore can be recovered from by using this feature.
Stop reason	An administrator that stops a service can now specify the reason for stopping the service. This allows postmortem reliability analysis to find out why a service is failing. If the administrator specifies the stop reason using the sc.exe stop option, the SCM logs an event with the stop reason to the event log. A new API called *ControlServiceEx* has also been added to accept the stop reason.
Localization	A service designer can now configure a service property such as display name or description as a localizable string and have the SCM load the specified resource from a resource DLL when a user queries the service property. The name is in the form *@resource_dll,-resource_ID*.

> **More Info**   For a more detailed description of the changes to the Windows Services Model in Windows Vista, see the white paper "Services in Windows Vista" available at *http://www.microsoft.com/whdc/system/vista/Vista_Services.mspx*.

Managing Services

Windows Vista provides four main tools for managing services:

- The Services snap-in (Services.msc)
- Task Manager
- Group Policy
- The sc.exe command

Using the Services Snap-in

The Services snap-in is mostly unchanged in Windows Vista from previous versions of Windows. One significant change is that the Startup value for a service can now be configured as Automatic (Delayed Start) on the General tab of the properties sheet for the service (Figure 16-4).

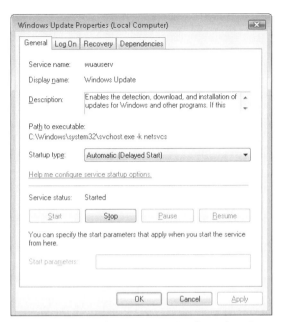

Figure 16-4   Configuring a service for Delayed Auto-Start.

> **Caution**   Before configuring a service for Delayed Auto-Start, be sure that you understand
> the possible ramifications. Delayed Auto-Start does not provide any time guarantee for when
> a delayed service will start after the boot process finishes, and if a client application attempts
> to use the service before it starts, the client application may fail. This means that client appli-
> cations should be designed to start up the service on demand if they need the service before
> the delayed autostart sequence starts it up. In addition, if a particular service is configured for
> Delayed Auto-Start and the SCM detects other services that depend on this service, SCM will
> ignore the Delayed Auto-Start setting on the service and will start it during the boot process.

The only other significant change in the Services snap-in is the option of enabling actions for
stops with errors. This option can be configured on the Recovery tab and configuring it
enables detection of and recovery from nonfatal errors. (See Table 16-6 for more information.)

Using Task Manager

A new Services tab has been added to Task Manager in Windows Vista (Figure 16-5). This tab
allows you to:

- View the name, process identifier (PID), description (which is actually the service's
  friendly name), status (running or stopped), and service group for all services running
  on the system.

- Stop or start a service by right-clicking it and then selecting the appropriate option.

- View the process within which a service is running by right-clicking the service and then
  selecting Go To Process.

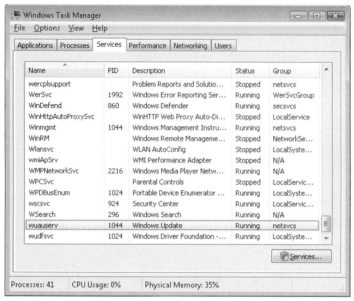

Figure 16-5 The new Services tab in Task Manager.

Note To view the process associated with a service, you should first click the Show Processes From All Users button on the Processes tab. This is a necessary step because many services run within an svchost.exe process to reduce the memory footprint that would result if each service ran separately. After processes for all users are displayed on the Processes tab, right-click a service that has a PID number on the Services tab and then select Go To Process. The focus will switch to the Processes tab and highlight the svchost.exe process used to host that particular service.

Using Group Policy

You can use Group Policy to configure the Startup state (Automatic, Manual, or Disabled) and ACLs for services in the same way that you do this on previous versions of Windows. A policy setting for each system service on the computer can be found under the following node:

Computer Configuration\Policies\Windows Settings\Security Settings\System Services

Using the sc.exe Command

You can use the sc.exe command to start, stop, configure, and manage various aspects of services in the same way that you can on earlier versions of Windows. On Windows Vista, however, the sc.exe command has been enhanced with new command-line switches.

New switches for specifying required privileges for a service include:

- **-privs** Sets the required privileges for a service.
- **-qprivs** Queries for the required privileges of a service.

New switches that support per-service SIDs include:

- **-sidtype**   Changes a service's SID.

- **-qsidtype**   Retrieves the setting for service's SID.

New switches to enable configuration of the FailureActionsOnNonCrashFailures setting include:

- **-failureflag**   Changes the setting of the *FailureActionsOnNonCrashFailures* flag.

- **-qfailureflag**   Retrieves the setting for the *FailureActionsOnNonCrashFailures* flag.

- **-showsid**   Displays the service SID string corresponding to an arbitrary name.

- **-stop**   This is an old setting that has been enhanced in Windows Vista to specify the stop reason. This enables postmortem reliability analysis to find out reasons (by examining the event logged by the SCM with the stop reason) an administrator would stop a service.

For more information about these new command-line switches for sc.exe, type **sc /?** at a command prompt. You can find additional information concerning these switches in the white paper "Services in Windows Vista" available from *http://www.microsoft.com/whdc/ system/vista/Vista_Services.mspx*.

Direct from the Source: Troubleshooting Service Issues

Here are a few troubleshooting tips for IT administrators and service developers:

- **Performance issues**   Sluggish service performance is one of the primary culprits for lengthier logon times and being unable to elevate programs after logon. If you experience these symptoms, check the System log using Event Viewer for warning or error messages from the Service Control Manager. In addition, you can use the sc.exe inbox tool to run commands such as sc.exe queryex that will allow you to see which services are blocked in START_PENDING state. You can also use the Services MMC snap-in to check the status of services. Such blocked services are likely causes of sluggish system performance.

- **Services tab in Task Manager**   In Windows Vista, the Task Manager has a new Services tab that can display various service-related information. This can be particularly useful for identifying services that chew up significant amounts of CPU or other resources. You could then choose to right-click the culprit services and stop them to solve the problem for the moment before contacting the service vendor for support.

- **General tip**   If some scenario is not working, it is useful to check the state of any services that might implement parts of the feature. For instance, if antivirus real-time monitoring is not working, perhaps the real-time monitoring service has failed to start up. Check the System log in Event Viewer for warning or error

> messages from the Service Control Manager related to the service. In addition, you can use the sc.exe inbox tool to run commands such as **sc.exe queryex** *service_short_name* and see details of the service status. The Services MMC snap-in can also help.
>
> *Chittur Subbaraman, Software Design Engineer*
>
> *Windows Kernel Development*

Summary

Windows Vista provides enhanced security, performance, and reliability for services using a new Windows Services Model and improved tools. Device support is also enhanced in Windows Vista, with device installation and power management now configurable using Group Policy. With these many enhancements, Windows Vista supports more devices, provides an improved user experience, and ensures the security and stability of applications and services running on the platform.

Additional Resources

The following resources contain additional information and tools related to this chapter.

Related Information

- "Windows Vista Hardware Compatibility List" found at *http://winqual.microsoft.com/HCL/Default.aspx*.

- "Microsoft Hardware Support for Windows Vista" found at *http://www.microsoft.com/hardware/windowsvista/support.mspx*.

- "Windows Logo Program V. 3.0" found at *http://www.microsoft.com/whdc/winlogo/WLP30.mspx*.

- "Driver Compatibility for Windows Vista" found at *http://download.microsoft.com/download/9/c/5/9c5b2167-8017-4bae-9fde-d599bac8184a/DrvCompat_Vista.doc*.

- "Step-by-Step Guide to Controlling Device Installation and Usage with Group Policy" found at *http://technet2.microsoft.com/windowsserver2008/en/library/9fe5bf05-a4a9-44e2-a0c3-b4b4eaaa37f31033.mspx?mfr=true*.

- "Step-by-Step Guide to Device Driver Signing and Staging" found at *http://technet2.microsoft.com/windowsserver2008/en/library/4bbbeaa0-f7d6-4816-8a3a-43242d71d5361033.mspx?mfr=true*.

- "Device Management and Installation Operations Guide" found at *http://technet2.microsoft.com/windowsserver2008/en/library/562ca3d1-7876-433f-82d3-15de1aaab6d81033.mspx?mfr=true*.

■ "Device Management and Installation Technical Reference" was not yet published at the time of writing, but a link to this will be found at *http://technet2.microsoft.com/ windowsserver2008/en/library/a8a66e55-c3b3-47b6-b7d2- 9805b13f73c81033.mspx?mfr=true.*

■ "Troubleshooting Device Management and Installation" found at *http://technet2.microsoft.com/windowsserver2008/en/library/927a0cf5-b0e6-4f77-848b- 5e19ffba25251033.mspx?mfr=true.*

■ "Device Installation Overview" (from the Windows Driver Kit) found at *http://msdn2.microsoft.com/en-us/library/ms791091.aspx.*

■ "Device and Driver Technologies" (from the Windows Driver Kit) found at *http://msdn2.microsoft.com/en-us/library/aa972913.aspx.*

■ "Device Identification Strings" (from the Windows Driver Kit) found at *http://msdn2.microsoft.com/en-us/library/ms791083.aspx.*

■ The white paper "Debugging Device Installation in Windows Vista" found at *http://www.microsoft.com/whdc/driver/install/diagnose.mspx.*

■ The white paper "Driver Package Compatibility for Windows Vista" found at *http://www.microsoft.com/whdc/driver/install/drvpkgerrors.mspx.*

■ "How Setup Ranks Drivers (Windows Vista)" found at *http://msdn2.microsoft.com/ en-us/library/aa477022.aspx.*

■ "Services in Windows Vista" found at *http://www.microsoft.com/whdc/system/vista/ Vista_Services.mspx.*

■ "Power Policy Configuration and Deployment in Windows Vista" found at *http://www.microsoft.com/whdc/system/pnppwr/powermgmt/PMpolicy_Vista.mspx.*

■ KB 930061, "Unified Extended Firmware Interface support in Windows Vista," found at *http://support.microsoft.com/kb/930061.*

■ KB 934801, "Description of the technical support policy for systems that have not been confirmed as meeting the requirements of Windows Vista or of Windows XP," found at *http://support.microsoft.com/kb/934801.*

■ KB 555927, "Description of the default behavior of a Windows Vista–based desktop computer when it wakes up from sleep," found at *http://support.microsoft.com/ default.aspx/kb/937556.*

■ KB 920730, "How to disable and re-enable hibernation on a computer that is running Windows Vista," found at *http://support.microsoft.com/kb/920730.*

■ KB 934539, "Error message when a system service on a Windows Vista–based computer connects to a system service on another Windows Vista–based computer: 'Cannot connect to machine'," found at *http://support.microsoft.com/kb/934539.*

On the Companion CD

- The batch file PreventCpuActivityFromIdlingToSleep.bat described in the sidebar titled "Direct from the Source: Problems with Automatic Sleep" in this chapter.

- ChangeServiceAccountLogon.vbs

- ChangeServiceAccountPassword.vbs

- ChangeServiceAccountStartUp.vbs

- ListComputerUsingParticularService.vbs

- ListDevicesAndDrivers.vbs

- ListPnpDevices.vbs

- ListServiceDependencies.vbs

- ListServicesUsingParticularAccount.vbs

- StartStopDisableAservice.vbs

Chapter 17

Managing Sharing

In this chapter:

Windows Vista includes both new ways for users to share information and enhancements to existing sharing technologies. File sharing has now been enhanced to include built-in support for Access-Based Enumeration (ABE), a technology that was first included in Service Pack 1 for Windows Server 2003. A redesigned file sharing user interface also makes it easier than ever for users to share files with each other. Administrators can now publish shared folders in Active Directory more easily by using Computer Management to connect to a file server from their Windows Vista workstations. And Windows Vista's Windows Media Player 11 includes support for sharing media libraries based on enhancements of Windows Media Connect technology previously introduced in Windows XP.

This chapter describes how file sharing has changed in Windows Vista compared to previous versions of Windows and how to manage this feature in different networking environments. Also included is a brief description of the new Media Sharing capabilities included in Windows Media Player 11 and how to manage them.

Managing File Sharing

File sharing has undergone significant changes in Windows Vista compared to the earlier Windows XP platform. This section describes these changes and explains how to share files in Windows Vista both for other users of a computer (*local sharing*) and for users on other computers on a network (*network sharing*) in both domain and workgroup environments. The section also looks at how file sharing in Windows Vista compares with earlier platforms such as Windows XP and explains how to manage file sharing using Group Policy and scripts.

More Info   For background information on some of the networking concepts and features discussed in this chapter, see Chapter 26, "Configuring Windows Networking."

Understanding Local Sharing

Local sharing, also known as *same computer sharing*, refers to sharing files so that all users on the same computer can access them. Local sharing is generally used on standalone computers that are used as shared computers for kiosk purposes. Local sharing has undergone several changes in Windows Vista compared to the earlier Windows XP platform. To understand these changes, let's first review how local sharing works in Windows XP.

Local Sharing in Windows XP

In Windows XP, files can be shared between users on the same computer by copying or moving them to the Shared Documents folder, which is found under the Files Stored On This Computer heading in My Computer. Shared Documents is actually a junction point that maps to the Documents folder in the All Users user profile found at %SystemDrive%\Documents and Settings\All Users\Documents. By default, all files and folders created under Shared Documents inherit the permissions shown in Table 17-1.

Table 17-1 Permissions on Shared Documents Folder in Windows XP

Identity	Permission	Applies To
SYSTEM	Full Control	This folder, subfolders, and files
Administrators	Full Control	This folder, subfolders, and files
CREATOR OWNER	Full Control	Subfolders and files only
Power Users	Modify	This folder, subfolders, and files
Users	Read & Execute	This folder, subfolders, and files
Users	Write	This folder and subfolders

The effective result of these permissions is that ordinary users can read and execute files saved by other users under Shared Documents or one of its subfolders (My Pictures, My Music, and My Videos), but they cannot modify or delete these files unless they are local Administrators or Power Users, or unless the user who created a file has explicitly granted the Users group additional permissions, such as Modify. It also means that users can create additional subfolders under Shared Documents, and other users can store their files in these subfolders but cannot modify them unless explicitly granted permission to do so.

Local Sharing in Windows Vista

In Windows Vista, users of the same computer can still share files, but the model has changed both in terms of how it works and in the collaborative experience itself. The underlying change in how it works has to do with the way user profile information is stored in Windows Vista. In the earlier Windows XP platform, user profile information for all users is stored in the %SystemDrive%\Documents and Settings\All Users folder. Two types of information are stored here:

- Application data for all users of the computer, which is typically stored in the hidden \All Users\Application Data subfolder

- User data for all users of the computer, which is stored in the \All Users\Documents folder

In Windows Vista, local user profiles are now stored in the %SystemDrive%\Users folder instead of %SystemDrive%\Documents and Settings, as in Windows XP. (A hidden junction point mapping %SystemDrive%\Documents and Settings to %SystemDrive%\Users is present in Windows Vista.) In addition, application and user data for the All Users user profile has now been separated in Windows Vista to provide better security. Specifically:

- Application data for all users of the computer is now stored in the %SystemDrive%\ProgramData hidden folder.

- User data for all users of the computer is now stored in the %SystemDrive%\Users\Public folder.

Understanding the Public Folder

The Public folder is new to Windows Vista and replaces the Shared Documents folder of Windows XP. Any files that a user copies or moves to the Public folder become available to all users on the computer—that is, by an interactive user on the computer. By default, all files and folders created within the Public folder on a standalone computer inherit the permissions shown in Table 17-2.

Table 17-2   Permissions on the Public Folder in Windows Vista

Identity	Permission	Applies To
Administrators	Full Control	This folder, subfolders, and files
CREATOR OWNER	Full Control	Subfolders and files only
SYSTEM	Full Control	This folder, subfolders, and files
INTERACTIVE	Read & Execute	This folder, subfolders, and files
INTERACTIVE	Special[1]	Subfolders only
INTERACTIVE	Special[2]	Files only
INTERACTIVE	Special[3]	This folder only
SERVICE	Read & Execute	This folder, subfolders, and files
SERVICE	Special[1]	Subfolders only
SERVICE	Special[2]	Files only
SERVICE	Special[3]	This folder only
BATCH	Read & Execute	This folder, subfolders, and files
BATCH	Special[1]	Subfolders only
BATCH	Special[2]	Files only
BATCH	Special[3]	This folder only

The special permissions listed in Table 17-2 are as follows:

1.   Create files/write data, create folders/append data, write attributes, write extended attributes, delete subfolders and files

2.   All special permissions except take ownership, change permissions, and full control

3.   Create folders/append data

Users can share files and folders with other users of their computers by storing the files and folders in one of the many subfolders under the Public folder, such as Public Documents, Public Downloads, Public Pictures, Public Music, and so on. Standard users can copy or move files or folders into the Public folder or any other subfolder of Public with the exception of the hidden Public Desktop folder, which requires local administrator credentials to access.

The effective result of the permissions listed in Table 17-2 is that users can read, execute, modify, and even delete files saved by other users to Public Documents and other subfolders of Public, regardless of whether they are standard users or administrators on the computer. Users can also create subfolders under Public Documents and other subfolders of Public, and other users can store their files in these subfolders. The basic difference, therefore, in user experience on standalone computers between using Shared Documents in Windows XP and Public in Windows Vista is that all Windows Vista users on the same computer are able to collaborate more effectively with respect to files stored in the Public folder than they can in Windows XP using the Shared Documents folder.

Using the Public Folder

To use the Public folder to share a file with other users on the same computer, simply drag the file into Public Documents or some other subfolder of Public. To make using the Public folder easier, Windows Vista includes a new environment variable called *%Public%* that maps to %SystemDrive%\Users\Public. This means that to open the Public folder, a user can simply type **%public%** in the Start Search box or type **start %public%** at the command prompt.

By creating a shortcut to %Public%\Documents (which maps to %SystemDrive%\Users \Public\Public Documents) on the user's desktop, the user can easily share files and folders with other users on the same computer by dragging them onto the shortcut. You can create such a shortcut on a user's desktop by running the script named CreateShortcutToPublic-Docs.vbs, which is found on the companion CD for this book. In an Active Directory environment, you can use Group Policy to assign this script as a logon script for a group of Windows Vista users within an organizational unit (OU). For more information on how to do this, see the topic titled "Assign user logon scripts" on Microsoft TechNet, which can be found at *http://technet2.microsoft.com/windowsserver/en/library/923c5070-528a-4a8c-8937-2d71ca4721701033.mspx?mfr=true.*

Note that for CreateShortcutToPublicDocs.vbs to be able to run as a logon script, the users targeted by the GPO must first have Cscript.exe configured as the default script host on their computers. To learn how to do this, see the subsection titled "Further Remarks" in the section titled "Script for Creating Multiple Shared Folders" in this chapter.

> **Note**   You can also leave Wscript.exe as the default script host on the computers of the users you are targeting and edit the CreateShortcutToPublicDocs.vbs script to comment out or remove all Wscript.Echo statements.

Understanding Network Sharing

Network sharing, usually called *file sharing* or just *sharing*, refers to sharing files stored on a networked computer so that users on other computers on the network can access them. Network sharing has undergone significant changes in Windows Vista compared to the earlier Windows XP platform. To understand these changes, let's first review how network sharing works in XP.

Network Sharing in Windows XP

Network sharing in Windows XP has the following characteristics:

- Only folders can be shared over the network, not individual files.

- Only members of the Administrators, Power Users, and Server Operators built-in groups can share folders.

- When a folder is shared, a hand appears under its icon in Windows Explorer.

- When a folder is shared, all users on the network can see the shared folder even if they don't have permission to list its contents or access any files stored in it.

The experience of sharing folders in Windows XP also differs depending on whether the computer belongs to a domain or a workgroup. Specifically, in a domain environment the following conventions apply:

- Folders are shared by configuring settings on the Sharing tab of the folder's properties sheet. This involves choosing to share the folder, specifying a share name and share permissions, and specifying caching settings. This is because Simple File Sharing is enabled by default on standalone Windows XP computers but disabled on domain-joined computers. (Simple File Sharing can optionally be disabled on standalone computers.)

- The effective permissions for accessing shared folders over the network are the most restrictive of the NTFS and shared folder permissions on the folder, with the default shared folder permissions being Read access for Everyone. Also, creating a share does not automatically modify the file system ACLs to allow access to the underlying folder and its contents.

■ Sharing a folder automatically causes an exception to be opened for File And Printer Sharing in Windows Firewall if this exception is not already open.

In a workgroup environment, however, there are two different ways of configuring network sharing:

■ The method used in domain environments as described earlier, which was the standard sharing interface used in Windows 2000.

■ The Simple File Sharing method described in the following section, which involves using ForceGuest (described in the How It Works sidebar).

Simple File Sharing in Windows XP

By default, Windows XP computers that belong to a workgroup are configured to use Simple File Sharing. This means that all incoming network connections are forced to use the Guest account to access resources on the computer, a mechanism called *ForceGuest*. Since the Guest account is a member of the Everyone built-in group, this means that access to a shared folder can be controlled by assigning permissions to either the Guest account, the Guests built-in group, or to Everyone.

When Simple File Sharing is turned off (that is, when ForceGuest is disabled) the standard sharing interface used in Windows 2000 appears. Simple File Sharing can be turned off in two ways:

■ In the GUI, by opening My Computer, selecting Tools, selecting Folder Options, selecting the View tab, and clearing the check box labeled User Simple File Sharing (Recommended). Note that this method disables the Simple File Sharing user interface but leaves ForceGuest behavior running.

■ By opening Local Security Policy and navigating to Computer Configuration\Policies\ Window Settings\Security Settings\Local Policy\Security Options and changing the policy setting Network Access: Sharing And Security Model For Local Accounts from Guest Only to Classic. Note that configuring this policy setting to Guest Only has no effect in a domain environment—in other words, Simple File Sharing can be used only in a workgroup environment. Note also that this method both disables the Simple File Sharing user interface and turns ForceGuest behavior off.

The intention of Simple File Sharing was to simplify the sharing of folders on small networks that are configured as workgroups, not domains. To share a folder using Simple File Sharing, users run the Network Setup Wizard, which does the following:

- Verifies that the computer is connected to a network

- Verifies the name of the computer and the workgroup it belongs to

- Opens the File And Printer Sharing exception in Windows Firewall

- Optionally allows the user to create a Network Setup disk to configure other computers on the network

After the user has run the wizard and rebooted her computer, she can use the Sharing tab on the folder's properties sheet to share the folder on the network.

By default, when a user shares a folder using Simple File Sharing, the level of access provided to other users on the network is Read, which allows them to access files in the folder but not to modify or delete them. This is because the wizard sets the shared folder permissions on the folder to Read and the NTFS permissions on the folder to Read & Execute. When the user shares the folder, however, she has an option to grant network users greater access to the folder by selecting the check box labeled Allow Network Users To Change My Files. Doing this sets the shared folder permissions on the folder to Change and the NTFS permissions on the folder to Modify, allowing network users to modify and delete files in the folder in addition to reading them.

In addition, when using Simple File Sharing, if a folder resides within a shared folder under the user's profile (for example, the folder resides within the user's shared My Documents folder) the user has the additional option of choosing whether or not to allow other users to access the contents of this folder. This is done by selecting or deselecting the check box labeled Make This Folder Private on the Sharing tab of the folder being considered. For more information on how file sharing is configured in Windows XP, see the article "How to configure file sharing in Windows XP" in the Microsoft Knowledge Base on Microsoft TechNet, found at *http://support.microsoft.com/kb/304040/*.

How It Works: ForceGuest

ForceGuest (also called *forced guest*) is a common term for one of the network access models used by Windows XP. This setting can be toggled on and off by using the local security policy editor (secpol.msc) and looking for the security option Network Access: Sharing And Security Model For Local Accounts. With Windows Vista, however, forced guest is no longer a supported setting; toggling this setting on is not recommended.

In Windows XP Professional, the default behavior for workgroup computers is to turn on the forced guest behavior by default. (Forced guest cannot be turned off for Home SKU versions of Windows XP.) This has a significant number of downfalls and makes both remote administration and allowing different levels of access very difficult. In Windows Vista, however, the default has changed. Windows Vista sets the default to force users to have a password to connect to a share remotely, just as it requires a password for remote desktop to work. (In a domain environment, of course, the user's credentials are supplied by the domain controller.)

Three different methods allow seamless access to shares in a workgroup: synchronizing user accounts and passwords across computers, using Password Manager and a master account (Password Manager is an associated task of the User Accounts Control Panel utility), or turning off Password Protected Sharing in the Network And Sharing Center. When the user credentials (a combination of user name and password) on a client computer and a server computer do not match, a user will be prompted to enter credentials for the server computer. If a user has the same account and password on both the client and server, the user will be able to automatically access folders shared to him.

If there are not matching accounts, an administrator can create a master sharing account on the server computer, and the user on the client computer can use Password Manager to automatically use those credentials when accessing the server. To use Password Manager, go to Control Panel\User Accounts\User Accounts and click Manage Your Network Passwords.

The final option for managing access to shares in a workgroup is to turn off sharing password protection. This is the behavior in Windows Vista that most closely matches forced guest behavior in Windows XP. Password Protected Sharing can be turned off via the Network And Sharing Center. This allows users to access shares that are permissioned to Everyone. (Both public and printers shares are shared to Everyone when they are shared.) This should be done, however, only in environments in which all the users on the network are trusted and do not want to use passwords. Some home environments could opt for this setting, but it is recommended that users always have a password for their accounts.

ForceGuest in Windows XP vs. Password Protected Sharing in Windows Vista

There is a slight difference between the way forced guest mode works and the way turning off password protected sharing works. In Windows XP, forced guest mode automatically forces any user on the network to connect as a guest remotely. Thus all users are treated exactly the same way remotely because they can't be differentiated. Additionally, administrators can't connect to the hidden $ shares because they cannot authenticate, and if a folder is shared to a specific user, he can't access it.

Turning password protection off in Windows Vista works differently than forced guest because it still allows a user to authenticate with credentials before it authenticates the user as guest. This means that if a folder is shared to a specific user or to users with different permissions, each user can connect and be allowed different permissions on the folder. Having users with different permission levels will be more and more common in Windows Vista, because the new File Sharing Wizard optimizes for distinguishing permission levels between different users.

Ed Averett, Program Manager

Windows Shell

Network Sharing in Windows Vista

Because of the confusing interface used by Simple File Sharing in Windows XP, and because a wizard-based approach to folder sharing is available only for workgroup users and not domain users, the file sharing interface has been revamped in Windows Vista to make it an easier-to-use, more integrated experience. In particular, the following enhancements have been made to file sharing in Windows Vista:

■ Just as in Windows XP, file and folder sharing in Windows Vista is blocked by default by Windows Firewall. In Windows Vista, however, the first time a file or folder is shared, a UAC prompt appears. This means that to allow other users to share files on her computer, the user must either be a local administrator on her computer, or an administrator must intervene to provide credentials for the prompt (a process called *opting in*). See the section titled "Enabling Network Sharing" later in this chapter for more information.

■ Users can now share individual files–not just folders–over the network, provided that these files are shared from within their user profiles. Outside their profiles, however, users can share only folders, not individual files.

■ Standard users can now share files and folders, provided that they share them from within their user profiles. (In Windows XP, you have to be a member of the Administrators, Power Users, or Server Operators group to share folders.) Outside their profiles, however, standard users must provide administrator credentials to share a folder.

■ A new File Sharing Wizard makes the experience of sharing a file or folder easier and more integrated, while the traditional ACL interface for sharing is still available for advanced users. This wizard-based approach for sharing works in both workgroup and domain environments and is explained in the section titled "Sharing a File or Folder Using the File Sharing Wizard" later in this chapter.

■ The Public folder, which is normally used to share files between different interactive users of the same computer, also can be shared on the network to simplify the sharing of files with users on other computers on the network. For more information, see the section titled "Using the Public Folder to Share Files" later in this chapter.

■ When a file or folder is shared on the network, only those users with whom it has been shared are able to see it. Explicit high-level Server Message Block (SMB) shares can still be seen by all users, including anonymous users. This is how sharing works in earlier versions of Windows. However, in Windows Vista, users won't be able to see files and folders within an SMB share unless they have NTFS permissions for accessing the particular file or folder. This change in behavior is a result of Access-Based Enumeration (ABE) technology being built into Windows Vista and is described in the section titled "Controlling Share Visibility with Access-Based Enumeration" later in this chapter.

- A hand icon is no longer superimposed on the icon for a folder that has been shared. Instead, two small people are superimposed on the folder icon to indicate it has been shared:

Public

Let's examine these enhancements in detail.

Direct from the Source: The Missing Hand

The hand overlay was retired in Windows Vista and replaced with people for multiple reasons. Windows users continually find it hard to understand that a hand means shared. Most often, people identify sharing with other people, so it was a clear transition. In addition, the entire overlay model in Windows has been given a new look and feel, and the hand did not fit with the design change.

Ed Averett, Program Manager

Windows Shell

Enabling Network Sharing

By default, standard users cannot share files on their computers with other network users unless an administrator first intervenes to provide credentials. This is because the first time a file or folder is shared, a UAC prompt appears. Users who are administrators on their computers can click Continue to configure sharing, but standard users will need an administrator to provide credentials as prompted. There are several reasons for this behavior:

- Sharing files and folders over the network requires that an exception for File And Printer Sharing be opened in Windows Firewall on the computer. Since this action can affect the security of the computer, only a local administrator on the computer is allowed to do this. However, even if you use Group Policy to open the File And Printer Sharing exception remotely on Windows Vista computers, users of these computers will still need elevated privileges or the intervention of an administrator, since the task of creating a Server Message Block (SMB) share on a Windows Vista computer requires administrator credentials.

- Sharing files and folders on desktop computers is generally not recommended in business environments. This is because files stored on network servers are usually backed up, but files stored on desktop computers generally aren't. Centralizing storage of user data files on network servers makes business data easier to manage and back up, whereas distributing business data across multiple desktop computers makes this information more difficult to manage and back up. For this reason, the default configuration of Windows Vista is not to allow users to share files unless they have administrator credentials on their computers.

If you do want to give some users in your enterprise the ability to share files on their computers, you can do one of the following:

- Make those users administrators on their computers instead of standard users. This will give them additional privileges on their computers, however, so do this only for advanced users who have basic knowledge of how to troubleshoot their computers and who understand and adhere to your corporate security policy as it applies to client computers.

- Manually turn on file sharing on these users' computers, either by sharing a folder on the computer or by turning on sharing for the Public folder on the computer. Opting users into the sharing experience like this can be done by "touching" each computer involved, or by creating a Remote Desktop connection to each computer (provided that Remote Desktop has previously been enabled on these computers, which by default is not the case), or by using Remote Assistance.

- Build an image of Windows Vista that has file sharing pre-enabled and use this image for deployment to the computers of users who require this functionality.

Note   There is no way to use Group Policy to enable sharing remotely on a Windows Vista computer. This is because sharing requires responding to a UAC prompt, and Group Policy cannot provide credentials to the Secure Desktop.

For information on how to enable sharing for the Public folder, see the section titled "Using the Public Folder to Share Files" later in this chapter. For information on how to create an image of Windows Vista for deployment, see Chapter 6, "Developing Disk Images."

Windows Firewall and Network Sharing

By default, when the first shared folder is created, the File And Printer Sharing exception is automatically opened in Windows Firewall on the computer. This allows other computers on the network to send inbound SMB traffic through Windows Firewall to access the shares.

The File And Printer Sharing exception opens the inbound ports shown in Table 17-3. (The scope of these rules is LocalSubnet except for the ICMP rules, where the scope is Any IP Address.)

Table 17-3 Firewall Rules for File and Printer Sharing

Rule Name	Port	Protocol	Process	Notes
File And Printer Sharing (NB-Name-In)	137	UDP	System	Used for NetBIOS Name Resolution
File And Printer Sharing (NB-Datagram-In)	138	UDP	System	Used for enabling NetBIOS Datagram transmission and reception
File And Printer Sharing (NB-Session-In)	139	TCP	System	Used for enabling NetBIOS Session Service
File And Printer Sharing (SMB-In)	445	TCP	System	Used for enabling Server Message Block transmission and reception via Named Pipes
File And Printer Sharing – Echo Request (ICMPv4-In)	All ports	ICMPv4	System	Used for enabling ICMPv4 echo requests using ping
File And Printer Sharing – Echo Request (ICMPv6-In)	All ports	ICMPv6	System	Used for enabling ICMPv6 echo requests using ping

Additional ports are also opened by this exception to allow shared printers on the computer to be accessed from other computers on the network. If shared folders on the computer are to be accessed from other computers and a third-party firewall is being used on the computer instead of Windows Firewall, the first four firewall rules listed in Table 17-3 will need to be opened on the firewall.

Note If network sharing has been inadvertently or maliciously enabled on some Windows Vista computers, you can block users on the network from accessing shares created on these computers by using Group Policy to close the File And Printer Sharing exception in Windows Firewall on these computers. For information on how to do this, see Chapter 27, "Configuring Windows Firewall and IPsec."

Implementing File Sharing

Files and folders can be shared from the user interface in Windows Vista in three ways:

- By sharing the file or folder from within the user's profile. This makes use of the Users share, a SMB share for the %SystemDrive%\Users directory. Files and folders within your profile can be shared using either the File Sharing Wizard or the Advanced Sharing interface, as described in the following sections of this chapter. Sharing a file or folder from within your user profile is sometimes called *in profile sharing* or *in place sharing*.

■ By enabling SMB sharing on the %SystemDrive%\Public folder and dragging, moving, or copying files you want to share into this folder. (The Public folder is a subfolder of the %SystemDrive%\Users directory.) For more information on this method, see the section titled "Using the Public Folder to Share Files" later in this chapter.

■ By creating an explicit SMB share to any folder outside your user profile. This method can use either the File Sharing Wizard or the Advanced Sharing interface.

Note   Administrators can use Group Policy to prevent sharing of files from within a user's profile. For more information, see the section titled "Managing File Sharing Using Group Policy" later in this chapter.

The first time a file or folder is shared on a Windows Vista computer, the SMB share named Users is automatically created for the %SystemDrive%\Users folder. Tables 17-4 and 17-5 list the share permissions and NTFS permissions assigned to this shared folder by default.

Table 17-4   NTFS Permissions Assigned to %SystemDrive%\Users

Identity	NTFS Permission	Applies To
SYSTEM	Full Control	This folder, subfolders, and files
Administrators	Full Control	This folder, subfolders, and files
Users	Read & Execute	This folder, subfolders, and files
Everyone	Read & Execute	This folder, subfolders, and files

Table 17-5   Share Permissions Assigned to Users

Identity	Share Permission
Administrators	Full Control
Authenticated Users	Full Control

Files and folders shared from within Users (typically from within Documents or some other subfolder of the user's profile) are not shared as explicit high-level SMB shares. In other words, they don't show up when you browse Network and view the SMB shares on the computer. Instead, files and folders shared from within Users make use of Access-Based Enumeration (ABE) to control which users on the network are able to view and access them.

For example, if the folder Reports is shared from within your Documents folder for some other users to access, those users will be able to access the folder by using the path *computername*\Users*username*\Documents\Reports instead of the path *computername*\Reports, which would be used if Reports were an explicit SMB share. Similarly, if the file Budget.doc is shared from within your Documents folder, the users you are sharing it with will be able to access the file using the path *computername*\Users*username*\Documents\Budget.doc. The File Sharing Wizard accomplishes this by changing the NTFS permissions, beginning from the file or folder shared and up until the top-level *computername*\Users SMB share. ABE is thus used here to hide access to all other files and folders that the user doesn't have permission to access. For more information on how ABE is used to control network sharing in Windows Vista, see the section titled "Controlling Share Visibility with Access-Based Enumeration" later in this chapter.

> **Caution**   If you stop sharing the C:\Users folder, you won't be able to share files or folders from within your user profile with other users on the network. In addition, changing the shared folder permissions or NTFS ACLs on the C:\Users folder may change how sharing files and folders from your profile works in ways you don't expect.

Direct from the Source: The Users Share and Roaming Profiles

After the Users share is created, files and folders shared under a user's profile are shared by modifying the NTFS file system ACLs up to the Users share. Note, however, that users with roaming user profiles or redirected documents will not experience this behavior. In profile sharing and roaming, user profiles are mutually exclusive. This is because with roaming user profiles, the data is physically on a server somewhere else, so creating a local share won't do any good. The same goes for folders that are redirected. If you redirect your Documents folder, you won't be able to share files via the File Sharing Wizard from within your Documents folder. Just modifying access like this allows for a single access point for sharing and also allows standard users to share files after an administrator has first created the Users share by running the wizard.

Ed Averett, Program Manager

Windows Shell

Sharing a File or Folder Using the File Sharing Wizard

You can use the new File Sharing Wizard in Windows Vista to share both files and folders in either a domain or workgroup environment. These files and folders can be stored either inside or outside the user's profile, although sharing of individual files is allowed only within a user's profile. If a user tries to share a folder outside her user profile, a UAC prompt will appear requiring administrator credentials. However, certain system folders, such as %Windir% and

%ProgramFiles%, can be shared only by using the advanced sharing interface. This is because sharing them using the wizard would adversely affect the security of these folders by changing their ACLs. See the section titled "Sharing a Folder Using the Advanced Sharing Interface" later in this chapter for more details.

> **Note**   You must also use the Advanced Sharing properties page if you want to share the root of your system volume (%SystemDrive%) on the network.

To enable sharing from within your user profile folder, follow these steps:

1. Open the Network And Sharing Center from Control Panel.

2. Expand the File Sharing option under Sharing And Discovery.

3. Select the option labeled Turn On File Sharing.

4. Respond to the UAC prompt as required. A UAC prompt is required here because enabling file sharing requires that the File And Printer Sharing exception be opened in Windows Firewall.

Completing this procedure shares the folder %SystemDrive%\Users as a high-level SMB share named Users. This means that other users on the network will be able to see this share in Network, but they won't be able to see anything within the share unless you explicitly share a file or folder from within your user profile, as described next.

To share a file or folder from within your user profile (for example, the file Budget.doc within your Documents folder) or a folder outside your profile (for example, C:\Test) follow these steps:

1. Right-click the file or folder and select Share. This starts the File Sharing Wizard.

2. On the Choose People To Share With page, do one of the following:

    ❑ Type the name of the user or group you want to share the file with and click Add. Note that the Everyone built-in group is available from the drop-down list to make it easy to share files or folders with all users on the network. Additionally, in a workgroup scenario, all local accounts on the computer are also available.

    ❑ Click the drop-down arrow and select Find, then use the Select Users And Groups dialog box to find the user account for the user you want to share the file with. For example, you can specify part of the user's name (such as his first name) and click Check Names to find his account. In an Active Directory environment, you can search for users in Entire Directory or within a specific domain or OU. In a workgroup scenario, you can only search for local user accounts on the computer.

    ❑ Click the drop-down arrow and select Everyone if you want to share the file with everyone on the network.

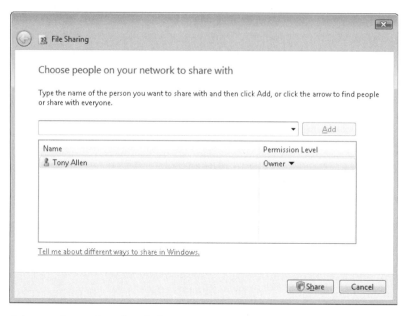

3. Select each user listed and change their permission levels as desired to control the level of access each user should have to the shared file or folder. The permission levels you can choose from are shown in Table 17-6. (The permissions shown in this table are the effective permissions for users accessing the file or folder over the network.)

4. Click Share. If you are trying to share a folder outside your user profile, a UAC prompt will appear. If you are an administrator, click Continue. If you are a standard user, you will need to provide administrator credentials on the computer to proceed.

5. Confirm that the actions that will be taken comply with what you intend and then click Next.

6. Copy the link to the shared folder or file for reference purposes or e-mail the link to other users who need to access the file over the network. Click Done to finish the wizard.

Table 17-6   Permission Levels Assignable Using the File Sharing Wizard

Permission Level	Effective Permission
Owner	Full Control
Co-owner	Full Control[1]
Contributor (Folders Only)	Special[2]
Reader	Read

[1]Windows Vista introduces the idea of a *co-owner*—someone who has full control over what he or she can do with a file but is not ACLed as the NTFS owner of the file.

[2]Making a user a Contributor for a folder that you are sharing gives the user permissions to create new files and read existing files in the folder but not to modify files added by other users.

After you've used the File Sharing Wizard to share a file or folder, you can change who has access to the shared file or folder and the level of access by following these steps:

1. Right-click the shared file or folder, select Share, and then do one of the following:

    ❑ Click Change Share Permissions to access the File Sharing Wizard so that you can add or remove users from the share permissions list or modify their level of access to the file or folder.

    ❑ Click Stop Sharing to stop sharing the file or folder over the network.

2. Respond to the UAC prompt if one appears.

> **Note** Sharing a file or folder will automatically open the File And Printer Sharing exception in Windows Firewall if this exception has not been previously opened. Stopping the sharing of all shared files and folders will not close this exception—you must close it manually using the Windows Firewall CPL in Control Panel.

Sharing a Folder Using the Advanced Sharing Interface

Experienced users who don't want to use the File Sharing Wizard to share folders can also use the Advanced Sharing interface to configure share permissions manually on the folder. The problem with this approach is that the Advanced Sharing interface configures only shared folder permissions on the folder and not the corresponding NTFS permissions that may be needed to provide users with the level of access you want to give them.

Furthermore, using the Advanced Sharing interface always generates a UAC prompt, even if the folder being shared resides in the user's profile. This means that Advanced Sharing is available only to users who are administrators on the local computer or who have administrator credentials they can supply when prompted.

Finally, the Advanced Sharing interface is the only method for sharing system folders like %Windir% and %ProgramFiles%, as these folders are not normally shared by ordinary users. Of course, sharing these folders is not recommended anyway because it exposes additional attack surface on the computer.

To use the Advanced Sharing interface to configure sharing for a folder, follow these steps:

1. Right-click the folder and select Properties.

2. Click the Sharing tab and then click Advanced Sharing.

3. Respond to the UAC prompt. This will open the Advanced Sharing interface:

4. Select the check box labeled Share This Folder.

5. Click Permissions and configure shared folder permissions for the users and groups that you want to be able to access the folder.

When you are finished sharing the folder, open its Properties again, select the Security tab, and configure the NTFS permissions on the folder to provide the level of access you want each user or group to have on the folder.

You can also configure the user interface so that only Advanced Sharing is available by default. Follow these steps:

1. Open Windows Explorer and press the Alt key to display the menu bar.

2. Select Tools and then select select Folder Options.

3. Click the View tab.

4. Scroll down and clear the option labeled Use Sharing Wizard (Recommended).

Note that when you follow this procedure, you will no longer be able to share individual files from within your user profile.

Note   In addition to using the File Sharing Wizard and Advanced Sharing interface, you can also share files and folders from the command line and by using scripts. For more information, see the section titled "Creating and Managing Shares Using Scripts" later in this chapter.

Using the Public Folder to Share Files

The other way that users can share files and folders on the network is to use the Public folder. Before users can use the Public folder to share files, however, sharing must be enabled for this folder. (By default, the Public folder is not shared on the network and can be used only for sharing files between different interactive users on the same computer.) Note that enabling sharing of the Public folder requires administrative credentials for the computer.

To enable sharing using the Public folder, follow these steps:

1. Open the Network And Sharing Center from Control Panel.

2. Expand the Public Folder Sharing option under Sharing And Discovery.

3. Choose one of the following two options, depending on the level of access to the contents of your Public folder you want to give network users:

   ❑ Turn On Sharing So Anyone With Network Access Can Open Files. This option assigns the Everyone special identity Read share permission on the folder and assigns the Administrators group Full Control share permission on the folder.

   ❑ Turn On Sharing So Anyone With Network Access Can Open, Change, And Create Files. This option assigns the Everyone special identity Full Control share permission on the folder.

4. Click Apply and then respond to the UAC prompt as required.

More Info   For more information on using the Network And Sharing Center, see Chapter 26.

Note that enabling sharing for the Public folder as described in the preceding procedure causes a new SMB share named Public to be created at C:\Users\Public, regardless of whether or not the Users folder is already shared. In other words, if Public folder sharing is enabled on a user's computer and the user has also shared a file from within her Documents folder (or another location from within her user profile), two shares (Users and Public) will appear when the user browses Network or types **net view localhost** from the command line. Additional shares may be displayed if the user is an administrator on her computer and has created other SMB shares outside her profile.

Note   Sharing the Public folder changes the ACL on this folder by adding an ACE for the Everyone group that assigns Read & Execute permission to this folder, subfolders, and files.

After your Public folder has been enabled for sharing, you can share files with other users on the network by copying or moving the files into Public (or some subfolder of Public such as Public Documents or Public Music) or by dragging them into the folder.

> **Note** All users on the network will have the same level of access to the files you've shared using your Public folder. If you want greater control over which users can access your shared files and the level of access they have to these files, you have two options: You can share your files from your user profile by using the File Sharing Wizard to assign different levels of access to each user (the preferred method), or you can create new SMB shares to contain your files and control access to the files by configuring NTFS permissions on them.

Determining Which Files and Folders Are Being Shared

To determine which files and folders are currently shared on the computer, you can use the Network And Sharing Center in Control Panel, shown in Figure 17-1.

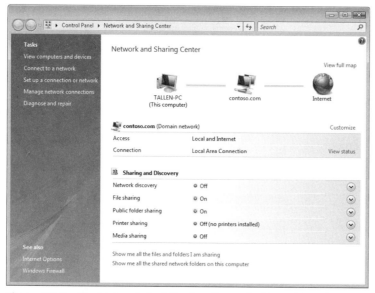

Figure 17-1 The Network And Sharing Center in Control Panel.

The Network And Sharing Center is the centralized place for users in home and small office environments to be able to configure key aspects of network sharing on their computers. Using this utility, users can do the following on their computers:

- Enable Network Discovery to make browsing the network faster and more reliable
- Enable the sharing of files and folders from within their user profiles
- Enable the Public folder as an easy means of sharing files with other users on the network
- Allow other users on the network to use a locally attached printer
- Enable sharing of media files stored in their media libraries

> **Note**   In an enterprise environment, many of the features in the previous list can be controlled using Group Policy. See the sections titled "Managing File Sharing Using Group Policy" and "Managing Media Sharing with Group Policy" later in this chapter for more information.

You can use the Network And Sharing Center in two ways to find out what files and folders are currently being shared on a computer:

- Click the link labeled Show Me All The Files And Folders I Am Sharing. This opens a saved search named Shared By Me that displays all nonstandard folders and individual files that are currently shared on the computer. Note that only files that reside in your user profile and which have been specifically shared using the File Sharing Wizard are displayed here. For instance, files within a folder that has been shared are not listed separately as being shared. For more information about saved searches, see Chapter 20, "Managing Search."

- Click the link labeled Show Me All The Shared Network Folders On This Computer. This opens a view of Network focused on your local computer (*computername*) showing all the shared folders and printers on the computer. By right-clicking any shared folder visible here and then selecting Properties, you can modify its share permissions, ACLs, and other settings.

Another way to view shared folders on a computer is to use Computer Management. (Using this tool requires administrative privileges on the computer.) Computer Management has been enhanced in Windows Vista not only to display all folders shared on the computer (including hidden administrative shares) but also to let you configure properties of these shares such as share permissions, offline settings, and the NTFS permissions on the folder underlying the share.

To use Computer Management to view or configure shared folders on a computer, follow these steps:

1. Open Computer Management from Administrative Tools in Control Panel and respond to the UAC prompt that appears.

2. Expand System Tools and then expand Shared Folders. Click Shares to display a list of SMB shares on the computer.

3. Right-click a share and click Properties to view or configure its share permissions, NTFS permissions, and other settings.

> **Note**   Computer Management can display only SMB shares on the computer; it cannot display files or folders shared from within your user profile.

To view shared files and folders on a different computer on the network, do one of the following:

- Open Network from the Start menu, find the computer you are interested in, and double-click it to display the shared folders and printers on it. This approach is most useful in a workgroup environment.

- Open a command prompt window and type **net view computername**, where *computername* is the host name, FQDN, or IP address of the remote computer.

- Search for shared folders that have been published to Active Directory. This is the usual approach to finding shared resources in a domain environment. See the section titled "Best Practices for Implementing File Sharing in a Domain Environment" later in this chapter for more information.

- Use Computer Management to connect to the computer whose shares you want to enumerate. To do this, you will need to be logged on to the computer using an account that has administrator rights on the remote computer. (This typically means you must log on as a member of the Domain Admins group.) Then follow these steps:

  a. Open Computer Management from Administrative Tools in Control Panel.

  b. Right-click the root node of the console and select Connect To Another Computer.

  c. Type the name (host name, FQDN, or IP address) of the remote computer or browse/search to locate and select it. Then click OK.

  d. Expand System Tools, Shared Folders, Shares as described in step 2 of the previous procedure.

For more information on using Computer Management to view and manage shares, see the section titled "Publishing Shares in Active Directory" later in this chapter.

Important   The fact that the Users folder can easily be shared on Windows Vista computers is an added bonus for administrators, because it allows users to access the contents of their profiles remotely. But if you want to prevent your users from accessing their profiles over the network, you can use Group Policy to prevent them from sharing the Users folder on their computers. (See the section titled "Managing File Sharing Using Group Policy" later in this chapter for information on how to do this.) Note that if you have roaming profiles configured on your network, your users will automatically be unable to share files from within their profiles—regardless of whether or not sharing the Users folder has been disabled on their computers using Group Policy.

How It Works: Administrative Shares in Windows Vista

When a user with administrator credentials opens Computer Management and views the SMB shares on his computer, he sees certain special shares with dollar signs ($) appended to them. These administrative shares are hidden shares (shares with $

appended to them are not visible when users browse the network using Windows Explorer) and include ADMIN$, C$, IPC$, and possibly others. These administrative shares are important for enabling remote administration of the computer by some enterprise management software. In addition, some backup programs utilize hidden volume shares, and certain services in Windows require these shares to function properly over the network. So, you should know that you should not try to delete these shares. (Even if you do delete an administrative share such as C$, Windows will re-create it the next time the Server service is restarted or the computer is rebooted.)

One common way that administrators in domain environments make use of such shares is to enable them to connect to the file system on a remote computer. For example, when you type *computername*\C$ in the Start Search box (where *computername* is the host name, FQDN, or IP address of a remote computer on your network), you are soon presented with a Connect To *computername* logon box asking you to provide credentials for accessing the C$ share on the remote computer. By entering administrator credentials (or Domain Admin credentials) on the remote computer, you can open the remote computer's C volume in Windows Explorer and copy files to the volume or perform some other administrative task. In Windows XP, you can do this regardless of whether the remote computer belongs to a workgroup or domain.

However, one of the ways that security has been enhanced in Windows Vista is that in workgroup scenarios this no longer works—you cannot connect to administrative shares on remote computers in a workgroup environment, regardless of whether or not you have administrator credentials for the remote computer.

Controlling Share Visibility with Access-Based Enumeration

One of the biggest complaints from administrators migrating from other platforms to Microsoft Windows is that when folders are shared on the network, users can see the contents of these folders even if they don't have any permissions to access portions of these contents. For example, say an Administrator on a file server running Windows Server 2008 shares the folder C:\Budgets as BUDGETS and grants Read permission to Everyone. Within this folder are two documents named C:\Budgets\Public.doc and C:\Budgets\Secret.doc, and while the Users group has Allow Read & Execute ACL on Public.doc, they have Deny Read & Execute ACL on Secret.doc (or just no ACL on Secret.doc). The idea is that ordinary domain users should be able to read the public form of the budget, which contains only summary information, but they should not have access to the secret budget, which contains sensitive business information that has not yet been made public.

In the preceding scenario, a curious user who is logged on to his Windows XP computer might stumble across the BUDGETS share by browsing the network as follows: opening My Network Places, then Entire Network, then Microsoft Windows Network, then the domain, and finally the file server. When the user double-clicks the BUDGETS share, he sees both files,

Public.doc and Secret.doc. He can open and read Public.doc but the Deny ACL on Secret.doc (or lack of an ACL on Secret.doc) prevents him from reading this file's contents. Although this might not seem like much of a security issue, remember that the user does at least have one possibly significant piece of information—the existence of a protected financial file named Secret.doc. In this case, a malicious user would expect that this file contains sensitive company information (such as highly confidential financial information) and could therefore focus an attack more effectively by concentrating his efforts on gaining access to this particular file.

To eliminate this kind of footprinting attack by malicious users (and unauthorized access attempts by curious employees), Service Pack 1 for Windows Server 2003 included a new feature called Access-Based Enumeration (ABE), which allows users to see only those files and folders within a network share that the user actually has permissions to access. In other words, with ABE an administrator can share C:\Budgets and assign ACLs as before, but ordinary users who browse the BUDGETS share will see only the Public.doc file. The Secret.doc file will not be visible to them—they won't even know of its existence. ABE thus increases the security of shared data and also helps protect its privacy.

ABE functionality was first included with Service Pack 1 for Windows Server 2003, but to realize this functionality, administrators have to first download and install the shell extension found at *http://www.microsoft.com/downloads/details.aspx?FamilyID=04a563d9-78d9-4342-a485-b030ac442084*. This download adds a new tab named Access-Based Enumeration to the Properties sheet for shared folders, allowing administrators to toggle ABE on or off on for each share. The download also includes a new command-line tool named abecmd.exe that can be used to enable ABE on a shared folder from the command line.

With Windows Vista and Windows Server 2008 however, ABE is built directly into the operating system. This means, for example, that when a user on a Windows Vista computer shares a file or folder located within the Users or Public folder to a user on another Windows Vista computer, the second user will see the shared file or folder on the network only if the first user has granted him permission to access it. For information about enabling ABE for shares on Windows Server 2008, see the sidebar that follows.

Direct from the Source: ABE in Windows Server 2008

The following options are available for managing Access-Based Enumeration in Windows Server 2008:

- **GUI**   Configuration is exposed through the advanced share properties of the new Share And Storage Management snap-in (storagemgmt.msc) on Windows Server 2008. A check box in the Advanced properties of a share allows you to enable ABE (see Figure 17-2). We no longer expose an ABE tab in the standard folder properties of shares as we did with ABE in Windows Server 2003.

- **API**   The ABE API referenced in the white paper titled "Access-Based Enumeration" is also unchanged since Windows Server 2003. You can find the white paper at *http://www.microsoft.com/windowsserver2003/techinfo/overview/abe.mspx.*

- **Command Line**   The abecmd command-line tool referenced in the preceding white paper will function on Windows Server 2008. You can copy the tool from a Windows Server 2003 computer or download it via this link: *http://www.microsoft.com/downloads/details.aspx?FamilyId=04A563D9-78D9-4342-A485-B030AC442084&displaylang=en.*

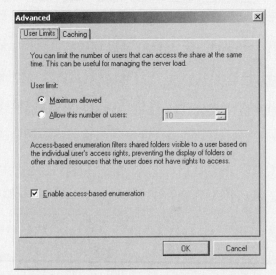

Figure 17-2   Enabling Access-Based Enumeration in Windows Server 2008.

Finally, there are no differences in functionality between the ABE implementations in Windows Server 2003 and Windows Server 2008.

Kapil Mehra

Windows Server 2008 Beta Lead

Accessing Shared Files and Folders

To access a shared file or folder on a computer from another computer on the network, you can use the UNC path to the file or folder. Table 17-7 shows several examples based on the following scenario:

- A computer is named TALLEN-PC with IP address 10.0.0.100, and it belongs to the Contoso.com domain.

- A user is named Tony Allen and has the UPN name tallen@contoso.com.

Table 17-7   Examples of UNC Sharing Syntax

Type of Share	Directory Path	UNC Path
A file named Budget.doc shared from within Tony's Documents folder	C:\Users\tallen\ Documents\Budget.doc	\\TALLEN-PC\Users\tallen\ Documents\Budget.doc
A folder named C:\Software shared as an explicit SMB share	C:\Software	\\TALLEN-PC\Software
A folder named Stuff that is dragged into the Public Documents folder (sharing has been enabled on Public)	C:\Users\Public\Public Documents\Stuff	\\TALLEN-PC\Public\Public Documents\Stuff

To access a shared file or folder on another computer using its UNC path, do one of the following:

- Type the UNC path into the Start Search box.

- Type **start** followed by the UNC path at a command prompt.

- Right-click Computer, select Map Network Drive, and then specify the UNC path to the shared folder.

- Open a Command Prompt window and use the *net use* command.

- Create a shortcut to a network location by clicking Start, clicking Computer, and then right-clicking an open space in Computer and selecting Add A Network Location. This starts the Add Network Location Wizard, which you can use to create a shortcut to a network location for easier access.

In addition to accessing shared files or folders directly using their UNC paths, users also can browse the network to find shared resources on their networks, or they can search Active Directory for the shared folder if it has been published. See the section titled "Publishing Shares in Active Directory" later in this chapter for more information.

How It Works: Network Discovery and File Sharing

One of the networking improvements in Windows Vista is in the area of Network Discovery and location awareness. To enable Windows Vista to accurately and reliably discover the presence of network nodes, or attached devices that support Universal Plug and Play (UPnP) broadcasts, special communication protocols such as Link Layer Topology Discovery (LLTD), Function Discovery (FD), and Web Services for Devices (WSD) are used. Network Discovery refers to the capability of Windows Vista to discover the presence of other computers and devices on the network; think of Network Discovery as another layer on top of file sharing functionality that helps to improve sharing from the user's point of view.

In Windows XP, for example, shared folders created on computers are sometimes slow to appear, possibly even taking a day or two before they become visible on the network. This is because of the way XP computers browse the network using a service called the Computer Browser service. In certain circumstances, the browse list may become inaccurate on master browsers on your network.

Network Discovery in Windows Vista solves this problem by broadcasting out the discoverability of shared folders on a computer so that other Windows Vista users on the network can quickly and accurately access your shared folders. In Windows Vista, your current network category is private, public, or domain, and Network Discovery is on by default for private networks so that users on home networks or in other work-group scenarios are able to easily find shared resources on their networks. On public networks, Network Discovery is off by default so that users who are sharing files on their computers don't broadcast the presence of these files to untrusted users on a public network—for example, at a WiFi hotspot in a coffee shop. In domain-based sce-narios, Network Discovery is off by default and should not be turned on, because it adds considerable broadcast traffic to your network, and in an Active Directory environment, you can publish shares anyway. Users who need to find them can search for them in the directory (fast) instead of browsing the network (slow).

Turning Network Discovery on or off can be done from the Network Center CPL and requires administrative privileges on the computer. Domain administrators can block Network Discovery from being enabled on their Windows Vista computers by using Group Policy to configure Windows Firewall to block Network Discovery on the computers targeted by the GPO.

Publishing Shares in Active Directory

In a workgroup environment, the only way for users themselves to find out about the presence of shared folders on their networks is by using Network Explorer to browse the network. Alternatively, you can provide users with the UNC path to the shared folders so that they can open the folders or map a drive to them. In a domain environment with hundreds of shares or more, browsing the network becomes impractical. Fortunately, Windows Server 2003 allows administrators to publish shared folders in Active Directory so that users can search for them in the directory and access them.

Windows XP users have no native capability to publish shared folders on their own comput-ers. With Windows Vista, however, the capability to publish shares in Active Directory is now present within the user interface, but only users who are members of the Domain Admins group can do this. Typically, this feature will be used by Domain Admins to publish shares on file servers while logged on to their Windows Vista administrative workstations. This makes it possible for domain administrators to publish shares from their workstations instead of having to do so directly from a server or from an RDP session with a server.

To publish a shared folder in Active Directory, follow these steps:

1. Log on to the computer as a member of the Domain Admins group.

2. Open Computer Management from Administrative Tools in Control Panel.

3. Right-click the root node and select Connect To Another Computer. Specify the name of the remote computer or browse the directory to find it.

4. Expand System Tools, then Shared Folders, and then click Shares to display a list of SMB shares on the remote computer.

5. Right-click a share and select Properties.

6. Switch to the Publish tab and select the check box labeled Publish This Share In Active Directory.

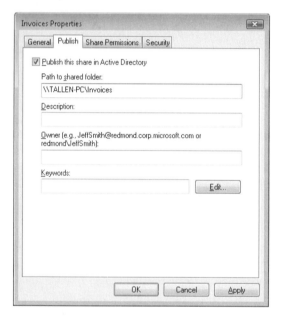

7. Configure the remaining publishing settings as required.

> **Note** The Publish tab of a shared folder's properties sheet in Computer Management will be visible only if the logged-on user is a member of the local Administrator's group on her computer and the computer is a member of a domain. Standard users will not see this tab.

When shared folders have been published in Active Directory, users can search the directory to quickly find them and access them. This method of finding shared resources on the network is much easier than browsing the network in most large domain-based environments.

To find a shared folder that has been previously published in Active Directory, follow these steps:

1. Click Start and then click Network.

2. Click Search Active Directory on the toolbar.

3. Click the drop-down arrow next to Find and then select Shared Folders.

4. Type the name of the share. (You can also type the first portion of the name and use wildcards.)

5. Click Find Now. If the share you are looking for appears, do one of the following:

   ❑ Double-click the share to open it in Windows Explorer.

   ❑ Right-click the share and select Map Network Drive to map a drive letter to the share.

If you want to prevent targeted users from being able to publish shared folders on their computers in Active Directory, you can disable the following Group Policy setting:

User Configuration\Policies\Administrative Templates\Shared Folders\Allow Shared Folders To Be Published

This setting works in Windows XP, Windows Server 2003, Windows Vista, and Windows Server 2008.

Note   Only shared folders can be published in the directory; individual files shared from within a user's profile cannot be published.

Managing File Sharing Using Group Policy

Administrators who want to prevent users from sharing files and folders from within their user profiles or the Public folder can use the following Group Policy setting:

User Configuration\Policies\Administrative Templates\Windows Components\Network Sharing\Prevent Users From Sharing Files Within Their User Profile

Enabling this policy setting will prevent users from sharing individual files or folders from within their user profiles, and it will also prevent the File Sharing Wizard from creating an SMB share at %SystemDrive%\Users. Users can still use the File Sharing Wizard to create other new SMB shares, and they can also still use the Advanced Sharing interface to share %SystemDrive%\Users. Note that this setting can be specified only on a per-user—not per-computer—basis for all users on the computer.

As described earlier in this chapter, the following policy is no longer supported in Windows Vista:

Computer Configuration\Policies\Windows Settings\Security Settings\Local Policies\Security Options\Network Access: Sharing And Security Model For Local Accounts

It is recommended that you leave this policy setting configured as Classic: Local Users Authenticate At Themselves, because the ForceGuest model of allowing local users to authenticate as Guest is no longer supported in Windows Vista. See the earlier sidebar titled "How It Works: ForceGuest" for more information.

Creating and Managing Shares Using the Net Commands

Network shares can also be created and managed in Windows Vista from the command line. For example, the Net commands can be used in Windows Vista to view a list of shares (Net view), create a new share (Net share), map a drive letter to a share (Net use), and so on. The caveat is that the Net share command must be run from a command prompt with elevated privileges so that only users who are local administrators on their computers or who know the credentials for an administrator account on their computers are able to create and manage shares using these commands.

For example, the following steps are for creating a share named TOMES for the %SystemDrive%\Books folder and assigning the share permission Change to user Tony Allen (tallen@contoso.com):

1. Type **cmd** into the Start Search box, right-click cmd in the Start menu, and then select Run As Administrator.

2. Respond to the UAC prompt as required.

3. Type **mkdir %SystemDrive%\Books** to create the Books folder.

4. Type **net share TOMES=%SystemDrive%\Books /grant:tallen,CHANGE** to create the share and assign Change permission to user Tony Allen.

You can now use the File Sharing Wizard to verify that the share has been created and configured as desired. To do this, follow these steps:

1. Open Windows Explorer and find the Books folder.

2. Right-click Books and select Share.

3. Click Change Sharing Permissions.

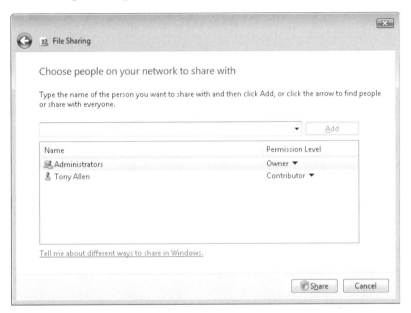

Note that using Net share will configure share permissions but not NTFS permissions for the underlying folder. To configure NTFS permissions on a folder, you can use the Sharing Wizard, the Security tab of the folder's properties, or the icacls.exe command from the command line.

Note   The cacls.exe command is deprecated in Windows Vista; use the icacls.exe command instead. For more information, type **icacls /?** at the command line.

Creating and Managing Shares Using Scripts

Many file sharing tasks can be performed using scripts. This can be a useful way of automating tasks that need to be repeated or involve many steps when using the user interface. The companion CD for this book includes a number of scripts you can use and/or customize to perform various tasks related to file sharing. The following sections describe two of these scripts.

Script for Creating Multiple Shared Folders

The script CreateMultipleSharedFolders.vbs provides an easy way to share multiple folders quickly.

Example Usage   To create the folders C:\Test1 and C:\Test2 on the local computer and share these folders as TEST1 and TEST2, type **Cscript CreateMultipleSharedFolders.vbs /f:C:\Test1,C:\Test2** at the Command Prompt window or use this line within a logon script. Note that the following permission levels are assigned to these shares:

- User whose credentials were used to run the script: Owner
- Everyone: Reader

Using Cscript.exe   Most of the VBScript scripts on the companion CD should be run using Cscript.exe as the default script host. To configure this manually on a single computer, follow these steps:

1. Type **cmd** in the Start Search box to display cmd under Programs.

2. Right-click cmd under Programs and select Run As Administrator. This opens an admin-level command window, which you can distinguish from other open command windows because of the word *Administrator* at the start of the title bar.

3. Type **cscript //h:cscript**.

> **Note**   If a script doesn't generate any command-line output, you can also run it using Cscript.exe by right-clicking it and selecting Open With Command Prompt. This causes a command-line window to open briefly to run the script, and then the window closes when the script is finished. Using this approach, a user could use the script CreateShortcutToPublicDocs.vbs described earlier in this chapter to create a shortcut on her desktop to her Public Documents folder. This method wouldn't work, however, with a script like ListSharedFolders.vbs, because the script output would be displayed only briefly before the command window closes.

In an Active Directory environment in which Group Policy is being used to manage desktop computers, you can change the default script host from Wscript.exe to Cscript.exe on all computers in an OU by following these steps:

1. Use Notepad to create a text file named ChangeToCscript.bat with the following two lines of text in it:

```
@echo off
cscript //h:cscript //s
```

2. Open the GPO that is linked to the OU and navigate to Computer Configuration\Policies\Windows Settings\Scripts\Startup.

3. Double-click the Startup policy setting to open its properties sheet.

4. Click the Show Files button and copy and paste ChangeToCscript.bat from Windows Explorer to the subfolder of SYSVOL where Startup scripts must be located.

5. Click the Add button on the properties sheet for the Startup policy setting.

6. Click the Browse button and select ChangeToCscript.bat.

7. Close all properties sheets.

Adding this startup script will cause the default script host on the targeted computers to be changed from Wscript.exe to Cscript.exe on the next reboot of these computers, and this will work regardless of whether the targeted users are standard users or local admins on their computers.

> **Note**   ChangeToCscript.bat must be run as a Startup script and not a Logon script. If you run it as a Logon script, it will work only when the targeted users are local admins on their computers.

Further Remarks   Like most of the scripts on the companion CD, the CreateMultipleShared-Folders.vbs script must be run using administrative credentials to perform as intended. This can be done by opening an admin-level command window as described earlier and typing **path\CreateMultipleSharedFolders.vbs**, where *path* is the location of the script in your file system.

Many of these scripts can be run against a remote computer—provided that Windows Firewall allows this on the remote computer. (See the next script in this section for more information.) For example, you can customize the CreateMultipleSharedFolders.vbs script to run against a remote computer by editing the following line within the script to change the period to the name (host name, FQDN, or IP address) of the remote computer:

```
strTargetComputer= "."  'computer to run script on.
```

Sometimes when these scripts are run against a remote computer, they have reduced functionality. For example, the script CreateMultipleSharedFolders.vbs can create folders on the local computer and share them, but when run against a remote computer, the folders to be shared must already be present. This limitation is documented in the comments included in the script.

Finally, only a few of the possible parameters for each task CreateMultipleSharedFolders.vbs can perform are exposed in the command-line syntax of the script. For quick usage of this script, type **CreateMultipleSharedFolders.vbs /?** at a command prompt to display simple syntax sufficient for most ordinary usage. For a detailed description of the possible parameters you can use by customizing the script, open the script in Notepad and view the comments. Most of the scripts on the Companion CD respond to this /? syntax and are heavily commented to help you customize them if required.

> **More Info**   For more information on how UAC can affect logon script processing in Windows Vista and how to work around this issue, see the section titled "Group Policy Scripts can fail due to User Account Control" in the topic titled "Deploying Group Policy Using Windows Vista" in the Windows Vista Technical Library at *http://technet2.microsoft.com/ WindowsVista/en/library/5ae8da2a-878e-48db-a3c1-4be6ac7cf7631033.mspx?mfr=true*.

Script for Configuring Windows Firewall to Allow Remote Scripting

Before you can run a script like CreateMultipleSharedFolders.vbs against a remote computer to share folders on that computer, you first need to ensure that Windows Firewall is configured on the remote computer to allow remote scripting. This involves opening the Remote Administration exception in Windows Firewall on the remote computer. Since this exception is disabled by default in Windows Vista, and standard users cannot configure Windows Firewall unless they know their computers' administrator credentials, enterprises that use standard users for Windows Vista desktops must first open the Remote Administration exception on target computers before admin scripts can be run remotely against these computers. Although you can use Group Policy to configure Windows Firewall on remote computers, another way is to use a logon script like ConfigureFirewallForRemoteScripting.vbs.

Additional Scripts

Additional scripts for performing tasks related to file sharing can be found on the companion CD. A complete listing of these scripts can be found in the section titled "On the Companion CD" at the end of this chapter.

Troubleshooting File Sharing

Troubleshooting file sharing involves two types of activity:

- Troubleshooting a computer that cannot access a shared folder that other computers can successfully access. In this case, troubleshooting efforts should be concentrated on the client—the computer that cannot access the share.

- Troubleshooting a computer that is sharing a folder when no other computers can access this share. In this case, troubleshooting efforts should be concentrated on the server—the computer on which the folder is being shared.

Troubleshooting Sharing on the Client Side

Tips for troubleshooting a client computer that cannot access a shared folder on a server include the following:

- Verify that you have basic network connectivity between the client and the server by using the ping command. If you can't ping the server from the client, check your physical connection to the network by ensuring that your network cable is securely plugged into the computer. If your physical network connection seems secure, try running Windows Network Diagnostics on the computer. For more information on using Windows Network Diagnostics, see Chapter 32, "Troubleshooting Network Issues."

■ If you have basic network connectivity and you are trying to access a shared file or folder on the network using its UNC path, verify that the name of the remote computer and the share name are correct. If these are correct, try using the IP address of the server instead of its host name or FQDN. If you can connect to the share using the IP address of the server but not its host name or FQDN, you have a name resolution problem— verify that NetBIOS over TCP/IP is enabled on the client and that the DNS settings for the client are correct.

■ If you can connect to the share on the server but a Connect To *servername* logon box appears, and the computer belongs to a domain, ensure that the server you are trying to connect to also belongs to a domain (the same domain or a trusted domain). If the server belongs to the same domain as the client, make sure that you are currently logged on to the client using domain credentials and not computer credentials. If you can connect to the share on the server but a Connect To *servername* logon box appears, and the computer belongs to a workgroup, you may need to enter credentials in the Connect To *servername* logon box before you can access the share—see the sidebar titled "How It Works: ForceGuest" earlier in this chapter for more information.

■ If you are trying to browse the network using Windows Explorer on the client and you cannot find the shared folder, the browse list might not be up to date. You can either wait and try again later or try connecting to the share using its UNC path if you know this.

■ If you are trying to search for the share in the directory but can't find it, verify that the share has been published in Active Directory. If the share has been previously published, verify that you are logged on to the domain and not using cached credentials by checking the System log for an occurrence of event 5719 at the time you last logged on to the computer. If this event is present, the computer was unable to contact the domain controller and you are logged on to the computer using cached credentials. In this case, check that the domain controller is running and verify your connectivity with the network.

Troubleshooting Sharing on the Server Side

Tips for troubleshooting a server computer (specifically, in this example, a Windows Vista computer that an administrator has opted in for file sharing) when client computers cannot access shares on the server include the following:

■ Open the properties of your network connection on the server and make sure that File And Printer Sharing For Microsoft Networks is selected. If this component is not selected, you will not be able to share from the computer.

- Open a command prompt on the server and type **sc query lanmanserver** to verify that the Server service is running. If the Server service is not running, you will not be able to share from the computer.

- Open Windows Firewall on the server and verify that the File And Printer Sharing exception has been opened. If this exception has not been opened, client computers will not be able to establish SMB connectivity with the server.

- Verify that the share permissions and ACLs on the share the client is trying to connect to grant the appropriate level of permissions to the user on the client. If the user does not have at least Read permission for the shared file or folder, Access-Based Enumeration (if the server is a Windows Vista computer or a Windows Server 2003 file server with ABE configured) will prevent the user from even seeing the share on the server.

- Verify that the client computer and user have the Access This Computer From The Network user right. This user right enables users and computers to access network shares and also Active Directory. By default, all Authenticated Users have this user right, but if it is removed from a user or computer, that user or computer will be unable to access shares on the network. For more information, see Microsoft Knowledge Base article 823659, "Client, service, and program incompatibilities that may occur when you modify security settings and user rights assignments" at *http://support.microsoft.com/ kb/823659*.

 More Info   For more information on troubleshooting file sharing, see Chapter 32.

Best Practices for Implementing File Sharing in a Workgroup Environment

In a home office or other workgroup environment, best practices for sharing files on Windows Vista computers include the following:

- Enable sharing on your Public folder to share files with other users on the network when all users should have the same level of access to these files. Then drag your files and folders into Public to share them easily.

- Share files from within your user profile when you want to have greater control over who can see and access shared files on the network. Windows Vista's Access-Based Enumeration technology means that users can see only the shared files for which they have a minimum of Read permission—if they don't have Read permission, they won't even know the file is shared.

- If you share files from within your user profile, share them from the appropriate folder: Share documents from within your Documents folder, share music from within your Music folder, and so on.

- If you share a file or folder, e-mail or otherwise communicate the UNC path to your share to network users whom you want to be able to access the share. Otherwise, users will have to browse the network using Windows Explorer to find any new shares present on the network.

- Make sure Network Discovery is turned on for all Windows Vista computers on your network. Network Discovery makes browsing for shared resources faster and more reliable.

- Make sure if you are setting up a work workgroup or a home network that your network type is a private network. This will allow you to enable things such as discovery and sharing on this network, but when you pick up your laptop and take it to a wireless hotspot, the computer will be less exposed, because your network type will switch to the public profile, which won't have services such as discovery and sharing turned on. Additionally, the Windows Firewall exceptions will apply only to your private network, blocking incoming requests when connected to public networks.

Caution   If you don't want your user profile folder visible from the network, don't share any files from within your profile. Sharing a file from within your profile automatically causes the %SystemDrive%\Users folder to be shared on the computer, and this means that other users on the network will be able to see your user profile folder on the computer. Of course, they won't be able to look inside your profile folder unless they somehow have administrator credentials on the computer. But simply knowing the names of profile folders on the computer can give malicious users knowledge that can help them footprint your network, because these folder names correspond to logon names for users either on the computer or on the network.

Best Practices for Implementing File Sharing in a Domain Environment

In an Active Directory environment, best practices for sharing files on Windows Vista computers include the following:

- Turn off Network Discovery in a domain environment, as it can generate excessive network traffic that can interfere with normal network activities.

- Publish shared folders in Active Directory so that users can search for them in the directory and access them instead of having to browse the network to find them.

- Use Group Policy to prevent users on Windows Vista computers from sharing files on their computers from their user profiles unless they are local administrators on their computers. For more information, see the section titled "Managing File Sharing Using Group Policy" earlier in this chapter.

- Allow only advanced users the ability to share folders on their computers by giving them administrative rights on their computers.

Caution   Do not make users local administrators on their computers unless you understand the consequences of doing so. One consequence is that they will be able to share folders and open firewall exceptions on their computers. Sharing folders from desktop computers in a domain environment may mean that important documents are being stored on computers instead of on network file servers, and since desktop computers are not normally backed up, this can mean lost work. Educate users to store files instead within shared folders on network file servers where their work can be centrally backed up regularly.

Managing Media Sharing

Windows Media Sharing is a feature of Windows Vista that lets users share the media files on their computers so that other users on the network can play or view them. This includes music files, video files, images, and playlists that are normally stored in the Music, Pictures, and Video folders within the user's profile. When Media Sharing is enabled, other users can play or view your files but cannot add, modify, or delete files in these folders. Windows Media Sharing is disabled by default and can be enabled in Network And Sharing Center and in Windows Media Player for private or domain networks.

Windows Vista's Media Sharing functionality is an evolution of the earlier Windows Media Connect technology developed for the Windows XP platform. Windows Media Connect was designed to allow users to experience music, photos, and videos stored on their Windows XP SP2–based computers on any compatible digital media receiver (DMR) device. Windows Media Connect accomplished this by streaming media information over HTTP from the computer to the target media device. But whereas Windows Media Connect enabled Windows computers to share their media libraries with other devices, it didn't allow them to consume shared media. For example, it didn't enable one Windows XP computer to find and play videos stored on another Windows XP computer using Windows Media Player.

With Windows Vista, however, Media Sharing capability is built into Windows Media Player 11 and lets you both share out your Windows Vista computer's media library and find and access media libraries shared by other Windows Vista computers. This functionality is built directly into Windows Media Player 11 in Windows Vista, and Media Sharing has been enhanced in Windows Vista by adding support for Real Time Streaming Protocol (RTSP) media streaming in addition to HTTP media streaming. RTSP is an industry-standard protocol developed by the IETF and is defined by RFC 2326, found at *http://www.ietf.org/rfc/rfc2326.txt*.

Note   Media Sharing capability in Windows Vista is targeted mainly toward home users, but this functionality is also included in the Business, Enterprise, and Ultimate SKUs for businesses that want to use this feature. Note also that although you can install Windows Media Player on Windows Server 2008 SKUs by adding the Desktop Experience feature, you cannot enable Media Sharing on server SKUs.

How It Works: Media Sharing

Windows Media Player (WMP) has two modes of operation for Media Sharing: client mode and host mode. Client mode is enabled by turning on Find Media That Others Are Sharing in the Media Sharing dialog box, and host mode is enabled by turning on Share My Media in the Media Sharing dialog box. As a client, WMP will stream media from other Windows Vista hosts that it finds on the network. As a host, WMP will stream media to other Windows Vista computers and devices on the network. It's important to note that Windows Media Sharing is completely separate from file and printer sharing. It uses a different set of protocols, only shares media files, and offers only read access to the files that are shared. Users cannot update files over Media Sharing.

When a user enables Media Sharing in host mode (Share My Media), a UPnP-based Media Server and Content Directory Service (CDS) are exposed on the network. These services respond to requests from DMR devices (or other WMPs in client mode) that are looking for Media Servers. To find a Media Server, a device will send out UPnP M-Search commands over UPnP multicast. When a server sees this on the network, it will respond directly to the device, notifying it that it is a Media Server. When the DMR has found a server, it will query that server directly using UPnP browse and search commands. The server responds to the browse and search commands, telling the DMR what content is available for playback on the device, and at what URL to access that content. The DMR can then request the content to be streamed from the server using the URL provided.

When a user enables Media Sharing in client mode (Find Media That Others Are Sharing), WMP will send out UPnP M-Search commands looking for available Media Servers that are sharing out content. After they are found, WMP will display these in the tree view pane of the player. Clicking the nodes will show available media that can be played.

UPnP is used for discovery of services and for browsing and searching the content of the discovered servers. In Windows Vista, the CDS will expose two transports for playing audio and video content: HTTP and RTSP/RTP. HTTP is always an offered transport for all types of media files. RTSP/RTP is offered when the server understands the format. For example, Windows Vista also offers MP3, WMA, and WMV over RTSP/RTP.

Windows Media Player by default will choose to play music files using HTTP and video files over RTSP/RTP. Streaming video over RTSP/RTP allows the video to be displayed better because it can offer better performance in home networks. If for some reason RTSP/RTP is not working (perhaps the required ports are blocked by a firewall), WMP will silently roll over to HTTP and try to receive the stream. It will then remember that RTSP/RTP failed, and always try HTTP for future requests, as long as WMP is running. To retry RTSP/RTP, just restart WMP.

James Walter, Lead Program Manager

Windows Media

Media Sharing and Windows Firewall

Enabling Media Sharing on a computer causes the following exceptions to be opened in Windows Firewall:

■ Windows Media Player (WMP)

■ Windows Media Player Network Sharing Service (WMPNSS)

Because enabling Media Sharing opens firewall exceptions, this task can be performed only by users who are administrators on their computers. A UAC prompt ensures that standard users cannot enable this feature unless they have been provided with the credentials for a local administrator account on their computers.

Caution   Because enabling Media Sharing opens firewall exceptions, this feature should be enabled only after consideration of the potential security risks.

The WMP exception opens inbound UDP traffic for all ports and for any IP address, as long as this traffic is directed to the process wmplayer.exe. The server-side firewall rules for WMPNSS are summarized in Table 17-8. Note that the scope for all the rules in this table is Local Subnet unless otherwise specified.

Table 17-8   Firewall Rules for the Server Side of the Windows Media Player Network Sharing Service (WMPNSS)

Rule Name	Port	Protocol	Binary	Notes
Windows Media Player Network Sharing Service (qWave-TCP-In)	2177	TCP	svchost.exe	Enables use of Quality Windows Audio Video Experience Service
Windows Media Player Network Sharing Service (qWave-UDP-In)	2177	UDP	svchost.exe	Enables use of Quality Windows Audio Video Experience Service
Windows Media Player Network Sharing Service (TCP-In)	Any	TCP	wmpnetwk.exe	Allows sharing traffic
Windows Media Player Network Sharing Service (UDP-In)	Any	UDP	wmpnetwk.exe	Allows sharing traffic
Windows Media Player Network Sharing Service (SSDP-In)	1900	UDP	svchost.exe	Allows use of Simple Service Discovery Protocol
Windows Media Player Network Sharing Service (UPnP-In)	2869	TCP	System	Allows use of Universal Plug and Play
Windows Media Player Network Sharing Service (Streaming-UDP-In)	*	UDP	wmplayer.exe	Allows UDP Media Streaming
Windows Media Player Network Sharing Service (HTTP-Streaming-In)	10243	TCP	System	Allows HTTP Media Streaming

In addition to the preceding firewall rules, note that ports 10243 and 2869 listed in Table 17-8 are used via HTTP.sys.

> **Note**   If you are using a third-party, host-based firewall on your Windows Vista computer, you might need to open the necessary ports manually to allow Windows Media Player Library Sharing to work properly.

Media Sharing and Windows Firewall in Windows XP

Windows Media Player 11 on Windows XP can also act as a Media Sharing host with the ability to share its library with DMR devices or Windows Vista computers (but not with other Windows XP computers—these can only share media, not consume it). However, Windows Vista's version of WMPNSS adds new features such as Quality of Service (QoS) using qWAVE and also advanced streaming using RTSP. (WMPNSS is version 4 on Windows Vista, compared to version 3 on XP.) The firewall rules for WMPNSS on XP are simpler than those needed for Windows Vista; these rules are summarized in Table 17-9. (The scope of these rules is again Local Subnet.)

Table 17-9   Firewall Rules for WMPNSS for Host-Side Windows Media Player 11 Running on Windows XP

Port	Protocol	Process	Notes
1900	UDP	SSDPsrv	Used for sending and receiving multicast announcements to enable device and service discovery
2869	TCP	SSDPsrv, UPnPHost	Used for retrieving device description and for making UPnP method invocations
10280–10284	UDP	wmpnetwk.exe	Used for determining Round Trip Time (RTT) between host and client
10243	TCP	wmpnetwk.exe	Used for HTTP streaming connections

Limitations of Media Sharing

Implementing Media Sharing in Windows Vista has limitations. In particular:

- Windows Vista computers must be on the same IP subnet to share media with one another. Media Sharing will not work across routers the way it is implemented in Windows Vista.

- Media Sharing requires *proximity* between the two computers involved (the computer sharing the media and the computer consuming the media) to share protected content within the local subnet. For clear content (in other words, not DRM-protected), however, proximity is not applicable and Media Sharing will share clear content to any device on the local subnet. Proximity is determined by exchanging a series of User Datagram Protocol (UDP) packets between the two computers to verify that the Round Trip Time (RTT) between the two computers over the network averages less than 7 milliseconds (msec). This limitation means that Media Sharing in Windows Vista can't be used for streaming media over a very large subnet, such as around a university campus. This RTT exchange between Windows Vista computers sharing and consuming media is known as Proximity Detection.

■ IPsec can prevent Proximity Detection from working on a network, which means that Media Sharing would be prevented from streaming content between Windows Vista computers.

 Note   Only protected content and music album art are restricted to WMDRM-ND validated devices. Device validation includes the RTT test.

What these limitations mean is that for small businesses or departments, Media Sharing in Windows Vista may be a useful tool for certain kinds of media streaming activities such as sharing training videos within an office. Enterprises that have more robust Media Sharing needs, however, should use Windows Media Services instead. Windows Media Services is a component of Windows Server 2003 and can be installed by adding the Streaming Media Server role using the Manage Your Server Wizard. For more information on how to configure this role in Windows Server 2003, see *http://technet2.microsoft.com/WindowsServer/en/ Library/f70088cc-f26b-4847-825b-28db053a92c51033.mspx?mfr=true* on Microsoft TechNet.

 Note   Media Sharing in Windows Vista is fully supported on both IPv4 and IPv6 networks.

Media Sharing and Network Categories

The initial configuration of Media Sharing in Windows Vista depends upon the current network category of the computer, which may be private, public, or domain. Specifically:

■ Media Sharing is never turned on by default; a user must always opt in. However, if the network category of the computer is Private, the Find Media That Others Are Sharing feature of Media Sharing is turned on, along with a notification process (wmpnscfg.exe). This is done primarily for home networks so that users can more easily find the Share Media feature and then share content between Windows Vista computers and DMR devices on a home network.

■ If the network category is public, turning on Media Sharing is dimmed in the sharing dialog box. If Media Sharing was previously turned on (when the network category was Private, for example) and the network category of the computer is switched to Public (traveling laptop), Media Sharing services are left running on the computer but the WMPNSS exception in Windows Firewall is automatically turned off to block sharing of media on the computer. The reason for this is that in public network situations—for example, at a WiFi hotspot in a coffee shop—the computer should not be sharing media files with other untrusted users on the network or over the Internet. However, an advanced user can share her media library on a Public network by manually opening the required firewall exceptions. For more information, see the sidebar titled "Direct from the Source: Media Sharing on Public Networks" later in this chapter.

■ If the network category of the computer is Domain, Media Sharing and Find Media That Others Are Sharing are turned off by default, but users with elevated privileges on their computers can manually turn Media Sharing on unless otherwise disabled by Group Policy. See the section titled "Managing Media Sharing with Group Policy" later in this chapter for more information. Note that with Media Sharing turned off by default, domain users will not receive the toast notifications that other computers or devices on the network have shared libraries they can access.

Caution   By default, Network And Sharing Center does not let you enable Media Sharing when your network category is Public. However, by manually opening the two firewall exceptions described previously, you can enable Media Sharing from a computer even when your network category is Public.

Direct from the Source: Media Sharing on Public Networks

Media Sharing in Windows Media Player is allowed in Private and Domain network categories. If the category is public, Windows Vista checks that the firewall is still set with the Windows Media Player (WMP) and Windows Media Player Network Sharing Service (WMPNSS) firewall exceptions to off. If that is the case, Windows Vista alerts the user that sharing is not permitted and explains the concerns of sharing on a public network. If the firewall ports have been opened (presumably by an advanced user who knows about firewalls), Windows Vista allows the user to share. This effectively allows the user to override defaults by manually opening the WMP and WMPNSS firewall exceptions.

James Walter, Lead Program Manager

Windows Media

Using Media Sharing

To enable media library sharing on a Windows Vista computer, follow these steps:

1. Open Windows Media Player.

2. On the Library tab, click the arrow to expose the options and then click Media Sharing.

3. Here you will see two options: Find Media That Others Are Sharing and Share My Media. Selecting the Find option shows other Windows Vista Media Servers on your network; selecting the Share option exposes your media library to others on your network.

4. Select the Share My Media check box and click OK.

5. Click Continue when the UAC prompt appears (for an administrator) or enter the password for an administrator account (for a standard user).

When media library sharing is enabled on a computer, a media device icon displaying both the computer name and user name appears in your Network folder. To view the properties of this icon, click Start, select Network, right-click the icon, and select Properties.

Additionally, you can start Media Sharing in three other places:

■ In the Windows Photo Gallery, under the File menu, choose Share With Devices.

■ In the Network And Sharing Center, in the Media Library Sharing area, click the Change button.

■ If the PC is on a private network, the notification process will start automatically (unless WMP has never been run). If we see a Digital Media Renderer on the network, we will display a notification. Clicking this notification and selecting Allow (to authorize that you want to share with the device) will also turn on Media Sharing.

Finding and Sharing Media

To find or share media that other Windows Vista users are sharing from their computers, follow these steps:

1. Start Windows Media Player.

2. Go through Windows Media Player Setup if you have not already done so.

3. From the toolbar, select Library and then select Media Sharing.

4. Do one of the following:

❑ Click Settings to choose which media you will share by default with other Windows Vista computers and DMR devices on your network. If you select the check box labeled Allow New Devices And Computers Automatically, any Windows Vista users or DMR devices on the network will be able to experience media files stored on the computer (provided that there are no DRM issues preventing them from doing so).

❑ Select the check box labeled Find Media That Others Are Sharing to locate other media libraries that have been shared on Windows Vista computers on your network (see Figure 17-3). You will be able to locate only media libraries for which the user of the remote computer has explicitly chosen to allow you to access (see the next option). This option is called the Browse function of Media Sharing (the computer acts as a client that consumes media libraries on host computers) and utilizes the UPnP protocol.

❑   Select the check box labeled Share My Media To in order to share your library with specific devices on your network. If no devices are currently visible in the box below this setting, no other DMR devices or Windows Vista computers with Media Sharing enabled are present on your network. This option is called the Share function of Media Sharing (the computer acts as a host that shares its media library with other client computers) and utilizes either the HTTP or RTSP protocols.

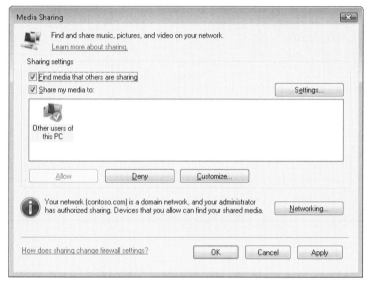

Figure 17-3   Sharing your media library.

Note that Windows Vista will usually automatically detect the presence of other Windows Vista computers on your network that have Media Sharing enabled and lead you through the steps of sharing your media library for users of those other computers to experience. A balloon tip will appear over the status area when Windows Vista has detected another Windows Vista computer that is trying to find shared libraries on the network. Clicking this balloon will bring up a dialog box saying that another device on the network wants to play content from your Windows Media Player library. By clicking Customize Sharing, you can allow or deny specific devices on your network to experience your media library; simply clicking Allow or Deny lets you choose whether to share your library with the device presently contacting you.

After you have shared your library with a device (see Figure 17-4), you can select the device and click Customize to specify what types of media should be shared with that particular device. You can also select the device and click Allow or Deny to allow or deny sharing of your media library with that particular device. You can also select the Other Users Of This PC icon and click Allow or Deny to allow or deny other users on the computer access to your media library.

Figure 17-4   Sharing your library with a specific device.

To play media from a shared library on another computer, follow these steps:

1. Expand the *Username* On *Computername* node representing the remote media library, which should be visible in the Navigation pane on the left side of Windows Media Player.

2. Select the type of media to play, such as All Video.

3. Double-click the media file you want to play.

Media Sharing and Network Traffic

Media Sharing is disabled by default for Windows Vista computers joined to a domain. Users can still enable Media Sharing, but administrators can choose to block users from enabling it. Some consideration must be given to how much network bandwidth this feature uses.

When users enable the Browse function of Media Sharing, their computers send out multicast UPnP announcements onto the network every few minutes. These announcements have a TTL of 1, however, so they are confined to the local subnet and are not likely to amount to a significant amount of traffic even if hundreds of computers are participating.

When a Windows Vista computer responds to multicast UPnP announcements from a Windows Vista computer that has its media library shared, a series of unicast UPnP exchanges takes place between the computers to exchange device documents and other information. While this adds to the previous traffic level, it is not significant enough to impact network performance.

But when users begin streaming media from shared libraries on other Windows Vista computers, the resulting HTTP or RTSP traffic can be excessive for some enterprise environments. For this reason, administrators of some enterprises may want to disable Media Sharing on Windows Vista computers, which can be done using Group Policy, as explained in the following section.

Direct from the Source: Media Sharing Notifications

Windows Vista will attempt to alert users that Media Sharing is a feature that is available, if Windows Vista finds DMRs on the network. The notification process is an .exe that runs as the local user. When a device sends out a UPnP M-Search command (to find media servers), Windows Vista will receive it, and the notification process will display a balloon alerting the user that WMP can share with the device. This is fantastic for a home network, but we cannot always be sure that a computer is on a home network.

Windows Vista will start the notification process every time a user connects to a Private network, including logging on while connected to a Private network. If the computer is joined to a domain, the notification process will not start. When a device is found, the notification process will wait 10 seconds before displaying a balloon and will only display a balloon once for any device found.

To make these notifications go away, the user can simply click the notification and select the Disable Future Notifications check box in the resultant dialog box. The user can also right-click the notification icon in the tray and choose Disable Future Notifications.

James Walter, Lead Program Manager

Windows Media

Managing Media Sharing with Group Policy

Media library sharing can be disabled in a domain environment by using Group Policy. To do this, open the GPO linked to the OU containing the targeted computers and enable the following policy setting:

Computer Configuration\Policies\Administrative Templates\Windows Components\Windows Media Player\Prevent Media Sharing

Enabling this policy prevents any users of the targeted computers from sharing their media libraries with other Windows Vista computers or with any other DMR devices on the network. This is the recommended setting in a domain environment unless an enterprise sees some specific need for enabling Media Sharing functionality on their network.

Troubleshooting Media Sharing

If a Windows Vista computer is experiencing difficulties sharing its media library or browsing other shared media libraries, you can troubleshoot by using the following procedure:

1. Check the System log in Event Viewer for events having Windows Media Player Network Sharing Service as the Source. These events can be used to determine whether or not the Media Sharing service has been successfully enabled on the computer, whether or not Proximity Detection has verified that the computer has proximity with a shared library, and so on. For example, the best RTT achieved is logged-on event ID 14208, and this information can be used to help you determine if network delays may be preventing media streaming from working properly on your network. If the events recorded in the System log indicate that Media Sharing is not enabled on the computer, try enabling it again using Network And Sharing Center or from Windows Media Player. If the best RTT recorded in event ID 14208 exceeds 7 msec, look for causes of excessive network latency on the subnet where the affected computers reside.

2. Verify that the appropriate exceptions are opened in Windows Firewall. If you are using a third-party, host-based firewall, be sure that the appropriate ports are opened as described in the section titled "Media Sharing and Windows Firewall" earlier in this chapter. If Media Sharing is still not working properly, try temporarily disabling the firewall on the affected computers and see if this resolves the problem. After you determine if the firewall is the source of the problem, re-enable the firewall and reconfigure the exceptions.

3. If Media Sharing still doesn't work properly, try stopping and starting the Windows Media Player Network Sharing Service on the affected computers. You can do this a couple of different ways. In WMP, in the Media Sharing dialog box, clear the Share check box and click OK. Wait a minute, go back into the dialog box, select the Share check box, and click OK. This will do more than just stop and start the service—it will also try to open the firewall ports in the Windows Firewall and try to set the ACLs on the files being shared so that the Network Service account has read access. (The Media Sharing Service runs as Network Service for security purposes.) You can also manually restart just the service, using either Services in Computer Management or by typing **net stop WMPNetworkSvc** followed by **net start WMPNetworkSvc** at the command prompt. Note that to stop and start the WMPNSS service, you must have administrator credentials on the computer.

4. If Media Sharing still doesn't work properly, it's probably because of Digital Rights Management (DRM) issues involving the media you're trying to experience. For example, the licenses for the media may not be updated on the computer where the media is stored. To check this, try playing the media file locally from the computer on which it is stored before sharing it out over the network. If the media can't be experienced locally because of DRM issues or any other reasons, it won't be accessible as shared media over the network either.

5. Check that the files you are trying to share to remote clients are in fact located on the local computer. Be sure that they are not on a remote file share. Remember that the Media Sharing Service runs as Network Service, whereas WMP runs as the current user. If the files are on a remote computer that the user has access to, they will play, but (most likely) the Network Service account will not have access to the remote file share.

Best Practices for Media Sharing

Although Media Sharing can be a useful tool for certain kinds of media streaming activities, such as sharing training videos within an office, enterprises that have more robust Media Sharing needs should use Windows Media Services instead to meet their media streaming needs. Windows Media Services is a component of Windows Server 2003 and can be installed by adding the Streaming Media Server role using the Manage Your Server Wizard.

Network traffic created by the Media Sharing feature itself is usually not a significant consideration in most environments. However, when users begin streaming media from shared libraries on other Windows Vista computers, the resulting HTTP or RTSP traffic can be excessive for some enterprise environments. For this reason, administrators of some enterprises may want to disable Media Sharing on Windows Vista computers, which can be done using Group Policy.

Summary

Windows Vista includes numerous enhancements in the area of file sharing functionality, and Windows Media Player 11, which is included with Windows Vista, has built-in support for media library sharing with nearby computers on the same subnet.

Additional Resources

The following resources contain additional information and tools related to this chapter.

Related Information

- Expert Zone Support WebCast "New Microsoft Windows Media Player 11" found at *http://support.microsoft.com/kb/919103/en-us* has more information about Media Sharing.

- "Access-Based Enumeration" white paper found at *http://www.microsoft.com/ windowsserver2003/techinfo/overview/abe.mspx*.

- KB 937624, "After you turn on User Account Control in Windows Vista, programs may be unable to access some network locations," found at *http://support.microsoft.com/kb/ 937624*.

- KB 934430, "Network connectivity may fail when you try to use Windows Vista behind a firewall device," found at *http://support.microsoft.com/kb/934430*.

- KB 947232, "Error message when you try to access an administrative share on a Windows Vista-based computer from another Windows Vista-based computer that is a member of a workgroup: 'Logon unsuccessful: Windows is unable to log you on'" found at *http://support.microsoft.com/?kbid=947232*.

On the Companion CD

- ConfigureFirewallForRemoteScripting.vbs
- ConfigureFirewallForSharedFolders.vbs
- CreateMultipleSharedFolders.vbs
- CreateMultipleSharedFoldersInActiveDirectory.vbs
- CreateShare.vbs
- CreateSharedFolders.vbs
- CreateShortcutToPublicDocs.vbs
- DeleteMultipleSharedFolders.vbs
- DeleteMultipleSharedFoldersInActiveDirectory.vbs
- DeleteSharedFolderInActiveDirectory.vbs
- DeleteSharedFolders.vbs
- ListSharedFolders.vbs
- ListSharedFoldersInActiveDirectory.vbs
- LogonScript.vbs
- ModifySharedFolders.vbs
- PublishSharedFolderInActiveDirectory
- SearchingForSharedFolderInActiveDirectory
- SharedFoldersAndLocalFolders

Chapter 18
Managing Windows Meeting Space

Windows Meeting Space is a lightweight collaboration tool that is built on the latest version of Microsoft's peer-to-peer (P2P) collaboration services included in Windows Vista. Meeting Space is designed to allow users to easily initiate and join collaboration sessions in domain, workgroup, and ad hoc wireless networking environments and is particularly intended for use by mobile users running Windows Vista on their wireless-enabled mobile PCs. Participants in a Meeting Space session can share files with each other and edit the files within a common work area, project their desktops or a selected application into the meeting space of another participant, project their desktops or a selected application onto a Windows Vista–ready network projector, and more. Meeting Space is designed to allow small groups of users to collaborate anytime and anywhere, and to do so more easily than if they were using traditional collaboration methods such as e-mailing or messaging documents to each other, uploading files to a network share or FTP site, exchanging documents using a USB key drive, and similarly cumbersome approaches. In addition, Meeting Space is designed to limit the risk of man-in-the-middle attacks and other forms of attacks against network sessions.

This chapter looks at how Meeting Space works and how to deploy, manage, and use it in enterprise environments. The chapter examines how Meeting Space interacts with Windows Firewall and People Near Me; how meetings are started and joined; and how Meeting Space is managed in domain, workgroup, and ad hoc wireless environments.

Understanding How Meeting Space Works

Meeting Space is built on three major Microsoft technologies:

- **Microsoft P2P Collaboration Services**   These services provide Meeting Space with the underlying technologies for peer discovery, group communication, and identifier to address resolution within the network environment. For more information on these services, see the section titled "Meeting Space and Microsoft P2P Collaboration Services" later in this chapter.

- **Distributed File Replication Services (DFRS)**   DFRS is the multithreaded, multiple-master replication engine originally used by the Windows Server platforms for server synchronization. It is now available on the client, and Meeting Space uses DFRS to enable meeting participants to share files with each other by replicating copies and any subsequent changes of the file to each participant.

- **Terminal Services**   These services provide Meeting Space with support for the Remote Desktop Protocol (RDP). This enables meeting participants to project applications or their entire desktops to other participants in a meeting by using Terminal Services Application Sharing. Meeting Space presentations use the Terminal Services ActiveX control to allow one participant to present an application or a desktop to other participants of a meeting.

 Note   Meeting Space uses Terminal Services to project applications onto another user's desktop. Meeting Space does not take over the other user's desktop when projecting applications, however.

Meeting Space and Microsoft P2P Collaboration Services

Microsoft's P2P network and collaboration technologies are designed to enable the next generation of peer-to-peer scenarios, including shared workspaces (such as Windows Meeting Space), distributed computing, and even load balancing. The P2P technologies allow users to securely communicate and share information with each other without requiring a central server to be involved. Microsoft's P2P networking services were first released as part of the Advanced Networking Pack for Windows XP, and were later included in Windows XP Service Pack 2 as an optional Windows component named Peer-to-Peer Networking. In Windows XP, Peer-to-Peer is found under Networking Services in Add/Remove Windows Components of the Add or Remove Programs CPL in Control Panel.

Because P2P technologies are designed to work in networking environments with transient connectivity—such as an ad hoc wireless network established between several laptops at a coffee shop—they cannot rely on the server-based Domain Name System (DNS) to perform name resolution between peers. Instead, P2P name resolution is based on the Peer Name Resolution Protocol (PNRP), a mechanism for distributed, serverless name resolution of peers in a P2P network. For more information on PNRP, see the section titled "Meeting Space and the Peer Name Resolution Protocol (PNRP)" later in this chapter.

Another P2P technology used by Meeting Space is P2P Grouping. Whereas PNRP is used for discovery of peers, P2P Grouping enables the actual communication between peers via a partition-detecting, secure mesh. P2P Grouping allows users to create secure "spheres of trust" that can be used for encrypted multiparty communications. For more information on this topic, see the section titled "How a Meeting Works" later in this chapter.

Direct from the Source: Windows Internet Computer Naming

Windows Meeting Space is just one of many experiences in Windows Vista that take advantage of the Windows Peer-to-Peer Networking Technologies. Another one is Windows Internet Computer Naming (WICN). With Windows Internet Computer Naming, you can make your computer resolvable over the Internet, much like DNS or DynDNS, but without having to sign up for a service. Windows Internet Computer Naming allows you to remote desktop into your own computer over the Internet, or even host your own website via IIS. A Windows Internet Computer Name works in most fields of Windows Vista that accept a resolvable name (such as Run dialog box, Internet Explorer, or ping). Learn more and try out this powerful feature today at *http://technet.microsoft.com/en-us/network/bb545868.aspx.*

Todd Manion, Program Manager

Windows Networking and Device Technologies

Meeting Space and IPv6

Since PNRP and P2P Grouping use IPv6 for network transport, Meeting Space is fundamentally an IPv6-only platform and one of the first Windows features that is IPv6-only in operation. However, because of the nature of IPv6 addressing and the IPv4/v6 transition technologies included in Windows Vista, Meeting Space also works without any further configuration on both wired and wireless IPv4 networks. Since the IPv6 protocol auto-assigns unique link-local addresses to all network interfaces of Windows Vista computers on the same network segment, all Windows Vista users on the same IPv4 subnet can join and participate in the same meeting. Users on different IPv4 subnets, however, cannot join the same meeting unless one of the following conditions is also met:

- Routers and gateways connecting subnets must be upgraded to support IPv6 or be replaced with IPv6-capable routers and gateways.

- An Intra-Site Automatic Tunnel Addressing Protocol (ISATAP) server must be deployed on your network to enable you to assign global IPv6 addresses to computers on your existing IPv4 network without having to upgrade any of your routers or any other

IPv4 networking support infrastructure. An ISATAP server essentially functions as a global IPv6 DHCP server and allows meeting participants to discover each other across IPv4 subnets by using global IPv6 addresses instead of link-local IPv6 addresses.

> **Note**   Windows Server 2003 can easily be deployed as an ISATAP server to provide global IPv6 connectivity that will enable Meeting Space to work across an enterprise. For more information on deploying ISATAP servers using Windows Server 2003, see the white paper "Intra-site Automatic Tunnel Addressing Protocol Deployment Guide" at *http://www.microsoft.com/downloads/details.aspx?familyid=0f3a8868-e337-43d1-b271-b8c8702344cd&displaylang=en*.

In addition, Meeting Space participants can join each other in meetings across the Internet using Teredo, another IPv4/v6 transition technology included in Windows Vista that enables IPv6 connectivity across the IPv4 Internet between computers that are located behind network address translators (NATs).

Meeting Space is built entirely upon IPv6 technologies for numerous reasons:

- Using IPv6 ensures that every meeting participant has a globally unique address, which facilitates holding meetings throughout an enterprise or across the Internet.

- IPv6 provides improved connectivity without the need for developers to code Teredo or other IPv4/v6 transition technology functionality into their collaborative applications.

- The ability of IPv6 to auto-assign link-unique IPv6 addresses without waiting for Auto-IP makes it possible for meetings to take place in ad hoc networking environments, such as in a workspace that has neither LAN nor wireless access point available.

- The native support in IPv6 for Security (IPsec) and Quality of Service (QoS) ensure that communications are secure and utilize bandwidth effectively.

- Using IPv6 ensures compliance with future national standards that mandate transition from IPv4 to IPv6 on government networks.

For more information on IPv6 support in Windows Vista, see Chapter 29, "Deploying IPv6."

> **Note**   Meeting Space cannot work across a router that uses Symmetric Network Address Translation (NAT). This is because Symmetric NAT is incompatible with IPv6. For more information, see *http://support.microsoft.com/kb/932134*.

Direct from the Source: Windows Meeting Space and IPv6

Though Windows Meeting Space is an IPv6 experience, don't think you need to upgrade your entire networking infrastructure! Windows Meeting Space was designed with IPv4 networks in mind, and it will work over your existing network. If your infrastructure does not have IPv6 capability yet, Windows Meeting Space will take advantage of the fact that Windows Vista has native support for IPv6 in the networking stack. This means that on your network, people will be able to use Windows Meeting Space with those nearby (on the same local subnet).

If you need to extend Windows Meeting Space and allow for remote participants, but don't want to buy new networking hardware, Windows Server 2003 has a solution: ISATAP, which assigns globally routable IPv6 addresses to a Windows Vista client. This solution allows Windows Meeting Space to be used by local and remote attendees in your corporate intranet. ISATAP is as scalable as DHCP, and just as low-maintenance—and you don't have to deploy DHCPv6 or enable IPv6 routing in your routers. For more information about ISATAP and how to set up an ISATAP router, please see the Microsoft TechNet Support WebCast "IPv6 Transition Technologies" found at *http://support.microsoft.com/ kb/923006* and the white paper of the same name found at *http://www.microsoft.com/ downloads/details.aspx?familyid=AFE56282-2903-40F3-A5BA-A87BF92C096D& displaylang=en.*

Todd Manion, Program Manager

Windows Networking and Device Technologies

Meeting Space and the Peer Name Resolution Protocol (PNRP)

PNRP works by utilizing multiple groupings of computers called *clouds*. These clouds correspond to two different scopes of IPv6 addresses:

- **Global clouds**   Any given computer will be connected to a single Global cloud. For computers with IPv6 Internet connectivity, the Global cloud is Internet-wide. In networks where computers do not have IPv6 Internet connectivity, but still have Global IPv6 addresses (such as firewalled corporate environments), the Global cloud is network-wide.

- **Link-local clouds**   One or more clouds, each corresponding to nodes within the same subnet or network link (link-local addresses and the link-local address scope).

Peer names in PNRP are static identifiers of endpoints that can be resolved to changing IP addresses, enabling P2P communications. Peer names can be computers, users, devices, groups, services, or anything that can be identified by an IPv6 address and port. Peer names are represented by *identifiers* (IDs) that are 32 bytes long and can be either unsecured (names that can be spoofed) or secured (names that cannot be spoofed because they are derived from a public/private key pair owned by the publisher).

Note   Windows Meeting Space uses only secured names.

The underlying name resolution functions on PNRP IDs within a cloud are stored in a distributed fashion in a cache on each peer within the cloud, with each peer's cache containing only a portion of the names for all the peers in the cloud. When a peer (the issuing peer) wants to resolve the name of another peer (the targeted peer) to its published address and port number, it follows these steps:

1. The issuing peer first consults its own PNRP cache for this information. If it finds this information, it sends a PNRP Request message to the targeted peer and waits for a response. These Request messages serve the function of enabling peers to communicate to other peers their active involvement within the cloud.

2. If the issuing peer does not find this information, it sends the Request message to the peer whose ID most closely matches (is closest numerically to) that of the targeted peer. The peer that receives this message then consults its own cache. If it finds a closer match or the match itself, it returns this information to the requesting peer. The requesting peer then goes to the returned peer and the process continues until the resolution succeeds or fails.

3. If the peer that receives this message does not find closer information in its cache, it returns the message to the issuing peer, indicating that it does not know the targeted peer. The issuing peer then repeats the previous step by sending a message to the peer whose ID next most closely matches that of the targeted peer. This process continues until the targeted peer is found (if present on the network) or not found (is no longer present within the cloud).

Looping is prevented by including in the Request message the list of peers that have already forwarded requests.

> **Note**   For more information on how Peer Name Resolution Protocol works, see the article titled "Introduction to Windows Peer-to-Peer Networking" found at *http://www.microsoft.com/technet/prodtechnol/winxppro/deploy/p2pintro.mspx* on Microsoft TechNet.

Meeting Space and People Near Me

Meeting Space makes use of People Near Me, a new feature of Windows Vista. People Near Me is a subnet-level system that enables users who are signed onto this service to automatically publish their availability onto the local subnet and discover other users using the Web Services Discovery (WS-Discovery) protocol. After users are published using People Near Me, they can be invited to start activities such as Windows Meeting Space.

People Near Me provides a framework for publication and discovery of identifying information that can be used to initiate and join collaboration activities such as Meeting Space. These collaboration activities are based upon Microsoft's Collaboration API as described in the

Windows SDK. (See *http://msdn2.microsoft.com/en-us/library/aa371044(VS.85).aspx* for more information.) By default, the identifying information published by People Near Me for a person includes:

- The person's nickname (human-readable text)
- The IPv6 address and port of the person's computer
- Computer name
- Any objects published via the API (by default, this is none)

> **Note**   For more information about People Near Me, see *http://technet.microsoft.com/en-us/library/bb726969.aspx* on Microsoft TechNet and *http://msdn2.microsoft.com/en-us/library/aa816479(VS.85).aspx* on MSDN.

Meeting Space Services

When Meeting Space is first set up on a Windows Vista computer, the following Peer-to-Peer services are started:

- Peer Networking Identity Manager service (p2pimsvc)
- Peer Networking Grouping service (p2psvc)
- Peer Name Resolution Protocol service (PNRPsvc)

Other services may also be started on demand during the meeting. For example, when a meeting is started, the user is signed into People Near Me, which starts the user-level service P2PHost. And when a meeting is created, the DFS Replication service (DFSR.exe) is started to handle the replication folder for the length of the meeting. (When a meeting is finished, the DFS Replication service continues listening if some other running application or service is using the service; otherwise, the service does not listen.)

> **Note**   P2Psvc and PNRPsvc will also stop listening if they are not in use. People Near Me will remain active until the user chooses to sign out of the service.

Meeting Space and Windows Firewall

Using Meeting Space on Windows Vista computers requires that several exceptions be opened in Windows Firewall:

- **Windows Peer To Peer Collaboration Foundation**   This exception is enabled when you first sign in to People Near Me so that your peer name can be published for others to see, and so that you can see names of others who are available for collaboration. This

exception must be enabled for the following two P2P protocols to function properly
(see Table 18-1 for more details of the firewall rules involved in this exception):

❑ **Peer Name Resolution Protocol (PNRP)**   Discussed earlier in this chapter, this
protocol enables peer names to find each other in ad hoc environments without
the need for centralized name resolution services such as DNS.

❑ **Simple Service Discovery Protocol (SSDP)**   This protocol forms the basis of the
discovery protocol used by Universal Plug and Play (UPnP) and is used by PNRP.

■ **Windows Meeting Space**   This exception is enabled when you first set up Meeting
Space by running Meeting Space for the first time on your computer. This exception
must be enabled for Meeting Space participants to join meetings and collaborate.
(See Table 18-2 for more details of the firewall rules involved in this exception.) For
information on how to set up Meeting Space, see the section titled "Using Meeting
Space" later in this chapter.

■ **Connect To A Network Projector**   This exception is enabled when you first set up
Meeting Space by running Meeting Space for the first time on your computer. This
exception must be enabled for Meeting Space participants to use Web Services Discovery
Application Programming Interface (WS-Discovery API or WSDAPI) to connect to a
network projector over wired or wireless networks. (See Table 18-3 for more details of
the firewall rules involved in this exception.)

**Table 18-1   Firewall Rules for the Windows Peer To Peer Collaboration Foundation
Exception**

Rule Name	Port	Protocol	Process	Notes
Windows Peer to Peer Collaboration Foundation (PNRP-In)	3540	UDP	svchost.exe (prnpsvc)	Used for enabling peer name resolution using PNRP
Windows Peer to Peer Collaboration Foundation (SSDP-In)	1900	UDP	svchost.exe (ssdpsrv)	Used for enabling SSDP
Windows Peer to Peer Collaboration Foundation (TCP-In)	All TCP ports	TCP	p2phost.exe	Used for enabling inbound TCP connections
Windows Peer to Peer Collaboration Foundation (WSD-In)	3702	UDP	p2phost.exe	Used for enabling device discovery using WSDAPI

Table 18-2   Firewall Rules for the Windows Meeting Space Exception

Rule Name	Port	Protocol	Process	Notes
Windows Meeting Space (DFSR-In)	5722	TCP	dfsr.exe	Used for enabling inbound DFS replication traffic
Windows Meeting Space (P2P-In)	3587	TCP	svchost.exe (p2psvc)	Used for enabling inbound P2P traffic

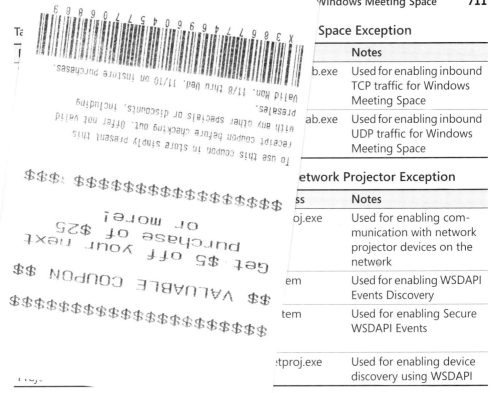

	Space Exception
	Notes
b.exe	Used for enabling inbound TCP traffic for Windows Meeting Space
ab.exe	Used for enabling inbound UDP traffic for Windows Meeting Space

	etwork Projector Exception
ss	**Notes**
oj.exe	Used for enabling communication with network projector devices on the network
em	Used for enabling WSDAPI Events Discovery
tem	Used for enabling Secure WSDAPI Events
tproj.exe	Used for enabling device discovery using WSDAPI

Receipt coupon (upside-down):

$$ VALUABLE COUPON $$
Get $5 off your next
purchase of $25
or more!

To use this coupon in store simply present this receipt coupon before checking out. Offer not valid with any other specials or discounts, including presales.

Valid Mon. 11/8 thru Wed. 11/10 on in store purchases.

Meeting Space and Security

Besides the Windows Firewall exceptions that must be opened to enable Meeting Space to work, security is built into Meeting Space in several ways. The fundamental, or root level, of security in Meeting Space is the passphrase specified by a user when he creates a new meeting. Meeting Space is thus comparable to a telephone conference call in which the person initiating the call communicates a passcode to the others who need to join the call. The passphrase for a Meeting Space meeting must be communicated ahead of time and out-of-band from the actual meeting, in the same way that the passcode for a conference call must be communicated ahead of time and out-of-band from the conference call. It is important to note that by default this passphrase must be as secure as a passphrase a user must use for a login and/or at least eight characters.

Another layer of security in Meeting Space is that all communication channels between participants of a meeting are encrypted. Secure Sockets Layer (SSL) encryption technologies are used to encrypt these channels to provide private communication between participants of a meeting. In addition, each piece of data sent via the P2PGrouping channel is signed by the publisher.

The final layer of security comes into play when ad hoc wireless network connections are established between participants of a meeting—for example, in a meeting room where no access point is present. Wired Equivalent Privacy (WEP) encryption is used in this situation, and WEP is then encrypted again using other technologies to ensure that the session is secure.

Direct from the Source: Windows Meeting Space Security

Important aspects of security in Meeting Space include encryption, password strength, controlling what can be shared, and how the file sharing part handles the issue of viruses. Let's look briefly at each of these issues.

Encryption

Windows Meeting Space security roots to the password created by the creator at the beginning of a meeting. When they are in the meeting, users communicate with each other over the metadata and file channels using 128-bit SSL to ensure that other individuals on the network cannot view their unencrypted communications. The streaming channel uses the same security encryption as Remote Desktop and is just as secure. All 1:1 communication (via sending notes) is encrypted from the other participants using the participant's security credentials (public/private key pairs), also over 128-bit SSL. Finally, when using ad hoc wireless, the layer 2 security protocol is WEP, and all other communication is again encrypted using the aforementioned security scheme.

Password Strength

By default, Windows Meeting Space requires passwords to be the equivalent strength of a domain user account password. This requirement can be turned off for the entire Peer Grouping infrastructure and thus for Windows Meeting Space. When this requirement is disabled, passwords for meetings must be at least eight characters in length. Note also that changing your password strength domain policy will change the password strength requirement for Windows Meeting Space and the Peer Group infrastructure.

Controlling What Can be Shared

Windows Meeting Space abides by the rules set up for the Attachment Manager. This allows you to limit the file types that can be shared via Windows Meeting Space in the same way that you limit the file types that can be sent via an e-mail client such as Windows Mail. For more information on configuring the file types that can be shared via the Attachment Manager, see Microsoft Knowledge Base article 883260 at *http://support.microsoft.com/kb/883260*.

File Sharing Part and Viruses

The file sharing part replicates every aspect of the file at the file driver level. This means that if a virus is detected in a file, an installed virus scanner will have an opportunity to clean the file before it writes to disk. What's even better is that the cleaned file will then be replicated to all participants—each user will have the clean file in his or her Windows Meeting Space instance.

Todd Manion, Program Manager

Windows Networking and Device Technologies

How a Meeting Works

Communication channels (or *channels*) form the basis for participation between participants of a meeting. Meeting Space utilizes three different kinds of channels:

- **Metadata Channel**   Used for overall communication and coordination of presence information in a meeting, ghosting information for files, and distribution of any setup information for the other two channels. This channel utilizes the P2P Grouping technology.

- **File Channel**   Used for replicating user documents and other files between participants using FRS so that they can collaborate by jointly editing copies of these files.

- **Streaming Channel**   Used for projecting applications or a user's desktop to other participants in a meeting or to a nearby network projector device using a Terminal Services stream.

The process for starting a meeting and using it to collaborate with other participants works as follows:

1. A metadata channel is created to publish presence for the new meeting. Simultaneously, a file channel is created to facilitate document sharing between participants.

2. The file channel password is put into the metadata channel so that users who join the meeting can share and receive shared files.

3. When another user joins the meeting, he presents his password and is then authorized to join the metadata channel.

4. The user then queries the metadata channel for the file channel password (a GUID) and then joins the file channel.

5. When a user shares a file, the file is put into the file channel and the metadata for the file is replicated via the metadata channel to everyone so that they can see a description of the file displayed.

6. When a user projects an application or her desktop, a streaming channel is created for that application. RDP projects the application to a participant only if the participant chooses to tune in to the presentation.

For more information, see the section titled "Using Meeting Space" later in this chapter.

Note   Meeting Space is included in all Windows Vista SKUs except for the Starter Edition. In addition, users with the Home Basic Edition can join an existing meeting but cannot start a new meeting.

Direct from the Source: How Windows Meeting Space Works

Windows Meeting Space is actually based on the Windows Peer-to-Peer Grouping technology. A meeting starts with a name and a password set by the creator of the meeting. This password must be at least eight characters in length and by default must meet the security policy of the computer the meeting is being created on. After the meeting is created, a Peer Group and associated metadata channel is created. This channel acts as the overall control channel for activities in the meeting. After the metadata channel is created, the creator also creates a file channel and puts the file channel password into the metadata channel. (A file channel password is a GUID.) The meeting is now ready for people to join.

When someone joins a meeting, he presents the password to the creator (or someone else in the meeting if there are multiple participants), and the creator does a password check. If the password is correct, the creator issues the invitee a Peer Group certificate to join the meeting. The invitee then uses that certificate to connect to the metadata channel, publishing his presence and user tile information. Next, he joins the file channel using the password specified in the metadata channel. This process repeats for each person joining the meeting.

During a meeting, participants can do one of three activities: add a file, share an application or desktop, or pass notes. When a user adds a file, she first adds a metadata record to the metadata channel to alert participants that the file is coming. Then she adds the file to the file channel. The file is then replicated using the Distributed File System Replication (DFSR) technology. The file is then replicated to each person's computer. If a user decides to share an application or her desktop, the user first creates a streaming channel. Then she publishes a sharing record to the metadata channel. This record contains the ticket needed to join the streaming channel. All participants receive the ticket and then connect to the streaming channel using the Terminal Services Collaboration technology and Remote Desktop Protocol. Finally, when a user sends a note to another participant, a 1:1 connection is made based on the metadata channel, and the text is then sent to a particular participant.

Todd Manion, Program Manager

Windows Networking and Device Technologies

Limitations of Meeting Space

Meeting Space is essentially a lightweight collaboration tool that has the following limitations:

- Meetings are limited to about 10 participants.
- Participants must be on the same IPv4 subnet if their computers do not have globally routable IPv6 addresses.

- Participants cannot share audio or video information—Meeting Space is optimized only for file transport and application sharing, not audio/video sharing.

- Remoting of DirectX is not supported.

- Sessions cannot be saved for later replay.

- Webcams and VOIP are not supported.

- Meetings cannot be moderated—that is, the meeting initiator cannot prevent participants from sharing files or launching presentations and cannot eject an unruly participant from a meeting.

- Interoperability with Microsoft NetMeeting is not supported.

Enterprises that need a more robust and scalable collaboration platform than Meeting Space can use either Microsoft Office Communications Server 2007 (*http://office.microsoft.com/ en-us/communicationsserver/default.aspx*) or Microsoft Office Live Meeting 2007 (*http://office.microsoft.com/en-us/livemeeting/FX101729061033.aspx*).

Note   Although Microsoft recommends that Meeting Space sessions include no more than 10 participants, this is not a hard limit built into the technology. This limitation to 10 participants is mainly a recommendation based on the performance limitations of using Meeting Space on typical Windows Vista computers and on the complexity of accomplishing useful work through serverless collaboration when too many individuals are involved.

Windows Meeting Space vs. Microsoft Office Live Meeting

The big brother of Windows Meeting Space within the sphere of Microsoft's P2P collaborative applications is Microsoft Office Live Meeting. A good way to compare these two platforms is to think of Live Meeting as the "Microsoft Office Word" of Windows collaborative technologies, while Meeting Space is the "Notepad" of these technologies. Live Meeting is intended mainly for structured collaboration between groups of remote participants over the Internet, and its fee-based structure and close integration with Microsoft Office products make it an excellent choice for businesses that need a collaboration tool that supports up to 2,500 users. (Live Meeting requires a live Internet connection for each user, because it uses a central server to provide collaboration services to clients.)

Meeting Space, on the other hand, supports only about 10 concurrent users, doesn't require live Internet connectivity (ad hoc wireless will do), is free, and is not integrated with Microsoft Office. Meeting Space is thus intended more for informal collaboration between small groups of users, but it can still be useful within many enterprise environments. In addition, there can be no presence relationship between participants using Meeting Space and Live Meeting, so these two platforms cannot interoperate. Finally, Meeting Space cannot interoperate with Microsoft NetMeeting, an older Microsoft collaboration technology that has been removed with Windows Vista.

Deploying and Managing Meeting Space

Meeting Space is designed to work out of the box with little or no configuration. This section covers deploying and managing Meeting Space in workgroup, domain, and ad hoc environments.

Managing Meeting Space in a Workgroup Environment

Implementing Meeting Space in a workgroup environment requires no initial configuration other than configuring People Near Me on users' computers and performing the initial Meeting Space setup. See the section titled "Using Meeting Space" later in this chapter for more information.

Managing Meeting Space in a Domain Environment

The primary tool for configuring Meeting Space in a domain environment is Group Policy. Tables 18-4 and 18-5 list the computer and user policies that can be used to configure Meeting Space. This includes two kinds of policies:

- **Policies for configuring Meeting Space**   Both computer and user policies are available, and these are found under Computer Configuration\Policies\Administrative Templates \Windows Components\Windows Meeting Space and under User Configuration\ Policies\Administrative Templates\Windows Components\Windows Meeting Space. See Table 18-4 for a description of these policies.

- **Policies for configuring Microsoft Peer-to-Peer Networking Services**   The computer policies for configuring the P2P services that underlie the operation of Meeting Space are found under Computer Configuration\Policies\Administrative Templates\ Network\Microsoft Peer-to-Peer Networking Services. See Table 18-5 for a description of these policies.

Table 18-4   Computer and User Policies for Configuring Meeting Space

Policy	Description
Turn Off Windows Meeting Space	Enable this policy to prevent users from using Meeting Space to collaborate. Use this policy if you are using a different collaboration tool or want to ensure that users only share information using other methods, such as storing documents on network shares or sending them as attachments by e-mail. The default is for users to be allowed to run Meeting Space on their computers.
Turn On Meeting Space Auditing	Enable this policy to log events such as starting a meeting, joining a meeting, or launching a presentation. These events have the Source name Meeting Space and are logged in the Operational Log for Meeting Space in Event Viewer, which is found under Applications and Services Logs\Microsoft\Windows\MeetingSpace. For more information about using Event Viewer, see Chapter 22, "Maintaining Desktop Health."

Table 18-5   Policies for Configuring Microsoft Peer-to-Peer Networking Services and Peer Name Resolution Protocol

Policy	Description
Disable Password Strength Validation For Peer Grouping	By default, this policy is disabled, which means Meeting Space tests the strength of the passphrase specified for a new meeting against the password policy for the domain, and passphrases that are weaker than those that are allowed for domain logon passwords are not allowed. Enable the policy if you want to allow a weak passphrase (minimum of eight characters) to be used for launching meetings. Note that this policy applies to any application that uses P2P Grouping technology.
Turn Off Microsoft Peer-To-Peer Networking Services	Enabling this policy will prevent Meeting Space from running. However, the preferred method of doing this is to use the Turn Off Windows Meeting Space policy.
Peer Name Resolution Protocol\Link-Local Clouds\Turn Off Multicast Bootstrap Site-Local Clouds\Turn Off Multicast Bootstrap Global Clouds\Turn Off Multicast Bootstrap	This policy setting is not supported at this time and may be supported in future platform versions.
Peer Name Resolution Protocol\Link-Local Clouds\Set The Seed Server Site-Local Clouds\Set The Seed Server Global Clouds\Set The Seed Server	This policy is not supported at this time and may be supported in future platform versions.

> **Note**   To display your current seed server configuration, type **netsh p2p pnrp cloud show initialization** at a command prompt.

Additional Group Policy Settings for Meeting Space

If you want to allow users to use Meeting Space to collaborate, but you want to prevent them from replicating copies of files to each other, use Group Policy to disable the DFSR service on their computers. To do this, navigate to Computer Configuration\Policies\Windows Settings\Security Settings\System Services and set the DFS Replication service to Disabled.

If you want to prevent meeting participants from connecting to a network projector device on your network, use Group Policy to navigate to User Configuration\Policies\Administrative Templates\Windows Components\Network Projector and enable the policy setting Turn Off Connect To A Network Projector. A machine version of this policy is also presented in the corresponding location.

Managing Meeting Space in an Ad Hoc Wireless Environment

In Windows Vista, the process of establishing an ad hoc wireless network has been integrated into the Meeting Space experience. This means that users who want to collaborate wirelessly without the presence of an access point can simply use the Meeting Space user interface to set up a new session and have other users join them by using Meetings Near Me—all without having to start the experience from the networking user interface or configure anything. Users who want to collaborate wirelessly using Meeting Space in an ad hoc environment are not required to understand ad hoc wireless networking or how it is configured.

> **Note**   Ad hoc meetings are possible only if your computer's wireless network adapter supports computer-to-computer connections and if IPv6 has not been disabled on your computer. (IPv6 is enabled by default in Windows Vista.) Also, ad hoc meetings can be joined only by using Meetings Near Me—you cannot invite others to join an ad hoc meeting because the network doesn't exist yet, and you have no way to identify it in the invitation.

How It Works: Ad Hoc Wireless Meetings

One of the features asked about most is our integration with ad hoc wireless. This is a very cool feature that allows users to use Windows Meeting Space any time, anywhere—as long as they have an ad hoc wireless–capable NIC (which is almost every wireless card). The flow for creating/joining an ad hoc wireless meeting is the same from a user experience standpoint as on a wired network, but it differs during the creation/joining technical process.

When a user creates an ad hoc wireless meeting, he first creates an ad hoc wireless network. This network name is always the bar character ("|") plus the meeting name. The user doesn't enter the bar character; Windows Meeting Space inserts it automatically. When a user attempts to join a meeting, the user starts Windows Meeting Space and his computer starts to look for meetings nearby. Meetings Near Me looks for meetings on the network and for ad hoc wireless networks that start with the "|" character. This indicates to the Meetings Near Me infrastructure that this ad hoc wireless network has a meeting on it. The user then enters the password and joins the meeting.

Todd Manion, Program Manager

Windows Networking and Device Technologies

Using Meeting Space

Using Meeting Space involves initiating new sessions and having others join the meeting using Meetings Near Me or by sending them a meeting invitation that they can respond to. After a session is underway, participants can collaborate by sharing files, projecting applications, and so on. Prior to using Meeting Space on your computer, you must first set it up and configure settings for People Near Me on your computer.

Setting Up Meeting Space

Before Meeting Space can be used on a Windows Vista computer, it must first be set up. Setting up Meeting Space involves opening exceptions in Windows Firewall, and this can only be done by an administrator. After Meeting Space is set up, users can run Meeting Space without administrative credentials.

Meeting Space can be set up in two ways:

- Manually by a user on the computer (requires administrator credentials on the local computer)

- Remotely by a network administrator

Caution   Setting up Meeting Space on Windows Vista computers requires administrative privileges on these computers. This is because exceptions need to be opened in Windows Firewall and only an administrator (or a standard user who has access to administrator credentials) can do this. Opening additional ports in your firewall increases the attack surface of your system and should be done only after careful consideration.

Manually Setting Up Meeting Space

To set up Meeting Space manually on a computer, follow these steps:

1. Click Start, click All Programs, and then click Windows Meeting Space.

2. Confirm that you want to set up Meeting Space by clicking Yes, Continue Setting Up Meeting Space.

3. Respond to the UAC prompt displayed after the previous step. If you are an administrator on your computer, click Continue; if you are a Standard user, you need to specify credentials for an Administrator account on your computer.

You can also set up Meeting Space by typing "**C:\Program Files\Windows Collaboration\WinCollab.exe**" at a command prompt.

Note   Note that if you have previously set up Meeting Space and then closed one or more of the Windows Firewall ports needed by this application, running Meeting Space will begin the Meeting Space setup process again, which reopens the ports needed.

Remotely Setting Up Meeting Space

Setting up Meeting Space remotely involves two steps. (These steps can be done in either order.)

■ Use Group Policy to enable the Windows Firewall exceptions needed by Meeting Space. See the section titled "Meeting Space and Windows Firewall" earlier in this chapter for more information on the firewall exceptions used by Meeting Space. See Chapter 27, "Configuring Windows Firewall and IPsec," for more information on how to configure Windows Firewall using Group Policy.

■ Configure file replication permissions by configuring the Windows Management Instrumentation (WMI) service on the remote computer. To configure this, follow these steps:

1. Open Computer Management on the local computer.

2. Right-click the root node and select Connect To Another Computer.

3. Type the name of the remote computer or browse Active Directory to select it.

4. Expand the Services And Applications node to show WMI Control.

5. Double-click WMI Control. Then, right-click WMI Control and click Properties.

6. Click the Security tab and expand the Root node.

7. Select the MicrosoftDfs node and click the Security button.

8. Click Add, type **INTERACTIVE**, click Check Names, and click OK.

9. Select the ACE for INTERACTIVE.

10. Select the Allow check boxes for the following permissions: Execute Methods, Provider Write, Enable Account, and Read Security.

11. Close all properties pages by clicking OK.

> **Note**   A script can be created to automate the preceding process. For more information on creating such scripts, please see Microsoft Knowledge Base article 325353 at *http://support .microsoft.com/kb/325353.*

Configuring People Near Me

People Near Me is the discovery and publishing framework used by Meeting Space to find other users who are available for meetings and also to publish your own availability to accept invitations to meetings initiated by others. Configuring People Near Me requires administrative rights; however, standard users can run People Near Me after it has been configured. Configuring People Near Me can be done manually prior to starting or joining your first meeting, or it can be done automatically as part of the process of starting or joining your first meeting.

To configure People Near Me manually on your computer, follow these steps:

1. Open Control Panel and select the Network And Internet group of CPLs.

2. Click the People Near Me CPL and then click the Settings tab.

3. Specify a display name that will be used to represent you in Meeting Space meetings. Note that there is no restriction on display names in People Near Me, and two users on the same network can have the same display names. So when you invite someone from your People Near Me list to a meeting, be sure that you are inviting the right person.

4. Optionally, specify a picture that will be sent to trusted contacts when you invite them to a meeting.

5. Select which users are allowed to send you invitations. This can include:

   ❏ **Anyone**   Any user can invite you to a meeting.

   ❏ **Trusted Contacts**   These are users from whom you have received .contact files and have imported these files into your Windows Contacts folder, the successor to the Windows Address Book (WAB) on earlier versions of Windows. For more information about sharing contacts, see the sidebar titled "How It Works: Trusted Contacts" later in this chapter.

   ❏ **No One**   No user can invite you to a meeting.

6. Specify whether you want to be notified when someone invites you to a meeting.

7. Select the Sign Me In Automatically When Windows Starts check box if you want Windows to sign you in to People Near Me whenever you start your computer. Selecting this check box will enable you to receive invitations to meetings whenever you are logged on to Windows, provided that you have specified earlier that receiving invitations from others is allowed.

8. Click the Sign In tab of the properties sheet.

9. Select the option labeled Sign In To People Near Me if you want to sign in to the service immediately so that you can begin sending out invitations or responding to invitations from others.

10. Click OK twice.

11. If prompted, respond to the UAC prompt displayed after you click OK in the previous step. If you are an administrator on your computer, click Continue; if you are a Standard user, you need to specify credentials for an Administrator account on your computer.

An icon representing People Near Me will now be visible in the System Tray to indicate that you are signed on to this service. Double-clicking this icon lets you reconfigure People Near Me as desired.

Enabling People Near Me on Windows Vista computers requires administrative privileges on these computers. This is because an exception needs to be opened in Windows Firewall and only an administrator (or a Standard user who has access to Administrator credentials) can do so. If desired, a domain administrator can allow users to configure People Near Me manually on their computers without the intervention of a UAC prompt by using Group Policy to open the Windows Peer-To-Peer Collaboration Foundation exceptions in Windows Firewall on the computers targeted by the GPO.

Caution   Opening additional ports in your firewall increases the attack surface of your system and should be done only after careful consideration.

How It Works: Trusted Contacts

The People Near Me and Application Invitation platform components allow users to invite people nearby into activities or applications like Windows Meeting Space. The People Near Me platform allows you to discover both people you know (trusted contacts) or people you don't know (untrusted contacts). During an invitation experience, like the Invitation experience in Windows Meeting Space, the platform is able to disambiguate invitations from individuals and let the user know if a contact is trusted. This is a great security feature of the platform and allows users to accept only invitations from people they trust rather than from those they don't.

To make a person a trusted contact, you need to do two things:

1. Export your "me" contact from the Windows Contacts Explorer.

2. Have someone add your contact to his or her Windows Contacts folder. By importing the received contact, the person is implicitly making the received contact a trusted contact in the People Near Me platform.

To export the "me" contact, follow these steps:

1. Click Start, click Control Panel, click Network And Internet, and then click People Near Me.

2. Set up People Near Me.

3. Click Start, click All Programs, and then click Windows Contacts.

4. Do one of the following:

   ❑ Right-click the "me" contact (the contact with the generic person as an overlay) and select Send Contact. This will place the contact in an e-mail so that you can send it to someone else.

   ❑ Select the "me" contact and drag it into a file share or an instant messaging program such as Windows Live Messenger.

To import the contact to make him or her a trusted contact, follow these steps:

1. Click Start, click All Programs, and then click Windows Contacts.

2. Go to the location of the received contact.

3. Select the received contact and drag it into the Windows Contacts folder.

After you have followed these steps, the contact will be labeled as a trusted contact in the preview pane of the Windows Contacts explorer. The platform will now recognize that contact as a trusted contact, and the user can be sure the person inviting him is really the person he trusts in his Windows Contacts.

Todd Manion, Program Manager

Windows Networking and Device Technologies

Starting a New Meeting

After People Near Me has been configured and Meeting Space is set up, starting Meeting Space will display the Meeting Space user interface and give you the choice of either starting a new meeting or joining an existing meeting nearby (Figure 18-1).

Figure 18-1   The opening screen of the Meeting Space user interface.

To start a new meeting, follow these steps:

1. Click Start A New Meeting.

2. Accept the default display name for the meeting (your name followed by the current time) and type a passphrase for the meeting.

3. Click Options and configure visibility and networking options as needed. Visibility options let you hide the meeting from others, so that only those who receive your invitations know of its existence. Networking options let you create a private ad hoc

wireless network with other Meeting Space users in your location, provided that your computer has the necessary wireless networking capability.

4. Click the green Go button to start the new meeting.

Joining a Meeting

The easiest way to join a meeting is by using Meetings Near Me. When you start Meeting Space, the Join A Meeting Near Me option is selected by default. If any meetings are currently underway nearby, a list of available meetings will be displayed on the right side (Figure 18-2). This list will include any ad hoc wireless meetings that are available to join. To check any time whether additional meetings have become available to join, click Update List. To join the meeting, simply select the item and enter the password communicated by the creator.

Figure 18-2   Joining a meeting using Meetings Near Me.

Another way to join a meeting is to respond to the prompt that appears when you receive a notification concerning a meeting you've been invited to. This notification says, "Someone is inviting you to use Windows Meeting Space" and can be either viewed (in case you want to accept), declined (the sender is told that you have declined), or dismissed (the sender is not informed that you have not accepted the invitation). Clicking View displays the details of the invitation, which show who it is from. Note that you have only a limited time (5 minutes) to respond to an invitation before it expires and your only option becomes Dismiss. To accept the invitation and enter the meeting, click Accept. See the next section in this chapter for information on how to invite others to your meeting.

> **Note**   To reconfigure your People Near Me settings at any time from within a meeting, click the drop-down arrow beside your name in the Participants section of the Meeting Space user interface and then select Personal Settings.

You can also join a meeting by double-clicking a meeting invitation you've received via e-mail or instant messaging, or one that is stored in a shared folder on the network.

To leave a meeting you've joined, click Meeting and then click Leave Meeting from the Meeting Space toolbar. Anyone can leave a meeting after he or she has been initiated, including the individual who started the meeting.

> **Note**   People Near Me and Meetings Near Me work only on the local subnet. To join a meeting that isn't on your subnet, you will need a file- or e-mail–based invitation from the meeting creator.

Inviting Others to Your Meeting

When you start a new meeting, you can invite others to join it. To send an invitation to someone in your People Near Me list from your initial meeting screen, follow these steps:

1.   In Windows Meeting Space, click Invite.

2.   In the Invite People dialog box, select the check boxes beside the people you want to invite. The people displayed in this dialog box are those currently in your People Near Me list—nearby Windows Vista users who are signed in to People Near Me.

3.   If you want people to be able to accept your meeting invitation without knowing the passphrase for the meeting, clear the check box labeled Require Participants To Type The Meeting Passphrase. Leaving this check box selected means that you will need to tell the participants the password. If you clear the check box, someone else on your network might be able to impersonate the intended invitee, because People Near Me does not provide security. However, because you will typically be communicating with the people in the meeting and they might even be in the same room, the risk of this is minimal.

4.   Click Send Invitations to send out invitations to the people you select. A notification will be received by the targets of your invitation. See the section titled "Joining a Meeting" earlier in this chapter for more information.

Meeting participants can also invite others to join a meeting by sending their initiations using e-mail or by saving invitations as a file and sending it using Windows Messenger or storing it on a network share. Invitation (*.wcinv) files are Unicode XML files that contain information such as the peer name, the PNRP cloud to which the peer belongs, and the IPv6 address of the peer (this is the address for the Teredo Tunneling Pseudo-Address if Meeting Space is being used on an IPv4 LAN). An example of an invitation file follows:

```
1.0 JackyChen 7d6/7/4/14/11/1f/37/121
<PEERINVITATIONVERSION="1.1">
    <CLOUDNAME>Global_</CLOUDNAME>
    <SCOPE>GLOBAL</SCOPE>
    <CLOUDFLAGS>1</CLOUDFLAGS>
    <GROUPPEERNAME>aa33253f6a621e1a877724e784632f4da7fbc3c7.WindowsCollaboration
        </GROUPPEERNAME>
    <GROUPFRIENDLYNAME>JackyChen12:31PM</GROUPFRIENDLYNAME>
</PEERINVITATION>1[3ffe:831f:4136:e37e:28d4:53:31d2:bfce]:3587;
```

Collaborating Within a Meeting

After a meeting has been started and joined by others, participants can use the Meeting Space user interface to share documents from your PC and edit copies of them together (only one participant at a time can edit a shared document, and only the copy of the document in the meeting space is modified during the process), start a shared session to share a program or your desktop, connect to a network projector to do a presentation, double-click a participant's People Near Me icon to create a quick note (you can even use Ink if you have a Tablet PC) and privately send it to that participant, invite others to join the meeting, change your availability status (to Busy, for example), and more. For more information on using Meeting Space to collaborate with others, search Help And Support on your computer for the topic Windows Meeting Space.

Note   The File And Printer Sharing exception in Windows Firewall does not need to be opened for meeting participants to share documents with one another. This is because Meeting Space uses the Distributed File Service Replication (DFSR) service for sharing files between meeting participants, not the Server service.

Troubleshooting Meeting Space

If a Windows Vista computer is experiencing difficulties initiating a new meeting or joining an existing meeting, you can troubleshoot your situation by following this procedure:

1.   Make sure you are on the same subnet as the user who initiated the meeting. (In a networking environment that has IPv6-enabled routers or an ISATAP server, this is not an issue.) Verify that you have basic network connectivity with the other computer using ping -6 *remote_address*, where *remote_address* is the link-local IPv6 address of the remote computer. (To determine a computer's link-local IPv6 address, open a command prompt and type **ipconfig**, then look for an address that begins with an fe80:: prefix.) Be sure to verify your IPv6 connectivity in both directions between the computers.

2. If your computers can see each other on the network using IPv6, try using Group Policy to turn on Meeting Space auditing. (See the section titled "Managing Meeting Space in a Domain Environment" earlier in this chapter for information on how to do this.) Then check Event Viewer for events having Meeting Space as Source. These events can be used to determine if meetings have been successfully created or joined, if presentations have been launched, and so on.

3. Verify that the appropriate exceptions are opened in Windows Firewall. If you are using a third-party, host-based firewall, be sure that the appropriate ports are opened, as described in the section titled "Meeting Space and Windows Firewall" earlier in this chapter. If Meeting Space is still not working properly, try temporarily disabling the firewall on the affected computers and see if this resolves the problem.

4. If Meeting Space still doesn't work properly, try stopping and starting the various services associated with it. (See the section titled "Meeting Space Services" earlier in this chapter for a list of these services.) Note that to stop and start service, you must have Administrator credentials on your computer.

For additional tips on troubleshooting problems using Meeting Space after a meeting has been initiated and joined, search Help And Support on your computer for the topic titled Troubleshooting Windows Meeting Space. For more information about network trouble-shooting, see Chapter 32, "Troubleshooting Network Issues."

Summary

Windows Vista includes Meeting Space, a lightweight, IPv6-based collaboration tool built on Microsoft P2P technologies and industry-standard protocols. Some best practices for implementing Meeting Space in an enterprise environment include the following:

■ Deploy an ISATAP server to allow collaboration across subnet boundaries when your routing hardware is not configured for native IPv6 routing.

■ Use Group Policy to disable Meeting Space in environments where use of this tool does not accord with company policy.

■ Use Group Policy to enable Meeting Space auditing to ensure that users cannot delete meeting logs from their computers in environments where auditing of user communications is required for policy reasons.

■ Upgrade to Microsoft Live Communication Server 2005 or Microsoft Office Live Meeting if more scalable and robust collaboration solutions are required.

Additional Resources

The following resources contain additional information and tools related to this chapter.

Related Information

- Chapter 27, "Configuring Windows Firewall and IPsec," includes more information about Windows Firewall exceptions.

- Chapter 29, "Deploying IPv6," includes more information about Teredo support in Windows Vista and deploying ISATAP using Windows Server 2003.

- "Windows Vista Windows Meeting Space Step-by-Step Guide" at *http://technet2.microsoft.com/WindowsVista/en/library/8a70907e-9137-4426-a46f-a2d1eeadbd5a1033.mspx?mfr=true.*

- "Windows Peer-to-Peer Networking" on Microsoft TechNet at *http://www.microsoft.com/technet/itsolutions/network/p2p/default.mspx* includes more information on Microsoft P2P technologies.

On the Companion CD

- Links to additional information on Microsoft TechNet about the following Microsoft peer-to-peer technologies: People Near Me, Peer Name Resolution Protocol, and Windows Internet Computer Names

- MeetingSpaceDiag.vbs

Chapter 19

Managing Printing

Windows Vista includes new and enhanced capabilities for printing that provide high-fidelity print output, better print performance, improved manageability of printers and print servers, integrated support for the new XML Paper Specification (XPS), and a new Windows Color System that provides a richer color-printing experience. This chapter describes Windows Vista's new printing features and how to manage printers in enterprise environments.

Enhancements to Printing in Windows Vista

Table 19-1 highlights some of the key improvements to printing in Windows Vista as compared to earlier versions of Windows.

Table 19-1   Enhancements to Printing in Windows Vista

Feature	Description
Integrated support for XPS	Windows Vista includes support for the new XML Paper Specification (XPS), a set of conventions for using XML to describe the content and appearance of paginated documents.
XPS print path	In addition to supporting the legacy Graphics Device Interface (GDI) print path used by earlier versions of Windows, the printing architecture of Windows Vista also includes the new XPS print path that uses XPS as a document format, a Windows spool file format, and a page description language (PDL) for printers.

Table 19-1   Enhancements to Printing in Windows Vista

Feature	Description
XPS document graphics fidelity and performance	The XPS document printing capability in Windows Vista supports vector-based graphics that can be scaled up to a high degree without creating jagged or pixilated text, producing high-fidelity print output for graphics-rich documents. An XPS document is created by default when you print from any application running on Windows Vista, and you can print this document without rerendering it to an XPS-capable printer; therefore, you can reduce print processing time by as much as 90 percent compared with printing in previous versions of Windows, depending on the richness of the content being printed and the capabilities of the printer.
Microsoft XPS Document Writer	Windows Vista includes the Microsoft XPS Document Writer, which you can use through any Windows application to print graphics-rich application output as XPS documents. You can then view these documents in Microsoft Internet Explorer by using the Microsoft XPS Viewer or by printing them directly to an XPS-capable printer without rerendering.
Client-Side Rendering (CSR)	By default, Windows Vista renders print jobs on the client instead of the print server. This can significantly reduce print processing times when printing to XPS-capable printers. CSR works on non-XPS printers as well, and CSR is useful for reducing CPU/memory load on the server (servers can host more queues); it also reduces network traffic for some drivers.
Resource Reuse	XPS documents include the capability of rendering images once and reusing the rendered image when it appears on multiple pages of a print job. This can reduce the print processing time for documents that have graphics-rich corporate logos and reduces the amount of data sent over the network to remote printers.
Windows Color System	The new Windows Color System (WCS) works together with the Windows Vista print subsystem to provide a richer color-printing experience that supports wide-gamut printers (inkjet printers that use more than four ink colors) for lifelike printing of color photos and graphics-rich documents.
Print Management	Print Management, a MMC snap-in first included in Windows Server 2003 R2, is installed by default on Windows Vista, allowing administrators to manage printers, print servers, and print jobs easily across an enterprise. Print Management in Windows Vista has also been enhanced with new capabilities.
Network Printer Installation Wizard	Windows Vista replaces the Add Printer Wizard that was used in previous versions of Windows with a new Network Printer Installation Wizard that is easier to use and has new capabilities, making it easier for users to connect to remote printers and to local printers that are not Plug and Play.
Non-admin printer installation	Standard users (users who are not local administrators on their computers) can install printers without requiring administrative privileges or elevation at a User Account Control (UAC) prompt.

Table 19-1   Enhancements to Printing in Windows Vista

Feature	Description
Deploy and manage printers Group Policy	Using Group Policy to deploy printer connections—first introduced in Windows Server 2003 R2—has been enhanced in Windows Vista by eliminating the requirement to prepare client computers first using a startup script that installs PushPrinterConnections.exe client software on them. New policy settings have also been added in Windows Vista to enhance the capability of managing printers and printing using Group Policy. You can also use the Group Policy Results Wizard in the Group Policy Management Console to display Resultant Set of Policy (RSoP) for deployed printers.
Assign printers based on location	In Windows Vista, you can assign printers based on location by deploying printers using Group Policy and linking Group Policy Objects to sites. When mobile users move to a different site, Group Policy updates their printer connections for the new location, and when the users return to their primary site, their original default printers are restored.
Migrate printers	You can use a new Printer Migrator tool (including a command-line version called Printbrm.exe) to back up printer configurations on print servers, move printers between print servers, and consolidate multiple print servers onto a single server.

Understanding Printing in Windows Vista

Understanding how printing works in Windows Vista is important for administrators who need to know how to configure, manage, and troubleshoot printers and printing on this platform. The key topics to understand are:

- The XML Paper Specification (XPS)
- The Windows Vista Print Subsystem

Understanding the XML Paper Specification

XPS is a platform-independent, royalty-free, open-standard document format developed by Microsoft that uses XML, Open Packaging Conventions (OPC), and other industry standards to create cross-platform documents. XPS was designed to simplify the process for creating, sharing, viewing, printing, and archiving digital documents that are accurate representations of application output. Using application programming interfaces (APIs) provided by the Windows SDK and the Microsoft .NET Framework 3.0, developers can create Windows Presentation Foundation (WPF) applications that take advantage of XPS technologies.

XPS support, which is native on Windows Vista, allows users to open XPS documents in Internet Explorer 7.0 or higher and to generate XPS documents from any Windows application using the Microsoft XPS Document Writer. When you install additional components, some earlier versions of Windows can also use some of the capabilities of XPS:

- By installing the Microsoft .NET Framework 3.0 redistributable on Windows XP Service Pack 2 or Windows Server 2003, users of these platforms can open XPS documents using Internet Explorer 6.0 or higher.

- By installing Microsoft Core XML Services 6.0 on Windows XP Service Pack 2 or later, users can generate XPS documents from any Windows application using the Microsoft XPS Document Writer.

- By installing the Microsoft XPS Essentials Pack and Microsoft Core XML Services 6.0 on Windows 2000, Windows XP, or Windows Server 2003, users can open XPS documents in a standalone XPS viewer application.

Note You can download these additional components from the Microsoft Download Center at *http://www.microsoft.com/downloads*.

You can find detailed information on the XML Paper Specification in the version 1.0 document for this specification at *http://www.microsoft.com/whdc/xps/downloads.mspx* on Microsoft Windows Hardware Developer Central (WHDC). You can find additional news concerning this specification on the XPS Team Blog at *http://blogs.msdn.com/xps/*.

Understanding the Windows Vista Print Subsystem

The print subsystem on earlier versions of Microsoft Windows uses the Graphics Device Interface (GDI) print path. The GDI print path processes print jobs as follows:

- **Client processes** When a user on a client computer sends a print job from an application, the application calls the GDI, which then calls the printer driver for information about how to render the print job in a format that the printer can understand. The printer driver resides on the user's computer and is specific to the type of printer being used. After the GDI has rendered the print job, it sends the job to the spooler. By default, on Windows 2000 and later, the GDI renders print jobs using the Enhanced Metafile (EMF) format, a standard print job format that is highly portable but needs to be further rendered by the spooler before being sent to the printer. When an EMF print job has been sent to the spooler, control returns to the user and the spooler then completes rendering the job for printing. (Because the EMF job is quickly handed off to the spooler, the time the user's computer is busy is minimized.)

- **Spooler processes** The print spooler is a collection of components that reside on both the client computer that sends the print job and a network print server that receives the job for printing. The spooler takes the job as rendered by the GDI and if necessary renders it further to ensure that it prints correctly. The spooler then hands the job off to the printer.

- **Printer processes** The printer receives the print job from the spooler, translates it into a bitmap, and prints the document.

Windows Vista still includes a GDI print path (for Type 3 – User Mode) to support printing to existing printers. Kernel-mode GDI (Type 2 – Kernel Mode) drivers are no longer supported.

Note   Type 3 (User Mode) means that the driver is compatible with Windows 2000, Windows XP, Windows Server 2003, Windows Server 2003 R2, Windows Vista, and Windows Server 2008.

Windows Vista also includes a second print path that is based on the XML Paper Specification. This additional print path, called the XPS print path, is built on the XPS printer driver model (XPSDrv) and provides the following benefits over the GDI model:

■ Maintains the XPS document format from the point where an application sends a print job to the final processing by the print driver or device. By comparison, the GDI print path first renders the job into EMF and then the print driver or device renders the job a second time into the language the printer can understand.

■ The XPS print path can be more efficient and can provide support for advanced color profiles, which include 32 bits per channel (bpc), CMYK, named colors, n-inks, and native support of transparency and gradients when XPS-capable printers are being used.

■ Provides "what you see is what you get" (WYSIWYG) printing.

Applications can print documents in Windows Vista using either the GDI or XPS print path. For example, if a Win32 application sends the print job to a print queue that uses a GDI-based print driver, the print job is processed using the same GDI print path used in previous versions of Microsoft Windows. However, if a WPF application sends the job to a print queue that uses a new XPSDrv print driver, the job is spooled using the XPS Spool File format and is processed using the XPS print path. The print path that the print job takes is therefore determined by the type of printer driver (GDI-based or XPSDrv) installed on the target print queue.

Figure 19-1 illustrates the two print paths (GDI and XPS) available in Windows Vista. Although not shown in the diagram, both of these paths use the same Print Spooler service (%SystemRoot%\System32\spoolsv.exe).

Depending on the presentation system of the application from which the document is being printed, the print job may need to be converted before being spooled in the target print path. For example, when you print from a Win32 application to an XPS-capable printer, GDI spooling functions must perform GDI-to-XPS conversion, which simulates a Windows Presentation Foundation (WPF) application and spools the job in XPS Spool File format. Similarly, when you print from a WPF application to a legacy GDI-based printer, the WPF Print Support functions must perform XPS-to-GDI conversion, which simulates GDI calls by a Win32 application and spools the job in EMF format. These two conversion technologies are built into Windows Vista for maximum application compatibility when printing from different kinds of applications to either legacy or XPS-capable printers.

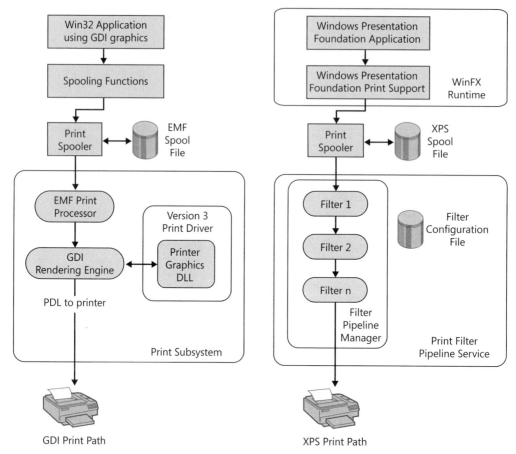

Figure 19-1   GDI and XPS print paths in Windows Vista.

For more information on the XPS print path and XPSDrv print drivers, see the white paper titled "The XPSDrv Filter Pipeline" on Microsoft Windows Hardware Developer Central (WHDC) at *http://www.microsoft.com/whdc/device/print/XPSDrv_FilterPipe.mspx.*

Understanding Print Management

Print Management is a snap-in for the Microsoft Management Console (MMC) that administrators can use to manage multiple printers and print servers on a network. Using Print Management, an administrator can manage hundreds of print servers and thousands of print queues on Windows 2000 Server, Windows Server 2003, and Windows Server 2008.

> **Note**   Print Management is designed as a general systems-management tool for administering print servers and print queues. For help-desk scenarios or printer-specific troubleshooting, however, enterprises may need to use vendor-supplied tools from printer manufacturers.

Enhancements to Print Management in Windows Vista

Print Management was first introduced in Windows Server 2003 R2 and has been enhanced in a number of ways in Windows Vista:

- **Network Printer Installation Wizard**   The Add Printer Wizard used in earlier versions of Windows has been replaced by a new Network Printer Installation Wizard that can automatically search the network for TCP/IP printers and Web Services for Devices (WSD) printers and add them to the print server. You can also use the wizard to manually add TCP/IP and WSD printers, add printers to an existing port, or add a new port and a new printer.

- **All Drivers filter**   The new All Drivers filter displays details concerning all installed printer drivers for all print servers managed by Print Management. The All Drivers filter shows the version of printer drivers on multiple servers, which allows administrators to quickly and easily see which print servers have to get updated drivers (when they are updating printer drivers in their organization). The All Drivers filter also allows administrators to easily remove printer driver packages from the driver store when they are no longer needed.

- **Export/Import print queues and printer drivers**   You can now use Print Management to export the configuration of all print queues and printer drivers on a print server to a Printer Migration (*.printerExport) file, which you can then import on either the same print server or a different one. This is useful for administrators who want to back up printer configurations or migrate printers to a different print server.

- **Comma-separated list in Add/Remove Servers**   Administrators can now quickly add multiple print servers to Print Management by specifying a comma-separated list of print servers in the Add/Remove Servers dialog box. Administrators can also copy and paste a list of servers (one per line) to the text box in the dialog box. In addition, the print servers being specified in this dialog box no longer need to be online when added to Print Management.

- **More filter conditions**   When creating a new custom filter, administrators now have the option of specifying up to six filter conditions instead of only three as supported previously.

- **Less detailed logging by default**   By default, only Error and Warning events are now logged in the event logs for the Spooler Service. If desired, however, administrators can still enable logging of Information events for detailed logging purposes such as auditing print queue activity.

- **Migrate Printers option**   By right-clicking the root node in Print Management, administrators now have the option of using the new Printer Migration Wizard to export or import print queues and printer drivers to move printers to a different print server—for example, for consolidation purposes.

> **Note**   To use Print Management directly on a remote computer (for example, on a remote print server), connect to the computer using Remote Desktop. The remote computer must be running Windows Server 2003 R2 or later and Print Management must be installed on the computer to use it. You may need to use this approach if the computer you are running Print Management on does not have all the printer drivers needed to manage the printers, because Print Management pulls its printer drivers from the computer that Print Management is running on.

The Print Management Console

As shown in Figure 19-2, Print Management displays a root node and three main subnodes. You expose the functionality of these different nodes in the Action pane (or by right-clicking a node). They can be summarized as follows:

- **Print Management (root) node**   Adds or removes print servers to/from the console and launches the Printer Migration Wizard to export or import printer configurations

- **Custom Filters node**   Displays all custom filters, including four default filters:

    ❑ **All Printers**   Displays all printers on all print servers and allows administrators to open the printer queue for a selected printer, pause or resume printing, print a test page from a printer, configure printer properties, and deploy a printer connection using Group Policy.

    ❑ **All Drivers**   Displays all printer drivers for all printers and allows administrators to view driver properties and remove driver packages from the driver store.

    ❑ **Printers Not Ready**   Displays all print queues that are in a Not Ready state for any reason.

    ❑ **Printers With Jobs**   Displays all print queues that currently have jobs pending in them.

    When you create a new custom filter using the New Printer Filter Wizard, you can configure an e-mail notification for troubleshooting purposes to alert administrators when a printer matches the filter conditions. You can also configure a script action so that a specified script can be run when a printer matches the condition—for example, a script to restart the spooler service on a print server.

    In addition, the Show Extended View option (available by right-clicking a custom filter) displays jobs pending on the print queue and—if supported by the print device—the web page from which the printer can be managed.

- **Print Servers node**   Displays all print servers being managed by Print Management, together with a manageable view of their drivers, forms, ports, and print queues. You can also use this node to export/import print queues and printer drivers, configure e-mail notifications or script actions for when the spooler or server is down, and launch the Network Printer Installation Wizard to add new printers manually or automatically search for TCP/IP and WSD printers and add them to the list of printers being managed by Print Management.

■ **Deployed Printers node**   Displays printer connections that have been deployed using Group Policy. For more information, see the section titled "Deploying Printers Using Group Policy" later in this chapter.

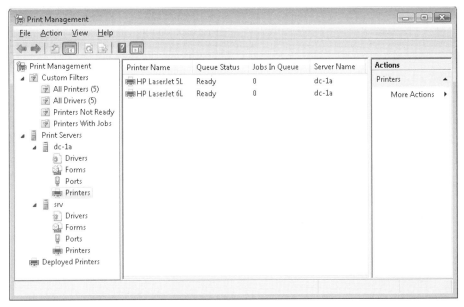

Figure 19-2   Overview of Print Management.

Note   Print Management also lets you view print queues on a UNIX or Linux server running SAMBA and print queues on Apple Macintosh computers. You can view these queues and also monitor these print servers by receiving notifications when they go down, but you cannot use Print Management to add or remove printers to such servers. To view print queues on UNIX or Linux servers, you must first authenticate to *server_name*\ipc$ before you can add the server to the list of print servers you want to monitor.

Adding and Removing Print Servers

To add or remove print servers so that Print Management can manage them, follow these steps:

1. Click Start, point to All Programs, click Administrative Tools, and then click Print Management.

2. Respond to the UAC prompt either by clicking Continue or by supplying administrator credentials as required.

3. Right-click either the root node or the Print Servers node, select Add/Remove Servers to open the Add/Remove Servers dialog box, and then do one of the following:

    ❏ Click Add The Local Server to add the local computer to the list of managed print servers.

    ❏ Click Browse to open Network Explorer and browse to select print servers on the network.

    ❏ Type a comma-separated list of print servers and click Add To List.

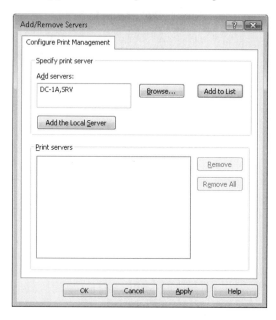

To remove a print server from the list of managed print servers, open the Add/Remove Services dialog box, select the print server, and then click Remove. You can also remove all print servers by clicking Remove All.

Adding Printers Using the Network Printer Installation Wizard

To add printers using the Network Printer Installation Wizard, follow these steps:

1. Add at least one print server to the list of managed print servers.

2. Right-click a print server and select Add Printer to start the Network Printer Installation Wizard.

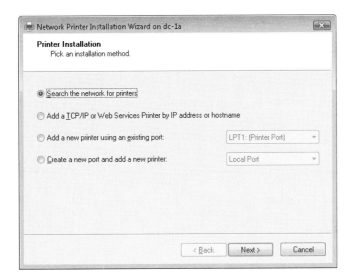

3.   Do one of the following:

- To automatically scan the local subnet for TCP/IP or WSD network printers, select Search The Network For Printers and then click Next. As the scan progresses, Windows will display a list of available network printers and will install them automatically on the selected print server. (You may be required to specify a driver for a printer manually if Windows Vista cannot find one automatically.)

- To manually add a specific TCP/IP or WSD network printer to the list of printers managed by the print server, select Add A TCP/IP Or Web Services Printer By IP Address Or Hostname, specify the name or IP address of the printer, and then click Next.

- To add a new printer using an existing port, which can be either a local port (LTP or COM) or a previously added TCP/IP port, select Add A New Printer Using An Existing Port, click Next, and either install the printer driver automatically selected by the wizard, select an existing driver, or install a new driver.

- To create a new local port and install a printer on it, select Create A New Port And Add A New Printer, click Next, specify a name for the new port, and then either install the printer driver automatically selected by the wizard, select an existing driver, or install a new driver.

Note   The option for automatically detecting printers on the local subnet using Search The Network For Printers cannot work across a firewall. If you want to use this feature to detect printers for another location, such as a remote subnet at a branch office location that is located behind a firewall, use Remote Desktop to connect to a Windows Server 2003 R2 or later computer at the remote location, start Print Management, and then select Search The Network For Printers as described previously.

In addition to the new Network Printer Installation Wizard, the end-user Add Printer Wizard is still present in Windows Vista and has been enhanced to allow users to add local, network, wireless, and Bluetooth printers. For more information on this topic, see the section titled "Client-Side Management of Printers" later in this chapter.

How It Works: WSD Printers

Web Services for Devices (WSD) is a new type of network connectivity supported by Windows Vista. With WSD, users can have a plug-and-play experience similar to that with USB devices, except over the network instead of for locally connected devices.

In Windows Vista, WSD printer ports are serviced by the WSD Port Monitor (WSDMon) instead of the Standard Port Monitor (TCPMon) used to service TCP/IP ports. WSDMon is used by default if a printer supports it; otherwise, it defaults to TCPMon.

For more information about the various Web Services specifications and their support on Microsoft Windows platforms, see *http://msdn2.microsoft.com/en-us/webservices/aa740689.aspx* on MSDN. You can find additional information on WSD printer support in Windows Vista on Windows Hardware Developer Central at *http://www.microsoft.com/whdc/device/print/default.mspx*.

Creating and Using Printer Filters

You can use Print Management to create custom printer filters to simplify the task of managing hundreds of print servers and thousands of printers. To create a custom filter, follow these steps:

1. Right-click the Custom Filters node in Print Management and select Add New Printer Filter.

2. Type a name and description for the new filter. For example, type **All HP Printers** for a filter that displays printers whose driver names begin with HP, indicating Hewlett-Packard printers. If desired, select the check box labeled Display The Total Number Of Printers Next To The Name Of The Printer Filter and then click Next.

3. Specify up to six filter criteria for your new filter. (See Table 19-2 for a list of filter criteria fields, conditions, and possible values you can specify.) For example, to filter printers whose driver names begin with HP, select the Driver Name field and the Begins With condition and type **HP** as the value.

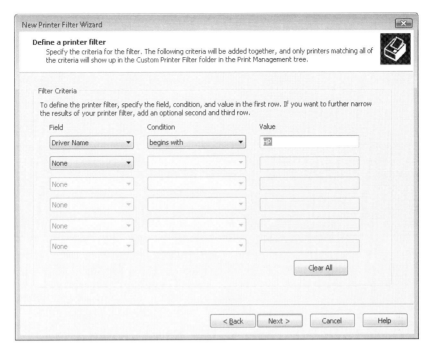

4. Click Next and configure an e-mail notification or script action that occurs when a printer matches the filter criteria specified by the filter. Configuration notification is optional and is described further in the section titled "Monitoring and Troubleshooting Printers" later in this chapter.

5. Click Finish to create the new filter. Select the new filter to activate it and display printers that meet the criteria specified by the filter.

Table 19-2 Fields, Conditions, and Possible Values for Printer Filter Criteria

Field	Conditions	Value
Printer Name	Is exactly, is not exactly, begins with, not begin with, ends with, not end with, contains, not contains	(type a value to specify)
Server Name		
Comments		
Driver Name		
Location		
Shared Name		

Table 19-2   Fields, Conditions, and Possible Values for Printer Filter Criteria

Field	Conditions	Value
Queue Status	Is exactly, is not exactly	Ready, paused, error, deleting, paper jam, out of paper, manual feed required, paper problem, offline, IO active, busy, printing, output bin full, not available, waiting, processing, initializing, warming up, toner/ink low, no toner/ink, page punt, user intervention required, out of memory, door open
Jobs in queue	Is exactly, is not exactly, is less than, is less than or equal to, is greater than, is greater than or equal to	(type a value to specify)
Is Shared	Is exactly, is not exactly	False, true

Note   To modify a printer filter after you create it, right-click the filter and then select Properties.

Managing Printers Using Print Management

After you have added print servers to Print Management and created printer filters to display and easily select different types of printers, you can begin managing these printers and print servers. Printer management tasks you can perform using Print Management include:

- Configuring properties of printers.
- Publishing printers in Active Directory so that users can find them easily.
- Adding, removing, and managing printer drivers.
- Exporting and importing printer configurations.
- Performing bulk actions such as pausing all print queues on a print server.

Configuring Properties of Printers

You can use Print Management to configure the properties of printers on your network. To do this, you may be required to install additional printer drivers locally on the Windows Vista computer from which you are running Print Management. This is because some printer properties may not be configurable unless the printer's driver is installed on the local computer, so if the in-box (default) printer drivers included with Windows Vista do not include a driver for a network printer you want to manage, you must first download and install a driver for the printer from the print server before you can configure the printer's properties using Print Management.

To configure the properties of a printer, follow these steps using Print Management:

1. Right-click the printer you want to configure and then select Properties.

2. Respond to one of the following messages if they appear:

   ❑ A message may appear saying "To use the shared printer *server_name*\ *printer_sharename*, you need to install the printer driver on your computer. If you do not recognize or trust the location or name of the printer, do not install the driver." If this message appears and you want to manage the printer, click Install Driver to automatically download and install the printer's driver from the print server.

   ❑ A message may appear saying "The *printer_sharename* driver is not installed on this computer. Some printer properties will not be accessible unless you install the printer driver. Do you want to install the printer driver now?" If this message appears and you want to manage the printer, click Yes to open the Add Printer Wizard. Follow the steps of the wizard to manually install the printer driver for the printer by supplying the necessary driver media.

   ❑ If no message appears and the printer's Properties dialog box appears, the printer driver is either already installed on the local computer or is included as an in-box driver in Windows Vista.

3. Configure the settings on the various tabs of the printer's Properties dialog box as desired. See Help And Support for addition information about configuring printer properties in Windows Vista.

Publishing Printers in Active Directory

By default, when printers are installed on Windows Server 2003 or later print servers and shared over the network, they are also automatically listed in Active Directory. However, other network printers—such as standalone TCP/IP or WSD network printers—may not be listed in Active Directory; you will need to add them manually to the directory so that users can search for them in the directory.

To manually add a network printer to Active Directory, do one of the following using Print Management:

- Right-click the printer and select List In Directory.

- Open the printer's Properties dialog box, click the Sharing tab, and then select the List In The Directory check box.

You can also remove printers from Active Directory either by clearing the List In The Directory check box or by right-clicking the printer and selecting Remove From Directory. You can remove printers from Active Directory to prevent users from installing them manually using the Add Printer Wizard from the Printers CPL.

After a printer is published in Active Directory, users can search Active Directory using the Add Printer Wizard and manually install a printer connection on their computers. This allows users to print to a network printer. For more information, see the section titled "Searching for Printers" later in this chapter.

Managing Printer Drivers

If client computers need additional printer drivers, you can use Print Management to add them to print servers, and you can also remove print drivers from print servers when clients no longer need them. For example, you can add additional printer drivers for network printers to support 64-bit Windows client computers by following these steps:

1. Open Print Management and expand the console tree to select the Drivers node beneath the print server to which you want to add additional drivers.

2. Right-click the Drivers node, select Add Driver to open the Add Printer Driver Wizard, and then click Next.

3. Select the types of system architectures for which you need to install additional drivers.

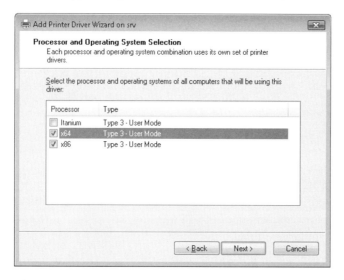

4. Click Next. If the drivers you need to install are not already staged within the driver store on the local computer, you will need to provide driver media or a network location where the driver packages are available. Then continue stepping through the wizard to add the drivers to the print server and make them available for clients that need them.

The following considerations apply when adding additional drivers using Print Management:

■ Using the Add Printer Drivers Wizard from Print Management running on Windows Server 2003 R2 or later lets you add additional x86, x64, and Itanium drivers for versions of Microsoft Windows prior to Windows Vista.

- Using the Add Printer Drivers Wizard from Print Management running on Windows Vista lets you add Type 3 (User Mode) printer drivers only for x86, x64, and Itanium systems running Windows Vista or Windows Server 2008. To add additional drivers for earlier versions of Windows, use Print Management on Windows Server 2003 R2 or later instead of on Windows Vista.

> **Note**   There are no differences in the installation method for adding 32-bit and 64-bit drivers.

You can also remove printer drivers from print servers when client computers no longer need these drivers. To remove a printer driver from a print server, follow these steps:

1. Open Print Management and expand the console tree to select the Drivers node beneath the print server from which you want to remove drivers.

2. Right-click a driver under the Drivers node and select Delete.

3. Click Yes to confirm your action.

> **Note**   When you use the preceding steps to try to remove a printer driver from the local print server (when using a Windows Vista or Windows Server 2008 computer as a print server), the driver package is uninstalled but remains staged in the driver store. Windows will pick and install the driver again when a compatible TCP/IP or Plug and Play printer is added to the system. If you selected Remove Driver Package instead of Delete, however, Windows will remove the package, not use the driver again.

You can display detailed information for all printer drivers installed on a print server by following these steps:

1. Open Print Management and expand the console tree to select the Drivers node beneath a print server.

2. From the View menu, select Add/Remove Columns.

3. Add additional columns from the list of available columns to display more detail concerning each driver installed on the server.

To save detailed information concerning each driver installed on a print server and import it into Microsoft Office Excel for reporting purposes, follow the preceding procedure to add the columns desired and then right-click the Drivers node and select Export List. Save the detailed driver as a comma-separated (*.csv) file and import it into Office Excel. The Export List command is available for any node in an MMC snap-in.

> ### Direct from the Field: Is Your Printer Compatible with Windows Vista?
>
> Let's say your company is thinking of upgrading your XP clients to Windows Vista. Question: Will the printers you currently have installed on your Windows Server 2003 R2 print server work for users when their computers are upgraded?
>
> Here's a quick way to determine this: Use Print Management to examine the version of each printer driver on your print server. If a driver says Windows XP or 2003 (that is, Type 3 drivers), the associated printer will be compatible with Windows Vista. If the driver says Windows NT 4.0 (Type 2), however, the printer uses a Kernel Mode driver and you will need an update for the driver before Windows Vista clients can use that printer.
>
> *Mitch Tulloch, MVP*
>
> *http://www.mtit.com*

Exporting and Importing Print Server Configurations

You can export the configuration of all print queues and printer drivers on a print server to a Printer Migration file (*.printerExport), which you then import on either the same print server or a different one. This is useful for administrators who want to back up printer configurations or migrate printers to a different print server. Exporting print queue configuration settings and printer drivers is also a useful method for backing up the configuration of a print server as part of your organization's Business Continuity Plan (BCP).

To export all printer drivers and the configuration of all print queues for a print server, right-click the print server's node in Print Management and select Export Printers To A File. This opens the Printer Migration tool, which displays a list of print queues and printer drivers that will be exported. Save the resulting *.printerExport file on a network share so that you can import it again during a disaster recovery scenario or when consolidating print servers.

You can import previously exported print server configurations by using the following methods:

- Right-click the print server's node in Print Management, select Import Printers From A File, and then browse to select a *.printerExport file and import it.

- Double-click a *.printerExport file while logged on to the print server into which you want to import the configuration information to start the Printer Migration tool and import the configuration.

For more information on using the Printer Migration tool, see the section titled "Migrating Print Servers" later in this chapter.

> **Note**   The Printbrm.exe command-line tool can also be used in Task Scheduler to perform nightly backups of your print server configurations.

How It Works: Printer Export Files

The printer export file has a .printerExport file extension and is essentially a compressed cabinet (.cab) file that contains XML definition files for the drivers, ports, forms, and printers on a computer. It also contains all of the driver files for each printer.

The following files are part of the printer export file:

- **BrmDrivers.xml**   Printer Driver description file. This file contains a list of every driver installed on the computer and the driver files for each driver.

- **BrmForms.xml**   Forms description file. This file contains a list of all of the installed forms.

- **BrmLMons.xml**   Port monitor definition file. This file usually contains either Windows NT x86 or Windows x64 as the architecture and a list of port monitors and the port monitor files installed on the computer.

- **BrmPorts.xml**   Printer ports definition file. This file contains a list of all printer ports that have been installed on the computer. This list does *not* include printer connections.

- **BrmPrinters.xml**   Printer definition file. This file contains a list of all printers that have been installed on the computer. This list does *not* include printer connections.

- **BrmSpoolerAttrib.xml**   Spooler attributes definition file. This file contains information about the spooler directory path and a value that determines whether the source computer was a cluster server.

Microsoft Global Technical Readiness Platforms Team

Performing Bulk Actions Using Print Management

You can also use Print Management to perform these bulk actions for printers and printer drivers on a print server:

- You can perform the following bulk actions on printers by multi-selecting printers on a print server or as displayed within a printer filter:
    - ❏ Pause Printing
    - ❏ Resume Printing
    - ❏ Cancel All Jobs

- ❑ List In Directory
- ❑ Remove From Directory
- ❑ Delete
- ■ You can perform the following bulk actions for printer drivers by multi-selecting printer drivers for a printer or as displayed within a printer filter such as the All Drivers default filter:
  - ❑ Remove Driver Package
  - ❑ Delete

Direct from the Source: Managing Print Queues and Servers with the Print Management Console

With Windows Vista client computers and the Windows Vista Print Management console, printer administrators can easily provide users with high printer availability. This can be achieved by moving users from the print queues on one server to identical print queues (for the same physical printers) on another server when the first server is unavailable.

First, use the Print Management console to deploy printers to a number of users using a Group Policy object (let's say \\ServerA\ColorPrinter, with GPO1) and link GPO1 to an OU with a number of users or computers.

Then, using the Print Server import/export tool, do a backup of a print server. In the Print Management console, right-click a print server and select Export Printers To A File. All the print queues and printer drivers will be exported to a .printerExport file. Alternatively, you can use the command-line tool Printbrm.exe (in %WinDir%\ System32\spool\tools), either from the command line or from Task Scheduler, to do periodic backups of the print server.

When a print server goes down because of a hardware failure, the administrator can easily move users to a new server. On the new server (Server2), use the Print Management console to import the .printerExport file. New print queues will now be created (such as \\Server2\ColorPrinter, if the old server had \\Server1\ColorPrinter).

Using the deployed printers functionality in the Print Management console, deploy the printers using GPO2. With the Group Policy Management tool, disable the link to GPO1. The print queues from Server1 will be undeployed and the print queues from GPO2 (Server2) will be installed.

When the old print server is online again, the link to GPO2 can be disabled, and the link to GPO1 can be enabled.

Frank Olivier, User Experience Program Manager

Windows Client

Client-Side Management of Printers

Depending on Group Policy settings, end users of Windows Vista computers in managed environments may be able to find and install their own printers when needed. See the section titled "Managing Client-Side Printer Experience Using Group Policy" later in this chapter for more information on the policy settings that apply.

Installing Printers Using the Printers CPL

In addition to the new Network Printer Installation Wizard used in Print Management, the end-user Add Printer Wizard is still available in Windows Vista, and it has been enhanced to allow users to easily add local, network, wireless, and Bluetooth printers. This wizard is not needed when installing USB printers, however, because the user can simply attach the printer to a USB port on the computer and the printer is automatically installed.

In earlier versions of Windows, the Add Printer Wizard is available from the Start menu by clicking Printers And Faxes and then clicking Add A Printer. To start the Add Printer Wizard in Windows Vista, follow these steps:

1. Click Start and then click Control Panel.

2. Click the Printer link under Hardware And Sound to open Printers Explorer.

3. Click Add A Printer on the toolbar to start the Add Printer Wizard.

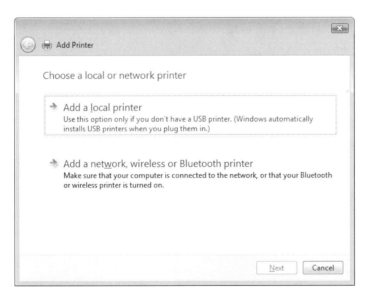

4. Do one of the following:

   ❏ To install a local (non-USB) printer, click Add A Local Printer and specify the port, printer driver, and other information required by the wizard. Installing a local printer manually like this is needed only for non–Plug and Play printers–USB printers are detected and installed automatically when they are connected to a USB port on the computer.

❑   To install a network, wireless, or Bluetooth printer, click Add A Network, Wireless Or Bluetooth Printer, select the printer you want to install from the list of found printers, and then click Next to install the printer.

On a managed network where Active Directory has been deployed, the Add A Network, Wireless Or Bluetooth Printer option in the Add Printer Wizard finds network printers published in Active Directory as well as available wireless Bluetooth printers. On an unmanaged network without Active Directory, selecting this option causes the Add Printer Wizard to scan the local subnet for TCP/IP printers, WSD printers, wireless printers, and Bluetooth printers.

> **Note**   Network administrators can also set the number and type of printers to find using Group Policy settings found under Computer Configuration\Policies\Administrative Templates\Printers. If you do not want a printer to show up, set the number of printers of each type to 0 in either Add Printer Wizard – Network Scan Page (Managed Network) or Add Printer Wizard – Network Scan Page (Unmanaged Network).

Searching for Printers

After a printer has been published in Active Directory, users use the Add Printer Wizard to search for network printers in Active Directory and manually install a printer connection on their computers so that they can print to the printer. To search for a published printer to install, the user can follow these steps using Printers in Control Panel:

1.   Click Add A Printer on the toolbar of the Printers Explorer.

2.   In the Add Printer Wizard, on the Choose A Local Or Network Printer page, click Add A Network, Wireless Or Bluetooth Printer to display a list of printers published in Active Directory.

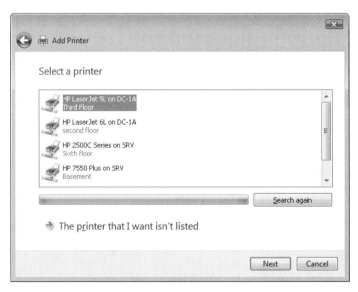

3. Select the published printer for which you want to install a connection and click Next to continue stepping through the wizard and install the printer connection on the local computer.

4. If the printer you want to install is not listed in the directory, or if the number of published printers displayed is very large and the user wants to search for a specific type of printer in Active Directory, click The Printer That I Want Isn't Listed to open the Find A Printer By Name Or TCP/IP Address page of the Add Printer Wizard.

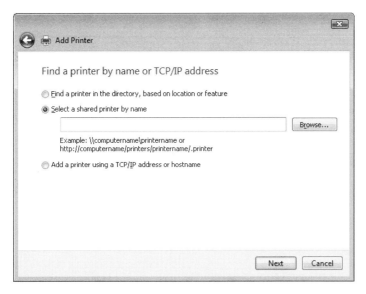

5. Select one of the following options:

   ❑ To browse for a shared printer using Network Explorer, select the Select A Shared Printer By Name check box and then click Browse. You can also type the UNC path to the shared printer if you know the path.

   ❑ To install a printer connection to a standalone TCP/IP or WSD network printer, select the Add A Printer Using A TCP/IP Address Or Hostname check box and then click Next. Type the IP address or host name of the printer, select Autodetect to automatically detect whether the printer is TCP/IP or WSD type, select Query The Printer And Automatically Select The Driver To Use, and then click Next to install a printer connection to the network printer.

   ❑ To search Active Directory for a printer that meets specified criteria, select the Find A Printer In The Directory Based On Location Or Feature check box and click Next to open the Find Printers dialog box. Specify the criteria for the type of printer you want to search for and then click Find Now to query Active Directory. Double-click the desired printer to install a printer connection for it.

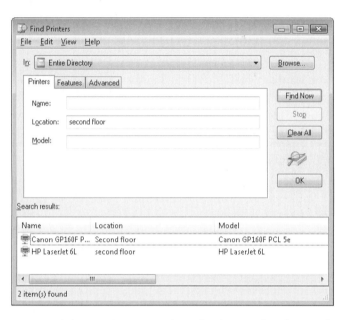

You can control the maximum number of printers of each type that the Add Printer Wizard will display on a computer on a managed network by using the following Group Policy setting:

Computer Configuration\Policies\Administrative Templates\Printers\Add Printer wizard - Network scan page (Managed network)

For more information on this policy setting, see the section titled "Managing Client-Side Printer Experience Using Group Policy" later in this chapter.

> **Note**   Advanced users can also search for printers to install by opening a command prompt, typing **rundll32 dsquery.dll,OpenQueryWindow**, selecting Printers from the Find list box, and continuing as described in the preceding steps.

Installing Printers Using Point and Print

End users can also use Point and Print to install printers over a network. When using Point and Print, the print server sends the client computer the following information concerning the printer being installed:

- The name of the server on which printer driver files are stored
- Printer model information that specifies which printer driver to install
- The actual printer driver files needed by the client

End users can install printer connections using Point and Print by browsing Network Explorer to find a print server, double-clicking the print server to display its shared printers, right-clicking a shared printer, and then clicking Connect. If a driver for the printer is not found in the Driver Store on the local computer, the user will need administrator credentials to respond to the UAC prompt that appears when the driver is being copied from the print server to the local computer. For more information about the Driver Store, read Chapter 16, "Managing Devices and Services."

Using Printers Explorer

Selecting a printer connection in the Printers Explorer folder causes toolbar buttons to appear in Printers Explorer. The user can click these buttons to perform a number of client-side management tasks for the selected printer, including:

- **See What's Printing**   Opens the print queue for the selected printer and displays documents currently being printed and pending print jobs.

- **Set As Default**   Sets the printer as the default printer for the user's computer. (Note that some client applications can maintain their own "Default Printer" setting that overrides the one set here.)

- **Select Printing Preferences**   Allows the user to select page layout and paper/quality options for the printer.

- **Delete This Printer**   Removes the printer connection from the user's computer.

- **Rename This Printer**   Lets the user specify a new name for the print queue.

- **Pause Printing**   Pauses printing of the current print job and holds all pending jobs until Resume Printing is selected.

- **Share**   Allows the user to share the printer so that other network users can print to it.

- **Set Printer Properties**   Lets the user configure different properties of the printer connection.

- **Go To The Manufacturer Website**   Lets the user visit the printer manufacturer's website to look for updated drivers and documentation for the printer.

> **Note**   Local administrator credentials for the computer are required to share a printer connection displayed in Printers Explorer. These credentials are required so that the end user can respond to the UAC prompt that appears when this action is selected. End users who have local administrator credentials on the computer can also use the Network And Sharing Center to turn on printer sharing and automatically share installed printers for other network users to use.

Using the Color Management CPL

Windows XP includes support for Image Color Management (ICM) version 2.0 to ensure that colors printed from a color printer are accurately reproduced. In Windows Vista, ICM functions have been enhanced to use the new Microsoft Windows Color System (WCS), which provides applications with the ability to perform wide-gamut, high-dynamic-range color processing of spool file data in a way that exceeds the possibilities of ICM in previous versions of Windows.

Windows Vista also includes a new Color Management CPL that end users can use to manage the following aspects of color printing:

- Add or remove color profiles and specify a default color profile for each printer and display device used by the local computer

- Configure advanced color management settings to ensure accurate display or printing of color information

For more information on using the Color Management CPL, open Color Management in Control Panel and click Understanding Color Management Settings on the Devices tab to access Help And Support information on this topic.

Managing Client-Side Printer Experience Using Group Policy

In managed environments where Active Directory is deployed, administrators can use Group Policy to manage different aspects of the end user's experience of installing, configuring, and using printer connections.

You can find Group Policy settings for managing the client-side printer experience in the following two locations in Group Policy Object Editor:

- Computer Configuration\Policies\Administrative Templates\Printers
- User Configuration\Policies\Administrative Templates\Control Panel\Printers

The following sections describe printer policy settings new to Windows Vista. For general information concerning printer policy settings introduced in earlier versions of Windows that still apply to Windows Vista, see the Group Policy Settings Reference Windows Vista at *http://www.microsoft.com/downloads/details.aspx?FamilyID=41DC179B-3328-4350-ADE1-C0D9289F09EF &displaylang=en.*

Configuring the Add Printer Wizard

You can find the following two policies that control how the Add Printer Wizard works on client computers under Computer Configuration\Policies\Administrative Templates\Printers:

- **Add Printer Wizard – Network Scan Page (Managed Network)**   This policy sets the maximum number of printers (of each type) that the Add Printer Wizard will display on a computer on a managed network (when the computer is able to reach a domain controller, such as a domain-joined laptop on a corporate network).

If this setting is disabled, the network scan page is not displayed. If this setting is not configured, the Add Printer Wizard displays the default number of printers of each type:

❑ Directory printers: 20

❑ TCP/IP printers: 0

❑ Web Services Printers: 0

❑ Bluetooth printers: 10

If you don't want to display printers of a certain type, enable this policy and set the number of printers to display to 0. You can control the number of printers of each type that are displayed by configuring the settings contained in this policy, as shown in Figure 19-3.

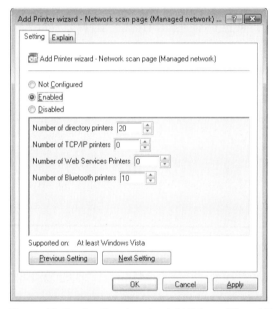

Figure 19-3   Configuring the Add Printer Wizard Network Scan Page (Managed Network) policy setting.

■ **Add Printer Wizard – Network Scan Page (Unmanaged Network)**   This policy sets the maximum number of printers (of each type) that the Add Printer Wizard will display on a computer on an unmanaged network (when the computer is not able to reach a domain controller, such as a domain-joined laptop on a home network).

If this setting is disabled, the network scan page is not displayed. If this setting is not configured, the Add Printer Wizard displays the default number of printers of each type:

❑ TCP/IP printers: 50

❑ Web Services Printers: 50

❑ Bluetooth printers: 10

Again, if you don't want to display printers of a certain type, enable this policy and set the number of printers to display to 0.

Disable Client-Side Printer Rendering

Administrators can also use Group Policy to prevent printer rendering from occurring on client computers. By default, when an application running on a Windows Vista computer sends a job to a printer hosted on a print server, the job is rendered on the client computer before it is sent to the print server. The following policy setting controls print job rendering behavior on Windows Vista computers:

Computer Configuration\Policies\Administrative Templates\Printers\Always Render Print Jobs On The Server

When printing through to printers hosted on a print server, this policy determines whether the print spooler on the client will process print jobs itself or will pass them on to the server to do the work. This policy setting only affects printing to a Windows print server.

If you enable this policy setting on a client computer, the client spooler will not process print jobs before sending them to the print server. This decreases the workload on the client at the expense of increasing the load on the server.

If you disable this policy setting on a client computer, the client itself will process print jobs into printer device commands. These commands will then be sent to the print server, and the server will simply pass the commands to the printer. This increases the workload of the client while decreasing the load on the server. If you do not enable this policy setting, the behavior is the same as disabling it.

Keep the following considerations in mind when using this policy:

- This policy does not determine if offline printing will be available to the client. The client print spooler can always queue print jobs when not connected to the print server. Upon reconnecting to the server, the client will submit any pending print jobs.

- Some printer drivers require a custom print processor. In some cases, the custom print processor may not be installed on the client computer, such as when the print server does not support transferring print processors during Point and Print. In the case of a print processor mismatch, the client spooler will always send jobs to the print server for rendering. Disabling the preceding policy setting does not override this behavior.

- In cases in which the client print driver does not match the server print driver (mismatched connection), the client will always process the print job, regardless of the setting of this policy.

Configuring Package Point and Print Restrictions

Windows XP Service Pack 1 and Windows Server 2003 introduced the following Group Policy setting:

User Configuration\Policies\Administrative Templates\Control Panel\Printers\Point and Print Restrictions

This policy setting controls the servers that a client computer can connect to for Point and Print. A new feature of this policy setting for Windows Vista is the ability to control the behavior of UAC prompts when installing printer drivers on Windows Vista computers using Point and Print (see Figure 19-4). This policy setting applies only to non–Print Administrators clients and only to computers that are members of a domain.

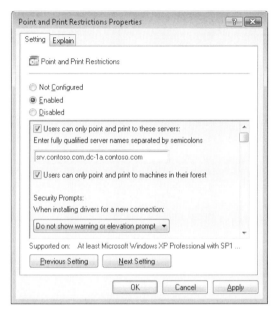

Figure 19-4   Controlling the behavior of security prompts using the Point And Print Restrictions policy setting when installing printers using Point and Print.

When you enable the policy setting, the client is restricted to only Point and Print to a list of explicitly named servers. You can configure Windows Vista clients to not show security warnings or elevation prompts when users point and print or when drivers for printer connections need to be updated.

When you do not configure the policy setting:

- Windows XP and Windows Server 2003 client computers can point and print to any server in their forest.

- Windows Vista client computers can point and print to any server.

- Windows Vista computers will show a warning and an elevation prompt when users point and print to any server.

- Windows Vista computers will show a warning and an elevation prompt when a driver for an existing printer connection needs to be updated.

When you disable the policy setting:

- Windows XP and Windows Server 2003 client computers can point and print to any server.

- Windows Vista client computers can point and print to any server.

- Windows Vista computers will not show a warning or an elevation prompt when users point and print to any server.

- Windows Vista computers will not show a warning or an elevation prompt when a driver for an existing printer connection needs to be updated.

Note that the Users Can Only Point And Print To Machines In Their Forest setting applies only to Windows XP SP1 (and later service packs) and Windows Server 2003.

In addition to this updated Point And Print Restrictions policy setting, Windows Vista includes two new policy settings related to Point and Print:

- **Only Use Package Point And Print**   This policy restricts clients' computers to use Package Point and Print only. If you enable this setting, users will only be able to point and print to printers that use package-aware drivers. When using Package Point and Print, client computers will check the driver signature of all drivers that are downloaded from print servers. If you disable or don't configure this setting, users will not be restricted to package-aware Point and Print only.

- **Package Point And Print – Approved Servers**   Restricts Package Point and Print to approved servers. If you enable this setting, users will only be able to Package Point and Print to print servers approved by the network administrator. When using Package Point and Print, client computers will check the driver signature of all drivers that are downloaded from print servers. If you disable or don't configure this setting, Package Point and Print will not be restricted to specific print servers.

In Package Point and Print, the complete driver package is put in the driver store on the Windows Vista client computer. All components of the printer driver are installed on the client and the installation process ensures that the package has been digitally signed properly before adding it to the store. This result is a more secure form of Point and Print than on previous versions of Windows.

 Note   Printing from Windows Vista to print servers running earlier versions of Windows uses legacy Point and Print.

Deploying Printers Using Group Policy

The ability to deploy printer connections to Windows-based client computers using Group Policy was first introduced in Windows Server 2003 R2. You can use Group Policy to deploy printer connections in two ways:

- As per-computer printer connections available for all users who log on to the client computer. You can deploy per-computer printer connections to computers running Windows XP or later.

- As per-user printer connections available to the user on any client computer the user logs on to. You can deploy per-user printer connections to users of computers running Windows 2000 or later.

Deploying printers using Group Policy is useful in scenarios where every user or computer in a room or office needs access to the same printer. Deploying printers using Group Policy can also be useful in large enterprises where users and computers are differentiated by function, workgroup, or department.

Direct from the Field: Configuring Printer Connections Using Group Policy Preferences

Group Policy Preferences, a new feature of Windows Server 2008, provides administrators with another means of deploying, configuring, and managing printer connections on Windows Vista computers. Configuring printer connections is a common task that administrators typically perform by writing logon scripts. The Printers preference extension, however, enables you to easily create, update, replace, or delete shared printers, TCP/IP printers, and local printers to multiple, targeted users or computers. Using preference targeting, you can deploy printer connections based on location, department, computer type, and so on.

Windows Vista Group Policy provides native support for deploying printers. However, it supports only shared printers and requires Active Directory schema extensions. In contrast, the Printers extension supports shared, local, and TCP/IP printers on Windows XP with SP2 and Windows Vista. It also allows you to set the default printer and map shared printers to local ports.

Jerry Honeycutt, Deployment Forum

http://www.deploymentforum.com

Note   For more information about Group Policy Preferences, see Chapter 13, "Managing the Desktop Environment."

Preparing to Deploy Printers

Deploying printers using Group Policy requires you to perform the following preparatory steps:

- If you are not using Windows Server 2008 domain controllers, your Active Directory schema must first be upgraded to Windows Server 2003 R2 level or later. This means the schema revision number must be 9 (for Windows Server 2003) and the schema version number must be 31 (for the R2 schema update). You can use ADSI Edit to determine your current schema version number by looking under the Schema node, right-clicking the object named *CN=Schema,CN=Configuration,DC=forest_root_domain*, selecting Properties, and then examining the value of the *objectVersion* attribute. The R2 schema update is required so that Print Management can create the following two objects in Active Directory:

    ❏ *CN=Schema,CN=Policies,CN=GPO_GUID,CN=Machine,CN=PushPrinterConnections*

    ❏ *CN=Schema,CN=Policies,CN=GPO_GUID,CN=User,CN=PushPrinterConnections*

- If your client computers are running an earlier version of Windows, you must deploy the PushPrinterConnections.exe utility to these clients prior to using Group Policy to deploy printer connections to these computers. The PushPrinterConnections.exe utility reads the Group Policy Objects (GPOs) that are used to deploy printer connections and adds or removes these connections on the client as needed. The easiest way to deploy PushPrinter-Connections.exe is to use a GPO as follows:

    ❏ As a user logon script for deploying per-user printer connections

    ❏ As a computer startup script for deploying per-computer printer connections

    The simplest approach is to use the same GPO to deploy both PushPrinterConnections.exe to targeted users and/or computers using startup/logon scripts, and for deploying the actual printer connections themselves to those users and/or computers. With Windows Vista, however, you do not need to first deploy PushPrinterConnections.exe to client computers, because Windows Vista includes this capability in the operating system.

Deploying a Printer Connection

After you have completed the preceding preparatory steps, you can deploy a printer connection by following these steps:

1. Create a new GPO for deploying the connections or use an existing GPO linked to the organizational unit (OU), domain, or site where the users or computers being targeted reside.

2. Open Print Management, right-click the printer you want to deploy, and select Deploy With Group Policy.

3.   In the Deploy With Group Policy dialog box, click Browse, find and select the GPO you
will use to deploy the printer, and then click OK.

4.   Choose whether to deploy the printer as a per-computer connection, a per-user
connection, or both.

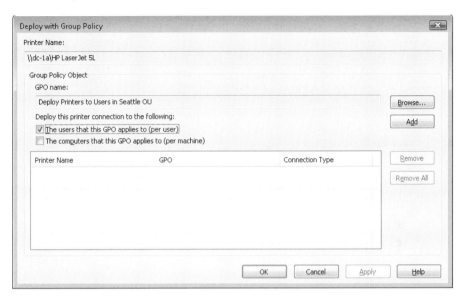

5.   Click Add to add the printer connection settings to the GPO.

6.   If needed, repeat steps 3 through 5 to deploy the same printer to additional GPOs.

7.   Click OK when finished. The printer connection to be deployed using Group Policy will
be displayed under the Deployed Printers node in Printer Management.

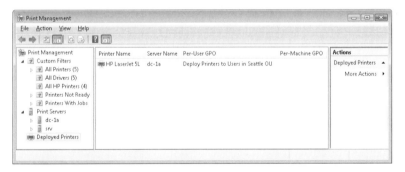

Per-user printer connections can be deployed immediately using Group Policy if the user next
logs off and then on again to a targeted client computer. Per-computer printer connections can
also be deployed immediately if the user's computer is restarted. Neither type of connection
will be deployed on earlier versions of Windows during normal background refresh of Group
Policy. On Windows Vista clients, however, background policy refresh can also deploy both
per-user and per-computer printer connections.

> **Note**   On Windows Vista, users can also force printer connections to be deployed immediately by typing **gpupdate /force** at an elevated command prompt.

The deployed printer connection is also displayed in the GPO used to deploy the connection. To view this, open the Group Policy Management Console (GPMC), right-click the GPO you used to deploy the connection, and then click Edit to open the GPO using the Group Policy Object Editor (Figure 19-5). To remove the deployed printer connection from the targeted users or computers during the next background refresh of Group Policy, right-click the connection and then click Remove. Unlinking the GPO from the OU, domain, or site where the targeted users or computers reside also removes the deployed connections.

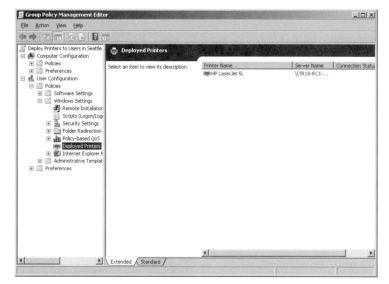

Figure 19-5   Viewing a deployed printer connection in a GPO.

> **Note**   You can also use the Group Policy Results Wizard in the GPMC to collect Resultant Set of Policy (RSoP) information to verify the success or failure of deploying printers using Group Policy. For more information on using Group Policy with Windows Vista, see Chapter 13.

Limitations of Deploying Printers Using Group Policy

The following limitations apply when deploying printer connections to Windows Vista clients using Group Policy:

■ You cannot configure the default printer on the targeted client using Group Policy.

■ Loopback mode is not supported.

Assigning Printers Based on Location

A new feature of Windows Vista is the ability to assign printers based on location. This can be useful in large enterprises that span more than one geographical location, allowing mobile users to update their printers as they move to new locations. When mobile users return to their primary locations, their original default printers are restored.

To assign printers based on location, deploy printers using GPOs linked to Active Directory sites. When a mobile computer moves to a new site, the printer connections for the computer are updated using normal Group Policy processing.

Direct from the Source: Managing Deployed Printer Connections

There are two ways of managing deployed printer connections in Windows Vista:

- Using the Print Management Console
- Using the Group Policy Editor

The following sections describe the differences between these two approaches.

Managing Deployed Printer Connections Using the Print Management Console

Deployed printer connections will be displayed in Print Management's Deployed Printers node for the connections hosted by the current list of monitored servers when the Print Management operator has read access to the domain policies in which printer connections are deployed.

To deploy connections to a Group Policy using the Print Management Console, you must have Write access to the domain policy, and the server that shares the printer must be added to the list of servers that Print Management is monitoring. The operator in charge of printer deployment does not need to have administrative rights on the print server.

The deployed printer connections feature is not used to create local printers, but anyone with administrative rights can add printer connections to the local policy of a computer. Local Policy deployed printer connections is useful when Active Directory is not fully implemented or when setting up systems in a workgroup environment. Some form of peer-to-peer authentication is required when the workgroup computers or users cannot authenticate to a domain controller.

Deployed printers connections do not need to be published to the Active Directory.

Deployed printers do not require any driver download prompts during installation. The user does not have access to delete deployed printer connections. The printer needs to be removed from the policy or the user must be unlinked from the policy for the printer removal to occur.

Managing Deployed Printer Connections Using the Group Policy Editor

This tool has a few advantages over the Print Management snap-in. You don't need to monitor the server sharing the deployed printers. You can deploy printer shares that have yet to be created. The user interface works directly within the selected Group Policy Object. The user does not need to be logged on to the same domain as the Group Policy Object.

The big disadvantage when using this tool rather than the Print Management snap-in is the lack of any print share validation. If valid server and share information is improperly entered, the connection will fail. The advantage, when no share validation is performed, is that this allows for deployment of connections prior to creating the share. After the share is created, the connections will be added for the user during the next policy refresh on Windows Vista clients and the next time PushPrinterConnections.exe is run on previous version clients.

Printers hosted on a server in one domain can easily be deployed to clients in another trusted domain.

Another important use of the Group Policy Editor is in the removal of deployed printers after a print server has been retired. The Group Policy Editor will display the printers deployed to a policy and allow the operator to remove them after the server is no longer available on the network.

Alan Morris, Software Design Engineer

Test, Windows Printing

Migrating Print Servers

You can use either the Printer Migration Wizard or the Printbrm.exe command-line tool to export print queues, printer settings, printer ports, and language monitors and then import them on another print server running Windows. This is an efficient way to consolidate multiple print servers onto a single computer or to replace an older print server with a newer system. The Printer Migration Wizard and the Printbrm.exe command-line tool are new to Windows Vista and replace the earlier Print Migrator 3.1 tool available from the Microsoft Download Center.

 Note   The Printer Migration Wizard can also be useful for backing up print server configurations for disaster recovery purposes. For more information on this topic, see the section titled "Exporting and Importing Print Server Configurations" earlier in this chapter.

Migrate Print Servers Using Print Management

To migrate print servers using Print Management, follow these steps:

1. Open Print Management, right-click the printer server that contains the print queues and printer drivers that you want to export, and then click Export Printers To A File. This launches the Printer Migration Wizard.

2. Review the list of items to be exported and then click Next.

3. Click Browse to specify the location where you want to save your printer export file (*.printerExport), type a name for this file, and then click Open.

4. Click Next to export the print server's print queues and printer drivers as a compressed cabinet (CAB) file with the .printerExport extension.

5. If errors are reported during the export process, click Open Event Viewer to view the related events.

6. Click Finish to complete the export process.

7. Right-click the destination print server to which you want to import the previously exported print queues and printer drivers and then click Import Printers From A File.

8. Click Browse, find the previously saved printer export file, and double-click it.

9. Click Next, review the items to be imported, and then click Next again.

10. Choose the options you want to select on the Select Import Options page of the wizard (these options are described following this procedure).

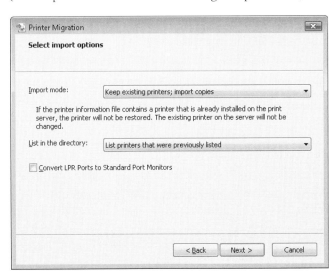

11. Click Next. If errors are reported during the import process, click Open Event Viewer to view the related events.

12. Click Finish to complete the export process.

> **Note** If the printers being migrated were deployed using Group Policy, use Group Policy to remove the deployed printer connections from users' computers before migrating your print server. When the migration is complete, use Group Policy to redeploy the migrated printers.

The available options on the Select Import Options page are:

- **Import Mode** Specifies what to do if a specific print queue already exists on the destination print server. The possible choices are:
  - ❑ Keep Existing Printers; Import Copies (the default)
  - ❑ Overwrite Existing Printers
- **List In The Directory** Specifies whether to publish the imported print queues in Active Directory. The possible choices are:
  - ❑ List Printers That Were Previously Listed (the default)
  - ❑ List All Printers
  - ❑ Don't List Any Printers
- **Convert LPR Ports To Standard Port Monitors** Specifies whether or not to convert Line Printer Remote (LPR) printer ports in the printer settings file to the faster Standard Port Monitor when importing printers.

Migrating Print Servers Using Printbrm.exe

To migrate print servers using Printbrm.exe from the command line, follow these steps:

1. Open an elevated command prompt by clicking Start, pointing to All Programs, clicking Accessories, right-clicking Command Prompt, and then clicking Run As Administrator.

2. To export the print server configuration to a file, type the following commands:

   cd %WinDir%\System32\Spool\Tools

   Printbrm -s \\print_server_name -b -f file_name.printerExport

3. To import the previously saved print server configuration file, type the following commands:

   Printbrm -s \\print_server_name -r -f file_name.printerExport

Monitoring and Troubleshooting Printers

Printer troubleshooting can involve numerous considerations, including device problems such as paper jams, incompatible printer drivers, misconfigured printer settings, problems with the spooler service on the client or the print server, and more. Detailed procedures for troubleshooting printer problems are beyond the scope of this chapter and are not presented here. Instead, the following are some general considerations and recommendations regarding monitoring printers so that support personnel can quickly identify and respond to problems.

For general guidance on how to troubleshoot hardware issues, see Chapter 31, "Troubleshooting Hardware, Driver, and Disk Issues." For additional information about how device drivers are implemented and managed on Windows Vista, see Chapter 16.

Note   You can find additional help on troubleshooting printing in Windows Vista in the white paper "Testing and Troubleshooting the Print Subsystem" at *http://www.microsoft.com/ whdc/device/print/PrtTrblSh.mspx*.

Configuring E-Mail Notifications

When you create a custom printer filter, you have the option of sending an automatic e-mail notification to someone when the conditions of the filter are met. This can be useful for resolving printer problems, particularly in an organization with multiple buildings and administrators. For example, you could set up a view of all printers managed by a particular print server where the status does not equal Ready. Then, if a printer changes from the Ready status to another status, the administrator could receive a notification e-mail from Print Management. (You can also configure e-mail notifications for existing printer filters, including the Printers Not Ready and Printers With Jobs default filters.) To send e-mail notifications, you must specify an SMTP server that can forward these e-mail messages.

To configure e-mail notifications, follow these steps:

1. To set a notification on an existing printer filter, open Printer Management, right-click a printer filter, click Properties, and then click the Notification tab.

2. Select the Send E-mail Notification check box.

3. Specify the following information:

   ❑ In the Recipient E-mail Address(es) text box, type the e-mail address(es) of the recipient(s) using the format *account@domain*. (Use semicolons to separate multiple accounts.)

   ❑ In the Sender E-mail Address text box, type the e-mail address of the sender using the format *account@domain*.

   ❑ In SMTP Server text box, type the fully qualified host name or IP address of the SMTP server that will forward the e-mail notifications.

   ❑ In the Message text box, type a text message describing the conditions of the printer problem.

4. Click Test to verify your SMTP configuration for sending e-mail notifications and then click OK if the test was successful.

Configuring Print Server Notifications

In addition to setting notifications on a custom set of printers by using a printer filter, you can also set notifications for print servers. For example, if the print server is offline or the spooler goes down, an e-mail notification can be sent.

To configure print server notifications, right-click a print server in Print Management, select Set Notifications, and then follow the steps described previously to configure e-mail message parameters.

Configuring Script Actions

When you create custom printer filter for specific printer criteria, you have the option of running a script when the conditions of the filter are met. Script notifications are also defined in the previously described Notifications tab of the printer filter's Properties dialog box.

Setting script notifications can be useful for resolving printer problems and troubleshooting. For example, you could automatically run a script to restart the Spooler service on a print server when its printers go offline. You could also automatically run a script that prints a test page or that notifies your internal monitoring system of a potential problem. Scripts can be written in VBScript or any scripting language available on the computer. The script has to be on the computer that is running Print Management, and the script should be running with suitable credentials and have the permissions needed to do whatever it is that you want the script to do.

An example of a command that you might use in a script to start the Spooler service is the net start spooler command. For sample scripts that you can use and customize to manage print queues, see the list in the section titled "On the Companion CD" at the end of this chapter. You can also find additional scripts on Microsoft TechNet at *http://www.microsoft.com/technet/scriptcenter/scripts/printing/default.mspx*.

Configuring Detailed Event Logging

To save a record of print jobs and their details, you can enable detailed Information event logging as follows:

1. Right-click a print server in Print Management and then select Properties.

2. Click the Advanced tab.

3. Select the Log Spooler Information Events check box.

You can use Event Viewer to view the resulting Information events and then use them either for troubleshooting or auditing purposes. For example, if a bad printer driver is causing reams of paper to be printed with random data on them, you can use these events to identify the user name, print queue, document title, size in pages, and other useful information to determine the possible cause of the problem.

Note   For troubleshooting information about Event Log events related to printing issues, see *http://technet2.microsoft.com/windowsserver2008/en/library/734410f8-de07-465f-ab98-5ba09e3b83fd1033.mspx?mfr=true.*

Summary

Windows Vista includes numerous enhancements in printing technologies and new tools for managing print queues and migrating print servers. Using these new features and tools can provide a more satisfying printing experience for end users and make the job of managing printers within an enterprise easier.

Additional Resources

The following resources contain additional information and tools related to this chapter.

Related Information

- If you have problems with printing or managing printers in Windows Vista and you need help, try posting your questions to the Windows Vista Printing forum on Microsoft TechNet at *http://forums.microsoft.com/TechNet/ShowForum.aspx?ForumID=717&SiteID=17.*

- The Windows Server 2008 Print Services section on Microsoft TechNet at *http://technet2.microsoft.com/windowsserver2008/en/servermanager/printservices.mspx.*

- The "Printing-Architecture and Driver Support" page on Windows Hardware Developer Central (WHDC) at *http://www.microsoft.com/whdc/device/print/default.mspx.*

- The white paper "Point and Print Security on Windows Vista" at *http://www.microsoft.com/whdc/device/print/VistaPnPSec.mspx.*

- The topic "Control printer driver installation security" at *http://technet2.microsoft.com/windowsserver2008/en/library/173ea6f2-3231-404b-92f5-a5d20bb6bed91033.mspx?mfr=true.*

- KB 931477, "Printers that were installed in Windows XP no longer appear to be installed after you upgrade the computer to Windows Vista," at *http://support.microsoft.com/kb/931477.*

- KB 946225, "You are prompted to install a new printer driver in Windows Vista when you try to print to a Windows Server 2008-based print server or to a Windows Server 2003-based print server," at *http://support.microsoft.com/kb/946225.*

- Chapter 13, "Managing the Desktop Environment," for more information about Group Policy in Windows Vista.

- Chapter 16, "Managing Devices and Services," for more information about the driver store and driver packages.

- Chapter 32, "Troubleshooting Network Issues," for more information on troubleshooting procedures.

On the Companion CD

- DisplayPrintQueueStats.vbs

- ListPrinterPorts.vbs

- PrintersAndShares.vbs

- WorkWithPrinters.vbs

Chapter 20

Managing Search

Search in Windows Vista has been enhanced and extended in many ways from previous Windows platforms. A new search-engine architecture provides improved performance and better query capabilities for faster and more focused information retrieval. Integration of the search feature throughout the user interface makes it easier to search for files, e-mail, and other information from within the currently open window. Instant Search produces nearly instantaneous search results as users type their queries, so that they can better focus their queries and narrow search results on the fly, as they type. And Search Folders provide users with a simple way of saving the results of their queries so that they can quickly access frequently needed data, which reduces the need for users to manually organize how they store information on their computers. This chapter explains how search and indexing work in Windows Vista and how to use Group Policy to manage these capabilities from within the user interface.

Search and Indexing Enhancements in Windows Vista

Rapidly growing storage capabilities in enterprise environments mean that the ability to quickly and efficiently find information is essential for knowledge workers. To meet these growing requirements, search capabilities have been enhanced several ways in Windows Vista to overcome limitations in search functionality in earlier versions of Windows.

Issues in Previous Windows Platforms

Search and indexing capabilities in the previous Windows XP Professional platform were limited in several ways:

- Using the Search Companion to search for files was often a slow process. As a result, users often had to spend much of their time organizing their data into hierarchical sets of folders to make information easier to find through folder-specific searches.

- Searching for text within files required enabling Indexing Service (cisvc.exe) on the computer, and by default this service is stopped and set for manual startup.

- The Indexing Service, when enabled, tended to be intrusive in its operation by being CPU- and I/O-intensive, which sometimes interfered with other user activity on the system.

- E-mail search capabilities in applications such as Microsoft Office Outlook were not integrated with the way search and indexing worked in Windows.

- The search query syntax was limited in scope and capabilities. Specifically, there was no support for keywords such as From: and the Indexing Service was restricted to file content.

Design Goals and New Features

To resolve these and other issues, search and indexing functionality in Windows Vista has been extended and enhanced. A completely new search-engine architecture replaces the Indexing Service to provide better performance and improved query capabilities. Indexing of content is now enabled by default and provides support for querying both the full text and also metadata (properties) of common document formats. The engine's extensibility also allows independent software vendors (ISVs) to provide plug-ins that allow users to search third-party document formats, such as Adobe Portable Document Format (PDF), as well as other storage repositories such as the offline files cache and MAPI stores such as Outlook .pst files by enabling such files and stores to be indexed. Search-engine activity is now also less intrusive, allowing indexing to occur during idle periods and interfere less with other user activity on the system.

With word-wheeled search (or search-as-you-type) functionality, Windows Vista users can watch the results of their queries narrow as they type the filename or word they are looking for. This makes the search experience for the user much more responsive than in earlier platforms, where users had to type their search string and click Search each time they wanted to run a query.

Search capability is now integrated into the shell in numerous places, making search easy to perform because of the ubiquitous presence of the Instant Search box within the Start menu, Control Panel, any Explorer window, and other Windows Vista experiences. In addition, each instance of the Instant Search box is tuned to provide the most suitable results for the types of queries that users might perform. For example, the Instant Search box integrated into the Start menu is best suited for searching for programs installed on the system.

New capabilities such as Search Folders; enhanced column headers; the ability to sort, group, and stack files and folders; and the ability to tag files and folders with descriptive keywords all make it much easier for users to find files on their computers without having to spend a lot of time organizing them into hierarchical sets of folders. In addition to being able to search for content within more than 200 common types of files (and to search for basic properties like filename and size for any file type), users can also search for e-mail messages in Windows Mail or Office Outlook (if installed, either from within Windows Mail or from the Start menu or Windows Explorer). Users who store documents on removable drives, such as USB drives, can also do indexed searches of content stored on these drives so that they can search this content for files and text. OneNote 2007 also takes advantage of Windows Vista's Windows Search service.

Using Advanced Search and the new Advanced Query Syntax (AQS) and Natural Language (NL) query functionality, users can easily create complex queries to return highly focused results and then save these queries for future use. Windows Vista also includes a number of preconfigured Search Folders that help users to quickly find recently changed documents and recent e-mail messages. Users can also create their own Search Folders by saving the results of frequently used queries to save time and provide easy access to needed documents. All of these new search features simplify the job of managing the large amounts of data typically found on computers used by today's information workers.

By default, client-side caching is enabled in Windows Vista so that redirected folders are accessible to users when their computers are not connected to the network. These redirected folders are now indexed locally so that users can search their contents even when their computers are not on the network or when the server to where their user profile folders have been redirected is down. The cached versions of offline folders are also indexed locally so that network shares marked offline can even be searched when the user's computer is not connected to the network. Using Windows Vista together with the 2007 Microsoft Office system also lets users take Microsoft Windows SharePoint Services version 3 (WSS v3) libraries and documents offline using Microsoft Office Outlook 2007 and search these libraries and documents while they are offline.

Users of Windows Vista computers can now use distributed search to easily search for shared information on other computers running Windows Vista and Windows Server 2008. (This is also known as computer-to-computer search.) The results of such a search are security-trimmed so that search results display only those files and documents that the user has permission to access. At the time of this writing, distributed search is limited to Windows Vista and Windows Server 2008. However, Windows Search 4.0 (set for release in 2008 H2) will also support distributed search for the Windows XP and Windows Server 2003 platforms.

Note   To remote search content on a Windows Server 2008 server, the optional Windows Search service must be installed on the server, which can be done by adding the File Services role to the server and including the Windows Search Service role service for this role. For more information on the File Services role in Windows Server 2008, see *http://technet2.microsoft.com/windowsserver2008/en/library/9913d3a3-bf49-4bf4-b1b9-7c4896152c701033.mspx?mfr=true*.

How Search and Indexing Works in Windows Vista

The underlying architecture and operation of indexing has changed considerably in Windows Vista compared with search capabilities built into earlier versions of Windows. Understanding how search and indexing works in Windows Vista is essential to configuring, maintaining, and troubleshooting search and indexing.

Understanding Search Engine Terminology

The following terminology relates to search and indexing as it has been implemented in Windows Vista:

- **Catalog**   The system index together with the property cache.

- **Crawl scopes (inclusions and exclusions)**   Included and excluded paths within a search root. For example, if a user wants to index the D drive but exclude D:\Temp, he would add a Crawl Scope (inclusion) for "D:*" and a Crawl Scope (Exclusion) for "D:\Temp*". The Crawl Scope Manager would also add a start address for "D:\".

- **Gathering**   The process of discovering and accessing items from a data store using protocol handlers and IFilters.

- **IFilter**   A component of the Windows search engine that is used to extract the text from the properties and contents of documents so that they can be indexed. IFilters are also responsible for extracting a number of format-dependent properties such as Subject, Author, and Locale. Microsoft provides IFilters for many common document formats by default, and third-party vendors such as Adobe provide their own IFilters for indexing other types of content.

- **Property handler**   A component of Windows that is used to extract format-dependent properties. This component is used both by the Windows search engine to read and index property values and also by Windows Explorer to read and write property values directly in the file. Microsoft provides property handlers for many common formats by default.

- **Indexing**   The process of building the system index and property cache, which together form the catalog.

- **Master index**   A single index formed by combining shadow indexes together using a process called the master merge. The master index is a content index and conceptually it maps words to documents or other items.

- **Master merge**   The process of combining index fragments (shadow indexes) together into a single content index called the master index.

- **Property cache**   The persistent cache of properties (metadata) for indexed items. This metadata can include the title or author of a document, and indexing this information allows search results to return this information when the index is queried.

- **Property store**   Another name for the property cache.

- **Protocol handler**   A component of the Windows search engine that is used to communicate with and enumerate the contents of stores such as the file system, Messaging Application Program Interface (MAPI) e-mail database, and the client-side cache (CSC) or offline files database. Like IFilters, protocol handlers are also extensible.

- **Start address**   A URL that points to the starting location for indexed content. When indexing is performed, each configured starting address is enumerated by a protocol handler to find the content to be indexed.

- **Search root**   The base namespace of a given protocol handler.

- **Search defaults**   The default crawl scope(s) for a given search root.

- **Shadow indexes**   Temporary indexes that are created during the indexing process and then combined into a single index called the master index.

- **Shadow merge**   The process of combining index fragments (shadow indexes) together into next level of index. The resulting index file will still be a shadow index, but merging indexes into bigger entities improves query performance.

- **System index**   The entire index on the system, including the master index, shadow indexes, and various configuration files, log files, and temporary files.

Note   IFilters can also be registered to new file types. For example, you can register the Plain Text filter for use with .cpp files.

Direct from the Source: The Evolution of Windows Desktop Search (WDS)

Content indexing was first introduced by Index Server in the NT4 Option Pack and then was included in every version of Windows beginning with Windows 2000. The Index Server name was later changed to Indexing Service. This component includes a file indexer but no gathering or crawling functionality, and it was not extensible to nonfile system content. Site Server introduced the first Microsoft gatherer (or crawler) and reused the content index technology from Index Server. At the same time, content indexing was also added to SQL Server 7 and has been enhanced in later versions of SQL Server (as well as Exchange Server). The indexing pipeline was rewritten for SQL Server 2005 to provide enormous increases in indexing throughput and scale for large databases.

SharePoint Portal Server 2001 and later versions built on the gathering and content indexing components from SQL Server 2000 and Exchange 2000 Server to provide aggregated gathering for portal and nonportal content. Eventually, this code base was retuned for the client desktop by the MSN team that produced Windows Desktop

> Search (WDS). Finally, WDS 3.0 was integrated into Windows Vista as a system service and platform for use by applications (including the 2007 Microsoft Office system).
>
> Note for trivia buffs: Microsoft Office XP shipped a version of the indexing engine for use on NT4 and Windows 98 (but would use the Indexing Service on Windows 2000).
>
> *Joe Sherman, Principal Program Manager*
>
> *Windows Experience, Find & Organize Team*

Windows Search Engine Processes

The new Windows search engine in Windows Vista is based on the MSSearch indexing and search engine developed previously for Microsoft SQL Server, Microsoft SharePoint Portal Server, Microsoft Office SharePoint Server, and other Microsoft products. The new Windows search engine replaces the Indexing Service (cisvc.exe) used in downlevel Windows platforms, including Windows XP and Windows Server 2003.

The new Windows search engine in Windows Vista logically consists of the following four processes:

■ **Indexer process**   The indexer process (SearchIndexer.exe) is the main component of the Windows search engine and is responsible for core indexing and searching activity on the system. This process is implemented as a Windows service named Windows Search service (WSearch) and is exposed for management in the shell through the Service Control Manager (Services.msc), as shown in Figure 20-1. This service runs in the context of the LocalSystem account but has all privileges removed except for the following two privileges:

❑ **SE_BACKUP_PRIVILEGE**   This privilege allows the service to read every file on the system so that they can be indexed.

❑ **SE_MANAGE_VOLUME_PRIVILEGE**   This privilege allows the service to interact with the NTFS change journal.

■ **System-wide Protocol Host**   The system-wide Protocol Host (SearchProtocolHost.exe) is a separate process that hosts Protocol Handlers, which are plug-ins assessing different stores, retrieving documents, and pushing the information to the SearchFilterHost process for filtering. The system-wide Protocol Host runs within the same LocalSystem context as the main indexer process. This security context is needed because the Protocol Host requires access to all files on the system. The system-wide Protocol Host also supports cross-user notifications and enumeration of per-computer data stores such as the local file system.

- **Per-user Protocol Host**   The per-user Protocol Host (also SearchProtocolHost.exe) is another separate process that hosts Protocol Handlers to isolate them from the main indexer process. The difference between this process and the system-wide Protocol Host is that this process runs within the security context of the logged-on user. (If two users are logged on to the computer and are using Fast User Switching, it is likely that two per-user Protocol Hosts will be running.) A per-user Protocol Host is necessary because some data stores must be accessed using the credentials of the logged-on user to be indexed. Examples of such stores include Outlook e-mail (using MAPI), the client-side cache (CSC), and remote file shares.

> **Note**   Locally indexing remote file shares requires installing the separately download-able UNC Protocol Handler on your computer. For more information concerning this, see the sidebar titled "Understanding the UNC Protocol Handler" later in this chapter.

- **Search Filter Host Process**   This process (which runs as SearchFilterHost.exe) hosts IFilters, which are used to extract text from files and other items. IFilters are hosted within a separate process instead of within the main indexer process to ensure the stability of the indexing engine because IFilters are generally considered to be untrusted code and are run within a separate process to protect the Windows Search service from possible crashes. This is needed because although many IFilters are written by Microsoft, some IFilters may be written by third-party vendors. Hosting IFilters within a separate process (a filtering host) that has very restricted permissions (a restricted token) provides a level of isolation that protects the main indexer process if an IFilter crashes. The indexer process runs a single instance of SearchFilterProcess.exe, and this process holds all IFilters parsing documents that come from the system-wide and per-user SearchProtocolHost processes. This Search Filter Host process only reads streams of content, runs IFilters, and returns text to the Indexer process.

In normal operation, each of these processes starts immediately after Windows Vista boots and the desktop appears. The main indexer process (SearchIndexer.exe) is the only one that always continues to run, however—the other processes may or may not be running, depending on the immediate needs of the Windows search engine. The main indexer process uses the standard service mechanism (SCM) to detect when the service is not running and then restart itself.

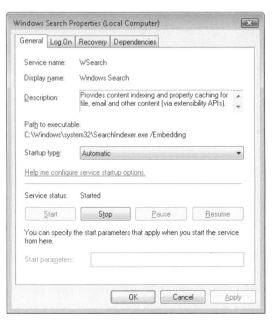

Figure 20-1 Properties of the Windows Search service (WSearch).

Enabling the Indexing Service

The Indexing Service (cisvc.exe) used in previous Windows platforms is still available in Windows Vista as an optional component that administrators can turn on if needed by following these steps:

1. Select Programs from Control Panel.

2. Under Programs And Features, click Turn Windows Features On Or Off and respond to the UAC prompt that appears.

3. In the Turn Windows Features On Or Off dialog box, select the Indexing Service check box and then click OK.

The main reason enterprises might need to enable the previous Indexing Service would be for application compatibility reasons. For example, if enterprises develop applications that depend on cisvc.exe, they can enable this service to support those applications. Microsoft Office Visio shape finding also uses cisvc.exe to index shapes, so if you need fast shape search in Visio on some computers, you could enable cisvc.exe on those computers after they have been upgraded to Windows Vista.

Note that Microsoft does not recommend running the Indexing Service on Windows Vista computers unless there is a compelling need to do so, and the next version of Microsoft Windows will not include this legacy service.

Windows Search Engine Architecture

The architecture of the Windows search engine in Windows Vista, shown in Figure 20-2, illustrates the interaction between the four search-engine processes described previously, the user's desktop session and client applications, user data (including local and network file stores, MAPI stores, and the CSC), and persistent index data stored in the catalog. The sections that follow outline in detail how the indexing service works and how the catalog is created and configured.

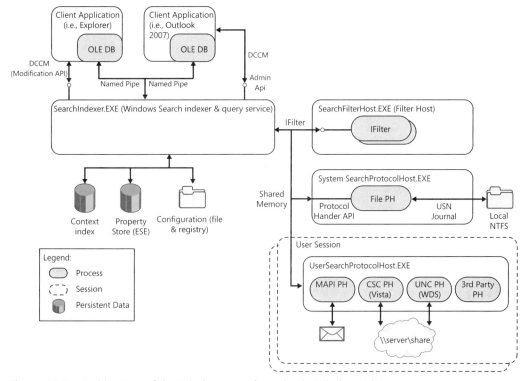

Figure 20-2   Architecture of the Windows search engine in Windows Vista.

Understanding the Catalog

The catalog contains the results of the indexing process running on the local computer. Each Windows Vista computer has a single catalog that is located by default in the Search subfolder under the %SystemDrive%\ProgramData\Microsoft folder. (You must make hidden files visible to view the ProgramData folder and its contents.) The catalog contains three main types of information:

■ The full-text index of all content that has been crawled by the indexer.

■ The property store, which is a Jet database that contains the properties of files that have been indexed. (The Windows Vista property schema is used to decide which properties are cached.)

■ Configuration files that control how the indexer works. (Additional configuration settings are stored in the registry.)

Although the catalog indexes items for all users who use the computer, the property store contains security descriptors for each item. Thus the indexer can security-trim the results of queries against the index so that the results returned include only documents that the user who is performing the query can access.

Note The location of the catalog can be changed either using Indexing Options in Control Panel or using Group Policy. For more information, see the section titled "Configuring the Catalog" later in this chapter.

Direct from the Source: Windows Vista Desktop Search Service Files and Subfolders Structure

The configuration and data files of the Windows Search service are kept under %SystemDrive% \ProgramData\Microsoft\Search. There are two subfolders: Config and Data.

\ProgramData\Microsoft\Search\Config

The only file kept in the Config folder is Msscolmn.txt. This is a configuration file describing human-readable names for the properties associated with documents and corresponding full property specification and property type.

\ProgramData\Microsoft\Search\Data

There are three subfolders under Data: Config, Temp, and Applications.

\ProgramData\Microsoft\Search\Data\Config

This Config folder contains two files: Gathrprm.txt and Schema.txt. Gathrprm.txt keeps Windows Search service parameters, the mappings between GUID+Name full property specifications to GUID+Number mentioned in Msscolmn.txt. Schema.txt describes the property schema used for indexing—the set of properties, their corresponding identifiers, property types, whether the property is indexed and/or retrievable (property value is saved to the Property Store), and a number of other options. The three .txt files mentioned here (Msscolmn.txt, Gathrprm.txt, and Schema.txt) are the minimal configuration file set required for the Windows Search service to function. The rest of the files under \ProgramData\Microsoft\Search are not so critical, because they can be re-created during catalog reset, so their corruption can cause current index content loss but won't block the Windows Search service from functioning completely.

\ProgramData\Microsoft\Search\Data\Temp

The Temp folder is used by Windows Search for temporary files creation.

\ProgramData\Microsoft\Search\Data\Applications

The Applications folder contains subfolders corresponding to the applications in the Windows Search service. In this context, "Applications" is not equivalent to "program" but rather refers to a logical entity bound to a specific Property Store. The only application supported in Windows Vista is Windows, so the only subfolder under Applications is Windows.

\ProgramData\Microsoft\Search\Data\Applications\Windows

The Windows folder contains the subfolders Config, GatherLog, and Projects, along with a number of *.edb and MSS*.* files. These are Jet database data files and logs that contain the Property Store.

\ProgramData\Microsoft\Search\Data\Application\Windows\Config

The Config folder is an exact copy of \ProgramData\Microsoft\Search\Config.

\ProgramData\Microsoft\Search\Data\Application\Windows\GatherLog

The GatherLog folder contains the single subfolder SystemIndex, which corresponds to the only catalog supported by the Windows Search service. (See the following Projects folder description for details.)

\ProgramData\Microsoft\Search\Data\Application\Windows\GatherLog\SystemIndex

The SystemIndex folder contains a number of SystemIndex.*.Crwl and System-Index.*.gthr files. The .Crwl files are log files tracking crawl transaction processing results. The .gthr files contain processing results for the notification transactions.

\ProgramData\Microsoft\Search\Data\Applications\Windows\Projects

The Projects folder contains subfolders corresponding to the different catalogs (projects). Catalogs are how the index is partitioned. The only catalog supported by the Windows Search service is SystemIndex, so this SystemIndex folder is the only subfolder under Projects.

\ProgramData\Microsoft\Search\Data\Applications\Windows\Projects\SystemIndex

The SystemIndex folder contains the subfolders Indexer, PropMap, SecStore, and a number of SystemIndex.chk*.gthr and SystemIndex.Ntfy*.gthr files. The System-Index.Ntfy*.gthr files are transaction logs. For a situation in which the document change event rate is higher than the document indexing rate (for example, when Outlook mailbox initial indexing happens or when there is considerable file churn on a file system), the number of events queued in memory for processing grows and the Windows Search service preempts some event records waiting to be processed from memory to the transaction log files to reduce system memory usage. As soon as the notification rate decreases, the Windows Search service will load the notifications from transaction log files back into memory and complete their processing. The System-Index.chk1.gthr and SystemIndex.chk2.gthr files work as persistent storage for gatherer checkpoint information. On system start, this checkpoint information indicates whether or not Windows Search was shut down properly and helps to roll back to a consistent state in case a crash happened.

\ProgramData\Microsoft\Search\Data\Applications\Windows\Projects\SystemIndex\PropMap

The PropMap folder contains data files of the proprietary database used for mapping full property specifications to internal property identificators.

\ProgramData\Microsoft\Search\Data\Applications\Windows\Projects\SystemIndex\SecStore

The SecStore folder contains data files of the proprietary database used for keeping access permissions in the form of SIDs for all indexed documents.

\ProgramData\Microsoft\Search\Data\Applications\Windows\Projects\SystemIndex\Indexer

The Indexer folder contains only one subfolder: CiFiles.

\ProgramData\Microsoft\Search\Data\Applications\Windows\Projects\SystemIndex\Indexer\CiFiles

The CiFiles folder contains the index files themselves, including shadow indexes and the master index. These index files include:

- The SETTINGS.DIA file, which contains diacritic settings.
- The *.ci files, which are index files containing indexed words, occurrence information, and references to the documents containing these words.
- The *.dir files, which are index directory files containing lookup tables for the *.ci files content to enable fast positioning inside the index without scanning the index file from the very beginning.
- The *.wid and *.wsb files, which are the *fresh test*, meaning a table of the documents specifying which information is up to date in the corresponding *.ci file. The trick is to write every *.ci file only once when it is created and never modify it later. If the information in the *.ci file concerning some document is no

> longer valid, the indexer just marks the document as invalid for this particular *.ci file.
>
> - The files INDEX.000, INDEX.001, INDEX.002, which implement fault-resistible persistent storage for the index table keeping records concerning all index files in use.
>
> - The CiMG*.* files, which are merge progress logs that enable the index merge process to continue when interrupted by service shutdown (or even a crash) without having to restart indexing from the very beginning.
>
> - The CiAD*.* and CiAB*.* files, which are average document length logs that are used for relevance metric calculations.
>
> *Max Georgiev, Software Development Engineer*
>
> *File & Organize Group of Windows Client Division*

Default System Exclusion Rules

System exclusion rules define which files will be excluded from being indexed. By default, the following folders and files are excluded:

- %SystemDrive%\ProgramData* (with some exceptions, such as %SystemDrive%\programData\Windows\StartMenu)
- %SystemDrive%\users\default*
- *\system volume information*
- *\$Recycle.bin*
- *\Temp*
- *\Windows.**
- *\dfsrprivate*

In addition, super-hidden files (protected operating system files that have both the hidden and system attributes set on them) and files that have their FILE_ATTRIBUTE_NOT_CONTENT_INDEXED attribute (FANCI bit) set are not indexed.

> ### How It Works: Understanding the FANCI Attribute
>
> When the FILE_ATTRIBUTE_NOT_CONTENT_INDEXED attribute (also known as FANCI bit) is set on a file, the file will *not* be indexed even if the location is an indexed location. Removing this attribute (when the check box is selected) allows the file to be indexed if it is in an indexed location, but it does not automatically make that location an indexed location. The attribute never indicates if a file is indexed, only whether it

should be indexed if it is in an indexed location. The order of operation at indexing time is to first look in the set of indexed locations, and then only to index items that do not have the FANCI attribute set. If the attribute is set (or removed) on an item outside of an indexed location, it has no effect.

Just to be clear: To *set* the FANCI bit on a file (or folder or volume), right-click the item, select Properties, click Advanced, and clear the check box labeled Index This File [or Folder or Volume] For Faster Searching. To *clear* the FANCI bit on the item, right-click, select Properties, and then select the check box. You can also toggle the FANCI bit using the attrib +i command from the command prompt.

If the FANCI bit is set this attribute on a folder (or drive), you will be given the options either to set only the attribute on the root location or to also cascade the change down to all subfolders and files. In addition, any new files created within the directory will inherit the FANCI bit. Existing files that are copied into the directory, however, will retain the current state of their FANCI bit (set or cleared). You can also set the attribute on a directory, and when applying the change, have it propagate recursively to all descendent files and folders.

Note that selecting the Index This Drive [or Folder] For Faster Searching check box for a volume or directory only *enables* the Windows Search service to index the volume or directory; it doesn't actually *cause* the contents of the volume or directory to be indexed. To do that, you need to add the volume or directory to the list of indexed locations using Indexing Options in Control Panel. For example, if you want to index the contents of a volume or directory, open Indexing Options in Control Panel, click Modify, click Show All Locations if you are running as a Standard user, and examine the check box under Change Seleted Locations for the volume or directory:

- If the check box is selected, the volume or directory is already being indexed.

- If the check box is cleared but available, the volume or directory is not yet being indexed. To index the volume or directory, select the check box to clear the FANCI bit and then click OK.

- If the check box is cleared and the volume or directory name appears dimmed (unavailable), the volume or directory does not have its FANCI bit set and so can't be indexed. To index the volume or directory, right-click the dimmed volume or directory name, select Properties, and then click Advanced and select the Index This Drive [or Folder] For Faster Searching check box. Close all properties pages by clicking OK several times, then reopen the Indexed Locations dialog box from Indexing Options and select the check box for the volume or directory.

Be cautious about changing the FANCI attribute for locations that by default have the FANCI bit set, because this can have a negative impact on the indexer. Some locations (such as the location for indexer data files, \ProgramData\Microsoft\Search) should *never* have the FANCI bit removed. Other locations, such as the ProgramData directory, may contain files that are updated on a very frequent basis. Having these files within the indexing scope will cause the indexer to index them each time they are updated, and this could adversely affect system performance.

A quick way to see *all* files that have the FANCI bit set for a drive is to make use of the dir command. For example, to find all FANCI files under the C:\ directory and all subdirectories, and to save the results to the file C:\fanci.txt, you can run **dir C:\ /AI /S >C:\fanci.txt** from an elevated command prompt.

Note   Windows Search does index hidden files (and also system files, but not files that are marked as both system and hidden). However, because hidden files are marked as hidden in the index, they are displayed in search results only if the user's folder settings are set to Show Hidden Files/Folders.

Default Start Addresses

Start addresses (also called indexing scopes) are URLs that point to the starting locations for indexed content. When indexing is performed, each configured start address is enumerated by the appropriate protocol handler so that the indexing engine can find the content that needs to be indexed. By default, the following locations are indexed for the local volume:

■ The Start menu (file:///%SystemDrive%\ProgramData\Microsoft\Windows\Start Menu)

■ The Users folder ((file:///%SystemDrive%\Users) and all user profile folders within it except for the Default user profile folder)

■ The Offline Files cache (csc://{user's SID}) for all users who use the computer

By default, all files and folders within these locations are indexed unless they are specifically excluded by a system exclusion rule as described previously.

Note   You can add additional crawl scopes by using Indexing Options in Control Panel. See the section titled "Configuring the Catalog" later in this chapter for more information. If Office Outlook 2007 is installed on the computer, this also appears as a default indexed location.

Initial Configuration

When Windows Vista is installed on a computer, the Windows search engine configuration code performs the following steps:

1. The Windows Search service is started.

2. The system catalog is created (first time).

3. The file, MAPI, and CSC protocol handlers are registered.

4. Predefined system exclusion and inclusion rules are added (first time).

5. Predefined start addresses are added (first time).

How It Works: Internationalization

Windows Vista search is language-agnostic, but the accuracy of searches across languages may vary because of the tokenization of text performed by components called *wordbreakers*. Wordbreakers implement the variable tokenization rules for languages. Wordbreakers will break down both the language of the indexed text and the query string; a mismatch between query and indexed language can cause unpredictable results.

Windows Vista ships with a well-defined set of wordbreakers and includes new tokenization code based on the Lexical Service Platform (LSP) for some languages. For others, LSP will delegate to the class wordbreakers. If no wordbreaker is installed for a language, a neutral white-space breaker will be used. (Windows Vista provides wordbreakers for 43 different languages.)

Windows Vista Search does not attempt to examine and detect the language of a text chunk. At index time, the IFilter should determine the language of a property or chunk. If a file format does not encode language information, the system locale typically is used as a default. At query time, the calling application (the shell, for example) designates the locale of the query.

Microsoft Global Technical Readiness Platforms Team

Understanding the Indexing Process

Understanding how the indexing process works is helpful for troubleshooting issues regarding searching and indexing in Windows Vista. The sections that follow outline different aspects of this process.

Types of Files Indexed

IFilters, property handlers, and the Windows Vista property system are used to extract text from documents so that they can be indexed. Microsoft provides IFilters and property handlers for many common document formats by default, while installing other Microsoft applications may also install additional IFilters and property handlers to allow indexing of additional properties and content for documents created by these applications. In addition, third-party vendors may provide their own IFilters and property handlers for indexing proprietary document formats.

IFilters and property handlers are selected on the basis of the file's extension. IFilters understand file formats, whereas property handlers typically just understand file properties. For example, files with the extension .txt are scanned using the Plain Text filter; files with the .doc extension are scanned using the Microsoft Office filter; and files with the .mp3 extension are scanned using the Audio property handler. All of these extensions are additionally scanned with the Windows Vista property system to extract basic properties such as filename and size. The Plain Text filter emits full-text content only because text files do not have extended properties (metadata). The Microsoft Office filter, however, emits both full-text content and metadata because .doc files and other Microsoft Office files can have extended properties such as Title, Subject, Authors, Date Last Saved, and so on.

Table 20-1 lists common document formats, their associated file extensions, and the IFilter DLL included in Windows Vista that is used to scan each type of document. (Table 20-2 then provides similar information for property handlers.) Note that the indexer scans files based on their file extension, not the type of content within the file. For example, a text file named test.txt will have its contents scanned and indexed by the Plain Text filter, but a text file named Test.doc will not—the Microsoft Office filter will be used to scan the file and will expect the file to be a .doc file and not a text file.

> **Note**   The following file extensions are excluded by default from being indexed: .386, .aps, .bin, .bk1, .bk2, .bkf, .blf, .bsc, .btr, .cat, .cfg, .cgm, .chk, .ci, .crwl, .cur, .dat, .dbg, .dct, .dir, .dl_, .el, .evt, .ex_, .exp, .eyb, .fnt, .fon, .ghi, .gthr, .hqx, .icm, .idb, .idx, .ilk, .imc, .in_, .inl, .inv, .ipp, .jbf, .lib, .local, .log, .log1, .log2, .m14, .mac, .man, .manifest, .map, .MAPIMail, .mmf, .mui, .muimanifest, .mv, .ncb, .obj, .oc_, .ocx, .onecache, .onetoc, .onetoc2, .ost, .pch, .pdb, .pds, .pf, .pic, .pma, .pmc, .pml, .pmr, .pst, .res, .rmp, .rpc, .rsp, .sbr, .sc2, .sit, .sr_, .sy_, .sym, .tlb, .tlh, .TMCONTAINER00000000000000000001, .TMCONTAINER00000000000000000002, .tmf, .tmp, .ttc, .ttf, .ttx, .ufm, .vbx, .vxd, .wll, .wlt, .xbm, .xix, .z96, and .ZFSendToTarget.

Table 20-1   IFilters Included in Windows Vista by Document Format and File Extension

Document Format	File Extensions	IFilter DLL
Plain Text	.a, .ans, .asc, .asm, .asx, .bas, .bat, .bcp, .c, .cc, .cls, .cmd, .cpp, .cs, .csa, .csv, .cxx, .dbs, .def, .dic, .dos, .dsp, .dsw, .ext, .faq, .fky, .h, .hpp, .hxx, .i, .ibq, .idl, .idq, .inc, .inf, .ini, .inl, .inx, .jav, .java, .js, .kci, .lgn, .log, .lst, .m3u, .mak, .map, .mdb, .mk, .msg, .odh, .odl, .pl, .prc, .rc, .rc2, .rct, .reg, .rgs, .rul, .s, .scc, .sol, .sql, .tab, .tdl, .tif, .tiff, .tlh, .tli, .trg, .txt, .udf, .udt, .usr, .vbs, .viw, .vspscc, .vsscc, .vssscc, .wri, .wtx	query.dll
RTF	.rtf	RTFfilt.dll
Microsoft Office Document	.doc, .dot, .pot, .pps, .ppt, .xlb, .xlc, .xls, .xlt	offfilt.dll
Microsoft Ics	.ics	icsfiltr.dll
HTML	.ascx, .asp, .aspx, .css, .hhc, .hta, .htm, .html, .htt, .htw, .htx, .odc, .shtm, .shtml, .sor, .srf, .stm, .user, .vcproj	nlhtml.dll

Table 20-1   IFilters Included in Windows Vista by Document Format and File Extension

Document Format	File Extensions	IFilter DLL
MIME HTML	.mht, .mhtml	mimefilt.dll
XML	.xml, .xsd, .xsl, .xslt	xmlfilt.dll
Journal	.jnt	jntfiltr.dll
XPS	.xps	mscoree.dll

Table 20-2   Property Handlers Included in Windows Vista by Document Format and File Extension

Document Format	File Extensions	Property Handler DLL
Contacts	.contact	wab32.dll
System	.cpl, .dll, .exe, .ocx, .rll, .sys	shell32.dll
Fonts	.fon, .otf, .ttc, .ttf	shell32.dll
.Group Shell Extension	.group	wab32.dll
Audio Media	.mp3, .wav, .wma	Mediametadatahandler.dll
Internet Shortcut	.url	Ieframe.dll
Games	.ChessTitansSave-ms, .ComfyCakesSave-ms, .FreeCellSave-ms, .HeartsSave-ms, .HoldemSave-ms, .MahjongTitansSave-ms, .MinesweeperSave-ms, .PurblePairsSave-ms, .PurbleShopSave-ms, .SolitaireSave-ms, .SpiderSolitaireSave-ms	
Images	.bmp, .dib, .gif, .ico, .jfif, .jpe, .jpeg, .jpg, .png, .rle, .tif, .tiff	PhotoMetadataHandler.dll
Microsoft XPS	.xps	Xpsshhdr.dll
Microsoft Office Document	.doc, .dot, .msi, .msp, .pot, .ppt, .xls, .xlt	Propsys.dll
Property Labels	.label	Shdocvw.dll
Search Folder	.search-ms	Shdocvw.dll
Shell Messages	.eml, .nws	Inetcomm.dll
Shortcut	.lnk	Shell32.dll
Video Media	.asf, .avi, .dvr-ms, .wmv	Mediametadatahandler.dll

Note that not all of the file types (extensions) listed in the Table 20-1 are enabled for indexing by default. For example, by default the Plain Text filter will scan files with the extension .txt but not files with the extension .log, even though the filter supports scanning of .log files. To configure the indexer to scan such files using the default filter, see the section titled "Modifying IFilter Behavior" later in this chapter.

Two additional (implicit) IFilters and their extensions are not shown in Table 20-1:

■ **File Properties filter**   This filter is used to index the system properties only of files for which there is no registered IFilter, or for which there is a registered IFilter but one has explicitly gone into Control Panel and selected the "Index Properties Only" option for the extension. File extensions that use this filter include .cat, .cfg, .evt, .idx, .mig, .msi, .ost, .pif, and so on. Note that the File Properties filter isn't really a filter per se, but instead represents the absence of a registered filter for these extensions. In other words, it relies on the File System Protocol Handler to provide the file properties.

■ **Null filter**   This filter extracts the same properties as the File Properties filter and is used to deal with backward compatability issues with legacy methods for registering IFilters. Again, this is not really a filter per se, and it relies on the File System Protocol Handler to provide the file properties. The file extensions that use the Null filter are .386, .aif, .aifc, .aiff, .aps, .art, .asf, .au, .avi, .bin, .bkf, .bmp, .bsc, .cab, .cda, .cgm, .cod, .com, .cpl, .cur, .dbg, .dct, .desklink, .dib, .dl_, .dll, .drv, .emf, .eps, .etp, .ex_, .exe, .exp, .eyb, .fnd, .fnt, .fon, .ghi, .gif, .gz, .hqx, .icm, .ico, .ilk, .imc, .in_, .inv, .jbf, .jfif, .jpe, .jpeg, .jpg, .latex, .lib, .m14, .m1v, .mapimail, .mid, .midi, .mmf, .mov, .movie, .mp2, .mp2v, .mp3, .mpa, .mpe, .mpeg, .mpg, .mpv2, .mv, .mydocs, .ncb, .obj, .oc_, .ocx, .pch, .pdb, .pds, .pic, .pma, .pmc, .pml, .pmr, .png, .psd, .res, .rle, .rmi, .rpc, .rsp, .sbr, .sc2, .scd, .sch, .sit, .snd, .sr_, .sy_, .sym, .sys, .tar, .tgz, .tlb, .tsp, .ttc, .ttf, .url, .vbx, .vxd, .wav, .wax, .wll, .wlt, .wm, .wma, .wmf, .wmp, .wmv, .wmx, .wmz, .wsz, .wvx, .xix, .z, .z96, .ZFSendToTarget, and .zip.

Note   Files that have no file extension have only their properties indexed, not their contents.

Get the Microsoft Filter Pack

The Windows Search service can be enhanced by installing the Microsoft Filter Pack, which provides additional IFilters to support critical search scenarios across multiple Microsoft Search products. The Filter Pack includes the following IFilters:

■ Metro (.docx, .docm, .pptx, .pptm, .xlsx, .xlsm, .xlsb)

■ Visio (.vdx, .vsd, .vss, .vst, .vdx, .vsx, .vtx)

■ OneNote (.one)

■ Zip (.zip)

These IFilters are designed to provide enhanced search functionality for the following products: SPS2003, MOSS2007, Search Server 2008, Search Server 2008 Express, WSSv3, Exchange 2007, SQL 2005, SQL 2008, and Windows Desktop Search 3.01.

When you install the Filter Pack, the IFilters in the preceding list are installed and registered with the Windows Search service. The Filter Pack is available from

> *http://www.microsoft.com/downloads/details.aspx?FamilyId=60C92A37-719C-4077-B5C6-CAC34F4227CC&displaylang=en* for both x86 and x64 versions of Windows Vista, Windows Server 2008, Windows XP, and Windows Server 2003.

Modifying IFilter Behavior

When the indexer is crawling the file system, each IFilter has three options to choose from for a file that has one of the file extensions associated with the IFilter:

- Index both the contents of the file and the file's properties
- Index only the properties of the file
- Do not index files of this type

> **Note**   The indexer will always try to index properties from a property handler (IProperty-Store) shell implementation. IFilter properties are overridden if there is a property handler.

To modify how a particular file type (extension) is handled during indexing by its associated IFilter, follow these steps:

1. Open Indexing Options in Control Panel.

2. Click Advanced and respond to the UAC prompt to open the Advanced Options properties sheet.

3. Click the File Types tab and select or clear the check box for the file extension. (See Figure 20-3.)

Figure 20-3   Configuring how file extensions are handled by their associated IFilters.

How Indexing Works

To illustrate the indexing process, consider what happens when a new document is added to an indexed location (a location that is configured for being indexed). The following high-level description explains the steps that take place during the indexing of new file system content:

1. The NTFS change journal detects a change to the file system and notifies the main indexer process (SearchIndexer.exe), provided that the flag Index This File For Faster Searching (FILE_ATTRIBUTE_NOT_CONTENT_INDEXED) is set on the file. To view the state of this flag for a file, open the file's properties in Explorer and click Advanced. The way this works is that a file change notification is recorded in the USN journal, and the file protocol handler listens to these notifications.

2. The indexer process launches the search filter host process (SearchFilterHost.exe) if it isn't currently running, and the system protocol handler loads the file protocol handler.

3. The file's URL is sent to the gatherer's queue. When the indexer retrieves the URL from the queue, it picks the file protocol handler to access the item (based on the file: scheme in the URL). The file protocol handler accesses the system properties (name), calls the property handler if one is available, and then reads the stream from the file system and sends it to the filter host.

4. In the filter host, the appropriate filter is loaded and the filter returns text and property chunks to the indexer.

5. Back in the indexer process, the chunks are tokenized using the appropriate language wordbreaker (each chunk has a locale ID), and the text is sent into the indexing pipeline.

6. In the pipeline, the indexing plug-in sees the data and creates the in-memory word lists (word to item ID/occurrence counts index). Occasionally these are written to shadow indexes and then to the master index via master merge.

7. Another plug-in reads the property values and stores them in the property cache.

8. If you have a Tablet PC, you may have activated another plug-in that looks for text you wrote and uses it to help augment handwriting recognition.

> **Note**   In Windows Vista, both NTFS and FAT32 volumes support notification-based indexing (crawling or pull-type indexing). For NTFS volumes, the NTFS change journal enables notification-based indexing. For FAT volumes, an initial crawl is performed when the location is added and then recrawl is done whenever the location is disconnected (for example, when using an external USB drive formatted with FAT) or when the system is rebooted. When the crawl is complete, however, the ReadDirectoryChangesW API can be used to listen for any updates. This means that scheduled indexing is not used for FAT volumes on Windows Vista as it was on previous versions of Windows.

Rebuilding the catalog can also be forced on demand, but doing so can take a long time. To force a catalog rebuild, follow these steps:

1.   Open Indexing Options in Control Panel.

2.   Click Advanced and then respond to the UAC prompt to open the Advanced Options properties sheet.

3.   Click Rebuild and then click OK.

> **Note**   You should rebuild the index only if your searches are producing inconsistent results or your search results are often out of date. Rebuilding the index can take a long time on a computer that has a large corpus (collection of files to be indexed). For information about what the Windows Search service does to reduce its impact on other operating system functionality, see the white paper "Good citizenship when developing background services for Windows Vista" at *http://www.microsoft.com/downloads/details.aspx?familyid=f8e87c7d-9404-4914-92ae-dde09389a64e&displaylang=en&t/.*

You can view indexing progress from the message displayed in Indexing Options in Control Panel. (See Figure 20-4.) When user activity is present on the system, the search engine throttles back so as not to interfere with what the user is doing. When this happens, the message "Indexing speed is reduced due to user activity" is displayed. When all indexed locations have been indexed and no more items remain in the gather queue, the message "Indexing complete" is displayed.

Figure 20-4   Using Indexing Options in Control Panel to view indexing progress.

Note   The Pause button shown in Figure 20-4 is a new feature that was added in Service Pack 1. Clicking this button causes the Windows Search service to stop indexing new content for 15 minutes.

You can also view indexing progress by using Reliability And Performance Monitor. For example, the Search Indexer\Documents Filtered counter displays the number of documents that have been scanned for indexing, whereas the Search Indexer\Master Merge Progress counter indicates progress made during a master merge on a scale of 0 to 100 percent completed. Performance objects for monitoring the indexer include Search Indexer, Search Gatherer, and Search Gatherer Projects. For more information on using Reliability And Performance Monitor, see Chapter 22, "Maintaining Desktop Health."

Direct from the Source: The Windows Desktop Search Backoff Logic

Backoff logic was implemented in the Windows Desktop Search (WDS) service to reduce the impact of the indexing process on activities performed by users and applications running on the same computer. The main goal of the WDS backoff system is to allow the indexing process to consume all available system resources at moments when the computer is not being used by anyone, so that the WDS can process incoming document change notifications as soon as possible and keep the index up to date, but also slow down or even suspend indexing to minimize system performance impact in case someone wants to use the computer. A special scenario is an interactive user performing some UI activities that are consuming just a small portion of the available system resources but that require fast UI response. This could be Internet browsing, mail reading, document editing, and so on. In this case, the approach of the WDS backoff system is to not fully pause but rather slow down the indexing process. This allows Windows Search to update the index with recently incoming e-mails and edited file documents without killing UI responsiveness.

As a way of detecting the presence of other agents pretending to access system resources, the Windows Search service monitors a number of system parameters such as the amount of free memory and disk space. The full list of monitored parameters is described in the section titled "Overview of Supported Backoff Types" in this sidebar. A threshold is associated with every monitored parameter, and when the parameter reaches this threshold, the Windows Search service switches to the backoff state. Backoff thresholds are initialized from the registry on service startup. You can also disable some backoff conditions by using Group Policy.

When a backoff condition is detected, the backoff controller (a piece of code in WDS that implements the backoff logic) pauses the WDS indexing thread and all threads that are processing merges. Thread pausing here means slowing down execution if the back-off condition was caused by detecting user activity and coming to a full stop in all other cases.

Overview of Supported Backoff Types

This section lists all default backoff conditions with their descriptions.

- **User Activity**   Indexing will be paused if user activity is detected. Any key press or mouse movement made by the user logged in from either the console or a Remote Desktop session is recognized as a User Activity event. Upon this event, indexing will be reduced to consume not more than 30 percent of CPU. One minute after the last user activity event is detected, the maximum CPU consumption will be increased to 60 percent, and after 30 more seconds, indexing will resume at full speed. The 30 percent and 60 percent CPU consumption limits can be configured using the registry values BackOffOnUserActivityInterval1 and BackOffOnUserActivityInterval2 correspondingly. This backoff on user activity feature is enabled by default and can be disabled using the Disable Indexer Backoff policy setting.

- **Low battery**   Indexing is paused when the box is low on battery power. This feature doesn't have a corresponding disabling flag.

- **Low memory**   Indexing is paused when the system is low on memory. The backoff controller monitors available space for the system page file (this can be examined using the Systeminfo.exe command-line utility) and pauses indexing when available space becomes less than the threshold configured. The default threshold value for this setting is 5,120 kilobytes (KB). This feature doesn't have a corresponding disabling flag.

- **Low disk space**   Low free disk space on the partition where the index resides (the system partition in the default configuration) can block the indexing process and the Windows Search service pauses if the index home partition is short on space. The default threshold valude for this setting is 200 megabytes (MB). This setting can be adjusted by the Stop Indexing On Limited Hard Drive Space policy setting. This feature doesn't have a disable flag, so the only way to disable it is to set the threshold value to 0.

Max Georgiev, Software Development Engineer

File & Organize Group of Windows Client Division

Direct from the Source: The Windows Desktop Search Power Policy Settings

When a computer is running on battery power, processing URLs from the indexer's gatherer queues is reprioritized to help conserve battery life. The following three gatherer queues are used to track all URLs that are pending processing by the indexer:

- **High priority notification queue**   This queue contains URLs that should be processed with high priority. URLs in this queue are processed before URLs in the other two queues. These URLs are added by applications using the indexer's notification APIs. The notification APIs enable an application to both notify the indexer that an URL has been added, deleted, or modified, and also to indicate to the indexer whether the URL should be processed with normal priority or high priority.

- **Normal priority notification queue** This queue contains URLs that should be processed with normal priority. These URLs are added by either the Indexer or other applications using the indexer's notification APIs. URLs in this queue are processed after items in the high-priority notification queue and before items in the crawl queue.

- **Crawl queue** This queue contains URLs added as a result of a protocol handler's enumerating all items in a particular location. This process can be very resource-intensive.

All queues are processed in a first in, first out (FIFO) order. The following three indexing policies are available to control processing of URLs when on battery power:

- **High Performance** With this policy, URLs are processed from all three gatherer queues.

- **Balanced** With this policy, crawls are disabled and only URLs from the two notification queues are processed. Most sources rely on notifications after the initial crawl, so this policy does not affect them, with the notable exception of Office Outlook. A crawl is initiated each time an Office Outlook client reconnects to the server in the following situations:

  ❑ For Office Outlook 2007 clients that are configured to run in online mode

  ❑ For Outlook 2003 and previous versions' clients (clients that are configured to run in either online or offline mode)

  As a result, for the preceding situations, this power setting disables indexing of any Office Outlook items that have changed while the client was disconnected.

- **Power saver** With this policy, only URLs from the high-priority notification queue are processed. High-priority notifications are used to notify the indexer that URLs should be processed immediately. In Windows Vista, high-priority notifications are used to notify the indexer only when updates are made in any Explorer window to 25 or fewer URLs. Because high-priority notifications are used infrequently, use of this policy effectively disables the majority of indexing.

Power management policy settings for Windows Vista contain both On Battery settings and Plugged In settings. The On Battery settings are relevant only on computers with batteries and will show up in the Advanced Settings tab for Power Options only on computers with batteries. Computers that don't have batteries will display only the Plugged In settings. For the indexer policies (as of Windows Vista SP1), changes to the

Plugged In settings will not change the behavior of the indexer. When a computer is plugged in, URLs from all gatherer queues will always be processed. The following table details the default configuration for the relationship between the default power plans and the different indexer power policies.

Power Plan Name	Indexer Power Policy	
	Plugged In Setting	**On Battery Setting**
High Performance	High Performance	High Performance
Balanced Power	High Performance	Balanced
Power Saver	High Performance	Power Saver

To change the association of the three indexing polices to a specific power plan for computers with batteries, use Power Options in Control Panel as follows:

1. Click Change Plan Settings under a power plan you choose and then click Change Advanced Power Settings.

2. Scroll down and expand Search And Indexing, expand Power Savings Mode, and click On Battery to associate a different indexing policy with the selected power plan.

Remember that although you can also change the Plugged In setting as of Windows Vista SP1, doing so will not have any impact on the indexer's behavior.

Anton Kucer, Senior Program Manager

Windows Experience, Find & Organize Team

Understanding Remote Search

Windows Search supports queries against a remote index across Windows Vista and Windows Server 2008 computers. Remote search is supported against content stored in shared directories on remote computers under the following conditions:

- The remote computer must be running either Windows Vista or Windows Server 2008.

- The Windows Search (WSearch) service must be running on the remote computer (on Windows Server 2008 you can do this by adding the Windows Search Service role service to the File Services role).

- The shared directory on the remote computer must be included in the indexed scope on the remote computer.

Remote search performed from the local computer uses the Windows Search service on the remote computer to perform the query against the index on the remote computer. The following example illustrates how you can use a Windows Vista computer to search for text within documents stored in a shared folder on a Windows Server 2008 file server:

1. Install the File Services role on the Windows Server 2008 computer, being sure to add the Windows Search Services role service.

2. Add some documents to a folder named Data that is in the indexing scope for the Windows Server 2008 computer. These should include a text file named findme.txt that contains the text "Hello world".

3. Share the Data folder as DATA, granting Read permissions to Domain Users.

4. Log onto a Windows Vista computer using a domain user account and press Windows Logo Key+R.

5. Type the UNC path to the remote share (*SERVERNAME***DATA**) and press Enter.

6. In the Explorer window that opens, type **Hello** in the Instant Search box. You should immediately see findme.txt in the results set for your search.

Note   If a yellow information bar appears saying, "Network locations and connected devices are searched more slowly than indexed locations," the remote location is not being indexed, and the slower GREP method is being used to search the remote directory.

Understanding the UNC Protocol Handler

Remote search is not the only way of searching network locations. Another approach is to use the UNC Protocol Handler, which is also known as the Add-in for Files on Microsoft Networks. When you install the UNC Protocol Handler on your computer, the local indexer will crawl any remote share you specify and add the results to the catalog on your local computer. This is different from remote search, where the query is issued against the indexer on the remote computer.

When you install the UNC Protocol Handler on your computer, it adds an extra tab named Add UNC Location to the Advanced Options dialog of the Indexing Options control panel:

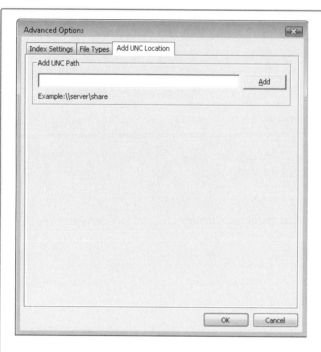

To add the remote location to the list of locations your local index will crawl, enter the UNC path to the remote location and click Add.

The main advantage of using the UNC Protocol Handler is that searches performed using the local index will generally be faster than remote searches. The downside is the additional impact on network bandwidth to index the remote location, especially if multiple users index the same location or many users are making use of this capability.

The UNC Protocol Handler is supported for Windows Desktop Search 3.x running on Windows Vista, Windows XP, and Windows Server 2003, and it can be obtained from the Microsoft Download Center at *http://www.microsoft.com/downloads/ details.aspx?familyid=F7E981D9-5A3B-4872-A07E-220761E27283&displaylang=en*. Note that at the time of this writing, the Add-in for Files on Microsoft Networks is only available for x86 versions of Windows and not x64 versions.

Managing Indexing

You can configure and manage the Windows search engine in two ways:

- Locally, using Indexing Options in Control Panel
- Remotely, using Group Policy by configuring policy settings in Group Policy Objects (GPOs) linked to organizational units (OUs) where targeted Windows Vista computers reside

You can only use Group Policy to configure a limited number of indexer settings, as described in the following sections.

Note   All of the Group Policy settings for configuring search and indexing in Windows Vista are computer settings and also apply to earlier Windows platforms that have previous versions of Windows Desktop Search (WDS) installed on them, with the exception of the policy for preventing indexing of the offline file cache. (This policy applies only to Windows Vista or later.)

Configuring the Catalog

Administrative tasks for configuring the catalog include:

- Changing the locations indexed (modifying start addresses and/or inclusion/exclusion rules for indexing).
- Moving the catalog to a new location.
- Rebuilding the index.
- Restoring the index to its original settings.
- Changing how file types are indexed.

Note   For information on how to rebuild the index, see the section titled "How Indexing Works" earlier in this chapter. For information on how to change how file types are indexed, see the section titled "Types of Files Indexed" earlier in this chapter.

Configuring the Catalog Using Control Panel

You may need to change the location of the catalog if the system drive is running low on free space. To change the location of the catalog using Indexing Options in Control Panel, follow these steps:

1. Click Advanced and respond to the UAC prompt to open the Advanced Options properties sheet.
2. Click Select New and choose a new volume or folder for storing the catalog on the system.
3. Restart the Windows Search service on the computer.

Note   The catalog can be located only on a fixed disk. You cannot move the catalog to a removable or network-attached disk.

To restore the index to its original settings using Indexing Options in Control Panel, open the Advanced Options properties sheet and click Restore Defaults. This will delete the existing index, including custom indexing locations (start addresses) the next time the system restarts and rebuild the catalog from scratch.

To change the locations that are indexed by adding or removing start addresses, open Indexing Options in Control Panel, click Modify, click Show All Locations, and then respond to the UAC prompt to open the Indexed Locations dialog box. (See Figure 20-5.)

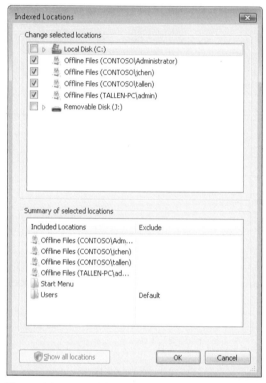

Figure 20-5   Modifying the locations that are indexed.

For example, to index the entire system volume, select the check box for this volume (usually C). This adds the system drive to the list of start addresses for the indexer, with the following default exclusions:

- %SystemRoot%\Program Files
- %SystemRoot%\Windows

> **Note**   Additional items are excluded, but these don't show up by default because they are either system or hidden directories, such as %SystemRoot%\ProgramData and %System-Root%\Users\Default. Making these directories visible in Windows Explorer will also result in their being visible in the Indexing control panel.

You can override these exclusions by expanding System Volume in the folder tree and selecting each folder, but this is not recommended because adding program and operating files to the corpus being indexed can slow search queries and degrade the search experience for users. In addition, if the FANCI bit is set on a directory, the directory will appear dimmed and you will be unable to select it. Selecting the Users item from the lower section of the Indexed Locations dialog box displays additional indexing locations you can select (see Figure 20-6).

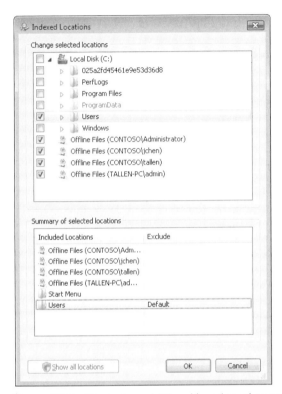

Figure 20-6   Displaying additional locations that can be indexed.

Note that the ProgramData location appears dimmed, indicating that the FANCI bit is set on the directory. If you rest your mouse pointer on this unavailable location, a tooltip will appear indicating this. To clear the FANCI bit for this unavailable location, right-click the location and select Properties, click Advanced, and then select the Index This Folder For Faster Searching check box.

Configuring the Catalog Using Group Policy

To change the location of the catalog using Group Policy, configure the following policy setting:

*Computer Configuration\Policies\Administrative Templates\Windows Components\Search\
Indexer data location*

Enable the policy and type a path for the new location of the catalog, up to a maximum of 250 characters.

Configuring Offline Files Indexing

Indexing of offline content in the CSC store is enabled by default, but you can disable it by using Indexing Options in Control Panel or by using Group Policy. Only the entire per-user offline cache can be indexed—individual files within the cache cannot be included or excluded from being indexed.

Configuring Offline Files Indexing Using Control Panel

To disable indexing of the offline files cache using Indexing Options in Control Panel, follow these steps:

1. Click Modify to open the Indexed Locations dialog box.

2. Clear the check box labeled Offline Files.

The preceding procedure disables indexing of offline files for the current user. To disable indexing of offline files for a different user of the computer using Indexing Options in Control Panel, follow these steps:

1. Click Modify to open the Indexed Locations dialog box.

2. Click Show All Locations and respond to the UAC prompt.

3. Clear the check box for the particular user's offline files cache.

 Note   To disable offline files indexing for all users of a computer, you must disable it using Group Policy, as explained in the next section.

Configuring Offline Files Indexing Using Group Policy

Using Group Policy, you can disable indexing of offline files only for all users of the computer, not for a particular user. To disable indexing of offline files for all users, enable the following policy setting:

Computer Configuration\Policies\Administrative Templates\Windows Components\Search\ Prevent indexing files in Offline Files cache

Configuring Indexing of Encrypted Files

Indexing of encrypted files is disabled by default in Windows Vista, but you can enable it by using Indexing Options in Control Panel or by using Group Policy. Note, however, that the ability to index items that have been encrypted with EFS is only available for items that you have made available to work offline using Offline Files (typically in a scenario where you are using Folder Redirection). The Windows Search service in Windows Vista cannot index local file system items that have been encrypted using EFS.

Configuring Indexing of Encrypted Files Using Control Panel

To enable indexing of encrypted files using Indexing Options in Control Panel, follow these steps:

1. Click Advanced and respond to the UAC prompt to open the Advanced Options properties sheet.

2. Select the Index Encrypted Files check box.

Configuring Indexing of Encrypted Files Using Group Policy

To enable indexing of encrypted files using Group Policy, enable the following policy setting:

Computer Configuration\Policies\Administrative Templates\Windows Components\Search\Allow indexing of encrypted files

If you enable this policy setting, indexing disregards encryption flags (although access restrictions will still apply) and will attempt to decrypt and index the content. If you disable this setting, the Windows Search service (including third-party components) should not index encrypted items such as files or e-mails to avoid indexing encrypted stores.

> **Note**   Windows Vista also supports indexing of drives that have BitLocker Drive Encryption enabled on them. Support for BitLocker Drive Encryption is included in the Enterprise and Ultimate SKUs.

Direct from the Source: Encrypting Your Index

By default, the index is obscured so that it is not easily readable if someone tries to open the index files. Additionally, only the following users have access rights to the index files by default: BUILTIN\Administrators and NT Authority\System. It is strongly recommended that any time you enable indexing of encrypted files, you additionally protect the index files by encrypting them using the Encrypting File System (EFS). You can also enable additional protection by using BitLocker Drive Encryption for the volume that contains the index files.

To strongly encrypt the index, use the Encrypting File System (EFS). Using EFS provides protection for the index files from intruders who might gain unauthorized physical access to the index files (for example, by stealing a portable computer or an external disk drive). For more information on EFS and Bitlocker, see Chapter 15, "Managing Disks and File Systems."

To encrypt the index, follow these steps:

1. Create a new folder for the catalog (for instance, %SystemDrive%\ProgramData\Microsoft\EncryptedIndex).

2. Right-click the new folder, select Properties, click Advanced, and then select the Encrypt Contents To Secure Data check box.

3. Open Indexing Options in Control Panel, click Advanced, and then click Select New to move the index to a new folder. Specify the folder you just encrypted.

4. Restart the Windows Search service on the computer to move it to the new location.

5. When the Windows Search service has restarted, verify that the new index location is being used by opening Indexing Options in Control Panel, clicking Advanced, and then verifying that the current location specified for the index is correct.

The index has now been moved and is now encrypted and usable.

Anton Kucer, Principal Program Manager

Windows Experience, Find & Organize Team

Configuring Indexing of Similar Words

By default, words that differ only in diacritics (accents) are considered the same word by the indexer (at least for English and some other languages). If you want such words to be treated as different words by the indexer, you can use Indexing Options in Control Panel or you can use Group Policy. Note that changing this policy results in a full rebuild of the index, because it changes the internal structure of the content index.

Note   The default setting for how diacritics are handled varies by language. For example, the default is Off in English, but it is On in several other languages.

Configuring Indexing of Similar Words Using Control Panel

To cause words that differ only in diacritics to be indexed as different words using Indexing Options in Control Panel, follow these steps:

1. Click Advanced and respond to the UAC prompt to open the Advanced Options properties sheet.

2. Select the check box labeled Treat Similar Words With Diacritics As Different Words.

Configuring Indexing of Similar Words Using Group Policy

To cause words that differ only in diacritics to be indexed as different words using Group Policy, enable the following policy setting:

Computer Configuration\Policies\Administrative Templates\Windows Components\Search\Allow using diacritics

Other Configuration Options

Table 20-3 lists additional search and indexing configuration settings that you can perform by using Group Policy. All of the policy settings listed in this table are found under Computer Configuration\Policies\Administrative Templates\Windows Components\Search.

Table 20-3   Additional Group Policy Settings for Windows Search

Policy	Description
Prevent Indexing E-mail Attachments	Enabling this policy setting prevents the indexing of the content of e-mail attachments.
Prevent Indexing Microsoft Office Outlook	Enabling this policy setting prevents the indexing of all Office Outlook items, including messages, contacts, calendar items, notes, and so on.
Prevent Indexing Public Folders	Enabling this policy setting prevents the indexing of Exchange public folders in Microsoft Outlook version 2003 or later when the user is running in cached mode and the Download Public Folder Favorites option is turned on. When this policy setting is set to Disabled or Not Configured, Outlook users have the option of indexing cached public folders.
Prevent Indexing Uncached Exchange Folders	Enabling this policy setting prevents the indexing of mail items on a Microsoft Exchange Server when Outlook 2003 or later is running in uncached mode. In earlier versions of Outlook, enabling this policy setting will index only local items such as PST files. When this policy is not configured, the default state is Enabled.
Prevent Displaying Advanced Indexing Options In The Control Panel	Enabling this policy setting will prevent users of targeted computers from being able to open Indexing Options in Control Panel to locally configure search and indexing settings on their computers.

Using Search

Managing the search experience for end users mainly requires educating them about the powerful new search capabilities built into Windows Vista. The sections that follow provide an overview of these search capabilities and how to use search effectively.

Configuring Search Using Folder Options

Using the new Search tab found in Folder Options in Control Panel (Figure 20-7), end users can configure different aspects of the Windows search experience to meet their needs, including what to search, how to search, and what should happen when searching nonindexed locations.

Figure 20-7   Configuring the end user's search experience using the Search tab found in Folder Options in Control Panel.

Configuring What to Search

By default, Windows Vista search is configured to search for both filenames and the contents of files when searching indexed locations. When searching nonindexed locations, only filenames are searched for. For example, searching the %WinDir% folder for *log* will return all files and subfolders under %WinDir% that satisfy any of these conditions:

- The files are named "log" or "Log" (case-insensitive).

- The filenames use *log* as a prefix. This means, for example, that searching for *log* might return *logger* or *logarithm* or even *fire-log* (the hyphen acts as a word separator), but won't return *blog* or *firelog* because these filenames do not have *log* as a prefix.

- The files have the .log file extension.

The %WinDir% folder is not indexed by default, so searching this folder will be slow because it uses the grep method instead of the Windows Search service. (This method was used by the Search Assistant in previous Windows platforms.) On the other hand, searching the user's Documents folder (%SystemDrive%\Users*username*\Documents) will return results almost instantaneously, because the user's Documents folder is indexed by default. Windows Search service simply has to query the catalog to obtain the results.

By configuring the What To Search option, users can modify this default search behavior with the following options:

- **Always Search File Names And Contents (Might Be Slow)**   Selecting this option causes Windows to search both filenames and the contents of files, even when searching locations that are not being indexed. This can slow down the search process considerably for such locations. A better approach is to mark these locations for indexing. When searching a nonindexed folder in this way using Explorer, a yellow notification bar will be displayed that says "Searching might be slow for non-indexed locations: foldername. Click to add to index." By clicking this notification bar and selecting Add To Index, computer administrators can cause the selected folder to be marked for indexing. For more information on adding locations to be indexed, see the section titled "Configuring the Catalog Using Control Panel" earlier in this chapter.

- **Always Search File Names Only**   Selecting this option causes Windows to search for filenames only when searching all locations, regardless of whether or not that location has been indexed. This has two effects: The results of the query are narrowed to matching filenames only, which shrinks the result set, and the query is much faster when searching non-indexed locations. Users who need to search only for filenames and who never need to search for files that contain specific words can choose this option to speed up searching.

Configuring How to Search

The following options configure how searching is performed:

- **Include Subfolders When Typing In The Search Box**   This option is enabled by default and causes Windows to search within subfolders when you use Instant Search from any Explorer window. Clearing this option will cause Windows to search only within the selected folder.

- **Find Partial Matches**   This option is enabled by default and causes Windows to display results as you type your search. For example, if you type **fi** in the Instant Search box on the Start menu, one of the results returned will be "Windows Firewall" because the second word in this program name begins with *fi*. If you disable this option, however, you will need to type the entire word **Firewall** before it will be displayed in your search results.

- **Use Natural Language Search**   Selecting this option causes Windows to interpret the search string as natural language. For example, searching for "email from Karen" would return all mail messages received from users named Karen.

- **Don't Use The Index When Searching The File System (Might Be Slow)**   Selecting this option causes Windows to always use the slower "grep" method for searching filenames, and the contents of files are not searched when this is selected and the setting Always Search File Names And Contents (Might Be Slow) is also selected.

Configuring What Happens When Searching Nonindexed Locations

Users can enable the following search behaviors when they are searching nonindexed locations:

- **Include System Directories**   Selecting this option causes system directories to be included when searching a volume or folder using the "grep" method of searching.

- **Included Compressed Files (ZIP, CAB...)**   Selecting this option causes compressed files to have their contents searched both for matching filenames and for matching content within these files.

Search Integration in Windows Explorer

Search capability is fully integrated into the Explorer shell in Windows Vista. The sections that follow describe some of the ways that users can perform a search from the Start menu, from any Explorer window, and using the Search Explorer.

Using Instant Search

Instant Search is a search box that enables instant filtering of search results currently in view. In Windows Vista, Instant Search boxes are integrated into the Start menu, present at the upper right of all Explorer windows, available in Control Panel, and integrated into some Windows applications such as Windows Media Player. In addition, Instant Search is contextualized so that the location from which you use it returns results most applicable for that location and listed first in the search results. You can see how this works by using different Instant Search boxes to search for programs, settings, and files as described in the sections that follow.

> **Note**   The Search option on the right side of the Start menu was removed with Service Pack 1. For more information, see *http://support.microsoft.com/kb/941946*.

Searching for Programs

Using Instant Search from the Start menu, users can quickly search for programs, Favorites, files, e-mails, and more. Start menu Instant Search is optimized to return programs first in response to a query. The results of performing a query are organized into four categories:

- **Programs**   Applications installed on the system. You can search either for program names or for link (.lnk) files, which are found within the %SystemDrive%\ProgramData\ Microsoft\Start Menu folder. However, you can't search for the actual executables within the %SystemDrive%\Program Files folder.

- **Favorites/Internet History**   Internet Favorites and recently visited web pages whose locations have been cached in the History folder.

- **Files**   Files located within the user's profile folder (searches both for filenames and for files that contain specified content).

- **Communications**   E-mail messages, events, tasks, and contacts (including e-mail messages that contain specific content).

> **Note**   In addition to prefix matching, anything that can be run at a command prompt (including executables, anything in your %PATH% variable, MMC consoles, and so on) can be run from the Start menu search box. However, Search doesn't support prefix matching for these items, so you will need to type the full name including file extension to see them in your results here.

Searching for Settings

Using Instant Search from the upper-right corner of Control Panel, users can quickly search for Control Panel items, configuration settings, or configuration tasks. For example, searching for "remote" returns the System applet and also links for enabling Remote Desktop, adding users to the Remote Desktop group, and enabling Remote Assistance on the computer. Clicking any of these links opens the System applet with the focus on the Remote tab.

Searching for Files

Using Instant Search from the upper right of any Explorer window, users can quickly search for filenames and for files that have specific content within the selected folder (and subfolders, depending on the subfolder option selected), provided that the folder has been marked for indexing.

> ### Direct from the Source: Search Protocols
>
> Two application protocols are related to search:
>
> - search:
> - search-ms:
>
> The search: protocol is new to Windows Vista Service Pack 1 and is intended to be the protocol for calling the default desktop search application. This can be any installed application a user has set as his default. For example, the default application can be Windows Search Explorer or another third-party application.
>
> By default, Windows Search Explorer is the default desktop search application for the search: protocol. You can change this, however, to any other desktop search application that supports the search: protocol by using the Programs control panel item. (See *http://support.microsoft.com/kb/941946* for more information.)

The search: protocol does not replace the proprietary search-ms: protocol. The search-ms: protocol is the way to start Window Search Explorer or to silently query the Windows Search indexer. Using the search-ms: protocol is the recommended way to always access the Windows search platform. You should not write scripts or programs against the search: protocol if you want to guarantee a specific search application is launched.

To learn more about the syntax for the search: and search-ms: protocols, see *http://msdn2.microsoft.com/en-us/library/bb776808.aspx* and *http://msdn2.microsoft.com/en-us/library/bb266520.aspx* respectively.

Ed Averett, Program Manager

Windows Experience, Find & Organize Team

Using the Search Explorer

Search Explorer (see Figure 20-8) is a specialized search tool that can be opened in any of the following ways:

- By pressing Windows Logo Key+F
- By clicking Start and then pressing F3
- By pressing Ctrl+F from Windows Explorer
- By using the Search Everywhere option that appears on the toolbar in Windows Explorer as soon as a search starts (this will appear only if you have another default desktop search engine installed)

Note that performing any of the preceding steps will open Search Explorer with the focus on no specific volume or folder (that is, the scope of your search will be All Indexed Locations). At that point, when you search for something and the results are displayed, the address bar will display Search Results In Indexed Locations.

If you already have a particular folder open in Windows Explorer, however, you can begin your search from within that folder by simply pressing F3 (that is, you can restrict the scope of your search to the selected folder). Then, when you search for something and the results are displayed, the address bar will display Search Results In <*folder_name*>. If the folder you have selected is not an indexed location, a yellow Information Bar will appear that says "Searches might be slow in non-indexed locations: <*folder_path*>. Click to add to index." By clicking the Information Bar and selecting Add To Index, you can add the folder to the list of folders that are indexed so that future searches will be faster.

Note   The option of right-clicking a volume or folder in Windows Explorer and selecting Search was removed in Service Pack 1.

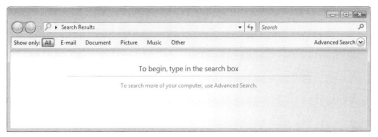

Figure 20-8 Using Search Explorer.

Note You can also open Search Explorer by pressing the Windows logo+F keystroke combination from within any Explorer window.

By selecting an appropriate option from the Search pane, users can narrow the focus of their search to e-mail messages, documents, pictures, music, or other types of files when they start typing their search string into an Instant Search box.

Using Advanced Search

Users can perform more focused queries by clicking Advanced Search to display the Advanced Search options in Search Explorer (Figure 20-9).

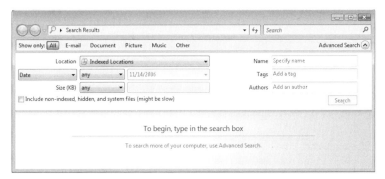

Figure 20-9 Using Advanced Search.

Using Advanced Search, users can specify additional search criteria such as the location from which to begin the search (the scope of the search); whether the file was created or modified before, after, or on a specified date; whether the file is larger, smaller, or equal to a specified size in kilobytes; and whether the properties (metadata) for the file match a specified Name, Authors, or Tag. (Tags are user-assigned metadata that make it easier to find files that have certain things in common. For example, a tag of "Sunset" might be assigned to all digital photos that were taken around sunset.)

When the user configures any of these Advanced Search criteria and performs a query, the syntax of the query is displayed using the Advanced Query Syntax. (See the Instant Search box in Figure 20-10.)

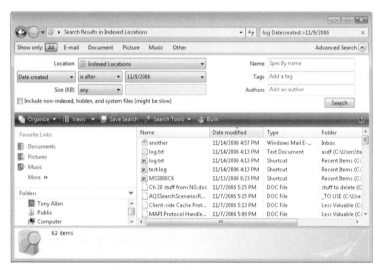

Figure 20-10   An Advanced Search query showing Advanced Query Syntax in the Instant Search box.

For more information on the Advanced Query Syntax, see the sidebar titled "Using the Advanced Query Syntax" later in this chapter.

Using Saved Searches

After the user has created a query that returns the desired result set, the user can save the search by clicking Save Search in the Search pane. Doing this opens the Save As dialog box, with a suggested name displayed for the saved search (Figure 20-11). Saved searches are saved as Search Folders within the Searches subfolder of the user's profile (%SystemDrive%\Users*username*\Searches) and have the file extension .search-ms.

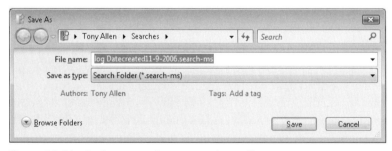

Figure 20-11   Saving a search as a .search-ms file.

By selecting a previously created saved search, users can instantly rerun a query to display its result set (Figure 20-12). Using this powerful feature, users who store large numbers of documents on their computers no longer have to create and manage hierarchical trees of folders to organize their files by different criteria. Instead, they can (if desired) store all their documents within a single physical folder and then create multiple "virtual folders" (also called Search Folders) that they can use to instantly access documents using the complex criteria supported by the Advanced Query Syntax.

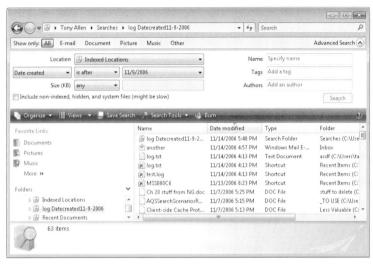

Figure 20-12   Rerunning a saved search by selecting a Search Folder in Explorer.

Using the Advanced Query Syntax

Advanced Query Syntax (AQS) is a syntax used for creating complex search queries using the search feature of Windows Vista. AQS is not case-sensitive (except for the Boolean operators "AND," "OR," and "NOT") and uses "implicit AND" when multiple search terms are specified. Supported syntax includes:

- Logical operators: *AND* (or + prefixed to term), *OR*, and *NOT* (or − prefixed to term) plus parentheses for grouping.

- Exact phrases enclosed in double quotation marks.

- The wildcard character (*) embedded anywhere in a search term.

- The single wildcard character (?) embedded anywhere in a search term. Note that this is supported only in property match queries and not in full-text (content) queries. For example, searching for author:?oe will return items with "joe" or "moe" in the Author property, but a search for ?oe won't return items with "joe" or "moe" in the contents.

- The tilde (~) operator, which can be used to search file properties (but not contents) for exact string matches. For example, the query name:~"this_that.txt" won't match a file named this-that.txt.

- Comparison operators (>, >=, <, <= and =) dates, times, and file sizes.

- Numerous kinds of Property:Value conditions (colon syntax). For example:

  - **Author:John** returns all documents whose Author property contains the word *John*.

  - **Year:>2000** returns all documents whose Year property is greater than 2000.

  - **Subject:="Are you home?"** returns all e-mail messages whose subject phrase is exactly "Are you home?"

  - **Tag:""** returns all documents whose Tag property is not set (null value).

  - **Kind:NOT Music** (or **–kind:music**) returns all items that are not music files.

  - **Filename:mydoc*.doc** returns all Word documents whose filenames begin with mydoc, such as mydoc1.doc, mydoc2.doc, mydocumentation.doc, and so on. This is where the **?** wildcard can be handy. For example, filename: mydoc?.doc will only return items with a single additional character.

  - **Folder:"My Stuff"** returns all documents within the folder named My Stuff.

  - **FolderPath:"C:\Budgets\2006"** returns all documents within the C:\Budgets\2006 path.

  - **Modified:Last Week** returns all documents that were modified within the past week (relative date syntax).

  - **Size:<=1 MB** returns all documents that are less than or equal to 1 MB in size.

  - **Music by REM** returns all music items featuring R.E.M.

For more information on AQS in Windows Vista (that is, in WDS 3.x), see *http://msdn2.microsoft.com/en-us/library/bb266512(VS.85).aspx* on MSDN and *http://www.microsoft.com/windows/desktopsearch/addresources/advanced.mspx*. And finally, to build complex search queries *without* using AQS, use the Advanced Search pane described previously in this chapter.

Other Search and Organization Features

Other search and organization features in Windows Vista include:

- Enhanced column headers in Explorer views for sorting and grouping documents in different ways. For example, files can be sorted according to name, date modified, type, size, and tag. Documents can also be grouped according to any of these properties and each group can be filtered (hidden or displayed) as desired.

■ Documents can also be stacked according to name, date modified, type, size, and tag. Stacked documents include all documents having the specified property and located within any subfolder of the selected folder.

■ Documents can also be tagged with keywords to group them by custom criteria defined by the user.

For more information on using these features, use Help And Support.

Troubleshooting Search

Computer administrators may have to deal the following troubleshooting issues with Windows Search.

Problem: The Windows Search service will not start.

Troubleshooting Steps:

■ Use Services.msc to verify that WSearch is set to Automatic startup type and uses the Local System account as its security context.

■ Verify that the permissions on the hidden catalog folder (*%SystemDrive%*\Program-Data\Microsoft\Search) are as follows:

❑ Everyone has Read & Execute permission

❑ SYSTEM has Full Control permission

❑ Administrators has Full Control permission

❑ Currently logged-on user has Read & Execute permission

Problem: Missing or corrupted index.

Troubleshooting Steps:

■ Rebuild the index.

■ Move the index to a new location.

Problem: Search results are not as expected.

Troubleshooting Steps:

■ Verify that the location being searched is marked for indexing.

■ Verify that the file extensions of the documents being searched for are enabled for indexing.

■ Verify that the syntax of the search query is correct.

- Verify that indexing is complete on the system.

- For additional help on this issue, see KB 932989, "You cannot find files when you search a Windows Vista–based computer even though the files exist on the computer," at *http://support.microsoft.com/kb/932989*.

Summary

Search and indexing has been enhanced in Windows Vista in numerous ways, making it much easier for users to manage large amounts of information stored on their computers. Administrators can use Group Policy to manage how indexing works, and users who are computer administrators can use Indexing Options and Folder Options in Control Panel to fine-tune the operation of search and indexing on their systems.

Additional Resources

The following resources contain additional information and tools related to this chapter.

Related Information

- For more information about Windows Desktop Search 3.x (the version of Windows Search included in Windows Vista and Windows Server 2008 and available as a separate download for Windows XP and Windows Server 2003), see the Windows Desktop Search 3.01 Administration Guide, which is available from the Microsoft Download Center at *http://www.microsoft.com/downloads/details.aspx?FamilyID= 00645e54-70a8-4d05-906d-af8773cbc728&DisplayLang=en*.

- For information about the Advanced Query Syntax in Windows Desktop Search 3.x (the version included in Windows Vista), see the following MSDN page: *http://msdn2.microsoft.com/en-us/library/bb266512(VS.85).aspx*. See also *http://www.microsoft.com/windows/desktopsearch/addresources/advanced.mspx*.

- The 2007 Office System Converter: Microsoft Filter Pack is available from *http://www.microsoft.com/downloads/details.aspx?FamilyId=60C92A37-719C-4077-B5C6-CAC34F4227CC&displaylang=en*.

- "Expert Zone Support WebCast: Access and manage information more easily with the search and organization tools in Microsoft Windows Vista" at *http://support.microsoft.com/kb/919206*.

- "The Windows Vista Developer Story: Search and Organize" at *http://msdn2.microsoft.com/en-us/library/aa480206.aspx*.

- KB 941946, "Overview of Windows Vista desktop search changes in Windows Vista Service Pack 1," at *http://support.microsoft.com/kb/941946*.

- KB 918996, "Availability of the Windows Desktop Search: Add-in for Files on Microsoft Networks," at *http://support.microsoft.com/kb/918996*.

- KB 918998, "Availability and functionality of the Windows Desktop Search: Add-in for Internet Explorer History," at *http://support.microsoft.com/kb/918998*.

- KB 917402, "Availability of the Windows Desktop Search: Add-in for Outlook saved mail (.msg file) indexing," at *http://support.microsoft.com/kb/917402*.

- KB 927320, "Availability of the Windows Desktop Search Add-in for Lotus Notes," at *http://support.microsoft.com/kb/927320*.

- KB 932989, "You cannot find files when you search a Windows Vista–based computer even though the files exist on the computer," at *http://support.microsoft.com/kb/932989*.

- KB 928219, "A search for communications items in Windows Vista returns no results when you use elevated permissions to run Outlook 2007," at *http://support.microsoft.com/kb/928219*.

- KB 930010, "Windows Desktop Search 3.0 does not return Outlook 2007 e-mail items, and event ID 3036 is logged in the Application log," at *http://support.microsoft.com/default.aspx/kb/930010*.

- KB 927595, "You cannot search RTF e-mail messages in Outlook 2007," at *http://support.microsoft.com/kb/927595*.

- KB 923937, "You cannot index e-mail messages or search e-mail messages when you run Outlook 2007 by using elevated user rights on a computer that is running Windows Vista," at *http://support.microsoft.com/kb/923937*.

- KB 929735, "You may not find the file that you want when you use Advanced Search to search by date and you use a non-Gregorian calendar format in Windows Vista," at *http://support.microsoft.com/kb/929735*.

- KB 934646, "The Advanced tab is unavailable in the Indexing Options item in Control Panel," at *http://support.microsoft.com/kb/934646*.

On the Companion CD

- ListStatusOfSearchService.vbs

- ManageStatusOfSearchService.vbs

- SettingSearchStartOptions.vbs

Chapter 21
Managing Internet Explorer

For many users, accessing websites is a critical part of their jobs. The web browser—Microsoft Internet Explorer specifically—provides the graphical user interface for many vital intranet and Internet web applications. Additionally, many users must access websites for research and communications purposes.

Microsoft offers Internet Explorer 7.0 with Windows Vista to make accessing the web as productive as possible. With new features—especially tabbed browsing, integrated searching, and improved printing—users can work more efficiently. Internet Explorer's security features help to significantly reduce security threats posed by potentially malicious websites, which might attempt to install malware on your organization's computers.

For administrators, Internet Explorer 7.0 is more manageable than earlier versions, because almost any aspect of Internet Explorer can now be configured by using Group Policy settings.

Non-Security Internet Explorer Improvements

Internet Explorer provides improvements to the user interface, browsing capabilities, security, and manageability. The sections that follow provide only a high-level overview of the Internet Explorer features that affect users. The remainder of the chapter provides information relevant to managing Internet Explorer in enterprise environments.

User Interface Changes

The Internet Explorer user interface has been redesigned to minimize space required for menus, toolbars, the status bar, and display of Favorites, Feeds, and History. This allows more screen space for the web page itself.

Tabbed Browsing

The introduction of tabbed browsing, as shown in Figure 21-1, allows users to keep several web pages open within a single browser window. Though in previous versions of Internet Explorer, users could open multiple windows to view different pages simultaneously, tabbed browsing reduces taskbar clutter.

Figure 21-1   With tabbed browsing, users can keep multiple web pages open without opening multiple browsers.

To turn off tabbed browsing, enable the Turn Off Tabbed Browsing Group Policy setting, located in User Configuration\Administrative Templates\Windows Components\Internet Explorer\ or Computer Configuration\Administrative Templates\Windows Components\ Internet Explorer\. You can also configure Internet Explorer to open pop-up windows in either new windows or new tabs by defining the Turn Off Configuration Of Tabbed Browsing Pop-Up Behavior setting. Finally, you can configure how new tabs open by defining the Turn Off Configuration Of Default Behavior Of New Tab Creation setting.

Search Bar

A Search bar has been added to Internet Explorer 7 toolbar. The Search bar allows users to perform Internet searches from their current windows using a variety of predefined search engines. By default, Internet Explorer 7 is configured to use the Microsoft Live Search engine. You can also add search engines—including almost any public search engine or even a search engine on your intranet—to the Search bar selection menu.

You can configure other search providers on individual computers by visiting *http:// www.microsoft.com/windows/ie/searchguide/en-en/default.mspx*. The sections that follow describe different techniques for configuring computers within your organization.

How to Create a Web Link to Add a Custom Search Provider

You can publish a link on a web page to allow users to add a custom search engine. First, create an OpenSearch 1.1 XML file that describes your search engine. For example, the following XML file describes a search engine that could be used to search the Microsoft.com website:

```
<?xml version="1.0" encoding="UTF-8" ?>
<OpenSearchDescription xmlns="http://a9.com/-/spec/opensearch/1.1/">
    <ShortName>Microsoft.com</ShortName>
    <Description>Microsoft.com provider</Description>
```

```
    <InputEncoding>UTF-8</InputEncoding>
    <Url type="text/html"
    template="http://search.microsoft.com/results.aspx?q={searchTerms}" />
</OpenSearchDescription>
```

To create your own OpenSearch XML document, simply replace the *template* attribute in the *<URL>* element with the URL of your search engine, inserting {*searchTerms*} at the location in the URL where search terms appear.

> **Note**   For detailed information about OpenSearch documents, visit *http://www.opensearch.org/home*.

After you create an OpenSearch XML document, you can allow users to add it from a web page by using a window.external.AddSearchProvider("*<url>*") call within a link. When users click the link, they will be prompted to add the search engine. The following example demonstrates the required HTML. (You must replace "*<URL>*" with the location of your OpenSearch XML document.)

```
<a Href="#"
    onClick="window.external.AddSearchProvider(&quot;<URL>&quot;);">Add Search Engine
</a>
```

How to Configure Custom Search Providers Using the Registry

Search providers are stored in the registry in either the HKEY_CURRENT_USER or HKEY_LOCAL_MACHINE hives, at Software\Microsoft\Internet Explorer\SearchScopes. To automate the process of adding search providers to computers, use a test computer to manually configure the search engines, including specifying the default search engine. Then, create a .REG file based on this registry key and its subkeys and distribute it to your client computers.

To create a .REG file, follow these steps:

1.   To launch the Registry Editor, click Start, type **Regedit**, and then press Enter.

2.   To configure search engines for individual users, select HKEY_CURRENT_USER\ Software\Microsoft\Internet Explorer\SearchScopes. To configure search engines for all users on a computer, select HKEY_LOCAL_MACHINE\Software\Microsoft\Internet Explorer\SearchScopes.

3.   Click the File menu and then click Export. Save the .REG file.

You can now distribute the .REG file to computers in your organization. To configure the search engines, double-click the .REG file to open the Registry Editor and apply the settings. Unfortunately, this requires administrative credentials. If you need to distribute the updated settings without explicitly providing administrative credentials, have a developer create a

Windows Installer package that creates the registry values and distribute the Windows Installer package by using Group Policy software distribution.

How to Configure Custom Search Providers Using Group Policy

You can provide a search provider list by using Group Policy settings. However, by default, this policy setting is not available. To include it, you must create administrative template files that update the proper registry keys on client computers. For detailed instructions, read Microsoft Knowledge Base article 918238 at *http://support.microsoft.com/kb/918238*.

If you do not want the Search bar to appear, disable the Prevent The Internet Explorer Search Box From Displaying Group Policy setting in User Configuration\Administrative Templates\ Windows Components\Internet Explorer\ or Computer Configuration\Administrative Templates\Windows Components\Internet Explorer\.

How to Use the Internet Explorer Administration Kit to Configure Custom Search Providers

If you plan to use the Internet Explorer Administration Kit (IEAK), you can use that tool to configure search providers. First, configure the computer you are using with the desired search providers. Then, when you reach the page (as shown in Figure 21-2), click Import to copy the configured search providers. For more information, see the section titled "Using the Internet Explorer Administration Kit" later in this chapter.

Figure 21-2   Use the IEAK to easily configure custom search providers.

RSS Feeds

Today, Really Simple Syndication (RSS) is used to distribute updates from news sites, blogs, and other regularly updated sources. Internet Explorer 7 includes a new Feed Discovery feature and integrates feed display into the web browser. With RSS, users can easily keep track of updates to many different websites, including your intranet sites.

If you have internal blogs or news sites that publish an RSS feed, you can add them to Internet Explorer on the computers in your organization. The easiest way to configure custom feeds is to use the Favorites, Links, And Feeds page of the Internet Explorer Administration Kit, as shown in Figure 21-3.

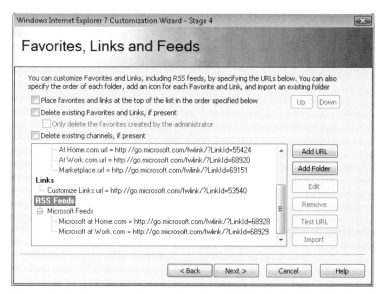

Figure 21-3   Use the IEAK to add custom RSS feeds.

Feeds are stored in the %LocalAppData%\Microsoft\Feeds folder. For example, the feeds for a user named Jane with the default file locations would be C:\Users\Jane\AppData\Local\Microsoft\Feeds. The FeedsStore.feedsdb-ms file is a set of Object Linking and Embedding (OLE) documents that stores the settings for each feed and the last time each feed was synchronized. The *.feed-ms files are used to cache content downloaded from each feed. To copy a feed to other computers, simply copy the *.feed-ms file.

Note   Developers: If you want to create a program that views or modifies feeds to Internet Explorer by editing the FeedsStore.feedsdb-ms file, examine the sample program at *http://www.codeproject.com/KB/XML/rssstoreviewer.aspx*.

You can configure several aspects of RSS feed behavior using Group Policy. Feeds-related Group Policy settings are located within both Computer Configuration and User Configuration, at Administrative Templates\Windows Components\RSS Feeds.

Improved Standards Support

Web developers have expressed some frustration with certain peculiarities in the behavior of Internet Explorer 6, especially in the areas of standards support. In Internet Explorer 7, the browser architecture has been reengineered to address standards compatibility problems and will offer additional support for popular standards.

- **CSS Improvements**   CSS is a widely used standard for creating web pages. Internet Explorer 7 is prioritizing compliance to CSS standards by first implementing the features that developers have said are most important to them. The work Microsoft has done includes fixing some positioning and layout issues related to the way Internet Explorer 6 handles <*div*> tags.

- **Transparent PNG support**   Internet Explorer 7 supports rendering of Portable Network Graphics (PNG) format images, including the optional alpha channel transparency. PNG files use a typographical file format that may include an indication of the exact degree of transparency a picture should have through a measurement called the *alpha channel*. With an alpha channel, designers can use special effects that were not previously supported. For instance, they can create web page images that have shadows but do not obscure the background image behind them.

Expanded Group Policy Settings

Internet Explorer 7 includes more than 1,200 Group Policy settings, enabling administrators to manage even the smallest aspects of Internet Explorer behavior. For detailed information about Internet Explorer Group Policy settings, read the section titled "Managing Internet Explorer with Group Policy" later in this chapter.

Internet Explorer 7 Security Features

Many of the most significant improvements to Internet Explorer 7 are security-related, including:

- Defending against malware
- Protecting against data theft
- Controlling browser add-ons
- Exposing malicious websites

The sections that follow describe improvements to each of these areas. For more information, view "Windows Vista Virtual Lab Express: Browse with Enhanced Security" at *http://go.microsoft.com/?linkid=6478946*.

Direct from the Source: How Internet Explorer 7 Strikes a Balance Between Security and Compatibility

We've worked to make sure that Internet Explorer 7 is as secure as possible but still compatible with the Internet. The principle that helps us balance security and compatibility is to not affect existing websites unless we need to change Internet Explorer to help protect end users. As we asked web developers and server administrators to make changes, they spoke frankly with us about what they could change and what they couldn't change. Here are some examples of how this principle played out in Internet Explorer 7.

SSL 2.0 Deprecated

One area where we faced a tough decision was with SSL 2.0. Contrary to what we expected, SSL 2.0 is still in use on a number of web servers around the world. The problem is that if a site chooses to use SSL 2.0, an attacker could decrypt a transaction between Internet Explorer and an SSL 2.0 web server. We've never heard any reports of SSL 2.0 sites or users being exploited, but we decided to keep SSL 2.0 disabled in Internet Explorer 7 to protect users from that threat. When we did hear of web servers running SSL 2.0, we contacted server administrators about upgrading to newer servers.

It's important that your web server administrator upgrade from SSL 2.0 if you haven't already. If for some reason you still need to use SSL 2.0, you can ask your users to re-enable SSL 2.0 on the Advanced tab of the Internet options control panel.

Obsolete Controls Disabled Through ActiveX Opt-in

An important part of the ActiveX opt-in feature is maintaining good housekeeping of the ActiveX controls that come with Windows. Many sites will benefit from Internet Explorer 7's new native XMLHTTP control, and sites can continue to use the MSXML 6.0 and 3.0 controls. The MSXML 5.0 control will not be enabled by default. The Windows Media Player 6.4 player is also disabled; it has been replaced by the Windows Media Player 7+ generation controls.

Because this should be a straightforward change for most sites, we're asking for your help in moving your pages toward the native object XMLHTTP, the latest version of MSXML, or the newer WMP control. In the best-case scenario, the change might be to simply swap in the native object for XMLHTTP or the newer CLSID for the current Windows Media Player control.

Warning About Rather Than Blocking Mixed Content for Compatibility with Web Applications

Mixed content refers to a secure page, hosted over HTTPS, that also includes unsecured http content. Since the plain HTTP content isn't protected with encryption, browsers have to warn users about the unencrypted content because it could be hijacked and rewritten by an attacker. In practice, many websites still mix HTTP content into HTTPS pages, typically to carry nonconfidential information such as logo images.

In early betas of Internet Explorer 7, we blocked the unencrypted HTTP content outright to give users the most secure default experience, not even allowing them to decide if they wanted the protection. Pages with mixed content showed the information bar, and the HTTP content simply didn't come through unless the user clicked the information bar to reload the full page. We've spoken with the people responsible for many major commercial websites and explained the problem with the user experience. As a result, you should see many fewer sites hosting mixed content.

At the same time, many of today's blog-publishing packages depend on the ability to mix HTTP content into an HTTPS-based outer page. Blocking the plain HTTP content on page load forced the blogger to reload the page and many folks lost draft posts. Getting updated blog software isn't an easy task and blogging is now common practice for folks who aren't necessarily part-timing as web server administrators.

Because mixed content is important for some web applications, and straightforward fixes are not always available, we made a hard decision to revert to the warning prompt for mixed content in Internet Explorer. That means your banking site, your blog software, or other secure sites might show a modal prompt for mixed content, as they do in Internet Explorer 6.

The responsibility for using mixed content wisely, if needed, rests on web developers and web server administrators. We still hope to address the mixed content prompt in a future release. As Transport Layer Security (TLS) improves the performance and economy of HTTPS web servers, we hope the industry can move away from mixed content completely.

TLS 1.0 Can Fall Back to SSL 3.0 for Compatibility with Legacy Web Servers

One of the new features in Windows Vista is support for TLS 1.0 extensions. Web servers that support TLS extensions open up new scenarios in HTTPS—such as the ability to have multiple hosts on a single server—and will allow servers and clients to negotiate more secure connections with improved performance. The problem we found is that some legacy web servers will simply reject connections that include a TLS 1.0 extension. Server updates are usually available to correct this problem, but those updates need to be deployed extensively, which can take time.

Rather than have end users locked out of important websites because of TLS extensions, we worked with the Windows Networking team on a simple fallback mechanism that will allow the legacy servers to keep working. In the final RTM version of Windows Vista, if the server hangs up the connection after Internet Explorer sends TLS extensions, Internet Explorer will simply retry the connection using SSL 3. SSL 3 remains a secure fallback alternative, and we found the workaround to be effective. Server operators should still ensure that they are running the latest updates on their servers for best performance.

Rob Franco, Lead Program Manager

Federated Identity Group

Defending Against Malware

Malware, a term used to describe malicious software such as spyware and adware, has had a significant negative impact on IT departments in recent years. Often malware has been distributed through websites that either trick users into installing the software or bypass the web browser's security features to install the software without the user's consent. Internet Explorer 7 has been hardened to reduce the potential for malicious websites to compromise a user's browser or the rest of the operating system. The sections that follow describe other improvements that reduce security risks when users browse the web.

Protected Mode

In Windows Vista, Internet Explorer 7 runs in Protected Mode, which helps protect users from attacks by running the Internet Explorer process with greatly restricted privileges. Protected Mode significantly reduces the ability of an attacker to write, alter, or destroy data on the user's computer or to install malicious code. Protected Mode is not available when Internet Explorer 7 is installed on Windows XP, because it requires several security features unique to Windows Vista.

How Protected Mode Improves Security   When Internet Explorer runs in Protected Mode, Mandatory Integrity Control (MIC), a Windows Vista feature, forces Internet Explorer to be a low-integrity process. MIC does not allow low-integrity processes to gain write access to high-integrity level objects, such as files and registry keys in a user's profile or system locations. Low-integrity processes can write only to folders, files, and registry keys that have been assigned a low-integrity MIC access control entry (ACE) known as a *mandatory label.* Table 21-1 describes the different integrity levels.

Table 21-1   Mandatory Integrity Control Levels

Integrity Access Level (IL)	System Privileges
High	Administrative. Processes can install files to the Program Files folder and write to sensitive registry areas such as HKEY_LOCAL_MACHINE.
Medium	User. Processes can create and modify files in the user's Documents folder and write to user-specific areas of the registry, such as HKEY_CURRENT_USER. Most files and folders on a computer have a medium-integrity level, because any object without a mandatory label has an implied default integrity level of Medium.
Low	Untrusted. Processes can write only to low-integrity locations, such as the Temporary Internet Files\Low folder or the HKEY_CURRENT_USER\Software\Microsoft\Internet Explorer\LowRegistry key.

As a result of being a low-integrity process, Internet Explorer and its extensions run in Protected Mode, which can only write to low-integrity locations, such as the new low-integrity temporary Internet files folder, the History folder, the Cookies folder, the Favorites folder, and the Windows temporary file folders. By preventing unauthorized access to sensitive areas of a user's system, Protected Mode limits the amount of damage that a compromised Internet Explorer process can cause. An attacker cannot, for example, silently install a keystroke logger to the user's startup folder.

Furthermore, the Protected Mode process runs with a low desktop integrity level. Therefore, because of User Interface Privilege Isolation (UIPI), a compromised process cannot manipulate applications on the desktop through window messages, helping to reduce the risk of *shatter attacks*. Shatter attacks compromise processes with elevated privileges by using window messages.

If a web page or add-on does require more privileges than provided by Protected Mode or the compatibility layer, it will prompt the user to grant those privileges using User Access Control. This will occur, for example, if the user needs to install an add-on that requires elevated rights, as shown in Figure 21-4. Most add-ons can run within Protected Mode, however, and loading them will not prompt the user.

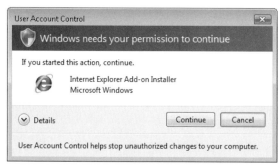

Figure 21-4   Internet Explorer protects elevated privileges.

Because Protected Mode also protects extensions, vulnerabilities in extensions such as buffer overflows cannot be exploited to access any part of the file system or other operating system object that Protected Mode would not normally have access to. Therefore, the damage that a successful exploit can cause is very limited.

> ## Defense-in-Depth
>
> Protected Mode is not the first line of defense against malware; it's a form of defense-in-depth. Protected Mode offers protection in the event a malicious web page successfully bypasses Internet Explorer's other security measures. In the case of a successful exploit, Protected Mode restricts the processes' privileges to limit the damage that malware could do. In other words, even if your browser gets hacked, Protected Mode might still keep your computer safe.

How the Protected Mode Compatibility Layer Works   To minimize the impact of the strict security restrictions, Protected Mode provides a compatibility architecture that redirects some requests to protected resources, and prompts the user to approve other requests. Figure 21-5 illustrates this behavior.

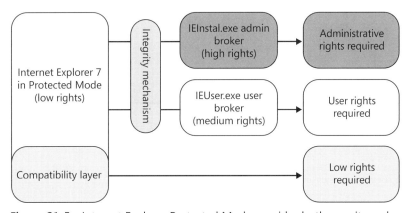

Figure 21-5   Internet Explorer Protected Mode provides both security and compatibility.

The *compatibility layer* handles the needs of extensions written for earlier versions of Windows that require access to protected resources by redirecting the requests to safer locations. Specifically, the Documents folder is redirected to \%UserProfile%\ AppData\Local\Microsoft\Windows\Temporary Internet Files\Virtualized, and the HKEY_CURRENT_USER registry hive is redirected to HKEY_CURRENT_USER\Software\ Microsoft\InternetExplorer\InternetRegistry.

The first time an add-on attempts to write to a protected object, the compatibility layer copies the object, and then modifies the copy. After the first modification is made, the compatibility layer forces add-ons to read from the copy. The Internet Explorer compatibility layer virtualization is used instead of the Windows Vista UAC virtualization.

> **Note**   Add-ons developed for Windows Vista can bypass the compatibility layer to save a file
> by calling the *SaveAs* API, so no functionality is lost. To allow the user to select a location to
> save a file, call *IEShowSaveFileDialog* to prompt the user for a folder, and then call *IESaveFile* to
> write the file. Use *IEGetWriteableFolderPath* and *IEGetWriteableHKCU* to find low-integrity
> locations that your add-on can write to. To determine whether Protected Mode is active, call
> the *IEIsProtectedModeProcess* method. For more information, visit *http://msdn.microsoft.com/
> en-us/library/ms537319.aspx.*

Two higher-privilege *broker* processes allow Internet Explorer and extensions to perform
elevated operations given user consent:

- The User Broker (IEUser.exe) process provides a set of functions that lets the user save
  files to areas outside of low-integrity areas.

- The Admin Broker (IEInstal.exe) process allows Internet Explorer to install ActiveX
  controls.

How to Solve Protected Mode Incompatibilities   Some applications that were designed
to work with Internet Explorer 6 may not work with Internet Explorer 7 on Windows Vista
because of restrictions imposed by Protected Mode. Applications that are failing because of
Protected Mode have the following characteristics:

- Applications that use IExplore.exe cannot write directly to disk while in the Internet
  Zone.

- Applications might not know how to handle new Internet Explorer 7 and Windows
  Vista prompts.

Before upgrading users to Internet Explorer 7, whether upgrading the browser on Windows
XP or upgrading users to Windows Vista, you need to ensure that critical web applications
still work correctly. Because Internet Explorer has a different rendering engine and higher
security, some applications might not work correctly using the standard settings.

If you do identify a compatibility problem, you should enable compatibility logging to help
you isolate the exact cause of the problem. To enable Compatibility Logging using a Group
Policy setting, enable the Turn On Compatibility Logging setting in Computer Configuration\
Administrative Templates\Windows Components\Internet Explorer or User Configuration\
Administrative Templates\Windows Components\Internet Explorer.

For more information about compatibility logging, read "Finding Security Compatibility
Issues in Internet Explorer 7" at *http://msdn.microsoft.com/en-us/library/bb250493.aspx.*

After using logging to identify the problem, you might be able to resolve Protected Mode
incompatibilities using the following techniques:

- **Add the site in question to the Trusted Sites zone**   Sites in the Trusted Sites zone have
  more privileges than sites in other zones. For more information, read the section
  titled "Security Zones" later in this chapter.

■ **Change the application to handle Protected Mode, including responding to any related prompts that may be displayed**   Most applications can run successfully in Protected Mode if they are written to follow Microsoft best practices and use minimal privileges. However, many existing applications might not have been created to follow these guidelines. Work with your developers to design applications for Protected Mode. For more information, read "Understanding and Working in Protected Mode Internet Explorer" at *http://msdn.microsoft.com/en-us/library/bb250462.aspx.*

■ **Disable Protected Mode (not recommended)**   Protected Mode is an important security feature that can reduce the damage caused by malicious sites and malware. If Protected Mode is causing problems that cost you more than the security improvements benefit you, you can disable Protected Mode for individual security zones. To disable Protected Mode, open the Internet Options dialog box, click the Security tab, select the zone, and clear the Enable Protected Mode check box. Then restart Internet Explorer. Protected Mode is disabled by default for the Trusted Sites zone. You can also disable Protected Mode using the Group Policy setting named Turn On Protected Mode. For more information, read the section titled "Security Zones" later in this chapter.

> **Note**   If you disable Protected Mode, Internet Explorer runs at the medium-integrity level.

To confirm compatibility with key web applications, use the Application Compatibility Toolkit (ACT). For more information about ACT, visit *http://www.microsoft.com/technet/windowsvista/ appcompat/.* In addition to ACT, the Internet Explorer 7 Readiness Toolkit has detailed information and tools to identify and resolve compatibility issues. To download the Internet Explorer 7 Readiness Toolkit, visit *http://www.microsoft.com/downloads/details.aspx?familyid= D13EE10D-2718-47F1-AA86-1E32D526383D.* For more information about web page problems caused by security settings, read "Finding Security Compatibility Issues in Internet Explorer 7" at *http://msdn.microsoft.com/en-us/library/bb250493.aspx.*

Windows Defender

Extending the protections against malware at the browser level, Windows Defender helps prevent malware entering the computer via a "piggy-back" download, a common mechanism by which spyware is distributed and installed silently along with other applications. Although the improvements in Internet Explorer 7 cannot stop non-browser–based spyware from infecting the computer, using it with Windows Defender will provide a solid defense on several levels. For more information about Windows Defender, read Chapter 25, "Managing Client Protection."

URL-Handling Protection

Historically, many browser-based attacks used intentionally malformed URLs to perform a buffer overflow attack and execute malicious code. Internet Explorer 7 benefits from these experiences and the analysis of attack signatures. Microsoft drastically reduced the internal attack surface of Internet Explorer 7 by rewriting certain sections of the code and by defining a single function to process URL data. This new data handler ensures higher reliability and provides better features and flexibility to address the changing nature of the Internet, URL formats, domain names, and international character sets.

How It Works: Buffer Overflow Attacks

A buffer overflow (also known as a buffer overrun) occurs when an application attempts to store too much data in a buffer, and memory not allocated to the buffer is overwritten. A particularly crafty attacker can even provide data that instructs the operating system to run the attacker's malicious code with the application's privileges.

One of the most common types of buffer overflows is the stack overflow. To understand how this attack is used, you must first understand how applications normally store variables and other information on the stack. Figure 21-6 shows a simplified example of how a C console application might store the contents of a variable on the stack. In this example, the string "Hello" is passed to the application and is stored in the variable *argv[1]*. In the context of a web browser, the input would be a URL instead of the word "Hello".

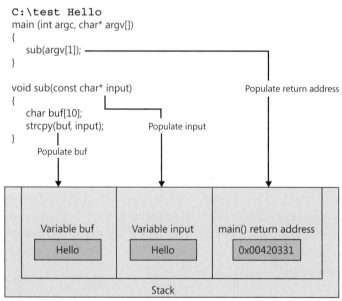

Figure 21-6   A simple illustration of normal stack operations.

Notice that the first command-line parameter passed to the application is ultimately copied into a 10-character array named *buf*. While the program runs, it stores information temporarily on the stack, including the return address where processing should continue after the subroutine has completed and the variable is passed to the subroutine.

The application works fine when fewer than 10 characters are passed to it. However, passing more than 10 characters will result in a buffer overflow.

Figure 21-7 shows that same application being deliberately attacked by providing input longer than 10 characters. When the line *strcpy(buf, input);* is run, the application attempts to store the string "hello-aaaaaaaa0066ACB1" into the 10-character array named *buf*. Because the input is too long, the input overwrites the contents of other information on the stack, including the stored address that the program will use to return control to *main()*. After the subroutine finishes running, the processor returns to the address stored in the stack. Because it has been modified, execution begins at memory address 0x0066ACB1, where the attacker has presumably stored malicious code. This code will run with the same privilege as the original application. After all, the operating system thinks the application called the code.

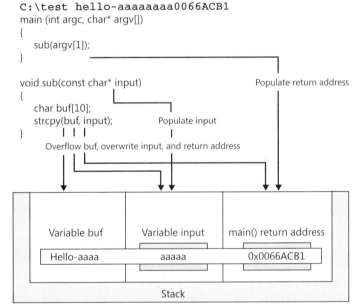

Figure 21-7   A simplified buffer overflow attack that redirects execution.

Address Bar Visibility

Attackers commonly rely on misleading users into thinking they are looking at information from a known and trusted source. One way attackers have done this in the past is to hide the true URL information and domain name from users by providing specially crafted URLs that appear to be from different websites.

To help limit this type of attack, all Internet Explorer 7 browser windows now require an Address bar. Attackers often have abused valid pop-up window actions to display windows with misleading graphics and data as a way to convince users to download or install their malware. Requiring an Address bar in each window ensures that users always know more about the true source of the information they are seeing.

Cross-Domain Scripting Attack Protection

Cross-domain scripting attacks involve a script from one Internet domain manipulating content from another domain. For example, a user might visit a malicious page that opens a new window containing a legitimate page (such as a banking website) and prompts the user to enter account information, which is then extracted by the attacker.

Internet Explorer 7 helps to deter this malicious behavior by appending the domain name from which each script originates and by limiting that script's ability to interact only with windows and content from that same domain. These cross-domain–script barriers will help ensure that user information remains in the hands of only those to whom the user intentionally provides it. This new control will further protect against malware by limiting the potential for a malicious website to manipulate flaws in other websites and initiate the download of some undesired content to a user's computer.

Controlling Browser Add-ons

Browser add-ons can add important capabilities to web browsers. Unreliable add-ons can also reduce browser stability, however. Even worse, malicious add-ons can compromise private information. Internet Explorer 7 provides several enhancements to give you control over the add-ons run by your users. The sections that follow describe these enhancements.

Internet Explorer Add-ons Disabled Mode   Internet Explorer 7 includes the No Add-ons mode that allows Internet Explorer to temporarily run without any toolbars, ActiveX controls, or other add-ons. Functionality in this mode reproduces that of manually disabling all add-ons in the Add-on Manager, and it is very useful if you are troubleshooting a problem that might be related to an add-on.

To disable add-ons using the Add-ons Disabled mode, follow these steps:

1. Open the Start menu and point to All Programs.

2. Point to Accessories, click System Tools, and then click Internet Explorer (No Add-ons).

3. Note the Information bar display in your browser that indicates add-ons are disabled, as shown in Figure 21-8.

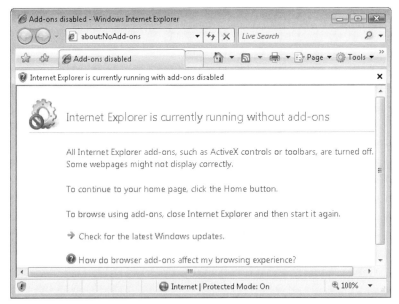

Figure 21-8   You can disable add-ons to troubleshoot Internet Explorer problems.

Running Internet Explorer from the standard Start menu shortcut will return the functionality to its prior state.

Add-on Manager Improvements   The Add-on Manager provides a simple interface that lists installed add-ons, add-ons that are loaded when Internet Explorer starts, and all add-ons that Internet Explorer has ever used. By reviewing these lists, you can determine which add-ons are enabled or disabled and disable or enable each item by simply clicking the corresponding item.

To disable specific add-ons, follow these steps:

1.   In your browser, open the Tools menu, click Manage Add-ons, and then click Enable Or Disable Add-ons.

2.   Click the Show list and select the set of add-ons that you want to manage.

3.   Select the add-on that you want to disable, as shown in Figure 21-9, and then click Disable.

4.   Click OK to close the Manage Add-ons dialog box.

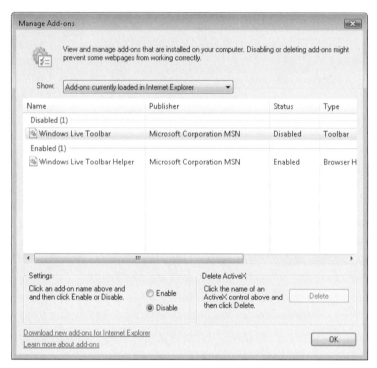

Figure 21-9 The Manage Add-ons dialog box makes it easy to disable problematic add-ons.

In troubleshooting scenarios, disable add-ons one by one until the problem stops occurring.

Controlling Add-ons Using Group Policy   As with earlier versions of Internet Explorer, you can use the Group Policy settings in User Configuration\Administrative Templates\ Windows Components\Internet Explorer\Security Features\Add-on Management to enable or disable specific add-ons throughout your organization.

Protecting Against Data Theft

Most users are unaware of how much personal, traceable data is available with every click of the mouse while they browse the web. The extent of this information continues to grow as browser developers and website operators evolve their technologies to enable more powerful and convenient user features. Similarly, most online users are likely to have trouble discerning a valid website from a fake or malicious copy. As described in the following sections, Internet Explorer provides several features to help give users the information they need to determine whether a site is legitimate.

Security Status Bar

Although many users have become quite familiar with Secure Sockets Layer (SSL) and its associated security benefits, a large proportion of Internet users remain overly trusting that any website asking for their confidential information is protected. Internet Explorer 7 addresses this issue by providing clear and prominent visual cues to the safety and trustworthiness of a website.

Previous versions of Internet Explorer place a gold padlock icon in the lower-right corner of the browser window to designate the trust and security level of the connected website. Given the importance and inherent trust value associated with the gold padlock, Internet Explorer 7 displays a new Security Status bar at the top of the browser window to highlight such warnings. By clicking this lock, users can quickly view the website identification information, as shown in Figure 21-10.

Figure 21-10   The gold lock that signifies the use of SSL is now more prominent.

In addition, Internet Explorer displays a warning page before displaying a site with an invalid certificate, as shown in Figure 21-11.

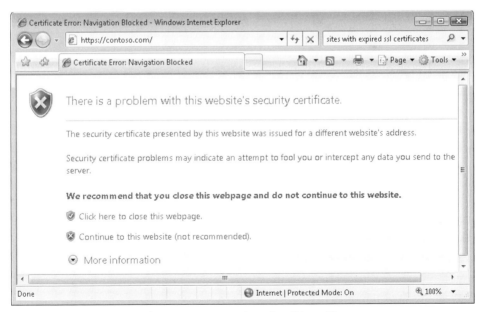

Figure 21-11   Internet Explorer warns users about invalid certificates.

Finally, if a user continues on to visit a site with an invalid certificate, the Address bar now appears on a red background, as shown in Figure 21-12.

Figure 21-12   The red background leaves no doubt that the site's SSL certificate has a problem.

Phishing

Phishing—a technique used by many malicious website operators to gather personal information—is the practice of masquerading online as a legitimate business to acquire private information such as social security numbers or credit card numbers. These fake websites, designed to look like the legitimate sites, are referred to as *spoofed* websites. The number of phishing websites is constantly growing, and the Anti-Phishing Working Group received reports of more than 10,000 different phishing sites in August 2006 that were attempting to hijack 148 different websites.

> **Note**   For more information about the Anti-Phishing Working Group, visit *http://www.antiphishing.org/*.

Unlike direct attacks, in which attackers break into a system to obtain account information, a phishing attack does not require technical sophistication but instead relies on users willingly divulging information such as financial account passwords or social security numbers. These socially engineered attacks are among the most difficult to defend, because they require user education and understanding rather than merely issuing an update for an application. Even experienced professionals can be fooled by the quality and details of some phishing websites, as attackers become more experienced and learn to react more quickly to avoid detection.

How the Phishing Filter Works   Phishing and other malicious activities thrive on lack of communication and limited sharing of information. To effectively provide anti-phishing warning systems and protection, the new Phishing Filter in Internet Explorer 7 consolidates the latest industry information about the ever-growing number of fraudulent websites spawned every day in an online service that is updated several times an hour. The Phishing Filter feeds this information back to proactively warn and help protect Internet Explorer 7 customers.

The Phishing Filter is designed around the principle that an effective early-warning system must ensure that information is derived dynamically and updated frequently. This unique system combines client-side scanning for suspicious website characteristics with an opt-in Phishing Filter that uses three checks to help protect users from phishing:

- Compares addresses of websites a user attempts to visit with a list of reported legitimate sites stored on the user's computer

■ Analyzes sites that users want to visit by checking those sites for characteristics common to phishing sites

■ Sends website addresses to a Microsoft online service for comparison to a frequently updated list of reported phishing sites

The service checks a requested URL against a list of known, trusted websites. If a website is a suspected phishing site, Internet Explorer 7 displays a yellow button labeled Suspicious Website in the Address bar. The user can then click the button to view a more detailed warning.

If a website is a known phishing site, Internet Explorer 7 displays a warning with a red status bar, as shown in Figure 21-13. If the user chooses to ignore the warnings and continue to the website, the status bar remains red and prominently displays Phishing Website.

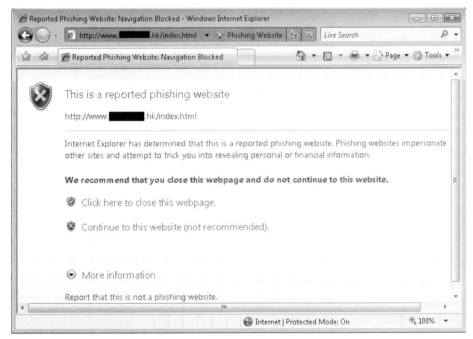

Figure 21-13   Internet Explorer can detect phishing websites and warn users before they visit them.

Internet Explorer first checks a website against a *legitimate list* (also known as an *allow list*) of sites stored on your local computer. This legitimate list is generated by Microsoft based on websites that have been reported as legitimate. If the website is on the legitimate list, the website is considered safe, and no further checking is done. If the site is not on the legitimate list or if the site appears suspicious based on heuristics, Internet Explorer can use two techniques to determine if a website might be a phishing website:

■ **Local analysis**   Internet Explorer examines the web page for patterns and phrases that indicate it might be a malicious site. Local analysis provides some level of protection against new phishing sites that are not yet listed in the online list. Additionally, local analysis can help protect users who have disabled online lookup.

- **Online lookup**   Internet Explorer sends the URL to Microsoft, where it is checked against a list of known phishing sites. This list is updated regularly.

When you use the Phishing Filter to check websites automatically or manually, the address of the website you are visiting will be sent to Microsoft (specifically, to *https://urs.microsoft.com*, using TCP port 443), together with some standard information from your computer such as IP address, browser type, and the Phishing Filter version number. To help protect your privacy, the information sent to Microsoft is encrypted using SSL and is limited to the domain and path of the website. Other information that may be associated with the address, such as search terms, data you entered in forms, or cookies, will not be sent.

> **Note**   Looking up a website in the online Phishing Filter can require transferring 8 kilobytes (KB) of data or more. Most of that is required to set up the encrypted HTTPS connection. The Phishing Filter will send a request only once for each domain you visit within a specific period of time. However, a single web page can have objects stored in multiple servers, resulting in multiple requests. Requests for different web pages require separate HTTPS sessions.

For example, if you visited the MSN search website at *http://search.msn.com* and entered **MySecret** as the search term, instead of sending the full address *http://search.msn.com/results.aspx?q=MySecret&FORM=QBHP*, the Phishing Filter would remove the search term and only send *http://search.msn.com/results.aspx*. Address strings might unintentionally contain personal information, but this information is not used to identify you or contact you. If users are concerned that an address string might contain personal or confidential information, users should not report the site. For more information, read the Phishing Filter privacy statement at *http://www.microsoft.com/windows/ie/ie7/privacy/ieprivacy_7.mspx*.

Direct from the Source: Real-Time Checking for Phishing Sites

Readers asked why we decided to use real-time lookups against the anti-phishing server as opposed to an intermittent download list of sites in the way that an antispyware product might. We included real-time checking for phishing sites because it offers better protection than using only static lists and avoids overloading networks.

The Phishing Filter does have an intermittently downloaded list of "known-safe" sites, but we know phishing attacks can strike quickly and move to new addresses, often within a 24- to 48-hour time period, which is faster than we could practically push out updates to a list of "known-phishing" sites. Even if the Phishing Filter downloaded a list of phishing sites 24 times a day, you might not be protected against a confirmed, known phishing site for an hour at a time, at any time of day.

> Because the Phishing Filter checks unknown sites in real time, you always have the latest intelligence. Requiring users to constantly download a local list would also cause network scale problems. We think the number of computers that could be used to launch phishing attacks is much higher than the number of spyware signatures that users deal with today. In a scenario where phishing threats move rapidly, downloading a list of new reported phishing sites every hour could significantly clog Internet traffic.
>
> *Rob Franco, Lead Program Manager*
>
> *Federated Identity Group*

Anonymous statistics about your usage of the Phishing Filter will also be sent to Microsoft, such as the time and total number of websites browsed since an address was sent to Microsoft for analysis. This information, along with the information described earlier, will be used to analyze the performance and improve the quality of the Phishing Filter service. Microsoft will not use the information it receives to personally identify you. Some URLs that are sent may be saved to be included in the legitimate list and then provided as client updates. When saving this information, additional information—including the Phishing Filter and Operating System version and your browser language—will be saved.

Although the online list of phishing sites is regularly updated, users might find a phishing site that is not yet on the list. Users can help Microsoft identify a potentially malicious site by reporting it. Within Internet Explorer 7, click Tools, click Phishing Filter, and then click Report This Website. Users are then taken to a simple form they can submit to inform Microsoft of the site.

How to Configure Phishing Filter Options   To configure Phishing Filter options, follow these steps:

1. In your browser, click Tools and then click Internet Options.

2. In the Internet Options dialog box, click the Advanced tab, scroll down to the Security group in the Settings list, and then select the desired Phishing Filter settings, as shown in Figure 21-14.

By default, users will be prompted to decide the mode used by the Phishing Filter the first time they visit a site that is not on the legitimate list. You can use the following Group Policy settings to configure whether or not users need to configure the Phishing Filter:

- Computer Configuration\Administrative Templates\Windows Components\Internet Explorer\Turn Off Managing Phishing Filters

- User Configuration\Administrative Templates\Windows Components\Internet Explorer\Turn Off Managing Phishing Filters

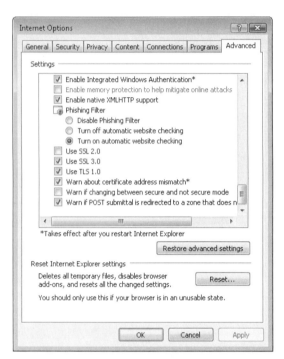

Figure 21-14   The Phishing Filter is enabled by default, but you can disable it.

If you enable the setting, you must choose one of three modes:

- **Automatic**   The Phishing Filter will automatically send the website address to Microsoft to help determine whether a website might be malicious (unless the website is on the legitimate list). Note that this communication might reveal some information about which websites your users visit.

- **Manual**   The Phishing Filter performs local analysis of websites and prompts users before sending any information to Microsoft.

- **Off**   The Phishing Filter performs local analysis of websites and prompts the user before sending information to Microsoft. Users can manually check a website by clicking Tools, clicking Phishing Filter, and then clicking Check This Website.

Direct from the Source: Anti-Phishing Accuracy Study

As we worked on the new Phishing Filter in Internet Explorer 7, we knew the key measure would be how effective it is in protecting customers. In addition to our internal tests, we wanted to find some external measure of our progress to date as well as pointing to ways we could improve. We didn't know of a publicly available study covering the area, only some internal and media product reviews.

To help us answer this question, we asked 3Sharp LLC to conduct a study of the Phishing Filter in Internet Explorer 7 along with seven other products designed to protect against phishing threats. 3Sharp LLC tested eight browser-based products to evaluate their overall accuracy in catching 100 live, confirmed phishing websites over a six-week period (May through July 2006), and also to understand the false-positive error rate on 500 good sites. We were pleased to see that Internet Explorer 7's Phishing Filter finished at the top of 3Sharp's list as the most accurate anti-phishing technology, catching nearly 9 out of 10 phishing sites while generating no warning or block errors on the 500 legitimate websites tested.

It's great to see so many companies looking for different ways to address the significant problem of phishing. We think that the results reported by 3Sharp validate the unique approach we've taken of combining a service-backed block list with client-side heuristics. That said, we understand that the threat posed by phishing is constantly evolving, as are the tools designed to protect users. This set of results represents only the relative performance during that period. We know we need to keep working to keep up with the changes in the attacks, and we are already using the results of this test to further improve the efficacy of the Phishing Filter.

Tony Chor, Group Program Manager

Internet Explorer Product Team

Deleting Browsing History

Browsers store many traces of the sites users visit, including cached copies of pages and images, passwords, and cookies. If a user is accessing confidential information or authenticated websites from a shared computer, the user might be able to use the stored copies of the website to access private data. To simplify removing these traces, Internet Explorer 7 provides a Delete Browsing History option that allows users to initiate cleanup with one button, easily and instantly erasing personal data.

To delete browsing history, follow these steps:

1. In your browser, click Tools and then click Internet Options.

2. In the Internet Options dialog box on the General tab, click Delete in the Browsing History group.

3. In the Delete Browsing History dialog box, shown in Figure 21-15, delete only the objects you need to remove. Alternatively, you can click Delete All.

Figure 21-15 The Delete Browsing History dialog box provides a single interface for removing confidential remnants from browsing the web.

If you don't want users to be able to delete their browsing history, form data, or passwords, you can enable the following group policy settings located in both Computer Configuration\ Administrative Templates\Windows Components\Internet Explorer\ and User Configuration\ Administrative Templates\Windows Components\Internet Explorer\:

- Turn off "Delete Browsing History" Functionality

- Turn off "Delete Forms" Functionality

- Turn off "Delete Passwords" Functionality

Blocking IDN Spoofing

Look-alike attacks (sometimes called *homograph* attacks) are possible within the ASCII character set. For example, www.alpineskihouse.com would be a valid name for Alpine Ski House, but www.a1pineskihouse.com would be easily mistaken for the valid name—even though the L has been replaced with the number 1. However, with IDN (International Domain Name), the character repertoire expands from a few dozen characters to many thousands of characters from all of the world's languages, thereby increasing the attack surface for spoofing attacks immensely.

The design of the anti-spoofing mitigation for IDN aims to:

- Reduce attack surface.

- Treat Unicode domain names fairly.

- Offer a good user experience for users worldwide.

- Offer simple, logical options with which the user can fine-tune the IDN experience.

One of the ways Internet Explorer reduces this risk is by using *Punycode*. Punycode, as defined in RFC 3492, converts Unicode domain names into a limited character set. With Punycode, the domain name soüth.contoso.com (which might be used to impersonate south.contoso.com) would become soth-kva.contoso.com. There is little doubt that showing the Punycode form leaves no ground for spoofing using the full range of Unicode characters. However, Punycode is not very user-friendly.

Given these considerations, Internet Explorer 7 imposes restrictions on the character sets allowed to be displayed inside the Address bar. These restrictions are based on the user's configured browser-language settings. Using APIs from Idndl.dll, Internet Explorer will detect which character sets are used by the current domain name. If the domain name contains characters outside of the user's chosen languages, it is displayed in Punycode form to help prevent spoofing.

A domain name is displayed in Punycode if any of the following are true:

- The domain name contains characters that are not a part of any language (such as www.❑.com).

- Any one of the domain name's labels contains a mix of scripts that do not appear together within a single language. For instance, Greek characters cannot mix with Cyrillic within a single label.

- Any of the domain name's labels contain characters that appear only in languages other than the user's list of chosen languages. Note that ASCII-only labels are always permitted for compatibility with existing sites. A label is a segment of a domain name, delimited by dots. For example, *www.microsoft.com* contains three labels: *www*, *microsoft*, and *com*. Different languages are allowed to appear in different labels, as long as all of the languages are in the list chosen by the user. This is to support domain names such as *name.contoso.com* where *contoso* and *name* are composed of different languages.

Whenever Internet Explorer 7 has prevented an IDN domain name from displaying in Unicode, an Information bar notifies the user that the domain name contains characters that Internet Explorer is not configured to display. It is easy to use the IDN Information bar to add additional languages to the Allow list. By default, the user's list of languages will usually contain only the currently configured Windows language.

The language-aware mitigation does two things:

- It disallows nonstandard combinations of scripts from being displayed inside a label. This takes care of attacks such as *http://bank.contoso.com*, which appears to use a single script but actually contains two scripts. That domain name will always be displayed as *http://xn--bnk-sgz.contoso.com*, because two scripts (Cyrillic and Latin) are mixed inside a label. This reduces the attack surface to single-language attacks.

- It further reduces the surface attack for single-language attacks to only those users who have chosen to permit the target language.

Users who allow Greek in their language settings, for example, are as susceptible to Greek-only spoofs, as the population using English is susceptible to pure ASCII-based spoofs. To protect against such occurrences, the Internet Explorer 7 Phishing Filter monitors both Unicode and ASCII URLs. If the user has opted into the Phishing Filter, a real-time check is performed during navigation to see if the target domain name is a reported phishing site. If so, navigation is blocked. For additional defense-in-depth, the Phishing Filter Web service can apply additional heuristics to determine whether the domain name is visually ambiguous. If so, the Phishing Filter will warn the user via the indicator in the Internet Explorer Address bar.

Whenever a user is viewing a site addressed by an International Domain Name, an indicator will appear in the Internet Explorer Address bar to notify the user that IDN is in use. The user can click the IDN indicator to view more information about the current domain name. Users who do not want to see Unicode addresses may select the Always Show Encoded Addresses check box on the Advanced tab of the Internet Options dialog box.

Security Zones

Web applications are capable of doing almost anything a standard Windows application can do, including interacting with the desktop, installing software, and changing your computer's settings. However, if web browsers allowed websites to take these types of actions, some websites would abuse the capabilities to install malware or perform other malicious acts on computers.

To reduce this risk, Internet Explorer limits the actions that websites on the Internet can take. However, these limitations can cause problems for websites that legitimately need elevated privileges. For example, your users might need to visit an internal website that uses an unsigned ActiveX control. Enabling unsigned ActiveX controls for all websites would be very dangerous, however.

Understanding Zones

To provide optimal security for untrusted websites while allowing elevated privileges for trusted websites, Internet Explorer provides multiple security zones:

- **Internet**   All websites that are not listed in the trusted or restricted zones. Sites in this zone are restricted from viewing private information on your computer (including cookies or temporary files from other websites) and cannot make permanent changes to your computer.

- **Local Intranet**   Websites on your intranet. Internet Explorer can automatically detect whether or not a website is on your intranet. Additionally, you can manually add websites to this zone.

- **Trusted Sites**   Websites that administrators have added to the Trusted Sites list because they require elevated privileges. Trusted Sites do not use Protected Mode, which could introduce security weaknesses. Therefore, you need to select the websites added to the

Trusted Sites zone carefully. You don't need to add all sites you trust to this zone; instead, you should add only sites that you trust *and* that cannot work properly in the Internet or intranet zones. By default, this zone is empty.

■ **Restricted Sites**   Websites that might be malicious and should be restricted from performing any potentially dangerous actions. You need to use this zone only if you plan to visit a potentially malicious website and you need to minimize the risk of a security compromise. By default, this zone is empty.

> **Note**   When moving from a trusted site to an untrusted site, or vice versa, Internet Explorer warns you and opens a new window. This reduces the risk of accidentally trusting a malicious site.

Configuring Zones on the Local Computer

You can configure the exact privileges assigned to each of these security zones by following these steps:

1.   Click Tools and then click Internet Options.

2.   In the Internet Options dialog box, click the Security tab.

3.   Click the zone you want to modify. In the Security Level For This Zone group, move the slider up to increase security and decrease risks, or move the slider down to increase privileges and increase security risks for websites in that zone. For more granular control over individual privileges, click Custom Level. To return to the default settings, click Default Level.

4.   Click OK to apply your settings.

> **Note**   Application developers can use the *IInternetSecurityManager::SetZoneMapping()* method to add sites to specific security zones.

To configure the websites that are part of the Local Intranet, Trusted Sites, or Restricted Sites zone, follow these steps:

1.   In Internet Explorer, visit the web page that you want to configure.

2.   Click Tools and then click Internet Options.

3.   In the Internet Options dialog box, click the Security tab.

4.   Click the zone you want to modify and then click Sites.

5.   If you are adding sites to the Local Intranet zone, click Advanced.

6. If you are adding a site to the Trusted Sites zone and the website does not support HTTPS, clear the Require Server Verification (HTTPS:) For All Sites In This Zone check box.

7. Click Add to add the current website to the list of Trusted Sites. Then click Close.

8. Click OK to close the Internet Options dialog box. Then close Internet Explorer, reopen it, and visit the web page again. If the problem persists, repeat these steps to remove the site from the Trusted Sites zone. Continue reading this section for more troubleshooting guidance.

You need to add sites to a zone only if they cause problems in their default zone. For more information, read the section titled "Troubleshooting Internet Explorer Problems" later in this chapter.

Configuring Zones Using Group Policy

To manage security zones in an enterprise, use the Group Policy settings located at Administrative Templates\Windows Components\Internet Explorer\Internet Control Panel\Security Page within both Computer Configuration and User Configuration. Using these settings, you can configure the exact rights applied to each zone. To assign a standard security level (Low, Medium Low, Medium, Medium High, or High) to a zone, enable one of the following settings:

- Internet Zone Template
- Intranet Zone Template
- Local Machine Zone Template
- Restricted Sites Zone Template
- Trusted Sites Zone Template

If none of the standard security levels provides the exact security settings you need, you can edit the settings in the appropriate zone's node within the Security Page node. In particular, notice the Turn On Protected Mode setting located in each zone's node.

To specify that a URL is part of a specific zone, enable the Site To Zone Assignment List setting in the Security Page node. After you have enabled a URL, you can assign it (using the *Value Name* field, with an optional protocol) to a specific zone (using the *Value* field) using the zone's number:

- 1: Local Intranet Zone
- 2: Trusted Sites Zone
- 3: Internet Zone
- 4: Restricted Sites zone

For example, Figure 21-16 shows the Group Policy setting configured to place any requests to *contoso.com* (regardless of the protocol) in the Restricted Sites zone (a value of 4). Requests to *www.fabrikam.com*, using either HTTP or HTTPS, are placed in the Intranet Zone (a value of 1). HTTPS requests to *www.microsoft.com* are placed in the Trusted Sites zone (a value of 2). In addition to domain names, you can specify IP addresses, such as 192.168.1.1, or IP address ranges, such as 192.168.1.1-200.

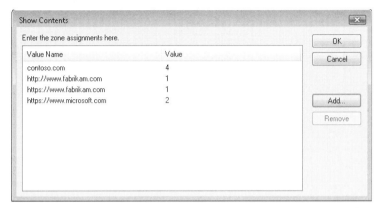

Figure 21-16   Use the Site To Zone Assignment List setting to override security zone assignment for specific URLs.

Network Protocol Lockdown

Sometimes you might want to apply different security settings to specific protocols within a zone. For example, you might want to configure Internet Explorer to lock down HTML content hosted on the Shell: protocol if it is in the Internet Zone. Since the Shell: protocol's most common use is for local content and not Internet content, this mitigation can reduce the attack surface of the browser against possible vulnerabilities in protocols less commonly used than HTTP.

By default, Network Protocol Lockdown is not enabled, and this setting is sufficient for most environments. If you choose to create a highly restrictive desktop environment, you might want to use Network Protocol Lockdown to mitigate security risks. Configuring Network Protocol Lockdown is a two-phase process:

- **Configure the protocols that will be locked down for each zone**   Enable the Group Policy setting for the appropriate zone and specify the protocols that you want to lock down. The Group Policy settings are located in both User Configuration and Computer Configuration, at Administrative Templates\Windows Components\Internet Explorer\Security Features\Network Protocol Lockdown\Restricted Protocols Per Security Zone.

- **Configure the security settings for the locked-down zones**   Enable the Group Policy setting for the zone and specify a restrictive template or configure individual security settings. The Group Policy settings are located in both User Configuration and Computer Configuration, at Administrative Templates\Windows Components\ Internet Explorer\Security Page\.

Managing Internet Explorer with Group Policy

Internet Explorer has hundreds of settings, and the only way to manage it effectively in an enterprise environment is to use the more than 1,200 settings Group Policy provides. Besides the security settings discussed earlier in the chapter, you can use dozens of other Group Policy settings to configure almost any aspect of Internet Explorer. Table 21-2 shows some examples of the more useful settings. Settings marked with CC can be found at Computer Configuration\ Administrative Templates\Windows Components\Internet Explorer\. Settings marked with UC can be found at User Configuration\Administrative Templates\Windows Components\ Internet Explorer\.

Table 21-2   Internet Explorer 7 Group Policy Settings

Setting	CC	UC	Description
Add A Specific List Of Search Providers To The User's Search Provider List	X	X	With the help of custom registry settings or a custom administrative template, you can configure custom search providers that will be accessible from the Search toolbar.
Turn Off Crash Detection	X	X	Allows you to disable Crash Detection, which automatically disables problematic add-ons. Only enable this setting if you have an internal add-on that is unreliable but still required.
Do Not Allow Users To Enable Or Disable Add-ons	X	X	Enable this setting to disable the Add-on Manager.
Turn On Menu Bar By Default	X	X	By default, Internet Explorer 7 does not display a menu bar. Users can display the menu bar by pressing the Alt key. Enable this setting to display the menu bar by default.
Disable Caching Of Auto-Proxy Scripts		X	If you use scripts to configure proxy settings, you can use this setting if you experience problems with script caching.
Disable External Branding Of Internet Explorer		X	Prevents the customization of logos and title bars in Internet Explorer and Outlook Express. This custom branding often occurs when users install software from an Internet service provider.

Table 21-2   Internet Explorer 7 Group Policy Settings

Setting	CC	UC	Description
Disable Changing Advanced Page Settings		X	Enable this policy to prevent users from changing security, multimedia, and printing settings from the Internet Options Advanced tab.
Customize User Agent String	X	X	Changes the user-agent string, which browsers use to identify the specific browser type and version to web servers.
Use Automatic Detection For Dial-Up Connections		X	Disabled by default, you can enable this policy setting to allow Automatic Detection to use a DHCP or DNS server to customize the browser the first time it starts.
Move The Menu Bar Above The Navigation Bar		X	Enable this policy setting to control the placement of the menu bar. If you don't set this, users can configure the location of the menu bar relative to the navigation bar by dragging it.
Turn Off Managing Pop-Up Filter Level	X	X	Use this setting to configure whether or not users can set the Pop-up filter level. You can't set the Pop-up filter level directly with this setting; you can only define whether or not users can manage the setting.
Turn Off The Security Settings Check Feature	X	X	By default, Internet Explorer will warn users if settings put them at risk. If you configure settings in such a way that Internet Explorer would warn the users, enable this setting to prevent the warning from appearing.
Turn On Compatibility Logging	X	X	Enable this setting to log the details of requests that Internet Explorer blocks. Typically, you need to enable this setting only when actively troubleshooting a problem with a website.
Enforce Full Screen Mode	X	X	Enable this policy only if using a computer as a web-browsing kiosk.
Configure Media Explorer Bar		X	Enable this policy if you want to be able to disable the Media Explorer Bar. The Media Explorer Bar plays music and video content from the Internet. Keep in mind that multimedia content is used for legitimate, business-related websites more and more often, including replaying meetings and webcasts.

Table 21-2   Internet Explorer 7 Group Policy Settings

Setting	CC	UC	Description
Prevent The Internet Explorer Search Box From Displaying		X	Enable this policy to hide the Search box.
Restrict Changing The Default Search Provider	X	X	Enable this policy to force users to use the search provider you configure.
Pop-Up Allow List	X	X	Enable this policy and specify a list of sites that should allow pop-ups if you have internal websites that require pop-up functionality.
Prevent Participation In The Customer Experience Improvement Program	X	X	Microsoft uses the Customer Experience Improvement Program (CEIP) to gather information about how users work with Internet Explorer. If you enable this policy, CEIP will not be used. In some organizations, you might need to disable CEIP to meet confidentiality requirements. If you disable this policy, CEIP will always be used. For more information about CEIP, visit *http://www.microsoft.com/products/ceip/*.

In addition to the settings in Table 21-2, several subnodes contain additional Internet Explorer–related settings. With the policy settings located in \Administrative Templates\ Windows Components\Internet Explorer\Administrator Approved Controls (within both User Configuration and Computer Configuration), you can enable or disable specific controls throughout your organization.

With the policy settings located in \Administrative Templates\Windows Components\ Internet Explorer\Application Compatibility (within both User Configuration and Computer Configuration), you can control cut, copy, and paste operations for Internet Explorer. Typically, you do not need to modify these settings.

With the policy settings located in \Administrative Templates\Windows Components\ Internet Explorer\Browser Menus (within both User Configuration and Computer Configuration), you can disable specific menu items.

With the policy settings located in \Administrative Templates\Windows Components\ Internet Explorer\Internet Control Panel (within both User Configuration and Computer Configuration), you can disable specific aspects of the Internet Options dialog box, including individual tabs and settings. Change these settings if you want to prevent users from easily modifying important Internet Explorer settings. This will disable the user interface only and will not prevent users from directly changing registry values.

With the policy settings located in \Administrative Templates\Windows Components\ Internet Explorer\Internet Settings (within both User Configuration and Computer

Configuration), you can configure user interface elements, including AutoComplete, image resizing, smooth scrolling, link colors, and more. You need to change these settings only if one of the default settings proves problematic in your environment.

With the policy settings located in \Administrative Templates\Windows Components\ Internet Explorer\Offline Pages (within both User Configuration and Computer Configuration), you can disable different aspects of offline pages, which allows users to keep a copy of web pages for use while disconnected from a network. Typically, you do not need to change these settings.

With the policy settings located in \Administrative Templates\Windows Components\ Internet Explorer\Persistence Behavior (within both User Configuration and Computer Configuration), you can configure maximum amounts for DHTML Persistence storage on a per-zone basis. Typically, you do not need to change these settings.

With the policy settings located in \Administrative Templates\Windows Components\ Internet Explorer\Security Features (within both User Configuration and Computer Configuration), you can configure all aspects of Internet Explorer security.

With the policy settings located in \Administrative Templates\Windows Components\ Internet Explorer\Toolbars (within both User Configuration and Computer Configuration), you can configure toolbar buttons and disable user customization of these buttons. Users will probably be most familiar with the default button configuration. However, you can modify the default settings to better suit your environment.

Using the Internet Explorer Administration Kit

Internet Explorer has dozens of settings. To simplify the process of configuring and customizing Internet Explorer for your organization, you can use the Internet Explorer Administration Kit (IEAK).

IEAK allows you to:

- Establish version control across your organization.
- Centrally distribute and manage browser installations.
- Configure automatic connection profiles for users' computers.
- Customize virtually any aspect of Internet Explorer, including home pages, search engines, RSS feeds, favorites, security, communications settings, and other important elements.

Naturally, you can also use Group Policy settings to configure each of these settings. In Active Directory environments, configuring Group Policy is more efficient than using IEAK. IEAK is extremely useful for configuring workgroup computers, however, and nothing prevents you from using IEAK to help deploy Internet Explorer in Active Directory environments.

You can download IEAK from Microsoft at *http://www.microsoft.com/technet/prodtechnol/ie/ieak/*. After installing IEAK, launch the Customization Wizard by clicking Start, pointing to All Programs, clicking Microsoft IEAK 7, and then clicking Internet Explorer Customization Wizard. The wizard prompts you for detailed information about your organization and how you want to configure Internet Explorer. Most of the wizard pages are self-explanatory. The following pages deserve some extra explanation:

- **Media Selection**   On this page, if you are deploying the settings to only Windows Vista computers, you can create a Configuration-Only Package. Select CD-ROM or File if you need to deploy it to earlier versions of Windows also.

- **Additional Settings**   The Control Management settings do not apply to Windows Vista. Instead, you should use the Group Policy settings located in \Administrative Templates\Windows Components\Internet Explorer\Administrator Approved Controls (within both User Configuration and Computer Configuration) to enable or disable specific controls throughout your organization.

After you complete the wizard, it saves your settings to the location you specify. You can edit them later using the IEAK 7 Profile Manager. This is useful if you need to make several slightly different variations of your Internet Explorer customizations.

To deploy the customized version of Internet Explorer, run the BrndOnly\WIN32\EN\ Setup.exe file on your Windows Vista client computers. If you created a version for earlier versions of Windows that includes the browser installation files, run INS\WIN32\EN\ IE7Setup.exe.

Troubleshooting Internet Explorer Problems

Because web pages are complex and change frequently, you might occasionally have problems using Internet Explorer. The sections that follow provide troubleshooting guidance for the following types of problems:

- Internet Explorer does not start.

- An add-on does not work properly.

- Some web pages do not display properly.

- An unwanted toolbar appears.

- The home page or other settings have changed.

Note   If you need to study the communications between Internet Explorer and a website, try Fiddler. Fiddler analyzes web communications and is much easier to understand than Network Monitor. For more information about Fiddler (a free download), visit *http://www.fiddlertool.com/fiddler*.

Internet Explorer Does Not Start

If Internet Explorer does not start, or starts but appears to be frozen, the problem is probably caused by a problematic add-on. Often, you can simply terminate the Internet Explorer process (iexplore.exe) with Task Manager and restart Internet Explorer. If restarting Internet Explorer does not solve the problem, start Internet Explorer in No Add-ons mode, as described in the section titled "Internet Explorer Add-ons Disabled Mode" earlier in this chapter.

An Add-on Does Not Work Properly

Occasionally, a web page might require you to have a specific add-on. If the web page displays a message indicating that you need to install the add-on, you should carefully consider the security risks before installing it.

If the page continues to display improperly after you install the add-on, the add-on may be disabled. Users can disable add-ons manually, or Internet Explorer might automatically disable a problematic add-on. To enable an add-on, follow these steps:

1. In your browser, open the Tools menu, click Manage Add-ons, and then click Enable Or Disable Add-ons.

2. Click the Show list and then click Add-ons That Have Been Used By Internet Explorer.

3. Select the add-on that you need to enable and then click Enable.

4. Click OK.

If the add-on later becomes disabled again, Internet Explorer probably disabled it because it is crashing. Visit the add-on developer's website and download the latest version—an update might be available that solves the problem. If no update is available or the problem persists, you can disable Internet Explorer's ability to automatically disable the plug-in. To disable crash detection, enable the Turn Off Crash Detection Group Policy setting in either Computer Configuration\Administrative Templates\Windows Components\Internet Explorer\ or User Configuration\Administrative Templates\Windows Components\Internet Explorer\. If the problem occurs on a single computer, edit the setting in local Group Policy. If the problem occurs on all computers in a domain, edit the domain Group Policy settings.

Some Web Pages Do Not Display Properly

Most website developers test their web pages using Internet Explorer's default settings. If you modify the default settings, you might cause pages to display incorrectly. In particular, enabling restrictive security settings or disabling components such as scripts can cause rendering problems.

If the problem occurs on a small number of trustworthy websites, your first troubleshooting step should be to add the sites to the Trusted Sites zone by following these steps:

1. In Internet Explorer, visit the web page.

2. Click Tools and then click Internet Options.

3. In the Internet Options dialog box, click the Security tab.

4. Click Trusted Sites and then click Sites.

5. If the website does not support HTTPS, clear the Require Server Verification (HTTPS:) For All Sites In This Zone check box. Click Add to add the current website to the list of Trusted Sites and then click Close.

6. Click OK to close the Internet Options dialog box. Then, close Internet Explorer, reopen it, and visit the web page again. If the problem persists, repeat these steps to remove the site from the Trusted Sites zone. Continue reading this section for more troubleshooting guidance.

If many different websites have the same symptoms, it might be more effective to modify the browser security settings for all websites.

1. In Internet Explorer, click Tools and then click Internet Options.

2. In the Internet Options dialog box, click the Security tab.

3. Click Internet. If the Default Level button is enabled, make note of the current security level for the Internet Zone and then click Default Level.

4. Click OK to close the Internet Options dialog box. Close Internet Explorer, reopen it, and visit the web page again. If the problem persists, repeat these steps to return the Internet security zone settings to their previous level. Continue reading this section for more troubleshooting guidance.

If changing zone security settings does not solve the problem, return your security settings to their previous state. Then, examine the advanced settings by following these steps:

1. Click Tools and then click Internet Options.

2. In the Internet Options dialog box, click the Advanced tab.

3. Browse the Settings list, and look for any settings that might cause your problem. Change one setting at a time and then test the web page to determine if the problem is solved. If the change does not solve the problem, return the setting to its original state and change another setting.

Because website developers tend to test pages using the browser's default settings, default settings will work correctly for most people. Before you restore settings, evaluate the risks—settings changes were probably made deliberately, and restoring the original settings might increase your security risks. If you determine that the risks are minimal, you can restore advanced settings by following these steps:

1. Click Tools and then click Internet Options.

2. In the Internet Options dialog box, click the Advanced tab.

3. Click Restore Advanced Settings.

4. Click OK and then restart Internet Explorer.

If problems persists, you can reset all browser settings except for Favorites, Feed, Internet Connection Settings, Group Policy Settings, and Content Advisor Settings by following these steps:

1. Close all windows except for one Internet Explorer window.

2. Click Tools and then click Internet Options.

3. In the Internet Options dialog box, click the Advanced tab.

4. Click Reset.

5. In the warning box that appears, click Reset.

6. Click Close and then click OK twice. Restart Internet Explorer.

If problems persist, you may have nonstandard settings defined by Group Policy. You can use the Resultant Set Of Policy tool to determine if any Internet Explorer Group Policy settings are overriding the defaults. To use this tool, follow these steps:

1. Click Start, type **Rsop.msc**, and then press Enter.

2. Check the following locations for Internet Explorer–related settings:

    ❑ Computer Configuration\Administrative Templates\Windows Components\ Internet Explorer\

    ❑ User Configuration\Administrative Templates\Windows Components\Internet Explorer\

    ❑ User Configuration\Windows Settings\Internet Explorer Maintenance

If you determine that Group Policy settings are causing problems, contact the administrator responsible for the effective Group Policy to discuss the problem.

As an alternative to changing Internet Explorer settings, you can contact the website adminis- trator to discuss the problem. Most website administrators want the website to work well with as many browsers as possible and will be happy to work with you to troubleshoot any problems. When you contact the website administrator, send a screenshot of how the website appears in your browser. To e-mail a screenshot of a website, follow these steps:

1. Open the website in Internet Explorer.

2. Press Alt+Print Screen to capture the current window to the clipboard.

3. Create an HTML e-mail to the website administrator.

4. In the body of the message, press Ctrl+V to paste the screenshot into the e-mail.

An Unwanted Toolbar Appears

Internet Explorer and Windows Vista include several layers of defense to prevent unwanted software from modifying the Internet Explorer configuration. However, if an unwanted toolbar appears in Internet Explorer, you can disable it using the Add-on Manager. For more information, read the section titled "Add-on Manager Improvements" earlier in this chapter. If the problem persists, start Internet Explorer in No Add-ons mode, as described in the section titled "Internet Explorer Add-ons Disabled Mode" earlier in this chapter. Then use the Add-on Manager to disable all add-ons that you have not intentionally installed.

To prevent unwanted software, ensure that you have all Microsoft Security Updates installed and are using anti-malware software such as Microsoft Forefront or Windows Defender. For more information about installing security updates, read Chapter 24, "Managing Software Updates." For more information about Microsoft Forefront and Windows Defender, read Chapter 25.

The Home Page or Other Settings Have Changed

If the home page or other settings have changed, you can reset all browser settings except for Favorites, Feed, Internet Connection Settings, Group Policy Settings, and Content Advisor Settings by following these steps:

1. Close all windows except for one Internet Explorer window.

2. Click Tools and then click Internet Options.

3. In the Internet Options dialog box, click the Advanced tab.

4. Click Reset.

5. In the warning box that appears, click Reset.

6. Click Close and then click OK twice. Restart Internet Explorer.

To prevent unwanted changes in the future, ensure that you have all Microsoft Security Updates installed and are using anti-malware software such as Microsoft Forefront or Windows Defender. For more information about installing security updates, read Chapter 24. For more information about Microsoft Forefront and Windows Defender, read Chapter 25.

Summary

To address the changing web, Internet Explorer 7 includes significant improvements over earlier versions of the web browser. The most visible changes are to the user interface: Internet Explorer now has a much cleaner interface and support for tabs. This allows users to work with multiple sites simultaneously, thus improving efficiency. Searching is integrated directly into the Internet Explorer toolbar so that users can search the web without opening a search engine web page.

Microsoft made many security improvements to Internet Explorer to reduce the risk of malware and data theft. Protected Mode, a feature not available when using Internet Explorer 7 on earlier versions of Windows, uses the new Windows Vista security features to run websites and add-ons with limited privileges. Therefore, even if attackers successfully exploit a security vulnerability, the damage they can do is very limited. Phishing filters help to inform users of potentially malicious websites, reducing the risk of data theft.

Additional Resources

These resources contain additional information and tools related to this chapter.

Related Information

- "How to create custom .adm or .admx files to add search providers to the toolbar search box in Internet Explorer 7" at *http://support.microsoft.com/kb/918238*.

- "Understanding and Working in Protected Mode Internet Explorer" at *http://msdn.microsoft.com/en-us/library/bb250462.aspx*.

- "Protected Mode Internet Explorer Reference" at *http://msdn.microsoft.com/en-us/ library/ms537319.aspx* for information about creating add-ons that work with Protected Mode.

- Chapter 24, "Managing Software Updates," includes information about deploying security updates in your organization.

- Chapter 25, "Managing Client Protection," includes more information about User Access Control and Windows Defender.

On the Companion CD

- A link where you can download the latest version of the Internet Explorer Administration Kit 7 (IEAK 7) and accompanying documentation

Part IV
Desktop Maintenance

Maintaining Desktop Health

Windows Vista includes numerous new tools and enhancements for monitoring and maintaining desktop health. This chapter deals with the following topics:

- Monitoring reliability and performance
- Using Event Viewer
- Using the Windows System Assessment Tool (WinSAT)
- Using the Performance Information and Tools Control Panel item
- Understanding Windows Error Reporting
- Using Task Scheduler

Monitoring Reliability and Performance

The Reliability And Performance Monitor is new in Windows Vista and provides new features as well as improvements to existing features. The key objective of the Reliability And Performance Monitor in Windows Vista is to provide an interface that makes it easier for users to visually find and isolate the cause of performance problems rather than just obtain and view performance data.

The Windows Vista Reliability And Performance Monitor contains the following components:

- Resource Overview
- Performance Monitor
- Reliability Monitor

- Data Collector Sets
- Reports

Component Binaries

The Reliability And Performance Monitor is a Microsoft Management Console (MMC) snap-in that is implemented in perfmon.msc. The following component-specific binaries are loaded when you start the Reliability And Performance Monitor MMC:

- **pdh.dll**   Used to interact with various performance counter sources
- **pdhui.dll**   Provides the new Add Counter dialog boxes (formerly in pdh.dll)
- **pla.dll**   Determines if the user has permission to view/modify performance data and provides logging of performance data
- **perfctrs.dll**   Acts as a performance counters interface
- **perfdisk.dll**   Acts as a disk performance object interface
- **relmon.dll**   Reliability Monitor
- **tdh.dll**   Event Trace Helper
- **wdc.dll**   Includes all Perfmon user interface elements

Opening the Reliability And Performance Monitor

You can open the Reliability And Performance Monitor by using any of the following methods:

- Open the Computer Management console (compmgmt.msc), expand System Tools, and click Reliability And Performance.
- From within Administrative Tools, open Reliability And Performance Monitor.
- Add the Reliability And Performance Monitor snap-in to a Microsoft Management Console (MMC).
- Type **perfmon.exe** or **perfmon.msc** and press Enter at the Start menu.

You can also open the Resource Overview And Performance Monitor alone from the command prompt (without opening the Reliability And Performance Monitor) as follows:

- Type **perfmon /sys** to launch the Reliability And Performance Monitor in standalone Performance Monitor mode (formerly System Monitor).
- Type **perfmon /report** to launch the Reliability And Performance Monitor in a standalone window, run the Diagnosis report for 60 seconds, and display the resulting report (new for Windows Vista).
- Type **perfmon /rel** to launch the Reliability And Performance Monitor in standalone Reliability Monitor mode (new for Windows Vista).
- Type **perfmon /res** to launch the Reliability And Performance Monitor in standalone Resource Monitor mode (new for Windows Vista).

To open Reliability Monitor outside of the Reliability And Performance Monitor, you can add the Reliability Monitor snap-in to a MMC console.

> **Note** When you open the Resource Overview using **/res** or Performance Monitor using **/sys**, these components are hosted in perfmon.exe rather than in mmc.exe. The parent window for Resource Overview is titled Resource Monitor when you open it with the command **perfmon / res**. In addition, Performance Monitor no longer supports collecting data from Windows Management Instrumentation (WMI), so the command **perfmon /wmi** is no longer supported.

Using Resource Overview

When you open the Reliability And Performance Monitor, the Performance Diagnostics node is highlighted by default, and the new Resource Overview is displayed in the main MMC pane, as shown in Figure 22-1.

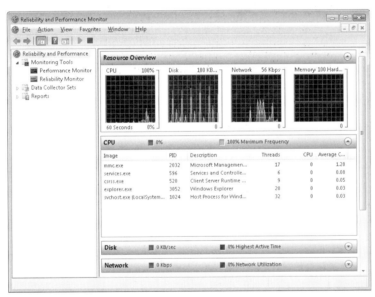

Figure 22-1 Resource Overview showing expandable details for CPU graph.

The Resource Overview provides a resource utilization summary for the four main performance metrics:

- CPU
- Disk
- Network
- Memory

Four scrolling graphs in the Resource Overview pane display the real-time resource usage in one-second intervals. Beneath the scrolling graphs are four expandable sections that provide more granular detail about each resource. You can expand the details sections to show more resource information by clicking the resource graph or by clicking the down arrow on the right side of the desired details section.

The Resource Overview is implemented in wdc.dll and is hosted in either an MMC console (mmc.exe) or perfmon.exe, depending on the method that you use to start the component. Resource Overview components are discussed in more detail in the following sections.

> **Note**   You can use the Resource Overview to monitor resources only on the local computer. You cannot obtain Resource Overview information for a remote computer.

CPU Graph

The CPU graph shows the overall CPU utilization. The expandable CPU details section shows the per-process CPU utilization along with a mini graph that displays the current CPU usage. The CPU details section (shown in Figure 22-1) includes the following information:

- **Image**   The application using CPU resources
- **PID**   The process ID of the application instance
- **Threads**   The number of threads currently active from the application instance
- **CPU**   The CPU cycles currently active from the application instance
- **Average CPU**   The average CPU load resulting from the application instance, expressed as a percentage of the computer's total processing capacity

Disk Graph

The Disk graph displays the total current disk I/O rate. The expandable Disk section shows the per-process disk utilization along with a mini graph showing current total disk usage in kilobytes per second (KB/sec). The Disk section includes the following information:

- **Image**   The application using disk resources
- **PID**   The process ID of the application instance
- **File**   The file being read and/or written by the application instance
- **Read**   The current speed (in bytes/min) at which data is being read from the file by the application instance
- **Write**   The current speed (in bytes/min) at which data is being written to the file by the application instance
- **IO Priority**   The priority of the I/O task for the application
- **Response Time**   The response time in milliseconds for the disk activity

Network Graph

The Network graph displays the current total network traffic in kilobits per second (Kbps). The expandable Network section shows the per-process network usage along with a mini graph showing current network utilization. The Network section includes the following information:

- **Image**   The application using network resources.
- **PID**   The process ID of the application instance.
- **Address**   The network address with which the local computer is exchanging information. This may be expressed as a computer name when referring to other computers on the same local area network, an IP address, or a hostname.
- **Send**   The amount of data (in bytes per minute) the application instance is currently sending from the local computer to the address.
- **Receive**   The amount of data (in bytes per minute) the application instance is currently receiving from the address.
- **Total**   The total bandwidth (in bytes per minute) currently being sent and received by the application instance.

Memory Graph

The Memory graph displays the current hard faults per second and the percentage of physical memory currently in use. The expandable Memory section shows the per-process memory usage and two mini graphs showing hard page faults per second and the percentage of physical memory in use. The Memory section includes the following information:

- **Image**   The application using memory resources
- **PID**   The process ID of the application instance
- **Hard Faults/min**   The number of hard faults per minute resulting from the process instance
- **Commit**   The amount of memory committed by the process
- **Working Set**   The amount of physical memory, in kilobytes (KB), currently in use by the process instance
- **Shareable**   The current size of memory, in KB, that a process has allocated and that can be shared with other processes
- **Private**   The current size of memory, in KB, that a process has allocated and that cannot be shared with other processes

Note   Hard page faults are a better indicator of memory starvation than soft page faults. A hard page fault occurs when the referenced memory page is no longer in physical memory and has been paged to the disk. A hard page fault is not an error, but it can indicate that more memory is needed to provide optimal performance.

Using Performance Monitor

Performance Monitor in Windows Vista has been enhanced to provide better visualizations, easier navigation, and more granular control than was available in previous versions. When you select the Performance Monitor node in the Reliability And Performance Monitor, the System Monitor ActiveX control sysmon.ocx is loaded into the host MMC process. System Monitor depends on the Performance Data Helper library pdh.dll to interact with the various counter sources such as real-time performance counters, stored binary files, and other older counter log formats. The control also provides a scriptable interface to display the performance counters.

The Performance Logs and Alerts (PLA) service is an on-demand service that starts when needed for logging performance data. This service is now implemented in pla.dll and runs in a shared host process (svchost.exe) with the short name PLA. The PLA service configuration information is located in the following registry key:

HKEY_LOCAL_MACHINE\SYSTEM\CurrentControlSet\Services\PLA

Because PLA now runs in a svchost process, exceptions that occur in the other services that share the svchost process can also affect the PLA service.

The following sections discuss the new features of Performance Monitor.

> **Important**   When you use the Reliability And Performance Monitor on a Windows Vista computer to remotely monitor earlier systems, only the features that Performance Monitor supports on the earlier version of Windows will be supported for the monitoring session.

New Features in Performance Monitor

New features in Performance Monitor include time-based algorithms, scale to fit, drag and drop, new time range controls, tool tips, and zoom functionality. The following sections describe these new Windows Vista Performance Monitor features.

New Classes for Individual Data Sources   Performance Monitor has been divided into three modules, all implemented within ActiveX control sysmon.ocx classes:

- **Frame class**   Handles interactions such as COM-based interfacing and property dialog boxes

- **Data Source class**   Handles input/output of data source (log file, real-time data)

- **View class**   Interfaces with the charting class for visualization

This feature was implemented to modularize the Performance Monitor code and to make it more extensible and scalable, but it does not introduce any additional functionality.

Time-Based Algorithms   Time-based sample collection allows you to collect performance-counter data based on a given time range. Previously, if a logging session failed to collect data for some period of time, the assumption was that all of the data was continuously collected and showed no missing data points. This resulted in the display of inaccurate data. The new time-based algorithms display gaps in graphs when a log file has missing samples. This feature does not introduce any new chart type.

Scale to Fit   Previously, because the values of some performance counters might have exceeded the current graph scale, not all of the data was visible and changing the graph or counter scales required several steps. The scale-to-fit feature allows the scaling of performance data to the current graph view on a counter-by-counter basis without changing the overall graph scale or performing numerous steps to change a particular counter's scale. The scale-to-fit feature is applicable to line and bar types of charts for both real-time and logged data sources.

When a user selects counters and applies the scale-to-fit feature to them, Performance Monitor automatically scales the selected counters to the current graph view based on the range of values for the counters. The view is updated to draw the graph with the new scale factor so that the values fall within the graph's current vertical minimum and maximum ranges. The scale-to-fit feature does not change the graph's vertical minimum or maximum ranges. You can determine the current scale factor for each counter from the Scale column in the counter list pane.

To use the scale-to-fit feature, select the counters you want to modify, right-click the counters at the bottom of Performance Monitor, and select Scale Selected Counters. When you use the scale-to-fit feature, you can select multiple counters by using Ctrl+left-click to individually select multiple counters or by using Shift+left-click to highlight a contiguous range of counters. Performance Monitor uses an algorithm to determine the best scale factor for each selected counter based on its current range of values and the graph scale. It then recalculates the data sample values and displays them in the graph, using the new scale factor.

> **Note**   Because the vertical minimum and maximum ranges are configurable and scaling uses a factor of 10, it is possible that the selected counter data still cannot be displayed within the configured vertical graph range, depending on the selected counter's values.

Drag and Drop   This feature allows a user to drag any Performance Monitor–related file into the display area to open the file. The Performance Monitor display will change to reflect the actions relevant to the opened file type. Supported file types include:

- Templates (html, xml)
- Logs (blg)
- Comma-separated or tab-separated value files (csv, tsv)

You can also drag multiple binary log files (*.blg) into the Performance Monitor window. However, you cannot drag multiple .html, .xml, .csv, or .tsv files; attempting to do so will generate an error.

Time Range Control Each performance counter data sample has a timestamp that identifies when the data was collected. In previous versions of Performance Monitor, users needed to view and change the properties of a loaded log file to adjust the log's visible timeframe (on the x-axis). With Windows Vista, when the graph is a line chart, time labels are now automatically displayed along the horizontal time axis in the main Performance Monitor view.

The timestamps for the first and last samples are always displayed. Because of limited x-axis space, time labels cannot be displayed for all data points. The displayable time labels are determined based on the sample interval time and the currently visible time range. The actual number of time labels displayed varies as the size of the System Monitor graph window is resized or if the chart area scale is changed.

Tool Tips Tool tips are now displayed when you pause the mouse on a data element in the Performance Monitor graph. The tool tips will show performance-counter data for the element nearest to the mouse pointer. This will be either the previous data point or the next data point, whichever is closest to the mouse pointer. Tools tips appear only for visible chart data elements.

Zoom The new zoom feature in Performance Monitor provides you with the ability to easily view logged data in more detail. (You cannot zoom into real-time performance data.) Users can select a time range that they want to view in more detail and then use the new Zoom To shortcut menu item to clear the current log view and replace it with the zoomed time range. Fewer samples are displayed in the zoomed time range, but you can obtain more detail from the samples that are displayed.

You can use the following methods to select a range of time to zoom in on:

- Using the left mouse button, click the graph to select the first time point, drag the mouse to the second time point, and then release the mouse button. The selected time range will be shadowed in the graph view. Click the right mouse button to open the shortcut menu and select Zoom To.

- Use the time range slider control (visible under the graph) to select the desired time range. You can use each end of the slider control to change the time window you want to display. The selected time range will be shadowed in the graph view. Click the right mouse button to access the shortcut menu and then select Zoom To.

To zoom out, reset the time range using the slider control and then select Zoom To again to zoom to the currently selected time range. You can also use the left and right arrows on the slider control to scroll the time range in the graph.

New Legend Control The new Performance Monitor Legend Control provides two features that allow easier, more granular control of the displayed performance counters:

- Multiple counter selection
- Show/Hide counters

Previously, performance counter operations, such as changing the scale factor, could be performed only on a single counter, and the only way to hide a performance counter was to delete it from the System Monitor view.

Now you can simultaneously select multiple counters for manipulation. The possible operations on multiple selected counters are Show Selected Counters, Hide Selected Counters, or Scale Selected Counters. You can select multiple counters in the legend, report, or chart window using standard keyboard or mouse functions (Ctrl+left-click or Shift+left-click). The selected counter items will be highlighted for ease of identification.

You can also temporarily hide performance counters from a graph or report view using the menu options. This provides a convenient method for quickly hiding a counter to make a graph more readable. To hide or show counters, users can either select or clear the Show check box next to the desired counters, or they can select the counter (or counters) and use the shortcut menu to show or hide the selected counters. Note that the Show and Hide options do not apply to the report view. Previously, the only way to remove a performance counter from the current view was to delete it from the System Monitor legend.

Add Counters Dialog Box   The Performance Monitor Add Counters dialog box has been redesigned based on user feedback to improve usability. The design of the previous Add Counters dialog box made it difficult for users to confirm the performance counters that were being added. The new interface, shown in Figure 22-2, has a hierarchical design that allows you to instantly see the counters that are being added to a log.

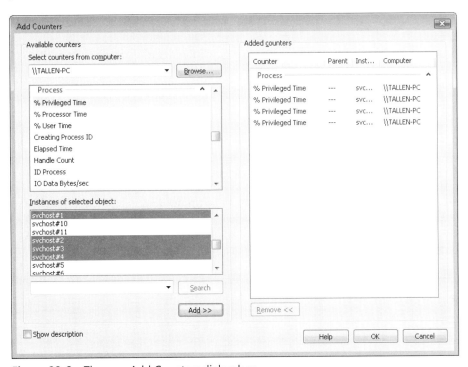

Figure 22-2   The new Add Counters dialog box.

The Add Counters window contains a list of available objects on the left side just below the Computer Name field. You can view and select the counters for the selected object by clicking the down arrow to the right of the object name. The instances associated with the selected object are displayed in the Instances Of Selected Object list. You can add any combination of objects, counters, and instances by clicking the Add button with the desired elements highlighted. The added elements are immediately displayed in the Added Counters list. The Objects, Counters, and Instances windows support multi-select so that you can select multiple items by using standard keyboard or mouse functions (Ctrl+left-click or Shift+left-click) and then adding to the log with one click of the Add button.

A search function is also available when the All Instances option is present for a performance object. The search feature provides you with the ability to search the available instances for the selected object. The search results will be grouped into the *<All searched instances>* instance item; you can add them to the log by clicking Add with the *<All searched instances>* item selected.

Transportable Configuration Files   In Windows 2000, Windows XP, and Windows Server 2003, the configuration of each performance log or alert can be saved to an HTML file, edited to change the computer name, and used as a template to create a log for another computer. In Windows Vista, the default configuration file format is changed to XML.

End of File Command   Performance Monitor previously used *CreateProcess* to execute an End of File command to launch the specified process when a log ended. To improve security and allow for flexibility of the execution context (credentials), this feature has been replaced by the ability to start an existing Task Scheduler job when a log file completes.

Compare Feature   Performance Monitor now includes a Compare feature that you can use to overlay multiple log files for relative comparison. An adjustable level of transparency is added to the logs being compared so that you can see through the logs that have been overlaid. This feature is useful if, for example, a user wants to compare server-resource utilization between 8:00 A.M. and 9:00 A.M. over a week-long period. The Compare feature is discussed in more detail in the section titled "Comparing Performance Monitor Logs" later in this chapter.

Working with Performance Monitor

Overall performance-monitoring concepts have changed very little since Windows NT 4.0. Windows Vista Performance Monitor is now part of the Reliability And Performance Monitor, but gathering performance data is in many ways unchanged from previous versions. Real-time performance monitoring and performance monitor log generation have changed slightly for Windows Vista, with most of the changes occurring in the user interface.

Real-Time Performance Monitoring   As they did with previous versions of Performance Monitor, users may perform real-time monitoring of the performance characteristics of their systems in a one-second data sample interval. The real-time monitoring interface, which you access by clicking the Performance Monitor node under Monitoring Tools in the Reliability

And Performance Monitor interface, is often referred to as System Monitor because it uses the ActiveX control sysmon.ocx. You can add and view real-time performance counters for the local computer or for a remote computer. Performance Monitor's real-time monitoring feature uses the new features discussed previously but otherwise has not changed. You can add performance counters to a real-time line chart view using one of two methods:

- Click the Add Counter icon (**+**) on the toolbar.
- Right-click the chart anywhere and then select Add Counters from the shortcut menu.

You can open a saved Performance Monitor file for viewing by dragging the file into the Performance Monitor window or, as in previous versions, by clicking the View Log Data cylinder on the toolbar or pressing Ctrl+L. Another enhancement is the addition of the Save Image As shortcut menu item that allows you to save the current view as a GIF image file for later reference.

Performance Monitor Logging   In Windows XP, you created Performance Monitor logs or alerts by using the Report Type node under Performance Logs And Alerts in the Performance interface. You could configure each log to contain a single data collection entity (counter log, trace log, or alert). Performance Monitor in Windows Vista now uses the concept of Data Collector Sets. In Windows Vista, a data collection entity is referred to as a *data collector* and must now be a member of a Data Collector Set (DCS). A DCS can contain any number of data collectors, allowing for greater control over performance monitoring and data organization tasks.

> **Note**   Log files created from Data Collector Sets in Windows Vista are not backward-compatible with earlier versions of Windows. However, you can view logs created in earlier versions of Windows in Performance Monitor in Windows Vista.

Data Collector Sets have been implemented to provide support for performance reports that require data from multiple log files of different types. These data collectors include counter, trace, alerts, and system configuration logs. You can add an arbitrary number of data collectors to a single DCS. Before Windows Vista, each data collection entity contained its own scheduling properties to be used by the Performance Logs And Alerts service. In Windows Vista, all members of a DCS use the scheduling properties—and other common properties— that have been specified for the parent DCS. The DCS is implemented as a single Task Scheduler object, and you can specify a single task to execute after all of the included data collectors have completed.

There are three types of Data Collector Sets:

- **User-defined**   Most, if not all, user-configured Data Collector Sets fall into this category.
- **System**   XML Data Collector Set templates that have been saved to Windows\PLA\System are displayed here. You cannot create these; they are included with Windows Vista.
- **Event trace sessions**   These are Data Collector Sets configured for Event Tracing for Windows (ETW) tracing.

The DCS concept provides the following features:

- A DCS is the unit of scheduling for all of the data collectors in the DCS.

- Log file properties are divided between the DCS and individual data collectors. Log file folder and subfolder properties are maintained by the DCS so that they are consistent across all data collectors in the set. Filename properties and other file options are maintained for individual data collectors.

- The DCS manages keyword and description metadata. You can locate the individual data collectors by using the Windows Vista Search engine to search by keyword.

- Security is implemented at the DCS level. A single Run As account is used for all data collectors in the set.

- A new type of data collector is introduced, called a System Configuration Data collector. The System Configuration Data collector gathers specified data from the registry.

- Each DCS has a description field. The DCS description will be a recognized Performance Logs And Alerts attribute.

Creating a Data Collector Set   You create a DCS by using a wizard or a preconfigured XML template. The data can be a single performance log, event trace, or system configuration data set, or any combination of the three. You can also configure Performance Counter Alerts from this interface.

To create a new DCS, follow these steps:

1. Open the Reliability And Performance Monitor and select the User Defined node beneath the Data Collector Sets node.

2. Right-click the User Defined node, select New, and then select Data Collector Set to start the Create New Data Collector Set Wizard.

3. Provide a name for the data collector set and choose to create from a template or create manually by following the remaining steps of the wizard.

When you create a new DCS, it is simplest to use the Create From A Template option in the Create New Data Collector Set Wizard. You can create templates for common monitoring scenarios and use them to quickly configure and start a new logging session using the template settings. The templates are in XML format; all settings for the DCS are specified in the template. Windows Vista includes three preconfigured templates for creating new Data Collector Sets:

- Basic
- System Diagnostics
- System Performance

You can also export a DCS as a template that can be modified and imported to create new Data Collector Sets. To export a DCS configuration XML file, right-click the Data Collector Set name in the Data Collector Sets node in System Monitor and then select Export Settings from the shortcut menu. The template files are not saved to a template store; you must import them each time you use them. You can save the XML template files to any folder you have access to.

Generally, a template is exported from a manually configured DCS. After you export the DCS template, you can edit the template to customize it for particular scenarios (different computer, different folder, and so on). After you have exported the template, you can import it into the DCS by selecting Create From A Template in the Create New Data Collector Set Wizard and browsing to the location of the XML file.

> **Note**   Performance Monitor no longer installs a default System Overview log. However, it does provide a System Diagnostics Data Collector Set template.

To manually create a DCS, follow these steps:

1. In the Create New Data Collector Set Wizard, select Create Manually and then click Next.

2. Select the desired data collector(s) and then click Next.

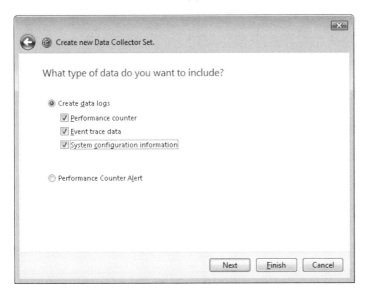

3. Select the performance counters, if any, that will be collected in the data collector and then click Next.

4. Select the event trace providers, if any, that will be used and then click Next.

5. Select registry keys to be monitored, if any, and then click Next.

6. Choose the path to the DCS and then click Next. All of the data files for the DCS will use this path and will share the parent folder that you specify. The default path for data collector sets is %SystemDrive%\perflogs\<*Data Collector Set name*>.

7. Click Change and then select the user account that will run this data collector set.

8. Before completing the wizard, you can select options to open the properties of the data set when completing the wizard and start the data collection immediately after completing the wizard.

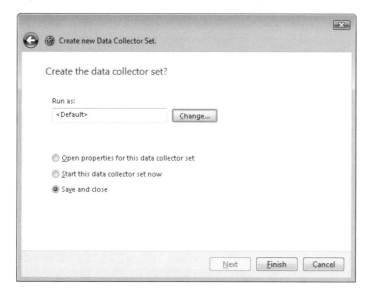

9. Click Finish to display the DCS in the Reliability And Performance Monitor. You can view the status of all of the configured Data Collector Sets by selecting the desired parent node under the Data Collector Sets node.

10. To view the data collector(s) contained within a DCS in the Reliability And Performance Monitor, expand the User Defined node in the left pane. Then, either click the Data Collector Set name under the User Defined node or double-click the Data Collector Set name if it appears in the right pane.

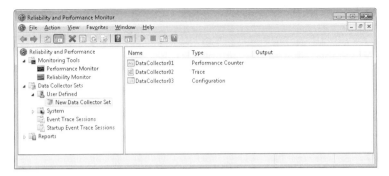

To start the Data Collector Set, click to highlight the DCS name and either click the green arrow on the toolbar to start logging or right-click the Data Collector Set name and then select Start from the shortcut menu.

Configuring a Data Collector Set   To access the properties for a DCS, right-click the Data Collector Set's name and select Properties from the shortcut menu. All of the properties for a data collector are configured from this interface. Properties available on each tab are:

- **General Tab**   Configure the data collector description, any keywords that are desired for Search purposes, and the Run As properties that determine under what user context this DCS will run. Click Change to change the user context for the collector. The default is the Local System account.

- **Directory Tab**   Configure the root directory for the DCS and specify a separate subdirectory if desired. The default is %SystemDrive%\perflogs\<*Data Collector Set name*>. You can also specify the format of the subdirectory name based on the following options:

    - **Date and time**   Choose from the available subdirectory name formatting options that are displayed.

    - **Computer name**   You can also prefix the subdirectory with the computer name by selecting the Prefix Subdirectory With Computer Name check box.

    - **Serial Number**   You can use the Serial Number format (N) to create a unique sub-folder name each time the DCS is started. This allows multiple logs of the same data collectors to be saved within different subfolders in the parent DCS folder. You can edit the serial only in the Data Collector Set Properties, but the serial number format may also be specified to be used by individual data collectors. The default DCS subdirectory naming convention is NNNNNN, which results in Data Collector Set subfolders named 00000*x* (where *x* is the serial number).

      For example, a Data Collector Set with a serial number of 8 that was run on January 31, 2003 at 4:20 A.M. would have the following results based on the selected subdirectory name format:

        - Subdirectory name format: yyyyMMddNNNN; Actual subdirectory name: 200301310008

- Subdirectory name format: yyDDD NN; Actual subdirectory name: 03031 08
- Subdirectory name format: MMMM MM\, yyyy \a\t h mmtt \- N; Actual subdirectory name: January 31, 2003 at 4 20 AM – 8

- **Security Tab**   Specific security parameters on the DCS. Default permissions are granted to SYSTEM, Administrators, Performance Log Users, and the data collector creator/owner.

- **Schedule Tab**   Configure the beginning date, expiration date, and launch time and day. Click Add to configure a schedule.

- **Stop Condition Tab**   Defines when the data collection will stop. Options available on this tab include:

  - **Overall Duration**   Configures the log to stop after a defined duration in seconds, minutes, days, hours, or weeks.

  - **Limits**   Defines limits for the log size or duration and whether or not to restart the Data Collector Set when those limits are reached. You can set the time duration or maximum size limit.

- **Task Tab**   Allows configuration of a specific task to run when a Data Collector Set stops. The specified task must be an existing Task Scheduler task. You can also specify the task arguments and the working directory.

> **Note**   You can also view and edit the properties of each data collector within a DCS by using the shortcut menus for each data collector. The configuration settings for a data collector vary depending on whether the data collector is used for collecting performance counter, event tracing, or registry information.

Using Data Manager to View Performance Data   The Data Manager was introduced in Windows Vista as a central location to manage logged performance data files. Each DCS has an associated Data Manager that controls the data management tasks, including report generation, data retention policy, conditions/actions, and data transfer, for the data in all of the subfolders in the Data Collector Set's root path.

By default, the Data Manager is disabled for a Data Collector Set. When you enable the Data Manager for a DCS, the Data Manager creates a Server Performance Advisor (SPA) overview report to summarize the data results when the data collection is completed. If you don't enable the Data Manager for a DCS, the DCS is still listed under the Reports node in the Diagnostic Console, but a SPA report is not generated for the DCS. This is discussed later in this section.

> **Note**   For more information concerning Server Performance Advisor (SPA), see *http://www.microsoft.com/downloads/details.aspx?FamilyID=09115420-8c9d-46b9-a9a5-9bffcd237da2&DisplayLang=en* and *http://www.microsoft.com/technet/prodtechnol/exchange/guides/ExMgmtGuide/9454ec83-c05f-4015-8c2d-f814915ba14a.mspx?mfr=true*.

To access the Data Manager Properties for a Data Collector Set, right-click the DCS name in the Data Collector Sets node in Performance Monitor and then select Data Manager from the shortcut menu. To enable the Data Manager for the DCS, select the Enable Data Management And Report Generation check box on the Data Manager tab (Figure 22-3). Note that by default, the Data Manager does not act on the selected options until the DCS has completed. To enforce the selected Data Manager options before the DCS starts, select the Apply Policy Before The Data Collector Set Starts check box. When you select this option, previous data is deleted based on the configured Data Manager conditions before the DCS creates the next log file.

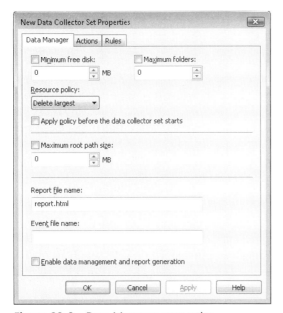

Figure 22-3   Data Manager properties.

The available Data Manager conditions are:

- **Minimum Free Disk**   The amount of disk space that must be available on the drive where log data is stored. If you select this condition, previous data is deleted according to the Resource Policy that you choose when the limit is reached.

- **Maximum Folders**   The number of subfolders that can be in the DCS data directory. If you select this condition, previous data is deleted according to the Resource Policy that you choose when the limit is reached.

- **Maximum Root Path Size**   The maximum size of the data directory for the DCS, including all subfolders. If you select this condition, this maximum path size overrides the Minimum Free Disk and Maximum Folders limits, and previous data will be deleted according to the Resource Policy that you choose when the limit is reached.

You can configure the Resource Policy to perform the following actions on the folders in the Data Collector Set's root folder if one of the preceding limits is exceeded:

- **Delete Largest**   The largest folder within the DCS root folder is deleted when one of the limits is exceeded.

- **Delete Oldest**   The oldest folder within the DCS root folder is deleted when one of the limits is exceeded.

> **Note**   These Resource Policy actions are performed on a folder basis, rather than a file basis.

You can use the Actions tab to define the folder actions to be performed when specified Data Manager conditions are met. The actions defined for the DCS are displayed in the Folder Actions section of the Actions tab window. Using this tab, you can add, edit, or remove folder actions for a DCS. Folder actions allow a user to choose how data is archived before it is permanently deleted according to the selected Resource Policy. You may also elect to not use the Data Manager limits in favor of managing all logged data according to the selected folder action rules. The following folder action options are available:

- **Age**   The age of the data file in days or weeks. If the value is 0, the criterion is not used.

- **Folder size**   The size, in megabytes (MB), of the folder where log data is stored. If the value is 0, the criterion is not used.

- **Actions**   Allows you to select which action to take when either the Resource Policy or Folder Action condition(s) are met. The actions include deletion of the raw data files and/or the report, as well as several cab file options. Cab files can be created, deleted, or sent (moved) to a local or shared folder.

Starting and Stopping Data Logging   The DCS will automatically start logging as soon as you create it if you select the Start This Data Collector Set Now option in the Create New Data Collector Set Wizard. If you don't select the Start This Data Collector Set Now option, logging must be started manually.

After you create the DCS, use the following methods to start and stop logging:

- Right-click the Data Collector Set name in the User Defined Data Collector Sets node and select Start or Stop action from the shortcut menu.

- Highlight the Data Collector Set name in the User Defined Data Collector Sets node and click the Start the Data Collector Set button or the Stop the Data Collector Set button on the Diagnostic Console toolbar.

> **Note**   To start performance counter logging automatically when the system reboots, create a scheduled task to run using System Startup as the condition and use Logman to start the log.

Viewing Performance Data   After you create the DCS, it is listed in the Reports section of Performance Monitor, as shown in Figure 22-4.

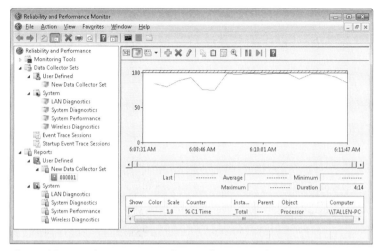

Figure 22-4   Using reports to view performance data.

You can still open Performance Monitor logs for viewing by using the same methods that you used in Windows 2000, Windows XP, and Windows Server 2003. However, you can now use three additional methods to open the logged performance data:

- Double-click a Performance Monitor log file (BLG) to open the log in Performance Monitor with all configured counters shown.

- Use the shortcut menu for the data collectors listed under Data Collector Sets in the Reports node in the Diagnostic Console.

- Right-click a data collector listed under the DCS name in the Reports node and select the desired view mode.

You can select the following three view modes from the Data Collector shortcut menu:

- **Report View**   If you enabled the Data Manager for the DCS, the Report menu item is available when you right-click the data collector in the Reports node. If you did not enable the Data Manager, the Reports menu option will be inaccessible. The Data Manager report is a Server Performance Advisor (SPA) report that provides a summary of the logged performance data, as shown in Figure 22-5. You can expand the Application Counters section to show a summary view of the Mean, Minimum, and Maximum data values from the data collector. The report is saved as an XML file in the DCS folder associated with the selected Data Collector.

- **Performance Monitor View**   If you select the Performance Monitor menu item, the Performance Monitor log file is displayed in the line chart with all configured counters.

■ **Folder View**   If you select the Folder menu item, the folder containing the selected data collector's files is displayed.

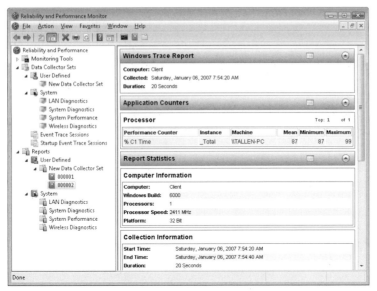

Figure 22-5   Server Performance Advisor report.

If a user clicks a log that is currently started, the main System Monitor window displays a green status bar with a Collecting Data label. To view the log, you must first stop the DCS for the log. Log files are listed under the Data Collector Set node in the Reports node. Filenames follow the default naming convention of NNNNNN (serial number). The serial number is incremented each time the DCS is restarted.

Comparing Performance Monitor Logs   You can use System Monitor's new Compare feature to overlay multiple log files for comparison. This feature is most useful for comparing multiple log files that have been configured to log the same data points for the same amount of time. To access the Compare feature, you must start Performance Monitor with the /**sys** parameter (perfmon /sys) from Run or from a command prompt. After Performance Monitor is open, you can view and compare log files as illustrated by the following steps:

1. To open the first log file, click the cylinder on the toolbar to open the System Monitor Properties dialog box.

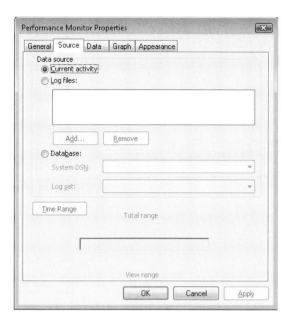

2. Click the Log Files radio button and then click Add to open the Select Log File window.

3. Locate the log file that you want to open and then click Open. The log file will be added to the System Monitor instance, but no counters will be added by default.

4. To add the desired counters, click the plus sign on the toolbar to open the Add Counters window. The counter data will be displayed in the main System Monitor window.

5. Repeat steps 1 through 3 to open the second log by opening another Performance Monitor instance with the **perfmon /sys command** and adding the desired counters.

6. After you open the logs for comparison, two opaque Performance Monitor windows will open on the desktop. Position and size the anchor window—which may be any of the Performance Monitor logs being compared—in the desired location. This will be the Performance Monitor window upon which you overlay the other windows.

7. Select the second Performance Monitor window—which will be overlaid on top of the first window—to bring it into focus, click the Compare menu, point to Set Transparency, and then select the desired transparency level. Note that transparency here is not related to the Windows Vista Aero Glass feature and will work on systems that are not capable of supporting Aero Glass.

    The Set Transparency option sets the transparency of the window to be overlaid on the anchor window. The transparency options are No Transparency, 40% Transparency, and 70% Transparency. When you set the transparency to 40%, the desktop background remains visible through the second window.

8. Select the Compare menu item and then click the Snap To Compare option.

    The second window is resized to the same size as the anchor window and is overlaid on top of the anchor window.

Note   You can still interact with both Performance Monitor windows individually to change properties; select menu items; and minimize, maximize, or close the windows.

Performance Monitor User Rights   Performance Monitor user rights are specified as follows:

- **Administrator**   Has local and remote full control

- **Performance Log Users**   Can access and log performance counter data locally and remotely (create, manipulate, and view logs)

- **Performance Monitor Users**   Can access performance counter data locally and remotely (view logs)

Note   On earlier versions of Windows, Performance Monitor can be used to monitor Windows Vista computers with options previously available on earlier versions of Windows but without support for new Windows Vista features. The user of the earlier version of Windows must also be in the local administrator group on the Windows Vista computer.

Table 22-1 summarizes the privileges needed to view and log counter data using Performance Monitor.

Table 22-1   Privileges Needed for Viewing and Logging Counter Data

Type of User or Group Membership	Elevation Prompt to Query Counter Data	Able to View Counters	Able to Log Counter Data
Standard user	No	No	No
Admin	Yes	Yes	Yes
PLUG (Performance Logs User Group)	No	Yes	Yes
PMON (Performance Monitoring User Group)	No	Yes	No

Remote Data Collection   To enable all remote Performance logging and alerting, you must perform the following actions:

- Enable the Performance Logs And Alerts firewall exception on the user's computer.

- Add the user to the Event Log Readers group. (This only applies when the user belongs to the Performance Log Users group.)

Managing Performance Logs and Event Trace Sessions with Logman   Logman.exe creates and manages Event Trace Session and Performance logs and supports many functions of Performance Monitor from the command line. Logman has been enhanced in Windows Vista and uses the following syntax from an elevated command prompt:

logman [create | query | start | stop | delete| update | import | export | /?] [options]

Logman commands include the following:

- **logman create**   Creates a counter, trace, configuration data collector, or API
- **logman query**   Queries data collector properties
- **logman start | stop**   Starts or stops data collection
- **logman delete**   Deletes an existing data collector
- **logman update**   Updates the properties of an existing data collector
- **logman import | export**   Imports a data collector set from an XML file or exports a data collector set to an XML file
- **logman /?**   Displays help for logman

The following usage examples illustrate logman syntax.

```
logman create counter perf_log -c "\Processor(_Total)\% Processor Time"

logman create trace trace_log -nb 16 256 -bs 64 -o c:\logfile

logman start perf_log

logman update perf_log -si 10 -f csv -v mmddhhmm

logman update trace_log -p "Windows Kernel Trace" (disk,net)
```

For detailed syntax of logman commands and more examples of usage, see *http://technet2.microsoft.com/windowsserver2008/en/library/574a5203-5b3b-4759-a678-f26d00dde4471033.mspx?mfr=true.*

Using Reliability Monitor

Reliability Monitor is a new MMC snap-in for Windows Vista that provides a system stability overview and trend analysis with detailed information about individual events that may affect the overall stability of the system. Reliability Monitor begins to collect data at the time of system installation. It then presents that data in a chart format that administrators and users can utilize to identify drivers, applications, or hardware that are causing stability or reliability problems on the computer.

Reliability Monitor tracks the following categories of events:

- Software installations and removals
- Application failures
- Hardware failures
- Windows failures
- Miscellaneous failures

The events tracked by Reliability Monitor are discussed in the section titled "System Stability Report" later in this chapter. You can access Reliability Monitor through the Diagnostic Console, or you can add it as a standalone MMC snap-in.

Reliability Monitor Features

Reliability Monitor provides the following features:

- Automatic data collection and processing
- System stability chart
- System stability report

Automatic Data Collection and Processing   Reliability Monitor gathers and processes data with the Reliability Analysis Component (RAC). Data is automatically collected by the reliability analysis metrics calculation executable (RACAgent.exe), also known as the RACAgent process. The RACAgent analyzes, aggregates, and correlates user disruptions in the operating system, services, and programs and then processes the data into reliability metrics. The RACAgent runs as a hidden scheduled task named RACAgent to collect specific events from the event log. The RACAgent runs once every hour to collect relevant event log data and processes data once every 24 hours, so stability data will not be available immediately after installation.

After the data is collected, the RACAgent processes this information using a weighted algorithm. The result of the data processing is a stability index number that can vary on a scale from 0 to 10, with 0 being the least reliable and 10 being the most reliable. The reliability index and the results of the event tracing are then displayed in the System Stability Chart, which you can view by clicking Reliability Monitor in the Diagnostic Console.

Direct from the Source: RACAgent Scheduled Task

The RACAgent is a hidden scheduled task that is automatically configured during system installation. This task is responsible for gathering the reliability data and displaying it in the chart view. The RACAgent task typically runs once every hour and will not wake the computer if it is sleeping. If the computer is a laptop on battery power, RACAgent.exe will immediately exit if the battery capacity is at less than 33 percent. To view the RACAgent task in Task Scheduler, select RAC within the Task Scheduler library and then right-click and select View – Show Hidden Tasks in the MMC action pane.

If you do not want to track system stability, you can disable the RACAgent task by selecting the Disable option, which is accessible in any of the following ways when the RACAgent task is highlighted in the main MMC pane:

- Via the action menu
- Via the action pane
- Via the shortcut menu for the task

Microsoft Global Technical Readiness Platforms Team

System Stability Chart   The top half of the Reliability Monitor window contains the System Stability Chart and a calendar control that you can use to select the time range to be viewed. A scroll bar at the bottom of the graph allows you to move forward or backward in time to view the stability history. Users will view the System Stability Chart to identify one or more days when the stability index has decreased from a previous level. Reliability Monitor maintains a year of history for system stability and reliability events.

The Reliability Monitor information is displayed in the System Stability Chart as data points that represent the reliability index of the system for a specific day. If the system clock is ever shifted significantly, the data point for that particular day is replaced by a blue information icon. The x-axis displays the date range and the y-axis displays the Stability Index number. The chart also indicates, with a circular red error icon or a yellow warning icon, if a failure occurred in one of the major categories on a given day. You can access the failure details from the expandable items in the System Stability Report section of the Reliability Monitor below the chart. Figure 22-6 shows the System Stability Chart and Report section.

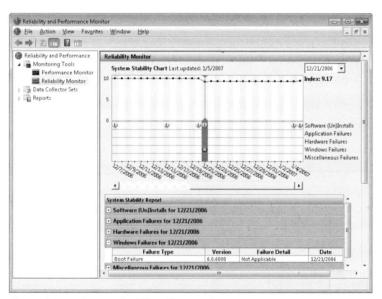

Figure 22-6   System Stability Chart and Report.

Stability Index   The Stability Index is the primary indicator of system stability (or reliability) over time, based on the data that has been gathered and processed by Reliability Monitor.

Reliability Monitor tracks the number of user disruptions per day over a 28-day rolling window of time, with the latest day of the rolling window being the current day. The Stability Index algorithm processes the information and calculates the stability index relative to the current day. Until the Reliability Monitor has collected 28 days of data, the Stability Index is displayed as a dotted line on the graph, indicating that it has not yet established a valid baseline for the measurement. The Stability Index is represented as a real number between 1.0 and 10.0, with 1.0 being the least stable and 10.0 being the most stable.

System Stability Report   After you select a day or date range, you can view the report items for that day by using the expandable items in the System Stability Report section. The report will specify the application, driver, or other system component that is causing the drop in the System Stability Index. This information helps you identify changes in system state that may be causing decreased system stability.

Reports focus on the following categories:

- Software (Un)installs
- Application Failures
- Hardware Failures
- Windows Failures
- Miscellaneous Failures
- System Clock Changes (will only appear if a system clock change has occurred)

The reports are sorted first by date in descending order (most recent date first) and then by application or driver name in ascending alphabetical order. The System Stability Reports are based on specific event data gathered by the RACAgent. Details for each event category are described in the following sections.

Software (Un)installs   This category tracks software installations, updates, configuration changes, and removals, including the operating system, Windows updates, drivers, and applications. The report contains the following information:

- **Software**   Operating system, name of application, Windows update name, or driver name
- **Version**   Version of the operating system, application, or driver (This field is not available for Windows updates.)
- **Activity**   Indicates the software change
- **Activity status**   Indicates success or failure for the action
- **Date**   The date of the action

The events that the RACAgent parses to generate the Software (Un)installs report are:

- Application installation and removal: MsiInstaller 1033, 1034, 1035, 1036, 1037, 1038
- Driver installation: User-PnP 20001
- Driver removal: User-PnP 20002
- Update installation and removal: Automatic Update / Windows Update 19, 20, 21, 23, 24 and SUS 183, 184, 190, 193, 194
- Operating system upgrade, service pack, or hotfix: NTServicePack 4353, 4354, 4363

> **Note**   User-PnP 20002 was not implemented for Windows Vista RTM and may be part of a future Windows release.

Application Failures   This category tracks application hangs (including the termination of a nonresponding application) and crashes. The report contains the following information:

- **Application**   Executable program name of the application that hung or crashed
- **Version**   Version number of the application
- **Failure type**   Indicates whether the application failed as a result of a hang or crash
- **Date**   The date of the application failure

The events that the RACAgent parses to generate the Application Failures report are:

- Application hang: Application Hang 1002
- Application crash: Application Error 1000

Hardware Failures   Disk (Disk Failure Diagnostic) and Memory (Windows Memory Diagnostic) failures are tracked in this category. The report contains the following information:

- **Component type**   Indicates whether the failure occurred on the hard drive or in memory
- **Device**   Identifies the device that is failing
- **Failure type**   Indicates whether a hard drive failure resulted from a bad disk or a bad block, or indicates that a memory failure resulted from bad memory
- **Date**   The date of the hardware failure

The events that the RACAgent parses to generate the Hardware Failures report are:

- Windows Memory Diagnostic: Microsoft-Windows-MemoryDiagnostics-Results 1102
- Disk Failure Diagnostic: Microsoft-Windows-DiskDiagnostic 1

Windows Failures   Operating system crashes, boot failures, and sleep failures are tracked in this category. The report contains the following information:

- **Failure type**   Indicates whether the event is a boot failure, operating system crash, or sleep failure
- **Version**   Versions of the operating system and service pack
- **Details**   Possible failure details are:
    - ❏ **OS Crash**   Indicates the stop code for the crash
    - ❏ **Boot Failure**   Indicates the detected problem
    - ❏ **Sleep Failure**   Indicates the component veto or failure to enter hibernation
- **Date**   The date of the Windows failure

The events that the RACAgent parses to generate the Windows Failures report are:

- Microsoft-Windows-StartupRepair; the failure types are:
    - ❑ 1101: Master boot record was corrupt
    - ❑ 1102: Partition table was corrupt
    - ❑ 1103: Corrupt boot sector
    - ❑ 1104: Corrupt system volume
    - ❑ 1105: No Windows startup files
    - ❑ 1106: No hard drive
    - ❑ 1107: No valid system partition
    - ❑ 1108: Missing boot manager
    - ❑ 1109: Corrupt boot manager
    - ❑ 1110: Missing Windows loader
    - ❑ 1112: Corrupt Windows loader
    - ❑ 1113: Corrupt boot config
    - ❑ 1114: Corrupt firmware boot config
    - ❑ 1115: Missing boot config
    - ❑ 1116: No boot failure
    - ❑ 1117: Bad RAM
    - ❑ 1118: Unknown
    - ❑ 1119: Failure during installation
    - ❑ 1120: Missing installation files
    - ❑ 1121: Corrupt installation files
    - ❑ 1122: Corrupt registry
    - ❑ 1123: Unknown
    - ❑ 1124: Bad driver
    - ❑ 1125: Bad software patch
    - ❑ 1126: Bad disk
    - ❑ 1127: Bad ACL
    - ❑ 1128: Security settings prevented boot
    - ❑ 1129: Low disk space
    - ❑ 1130: Unrecognized system partition
    - ❑ 1131: Corrupt boot entry

❑   1132: OS version mismatch

❑   1133: Incompatible BIOS

❑   1134: Incompatible boot sector

❑   1135: Detected file corruption

■   Bug check: 1000, 1001

System Clock Changes   This category displays information on any significant clock changes that have occurred on the system. Information on clock changes is shown only if the system has experienced at least one significant clock change.

■   **Old Time**   Previous time (before time change)

■   **New Time**   New time (after time change)

■   **Date**   Date of time change

The event that will be parsed by the RACAgent to generate the System Clock Changes report is:

■   Time change: Microsoft-Windows-Kernel-General 1

Miscellaneous Failures   This category displays information on any shutdown that was unexpected or where the system does not have a record of any user or process requesting system shutdown. The report contains the following information:

■   **Failure type**   Disruptive shutdown

■   **Version**   Version of the operating system and service pack

■   **Details**   The computer was not cleanly shut down

■   **Date**   Date of failure

The event that the RACAgent parses to generate the Miscellaneous Failures report is:

■   Disruptive shutdown: USER32 6008

Reliability Monitor Data Files

The data files that Reliability Monitor creates and uses to determine the stability information are stored in the following folders:

■   \ProgramData\Microsoft\RAC\PublishedData

■   \ProgramData\Microsoft\RAC\StateData

To reset Reliability Monitor to its default state, where no stability information is displayed, delete all of the files in these two folders. The files will be re-created with only current stability information the next time the RACAgent scheduled task runs.

The data that Reliability Monitor presents in the default view—as well as the time-specific views—is from HTML pages that Reliability Monitor creates before displaying the particular view. Reliability Monitor creates the HTML files, named Rmo*xxxx*.tmp.htm (where *xxxx* is a random number) in the Temp folder in the user's profile folder:

\Users\<username>\AppData\Local\Temp

You can obtain this file for trend analysis if desired; however, it will be deleted automatically when Reliability Monitor is closed.

Understanding Windows Eventing

Administrators, developers, and technical support personnel use Windows Eventing to gather information about the state of the hardware, the software, and the system, as well as to monitor security events. To provide these users with useful information, you need to give an event the right level or severity, raise it to the appropriate log, provide it with the correct attributes, and give it a useful and actionable message.

The Event Viewer in Windows Vista now contains component-specific logs and events. Components that write events to the system or application event logs in Windows XP can also write events to their own event logs, also known as a *channel*. These component-specific logs generally contain nonadministrative events, either operational, analytic, or debug events. These events are usually nonactionable and more verbose and are logged for tracing of normal operation or more details concerning potential problems. Administrative (actionable) events, however, are still usually logged in the application or system log. An exception may be large components or applications with a significant volume of administrative events, in which case there may be a separate component-specific administrative log. Because of these changes, the Windows Vista Event Viewer is easier to read and contains many more events with detailed information than on previous Windows platforms.

Overview of Windows Eventing

Windows Eventing 6.0 is the next generation of the Windows Event Log service in Windows Vista and Windows Server 2008. Whereas the system as a whole provides an end-to-end solution for various needs related to tracing and organizing events, Windows Eventing specifically offers services for administrators, IT professionals, and developers. It allows users to query and select events for analysis, diagnostics, and monitoring; it provides powerful local and remote subscriptions to events; and it allows you to forward events using industry-standard protocols.

Windows Eventing Capabilities

Windows Eventing includes the following capabilities:

- Windows Eventing provides a hierarchy of channels:
    - Global channels (displayed in Event Viewer as Windows Logs) that correspond to the NT Event Log standard channels (System, Application, Security)

- ❑ Installation channel (displayed in Event Viewer as Setup) for the events describing installation and setup history

- ❑ Global channels that correspond to the NT Event Log application private channels (some Windows components such as Active Directory use these channels for backward compatibility reasons)

- ❑ Manifest-defined private channels within the Applications subspace

■ Enhancements associated with these channels include:

- ❑ Log files associated with every channel

- ❑ Access control list (ACL)–based read/write/clear security for the channels and associated log files

- ❑ A significant improvement in logging performance and scalability over the NT Event Log

■ Windows Eventing provides the following capabilities to Event Publishers:

- ❑ The ability to log their events into global and private channels (with write security)

- ❑ The ability to raise structured and schematized events efficiently from user and kernel mode

- ❑ The ability to describe and register the structure and constant values in their events ahead of time to increase discoverability by allowing users (administrators) to discover events and their shape before these events are published as described later

- ❑ The auto-generation of various system properties in the event, extending similar capabilities of the NT Event Log

■ Windows Eventing provides the following capabilities to Event Consumers:

- ❑ The ability to discover which events a given Event Publisher is capable of reporting, where these events go, and the shape and meaning of each event

- ❑ The ability to select events from one or more channels using queries (with read security)

- ❑ The ability to register subscription filters to receive event notifications (with read security)

- ❑ The ability to configure the forwarding of events across computers

■ Windows Eventing provides the following configuration and maintenance capabilities:

- ❑ The ability to configure the size, retention policy, and security of event logs

- ❑ The ability to configure subscriptions

- ❑ The ability to save archive events from one or more channels using a query

- ❑ The ability to clear an event log file

Channels

A *channel* is a named stream of events; conceptually, this is no different from a television channel. Just as TV channels are directed at particular audiences, event channels are intended for specific audiences.

> **Note**   In Windows Eventing 6.0, each channel has its own event log file associated with it. This means that you can use the terms *channel* and *event log* interchangeably in Windows Vista.

A channel serves as a logical pathway for transporting events from the event provider to a log file and possibly to an event consumer. Channels have a number of properties defining their behavior. These properties can be divided into two groups: publishing properties and logging properties.

Publishing Properties   When events leave the provider, they are transported through an ETW session within the Windows kernel. The physical session can carry multiple channels and the publishing properties of the channel determine the properties of the session that must be used to transport the events in this channel. Channels that share publishing properties can share a single session.

Publishing properties include the security settings that specify which providers can publish events into the channel and the filtering parameters that control event filtering at the source.

Logging Properties   The second set of properties defines how the events in this channel are to be consumed. Based on these properties, the channels can be divided into two groups: Serviced Channels and Direct Channels. Table 22-2 describes the properties associated with each group.

Table 22-2   Logging Properties for Channels

Serviced Channels	Direct Channels
Consumers can subscribe for reliable delivery of events in the Serviced Channels. The subscriptions are based on XPath queries so that only events that match the query are delivered to the subscribers.	Consumers cannot subscribe to these channels easily.
Events can be forwarded to other systems. Forwarding is subscription-based so that selected events from any number of channels can be forwarded.	These channels are performance-oriented. The events are not processed in any way by the eventing system. This allows these channels to support a high volume of events.

Each channel belongs to one of the two groups. The requirements on the events determine which channel group would best serve as the destination of the events.

Channel Types   Two channel types are defined within each group, for a total of four channel types. The channel types are based on the event audiences. Table 22-3 describes the channel types in more detail.

Table 22-3   Channel Types

Type	Group	Description
Admin	Serviced	These channels are primarily targeted at end users, administrators, and support personnel. The events found in Admin channels indicate a problem and are well-documented or have a message associated with them that gives the reader direct instruction on what needs to be done to rectify the problem.
Debug	Direct	The events in the Debug channels are created by developers for developers. They are typically used during development or may be turned on to provide information to the developers to help diagnose a problem. The structure of those events may change often and cannot be relied on to stay unchanged for a significant period of time.
Operational	Serviced	All other events describe program operation and indicate problems that cannot be handled by user intervention. The main consumers of these events are tools; many of these events are used for problem analysis and diagnosis.
Analytic	Direct	

The Admin channels have a special place on every system. Administrators and users refer to these channels to see if their systems are having problems. The contents of these channels are normally highly visible and easy to find. Two standard channels—System and Application—are well-established targets of such error and warning events. System services publish global error and warning events into the System channel. All other programs publish such events into the Application channel. Programs normally avoid creating Admin channels of their own.

Event Log Files

A log file is attached to every channel. Applications direct the events into the channels, and these events are typically recorded in a log file. Figure 22-7 shows the structure of event logs in Windows Vista.

Naming Providers and Channels

A provider's distinguished name must be specified in the manifest. In most cases, the name is composed of three parts:

```
<Company>-<Product>-<ProgramName>
```

The last component may also include a version number (useful when multiple versions may be running side by side), as in the following example:

```
Microsoft-Windows-TaskScheduler
Microsoft-Windows-Eventlog
Microsoft-Windows-SqlServer-10
```

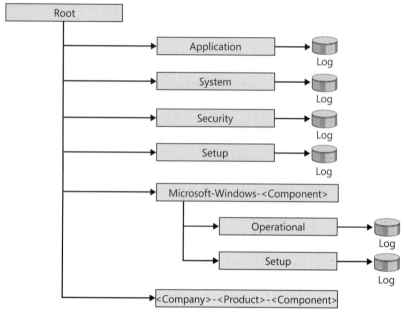

Figure 22-7   Event Log structure in Windows Vista.

The unique names of the channels created using manifests are designed to provide maximum information to the administrator about the purpose of the channel. The name for a channel is usually based on the provider name:

```
<Provider Name>/<Channel Name>
```

The channel names thus look like the following example:

```
Microsoft-Windows-SqlServer/Operational
Microsoft-Windows-TaskScheduler/CompletedJobs
```

Event Level

Event level is used to indicate the seriousness of an issue with regard to the functionality delivered by the service or component. It is also used to describe the verbosity of events logged in tracing scenarios.

The following event levels are predefined and known to all event providers in the Windows Event Log (event providers can also define custom levels):

- **Information events**   Indicate a change in the application's or component's state as a part of normal operation (an operation has been completed successfully, a resource has been created, or a service started) or that the component has recovered from a problem and returned to a healthy state.

- **Warning events**   Notify the user of degradation in service or of other issues that can affect service level or result in a more serious problem or failure unless action is taken.

■ **Error events**   Provide information about a problem that might affect functionality external to the component raising the event, or that is not core to the capabilities that the service or application provides to users.

■ **Critical events**   Provide information about a catastrophic loss of functionality in the application or component itself. The failure is about the component raising the event (in other words, failure has already occurred) and cannot be automatically recovered from Deployment and Configuration.

Event Logs

The unified event-publishing Application Programming Interface (API) in Windows Vista supports raising events to four types of logs:

■ **Admin logs**   Administrator logs or tools use Admin to determine the health of a component. Error and warning events, being most critical, are always raised to an Admin log. Information events that indicate a service's return to a healthy state are also appropriate for the Admin logs. To help administrators find these important events, they are normally only raised to the System and Application logs, which are common admin logs shared by system components and applications. In most scenarios, private Admin logs are not created.

■ **Operational logs**   Operational logs are typically private logs in which components can raise events that are useful for troubleshooting or launching automated actions, but are not actionable by themselves. Most Information events belong in Operational logs, which are enabled by default.

■ **Analytic logs**   Analytic logs contain events primarily used by tools for scenarios such as problem diagnosis or performance analysis. Analytic logs are also known as Trace logs and are generally disabled by default. Messages for events in Analytic logs are not necessarily written for administrators.

■ **Debug logs**   Debug logs contain events raised by developers for developers. Debug logs are hidden and disabled by default. Messages for events in debug logs are designed for developers and support personnel.

Event Attributes

Other event properties help administrators and tools filter events and automate tasks. Some properties are displayed on the event summary page, and others are available on the details page or programmatically.

■ **Source**   Source is the name of the component that published the event. Windows components normally use their assembly names as the name of the main provider in the manifest, for example, Microsoft-Windows-TaskScheduler.

■ **Value**   Value is the numeric ID unique to a specific event and source. An event ID is normally used for that event for each version.

■ **Keyword** Keyword is a set of categories or tags that can be used to filter or search on events. Examples include Network, Security, or Resource Not Found.

■ **Task Category** Task Category represents a subcomponent or activity of the event publisher. Task Category is only supported when you use the Windows Vista Event Publishing API.

Event Messages

Every event report displayed in Event Viewer contains a message, which is located in the Description box of the event's property sheet as well as on the preview pane. The event message provides context for what happened to the resource about which the event was raised. Messages for events in an admin log (the System or Application log) are generally actionable by an administrator. (There can be additional admin logs for certain applications that are application-specific.)

In addition to the description message, the Event Viewer can display event structure using XML (in XML view) and text (in Friendly View). The following example illustrates an event in XML format:

```xml
- <Event xmlns="http://schemas.microsoft.com/win/2004/08/events/event">
- <System>
 <Provider Name="Microsoft-Windows-TaskScheduler" Guid="{de7b24ea-73c8-4a09-985d-
5bdadcfa9017}" />
 <EventID>301</EventID>
 <Version>0</Version>
 <Level>4</Level>
 <Task>300</Task>
 <Opcode>2</Opcode>
 <Keywords>0x8000000000000000</Keywords>
 <TimeCreated SystemTime="2006-03-17T18:48:36.635Z" />
 <EventRecordID>530</EventRecordID>
 <Correlation />
 <Execution ProcessID="2916" ThreadID="1156" />
 <Channel>Microsoft-Windows-TaskScheduler</Channel>
 <Computer>user1_PC</Computer>
 <Security UserID="S-1-5-19" />
 </System>
- <UserData>
- <TaskEngineExitEvent xmlns="http://manifests.microsoft.com/win/2004/08/windows/
eventlog">
 <TaskEngineName>S-1-5-19:NT AUTHORITY\Local Service:Interactive:LUA</TaskEngineName>
 </TaskEngineExitEvent>
 </UserData>
 </Event>
```

Event Viewer User Interface

The Windows Vista Event Viewer interface is new for Windows Vista and has many new features. The Event Log service in Windows Vista introduces many more event logs and event log types to the operating system. The increase in the number of events, increased verbosity of events, and the dramatic increase in the number of component-specific event logs necessitates a much more intuitive user interface. The new Event Viewer contains powerful filtering and view customization features, as well as many new actions that can be performed on events or groups of events. The following sections explain the new features of the Windows Vista Event Viewer.

Accessing Event Viewer

You can open Event Viewer by using any of the following methods:

- Click Start, click All Programs, click Administrative Tools, and then click Event Viewer.

- Open the Computer Management console by right-clicking Computer from the Start menu and clicking Properties. Expand System Tools and click Event Viewer.

- From Run or from a command prompt, type **eventvwr.exe** or **eventvwr.msc**.

- Add the Event Viewer MMC snap-in to an MMC console.

Figure 22-8 shows the default Event Viewer interface.

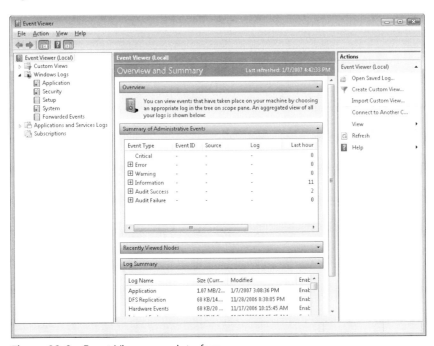

Figure 22-8   Event Viewer user interface.

Overview And Summary View

The Event Viewer opens to the Overview And Summary page, which shows all events across all Windows Logs. The total number of events for each type that have occurred are displayed, with additional columns that will display the number of events of each type that have occurred over the last seven days, the last 24 hours, or the last hour. Clicking on the + (plus) sign allows you to drill down into each event type and display the Event ID, Source, and Log that the event occurred in. Double-clicking a specific event summary will take you directly to that event in the log and automatically creates a filtered view, showing all individual events with that event source and event ID, which can be accessed from the left pane.

Note When you scroll to the bottom of the Summary page, a Log Summary is presented that lists the name of each event log on the system, the current size and maximum size, the last modified date, whether the log is enabled or disabled, and the retention policy. The Summary page includes events from all administrative logs, which includes both the Windows Logs and any application-specific administrative logs, if they exist.

Custom Views

You can configure and persist event filters by using the Custom Views node in Event Viewer. You can automatically create views by double-clicking events in the summary view, or you can create views manually. In Windows Vista, a built-in custom view named Administrative Events shows all events on the system that may require administrative action by filtering errors and warnings across all admin logs on the system.

Create a View Manually

To create a view (filter) manually, follow these steps:

1. Right-click Custom Views and then select Create Custom View.

2. In the Create Custom View dialog box, enter the criteria for which you want events displayed.

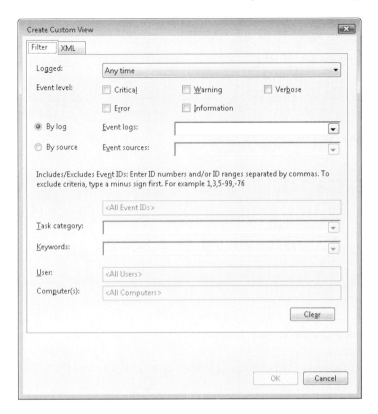

> **Note**   You can also click the XML tab and enter the XML filter directly. This may be useful if you are creating an advanced query for which the GUI options in the Filter tab are insufficient. Note that when you have edited a filter in the XML tab, you cannot return to the Filter tab for that filter.

3. Select the fields used to filter events using the following criteria:

   ❏ **By Log**   If you are filtering by log, first select the logs you are interested in. The event logs drop-down list adjusts to the list of logs relevant for those sources.

   ❏ **By Source**   If you are filtering by source, pick the sources of interest first. The sources drop-down list adjusts to just the sources available in those logs.

   ❏ **Logged**   Last Hour, Last 12 Hours, Last 24 Hours, Last 7 Days, or Last 30 Days. Selecting Custom Range brings up the Custom Range dialog box, allowing you to select a much more specific date range, including when events start and when they stop.

   ❏ **Event Level**   Select Critical, Warning, Verbose, Error, or Information.

❑ **Event Logs** Click the drop-down arrow to open the Event Log Selection window. Select the event log or event logs that you want to include in the view.

❑ **Event Sources** Click the drop-down arrow to display a list of available sources for the selected log so that you can specify which event source(s) to include in the view. In some cases, certain sources may not be listed (usually this can happen for legacy sources), in which case you can type in the source name manually.

❑ **Include/Exclude Event IDs** Enter Event ID numbers or ranges to be included or excluded, separated by commas. To exclude, include a minus sign in front of the number. For example, typing 1,3,5-99,-76 will include event IDs 1,3,5 through 99 and exclude 76.

❑ **Task Category** Select a task category to filter for events that specify that task category.

❑ **Keywords** Enter task keywords to be included in the filter.

❑ **User** Enter the user name by which to filter the events.

❑ **Computer** Enter the computer name by which to filter events. This will likely be used when filtering saved logs from other computers, or when filtering events forwarded from several computers on to a centralized log.

4. Click OK, name the View, and then select where the view will be saved. Create a new folder, if needed, to better categorize your custom views you create for various purposes. By default, custom views defined on a computer will be available to all users on that computer. To define a custom view private to the current user, clear the All Users check box before saving the view. Custom Views are saved and you may reuse them any time you run Event Viewer in the future. Furthermore, you can also export custom views into an XML file at a specified location, or imported from an XML file. This allows administrators to share interesting event views by exporting them to a shared location and importing into various Event Viewer consoles as needed.

Figure 22-9 shows the default Administrative Events custom view.

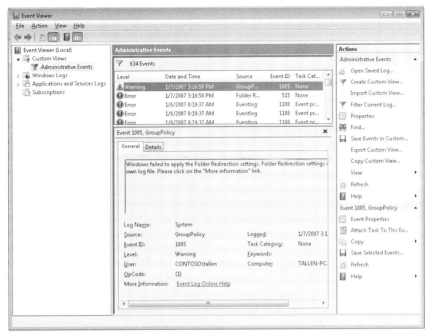

Figure 22-9   The default Administrative Events custom view.

Windows Logs

The Application, System, Security, and Setup logs are now located under the Windows Logs node in the Event Viewer tree view. An event summary view including the name, type, number of events, and size of each log is displayed when this node is selected. To view events in a log, select the log you want to view in the left pane.

Applications and Services Logs

Hardware Events, Internet Explorer, and other Windows components and applications events are accessible under the Applications And Services Logs node. Applications And Services Logs are a new category of event logs that store events from a single application or component rather than events that might have system-wide impact. Normally, available application or service logs will be listed in a hierarchy under the manufacturer and product name. (Some event providers that do not follow the naming convention that allows such categorization may show up directly under the Applications And Services node). A summary view including the name, type, number of events, and size of each log is displayed when the Applications And Services node, or any subnode that contains logs, is selected in the Event Viewer tree view as shown in Figure 22-10.

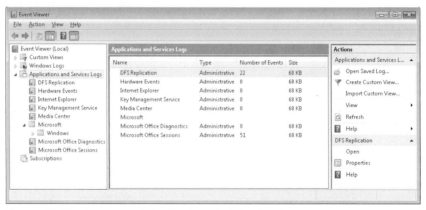

Figure 22-10   Summary of Applications And Services Logs.

Note   If other applications are installed, such as the 2007 Microsoft Office system applications, additional Applications And Services Logs may be displayed, as shown in Figure 22-10.

This category of logs includes four subtypes: Admin, Operational, Analytic (trace), and Debug logs. Events in Admin logs are of particular interest to IT professionals who use Event Viewer to troubleshoot problems, because events in the Admin log provide guidance on how to respond to the event. Events in the Operational log are also useful for IT professionals, but sometimes require more interpretation.

Analytic and Debug logs are not as user-friendly and are mostly oriented to be used by tools or advanced administrators and developers. Analytic logs store events that trace an issue, and often a high volume of events are logged. Debug logs are used by developers when debugging applications. Both Analytic and Debug logs are hidden by default. If you will be working with these types of logs and want to see them in the Event Viewer, select the Show Analytic and Debug Logs menu option from the View item on the action pane. Then, to turn on/off logging into a particular analytic or debug log, select the log of interest and click Enable Log or Disable Log in the Actions pane. Alternatively, you can also enable or disable Analytic and Debug logs by typing **wevtutil sl** *logname* **/e:true** at an elevated command prompt. For more information concerning wevtuti.exe, see the sidebar titled "How It Works: The Windows Events Command Line Utility."

Caution   When you enable Analytic (trace) and Debug logs, they usually generate a large number of entries. For this reason, you should only enable them for a specified period to gather troubleshooting data and then turn them off to reduce the associated overhead.

You can view events by highlighting the log you want to view in the left pane. Most Microsoft components that have their own channel in Windows Vista are displayed under the Microsoft section, as shown in Figure 22-11. (This is true for all events whose publishers follow the *<manufacturer>-<product>-<publisher>* naming convention described previously.)

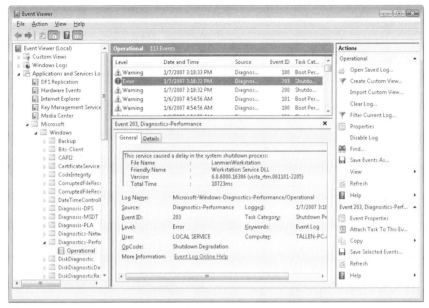

Figure 22-11   Events for different Microsoft components.

How It Works: The Windows Events Command Line Utility

The Windows Events Command Line Utility (Wevtutil.exe) lets you retrieve information about event logs and publishers; install and uninstall event manifests; run queries; and export, archive, and clear logs from an elevated command prompt. (The usage for this command is described later in this sidebar.) Note that you can use either the short (ep /uni) or long (enum-publishers /unicode) version of the command and option names, and all commands, options, and option values are case insensitive.

The general syntax for Wevtutil.exe is as follows:

wevtutil *command [argument [argument] ...] [/option:value [/option:value] ...]*

Here *command* can be any of the following:

- **al (archive-log)**   Archives an exported log.
- **cl (clear-log)**   Clears a log.
- **el (enum-logs)**   Lists log names.
- **ep (enum-publishers)**   Lists event publishers.
- **epl (export-log)**   Exports a log.

- **gl (get-log)**   Gets log configuration information.
- **gli (get-log-info)**   Gets log status information.
- **gp (get-publisher)**   Gets publisher configuration information.
- **im (install-manifest)**   Installs event publishers and logs from manifest.
- **qe (query-events)**   Queries events from a log or log file.
- **sl (set-log)**   Modifies configuration of a log.
- **um (uninstall-manifest)**   Uninstalls event publishers and logs from manifest.

Common options are as follows:

- **/r:*value* (remote)**   If specified, runs the command on a remote computer named *value*. Note that im (install-manifest) and um (uninstall-manifest) do not support remote operation.
- **/u:*value* (username)**   Specifies a different user to log on to remote computer. Here *value* is a user name in the form *domain\user* or *user*. This option is only applicable when option /r (remote) is specified.
- **/p:*value* (password)**   Specifies a password for the specified user. If not specified or *value* is "*", the user will be prompted to enter a password. This option is only applicable when /u (username) option is specified.
- **/a:*value* (authentication)**   Specifies an authentication type for connecting to a remote computer. *Value* can be Default, Negotiate, Kerberos, or NTLM. The default is Negotiate.
- **/uni:*value* (unicode)**   Displays output in Unicode. *Value* can be true or false (if true, output is in Unicode).

To learn more about a specific command, type **wevtutil command /?** at an elevated command prompt. For additional information concerning Wevtutil.exe, see *http://technet2.microsoft.com/windowsserver2008/en/library/d4c791e0-7e59-45c5-aa55-0223b77a48221033.mspx?mfr=true.*

Saving and Opening Event Logs

You can use Event Viewer to save events and open saved event logs for archiving and analysis purposes. The context menu options are as follows:

Save Events As   Save the selected channel (log file) in one of the following formats:

- Event Files (.evtx) (the default)
- XML (XML File) (.xml)
- Text (Tab delimited) (.txt)
- CSV (Comma separated) (.csv)

Open Saved Log   Open the saved events to display them in Event Viewer. The supported formats are:

- Event Log Files (.evtx, .evt, .etl) (the default)
- Event Files (.evtx)
- Legacy Event Files (.evt)
- Trace Log Files (.etl)

These actions are commonly used by administrators and support individuals to troubleshoot problems on computers where a direct live connection is not available.

Subscriptions

Using Event Viewer, you can view events on a single remote computer. However, troubleshooting an issue might require you to examine a set of events stored in multiple logs on multiple computers.

Windows Vista includes the ability to collect copies of events from multiple remote computers and store them locally. To specify which events to collect, you create an event subscription. Among other details, the subscription specifies exactly which events will be collected and in which log they will be stored locally. When a subscription is active and events are being collected, you can view and manipulate these forwarded events as you would any other locally stored events.

Using the event-collecting feature requires that you configure both the forwarding and the collecting computers. The functionality depends on the Windows Remote Management (WinRM) service and the Windows Event Collector (Wecsvc) service. The WinRM service must be running on both computers participating in the forwarding and collecting process. The Wecsvc service needs to be running only on the collector computer because the source computer has a forwarding plug-in that runs in-process to WinRM.

To define a subscription, you must be administrator on the collector computer. As part of the subscription definition, you define what security context should be used when accessing the logs on the source computers. This can be either a specific user account or the collector computer account. The specified account must have Read access to the logs on the source computers that are participating in the subscription. One way to set this up is to use a new built-in group called Event Log Readers, to which you can add any accounts you want to give access to reading logs.

To configure computers to forward and collect events, follow these steps:

1. Log on to all collector and source computers. If the computers are members of a domain, it is a best practice to use a domain account with administrative privileges.

2. On each source computer, type **winrm quickconfig** at an elevated command prompt. When prompted, confirm that the changes should be made. To skip the prompt (for example, if you are using this command in a script), add the –*q* parameter.

3. On the collector computer, type **wecutil qc** at an elevated command prompt. (If you use Event Viewer, this will be done automatically for you on the collector.) When prompted, confirm that the changes should be made. To skip the prompt, add the /*q:true* parameter.

4. Add the computer account of the collector computer to the Event Log Readers group on each of the source computers if you will be using the computer account as the account to be used when collecting events. The advantage of using the collector computer account is that you don't need to deal with expiring passwords. However, if you do use a specific user account, you will need to add that account to the Event Log Readers instead of the collector computer account.

> **Note**   By default, the Local Users And Groups MMC snap-in does not allow you to add computer accounts. In the Select Users, Computers, Or Groups dialog box, click Object Types and then select the Computers check box. You will now be able to add computer accounts.

The computers are now configured to forward and collect events. Follow the steps described in the section titled "Creating a New Subscription" later in this chapter to specify the events you want to have forwarded to the collector.

Additional Considerations   In a workgroup environment, you can follow the same basic procedure described in the previous section to configure computers to forward and collect events. However, workgroups require some additional steps and considerations:

■   You can use only Normal mode (Pull) subscriptions.

■   You must add a Windows Firewall exception for Remote Event Log Management on each source computer.

■   You must add an account with administrator privileges to the Event Log Readers group on each source computer. You must specify this account in the Configure Advanced Subscription Settings dialog box when you create a subscription on the collector computer.

■   Type **winrm set winrm/config/client @{TrustedHosts="<*sources*>"}** at a command prompt on the collector computer to allow all of the source computers to use NTLM authentication when communicating with WinRM on the collector computer. Run this command only once. Where <*sources*> appears in the command, substitute a comma-separated list of the names of all of the participating source computers in the workgroup. Alternatively, you can use wildcards to match the names of all the source computers. For example, if you want to configure a set of source computers that each has a name that begins with *msft*, you could type the command **winrm set winrm/config/ client @{TrustedHosts="msft*"}** on the collector computer. To learn more about this command, type **winrm help config** at a command prompt.

■   If you configure a subscription to use the HTTPS protocol by using the HTTPS option in Advanced Subscription Settings, you must also set corresponding Windows Firewall exceptions for port 443. For a subscription that uses Normal (PULL mode) delivery optimization, you must set the exception only on the source computers. For a subscription that uses either Minimize Bandwidth or Minimize Latency (PUSH mode) delivery optimizations, you must set the exception on both the source and collector computers.

■   If you intend to specify a user account by selecting the Specific User option in Advanced Subscription Settings when creating the subscription, you must ensure that the account is a member of the local Administrators group on each of the source computers in step 4 in the previous procedure instead of adding the machine account of the collector computer. Alternatively, you can use the Windows Event Log command-line utility to grant an account access to individual logs. To learn more about this command-line utility, type **wevtutil -?** at a command prompt.

Creating a New Subscription   To configure a new subscription, follow these steps:

1.   Right-click Subscriptions in the Event Viewer tree view and then select Create Subscription, or select the Subscriptions node and click the Create Subscription action in the Actions pane.

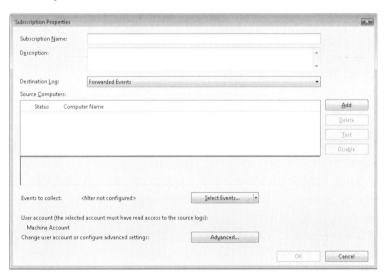

2.   In the Subscription Properties dialog box, enter the Subscription Name.

3.   Select the Destination Log name to save the subscribed events to. By default, the event subscriptions will be collected in the ForwardedEvents log.

4. Add the Source Computers that the subscription will pull data from. The Test button can be used to test connectivity to the selected computer and ensure that the collector will have access to that computer to collect events.

5. Click Select Events to configure the specific events that you want to collect. The Select Events button presents two options when you click the drop-down list:

   ❑ **Edit**   Opens the Query Filter dialog box to allow the creation of an event filter to be used for the subscription.

   ❑ **Copy From Existing Custom View**   Allows the selection of an existing Custom View to be used for the subscription.

6. Click Advanced to configure the options shown in the following dialog box.

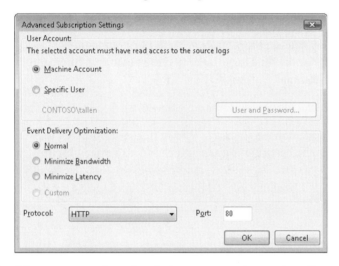

7. After you create the subscription, you can view and configure it from the middle pane of Event Viewer. For each subscription, you can see its name, status, participating source computers, and description. To view detailed status for each source computer participating in a subscription, open the Subscription Properties dialog box for the subscription of interest. The Source Computers list displays the list of participating computers and the status for each. Selecting a specific computer in the list will display detailed status in the box underneath the computer list, and if there is a problem with that computer, the detailed status also includes possible causes and remedies. You can temporarily disable individual computers from participating in the subscription by selecting the computer in the list and clicking Disable. In addition, you can temporarily disable an entire subscription by selecting the subscription in the Subscriptions list in the main MMC middle pane and clicking the Disable action. You can also retry individual computers or the entire subscription (to check if previous problems have been remedied, for example) by selecting the computer or entire subscription, respectively, and clicking Retry.

The Advanced button lets you configure how collected events are delivered and also lets you specify the account used to manage the process of collecting events. Event Viewer provides three event delivery optimization options: Normal, Minimize Bandwidth, and Minimize Latency. Table 22-4 describes each of these three options.

Table 22-4   Optimization Delivery Options for Configuring Event Collection

Event Delivery Optimization Method	Description
Normal	Ensures reliable delivery of events and does not attempt to conserve bandwidth. This is the appropriate choice unless you need tighter control over bandwidth usage or need forwarded events delivered as quickly as possible. This method uses pull delivery mode, batches 5 items at a time, and sets a batch time-out of 15 minutes.
Minimize Bandwidth	Ensures that the use of network bandwidth for event delivery is strictly controlled. This is an appropriate choice if you want to limit the frequency of network connections made to deliver events. This method uses push delivery mode and sets a batch time-out of six hours. This method also uses a heartbeat interval of six hours.
Minimize Latency	Ensures that events are delivered with minimal delay. This is an appropriate choice if you are collecting alerts or critical events. This method uses push delivery mode and sets a batch time-out of 30 seconds.

Actions Pane

Previous versions of Event Viewer were MMC 2.0 snap-ins and thus did not have the Actions pane. Event Viewer in Windows Vista and Windows Server 2008 is an MMC 3.0 snap-in and contains an all-new Actions pane on the far right side of the user interface. This pane displays actions that can be performed on the currently selected item in the left pane (tree view). The Actions pane changes based on what is highlighted in the tree view. The actions that can be performed normally will be the same as the shortcut menu actions.

Table 22-5 lists and describes the actions that you can perform on an event. Note that some of the object-specific actions in the actions pane will change (show up or hide) depending on the context you are in—in other words, whether the node that you have selected is in the scope pane (tree) or results pane (middle). So this list is relevant only when you have a log selected in the tree and an event selected in the middle pane. Also note that the actions are categorized in several groups; mainly the top group applies globally (no selection required) or to the selected tree node (the log), whereas the bottom group applies to the selected middle-pane object (the specific event).

Table 22-5   Available Actions That Can Be Performed on Events

Action	Description
Open Saved Log	Opens a new log file in the current view. Log file must be EVTX, EVT, or ETL format.
Create Custom View	Opens the Create Custom View (filter) Wizard.
Import Custom View	Allows the user to import a view that has been saved in XML format.
Clear Log	Clears the selected event log of all events.
Filter Current Log	Opens the Filter Wizard. You create filters the same way that you create views.
Properties	Opens the properties of the currently selected event.
Find	Offers a generic Find dialog box to search for text.
Save Events As	Allows the user to save a log file in ELF or XML format.
View	Provides options to customize the MMC view and to show Analytic and Debug Logs.
Refresh	Refreshes the Event Log.
Help	Activates the Help menu.
Event Properties	Active only when an event is selected. This is the same as the Properties action.
Attach Task To This Event	Opens the Task Scheduler Wizard with the Event Log, Event Source, and Event ID automatically populated. The user can attach any task to an event using Task Scheduler.
Copy	Copies the XML event text to the clipboard.
Save Selected Event(s)	Saves only selected events to ELF or XML format.

Understanding the Windows System Assessment Tool

You can use the Windows System Assessment Tool (WinSAT) to assess the features, capabilities, and attributes of a Windows Vista PC. WinSAT executes during out-of-box-experience (OOBE) and when the Rate This Computer option is selected in the Performance Information And Tools control panel. This section discusses the Performance Information And Tools control panel in more detail. This section also describes how Desktop Window Manager performs composition and how Windows Vista determines which level of Aero Glass can be supported given the system's hardware configuration.

Overview of WinSAT

Each assessment name has a set of assessment parameters that it will accept. For brevity, the assessment parameters are not provided here. To see the available assessment parameters, type **winsat /?** from an elevated command prompt.

Assessment Names

WinSAT assessment names include:

- **dwm**   The Desktop Window Manager (DWM) assessment is targeted at assessing a system's ability to run a Windows Vista–composited desktop, usually referred to as Aero Glass. Note that these are names of Aero themes. You can only run this assessment on computers with WDDM video drivers.

- **d3d**   The Direct3D (D3D) assessment is targeted at assessing a system's ability to run games.

- **mem**   Runs system memory bandwidth tests. This is intended to be reflective of large memory-to-memory buffer copies, like those used in multimedia processing (video, graphics, imaging, and so on).

- **disk**   Measures the performance of disk drives.

- **cpu**   Measures the computation ability of the processor.

- **media**   Measures the performance of video encoding and decoding.

- **features**   Enumerates relevant system information. This assessment is automatically run once for each invocation of WinSAT and the data saved in the XML output.

- **formal**   Runs the full set of assessments and saves the result.

- **mfmedia**   Runs the Media Foundation–based assessment.

Examining the Features Assessment

WinSAT automatically runs the Features assessment each time it runs. This assessment enumerates system information relevant to the assessments, including:

- The name of the computer. Note that this information is supported only in private builds of WinSAT and will not be present in the retail version of the product.

- An optional globally unique identifier (GUID) if the *–igCid* command-line switch is used. This ensures that each XML file has a unique identifier.

- The iteration value from the *–iter <n>* command-line switch.

- The number of processors, cores, and CPUs.

- The presence of CPU threading technology.

- x64 capability.

- The processor signature.

- The size and other characteristics of the processor's L1 and L2 caches.

- The presence of MMX, SSE, and SSE2 instructions.

- Information on the memory subsystem. (Note that this is very system-dependent: Some systems will produce good detail here; others will not.)

- Graphics memory.

- Graphics resolution.

- Graphics refresh rate.

- Graphics names and device IDs.

Direct from the Source: WinSAT Data Files

Advanced users may want more information regarding the Windows Experience Index and system performance than is available in the Performance Information And Tools Control Panel item. The underlying technology that supports the Windows Experience Index is the Windows System Assessment Tool (WinSAT). This tool stores the 10 most recent assessments in a data store folder located at

%WinDir%\Performance\WinSAT\DataStore

The data store consists of XML files that contain information regarding each assessment. These XML files contain advanced details regarding system performance and the Windows Experience Index. The files are named by the date and time the assessments ran.

Quais Taraki, Program Manager

Windows Performance

Command-Line Usage

Although in most cases, WinSAT will not be executed manually from a command prompt, the general format of the command line is

```
winsat <assessment name> <assessment parameters>
```

The WinSAT command-line options are not case sensitive. The command line does not require a dash for forward slash for the assessment name, but does support either a leading dash (–) or a leading forward-slash (/) character to designate an assessment parameter. An error will be reported if any options or switches are not supported.

The WinSAT tool also supports several command-line switches in addition to the assessment parameters. These are parsed by WinSAT before it passes control to one or more of the assessments. Some of these parameters are also supported by one or more assessments. Parameters that are not handled by assessments are stripped from the command line before the command line is processed by the assessments.

The command-line parameters recognized by WinSAT are:

- **–help or –?**   Displays the help content.

- **–v**   This specifies that WinSAT should produce verbose output. This output includes progress and status information, and possibly error information. The default is for no verbose output. This switch is passed to all of the specified assessments.

- **–xml <file name>**   This specifies that the XML output from the assessment is to be saved in the specified filename. All assessments support the *–xml* command-line switch; a pre-existing file with the same name will be overwritten.

- **–idiskinfo**   Information on the disk subsystem (logical volumes and physical disks) is not normally saved as part of the *<SystemConfig>* section in the XML output.

- **–iguid**   Generates a globally unique identifier in the XML output file. Note that this is not valid with the formal assessment.

- **–iter <n>**   Includes the iteration number *<n>* in the XML output file.

- **–ssc**   This causes WinSAT to skip checking the XML output against the WinSAT XML schema. Note that this command-line switch will be deprecated in release candidate versions.

- **–csv**   This causes WinSAT to save the top-level measured metrics to a CSV file.

Binary Components

WinSAT contains the following files:

- **Winsat.exe**   The executable. This file is located in the %WinDir%\system32 folder.

- **WinSAT.wmv**   The recommended video clip for use with the media decode assessment. This file is located in the %WinDir%\Performance\Winsat folder.

- **WinSAT.prx**   The recommended encode configuration file to use with the media encode assessment. This file is located in the %WinDir%\Performance\Winsat folder.

Exit Values

WinSAT provides the following exit values:

- **0** indicates all requested assessments were completed successfully.

- **1** indicates one or more assessment did not complete because of an error.

- **2** indicates one or more assessments did not complete because of interference.

- **3** indicates that WinSAT was canceled by the user.

- **4** indicates that the command given to WinSAT was invalid.

- **5** indicates that WinSAT did not run with administrator privileges.

- **6** indicates that another instance of WinSAT is running.

Registry Locations

WinSAT writes the assessment results to the following registry key:

HKLM\Software\Microsoft\Windows NT\CurrentVersion\WinSAT

Value: VideoMemorySize – Size of the video memory, in bytes

Value: VideoMemoryBandwidth – Derived from compilation of video memory and display resolution

If these registry keys do not exist, WinSAT did not run during the installation or upgrade the operating system. To create these registry keys, run WinSAT from the command line or from Performance Information And Tools, discussed in the next section.

> **Note**   You can also run WinSAT on earlier versions of Windows by installing the Windows Vista Upgrade Advisor, which can be downloaded from *http://www.microsoft.com/downloads/ details.aspx?familyid=42B5AC83-C24F-4863-A389-3FFC194924F8&displaylang=en.*

How Desktop Window Manager Performs Composition

The new Windows Vista desktop composition feature fundamentally changes the way Windows displays pixels on the screen. When you enable desktop composition, individual windows no longer draw directly to the screen or primary display device as they did in previous versions of Windows. Instead, their drawing is redirected to off-screen surfaces in video memory, which are then rendered into a desktop image and presented on the display.

Desktop composition is performed by a new component in Windows Vista, the Desktop Window Manager (DWM). Through desktop composition, DWM allows for visual effects on the desktop as well as various features such as glass window frames, 3D window transition animations, Windows Flip and Windows Flip3D, and high-resolution support.

Desktop Window Manager Components

The Desktop Window Manager consists of two main components: the Desktop Window Manager Session Manager service and the Desktop Window Manager process. The following section discusses these components in detail.

Desktop Window Manager Session Manager Service   The Desktop Window Manager Session Manager service starts and manages one Desktop Window Manager process for each user session on the computer. The Desktop Window Manager process runs as %SystemRoot%\system32\dwm.exe. If the process is ever terminated unexpectedly, it is restarted by the Desktop Window Manager Session Manager service.

The Desktop Window Manager process loads two important modules:

- **Udwm.dll**   Microsoft Desktop Window Manager DLL
- **Milcore.dll**   Microsoft Media Integration Library (MIL) Core Library

Windows Presentation Foundation   The Microsoft Windows Presentation Foundation (formerly code-named Avalon) provides the foundation for building applications and high-fidelity experiences in Windows Vista and Windows Server 2008, blending together application UI, documents, and media content. The functionality extends to support for Tablet and other forms of input, a more modern imaging and printing pipeline, accessibility and UI automation infrastructure, data-driven UI and visualization, and the integration points for weaving the application experience into the Windows shell. The WPF components pf.dll and pc.dll are also clients to milcore.dll, which is loaded by the DWM service.

All of the Windows Aero and Glass features of the desktop are implemented through the Desktop Window Manager Session Manager service. This service is also known as the User Experience Session Manager Service (UxSms) and is implemented as a service that runs under the generic service host process Svchost.exe.

WinSAT and the Desktop Windows Manager

WinSAT queries the system hardware and assesses the hardware capabilities of the computer. The Desktop Window Manager uses the data that WinSAT gathers to determine if the computer is capable of displaying the Aero Glass interface. WinSAT runs once during the out-of-box experience, but it can also be run manually by running WinSAT.exe from the command line or from the Performance Rating And Tools user interface, as described in the section titled "Forcing WinSAT to Reassess the Computer" later in this chapter.

Table 22-6 lists the VideoMemoryBandwidth threshold values, in MB/s, above which composition is enabled. If your value is above the threshold value required for Transparent Glass, you'll get Transparent Glass. If your value is below the Aero Glass threshold value but above the Opaque Glass value, you'll get Opaque Glass. Otherwise, you will not get glass composition.

The values shown in the table are dependent on the resolution setting and availability of the Required Video Memory shown for each resolution setting to get composition.

Table 22-6   Thresholds for Aero Glass Composition

Resolution	Threshold for Transparent Glass	Threshold for Opaque Glass	Required Video Memory for Transparent Glass	Required Video Memory for Opaque Glass
Single Monitor				
800x600	288,234	58,457	32 MB	32 MB
1024x768	388,848	94,735	32 MB	32 MB
1280x1024	526,766	156,481	64 MB	32 MB
1600x1200	687,589	228,037	128 MB	64 MB
1920x1200	814,702	273,150	128 MB	64 MB
Dual Monitor				
800x600	376,218	88,998	32 MB	32 MB
1024x768	512,165	144,523	64 MB	64 MB

Table 22-6 Thresholds for Aero Glass Composition

Resolution	Threshold for Transparent Glass	Threshold for Opaque Glass	Required Video Memory for Transparent Glass	Required Video Memory for Opaque Glass
1280x1024	701,979	239,123	128 MB	64 MB
1600x1200	923,249	348,809	128 MB	128 MB
1920x1200	1,094,897	417,957	256 MB	128 MB

These thresholds may be overridden, as explained in later in this section.

Troubleshooting Aero Glass

If your system is not displaying with Aero Glass, and you have met the minimum system requirements, you can use the following steps to diagnose the problem.

First, determine what display mode your system is currently in. The Windows Vista desktop has three distinct looks: transparent glass, opaque glass, and no composition, as demonstrated graphically in Chapter 1, "Overview of Windows Vista Improvements." Are you seeing opaque glass or are you simply not getting composition at all? A quick way to determine the level of composition is to look at the Minimize, Restore, and Close buttons on a window to see if they are docked at the top edge of the window:

■ Extended rectangular buttons indicate transparent or opaque glass.

■ Smaller square buttons indicate no composition.

Transparent glass is fully functional Windows Aero Glass. If you're getting opaque glass, in all likelihood your computer has been assessed by WinSAT as not powerful enough to recommend transparent glass. The accuracy of the model by which this is evaluated will be increased in RC1 and RTM builds of Windows Vista, which may allow more computers to achieve an assessment that automatically enables transparent glass display.

WinSAT will write the following values to the registry during install if the computer is using a WDDM video driver. Computers with legacy video drivers will not generate these registry keys. These registry keys indicate what WinSAT detected for the video hardware:

HKLM\Software\Microsoft\Windows NT\CurrentVersion\WinSAT\VideoMemoryBandwidth

HKLM\Software\Microsoft\Windows NT\CurrentVersion\WinSAT\VideoMemorySize

WinSAT generally assesses graphics subsystems correctly. However, in some cases, the amount of textures and render targets WinSAT allocates causes the performance metric to be too low. This predominantly happens on cards with 64 MB or less of graphics memory.

If you're not getting composition at all, the first step is to look at the Event Log to see what the problem is. Run Event Viewer, choose Windows Logs, and then choose the Application log.

Look for entries with Desktop Window Manager as the Source. A recent entry should indicate why the Desktop Window Manager didn't start. Possibilities include:

- Not running a WDDM/LDDM driver.

- Not running with 32 bits per pixel color. (To fix this, change your Display Settings and then log off and log on again.)

- The monitor frequency is too low. (Realistically, this only happens with a faulty KVM, or if the computer was booted without a monitor.)

- A mirroring device driver is in use.

- An analysis of the hardware and configuration indicated it would perform poorly. In this case, the system may have been incorrectly assessed. If you believe it was, you can override this assessment, as explained in the next section.

Overriding Windows Vista Automatic Detection Mechanisms

On computers with WDDM-capable drivers, you can set the composition policy manually by setting two registry keys and then restarting the DWM. First, ensure that the following registry values are set:

- **Composition**   HKCU\Software\Microsoft\Windows\DWM\Composition

  Set to 1 (32-bit DWORD)

  The *Composition* key indicates whether composition is enabled or disabled. Setting this value to 1 will enable composition.

- **CompositionPolicy**   HKCU\Software\Microsoft\Windows\DWM\CompositionPolicy

  Set to 2 (32-bit DWORD)

  The *CompositionPolicy* key determines whether you can use the WinSat assessment to enable or disable composition. Values are:

  - ❏   USE ASSESSMENT = 0

  - ❏   IGNORE ASSESSMENT AND DISABLE = 1

  - ❏   IGNORE ASSESSMENT AND ENABLE = 2

  Setting *CompositionPolicy* to 2 forces the system to ignore the WinSat assessment and enable composition.

> **Note**   You may need to create the DWM key and the *Composition* and *CompositionPolicy* values if they are not already present.

Now restart the Desktop Window Manager Session Manager service by opening an elevated Command Prompt window with administrative privileges and typing **net stop uxsms** followed by **net start uxsms** at the command prompt.

Forcing WinSAT to Reassess the Computer

If WinSAT has not assessed the system at all or has incorrectly assessed the system hardware during install or upgrade, the Windows Aero Glass features will not be available. If you have installed new video hardware or other hardware that might affect the system rating, you may force WinSAT to reassess the computer.

To force WinSAT to run again and reassess the hardware, follow these steps:

1. Click Start, click Control Panel, and then click System And Maintenance.

2. Click Performance Information And Tools. From the Performance Rating And Tools control panel, click Rate This Computer or Update My Score. User Account Control will prompt you for permission to run the System Assessment Tool.

The Rating dialog box will be displayed with a status bar. This process can take a few minutes. The screen may flash while the system is being assessed.

Examining Desktop Window Manager Performance

When the DWM process starts, it detects the video bandwidth and screen resolution to determine if the computer can hit the target requirement of 30 frames per second and then determines the state to start in—no composition, opaque glass, or transparent glass.

The desktop is normally rendered at 60 frames per second. If the DWM detects that it is taking longer than normal to render the desktop, a dialog displays, indicating a performance decrease has been detected. You will be prompted to take the one of the following actions:

- **Disable Desktop Composition**   Disable all desktop composition by the Desktop Window Manager service until the system is restarted or explicitly enabled.

- **Do Not Disable Desktop Composition, But Keep Monitoring**   Ignore the problem now and do not disable desktop composition. Inform the user again the next time a performance drop is detected.

- **Do Not Disable Desktop Composition, And Stop Monitoring**   Ignore the problem now and stop detecting performance reductions until the next system restart.

Note   For more information on troubleshooting Aero on Windows Vista, see *http://www.microsoft.com/whdc/device/display/aero_rules.mspx*.

Using Performance Information And Tools

Performance Information And Tools is a new Control Panel item that allows users to view performance information about their computers, diagnose and resolve performance-related issues, and make better purchasing decisions by comparing system metrics to software requirements using the System Performance Rating (SPR) score.

Accessing Performance Information And Tools

Figure 22-12 shows the Performance Information And Tools user interface.

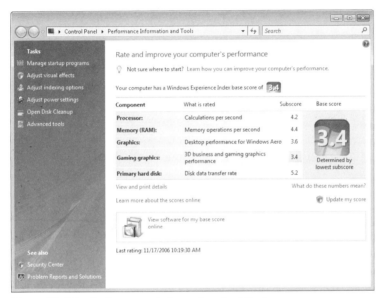

Figure 22-12   Performance Information And Tools.

You can access Performance Information And Tools by using any of the following methods:

■ From the Control Panel default view, select System And Maintenance and then select Performance Information And Tools.

■ From the Control Panel classic view, select Performance Information And Tools.

■ From System Properties, click Windows Experience Index.

> **Note**   You cannot use Performance Information And Tools in Safe Mode; you can also disable it using Group Policy.

Entry points on the left side of this tool include:

■ **Manage Startup Program**   Opens Windows Defender

- **Adjust Visual Effects**   Opens Personalization

- **Adjust Indexing Options**   Opens Indexing Options

- **Adjust Power Settings**   Opens Power Options

- **Open Disk Cleanup**   Opens Disk Cleanup Options

- **Security Center**   Opens Windows Security Center

- **Solutions To Problems**   Opens Problem Reports And Solutions

- **Advanced Tools**   Opens Advanced Tools to access other performance-related tools, as shown in Figure 22-13

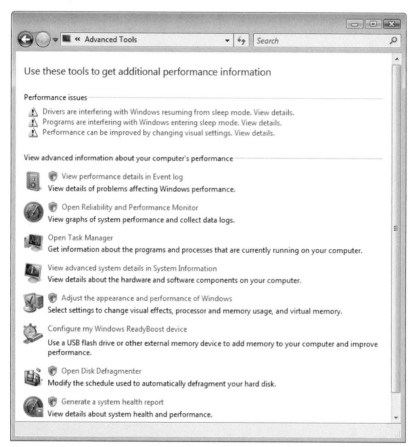

Figure 22-13   Advanced Tools.

Configuring Performance Information And Tools Using Group Policy

You can configure the Performance Information And Tools control panel using Group Policy to configure the policies in the following location:

Computer Configuration\Policies\Administrative Templates\System\Performance Control Panel

Understanding Each Section of the Tool

The main screen of Performance Information And Tools (see Figure 22-12 previously) includes the following three sections (from top to bottom):

- Performance Issues
- System Capabilities
- OEM Upsell And Help

The following sections describe these different sections of Performance Information And Tools.

Performance Issues

The Performance Issues section (if displayed) will list potential performance issues detected for the following scenarios:

- Startup (boot)
- Logon
- Logoff
- Shutdown
- Hybrid-sleep (standby/hibernate)
- Resume from hybrid-sleep
- Start menu
- Shell responsiveness

The following three levels of severity are assigned to these performance scenarios:

- **Minor**   Performance issues detectable by computer, but they do not cause major functional issues. The user might not detect the issues. Displayed only in the global Event Logs.

- **Bad**   Performance issues that customers notice and that may be annoying. Displayed in Performance Information And Tools (and Problem Reports And Solutions) if the root cause was determined and a solution is available. Otherwise, these issues are displayed in the global Event Log and the Diagnostics – Performance Event Log channel.

- **Serious**   Performance issues that cause major functional issues and potential customer dissatisfaction. Displayed in Performance Information And Tools (and Problem Reports And Solutions) if the root cause was determined and either a solution or Help content was available. Otherwise, these issues are displayed in the Event Log and the Diagnostics – Performance Event Log channel.

> **Note**   The Diagnostics – Performance Event Log channel is the filtered Event Log view that shows only performance-related error and diagnostic events (no informative events).

Table 22-7 provides the metrics used to determine the severity levels.

Table 22-7   Severity-Level Metrics

Scenario	Minor	Bad	Serious
Boot time (excluding logon and post boot time)	< 15 seconds	>= 15 seconds and <= 1 minute	> 1 minute
Logon time	< 15 seconds	>= 15 seconds and <= 1 minute	> 1 minutes
Post boot time (time after logon)	< 30 seconds	>= 30 seconds and <= 1 minute	> 1 minute
Logoff time	< 30 seconds	>= 30 seconds and <= 1 minute	> 1 minute
Shutdown time (including logoff)	< 1 minute	>= 1 minute and <= 2 minutes	> 2 minutes
Standby/hybrid-sleep time	< 7 seconds	>= 7 seconds and <= 20 seconds	> 20 seconds
Resume from hybrid-sleep	< 5 seconds	>= 5 seconds and <= 15 seconds	> 15 seconds
Start menu launch time	< 2 seconds	>= 2 seconds and <= 10 seconds	> 10 seconds
Shell responsiveness time	< 1 Second	>= 1 second and <= 10 seconds	> 10 seconds
Shell folder open time	< 10 seconds	>= 10 second and <= 2 minutes	> 2 minutes

When the listed Performance Issues are clicked, Problem Reports And Solutions will open. When a specific solution is viewed, that solution will be marked as viewed, and will no longer be shown in the Performance Information And Tools control panel. This list will display only high-priority items (Bad or Severe severity) and will not display duplicate solutions. The maximum size of the list at this time is six items.

System Capabilities

The System Capability details section contains the Windows System Assessment Tool (WinSAT) data and provides System Performance Rating (SPR) information details. The specific components of the SPR are displayed along with a single unitless metric.

The System Performance Rating consists of one main rating number and the following subattributes:

- Processor
- Memory (RAM)
- Primary hard disk
- Graphics
- Gaming graphics

The overall rating number is a positive integer that starts at 1 and can continue to grow as new technology comes out. Each of the subattributes also has a rating, and the System Properties related to these subattributes are listed as reference to make it easier to understand the System Performance Rating user interface.

The System Capabilities section can be shown in three different modes:

- **Unrated**   The computer has not yet been rated.

- **Normal**   The computer has been rated and the rating is up to date.

- **Dirty**   Hardware configuration was changed and System Performance Rating number should be updated.

How It Works: Understanding the System Performance Rating

It is important to note that the System Performance Rating number indicates the general speed and power of a computer running Windows Vista. The rating pertains only to the performance aspects that affect how well features in Windows and other programs will run on this computer and does not reflect the overall quality of the computer. A higher performance rating means the computer will perform better and faster—especially when performing more advanced and resource-intensive tasks—than a computer with a lower performance rating. In the future, programs will be rated using the same scale as the System Performance Rating, so users will be able to confidently buy programs and other software that are rated to match the computer's performance level. For example, if a user's computer has a System Performance Rating of 3, she can confidently purchase any software designed for this version of Windows that requires a computer with a rating of 3 or less.

The rating system is designed to accommodate future advances in computer technology, so the standards for each level of the rating system stay the same. For example, a computer that is rated as a 4 should remain a 4 unless the computer's hardware is upgraded. As technology continues to improve, additional System Performance Ratings will be introduced and will be available for download.

Because System Performance Rating calls for WinSAT APIs to gather information and launch tests, failures in retrieving the ratings will need to be investigated as a problem with WinSAT. This will normally be indicated by an error message similar to the following: "Windows was unable to refresh your Windows System Performance Rating."

Microsoft Global Technical Readiness Platforms Team

OEM Upsell And Help

The OEM Upsell And Help section provides the following features:

- An area for original equipment manufacturer (OEM) suppliers to place their logos and a link to a local page or their websites.

- An area for software links that is available for the System Performance Rating as determined for the computer by WinSAT.

- At this time, the default links point to the following default locations:

  ❏ View software available for my rating online at *http://www.windowsmarketplace.com*.

  ❏ Get more information online about my system's performance from *http://www.microsoft.com*.

Understanding Windows Error Reporting

Windows Error Reporting (WER) is the client component for the overall Watson Feedback Platform (WFP), which allows Microsoft to collect reports about failure events that occur on a user's system, analyze the data contained in those reports, and respond back to the user in a meaningful and actionable manner.

WER is the technology that reports user-mode hangs, user-mode faults, and kernel-mode faults to the back-end servers at Microsoft and replaces Dr. Watson as the default application exception handler.

Note WER in Windows Vista has support for any kind of problem event as defined by the developer, not just critical failures as in Windows XP.

Overview of Windows Error Reporting

The Watson Feedback Platform is illustrated in the high-level flow diagram in Figure 22-14, with Windows Error Reporting labeled as the Watson Client.

Note A more detailed diagram illustrating WER flow can be found in the folder for this chapter on the Companion CD.

In Windows Vista, the user interface for Windows Error Reporting is the Problem Reports And Solutions Control Panel applet. When installing Windows Vista, you can choose if you would like WER to send basic problem reports automatically. Basic problem reports include only the minimum amount of information necessary to search for a solution. Later you can choose to send additional information automatically as well. The goal of the Problem Reports And Solutions control panel is to provide you with one location to simply and efficiently view the problem events that have occurred on your computer, track your reports, manage responses from Microsoft, and act on these responses to prevent failures in the future.

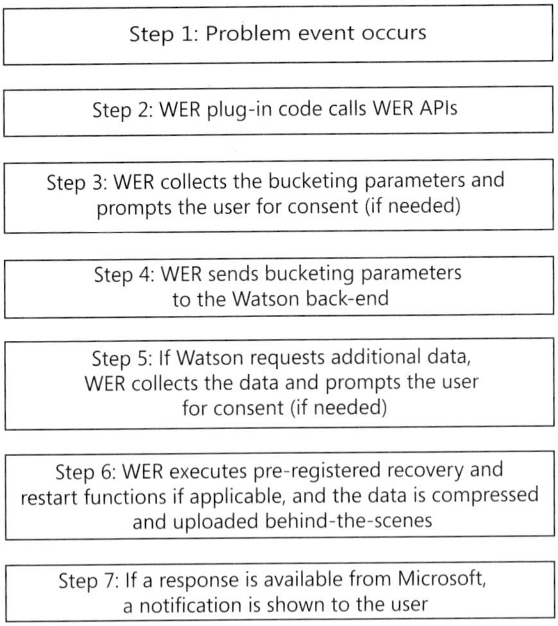

```
┌─────────────────────────────────────────────────┐
│         Step 1: Problem event occurs            │
└─────────────────────────────────────────────────┘

┌─────────────────────────────────────────────────┐
│      Step 2: WER plug-in code calls WER APIs    │
└─────────────────────────────────────────────────┘

┌─────────────────────────────────────────────────┐
│   Step 3: WER collects the bucketing parameters and │
│      prompts the user for consent (if needed)   │
└─────────────────────────────────────────────────┘

┌─────────────────────────────────────────────────┐
│      Step 4: WER sends bucketing parameters     │
│             to the Watson back-end              │
└─────────────────────────────────────────────────┘

┌─────────────────────────────────────────────────┐
│      Step 5: If Watson requests additional data,│
│    WER collects the data and prompts the user   │
│              for consent (if needed)            │
└─────────────────────────────────────────────────┘

┌─────────────────────────────────────────────────┐
│   Step 6: WER executes pre-registered recovery and │
│ restart functions if applicable, and the data is compressed │
│            and uploaded behind-the-scenes       │
└─────────────────────────────────────────────────┘

┌─────────────────────────────────────────────────┐
│   Step 7: If a response is available from Microsoft, │
│       a notification is shown to the user       │
└─────────────────────────────────────────────────┘
```

Figure 22-14 Watson Feedback Platform flow diagram.

One significant improvement of Windows Error Reporting in Windows Vista is the concept of queuing. In Windows XP, WER reports could only be sent at the time the event occurred, with few exceptions. In Windows Vista, WER provides a flexible queuing architecture where users, administrators, or WER integrators can determine the queuing behavior of their WER events.

For more information about Problem Reports And Solutions, see the section titled "Using the Problem Reports And Solutions Control Panel" later in this chapter.

Error Reporting Cycle

The cycle begins when a report is generated on a user's system and completes when a response is returned to the user. Overall, five primary steps are involved in this process: reporting, categorization, investigation, resolution, and response. The following sections explain what is involved in each of these steps.

Reporting

The first step is the creation and submission of the report. This can be triggered by a number of events, including an application crash, application hang, or stop error (blue screen). In Windows Vista, applications can also be designed to define their own custom event types, allowing them to initiate the reporting process when any type of problem occurs.

Categorization

After the back-end servers at Microsoft receive the report, it is categorized by problem type. Categorization may be possible with only the event parameters (text descriptors of the event), or it may require additional data (dumps). The end result of categorization is that the event reported by the customer becomes a Watson Bucket ID. This allows the developers investigating the events to determine the most frequently reported problems and focus on the most common issues.

Investigation

After the problem is categorized, development teams may view the report data via the Watson portal. The Watson portal provides the data necessary to understand high-level trends and aggregate data, such as the top errors reported against an application. It also provides a mechanism to investigate the low-level data that was reported to debug the root cause of the problem.

Resolution

After a developer has determined the root cause of a problem, ideally a fix, workaround, or new version will be created that can be made available to the customer.

Response

The final step is to close the loop with the customer that reported the problem by responding to his report with information he can use to mitigate the issue. A customer may receive a response in two ways:

- If the issue is understood at the time an error report is submitted, the customer can receive a response in the form of a balloon notification immediately after the categorization step.

- If the issue is not understood at the time an error report is submitted but is resolved some time after the report, the customer will be able to query for updated knowledge of the problem at a later time. Users can also elect to check for new solutions manually using the Problem Reports And Solutions control panel.

Report Data Overview

To optimize the reporting process, the WER error data is divided into first- and second-level data. During first-level communication with the back-end servers, WER determines if more data is needed. If the server returns a request for more data, collection of the second-level data begins immediately. Simultaneously, a second-level consent dialog is displayed. The WER user interface is discussed later in this chapter.

First-Level Data

First-level data consists of up to 10 string parameters that identify a particular classification of the problem. This data is stored in the report manifest file, Report.wer, and is initially submitted to the Watson back-end servers. (The Report.wer file is not itself sent—only the parameters are sent.) The included parameters are used to identify a class of problems. For example, the parameters for a crash (Application Name, Application Version, Module Name, Module Version, Module Offset, AppTimeStamp, ModTimeStamp, and ExceptionCode) provide a unique way to accurately classify a crash. The parameters are the only data submitted to the Watson back-end during first-level communication.

Reports are stored in an archive as a folder structure on the system. Each report subfolder contains, at a minimum, the report manifest text file (Report.wer), which describes the contents of the error report. Although the Report.wer file is a simple text file, it is not meant to be human-readable or editable. Any files referenced by the report are also placed in this folder. The following major sections appear in most Report.wer files:

- Version
- Event Information
- Signature
- UI
- State
- Files
- Response

Second-Level Data

Second-level data is additional data that may be needed to diagnose and resolve a particular bucket. Because Microsoft usually needs only a small sample of this verbose data, the second-level data is submitted only if the back-end server requests it and the user consents to sharing the data. Second-level data is split into two categories:

- **Safe data**   This is information that the developer feels is unlikely to contain any personal information, such as a small section of memory, a specific registry key, or a log file.
- **Other data**   This encompasses everything else, which may or may not contain personal information.

You have the option to always send safe data automatically. Second level data is specified by the back-end Watson servers and can include but is not limited to the following items:

- Files
- Minidump

- Heap

- Registry Keys

- WMI queries

For more information about what information can be sent with Windows Error Reporting, see the Windows Vista WER Privacy Statement at *http://go.microsoft.com/fwlink/?linkid=50163*

> **Note**   WER in Windows Vista generates minidump files and heap dump files; it does not generate user-mode process dump files. For information about how to generate user-mode process dump files, see KB 931673, "How to create a user-mode process dump file in Windows Vista," at *http://support.microsoft.com/kb/931673*.

> **Note**   For security reasons, report manifests are not allowed to reference files outside the report directory.

Conceptual Components

Windows Error Reporting consists of the following conceptual components:

- Report Processor

- Data Collection Module

- Transport System

- Queue Management System

Each of the components is discussed in the following sections.

Report Processor

The Report Processor is a conceptual component that is responsible for managing the state of a report after it has been sent to WER. Applications use WER APIs to create and submit reports. At that point, the Report Processor decides whether to queue the report or submit the report. The Report Processor will attempt to hand over the report to the Transport System if the following conditions are met: there is network connectivity, the report is for an interactive application, and a user interface can be shown. Otherwise, the Report Processor will hand over the report to the Queue Management system. The Report Processor will also invoke the user interface component if applicable.

Data Collection Module

The Data Collection Module is responsible for collecting the following data:

- Heap dump data

- WMI query results

- Registry key data

- Registry tree data

- Files

- File version information

- User documents

- Minidump

- Microdump (A minidump that has been stripped of all other information except the faulting stack trace)

Transport System

WER uses two separate modes of transport:

- **Live Watson Mode**   In this mode, WER uses a four-stage protocol based on top of HTTP to communicate with the live Watson back-end servers.

- **Agentless Exception Monitoring (AEM)**   Support for the file share based Corporate Error Reporting (CER) transport mode used in previous versions of Windows has been discontinued in Windows Vista. Instead, support for Agentless Exception Monitoring (AEM) has been added to Windows Vista for use in corporate environments. AEM is a component of the Client Monitoring feature in Microsoft System Center Operations Manager 2007 that lets you monitor operating systems and applications for errors within your organization. For more information about AEM, see *http://technet.microsoft.com/en-us/library/bb309493.aspx.*

Store Management System

The WER Store Management System component is responsible for maintaining the error report stores (folders) and for scheduling the prompts that a user will see when there are unsent queued error reports. WER uses user stores for user-level problems and machine stores for system-level problems. The type of store affects the WER prompts that a user sees and the location that the error report data is stored.

> **Note**   NTFS file compression is enabled by default on the store root folders.

In addition, user and machine stores contain two subfolders named ReportQueue and Report-Archive. These folders store the queued (unsent) and archived report contents, respectively. The actual data for each error report is stored in individual subfolders within the Report-Queue and ReportArchive folders. When an error report is generated, the queue subsystem evaluates the WER configuration and connection status to determine the appropriate store to use. The WER queuing structure and behavior is discussed later in this section.

User Store   The WER user queue is located in the following folder:

Users\<username>\AppData\Local\Microsoft\Windows\WER

The default WER behavior is to store error report data in user stores. Error reports are written to the current user's store if the following conditions are true:

- Reporting failed for any reason other than the user clicking the Cancel button.
- The application developer designed the application using WER APIs to specify queuing as the default behavior.
- The ForceAdminQueue policy is not enabled.

Computer Store   The WER machine store is located in the following folder:

ProgramData\Microsoft\Windows\WER

You can configure WER by using Group Policy or the registry to force all error report data to be written to the machine store. Reports are written to the machine store if either of the following conditions is true:

- The process submitting the report is not running in an interactive desktop (includes system services).
- The ForceAdminQueue policy is enabled.

ReportQueue Folder   The ReportQueue folder contains reports that are queued for sending at a later time. These reports have either the necessary consent and are pending a network connection for upload, or they need consent from the user before they can be uploaded. When a report has been successfully uploaded, it is removed from the ReportQueue folder. This folder is referred to as the Upload or Signoff queue. After a report is successfully submitted, the report, along with any uploaded data, is copied into the ReportArchive Folder.

The location of the ReportQueue folder is:

- Users\<*username*>\AppData\Local\Microsoft\Windows\WER\ReportQueue (for reports in the user store)
- ProgramData\Microsoft\Windows\WER\ReportQueue (for reports in the computer store)

Note that when the error data is collected initially and before it is queued in the ReportQueue folder, the collected error report files are stored in subfolders within the following folder:

Users\<username>\AppData\Local\Temp

ReportArchive Folder   The ReportArchive folder contains reports that have been uploaded or denied upload (via policy or explicit user action). This folder is referred to as the Archive store. Reports that are successfully submitted from the queue store(s) are automatically transferred to the archive store.

You also can create an Event Reporting Console (ERC) folder in the WER store folder(s). The subfolders in the ERC folder store response metadata and templates used for displaying the response data in the Problem Reports And Solutions control panel. You don't need to modify the data in the ERC folder, and modifying the data is not supported. The location of the ReportArchive folder is:

- Users\\<*username*>\\AppData\\Local\\Microsoft\\Windows\\WER\\ReportArchive (for reports in user store)

- ProgramData\\Microsoft\\Windows\\WER\\ReportArchive (for reports in the computer store)

Queue Reporting   When a new error report is successfully submitted to any of the queues or directly to the Watson back-end servers, WER launches into a queue reporting mode. In queue reporting mode, WER will prompt you to send the queued report(s) if conditions permit. If conditions are not optimal for reporting, WER schedules itself to be launched when a network connection is established (SENS) or when the current user logs on the next time (HKCU\\Run). This ensures that at some point in the future when conditions are right for reporting, infrastructure will be able to show the queued reporting console.

In queue reporting mode, WER performs the following checks in the following order:

1. Is the failing process running in an interactive desktop? If not, WerMgr.exe terminates. This is necessary because WER dialogs should not be shown for noninteractive desktops, such as the ones that the service accounts own.

2. Does the current user have reports in her queue, or is the current user an administrator and is administrative queuing enabled? If neither of the conditions is true, the current user has no reports to report. In this case, WER will ensure that network and logon triggers for the current user are removed, and it will exit immediately. If either of the conditions is true, WER attempts to prompt you to report entries in the queue.

3. Set the network and logon triggers for the current user in case conditions are not optimal for reporting at this time.

4. Check network access and see if the last pester time has expired. If either of these checks fails, WerMgr.exe terminates.

5. Launch the Problem Reports And Solutions control panel to prompt you and update the last pester time.

Store Maintenance   By default, the Queue Management System performs maintenance such as deleting stale data and trimming the size of the queue on a report store whenever 50 saved reports are in the store. When the total queued report count exceeds the number defined in the registry value MaxQueueCount or the registry value MaxArchiveCount for archive stores, the queue subsystem deletes the oldest CAB files from the queues in the following order until the size of the queue reaches MaxQueueCount or no more CABs remain to delete:

1. Archive Store

2. Signoff Queue

3. Upload Queue

The metadata for a report is persisted for one calendar year unless the user has disabled the archive via the DisableArchive setting.

WER queue data retention policies can be configured using Group Policy. If no queuing policies are configured, the Archive queue will retain 1,000 reports and the Upload/Signoff queue will retain 50 reports. If a queue becomes full and a new report is created, the new report will overwrite the oldest report in the respective queue (FIFO).

Queue Triggers   This section describes the launch triggers that WER uses to ensure that the queued reporting prompt is launched for users when they have unsent reports in their queues. Triggers are persistent across reboots.

WER launch triggers include:

- **Network trigger**   This trigger launches WerMgr.exe in queue reporting mode for a specific user when a network connection is established. The network trigger is implemented through the SENS API that senses the presence of a network connection.

- **Logon trigger**   This trigger launches WerMgr.exe in queue reporting mode for a specific user when the user logs on. Currently, the shell HKCU Run key is used to implement this feature.

- **Administrator trigger**   The administrator trigger notifies an administrator of unsent entries in the machine queue. This trigger only occurs for administrators on the system.

A System Tray popup that says "Check for solutions: Click to have Windows check online for solutions to computer problems" will be displayed when queued reports are available to send.

Architecture of Windows Error Reporting

This section discusses the main Windows Error Reporting components.

Wer.dll

Wer.dll contains the major parts of the WER infrastructure and is responsible for showing the user interface (dialogs), exposing the WER APIs, and report management.

WerMgr.exe

WerMgr.exe is responsible for WER error queue management.

Problem Reports And Solutions Control Panel

The Problem Reports And Solutions control panel provides a user interface to access the following actions:

- View any solutions to your problems
- Configure Windows Error Reporting
- View problem history
- Check for new solutions (to sent or unsent reports)
- Clear solutions and problem history
- Learn more about WER Privacy
- Change your Customer Experience Improvement Program Settings

The Problems And Reports control panel is implemented entirely within the following binaries:

- Wercon.exe
- Wercplsupport.dll

> **Note**   You can access Problem Reports And Solutions from the Control Panel or by running Wercon.exe.

Problem Reports And Solutions Control Panel Support Service

You use the Problem Reports And Solutions Control Panel Support service to manage error reports in the Problem Reports And Solutions control panel when needed for UAC support. This service is set to a Manual startup type and starts on demand when called by WER.

Windows Error Reporting Service

The Windows Error Reporting Service is responsible for obtaining the information that is provided to the back-end Watson servers when an application exception occurs. The service library, wersvc.dll, is hosted in its own Svchost.exe process. When a process crashes, the Windows Error Reporting service calls Werfault.exe (or Werfaultsecure.exe, discussed later in this section) to obtain all of the necessary data for the crashing/hanging process. Werfault.exe loads dbgeng.dll and dbghelp.dll to collect the application error data. It also loads faultrep.dll to perform the reporting to the back-end Watson servers. If the Windows Error Reporting

Service is not started when an application exception occurs, Werfault.exe and the dependent libraries will still be started to perform the data collection and reporting tasks for the fault.

WER in Windows Vista also supports error reporting for secure processes. Secure processes are processes that contain data encrypted with a private key and restricted permission. If a crash occurs in a secure process, the Windows Error Reporting service uses Werfault-secure.exe to obtain the necessary data for the crashing/hanging process. The report is encrypted when created and queued automatically to prevent any possibility of exploitation through the user interface. The encrypted data is then sent to the back-end Watson servers, where it is decrypted and analyzed.

The following components have been removed because of the error-reporting redesign for Windows Vista and no longer install as part of the operating system:

- ErSvc.dll
- Drwtsn32.exe
- Dwwin.exe
- Dumprep.exe

Store.lock

To ensure that WER and the Problem Reports And Solutions control panel are synchronized, Wercon.exe creates a store.lock file in each of the four report folders when the Problems Reports And Solutions control panel is open. WER will still function to obtain the error report data even though the stores (report folders) are locked, but it will not write the data to any of the stores. The collected report data remains in the user's Temp folder when the stores are locked.

The store.lock file is deleted when the Problems Reports And Solutions control panel is closed; the report data is then written to the destination store folder. Because of this locking feature, errors that occur when the Problems Reports And Solutions control panel is open will not be immediately displayed but will be displayed when the Problems Reports And Solutions control panel is closed and then reopened.

Configuring Windows Error Reporting

You can configure Windows Error Reporting by selecting options in the Problem Reports And Solutions control panel, by directly editing the registry, or by using Group Policy settings. This section describes the registry keys used to store per-computer, per-user, and Group Policy settings.

Per-Computer Registry Settings

Per-computer settings are stored in the following registry key:

HKEY_LOCAL_MACHINE\Software\Microsoft\Windows\Windows Error Reporting

Per-User Registry Settings

Per-user settings are stored in the following registry key:

HKEY_CURRENT_USER\Software\Microsoft\Windows\Windows Error Reporting

Group Policy Registry Settings

Each WER registry setting has a corresponding Group Policy setting.

Per-Computer Group Policy Settings   The per-computer WER Group Policy settings are located in the following Group Policy container:

Computer Configuration\Policies\Administrative Templates\Windows Components\Windows Error Reporting

These settings are stored in the following registry key:

HKEY_LOCAL_MACHINE\SOFTWARE\Policies\Microsoft\Windows\Windows Error Reporting

Per-User Group Policy Settings   The per-user WER Group Policy settings are located in the following Group Policy container:

User Configuration\Policies\Administrative Templates\Windows Components\Windows Error Reporting

These settings are stored in the following registry key:

HKEY_CURRENT_USER\Software\Policies\Microsoft\Windows\Windows Error Reporting

WER Registry Values

WER uses the same registry value names for per-computer, per-user, and Group Policy settings described in the preceding section. Table 22-8 describes WER registry values.

Table 22-8   WER Registry Values

Key/Value Description	Type	Values
Disabled		
Enable error reporting.	DWORD	0 = Reporting Enabled
		1 = Reporting Disabled
Consent\DefaultConsent		
Default consent choice for the user.	DWORD	1 = Always Ask
		2 = Params Only
		3 = Params + Safe second Level
		4 = Send Everything

Table 22-8 WER Registry Values

Key/Value Description	Type	Values
Consent\DefaultOverride-Behavior		
Whether or not the default consent should override the vertical consents.	DWORD	0 = Do Not Override [Default] 1 = Override
Consent\<VerticalName>\ Consent		
Consent choice for the user for that vertical.	DWORD	Same as Consent\DefaultConsent
ConfigureArchive		
Configure whether the archive will store parameters only or all data.	DWORD	1 = Store Parameters Only (no CAB) 2 = Store everything (Default)
DisableArchive		
Disable the archival of WER reports.	DWORD	0 = Disabled (Archive is enabled) 1 = Enabled (Archive is disabled)
MaxArchiveCount		
Maximum size of the computer archive.	DWORD	File Count (min 1, default 1000, max 5000)
DisableQueue		
Disable queuing of WER reports.	DWORD	0 = Disabled (Queue is enabled) 1 = Enabled (Queue is disabled)
MaxQueueCount		
Maximum size of the computer queue.	DWORD	File Count (min 1, default 50, max 500)
LoggingDisabled		
Enable event logging.	DWORD	0 = Enabled [Default] 1 = Disabled
ExcludedApplications\ <Application Name>		
List of applications that do not support error reporting (based on APIs used).	STRING	
DebugApplications\ <ExeName>		
List of executable names that will always require the user to choose between Debug and Continue. A value of "*" (asterisk) prompts for all executables.	STRING	
ForceQueue		
Send all reports to the user's queue.	DWORD	0 = Disabled [Default] 1 = Enabled

Table 22-8   WER Registry Values

Key/Value Description	Type	Values
ForceAdminQueue		
Send all reports to the administrator's queue.	DWORD	0 = Disabled [Default]
		1 = Enabled
DontSendAdditionalData		
Prevent any second-level data from being sent from the computer. Takes precedence over consent settings.	DWORD	0 = Disabled [Default]
		1 = Enabled
DoNotShowUI		
Prevent any WER dialog UI from being shown to the user.	DWORD	0 = Disabled [Default]
		1 = Enabled
QueuePesterInterval		
Time between notification reminders to tell the user to check for solutions.	DWORD	Time in days [Default = 2 weeks]
CorporateWERServer		
Name of corporate server.	STRING	Server name
CorporateWERUseSSL		
Whether or not to use SSL.	DWORD	0 = Disabled [Default]
		1 = Enabled
CorporateWERPortNumber		
Port number to use with corporate server.	DWORD	Port number
CorporateWERDirectory		
Name of target directory on server.	STRING	Directory name
CorporateWERUse-Authentication		
Whether or not to use Windows Integrated Authentication.	DWORD	0 = Disabled [Default]
		1 = Enabled

The order of preference for applying the configured settings is:

1. Per-computer Group Policy settings (overrides all other configured settings)

2. Per-computer settings

3. Per-user Group Policy settings

4. Per-user settings

5. User interface settings

If WER has been configured using Group Policy settings, the Problems And Reports user interface will appear dimmed and will be unavailable.

> **Note**   The following registry key is no longer used for error reporting:
> HKEY_LOCAL_MACHINE\SOFTWARE\Microsoft\PCHealth\ErrorReporting.

Direct from the Source: WER and System Center Operations Manager 2007

All versions of Windows have a service called Windows Error Reporting, which uses the Windows Error Reporting client (on Windows Vista or later) or the Watson client (on earlier versions of Windows) to gather information about application and operating system crash. Windows Error Reporting then forwards the crashes on to Microsoft for analysis. Microsoft System Center Operations Manager 2007 allows Windows Error Reporting to first forward those errors to a management server operated by the organization. The administrator can then decide if she wants to send the data to Microsoft for analysis and to see if a resolution to the problem exists. Having access to this information gives the client administrators visibility into their system errors as they have never had before, through built-in reports that aggregate crash information from all WER clients. Using these reports, administrators can identify the top crashing applications, the top crashes, and any available solutions on Windows Error Reporting Service.

Agentless Exception Monitoring (AEM), a feature of System Center Operations Manager 2007, offers the flexibility of sending no information, error IDs only, or full crash information including memory images for analysis. If an error ID or full crash information is sent, Microsoft will search its knowledge base of errors and return a resolution if one exists. Microsoft uses crash information submitted by Windows Error Reporting to improve the quality of its products. By having access to this crash data, administrators can use it to improve the quality of their own internal applications as well. AEM has very little overhead, and because crashes happen infrequently and it can easily be deployed across all of the client systems within an enterprise, without a large data storage burden. Typically, a single server can collect, aggregate, and analyze crashes from 100,000 desktops with "normal" crash rates.

Dhananjay Mahajan, Senior Program Manager

Enterprise Management Division

Using the Problem Reports And Solutions Control Panel

This section describes the Problem Reports And Solutions Control Panel item. When you open the Problem Reports And Solutions control panel, the solutions overview page is displayed as shown in Figure 22-15.

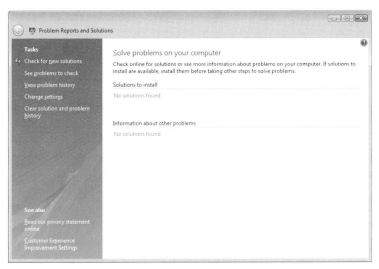

Figure 22-15   Problem Reports And Solutions control panel.

The main pane of the solutions overview shows responses that have been received for previously reported problems. The Solutions To Install section will list any updates that can be installed to address an issue. The Information About Other Problems section will list any information, such as Knowledge Base articles, that may help resolve an issue. Use the items in the Tasks pane on the left to further explore the errors that have been reported, as explained in the following sections.

Check For New Solutions

Clicking the Check For New Solutions link will force WER to check for solutions to previously reported issues that had no solution at that time, as well as unsent issues. If a new solution is received from the Watson servers, it will appear in the main pane of the solutions overview. If a new solution is received at the time the problem event occurs, the response dialog box that is displayed will depend on the priority of the response. Three levels of response priority are set by the developers working with the Watson back-end servers:

- Low priority
- Medium priority
- High priority

Low-Priority Response   Low-priority responses do not present a dialog box. The response will be displayed in either the Solutions To Install section or the Information About Other Problems section on the main page of Problem Reports And Solutions.

Medium-Priority Response   Medium-priority responses display a System Tray icon and balloon notification. If you click the notification or the System Tray icon, a formatted response will be opened in Problem Reports And Solutions.

High-Priority Response   High-priority responses immediately open the formatted response in Problem Reports And Solutions.

Response Notification   For medium- and high-priority responses, a notification is displayed in Problem Reports And Solutions that describes the problem and provides more information.

No New Solution Found   If a previously checked problem is checked again for a solution, but a new solution is not found, a dialog box saying "No new solutions found: Please check for solutions again later" will be displayed.

See Problems To Check

The See Problems To Check link on the Problems And Solutions Task pane opens the Check For Solutions To These Problems window that displays a list of problems that have not been checked for a solution (see Figure 22-16). In this window, you can select which problems to check for a solution and which to omit. Users can also select Check Again For Solutions To Other Problems to cause WER to check previously checked problems where a solution was not found.

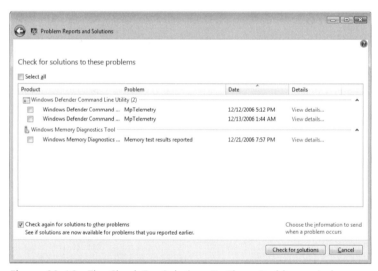

Figure 22-16   The Check For Solutions To These Problems window.

Each listed problem has a shortcut menu that you can use to delete the problem, view problem details, or group the problem among other listed problems.

The Choose The Information To Send When A Problem Occurs link in the Problems And Solutions menu opens a dialog box saying "Do you want to automatically send more information about unsolved problems?" that allows you to either automatically send safe additional information requested by the Watson back-end servers or to be asked each time the additional data is requested. If you choose to automatically send safe data, you will still be prompted when other data is requested.

View Problem History   The View Problem History link in the Problems and Solutions menu switches to a window that lists a history of problems that have occurred on the computer (Figure 22-17). By default, a user will see his or her own history of problems. If the user is an administrator, he will also be able to see system-level problems.

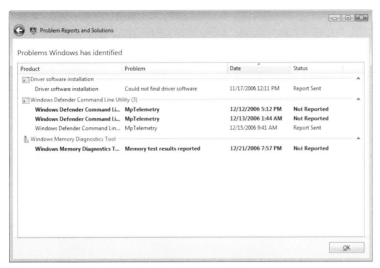

Figure 22-17   The View Problem History window.

Each listed problem has a shortcut menu that you can use to check for a solution, delete the problem, view the solution, view the problem details, or group the problem among other listed problems.

Change Settings   The Change Settings link in the Problems And Solutions Tasks pane switches to the Choose How To Check For Solutions To Computer Problems window shown in Figure 22-18. From this window, you can select the desired Opt In option, either to check for solutions automatically (Opted In) or prompt for consent to check for a solution (Not Opted In).

The WER dialog boxes that a user sees when a failure occurs depend on the Opt In option selected in the Choose How To Check For Solutions To Computer Problems window.

If you chose to automatically check for solutions during installation, the Check For Solutions Automatically (Recommended) option is selected.

Advanced Settings   Advanced Settings (which you can open by opening Problem Reports And Solutions, clicking Change Settings, and then clicking Advanced Settings) switches to the Advanced Settings For Problem Reporting window, where you can configure more advanced WER options. You can configure the options shown in Table 22-9 from the Advanced Settings For Problem Reporting window.

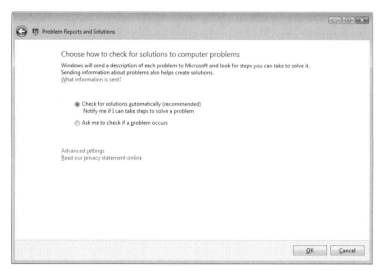

Figure 22-18   The Choose How To Check for Solutions To Computer Problems window.

Table 22-9   Advanced Problem Reporting Settings

Setting	Possible Values
For My Programs, Problem Reporting Is	On (default)
	Off
For All Users And Programs, Problem Reporting Is Set To	Allow Each User To Choose Settings (default)
	On
	Off
For All Users, Windows Is Set To	Allow Each User To Choose Reporting Settings (default)
	Ask Each Time A Problem Occurs
	Automatically Check For Solutions (recommended)
	Automatically Check For Solutions And Send Additional Information, If Needed
Automatically Send More Information If It Is Needed To Help Solve Problems	Enabled
	Disabled (default)
Don't Send Information About The Following Programs	Specify a block list of programs (none specified by default)

Using Task Scheduler

Task Scheduler in Windows Vista is more reliable, more scalable, and much easier to use than in previous versions of Windows. The following sections describe the features and enhancements of this tool.

Task Scheduler Enhancements and Improvements

The new Task Scheduler version provides significant improvements in the following areas:

- User Interface
- Scheduling
- Security
- Administrative
- Platform and Manageability

User Interface Improvements

The Windows Vista Task Scheduler features a completely new user interface based on Microsoft Management Console (MMC). The interface includes a number of new conditions and filters to assist administrators in defining and managing scheduled tasks.

Scheduling Improvements

Time-based task launch in Windows Vista Task Scheduler has been improved with higher granularity and enhanced scheduling options. One key improvement allows you to chain a series of actions together instead of having to create multiple scheduled tasks.

You can schedule tasks on demand for execution when a specified event is logged to an event log. You can configure scheduled tasks to wake a computer from sleep or hibernation or to run only when the computer is idle. You can also run previously scheduled tasks when a powered-down computer is turned back on.

Scalability has been improved by removing limitations on the number of registered tasks and allowing multiple instances of a task to run in parallel or in sequence.

Security Improvements

New security features include use of Windows Vista's new Credentials Manager (CredMan) to securely store passwords needed for running tasks, and also supporting Service for User (S4U) for many scenarios such that passwords do not need to be stored at all.

To further increase security, scheduled tasks are executed in their own session instead of the same session as system services or the current user:

- Separate per-user credentials are required for Winstations and Desktops.
- System tasks run in the system session (session 0), while user tasks run in the user's session.

Improved credentials management provided by S4U and Credentials Manager also increases reliability and reduces maintenance overhead.

Administrative Improvements

Windows Vista also includes features to enhance the administration experience for scheduled tasks.

Scheduled tasks may be activated by Event Log events and may be synchronized using operational events fired by the service. (You can view these in Event Viewer under Applications And Services Logs/Microsoft/Windows/Task Scheduler/Operational log.) Tasks may be configured to retry on failure and activated when resources become available, as in the case of mobile devices that may miss run times of scheduled tasks.

Control and task status monitoring has been improved and now provides detailed failure reporting and task history. Status feedback has been significantly improved. For example, using the detailed events logged by the Task Scheduler about task operation, an administrator can set up an e-mail to be sent to her when a failure occurs, including a complete run-time history of the event. In addition, the complete history of executed scheduled tasks can be easily reviewed, and at any time the administrator can view the list of currently running tasks and run or stop tasks on-demand.

To assist administrators in scripting complex tasks, the Task Scheduler API is now fully available to scripting languages.

Platform and Manageability Improvements

Windows Vista Task Scheduler enables several new features that improve platform operations and manageability. Infrastructure features for application monitoring now allow hosting and activation of troubleshooters and other corrective actions. Periodic data collection has been implemented to improve event detection. Task process prioritization has been improved and quotas may be assigned. Computer resources are used more efficiently by activating tasks based on a *true idle state*, defined by a combination of the following criteria:

- CPU, memory, and I/O usage
- User presence
- Nonpresentation mode

Default Tasks

A default installation of Windows Vista creates a number of scheduled tasks used to maintain various aspects of your system. For more information concerning these default tasks, see KB 939039, "Description of the scheduled tasks in Windows Vista," at *http://support.microsoft.com/kb/939039*.

Operational Overview

A task has a set of one or more triggers, execution conditions named settings, and an execution body named actions.

Task Triggers

A task trigger is the condition or conditions under which a task is launched. A task trigger defines when a task will begin and can include conditions such as running a task when a system is started, when a user logs on to a computer, or when a specific event is logged in the event log. A task may have one or more triggers defined. This means that the task will be launched whenever one of the triggers' conditions is met.

Task Settings

Task settings are conditions besides the trigger under which a task will execute, and they also control the behavior of the task. Task settings include conditions such as running the task only if the computer is idle, or running it only if the computer is connected to a specific network. Other task settings include allowing a task to run on demand, allowing a user to end a task forcefully, defining actions to take when a task fails, and deleting a task after it runs.

Task Actions

A task action is the code that executes when the task is run. The body of a task can be a script, batch file, executable, or a component written as a handler to the Task Scheduler interface. (This applies to operating system components only.) The execution hosts for task actions are called *task scheduler engines*. A task may define one or more actions to be run consecutively as part of the task execution.

User Interface

The Task Scheduler user interface has been integrated as an MMC console and provides an intuitive experience for administrators. Command-line capabilities include use of JOB.EXE in the current shell, the SchTasks.exe command-line tool for administrative and scripting use, and the legacy command-line task interface known as AT.

Task Scheduler Architecture

Task Scheduler supports an isolation model in which each set of tasks running in a specific security context is launched in a separate session. Task scheduler engines running in transient processes in the user or computer context process the execution defined for launch by a trigger. Tasks can be launched in a computer account context such as LocalSystem, LocalService, or NetworkService, or they may be launched in a specified user context. Task Scheduler also attempts to ensure task integrity even when a user's domain credentials are updated (applies to Windows Server 2003 domains only).

Tasks can be launched either locally or remotely. Each task may contain multiple actions running in series. Multiple tasks can be launched in parallel or serially to perform a series of synchronized operations using the events logged by the service. A set of predefined events in the System Event Log as well as the private Task Scheduler Operational Event Log are used to record each action's execution status for monitoring, synchronization, and health management.

The simplified block diagram shown in Figure 22-19 illustrates the high-level architecture implemented in Task Scheduler.

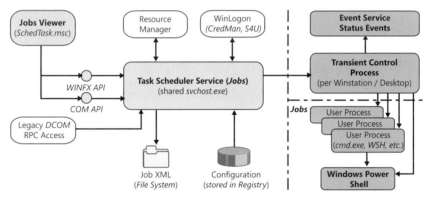

Figure 22-19   Task Scheduler architecture.

Task Scheduler combines several components that work together to provide the Task Scheduler user interface, the task execution engine, and event tracking and management.

The Task Scheduler user interface has been redesigned in the MMC .NET snap-in SchedTask.msc. This graphical user interface includes a wizard for creating and configuring tasks and property pages that accesses the Task Scheduler service through its COM API.

A shared Svchost.exe loads the Task Scheduler Service DLL SchedSvc.dll using a LocalSystem account, uses the TaskSchd.dll component to interface with the Resource Manager, and uses S4U to obtain the required credentials. This service DLL also reads configuration information from the registry and writes job tasks to the disk in XML format.

The Transient Control Process engine TaskEng.exe runs in the context of the task-defined user account, logs Event Log status events, and generates user processes that execute actions defined by the task.

The TaskComp.dll component provides backward compatibility for management and execution of tasks that were created in previous versions of Windows.

Task Scheduler Security

In the Windows Vista Task Scheduler, security is vastly improved. Task Scheduler supports a security isolation model in which each set of tasks running in a specific security context starts in a separate session. Tasks executed for different users are launched in separate window sessions, in complete isolation from one other and from tasks running in the machine (system) context. Passwords are stored (when needed) with the Credentials Manager (CredMan) service. Using CredMan prevents malware from retrieving the stored password, tightening security further.

In Windows Vista, the burden of credentials management in Task Scheduler is lessened. Credentials are no longer stored locally for the majority of scenarios, so tasks do not "break" when a password changes. Administrators can configure security services such as S4U and CredMan, depending on whether the task requires remote or local resources. S4U relieves the need to store passwords locally on the computer, and CredMan, though it requires that passwords be updated once per computer, automatically updates all scheduled tasks configured to run for the specific user with the new password.

Credentials Management

The Credentials Manager stores the target/credentials pair locally in the user profile CredMan store. Upon registration, Task Scheduler impersonates the user and stores the target/credentials pair. This process is also used to access resources that require non-Windows credentials. The Credentials Manager also manages credentials for service accounts and extends credentials handling for computer accounts.

User Security

You can locally and remotely activate tasks and run them on behalf of a user who is not logged on. Credentials on distributed tasks can be updated when credentials are changed in the authentication authority. User security has been extended to function in a non-Microsoft Active Directory environment across forests and across firewalls. These features allow tasks to be launched even if the task accesses a resource that requires non-Windows credentials.

Security Concepts

Task Scheduler uses standard Windows security functions provided by Service for Users (S4U). Upon registration, Task Scheduler authenticates credentials as a trusted service and stores identity only in a *domain\user* name format. Upon execution, S4U provides restricted token access based on the identity provided by Task Scheduler. S4U2Self implements the same functions as S4U for workgroups, standalone computers, and computers that belong to a domain but are not currently connected to that domain.

Note For more information about S4U, see RFC 1510: The Kerberos Network Authentication Service (V5) at *http://www.ietf.org/rfc/rfc1510.txt*.

Securing Running Tasks

Task Scheduler supports an isolation model in which each set of tasks running in specific security contexts are launched in separate Desktops. The execution defined and launched by the trigger is handled by engines running in transient processes in a user or computer context. Tasks can be launched in a system account context, such as LocalSystem, LocalService, or NetworkService, or in a specified user account context. Tasks launched in a system account context will always run noninteractively in Session 0.

The *CreateProcess* function used to create tasks ensures that any Winstation created in a user context will run in a different session than Session 0. By default, all Winstations will be created in the same session.

Registration Permissions Matrix

The Task Scheduler service adheres to the following task registration permissions rules:

- Any user can schedule any task for herself.
- Any user can schedule any task for anyone whose password he supplies at registration.
- An administrator or system account can schedule tasks for other users or security groups without supplying a password, with the following restrictions:
  - ❏ Only with the Run Only If Logged On flag set, which is similar to a logon script and consistent with current behavior
  - ❏ Only running in interactive mode
- Tasks scheduled with *RunOnlyIfUserLoggedon* with no password will run only in interactive mode.
- Tasks scheduled to run in system contexts such as LocalSystem, LocalService, or NetworkService will not run in interactive mode.

AT and Task Scheduler v1.0 Compatibility Modes

Task Scheduler provides two backward-compatibility modes:

- **AT Compatibility Mode**   Tasks registered through AT.exe are visible and can be modified by the Task Scheduler v1.0 GUI and the Task Scheduler command-line utility SchTasks.exe.
- **Task Scheduler v1.0 Compatibility Mode**   Tasks created or modified in the Task Scheduler v1.0 user interface and the Task Scheduler command-line utility SchTasks.exe are *not* accessible or visible through AT.exe.

The Task Scheduler parser will determine at registration time if the task can be converted to either of these compatibility modes.

Task Scheduler User Interface

The Task Scheduler user interface is now an MMC 3.0 snap-in, as shown in Figure 22-20.

Figure 22-20   Task Scheduler user interface.

The scope pane on the left contains the Scheduled Tasks Library subnode under the root Task Scheduler node by default. The Library subnode has all currently defined tasks listed under it, in a hierarchy of folders. The Microsoft subnode under the Scheduled Tasks Library contains a Windows subnode with default Windows system tasks used by operating system components, such as Reliability Monitor (RAC) and System Restore. Default system tasks are normally not modified.

The Results Pane in the center shows the task name and other relevant information about the currently selected task. The bottom part of the center pane contains a preview pane showing the definition details of the currently selected task in the list at top. You can modify task definitions by either double-clicking the task name in the list or by selecting and right-clicking or clicking the Properties action in the Actions Pane at right.

The Actions Pane on the right shows relevant actions for a selected task or scope node. New tasks can be created using the Create Basic Task action for wizard-based simple tasks or using Create Task for full-featured tasks.

The Summary (home) page that shows up whenever you start Task Scheduler and have the top node selected displays a summary of task status for the system that includes how many tasks ran, how many succeeded or failed, and a list of currently active tasks that are not disabled or expired.

Creating New Tasks

Before you create a task, you should create a new folder under the Task Scheduler Library to store the new task. To create a new Scheduled Tasks folder, follow these steps:

1. Select the Task Scheduler Library and either right-click and then select New Folder or click New Folder in the Actions pane.

2. Enter the name of the new folder and click OK to complete creation of the new subnode.

3. Select the new folder to start creating a new task.

You can create tasks by using the Create Basic Task Wizard or by manually using the Create Task interface. To create a new task using the Create Basic Task Wizard, follow these steps:

1. Right-click the folder you created to store your tasks and select Create Basic Task to display the Create Basic Task Wizard, or select Create Basic Task in the Actions pane.

2. Enter the name of the task, provide an optional description, and then click Next.

3. On the Task Trigger page, specify when you want the task to start and then click Next. Some choices may require additional information to further define the trigger.

4. On the Task Action page, specify an action for your task to perform and then click Next to specify action details.

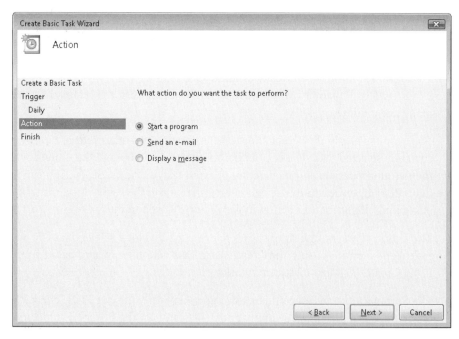

5. Options displayed on the next page depend on the action you selected on the previous page.

6. After specifying the appropriate action details, click Finish to create the task and close the wizard.

To create a new task manually, follow these steps:

1. Select the folder that the task will reside in and either right-click the folder and select Create Task or select Create Task in the Actions pane. Either action will display the Task Properties dialog box with several tabs for the different task details. The General tab defines general information about the task.

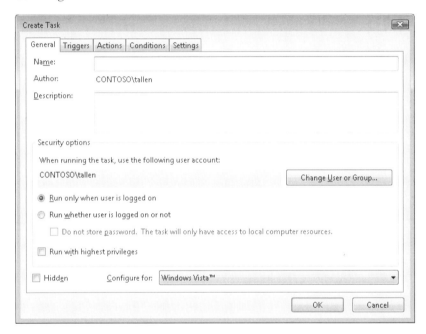

2. In the Name text box, enter a name for the task.

3. In the Description text box, you can enter an optional task description or leave the box entry blank.

4. Under Security options, select the appropriate options for the task:

   ❑ By default, the task will run under the security context of the currently logged-on user. To select a different security context, click Change User Or Group.

   ❑ Select either Run Only When User Is Logged On or Run Whether User Is Logged On Or Not. If you select Run Whether User Is Logged On Or Not and check the box Do Not Store Password, the task will use S4U and will not be able to access any resources outside the local computer.

❑ Select Run With Highest Privileges if the task must run with the highest privileges that the specified user account can obtain. If left unchecked, and if the user account is an administrative account, the task will run under User Account Control (UAC) with partial privileges.

5. To hide the task from view by default, select the Hidden check box. You can still view hidden tasks by opening the View menu and selecting Show Hidden Tasks.

6. By default, tasks are configured for Windows Vista, Task Scheduler compatibility. For backward compatibility, the list allows you to select Windows Server 2003, Windows XP, or Windows 2000 to define a task that is compatible with Task Scheduler v1.0.

Options on other tabs that are used to define task details are discussed in later sections of this chapter.

Defining Triggers

The Triggers tab shown in Figure 22-21 allows users to view and configure one or more triggers that will launch the task. To define a new trigger, click the New button. To edit an existing trigger, select the trigger in the list and click Edit. To delete an existing trigger, select the trigger and click Delete.

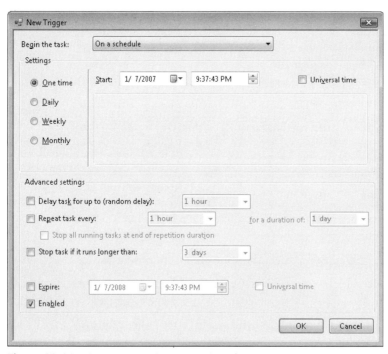

Figure 22-21   Create New Trigger user interface.

In the New Trigger dialog box, the Begin The Task drop-down list allows you to configure a task to begin based on the following trigger types:

- On A Schedule
- At Logon
- At Startup
- On Idle
- On An Event
- At Task Creation/Modification
- On Connection To or Disconnect From User Session
- On Workstation Lock or Unlock

The following sections explain trigger types and their corresponding settings in detail.

On A Schedule Trigger   The On A Schedule trigger configures the task to start on a defined schedule. Selecting the On A Schedule trigger type in the Begin The Task list displays the controls in the Settings group box to configure schedule parameters. Table 22-10 describes these controls.

Table 22-10   On A Schedule Trigger Settings

Setting	Description
One time	Configures the task to run once at the specified date and time
Daily	Configures the task to run on a schedule based on days
Weekly	Configures the task to run on a schedule based on weeks
Monthly	Configures the task to run on a schedule based on months
Universal Time	Configures the task to run using UTC instead of the local time

At Log On Trigger   The At Log On trigger allows you to define a task to run when someone logs on to the computer. Selecting the At Log On trigger type in the Begin The Task list displays the controls in the Settings group box to configure schedule parameters. Table 22-11 describes these controls.

Table 22-11   At Logon Trigger Settings

Setting	Description
Any User	Configures the task to start at logon of any user.
Specific User Or Group	Configures the task to start at logon of the specified user or group.
<domain\user>	Read-only display of the currently selected user or group.
Change User Or Group	Launches the standard Windows Select User Or Group dialog box to allow the user to change the selected user or group. If the user makes a different selection in the dialog box and clicks OK to accept, the *<domain\user>* read-only text box should change to display the new selection.

At Startup Trigger   This trigger causes the task to run when the computer starts up. The only settings for this trigger are the advanced settings described in the Advanced Settings section later in this section.

On Idle Trigger   The On Idle trigger configures the task to run when the computer becomes idle. To complete configuration for this trigger, you must also select the Conditions tab and configure Idle settings; see the section titled "Defining Conditions" later in this chapter for more information about these settings.

On An Event Trigger   The On An Event trigger type allows a user to define a task to execute on a specified Event Log event. To define the event trigger, the Settings group box provides two options:

- The Basic option allows for simple selection of a single event to be used as a trigger (by choosing the log, source, and event ID identifiers for the event).

- The Custom option allows defining a more complex event filter by providing the New Event Filter button. Click the button to launch the Event Filter dialog box (same as in Event Viewer) and define a more detailed event filter by time, level, source, and so on.

At Task Creation/Modification Trigger   Selecting the At Task Creation/Modification trigger type in the Begin The Task list configures the task to start immediately when it is created or modified. No other condition is required and no further settings are displayed for this trigger.

On Connection To or Disconnect From User Session Triggers   The user session triggers cause a task to run when a user session is connected to or disconnected from the local computer or from a remote desktop connection. For example, when you connect to a user session on the local computer by switching users on the computer, this trigger will cause the task to run. Another example that can trigger a task to run is when a user connects to a user session by using the Remote Desktop Connection program from a remote computer. The trigger's settings allow you to specify that the task should be triggered when any user connects or disconnects to a user session or when a specific user or user group member connects or disconnects.

Selecting the On Connection To User Session or the On Disconnect From User Session trigger types in the Begin The Task list displays the controls listed in Table 22-12 in the Settings group box.

Table 22-12   On Connection To or Disconnect From User Session Trigger Settings

Setting	Description
Any User	Configures the task to start when any user makes a connection to a user session.
Specific User Or Group	Configures the task to start when the specified user or group makes a connection to a user session.

Table 22-12   On Connection To or Disconnect From User Session Trigger Settings

Setting	Description
<domain\user>	Read-only display of the currently selected user or group.
Change User Or Group	Launches the standard Windows Select User Or Group dialog box to allow the user to change the selected user or group. If the user makes a different selection in the dialog and clicks OK to accept, the *<domain\user>* read-only text box should change to display the new selection.
Connection From Local Computer	Configures the task to start when the specified user connects locally.
Connection From Remote Computer	Configures the task to start when the specified user connects remotely.

On Workstation Lock or Unlock Triggers   Selecting the On Workstation Lock or the On Workstation Unlock trigger type in the Begin The Task list displays the controls listed in Table 22-13 in the Settings group box.

Table 22-13   On Workstation Lock and Unlock Trigger Settings

Setting	Description
Any User	Configures the task to start when any user locks or unlocks the workstation.
Specific User Or Group	Configures the task to start when the specified user or member of the specified group locks or unlocks the workstation.
<domain\user>	Read-only display of the currently selected user or group.
Change User Or Group	Launches the standard Windows Select User Or Group dialog box to allow the user to change the selected user or group. If the user makes a different selection in the dialog and clicks OK to accept, the *<domain\user>* read-only text box should change to display the new selection.

Defining Actions

When you create a task, you must configure one or more actions to run a program, script, or batch file; send an e-mail; or pop up a message when your task starts. The Actions tab allows you to define, view, or modify actions for this task. To configure actions, click the Actions tab and then click New to display the New Action dialog box, as shown in Figure 22-22.

Figure 22-22   Create New Action – Start a Program.

To configure an action to start a program, script, or batch file, follow these steps:

1. Open the Action list and then select Start A Program to display configuration options shown in Figure 22-22.

2. In the Settings group box, under Program/Script, provide the path to the program or script or select Browse to choose a program, script, or batch file on the local computer.

3. If the directory that contains the program, script, or batch file is not included in the local computer path, enter the starting directory in the Start In text box.

4. If the program, script, or batch file requires additional arguments to be passed to it at launch, enter these arguments in the Add Arguments (Optional) text box.

To configure an action to send e-mail, follow these steps:

1. Open the Action list and select Send An E-mail to display the configuration options:

2. In the Settings group box, enter the required information listed in Table 22-14.

Table 22-14   Send E-Mail Settings

Setting	Description
From	Specifies the e-mail address of the sender.
To	Specifies one or more e-mail addresses for recipients. When you enter multiple addresses, separate each address with a semicolon (;).

Table 22-14   **Send E-Mail Settings**

Setting	Description
Subject	Specifies a subject for the e-mail.
Text	Allows the user to enter a formatted message to be included in the content of the e-mail.
Attachment	Displays a File Open dialog box that allows the user to select one or more files to attach to the e-mail.
SMTP Server	Allows the user to enter the DNS or NETBIOS name for the SMTP server to be used to send the e-mail.

Note   To configure the task to pop up a message, choose Display A Message in the Action drop-down list and then enter a title and a message to be displayed when the task runs.

Defining Conditions

The Conditions tab displays different conditions for running tasks and allows you to define settings for these conditions. If you do not specify condition settings, designated defaults will be applied to the task. Conditions on this page are optional unless you have selected the On Idle trigger type. If you have selected this trigger type, you must configure Idle settings as described in this section.

To configure task conditions, click the Conditions tab and configure the desired options as described in Table 22-15.

Table 22-15   **Conditions Tab Options**

Setting	Description
Idle	Groups all conditions related to idle that affect the starting of the task.
Start The Task Only If The Computer Is Idle For	Configures the task to start only if the computer has been idle for a certain amount of time.
Wait For Idle	Enabled only by selecting the Start Only If Computer Is Idle For option; configures how long to wait for the idle condition to be satisfied.
	Options in the list include Indefinitely, 1 Minute, 5 Minutes, 10 Minutes, 15 Minutes, 30 Minutes, 1 Hour, and 2 Hours.
	Default value: 30 Minutes
	You can also enter other values using the following formats:
	<ss> s[econds]
	<mm>[:<ss>] m[inutes]
	<hh>[:<mm>:<ss>] h[ours]
Stop If The Computer Ceases To Be Idle	Configures the task to stop if the computer ceases to be idle.
	Default value: Selected

Table 22-15   Conditions Tab Options

Setting	Description
Restart If The Idle State Resumes	Enabled only by selecting the Stop If Computer Ceases To Be Idle option. Configures the task to restart if the computer re-enters the idle state.
	Default value: Cleared
Start The Task Only If The Computer Is On AC Power	Configures the task to start only if the computer is on AC power and not on battery power.
	Default value: Cleared
Stop If The Computer Switches To Battery Power	Configures the task to stop if the computer switches to battery power.
	Default value: Cleared
Wake The Computer To Run This Task	Specifies that the computer should be brought out of hibernation or standby to run this task.
	Default value: Cleared
Start Only If The Following Network Connection Is Available	Sets a condition to run the task only if a specific named network connection is available or if any network connection is available when the task's trigger is activated.
	Default value: Cleared

Defining Settings

The Settings tab displays additional global settings for the task and allows you to define these settings. All settings on this page are optional. If you do not specify these settings, designated default values will be applied to the task.

To configure global settings using the Settings tab, click the Settings tab and configure the desired settings as described in Table 22-16.

Table 22-16   Global Settings Defined on the Settings Tab

Setting	Description
Allow Task To Be Run On Demand	Defines whether the task supports Run Now functionality that allows tasks to be run on demand from the user interface or command-line utilities.
	Default value: Selected
Run Task As Soon As Possible After A Scheduled Start Is Missed	Configures the task to run immediately if the service detects that a scheduled activation was missed. For example, the computer was turned off when the trigger condition occurred.
	Default value: Cleared
If The Task Is Already Running, Then The Following Rule Applies	Configures action to be taken if the trigger for a task fires, while an instance of that task is already running. Options include Do Not Start A New Instance, Stop The Existing Instance, Run A New Instance In Parallel, And Queue A New Instance.
	Default value: Do Not Start A New Instance

Table 22-16   Global Settings Defined on the Settings Tab

Setting	Description
If The Task Fails	Use this setting to restart a task if the task fails to run. (The last run result of the task was not a success.) The user specifies the time interval that takes place between task restart attempts and the number of times to try to restart the task.
	Default value: Cleared
Restart Every	Enabled only by selecting the If Task Fails option. Specifies how often a retry should be attempted.
	Options in the list include Indefinitely, 1 Minute, 5 Minutes, 10 Minutes, 15 Minutes, 30 Minutes, and 1 Hour
	Default value: 1 Minute
	You can also enter other values using the following formats:
	<ss> s[econds]
	<mm>[:<ss>] m[inutes]
	<hh>[:<mm>:<ss>] h[ours]
Attempt To Restart Up To	Enabled only if you select the If Task Fails option. Specifies the number of times to restart the task upon failure (number of retries).
Stop The Task If It Runs Longer Than	Configures the task to stop if it has been running for longer than the specified time.
	Default value: Selected
<Execution Time Limit>	Enabled only if you select the Stop The Task If It Runs Longer Than check box. Configures the task to be stopped after the specified amount of time specified by Execution Time Limit. Options include 1 Hour, 2 Hours, 4 Hours, 8 Hours, 12 Hours, 1 Day, and 3 Days
	Default value: 3 Days
	You can also enter other values using the following formats:
	<ss> s[econds]
	<mm>[:<ss>] m[inutes]
	<hh>[:<mm>:<ss>] h[ours]
If The Running Task Does Not End When Requested, Force It To Stop	If this setting is selected, the task will be forced to stop if the task does not respond to a request to stop.
	Default value: Selected
If The Task Is Not Scheduled To Run Again, Delete It	Configures the task to be deleted if it is not scheduled to run again.
	Default value: Cleared

Table 22-16   Global Settings Defined on the Settings Tab

Setting	Description
After	Enabled only if you select the Delete Task option. Specifies the amount of time to wait, after the task completes its last run, before deleting it. Options include Immediately, 30 Days, 90 Days, 180 Days, or 365 Days.
	Default value: 30 Days
	You can also enter other values using the following formats:
	<ss> s[econds]
	<mm>[:<ss>] m[inutes]
	<dd> d[ays]
	<mm> months

Managing Tasks

Task Scheduler simplifies task management and monitoring. This section explains how to view task history, export tasks, and import tasks.

Display Running Tasks

To display all tasks currently running on the system, open Task Scheduler and select Display All Running Tasks from the Action menu. This opens the All Running Tasks window, and you can click Refresh to manually refresh the display. You can also select one or more tasks and click End Task to stop tasks on demand.

Viewing History

The History tab of a task displays all the known events for that task and allows you to quickly see the last time the task ran and its status. Only events that relate to the currently selected task will be shown, eliminating the need to scour the Task Scheduler event log for individual events from specific tasks.

To view the history of a task, do the following:

1. If Task Scheduler is not open, start Task Scheduler.

2. Find and click the task folder in the console tree that contains the task you want to view.

3. In the console window, click the task that you want to view.

4. Click the History tab to view the task's history. Click an event, in the list of events on the History tab, to view the description of the event.

Exporting Tasks

You can export tasks to an .xml file and then import them at some later time, on either the same computer or a different computer. This feature allows for easy portability of tasks from computer to computer.

To export a task, follow these steps:

1. Right-click the task that you want to export and then select Export, or select Export in the Action pane.

2. Browse to where you want to save the file, enter the name of the file, and then click Save.

3. The task will be saved in .xml format. The following example shows a simple task:

```xml
<?xml version="1.0" encoding="UTF-16"?>
<Task version="1.2" xmlns="http://schemas.microsoft.com/windows/2004/02/mit/task">
  <RegistrationInfo>
    <Date>2006-04-11T13:54:51</Date>
    <Author>USER1-VISTA\user1</Author>
    <Description>Test Task</Description>
  </RegistrationInfo>
  <Triggers>
    <TimeTrigger id="1a08ebe4-0527-4e7a-af76-84f2ef1dbfa0">
      <StartBoundary>2006-04-11T13:55:23</StartBoundary>
      <Enabled>true</Enabled>
    </TimeTrigger>
  </Triggers>
  <Principals>
    <Principal id="Author">
      <UserId>USER1-VISTA\user1</UserId>
      <LogonType>InteractiveToken</LogonType>
      <RunLevel>LeastPrivilege</RunLevel>
    </Principal>
  </Principals>
  <Settings>
    <IdleSettings>
      <Duration>PT10M</Duration>
      <WaitTimeout>PT1H</WaitTimeout>
      <StopOnIdleEnd>true</StopOnIdleEnd>
      <RestartOnIdle>false</RestartOnIdle>
    </IdleSettings>
    <MultipleInstancesPolicy>IgnoreNew</MultipleInstancesPolicy>
    <DisallowStartIfOnBatteries>true</DisallowStartIfOnBatteries>
    <StopIfGoingOnBatteries>true</StopIfGoingOnBatteries>
    <AllowHardTerminate>true</AllowHardTerminate>
    <StartWhenAvailable>false</StartWhenAvailable>
    <RunOnlyIfNetworkAvailable>false</RunOnlyIfNetworkAvailable>
    <AllowStartOnDemand>true</AllowStartOnDemand>
    <Enabled>true</Enabled>
    <Hidden>false</Hidden>
    <RunOnlyIfIdle>false</RunOnlyIfIdle>
```

```
      <WakeToRun>false</WakeToRun>
      <Priority>7</Priority>
    </Settings>
    <Actions Context="Author">
      <Exec>
        <Command>C:\Windows\System32\calc.exe</Command>
      </Exec>
    </Actions>
  </Task>
```

Importing Tasks

Tasks that have been exported can also be easily imported to another computer or the same computer.

To import a task, follow these steps:

1. Right-click a task folder under the Task Scheduler Library and then select Import Task, or select Import Task in the Action pane.

2. Browse to where the .xml file is located and click Open. The task will be automatically imported into the library using the settings contained in the .xml file.

> **Note** To ensure that the task runs properly, it is recommended that you verify the properties of the task after you import it.

Using the SchTasks.exe Command

This section describes the SchTasks.exe command-line syntax and parameters. The Schtasks.exe command-line interface utility allows an administrator to create, delete, query, change, run, and end scheduled tasks on a local or remote system through the command shell.

Command Syntax

The SchTasks.exe command interface uses the following syntax:

```
schtasks /<parameter> [arguments]
```

Command Parameters

- **/Create** Creates a new scheduled task
- **/Delete** Deletes the scheduled task(s)
- **/Query** Displays all scheduled tasks
- **/Change** Changes the properties of scheduled task

- ■   **/Run**   Runs the scheduled task immediately
- ■   **/End**   Stops the currently running scheduled task
- ■   **/?**   Displays this help message

Creating Tasks

The general syntax for Schtasks.exe is as follows:

SCHTASKS /Create [/S system [/U <username> [/P [<password>]]]] [/RU <username> [/RP <password>]] /SC schedule [/MO <modifier>] [/D <day>] [/M <months>] [/I <idletime>] /TN <taskname> /TR <taskrun> [/ST <starttime>] [/RI <interval>] [[/ET <endtime> | /DU <duration>] [/K] [/XML <xmlfile>] [/V1]] [/SD <startdate>] [/ED <enddate>] [/IT] [/Z] [/F]

Example command:

```
SCHTASKS /Create /S system /U user /P password /RU runasuser /RP runaspassword
  /SC HOURLY /TN rtest1 /TR notepad
```

Deleting Tasks

Syntax:

SCHTASKS /Delete [/S <system> [/U <username> [/P [<password>]]]] /TN <taskname> [/F]

Example command:

```
SCHTASKS /Delete /TN "Backup and Restore"
```

Running Tasks

Syntax:

SCHTASKS /Run [/S <system> [/U <username> [/P [<password>]]]] /TN <taskname>

Example command:

```
SCHTASKS /Run /TN "Start Backup"
```

Ending Tasks

Syntax:

SCHTASKS /End [/S <system> [/U <username> [/P [<password>]]]] /TN <taskname>

Example command:

```
SCHTASKS /End /TN "Start Backup"
```

Querying Tasks

Syntax:

SCHTASKS /Query [/S <system> [/U <username> [/P [<password>]]]] [/FO <format>]
[/NH] [/V] [/?]

Example commands:

```
SCHTASKS /Query /S system /U user /P password
SCHTASKS /Query /FO LIST /V
```

Changing Tasks

Syntax:

SCHTASKS /Change [/S <system> [/U <username> [/P [<password>]]]] /TN <taskname>
{ [/RU <runasuser>] [/RP <runaspassword>] [/TR <taskrun>] [/ST <starttime>] [/RI <interval>]
[{/ET <endtime> | /DU <duration>} [/K]] [/SD <startdate>] [/ED <enddate>] [/ENABLE |
/DISABLE] [/IT] [/Z] }

Example command:

```
SCHTASKS /Change /RP password /TN "Backup and Restore"
```

Scheduled Tasks Events

In Windows Server 2003 and earlier versions of the Windows operating system, scheduled tasks used a Schedlgu.txt log file to track tasks and their status. Windows Vista implements all new event logs for applications and Task Scheduler now logs all operational information about scheduled tasks into its own event log. The Scheduled Tasks event log Microsoft-Windows-TaskScheduler is located under Application Logs. Important errors or warnings about task or service failures are logged to the System log so that administrators can readily see them and take action.

The Windows Vista Scheduled Tasks component will normally log an event on task registration (at creation), at task launch, and when the task instance has been sent to the engine. Events will also be logged on task failures and any task-related problems.

This section provides examples of typical events that are logged by the Scheduled Tasks service.

Task Registration

An Event ID 106 is logged when a task is created. This event is also referred to as *task registration*.

Task Launch

Tasks can be launched by either a user request or by a trigger. An Event ID 110 is normally logged when a user manually launches a task. An Event ID 107 is normally logged when a task is launched as the result of a trigger.

Task Execution

An Event ID 319 indicates that the Task Engine received a message from the Task Scheduler service requesting task launch, and it is the best indicator of a task launch. In these events, the Task Engine is identified by the user SID, and the task name is also logged.

Task Completion

An Event ID 102 is normally logged when a task completes successfully.

Troubleshooting Task Scheduler

Task or service failures are logged to the system event log. It is important to note that the events will vary and will be based on what specifically failed. A user will see different events based on whether a task failed to start or if the task started successfully but the action failed.

The key to troubleshooting Task Scheduler is understanding specifically where the failure occurred in the process. A task is defined as an action, the trigger for the action, the conditions under which the task will run, and additional settings. The event log will show whether the failure is in the trigger, the task action, the conditions, or the settings of the task.

Tasks Won't Run If the Service Is Not Started

If you are having problems scheduling tasks or getting tasks to run correctly, first ensure that the Task Scheduler service is running. You can run services.msc to verify that the Task Scheduler service status is Started.

The Task Did Not Run at the Expected Time

If a scheduled task does not run when you expect it to run, ensure that the task is enabled and also check the triggers on the task to ensure that they are set correctly. Also, check the history of the task, as shown in Figure 22-23, to see when the task was started and to check for errors.

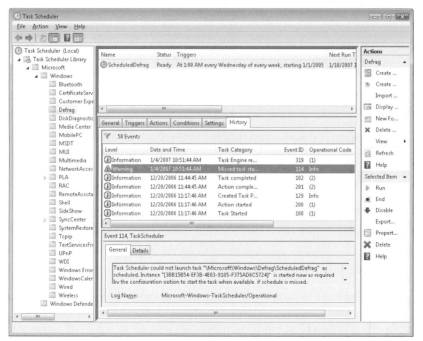

Figure 22-23   Task Scheduler History Tab.

The Task Will Run Only If All Conditions Are Met

You can set task conditions on the Conditions tab of the Task Properties dialog box. If conditions are not met or are set up incorrectly, the task will not execute.

The Task Will Only Run When a Certain User Is Logged On

If a scheduled task does not run when you expect it to run, review the Security Options settings in the Task Properties dialog box on the General tab.

The Task Executed a Program But the Program Did Not Run Correctly

If a task attempts to execute a program, but the program does not run correctly, first try running the program manually (not from a task) to ensure that the program works correctly. You may need to add arguments to the program command or define the Start In path using the *Add Arguments* and/or *Start In* optional fields.

The Task Failed to Start

An Event ID 101 is normally logged when a task fails to start. In these events, the result code is also displayed. For more information about result and return codes, see the section titled "Interpreting Result and Return Codes" later in this chapter.

The Task Action Failed to Execute

When a task starts but the action configured for the task fails to execute, an Event ID 103 or an Event ID 203 is normally logged. These events also display the return code. For more information about result and return codes, see the section titled "Interpreting Result and Return Codes" later in this chapter.

The Program Specified in the Task Requires Elevated Privileges

If a task is running a program that requires elevated privileges, ensure that the task runs with the highest privileges. You can set a task to run with the highest privileges by changing the task's security options on the General tab of the Task Properties dialog box.

Interpreting Result and Return Codes

To interpret return codes, you can use a tool such as Err.exe, which you can obtain from the Microsoft Download Center. Err.exe parses source-code header files until it finds a match for the error. In this regard, the Scheduled Tasks service in Windows Vista still functions quite similarly to previous versions of Windows. Return codes from events that occur internally are always translated into hresult code. For example, the logon failed event will contain a result code that can be interpreted as a hresult. Task handler tasks also return result codes that you can interpret using the same tools.

However, when an executable is launched and fails for an unknown reason, you have no way of knowing what the result code might mean. The hresult logged in the event log will typically indicate the value returned to the service from the executable itself, and additional research and documentation may be required for accurately interpreting the code.

 Note You can download Err.exe from the Microsoft Download Center at *http://www.microsoft.com/downloads/details.aspx?familyid=be596899-7bb8-4208-b7fc-09e02a13696c*. Although this tool is called the Microsoft Exchange Server Error Code Look-up tool, it actually looks up any Windows operating system error codes.

Summary

This chapter has covered new tools and enhancements for monitoring and maintaining desktop health of Windows Vista computers. Using these tools, users can monitor event logs, manage tasks, monitor reliability, obtain performance information for their systems, and configure Windows Error Reporting as needed.

Additional Resources

The following resources contain additional information and tools related to this chapter.

Related Information

- Chapter 31, "Troubleshooting Hardware, Driver, and Disk Issues," includes more information about troubleshooting issues using Event Viewer, Reliability Monitor, and Problem Reports And Solutions.

- The Reliability And Performance section of the Windows Vista TechCenter, at *http://technet.microsoft.com/en-us/windowsvista/aa905077.aspx.*

- "Windows Vista Performance and Reliability Monitoring Step-by-Step Guide" in the Windows Vista Technical Library at *http://technet2.microsoft.com/WindowsVista/en/library/ab3b2cfc-b177-43ec-8a4d-0bfac62d88961033.mspx?mfr=true.*

- "Windows Reliability And Performance Monitor" in the Windows Vista Technical Library at *http://technet2.microsoft.com/windowsserver2008/en/library/ec5b5e7b-5d5c-4d04-98ad-55d9a09677101033.mspx?mfr=true.*

- "Event Viewer" in the Windows Vista Technical Library at *http://www.microsoft.com/technet/WindowsVista/library/ops/4229f239-16a6-4ecd-b3cf-aec03dc08cd5.mspx?mfr=true.*

- "Task Scheduler Overview" in the Windows Vista Technical Library at *http://technet2.microsoft.com/WindowsVista/en/library/61e2eb14-d71d-4a60-9eab-ba7bdd422b941033.mspx?mfr=true.*

- KB 281884, "The Process object in Performance Monitor can display Process IDs (PIDs)," at *http://support.microsoft.com/kb/281884.*

- KB 927823, "The WFP provider counter displays more providers than expected in Windows Vista," at *http://support.microsoft.com/kb/927823.*

- KB 931705, "Error message on a Windows Vista–based computer when you try to update the user credentials of a Data Collector Set on a remote computer: 'Collection already exists,'" at *http://support.microsoft.com/kb/931705.*

- KB 931706, "The name of the trace session is incorrectly set to NT Kernel Logger in the Windows Vista 'Reliability And Performance Monitor,'" at *http://support.microsoft.com/kb/931706.*

- KB 926098, "How to enable COM+ and COM diagnostic tracing," at *http://support.microsoft.com/kb/926098.*

- KB 942910, "'Error, Warning, or Critical' events are logged in the Diagnostic Performance/Operational event log on a Windows Vista–based computer," at *http://support.microsoft.com/kb/942910.*

■ KB 934640, "In Windows, Event Viewer incorrectly displays IPv6 addresses in event descriptions," found at *http://support.microsoft.com/kb/934640.*

■ KB 932579, "The event log is not saved when you click 'Save and Clear' after you click Clear Log in Event Viewer in Windows Vista," at *http://support.microsoft.com/kb/932579.*

■ KB 930857, "An update is available for Windows Error Reporting in Windows Vista to make sure that problem reports are sent only after you have granted permission," at *http://support.microsoft.com/kb/930857.*

■ KB 931673, "How to create a user-mode process dump file in Windows Vista," at *http://support.microsoft.com/kb/931673.*

■ KB 939039, "Description of the scheduled tasks in Windows Vista," found at *http://support.microsoft.com/kb/939039.*

■ KB 927014, "How to disable the backup-related scheduled tasks in Windows Vista," at *http://support.microsoft.com/kb/927014.*

■ KB 939615, "You cannot change the settings for a file backup operation or use Windows Task Scheduler to change the defrag schedule in Windows Vista," at *http://support.microsoft.com/kb/939615.*

■ KB 930133, "A task does not run as expected after you wake a Windows Vista–based computer," at *http://support.microsoft.com/kb/930133.*

■ KB 929463, "The Task Scheduler does not wake the computer to run a scheduled task in Windows Vista," at *http://support.microsoft.com/kb/929463.*

On the Companion CD

■ Vista WER UI Flow.pdf

■ MeasureWinSAT.vbs

■ BackupEventLog.vbs

■ ClearEventLog.vbs

■ CreateScheduledTask.vbs

■ ManageScheduledTasks.vbs

■ MemoryUtilization.vbs

■ MonitorIPstats.vbs

■ MonitorNetworkUtilization.vbs

■ MonitorServerOSstats.vbs

■ MonitorTCPstats.vbs

Chapter 23

Supporting Users Using Remote Assistance

Remote Assistance (RA) in Windows Vista includes a number of improvements in connectivity, performance, usability, and security along with feature enhancements that make it even more useful than RA in Windows XP. With increased Group Policy support, command-line scripting capabilities, session logging, bandwidth optimization, and more, Remote Assistance is now an essential tool for enabling enterprises to support users in Help Desk scenarios. This chapter examines how Remote Assistance works in Windows Vista, how to use it to support end users, and how to manage it using Group Policy and scripts.

Understanding Remote Assistance

Supporting end users is an essential function of IT departments and the corporate Help Desk. Unfortunately, conventional technical support provided over the telephone or using chat tools is generally cumbersome and inefficient. As a result, supporting users is often both time-consuming and costly for large enterprises to implement. For example, end users often have difficulty describing the exact nature of the problem they are having. Because of their general inexperience and lack of technical knowledge, end users may try to describe their problem using nontechnical, inexact language. As a result, Help Desk personnel are generally reduced to asking a series of simple questions to try to isolate the problem the user is having. The methodical nature of these questions sometimes causes users to feel as if Help Desk personnel are being condescending, and such misunderstandings can reduce the effectiveness of the support experience and can make users tend to avoid contacting support personnel when future problems arise.

End users also often have difficulty following instructions given to them by Help Desk personnel who are trying to assist them. Well-trained support personnel will try to avoid using technical jargon when communicating with end users, but although using plain language can improve the support experience, it may also mean that resolution steps become long and tiresome. For example, telling a user how to use Disk Cleanup from System Tools in Accessories can require several sentences or more, and this kind of communication can add time to support incidents, making them more costly to the company.

Remote Assistance (RA) solves these problems by enabling support personnel to view the user's desktop in real time. The user seeking assistance can demonstrate the nature of the problem to the support person. This is a quicker and more efficient way to communicate a problem than using words or e-mail. If necessary, the user can also give the support person permission to assume shared interactive control of the user's computer to show the user how to resolve the problem. The result of using Remote Assistance is faster problem resolution, an improved support experience, and a lower Total Cost of Ownership (TCO) for supporting end users in large, corporate environments.

Remote Assistance vs. Remote Desktop

Remote Assistance and Remote Desktop are different features of Windows Vista that have entirely different uses. Remote Desktop is based on Microsoft's Terminal Services and is a tool for remotely logging on to remote computers. When you use Remote Desktop to connect to a remote computer, a new user session is established. Remote Desktop can also establish sessions with computers that have no interactive sessions running (no users logged on locally), such as headless servers. For more information on Remote Desktop, see Chapter 28, "Connecting Remote Users and Networks."

Remote Assistance, on the other hand, is a tool for interactively helping users trouble-shoot problems with their computers. To use Remote Assistance, both the User (also called the Novice) and the Helper must be present on their computers. Unlike Remote Desktop, Remote Assistance does not create a new session. Instead, Remote Assistance allows the Helper to work in the existing session of the User. The User's desktop gets remoted to the Helper, who can then view the User's desktop and, with the User's consent, share control of the desktop.

Here is another way to summarize the difference between these two features: In Remote Assistance, both users involved are looking at the same desktop using the same logon credentials (those of the interactively logged-on User) and can share control of that desktop; in Remote Desktop, when the remote person logs on, the interactively logged-on user (if one exists) is logged out.

Improvements to Remote Assistance in Windows Vista

Windows Vista includes a number of new features and enhancements for Remote Assistance compared to the Remote Assistance available in Windows XP, including:

- Connectivity improvements with transparent NAT traversal using Teredo and IPv6.
- An improved user interface that is easier to launch and use

- A standalone executable (Msra.exe) that accepts command-line arguments and can easily be scripted

- Improved overall performance with a smaller footprint, quicker startup and connect times, and optimized bandwidth usage for screen updates

- Enhanced security with mandatory password and integration with UAC

- New Offer RA via IM scenario and an open API for integration with peer-to-peer applications

- Additional Group Policy settings for improved manageability

Remote Assistance in Windows Vista deprecates the following features that are available on XP:

- No more support for the MAILTO method of solicited Remote Assistance

- No more support for voice sessions

For information on interoperability between the Windows XP and Windows Vista versions of Remote Assistance, see the section titled "Interoperability with Remote Assistance in Windows XP" later in this chapter.

How Remote Assistance Works

In Remote Assistance, the person needing help is referred to as the *User* (or *Novice*), and the support person providing assistance is called the *Helper* (or *Expert*). You launch RA from the Start menu by navigating to All Programs, clicking Maintenance, and then selecting Windows Remote Assistance. You can also launch RA from a command prompt by typing **msra.exe**.

Remote Assistance has two basic modes of operation:

- **Solicited RA**   In *Solicited RA* (also known as *Escalated RA*) the User requests assistance from the Helper by initiating the RA session using e-mail, instant messaging, or by providing the Helper with a saved copy of an invitation file (*.MsRcIncident). Each of these methods uses a different underlying mechanism:

   ❏ **Solicited RA using e-mail**   This method requires that the e-mail clients being used by the User support Simple Mail Application Programming Interface (SMAPI). An example of an e-mail client that supports SMAPI is Windows Mail, which is included with Windows Vista. Other examples of SMAPI-compliant e-mail clients include Microsoft Outlook and other third-party clients. In this approach, the User launches the RA user interface to create an e-mail message that has an RA invitation file (*.MsRcIncident) attached to the message. The User must enter a password for the RA session, which must be communicated to the Helper using an out-of-band (OOB) method such as calling the Helper on the telephone. When the Helper receives the User's RA invitation, she opens the attached ticket, enters the password that was conveyed by the User, and the RA session starts. The Helper must respond to the invitation from the User within a specified time limit (the default is 6 hours), or the invitation will expire and a new one will need to be sent. In a domain environment, this ticket lifetime can also be configured using Group Policy. See the section titled "Managing Remote Assistance Using Group Policy" later in this chapter.

❑ **Solicited RA using file transfer**   This method requires that both the User and Helper have access to a common folder (such as a network share on a file server), or that they use some other method for transferring the file (for example, by using a USB key to manually transfer the file or by uploading the file to an FTP site). The user creates an RA invitation file and saves it in the shared folder. The User must provide a password that must be communicated to the Helper using an out-of-band (OOB) method such as a telephone call. The Helper retrieves the ticket from the shared folder, opens it, enters the password, and the RA session starts. Again, the Helper must respond to the invitation within a specified time, or the invitation will expire and a new one will be needed. (The expiration time is configurable through Group Policy.)

❑ **Solicited RA using Instant Messaging**   This method for soliciting assistance requires that the instant messaging (IM) applications being used by both the User and the Helper support Microsoft's new Rendezvous API. Windows Live Messenger is an example of an IM application that supports Rendezvous. Windows Live Messenger is available as a download. In this approach, the User requests assistance from someone on his buddy list. To ensure that the remote person is really the User's buddy (and not someone masquerading as the buddy), Remote Assistance requires that a password be relayed from the User to the Helper by other means (such as a phone call) before the Helper can connect. For more information on the Rendezvous API, see the Windows SDK on MSDN at *http://msdn2.microsoft.com/en-us/library/aa359213(vs.85).aspx.*

■ **Unsolicited RA**   In *Unsolicited RA* (also known as *Offer RA*), the Helper offers help to the User by initiating the RA session.

❑ **Offer RA using DCOM**   This is a typical corporate Help Desk scenario in which all the users are in a domain. The Helper enters either the fully qualified domain name (FQDN) or IP address of the User's computer to connect to the User's computer. This method requires that the Helper has been previously authorized a domain administrator to be able to offer Remote Assistance to the Users. (For information on how to authorize Helpers for offering RA, see the section titled "Managing Remote Assistance Using Group Policy" later in this chapter.) This method also requires that the Helper either knows the name (the host name on a local subnet; the fully qualified name otherwise) or address (IPv4 or IPv6) of the User's computer.

❏ **Offer RA using Instant Messaging**   This method for soliciting assistance requires that the instant messaging (IM) applications being used by both the User and the Helper support the Rendezvous API. In this approach, the Helper offers assistance to someone on her buddy list. If the buddy agrees, he must enter a password to be used by the Helper. The password must be relayed by an OOB mechanism to ensure that the remote person is really the User's buddy (and not someone masquerading as the buddy). For more information on the Rendezvous API, see the Windows SDK on MSDN at *http://msdn2.microsoft.com/en-us/library/ aa359213(vs.85).aspx.*

How It Works: RA Invitation Files

Remote Assistance invitation files (.MsRcIncident) are XML-formatted file documents that include information used by the Helper's computer that will attempt to connect. This ticket information is encrypted to prevent unauthorized users from accessing the information if e-mail or file transfer is used to send the invitation over an unsecured network.

If the e-mail method is used to send the invitation file to the Helper, the invitation file is sent as an e-mail attachment with a filename of RATicket.MsRcIncident. If the file transfer method is used instead, the invitation file is created by default on the desktop of the User's computer, and the filename of the invitation is Invitation.MsRcIncident.

Remote Assistance Operational States

Remote Assistance has three operational states:

■ **Waiting For Connect**   This state occurs when either:

❏ The Helper has offered RA to the User, but the User has not yet agreed to allow the Helper to connect to his computer.

❏ The User has sent the Helper an invitation but the Helper has not yet responded by opening the invitation, or the Helper has opened the invitation and the User has not yet agreed to allow the Helper to connect to his computer.

In the Waiting For Connect state, the Helper cannot view or control the screen of the User's computer until an RA connection has been established and both computers have entered the Screen Sharing state. After the RA application has been started and is running in the Waiting For Connect state, the application should not be closed until the other party responds and establishes the connection. For example, if the User uses the Solicit RA Using E-mail method and sends an invitation file to a Helper, the RA application opens on the User's computer and waits for the Helper to accept the invitation. If the User closes RA on her computer before the Helper accepts the invitation, the Helper will not be able to connect to the User's computer and the User will need to send a new invitation.

- **Screen Sharing** This state occurs when the User has consented to allow the Helper to connect to his computer—either after the User has sent the Helper an invitation or the Helper has offered RA to the User. In the Screen Sharing state, an RA session has been established and the Helper can view—but not control—the screen of the User's computer.

  When the User is prompted for consent to allow the Helper to connect to his computer, a warning message appears on the User's computer saying that the Helper wants to connect to his computer. This warning message is customizable using Group Policy. See the section titled "Managing Remote Assistance Using Group Policy" later in this chapter for more information.

- **Control Sharing** This state occurs after the Screen Sharing state, when the Helper has requested control of the User's computer and the User has consented to allow the Helper to have shared control of his computer. In the Control Sharing state, the Helper has the same level of access to the User's computer that the User has, and the Helper can use his own mouse and keyboard to remotely perform actions on the User's computer. Specifically:

  - ❑ If the User is a standard user on his computer, the Helper will be able to perform only those actions on the User's computer that can be performed by a standard user on that computer.

  - ❑ If the User is a local administrator on his computer, the Helper will be able to perform any actions on the User's computer that can be performed by a local administrator on that computer.

  For more information on the level of control that a Helper has on a User's computer, see the section titled "Remote Assistance and the Secure Desktop" later in this chapter.

User vs. Helper Functionality

After an RA connection has been established and both computers have entered the Screen Sharing state, the User and Helper are able to perform the tasks listed in Table 23-1.

Table 23-1 Tasks That Can Be Performed by User and Helper During an RA Session

Description of Task	User?	Helper?
Chat	Yes	Yes
Send files	Yes	Yes
Save a log of session activity	Yes (default)	Yes (default)
Configure bandwidth usage	Yes	No
Pause (temporarily hide screen)	Yes	No
Request shared control	No	Yes
Give up shared control	Yes	Yes
Disconnect	Yes	Yes
Disconnect using Esc key	Yes	No

Remote Assistance and NAT Traversal

Remote Assistance works by establishing a peer-to-peer connection between the User's computer and the Helper's computer. One challenge this poses is that it can be difficult to establish peer-to-peer connections if one or both of the computers involved are behind a gateway or router that uses Network Address Translation (NAT). NAT is an IP routing technology described by RFC 1631 that is used to translate IP addresses and TCP/UDP port numbers of packets being forwarded. NAT is typically used to map a set of private IP addresses to a single public IP address (or to multiple public addresses). Home networks using a wireless or wired router also use NAT technology.

To overcome this difficulty, Windows Vista includes built-in support for Teredo, an IPv6 transition technology described in RFC 4380 that provides address assignment and automatic tunneling for unicast IPv6 connectivity across the IPv4 Internet. The NAT traversal capability provided by Teredo in Windows Vista allows RA connectivity when one or both of the users involved in an RA session are hidden behind a NAT. The RA experience is transparent from the perspective of the users involved, regardless of whether or not NAT is being used on either user's network. For most small business and home user environments, RA in Windows Vista will seamlessly traverse a NAT-enabled router with no additional router configuration required. For information on enterprises that need to remotely support users who work from home, see the section titled "Other Possible Remote Assistance Usage Scenarios" later in this chapter.

 Note   Offering RA using DCOM is not usually a Teredo scenario, because enterprise users are behind a corporate firewall and are not separated from each other by NATs.

Remote Assistance will not connect in certain configurations. Specifically:

- Teredo cannot traverse a symmetric NAT. Remote Assistance can connect only across restricted NATs and cone NATs. In most cases, this is not a significant limitation, because the large majority of deployed NATs are either the restricted or cone variety. For more information on NAT traversal support in Windows Vista, see Chapter 29, "Deploying IPv6."

- RA will not work if the NAT-enabled router is configured to block the specific ports used by RA. See the section titled "Remote Assistance and Windows Firewall" later in this chapter for more information.

- Remote Assistance will not work if the user's NAT-enabled router is configured to block all UDP traffic.

 Note   To determine the type of NAT a network is using, open an elevated command prompt and type **netsh interface teredo show state**.

For more information on IPv6 support in Windows Vista, including built-in client support for Teredo and other IPv6 transition technologies, see Chapter 29.

To verify whether your NAT supports Remote Assistance, you can use the Internet Connectivity Evaluation Tool at http://www.microsoft.com/windows/using/tools/igd/default.mspx. If your NAT supports Universal Plug and Play (UPnP), then RA should be able to get a global IPv4 address that allows anyone to connect to you. If your NAT supports Teredo/IPv6 and you are running Vista, then an RA helper that is running Vista (and is Teredo enabled) should be able to connect to you.

Remote Assistance and IP Ports Used

The ports used by a Remote Assistance session depend on whether the session is between two Windows Vista computers or between a Windows Vista computer and a legacy Windows XP computer. Specifically:

- **Windows Vista to Windows Vista RA Session**   Dynamic ports allocated by the system in the range TCP/UDP 49152–65535

- **Windows Vista to XP RA Session**   Port 3389 TCP (local/remote)

In addition, the Offer RA via DCOM scenario uses Port 135 (TCP).

> **Note**   If you are concerned about opening the DCOM port (TCP port 135) on your corporate firewall and want to avoid doing this but still be able to offer RA to remote users, you can do so by using Authenticated IPsec Bypass as described in *http://technet2.microsoft.com/windowsserver/en/library/0e79765c-beb2-4e5e-8a74-ea7d07598f821033.mspx?mfr=true.*

Remote Assistance and Windows Firewall

The Windows Firewall is configured with a group exception for Remote Assistance. This group exception has multiple properties that are grouped together as part of the RA exception. The RA exception properties will change depending on the network location of the computer (private, public, or domain). For example, the default RA exception when the computer is in a public location is stricter than when the computer is in a private location. In a public location (such as an airport), the RA exception is disabled by default and does not open ports for Universal Plug-and-Play (UPnP) and Simple Service Discovery Protocol (SSDP) traffic. In a private network (a home or work network, for example) the RA exception is enabled by default and uPnP and SSDP traffic is permitted.

Table 23-2 summarizes the state of the Remote Assistance firewall inbound exception for each type of network location. The RA exception has outbound properties as well; however, the Windows Firewall is not by default configured to enable outbound properties.

Table 23-2   Default State of Remote Assistance Firewall Inbound Exception for Each Type of Network Location

Network Location	State of RA Exception	Default Properties of the RA Exception
Private (Home or Work)	Enabled by default	■ Msra.exe application exception ■ uPnP enabled for communications with uPnP NATs ■ Edge traversal enabled to support Teredo
Public	Disabled by default—must be enabled by user with Admin credentials	■ Msra.exe application exception ■ Edge traversal enabled to support Teredo
Domain	Disabled by default—typically enabled by Group Policy	■ Msra.exe application exception ■ RAServer.exe (the RA COM server) application exception ■ DCOM Port 135 ■ uPnP enabled for communications with uPnP NATs

In other Windows Firewall profiles, the default configuration of the Remote Assistance exception is as follows:

■ **Private profile**   The RA exception in the Windows Firewall is enabled by default when the computer location is set to Private. It is configured for NAT traversal using Teredo by default so that users in a private networking environment (for example, the home environment) can solicit help from other users who may also be behind NATs. The private profile includes the appropriate exceptions needed to allow communication with uPnP NAT devices. If a uPnP NAT is in this environment, Remote Assistance will attempt to use the uPnP for NAT traversal. Offer RA via DCOM is not configured in this profile.

■ **Public profile**   The RA exception is disabled by default and no inbound RA traffic is permitted. Windows Firewall is configured this way by default to better protect users in a public networking environment (such as a coffee shop or airport terminal). When the RA exception is enabled, NAT traversal using Teredo is enabled. However, traffic to uPnP devices is not enabled, and Offer RA via DCOM is not enabled.

■ **Domain Profile**   The RA exception when the computer is in a domain environment is geared toward the Offer RA scenario. This exception is disabled by default and is typically enabled via Group Policy. Teredo is not enabled in this profile because corporate networks typically have a corporate firewall that blocks Teredo UDP traffic. However, uPnP is enabled so that uPnP NATs can be communicated with.

Remote Assistance and the Secure Desktop

When a User consents to having a Helper share control of her computer during a Remote Assistance session, the User has the option of allowing the Helper to respond to UAC prompts (Figure 23-1). Typically, User Account Control (UAC) prompts appear on the Secure Desktop (which is not remoted), and consequently the Helper cannot see or respond to Secure Desktop prompts. The Secure Desktop mode is the same mode that a user sees when she logs on to her computer or presses the Secure Attention Sequence (SAS) keystroke (Ctrl+Alt+Delete). UAC elevation prompts are displayed on the Secure Desktop instead of the user's normal desktop to protect the user from unknowingly allowing malware to run with elevated privileges on her computer. The user must provide consent to a UAC prompt to return to her normal desktop and continue working. This consent requires either clicking Continue (if the user is a local administrator on her computer) or by entering local administrative credentials (if she is a Standard user on her computer).

Figure 23-1   The User has the option of allowing the Helper to respond to UAC prompts when the RA session is in Control Sharing State.

It is important to understand that the Secure Desktop on the User's computer is not remoted to the Helper's computer. In other words, the Helper can only respond to UAC prompts on the User's computer using the User's own credentials. This means that if the User is a Standard user on her computer and the Helper is a local administrator on the User's computer, the Helper can only have administrative privileges on the User's computer if the User can first supply those credentials.

Enforcing this limitation is essential to ensure the security of Windows Vista desktops. The reason behind this design decision is that if RA was architected to allow the Helper to remotely elevate the User's privileges, the User would be able to terminate the RA session and thus steal local administrative credentials from the Helper.

Remote Assistance Logging

Remote Assistance can generate a session log of RA-associated activity. Session logging is enabled by default and consists of timestamped records that identify RA-related activities on each computer. Session logs only contain information about activities that specifically relate to RA functionality, such as who initiated the session, if consent was given to a request for shared control, and so on.

Session logs do not contain information on actual tasks that the User or Helper performed during a session. For example, if the Helper is given Shared Control privileges, starts an Admin command prompt, and performs steps to reconfigure the TCP/IP configuration on the User's computer during an RA session, the session logs will not contain a record of this action.

Session logs do include any chat activity performed during an RA session. The log generated during a session is also displayed within the chat window so that both the User and the Helper can see what is being logged during the session. Session logs also include any file transfer activity that occurs during the session, and they also record when the session has been paused.

Purpose of RA Session Logging   Session logs for RA are mainly intended for enterprises that are required to maintain records of system and user activity for record-keeping purposes. They are not intended as a way to record every action performed by Help Desk personnel when troubleshooting problems with users' computers. A typical environment in which session logging might be required would be in a banking environment, where a financial institution is required by law to maintain records of who accessed a computer and at what time.

Because the ACLs on these session logs grant the User full control over logs stored on her own computer, by default, session logs are generated on both the User's computer and Helper's computer so that the Helper can archive them and protect them from tampering. The logs created on each side of an RA session are similar but not identical. This is because session logs are generated from the perspective of the computer involved—whether the User's computer or the Helper's computer—and therefore complement each other instead of being identical.

In an enterprise environment, Group Policy can be used to enable or disable session logging. If session logging is not configured using Group Policy, both the User and Helper are free to disable session logging on their own computers. For more information, see the section titled "Managing Remote Assistance Using Group Policy" later in this chapter.

Session Log Path and Naming Convention   Session logs are XML-formatted documents so that they can be easily integrated into other data sets—for example, by importing them into a database managed by Microsoft SQL Server 2005. All session logs are stored under each user's Documents folder within the following path:

Users\user_name\Documents\Remote Assistance Logs

A unique session log file is created for each RA session on the computer. Log files stored within this folder are formatted using XML and are named using the convention *YYYYMMD-DHHMMSS*.xml, where the time format is 24-hour. For example, a session log created at 3:45:20 P.M. on August 13, 2006, would be named 20060813154520.xml.

The XML content of a typical session log looks like this:

```
<?xml version="1.0" ?>
<SESSION>
  <INVITATION_OPENED TIME="3:24 PM" DATE="Wednesday, May 07, 2008" EVENT="A Remote
Assistance invitation has been opened." />
  <INCOMING_IP_ADDRESS TIME="3:26 PM" DATE="Wednesday, May 07, 2008">fe80::2856:e5b0:
fc18:143b%10</INCOMING_IP_ADDRESS>
  <CONNECTION_ESTABLISHED TIME="3:26 PM" DATE="Wednesday, May 07, 2008" EVENT="A Remote
Assistance connection has been established.">jdow</CONNECTION_ESTABLISHED>
  <EXPERT_REQUEST_CONTROL TIME="3:27 PM" DATE="Wednesday, May 07, 2008" EVENT="jdow has
requested to share control of the computer." />
  <EXPERT_GRANTED_CONTROL TIME="3:27 PM" DATE="Wednesday, May 07, 2008" EVENT="jdow has
been granted permission to share control of the computer." />
  <EXPERT_CONTROL_STARTED TIME="3:27 PM" DATE="Wednesday, May 07, 2008" EVENT="jdow is
sharing control of the computer." />
  <EXPERT_CONTROL_ENDED TIME="3:27 PM" DATE="Wednesday, May 07, 2008" EVENT="jdow is
not sharing control of the computer." />
  <CHAT_MESSAGE TIME="3:30 PM" DATE="Wednesday, May 07, 2008">jdow: test</CHAT_MESSAGE>
  <CHAT_MESSAGE TIME="3:30 PM" DATE="Wednesday, May 07, 2008">jchen: ok</CHAT_MESSAGE>
  <CONNECTION_ENDED TIME="3:30 PM" DATE="Wednesday, May 07, 2008" EVENT="The Remote
Assistance connection has ended." />
  <INVITATION_CLOSED TIME="3:30 PM" DATE="Wednesday, May 07, 2008" EVENT="A Remote
Assistance invitation has been closed." />
</SESSION>
```

Using Remote Assistance in the Enterprise

The main Remote Assistance scenario within a corporate networking environment is supporting desktop computers that are on the corporate network and joined to a domain. Users' computers must be configured appropriately before they can be offered RA. This is done via Group Policy, as explained in the section titled "Managing Remote Assistance Using Group Policy" later in this chapter. Additionally, the Remote Assistance exception in the Windows Firewall must be enabled. For more information, see the section titled "Remote Assistance and Windows Firewall" earlier in this chapter.

Because most corporate networks have a perimeter firewall blocking access from outside the internal network, supporting remote users who are connecting from outside the corporate network can be more difficult. However, most enterprises now use virtual private network (VPN) technologies to allow remote users to connect to their corporate networks over the Internet, and this kind of scenario generally poses no problem to RA functionality.

Using Remote Assistance in the Corporate Help Desk Environment

The standard approach to using Remote Assistance in an enterprise environment is for Help Desk personnel to offer Remote Assistance to users who telephone in to request assistance. A typical scenario might be as follows:

1. User Jane Dow (the User) is having problems configuring an application on her computer. She phones Help Desk, explains her problem briefly, and asks for help.

2. A Help Desk person named Jacky Chen (the Helper) asks Jane for the fully qualified name or IP address of her computer. She responds with the information, which she can get from computer properties or by running ipconfig.

3. Jacky starts Remote Assistance on his computer and uses the Offer RA feature to offer help to Jane. This causes a dialog box to appear on Jane's computer, asking her if she would like to allow Jacky to connect to her computer.

4. Jane accepts the offer, and at this point Jane's desktop may temporarily change to conserve network bandwidth used by the Remote Assistance session. The Remote Assistance window that opens on Jane's screen tells her that she is being helped by Jacky.

5. At this point, Jacky can see Jane's screen, but he can't control it. Jane then explains the problem she is having, either by using the Chat feature of Remote Assistance, or more likely over the telephone. Jacky asks Jane to perform a series of steps to correct the problem and watches her screen in his own Remote Assistance window as she does this.

6. If the instructions Jacky provides are too complex or if time is limited, Jacky can ask Jane if he can share control of her computer. If Jane agrees, Jacky clicks the Request Control button at the top of his Remote Assistance window. A dialog box appears on Jane's desktop asking her if she wants to allow Jacky to share control of her desktop. Jane accepts the prompt and also selects the option to allow Jacky to respond to User Account Control (UAC) prompts on Jane's computer.

7. Jacky is now connected to Jane's computer using Jane's credentials, and he can both view her screen and interact with it using his own mouse and keyboard. Jacky then proceeds to perform the steps needed to resolve the problem, either correcting the issue or demonstrating to Jane how to fix the problem if it occurs again in the future. If at any time Jane wants to force Jacky to relinquish control of her computer, she can click the Stop Sharing button or the Disconnect button, or she can press the Panic key (Esc).

> **Note** Offer RA needs preconfiguration of the User's computer via Group Policy. See the section titled "Managing Remote Assistance Using Group Policy" later in this chapter for more information.

Other Possible Remote Assistance Usage Scenarios

Other types of Remote Assistance scenarios are also possible for businesses ranging from large enterprises to Small Office/Home Office (SOHO) environments. Examples of possible usage scenarios include:

- A user who is having a problem with configuring an application on her computer can phone Help Desk for assistance. A support person can then use Offer RA to connect to the user's computer, ask for control of her screen, and show the user how to configure her application. This scenario is the standard one for enterprise Help Desk environments and is described in more detail in the section titled "Using Remote Assistance in the Corporate Help Desk Environment" later in this chapter.

- A user who is having trouble installing a printer sends an RA invitation to Help Desk using Windows Mail. A support person who is monitoring the Help Desk e-mail alias reads the message, opens the attached invitation file, and connects to the user's computer. The support person asks for control of the user's computer and walks him through the steps of installing the printer.

- A user is on the road and is connected to the internal corporate network using a VPN connection over the Internet. The user is having problems configuring Windows Mail on her computer, so she opens Windows Messenger and notices that someone she knows in Corporate Support is currently online. She sends an RA invitation to the support person using Windows Messenger, and that person responds to the invitation, asks for control, and shows the user how to configure Windows Mail.

The preceding list is not intended to be complete—other corporate support scenarios using RA are possible. Generally speaking, however, corporate environments will use Offer RA to provide assistance to users who phone Help Desk when they have problems. Some enterprises may also allow users to submit RA invitations either via e-mail or by saving invitation files to network shares that are monitored by support personnel. Others may use instant messaging applications that support Remote Assistance within the corpnet.

> **Note** Helpers can have multiple RA sessions open simultaneously—one session for each User they are supporting. However, Users can have only one RA session in the Waiting For Connect state. The invitation that was created could be sent to multiple recipients—any of whom may connect. All subsequent connect attempts will be blocked until the first helper disconnects, after which another helper may connect. If the user disconnects the session, the RA application terminates and no further connections will be allowed.

Interoperability with Remote Assistance in Windows XP

Remote Assistance in Windows Vista is backward-compatible with Remote Assistance in Windows XP, with the following limitations:

- Offer RA from Windows Vista to Windows XP is supported, but Offer RA from Windows XP to Windows Vista is not supported. This means that enterprises who want to implement Offer RA as a support solution for their Help Desk departments should ensure that computers used by support personnel who will help users running Windows Vista are themselves running Windows Vista (and not Windows XP).

- NAT traversal using Teredo and IPv6 is supported on Windows Vista to Windows Vista RA only, and not on Windows Vista to Windows XP.

- Voice support for RA in Windows XP is not supported by RA in Windows Vista, and any attempt by a User on an Windows XP computer to use this feature during an RA session with a Helper on a Windows Vista computer will cause a notification message regarding this limitation to appear.

- The MAILTO method of soliciting assistance that is supported by RA in Windows XP is not supported by RA in Windows Vista.

- Windows Messenger (which shipped with Windows XP) does not ship with Windows Vista. Users of RA with Windows Messenger in Windows XP will need to migrate to an IM vendor that supports Windows Vista and Remote Assistance. Windows Live Messenger currently supports Windows XP, Windows Vista, and Remote Assistance.

- Offer RA via Messenger is a new feature in Windows Vista and is not available in Windows XP.

Implementing and Managing Remote Assistance

Remote Assistance is a powerful and flexible feature that can be used in many different ways to support users within large enterprises, medium-sized businesses, and SOHO environments. This section outlines how to initiate Remote Assistance sessions from both the UI and the command line. This section also demonstrates how to use Remote Assistance in an enterprise Help Desk environment involving two common scenarios:

- Helper offers RA to User who has telephoned Help Desk with a problem.

- User creates an RA invitation and saves it on a network share that is monitored by Help Desk personnel.

For information on other scenarios for implementing Remote Assistance, including sending invitations with Windows Mail and Windows Messenger, search for the topic "Remote Assistance" within Windows Help And Support.

Initiating Remote Assistance Sessions

Remote Assistance sessions can be initiated either from the user interface or the command line. A significant usability enhancement, from the perspective of support personnel, is that Offer RA is no longer buried within Help And Support as it is in Windows XP, but instead is easily accessible now from the GUI.

Initiating Remote Assistance From the GUI

Initiating Remote Assistance sessions from the GUI can be done using any of several available methods:

- From the Start menu, click Start, click All Programs, click Maintenance, and then click Windows Remote Assistance. This launches the RA app.

- Click Start, click Help And Support, and then, under the Ask Someone heading, click Windows Remote Assistance.

- Click Start, type **assistance**, and when Windows Remote Assistance appears in the Programs list, click it.

Any of these methods will open the initial Remote Assistance screen, shown in Figure 23-2.

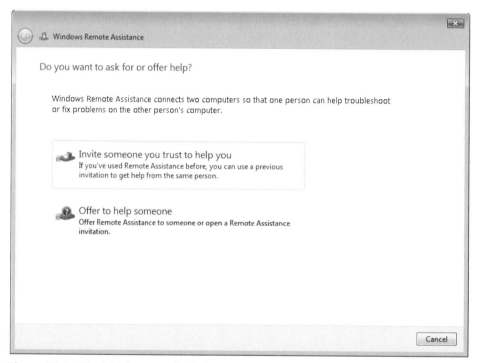

Figure 23-2   The initial screen of Windows Remote Assistance.

Initiating Remote Assistance from the Command Line

Remote Assistance in Windows Vista is implemented as a standalone executable called Msra.exe. You can initiate RA sessions directly from the command line or by using scripts. The syntax and usage for this command is explained in Table 23-3.

Table 23-3   Syntax and Usage for Command-Line Remote Assistance (Msra.exe)

Option	Description
/novice	Launches Remote Assistance as Novice (or User) in Solicited RA mode and presents the user with the choice of either sending an RA ticket using a SMAPI-enabled e-mail application such as Windows Mail or by saving the invitation as a file. After this choice has been made, Windows Remote Assistance opens on the User's computer in the Waiting For Connect state.
/expert	Launches Remote Assistance in the Helper mode and presents the user with the choice of either specifying the location of an RA ticket to open or specifying the User's computer name or address (Offer RA). The computer name can be either a host name (if the User is on the local subnet) or a fully qualified name (DNS name), and the address can be either an IPv4 address or an IPv6 address. Unsolicited RA without an invitation requires preconfiguration of the remote computer being helped.
/offerRA *computer*	Launches Remote Assistance as Helper in Unsolicited (Offer) RA mode and uses DCOM to remotely open Remote Assistance on the User's computer and then connect to the User's computer to initiate an RA session. The User's computer can be specified using either its computer name or address. The computer name can be either a host name (if the User is on the local subnet) or a fully qualified name (DNS name), and the address can be either an IPv4 address or an IPv6 address. This method is demonstrated in more detail in the section titled "Scenario 1: Offering Remote Assistance Using DCOM" later in this chapter.
/email *password*	Launches Remote Assistance as Novice (or User) in Solicited RA mode and creates a password-protected RA ticket that is attached to a new RA invitation message opened by the default SMAPI-enabled e-mail client (which by default is Windows Mail). The password must be six characters or more and must be relayed separately to the Helper. The e-mail client application launches a window with the invitation file attached. The User must enter the e-mail address of the Helper in the To field to send the message to the Helper.
/saveasfile *path* *password*	Launches Remote Assistance as Novice (or User) in Solicited RA mode and creates a password-protected RA ticket that is saved at the path specified. The path may be either a local folder or network share, and the User must have appropriate permissions on the destination folder to create the file. The path must include a filename for the ticket. (The .MsRcIncident file extension will be automatically added to the filename.) The password must be six characters or more. Use of this method is demonstrated in more detail in the section titled "Scenario 2: Soliciting Remote Assistance by Creating RA Tickets and Saving Them on Monitored Network Shares" later in this chapter.
/openfile *path* *password*	Launches Remote Assistance as Helper in Solicited RA mode and opens a previously created RA ticket that was saved within the path specified. The path may be either a local folder or network share, and the Helper must have appropriate permissions on the destination folder to open the file. The path must include the filename of a valid ticket that has the .MsRcIncident file extension. The password must be the same password that was used by the User to secure the ticket when it was created.

Note   There is no support for Windows Managing Instrumentation (WMI) scripting of Msra.exe.

Scenario 1: Offering Remote Assistance Using DCOM

Before you can offer Remote Assistance to other users, your user account must be authorized as a Helper on the User's computer. You can use Group Policy to do this in an enterprise environment. (See the section titled "Managing Remote Assistance Using Group Policy" later in this chapter for information on how to do this.)

After a support person (or group of individuals) has been configured as a Helper for all Windows Vista computers in a domain or OU, the support person can offer RA to users of those computers when they need assistance. For this scenario, let's say that Tony Allen (tallen@contoso.com) is a Windows Vista user who needs assistance with an issue on his computer. Tony telephones the Help Desk department, and the call is taken by Karen Berg (kberg@contoso.com), who asks Tony for the name or IP address of his computer. Tony provides Karen with his fully qualified computer name (TALLEN-PC.contoso.com) or IP address, and Karen then offers assistance to Tony by following these steps:

1. Start Remote Assistance using any of the methods described previously.

2. Click Offer To Help Someone.

3. Enter **TALLEN-PC.contoso.com** in the field labeled Type A Computer Name Or IP Address.

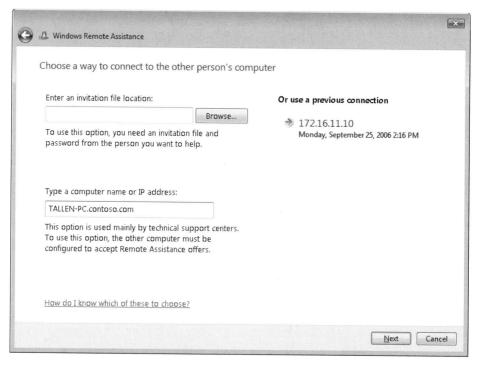

4. Click Next.

At this point, a dialog box will appear on Tony's computer asking if he would like to allow Karen to connect to his computer and view his desktop. Tony has two minutes to respond to this dialog box before the offer times out and the dialog box disappears, which will cause a message saying, "The person you are trying to help isn't responding" to appear on Karen's computer. If the offer to Tony times out, Karen can resubmit the offer by selecting it from the list of previous connections that are displayed in her RA application (Figure 23-3). If Tony accepts the offer (grants consent), the Remote Assistance session begins, and Tony's desktop will be viewable by Karen in a Remote Assistance application window.

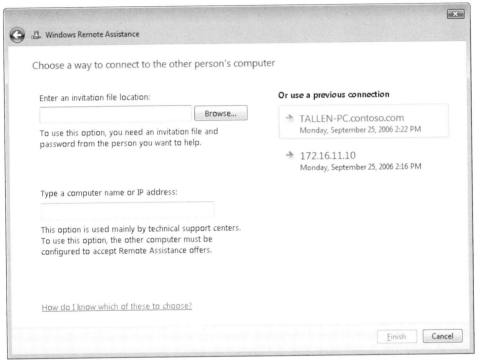

Figure 23-3 Recent RA invitations and offers listed under Or Use A Previous Connection can be reused.

At this point, the desktop properties of Tony's desktop may change (based on configurable settings) to optimize the network bandwidth used by RA for screen updates on Karen's computer. Karen can now request control from Tony, send files to Tony or receive files from him, chat with Tony, or disconnect the session. Tony can send and receive files, chat, or pause or disconnect the session.

Note If you are a User and a Helper has shared control of your computer, you can immediately terminate shared control and return the session to Screen Sharing state by pressing the Panic key (Esc).

Scenario 2: Soliciting Remote Assistance by Creating RA Tickets and Saving Them on Monitored Network Shares

Another way that you can use Remote Assistance in an enterprise environment is by having users create invitation files and save them on a network share that is monitored by Help Desk personnel. This way, when Help Desk determines that a new ticket has been uploaded to the share, a support person can call the user on the telephone to obtain the password for the ticket and then use the ticket to establish an RA session with the user who needs help.

To make the procedure easier, administrators can first deploy a script on users' desktops that uses command-line Remote Assistance (Msra.exe) to create the invitation file and save it on the network share. For example, let's say that users' invitation files should be uploaded to \\FILESRV3.contoso.com\Support\IncomingTickets, a folder in the Support share on the file server named FILESRV3. The following script, named SubmitTicket.vbs, could be deployed on each user's desktop to accomplish this task:

```
dim strPassword
dim strUser
dim strTicketName

strPassword = InputBox("Enter a password for your ticket")
Set WshShell = Wscript.CreateObject("Wscript.Shell")
strUser = WshShell.ExpandEnvironmentStrings("%username%")
strTicketName = strUser & "-" & Year(Now) & "-" & Month(Now) & "-" & Day(Now) & _
    "-" & Hour(Now) & "-" & Minute(Now) & "-" & Second(Now)
strRA = "msra.exe /saveasfile \\FILESRV3\Support\IncomingTickets\" & _
    strTicketName & " " & strPassword
WshShell.Run strRA
```

When the user double-clicks this script to run it, an Input box appears asking the user to provide a password to be used to secure the invitation. After the user supplies a password, a new RA ticket is created and saved in the target folder on the file server. The name of the ticket is unique and consists of the user's name followed by the date and time, such as tallen-YYYY-MM-DD-HH-MM-SS.MsRcIncident. When the support person monitoring the share has obtained the ticket's password using an OOB method such as a telephone call, the support person opens the ticket. After the User grants consent, the RA connection is established.

To monitor the IncomingTickets folder in the network share, Help Desk personnel can use the file-screening capabilities of file servers running Windows Server 2008. To do this, follow these steps to create a passive file screen that monitors the folder and sends an e-mail alert to a Help Desk alias whenever a new ticket is uploaded to the folder:

1. Install or upgrade the File Server role on the Windows Server 2008 computer where the Support folder is located.

2. Start the File Server Resource Manager console from Administrative Tools, right-click the root node, and select Configure Options.

3. Specify the DNS name of the IP address of an SMTP host that can be used to forward alert e-mails generated by the file screen you will create.

4. Click OK to close File Server Resource Manager Options and expand the console tree to select File Screens under File Screening Management.

5. Select the option Create File Screen in the Action pane.

6. Click Browse to select the Incoming folder for the File Screen Path.

7. Select the Define Custom File Screen Properties option and click Custom Properties.

8. Choose the option for Passive Screening so that uploaded tickets will only be monitored and not blocked by the screen.

9. Click Create to create a new file group called RA Tickets and use the Add button to add files of type *MsRcIncident to the group.

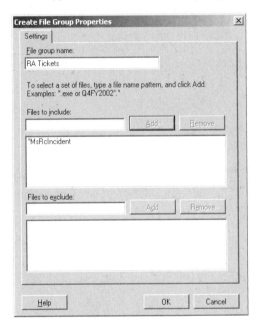

10. Click OK to return to the properties sheet for the new file screen and select the check box for the RA Tickets file group you just created.

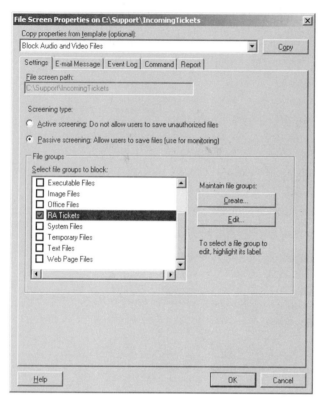

11. Click the E-mail tab and specify a support alias (such as support@contoso.com) that will be notified whenever a new ticket is uploaded to the folder. Configure a suitable subject and body for the message.

12. Click Create to create the new file screen and then choose the option to save the screen without creating a template.

13. Test the new file screen by opening a command prompt on a user's computer and then typing **msra.exe /saveasfile *path password*,** where *path* is the UNC path to the Incoming folder within the Support share on the file server, and *password* is any password of six or more characters that you specify.

For more information on how to implement file screening in Windows Server 2008, see the topic "Screening Files" on the Microsoft Windows Server TechCenter at *http://technet2.microsoft.com/windowsserver2008/en/library/c16070f8-25f6-4d22-8040-5299b08d6eea1033.mspx?mfr=true.*

Managing Remote Assistance Using Group Policy

In an enterprise environment, Remote Assistance can be managed using Group Policy. The policy settings for Remote Assistance are all machine settings and are found in the following policy location:

Computer Configuration\Policies\Administrative Templates\System\Remote Assistance

When these policy settings are written to the registry on targeted computers, they are stored under the following registry key:

HKLM\SOFTWARE\Policies\Microsoft\WindowsNT\Terminal Services

Remote Assistance policy settings are summarized in Table 23-4.

Table 23-4   Group Policy Settings for Remote Assistance

Policy	Description
Solicited Remote Assistance	Enabling this policy allows users of targeted computers to use Solicited RA to request assistance using e-mail, file transfer, or instant messaging. Disabling this policy prevents users from using Solicited RA. The default setting is Not Configured, which allows users to change their Remote Assistance settings using the Remote tab of the System CPL in Control Panel.
	If the policy is Enabled, you can further configure whether Helpers can be prevented from sharing control of the User's computer, the maximum ticket lifetime, and the method used for sending invitations by e-mail. (Windows Vista does not support the MAILTO method—select SMAPI instead if the targeted computers are running Windows Vista.) Ticket lifetime applies only to RA invitations sent by e-mail or file transfer. The default ticket lifetime when Group Policy is not being used is 6 hours.
	If this policy is Enabled, you must also enable the Remote Assistance exception in Windows Firewall to allow Solicited RA to work.
	In an unmanaged environment, this setting can also be configured using the Remote tab of the System CPL in Control Panel.
	This policy is also supported on Windows XP Professional and Windows Server 2003.
Offer Remote Assistance	Enabling this policy allows designated Helpers to use Offer RA to offer assistance to users of targeted computers. Disabling this policy or leaving it Not Configured prevents Offer RA from being used to offer assistance to users of targeted computers.
	If the policy is Enabled, you can further configure whether Helpers can view or control the Users' computers, and you must specify a list of Helpers who are allowed to Offer RA to the users of the targeted computers. Helpers can be either users or groups and must be specified in the form *domain_name\username or domain_name\groupname*.
	If this policy is Enabled, you must also enable the Remote Assistance exception in Windows Firewall to allow Offer RA to work.
	This policy is also supported on Windows XP Professional and Windows Server 2003. See the Explain tab of this policy setting for more details.

Table 23-4   Group Policy Settings for Remote Assistance

Policy	Description
Allow Only Vista Or Later Connections	The default Windows Vista invitation file includes a XP-specific node for backward-compatibility. This node is not encrypted and allows Windows XP computers to connect to the Windows Vista computer that created the ticket. Enabling this policy causes all RA invitations generated by users of targeted computers to *not* include the XP node, thereby providing an additional level of security and privacy. Disabling this policy or leaving it Not Configured leaves information such as IP address and port number unencrypted in RA invitations This policy setting applies only to RA invitations sent using e-mail or file transfer and has no effect on using instant messaging to solicit assistance or on using Offer RA to offer assistance.
	In an unmanaged environment, this setting can also be configured by clicking Advanced from the Remote tab of the System Properties dialog box.
	This policy is supported only on Windows Vista and later platforms.
Customize Warning Messages	Enabling this policy causes a specified warning to be displayed on targeted computers when a Helper wants to enter Screen Sharing State or Control Sharing State during an RA session. Disabling this policy or leaving it Not Configured causes the default warning to be displayed in each instance.
	If the policy is Enabled, you can further specify the warning message to be displayed in each instance.
	This policy is supported only on Windows Vista and later platforms.
Turn On Session Logging	Enabling this policy causes RA session activity to be logged on the targeted computers. For more information, see the section titled "Remote Assistance Logging" earlier in this chapter. Disabling this policy causes RA auditing to be disabled on the targeted computers. The default setting is Not Configured, in which case RA auditing is automatically turned on.
	This policy is supported only on Windows Vista and later platforms.
Turn On Bandwidth Optimization	Enabling this policy causes the specified level of bandwidth optimization to be used to enhance the RA experience over low-bandwidth network connections. Disabling this policy or leaving it Not Configured allows the system defaults to be used.
	If the policy is Enabled, you must specify the level of bandwidth optimization you want to use from the following options:
	■ No Optimization
	■ No Full Window Drag
	■ Turn Off Background
	■ Full Optimization (Use 8-Bit Color)
	If No Optimization is selected, the User's computer will use the Windows Basic theme with full background, and during a shared control session, the Helper will be able to drag full windows across the User's screen. Additional optimization turns off effects to allow a more responsive experience for the Helper.
	This policy is supported only on Windows Vista and later platforms.

Note In Windows XP, members of the Domain Admins group are implicitly granted Helper privileges even if they are not added to the Helpers list of the Offer Remote Assistance policy setting. This is no longer the case in Windows Vista, where the Domain Admins group must now be explicitly added to the Helpers list to grant them Helper privileges for Offer RA.

Configuring Remote Assistance in Unmanaged Environments

Users of unmanaged computers can enable and configure Remote Assistance using the Remote tab of the System CPL in Control Panel (Figure 23-4). Enabling or disabling Remote Assistance and configuring its settings this way requires local administrator credentials on the computer, so a UAC prompt will appear when the user tries to do this.

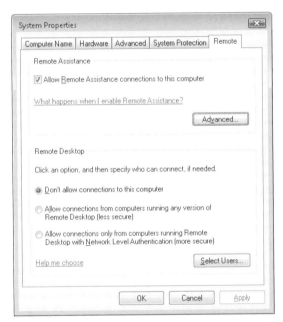

Figure 23-4 Configuring RA from the Remote tab of the System CPL in Control Panel.

Note that settings changes made this way will affect all users on the system. The per-computer registry settings for Remote Assistance are found under the following key:

HKLM\SYSTEM\CurrentControlSet\Control\Remote Assistance

In managed environments, when the following Group Policy setting is Enabled, the Control Panel settings for configuring Remote Assistance become unavailable (appear dimmed):

Computer Configuration\Policies\Administrative Templates\System\Remote Assistance\Solicited Remote Assistance

> **Note**   Group Policy settings always prevail over locally configured settings when they overlap.

Additional Registry Settings for Configuring Remote Assistance

Additional behavior for Remote Assistance can be configured by modifying certain registry settings. Specifically, per-user registry settings for Remote Assistance are found under the following key:

HKCU\Sofware\Microsoft\Remote Assistance

These settings are changeable when in the Waiting To Connect mode or when in the connected mode from the Settings button.

> **Caution**   If Group Policy is used to manage Remote Assistance settings and any configured policy settings overlap these registry settings, the policy settings prevail.

Direct from the Source: Troubleshooting Remote Assistance

The following are some tips for troubleshooting Remote Assistance in Windows Vista:

1. *When I attempt to create an invitation with e-mail or save-to-file, I see a warning message that says that the Windows Firewall is currently blocking Remote Assistance.*

   The Remote Assistance firewall exception will change depending on your network location (Private, Public, or Domain). If you are at home, your network location type should be set to Private, which enables the Remote Assistance firewall exception automatically. If your network location is set to Public, the Remote Assistance firewall exception is not enabled automatically for security purposes. It will need to be enabled by an administrator.

   If you are connected to a managed network (for example, when you are within a corporate domain), the network location is categorized as Domain, and the Remote Assistance exception is not enabled automatically. It is expected to be configured by Group Policy by your system administrator.

2. *I cannot use RA to connect from my home computer to a work computer.*

   RA uses Teredo (IPv6) to traverse NATs. However, Teredo cannot be used to traverse corporate edge firewalls that provide NAT for intranet clients and block dynamic ports or outbound UDP traffic. Because you do not have a globally reachable IPv4 address within the corpnet, RA cannot make a connection to you from outside the corpnet.

3. *If I disable the Windows Firewall, I cannot make an RA connection in certain cases. This is counterintuitive, because I expect connectivity to be less restrictive with the firewall disabled.*

    In Windows Vista, the Windows Firewall is IPv6-aware. The RA exception in the Windows Firewall enables Teredo for edge traversal. If the Windows Firewall is disabled, the ability to use Teredo for NAT traversal is also disabled. The Windows Firewall must be running with the RA exception enabled for RA to be able to traverse NATs using Teredo.

4. *I cannot use RA to connect from my work to my home computer.*

    Your corporate firewall may be configured to block outbound peer-to-peer connections. In a managed environment (domain-joined computers), which is typically found in a corporate network, the RA exception does not enable Teredo (edge traversal), because corporate firewalls typically block outbound UDP traffic. NAT traversal using Teredo is disabled by default in this scenario. If the person you are trying to help is behind a UPnP NAT or is connected directly to the Internet, you should be able to make a connection. Check with your network administrator to see whether outbound peer-to-peer connections through the corporate firewall can be enabled.

5. *When I move my laptop (or change my home network location) from a Private to Public location, I am not able to connect to certain computers.*

    If you have a laptop that moves between work and home, the properties of the RA firewall exception in the Windows Firewall will change depending on whether your network location is classified as Private, Public, or Domain. In a Private location, the RA exception is enabled by default, and if you are using a UPnP NAT, the RA exception will allow communications with the UPnP NAT to enable RA connections that make use of UPnP. In a Public network, the RA exception is not enabled by default and will need to be enabled using Administrator credentials. In addition, the default Public profile does not permit UPnP communication for security purposes, thereby restricting RA connectivity in certain cases.

6. *I am on a low-bandwidth connection, and the person helping me is experiencing slow screen refreshes.*

    Under Settings, set the Bandwidth Usage to Low to reduce the bandwidth used during a Remote Assistance connection. Keep in mind that display quality decreases as bandwidth usage is limited.

7. *Why can't I connect to Windows XP computers that are behind a NAT as easily as I can connect to Windows Vista computers?*

    RA in Windows XP does not support Teredo for NAT traversal. Consequently, a Windows Vista–to–Windows XP RA connection attempt may fail in cases where both computers are behind non-UPnP NATs.

8. *How does RA make a connection?*

When the RA invitation is created, the User's computer will set itself as a listener on all of its IP addresses (IPv4 and IPv6), including its Teredo address. All these listeners are waiting for a connection from the Helper's computer. The address and port information associated with these different listeners is relayed to the Helper's computer via the RA invitation (which gets transported by Messenger when Messenger is used to launch RA). The Helper's computer then tries to connect concurrently on all the address/port pairs in the invitation. The first successful connection that is made is used for the RA session and the rest of the connection attempts are terminated.

9. *How do I troubleshoot a connection failure between two home-based Windows Vista computers that are behind NATs?*

Refer to the RA Connectivity information in Tables 23-5 and 23-6 to verify that the network configuration you have is supported for RA connectivity. Then do the following:

❑ Confirm that the Windows Firewall on the computer of the person that is being helped is running and configured for RA:

- The Windows Firewall is IPv6 compatible and must be running to enable NAT traversal using Teredo.

- The network location of the computer must set to Private or Public, since Teredo is not enabled in Domain or Managed settings.

- The Remote Assistance exception in the firewall must be enabled to allow RA connections.

❑ Check that there is no edge firewall between User and Helper, since it may block peer-to-peer applications like RA.

❑ Confirm that the User and Helper are not behind a symmetric NAT and that Teredo is able to get to the Qualified state on both computers. To determine this, do the following:

1. First, initiate Teredo by forcing RA into the Waiting To Connect state. You can do this by typing **msra.exe /saveasfile myinvitation mypassword** at a command prompt.

2. Then, check to see if Teredo can be activated on both computers and goes into the Qualified state. Open an elevated command prompt window and type **netsh interface teredo show state** at the command prompt. The output should show Teredo in the Qualified state. If Teredo does not go to the Qualified state on both computers, an RA connection may not be possible between these two computers. Teredo

will not go into the qualified state if one of the following two conditions exists:

- ○ A global Teredo server could not be reached at teredo.ipv6.microsoft.com.

- ○ The computer is behind a symmetric NAT. To verify this, look at the output of netsh interface teredo show state and check the output on the NAT: line, which specifies NAT type.

10. *When I am helping someone who is a Standard user, I cannot run a program that needs Administrator privileges even though I have Administrator privileges to the User's computer.*

RA allows a User to share control of his computer with a remote Helper. If the User is a Standard user, the remote Helper is given the same privileges as the Standard user. If the Helper attempts to launch a program that requires Administrator credentials, by default these credentials must be entered locally (on the Secure Desktop) by the User and cannot be entered remotely by Helper. This is required to prevent a security loophole where Admin programs launched by a remote Helper could be hijacked by the local User simply by terminating the RA session. In managed environments where client computers are running Windows Vista Service Pack 1 or later, however, a new Group Policy setting can be enabled that allows RA to turn off the Secure Desktop during an RA session even if the User is a Standard user. As a result, the remote Helper can now enter administrator credentials when a UAC prompt appears during an RA session to perform Admin-level tasks on the User's computer. To configure this behavior, enable the following policy setting:

Computer Configuration\Policies\Windows Settings\Security Settings\Local Policies\ Security Options\User Account Control: Allow UIAccess Applications To Prompt For Elevation Without Using The Secure Desktop

Table 23-5   RA Connectivity for Expert on Windows XP

		Expert on XP			
		Directly Connected	Behind UPnP NAT	Behind non-UPnP NAT	Behind Corporate Edge Firewall[**]
Novice (User) on XP	Directly Connected	Yes	Yes	Yes	Yes
	Behind UPnP NAT	Yes	Yes	Yes	Yes
	Behind non-UPnP NAT	Yes, using Msgr Only	Yes, using Msgr Only	No	No
	Behind Corporate Edge Firewall[**]	Yes, using Msgr Only	Yes, using Msgr Only	No	Yes, if both are behind same firewall No, if both are behind different firewalls
Novice (User) on Vista	Directly Connected	Yes	Yes	Yes	Yes
	Behind UPnP NAT	Yes	Yes	Yes	Yes
	Behind non-UPnP NAT	Yes, using Msgr Only	Yes, using Msgr Only	No	No
	Behind Corporate Edge Firewall[**]	Yes, using Msgr Only	Yes, using Msgr Only	No	Yes, if both are behind same firewall No, if both are behind different firewalls

Table 23-6   RA Connectivity for Expert on Windows Vista

		Expert on Windows Vista			
		Directly Connected	Behind UPnP NAT	Behind non-UPnP NAT	Behind Corporate Edge Firewall**
Novice (User) on XP	Directly Connected	Yes	Yes	Yes	Yes
	Behind UPnP NAT	Yes	Yes	Yes	Yes
	Behind non-UPnP NAT	Yes, using Msgr Only	Yes, using Msgr Only	No	No
	Behind Corporate Edge Firewall**	Yes, using Msgr Only	Yes, using Msgr Only	No	Yes, if both are behind same firewall No, if both are behind different firewalls
Novice (User) on Vista	Directly Connected	Yes	Yes	Yes	Yes
	Behind UPnP NAT	Yes	Yes	Yes	Yes
	Behind non-UPnP NAT	Yes, using Teredo*	Yes, using Teredo*	Yes, using Teredo*	None
	Behind Corporate Edge Firewall**	No	No	No	Yes, if both are behind same firewall No, if both are behind different firewalls

*Teredo connectivity is not available if both computers are behind Symmetric NATs.

**Edge Firewall must permit outbound connection (e.g., using the Microsoft ISA Firewall Client).

John Thekkethala, Program Manager

Remote Assistance and the Remote Assistance Team at Microsoft

Summary

Remote Assistance has been enhanced in Windows Vista to provide better performance, improved usability, NAT-traversal flexibility, and increased security. Best practices for implementing Remote Assistance in an enterprise environment include:

- Use Group Policy to enable users of targeted computers in a domain or OU to receive offers of RA from Help Desk personnel.

- Use Group Policy to enable the RA exception in the Windows Firewall.

- Use Group Policy to deploy scripts to enable users to run the Msra.exe executable if you want to customize how they launch RA sessions—for example, to upload an invitation to a network share monitored by support personnel.

- If all of your support computers are running Windows Vista, use Group Policy to encrypt RA tickets to hide sensitive information such as users' IP addresses and computer names.

- If corporate policy requires RA records for auditing purposes, use Group Policy to enable RA logging on your company's desktop computers and run scripts to periodically move both Helper and User RA logs to a safe storage.

- To meet corporate privacy and security requirements, use Group Policy to customize the text message that users see before they allow the Helper to view their screens or share control.

Additional Resources

The following resources contain additional information and tools related to this chapter.

Related Information

- Remote Assistance FAQ from Windows Vista Help And Support can be found at *http://windowshelp.microsoft.com/Windows/en-US/help/398b5eda-aa7f-4078-94c5-1519b697bfa01033.mspx*.

- "Remote Assistance and Resulting Internet Communication in Windows Vista" at *http://technet2.microsoft.com/WindowsVista/en/library/cdfa2f21-56e5-44da-aa5a-f22987be13511033.mspx?mfr=true*.

- KB 937803, "During a Remote Assistance session in Windows Vista, the administrator who is trying to provide remote assistance receives a black screen," at *http://support.microsoft.com/kb/937803*.

- Remote Assistance Rendezvous API reference from the Windows SDK can be found at *http://msdn2.microsoft.com/en-us/library/aa359213(vs.85).aspx*.

Chapter 24
Managing Software Updates

Microsoft strives to make Windows Vista as secure and reliable as possible the day it is initially released. However, networked software will always require regular updates, because security threats on networks change constantly. To minimize the risk of new security threats, you need to regularly update Windows Vista using updates provided by Microsoft.

This chapter discusses new features added to Windows Vista that relate to software updates and describes how they will improve the efficiency of delivering updates in your organization. This chapter also explains the three primary ways to distribute Microsoft updates: the Windows Update client, Windows Server Update Services (WSUS), and Systems Management Server (SMS). A detailed description of Background Intelligent Transfer Service (BITS) 3.0 and how you can manage BITS is also provided in this chapter.

Because you can use Group Policy settings to manage the Windows Vista Windows Update client, this chapter describes useful Group Policy settings. Organizations that use proxy servers might require an additional configuration step to allow the Windows Update client to work properly, and this chapter describes how to perform that configuration. To verify that updates are being deployed correctly, you can use auditing tools such as Microsoft Baseline Security Analyzer (MBSA) and SMS.

Occasionally you may experience a problem with a Windows Vista client that fails to update properly. This chapter also provides troubleshooting information to allow you to diagnose and resolve the problem. Finally, the chapter provides a conceptual overview of the planning the software update process and a description of Microsoft's approach to updates.

Update Improvements to Windows Vista

Windows Vista includes several improved update capabilities when compared to Windows XP. Windows Update is now a standalone application that can download updates either directly from Microsoft or from an internal Windows Server Update Services (WSUS) server, as shown in Figure 24-1. Because Windows Update provides a single interface to updates downloaded either from Microsoft or from an internal server, users do not have to learn how to use two separate tools. Windows Update can also allow users to browse beta updates if you configure it to do so.

Figure 24-1   Windows Update is now a standalone application.

Windows Update also includes improvements to simplify deploying a new computer and for installing noncritical updates. First, Windows Update will by default connect immediately to an update server the first time Windows Vista connects to a network. This enables updates to be installed sooner, reducing the time period the new computer is without updates. Windows Update will automatically install drivers for devices that are using generic drivers or that do not have any driver installed. Additionally, you can configure Windows Update to automatically install recommended updates as well as critical updates.

Windows Update also includes improvements to simplify installation of updates. Now non-administrators can approve update installations without providing administrative credentials. Windows Update can also wake a computer from standby to install updates, so users no longer need to leave their computers running to enable updates to be installed overnight.

Windows Vista includes Background Intelligent Transfer Service (BITS) 3.0. BITS 3.0 includes several improvements over BITS 2.0 and 2.5. As of this writing, BITS 2.0 is available for download for Windows XP and earlier operating systems, and BITS 2.5 is under development, with future availability planned for Windows XP and Windows Server 2003. Compared to BITS 2.5, BITS 3.0 offers the following benefits:

■ Improves the efficiency of update downloads by allowing multiple Windows Vista computers on an intranet to share downloaded files. Windows Update can use this capability to allow a single Windows Vista computer to download updates from Microsoft and then share the updates across the local network, as shown in Figure 24-2. To safeguard against the transfer of malicious files, Microsoft signs all updates, and the Windows Update client will not install unsigned updates.

> **Note**   Although BITS 3.0 does contain the ability to share files among peers on the local network, this capability is disabled by default. Windows Update will not take advantage of the capability unless you have enabled the Allow BITS Peer-caching Group Policy setting and are connected to a Windows Server Update Services (WSUS) 3.0 infrastructure.

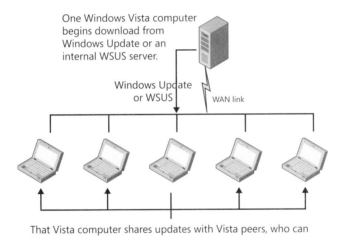

Figure 24-2   Peer-caching reduces Internet or wide area network (WAN) bandwidth usage.

■ Notifies users when a file is downloaded and provides them the option of installing it.

■ Calculates available bandwidth more accurately by communicating with routers using Internet gateway device counters (IGD, also known as IGDDC). This feature is typically useful only on home networks.

■ Allows downloads to be paused and restarted.

For more information, see the section titled "Managing BITS" later in this chapter.

Methods for Deploying Updates

To meet the needs of various types of organizations, Microsoft provides several different methods for applying updates. For home users and small businesses, Windows Vista is configured to automatically retrieve updates directly from Microsoft. The preferred method for deploying updates in medium and many large organizations is Windows Server Update Services (WSUS), which provides better control and performance. Finally, enterprises that use Microsoft Systems Management Server (SMS) can use SMS to deploy and manage updates.

Table 24-1 lists the advantages and disadvantages of each of the update distribution methods and the network size for which the method is effective. The sections that follow describe each of these methods in more detail.

Table 24-1   Comparison of Automated Update Distribution Methods

Update Distribution Method	Network Size	Advantages	Disadvantages
Windows Update client connecting directly to Microsoft	50 or fewer computers	Does not require that any infrastructure be deployed.	Does not allow administrators to centrally test or approve updates or manage installation errors. Wastes Internet bandwidth by downloading updates directly to each computer.
Windows Server Update Services	Any number of computers	Allows administrators to test, approve, and schedule updates. Reduces Internet bandwidth usage.	Requires an infrastructure server.
Systems Management Server	Any number of computers	Provides highly customizable, centralized control over update deployment, with the ability to audit and inventory client systems. Can be used to distribute other types of software. Supports Windows NT 4.0 and Windows 98.	Requires infrastructure servers and additional software licenses.

Windows Update Client

Whether a client computer is configured to retrieve updates directly from Microsoft or from a WSUS server on your intranet, the same client downloads and installs the updates: Windows Update. Windows Update can automatically notify users of critical updates and security updates available either at Microsoft or at a specified WSUS server.

The Windows Update client (implemented as both a service and a Control Panel application) in Windows Vista replaces the Automatic Updates client available in Windows 2000 Service Pack 3, Windows XP Home Edition, Windows XP Professional, and Windows Server 2003. Both Windows Update in Windows Vista and Automatic Updates in previous platforms are proactive "pull" services that allow for automatic detection, notification, download, and installation of important updates. Both clients will even reboot a computer at a scheduled time to ensure that updates take effect as soon as possible.

The Windows Update client provides for a great deal of control over its behavior. You can configure individual computers by using the Control Panel\Security\Windows Update\Change Settings page. Networks that use Active Directory can specify the configuration of each Windows Update client by using Group Policy. In non–Active Directory environments, you also can configure computers by changing local Group Policy settings or by the configuration of a set of registry values.

Systems administrators can configure Windows Update to automatically download updates and schedule their installation for a specified time. If the computer is turned off at that time, the updates can be installed as soon as the computer is turned on. Alternatively, Windows Update can wake a computer from standby and install the update at the specified time, if the computer hardware supports it. This will not work if a computer is shut down, however. Downloading updates will not affect a user's network performance, either, because the Windows Update agent downloads the updates by using BITS.

If complete automation is not acceptable, you can also give users control over when updates are downloaded and installed. The Windows Update client can be configured by using Group Policy to only notify the user that updates are available. The updates are not downloaded or applied until the user clicks the notification balloon and selects the desired updates. For more information, see the section titled "Windows Update Group Policy Settings" later in this chapter.

After the Windows Update client downloads updates, the client checks the digital signature and the Secure Hash Algorithm (SHA1) hash on the updates to verify that they have not been modified.

If Windows Update is configured to automatically download or check for updates, and Windows Server Update Services (WSUS), Systems Management Server (SMS), or Systems Center Configuration Manager 2007 (Configuration Manager 2007) are not being used to manage updates, the Windows Update client will always automatically update itself. This ensures that the Windows Update client will continue to function correctly.

Windows Server Update Services

Windows Server Update Services (WSUS) is a version of the Microsoft Update service that you can host on your private network. WSUS connects to the Windows Update site, downloads information about available updates, and adds them to a list of updates that require administrative approval.

After an administrator has approved and prioritized these updates, WSUS automatically makes them available to any computer running Windows Update (or the Automatic Updates client on earlier versions of Windows). Windows Update (when properly configured) then checks the WSUS server and automatically downloads and installs updates as configured by the administrators. As shown in Figure 24-3, WSUS can be distributed across multiple servers and locations to scale to enterprise needs. WSUS meets the needs of medium-sized organizations and many enterprises.

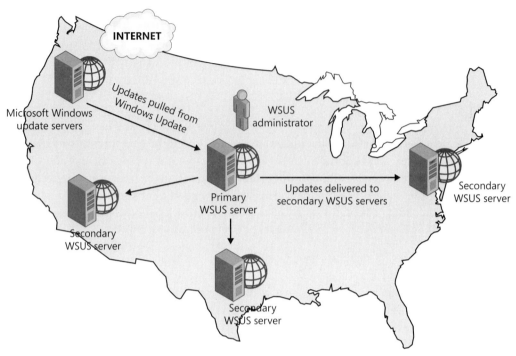

Figure 24-3   WSUS can scale for enterprises.

WSUS requires at least one infrastructure server: a Windows 2000 Server computer with Service Pack 3 or a Windows Server 2003 computer with Internet Information Services (IIS) installed. As shown in Figure 24-4, WSUS is managed using a web browser.

Figure 24-4   WSUS is managed using a web browser.

> **Important**   To deploy updates to Windows Vista computers, you must have WSUS Service Pack 1 or later.

The WSUS interface enables administrators to perform the following administrative tasks:

- Synchronize the WSUS server by downloading a list of updates from Microsoft

- Approve updates for distribution to client computers

- View a list of computers that successfully installed updates or experienced problems installing updates and drill down to determine exactly which updates have been installed

> **Note**   For more information about update management with WSUS and to download WSUS, visit *http://technet.microsoft.com/en-us/wsus/default.aspx*.

Systems Management Server

Microsoft Systems Management Server (SMS) 2003 is the most powerful and efficient way to distribute, manage, and inventory updates and applications in an organization. Whereas a combination of WSUS and MBSA are sufficient to meet the needs of medium-sized organizations, SMS is designed for enterprise organizations managing hundreds to thousands of computers. SMS does not replace WSUS and MBSA, but rather builds on those tools to improve manageability.

Most useful to the task of managing software updates is the ability of SMS to streamline the software update process using the SMS Distribute Software Updates Wizard. The Patch Distribution Wizard walks administrators through the end-to-end update deployment process, including identifying vulnerabilities to be addressed, downloading the updates from the Microsoft website, determining the systems that need to be updated, and reliably deploying the updates. SMS 2003 also provides the ability to install updates during selected service windows and to control reboots, minimizing disruption to end users. Comprehensive reporting allows you to track exactly which computers have been updated and which still require updates.

SMS 2003 R2 provides the following key update-related capabilities:

- Inventory tool for custom updates
  - ❑ Enables you to distribute custom updates (for example, for custom applications or other non-Microsoft applications) to computers in your organization using the same mechanism you use to distribute Microsoft updates
  - ❑ Provides a scanner for evaluating target clients for software update compliance

- Scan tool for vulnerability assessment

  - ❑ Uses the MBSA 2.0 engine to provide vulnerability assessment reporting

  - ❑ Provides MBSA capabilities integrated into SMS

Note   For more information about SMS, visit the SMS website at *http://www.microsoft.com/smserver/default.mspx*. For information about using SMS for update management, refer to "Patch Management Using Systems Management Server 2003" at *http://www.microsoft.com/technet/itsolutions/cits/mo/swdist/pmsms/2003/pmsms031.mspx*.

Systems Center Configuration Manager 2007

Microsoft Systems Center Configuration Manager 2007 (Configuration Manager 2007) is an updated version of SMS 2003. Like SMS 2003, Configuration Manager 2007 is primarily intended for enterprises to more efficiently manage their network infrastructure, including distributing software updates.

Configuration Manager 2007's software update distribution mechanism is based on WSUS. However, Configuration Manager 2007 also supports:

- Custom software update catalogs that you can use to distribute updates for third-party and custom applications.

- Wake-on-LAN capability to start and update computers outside of normal business hours.

- Internet-based update distribution for clients that are disconnected from the internal network.

- Integration with Network Access Protection (NAP) to require client computers to apply updates before connecting to the internal network.

- Flexible reporting to simplify analyzing update distribution in your organization.

Note   For more information about Configuration Manager 2007, visit the Configuration Manager 2007 website at *http://www.microsoft.com/sccm*. For information about using Configuration Manager 2007 for update management, refer to Software Updates In Configuration Manager at *http://technet.microsoft.com/en-us/library/bb680701.aspx*.

Manually Installing, Scripting, and Removing Updates

Most updates in your organization should be installed using WSUS or SMS. However, at times you may need to manually install, script, or remove updates. This section provides an overview of Windows Update files and describes how to work with updates.

Overview of Windows Vista Update Files

Windows Vista uses a new file type for installing updates: MSU files. MSU files are Microsoft Update Standalone Packages. MSU files are not executable files, as updates for earlier versions of Windows are. However, they function quite similarly to executable files, because you can double-click them to install an update.

 Security Alert   For security purposes, MSU files should be treated as executable files. Therefore, if you block executable files as e-mail attachments, you should also block MSU files.

MSU filenames have the following format:

<WindowsVersion>-KB<ArticleNumber>-[v<VersionNumber>-]<Platform>-<LanguageName>.MSU

The version number is listed only if an update is re-released with a version number higher than 1. For example, version 1 of a 32-bit Windows Vista update could be named Windows6.0-KB921590-x86-ENU.MSU. The 64-bit version of the same release of that update would be named Windows6.0-KB921590-v2-x64-ENU.MSU. The following section describes each of these placeholders:

- **WindowsVersion**   The version of Windows to which the update applies. For Windows Vista, this is Windows6.0. For Windows XP, this is WindowsXP.

- **ArticleNumber**   The Microsoft Knowledge Base article number that describes the update. You can look up the article at *http://support.microsoft.com/kb/<ArticleNumber>*. For example, if the update filename is Windows6.0-KB921591-v1-x86-ENU.MSU, you could look up the supporting Knowledge Base article at *http://support.microsoft.com/kb/921591*.

- **VersionNumber**   Occasionally, Microsoft may release multiple versions of an update. Typically, the version number will be 1.

- **Platform**   This value will be x86 for 32-bit operating systems, x64 for 64-bit versions of Windows, and ia64 for Itanium-based computers.

- **LanguageName**   The three-digit Windows language name for the version of the operating system that the update applies to. This could be ENU for U.S. English, DEU for German, ESP for Spanish, or dozens of other codes.

Standardized naming for updates simplifies update processing by allowing you to evaluate updates from a script using only the filename.

How to Script Update Installations

Windows Vista opens MSU files with the Windows Update Standalone Installer (Wusa.exe). To install an update from a script, run the script with administrative privileges, call Wusa, and provide the path to the MSU file. For example, you can install an update named Windows6.0-KB921590-v1-x86-ENU.MSU in the current directory by running the following command:

```
wusa Windows6.0-KB921590-v1-x86-ENU.MSU
```

Additionally, Wusa supports the following standard command-line options:

- **/?, /h, or /help**   Displays the command-line options.

- **/quiet**   Quiet mode. This is the same as unattended mode, but no status or error messages are displayed. Use quiet mode when installing an update as part of a script.

- **/norestart**   Does not restart when installation has completed. Use this parameter when installing multiple updates simultaneously. All but the last update installed should have the /**norestart** parameter.

Scripting is not usually the best way to install updates on an ongoing basis. Instead, you should use Automatic Updates, WSUS, or SMS. However, you might create a script to install updates on new computers, or to install updates on computers that cannot participate in your standard update distribution method.

How to Remove Updates

Some updates can cause application compatibility problems. Although this is rare, if you suspect that an update has caused a problem, you can remove the update to alleviate the problem. Then you should work with Microsoft and any other software vendors to resolve the problem so that you can install the update.

Security Alert   Before you remove an update, view the update's Knowledge Base article to determine if you can use a different countermeasure to remove the vulnerability that the update resolves. For example, you might be able to reduce the vulnerability by properly configuring your firewall. This will reduce the risk of being compromised while you work to resolve the problem with an update.

You can remove an update in two different ways:

- **WSUS**   You can remove some updates with WSUS, but many updates do not support being removed. To remove an update for a group of computers or all computers with WUSA, follow these steps:

  1. View the WUSA Updates page.

  2. Select the update and then click Change Approval under Update Tasks.

  3. Click the Approval list and then click Remove.

  4. Click OK.

■ **Add/Remove Programs** Manually uninstall an update from a client computer by following these steps:

1. Open Control Panel.

2. Click Uninstall A Program under Programs.

3. Click View Installed Updates under Tasks.

4. Click an update and then click Uninstall.

Note that removing an update from a single computer in a networked environment can temporarily alleviate problems caused by the update. However, depending on the distribution mechanism used to install the update, it may be automatically reinstalled. Additionally, when you intentionally remove an update, you should inform personnel responsible for auditing software updates that the missing update is intentional and that you have taken other measures to protect against the security vulnerability (if applicable).

Deploying Updates to New Computers

Microsoft will undoubtedly continue to release important updates for Windows Vista. When you deploy a new computer, it might not have those updates installed. Therefore, the new computer could have known, but unprotected, vulnerabilities.

Direct from the Source: How Windows Update Behaves on New Computers

Windows Vista will not wait for the scheduled time to install the first batches of applicable updates; they will be downloaded and installed, and the user will be prompted to reboot if necessary.

Also, the WSUS administrator can deploy the most critical updates with a deadline. Thus, new computers connecting to that WSUS server will immediately download and install those very critical updates and force the immediate reboot to make sure the computer is secure.

Gary Henderson, Lead Program Manager

Windows Update Agent

To minimize the risk of attack against computers that haven't been updated, you can use the following techniques:

■ **Integrate updates into the Windows Vista setup files** You can integrate service packs and other updates, including non-Microsoft updates, by installing Windows Vista and all updates on a lab computer and then using Windows PE and the XImage tool to create an operating system image (a .wim file) that you can deploy to new computers.

> **Note**   For more information about Windows PE and XImage, see Chapter 3, "Deployment Platform," and Chapter 6, "Developing Disk Images."

- **Include update files with your Windows Vista distribution and install them automatically during setup**   If you cannot integrate updates into setup files, you should automate their installation after setup. You have several ways to run additional commands during installation:

  - Use the Windows System Image Manager to add a RunSynchronous command to an Unattend.xml answer file. RunSynchronous commands are available in the Microsoft-Windows-Setup and the Microsoft-Windows-Deployment components.

> **Note**   For more information about System Image Manager, see Chapter 3 and Chapter 6.

  - Edit the %WinDir%\Setup\Scripts\SetupComplete.cmd file. This file runs after Windows Setup completes and any commands in this file are executed. Commands in the Setupcomplete.cmd file are executed with local system privilege. You cannot reboot the system and resume running SetupComplete.cmd; therefore, you must install all updates in a single pass.

- **Deploy updates to client computers using removable media**   If you cannot integrate updates into setup files, you should install them immediately after setup is complete. To minimize the risk of network attacks, set up Windows Vista computers without connecting them to a network. Then install all updates from removable media. When the computer has all critical updates, you can attach it to the network without unnecessary risk. The disadvantage to this technique is that it requires administrators to physically insert the removable media in each new computer.

- **Deploy updates to client computers across the network**   As a more efficient alternative to installing updates from removable media, you can install updates across the network. However, connecting computers to a network exposes them to a risk of attack across that network. Even if the network is internal, other computers on your internal network might have malicious software, such as worms, that can launch attacks. Often, malicious software is extremely efficient at contacting new computers and can infect an unprotected computer within a few seconds after you connect it to a network. Therefore, you cannot necessarily update a networked computer fast enough to protect it. If you install updates for new computers across the network, create a private, nonrouted network for updates; keep the number of computers on the network extremely limited; and audit the computers regularly to ensure that they do not contain malicious software. This type of network is illustrated in Figure 24-5.

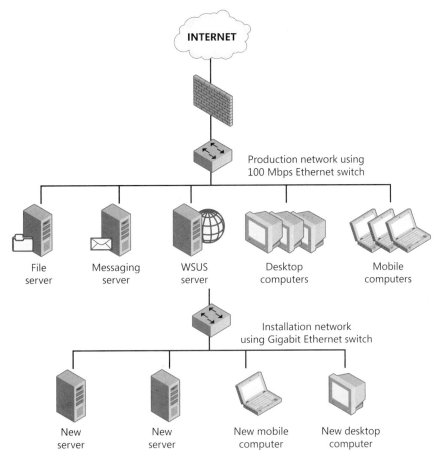

Figure 24-5   Create a separate subnet to protect new computers before installing updates.

Other Reasons to Use a Private Network for New Computers

Creating a separate network segment for installing new computers has benefits in addition to improved security. Installing an operating system across a network is extremely bandwidth-intensive, and, depending on your network configuration, the bandwidth consumed while installing a computer can negatively impact the network performance of other computers on the network. Additionally, you can significantly reduce the time required to install a new computer by using a higher-speed network for installations. For example, if your production network segment is 100 Mbps Ethernet, and you can't justify the cost of upgrading all computers to gigabit Ethernet, you might be able to justify the cost of a small gigabit Ethernet network switch and gigabit network interface cards, to be used only during the installation process.

> **Note**   For more information about designing setup architectures, see Chapter 3.

Managing BITS

Windows Vista includes Background Intelligent Transfer Service (BITS) 3.0. BITS is a file-transfer service designed to transfer files across the Internet using only idle network bandwidth. Unlike standard HTTP, FTP, or shared-folders file transfers, BITS does not use all available bandwidth, so you can use BITS to download large files without impacting other network applications. BITS transfers are also very reliable, and can continue when users change network connections or restart their computers.

BITS Network Protocol

BITS uses HTTP to transfer files the same way a web browser does. However, unlike standard HTTP transfers, BITS transfer speed is carefully throttled. Using the HTTP protocol enables BITS to work through proxy servers, to authenticate both clients and servers, and to provide encryption using SSL certificates. If you want to explicitly allow or block BITS transfers at your firewall, create filters for the HTTP or HTTPS protocol and the source or destination networks. For example, you could limit HTTP communications so that Windows Vista clients could connect only to your WSUS server.

How It Works: BITS File Storage

Because updates can be very large and have the potential to affect network performance, Windows Update uses BITS to download updates from Microsoft Update or from a WSUS server. Additionally, custom applications can make use of BITS to transfer files. To use BITS, the Background Intelligent Transfer Service must be running.

BITS Behavior

BITS (and thus Windows Update) does not initiate a demand-dial network connection at times when it would normally download updates. BITS will instead wait for the user or another application to initiate a network connection. If a computer stays disconnected or is otherwise unable to reach its update server for weeks or months at a time, the computer will not have recent updates and might be vulnerable to attack. To mitigate the risk of an unprotected computer spreading worms or viruses on your local network, use Network Access Protection.

> **Note**   For more information about network access protection, refer to Chapter 28, "Connecting Remote Users and Networks."

BITS stores the partially downloaded files in the destination folder under a temporary name; these files are marked hidden. When the job is complete, BITS renames the file with its final name and removes the file's hidden attribute. BITS impersonates the job owner before writing these files to preserve the file system security and quotas for the user.

BITS Group Policy Settings

You can use Group Policy settings from the Bits.admx administrative template to configure several aspects of BITS and control how much bandwidth BITS uses. These policies are located in the Computer Configuration\Administrative Templates\Network\Background Intelligent Transfer Service node of the Group Policy Object Editor. Unless otherwise noted, the following Group Policy settings apply only to Windows Vista computers:

- **Do Not Allow The Computer To Act As A BITS Peercaching Client**   When this setting and the Allow BITS Peercaching setting are both enabled, Windows Vista client computers will not attempt to download files from peers. Instead, they will download files from the origin source directly. By default, Windows Vista computers will act as a Peercaching client, and thus will first attempt to download peer-enabled BITS jobs from peer computers before reverting to the origin server. This setting requires Windows Vista.

- **Do Not Allow The Computer To Act As A BITS Peercaching Server**   When this setting and the Allow BITS Peercaching setting are both enabled, Windows Vista client computers will not attempt to share files with peers. However, they might still download files from other Windows Vista computers that are configured to act as Peercaching servers. By default, Windows Vista computers will act as Peercaching servers. This setting requires Windows Vista.

- **Allow BITS Peercaching**   By default, Windows Vista computers have Peercaching disabled, causing Windows Vista to always transfer files directly from the origin server. If you enable this setting, Windows Vista will also attempt to transfer files from other Windows Vista peers, potentially reducing bandwidth utilization on your Internet connection. This setting requires Windows Vista.

- **Timeout For Inactive BITS Jobs**   The number of days without successful download action or job property changes after which BITS will remove a pending job. After a job is considered abandoned, BITS deletes all downloaded files. This setting typically will not impact the Windows Update client, but it might affect other applications that use BITS. This setting is available for Windows 2000, Windows XP, and Windows Server 2003 with BITS 1.5 in addition to Windows Vista.

- **Maximum Network Bandwidth For BITS Background Transfers**   Enables you to limit the bandwidth that BITS uses. You can configure two different bandwidth limits for different times of the day. For example, you might limit the bandwidth to 10 Kbps per client computer during the day to minimize impact on the network during the busiest time, but allow up to 20 Kbps per client computer after normal working hours. If you specify a value that is less than 2 Kbps, BITS will still use up to 2 Kbps. To prevent transfers from occurring, specify 0 Kbps. Because BITS is designed to make use of idle bandwidth, you do not usually need to define this setting. Instead, consult with your network engineering group to monitor BITS bandwidth usage and adjust this setting only if bandwidth utilization becomes a problem. Setting bandwidth restrictions too low can interfere with the ability of Windows Update to retrieve updates. This setting is available for Windows 2000, Windows XP, and Windows Server 2003 with BITS 2.0 in addition to Windows Vista.

■ **Maximum Network Bandwidth Used For Peercaching**   The maximum bandwidth used when transferring files to peers across the local area network (LAN). By default, BITS uses 8 Mbps as the maximum bandwidth. If you have a LAN that is 10 Mbps or slower, you can decrease this setting to reduce the likelihood of BITS peer transfers affecting other network applications. This setting does not affect WAN or Internet bandwidth. This setting requires Windows Vista.

■ **Limit The BITS Peercache Size**   The minimum and maximum disk space to be used to cache BITS content. This setting requires Windows Vista.

■ **Limit Age Of Items In The BITS Peercache**   The maximum number of days before BITS removes cached content. This setting requires Windows Vista.

■ **Maximum BITS Job Download Time**   The number of seconds an active BITS download can run. By default, this setting is 54,000, or 90 minutes. This setting requires Windows Vista.

■ **Maximum Number Of Files Allowed In A BITS Job**   The maximum number of files that can be added to a BITS job. Typically, you do not need to define this setting. This setting requires Windows Vista.

■ **Maximum Number Of BITS Jobs For This Computer**   The maximum number of BITS jobs allowed for all users except services and administrators. This setting requires Windows Vista.

■ **Maximum Number Of BITS Jobs For Each User**   The maximum number of BITS jobs allowed for each user except services and administrators. This setting requires Windows Vista.

■ **Maximum Number Of Ranges That Can Be Added To The File In A BITS Job**   The maximum number of ranges that can be added to a file. Ranges allow a portion of a file to be downloaded. This setting requires Windows Vista.

Configuring the Maximum Bandwidth Served For Peer Client Requests Policy

This policy is configured in bytes per second, which is a different measurement than the Maximum Network Bandwidth That Bits Uses setting, which uses kilobits per second (Kbps). There are 8 bits in a byte, so the default setting of 1048576 converts to about 8 megabits per second (Mbps), and 8 Mbps is about 10% the usable bandwidth of a standard 100 Mbps fast Ethernet network.

The BITSAdmin.exe Tool

You can manage BITS from the command line or from a script by using the BITSAdmin.exe tool. This tool allows you to perform tasks that would otherwise require you to write a compiled application, including the following:

- Viewing BITS jobs, including Windows Update transfers
- Canceling BITS jobs
- Configuring BITS jobs to share files with peers on the same network
- Downloading custom files by using BITS

> **Note**   Whereas administrators will be more comfortable creating scripts with BITSadmin, developers can use BITS to transfer files using the *IBackgroundCopyManager* interface (implemented within a COM object). This enables applications to asynchronously transfer files while preserving the responsiveness of other applications. In other words, applications can use BITS to transfer a file without using all the available bandwidth and slowing down the network. BITS automatically resumes file transfers after network disconnects and computer restarts, making it perfect for low-priority transfers such as application updates. For more information about BITS development, visit MSDN at *http://msdn2.microsoft.com/en-us/library/aa362827.aspx*.

The most important BITSadmin parameters are:

- **/help | /?**   Displays command-line usage.
- **/list [/allusers] [/verbose]**   Lists transfer jobs. The */allusers* parameter lists jobs for all users on the system. The */verbose* parameter provides detailed information about jobs.
- **/monitor [/allusers] [/refresh *Seconds*]**   Monitors the copy manager. The */allusers* parameter monitors the copy manager for all users on the system. The */refresh* parameter reacquires copy manager data in the specified time interval in seconds.
- **/reset**   Deletes all jobs in the manager. If an administrator executes this parameter, all jobs are deleted. If a normal user executes this parameter, only the jobs owned by the user are deleted.
- **/create [*type*] *DisplayName***   Creates a job and assigns *DisplayName* to it. The type can be /Download, /Upload, or /Upload-Reply. After creating a job, you need to add a file to it using the */addfile* parameter.
- **/info *DisplayName* [/verbose]**   Displays information about the specified job. The */verbose* parameter provides detailed information about the job.
- **/addfile *DisplayName RemoteURL LocalName***   Adds a file to the specified job. *RemoteURL* specifies the file's source location, which can be HTTP, HTTPS, UNC (for example, "\\server\file"), or a file:// path. *LocalName* specifies the file's name on the local target computer.

- **/listfiles** *DisplayName*   Lists the files in the specified job.

- **/suspend** *DisplayName*   Suspends the specified job. The job will not be scheduled to run again until the */resume* parameter is executed.

- **/resume** *DisplayName*   Queues the job to the list of jobs enabled for transfer.

- **/cancel** *DisplayName*   Deletes the specified job.

- **/complete** *DisplayName*   Completes the job and makes the files available for the destination directory. This is normally executed after the job moves to the transferred state.

- **/gettype** *DisplayName*   Retrieves the job type of the specified job.

- **/getbytestotal** *DisplayName*   Retrieves the size of the specified job.

- **/getbytestransferred** *DisplayName*   Retrieves the number of bytes transferred for the specified job.

- **/getfilestotal** *DisplayName*   Retrieves the number of files in the specified job.

- **/getfilestransferred** *DisplayName*   Retrieves the number of files transferred for the specified job.

- **/getcreationtime** *DisplayName*   Retrieves the job creation time for the specified job.

- **/getmodificationtime** *DisplayName*   Retrieves the job modification time.

- **/getcompletiontime** *DisplayName*   Retrieves the job completion time for the specified job.

- **/getstate** *DisplayName*   Retrieves the job state for the specified job.

- **/geterror** *DisplayName*   Retrieves detailed error information for the specified job.

- **/getowner** *DisplayName*   Retrieves the job owner for the specified job.

- **/getdisplayname** *DisplayName*   Retrieves the display name for the specified job.

- **/setdisplayname** *CurrentDisplayName NewDisplayName*   Sets the display name for the specified job.

- **/getdescription** *DisplayName*   Retrieves the job description of the specified job.

- **/setdescription** *DisplayName NewDescription*   Sets the description for the specified job.

- **/getpriority** *DisplayName*   Retrieves the priority of the specified job.

- **/setpriority** *DisplayName NewPriority*   Sets the priority for the specified job. BITS supports four priority queues: FOREGROUND, HIGH, NORMAL, and LOW. Each priority queue is processed completely before any jobs at a lower priority. BITS does a round-robin scheduling within a priority queue with a time quanta of about 5 minutes, which ensures that one job cannot block the queue.

- **/getnotifyflags** *DisplayName*   Retrieves the notify flags for the specified job.

- ■ **/setnotifyflags** *DisplayName NotifyFlags*   Sets the notify flags for the specified job.

- ■ **/getnotifyinterface** *DisplayName*   Determines if notify interface is registered for the specified job.

- ■ **/getminretrydelay** *DisplayName*   Retrieves the retry delay, in seconds, for the specified job.

- ■ **/setminretrydelay** *DisplayName RetryDelay*   Sets the retry delay, in seconds, for the specified job.

- ■ **/getnoprogresstimeout** *DisplayName*   Retrieves the no progress timeout, in seconds.

- ■ **/setnoprogresstimeout** *DisplayName Timeout*   Sets the no progress timeout, in seconds, for the specified job.

- ■ **/geterrorcount** *DisplayName*   Retrieves an error count for the specified job.

- ■ **/getproxyusage** *DisplayName*   Retrieves the proxy usage setting for the specified job.

- ■ **/getproxylist** *DisplayName*   Retrieves the proxy list for the specified job.

- ■ **/getproxybypasslist** *DisplayName*   Retrieves the proxy bypass list for the specified job.

- ■ **/setproxysettings** *DisplayName <usage>*   Sets the proxy settings for the specified job. For usage, you can provide PRECONFIG, AUTODETECT, NO_PROXY, or OVERRIDE. If you choose OVERRIDE, you must specify an explicit proxy list and bypass list. Provide NULL to bypass the proxy list. The following examples demonstrate this parameter:

```
Bitsadmin /setproxysettings MyJob OVERRIDE proxy1:80 "<local>"
Bitsadmin /setproxysettings MyJob OVERRIDE proxy1,proxy2,proxy3 NULL
```

- ■ **/takeownership** *DisplayName*   Takes ownership of the specified job.

- ■ **/SetNotifycmdline** *DisplayName <command-line>*   Sets a command line for job notification.

- ■ **/GetNotifycmdline** *DisplayName*   Returns the job's notification command line.

- ■ **/GetReplyProgress** *DisplayName*   Gets the size and progress of the server reply. This is useful if your script needs to monitor the progress of a transfer.

- ■ **/GetReplyData** *DisplayName*   Gets the server's reply data in hex format. This is useful primarily for troubleshooting transfer problems.

Additionally, the BITSAdmin tool displays several parameters related to Peercaching. However, this functionality was not implemented when Windows Vista was released.

The following examples illustrate some common tasks that you might perform with BITSAdmin.

- ■ To view all list jobs:

```
Bitsadmin /list /allusers /verbose
```

■ To delete all BITS jobs:

```
Bitsadmin /reset
```

■ To cancel a job named MyJob:

```
Bitsadmin /cancel MyJob
BITSADMIN version 3.0 [ 6.7.5456.5 ]
BITS administration utility.
(C) Copyright 2000-2006 Microsoft Corp.

GUID: {A4AA2B7D-DDE5-471C-BB6C-446119B57E55} DISPLAY: 'GetFile'
TYPE: DOWNLOAD STATE: ERROR OWNER: HQ\administrator
PRIORITY: NORMAL FILES: 0 / 1 BYTES: 0 / UNKNOWN
CREATION TIME: 7/19/2006 6:38:38 PM MODIFICATION TIME: 7/19/2006 6:39:34 PM
COMPLETION TIME: UNKNOWN ACL FLAGS:
NOTIFY INTERFACE: UNREGISTERED NOTIFICATION FLAGS: 3
RETRY DELAY: 600 NO PROGRESS TIMEOUT: 1209600 ERROR COUNT: 1
PROXY USAGE: PRECONFIG PROXY LIST: NULL PROXY BYPASS LIST: NULL
ERROR FILE:    http://www.microsoft.com/ -> C:\destination_file.html
ERROR CODE:    0x80200011 - The server did not return the file size. The URL
might point to dynamic content. The Content-Length header is
not available in the server's HTTP reply.
ERROR CONTEXT: 0x00000005 - The error occurred while the remote
file was being processed.
DESCRIPTION:
JOB FILES:
        0 / UNKNOWN WORKING http://www.microsoft.com/ -> C:\destination_file.html
NOTIFICATION COMMAND LINE: none
USE PEER CACHE: false   ALLOW CACHING:  false
HTTP REDIRECT POLICY:  ALLOW_SILENT
ALLOW HTTPS TO HTTP REDIRECTIONS:  false
CUSTOM HEADERS: NULL
```

■ To use BITS to transfer the Microsoft.com logo to the root directory:

```
Bitsadmin /create GetLogo

Rem Change the URL in the following line to the file you want to transfer
Bitsadmin /addfile GetLogo http://www.microsoft.com/library/toolbar/3.0/images/
banners/ms_masthead_ltr.gif C:\logo.gif

Rem Jobs are suspended by default, so you must call /resume to begin the transfer
Bitsadmin /resume GetLogo

Rem Files are not saved in their permanent location until you call /complete
Bitsadmin /complete GetLogo
```

Windows Update Group Policy Settings

You can configure Windows Update client settings using local or domain Group Policy settings. This is useful for the following tasks:

- Configuring computers to use a local WSUS server
- Configuring automatic installation of updates at a specific time of day
- Configuring how often to check for updates
- Configuring update notifications, including whether non-administrators receive update notifications
- Configure client computers as part of a WSUS target group, which you can use to deploy different updates to different groups of computers

Windows update settings are located at Computer Configuration\Administrative Templates\Windows Components\Windows Update. The Windows Update Group Policy settings are:

- **Configure Automatic Updates**   Specifies whether or not this computer will receive security updates and other important downloads through the Windows automatic updating service. You also use this setting to configure if the updates are installed automatically and what time of day the installation occurs.
- **Specify Intranet Microsoft Update Service Location**   Specifies the location of your WSUS server.
- **Automatic Updates Detection Frequency**   Specifies how frequently the Automatic Updates client checks for new updates. By default, this is a random time between 17 and 22 hours.
- **Allow Non-Administrators To Receive Update Notifications**   Determines whether all users or only administrators will receive update notifications. Non-administrators can install updates using the Windows Update client.
- **Allow Automatic Updates Immediate Installation**   Specifies if Automatic Updates will immediately install updates that don't require the computer to be restarted.
- **Turn On Recommended Updates Via Automatic Updates**   Determines if client computers install both critical and recommended updates, which might include updated drivers.
- **No Auto-Restart For Scheduled Automatic Updates Installations**   Specifies that to complete a scheduled installation, Automatic Updates will wait for the computer to be restarted by any user who is logged on instead of causing the computer to restart automatically.

- **Re-Prompt For Restart With Scheduled Installations**   Specifies how often the Automatic Updates client prompts the user to restart. Depending on other configuration settings, users might have the option of delaying a scheduled restart. However, the Automatic Updates client will automatically remind them to restart based on the frequency configured in this setting.

- **Delay Restart For Scheduled Installations**   Specifies how long the Automatic Updates client waits before automatically restarting.

- **Reschedule Automatic Updates Scheduled Installations**   Specifies the amount of time for Automatic Updates to wait, following system startup, before proceeding with a scheduled installation that was missed previously. If you don't specify this amount of time, a missed scheduled installation will occur one minute after the computer is next started.

- **Enable Client-Side Targeting**   Specifies which group the computer is a member of. This option is useful only if you are using WUS; you cannot use this option with SUS.

- **Enable Windows Update Power Management To Automatically Wake Up The System To Install Scheduled Updates**   If people in your organization tend to shut down their computers when they leave the office, enable this setting to configure computers with supported hardware to automatically start up and install an update at the scheduled time. Computers will not wake up unless there is an update to be installed. If the computer is on battery power, the computer will automatically return to Sleep after 2 minutes.

Additionally, the following two settings are available at the same location under both Computer Configuration and User Configuration:

- **Do Not Display 'Install Updates And Shut Down' Option In Shut Down Windows Dialog Box**   Specifies if Windows XP with Service Pack 2 or later shows the Install Updates And Shut Down option.

- **Do Not Adjust Default Option To 'Install Updates And Shut Down' In Shut Down Windows Dialog Box**   Specifies if Windows XP with Service Pack 2 or later automatically changes the default shutdown option to Install Updates And Shut Down when Automatic Updates is waiting to install an update.

Finally, the last user setting is available at Administrative Templates\Windows Components\ Windows Update:

- **Remove Access To Use All Windows Update Features**   When enabled, prevents the user from accessing the Windows Update interface.

You should create separate Group Policy objects for groups of computers that have different update installation requirements. For example, if you deploy updates to the IT department first as part of a pilot deployment, IT computers should have their own Group Policy object with settings that place them in a specific WSUS target group for the pilot project.

Configuring Windows Update to Use a Proxy Server

Windows Update can use an HTTP proxy server. However, configuring Internet Explorer is not sufficient to configure Windows Update, because Windows Update uses Windows HTTP Services (WinHTTP) to scan for updates and BITS to download updates.

You can configure Windows Update to use a proxy server in two ways:

- Web Proxy Auto Detect (WPAD) settings are configured. The WPAD feature lets services locate an available proxy server by querying a DHCP option or by locating a particular DNS record.

- Use the Netsh command-line tool, which replaces the Proxycfg.exe tool.

To use the Netsh command-line tool, first switch to the Netsh Winhttp context. Then, use the show proxy command to view settings or the set proxy command to define your proxy server configuration settings. For example, you can run the following command to view current proxy server settings:

```
Netsh winhttp show proxy
```

The following commands demonstrate how to configure proxy server settings:

```
Netsh winhttp set proxy myproxy
Netsh winhttp set proxy myproxy:80 "<local>;bar"
Netsh winhttp set proxy proxy-server="http=myproxy;https=sproxy:88 bypass-list="*.contoso.com"
```

Alternatively, if you have configured Internet Explorer proxy server settings correctly, you can import settings from Internet Explorer into WinHTTP by using the following command:

```
Netsh winhttp import proxy source=ie
```

To reset your proxy server settings, run the following command:

```
Netsh winhttp reset proxy
```

Tools for Auditing Software Updates

One of the most important concepts in security is, "Trust, but audit." Auditing provides a critical layer of protection against human error and omission. In the case of software update management, auditing enables you to verify that updates have been distributed correctly and that updates are not removed after distribution.

Microsoft provides several tools for auditing software updates and the software update process:

- **WSUS**   Described earlier in this chapter, WSUS enables you to view which updates have been distributed to which computers. To detect updates that are removed after distribution and new computers that do not have the proper updates installed, use WSUS reporting in conjunction with one of the other tools in this list.

- **MBSA**   The Microsoft Baseline Security Analyzer (MBSA) actively connects to computers on your network and, with proper credentials, generates reports displaying the installed updates and a list of other security vulnerabilities. MBSA is a graphical tool that simplifies manual, interactive auditing. MBSACLI and SMS, described next, use the MBSA engine.

- **MBSACLI**   The MBSA command-line interface (MBSACLI) allows you to script MBSA auditing, enabling you to audit large numbers of computers in an automated fashion. You can generate XML-based reports that you can view with the MBSA interface, or you can create tools that process the XML-based MBSACLI reports. MBSACLI is included with MBSA.

- **SMS**   Microsoft Systems Management Server (SMS) is a tool that integrates with Active Directory to facilitate the software distribution and management. SMS uses the MBSA engine to simplify auditing and reporting.

WSUS was described earlier in this chapter. The sections that follow describe MBSA, MBSACLI, and SMS.

The MBSA Console

Microsoft Baseline Security Analyzer (MBSA) is used to analyze one or more computers for vulnerabilities. MBSA scans for two categories of vulnerabilities: weak security configurations and missing security updates. This section focuses on using MBSA to scan for updates that should have been installed but have not been.

After installing MBSA, you can use it to scan all computers on your network or domain for which you have administrator access. To scan all computers on a specific subnet using your current user credentials, follow these steps:

1. Start MBSA by clicking Start, pointing to All Programs, and then clicking Microsoft Baseline Security Advisor.

2. On the Welcome To The Microsoft Baseline Security Analyzer page, click Scan Multiple Computers.

3. On the Which Computers Do You Want To Scan page, type the domain or workgroup name, or the IP address range you want to scan. To speed up the scanning process, clear all check boxes except for Check For Security Updates. If you have a WSUS server on your network, you can further speed up the process by selecting the Advanced Update Services Options check box and the Scan Using Assigned Update Services Servers Only radio button to prevent unmanaged computers from being scanned. Figure 24-6 shows MBSA configured to scan the contoso.com domain for security updates.

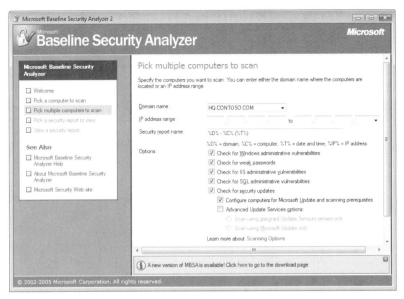

Figure 24-6 MBSA configured to scan a subnet.

4. Click Start Scan. While MBSA performs the scan, it will keep you updated on the progress.

5. After the scan is completed, the View Security Report page appears, listing the computers that were scanned.

Note   If you do not have sufficient credentials on a computer, MBSA will display the Internet Protocol (IP) address of the computer and the message, "User Is Not An Administrator On The Scanned Machine."

Missing security updates are marked by a red X, and missing service packs or update rollups are marked with a yellow X. A green check mark denotes a scan that was completed success-fully with no missing updates found. Scan reports are stored on the computer from which you ran MBSA in the %UserProfile%\SecurityScans folder. An individual security report is created for each computer that is scanned.

During the scanning process, MBSA uses NetBIOS over Transmission Control Protocol/ Internet Protocol (TCP/IP) and Common Internet File System (CIFS) protocols to connect to computers, which requires TCP ports 135, 139, and 445 and UDP ports 137 and 139. If a firewall blocks these ports between you and the target computers, or if the computers have Internet Connection Firewall enabled and these ports have not been opened, you will not be able to scan the computers.

At the beginning of the scan, MBSA must retrieve an updated MBSA detection catalog (Wsusscan.cab) that provides information about updates and security vulnerabilities. By default, this file is retrieved from the Microsoft website at *http://go.microsoft.com/fwlink/ ?LinkId=39043* and includes every current update available from Microsoft. If the computer is configured as a WSUS client, it will retrieve the file from your WSUS server instead.

MBSACLI

Scanning a large network should be done on a regular basis to find computers that have not been properly updated. However, scanning a large network is a time-consuming process. Although the MBSA console is the most efficient way to interactively scan a network, the MBSACLI command-line tool provides a way to script an analysis. By using scripts, you can schedule scanning to occur automatically, without your intervention. This way, you can have MBSACLI generate a report that you can refer to on demand.

> ## Scheduling MBSA
>
> It's convenient to schedule MBSACLI scans after business hours so that you don't consume network resources during working hours; however, if you do this, you won't be able to scan computers that users take home. It's a good idea to schedule scans at various times during the day.
>
> Another good reason to schedule scans by using MBSACLI is that you can scan from multiple points on your network. For example, if your organization has five remote offices, it is more efficient to scan each remote office by using a computer located in that office. This improves performance, reduces the bandwidth used on your wide area network, and allows you to scan computers even if a perimeter firewall blocks the ports that MBSACLI uses to scan.

As with the MBSA graphical console, you need administrative access to use MBSACLI to scan a computer. In a domain environment, simply log on to your computer using an account that has sufficient privileges. Otherwise, you can provide credentials at the command line by using the */u* and */p* parameters. However, you should avoid typing credentials in a script, because the script could be compromised, allowing an attacker to gain privileges on remote computers.

Table 24-2 lists the parameters available in MBSACLI's MBSA mode.

Table 24-2   MBSACLI's MBSA Mode Parameters

Parameter	Description
/target *domain*\computer-name | ipaddress	Scans the host with the specified computer name or IP address.
/r ipaddress1-ipaddress2	Specifies an IP address range to be scanned, beginning with ipaddress1 and ending with ipaddress2, inclusive.

Table 24-2   MBSACLI's MBSA Mode Parameters

Parameter	Description
/listfile *filename*	Scans hosts specified in a text file
/d domain_name	Scans all computers in a specified domain. Of course, your computer must be able to identify those computers. It uses the same mechanism as Network Neighborhood, so if you can browse computers in Network Neighborhood, this switch will work.
/u username /p password	Scans using the specified user name and password.
/n scans	Skips specific scans. You can choose OS, SQL, IIS, Updates, and Password. If you want to suppress multiple scans, separate them with a + sign. For example, to scan only for updates, use the command Mbsacli /n OS+SQL+IIS+Password.
/wa	Show only updates approved on the WSUS server.
/wi	Show all updates, even if they haven't been approved on the WSUS server.
/catalog *filename*	Specifies the MBSA detection catalog, Wsusscan.cab. You can download this file from *http://go.microsoft.com/fwlink/ ?LinkId=39043*.
/qp, /qe, /qr, /qt, /q	Does not display the scan progress, error list, and report list, the report following a single-computer scan, or any of these items, respectively.
/l, /ls	Lists all available reports, or just the reports created in the latest scan, respectively.
/lr "reportname", /ld "report-name"	Displays an overview or detailed report summary, given the filename of the report. You do not need to specify the full filename—only the name of the report. For example, the following command would show a report for Computer1: mbsacli /ld "Cohowinery.com – Computer1 (11-11-2003 07-46 AM)"
/nai, nm, nd	Prevents MBSACLI from updating the Windows Update components, configuring computers to use the Microsoft Update website, or downloading files from the Microsoft website, respectively.
/nvc	Prevents MBSACLI from checking for a new version of MBSA.
/xmlout	Provides XML-based output, which is more difficult to read as a text file, but easier to parse programmatically.
/o "template"	Uses a different template for the report filename. By default, the name is *%domain% - %computername% (%date%)*. If you put one or more spaces in the template, be sure to enclose it in quotation marks.

When scanning a single computer, MBSACLI outputs information about vulnerabilities directly to the console. To save the output to a file, redirect it using the standard ">" notation. For example, this command saves the report output to a file named output.txt:

```
Mbsacli > output.txt
```

When scanning multiple computers, MBSACLI displays only the computers scanned and the overall assessment. The details of the scan are stored in an XML report that is saved in your %UserProfile%\SecurityScans\ folder. By default, the filename for each report is set to *domain − computername (date)*.mbsa.

You can view the reports by using the graphical MBSA console, however. Simply start MBSA and then click View Existing Security Reports. MBSA will show the Pick A Security Report To View page, listing all of the available reports. You can also view them from the command line by using the /ld parameter and specifying the report's filename.

For more information about creating scripts with MBSACLI to perform parallel scans and aggregate multiple scan reports, download the MBSA 2.0 Scripting Samples at *http://www.microsoft.com/downloads/details.aspx?familyid=3B64AC19-3C9E-480E-B0B3-6B87F2EE9042&displaylang=en*.

SMS

SMS can use the MBSA scanning engine to scan computers in your organization for missing updates and other potential security vulnerabilities. Detailed coverage of SMS capabilities is outside the scope of this Resource Kit, however.

For more information about SMS, visit the SMS website at *http://www.microsoft.com/smserver/default.mspx*.

Troubleshooting the Windows Update Client

Occasionally, you might discover a client that isn't automatically installing updates correctly. Typically, such clients are identified during software update audits, as described in the section titled "Tools for Auditing Software Updates" earlier in this chapter. To identify the source of the problem, follow these steps:

1. Determine the last time the client was updated. This can be done in two different ways: by checking the client's registry (the most reliable technique) or, if you use WSUS, by checking the Reports page on the WSUS website.

   ❑ To check the client's registry, open the HKEY_LOCAL_MACHINE\SOFTWARE\ Microsoft\Windows\CurrentVersion\WindowsUpdate\Auto Update\Results registry key. In each of the Detect, Download, and Install subkeys, examine the LastSuccessTime entry to determine when updates were last detected, down-loaded, and installed.

   ❑ To check the WSUS server, visit the WSUS website at *http://<WSUSServerName>/ WSUSAdmin/Web page*. Click the Reports icon and then click Status Of Computers. Browse all computers and then click the computer name to open the Computer Properties window. The Details tab displays the Last Contacted time, as shown in Figure 24-7. The Status tab displays other useful information.

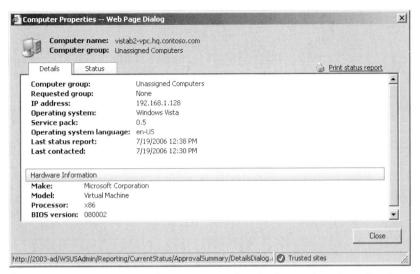

Figure 24-7 You can use WSUS reports to view the last update time of a client computer.

2. Examine any error messages returned by the Windows Update client by viewing the client's %SystemRoot%\WindowsUpdate.log file. This text file contains detailed output from the Windows Update client, including notifications for each attempt to find, download, and install updates. You can also use the WindowsUpdate.log file to verify that the client is attempting to access the correct update server. Search for any error messages in the Microsoft Knowledge Base for more troubleshooting information.

> **Note** For detailed information about how to read the WindowsUpdate.log file, refer to Microsoft Knowledge Base article 902093 at *http://support.microsoft.com/kb/902093/*.

3. If you are using WSUS, verify that the client can connect to the WSUS server. Open a web browser on the client and go to the URL http://<*WSUSServerName*>/iuident.cab. If you are prompted to download the file, this means that the client can reach the WSUS server and it is not a connectivity issue. Click Cancel. If you are not prompted to download the file, you could have a name resolution or connectivity issue, or WSUS is not configured correctly. Troubleshoot the problem further by identifying why the client cannot communicate with the WSUS server using HTTP.

4. If you can reach the WSUS server, verify that the client is configured correctly. If you are using Group Policy settings to configure Windows Update, use the Resultant Set of Policy (RSOP) tool (Rsop.msc) to check the computer's effective configuration. Within RSOP, browse to the Computer Configuration\Administrative Templates\Windows Components\Windows Update node and verify the configuration settings. Figure 24-8 shows the RSOP snap-in.

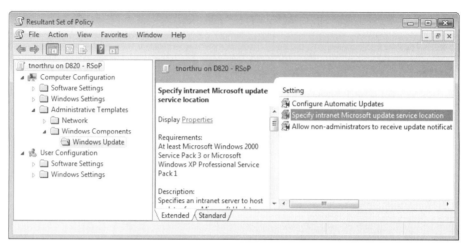

Figure 24-8   Use the RSOP snap-in to verify Windows Update configuration.

5. If you think WSUS is not configured correctly, verify the IIS configuration. WSUS uses IIS to automatically update most client computers to the WSUS-compatible Automatic Updates. To accomplish this, WSUS Setup creates a virtual directory named /Selfupdate, under the website running on port 80 of the computer where you install WSUS. This virtual directory, called the *self-update tree*, holds the latest WSUS client. For this reason, you must have a website running on port 80, even if you put the WSUS website on a custom port. The website on port 80 does not have to be dedicated to WSUS. In fact, WSUS uses the site on port 80 only to host the self-update tree. To ensure that the self-update tree is working properly, first make sure there is a website set up on port 80 of the WSUS server. Next, type the following at the command prompt of the WSUS server:

```
cscript <WSUSInstallationDrive>:\program files\microsoft windows server
update services\setup\InstallSelfupdateOnPort80.vbs
```

> **Note**   For more information about troubleshooting WSUS, visit *http://technet2.microsoft.com/WindowsServer/en/library/b23562a8-1a97-45c0-833e-084cd463d0371033.mspx?mfr=true.*

If you have identified a problem and made a configuration change that you hope will resolve it, restart the Windows Update service on the client computer to make the change take effect and begin another update cycle. You can do this using the Services console or by running the following two commands:

```
net stop wuauserv
net start wuauserv
```

Within 6 to 10 minutes, Windows Update will attempt to contact your update server.

The Process of Updating Network Software

You must plan to update every network component that uses software. This naturally includes client and server operating systems and applications, but it also includes routers, firewalls, wireless access points, and switches. To keep your systems up to date, follow these steps:

1. Assemble an update team.

2. Inventory all software in your organization. Then, contact each software vendor and determine its process of notifying customers of software updates. Some vendors will directly notify you of updates via e-mail, but others require you to check a website regularly. Assign individuals to identify software updates on a regular basis. For example, someone on your team should be responsible for checking every software vendor's website for new updates on at least a weekly basis.

3. Create an update process for discovering, evaluating, retrieving, testing, installing, auditing, and removing updates. Although most of the process will be the same for all vendors, you might have to customize parts of the process to accommodate different uptime and testing requirements for servers, clients, and network equipment. As an example, this chapter will thoroughly document the update process to use for Microsoft operating system updates.

This Resource Kit focuses on updating the Windows Vista operating system only. However, your process should include the ability to manage updates for other operating systems, applications, and network devices. The sections that follow discuss the these steps in more detail.

Assembling the Update Team

Identifying individuals with the right mix of technical and project management skills for deploying updates is one of the first decisions that you and your company's management will make. Even before staffing can begin, however, you need to identify the team roles, or areas of expertise, required for update management. Microsoft suggests using the Microsoft Solutions Framework (MSF) team model, which is based on six interdependent, multidisciplinary roles: product management, program management, development, testing, user experience, and release management. This model applies equally well to both Microsoft and non-Microsoft software.

- **Product management**   Product management is responsible for identifying the organization's business needs and the needs of the end users, and for making sure those needs are supported by the update process.

- **Program management**   The program management team's goal is to deliver updates within project constraints. Program management is responsible for managing the update schedule and budget, and for reporting status, managing project-related risk factors (such as staff illnesses), and managing the design of the update process.

- **Development**   The development team builds the update infrastructure according to specification. The team's responsibilities include specifying the features of the update infrastructure, estimating the time and effort required to deploy the update infrastructure, and preparing the infrastructure for deployment.

- **Testing**   The testing team ensures that updates are released into the production environment only after all quality issues have been identified and resolved. The team's responsibilities include developing the testing strategy, designing and building the update lab, developing the test plan, and conducting tests.

- **User experience**   The user experience team ensures that the update process meets the users' needs. The team gathers, analyzes, and prioritizes user requirements and complaints.

- **Release management**   The release management team is responsible for deploying the updates. In large environments, the release management team also designs and manages a pilot deployment of an update to ensure that the update is sufficiently stable for deployment into the production environment.

The MSF team roles are flexible; they can be adapted to your organization's own processes and management philosophy. In a small organization or a limited deployment, one individual might play multiple roles. In larger organizations, a team might be required to perform all of the tasks assigned to each role.

> **Note**   For more information about the MSF team model, see the MSF Team Model white paper at *http://www.microsoft.com/technet/itsolutions/msf/*.

Inventorying Software

After you create an update team, you must inventory the software on your network. Specifically, you need to know which operating systems and applications you have installed to identify updates that need to be deployed. You also need to understand the security requirements for each computer system, including which computers store highly confidential information, which are connected to the public Internet, and which will connect to exterior networks.

For each computer in your environment, gather the following information:

- **Operating system**   Document the operating system version and update level. Remember that most routers, firewalls, and switches have operating systems. Also document which optional components, such as IIS, are installed.

- **Applications**   Document every application installed on the computer, including versions and updates.

- **Network connectivity**   Document which networks the computer connects to, including whether or not the computer is connected to the public Internet, whether it connects to other networks across a virtual private network (VPN) or dial-up connection, and if it is a mobile computer that might connect to networks at other locations.

■ **Existing countermeasures**   Firewalls and virus checkers might protect a computer against a vulnerability, making the update unnecessary. For firewalls, document the firewall configuration, including which ports are open.

■ **Site**   If your organization has multiple sites, you can choose to deploy updates to computers from a server located at each site to optimize bandwidth usage. Knowing at which site a computer or piece of network equipment is located allows you to efficiently deploy the updates.

■ **Bandwidth**   Computers connected across low-bandwidth links have special requirements. You can choose to transfer large updates during non-business hours. For dial-up users, it might be more efficient to bypass the network link and transfer updates on removable media such as CD-ROMs.

■ **Administrator responsibility**   You must understand who is responsible for deploying updates to a particular device, and who will fix a problem if the device fails during the update process. If others are responsible for individual applications or services, make note of that as well.

■ **Uptime requirements**   Understand any service-level agreements or service-level guarantees that apply to a particular device, and whether or not scheduled downtime counts against the total uptime. This will enable you to prioritize devices when troubleshooting and testing updates.

■ **Scheduling dependencies**   Applying updates requires planning systems to be offline. This can be a disruption for users, even if the device requires only a quick reboot. Understand who depends on a particular device so that you can clear downtime with that person ahead of time.

Some of this information, including operating system and installed applications, can be gathered in an automated fashion. Most network management tools have this capability, including Microsoft Systems Management Server (SMS). You can also inventory Microsoft software on a computer by using Microsoft Software Inventory Analyzer (MSIA), a free download.

> **Note**   For more information about SMS, visit *http://www.microsoft.com/smserver/default.mspx*. For information about MSIA, visit *http://www.microsoft.com/resources/sam/msia.mspx*. To find non-Microsoft software inventory tools, visit *http://www.microsoft.com/resources/sam/aspx/findtool.aspx*.

Creating an Update Process

Deploying updates involves more than just choosing a technology to install the updates. An effective update process involves planning, discussion, and testing. Although you should use your organization's existing change-management process (if one exists), this section will describe the fundamental components of an update process.

The sections that follow describe each of these steps in more detail.

Discovering Updates

The security update process starts when Microsoft releases or updates a security bulletin. Reissued bulletins that have a higher severity rating should be evaluated again to determine if an already-scheduled security release should be reprioritized and accelerated. You might also initiate the security update process when a new service pack is released.

You can be notified of Microsoft-related security issues and fixes by subscribing to the Microsoft Security Notification Services. You can register for this service from the following website: *http://www.microsoft.com/technet/security/bulletin/notify.mspx*. If you subscribe to this service, you will receive automatic notification of security issues by e-mail. Note that you will never receive the update as an attachment from Microsoft. E-mail is easy to spoof, so Microsoft includes a digital signature that can be verified. However, it's generally easier to simply check the Microsoft website to ensure that the bulletin is officially listed.

In addition, use non-Microsoft sources to receive an objective opinion of vulnerabilities. The following sources provide security alert information:

- Security alert lists, especially SecurityFocus (*http://www.securityfocus.com*)
- Security websites such as *http://www.sans.org* and *http://www.cert.org*
- Alerts from antivirus software vendors

Evaluating Updates

After you learn of a security update, you need to evaluate the update to determine which computers at your organization, if any, should have the update applied. Read the information that accompanies the security bulletin and refer to the associated Knowledge Base article after it is released.

Next, look at the various parts of your environment to determine if the vulnerability affects the computers on your network. You might not be using the software component being updated, or you might be protected from the vulnerability by other means such as a firewall. For example, if Microsoft releases a security update for Microsoft SQL Server and your company doesn't use SQL Server (and it's not a component of other installed applications), you don't need to act. If Microsoft releases a security update for the Windows Messenger service, but you have blocked the vulnerable ports by using Windows Firewall, you don't necessarily need to apply the update (though applying the update will provide an important additional layer of protection). As an alternative, you might decide that applying the update is not the best countermeasure for a security vulnerability. Instead, you might choose to add a firewall or adjust firewall filtering rules to limit the vulnerability's exposure.

Determining whether or not an update should be applied is not as straightforward as you might think. Microsoft updates are free downloads, but applying an update does have a cost. You will need to dedicate time to testing, packaging, and deploying the update. In larger organizations, applying a software update to a server requires that many hours be dedicated to justifying the update and scheduling the associated downtime with the groups who use the server.

Any type of update also carries the risk of something going wrong when the update is applied. In fact, any time you restart a computer, there is a small risk that the computer won't start up successfully. There's also the very real risk that the update will interfere with existing applications. This risk, fortunately, can be offset by extensively testing the update before applying it. Deciding not to apply a security update also has a cost: an increased risk of a security vulnerability being exploited.

Besides testing, you can offset the risk that an update will cause problems by having a plan to roll back the update. When evaluating an update, determine if the release can be easily uninstalled if it causes a problem that isn't identified during testing. Functionality for uninstalling updates can vary from fully automated uninstall support to manual uninstall procedures to no uninstall. If an update cannot be uninstalled, your only option might be to restore the computer from a recent backup. Regardless of the uninstall method required for an update, ensure that you have a defined rollback plan in case the deployment doesn't match the success encountered in the test environment.

To be prepared for the worst, verify that you have recent backups of all computers that will be updated, and that you are prepared to restore those systems if the update cannot be successfully removed. It's not likely that an update will cause your systems to fail completely and require them to be restored from backup, but it is a circumstance you must be prepared to handle.

Choosing whether or not to apply an update is such a complicated, yet critical, decision that larger organizations should create a security committee that collectively determines which updates should be applied. The committee should consist of employees who are familiar with the update requirements of each different type of computer on your network. For example, if you have separate organizations that manage desktop and client computers, both organizations should have a representative in the committee. If separate individuals manage each of the web, messaging, and infrastructure servers on your network, each should have input into whether or not a particular update is applied. Ask members from your database teams, networking groups, and internal audit teams to play an active role—their experience and expertise can be an asset in determining risk. Depending on your needs, the committee can discuss each update as it is released, or it can meet on a weekly or biweekly basis.

If the committee determines that an update needs to be deployed, you then need to determine the urgency. In the event of an active attack, you must make every effort to apply the update immediately, before your system is infected. If the attack is severe enough, it might even warrant removing vulnerable computers from the network until the update can be applied.

> ### Speeding the Update Process
>
> If it usually takes your organization more than a few days to deploy an update, create an accelerated process for critical updates. Use this process to speed or bypass time-consuming testing and approval processes. If a vulnerability is currently being exploited by a quickly spreading worm or virus, deploying the update immediately could save hundreds of hours of recovery time.

Retrieving Updates

After you have decided to test and/or deploy an update, you must retrieve it from Microsoft. If you are using WSUS as your deployment mechanism, WSUS can automatically download the update. If you are deploying updates by using another mechanism, download the update from a trusted Microsoft server.

Testing Updates

After applying an update or group of updates to your test computers, test all applications and functionality. The amount of time and expense you dedicate to testing the update should be determined by the potential damage caused by a problematic update deployment. There are two primary ways you can test an update: in a test environment and in a pilot deployment. A test environment consists of a test lab or labs and includes test plans that detail what you will test and test cases that describe how you will test each component. Organizations that have the resources to test updates in a test environment should always do so because it will reduce the number of problems caused by update incompatibility with applications. Even if your organization does not have the resources to test critical updates and security updates, always test service packs before deploying them to production computers.

The test lab can be made up of a single lab or of several labs, each of which supports testing without presenting risk to your production environment. In the test lab, members of the testing team can verify their deployment design assumptions, discover deployment problems, and improve their understanding of the changes implemented by specific updates. Such activities reduce the risk of errors occurring during deployment and allow the members of the test team to rapidly resolve problems that might occur while deploying an update or after applying an update.

Many organizations divide their testing teams into two subteams: the design team and the deployment team. The design team collects information that is vital to the deployment process, identifies immediate and long-term testing needs, and proposes a test lab design (or recommends improvements to the existing test lab). The deployment team completes the process by implementing the design team's decisions and then testing new updates on an ongoing basis.

During the beginning of the lifetime of the update test environment, the deployment team will test the update deployment process to validate that the design is functional. Later, after your organization has identified an update to be deployed, the deployment will test the individual updates to ensure that all the updates are compatible with the applications used in your environment.

An update test environment should have computers that represent each of the major computer roles in your organization, including desktop computers, mobile computers, and servers. If computers within each role have different operating systems, have each operating system available on either dedicated computers, a single computer with a multiboot configuration, or in virtual desktop environment.

After you have a set of computers that represent each of the various types of computers in your organization, connect them to a private network. You will also need to connect test versions of your update infrastructure computers. For example, if you plan to deploy updates by using Windows Server Update Services, connect a WSUS server to the lab network.

Load every application that users will use onto the lab computers and develop a procedure to test the functionality of each application. For example, to test the functionality of Internet Explorer, you could visit both the Microsoft website and an intranet website. Later, when testing updates, you will repeat this test. If one of the applications fails the test, the update you are currently testing might have caused a problem.

> **Note**   If you will be testing a large number of applications, identify ways to automate the testing of updates by using scripting.

In addition to testing your implementation of an update, conducting a pilot deployment provides an opportunity to test your deployment plan and the deployment processes. It helps you to determine how much time is required to install the update and the personnel and tools needed to do so. It also provides an opportunity to train support staff and to gauge user reaction to the update process. For example, if a particular update takes an hour for a dial-up user to download, you might have to identify an alternative method for delivering the update to the user.

> **Note**   The more significant the update, the more important it is to use a pilot program. Service packs, in particular, require extensive testing both in and out of the lab.

Besides testing the update yourself, subscribe to mailing lists and visit newsgroups frequented by your peers. People tend to report problems with updates to these forums before an official announcement is made by Microsoft. If you do discover a problem, report it to Microsoft. Microsoft, historically, has fixed and re-released security updates that have caused serious problems. On the other hand, Microsoft support might be able to suggest an alternative method for reducing the vulnerability's risk.

Installing Updates

After you are satisfied that you have sufficiently tested an update, you can deploy it to your production environment. During the installation process, be sure to have sufficient support staff to handle problems that might arise. Have a method in place to monitor the progress of the updates, and have an engineer ready to resolve any problems that occur in the update deployment mechanism. Notify network staff that an update deployment is taking place so that they are aware of the cause of the increased network utilization.

Removing Updates

Despite following proper planning and testing procedures, problems can arise when you deploy an update to production computers. Before you deploy updates, have a plan in place to roll back updates from one, many, or all of the target computers. The main steps for the rollback and redeployment of updates are:

1. Stop the current deployment. Identify any steps necessary for deactivating release mechanisms used in your environment.

2. Identify and resolve any update deployment issues. Determine what is causing an update deployment to fail. The order in which updates are applied, the release mechanism used, and flaws in the update itself are all possible causes for a failed deployment.

3. Uninstall updates if necessary. Updates that introduce instabilities to your production environment should be removed if possible. For instructions, refer to the section titled "How to Remove Updates" earlier in this chapter.

4. Reactivate release mechanisms. After resolving update issues, reactivate the appropriate release mechanism to redeploy updates. Security bulletins issued by Microsoft will always indicate whether or not an update can be uninstalled. Because reverting computers to a previous state is not always possible, pay close attention to this detail before deploying an update that cannot be uninstalled.

When a simple uninstall process is not available for a security update, ensure that the necessary provisions are in place for reverting your critical computers back to their original state in the unlikely event that a security update deployment causes a computer to fail. These provisions might include having spare computers and data backup mechanisms in place so that a failed computer can be rebuilt quickly.

Auditing Updates

After you have deployed an update, it is important to audit your work. Ideally, someone who is not responsible for deploying the update should perform the actual auditing. This reduces the possibility that the person or group responsible for deploying the update would unintentionally overlook the same set of computers during both update deployment and auditing; it would also reduce the likelihood of someone covering up oversights or mistakes.

Auditing an update that resolves a security vulnerability can be done in one of two ways. The simplest way to audit is to use a tool such as MBSA to check for the presence of the update. This can also be done by checking the version of files that have been updated by an update and verifying that the version matches the version of the file included with the update.

Quarantine Control for Computers That Haven't Been Updated

You should require updates for remote computers connecting via dial-up and virtual private network solutions, because they might miss your update and auditing. Windows Vista and Windows Server 2008 both support Network Access Protection, which you can use to restrict access for computers that do not meet specific security requirements such as having the latest updates, and to distribute the updates to the client computer so that they can safely join the intranet. For more information about network access protection, refer to Chapter 26, "Configuring Windows Networking." With a Windows Server 2003 infrastructure, you can use Microsoft Network Access Quarantine Control, described at *http://technet.microsoft.com/en-us/library/bb726973.aspx.*

How Microsoft Distributes Updates

Microsoft continually works to reduce the risk of software vulnerabilities in Microsoft software, including Windows Vista. This section describes the different types of updates released by Microsoft. It also describes the Microsoft product life cycle, which affects update management, because Microsoft stops releasing security updates for a product at the end of its life cycle.

Security Updates

A security update is an update that the Microsoft Security Response Center (MSRC) releases to resolve a security vulnerability. Microsoft security updates are available for customers to download and are accompanied by two documents: a security bulletin and a Microsoft Knowledge Base article.

Note   For more information about the MSRC, visit *http://www.microsoft.com/security/msrc/default.mspx.*

A Microsoft security bulletin notifies administrators of critical security issues and vulnerabilities and is associated with a security update that can be used to fix the vulnerability. Security bulletins generally provide detailed information about whom the bulletin concerns, the impact of the vulnerability, the severity of the vulnerability, and a recommended course of action for affected customers.

Security bulletins usually include the following pieces of information:

- **Title**   The title of the security bulletin, in the format *MSyy-###*, where *yy* is the last two digits of the year and ### is the sequential bulletin number for that year.

- **Summary**   Information about who should read the bulletin, the impact of the vulnerability and the software affected, the maximum severity rating, and the MSRC's recommendation for how to respond to the bulletin. The severity rating of a bulletin gauges the maximum risk posed by the vulnerability that the update fixes. This severity level can be Low, Moderate, Important, or Critical. The MSRC judges the severity of a vulnerability on behalf of the entire Microsoft customer base. The impact a vulnerability has on your organization might be more or less serious than this severity rating.

- **Executive summary**   An overview of the individual vulnerabilities discussed in the security bulletin and their severity ratings. One security bulletin might address multiple, related vulnerabilities that are fixed with a single update.

- **Frequently asked questions**   Discusses updates that are replaced, whether or not you can audit the presence of the update using the Microsoft Baseline Security Analyzer (MBSA) or Microsoft Systems Management Server (SMS), life-cycle information, and other relevant information.

- **Vulnerability details**   The technical details of the vulnerabilities, a list of mitigating factors that might protect you from the vulnerability, and alternative workarounds that you can use to limit the risk if you cannot immediately install the update. One of the most important pieces of information in this section is if there are known, active exploits that attackers can use to compromise computers that haven't been updated. If you are unable to immediately install the update, you should read this section carefully to understand the risk of managing a computer that hasn't been updated.

- **Security update information**   Instructions for how to install the update and what files and configuration settings will be updated. Reference this section if you need to manually deploy updated files, or if you are configuring custom auditing to verify that the update has been applied to a computer.

Note   If you are not familiar with the format of security bulletins, take some time to read current bulletins. You can browse and search bulletins at *http://www.microsoft.com/technet/ security/current.aspx*.

In addition to security bulletins, Microsoft also creates Knowledge Base articles about security vulnerabilities. Knowledge Base articles generally include more detailed information about the vulnerability and step-by-step instructions for updating affected computers.

From time to time, Microsoft releases security advisories. Security advisories are not associated with a security update. Instead, advisories communicate to customers security guidance that might not be classified as a vulnerability.

Update Rollups

At times, Microsoft has released a significant number of updates between service packs. It is cumbersome to install a large number of updates separately, so Microsoft releases an update rollup to reduce the labor involved in applying updates. An update rollup is a cumulative set of hotfixes, security updates, critical updates, and other updates, all packaged together for easy deployment. An update rollup generally targets a specific area of a product such as security, or a component of a product such as IIS. Update rollups are always released with a Knowledge Base article that describes the rollup in detail.

Update rollups receive more testing from Microsoft than individual security updates, but less testing than service packs. In addition, because update rollups consist of updates that have been previously released and are being run by many other Microsoft customers, it is more likely that any incompatibilities associated with the update rollup have already been discovered. Therefore, the risk associated with deploying update rollups is typically lower overall than the risk of deploying security updates, despite the fact that rollups affect more code. However, you still need to test update rollups with critical applications before deploying them.

Service Packs

A service pack is a cumulative set of all the updates that have been created for a Microsoft product. A service pack also includes fixes for other problems that have been found by Microsoft since the release of the product. Service packs can also contain customer-requested design changes or features. Like security updates, service packs are available for download and are accompanied by Knowledge Base articles.

The chief difference between service packs and other types of updates is that service packs are strategic deliveries, whereas updates are tactical. That is, service packs are carefully planned and managed—the goal is to deliver a well-tested, comprehensive set of fixes that is suitable for use on any computer. In contrast, security updates are developed on an as-needed basis to combat specific problems that require an immediate response.

> **Note**   Service packs undergo extensive regression testing that Microsoft does not perform for other types of updates. However, because they can make significant changes to the operating system and add new features, they still require extensive testing within your environment.

Microsoft does not release a service pack until it meets the same quality standards as the product itself. Service packs are constantly tested as they are built, undergoing weeks or months of rigorous final testing that includes testing in conjunction with hundreds or thousands of non-Microsoft products. Service packs also undergo a beta phase during which customers participate in the testing. If the testing reveals bugs, Microsoft will delay the release of the service pack.

Even though Microsoft tests service packs extensively, they frequently have known application incompatibilities. However, they are less likely to have unknown application incompatibilities. It is critical that you review the service pack release notes to determine how the service pack might affect your applications.

Because service packs can make substantial changes to Windows Vista, thorough testing and a staged deployment are essential. After Microsoft releases a service pack for beta, begin testing it in your environment. Specifically, test all applications, desktop configurations, and network connectivity scenarios. If you discover problems, work with Microsoft to further identify the problem so that Microsoft can resolve the issues before the service pack is released. After the service pack is released, you need to carefully test the production service pack before deploying it.

While testing a newly released service pack, stay in touch with the IT community to understand the experiences of organizations that deploy the service pack before you. Their experiences can be valuable for identifying potential problems and refining your deployment process to avoid delays and incompatibilities. Microsoft security updates can be applied to systems with the current or previous service pack, so you can continue with your usual Microsoft update process until after you have deployed the new service pack.

 Note   For more information about the Microsoft TechNet IT Professional Community, visit *http://www.microsoft.com/technet/community/*.

After testing, you should use staged deployments with service packs, just like you would for any major change. With a staged deployment, you install the service pack on a limited number of computers first. Then, you wait days or weeks for users to discover problems with the service pack. If a problem is discovered, you should be prepared to roll back the service pack by uninstalling it. Work to resolve all problems before distributing the service pack to a wider audience.

Microsoft Product Life Cycles

Every product has a life cycle, and, at the end of the product life cycle, Microsoft stops providing updates. This doesn't mean that no new vulnerabilities will be discovered in the product, however. To keep your network protected from the latest vulnerabilities, you will need to upgrade to a more recent operating system.

Microsoft offers a minimum of five years of mainstream support from the date of a product's general availability. When mainstream support ends, businesses have the option to purchase two years of extended support. In addition, online self-help support, such as the Knowledge Base, will still be available.

Security updates will be available through the end of the extended support phase—seven years after the date of the product's general availability—at no additional cost for most products. You do not have to have an extended support contract to receive security updates during the extended support phase. This means that Microsoft will release security updates for Windows Vista until at least the fourth quarter of 2013. In all likelihood, your organization will have upgraded its Windows Vista–based computers to a newer operating system by then. However, when planning future operating system upgrades, you must keep the product life cycle in mind, particularly the period during which security updates will be released.

You have to stay reasonably current on updates to continue to receive Microsoft support, because Microsoft provides support only for the current service pack and the one that immediately precedes it. This support policy allows you to receive existing hotfixes or to request new hotfixes for the currently shipping service pack, the service pack immediately preceding the current one, or both during the mainstream phase.

Summary

Networks and the Internet are constantly changing. In particular, network security threats continue to evolve, and new threats are introduced daily. Therefore, all software must constantly change to maintain high levels of security and reliability.

Microsoft provides tools for managing Windows Vista software updates for home users, small organizations, and large enterprises. Regardless of the organization, the Windows Vista Windows Update client is responsible for downloading, sharing, and installing updates. Small organizations can download updates directly from Microsoft to a Windows Vista computer, which will then share the update with other computers on the same LAN. Larger organizations, and organizations that must test updates prior to installation, can use WSUS to identify, test, and distribute updates. Combined with Active Directory Group Policy settings, you can centrally manage updates for an entire organization.

Additional Resources

These resources contain additional information and tools related to this chapter.

Related Information

- See the MBSA 2.1 website at *https://www.microsoft.com/mbsa* for more information and to download MBSA.

- "MBSA 2.0 Scripting Samples" at *https://www.microsoft.com/downloads/ details.aspx?familyid=3B64AC19-3C9E-480E-B0B3-6B87F2EE9042&displaylang=en* includes examples of how to create complex auditing scripts using MBSA.

- The SMS website at *https://www.microsoft.com/smserver/default.mspx* includes more information about using SMS.

- The Configuration Manager 2007 website at *https://www.microsoft.com/sccm* includes more information about using Configuration Manager 2007.

- "Microsoft Update Product Team Blog" at *http://blogs.technet.com/mu/archive/2007/ 09/13/how-windows-update-keeps-itself-up-to-date.aspx* provides the latest Microsoft Update news direct from the Microsoft Update product team.

- "WSUS Product Team Blog" at *http://blogs.technet.com/wsus/default.aspx* has the latest WSUS news.

On the Companion CD

- AuditSoftwareUpdatesStatus.vbs

- ConfigureSoftwareUpdatesSchedule.vbs

- ListSoftwareUpdatesConfiguration.vbs

- ListWindowsUpdateVersion.vbs

- ReportSoftwareUpdatesLastRun.vbs

- SearchDownloadInstallWindowsUpdates.vbs

- SearchForUpdatesAndReport.vbs

- SetSoftwareUpdatesConfiguration.vbs

Chapter 25

Managing Client Protection

Networked client computers are constantly under attack. Sometimes people manually initiate these attacks, but the vast majority of attacks come from malware, such as spyware and viruses. In the past, repairing computers compromised by malware was a significant cost to IT departments. Windows Vista strives to reduce this cost by using a combination of technologies—including User Account Control (UAC) and Windows Defender—to help prevent malware compromises. Additionally, Microsoft offers Microsoft Forefront Client Security (FCS) separately from Windows Vista to provide better manageability of client security.

For an interactive demonstration of Windows Vista security, visit the Microsoft TechNet Virtual Lab at *http://go.microsoft.com/?linkid=6673522*.

Understanding the Risk of Malware

Malware (as described in Chapter 2, "Security in Windows Vista"), is commonly spread in several different ways:

- **Included with legitimate software**   Malware is often bundled with legitimate software. For example, a peer-to-peer file transfer application might include potentially unwanted software that displays advertisements on a user's computer. Sometimes, the installation tool might make the user aware of the malware (though users often do not understand the most serious compromises, such as degraded performance and compromised privacy). Other times, the fact that unwanted software is being installed might be hidden from the user (an event known as a *non-consensual installation*). Windows Defender, as described later in this chapter, can help detect both the legitimate software that is likely to be bundling and the potentially unwanted software bundled with it, and it will notify the user about the potential malware. Additionally, when UAC is active, Standard user accounts will not have sufficient privileges to install most dangerous applications.

■ **Social engineering** Users are often tricked into installing malware. A common technique is to attach a malware installer to an e-mail and provide instructions for installing the attached software in the e-mail. For example, the e-mail might appear to come from a valid contact and indicate that the attachment is an important security update. E-mail clients such as Microsoft Office Outlook now prevent the user from running executable attachments. Modern social engineering attacks use e-mail, instant messages, or peer-to-peer networks to instruct users to visit a website that installs the malware, either with or without the user's knowledge. The most effective way to limit the impact of social engineering attacks is to train users not to install software from untrustworthy sources and not to visit untrusted websites. Additionally, UAC reduces the user's ability to install software, and Windows Defender makes users more aware of when potentially unwanted software is being installed. For more information about social engineering, read "Behavioral Modeling of Social Engineering–Based Malicious Software" at *http://www.microsoft.com/downloads/details.aspx?FamilyID=e0f27260-58da-40db-8785-689cf6a05c73.*

> **Note** Windows XP Service Pack 2 and Windows Vista support using Group Policy settings to configure attachment behavior. The relevant Group Policy settings are located in User Configuration\Policies\Administrative Templates\Windows Components\Attachment Manager.

■ **Exploiting browser vulnerabilities** Some malware has been known to install itself without the user's knowledge or consent when the user visits a website. To accomplish this, the malware needs to exploit a security vulnerability in the browser to launch a process with the user's privileges, and then use those privileges to install the malware. The risk of this type of exploit is significantly reduced by Internet Explorer Protected Mode in Windows Vista. For more information about Microsoft Internet Explorer, read Chapter 21, "Managing Internet Explorer."

■ **Exploiting operating system vulnerabilities** Some malware might install itself by exploiting operating system vulnerabilities. For example, many worms infect computers by exploiting a network service to launch a process on the computer and then install the malware. The risks of this type of exploit are reduced by UAC, explained in this chapter, and Windows Service Hardening, described in Chapter 27, "Configuring Windows Firewall and IPsec."

User Account Control

Most administrators know that users should log on to their computers using accounts that are members of the Users group, but not the Administrators group. By limiting your user account's privileges, you also limit the privileges of any applications that you start—including software installed without full consent. Therefore, if you can't add a startup application, neither can a malicious process that you accidentally launch.

With earlier versions of Windows, however, not being a member of the Administrators group could be very difficult, for a few reasons:

- Many applications would only run with administrative privileges.

- Running applications with elevated privileges required users to either right-click the icon and then click Run As or create a custom shortcut, which is inconvenient, requires training, and requires that the user have a local administrator account (largely defeating the purpose of limiting privileges).

- Many common operating system tasks, such as changing the time zone or adding a printer, required administrative privileges.

UAC is a feature of Windows Vista that improves client security by making it much easier to use accounts without administrative privileges. At a high level, UAC offers the following benefits:

- **Most applications can now run without administrative privileges**   Applications created for Windows Vista should be designed to not require administrative credentials. Additionally, UAC virtualizes commonly accessed file and registry locations to provide backward compatibility for applications created for earlier versions of Windows that still require administrative credentials. For example, if an application attempts to write to a protected portion of the registry that will affect the entire computer, UAC virtualization will redirect the write attempt to a nonprotected area of the user registry that will affect only that single application.

- **Applications that require administrative privileges automatically prompt the user for administrative credentials**   For example, if a standard user attempts to open the Computer Management console, a User Account Control dialog box appears and prompts for administrative credentials, as shown in Figure 25-1. If the current account has administrative credentials, the dialog box prompts to confirm the action before granting the process administrative privileges.

Figure 25-1   UAC prompts standard users for administrative credentials when necessary.

■ **Users no longer require administrative privileges for common tasks**   Windows Vista has been improved so that users can make common types of configuration changes without administrative credentials. For example, in earlier versions of Windows, users needed administrative credentials to change the time zone. In Windows Vista, any user can change the time zone, which is important for users who travel. Changing the system time, which has the potential to be malicious, still requires administrative credentials, however.

■ **Operating system components display an icon when administrative credentials are required**   In earlier versions of Windows, users were often surprised when an aspect of the operating system required more privileges than they had. For example, users might attempt to adjust the date and time, only to see a dialog box informing them that they lack necessary privileges. In Windows Vista, any user can open the Date And Time properties dialog box. However, users need to click a button to change the time (which requires administrative privileges), and that button has a shield icon indicating that administrative privileges are required. Users will come to recognize this visual cue and not be surprised when they are prompted for credentials.

■ **If you log on with administrative privileges, Windows Vista will still run applications using Standard user privileges by default**   Most Windows Vista users should log on with only Standard user credentials. If users do log on with an account that has Administrator privileges, however, UAC will still launch all processes with only User privileges. Before a process can gain Administrator privileges, the user must confirm the additional rights using a UAC prompt.

Table 25-1 illustrates the key differences in the behavior of Windows Vista with UAC installed when compared to Windows XP.

Table 25-1   Behavior Changes in Windows Vista with UAC

Windows XP	Windows Vista with UAC
When logged on as a Standard user, administrators could run administrative tools by right-clicking the tool's icon, clicking Run As, and then providing administrative credentials.	Standard users open administrative tools without right-clicking. UAC then prompts the user for administrative credentials. All users can still explicitly launch an application with administrative credentials by right-clicking, but it is rarely necessary.
Using a Standard user account could be a nuisance, especially for technical or mobile users.	The same number of security prompts are required for standard and administrative accounts, and standard accounts can perform many tasks that previously required elevation.
When a user was logged on as a Standard user, an application that needed to change a file or setting in a protected location would fail.	When a user is logged on as a Standard user, UAC provides virtualization for important parts of the system, allowing the application to run successfully while protecting the operating system integrity. Some applications may still fail, however.
If a specific Windows feature required administrative privileges, the entire tool required administrative privileges.	Windows Vista displays the UAC shield on buttons to warn users that the feature requires elevated privileges.
When a user was logged on as an Administrator, all applications ran with administrative privileges.	When a user is logged on as an Administrator, all applications run with standard user privileges. UAC confirms elevated privileges before launching a tool that requires administrative privileges.

The sections that follow describe UAC behavior in more detail.

UAC for Standard Users

Microsoft made many changes to the operating system so that Standard users could perform almost any day-to-day task. Tasks Standard users can do without receiving a UAC prompt that requires administrative privileges in Windows XP include:

- View the system clock and calendar
- Change the time zone
- Connect to wired or wireless networks
- Connect to virtual private networks (VPNs)
- Change display settings and the desktop background
- Change their own passwords
- Install critical Windows Updates

- Add printers and other devices that have the required drivers installed on the computer or that have been allowed by an administrator in Group Policy

- Install ActiveX Controls from sites approved by an administrator

- Play or burn CDs and DVDs (configurable with Group Policy settings)

- Connect to another computer with Remote Desktop

- Configure battery power options on mobile computers

- Configure accessibility settings

- Configure and use synchronization with a mobile device

- Connect and configure a Bluetooth device

- Restore backed-up files from the same user

Additionally, disk defragmentation is scheduled to automatically happen in the background, so users do not need privileges to manually initiate a defragmentation.

Some of the common tasks standard users *cannot* do include:

- Install and uninstall applications

- Install device drivers

- Install noncritical Windows Updates

- Install ActiveX controls from sites not approved by an administrator

 Note To install ActiveX controls in Internet Explorer, launch Internet Explorer by right-clicking the icon and then clicking Run As Administrator. After installing the ActiveX control, close Internet Explorer and reopen it using standard privileges. After it is installed, the ActiveX control will be available to Standard users.

- Change Windows Firewall settings, including enabling exceptions

- Configure Remote Desktop access

- Create scheduled tasks

- Restore system files from a backup

The Power Users group still exists in Windows Vista. However, Windows Vista removes the elevated privileges. Therefore, you should make users members of the Users group and not use the Power Users group at all. To use the Power Users group on Windows Vista, you must change the default permissions on system folders and the registry to grant Power Users group permissions equivalent to Windows XP.

Direct from the Source: Bypassing UAC

The frequently asked question "Why can't I bypass the UAC prompt?" is often accompanied by statements like one or more of the following:

- "We want our application to run elevated automatically without prompting the user."

- "I don't get why I can't authorize an application *once* and be done with it."

- "Unix has setuid root, which lets you run privileged programs securely."

The designers of UAC expressly decided not to incorporate functionality like setuid/suid or sudo found in Unix and Mac OS X. I think they made the right decision.

As I'm sure everyone knows, large parts of the Windows ecosystem have a long legacy of assuming that the end user has administrative permissions, and consequently a lot of programs work correctly only when run that way. As computer security has become increasingly important, breaking that cycle with Windows Vista became absolutely imperative. Indeed, the primary purpose of the technologies that comprise UAC is to enable Standard user privileges to be the default for Windows, encouraging software developers to create applications that do not require administrative privileges.

If it were possible to mark an application to run with silently elevated privileges, what would become of all the existing applications that require administrative privileges? They'd all be marked to silently elevate. How would future software for Windows be written? To silently elevate. Few developers would fix their applications, and end-user applications would continue to require and run with full administrative permissions unnecessarily.

"Well, so what? We're only talking about applications I approved!" OK, let's say that's true, but how do you ensure that malware that has infected the user's session cannot drive an application programmatically to take over the system? Ensuring strict behavioral boundaries for complex software running with elevated privileges is incredibly difficult, and ensuring that it is free of exploitable design and implementation bugs is far beyond the capabilities of software engineering today. The complexity and risk compounds when you consider how many applications have extensibility points that load code that you or your IT administrator may not be aware of, or that can load code or consume data from user-writable areas with minimal if any validation.

We expect that in ordinary day-to-day usage, users should rarely, if ever, see elevation prompts, because most should rarely, if ever, have to perform administrative tasks—and never in a well-managed enterprise. Elevation prompts are to be expected when setting up a new system or installing new software. Beyond that, they should be infrequent enough that they catch your attention when they occur, and not simply trigger a reflexive approval response. This will increasingly be the case as more software conforms to least-privilege norms, and as improvements in the Windows user experience further reduces prompting.

Excerpted from *http://blogs.msdn.com/windowsvistasecurity/archive/2007/08/09/ faq-why-can-t-i-bypass-the-uac-prompt.aspx.*

Aaron Margosis, Senior Consultant

Microsoft Consulting Services

UAC for Administrators

UAC uses Admin Approval Mode to help protect administrators from malicious and potentially unwanted software. When an administrator logs on, Windows Vista generates two access tokens:

- **Standard user access token**   This token is used to launch the desktop (Explorer.exe). Because the desktop is the parent process for all user-initiated processes, any applications the user launches also use the Standard user access token, which does not have privileges to install software or make important system changes.

- **Full administrator access token**   This token has almost unlimited privileges to the local computer. This token is used only after the user confirms a UAC prompt.

> **Note**   As described in the section titled "How to Configure User Account Control" later in this chapter, you can change the default behavior to suit your needs.

If the administrator attempts to launch an application that requires administrative rights (as identified in the application's manifest, described later), UAC prompts the administrator to grant additional rights using the consent prompt, as shown in Figure 25-2. If the user chooses to grant elevated privileges to an application, the Application Information service creates the new process using the full administrator access token. The elevated privileges will also apply to any child processes that the application launches. Parent and child processes must have the same integrity level. For more information about integrity levels, read Chapter 21.

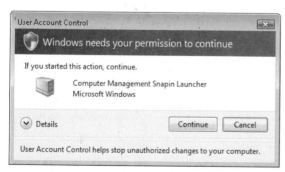

Figure 25-2   By default, Admin Approval Mode prompts administrators to confirm elevated privileges.

> **Note**   The Application Information service must be running to launch processes with elevated privileges.

Command prompts require special consideration, because UAC will not prompt you to elevate privileges if you attempt to run a command that requires administrative rights. To run a command with administrative rights, right-click Command Prompt on the Start menu and then click Run As Administrator. The command prompt that opens will include Administrator in the title, helping you identify the window on your taskbar.

Admin Approval Mode does not apply to the built-in Administrator account. To protect this account from attack, the built-in Administrator account is disabled by default.

UAC User Interface

Windows Vista uses a shield icon to indicate which features of an application require elevated rights. For example, Standard users can run Task Manager (shown in Figure 25-3), but they will need administrative credentials if they click the Resource Monitor button. The shield icon serves to warn users before they attempt to access a feature they might not have sufficient privileges for.

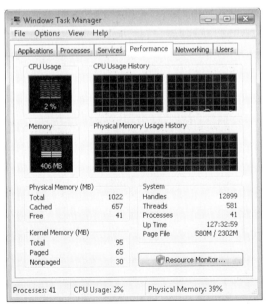

Figure 25-3   The shield icon on the Resource Monitor button indicates that this function requires elevation.

By default, the consent or credential prompt appears on the *secure desktop*. The secure desktop freezes and darkens the entire desktop except for the UAC prompt, making it very difficult for malware to trick you into providing consent.

> ### How It Works: Secure Desktop
>
> The secure desktop actually makes a bitmap copy of the current screen and then alpha-blends it to darken it. To prove that it's a bitmap copy, open Task Manager, click the Performance tab, and notice how the CPU Usage History chart updates. Then, attempt to open Computer Manager. When the UAC prompt appears, Task Manager stops updating. Task Manager continues to draw the graph in the background, even though it's not visible—this will be apparent if you wait a few seconds and then close the UAC prompt.

UAC prompts are color-coded to indicate the level of risk associated with the application:

- If the top portion of the dialog box is red, policy will prevent the application from running and users do not have the option of allowing it to run.

- If the top portion is yellow, as shown in Figure 25-4, the application is unsigned, or it's signed, but the certificate is not trusted.

Figure 25-4   UAC prompts are color-coded.

- If the top portion is green, it indicates that the application is a component of Windows Vista, such as the Microsoft Management Console (MMC), as shown earlier in Figure 25-2.

- If the top portion is gray, the application is signed and trusted by the local computer.

When training users, point out the color coding. Tell them to pay particular attention to yellow prompts, which indicate an increased risk of the application being malicious.

How Windows Vista Determines If an Application Needs Administrative Privileges

Windows Vista examines several aspects of an executable to determine if it should display a UAC prompt before running the application:

- **Application properties**   Users can select the Run As Administrator check box for executable files.

- **Application manifest**   A description of the application provided by the application developer, which can require Windows Vista to run the program as an administrator.

- **Application heuristics**   Aspects of the application that might indicate it requires administrative privileges, such as being named Setup.exe.

The sections that follow describe each of these aspects and show you how to configure applications so that they always require elevated privileges (which is important if an application does not work properly without elevated privileges, but UAC does not automatically prompt the user).

How to Control UAC Using Application Properties

If the application does not automatically run with administrative credentials, you can right-click the application and then click Run As Administrator. If you deploy an application to users, however, you should configure the application to automatically prompt the user if it does not automatically run with administrator credentials. To mark an application to always run with administrative credentials, follow these steps:

1. Log on using administrative credentials but do not use the built-in Administrator account.

2. Right-click the application and then click Properties.

3. Click the Compatibility tab. If you want other users on the same computer to run the application with administrative privileges, click Show Settings For All Users.

4. Under Privilege Level, select the Run This Program As An Administrator check box, as shown in Figure 25-5. Click OK. If the check box is not available, it means that the application is blocked from always running elevated, the application does not require administrative credentials to run, the application is part of the current version of Windows Vista, or you are not logged on to the computer as an administrator.

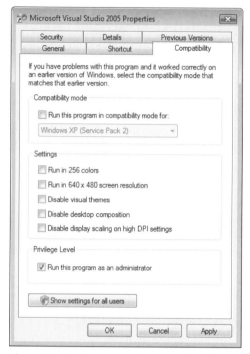

Figure 25-5   You can mark an application to always run with administrative credentials.

You need to mark only applications that require administrative credentials but do not cause UAC to automatically prompt the user. You cannot set privilege level for Windows components, such as the command prompt. Instead, you should always right-click them and click Run This Program As An Administrator.

How UAC Examines the Application Manifest

For applications to receive a Certified For Windows Vista logo, they must include an embedded *requested execution level manifest* that specifies the privileges required. The privilege level is one of the following:

■ **asInvoker or RunAsInvoker**   The application runs using the standard user privileges, and will not initiate a UAC prompt.

■ **highestAvailable or RunAsHighest**   The application requests privileges higher than Standard users and generates a UAC prompt. However, if the user does not provide additional credentials, the application will run anyway, using standard privileges. This is useful for applications that can adjust to either higher or lower privilege levels, or for applications that might need more privileges than a Standard user, but fewer than a full administrator. For example, backup applications typically need the user to be a member of the Backup Operators group but do not require the user to be a member of the Administrators group.

- **requireAdministrator or RunAsAdmin**   The application requires administrative privileges, generating a UAC prompt. The application will not run with standard privileges.

> **Note**   To add a manifest to existing applications, use the Application Compatibility Toolkit, which you can download at *http://go.microsoft.com/fwlink/?LinkId=23302*. The Application Compatibility Toolkit also includes the Microsoft Standard User Analyzer tool, which allows you to diagnose issues that would prevent a program from running properly as a standard user. For more information about Application Compatibility, read Chapter 8, "Deploying Applications."

UAC Heuristics

If you run an application setup file, UAC will prompt you for administrative credentials. This makes sense, because most installation routines require elevated privileges. However, installers created before Windows Vista do not include a manifest, so Windows Vista has to heuristically detect which executables are setup files.

To do this, Windows Vista examines 32-bit executables without a requested execution level manifest that would be run with standard privileges. If the executable meets those requirements and has a filename or metadata that includes keywords such as *install*, *setup*, or *update* (or several other indicators that it might be an installer), UAC prompts for elevated privileges before running the file. If UAC does not prompt you for administrator credentials for an install, right-click the setup file and then click Run As Administrator. Without administrative privileges, most installations will fail.

UAC Virtualization

By default, UAC virtualizes requests for protected resources to provide compatibility with applications not developed for UAC. This is important, because many applications written for Windows XP and earlier operating systems assume that the user has administrative privileges and attempt to write to protected resources such as the Program Files or System folders.

UAC virtualization redirects requests for the following resources to safer, user-specific locations:

- %Program Files%
- %WinDir%
- %WinDir%\System32
- HKEY_LOCAL_MACHINE\Software

When a user process attempts to add a file to a protected folder, UAC redirects the request to the \AppData\Local\VirtualStore\ folder in the user's profile. For example, if a user named MyUser runs an application that stores a log file at C:\Program Files\MyApps\Logs\Log.txt, the file write attempt will succeed. However, UAC will actually store the file at C:\Users\MyUser\AppData\Local\VirtualStore\Program Files\MyApps\Logs\Log.txt.

The application will be able to access the file at C:\Program Files\MyApps\Logs\Log.txt, but the user will need to browse to her profile to access the file directly, because virtualization affects only the application process itself. In other words, if the user browses to open the log file from within the application, it will appear to be under %Program Files%. If the user browses to open the log file using an Explorer window, it will be under her profile.

The first time an application makes a change to a virtualized resource, Windows Vista copies the folder or registry key to the location within the user's profile. Then, the change is made to the user's copy of that resource.

UAC virtualization is designed to allow already-installed applications to run successfully with Standard user privileges, even if they store temporary files or logs in a protected folder. UAC virtualization does not allow users to install applications that make changes to these resources; users will still need to provide administrative credentials to do the installation.

When an executable has a requested execution level manifest, Windows Vista automatically disables UAC virtualization. Therefore, virtualization should never be a factor for applications designed for Windows Vista. Native 64-bit applications are required to be UAC-aware and to write data into the correct locations and thus are not affected. Virtualization also does not affect applications that administrators run with elevated privileges.

If you plan to run applications that would support virtualization, and you specifically want to prevent UAC from virtualizing requests from the application, you can disable virtualization by using the Application Compatibility Toolkit to mark the application. Setting the NoVirtualization marking makes applications easier to debug (because you don't have to worry about file and registry requests being redirected), and it reduces the attack surface by making it more difficult for malware to infect an application (because that application's files would not be moved into the relatively unprotected user profile).

UAC and Startup Programs

By default, UAC blocks startup applications located in the Startup folder or identified in the Run registry key that require elevated privileges for both Standard and administrative users. It would simply be too annoying to have multiple UAC prompts when logging on, and forcing users to confirm the prompts would require them to blindly elevate processes they did not explicitly launch—a bad security practice.

Instead of a UAC prompt, UAC displays a notification bubble stating that Windows has blocked some startup programs. The user can click the bubble to view and launch the blocked programs within Windows Defender. (Windows Defender provides the user interface, but is not itself responsible for blocking startup programs.) As an administrator, you should ensure that no startup programs require elevated privileges.

Startup applications launched from the RunOnce registry key or specified in a Group Policy setting are unaffected by this feature; UAC will still prompt the user for administrative credentials. This allows applications that must make changes after restarting the computer to complete installation successfully.

Compatibility Problems with UAC

For applications to receive the Certified For Windows Vista logo, the application must be designed to work well for Standard users unless the tool is specifically intended for use by administrators. However, many applications were developed prior to Windows Vista and will not work correctly with UAC enabled. Some of the more significant applications that might experience problems with specific features include:

- **Microsoft SQL Server Desktop Engine (MSDE)**   MSDE is not supported on Windows Vista, but SQL Server 2005 Express is.

- **Microsoft Visual Studio 6.0 and Microsoft Visual Studio 2003**   Microsoft currently has no plans to support these versions of Microsoft Visual Studio on Windows Vista.

- **Microsoft Visual Studio 2005**   Windows Vista Service Pack 1 must be installed for compatibility with Windows Vista.

Additionally, some older antispyware, antivirus, firewalls, CD/DVD-authoring, disk-defragmentation, and video-editing tools designed for Windows XP will not work with Windows Vista.

Typically, most features of an application will work correctly with UAC enabled, but specific features might fail. You have several ways to work around this:

- **Run the application with administrative credentials**   As described in the section titled "How to Control UAC Using Application Properties" earlier in this chapter, you can specify that an application always requires administrative credentials.

- **Modify permissions on the computer**   If an application requires access to a protected resource, you can change the permissions on that resource so that Standard users have the necessary privileges. Instructions on how to isolate the protected resources are provided later in this section.

- **Run Windows XP (or an earlier version of Windows) in a virtual machine**   If the application fails with administrative privileges or you do not want to grant the application administrative privileges to your computer, you can run the application within a virtual machine. Virtual machines provide an operating system within a sandbox environment, allowing you to run applications within Windows XP without requiring a separate computer. You can maximize virtual machines so that they display full-screen, providing a similar experience to running the operating system natively. Virtual machines perform slightly slower than applications that run natively within Windows Vista, however. Virtual PC is a free download from Microsoft, and Windows Vista Enterprise and Windows Vista Ultimate include the right to install Windows XP in a virtual machine without paying additional fees. For more information about Virtual PC, read Chapter 4, "Planning Deployment."

■   **Disable UAC**   You can disable UAC to bypass most application-compatibility problems related to the permission changes in Windows Vista. However, this increases the security risks of client computers when running any application, and therefore is not recommended. To disable UAC, read the section titled "How to Configure User Account Control" later in this section.

To isolate the protected resources accessed by an application, follow these steps:

1. On a Windows Vista computer with UAC enabled, download and install the Microsoft Application Verifier from *http://www.microsoft.com/downloads/details.aspx?FamilyID= bd02c19c-1250-433c-8c1b-2619bd93b3a2*.

2. On the same computer, install the Application Compatibility Toolkit, which you can download at *http://go.microsoft.com/fwlink/?LinkId=23302*.

3. Start the Standard User Analyzer (which is installed with the Application Compatibility Toolkit). On the App Info tab, click Browse and then select the application's executable file.

4. Click Launch and then respond to any UAC prompts that appear. The Standard User Analyzer will start the application. Use the application, especially any aspects that might require elevated privileges, and then close the application.

5. Click the View menu and select Detailed Information.

6. Wait a few moments for the Standard User Analyzer to examine the application log file, as shown in Figure 25-6. Browse the different tabs to examine any errors. Errors indicate that the application attempted to perform an action that would have failed if it were not run with administrative privileges.

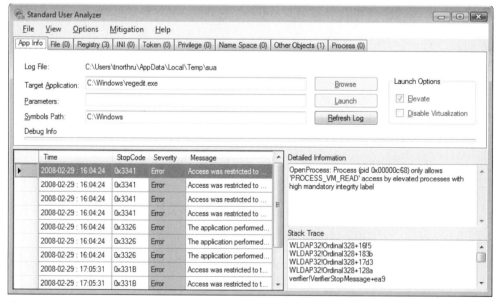

Figure 25-6   The Standard User Analyzer tool shows exactly which elevated privileges an application requires.

On the File tab and the Registry tab (shown in Figure 25-7), notice the Work With Virtualization column. If the entry in that column is Yes, that particular error will not cause a problem as long as UAC virtualization is enabled. If UAC virtualization is disabled, the error will still occur. If the entry in the column is No, it will always be a problem unless the application is run as an administrator.

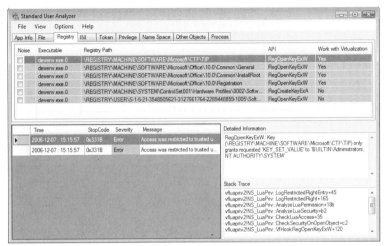

Figure 25-7   The Standard User Analyzer tool indicates which problems can be negated by UAC virtualization.

How to Configure User Account Control

You can use Group Policy settings to granularly configure UAC behavior. Additionally, you can disable UAC by using the Control Panel or Msconfig.exe, or by directly editing registry settings. The sections that follow describe each of these techniques in more detail.

Group Policy Settings

You can configure UAC using local or Active Directory Group Policy settings located in the following node:

Computer Configuration\Policies\Windows Settings\Security Settings\Local Policies\Security Options

You can configure the following settings:

- **User Account Control: Admin Approval Mode For The Built-in Administrator Account**   This policy applies only to the built-in Administrator account, and not to other accounts that are members of the local Administrators group. When you enable this policy setting, the built-in Administrator account has UAC Admin Approval Mode enabled, just like other administrative accounts. When you disable the setting, the built-in Administrator account behaves just like it does in Windows XP, and all processes run using Administrator privileges. This setting is disabled by default.

> **Note**   To minimize the risk of abusing the built-in Administrator account, the account is disabled by default. If Windows Vista determines during an upgrade from Windows XP that the built-in Administrator is the only active local administrator account, Windows Vista leaves the account enabled and places the account in Admin Approval Mode. The built-in Administrator account, by default, cannot log on to the computer in safe mode. If the last local administrator account is inadvertently demoted, disabled, or deleted, safe mode will allow the disabled built-in Administrator account to log on for disaster recovery.

- **User Account Control: Behavior Of The Elevation Prompt For Administrators In Admin Approval Mode**   By default, this setting is set to Prompt For Consent, which causes the UAC prompt to appear any time a process needs more than standard User privileges. Change this setting to Prompt For Consent to cause Admin Approval Mode UAC prompts to behave like prompts for Standard users, requiring the user to type an administrative password instead of simply clicking Continue. Change this setting to Elevate Without Prompting to automatically provide administrative privileges, effectively disabling UAC for administrative accounts. Choosing Elevate Without Prompting significantly reduces the security protection provided by Windows Vista, and might allow malicious software to install itself or make changes to the system without the administrator's knowledge.

- **User Account Control: Behavior Of The Elevation Prompt For Standard Users**   By default, this setting is Prompt For Credentials in workgroup environments and Automatically Deny Elevation Requests in domain environments. Prompt For Credentials causes UAC to prompt the user to enter an administrative user name and password. You can change this to Automatically Deny Elevation Requests to disable the UAC prompt. Disabling the prompt can improve security; however, the user might experience application failures because of denied privileges. If users do not have access to administrative credentials, you should disable the elevation prompt, because the user would not be able to provide credentials anyway. If you do not disable the prompt, users are likely to call the support center to ask for administrative credentials.

- **User Account Control: Detect Application Installations And Prompt For Elevation**   By default, this setting is enabled in workgroup environments and disabled in domain environments. When enabled, UAC will prompt for administrative credentials when the user attempts to install an application that makes changes to protected aspects of the system. When disabled, the prompt won't appear. Domain environments that use delegated installation technologies such as Group Policy Software Install (GPSI) or SMS can safely disable this feature because installation processes can automatically escalate privileges without user intervention.

- **User Account Control: Only Elevate Executables That Are Signed And Validated**   If your environment requires all applications to be signed and validated with a trusted certificate, including internally developed applications, you can enable this policy to greatly increase security in your organization. When this policy is enabled, Windows Vista will refuse to run any executable that isn't signed with a trusted certificate, such as a certificate generated by an internal Public Key Infrastructure (PKI). All software with the Certified For Windows Vista logo must be signed with an Authenticode certificate, though you might have to configure your domain PKI to trust the certificate. This setting is disabled by default, which allows users to run any executable, including potentially malicious software.

■ **User Account Control: Only Elevate UIAccess Applications That Are Installed In Secure Locations**   This setting, which is enabled by default, causes Windows Vista to grant user interface access (required for opening windows and doing almost anything useful) to only those applications launched from Program Files, from \Windows\System32\, or from a subdirectory. Enabling this setting effectively prevents non-Administrators from downloading and running an application, because non-Administrators won't have the privileges necessary to copy an executable file to one of those folders.

■ **User Account Control: Run All Administrators In Admin Approval Mode**   This setting, enabled by default, causes all accounts with administrator privileges *except* for the local Administrator account to use Admin Approval Mode. If you disable this setting, Admin Approval Mode is disabled for administrative accounts, and the Security Center will display a warning message.

■ **User Account Control: Switch To The Secure Desktop When Prompting For Elevation**   This setting, enabled by default, causes the screen to darken when a UAC prompt appears. If the appearance of the entire desktop changes, it is very difficult for malware that hasn't been previously installed to impersonate a UAC prompt. Some users might find the secure desktop annoying, and you can disable this setting to minimize that annoyance. However, disabling this setting decreases security by making it possible for other applications to impersonate a UAC prompt.

■ **User Account Control: Virtualize File And Registry Write Failures To Per-User Locations**   This setting, enabled by default, improves compatibility with applications not developed for UAC by redirecting requests for protected resources. For more information, read the section titled "UAC Virtualization" earlier in this chapter.

To disable UAC, set the User Account Control: Behavior Of The Elevation Prompt For Administrator In Admin Approval Mode setting to No Prompt. Then, disable the User Account Control: Detect Application Installations And Prompt For Elevation and User Account Control: Run All Administrators In Admin Approval Mode settings. Finally, set User Account Control: Behavior Of The Elevation Prompt For Standard Users setting to Automatically Deny Elevation Requests.

Additionally, you can configure the credential user interface using the following two Group Policy settings located at Computer Configuration\Policies\Administrative Templates\ Windows Components\Credential User Interface:

■ **Require Trusted Path For Credential Entry**   If you enable this setting, Windows Vista requires the user to enter credentials using a trusted path, which requires the user to press Ctrl+Alt+Delete. This helps prevent a Trojan horse program or other types of malicious code from stealing the user's Windows credentials. This policy affects non-logon authentication tasks only. As a security best practice, you should enable this policy to reduce the risk of malware tricking the user into typing her password. However, users who need elevated privileges regularly will find it annoying and time-consuming. Figures 25-8, 25-9, and 25-10 show the dialog boxes that appear each time a user must elevate privileges when this setting is enabled.

Figure 25-8   The first of three prompts that the user must respond to when you require a trusted path for administrative credentials.

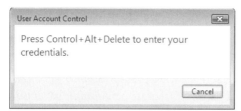

Figure 25-9   The second of three prompts that the user must respond to when you require a trusted path for administrative credentials.

Figure 25-10   The third of three prompts that the user must respond to when you require a trusted path for administrative credentials.

■ **Enumerate Administrator Accounts On Elevation**   By default, this setting is disabled, which causes the UAC prompt to list all administrator accounts displayed when a users attempts to elevate a running application. If you enable this setting, users are required to type both a user name and password to elevate their privileges.

Control Panel

Group Policy is the best way to configure UAC in Active Directory environments. In workgroup environments, you can disable UAC on a single computer by using Control Panel:

1. In Control Panel, click User Accounts And Family Safety.

2. Click User Accounts.

3. Click Turn User Account Control On Or Off.

> **Note**   Although the link appears on a single user's Control Panel page, it will affect all users.

4. Clear the Use User Account Control (UAC) To Help Protect Your Computer check box and then click OK.

5. When prompted, restart your computer.

To re-enable UAC, repeat these steps and select the Use User Account Control (UAC) To Help Protect Your Computer check box.

Msconfig.exe

Msconfig.exe is a troubleshooting tool that can be useful for temporarily disabling UAC to determine whether UAC is causing an application compatibility problem. To make the change, msconfig.exe simply modifies the registry value. To disable UAC with Msconfig.exe, follow these steps:

1. Click Start, type **msconfig**, and then press Enter. The System Configuration tool opens.

2. Click the Tools tab.

3. Click Disable UAC and then click Launch.

4. A command window appears, and shortly thereafter, a notification bubble appears informing you that UAC is disabled. Restart your computer to apply the change.

To re-enable UAC with Msconfig.exe, follow the preceding steps, clicking Enable UAC instead of Disable UAC.

Registry

To disable UAC using the registry, change the following registry value to 0:

HKEY_LOCAL_MACHINE\Software\Microsoft\Windows\CurrentVersion\Policies\System\EnableLUA

> **Note**   During the early Windows Vista beta period, UAC was known as Limited User Account or Limited User Access (LUA).

To re-enable UAC, change that registry value to 1. Restart the computer to apply the change.

How to Configure Auditing for Privilege Elevation

You can enable auditing for privilege elevation so that every time a user provides administrative credentials or an administrator clicks Continue at a UAC prompt, an event is added to the Security Event Log. To enable privilege elevation auditing, enable success auditing for both the Audit Process Tracking and Audit Privilege Use settings in the Local Policies\Audit Policy node of Group Policy. Note that you should enable auditing only when testing applications or troubleshooting problems; enabling these types of auditing can generate an excessive number of events and negatively affect computer performance.

To enable auditing on a single computer, use the Local Security Policy console. To enable auditing on multiple computers within a domain, use Group Policy settings. In Group Policy, auditing settings are located within Computer Configuration\Policies\Windows Settings\Security Settings\Local Policies\Audit Policy node. After changing auditing settings, you must restart the computer for the change to take effect.

After enabling Audit Privilege Use, you can monitor Event IDs 4648 and 4624 in the Security event log to determine when users elevate privileges using the UAC consent dialog box. Event ID 4648 will always precede 4624 and will have a process name that includes Consent.exe, the UAC consent dialog box. These events will not appear if a user cancels the UAC consent dialog box. Events with Event ID 4673 will appear if the user cancels a consent dialog box; however, that same event will appear under different circumstances as well.

After enabling Audit Process Tracking, you can monitor Event ID 4688 to determine when administrators make use of Admin Approval Mode to provide full administrator privileges to processes. The description for this event includes several useful pieces of information:

- **Security ID**   The user name and domain of the current user.
- **New Process Name**   The path to the executable file being run. For more information about the new process, look for an event with Event ID 4696 occurring at the same time.

- **Token Elevation Type** A number from 1 to 3 indicating the type of elevation being requested:

    - Type 1 (TokenElevationTypeDefault) is used only if UAC is disabled or if the user is the built-in Administrator account or a service account. This type does not generate a UAC prompt.

    - Type 2 (TokenElevationTypeFull) is used when the application requires (and is granted) elevated privileges. This is the only type that generates a UAC prompt. This type can also be generated if a user starts an application using RunAs, or if a previously elevated process creates a new process.

    - Type 3 (TokenElevationTypeLimited) is used when the application runs using standard privileges. This type does not require a UAC prompt.

Note that many events with Event ID 4688 won't be applications launched by the user. Most of these events are generated by background processes and services that require no interaction with the user. To find the most interesting events, filter the Security Event Log using Event ID 4688. Then, use the Find tool to search for the phrase "TokenElevationTypeFull". For more information about using Event Viewer, read Chapter 22, "Maintaining Desktop Health."

Other UAC Event Logs

Besides security auditing (which is not enabled by default), UAC provides two additional logs within Event Viewer:

- **Applications and Services Logs\Microsoft\Windows\UAC\Operational** Logs UAC errors, such as processes that fail to handle elevation requirements correctly

- **Applications and Services Logs\Microsoft\Windows\UAC-FileVirtualization\ Operational** Logs UAC virtualization details, such as virtualized files that are created or deleted

If you are experiencing a problem and you think it might be related to UAC, check these logs for any related information.

Best Practices for Using UAC

To receive the security benefits of UAC while minimizing the costs, follow these best practices:

- Leave UAC enabled for client computers in your organization.

- Have all users—especially IT staff—log on with Standard user privileges.

- Each end user should have a single account with only Standard user privileges. Do not give users accounts with administrative privileges to their local computers. If you follow this guideline, you should also disable the UAC elevation prompts as described in the section titled "How to Configure User Account Control" earlier in this section.

■ Domain administrators should have two accounts: a Standard user account that they use to log on to their computers, and a second Administrator account that they can use to elevate privileges.

■ Admin Approval Mode can slow down administrators by requiring them to frequently confirm elevation for administrative tools. If your administrators use Standard user account for day-to-day privileges and only log on with an Administrator account when managing a computer, your IT department might be more efficient if you disable the elevation prompt. To do this, configure the UAC policy setting Behavior Of The Elevation Prompt For Administrators In Admin Approval Mode to Elevate Without Prompting. However, changing this policy may increase the security risk in your environment, and the Windows Security Center will report it.

■ Train users with local administrative credentials *not* to approve a UAC prompt if it appears unexpectedly. UAC prompts should appear only when the user is installing an application or launching a tool that requires elevated privileges. A UAC prompt that appears at any other time might have been initiated by malware. Rejecting the prompt will help prevent the malware from making permanent changes to the computer.

■ Thoroughly test all applications with a Standard user account in Windows Vista prior to deploying Windows Vista. If a third-party application does not work properly with a Standard user account, contact the application developer and request an update for the application. If an internal application does not work properly, refer the developers to "Windows Vista Application Development Requirements for User Account Control Compatibility" at *http://www.microsoft.com/downloads/details.aspx?FamilyID= ba73b169-a648-49af-bc5e-a2eebb74c16b.*

■ Create Windows Firewall exceptions for users before deploying an application. For more information, read Chapter 27.

■ Use Group Policy software installation, Microsoft Systems Management Server, or another similar application-deployment technology to deploy applications. Disable application-installer detection using the User Account Control: Detect Application Installations And Prompt For Elevation setting, as described in the section titled "How to Configure User Account Control" earlier in this chapter.

■ When users do require elevated privileges, administrators can provide the necessary credentials using either Remote Assistance or by physically typing administrative credentials while at the user's computer.

■ Use UAC as part of a defense-in-depth, client-security strategy that includes antispyware and antivirus applications, update management, and security auditing.

Managing Client Certificates

Certificates are used for many different client security scenarios, including:

- Authenticating Web servers to the client, and authenticating the client to the Web server
- IPsec connection security authentication
- Encrypting File System (EFS) encryption

You can use the Certificates console to add, remove, back up, and configure client certificates. To run the Certificates console (which requires administrative privileges), click Start, type **certmgr.msc**, and then press Enter. The two most common certificate management tasks are:

- **Export certificates**   Right-click a certificate, click All Tasks, and then click Export. Then, use the Certificate Export Wizard to save the certificate to a file. This file can act as a backup, or you can transfer it to another computer and import it into the certificate store.
- **Import certificates**   If you have previously exported a certificate, you can import it by right-clicking the certificate container and then clicking Import. Then, use the Certificate Import Wizard to import the certificate into the certificate store.

Direct from the Source: Public Key Infrastructure (PKI) Enhancements

In Windows Vista and Windows Server 2008, the PKI team focused on four main investment pillars:

- **Crypto enhancements**   The Microsoft crypto and PKI platform now supports the most advanced crypto algorithms such as Elliptic Curve Certificate (ECC) and the SHA-2 hashing algorithm family out of the box. The Microsoft certificate authority (CA) can now issue ECC certificates and the Microsoft client can enroll and validate ECC and SHA-2 based certificates. Moreover, the platform is now dynamic enough to allow plugability of new algorithms much easily than before. The use of the new crypto and hash algorithms will be mandated by the U.S. government as well as some European governments in the next few years, making the operating system support key for Microsoft PKI success in those market segments.

- **Revocation enhancements**   OCSP (Online Certificate Status Protocol) is now supported natively in the Windows platform. The OCSP client is included as part of Windows Vista and Windows Server 2008, and a new OCSP Responder is available as part of the Certificate Server role. Additional revocation checking enhancements such as CRL pre-fetching, OCSP response stapling, and CAPI diagnostics are also introduced to improve our PKI revocation story as well as to improve the user experience when using PKI-aware applications. Revocation was always one of the biggest problems in PKI, especially in the Internet age. Introducing OCSP and enhancing the revocation platform will significantly assist deploying PKI for such large scale scenarios.

- **Management and monitoring**   This topic has been a major pain point in the past and we invested significant efforts on the server side to improve that experience. We made it very easy for administrators to deploy PKI and to manage their PKI from a single console. A new CA MOM Pack was created, the CA was armed with a bunch of new performance counters, and the PKI View monitoring console was added to the server default setup. Most important, the CA setup was written from scratch to allow simple and easy deployment of the CA and now provides one-click setup for deploying the CA.

- **Certificate Services Client**   On the client side of the Microsoft PKI we focused on both the UX (user experience) and on the developer experience. A completely new set of developer enrollment API is introduced (CertEnroll). This new COM-based library replaces the legacy XEnroll library, which been around for a long time and provides an object-oriented (OO) developer experience and the ability to practically modify any request extension or attribute. Pretty powerful stuff. By doing that we ensure that we give the proper developer support to enable PKI-aware applications development.

For more information, visit *http://www.microsoft.com/downloads/details.aspx? FamilyID=9bf17231-d832-4ff9-8fb8-0539ba21ab95.*

Avi Ben-Menahem, Lead Program Manager

PKI and Smart Card Technologies

Using Windows Defender

Windows Defender is a tool designed to reduce the risk of specific types of malware for small office and home users. Though Windows Defender is not designed for use in large enterprises, it does provide some integration with Active Directory Group Policy and can retrieve updates from an internal Windows Software Update Services (WSUS) server.

Windows Defender will interact with users if potentially unwanted software is detected. Therefore, users must be trained before Windows Defender is deployed so that they understand how to respond to the various prompts and can distinguish between genuine Windows Defender prompts and other software that might impersonate those prompts (a common social engineering technique).

For more information about Windows Defender, visit the Windows Defender Virtual Lab Express at *http://www.microsoftvirtuallabs.com/express/registration.aspx?LabId=92e04589-cdd9-4e69-8b1b-2d131d9037af.*

Understanding Windows Defender

Windows Defender provides two types of protection, both enabled by default:

- **Automatic scanning**   Windows Defender scans the computer for potentially malicious software on a regular basis. By default, Windows Defender is configured to download updated definitions and then do a quick scan daily at 2:00 A.M. You can configure scanning frequency on the Windows Defender Options page.

- **Real-time protection**   Windows Defender constantly monitors computer usage to notify you if potentially unwanted software might be attempting to make changes to your computer.

The sections that follow describe each type of protection in more detail.

Automatic Scanning

Windows Defender provides two different types of scanning:

- **Quick Scan**   Scans the portions of a computer most likely to be infected by malware, such as the computer's memory and portions of the registry that link to startup applications. This is sufficient to detect most malware applications.

- **Full Scan**   Scans every file on the computer, including common types of file archives as well as applications already loaded in the computer's memory. A full scan typically takes several hours, but it may take more than a day, depending on the speed of the computer and the number of files to be scanned. The user can continue to work on the computer during a quick scan or a full scan; however, these scans do slow the computer down, and will consume battery power on mobile computers very quickly.

By default, Windows Defender runs a quick scan daily. This is usually sufficient. If you think a user might have malware installed, you should run a full scan to increase the chances of removing every trace of the malware. In addition to quick scans and full scans, you can configure a custom scan to scan specific portions of a computer. Custom scans always begin with a quick scan.

If Windows Defender finds potentially unwanted software, it will display a warning, as shown in Figure 25-11.

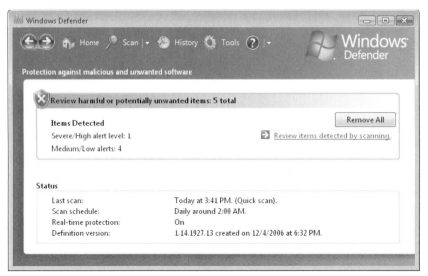

Figure 25-11   Windows Defender notifies the user of potentially unwanted software.

Most of the time, the user should simply choose to remove all of the potentially unwanted software. However, Windows Vista will display four options for each item detected:

- **Ignore**   Allows the software to be installed or run on your computer. If the software is still running during the next scan, or if the software tries to change security-related settings on your computer, Windows Defender will alert you about this software again.

- **Quarantine**   When Windows Defender quarantines software, it moves it to another location on your computer, and then prevents the software from running until you choose to restore it or remove it from your computer.

- **Remove**   Deletes the software from your computer.

- **Always Allow**   Adds the software to the Windows Defender allowed list and allows it to run on your computer. Windows Defender will stop alerting you to actions taken by the program. Add software to the allowed list only if you trust the software and the software publisher.

For more information about malware infections, read the section titled "How to Troubleshoot Problems with Unwanted Software" later in this chapter.

Real-Time Protection

Real-time protection might alert you when software attempts to install itself or run on your computer, as shown in Figure 25-12. Depending on the alert level, users can choose to remove, quarantine, ignore, or always allow the application, just as if the problem were encountered during a scan.

Figure 25-12 Windows Defender real-time protection warns the user if potential malware attempts to make changes to your computer.

If potentially unwanted software is allowed to run on your computer, it sometimes attempts to make changes to system settings so that it will automatically run the next time you start your computer. Of course, legitimate software also makes similar changes, so it's up to the user to determine if the change should be allowed. If Windows Defender real-time protection detects software attempting to make a change to important Windows Settings, the user will be prompted to Permit (allow the change) or Deny (block the change).

Real-time protection provides the following security agents, all of which are enabled by default:

- **Auto Start**   Monitors lists of programs that are allowed to automatically run when you start your computer. Malware typically wants to run after you restart your computer, and frequently adds itself to one of the several lists of autostart programs.

- **System Configuration (Settings)**   Monitors security-related settings in Windows. Malware often attempts to disable security software to make it more difficult for users to detect or remove the malware and to allow other applications to install without the user's permission.

- **Internet Explorer Add-ons**   Monitors programs that automatically run when you start Internet Explorer. Malware can masquerade as web browser add-ons and run without the user's knowledge.

- **Internet Explorer Configurations (Settings)**   Monitors browser security settings, which are your first line of defense against unwanted content on the Internet. Malware can try to change these settings without the user's knowledge to make it easier to make browser configuration changes.

- **Internet Explorer Downloads**   Monitors files and programs that are designed to work with Internet Explorer, such as ActiveX controls and software-installation programs. These files can be downloaded, installed, or run by the browser itself. Unwanted software is often included with these files and installed without the user's knowledge.

- **Services and Drivers**   Monitors services and drivers as they interact with Windows Vista and applications. Malware often attempts to use services and drivers to gain access to protected areas of the operating system.

- **Application Execution**   Monitors when programs start and any operations they perform while running. Malware can use vulnerabilities in previously installed applications to run unwanted software without the user's knowledge. For example, spyware can run itself in the background when a user starts another frequently used application. Windows Defender monitors applications and alerts the user if suspicious activity is detected.

- **Application Registration**   Monitors tools and files in the operating system where applications can register to run at any time, not just when you start Windows Vista or another program. Malware can register a program to start without notice and run at a scheduled time each day, for example. This allows the program to collect information about the user or gain access to important software in the operating system without the user's knowledge.

- **Windows Add-ons**   Monitors add-on programs (also known as software utilities) for Windows Vista. Add-ons are designed to enhance your computing experience in areas such as security, browsing, productivity, and multimedia. However, add-ons can also install programs that will collect information about users and expose sensitive, personal information, often to advertisers.

Windows Defender Alert Levels

When Windows Defender detects potentially malicious software, it assigns one of the following alert levels to it:

- **Severe**   Assigned to potentially unwanted software that can severely affect your computer or compromise your privacy. You should always remove this software.

- **High**   Similar to the severe rating, but slightly less damaging. You should always remove this software.

- **Medium**   Assigned to potentially unwanted software that might compromise your privacy, affect your computer's performance, or display advertising. In some cases, software classified as a medium alert level might have legitimate uses. Evaluate the software before allowing it to be installed.

- **Low**   Assigned to potentially unwanted software that might collect information about you or your computer or change how your computer works, but operates in agreement with licensing terms displayed when you installed the software. This software is typically benign, but it might be installed without the user's knowledge. For example, remote control software might be classified as a Low alert level, because it could be used legitimately, or it might be used by an attacker to control a computer without the owner's knowledge.

■ **Not yet classified**   Programs that haven't yet been analyzed. If you discover software that is not yet classified, you can submit it directly to Microsoft to be considered for classification. For more information, visit *http://www.microsoft.com/athome/security/ spyware/software/support/reportspyware.mspx.*

Understanding Microsoft SpyNet

Microsoft's goal is to create definitions for all qualifying software. However, hundreds of new malware applications are created and distributed every day. Because of the rapid pace of newly released software, users can possibly encounter malware that Microsoft has not yet classified. In these cases, Windows Defender should still warn the user if the malware takes a potentially malicious action such as configuring itself to start automatically each time the computer is restarted.

To help users determine whether or not to allow application changes (detected by real-time protection) when prompted, Windows Defender contacts Microsoft SpyNet to determine how other users have responded when prompted about the same software. If the change is part of a desired software installation, most users will have approved the change, and Windows Defender can use the feedback from SpyNet when informing the user about the change. If the change is unexpected (as it would be for most unwanted software), most users will not approve the change.

Two levels of SpyNet participation are available:

■ **Basic**   Windows Defender sends only basic information to Microsoft, including where the software came from (such as the specific URL) and whether the user or Windows Defender allowed or blocked the item. With basic membership, Windows Defender does not alert users if it detects software or changes made by software that has not yet been analyzed for risks. Although personal information might possibly be sent to Microsoft with either basic or advanced SpyNet membership, Microsoft will not use this information to identify or contact the user.

> **Note**   For more information about what information might be transferred and how Microsoft might use it, view the Windows Defender privacy statement online at *http://go.microsoft.com/fwlink/?linkid=55418.*

■ **Advanced**   Advanced SpyNet membership is intended for users who have an understanding of the inner workings of the operating system and might be able to evaluate whether or not the changes an application is making are malicious. The key difference between basic and advanced membership is that with advanced membership, Windows Defender will alert users when it detects software or changes that have not yet been analyzed for risks. Additionally, advanced membership sends additional information to SpyNet, including the location of the software on the local computer, filenames, how the software operates, and how it has affected the computer.

In addition to providing feedback to users about unknown software, SpyNet is also a valuable resource to Microsoft when identifying new malware. Microsoft analyzes information in SpyNet to create new definitions. In turn, this helps slow the spread of potentially unwanted software.

Configuring Windows Defender Group Policy

You can configure some aspects of Windows Defender Group Policy settings. Windows Defender Group Policy settings are located in Computer Configuration\Policies\ Administrative Templates\Windows Components\Windows Defender. From that node, you can configure the following settings:

- **Turn On Definition Updates Through Both WSUS And Windows Update**   Enabled by default, this setting configures Windows Defender to check Windows Update when a WSUS server is not available locally. This can help ensure that mobile clients, who might not regularly connect to your local network, can stay up to date on malware definitions. If you disable this setting, Windows Defender checks for updates using only the setting defined for the Automatic Updates client—either an internal WSUS server or Windows Update. For more information about WSUS and distributing updates, read Chapter 24, "Managing Software Updates."

> ### Direct from the Source: Malware Analysis
>
> Keeping up to date with the current malware definitions can help protect your computer from harmful or potentially unwanted software. Microsoft has taken several steps to create definition updates, including gathering new samples of suspicious files, observing and testing the samples, and performing a deep analysis. If we determine that the sample does not follow our criteria, its alert level is determined and the software is added to the software definitions and released to customers.
>
> For more information, visit *http://www.microsoft.com/athome/security/spyware/ software/msft/analysis.mspx.*
>
> *Sterling Reasor, Program Manager*
>
> *Windows Defender*

- **Check For New Signatures Before Scheduled Scans**   Disabled by default, you can enable this setting to cause Windows Defender to always check for updates prior to a scan. This helps ensure that Windows Defender has the most up-to-date signatures. When you disable this setting, Windows Defender still downloads updates on a regular basis but will not necessarily check immediately prior to a scan.

- **Turn Off Windows Defender**   Enable this setting to turn off Windows Defender Real-Time Protection and to remove any scheduled scans. You should enable this setting only if you are using different anti-malware software. If Windows Defender is turned off, users can still manually run the tool to scan for potentially unwanted software.

- **Turn Off Real-Time Protection Prompts For Unknown Detection**   If you enable this policy setting, Windows Defender does not prompt users to allow or block unknown activity. If you disable or do not configure this policy setting, by default Windows Defender prompts users to allow or block unknown activity on their computers.

- **Enable Logging Known Good Detections**   By default, Windows Defender adds an event to the Event Log only when it detects a potentially malicious file. If you enable this setting (it is disabled by default), Windows Defender will also log files that it determines are not a problem. You should enable this setting only if you are troubleshooting a problem. In fact, enabling this setting will cause a large number of events to be added to the computer's Event Log, causing performance problems.

- **Enable Logging Unknown Detection**   Enabled by default, this setting configures Windows Defender to add events to the Event Log when it finds a potentially malicious file during Real-Time Protection. Disable this setting if you do not find the events useful.

- **Download Entire Signature Set**   By default, this setting is disabled, which causes Windows Defender to download only incremental signature updates (in other words, just the new signatures since it downloaded them last). If you enable this setting, Windows Defender will download the full signature set, which could be very large. Because downloading the full signature set will use more network bandwidth, you should enable this setting only when troubleshooting a problem with signatures.

- **Configure Microsoft SpyNet Reporting**   Microsoft SpyNet is the online community that helps users choose how to respond to potential spyware threats that Microsoft has not yet classified by showing users how other members have responded to an alert. When enabled and set to Basic or Advanced, Windows Defender will display information about how other users responded to a potential threat. When enabled and set to Basic, Windows Defender will also submit a small amount of information about the potentially malicious files on the user's computer. When set to Advanced, Windows Defender will send more detailed information. If you enable this setting and set it to No Membership, SpyNet will not be used, and the user will not be able to change the setting. If you leave this setting Disabled (the default), SpyNet will not be used unless the user changes the setting on his local computer.

Windows Defender Group Policy settings are defined in WindowsDefender.admx, which is included with Windows Vista. For more information about using Group Policy administrative templates, read Chapter 13, "Managing the Desktop Environment."

Configuring Windows Defender on a Single Computer

Besides the settings that you can configure by using Group Policy, Windows Defender includes many settings that you can configure only by using the Windows Defender Options page on a local computer. To open the Options page, launch Windows Defender, click Tools, and then click Options. Some of the settings you can configure from this page include:

- Frequency and time of automatic scans

- Which security agents are automatically scanned

- Specific files and folders to be excluded from scans

- Whether non-administrators can run Windows Defender

Because you cannot easily configure these settings with Group Policy settings, Windows Defender might not be the right choice for enterprise spyware control.

Windows Defender Tools

Windows Defender includes several useful tools that you can access by clicking Tools on the Windows Defender toolbar:

- **Software Explorer**   It's very difficult to track software installed on a computer, because it can be installed in many different places. For example, startup programs can be installed as services, referenced in several different registry locations, or added to a user's (or all users') Startup group. Software Explorer, shown in Figure 25-13, allows you to browse and disable applications installed on your computer. You can also use Software Explorer to view and terminate running processes (much like Task Manager), to browse running processes that are currently networked, and to browse Winsock Service Providers.

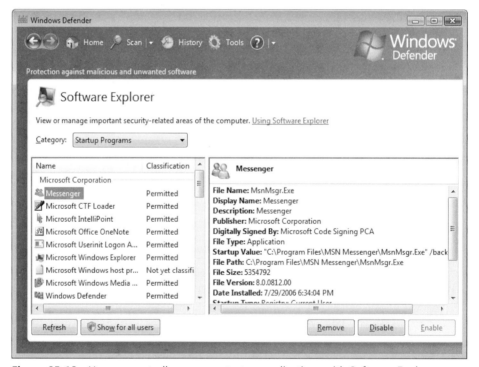

Figure 25-13   You can centrally manage startup applications with Software Explorer.

■ **Allowed Items**   Use the Allowed Items tool in Windows Defender to view items that an administrator has configured as safe. Windows Defender will not alert the user about changes made by items on this list.

■ **Quarantined Items**   Use the Quarantined Items tool in Windows Defender to view items that an administrator has configured as unsafe. If you are having a problem installing an application, it's possible that it has been mistakenly added to the Quarantined Items list. You need administrative privileges to manage this list.

■ **History**   Available by clicking History on the Windows Defender toolbar, this tool displays changes that Windows Defender either allowed or blocked, and whether or not Windows Defender prompted the user for approval. If you are experiencing problems installing an application or making system changes, you should check the history, as shown in Figure 25-14, to determine if Windows Defender might be involved.

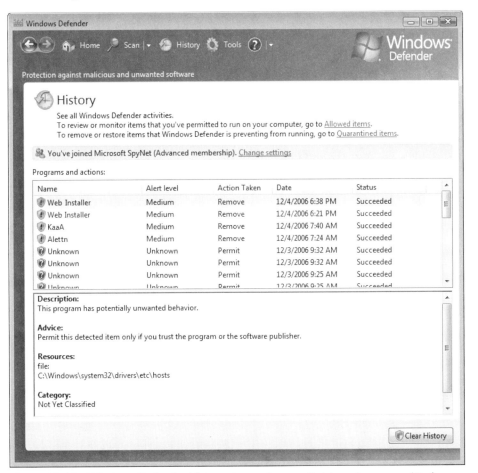

Figure 25-14   Windows Defender History shows changes that have been permitted or blocked.

How to Determine If a Computer Is Infected with Spyware

Several signs indicate if a computer is infected with spyware. You should train users in your environment to notice these changes and call your support center if they suspect a malware infection:

- A new, unexpected application appears.

- Unexpected icons appear in the system tray.

- Unexpected notifications appear near the system tray.

- The web browser home page, default search engine, or Favorites change.

- The mouse pointer changes.

- New toolbars appear, especially in web browsers.

- The web browser displays additional advertisements when visiting a web page, or pop-up advertisements appear when the user is not using the web.

- When the user attempts to visit a web page, he is redirected to a completely different web page.

- The computer runs more slowly than usual. This can be caused by many different problems; however, malware is one of the most common causes.

Some malware might not have any noticeable symptoms, but it still might compromise private information. For best results, run Windows Defender real-time protection with daily quick scans.

Requiring Windows Defender Using Network Access Protection

You can use Network Access Protection (NAP), as described later in this chapter, to restrict network access for client computers that do not have Windows Defender (or another antispyware tool) installed with up-to-date signatures. As shown in Figure 25-15, the Windows Security Health Validator (SHV), included with Windows Server 2008, works with the Windows Security Center in Windows Vista or Windows XP to verify security settings.

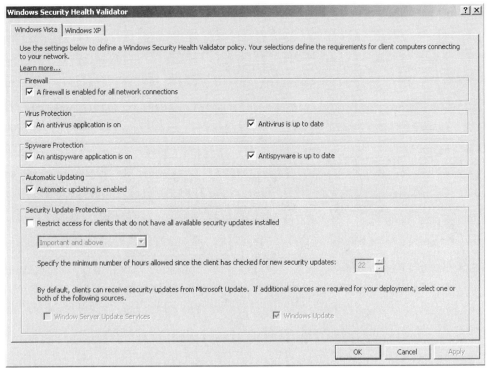

Figure 25-15 Windows Security Health Validator works with the Windows Security Center.

Best Practices for Using Windows Defender

To receive the security benefits of Windows Defender while minimizing the costs, follow these best practices:

- Teach users how malware works and the problems that malware can cause. In particular, focus on teaching users to avoid being tricked into installing malware by social engineering attacks.

- Before deploying Windows Vista, test all applications with Windows Defender enabled to ensure that Windows Defender does not alert users to normal changes the application might make. If a legitimate application does cause warnings, add the application to the Windows Defender allowed list.

- Change the scheduled scan time to meet the needs of your business. By default, Windows Defender scans at 2:00 A.M. If third-shift staff uses computers overnight, you might want to find a better time to perform the scan. If users turn off their computers when they are not in the office, you should schedule the scan to occur during the day. Although the automatic quick scan can slow down computer performance, it typically takes fewer than 10 minutes, and users can continue working. Any performance cost is typically outweighed by the security benefits.

- Use WSUS to manage and distribute signature updates.

- Use antivirus software with Windows Defender. Alternatively, you might disable Windows Defender completely and use client-security software that provides both antispyware and antivirus functionality.

- Do not deploy Windows Defender in enterprises. Instead, use Microsoft Forefront Client Security or a third-party client-security suite that can be more easily managed in enterprise environments.

How to Troubleshoot Problems with Unwanted Software

If a malware infection is found during a scan, Windows Defender will prompt the user to choose how to respond. Typically, the user should allow Windows Defender to attempt to remove the malware.

A malware infection is rarely a single application; most successful malware infections automatically install several, even dozens, of malicious applications. Some of those applications might be straightforward to remove. However, if even a single malicious application remains, that remaining malware application might continue to install other malware applications.

If you detect a malware problem, follow these steps to troubleshoot it:

1. Perform a quick scan and remove any potentially malicious applications. Then, immediately perform a full scan and remove any additional potentially malicious software. The full scan can take many hours to run. Windows Defender will probably need to restart Windows Vista.

2. If the malware has made changes to Internet Explorer, such as adding unwanted add-ons or changing the home page, refer to Chapter 21 for troubleshooting information.

3. Run antivirus scans on your computer. Often, spyware might install software that is classified as a virus, or the vulnerability exploited by spyware might also be exploited by a virus. Window Defender cannot detect or remove viruses. Remove any viruses installed on the computer.

4. If you still see signs of malware, install an additional antispyware and antivirus application. With complicated infections, a single anti-malware tool might not be able to completely remove the infection. Your chances of removing all traces of malware increase by using multiple applications, but you should not configure multiple applications to provide real-time protection.

5. If problems persist, shut down the computer and use the Startup Repair tool to perform a System Restore. Restore the computer to a date prior to the malware infection. System Restore will typically remove any startup settings that cause malware applications to run, but it will not remove the executable files themselves. Use this only as a last resort: Although System Restore will not remove a user's personal files, it can cause problems with recently installed or configured applications. For more information, see Chapter 30, "Configuring Startup and Troubleshooting Startup Issues."

These steps will resolve the vast majority of malware problems. However, once malware has run on a computer, you can never be certain that the software is completely removed. In particular, malware known as *rootkits* can install themselves in such a way that they are undetectable on a computer. In these circumstances, the only sure way to remove the malicious software is to reformat the hard disk, reinstall Windows Vista, and then restore user files using a backup created prior to the infection.

Network Access Protection

Many organizations have been affected by viruses or worms that entered their private networks through a mobile PC and quickly infected computers throughout the organization. Windows Vista, when connecting to a Windows Server 2008 infrastructure, supports NAP to reduce the risks of connecting unhealthy computers to private networks directly or across a VPN. If a computer running Windows Vista lacks current security updates or virus signatures—or otherwise fails to meet your requirements for computer health—NAP blocks the computer from having unlimited access to your private network. If a computer fails to meet the health requirements, it will be connected to a restricted network to download and install the updates, antivirus signatures, or configuration settings that are required to comply with current health requirements. Within minutes, a potentially vulnerable computer can be updated, have its new health state validated, and then be granted unlimited access to your network.

NAP is not designed to secure a network from malicious users. It is designed to help administrators maintain the health of the computers on the network, which in turns helps maintain the network's overall integrity. For example, if a computer has all the software and configuration settings that the health requirement policy requires, the computer is considered compliant, and it will be granted unlimited access to the network. NAP does not prevent an authorized user with a compliant computer from uploading a malicious program to the network or engaging in other inappropriate behavior.

Network Access Protection has three important and distinct aspects:

- **Network Policy Validation** When a user attempts to connect to the network, the computer's health state is validated against the network access policies as defined by the administrator. Administrators can then choose what to do if a computer is not compliant. In a monitoring-only environment, all authorized computers are granted access to the network even if some do not comply with health requirement policies, but the compliance state of each computer is logged. In an isolation environment, computers that comply with the health requirement policies are allowed unlimited access to the network, but computers that do not comply with health requirement policies or are not compatible with NAP are placed on a restricted network. In both environments, administrators can define exceptions to the validation process. NAP also includes migration tools to make it easier for administrators to define exceptions that best suit their network needs.

■ **Health Requirement Policy Compliance**   Administrators can help ensure compliance with health requirement policies by choosing to automatically update noncompliant computers with the required updates through management software, such as Microsoft Systems Center Configuration Manager. In a monitoring-only environment, computers will have access to the network even before they are updated with required software or configuration changes. In an isolation environment, computers that do not comply with health requirement policies have limited access until the software and configuration updates are completed. Again, in both environments, the administrator can define policy exceptions.

■ **Limited Access for Noncompliant Computers**   Administrators can protect network assets by limiting the access of computers that do not comply with health requirement requirements. Computers that do not comply will have their network access limited as defined by the administrator. That access can be limited to a restricted network, to a single resource, or to no internal resources at all. If an administrator does not configure health update resources, the limited access will last for the duration of the connection. If an administrator configures health update resources, the limited access will last only until the computer is brought into compliance.

NAP is an extensible platform that provides an infrastructure and an application programming interface (API) set for adding components that verify and remediate a computer's health to comply with health requirement policies. By itself, NAP does not provide components to verify or correct a computer's health. Other components, known as system health agents (SHAs) and system health validators (SHVs), provide automated system health reporting, validation, and remediation. Windows Vista and Windows Server 2008 will include an SHA and an SHV that allow the network administrator to specify health requirements for the services monitored by the Windows Security Center.

> **Note**   The NAP platform is not the same as Network Access Quarantine Control, which is a feature included with Windows Server 2003 to provide limited health policy enforcement only for remote access (dial-up and VPN) connections.

When troubleshooting client-side problems related to Network Access Protection, open Event Viewer and browse the Applications And Services Logs\Microsoft\Windows\Network Access Protection event log. For more information about configuring a NAP infrastructure with Windows Server 2008, read Chapters 14 through 19 of *Windows Server 2008 Networking and Network Access Protection* by Joseph Davies and Tony Northrup (Microsoft Press, 2008).

Microsoft Forefront Client Security

Microsoft Forefront Client Security (FCS) is enterprise security software that provides protection from malware in addition to many other threats. Whereas Windows Defender is designed for consumers and small businesses, FCS is designed to be deployed throughout large networks and managed efficiently. As shown in Figure 25-16, you can use FCS to centrally manage client security.

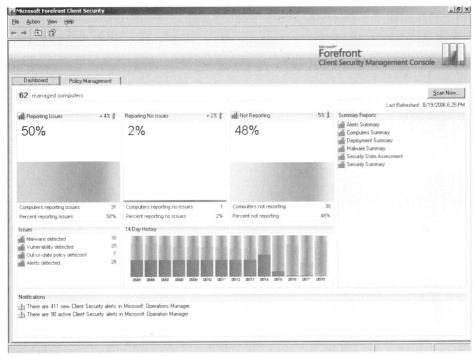

Figure 25-16   You can use FCS to centrally manage client security.

Microsoft Forefront products are designed to provide defense-in-depth by protecting desktops, laptops, and server operating systems. Forefront currently consists of the following products:

- Microsoft Forefront Client Security

- Microsoft Forefront Security for Exchange Server (formerly called Microsoft Antigen for Exchange)

- Microsoft Forefront Security for SharePoint (formerly called Antigen for SharePoint)

- Microsoft Forefront Security for Office Communications Server (formerly called Antigen for Instant Messaging)

- Microsoft Internet Security and Acceleration (ISA) Server 2006

Of these products, only FCS would be deployed to Windows Vista or Windows XP client computers. The other products would typically be deployed on servers to protect applications, networks, and infrastructure.

Enterprise management of anti-malware software is useful for:

- Centralized policy management.

- Alerting and reporting on malware threats in your environment.

- Comprehensive insight into the security state of your environment, including security update status and up-to-date signatures.

FCS provides a simple user interface for creating policies that you can automatically distribute to organizational units (OUs) and security groups by using Group Policy objects. Clients also centrally report their status so that administrators can view the overall status of client security in the enterprise, as shown in Figure 25-17.

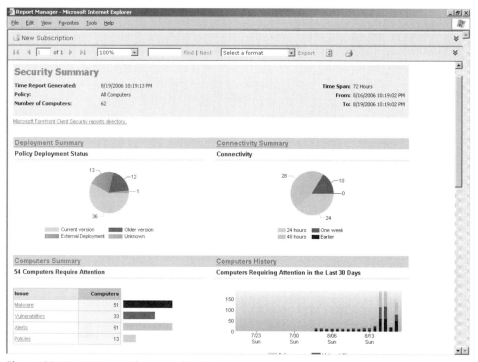

Figure 25-17   FCS provides centralized client security status.

With FCS, administrators can view statistics ranging from domain-wide to specific groups of computers or individual computers to understand the impact of specific threats. In other words, if malware does infect computers in your organization, you can easily discover the infection, isolate the affected computers, and then take steps to resolve the problems.

FCS also provides a client-side user interface. Similar to Windows Defender, FCS can warn users if an application attempts to make potentially malicious changes, or if it detects known malware attempting to run. The key differences between Defender and FCS are:

- **FCS is centrally managed**   FCS is designed for use in medium and large networks. Administrators can use the central management console to view a summary of current threats and vulnerabilities, computers that need to be updated, and computers that are currently having security problems. Windows Defender is designed for home computers and small offices only, and threats must be managed on local computers.

- **FCS is highly configurable**   You can configure automated responses to alerts, and, for example, prevent users from running known malware instead of giving them the opportunity to override a warning as they can do with Windows Defender.

- **FCS protects against all types of malware**   Windows Defender is designed to protect against spyware. Forefront protects against spyware, viruses, rootkits, worms, and Trojan horses. If you use Windows Defender, you need another application to protect against the additional threats.

- **FCS can protect a wider variety of Windows platforms**   FCS is designed to protect Windows 2000, Windows XP, Windows Server 2003, and Windows Vista computers. Windows Defender can protect only Windows XP and Windows Vista computers.

Like Windows Defender, FCS supports using WSUS to distribute updated signatures to client computers, but FCS also supports using third-party software distribution systems. For more information about FCS, visit *http://www.microsoft.com/forefront/default.mspx*. Also, explore the Microsoft TechNet Virtual Labs at *http://technet.microsoft.com/en-us/bb499665.aspx*.

Note   Microsoft offers a third client security solution: Windows Live OneCare. Windows Live OneCare is designed to help protect home computers and small businesses with antivirus protection, antispyware protection, improved firewall software, performance monitoring, and backup and restore assistance. For more information, visit *http://onecare.live.com/*.

Summary

Windows Vista is designed to be secure by default, but default settings don't meet everyone's needs. Additionally, the highly secure default settings can cause compatibility problems with applications not written specifically for Windows Vista. For these reasons, it's important that you understand the client-security technologies built into Windows Vista and how to configure them.

The most significant security improvement is User Account Control (UAC). By default, both users and administrators are limited to Standard user privileges, which reduces the damage that malware could do if it were to successfully launch a process in the user context. If an application needs elevated privileges, UAC prompts the user to confirm the request or to provide administrative credentials. Because UAC changes the default privileges for applications, it can cause problems with applications that require administrative rights. To minimize these problems, UAC provides file and registry virtualization that redirects requests for protected resources to user-specific locations that won't impact the entire system.

Microsoft also provides Windows Defender for additional protection from malware. Windows Defender is signature-based and heuristic antispyware detection. If it finds malware on a computer, it gives the user the opportunity to prevent it from installing or to remove it if it's already installed. Windows Defender isn't designed for enterprise use, however. For improved manageability and protection against other forms of malware (including viruses and rootkits), use Microsoft Forefront Client Security or another similar enterprise client-security solution.

Additional Resources

These resources contain additional information and tools related to this chapter.

Related Information

- Chapter 2, "Security in Windows Vista," includes an overview of malware.

- Chapter 4, "Planning Deployment," includes more information about application compatibility.

- Chapter 21, "Managing Internet Explorer," includes more information about protecting Internet Explorer.

- Chapter 24, "Managing Software Updates," includes information about deploying WSUS.

- Chapter 27, "Configuring Windows Firewall and IPsec," includes more information about Windows Service Hardening.

- Chapter 30, "Configuring Startup and Troubleshooting Startup Issues," includes information about running System Restore.

- "Behavioral Modeling of Social Engineering–Based Malicious Software" at *http://www.microsoft.com/downloads/details.aspx?FamilyID=e0f27260-58da-40db-8785-689cf6a05c73* includes information about social-engineering attacks.

- "Windows Vista Security Guide" at *http://www.microsoft.com/downloads/details.aspx?FamilyID=a3d1bbed-7f35-4e72-bfb5-b84a526c1565* includes detailed information about how to best configure Windows Vista security for your organization.

- "Microsoft Security Intelligence Report" at *http://www.microsoft.com/downloads/details.aspx?FamilyId=1C443104-5B3F-4C3A-868E-36A553FE2A02* includes information about trends in the malicious and potentially unwanted software landscape.

Part V
Networking

Chapter 26

Configuring Windows Networking

Windows Vista introduces many new networking features that are important for administrators to understand. Some of the features might require additional configuration, depending on how your organization uses them. This chapter discusses how Windows Vista addresses the concerns of a modern network, how you can configure and manage these new features, and how you can deploy Windows Vista to take advantage of modern, flexible networking.

Usability Improvements

Improving the usability of Windows Vista helps both end users and administrators. End users benefit because they can get more done in less time, and administrators benefit because end users make fewer support calls.

The sections that follow describe important networking usability improvements, including the new Network And Sharing Center, Network Explorer, the Network Map, and the Set Up A Connection Or Network Wizard. Understanding these features will help you to use them effectively and guide end users through many common network configuration and troubleshooting tasks.

Network And Sharing Center

Windows Vista's Network And Sharing Center, shown in Figure 26-1, provides a clear view of available wireless networks, a Network Map to show the surrounding network resources on a home or unmanaged network, and easy methods to create or join ad hoc wireless networks. Diagnostic tools built into Network And Sharing Center simplify troubleshooting connectivity problems. Users can also browse network resources with the new Network Explorer, which they can start by clicking View Computers And Devices.

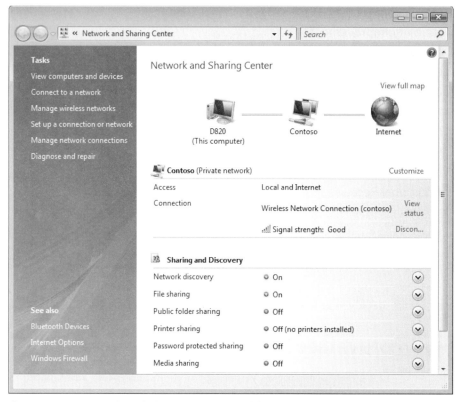

Figure 26-1   Network And Sharing Center simplifies network management for end users.

Network And Sharing Center is especially useful for traveling users who connect to wireless networks and virtual private networks (VPNs). With previous versions of Windows, connecting remotely can be complicated. Without direct access to IT support, troubleshooting these connection problems can be difficult. Network And Sharing Center should reduce the number of IT support calls related to remote connectivity.

If a network connection is not available, such as a failed Internet connection (even if the link connected to the computer is functioning), Network And Sharing Center detects this failure and displays it graphically on the abbreviated version of the Network Map, shown in Figure 26-2. Users can troubleshoot the problem simply by clicking the failed portion of the network map to launch Windows Network Diagnostics.

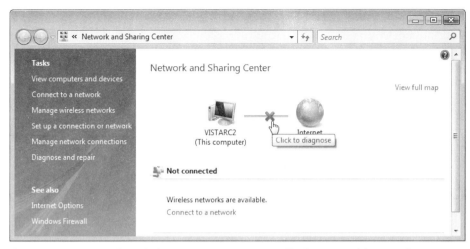

Figure 26-2   Network And Sharing Center automatically detects problems and can assist users with diagnosis and troubleshooting.

Figure 26-3 shows some of the suggestions that Windows Network Diagnostics can display when Windows Vista cannot reach the DNS server and domain controller (the specific suggestions will vary depending on network conditions and your computer configuration). Although the suggestions offered by Windows Network Diagnostics will not solve all network problems, they can provide useful information for further troubleshooting and might offer a link to resolve the problem without requiring the user to call Help Desk. If the user does choose to take an action, such as resetting the network adapter, Windows Network Diagnostics will automatically retest the connection and provide additional troubleshooting information to the user if the problem persists.

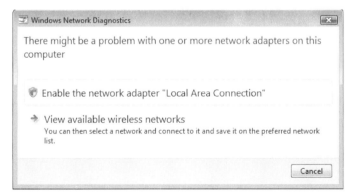

Figure 26-3   Windows Network Diagnostics can solve many common problems.

To open Network And Sharing Center, click Start, click Network, and then click Network And Sharing Center. Alternatively, you can click Start, right-click Network, and then click Properties.

Network Explorer

Like My Network Places in Windows XP, Network Explorer (also known as the Network folder) allows users to browse resources on the local network. However, Network Explorer is more powerful than My Network Places, largely because of the Network Discovery support built into Windows Vista (described later in this section).

To open Network Explorer, click Start and then click Network. As shown in Figure 26-4, Network Explorer displays other visible computers and network devices. Users can access network resources simply by double-clicking them.

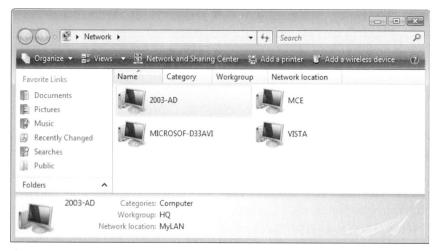

Figure 26-4   Network Explorer allows users to browse local resources.

The following sections discuss how different aspects of Network Explorer function, including Network Discovery and the Network Map.

How Windows Vista Finds Network Resources

Previous versions of Windows use NetBIOS broadcasts to announce their presence on the network to facilitate finding shared resources in workgroup environments. Windows Vista expands this capability with a feature called Network Discovery, or Function Discovery (FD). Network Discovery's primary purpose is to simplify configuring and connecting network devices in home and small office environments. For example, Network Discovery can enable the Media Center component of Windows Vista to detect a Media Center Extender device (such as an Xbox 360) when it is connected to the network.

Network Discovery can be enabled or disabled separately for different network location types. For example, Network Discovery is enabled by default on networks with the private location type, but it is disabled on networks with the public location type. By properly configuring network location types (described later in this chapter), Windows Vista computers in your environment can take advantage of Network Discovery when connected to your internal networks, but minimize security risks by disabling Network Discovery when connected to other networks such as the Internet. You might want to leave Network Discovery enabled for some network location types so that users can more easily find network resources on your intranet that aren't listed in the Active Directory, and so that users with mobile PCs can more easily configure network devices on their home networks or when traveling.

Though Network Discovery is preferred, Windows Vista continues to use the Computer Browser service and NetBIOS broadcasts to find earlier versions of Windows computers on the network. Additionally, Windows Vista uses the Function Discovery Provider Host service and Web Services Dynamic Discovery (WS-Discovery) to find other Windows Vista computers, and Universal Plug and Play (UPnP)/Simple Service Discovery Protocol (SSDP) to find networked devices that support the protocols. Therefore, enabling Network Discovery in Network And Sharing Center creates exceptions for each of these protocols through Windows Firewall.

WS-Discovery is a multicast discovery protocol developed by Microsoft, BEA, Canon, Intel, and webMethods to provide a method for locating services on a network. To find network resources, Windows Vista computers send a multicast request for one or more target services, such as shared folders and printers. Then, any computers on the local network with shared resources that match the request use WS-Discovery to respond to the message. To minimize the need for clients to regularly send requests to find new resources, newly published resources announce themselves on the network, as described in the next section.

WS-Discovery uses SOAP over UDP port 3702. The multicast address is 239.255.255.250 for IPv4, and FF2::C for IPv6.

How Windows Vista Publishes Network Resources

When you share a network resource, such as a folder or printer, Windows Vista communicates using several protocols to make other computers on the network aware of the resource. To communicate with earlier versions of Windows, the Server service notifies the Computer Browser service when new shares are created or deleted, and the Computer Browser service sends the announcements over NetBIOS.

To announce resources to other Windows Vista computers using WS-Discovery, Windows Vista uses the Function Discovery Resource Publication (FDRP) service. Although FD is responsible for discovering shared resources on a network when the computer is acting as a client, FDRP is responsible for announcing resources when the computer is acting as a server. The primary functions are:

- Sends a HELLO message for each registered resource on service startup.
- Sends a HELLO message whenever a new resource is registered. Responds to network probes for resources matching one of the registered resources by type.

- Resolves network requests for resources matching one of the registered resources by name.

- Sends a BYE message whenever a resource is unregistered.

- Sends a BYE message for each registered resource on service shutdown.

The HELLO message includes the following information:

- Name

- Description

- Whether the computer is part of a workgroup or domain

- Computer type, such as desktop, laptop, tablet, media center, or server

- Whether or not Remote Desktop is enabled and allowed through Windows Firewall

- Folder and printer shares with at least Read Access for Everyone if file sharing is enabled and allowed through Windows Firewall. Specifically, administrative shares are not announced. For each share, the following information is included:

  ❑ Path

  ❑ If applicable, the folder type (such as documents, pictures, music, or videos)

  ❑ The share permissions assigned to the Everyone special group

FDRP is primarily intended for home networks, where ease of use is typically a requirement and networks are unmanaged. In corporate computing environments, where there can be a large number of computers on a single subnet and the network is managed, FDRP is not recommended, because the traffic might become a nuisance. By default FDPS is enabled in a workgroup and disabled in a domain environment.

How Windows Vista Creates the Network Map

Windows Vista creates the Network Map in part by using the Link Layer Topology Discovery (LLTD) protocol. As the name suggests, LLTD functions at Layer 2 (the layer devices use to communicate on a local area network, or LAN) and enables network devices to identify each other, learn about the network (including bandwidth capabilities), and establish communications (even if devices have not yet been configured with IP addresses). Typically, you do not need to manage LLTD directly. However, you can configure two Group Policy settings located within Computer Configuration\Policies\Administrative Templates\ Network\Link Layer Topology Discovery:

- **Turn on Responder (RSPNDR) Driver**   This setting enables computers to be discovered on a network and to participate in Quality of Service (QoS) activities such as bandwidth estimation and network health analysis. You can choose to enable the responder driver while connected to networks of the domain, public, or private location type. Windows Vista enables the responder driver for all networks by default.

■ **Turn on Mapper I/O (LLTDIO) Driver**   This setting enables a computer to discover the topology of the local network and to initiate QoS requests. You can choose to enable the mapper driver while connected to networks of the domain, public, or private location type. This option is enabled for all networks by default. Windows Vista enables the mapper driver for all networks by default.

Figure 26-5 illustrates how the LLTD responder and mapper relate to other Windows Vista networking components.

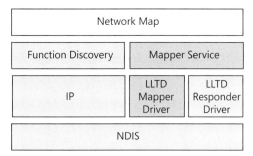

Figure 26-5   LLTD is implemented as a low-level mapper and responder.

Note   Windows Vista clients include an LLTD responder, but earlier versions of Windows do not. To find out how to download an LLTD responder that you can add to Windows XP, read Microsoft Knowledge Base article 992120 at *http://support.microsoft.com/kb/922120*. This will enable Windows XP computers to appear on the network maps in Windows Vista, but Windows XP computers still cannot generate the maps.

LLTD is not a secure protocol, and there is no guarantee that the Network Map is accurate. It is possible for devices on the network to send false announcements, adding bogus items to the map.

Because each user can have his or her own set of network profiles, Windows Vista creates network maps on a per-user basis. For each network profile that a user creates, Windows Vista actually generates two maps: the current map and a copy of the last functional map (similar to the Last Known Good recovery option). When displaying the Network Map to the user, Windows Vista combines these two maps.

Network Map

Network Map, shown in Figure 26-6, makes it simpler to visually examine how a computer is connected to one or more networks and to other computers on your intranet. Although the tool is primarily intended to simplify networking for end users, it is also a useful tool for administrators. A user can click the name of her computer to view her computer's properties, click a local network to view network resources with Network Explorer, or click the Internet icon to browse the web.

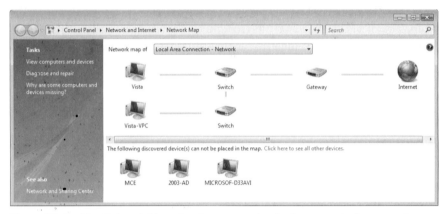

Figure 26-6   The Network Map visually represents all of a computer's connections.

For Windows Vista to create a full network map, the LLTD Mapper service must be running and network mapping must be enabled. This service is set to start manually by default; the Network Map will automatically start the service when required. You should avoid disabling the LLTD Mapper service unless you also want to disable network mapping. Network maps might not always be accurate; Windows Vista might not display devices that do not support LLTD.

Network mapping is disabled by default when a computer is connected to a domain. To enable Network Map, enable the Turn On Mapper I/O (LLTDIO) Driver Group Policy setting (described in the previous section) and select the Allow Operation While In Domain check box. To enable Windows Vista client computers to appear on other computers' maps, enable the Turn On Responder (RSPNDR) Driver setting.

Networking Icons in the System Tray

In Windows XP, each network adapter can have a separate icon in the system tray, and the icon only communicates whether or not the network adapter is connected to the local network. In Windows Vista, a single icon represents all network adapters, allowing users with multiple network adapters to quickly determine connectivity. As shown in Figure 26-7, the networking icon has four states:

- **No connectivity**   Represented by an icon with a red X, this indicates that no network adapters are connected to the local network.

- **Connectivity problem**   Represented by an icon with an exclamation point on a yellow triangle, this indicates a connectivity problem. When this icon is displayed, you can use network diagnostics to attempt to troubleshoot the problem.

- **Local connectivity only**   Represented by an icon without an X or a globe, this indicates that at least one network adapter is connected to the local network, but cannot reach the Internet.

■ **Internet connectivity**   Represented by an icon with a globe, this indicates that at least one network adapter is connected to the local network and that Windows Vista can reach the Internet.

Figure 26-7   The new networking icons communicate network connectivity separate from the status of individual network adapters.

If the computer has multiple network connections that have different levels of connectivity, the tray icon will only communicate the greatest level of connectivity. To display the status of individual network adapters, click the icon or pause the cursor on the icon.

The Set Up A Connection Or Network Wizard

Windows Vista includes a new network setup wizard to further simplify connecting to wired networks, wireless networks, dial-up connections, and VPNs. Typically, administrators should configure all required network connections before deploying a computer. However, users often need to add wireless connections, VPN connections, and dial-up connections after a computer is deployed.

For more information about setting up wireless networks, read the section titled "Manually Configuring Wireless Settings" later in this chapter. For more information about setting up dial-up connections and VPNs, see Chapter 28, "Connecting Remote Users and Networks."

Manageability Improvements

Windows Vista networking includes several improvements in manageability. First, network location types enable you to configure different security settings to better protect computers when connected to public networks, but still enable required functionality when connected to private networks. Administrators can configure policy-based QoS to make better use of available networks and ensure that the most critical network applications have the bandwidth they need. Windows Firewall and Internet Protocol security (IPsec) continue to provide network filtering, authentication, and encryption, but you can now manage both features using a single tool. Windows Connect Now simplifies end-user configuration of computers and network devices.

The sections that follow describe these features in more detail.

Network Location Types

Different types of networks require different levels of protection. For example, when connected to your internal Active Directory network, you might want Windows Vista computers to allow network management tools to establish incoming connections. However, you would not want to allow management connections if a user connects to a wireless hotspot at an airport or coffee shop.

Windows Vista provides three different network location types:

■ **Public** With public networks, such as wireless hotspots, protecting the computer from network attacks is vital. Network Discovery is disabled by default for public networks, and Windows Firewall blocks all unrequested, incoming traffic unless you specifically create exceptions.

■ **Private** Private networks are designed to be used for home or small office networks, where you may want to share resources with other computers on the LAN, but you do not have an Active Directory domain controller. Network Discovery is enabled by default on private networks.

■ **Domain** Anytime the Windows Vista computer can connect to and authenticate with an Active Directory domain controller of the domain for which it is a member, the network is considered a domain network. Windows Firewall and Network Discovery are disabled by default on domain networks, unless overridden by domain Group Policy settings. Administrators should use Group Policy settings to create Windows Firewall exceptions for internal monitoring and management software to the domain network.

It is important to understand network location types because any Windows Firewall exceptions you create apply to only the currently configured network location type. For example, if you want to allow Internet Information Services (IIS) to accept incoming connections when you are connected to your home network, you should specify that the home network is a private network prior to creating the exception. If your home network is configured as a public network when you create the exception, IIS will be available when you are connected to public networks such as wireless hotspots, thereby exposing IIS to attacks from the Internet.

Domain networks are configured automatically when a computer connects to a domain controller. All other networks are considered public networks by default. To specify a network as the private location type, follow these steps:

1. Connect your computer to the network you want to configure as private.

2. Open Network And Sharing Center. Click Customize, located next to your network connection.

3. The Customize Network Settings dialog box appears. Click Private and then click Next.

> **Note**   You can also use this dialog box to give a network a more meaningful name than simply Network, Network1, or Network2.

 4. Click Close.

Because Windows Vista might connect to many different networks, it stores profiles of each network using the network's DNS suffix and gateway MAC address. The gateway MAC address uniquely identifies a network adapter in your router.

Depending on your network configuration, Windows Vista might generate multiple network locations for a single network. To merge two or more network locations so that Windows Vista recognizes them as a single network location, follow these steps:

 1. Connect your computer to a network you want to merge.

 2. Open Network And Sharing Center. Click Customize, located next to your network connection.

 3. The Customize Network Settings dialog box appears. Click Merge Or Delete Network Locations.

 4. In the Merge Or Delete Network Locations dialog box, click the network locations that you want to merge and then click Merge.

 5. Click OK.

Policy-Based QoS

The cost of bandwidth has fallen significantly in the last several years, but network congestion is still a problem. As more people and organizations begin to use real-time networking services, such as Voice over IP (VoIP), multimedia streaming, and video conferencing, it is obvious that increasing bandwidth alone cannot solve network quality problems.

> **Note**   Windows Vista supports Quality Windows Audio Video Experience (qWAVE), which provides QoS support for streaming audio and video across home networks. Because this Resource Kit focuses on enterprise networking, qWave is not discussed in detail. Instead, all references to QoS refer to enterprise QoS, also known as eQoS.

Policy-based QoS in Windows Vista enables domain-wide management of how computers on your network use bandwidth. This technology can solve network problems and make possible the following scenarios:

 ■ Enable real-time traffic by prioritizing more important applications, such as VoIP, over lower priority traffic, such as browsing the web or downloading e-mail.

- Customize bandwidth requirements for groups of users and computers. For example, you can prioritize traffic for your IT support center over other users to increase responsiveness when managing and troubleshooting computers.

- Minimize the negative impact of high-bandwidth, low-priority traffic such as backup data transfers by using prioritization and throttling.

Network congestion problems occur because high-bandwidth applications tend to consume all available bandwidth, and applications are not written to give central bandwidth control to IT administrators. Adding more bandwidth does not usually solve these problems. Instead, adding more bandwidth only leads to applications consuming the newly available capacity. IT administrators need a central means to control and allocate bandwidth resources based on the needs of their business.

Policy-based QoS enables you to make the most of your current bandwidth by enabling flexible bandwidth management through Group Policy settings. With Policy-based QoS, you can prioritize and/or throttle outbound network traffic without requiring applications to be modified for QoS support. You can use Differentiated Services Code Point (DSCP) marking to configure QoS policies to outbound traffic so that network equipment can prioritize it or specify a maximum throttle rate. DSCP marking is useful only if prioritization is enabled in routers. Almost all enterprise-class routers support DSCP prioritization; however, it is usually disabled by default.

Each Windows Vista computer can prioritize or throttle outbound traffic based on a mix of any of the following conditions:

- Group of users or computers based on an Active Directory container, such as a domain, site, or organizational unit

- Sending application

- Source or destination IPv4 or IPv6 address (including network prefix length notation, such as 192.168.1.0/24)

- Source or destination TCP or UDP port number

> **Note**   Windows Vista includes a new implementation of the QoS component in the Pacer.sys NDIS 6.0 lightweight filter driver, located in %SystemRoot%\System32\Drivers. Pacer.sys replaces Psched.sys, which is used in the Windows Server 2003 and Windows XP operating systems. It continues to support the Generic QoS (GQoS) and Traffic Control (TC) APIs provided by Windows 2000, Windows XP, and Windows Server 2003. Therefore, existing applications that use QoS will work with Windows Vista. For more information about these APIs, see "The MS QoS Components" at *http://technet.microsoft.com/en-us/library/bb742475.aspx*.

Selecting DSCP Values

When sending packets, computers add a DSCP value that your network infrastructure can examine to determine how the packet should be prioritized. Although DSCP values can be arbitrary, depending on how your network infrastructure is configured, many organizations use a typical DSCP strategy with the following five queues:

- **Control traffic** Communications transmitted between routers. Typically these communications require minimal bandwidth, but they should be assigned a high priority because quick transmission can reduce downtime in the event of a hardware failure. You should also use this priority for VoIP control traffic. Use DSCP values of 26 for control traffic.

- **Latency-sensitive traffic** Traffic, such as VoIP, that must be delivered as quickly as possible. Typically, you should assign this a DSCP value of 46, known as Expedited Forwarding (EF).

- **Business critical traffic, also known as Better than Best Effort (BBE)** Communications that should receive priority treatment, such as customer service database queries from a line-of-business (LOB) application or streaming video, but that are not highly sensitive to latency. Use a DSCP value of 34.

- **Best effort traffic** Standard traffic, including any traffic not marked with a DSCP number, that should be handled after either of the preceding two queues. This traffic should have a DSCP value of 0, which is the default if no DSCP value has been specified.

- **Scavenger traffic** Low-priority traffic, such as backups, downloading of updates, noncritical file synchronization, and non–work-related traffic that employees might generate. Use a DSCP value of 10 or 8.

Note If you mark traffic from too many applications as high-priority, the high-priority queue on routers can grow long enough to add significant latency. This defeats the purpose of QoS. Therefore, you should reserve the highest priority DSCP marking for real-time communications such as VoIP.

Table 26-1 summarizes these values.

Table 26-1 DSCP Interoperability Values

Purpose	Common Uses	DSCP Value
VoIP	VoIP traffic, including signaling and control traffic	46
Interactive video	Two-way video conferencing	34
Mission-critical data	Database queries, line-of-business communications, video streaming	26
Best effort	All other traffic, including e-mail and Web browsing	0
Bulk data	Backups, nonbusiness applications, file transfers	10

Many networks use an even simpler structure, with only two priorities: one for latency-sensitive traffic and another for best effort traffic. However, if you have third-party tools that can use DSCP values to report on network performance for different types of traffic, it is advantageous to define a larger number of DSCP values even if your network infrastructure isn't configured to handle each DSCP value uniquely.

DSCP values might be lost when packets leave your network, because most organizations do not trust priorities provided by computers outside the organization. Because sending traffic labeled as high-priority could create a denial-of-service (DoS) attack, DSCP values from untrusted computers could be malicious.

Wireless Multimedia (WMM) includes four access categories for prioritizing traffic on 802.11 wireless networks. WMM uses DSCP values to set priority, so you can automatically take advantage of WMM by specifying DSCP values. Table 26-2 shows how DSCP values correspond to WMM access categories.

Table 26-2   DSCP Values and WMM Access Categories

DSCP Value	WMM Access Category
48–63	Voice (VO)
32–47	Video (VI)
24–31, 0–7	Best effort (BE)
8–23	Background (BK)

To fully support prioritizing traffic based on DSCP values, your network infrastructure must support the use of multiple queues as defined in RFC 2474.

Planning Traffic Throttling

Using DSCP values to prioritize traffic allows you to fully utilize your network's bandwidth while providing the best possible performance for your most important traffic. That's the ideal QoS scenario; however, not all network infrastructures support prioritizing traffic using DSCP values. If your network does not support traffic priorities, you can use traffic throttling to ensure that specific applications do not consume more than a specified amount of bandwidth.

Traffic throttling limits traffic on individual computers and cannot limit the aggregate bandwidth used by multiple computers. For example, if you have five web servers and you want to ensure that they never use more than half of your 1,000 kilobit-per-second (mbps) link, you must configure the QoS policy to throttle traffic at 100 kilobits per second (kbps) for each of the five computers, which would total 500 kbps if all five servers were sending traffic at their throttled maximum. Do not attempt to use traffic throttling to limit the bandwidth of every application or protocol; instead, use traffic throttling to limit only traffic from low-priority applications such as network backups or the downloading of large updates.

Traffic throttling does not have any network infrastructure requirements.

Configuring QoS Policies

To configure QoS using Group Policy, edit the Computer Configuration\Policies\Windows Settings\Policy-based QoS node or the User Configuration\Policies\Windows Settings\ Policy-based QoS node. Then, follow these steps:

1. Right-click the Policy-based QoS node and click Create New Policy.

2. The Policy-based QoS Wizard appears. On the Create A QoS Policy page, specify a name for the policy. Then, specify a DSCP value (which your network infrastructure can use to prioritize traffic) and a throttle rate (which Windows Vista will use to restrict outgoing bandwidth usage) as needed. Click Next.

> **Note**   Notice that throttle rate must be entered in kilobytes per second (KBps) or megabytes per second (MBps) rather than the more commonly used kilobits per second (Kbps) or megabits per second (Mbps)—notice the lowercase *b*. Eight bits equal one byte. Therefore, if you determine the Kbps or Mbps that you want to throttle at, divide that number by 8 when typing it into the Policy-Based QoS Wizard. For example, if you want to throttle at 128 Kbps, you would type **16 KBps**.

3. On the This QoS Policy Applies To page, select either All Applications or Only Applications With This Executable Name. If you are specifying an application, Windows Vista will apply the DSCP value or throttle rate to network traffic generated by that application. To identify the executable file used by a service, use the Services snap-in to check the service properties. Click Next.

4. On the Specify The Source And Destination IP Addresses page, you can configure the policy to apply to traffic between any two computers. Use network prefix length representation to specify networks—for example, specify 192.168.1.0/24 to indicate the entire 192.168.1.x network or 192.168.0.0/16 to indicate the entire 192.168.x.x network. For example, if you want to configure a QoS policy that applies a DSCP value for traffic sent to your e-mail server, you would select Only For The Following Destination IP Address Or Prefix and then type the e-mail server's IP address. (IPv4 and IPv6 addresses will both work.) Click Next.

> **Note**   QoS policies apply only to outgoing traffic, so the computer to which you're applying the policy will always be identified by the source address, and the remote computer or network will always be identified by the destination address.

5. On the Specify The Protocol And Port Numbers page, you can prioritize traffic based on TCP or UDP port numbers. For example, if you want to throttle all outgoing web requests, you would select TCP, select To This Destination Port Number Or Range, and then specify port 80. (The HTTP protocol uses TCP port 80.) Click Finish.

After creating a policy, you can edit it by right-clicking it in the details pane of the Group Policy Object Editor and then clicking Edit Existing Policy. You can configure system-wide QoS settings within the Computer Configuration\Administrative Templates\Network\QoS Packet Scheduler node of Group Policy. You need to modify these settings only if you need to limit the bandwidth that can be reserved, change the Packet Scheduler timer resolution, or configure nonstandard DSCP values for different traffic types.

Windows Vista applies QoS policies only for domain network location types. Therefore, if a user connects to a wireless network at a coffee shop (and your domain controller cannot be contacted), Windows Vista will not apply your QoS policies. However, if the user then connects to your internal network by using a VPN, Windows Vista will apply QoS policies to that VPN connection.

How It Works: Prioritizing QoS Policies

Much like applying Group Policy objects, the most specific QoS policy applies when multiple policies conflict. For example, if you create policies for both a specific IP address and a network that includes that IP address, the IP address policy will be applied instead of the network policy. Windows uses the following rules when applying QoS policies:

1. User-level QoS policies take precedence over computer-level QoS policies.

2. QoS policies that identify applications take precedence over QoS policies that identify networks or IP addresses.

3. QoS policies that specify IP addresses and more-specific networks take precedence over QoS policies that specify less-specific networks.

4. QoS policies that specify port numbers take precedence over QoS polices that specify port ranges, which take precedence over QoS policies that do not specify a port number.

5. If multiple QoS policies still conflict, policies that specify source IP addresses take precedence over policies that specify destination IP addresses, and policies that specify a source port take precedence over policies that specify a destination port.

QoS policies are not cumulative; only one QoS policy can be applied to any given connection.

Configuring System-Wide QoS Settings

You can configure system-wide QoS settings within the Computer Configuration\ Policies\Administrative Templates\Network\QoS Packet Scheduler node of Group Policy. You must modify these settings only if you must limit the outstanding packets, limit the bandwidth that can be reserved, or change the Packet Scheduler timer resolution. The following policies are available in the QoS Packet Scheduler node:

■ **Limit Outstanding Packets**   Specifies the maximum number of outstanding packets that can be issued to the network adapter at any given time. When this limit is reached, new packets are queued until the network adapter completes a packet, at which point a previously queued packet is removed from the Pacer.sys queue and sent to the network adapter. This setting is disabled by default, and you should never need to enable this setting.

■ **Limit Reservable Bandwidth**   Controls the percentage of the overall bandwidth that the application can reserve. By default, this is set to 20%, which provides 80 percent of bandwidth to processes that do not have reserved bandwidth.

■ **Set Timer Resolution**   This value is not supported and should not be set.

The QoS Packet Scheduler node also has the following three subnodes that you can use to manually configure the standard DSCP values:

■ **DSCP Value Of Conforming Packets**   These settings apply to packets that comply with flow specifications.

■ **DSCP Value Of Non-Conforming Packets**   These settings apply to packets that do not comply with flow specifications.

■ **Layer-2 Priority Value**   These settings specify default link-layer priority values for networks that support it.

You will need to change the values contained in these subnodes only if you have configured your network infrastructure to use nonstandard DSCP values.

Configuring Advanced QoS Settings

You can also configure advanced QoS settings for computers using Group Policy. Within the Group Policy Object Editor, right-click the Computer Configuration\Policies\Windows Settings\Policy-based QoS node and then click Advanced QoS Settings. You can use the Advanced QoS Settings dialog box to configure the following settings:

■ **Specify The Inbound TCP Throughput Level**   Most QoS policies relate to outbound traffic that the client computer sends. You can use this setting on the Inbound TCP Traffic tab to configure Windows Vista so that it will attempt to throttle incoming traffic. Although Windows Vista has direct control over the throughput of outbound traffic, it has indirect control only over the rate of incoming traffic. For TCP connections, you can configure a Windows Vista client computer to limit incoming traffic by specifying the maximum size of the TCP receive window. The TCP receive window is the amount of data that a receiver allows a sender to send before having to wait for an acknowledgment. A larger maximum window size means that the sender can send more data at a time, increasing network utilization and throughput. By limiting the maximum size of the TCP receive window, a receiver can indirectly control the incoming throughput for a TCP connection. Level 3 (Maximum Throughput) is for a 16-megabyte (MB) TCP receive window. Level 2 is for a 1-MB TCP receive window. Level 1 is for a 256-kilobyte (KB) TCP receive window. Level 0 is for a 64-KB TCP receive window. Unlike Policy-based QoS settings for outgoing traffic, this setting cannot control the rate of incoming traffic on a per-application, per-address, or per-port basis.

> **Note**   Because UDP traffic is not acknowledged, you cannot throttle UDP traffic from the receiving computer.

- **Control DSCP Marking Requests From Applications**   DSCP marking adds information to outgoing packets to identify the priority of the packet. If your network infrastructure supports DSCP-differentiated delivery, the infrastructure can use the DSCP value to select a priority for traffic. Use this setting to allow applications to specify their own DSCP values or to ignore application-specified values and only allow QoS policies to specify DSCP values.

For more information about Windows Vista and Policy-based QoS, visit the Quality Of Service home page at *http://technet.microsoft.com/en-us/network/bb530836.aspx*. Also, explore the QoS virtual lab at *http://go.microsoft.com/?linkid=6269134*. For detailed information, read Chapter 5, "Policy-Based Quality of Service," in *Windows Server 2008 Networking and Network Access Protection* by Joseph Davies and Tony Northrup (Microsoft Press, 2008).

Windows Firewall and IPsec

As the need for enterprises to share data within and outside their organizations increases, so does the need for greater security. Windows Vista provides strong, easy-to-configure security features. For example, the new Windows Firewall with the Advanced Security Microsoft Management Console (MMC) snap-in combines inbound and outbound firewall port management with IPsec for authentication and/or encryption. This powerful layer of security can also be managed via Group Policy or command-line scripting to provide a simple way to deploy firewall filtering and traffic protection rules that can limit access by specific users, computers, or applications, providing the administrator with an extremely granular level of control.

For more information about the Windows Firewall and improvements to IPsec, see Chapter 27, "Configuring Windows Firewall and IPsec."

Windows Connect Now

To simplify the creation and configuration of wireless networks and their security settings, Windows Vista supports Windows Connect Now, with which users can store network configuration information on a USB flash drive (UFD). To configure a wireless network, users first step through a network setup wizard that gathers their wireless network preferences. Then, Windows Vista configures the computer with authentication and encryption settings for a protected wireless network and stores the configuration on a UFD. Adding new computers (running Windows XP Service Pack 2 or later or Windows Vista) to the wireless network can be as simple as connecting the UFD to each computer. Although Group Policy is the preferred way to configure domain member computers for wireless networks, UFDs are an excellent way to grant guests access to an encrypted wireless network. Note, however, that the wireless network should be isolated from your internal networks to protect your intranet from your guests.

You can completely prevent users from accessing the Windows Connect Now Wizards using the Prohibit Access Of The Windows Connect Now Wizards in either the Computer Configuration\Policies\Administrative Templates\Network\Windows Connect Now node or the User Configuration\Policies\Administrative Templates\Network\Windows Connect Now Group Policy node. Additionally, the Computer Configuration\Policies\Administrative Templates\Network\Windows Connect Now node has the Configuration Of Wireless Settings Using Windows Connect Now setting, which provides the following options:

- **Turn Off Ability To Configure Using WCN Over Ethernet (UPnP)**   Prevents Windows Vista from being able to configure networked devices that support UPnP.

- **Turn Off Ability to Configure Using WCN Over In-band 802.11 Wi-Fi**   Prevents Windows Vista from being able to configure wireless networked devices.

- **Turn Off Ability To Configure Using A USB Flash Drive**   Prevents Windows Vista from being able to store Windows Connect Now configuration to a USB flash drive. Because the Windows Connect Now information stored on a flash drive contains information that can allow computers to access your protected wireless network, you might choose to disable this setting to improve the security of your wireless networks.

- **Turn Off Ability To Configure Windows Portable Device (WPD)**   Prevents Windows Vista from being able to configure WPDs, which include portable media players, digital cameras, and mobile phones.

- **Maximum Number Of WCN Devices Allowed**   Enables you to limit the number of Windows Connect Now devices that a Windows Vista computer can configure.

- **Higher precedence medium for devices discovered by multiple media**   Determines which networking type is used when a device is available across both wired and wireless networks.

If you do not plan to use Windows Connect Now, you can safely disable it. The default setting for the Windows Connect Now–related Group Policy settings enables all Windows Connect Now capabilities.

Core Networking Improvements

Windows Vista networking components have been designed to offer improved performance, security, and manageability. Most users will never notice many of the most important changes, however, because they function without user intervention or administrative configuration. For example, Windows Vista with its default settings will offer much better bandwidth utilization over high-bandwidth, high-latency satellite and wide area network (WAN) connections. Additionally, IPv6 and 802.1X are built in to Windows Vista. Server Message Block (SMB) 2.0, the protocol used for file and printer sharing, will improve performance when communicating with other SMB 2.0 clients.

The sections that follow describe changes to the core networking functionality in Windows Vista. Although these improvements offer significant benefits to those upgrading to Windows Vista—and administrators should be aware of these changes—you typically do not need to make management or design decisions because of these changes.

Efficient Networking

Most network communications—including downloading files, browsing the web, and reading e-mail—use the TCP (Transmission Control Protocol) Layer 3 protocol. TCP is considered a reliable network protocol because the recipient must confirm receipt of all transmissions. If a transmission isn't confirmed, it's considered lost and will be retransmitted.

However, confirming transmissions can prevent TCP transfers from using all available bandwidth. This happens because TCP breaks blocks of data into small pieces before transmitting them, and recipients must confirm receipt of each piece of the data. The number of pieces that can be sent before waiting to receive confirmation receipts is called the *TCP receive window size*.

When TCP was designed, network bandwidth was very low by today's standards, and communications were relatively unreliable. Therefore, waiting for confirmation for small pieces of a data block did not have a significant impact on performance. However, now that bandwidth is measured in megabits per second (Mbps) instead of kilobits per second (Kbps), a small TCP receive window size can significantly slow communication while the computer sending a data block waits for the receiving computer to send confirmation receipts. Figure 26-8 demonstrates how TCP confirms portions of a data block.

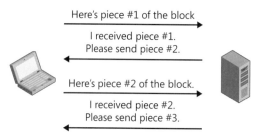

Here's piece #1 of the block

I received piece #1.
Please send piece #2.

Here's piece #2 of the block.

I received piece #2.
Please send piece #3.

Figure 26-8   TCP requires data transfers to be confirmed.

TCP works well and does indeed provide reliable transfers over a variety of networks. However, waiting to confirm each portion of a data block causes a slight delay each time a confirmation is required. Just how much delay depends on two factors:

- **Network latency**   Network latency is the delay, typically measured in milliseconds (ms), for a packet to be sent to a computer and for a response to be returned. Latency is also called the round-trip time (RTT). If latency is so high that the sending computer is waiting to receive confirmation receipts, latency has a direct impact on transfer speed, because nothing is being transmitted while the sending computer waits for the confirmations.

- **How much of the file can be transferred before waiting for confirmation (TCP receive window size)**   The smaller the TCP receive window size, the more frequently sending computers might have to wait for confirmation. Therefore, smaller TCP receive window sizes can cause slower network performance, because the sender has to wait for confirmations to be received. Larger TCP receive window sizes can improve performance by reducing the time spent waiting for confirmations.

What Causes Latency, How to Measure It, and How to Control It

Latency typically originates from two different sources: routers and distance.

Each router that a packet travels through has to copy the packet from one network interface to the next. This introduces a very slight delay—typically only a few milliseconds. However, traffic on the Internet might have to travel through more than fifty routers when making a round trip between two computers, so the delay does add up. Busy routers and networks that are near saturation can introduce more latency, because the router might have to wait several milliseconds before it can place a packet onto a network interface.

Distance also introduces latency. Packets travel across networks slightly slower than the speed of light. A rough estimate of the speed packets travel would be about 100,000 miles per second. Although the speed is still very fast, a packet that has to travel to the other side of the earth and back would have at least 250 milliseconds of latency (before you calculate latency introduced by routers). Satellite connections add about 500 milliseconds of latency sending the packet to and from the satellite. Additionally, network paths are often very indirect, and packets often travel several times farther than the distance of a straight line between two computers. VPNs, in particular, can cause extremely indirect routing between computers.

The most common tool to measure latency is the command-line tool Ping. Ping can give you a rough idea of the latency between two points, but it is less than perfect, because Ping does not transmit TCP-based data. Instead, Ping sends Internet Control Message Protocol (ICMP) messages that are designed for diagnostic purposes. Many routers give these ICMP messages a lower priority than other traffic, so Ping may report a higher latency than normal. Additionally, many routers and computers are configured to completely block the ICMP messages used by Ping. A related command-line tool, PathPing, provides approximate latency information for all routers between two hosts. PathPing uses the same ICMP messages as Ping.

If latency is causing a problem on your network, first determine the source of the latency. If distance is causing the latency, find ways to shorten the distance. For example, you might replace a satellite link with a terrestrial link. Alternatively, if you determine that the path being taken between two points is inefficient, you might be able to reconfigure your network to shorten the distance that the packets need to travel between the two points. If you determine that busy networks or routers are introducing latency, you can upgrade your routers or increase the available bandwidth. Alternatively, you can use Policy-based QoS to prioritize the most important traffic to reduce latency for time-sensitive transmissions such as streaming media and voice-over-IP.

As you can see, high network latency can hurt performance, especially when combined with small TCP receive window sizes. Computers can reduce the negative impact of high-latency networks by increasing the TCP receive window size. However, earlier versions of Windows used a static, small, 64-KB receive window. This setting was fine for low-bandwidth and low-latency links, but it offers limited performance on high-bandwidth, high-latency links. Figure 26-9 shows the throughput a TCP connection can get with various static values of the receive window over different latency conditions. As you can see, the maximum throughput of a TCP connection with the default receive window of 64 KB can be as low as 5 Mbps even within a single continent and can go all the way down to 1 Mbps on a satellite link.

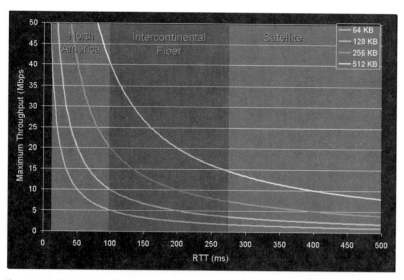

Figure 26-9 The TCP receive window size setting can significantly impact throughput.

Windows Vista includes an auto-tuning capability for TCP receive window size that is enabled by default. Every TCP connection can benefit in terms of increased throughput and decreased transfer times, but high-bandwidth, high-latency connections will benefit the most. Therefore, Windows Vista Receive Window Auto-Tuning can significantly benefit network performance across both satellite and WAN links. However, performance on high-speed LANs where latency is very low will benefit less.

Receive Window Auto-Tuning continually determines the optimal receive window size on a per-connection basis by measuring the bandwidth-delay product (the bandwidth multiplied by the latency of the connection) and the application retrieve rate, and it automatically adjusts the maximum receive window size on an ongoing basis. For auto-tuning to dramatically improve the throughput on a connection, all of the following conditions must be true:

- **High latency connection**   For example, round trip times of greater than 100 ms.

- **High bandwidth connection**   For example, greater than 5 Mbps.

- **Application does not specify a receive buffer size**   Some applications may explicitly specify a receive buffer size, which would override the Windows default behavior. This can offer similar benefits on older versions of Windows, but changing the receive buffer size is uncommon.

- **Application consumes data quickly after receiving them**   If an application does not immediately retrieve the received data, Receive Window Auto-Tuning may not increase overall performance. For example, if the application retrieves received data from TCP only periodically rather than continually, overall performance might not increase.

When TCP considers increasing the receive window, it pays attention to the connection's past history and characteristics. TCP won't advertise more than the remote host's fair share of network bandwidth. This keeps the advertised receive window in line with the remote host's congestion window, discouraging network congestion while encouraging maximum utilization of the available bandwidth.

TCP Receive Window Scaling

The ability to increase the receive window would be meaningless without window scaling. On its own, TCP allows a window size of only 64 KB. Operating systems back through Windows XP use this as their default value on fast links. The window scaling option is a way for window sizes to scale to megabytes and beyond. Starting with Windows Vista, window scaling is used by default.

During connection establishment, use of the window scaling option is negotiated with the remote host. If supported by the remote side, window scaling is enabled on the connection. Windows Vista uses a scale factor of 8, which means that the advertised receive window value should be multiplied by 256. Therefore, Receive Window Auto-Tuning uses a maximum receive window size of 16 MB.

The Windows Vista TCP/IP stack supports the following RFCs to optimize throughput in high-loss environments:

- **RFC 2582: The NewReno Modification to TCP's Fast Recovery Algorithm**   The NewReno algorithm provides faster throughput by changing the way that a sender can increase the sending rate when multiple segments in a window of data are lost and the sender receives a partial acknowledgment (an acknowledgment for only part of the data that has been successfully received). You can find this RFC at *http://www.ietf.org/rfc/ rfc2582.txt.*

- **RFC 2883: An Extension to the Selective Acknowledgment (SACK) Option for TCP**   SACK, defined in RFC 2018, allows a receiver to indicate up to four noncontiguous blocks of received data. RFC 2883 defines an additional use of the fields in the SACK TCP option to acknowledge duplicate packets. This allows the receiver of the TCP segment containing the SACK option to determine when it has retransmitted a segment unnecessarily and adjust its behavior to prevent future retransmissions. The fewer retransmissions sent, the better the overall throughput. You can find this RFC at *http://www.ietf.org/rfc/rfc2883.txt.*

- **RFC 3168: The Addition of Explicit Congestion Notification (ECN) to IP**   If a packet is lost in a TCP session, TCP assumes that it was caused by network congestion. In an attempt to alleviate the source of the problem, TCP lowers the sender's transmission rate. With ECN support on both TCP peers and in the routing infrastructure, routers experiencing congestion mark the packets as they forward them. This enables computers to lower their transmission rate before packet loss occurs, increasing the throughput. Windows Vista supports ECN but it is disabled by default. You can enable ECN support with the following command:

```
netsh interface tcp set global ecncapability=enabled
```

  You can find this RFC at *http://www.ietf.org/rfc/rfc3168.txt.*

- **RFC 3517: A Conservative Selective Acknowledgment (SACK)-based Loss Recovery Algorithm for TCP**   The implementation of TCP/IP in Windows Server 2003 and Windows XP uses SACK information only to determine which TCP segments have not arrived at the destination. RFC 3517 defines a method of using SACK information to perform loss recovery when duplicate acknowledgments have been received, replacing the fast recovery algorithm when SACK is enabled on a connection. Windows Vista keeps track of SACK information on a per-connection basis and monitors incoming acknowledgments and duplicate acknowledgments to recover more quickly when multiple segments are not received at the destination. You can find this RFC at *http://www.ietf.org/rfc/rfc3517.txt.*

- **RFC 4138: Forward RTO-Recovery (F-RTO): An Algorithm for Detecting Spurious Retransmission Timeouts with TCP and the Stream Control Transmission Protocol (SCTP)**   Spurious retransmissions of TCP segments can occur with a sudden and temporary increase in the RTT. The F-RTO algorithm prevents spurious retransmission of TCP segments. The result of the F-RTO algorithm is that for environments that have sudden and temporary increases in the RTT—such as when a wireless client roams from one wireless AP to another—F-RTO prevents unnecessary retransmission of segments and more quickly returns to its normal sending rate. You can find this RFC at *http://www.ietf.org/rfc/rfc4138.txt.*

Scalable Networking

As LAN bandwidth has increased beyond gigabit speeds, other components of a computer have become bottlenecks, limiting network performance. For example, a computer connected to a 10-gigabit network might not be able to fully saturate the link because the processor would be fully utilized processing network traffic.

Windows Vista and Windows Server 2008 support the following scalable networking technologies (which require compatible hardware):

- **TCP Chimney Offload**   The computer's processor must assemble data from multiple TCP packets into a single network segment. TCP chimney offload allows the network adapter to handle the task of segmenting TCP data for outgoing packets, reassembling data from incoming packets, and acknowledging sent and received data. TCP Chimney Offload is not compatible with QoS or adapter teaming drivers developed for earlier versions of Windows. TCP Chimney Offload does not change how non-TCP packets are handled, including Address Resolution Protocol (ARP), Dynamic Host Configuration Protocol (DHCP), Internet Control Message Protocol (ICMP), and UDP. TCP Chimney Offload still requires the operating system to process every application I/O. Therefore, it primarily benefits large transfers, and chatty applications that transmit small amounts of data will see little benefit. For example, file or streaming media servers can benefit significantly. However, a database server that is sending 100–500 bytes of data to and from the database might see little or no benefit.

> **Note**   To examine TCP Chimney Offload performance testing data, read "Boosting Data Transfer with TCP Offload Engine Technology" at *http://www.dell.com/downloads/global/power/ps3q06-20060132-broadcom.pdf* and "Enabling Greater Scalability and Improved File Server Performance with the Windows Server 2003 Scalable Networking Pack and Alacritech Dynamic TCP Offload" at *http://www.alacritech.com/Resources/Files/File_Serving_White_Paper.pdf.* For more information about TCP Chimney Offload, read "Scalable Networking: Network Protocol Offload—Introducing TCP Chimney" at *http://www.microsoft.com/whdc/device/network/TCP_Chimney.mspx.*

- **Receive-side scaling (RSS)**   With NDIS 6.0 and in Windows Vista and Windows Server 2008, incoming packets can be processed by multiple processors. In earlier versions of Windows, packets had to be processed by a single processor. Because more new computers have multiple cores and processors, this can alleviate an important bottleneck when used with a network adapter that supports RSS.

> **Note**   For detailed information about RSS, read "Scalable Networking: Eliminating the Receive Processing Bottleneck—Introducing RSS" at *http://download.microsoft.com/download/5/D/6/5D6EAF2B-7DDF-476B-93DC-7CF0072878E6/NDIS_RSS.doc.*

■ **NetDMA**   NetDMA moves data directly from one location in the computer's main memory directly to another location without requiring the data to be moved through the processor, reducing the processor overhead. NetDMA requires the underlying hardware platform to support a technology such as Intel I/O Acceleration Technology (Intel I/OAT). NetDMA and TCP Chimney Offload are not compatible. If a network adapter supports both NetDMA and TCP Chimney Offload, Windows Vista will use TCP Chimney Offload.

> **Note**   For more information about NetDMA, read "Introduction to Intel I/O Acceleration Technology and the Windows Server 2003 Scalable Networking Pack" at *http://www.intel.com/technology/ioacceleration/317106.pdf.*

■ **IPsec Offload**   IPsec authentication and encryption requires some processor overhead. Although the IPsec generated by a typical workstation will not significantly impact processor utilization, a workstation that is transferring large amounts of data (typically at greater than gigabit speeds) can dedicate a significant amount of processing time to IPsec. IPsec Offload moves IPsec processing to the network adapter, which typically has a processor optimized for handling authentication and encryption tasks.

Improved Reliability

The Windows Vista TCP/IP networking components also offer improvements designed to increase reliability when network conditions are less than optimal:

■ **Neighbor Unreachability Detection for IPv4**   Neighbor Unreachability Detection is a feature of IPv6 in which a node tracks whether or not a neighboring node is reachable, providing better error detection and recovery when nodes suddenly become unavailable. Windows Vista also supports Neighbor Unreachability Detection for IPv4 traffic by tracking the reachable state of IPv4 neighbors in the IPv4 route cache. IPv4 Neighbor Unreachability Detection determines reachability through an exchange of unicast Address Resolution Protocol (ARP) Request and ARP Reply messages or by relying on upper layer protocols such as TCP. With IPv4 Neighbor Unreachability Detection, IPv4-based communications benefit by determining when neighboring nodes, including routers, are no longer reachable and reporting the condition.

■ **Changes in Dead Gateway Detection**   Dead gateway detection in TC/IP for Windows Server 2003 and Windows XP provides a failover function, but it does not provide a failback function in which a dead gateway is tried again to determine if it has become available. Windows Vista, however, also provides failback for dead gateways by periodically attempting to send TCP traffic through the previously detected dead gateway. If the TCP traffic sent through the dead gateway is successful, Windows Vista switches the default gateway to the previously detected dead gateway. Support for failback to primary default gateways can provide faster throughput by sending traffic through the primary default gateway on the subnet.

■ **Changes in PMTU Black Hole Router Detection**   Path maximum transmission unit (PMTU) discovery, defined in RFC 1191, relies on the receipt of ICMP Destination Unreachable-Fragmentation Needed and Don't Fragment (DF) Set messages from routers containing the MTU of the next link. However, in some cases, intermediate routers silently discard packets that cannot be fragmented. These types of routers are known as black-hole PMTU routers. Additionally, intermediate routers might drop ICMP messages because of configured firewall rules. As a result, TCP connections can time out and terminate because intermediate routers silently discard large TCP segments, their retransmissions, and the ICMP error messages for PMTU discovery. PTMU black-hole router detection senses when large TCP segments are being retransmitted and automatically adjusts the PMTU for the connection, rather than relying on the receipt of the ICMP Destination Unreachable-Fragmentation Needed and DF Set messages. With TCP/IP in Windows Server 2003 and Windows XP, PMTU black-hole router detection is disabled by default because enabling it increases the maximum number of retransmissions that are performed for a given segment. However, with increasing use of firewall rules on routers to drop ICMP traffic, Windows Vista enables PMTU black-hole router detection by default to prevent TCP connections from terminating. PMTU black-hole router detection is triggered on a TCP connection when it begins retransmitting full-sized segments with the DF flag set. TCP resets the PTMU for the connection to 536 bytes and retransmits its segments with the DF flag cleared. This maintains the TCP connection, although at a possibly lower PMTU size than actually exists for the connection.

IPv6 Support

To solve problems with limited public IPv4 addresses, many governments, Internet Service Providers (ISPs), and other organizations are transitioning to IPv6, the next version of the Network layer protocol that drives the Internet. Windows Vista supports the following enhancements to IPv6 when compared to Windows XP:

■ **Dual IP layer stack enabled by default**   Windows Vista supports a dual IP layer architecture in which the IPv4 and IPv6 implementations share common transport (including TCP and UDP) and framing layers, as Figure 26-10 illustrates. Windows Vista has both IPv4 and IPv6 enabled by default. You don't need to install a separate component to obtain IPv6 support. You can disable either IPv4 or IPv6 for a network adapter, however.

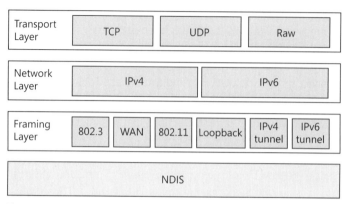

Figure 26-10   IPv4 and IPv6 work side by side in Windows Vista.

- **GUI-based configuration**   In Windows Vista, you can now manually configure IPv6 settings through a set of dialog boxes in the Network Connections folder (similar to the way you manually configure IPv4 settings). Additionally, you can configure both IPv4 and IPv6 using the Netsh command.

- **Integrated IPsec support**   In Windows Vista, IPsec support for IPv6 traffic is the same as that for IPv4, including support for Internet Key Exchange (IKE) and data encryption. The Windows Firewall with Advanced Security and IP Security Policies snap-ins now support the configuration of IPsec policies for IPv6 traffic in the same way as for IPv4 traffic. For example, when you configure an IP filter as part of an IP filter list in the IP Security Policies snap-in, you can now specify IPv6 addresses and address prefixes when specifying a specific source or destination IP address.

- **MLDv2**   Multicast Listener Discovery version 2 (MLDv2), specified in RFC 3810, provides support for source-specific multicast traffic. MLDv2 is equivalent to Internet Group Management Protocol version 3 (IGMPv3) for IPv4.

- **LLMNR**   Link-Local Multicast Name Resolution (LLMNR) allows IPv6 hosts on a single subnet without a DNS server to resolve each other's names. This capability is useful for single-subnet home networks and ad hoc wireless networks.

- **IPv6 over PPP**   The built-in remote access client now supports IPv6 over the Point-to-Point Protocol (PPP) (PPPv6), as defined in RFC 2472. Native IPv6 traffic can now be sent over PPP-based connections. For example, PPPv6 support allows you to connect with an IPv6-based ISP through dial-up or PPP over Ethernet (PPPoE)-based connections that might be used for broadband Internet access.

- **Random Interface IDs for IPv6 Addresses**   To prevent address scans of IPv6 addresses based on the known company IDs of network adapter manufacturers, Windows Server 2008 and Windows Vista by default generate random interface IDs for nontemporary, autoconfigured IPv6 addresses, including public and link-local addresses.

■ **DHCPv6 support**   Windows Server 2008 and Windows Vista include a DHCPv6-capable DHCP client that will perform stateful address autoconfiguration with a DHCPv6 server. Windows Server 2008 includes a DHCPv6-capable DHCP Server service.

For more information about IPv6, see Chapter 29, "Deploying IPv6."

802.1X Network Authentication

802.1X is a protocol for authenticating computers to your network infrastructure before allowing them access. 802.1X has commonly been used to protect IEEE 802.11 wireless networks: If a client computer cannot provide a set of valid credentials for a wireless network, the wireless access point will not allow the client to join the network.

802.1X can also be used to protect wired networks. For example, if you physically connect a computer to an Ethernet network, the Ethernet switch can use 802.1X to require the client computer to authenticate to the network infrastructure. If the computer passes the authentication requirements, the network infrastructure will freely forward network traffic to and from the client computer. If the client computer does not provide valid credentials or otherwise cannot meet specified requirements, it can be denied access or placed onto a restricted network.

Windows Vista supports 802.1X authentication for both wired and wireless networks. Clients can authenticate themselves using a user name and password or a certificate, which can be stored locally on the computer or on a smart card. With compatible network hardware and a Remote Authentication Dial-in User Service (RADIUS) authentication server (such as a Windows Server 2003 or Windows Server 2008 computer), you can centrally control both wired and wireless access to your intranet. This means that an attacker with physical access to your facilities cannot simply plug a computer into an available Ethernet port and gain access to your intranet. When you combine 802.1X authentication with NAP, you can ensure that computers have required security updates and meet other system health requirements before allowing them unlimited access to your intranet.

Although almost all wireless access points support 802.1X, only newer wired network switches support the authentication protocol. When a computer is connected to your network, the switch must detect this connection, initiate the authentication process with the connected computer, send an authentication request to the RADIUS server you have configured, and then use the server's response to determine whether the client computer should be connected to your private intranet, a restricted network, another virtual LAN (VLAN), or apply other restrictions. Figure 26-11 illustrates this process. In addition to restricting network access, 802.1X can be used to apply user-specific bandwidth or quality of service (QoS) policies.

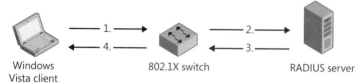

1. User connects a computer to a wired Ethernet port.
2. 802.1X switch notices the connection and initiates authentication by passing the request to the RADIUS server.
3. The RADIUS server authenticates the computer and sends a message to the switch.
4. The switch opens the Ethernet port to allow intranet access and enforces any restrictions or QoS policies.

Figure 26-11   You can use 802.1X to protect both your wired and wireless networks.

To configure 802.1X for a network adapter on a single computer, use the Authentication tab on the network adapter's properties. This tab enables you to configure the authentication type and the certificate to use for authentication. Additionally, you can configure 802.1X from the command line using the Netsh Lan command. The Authentication tab appears only if the Wired AutoConfig service is started, and the Netsh Lan command also requires this service to be running.

> **Caution**   802.1X improves security, but it is not foolproof. An attacker with both physical access to your network and a computer configured to authenticate successfully with 802.1X can insert a hub (or even a wireless access point) between the legitimate computer and the network. When the computer has authenticated the network port, the network infrastructure will allow all communications through that port, whether they originate from an unauthenticated computer connected to the hub or from the legitimate computer. For better security, require both 802.1X and IPsec.

To configure computers in an Active Directory domain to use 802.1X authentication, follow these high-level steps:

1. Configure Active Directory for accounts and groups. Set the remote access permission on the Dial-up tab of the user or computer account properties dialog box to either Allow Access or Control Access Through Remote Access Policy.

2. Configure primary and redundant Internet Authentication Service (IAS) servers. Then, create a wired remote access policy on the IAS server. (For more information about IAS, visit *http://www.microsoft.com/technet/itsolutions/network/ias/*.) For Windows Server 2008, IAS is replaced with the Network Policy Server (NPS).

3. Deploy and configure your authenticating switches. You will need to configure the switches with the IP addresses of your primary and secondary IAS servers.

4. Configure client computers. If necessary, configure a certificate infrastructure to issue certificates that client computers and users will use for authentication. Additionally, you should start the Wired AutoConfig service and configure it to start automatically.

For more information about configuring 802.1X, see "Deployment of IEEE 802.1X for Wired Networks Using Microsoft Windows" at *http://www.microsoft.com/downloads/ details.aspx?familyid=05951071-6b20-4cef-9939-47c397ffd3dd.*

802.1X Improvements in Windows Vista

In both Windows XP and Windows 2000 with Service Pack 4 wired 802.1X networks, a known problem can occur if all of the following conditions are true:

- You've configured 802.1X only for computer (not computer and user) authentication.
- You're using PEAP-MS-CHAP v2 (not EAP-TLS).
- Your computer's computer account password has expired.

If a computer meets all of these conditions, the computer won't be able to log on to the domain. However, this is fixed in Windows Vista, and you will be able to log on to the domain.

Note   Requiring 802.1X will eliminate your ability to use PXE boot, in which a client computer loads the operating system directly from the network, because PXE clients can't provide the necessary credentials—another good reason to have a separate network for deployment.

To manage 802.1X using Group Policy, extend the Active Directory schema as described in "Active Directory Schema Extensions for Windows Vista Wireless and Wired Group Policy Enhancements" at *http://technet.microsoft.com/en-us/library/bb727029.aspx.*

Additionally, Windows Vista also supports the new EAPHost architecture to enable easier development of 802.1X authentication mechanisms. For more information, see the section titled "EAPHost Architecture" later in this chapter.

Server Message Block (SMB) 2.0

Server Message Block (SMB), also known as the Common Internet File System (CIFS), is the file sharing protocol used by default on Windows-based computers. Windows includes an SMB client (the Client for Microsoft Windows component installed through the properties of a network connection) and an SMB server (the File and Printer Sharing for Microsoft Windows component installed through the properties of a network connection). SMB in versions of Windows prior to Windows Server 2008 and Windows Vista, known as SMB 1.0, was originally designed 15 years ago for early Windows-based network operating systems such as Microsoft LAN Manager and Windows for Workgroups and carries with it the limitations of its initial design.

SMB in Windows Server 2008 and Windows Vista also supports SMB 2.0, a new version of SMB that has been redesigned for today's networking environments and the needs of the next generation of file servers. SMB 2.0 has the following enhancements:

- Supports sending multiple SMB commands within the same packet. This reduces the number of packets sent between an SMB client and server, a common complaint against SMB 1.0.

- Supports much larger buffer sizes compared to SMB 1.0.

- Increases the restrictive constants within the protocol design to allow for scalability. Examples include an increase in the number of concurrent open file handles on the server and the number of file shares that a server can have.

- Supports durable handles that can withstand short interruptions in network availability.

- Supports symbolic links.

Computers running Windows Server 2008 or Windows Vista support both SMB 1.0 and SMB 2.0. SMB 2.0 can be used only if both the client and server support it, however. Therefore, both the client and the server must be using SMB 2.0 to benefit from the improvements. Windows Vista supports complete backward compatibility with SMB 1.0 and earlier versions of Windows.

As with other versions of Windows, server-side support for SMB (sharing files and printers) is provided by the Server service, and client-side support (connecting to shared resources) is provided by the Workstation service. Both services are configured to start automatically, and you can safely disable either service if you don't require it. The security risks presented by having the Server service running are minimized because Windows Firewall will block incoming requests to the Server service on public networks by default.

Strong Host Model

When a unicast packet arrives at a host, IP must determine whether the packet is locally destined (its destination matches an address that is assigned to an interface of the host). IP implementations that follow a weak host model accept any locally destined packet, regardless of the interface on which the packet was received. IP implementations that follow the strong host model accept locally destined packets only if the destination addresses in the packet matches an address assigned to the interface on which the packet was received.

The current IPv4 implementation in Windows XP and Windows Server 2003 uses the weak host model. Windows Vista supports the strong host model for both IPv4 and IPv6 and is configured to use it by default. However, you can revert to the weak host model using Netsh.

The weak host model provides better network connectivity, but it also makes hosts susceptible to multihome-based network attacks.

To change the host model being used, use the following Netsh commands (and specify the name of the network adapter):

```
Netsh interface IPv4 set interface "Local Area Connection" WeakHostSend=enabled
```

```
ok.
```

```
Netsh interface IPv4 set interface "Local Area Connection" WeakHostReceive=enabled
```

```
ok.
```

To return to the default settings, use the same command format but disable the WeakHost-Send and WeakHostReceive parameters.

Wireless Networking

In Windows Server 2003 and Windows XP, the software infrastructure that supports wireless connections was built to emulate an Ethernet connection and can be extended only by supporting additional Extensible Authentication Protocol (EAP) types for 802.1X authentication. In Windows Vista, the software infrastructure for 802.11 wireless connections, called the Native Wi-Fi Architecture (also referred to as Revised Native Wi-Fi MSM, or RMSM), has been redesigned for the following:

- IEEE 802.11 is now represented inside of Windows as a media type separate from IEEE 802.3. This allows hardware vendors more flexibility in supporting advanced features of IEEE 802.11 networks, such as a larger frame size than Ethernet.

- New components in the Native Wi-Fi Architecture perform authentication, authorization, and management of 802.11 connections, reducing the burden on hardware vendors to incorporate these functions into their wireless network adapter drivers. This makes the development of wireless network adapter drivers much easier.

- The Native Wi-Fi Architecture supports APIs to allow hardware vendors the ability to extend the built-in wireless client for additional wireless services and custom capabilities. Extensible components written by hardware vendors can also provide customized configuration dialog boxes and wizards.

Additionally, Windows Vista includes several important changes to the behavior of wireless auto configuration. Wireless auto configuration is now implemented in the WLAN AutoConfig service, which dynamically selects the wireless network to which the computer will automatically connect, based either on your preferences or on default settings. This includes automatically selecting and connecting to a more preferred wireless network when it becomes available. The changes include:

- **Single Sign-On**   To enable users to connect to protected wireless networks before logon (and thus, allow wireless users to authenticate to a domain), administrators can use Group Policy settings or the new Netsh wireless commands to configure single sign-on profiles on wireless client computers. After a single sign-on profile is configured, 802.1X authentication will precede the computer logon to the domain and users are prompted for credential information only if needed. This feature ensures that the wireless connection is placed prior to the computer domain logon, which enables scenarios that require network connectivity prior to user logon, such as Group Policy updates, execution of login scripts, and wireless client domain joins.

- **Behavior when no preferred wireless networks are available**   In earlier versions of Windows, Windows created a random wireless network name and placed the network adapter in infrastructure mode if no preferred network was available and automatically connecting to nonpreferred networks was disabled. Windows would then scan for preferred wireless networks every sixty seconds. Windows Vista no longer creates a randomly named network; instead, Windows Vista "parks" the wireless network adapter while periodically scanning for networks, preventing the randomly generated wireless network name from matching an existing network name.

- **Support for hidden wireless networks**   Earlier versions of Windows would always connected to preferred wireless networks that broadcast an SSID before connecting to preferred wireless networks that did not broadcast, even if the hidden network had a higher priority. Windows Vista connects to preferred wireless networks based on their priority, regardless of whether or not they broadcast an SSID.

- **WPA2 support**   Windows Vista supports WPA2 authentication options, configurable by either the user (to configure the standard profile) or by Active Directory domain administrators using Group Policy settings. Windows Vista supports both Enterprise (IEEE 802.1X authentication) and Personal (pre-shared key authentication) modes of operation for WPA2, and can connect to ad hoc wireless networks protected by WPA2.

- **Integration with NAP**   WPA2-Enterprise, WPA-Enterprise, and dynamic WEP connections that use 802.1X authentication can leverage the Network Access Protection platform to prevent wireless clients that do not comply with system health requirements from gaining unlimited access to a private network.

Additionally, troubleshooting wireless connection problems is now easier because wireless connections do the following:

- Support the Network Diagnostics Framework, which attempts to diagnose and fix common problems

- Record detailed information in the Event Log if a wireless connection attempt fails

- Prompt the user to send diagnostic information to Microsoft for analysis and improvement

For more information about troubleshooting wireless networks, see Chapter 32, "Troubleshooting Network Issues." For more information about configuring wireless networks, see "How to Configure Wireless Settings" later in this chapter.

Improved APIs

Windows Vista also includes improved APIs that will enable more powerful networked applications. Systems administrators will not realize immediate benefits from these improved APIs; however, developers can use these APIs to create applications that are more robust when running on Windows Vista. This enables developers to create applications faster, and to add more powerful features to those applications.

Network Awareness

More applications are connecting to the Internet to look for updates, download real-time information, and facilitate collaboration between users. However, creating applications that can adapt to changing network conditions has been difficult for developers. Network Awareness enables applications to sense changes to the network to which the computer is connected, such as closing a mobile PC at work and then opening it at a coffee shop wireless hotspot. This enables Windows Vista to alert applications of network changes. The application can then behave differently, providing a seamless experience.

For example, Windows Firewall with Advanced Security can take advantage of Network Awareness to automatically allow incoming traffic from network management tools when the computer is on the corporate network but block the same traffic when the computer is on a home network or wireless hotspot. Network Awareness can therefore provide flexibility on your internal network without sacrificing security when mobile users travel.

Applications can also take advantage of Network Awareness. For example, if a user disconnects from a corporate internal network and then connects to his or her home network, an application could adjust security settings and request that the user establish a VPN connection to maintain connectivity to an intranet server. New applications can automatically go offline or online as mobile users move between environments. Additionally, software vendors can more easily integrate their software into the network logon process because Windows Vista enables access providers to add custom connections for use during logon.

Network Awareness only benefits applications that take advantage of the new API and does not require any management or configuration. For Network Awareness to function, the Network Location Awareness and Network List Service services must be running.

Improved Peer Networking

Windows Peer-to-Peer Networking, originally introduced with the Advanced Networking Pack for Windows XP and later included in Windows XP Service Pack 2, is an operating system platform and API in Windows Vista that allows the development of peer-to-peer (P2P) applications that do not require a server. Windows Vista includes the following enhancements to Windows Peer-to-Peer Networking:

- **New, easy-to-use API**   APIs to access Windows Peer-to-Peer Networking capabilities such as name resolution, group creation, and security have been highly simplified in Windows Vista, making it easier for developers to create P2P applications.

- **New version of PNRP**   Peer Name Resolution Protocol (PNRP) is a name resolution protocol, like DNS, that functions without a server. PNRP uniquely identifies computers within a peer *cloud*. Windows Vista includes a new version of PNRP (PNRP v2) that is more scalable and uses less network bandwidth. For PNRP v2 in Windows Vista, Windows Peer-to-Peer Networking applications can access PNRP name publication and resolution functions through a simplified PNRP API that supports the standard name resolution methods used by applications. For IPv6 addresses, applications can use the *getaddrinfo()* function to resolve the Fully Qualified Domain Name (FQDN) *name*.prnp.net, in which *name* is peer name being resolved. The pnrp.net domain is a reserved domain in Windows Vista for PNRP name resolution. The PNRP v2 protocol is incompatible with the PNRP protocol used by computers running Windows XP. Microsoft is investigating the development and release of an update to the Windows Peer-to-Peer Networking components in Windows XP to support PNRP v2.

- **People Near Me**   People Near Me is a new capability of Windows Peer-to-Peer Networking for Windows Vista that allows users to dynamically discover other users on the local subnet, their registered People-Near-Me–capable applications, and to easily invite users into a collaboration activity. The invitation and its acceptance launches an application on the invited user's computer, and the two applications can begin participating in a collaboration activity such as chatting, photo sharing, or game playing.

- **P2P-based meeting application**   Windows Vista includes Windows Meeting Space, a new P2P-based meeting application that uses Windows Peer-to-Peer Networking functionality.

PNRPv2 is not backward-compatible with earlier versions of the protocol. Although PNRPv2 can coexist on a network with earlier versions, it cannot communicate with PNRPv1 clients. For more information about Windows Meeting Space and People Near Me, read Chapter 18, "Managing Windows Meeting Space."

Services Used by Peer-to-Peer Networking

Windows Peer-to-Peer Networking uses the following services, which by default start manually (Windows Vista will start services automatically as required):

- Peer Name Resolution Protocol
- Peer Networking Grouping

- Peer Networking Identity Manager
- PNRP Machine Name Publication Service

If these services are disabled, some peer-to-peer and collaborative applications, such as Windows Meetings, might not function.

Managing Peer-to-Peer Networking

Windows Peer-to-Peer Networking is a set of tools for applications to use, so they don't provide capabilities without an application. You can manage Windows Peer-to-Peer Networking using the Netsh tool or by using Group Policy settings:

- **Netsh tool**   Commands in the **netsh p2p** context will be used primarily by developers creating peer-to-peer applications. Systems administrators should not need to directly troubleshoot or manage Windows Peer-to-Peer Networking, so that aspect of the Netsh tool is not discussed further here.

- **Group Policy settings**   You can configure or completely disable Windows Peer-to-Peer Networking by using the Group Policy settings in Computer Configuration\Policies\ Administrative Templates\Network\Microsoft Peer-to-Peer Networking Services. You should need to modify the configuration only if an application has specific, nondefault requirements.

How It Works: Peer-to-Peer Name Resolution

In peer-to-peer networking, peers use Peer Name Resolution Protocol (PNRP) names to identify computers, users, groups, services, and anything else that should be resolved to an IP address. Peer names can be registered as unsecured or secured. Unsecured names are just automatically generated text strings that are subject to spoofing by a malicious computer that registers the same name. Unsecured names are therefore best used in private or otherwise secure networks. Secured names are digitally signed with a certificate and thus can be registered only by the owner.

PNRP IDs are 256 bits long and are composed of the following:

- The high-order 128 bits, known as the peer-to-peer ID, are a hash of a peer name assigned to the endpoint.

- The low-order 128 bits are used for the service location, which is a generated number that uniquely identifies different instances of the same ID in a cloud.

The 256-bit combination of peer-to-peer ID and service location allows multiple PNRP IDs to be registered from a single computer. For each cloud, each peer node manages a cache of PNRP IDs that includes both its own registered PNRP IDs and the entries cached over time.

When a peer needs to resolve a PNRP ID to the address, protocol, and port number, it first examines its own cache for entries with a matching peer ID (in case the client has resolved a PNRP ID for a different service location on the same peer). If that peer is found, the resolving client sends a request directly to the peer.

If the resolving client does not have an entry for the peer ID, it sends requests to other peers in the same cloud, one at a time. If one of those peers has an entry cached, that peer first verifies that the requested peer is connected to the network before resolving the name for the requesting client. While the PNRP request message is being forwarded, its contents are used to populate caches of nodes that are forwarding it. When the response is sent back through the return path, its contents are also used to populate node caches. This name resolution mechanism allows clients to identify each other without a server infrastructure.

EAPHost Architecture

For easier development of Extensible Authentication Protocol (EAP) authentication methods for IEEE 802.1X-authenticated wireless connections, Windows Vista supports a new EAP architecture called EAPHost. EAPHost provides the following features that are not supported by the EAP implementation in earlier versions of Windows:

- **Network Discovery**   EAPHost supports network discovery as defined in the "Identity selection hints for Extensible Authentication Protocol (EAP)" Internet draft.

- **RFC 3748 compliance**   EAPHost will conform to the EAP State Machine and address a number of security vulnerabilities that have been specified in RFC 3748. Additionally, EAPHost will support additional capabilities such as Expanded EAP Types (including vendor-specific EAP Methods).

- **EAP method coexistence**   EAPHost allows multiple implementations of the same EAP method to coexist simultaneously. For example, the Microsoft version of Protected EAP (PEAP) and the Cisco Systems, Inc. version of PEAP can be installed and selected.

- **Modular supplicant architecture**   In addition to supporting modular EAP methods, EAPHost also supports a modular supplicant architecture in which new supplicants can be added easily without having to replace the entire EAP implementation.

For EAP method vendors, EAPHost provides support for EAP methods already developed for Windows Server 2003 and Windows XP, and an easier method of developing new EAP methods for Windows Vista. Certified EAP methods can be distributed with Windows Update. EAPHost also allows better classification of EAP types so that the built-in 802.1X- and PPP-based Windows supplicants can use them.

For supplicant method vendors, EAPHost provides support for modular and pluggable supplicants for new link layers. Because EAPHost is integrated with NAP, new supplicants do not have to be NAP-aware. To participate in NAP, new supplicants only need to register a connection identifier and a callback function that informs the supplicant to re-authenticate.

For more information, read "EAP Host Extensibility in Windows" at *http://technet.microsoft.com/ en-us/magazine/cc162364.aspx*.

Layered Service Provider (LSP)

The Winsock Layered Service Provider (LSP) architecture resides between the Winsock DLL, which applications use to communicate on the network, and the Winsock Kernel Mode Driver (Afd.sys), which communicates with network adapter drivers. LSPs are used in several categories of applications, including:

- Proxy and firewalls
- Content filtering
- Virus scanning
- Adware and other network data manipulators
- Spyware and other data monitoring applications
- Security, authentication, and encryption

Windows Vista includes several improvements to LSPs to enable more powerful network applications and better security:

- Adding and removing LSPs is logged to the System Event Log. Administrators can use these events to determine which application installed an LSP and to troubleshoot failed LSP installations.

- A new installation API (*WSCInstallProviderAndChains*) that provides simpler, more reliable LSP installation.

- New facilities to categorize LSPs and allow critical system services to bypass LSPs. This can improve reliability when working with flawed LSPs.

- A diagnostics module for Network Diagnostics Framework that allows users to selectively remove LSPs that are causing problems.

Windows Sockets Direct Path for System Area Networks

Windows Sockets Direct (WSD) enables Windows Sockets applications that use TCP/IP to obtain the performance benefits of System Area Networks (SANs) without application modifications. SANs are a type of high-performance network often used for computer clusters.

WSD allows communications across a SAN to bypass the TCP/IP protocol stack, taking advantage of the reliable, direct communications provided by a SAN. In Windows Vista, this is implemented by adding a virtual switch between Winsock and the TCP/IP stack. This switch has the ability to examine traffic and pass communications to a SAN Winsock provider, bypassing TCP/IP entirely. Figure 26-12 illustrates this architecture.

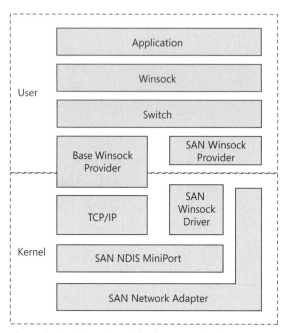

Figure 26-12   WSD enables improved performance across SANs by selectively bypassing TCP/IP using a virtual switch.

How to Configure Wireless Settings

Users want to stay constantly connected to their networks, and wireless LANs and wireless WANs are beginning to make that possible. However, managing multiple network connections can be challenging, and users often have difficulty resolving connectivity problems. As a result, users place more calls to support centers, increasing support cost and user frustration. You can reduce this by configuring Windows Vista client computers to connect to preferred wireless networks.

Windows Vista will automatically connect to most wired networks. Wireless networks, however, require configuration before Windows Vista will connect to them. You can connect Windows Vista computers to wireless networks in three different ways:

■ **Manually**   Windows Vista includes a new wizard-based user interface that makes it simple to connect to wireless networks. You can use this interface to manually configure intranet-based Windows Vista computers; end users can use this method to connect to public networks when they travel.

■ **Using Group Policy**   Group Policy settings are the most efficient way to configure any number of Windows computers in your organization to connect to your internal wireless networks.

■ **From the command line or by using scripts** Using the Netsh tool and commands in the netsh wlan context, you can export existing wireless network profiles, import them into other computers, connect to available wireless networks, or disconnect a wireless network.

After a wireless network is configured, the Wireless Single Sign-On feature of Window Vista executes 802.1X authentication at the appropriate time based on the network security configuration, while simply and seamlessly integrating with the user's Windows logon experience. The following sections describe each of these configuration techniques.

Manually Configuring Wireless Settings

To configure a wireless network that is currently available to the Windows Vista client computer, follow these steps:

1. Click Start and then click Connect To.

> **Note** The WLAN AutoConfig service must be started for wireless networks to be available. This service by default is set to start automatically.

2. The Connect To A Network Wizard appears, as shown in Figure 26-13. Click the wireless network you want to connect to and then click Connect.

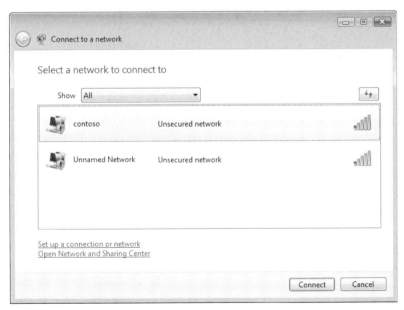

Figure 26-13 You can use the Connect To A Network Wizard to connect to a wireless network regardless of whether it broadcasts an SSID.

> **Note**   In Windows Vista, networks that are configured to not broadcast an SSID will appear as Unnamed Network, allowing you to connect to the network.

3. If the network does not broadcast an SSID, you will see the Type The Network Name (SSID) For The Network page. Type the network name and then click Next.

4. If the network is not encrypted, click Connect Anyway.

5. If the network is encrypted, you will see the Type The Network Security Key Or Passphrase page. Type the security key. Alternatively, if you have saved network settings to a USB flash drive, you can connect it now. Click Connect.

6. Windows Vista will connect to the network and then display the Successfully Connected To *SSID* page. Click Close.

Why Disabling SSID Broadcasting Doesn't Improve Security

Wireless networks broadcast an SSID that specifies the network name to help users who have not previously connected to the network to find it. However, disabling the SSID broadcast does not increase security, because the tools that a malicious attacker might use to find and connect to your wireless network do not rely on SSID broadcasts. The SSID broadcast does make it easier for legitimate users to find and connect to your wireless networks. By disabling the broadcasting of the SSID, you can negatively impact the people whom you do want to be able to connect.

Using Group Policy to Configure Wireless Settings

In Active Directory environments, you can use Group Policy settings to configure wireless network policies. For best results, you should have Windows Server 2003 with Service Pack 1 or later installed on your domain controllers, because Microsoft extended support for wireless Group Policy settings when they released Service Pack 1.

Before you can configure wireless networks for Windows Vista client computers, you need to extend the Active Directory schema using the 802.11Schema.ldf file included on the companion CD. If you do not have access to the companion CD, you can copy the schema file from *http://technet.microsoft.com/en-us/library/bb727029.aspx*. To extend the schema, follow these steps:

1. Copy the 802.11Schema.ldf file to a folder on a domain controller.

2. Log on to the domain controller with Domain Admin privileges and open a command prompt.

3. Select the folder containing the 802.11Schema.ldf file and run the following command (where *Dist_Name_of_AD_Domain* is the distinguished name of the Active Directory

domain whose schema is being modified; an example of a distinguished name is DC=wcoast,DC=microsoft,DC=com for the wcoast.microsoft.com Active Directory domain):

```
ldifde -i -v -k -f 802.11Schema.ldf -c DC=X Dist_Name_of_AD_Domain
```

4. Restart the domain controller.

After you have extended the schema, you can configure a wireless network policy from a Windows Vista client computer by following these steps:

1. Open the Active Directory Group Policy Object (GPO) in the Group Policy Object Editor.

2. Expand Computer Configuration, Policies, Windows Settings, Security Settings, and then click Wireless Network (IEEE 802.11) Policies.

3. Right-click Wireless Network (IEEE 802.11) Policies and then click Create A New Windows Vista Policy. The Wireless Network Properties dialog box appears, as shown in Figure 26-14.

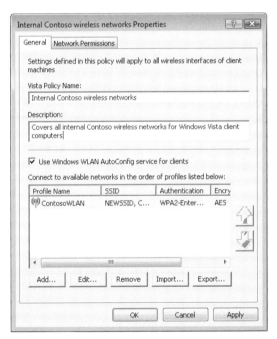

Figure 26-14   You can use Group Policy settings to configure Windows Vista wireless network clients.

4. To add an infrastructure network, click Add and then click Infrastructure to open the Connection tab of the New Profile Properties dialog box. In the Network Names list, click NEWSSID and then click Remove. Then, type a valid internal SSID in the Network Names box and then click Add. Repeat this to configure multiple SSIDs for a single

profile. If the network is hidden, select the Connect Even If The Network Is Not Broadcasting check box.

5. On the New Profile Properties dialog box, click the Security tab. Use this tab to configure the wireless network authentication and encryption settings. Click OK.

> **Note**   This Resource Kit does not cover how to design wireless networks. However, you should avoid using Wired Equivalent Privacy (WEP) whenever possible. WEP is vulnerable to several different types of attack, and WEP keys can be difficult to change. Whenever possible, use Wi-Fi Protected Access (WPA) or Wi-Fi Protected Access 2 (WPA2), which both use strong authentication and dynamic encryption keys.

The settings described in the previous process will configure client computers to automatically connect to your internal wireless networks, and to not connect to other wireless networks.

Configuring Wireless Settings from the Command Line or a Script

You can also configure wireless settings using commands in the netsh wlan context of the Netsh command-line tool, which enables you to create scripts that connect to different wireless networks (whether encrypted or not). To list available wireless networks, run the following command:

```
Netsh wlan show networks
```

```
Interface Name : Wireless Network Connection
There are 2 networks currently visible

SSID 1 : Contoso1
    Network Type           : Infrastructure
    Authentication         : Open
    Encryption             : None

SSID 1 : Contoso2
    Network Type           : Infrastructure
    Authentication         : Open
    Encryption             : WEP
```

Before you can connect to a wireless network using Netsh, you must have a profile saved for that network. Profiles contain the SSID and security information required to connect to a network. If you have previously connected to a network, the computer will have a profile for that network saved. If a computer has never connected to a wireless network, you need to save a profile before you can use Netsh to connect to it. You can save a profile from one computer to an XML file and then distribute the XML file to other computers in your network. To save a profile, run the following command after manually connecting to a network:

```
Netsh wlan export profile name="SSID"
```

```
Interface profile "SSID" is saved in file ".\Wireless Network
Connection-SSID.xml" successfully.
```

Before you can connect to a new wireless network, you can load a profile from a file. The following example demonstrates how to create a wireless profile (which is saved as an XML file) from a script or the command line:

```
Netsh wlan add profile filename="C:\profiles\contoso1.xml"
```

```
Profile contoso1 is added on interface Wireless Network Connection
```

To quickly connect to a wireless network, use the netsh wlan connect command and specify a wireless profile name (which must be configured or added previously). The following examples demonstrate different but equivalent syntaxes for connecting to a wireless network with the Contoso1 SSID:

```
Netsh wlan connect Contoso1
```

```
Connection request is received successfully
```

```
Netsh wlan connect Contoso1 interface="Wireless Network Connection"
```

```
Connection request is received successfully
```

Note that you need to specify the interface name only if you have multiple wireless network adapters—an uncommon situation. You can use the following command to disconnect from all wireless networks:

```
Netsh wlan disconnect
```

```
Disconnection request is received successfully
```

You can use scripts and profiles to simplify the process of connecting to private wireless networks for your users. Ideally, you should use scripts and profiles to save users from ever needing to type wireless security keys.

You can also use Netsh to allow or block access to wireless networks based on their SSIDs. For example, the following command allows access to a wireless network with the Contoso1 SSID:

```
Netsh wlan add filter permission=allow ssid=Contoso networktype=infrastructure
```

Similarly, the following command blocks access to the Fabrikam wireless network:

```
Netsh wlan add filter permission=block ssid=Fabrikam networktype=adhoc
```

To block all ad hoc networks, use the Denyall permission, as the following example demonstrates:

```
Netsh wlan add filter permission=denyall networktype=adhoc
```

To prevent Windows Vista from automatically connecting to wireless networks, run the following command:

```
Netsh wlan set autoconfig enabled=no interface="Wireless Network Connection"
```

You can also use Netsh to define the priority of user profiles (but not Group Policy profiles). Group Policy profiles always have precedence over user profiles. The following example demonstrates how to configure Windows Vista to automatically connect to the wireless network defined by the Contoso profile before connecting to the wireless network defined by the Fabrikam profile:

```
Netsh wlan set profileorder name=Contoso interface="Wireless Network Connection" priority=1
Netsh wlan set profileorder name=Fabrikam interface="Wireless Network Connection" priority=2
```

Netsh has many other commands for configuring wireless networking. For more information, run the following at a command prompt:

```
Netsh wlan help
```

Note When troubleshooting problems connecting to wireless networks, open Event Viewer and browse the Applications And Services Logs\Microsoft\Windows\WLAN-AutoConfig event log. You can also use this log to determine which wireless networks a Windows Vista client has connected to, which might be useful when identifying the source of a security compromise. For more information, see Chapter 32.

How to Configure TCP/IP

You can use several different techniques to configure TCP/IP for Windows Vista. Most environments use DHCP to provide basic settings. Alternatively, you can manually configure TCP/IP settings using graphical tools. Finally, some settings are most easily configured using scripts that call command-line tools such as Netsh. You can use logon scripts to automate command-line configuration. The following sections describe each of these configuration techniques.

> **Note** For wireless networks, you will need to first connect the wireless adapter to the wireless network and then configure the TCP/IP settings. However, wireless networks almost always have a DHCP server available.

DHCP

Almost all client computers should be configured using Dynamic Host Configuration Protocol (DHPC). With DHCP, you configure a DHCP server (such as a Windows Server 2003 computer) to provide IP addresses and network configuration settings to client computers when they start up. Windows Vista and all recent Windows operating systems are configured to use DHCP by default, so you can configure network settings by simply setting up a DHCP server and connecting a Windows Vista computer to the network.

As the number of mobile computers, traveling users, and wireless networks has increased, so has the importance of DHCP. Because computers may have to connect to several different networks, manually configuring network settings would require users to make changes each time they connected to a network. With DHCP, the DHCP server on the local network provides the correct settings when the client connects.

Some of the configuration settings you can configure with DHCP include:

- **IP address**   Uniquely identifies a computer on the network
- **Default gateway**   Identifies the router that the client computer will use to send traffic to other networks
- **DNS servers**   Internet name servers use to resolve host names of other computers
- **WINS servers**   Microsoft name servers use for identifying specific computers on the network
- **Boot server**   Used for loading an operating system across the network when configuring new computers or starting diskless workstations

Clients use the following process to retrieve DHCP settings:

1. The client computers transmit a DHCPDiscover broadcast packet on the local network.

2. DHCP servers receive this broadcast packet and send a DHCPOffer broadcast packet back to the client computer. This packet includes the IP address configuration information. If more than one DHCP server is on the local network, the client computer might receive multiple DHCPOffer packets.

3. The client computer sends a DHCPRequest packet to a single DHCP server requesting the use of those configuration settings. Other DHCP servers that might have sent a DHCPOffer broadcast will see this response and know that they no longer need to reserve an IP address for the client.

4. Finally, the DHCP server sends a DHCPACK packet to acknowledge that the IP address has been leased to the client for a specific amount of time. The client can now begin using the IP address settings.

Additionally, client computers will attempt to renew their IP addresses after half the DHCP lease time has expired. By default, Windows Server 2003 computers have a lease time of eight days. Therefore, Windows client computers attempt to renew their DHCP settings after four days and will retrieve updated settings if you have made any changes to the DHCP server.

Because client computers retrieve new DHCP settings each time they start up, connect to a new network, or a DHCP lease expires, you have the opportunity to change configuration settings with only a few days notice. Therefore, if you need to replace a DNS server and you want to use a new IP address, you can add the new address to your DHCP server settings, wait eight days for client computers to renew their DHCP leases and acquire the new settings, and then have a high level of confidence that client computers will have the new server's IP address before shutting down the old DNS server.

If a client computer does not receive a DHCP address and an alternate IP address configuration has not been manually configured, Windows client computers automatically configure themselves with a randomly selected Automatic Private IP Addressing (APIPA) address in the range of 169.254.0.1 to 169.254.255.255. If more than one Windows computer on a network has an APIPA address, the computers will be able to communicate. However, APIPA has no default gateway, so client computers will not be able to connect to the Internet, to other networks, or to computers with non-APIPA addresses. For information about IPv6, refer to Chapter 29.

You can use the following techniques to determine if a client has been assigned an IP address and to troubleshoot DHCP-related problems:

- **IPConfig** From a command line, run **IPConfig /all** to view the current IP configuration. If the client has a DHCP-assigned IP address, the *DHCP Enabled* property will be set to Yes, and the *DHCP Server* property will have an IP address assigned, as the following example demonstrates:

```
Ipconfig /all
```

```
Windows IP Configuration
        Host Name . . . . . . . . . . . . : Vista
        Primary Dns Suffix  . . . . . . . : hq.contoso.com
        Node Type . . . . . . . . . . . . : Hybrid
        IP Routing Enabled. . . . . . . . : No
        WINS Proxy Enabled. . . . . . . . : No
        DNS Suffix Search List. . . . . . : contoso.com

    Ethernet adapter Local Area Connection:

        Connection-specific DNS Suffix  . : contoso.com
        Description . . . . . . . . . . . : Broadcom NetXtreme 57xx Gigabit
```

```
Controller
   Physical Address. . . . . . . . . : 00-15-C5-08-82-F3
   DHCP Enabled. . . . . . . . . . . : Yes
   Autoconfiguration Enabled . . . . : Yes
   Link-local IPv6 Address . . . . . :
fe80::a1f2:3425:87f6:49c2%10(Preferred)
   IPv4 Address. . . . . . . . . . . : 192.168.1.242(Preferred)
   Subnet Mask . . . . . . . . . . . : 255.255.255.0
   Lease Obtained. . . . . . . . . . : Sunday, August 20, 2006 11:12:44 PM
   Lease Expires . . . . . . . . . . : Monday, August 28, 2006 11:12:44 PM
   Default Gateway . . . . . . . . . : 192.168.1.1
   DHCP Server . . . . . . . . . . . : 192.168.1.210
   DNS Servers . . . . . . . . . . . : 192.168.1.210
   NetBIOS over Tcpip . . . . . . . . : Enabled
```

> **Note**   If you are troubleshooting a client connectivity problem and notice that the IP address begins with 169.254, the DHCP server was not available when the client computer started. Verify that the DHCP server is available and the client computer is properly connected to the network. Then, issue the **ipconfig /release** and **ipconfig / renew** commands to acquire a new IP address. For more information about troubleshooting network connections, see Chapter 32.

■ **Network And Sharing Center**   In Network And Sharing Center, click View Status to open the connection status. Then, click the Details button to open the Network Connection Details, as shown in Figure 26-15. This dialog box provides similar information to that displayed by the IPConfig /all command.

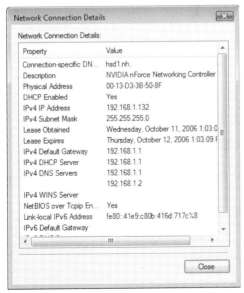

Figure 26-15   The Network Connection Details dialog box provides graphical access to IP configuration settings.

■ **Event Viewer**   Open Event Viewer and browse the Windows Logs\System Event Log. Look for events with a source of Dhcp-Client for IPv4 addresses, or DHCPv6-Client for IPv6 addresses. Although this technique is not useful for determining the active configuration, it can reveal problems that have occurred in the past.

Manually Configuring IP Addresses

The alternative to using DHCP is to manually configure IP address settings. However, because of the time required to configure settings, the likelihood of making a configuration error, and the challenge of connecting new computers to a network, manually configuring IP addresses is rarely the best choice for client computers.

To manually configure an IPv4 address, follow these steps:

1. Click Start, right-click Network, and then click Properties.

2. Click Manage Network Connections.

3. Right-click the network adapter and then click Properties.

4. In the Properties dialog box, click Internet Protocol Version 4 (TCP/IPv4) and then click Properties.

5. If you always want to use manually configured network settings, click the General tab and then click Use The Following IP Address. If you only want to use manually configured network settings when a DHCP server is not available, click the Alternate Configuration tab and then click User Configured. Then, configure the computer's IP address, default gateway, and DNS servers.

6. Click OK twice. The configuration changes will take effect immediately, without requiring you to restart the computer.

You should rarely need to configure an IPv6 address manually, because IPv6 is designed to automatically configure itself. For more information about IPv6 autoconfiguration, refer to Chapter 29. To configure an IPv6 address manually, follow these steps:

1. Click Start, right-click Network, and then click Properties.

2. Click Manage Network Connections.

3. Right-click the network adapter and then click Properties.

4. In the Properties dialog box, click Internet Protocol Version 6 (TCP/IPv6) and then click Properties.

5. Click Use The Following IPv6 Address and configure the computer's IP address, subnet prefix length, default gateway, and DNS servers. TCP/IPv6 does not support an alternate configuration, as TCP/IPv4 does.

6.   Click OK twice. The configuration changes will take effect immediately, without requiring you to restart the computer.

You can prevent users from accessing these graphical tools. Most important settings require administrative credentials, so simply not giving users local administrator access to their computers will prevent them from making most important changes. You can also use the Group Policy settings located in User Configuration\Policies\Administrative Templates\ Network\Network Connections to further restrict the user interface (but this will not necessarily prevent the user from using other tools to change).

Command Line and Scripts

You can also configure network settings from the command line or from a script using the Netsh tool and commands in the Netsh interface ipv4 or Netsh interface ipv6 contexts. For example, to configure the standard network interface to use DHCP and to use the DNS servers provided by DHCP, you could issue the following commands:

```
Netsh interface ipv4 set address "Local Area Connection" dhcp
Netsh interface ipv4 set dnsserver "Local Area Connection" dhcp
```

Note   Windows XP also included the Netsh tool. However, the Windows XP version of Netsh uses different commands. For example, you would use **Netsh interface ip set dns** to configure DNS settings for a Windows XP computer, instead of **Netsh interface ipv4 set dnsserver**, which you use to configure DNS settings for a Windows Vista computer. However, Netsh in Windows Vista is backward-compatible and will accept the older, Windows XP–compatible syntax.

Because DHCP is the default setting for network adapters, it is more likely that you will need to use Netsh commands to configure a static IP address. The following command demonstrates how to do this for IPv4:

```
Netsh interface ipv4 set address "Local Area Connection" source=static address=192.168.1.10
mask=255.255.255.0 gateway=192.168.1.1
Netsh interface ipv4 set dnsserver "Local Area Connection" source=static address=192.168.1.2
 register=primary
```

The following commands demonstrate configuring a static IP address and DNS server configuration for IPv6:

```
Netsh interface ipv6 set address "Local Area Connection" address=2001:db8:3fa8:102a::2
anycast
Netsh interface ipv6 set dnsserver "Local Area Connection" source=static address=2001:db8:
3fa8:1719::1 register=primary
```

You should avoid using scripts to configure production client computers because they are not tolerant of varying hardware configurations, and because DHCP provides most of the configuration capabilities required for production networks. However, scripts can be useful for quickly changing the network configuration of computers in lab environments. Instead of manually writing Netsh commands, you can configure a computer using graphical tools and use the Netsh tool to generate a configuration script.

Note You can generate a configuration script that can be run from within Netsh by running the command **Netsh interface dump > *script_filename***. In theory, you would be able to apply that script using the command **Netsh –f *script_filename***. Unfortunately, at the time of this writing, Windows Vista creates flawed configuration scripts that cannot be executed. This should be fixed in an update and may work properly by the time this book is released.

Netsh provides the ability to configure almost any aspect of Windows Vista networking. For detailed instructions, refer to Windows Vista Help And Support or run the following command from a command prompt:

```
Netsh ?
```

Note You can also configure static IP addresses using the SetStaticIP.vbs script from this book's companion CD.

Direct from the Source: Automate NIC Configuration Using Netsh

During the years I worked as a consultant, it was not uncommon to connect my laptop to several different networks in the same day. In some cases they were DHCP enabled, so connection was easy. For others, I would have to configure the network adapter manually. Ugh!

Enter the Netsh commands. You can use the Netsh command to modify the network configuration on Windows 2000 and later computers. It's not the friendliest syntax to use, but it is a real time-saver once you learn to use it. (I have noticed the version that ships with Windows Vista seems almost intuitive.) The following sample scripts are for using Netsh to set STATIC IP entries on an adapter and another script to set the adapter back to DHCP mode so the settings can be obtained automatically. To use the code, type it into a batch file and modify the "name=" to the name of the adapter in quotation marks and change the IP addresses.

Static IP

```
netsh interface ipv4 set address name="Wireless Network Connection" source=static addr
=192.168.0.100 mask=255.255.255.0 gateway=192.168.0.250 gwmetric=0
netsh interface ipv4 set dnsserver name="Wireless Network Connection" source=static ad
dr=192.168.0.2 register=NONE
REM netsh interface ipv4 set wins name="Wireless Network Connection" source=static add
```

```
r=10.217.27.9
REM  OR if no WINS server
netsh interface ipv4 set winsserver name="Wireless Network Connection" source=dhcp
ipconfig /all
```

DHCP

```
netsh interface ipv4 set address name="Wireless Network Connection" source=dhcp
netsh interface ipv4 set dnsserver name="Wireless Network Connection" source=dhcp
netsh interface ipv4 set winsserver name="Wireless Network Connection" source=dhcp
ipconfig /renew "Wireless Network Connection"
ipconfig /all
```

Don Baker, Premier Field Engineer

Windows Platform

How to Connect to Active Directory Domains

Most organizations with more than a few Windows client computers should use an Active Directory domain to simplify managing the computers. Typically, joining clients to a domain is one of the first steps in configuring a computer. The process you should use is slightly different if you have 802.1X authentication enabled.

How to Connect to a Domain When 802.1X Authentication Is Not Enabled

For networks without 802.1X authentication, follow these steps to join a domain:

1. Click Start. Right-click Computer and then click Properties.

2. Under Computer Name, Domain, And Workgroup Settings, click Change Settings.

3. From the System Properties dialog box, click Network ID.

4. The Join A Domain Or Workgroup Wizard appears. Select This Computer Is Part Of A Business Network; I Use It To Connect To Other Computers At Work. Click Next.

5. On the Is Your Company Network On A Domain page, click My Company Uses A Network With A Domain. Click Next.

6. On the You Will Need The Following Information page, verify that you have domain credentials available and that you know the domain name. Click Next.

7. On the Type Your User Name, Password, And Domain Name For Your Domain Account page, provide your domain credentials. Click Next.

8. If the Type The Computer Name And Computer Domain Name page appears, type the computer and domain name. Then click Next.

9. If prompted, type a user name, password, and domain. Click OK.

10. On the Do You Want To Enable A Domain User Account On This Computer page, click Do Not Add A Domain User Account. Click Next.

11. Click Finish.

12. Click OK and then restart the computer when prompted.

If you experience problems joining a domain, see Chapter 32.

How to Connect to a Domain When 802.1X Authentication Is Enabled

For networks with 802.1X authentication, joining a domain is slightly more complicated. During 802.1X authentication, the client authenticates the server's identity by ensuring that the server certificate is valid and was issued by a trusted certificate authority (CA). However, if you used an internal CA (such as one hosted by Windows Server 2003 certificate services) to issue the server certificate, the CA will not be trusted by default until the computer joins a domain. Therefore, to join the domain, you must temporarily configure the client computer to ignore the 802.1X authentication server's certificate.

> **Note**   If you have configured your 802.1X authentication servers with a server certificate issued by a public certification authority that is trusted by Windows Vista by default, you can leave the Validate Server Certificate check box selected.

To join a domain with 802.1X authentication enabled, follow these steps:

1. Launch the Services console, start the Wired AutoConfig service, and set the Wired AutoConfig service to start automatically.

2. Open Network And Sharing Center and then click Manage Network Connections.

3. Right-click the network adapter and then click Properties.

4. In the Properties dialog box, click the Authentication Tab. Click the Choose A Network Authentication Method list and then click Protected EAP (PEAP).

5. Click Settings. In the Protected EAP (PEAP) Properties dialog box, clear the Validate Server Certificate check box. Click OK twice.

6. Follow the standard instructions for joining the computer to a domain, as described in the previous section.

7. After the computer has joined the domain and restarted, perform steps 2 though 5. This time in step 5, select the Validate Server Certificate check box.

To partially automate this process, configure a Windows Vista computer to not validate the server certificate. Then use the Netsh lan export profile command to export a profile for the configured network adapter. You can create a script to import that profile on other client computers to allow them to join a domain without validating a server certificate. For more information about exporting and importing profiles, see the section titled "Configuring Wireless Settings from the Command Line or a Script" earlier in this chapter. For detailed instructions, see "Joining a Windows Vista Wired Client to a Domain" at *http://www.microsoft.com/technet/itsolutions/network/wifi/vista_bootstrap_wired.mspx.*

Summary

Windows Vista represents the most significant update to Windows networking since 1995. Users will find it easier to take advantage of both wired and wireless networks as they travel. With the new auto-tuning TCP/IP stack, file transfers and web access can be faster than before. Enterprises will appreciate the reduced security risks, including improved protection from threats introduced by mobile and wireless users. Systems administrators will find managing bandwidth easier with Windows Vista because they can create granular security policies for network traffic as well as QoS support for mission-critical applications. These changes let you do more with your network infrastructure while minimizing administration time and maximizing end-user productivity.

Additional Resources

The following resources contain additional information and tools related to this chapter.

Related Information

- Chapter 25, "Managing Client Protection," includes information about configuring the desktop.

- Chapter 27, "Configuring Windows Firewall and IPsec," includes information about Windows Firewall and improvements to IPsec.

- Chapter 28, "Connecting Remote Users and Networks," includes information about setting up dial-up connections and VPNs.

- Chapter 29, "Deploying IPv6," includes information about IPv6.

- Chapter 32, "Troubleshooting Network Issues," includes information about solving networking problems.

- "Active Directory Schema Extensions for Windows Vista Wireless and Wired Group Policy Enhancements" at *http://www.microsoft.com/technet/network/wifi/ vista_ad_ext.mspx* includes instructions on extending the Active Directory schema to support configuring wireless Windows Vista clients.

- "Deployment of IEEE 802.1X for Wired Networks Using Microsoft Windows" at *http://www.microsoft.com/downloads/details.aspx?familyid=05951071-6b20-4cef-9939-47c397ffd3dd* includes more information about 802.1X authentication.

- "Joining a Windows Vista Wired Client to a Domain" at *http://www.microsoft.com/technet/itsolutions/network/wifi/vista_bootstrap_wired.mspx* includes more information about joining a domain when you have required 802.1X authentication.

- "Active Directory Schema Extensions for Windows Vista Wireless and Wired Group Policy Enhancements" at *http://www.microsoft.com/technet/itsolutions/network/wifi/vista_ad_ext.mspx* includes information about extending the Active Directory schema to manage 802.1X.

- "TCP/IP Registry Values for Microsoft Windows Vista and Windows Server 2008" at *http://download.microsoft.com/download/c/2/6/c26893a6-46c7-4b5c-b287-830216597340/TCPIP_Reg.doc* includes a list of registry values that can be used to configure TCP/IP in Windows Vista.

- RFC 1191: *http://www.ietf.org/rfc/rfc1191.txt*

- RFC 2581: *http://www.ietf.org/rfc/rfc2581.txt*

- RFC 2582: *http://www.ietf.org/rfc/rfc2582.txt*

- RFC 2883: *http://www.ietf.org/rfc/rfc2883.txt*

- RFC 3517: *http://www.ietf.org/rfc/rfc3517.txt*

- RFC 4138: *http://www.ietf.org/rfc/rfc4138.txt*

On the Companion CD

- 802.11Schema.ldf
- ConfigureDNSsettings.vbs
- ManageDHCP.vbs
- ManageNetworkAdapter.vbs
- NetworkCardInventory.vbs
- ReportBandwidth.vbs
- SetStaticIP.vbs

Chapter 27

Configuring Windows Firewall and IPsec

Windows Vista includes a stateful, authenticating Windows Firewall (also called Windows Firewall With Advanced Security) that provides more granular firewall rules, can block both incoming and outgoing traffic, fully supports IPv6, uses location-aware profiles, enforces network service hardening, and provides integrated Internet Protocol security (IPsec) protection. This chapter examines how to configure and manage Windows Firewall and how to configure and manage IPsec protection using the new Windows Firewall With Advanced Security snap-in, Group Policy, and new netsh command contexts included with Windows Vista. The chapter also describes how the new Windows Firewall simplifies the implementation of server and domain isolation scenarios and Network Access Protection (NAP) using IPsec.

Understanding Windows Firewall

Windows Firewall in Windows Vista is a significant advance over the Windows Firewall first introduced in Windows XP Service Pack 2. Table 27-1 illustrates a feature comparison between these two firewalls.

Table 27-1 Feature Comparison Between Windows Firewall in Windows Vista and Windows XP SP2

Feature	XP SP2	Windows Vista
Filtering direction	Inbound only	Both inbound and outbound
Default filtering action	Block (fixed)	Configurable actions for inbound and outbound traffic
Protocols supported	TCP, UDP, ICMP (partial)	Any IANA IP protocols
Types of rules	Filter by port, application, or ICMP type	Filter by any combination or permutation of the following: protocol, local or remote port (TCP and UDP only), ICMPv4/v6 Type and code, local or remote IP addresses, interface type, programs, services, and IPsec metadata

Table 27-1   Feature Comparison Between Windows Firewall in Windows Vista and Windows XP SP2

Feature	XP SP2	Windows Vista
Possible rule actions	Allow only	Allow, block, bypass
Group Policy support	Provided by ADM files	Provided by a custom Group Policy extension snap-in that is the same as the snap-in used to configure local policy
Remote management	N/A	Use MMC snap-in or netsh.exe command
User interface and tools	Control panel tool (CPL) and netsh	MMC snap-in, CPL, and netsh
APIs	Public COM APIs	Enhanced public COM APIs

Other enhancements include:

- Integration with Internet Protocol Security (IPsec). This provides IPsec-aware firewall rules and simplifies the task of using IPsec to implement network protection strategies such as server and domain isolation and Network Access Protection (NAP).

- An expanded set of firewall profiles. These take advantage of Windows Vista's Network Location Awareness (NLA) feature to allow Windows Firewall to reconfigure itself depending on the categorization of connected networks it senses on the computer's network interfaces.

- Full support for IPv6.

> **Note**   Although Windows Firewall CPL in Windows XP lets you allow exceptions by selecting a check box, technically an unchecked rule in the CPL results in a block rule, because traffic will see it as disabled and match the default block inbound action.

Understanding the new features of Windows Vista's Windows Firewall requires an understanding of the underlying Windows Filtering Platform upon which Windows Firewall is based. It also requires an understanding of how Windows Service Hardening is implemented in Windows Vista to protect built-in network services.

> **Note**   Although Windows Vista's Windows Firewall supports stateful packet inspection, it does not support application-layer pluggable filters. This means, for example, that Windows Firewall cannot perform stateful inspection of HTTP traffic and can therefore not directly prevent root kit–based malware from being installed on a Windows Vista computer. Instead, other Windows Vista features provide malware protection, including User Access Control (UAC) and Windows Defender. For more information on protecting Windows Vista computers from malware, see Chapter 25, "Managing Client Protection."

Multiple Firewalls

Windows XP Service Pack 2 actually has three different firewalling (or network traffic filtering) technologies that you can separately configure, and which have zero interaction with each other:

- Windows Firewall, which was first introduced in Service Pack 2

- TCP/IP Filtering, which is accessed from the Options tab of the Advanced TCP/IP Properties sheet for the network connection

- IPsec rules and filters, which you can create using the IPsec Security Policy Management MMC snap-in

On top of this confusion, Windows Server 2003 had a fourth network traffic filtering technology that you could use: the Routing And Remote Access Service (RRAS), which supported basic firewall and packet filtering. The problem, of course, is that when more than one of these firewalls is configured on a computer, one firewall can block traffic that another allows. As a result, network services might not work as expected, and verifying the configuration of each of these firewalls can make troubleshooting a nightmare.

With Windows Vista, however, IPsec filtering has been integrated with Windows Firewall; TCP/IP Filtering on the Options tab has been removed. This means that Windows Vista users have only one place to configure for both traffic filtering and network protection, and the result is easier management and simplified troubleshooting.

Understanding the Windows Filtering Platform

The Windows Filtering Platform (WFP) is an architectural component of Windows Vista that allows access to TCP/IP packets as they are being processed by Windows Vista's Next Generation TCP/IP Stack. WFP is a collection of public APIs that provide hooks into the networking stack and the underlying filtering logic upon which Windows Firewall is built. Independent software vendors (ISVs) can use WFP to develop third-party firewalls, network diagnostic software, antivirus software, and other types of network applications. Using these APIs, a WFP-aware filtering application can access a packet at anywhere in the processing path to view or modify its contents (Figure 27-1).

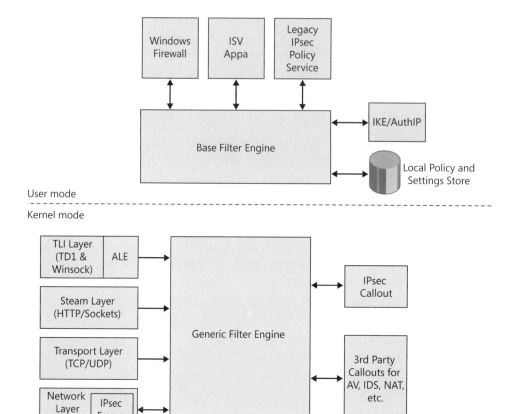

Figure 27-1 Simplified architecture of the new Windows Filtering Platform.

 Note Third-party vendors and network application developers should utilize the WFP APIs only for filtering applications or security applications.

The main components of the WFP are:

- **Base Filter Engine (BFE)** This component runs in user mode and receives filtering requests made by Windows Firewall, third-party applications, and the legacy IPsec policy service. The BFE then plumbs the filters created by these requests into the kernel mode Generic Filter Engine. The BFE (bfe.dll) runs within a generic Svchost.exe process.

- **Generic Filter Engine** This component receives the filters plumbed from the BFE and stores them so that the different layers of the TCP/IP stack can access them. As the stack processes a packet, each layer the packet encounters calls the GFE to determine whether the packet should be passed or dropped. The GFE also calls the various callout modules (defined next) to determine whether the packet should be passed or dropped. (Some callouts may perform an identical function, especially if multiple third-party firewalls are running concurrently.) The GFE (wfp.lib) is part of the kernel-mode Next Generation TCP/IP Stack (NetioTcpip.sys).

■ **Callout Modules**   These components are used for performing deep inspection or data modification of packets being processed by the pack. Callout modules store additional filtering criteria that the GFE uses to determine whether a packet should be passed or dropped.

> **Note**   The BFE can support multiple clients simultaneously. This means that a third-party, WFP-aware application can interact with and even override Windows Firewall if so designed.

The APIs of the BFE are all publicly documented so that ISVs can create applications that hook into the advanced filtering capabilities of the Next Generation TCP/IP Stack in Windows Vista and Windows Server 2008. Some of the filtering features of the WFP are implemented using callouts, but most filtering is performed using static filters created by the BFE as it interacts with Windows Firewall. The Windows Firewall service, which manages policies from Group Policy, uses interfaces and third-party applications and monitors the system to make sure the filters passed to BFE reflect at any given time the environment the system is in. These public WFP APIs do not replace the legacy COM APIs used by Windows Firewall in Windows XP. Windows Firewall in Windows Vista supports these APIs and provides new public APIs that are scriptable and expose the full configurability of the firewall, but they have some limitations. For instance, they have no IPsec integration and do not allow discrimination between IPv4 and IPv6.

For more information about the Windows Filtering Platform, see *http://msdn2.microsoft.com/ en-us/library/aa366510.aspx* on MSDN. You can find the Windows Filtering Platform API reference at *http://windowssdk.msdn.microsoft.com/en-us/library/aa364947.aspx*.

Understanding Windows Service Hardening

Windows Service Hardening (WSH) is a new feature of Windows Vista and Windows Server 2008 that is designed to protect critical network services running on a system. If a service is compromised, WSH reduces the potential damage that can occur by reducing the attack surface that could be potentially exploited by some forms of malicious code. Because network services (both those built into the operating system and those installed by third-party applications) are by their nature exposed to the network (which itself is usually connected to the Internet), they provide a vector by which attackers can try to compromise a system. WSH implements the following protection improvements over previous versions of Windows:

■ Configuring services run whenever possible within the lower-privileged LocalService or NetworkService context instead of the LocalSystem context favored by many services in previous versions of Windows.

■ Implementing a new type of per-service security identifier (Service SID) that extends the Windows access control model to services and the system resources they access. When a service is started by the SCM, the SID is added to secondary SIDs list of the process token if the service opted to do this.

■ Applying a write-restricted access token to the process for each service so that any attempt to access a system resource that does not have an explicit allow ACE for the Service SID will fail.

■ Tightening control over the generic Svchost.exe grouping and distribution of services.

■ Reducing the number of privileges assigned to services to only those needed by the service.

Understanding Service SIDs

Service SIDs are of the form S-1-5-80-{*SHA1 hash of short service name*} and complement the existing set of user, group, machine, and special SIDs used by previous versions of Windows. Service SIDs are secondary SIDs that are added to the SIDs list of the service process token when the Service Control Manager starts the service. The primary SID for a service is the built-in identity (LocalService, NetworkService, or LocalSystem) under which the service runs.

To have a Service SID added to its token, the service must first opt in to doing so. Opt-in is normally done by the operating system or application when the service is started. Administrators can manually opt in user-mode services by using the sc sidtype command, which can configure the Service SID as either RESTRICTED, UNRESTRICTED, or NONE. For example, sc sidtype *service_name* restricted will add the Service SID for the service to its service process token and also make it a write-restricted token. This means, for example, that any registry key used by the service must be explicitly ACLed to allow the service to access it. On the other hand, sc sidtype *service_name* unrestricted adds the SID of the service so that access check operations requesting that SID on the service token will succeed. Finally, sc sidtype *service_name* none does not include any SID in the token. For more information, type **sc sidtype ?** at a command prompt.

> **Note**   To query the sidtype of a service, you can use the sc qsidtype command.

Some services in Windows Vista ship out of box as UNRESTRICTED, and most services will fail to start if changed to RESTRICTED. Third-party applications, such as antivirus software, can be designed to opt in to having Service SIDs and can be designed to run either RESTRICTED or UNRESTRICTED. If the local administrator changes an existing service SID type from NONE to UNRESTRICTED, she gets the service having SID type with probably zero regression or issues with this service. (A SID type of UNRESTRICTED is sufficient for network traffic filtering.)

> **Note**   The service SIDs of all the configured services per process are always present in the
> process. Only the running services have their SIDs enabled; the SIDS of non-running services
> are there, but in a disabled state. However, for Windows Vista, the filtering platform considers
> all SIDs to be activated, regardless of whether or not the service is in a disabled state.

Windows Firewall and Windows Service Hardening

You can use Service SIDs to restrict ways that services can interact with system objects,
the file system, the registry, and events. For example, by ACLing the firewall driver object
using Windows Firewall's Service SID, this driver will accept communication only from the
Windows Firewall service.

WSH also protects services by using rules similar to those used by Windows Firewall. These
rules are called *service restriction rules* and are built into Windows Vista and can specify
things such as which ports the service should listen on or which ports the service should send
data over. An example of a built-in WSH rule might be "The DNS client service should send
data only over port UDP/53 and should never listen on any port." These rules add additional
protection to network services because network objects such as ports do not support ACLs.
ISVs can extend this protection to third-party services they develop by using the public COM
APIs for WSH, found at *http://msdn2.microsoft.com/en-us/library/aa365489.aspx*. However,
WSH rules don't actually allow traffic (assuming Windows Firewall is on); instead, they
define the restricted traffic that can be allowed to/from a service, regardless of the
administrator-created firewall rules. WSH rules are thus a sandbox for the service.

WSH rules are also merged into the filtering process performed when Windows Firewall
decides whether to pass or drop a packet. In other words, when making decisions about traffic
destined to or originating from services, Windows Firewall rules and WSH rules work closely
together to decide whether to allow or drop traffic. For more information on how service
restriction rules merge with Windows Firewall rules, see the section titled "Understanding
Windows Firewall Policy Storage and Rule Merge Logic" later in this chapter.

> **Note**   An assumption behind WSH is that the services being protected are running under
> either the NetworkService or LocalService accounts. Services running under the LocalSystem
> account are omnipotent: They can turn off Windows Firewall or mock its rules on the fly and
> are therefore not protected.

> ## Direct from the Source: Windows Firewall Stealth
>
> Windows Firewall comes with an always-on, nonconfigurable stealth feature. The
> purpose of this feature is to prevent fingerprinting attacks that remotely attempt to
> figure out which ports are open on the computer, which services are running, the
> update state of the computer, and so on.

When a remote computer tries to connect to a nonlistening TCP port (a TCP port that is not used on the local computer), the TCP/IP stack sends back a special TCP packet called TCP RESET (RST). However, if an application is listening on that port but a firewall is blocking it from receiving traffic, the remote computer will simply time out. This is a common technique to fingerprint the computer and see which ports are unused and which are used but blocked by the firewall. With the stealth feature of Windows Firewall, all TCP RST outbound packets are blocked so that the remote computer will time out when it connects to a port that is not allowed through the firewall, regardless of whether this port is in use.

For UDP ports and non-TCP/UDP sockets, a similar mechanism is used. Unlike TCP, these are not session-based protocols, so when a remote computer tries to connect to a non-listening UDP port (or a non-TCP/UDP socket), the stack replies back with an ICMP packet saying "nobody's home." For IPv4 traffic, the response is ICMPv4 (protocol 1)/type 3/code 3 (Destination Unreachable/Port Unreachable) or ICMPv4 (protocol 1)/type 3/code 2 (Destination Unreachable/Protocol Unreachable). For IPv6 UDP traffic, the response is ICMPv6 (protocol 58)/type 1.

With the stealth feature on, Windows Firewall blocks these outbound responses so that the remote computer can't tell the difference between a nonlistening UDP port (or non-TCP/UDP socket) and one that is listening but is blocked by the firewall.

Eran Yariv

Windows Firewall and IPsec Management Development Lead

Understanding Windows Firewall Profiles

The previous version of Windows Firewall in Windows XP Service Pack 2 uses two kinds of profiles, only one of which can be active at any given time:

- **Domain profile**   This profile is active whenever a domain DNS suffix is present. The domain profile is usually configured to be the less restrictive profile. For example, the domain profile may have a rule enabled that allows incoming remote management traffic from a network management application such as Microsoft Systems Center Operations Manager (SCOM).

- **Standard profile**   This profile is active in all other circumstances. For instance, if the computer belongs to a workgroup instead of a domain, the standard profile will be active. Or, if the computer belongs to a domain, is multihomed, and has authenticated over its LAN interface—but it is also connected to an unmanaged wireless LAN using a Wi-Fi interface—the standard profile will again be active. Administrators usually configure the standard profile to be the most restrictive profile (though both profiles are the same out of the box). For example, when a laptop is disconnected from the corporate network and taken to a coffee shop where a wireless hotspot is present, the standard profile can provide greater protection for the computer if configured accordingly. The computer's direct connection with the Internet makes this added protection necessary.

With Windows Vista, the number of profiles used by Windows Firewall has been expanded to three profiles, and the active profile at any given time is determined as follows:

- **Domain profile**   This profile is active only when the computer can authenticate with a domain controller on all active network interfaces (LAN, wireless, VPN, and so on). The domain profile may be more or less restrictive than the other two profiles depending on the management needs and security policy of the network.

- **Private profile**   This profile is active whenever the network type for all network active network connections on the computer are identified as Private networks. When a computer that is not joined to a domain connects to a new network for the first time, the user is presented with a choice of Home, Work, or Public for the type of network she is connecting to. If the user selects Home or Work, the network type for the connection is set to Private; otherwise, the network type for the connection is set to Public. The private profile is generally less restrictive than the public profile because the computer is usually on a home or SOHO network, where it may be connected to the Internet using a NAT or other gateway device with its own built-in firewall. For example, the Windows Firewall rules for Network Discovery are allowed by default in the private profile so that users on a home or SOHO network can easily find each other's computers on the network for file sharing and other purposes. The rules for Remote Assistance are likewise allowed by default in the private profile.

- **Public profile**   This profile is active in all other circumstances. For example, if a corporate laptop is taken to a coffee shop where a wireless hot spot is present, the public profile will be active on the computer. The public profile is generally more restrictive than the private profile because the computer usually has a direct connection to the Internet in a location that isn't secure. For example, the firewall rule group for Network Discovery is disabled by default in the public profile so that laptop users in a public place can avoid being discoverable by other computers connected to the same wireless access point. The rule group for Remote Assistance is likewise disabled by default in the public profile. (Traffic for these features is not actually blocked explicitly—the firewall rule action is not Block. Instead, the rules in the rule group for Network Discovery and Remote Assistance are disabled, which means that the rule does not match and so the default action is taken instead. All traffic is blocked by default because rule groups are disabled and the inbound default action is block.)

Note   Public is the default network categorization, and classification as Public Location/ Other or bypassing the categorization dialog box will result in the network being classified as public. For more information on network types (categories) in Windows Vista, see Chapter 26, "Configuring Windows Networking."

Using the following algorithm offers another way to understand which Windows Firewall profile is active in Windows Vista at any given time:

1. If all active network interfaces can be securely authenticated with the domain, the profile is Domain.

2. Otherwise, if all active network interfaces are either private or cannot be securely authenticated with the domain, the profile is Private.

3. Otherwise, the profile is Public.

> **Note**   Windows Firewall profiles also apply to Bluetooth interfaces if they are present on the computer—all network interfaces visible at the NDIS layer are also visible to Windows Firewall. If USB Remote NDIS (RNDIS) devices/networks identify themselves as terminated networks at driver install time, they will not be categorized or affect the categorization algorithm. Instead, they are simply omitted. However, Windows Firewall still enforces its rules on their interfaces.

Windows Vista selects the active profile at any given time by using a feature called Network Location Awareness (NLA). NLA is a set of network APIs that senses the state of each connected network on the computer. NLA queries each network that the computer is connected to in order to determine three things:

- The connectivity state of the network. For example, a network may be disconnected, connected to the local network only, or connected to the local network—and through it connected to the Internet.

- The network connections or interfaces used to connect to the network. For example, a multihomed computer may have both network connections authenticating to the domain, or one domain-authenticated connection and one unsecured connection.

- The network location type or category of the network. Network location types in Windows Vista can be Public, Private, or Domain.

NLA enables Windows Firewall to seamlessly switch between profiles as needed. For example, when a laptop on a corporate network is placed in standby mode, undocked from the network, and taken to a public hotspot off premises, NLA determines the network change that takes place when the computer resumes from standby and then switches the active profile for Windows Firewall from domain to public.

How It Works: Network Location Awareness

The Network Location Awareness service (NLASVC) monitors the local computer for changes in its connectivity to connected networks. When a Windows Vista computer connects to a new network for the first time, the Network List Service assigns a globally unique identifier (GUID) to the new network. If the Network Location Awareness service later detects a change in network connectivity on the computer, the NLA service notifies the Network List Service, which then notifies Windows Firewall to indicate whether the active profile should be changed. If such a change is required, it generally occurs within 200 milliseconds.

Note   Windows Firewall profiles are global and not per-interface. Only one profile can be active at any given time, even on multihomed computers with more than one network interface or type of interface.

For information on how to configure Windows Firewall profiles, see the section titled "Understanding Windows Firewall Profiles" later in this chapter.

Understanding Windows Firewall Policy Storage and Rule Merge Logic

Windows Firewall profiles contain the policy information (rules) that governs how Windows Firewall works on the computer. This policy information consists of inbound and outbound rules for normal traffic and connection security rules for IPsec traffic, together with Windows Firewall global settings. Profiles and their policy information are stored in several places:

- **Local Policy Store**   When a user with administrative privileges configures Windows Firewall settings on a computer, the resulting policy information is stored within the Windows Firewall local policy store. This store is found within the local registry hive on the computer.

- **Group Policy Object (GPO)**   In a domain environment, you can configure and maintain Windows Firewall settings in GPOs, which are stored in the SYSVOL share on domain controllers.

- **Group Policy Resultant Set of Policy (GP_RSoP)**   In a domain environment, GP_RSoP represents the cache of policies obtained from all domain controllers on which GPOs are linked to the organizational unit (OU) to which the computer belongs. This cache of policies is stored in the registry on the computers targeted by the GPOs.

In addition to these policy stores, Windows Firewall uses an additional policy store when determining whether to block or allow traffic. This additional store is where Windows Service Hardening (WSH) maintains its static and configurable service restriction rules; it is also located in the registry.

The Windows Firewall merge logic works as follows:

- **Firewall settings**   Windows Firewall settings are merged from the computer's Local store and the GP_RSoP store. In case of conflicts, each configuration option defines a way in which the setting will be merged. For example, for the Firewall Enabled setting, GP_RSOP will always win, whereas for the Block All Inbound Connections setting (also know as "shields up"), the store with the most secure option wins. (In other words, "shields up" wins above nothing.)

- **Connection security rules**   Connection Security Rules are merged according to *specificity*. Specificity is how granular and narrow a rule is. More specific rules—that is, more granular rules—will match first. This happens regardless of the store the rule originated from.

- **Firewall rules**   Firewall rules (inbound and outbound rules) are merged in the following manner:

  1. Allow-bypass rules are matched first.

  2. Block rules are matched second.

  3. Allow rules are matched last.

  This happens regardless of the store each rule originates from. If nothing matches, the default inbound or outbound action is taken as the decision (depending on whether the traffic is inbound or outbound). The default actions have their own merge logic.

- **WSH rules**   Simultaneously to the logic described for firewall rules, WSH rules act like a parallel firewall working side by side with Windows Firewall. Both WSH and Windows Firewall stores (GP_RSoP and Local) must agree to allow traffic to pass through. The merge logic waits for a decision from both WSH and Windows Firewall. It then compares the decisions, and a Block decision always wins as the final decision.

How It Works: Local Policy Store vs. LGPO

The local policy store sits in the registry and contains the out-of-box settings and the policy dictated by the local admins. It's there all the time, whether or not the computer is domain-joined. To manage the local settings, you can use netsh, scripts/COM APIs, the Windows Firewall Control Panel item, or the MMC snap-in (from the Administrative Tools folder).

The Local-GPO store is a domain-only concept. Basically, when your computer joins a domain, it is subject to policy coming from multiple GPOs in a hierarchy. At the bottom of the hierarchy you will find one or more local GPOs that are stored on the local computer (in the registry) and affect only the local computer. By default, local GPOs are empty of any policy. To manage the local GPO, you can use netsh (and point it to a GPO on the local host) or run Gpedit.msc and drill down to the Windows Firewall With Advanced Security node. You can find more information at *http://msdn2.microsoft.com/ en-us/library/aa374155.aspx*.

Eran Yariv

Windows Firewall and IPsec Management Development Lead

Understanding Windows Firewall Rules

Windows Firewall includes three kinds of rules that you can configure:

■ **Inbound rules**   These rules filter inbound traffic to the host and can either block or allow traffic based on specified conditions.

■ **Outbound rules**   These rules filter outbound traffic from the host and can either block or allow traffic based on specified conditions.

■ **Connection Security rules**   These rules can use IPsec to authenticate, sign (validate against tampering), and optionally encrypt traffic for different network protection scenarios.

> **Note**   For more information about connection security rules, see the section titled "Understanding Connection Security Rules" later in this chapter.

How It Works: Firewall Rules vs. Connection Security Rules

Firewall rules (also called inbound/outbound rules or block/allow rules) have similarities and differences with connection security rules. You can create and maintain both types of rules using the Windows Firewall With Advanced Security snap-in or Group Policy. However, whereas firewall rules are configured on the local computer and act unilaterally (independent of the remote computer), connection security rules, on some occasions, must be configured on both the local and remote computers for IPsec to secure network traffic between them. Although firewall rules allow or prevent traffic from entering or leaving the local computer, they do not secure this traffic—you must create connection security rules to do this. And though creating a connection rule creates the potential to secure network traffic entering or leaving the local computer, it does not allow or prevent traffic from entering or leaving this computer—you must create firewall rules to do this.

In addition to these three basic rule types, Windows Firewall supports the following additional types of rules:

■ **Windows Service Hardening rules**   These outbound and inbound rules are available out-of-box (OOB) to protect the different network services in Windows Vista and the applications that use them. WSH rules are configurable for third-party service providers. The main differences between Windows Firewall (inbound/outbound) rules and WSH rules are:

❑ Windows Firewall rules are created and managed by the computer or domain administrators to enforce a policy.

❑ WSH rules, on the other hand, are created and managed by Microsoft and ISVs, who install services on the computer with the purpose of sandboxing their services so that they cannot be used as a stepping stone for network attacks. WSH rules are not visible to or managed by computer or Group Policy administrators.

■ **Authenticated Bypass rules**   These inbound rules have been configured so that any traffic that specifically matches this rule will override any other rules that explicitly block this traffic. In other words, enabling authenticated bypass on an inbound rule means that the connection is allowed even if another rule is attempting to block the connection. Authenticated bypass is not available for outbound rules and can be used to enable authenticated (IPsec) traffic to bypass Windows Firewall while blocking unauthenticated traffic with the same criteria. You can also use authenticated bypass to enable network scanners and intrusion-detection systems to run on Windows Vista and not have Windows Firewall block their functionality.

A remote user (or more typically a group of domain users) and/or remote computer is a mandatory condition field in authenticated bypass rules. If this condition is not specified, you end up with a regular allow rule (not an allow bypass rule) that has some IPsec-related conditions in it. For allow bypass rules, however, you must specify a remote computer or remote user. Note that only users and computer objects in the same Active Directory forest can be permitted. Authenticated bypass rules don't work in workgroup or untrusted environments.

■ **Default rules**   These are rules that specify the default behavior when traffic does not match any other type of rule. The default rules for all three profiles (domain, private, and public) are:

❑ Block all inbound connections that do not match any other inbound rules.

❑ Allow all outbound connections that do not match any other outbound rules.

The default rules for inbound and outbound connections can also be modified as follows:

❑ The default rule for inbound traffic can be:

- Block (the default)
- Block All Connections
- Allow

> **Note**   From a practical standpoint, the default rule Block All Connections for inbound traffic means "shields up" or "ignore all allow and allow-bypass rules."

❑ The default rule for outbound traffic can be:

- Allow (the default)
- Block

Rules and Conditions

Windows Firewall can filter traffic based on a number of different conditions, as described in Table 27-2. (The generalized Windows Firewall rule is the logical AND of all these conditions.)

Table 27-2   Filtering Conditions for Windows Firewall Inbound/Outbound Rules

Condition	Possible Values
Protocol	Any
	IANA IP protocol number
	TCP or UDP
	ICMPv4 or ICMPv6
	Other protocols including IGMP, HOPOPT, GRE, IPv6-NoNxt, IPv6-Opts, VRRP, PGM, L2TP, IPv6-Route, IPv6-Frag
Local port (for TCP and UDP only)	All Ports
	Specific ports (comma-separated list)
	Dynamic RPC
	RPC Endpoint Mapper
	Edge Traversal
Remote port (for TCP and UDP only)	All ports
	Specific ports (comma-separated list)
ICMP Type Code (for ICMPv4 and ICMPv6)	All ICMP Types
	Specific types of ICMP traffic
Local IP address scope	A specific IPv4 or IPv6 address or list of addresses
	A range of IPv4 or IPv6 addresses or list of ranges
	An entire IPv4 or IPv6 subnet or list of subnets
Remote IP address scope	A specific IPv4 or IPv6 address or list of addresses
	A range of IPv4 or IPv6 addresses or list of ranges
	An entire IPv4 or IPv6 subnet or list of subnets
	A predefined set of computers—including local subnet, default gateway, DNS servers, WINS servers, or DNS servers—or a list of such items
Interface type	All interface types
	Local area network
	Remote access
	Wireless
Programs	All programs
	System, a special keyword that if used will restrict traffic to the System Process (This is useful for scoping traffic to any kernel mode driver such as http.sys, smb.sys, and so on.)
	Specify path and .exe name to program executable

Table 27-2   Filtering Conditions for Windows Firewall Inbound/Outbound Rules

Condition	Possible Values
Services	Apply to all programs and services
	Apply to services only
	Apply to a specified service or to a service with the specified short name

Note   Windows Firewall rules can allow or block services regardless of where their executables are located on the computer. Services can be specified by their service name, even if the service is implemented as a DLL. Programs are identified by specifying the application path. (Specifying DLLs is not supported.)

Note   When creating and configuring rules in Windows Firewall, use scope wherever possible. For example, if you do network backup and need to allow incoming connections from the backup service, configure the scope so that Windows Firewall allows connections only from the backup server's IP address or network. Similarly, refine the scope for network management and remote administration tools to just those networks that require it.

How It Works: Predefined Local Port Types

There are three special, predefined local ports: Dynamic RPC, RPC Endpoint Mapper, and Edge Traversal:

- **Dynamic RPC**   This port is utilized by applications and services that receive dynamic RPC traffic over TCP. Applications or services that receive RPC traffic over named pipes do not use this port.

- **RPC Endpoint Mapper**   This port is used only with the RPCSS service and allows traffic to the endpoint mapper. When no RPC server is registered with the endpoint mapper, this local port type automatically closes and traffic is not matched by the rule using it.

- **Edge Traversal**   This port is used only with the iphlpsvc (Teredo) service and allows the traffic that is to be decapsulated by the Teredo service on a dynamic port. When Teredo is not active, this port type automatically closes and traffic is not matched by the rule using it.

In addition to the conditions described in Table 27-2, if a rule is configured to allow secure connections only and a corresponding connection security rule (IPsec rule) exists for the users or computers specified in the rule, additional rule conditions are available for configuration, as shown in Table 27-3. Because of these additional configuration options, which integrate IPsec functionality with firewall rules, you can think of Windows Firewall rules in Windows Vista as "IPsec-aware" rules.

Table 27-3   Filtering Conditions for Windows Firewall Inbound/Outbound Rules When Allow Only Secure Connections Is Enabled for the Rule

Condition	Possible Values
Require encryption	Optionally select or leave unselected
Allow only connections from specified computers	Select from Active Directory
Allow only connections from specified users	Select from Active Directory

An additional condition is the ability to filter when traffic is secured by IPsec but not necessarily encrypted or from a specific computer. This is configured by selecting Allow Only Secure Connections on the General tab of the Inbound or Outbound rule's properties. If this condition does *not* have the Override Block Rules option selected, this condition is treated as an action, and traffic will be dropped if not secured.

> **Note**   Yet another condition is the option to locally restrict rules to specific interfaces (not interface types). Note that this is a local-only option available only via the APIs.

How It Works: Windows Firewall and Traditional Firewalls

Windows Vista's Windows Firewall is similar to traditional network firewalls in that you can create highly granular rules that filter traffic based on specified conditions. You can think of the collection of Windows Firewall rules as a database, with rules representing the different rows and conditions representing the columns. After they are created, these rules can be either enabled or disabled depending on the requirements of the network.

A significant difference between Windows Firewall and traditional network firewalls, however, is that traditional firewalls allow you to create an ordered list of rules that are then processed in order until a match occurs to allow or block traffic. Windows Firewall does not apply rule ordering in the way that traditional firewalls do.

In addition, Windows Firewall in Windows Vista is an authenticating firewall that integrates IPsec protection with traditional inbound/outbound filtering in two ways: first, by enabling you to create connection security rules that authenticate and, optionally, encrypt traffic; and second, by allowing you to further restrict firewall rules and match traffic only if specific IPsec protections are present.

Examples of Rules

The kinds of firewall rules that you can configure using Windows Firewall in Windows Vista include:

- Allow Microsoft Internet Explorer to send outbound traffic over TCP port 80.
- Allow a specified application to receive inbound UDP traffic if it arrives over any wireless network interface.
- Block the generic Svchost.exe process that hosts the MPSSVC service for all inbound traffic from a specified remote address.
- Allow the SSDP service to listen for inbound traffic from a specific interface, such as Local Area Connection 2.

For more information on configuring firewall rules, see the section titled "Managing Windows Firewall" later in this chapter.

Direct from the Source: Using RPC with Windows Firewall

RPC (Remote Procedure Call) is a common method for applications to receive traffic from the network, process it, and respond. RPC is very common in servers, whose role in part is to provide a service over the network for clients. Some primary examples are the Microsoft Exchange Server, Microsoft ISA server (for remote administration purposes), the Windows Fax service, and so on. RPC is even used in various scenarios for client computers. For example, the Windows Firewall Remote Management feature, when enabled, works by having the PolicyAgent service use an RPC over TCP (RPC/TCP) interface to answer remote management requests and proxy it locally to the Windows Firewall service. The purpose of this proxy approach is to keep the Windows Firewall service from directly accessing the network so that it can keep running in a secure, can't-touch-the-network account.

RPC can use multiple transports to communicate over the network. The most common ones are RPC over named pipes (RPC/NP) and RPC over TCP/IP (RPC/TCP). RPC/NP is a less-recommended transport because it lacks features such as mutual authentication and requires the server side to open up for SMB traffic, which has such additional side effects such as allowing file and printer share over the network. If a service is using RPC/NP to provide its interfaces to the network, you need to enable the built-in File and Printer Sharing group of rules for traffic to be allowed inbound.

There are two methods for RPC/TCP:

- **A fixed TCP port**   In this case, the port is usually known in advance to both the RPC server and client(s). The clients simply connect to the server using TCP with that port number. If you have an RCP server that uses RPC/TCP with a fixed port, all you need to do to allow traffic is add an Allow firewall rule to that application/

---

service for that specific local TCP port. Using a fixed TCP port is not recommended because it lacks the flexibility of avoiding port collisions with other networking applications. As a result, it's a less common method for RPC/TCP; only a few services actually use it (such as the RPCSS service).

- **A dynamic TCP port**   In this case, the actual port that the RPC server uses to expose its RPC/TCP interface is determined at run time from a pool of available ports. Because the RPC clients can't tell in advance which TCP port they need to connect to, they need to use a mediator in the form of the RPC end-point mapper. The process works like this:

  1. Application App1 (the RPC server) starts running and registers its RPC interface with the RPC subsystem for dynamic RPC/TCP.

  2. The RPC subsystem assigns a dynamic TCP port (denote port X) to that application and starts listening on port X from the process context of application App1.

  3. The RPCSS service, which acts as an endpoint mapper, listens for RPC endpoint mapping requests on a fixed port: TCP/135.

  4. The RPC client, from another computer, connects to TCP/135 and talks to the RPCSS service (the end-point mapper).

  5. The RPC client asks for a specific RPC interface. The end-point-mapper, being part of the RPC subsystem, knows about steps (a) and (b) and replies with port X.

  6. The RPC client connects to port TCP/X and starts the interface activation with the RPC server.

As you can see, two firewall rules are necessary to enable dynamic RPC/TCP:

- Allow the RPCSS service to receive traffic over TCP/135 for end-point mapping purposes.

- Allow application App1 to receive traffic over TCP/X.

Two problems come to mind:

1. You want to enable the RPCSS service inbound traffic only if RPC servers are registered on the computer. If none are, TCP/135 should not be open in the firewall—this might expose the computer to unnecessary attacks.

2. You can't tell in advance what port X is, and you can't create a firewall rule to allow it.

To address the first problem, Windows Firewall uses a special local port keyword called *RPC endpoint mapper*. You can use this local port keyword when creating the Allow The RPCSS Service To Receive Traffic Over TCP/135 For End-Point Mapping Purposes rule, replacing TCP/135 with the *RPC endpoint mapper* keyword. The Windows Firewall service keeps a special and secure interface with the RPCSS service. The RPCSS service notifies the Windows Firewall service whenever RPC servers are registered, and the

Firewall Service dynamically replaces the keyword with the actual port value (in this case, TCP/135, but it could also be TCP/593 for RPC/HTTP cases). If no RPC servers are registered with the RPC subsystem, the Windows Firewall service does not open port TCP/135.

To address the second problem, Windows Firewall uses a special local port keyword called *Dynamic RPC*. When this keyword is used, Windows Firewall makes sure that the socket receiving the TCP traffic (port X in this example) was actually acquired by the RPC subsystem and is used for RPC purposes. Instead of a firewall rule that says Allow Application App1 To Receive TCP Traffic Over Any Port, you use the *Dynamic RPC* local port keyword to create this rule: Allow application App1 to receive TCP traffic for RPC purposes only.

Eran Yariv

Windows Firewall and IPsec Management Development Lead

Rules Processing

When Windows Firewall inspects traffic to determine whether it should be allowed or blocked, the decision is made by ordered processing of rules by their actions. Rules with the same action are bucketed together and have no specific ordering among themselves.

Windows Firewall rules processing works as follows:

1. Allow-bypass rules (these are rules that *must* have IPsec conditions in them)

2. Block rules

3. Allow rules

4. The default inbound/outbound rules

Note   Allow-bypass rules are rules that must have IPsec conditions in them. Normal (block/allow) rules can also have IPsec conditions in them and still not be allow-bypass rules.

Two notes concerning the preceding description of rules processing:

- The preceding description applies only to block/allow rules and not to connection security rules.

- Block rules are evaluated before allow rules and therefore take precedence. However, you can use authenticated bypass to override block rules, as discussed in the next section.

For more information on how to configure Windows Firewall using Group Policy, see the section titled "Managing Windows Firewall Using Group Policy" later in this chapter.

Rule Groups

The Windows Firewall With Advanced Security MMC console in Windows Vista groups rules together into sets of rules called rule groups. A *rule group* is a collection of inbound/outbound rules that enables a particular experience or feature in Windows Vista. For example, the Remote Assistance rule group is a set of rules that enables the Remote Assistance feature to function. By enabling the rules within a specific rule group, the experience associated with that rule group can work transparently with respect to the Windows Firewall.

Rule groups are a management/UI concept only and they have no effect on the policy enforcement engine or on the processing of rules. Rule groups are there simply to support the notion of pre-canned rules, which are pre-tested with a lot of built-in experiences, and the user just needs to select a check box in the firewall's Control Panel to enable that experience. Rule group enablement and querying is also available through netsh and the APIs.

Table 27-4 describes all rule groups that are available in Windows Vista. Although a particular rule group might be available for a certain SKU, it won't be displayed in the Windows Firewall With Advanced Security console if the specific Windows role or component associated with that rule group is not installed.

Table 27-4   Rule Groups Available in Windows Firewall Based on SKU

Rule Group	Description	SKU
BITS Peercaching	This feature allows Background Intelligent Transfer Service (BITS) clients that are in the same subnet to locate and share files that are stored in the BITS cache (uses WSDAPI and RPC).	All SKUs
Connect To A Network Projector	This feature enables users to connect to projectors over wired or wireless networks to project presentations (uses WSDAPI).	Home Premium, Business, Enterprise, and Ultimate only
Core Networking	The firewall rules that are part of Core Networking are required for reliable IPv4 and IPv6 connectivity.	All SKUs
Distributed Transaction Coordinator	This feature coordinates transactions that update transaction-protected resources, such as databases, message queues, and file systems.	All SKUs
File And Printer Sharing	This feature is used for sharing local files and printers with other users on the network (uses NetBIOS, SMB, and RPC).	All SKUs
Key Management Service	This feature is used for machine counting and license compliance in enterprise environments. This group exists only on Business SKUs.	Business only
iSCSI Service	This feature is used for connecting to iSCSI target servers and devices.	All SKUs

Table 27-4 Rule Groups Available in Windows Firewall Based on SKU

Rule Group	Description	SKU
Media Center Extenders	This feature allows Media Center Extenders to communicate with a computer running Windows Media Center (uses SSDP and qWave).	Home Premium and Ultimate only
Network Discovery	This feature allows this computer to discover other devices and be discovered by other devices on the network (uses Function Discovery Host and Publication Services, UPnP, SSDP, NetBIOS, and LLMNR).	All SKUs
Performance Logs And Alerts	This feature allows remote management of the Performance Logs and Alerts service (uses RPC).	All SKUs
Remote Administration	This feature allows remotely manageable services to receive RPC traffic (uses Named Pipes and RPC).	All SKUs
Remote Assistance	This feature allows users of this computer to request remote assistance from other users on the network (uses UPnP, SSDP, and Teredo).	All SKUs
Remote Desktop	This feature is used for accessing the desktop from a remote system.	Business, Enterprise, and Ultimate only
Remote Event Log Management	This feature allows remote viewing and management of the local event log (uses Named Pipes and RPC).	All SKUs
Remote Scheduled Tasks Management	This feature allows remote management of the local task scheduling service (uses RPC).	All SKUs
Remote Service Management	This feature allows remote management of local services (uses Named Pipes and RPC).	All SKUs
Remote Volume Management	This feature provides remote software and hardware disk volume management (uses RPC).	All SKUs
Routing And Remote Access	This feature is used to allow incoming VPN and RAS connections.	All SKUs
SNMP Trap	Receives trap messages generated by local or remote Simple Network Management Protocol (SNMP) agents and forwards the messages to SNMP management programs running on this computer. If this service is stopped, SNMP-based programs on this computer will not receive SNMP trap messages. If this service is disabled, any services that explicitly depend on it will fail to start.	All SKUs
Windows Collaboration Computer Name Registration Service	This feature allows other computers to find and communicate with your computer using the Peer Name Resolution Protocol (uses SSDP and PNRP).	All SKUs except Starter

Table 27-4   Rule Groups Available in Windows Firewall Based on SKU

Rule Group	Description	SKU
Windows Firewall Remote Management	This feature allows remote management of the local Windows Firewall (uses RPC).	All SKUs
Windows Management Instrumentation (WMI)	This feature allows remote management of Windows by exposing a set of manageable components in a set of classes defined by the Common Information Model (CIM) of the distributed management task force (uses DCOM).	All SKUs
Windows Media Player	This feature allows users to receive streaming media over UDP.	Home Basic and Premium, Business, Enterprise, and Ultimate
Windows Media Player Network Sharing Service	This feature enables users to share media over a network (uses UPnP, SSDP, and qWave).	Home Basic and Premium, Business, Enterprise, and Ultimate
Windows Meeting Space	This feature is used for collaborating over a network to share documents, programs, or your desktop with other people (uses DFSR and P2P).	All SKUs except Starter
Windows Peer To Peer Collaboration Foundation	This feature is required to enable various peer-to-peer programs and technologies (uses SSDP and PNRP).	All SKUs except Starter
Windows Remote Management	This feature allows remote management of the system via WS-Management, a Web Services–based protocol for remote management of operating systems and devices.	All SKUs
Wireless Portable Devices	This feature allows the transfer of media from your network-enabled camera or media device to your computer using the Media Transfer Protocol, or MTP (uses UPnP and SSDP).	Home Basic and Premium, Business, Enterprise, and Ultimate
ActiveSync	Windows Mobile–based device connectivity.	Optional component
Digital Cable Receiver Device	This feature allows device discovery and video streaming from the cable receiver device to the PC (uses UPnP and SSDP).	Optional component
Internet Connection Sharing	This feature allows this computer to share its Internet connection with other computers on a private network (uses UPnP and SSDP).	Optional component
SNMP Service	This feature allows Simple Network Management Protocol (SNMP) traffic to be sent and received by this computer.	Optional component
TCP/IP Print Server	Opens the default port used by the Line Printer Daemon protocol.	Optional component
Telnet Server	This feature allows remote telnet clients to connect to this computer.	Optional component

Table 27-4   Rule Groups Available in Windows Firewall Based on SKU

Rule Group	Description	SKU
Telnet Server Remote Administration	This feature allows the local telnet server to be remotely managed (uses DCOM and RPC).	Optional component
World Wide Web Services (HTTP)	Enables/Disables firewall rules for World Wide Web Services HTTP.	Optional component
Secure World Wide Web Services (HTTPS)	Enables/Disables firewall rules for Secure World Wide Web Services HTTPS.	Optional component
FTP Server	Enables/Disables firewall rules for FTP Server.	Optional component
Services for NFS, Client for NFS	Rules to allow inbound and outbound UDP and TCP traffic for Services for NFS and Client for NFS.	Optional component

Note   To remotely manage Windows XP SP2 computers that have Windows Firewall enabled, an exception for remote administration needed to be opened in the firewall on these computers. This could be done by enabling the Windows Firewall: Allow Remote Administration Exception Group Policy setting for Windows XP SP2 computers in the targeted OU. However, you can remotely manage Windows Vista computers that have Windows Firewall without first opening an exception to allow for remote administration. If you are managing Group Policy from a Windows Vista computer in a mixed Windows Vista/Windows XP SP2 environment, you can enable the Remote Administration exception on targeted Windows XP SP2 computers by enabling the rules in the Remote Administration rule group using Windows Firewall With Advanced Security.

Rule groups as viewed within the Windows Firewall With Advanced Security snap-in correspond closely to exceptions on the Exceptions tab of the Windows Firewall CPL properties in Control Panel. For example, the Windows Firewall CPL exception named Remote Desktop corresponds to the Remote Desktop rule group in Table 27-4, and enabling this exception in the Windows Firewall CPL enables the rules in this rule group in the Windows Firewall With Advanced Security snap-in (but only for the current firewall profile). For more information on configuring rules using the Windows Firewall With Advanced Security snap-in, see the section titled "Managing Windows Firewall Using the Windows Firewall With Advanced Security Snap-In" later in this chapter.

Note   For simplicity, the Windows Firewall CPL applies to only the current profile. Enabling an exception using this CPL will enable it for only the current profile. For example, let's say that rule X is marked for the public and private profile, the current profile is public, and the user checks rule X in the CPL. The CPL will split that rule into rule X (public), which is active, and rule X (private, with the same name and conditions), which is inactive.

Not all rule groups have both inbound and outbound rules. For example, rule groups for remote management such as Remote Administration and Remote Event Log Management do not have outbound rules because remote management depends on the computer being managed being able to listen for traffic initiated by a central management station. Table 27-5 lists the available rule groups and whether they have inbound rules only, outbound rules only, or rules for both inbound and outbound traffic.

Table 27-5 Rule Groups and Whether They Have Inbound Rules, Outbound Rules, or Both

Rule Group	Inbound Rules	Outbound Rules
BITS Peercaching	✓	✓
Connect to a Network Projector	✓	✓
Core Networking	✓	✓
Distributed Transaction Coordinator	✓	✓
File And Printer Sharing	✓	✓
iSCSI Service	✓	✓
Media Center Extenders	✓	✓
Network Discovery	✓	✓
Performance Logs And Alerts	✓	
Remote Administration	✓	
Remote Assistance	✓	✓
Remote Desktop	✓	
Remote Event Log Management	✓	
Remote Scheduled Tasks Management	✓	
Remote Service Management	✓	
Remote Volume Management	✓	
Routing And Remote Access	✓	✓
SNMP Trap Service	✓	
Windows Collaboration Computer Name Registration Service	✓	✓
Windows Firewall Remote Management	✓	
Windows Management Instrumentation (WMI)	✓	✓
Windows Media Player	✓	✓
Windows Media Player Network Sharing Service	✓	✓
Windows Meeting Space	✓	✓
Windows Peer-To-Peer Collaboration Foundation	✓	✓
Windows Remote Management	✓	
Wireless Portable Devices	✓	✓

Rule Groups Enabled By Default

In a default install of Windows Vista, most rule groups are disabled in most profiles to reduce the attack surface. However, you can develop custom installation images that enable selected rule groups by default. For more information on building custom images of Windows Vista, see Part II of this book, "Deployment."

Table 27-6 lists the rule groups that are enabled by default for each profile. Users who are local administrators on their computers can enable additional rule groups, provided that Group Policy does not prevent them from doing so.

Table 27-6   Rule Groups Enabled by Default for Each Profile

Rule Group	Domain	Private	Public
Core Networking	Yes	Yes, except for Group Policy rules	Yes, except for Group Policy rules
Network Discovery	No	Yes	No
Remote Assistance	No	Yes	No
All other rule groups	No	No	No

Core Networking Rules

Core Networking Rules is the only rule group that is enabled by default in all three profiles. These rules are designed to allow reliable communications using IPv4 and IPv6 and should generally not be modified or disabled. Core Networking Rules includes inbound/outbound rules for the following networking capabilities:

- **DHCP**   Rules for allowing stateful auto-configuration using DHCP messages.

- **DNS**   Rules to allow DNS traffic.

- **Group Policy**   Rules to allow Group Policy updates to occur on the computer. This is enabled for only the Domain profile.

- **ICMPv4**   Rules to allow Destination Unreachable and Fragmentation Needed error messages.

- **ICMPv6**   Rules for allowing router advertisements, Router Solicitation messages, neighbor discovery advertisements, Neighbor Discovery Solicitation messages, Multicast Listener Query messages, Multicast Listener Report messages, Multicast Listener Done messages, and various ICMPv6 error messages including Destination Unreachable, Packet Too Big, Time Exceeded, and Parameter Problem.

- **IGMP Multicast**   Rules to allow IGMP messages to enable the computer to create, join, or leave a multicast group.

- **ISATAP/6to4 Tunneling**   Rules to allow traffic for ISATAP and 6to4 tunneling.

- **Teredo (IPv6 Edge Traversal)**   Rules for allowing Teredo edge traversal across a NAT.

Note   The rules for enabling Group Policy processing and outbound DNS traffic that are part of Core Networking Rules are available and enabled only in the domain profile. These rules were designed so that if an administrator decides to push a policy via Group Policy that changes the default outbound action from Allow to Block, the computer will still be able to get Group Policy, and every single system will not need to be manually reconfigured afterward. In other words, these rules are a safety mechanism to prevent administrators from being unable to push further policies. All other rules in the Core Networking Rules rule group are available and enabled in all three profiles: domain, private, and public.

Direct from the Source: Loose-Source-Mapping vs. Strict-Source-Mapping for Firewall Filtering and Its Use for DNS Lookups

In the TCP protocol, a session is established between two communicating computers. A third computer cannot join an existing session. In UDP and portless protocols, there is no session semantics. After an outbound packet is sent, the firewall engine is creating a virtual session allowing inbound responses for that packet within a timeout (60 seconds).

In Windows XP and Windows Server 2003, Windows Firewall used a Loose-Source-Mapping (LSM) policy. LSM means that inbound non-TCP responses need only match the protocol and ports of the outbound request to be allowed in. Practically speaking, in LSM you can send an outbound UDP request (for example, for DNS lookups sent to your primary DNS server) and receive the UDP response from another server (for example, one of your secondary DNS servers), and that response would be allowed by the firewall.

In Windows Vista, Windows Firewall moved to a Strict-Source-Mapping policy (SSM). In SSM, the remote IP address is also matched in the non-TCP responses, and if it's not the same as the request was sent to, the inbound packet gets dropped. This change increases the security of multiple protocols and reduces the chances of some spoofing and poisoning attacks.

The only exception to the SSM policy in Windows Vista is for DNS lookups. One of the core networking outbound firewall rules (CoreNet-DNS-Out-UDP) is set up in a special way to allow the UDP responses to arrive from any IP address (we apply the LSM policy model for that rule). This special way to configure outbound rules for LSM/SSM is currently not exposed in Windows Firewall in Windows Vista, but might be exposed in future versions of the operating system.

The DNS client service also applies some special restrictions that are new to Windows Vista. It ignores DNS responses from remote IP addresses that are not in the DNS servers list.

Eran Yariv

Windows Firewall and IPsec Management Development Lead

Tables 27-7 through 27-14 provide a detailed look at the rules that make up the Core Networking Rules rule group. Keep the following notes in mind regarding these tables:

■ The scope for all of these rules is any local or remote IP address, with the following exceptions:

❑ Rule names prefixed with one asterisk (*) have "Local Subnet" configured for their remote address.

❑ Rule names prefixed with two asterisks (**) have "Local Subnet, ff02::1, fe80::/64" configured for their remote address.

❑ The rule Core Networking-Router Advertisement (ICMPv6-In) has "fe80::/64" configured for its remote address.

❑ The rule Core Networking-Router Advertisement (ICMPv6-Out) has "fe80::/64" configured for its local address.

■ The program or service associated with each rule is System unless otherwise specified.

■ These are all Allow rules (no Block rules).

■ Override is No for all inbound rules.

■ Local and remote port is Any unless otherwise specified.

Table 27-7   Core Networking Rules for DHCP

Rule Name	Rule Description	Protocol / Local Port	Protocol / Remote Port	Direction
Core Networking – Dynamic Host Configuration Protocol (DHCP-In)	Allows DHCP messages for stateful auto-configuration	UDP/67	UDP/68	Inbound
Core Networking – Dynamic Host Configuration Protocol (DHCP-Out)	Allows DHCP messages for stateful auto-configuration	UDP/68	UDP/67	Outbound

Table 27-8   Core Networking Rule for DNS

Rule Name	Rule Description	Protocol / Remote Port	Direction	Binary (Service)
Core Networking – DNS (UDP-Out)	Outbound rule to allow DNS requests [UDP 53]	UDP/53	Outbound	Svchost.exe (dnscache)

Table 27-9   Core Networking Rules for Group Policy

Rule Name	Rule Description	Protocol / Remote Port	Direction	Binary (Service)
Core Networking – Group Policy (NP-Out)	Outbound rule to allow SMB traffic for Group Policy updates [TCP 445]	TCP/445	Outbound	System
Core Networking – Group Policy (TCP-Out)	Outbound rule to allow remote RPC traffic for Group Policy updates	TCP/*	Outbound	Svchost.exe
Core Networking – Group Policy (LSASS-Out)	Outbound rule to allow remote LSASS traffic for Group Policy updates [TCP]	TCP/*	Outbound	Lsass.exe

Table 27-10   Core Networking Rule for ICMPv4

Rule Name	Rule Description	ICMP Type/ Code	Direction
Core Networking – Destination Unreachable Fragmentation Needed (ICMPv4-In)	Destination Unreachable error messages are sent from any node that a packet traverses that is unable to forward the packet for any reason except congestion.	3:4	Inbound

Table 27-11   Core Networking Rules for ICMPv6

Rule Name	Rule Description	ICMP Type/Code	Direction
Core Networking – Destination Unreachable (ICMPv6-In)	Destination Unreachable error messages are sent from any node that a packet traverses that is unable to forward the packet for any reason except congestion.	1:*	Inbound
Core Networking – Packet Too Big (ICMPv6-In)	Packet Too Big error messages are sent from any node that a packet traverses that is unable to forward the packet because the packet is too large for the next link.	2:*	Inbound
Core Networking – Packet Too Big (ICMPv6-Out)	Packet Too Big error messages are sent from any node that a packet traverses that is unable to forward the packet because the packet is too large for the next link.	2:*	Outbound

Table 27-11 Core Networking Rules for ICMPv6

Rule Name	Rule Description	ICMP Type/Code	Direction
Core Networking – Time Exceeded (ICMPv6-In)	Time Exceeded error messages are generated from any node that a packet traverses if the Hop Limit value is decremented to zero at any point on the path.	3:*	Inbound
Core Networking – Time Exceeded (ICMPv6-Out)	Time Exceeded error messages are generated from any node that a packet traverses if the Hop Limit value is decremented to zero at any point on the path.	3:*	Outbound
Core Networking – Parameter Problem (ICMPv6-In)	Parameter Problem error messages are sent by nodes as a result of incorrectly generated packets.	4:*	Inbound
Core Networking – Parameter Problem (ICMPv6-Out)	Parameter Problem error messages are sent by nodes as a result of incorrectly generated packets.	4:*	Outbound
Core Networking – Router Solicitation (ICMPv6-In)	Router Solicitation messages are sent by nodes seeking routers to provide stateless auto-configuration.	133:*	Inbound
**Core Networking – Router Solicitation (ICMPv6-Out)	Router Solicitation messages are sent by nodes seeking routers to provide stateless auto-configuration (applies to LocalSubnet, fe80::/64 and ff02::2 remote addresses).	133:*	Outbound
Core Networking – Router Advertisement (ICMPv6-In)	Router Advertisement messages are sent by routers to other nodes for stateless auto-configuration (applies to fe80::/64 remote addresses).	134:*	Inbound

Table 27-11   Core Networking Rules for ICMPv6

Rule Name	Rule Description	ICMP Type/Code	Direction
**Core Networking – Router Advertisement (ICMPv6-Out)	Router Advertisement messages are sent by routers to other nodes for stateless auto-configuration (applies to fe80::/64 local addresses, and LocalSubnet, fe80::/64, ff02::1 remote addresses).	134:*	Outbound
Core Networking – Neighbor Discovery Solicitation (ICMPv6-In)	Neighbor Discovery Solicitation messages are sent by nodes to discover the link-layer address of another on-link IPv6 node.	135:*	Inbound
Core Networking – Neighbor Discovery Solicitation (ICMPv6-Out)	Neighbor Discovery Solicitation messages are sent by nodes to discover the link-layer address of another on-link IPv6 node.	135:*	Outbound
Core Networking – Neighbor Discovery Advertisement (ICMPv6-In)	Neighbor Discovery Advertisement messages are sent by nodes to notify other nodes of link-layer address changes or in response to a Neighbor Discovery Solicitation request.	136:*	Inbound
Core Networking – Neighbor Discovery Advertisement (ICMPv6-Out)	Neighbor Discovery Advertisement messages are sent by nodes to notify other nodes of link-layer address changes or in response to a Neighbor Discovery Solicitation request.	136:*	Outbound
*Core Networking – Multicast Listener Query (ICMPv6-In)	An IPv6 multicast-capable router uses the Multicast Listener Query message to query a link for multicast group membership.	130:*	Inbound
*Core Networking – Multicast Listener Query (ICMPv6-Out)	An IPv6 multicast-capable router uses the Multicast Listener Query message to query a link for multicast group membership.	130:*	Outbound

Table 27-11 Core Networking Rules for ICMPv6

Rule Name	Rule Description	ICMP Type/Code	Direction
*Core Networking – Multicast Listener Report (ICMPv6-In)	The Multicast Listener Report message is used by a listening node to either immediately report its interest in receiving multicast traffic at a specific multicast address or in response to a Multicast Listener Query.	131:*	Inbound
*Core Networking – Multicast Listener Report (ICMPv6-Out)	The Multicast Listener Report message is used by a listening node to either immediately report its interest in receiving multicast traffic at a specific multicast address or in response to a Multicast Listener Query.	131:*	Outbound
*Core Networking – Multicast Listener Report v2 (ICMPv6-In)	Multicast Listener Report v2 message is used by a listening node to either immediately report its interest in receiving multicast traffic at a specific multicast address or in response to a Multicast Listener Query.	143:*	Inbound
*Core Networking – Multicast Listener Report v2 (ICMPv6-Out)	Multicast Listener Report v2 message is used by a listening node to either immediately report its interest in receiving multicast traffic at a specific multicast address or in response to a Multicast Listener Query.	143:*	Outbound
*Core Networking – Multicast Listener Done (ICMPv6-In)	Multicast Listener Done messages inform local routers that no members remain for a specific multicast address on the subnet.	132:*	Inbound
*Core Networking – Multicast Listener Done (ICMPv6-Out)	Multicast Listener Done messages inform local routers that no members remain for a specific multicast address on the subnet.	132:*	Outbound

Table 27-12   Core Networking Rules for IGMP Multicast

Rule Name	Rule Description	Protocol	Direction
Networking – Internet Group Management Protocol (IGMP-In)	IGMP messages are sent and received by nodes to create, join, and depart multicast groups.	2	Inbound
Networking – Internet Group Management Protocol (IGMP-Out)	IGMP messages are sent and received by nodes to create, join, and depart multicast groups.	2	Outbound

Table 27-13   Core Networking Rules for ISATAP/6to4 Tunneling

Rule Name	Rule Description	Protocol	Direction
Core Networking – IPv6 (IPv6-In)	Inbound rule required to permit IPv6 traffic for ISATAP (Intra-Site Automatic Tunnel Addressing Protocol) and 6to4 tunneling services	41	Inbound
Core Networking – IPv6 (IPv6-Out)	Inbound rule required to permit IPv6 traffic for ISATAP and 6to4 tunneling services	41	Outbound

Table 27-14   Core Networking Rules for Teredo (Edge Traversal)

Rule Name	Rule Description	Protocol / Local Port	Direction	Binary (Service)
Core Networking – Teredo (UDP-In)	Inbound UDP rule to allow Teredo edge traversal, a technology that provides address assignment and automatic tunneling for unicast IPv6 traffic when an IPv6/IPv4 host is located behind an IPv4 network address translator	UDP/$TEREDO	Inbound	Svchost.exe (iphlpsvc)
Core Networking – Teredo (UDP-Out)	Inbound UDP rule to allow Teredo edge traversal, a technology that provides address assignment and automatic tunneling for unicast IPv6 traffic when an IPv6/IPv4 host is located behind an IPv4 network address translator	UDP	Outbound	Svchost.exe (iphlpsvc)

Note   For detailed information concerning rules for other rule groups, open the Windows Firewall With Advanced Security snap-in and filter to display the rules for that rule group.

Windows Firewall and the Startup Process

When a Windows Vista computer starts, boot-time filters are applied to all network interfaces to reduce the attack surface prior to the Windows Firewall service (MpsSvc) starting. The boot-time filters perform the following actions:

- Block all unsolicited inbound traffic to the computer.

- Allow all inbound DHCP traffic. (The ports are restricted, as shown earlier in Table 27-7.)

- Allow inbound ICMPv6 Type 135:* Neighbor Discovery traffic.

- Allow all outbound traffic.

- Block outbound TCP Resets.

- Block outbound ICMPv6 Type 1:3 and ICMPv4 Type 3:3 Destination Unreachable / Port Unreachable error messages.

After the BFE has initialized, Windows switches to using persistent filters until MpsSvc starts. These persistent filters are identical in policy to the boot-time filters. When MpsSvc starts, Windows Firewall policy is processed and applied to the computer. For more information on persistent filters, see the sidebar titled "Direct from the Source: Windows Firewall and Boot-Time Filtering" that follows.

Direct from the Source: Windows Firewall and Boot-Time Filtering

A new Windows Vista platform service called Windows Filtering Platform (WFP) performs Windows Firewall's filtering. Firewall rules and settings are implemented via three types of WFP filter:

- **Boot-time filters**   These filters are in effect from the time the TCP/IP stack starts until the BFE service starts. After the BFE starts, these filters are removed.

- **Persistent filters**   These filters are stored persistently in the BFE service (in the registry) and applied while the BFE is running.

- **Dynamic filters**   These filters are not persistent and are associated with an active API session. After the session ends, these filters are automatically removed.

This is what happens during Windows Vista startup:

1. The computer starts up. There's no networking yet.

2. The TCP/IP stack starts up and starts the WFP driver (Netio.sys).

3. Networking starts and the WFP boot-time filters are in effect.

4. The BFE service starts: Persistent filters replace the boot-time filters.

5. The Firewall Service starts, adding the current policy rules and settings (as filters) based on the current profile.

The boot-time filters (step 3) and the persistent filters (step 4) are identical and contain the following:

- Block All Unsolicited Inbound Traffic
- Allow Inbound Loopback Traffic
- Allow Inbound ICMPv6 Neighbor Discovery (also known as Neighbor Solicitation), which is used for mapping IPv6 addresses to the MAC address (equivalent of ARP in IPv4)

These filters are present at all times and are low priority. Higher-priority filters mask out these filters when Windows Firewall policy is in effect (step 5). When Windows Firewall is disabled, the WFP boot-time and persistent filters are removed. If Windows Firewall is enabled, but the Windows Firewall service is stopped or killed, the dynamic filters are automatically removed, and you end up with the persistent filters, which in effect block all inbound traffic.

Eran Yariv

Windows Firewall and IPsec Management Development Lead

Upgrading Windows Firewall

When a Windows XP Service Pack 2 computer is upgraded to Windows Vista, all existing Windows Firewall settings are preserved. For more information on performing upgrades, see Part II of this book, "Deployment."

Note   Windows PE 2.0—a bootable deployment tool that you can use for installation and troubleshooting purposes—includes full Windows Firewall functionality.

Understanding IPsec Integration

A major enhancement of Windows Firewall in Windows Vista is the integration of IPsec protection with firewall filtering. In addition, processing and creating IPsec policy in Windows Vista has been updated to reduce the number of rules necessary to create a practical IPsec policy. These policy-engine enhancements include simplified policy, AuthIP, new crypto algorithms, and other features described in the following sections.

Note   Both the IPsec service (PolicyAgent) and the Windows Firewall service (MpsSvc) are based on and supported by the Windows Filtering Platform.

In the previous Windows XP client platform (and in Windows Server 2003), configuring firewall settings and creating IPsec filters were done entirely independently of each other. This approach caused several issues:

- Conflicting filtering settings could be configured for Windows Firewall and IPsec, resulting in traffic being blocked when it should be allowed. In addition, the fact that filtering was configured in several places using different tools made troubleshooting such conflicts challenging.

- Using IPsec to protect internal server-to-server traffic and isolate servers from rogue clients involved creating and maintaining dozens or even hundreds of IPsec filters or rules. Additionally, using IPsec to protect client-to-domain controller traffic was almost impossible to configure and maintain because of bootstrap issues, among others. As a result, until today many enterprises have been reluctant to use IPsec internally to enhance the protection of their corporate networks because of the complexity, time, and labor involved.

In Windows Vista, however, updates to the IPsec policy integration and the integration of IPsec into Windows Firewall greatly simplify the creation and maintenance of IPsec filters and rules for implementing IPsec policy on the computer for different network protection scenarios. Instead of creating IPsec filters and rules using the IPsec Security Policy Management snap-in, the administrator can now create connection security rules using the Windows Firewall With Advanced Security snap-in (the same tool used to create Windows Firewall rules) to configure IPsec policy protection on the computer. The Windows Firewall With Advanced Security snap-in thus becomes the central tool for managing both firewall rules and IPsec policy on the computer.

> **Note**   The IPsec Security Policy Management snap-in is still included with Windows Vista for compatibility with legacy Windows IPsec implementations.

New IPsec Features in Windows Vista

In addition to the new user interface for managing IPsec policy, which lets you easily create connection security rules, Windows Vista IPsec enhancements include:

- New encryption and data integrity algorithms, credential types, and authentication methods.

- AuthIP, an enhanced version of the Internet Key Exchange (IKE) protocol used for negotiating security associations to secure Authentication Header (AH) and Encapsulating Security Payload (ESP) traffic.

- Negotiation Discovery, a new method of determining whether or not a peer is configured for IPsec protection. When configured to use IPsec, a Windows Vista client sends simultaneous outbound packets—for example, one IKE negotiation packet and one unsecured packet—when initiating a connection, and through this process is able to discover if a peer is able to negotiate the use of IPsec security. This allows administrators to deploy more simplified IPsec policies, which ease administrative overhead and reduce policy complexity.

■ Support for NIST Common Criteria (CC) compliance by enabling Windows Firewall to log audit events to the Security event log in addition to the default firewall log.

■ Domain IPsec policy is now fully integrated with Group Policy and is stored in policy (.pol) files in Sysvol instead of in the IPsec container in Active Directory. This makes it easier to manage firewall (block/allow) rules and IPsec filters and rules in a domain environment using Group Policy. Also, IPsec policy inherits from the dynamic per-profile approach of Windows Firewall. In other words, you can have different IPsec policies for each of the three profiles.

Most of these features are discussed further in the following sections. For information concerning general IPsec concepts and how to implement IPsec on different Windows platforms, see *http://technet.microsoft.com/en-us/network/bb531150.aspx* on Microsoft TechNet.

Note   Service Pack 1 for Windows Vista also enhances Windows Firewall and IPsec to support use of the new Suite B cryptographic algorithms. See the following sidebar titled "Direct from the Source: Windows Firewall and Suite B Cryptographic Algorithms" for more information.

Direct from the Source: Windows Firewall and Suite B Cryptographic Algorithms

Suite B is a set of cryptographic algorithms announced by the National Security Agency in February 2005 to protect national security information and systems. As such, Windows Vista supports Suite B cryptographic algorithms. In Windows Vista SP1, this support is present in Windows Firewall With Advanced Security.

Windows Firewall With Advanced Security allows the configuration of ECDSA256 and ECDSA384 as certificate-signing algorithms in addition to the default RSA signing on First and Second authentications of connection security. In addition, Windows Firewall With Advanced Security provides support in Main Mode and Quick Mode connection security for the GCM128, GCM192, and GCM256 encryption algorithms. Also in Main Mode and Quick Mode, Windows Firewall With Advanced Security supports the related GMAC128, GMAC 192, GMAC256, SHA256, and SHA384 hash algorithms.

All the Suite B algorithms can be managed through the netsh advfirewall consec context of the netsh.exe command. Unfortunately, Windows Vista SP1 does not include help or documentation changes to expose these new settings. Therefore, to help you configure these settings, we include the Suite B settings syntax:

```
Usage: set global mainmode (parameter) (value) | notconfigured

    mmsecmethods         - configures the main mode list of proposals
                         - Usage:
                           keyexch:enc-integrity,enc-integrity[,...]|default
                         - keyexch=dhgroup1|dhgroup2|dhgroup14|
                           ecdhp256|ecdhp384
                         - enc=3des|des|aes128|aes192|aes256
                         - integrity=md5|sha1|sha256|sha384


Usage: add rule name=<string>
    endpoint1=any|localsubnet|dns|dhcp|wins|defaultgateway|
       <IPv4 address>|<IPv6 address>|<subnet>|<range>|<list>
    endpoint2=any|localsubnet|dns|dhcp|wins|defaultgateway|
       <IPv4 address>|<IPv6 address>|<subnet>|<range>|<list>
    action=requireinrequestout|requestinrequestout|
       requireinrequireout|noauthentication
    [description=<string>]
    [mode=transport|tunnel (default=transport)]
    [enable=yes|no (default=yes)]
    [profile=public|private|domain|any[,...] (default=any)]
    [type=dynamic|static (default=static)]
    [localtunnelendpoint=<IPv4 address>|<IPv6 address>]
    [remotetunnelendpoint=<IPv4 address>|<IPv6 address>]
    [port1=0-65535|any (default=any)]
    [port2=0-65535|any (default=any)]
    [protocol=0-255|tcp|udp|icmpv4|icmpv6|any (default=any)]
    [interfacetype=wiresless|lan|ras|any (default=any)]
    [auth1=computerkerb|computercert|computercertecdsap256|
       computercertecdsap384|computerpsk|computerntlm|anonymous[,...]]
    [auth1psk=<string>]
    [auth1ca="<CA Name> [certmapping:yes|no] [excludecaname:yes|no] | ..."]
    [auth1healthcert=yes|no (default=no)]
    [auth1ecdsap256ca="<CA Name> [certmapping:yes|no]
       [excludecaname:yes|no] | ..."]
    [auth1ecdsap256healthcert=yes|no (default=no)]
    [auth1ecdsap384ca="<CA Name> [certmapping:yes|no]
       [excludecaname:yes|no] | ..."]
    [auth1ecdsap384healthcert=yes|no (default=no)]
    [auth2=computercert|computercertecdsap256|computercertecdsap384|
       userkerb|usercert|usercertecdsap256|usercertecdsap384|userntlm|
       anonymous[,...]]
    [auth2ca="<CA Name> [certmapping:yes|no] | ..."]
    [auth2ecdsap256ca="<CA Name> [certmapping:yes|no] | ..."]
    [auth2ecdsap384ca="<CA Name> [certmapping:yes|no] | ..."]
    [qmpfs=dhgroup1|dhgroup2|dhgroup14|ecdhp256|ecdhp384|mainmode|
       none (default=none)]
    [qmsecmethods=
       ah:<integrity>+esp:<integrity>-<encryption>+[valuemin]+[valuekb]
       |default]
```

```
Remarks:

    - Certsigning options ecdsap256 and ecdsap384 are only supported on
      Windows Vista SP1 and later.
    - Qmsecmethods can be a list of proposals separated by a ",".
    - For qmsecmethods, integrity=md5|sha1|sha256|aesgmac128|aesgmac192|
      aesgmac256|aesgcm128|aesgcm192|aesgcm256  and
      encryption=3des|des|aes128|aes192|aes256|aesgcm128|aesgcm192|aesgcm256.
    - If aesgcm128, aesgcm192, or aesgcm256 is specified, it must be used for
      both ESP integrity and encryption.
    - Aesgmac128, aesgmac192, aesgmac256, aesgcm128, aesgcm192, aesgcm256,
      sha256 are only supported on Windows Vista SP1 and later.
```

For a discussion of the complexity that Suite B algorithms can add to managing Windows Firewall in mixed environments containing legacy versions of Windows, see the sidebar titled "Direct from the Source: Mixed Mode Policies Support" later in this chapter.

Gerardo Diaz Cuellar

Software Developer Engineer Technical Lead, Core Networking

New Cryptographic Algorithms for IPsec Key Exchange, Data Integrity, and Encryption

Support for the following cryptographic algorithms has been added in Windows Vista:

- AES-128 encryption

- AES-192 encryption

- AES-256 encryption both in Main Mode and Quick Mode

- ECC-256 and ECC-384 for Diffie-Hellman in Main Mode

Tables 27-15 and 27-16 summarize the encryption and data integrity algorithms supported for IPsec in Windows Vista, listed in order of decreasing cryptographic strength.

Table 27-15   Encryption Algorithms Supported for IPsec in Windows Vista

Algorithm	Description
AES-256	Provides the strongest security
	Highest level of resource usage
	Compatible with Windows Vista or later only
AES-192	Less security and resource usage than AES-256
	Compatible with Windows Vista or later only
AES-128	Less security and resource usage than AES-192
	Compatible with Windows Vista or later only

Table 27-15   Encryption Algorithms Supported for IPsec in Windows Vista

Algorithm	Description
3DES	Less secure than AES-128 but stronger than DES
	Supported by IPsec in Windows XP and Windows Server 2003
DES	Least secure method and provided for backward-compatibility reasons only (not recommended)

Table 27-16   Data Integrity Algorithms Supported for IPsec in Windows Vista

Algorithm	Description
SHA1	Supported by IPsec in Windows Vista and also in Windows XP and Windows Server 2003
	Stronger than MD5 and uses slightly more resources
MD5	Least secure method and provided for backward-compatibility only (not recommended)

When negotiating IPsec Key Exchange (also known as Main Mode) in Windows Vista, the following encryption and data integrity algorithms are tried in the following order under the default IPsec configuration:

1. AES-128 for encryption and SHA1 for data integrity

2. 3DES for encryption and SHA1 for data integrity

By comparison, when negotiating IPsec Key Exchange on the legacy Windows XP and Windows Server 2003 platforms, the following algorithms are tried in order under the default IPsec configuration:

1. 3DES for encryption and SHA1 for data integrity

2. 3DES for encryption and MD5 for data integrity

3. DES for encryption and SHA1 for data integrity

4. DES for encryption and MD5 for data integrity

Note   The new defaults in Windows Vista for Key Exchange (Main Mode) negotiation are backward-compatible with the old defaults on legacy Windows platforms. Only the default crypto sets have been changed in Windows Vista; the algorithms specified in the defaults are used only if you create a connection security rule.

The following methods of data protection (also know as Quick Mode) are tried in order by Windows Vista to secure network traffic using IPsec:

- Order of methods tried when data integrity only is configured (no encryption):

    1. ESP using SHA1 for integrity

    2. AH using SHA1 for integrity

- Order of methods tried when both data integrity and encryption are configured:

    1. ESP using SHA1 for integrity and AES-128 for encryption

    2. ESP using SHA1 for integrity and 3DES for encryption

By comparison, the following data protection methods are tried in turn by Windows XP and Windows Server 2003 to secure network traffic using IPsec:

1. ESP using SHA1 for integrity and 3DES for encryption

2. ESP using MD5 for integrity and 3DES for encryption

3. ESP using SHA1 for integrity and DES for encryption

4. ESP using MD5 for integrity and DES for encryption

5. AH using SHA1 for integrity only

6. AH using MD5 for integrity only

Note The new defaults in Windows Vista for data protection (Quick Mode) negotiation are backward-compatible with the old defaults on legacy Windows platforms. Only the default crypto sets have been changed in Windows Vista.

Table 27-17 summarizes the key exchange algorithms that IPsec can use in Windows Vista, listed in order of decreasing cryptographic strength.

Table 27-17   Key Exchange Algorithms Available in Windows Vista

Algorithm	Description
Elliptic Curve Diffie-Hellman P-384	Provides the strongest security
	Highest level of resource usage
	Compatible with Windows Vista or later only
Elliptic Curve Diffie-Hellman P-256	Less security and resource usage than P-384
	Compatible with Windows Vista or later only
Diffie-Hellman Group 14	Stronger than the Group 2 used in Windows XP and Windows Server 2003
Diffie-Hellman Group 2	Supported by IPsec in Windows Vista and also in Windows XP and Windows Server 2003
Diffie-Hellman Group 1	Provided for backward-compatibility only

New Credential Types for IPsec Authentication

In addition to the default Computer (Kerberos v5 or NTLMv2), Computer (Certificate), and preshared key credential types used for IPsec authentication in previous versions of Windows, support for the following credential types has been added in Windows Vista:

- **User (Kerberos v5)**   Uses Kerberos v5 to authenticate a user account found in Active Directory

- **Computer And User (Kerberos v5)**   Uses Kerberos v5 to authenticate both a user account and a computer account found in Active Directory

- **User (NTLMv2)**   Uses NTLMv2 to authenticate a user account found in Active Directory if Kerberos cannot be used

- **User (Certificate)**   Uses a certificate from a trusted Certificate Authority (CA) to authenticate a user account

- **Computer (Health Certificate)**   Uses a NAP health certificate from a trusted CA to authenticate a computer account

Note   Computer And User (Kerberos v5) is actually not a separate credential type, but a combination of Computer (Kerberos v5), which is supported by IPsec on the legacy Windows XP and Windows Server 2003 platforms, and User (Kerberos v5), which is new to Windows Vista. In fact, in Windows Vista you can specify any supported IPsec credential types in a combination of up to two credentials, as explained later in this chapter. This chaining of credentials is another key IPsec feature new to Windows Vista.

Note   If you plan to use certificates for IPsec authentication, see Knowledge Base article KB922706 at *http://support.microsoft.com/default.aspx/kb/922706* for information about how to use Windows Server 2003 Certificate Services web enrollment pages together with Windows Vista.

In Windows Vista, IPsec authentication can take place in two steps:

- **First Authentication**   This is performed during the Main Mode phase of IPsec negotiation and authenticates the computer. First Authentication is optional: You can opt out of it in scenarios that require only user authentication. (Opting out of Second Authentication either causes user authentication to be performed using anonymous credentials or else no authentication is performed at all, depending on how you configure Extended Mode policy.)

- **Second Authentication**   This is performed using AuthIP during the Extended Mode of the Main Mode phase of IPsec negotiation and authenticates the user. Second Authentication is also optional; you can opt out of it in scenarios that require only computer authentication. (Opting out of Second Authentication causes user authentication to be performed using anonymous credentials.) For information about AuthIP, see the section titled "Understanding AuthIP" later in this chapter.

> **Note**   Opting out of both First Authentication and Second Authentication is allowed but not recommended, because it is equivalent to disabling IPsec authentication entirely.

Tables 27-18 and 27-19 summarize the different authentication methods available for First Authentication and Second Authentication. If more than one authentication method is configured, they are each tried in turn until either one succeeds or they all fail.

Table 27-18   Authentication Methods Available for First Authentication

Method	Description
Computer (Kerberos v5)	Uses a computer account in Active Directory to authenticate the computer using Kerberos. This is the default method used for First Authentication. Both peers must either belong to the same Active Directory domain or to separate domains that trust one another.
Computer (NTLMv2)	Uses a computer account for a standalone computer or a computer belonging to a lower-level Windows domain to authenticate the computer using NTLMv2.
Computer (Certificate)	Uses a computer certificate from a specified CA to authenticate the computer. This method is useful if the computers are not in a domain or are in separate domains that do not trust one another. Computer certificates can optionally be mapped to computer accounts in Active Directory, and they can also optionally be required to be NAP health certificates.
Preshared key	Uses a secret preshared key to authenticate the computer. This method requires manual configuration of the key and is therefore not recommended in an enterprise environment, because too much administrative overhead is involved, the key is stored in plaintext. Using a preshared key for First Authentication means that Second Authentication cannot be used.

Table 27-19   Authentication Methods Available for Second Authentication

Method	Description
User (Kerberos v5)	Uses a computer account in Active Directory to authenticate the user using Kerberos. This is the default method used for Second Authentication. Both peers must either belong to the same Active Directory domain or to separate domains that trust one another. By default, the Second Authentication is not specified.
User (NTLMv2)	Uses a user account for a standalone computer or a computer belonging to a legacy Windows domain to authenticate the user using NTLMv2.

Table 27-19 Authentication Methods Available for Second Authentication

Method	Description
User (Certificate)	Uses a user certificate from a specified CA to authenticate the user. This method is useful if the users are not in a domain or are in separate domains that do not trust one another. User certificates can optionally be mapped to user accounts in Active Directory.
Computer (Health Certificate)	Uses a computer certificate from a specified CA to authenticate the computer. This method is useful if the computers are not in a domain or are in separate domains that do not trust one another. Computer certificates must be NAP health certificates and can optionally be mapped to computer accounts in Active Directory.

The default configuration for IPsec authentication in Windows Vista is:

■ **First Authentication** Computer (Kerberos v5)

■ **Second Authentication** Not configured

> **Note** If you use a preshared key for First Authentication, you cannot specify a Second Authentication method.

Five predefined combinations of authentication methods are available from the Windows Firewall With Advanced Security snap-in. To display these options, follow these steps:

1. Open the Windows Firewall With Advanced Security snap-in using an account that has administrator credentials on the computer. Right-click the root node and select Properties.

2. Click the IPsec Settings tab and click Customize to open the Customize IPsec Settings dialog box.

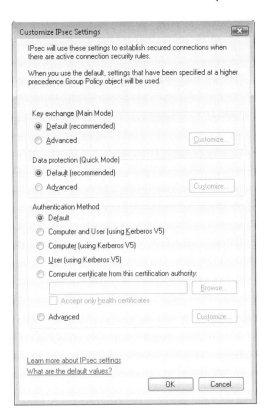

Table 27-20 summarizes the First Authentication and Second Authentication settings for each of these five predefined combinations of authentication methods.

Table 27-20   Predefined IPsec Authentication Methods and Their Corresponding First Authentication and Second Authentication Settings

Predefined Authentication Method	First Authentication Settings	Second Authentication Settings
Default	Computer (Kerberos v5)	None
Computer And User (Kerberos v5)	Computer (Kerberos v5)	User (Kerberos v5)
Computer (Kerberos v5)	Computer (Kerberos v5)	None
User (Kerberos v5)	Optional	User (Kerberos v5)
Computer Certificate From This Certification Authority	Computer (Certificate)	None
Advanced	Configurable	Configurable

Note When you create connection security rules, don't be confused by the first and third authentication methods shown in Table 27-20. Think of the Default option as being Not Configured in Group Policy. This Not Configured option allows you to configure it at one level of Group Policy and have it fall through the hierarchy with the highest-precedence GPO settings winning. If you have no GPO policy and you haven't configured these settings, the service default settings kick in, which are Computer (Kerberos).

Understanding AuthIP

Authenticated Internet Protocol (AuthIP) is a new key exchange/keying protocol that extends the Internet Key Exchange (IKE) protocol used by IPsec to negotiate security associations for the purpose of protecting AH and ESP traffic. AuthIP is an extension of the current version of IKE (IKEv1) and provides additional features for transport mode to make it more efficient and robust. Although an AuthIP key exchange is similar in operation to an exchange using IKE, AuthIP was designed to simplify key exchange by reducing option complexity and the number of round trips required.

AuthIP works by performing mutual authentication between two peers, establishing a security association that you can use to establish the security associations for both ESP and AH traffic. AuthIP operates as a request/response protocol in which the initiating peer sends a message to the responding peer and the responding peer then returns a message to the initiating peer. AuthIP is primarily used to negotiate ESP transport-mode traffic between two peers but can also be used to protect AH traffic. (AuthIP is currently not able to support VPN scenarios.)

Note The essential difference between IKE and AuthIP is that IKE supports only one authentication, whereas AuthIP supports two. If you specify the second authentication and don't specify it as optional, the exchange will be done with AuthIP. This means that AuthIP is not legacy platform–compatible.

IKEv1 and AuthIP negotiate authentication differently:

- **IKEv1 negotiation** If peers have multiple authentication methods in common, they negotiate the use of one of these common methods. If authentication using this method fails, IKE negotiation fails and no other other common authentication method is attempted.

- **AuthIP negotiation** If peers have multiple authentication methods in common, they negotiate the use of one of these common methods. If authentication using this method fails, AuthIP removes this negotiation method from its list of negotiation methods and attempts negotiation using another method common to both peers. This process repeats until either all negotiation methods have failed or authentication has succeeded using one of the common methods.

The traditional IKEv1 key exchange makes use of two different exchange modes:

■ **Main Mode (MM)**   Used for establishing the base security associations (SAs) for the key exchange, for authenticating the peers involved, and for all subsequent traffic flows. MM generally authenticates machine credentials of the peers involved.

■ **Quick Mode (QM)**   Used for establishing SAs for protecting individual traffic flows by providing data integrity and optional encryption of the flows. (QM is not used for authentication purposes.)

AuthIP adds a third mode to these two: User Mode (UM), which can optionally be used to authenticate user credentials of the peers involved and is the basis for the Second Authentication phase of IPsec authentication in Windows Vista described earlier in this chapter. This means that in Windows Vista, IPsec authentication generally takes one of the following two forms:

MM + QM

MM + UM + QM

The first form involves MM once to establish the base SA, and involves QM multiple times—once for each data-protection SA established. UM is not configured in this approach. The second form involves MM once followed by UM once (to establish the base SA) and then QM multiple times.

Note   The existing IKE protocol is currently under revision by the IETF. Although the planned IKEv2 protocol improves on many of the IPsec VPN usage issues associated with IKEv1, the plans for IKEv2 do not currently address deficiencies in how transport mode operates during IPsec key exchange.

Understanding Negotiation Discovery

Negotiation discovery is an enhancement to IPsec in Windows Vista that allows one peer (the initiator) to dynamically determine if it needs to use IPsec to protect a TCP connection when no prior SA exists with the peer (the responder). Previous versions of Windows use a different method, known as default responder, in which the initiator sends its request in the clear; if the responder does require IPsec, the responder must accept the inbound packet unsecured. Otherwise, traffic continues in the clear between the peers. Unfortunately, this "fallback to clear" approach, which allows outbound traffic to flow even if IKE authentication fails, often takes too long (three seconds by default) and introduces unacceptable delays in establishing IPsec communication between peers, especially when multiple delays are incurred because communication with multiple domain controllers is required.

Negotiating discovery resolves the delay problem by having the initiator simultaneously start a TCP session with the responder and begin negotiating an IKE session. As a result, negotiation discovery guarantees that client-initiated traffic will succeed without the three-second delay imposed by fallback to clear. The delay occurs in legacy IPsec implementations when the responder does not require IPsec to accept inbound network connections. If the responder does require IPsec to accept inbound connections, IKE/AuthIP will be used to negotiate an SA with the initiator; the only delay experienced for secure traffic is the normal delay of the IKE negotiation process. This means that in Windows Vista, the fallback to clear time-out value is virtually eliminated, because Windows Vista simultaneously sends two outbound packets (one IKE negotiation packet and one unsecured packet) when trying to establish a connection with a host that may require IPsec protection.

Note   If credential and policy mismatch failures occur, IPsec in Windows Vista can use fallback to clear and reduce the fallback delay from 3 seconds to 500 milliseconds. You can also enable this functionality in Windows XP and Windows Server 2003 by installing an update available from the Microsoft Download Center. For more information, see Knowledge Base article KB914841 at *http://support.microsoft.com/kb/914841*.

Understanding Connection Security Rules

Connection security rules let you use IPsec to authenticate and optionally encrypt traffic for different network-protection scenarios, including server isolation, secure server-to-server communications, domain isolation, and Network Access Protection (NAP) scenarios. Connection security rules can filter traffic based on a number of different conditions, as described in Table 27-21. (The generalized connection security rule is the logical AND of all these conditions.)

Table 27-21   Filtering Conditions for Windows Firewall Connection Security Rules

Condition	Possible Values
Endpoints (Represents the two sides of the connection.)	A specific IPv4 or IPv6 address or a list of addresses
	A range of IPv4 or IPv6 addresses or a list of ranges
	An entire IPv4 or IPv6 subnet or a list of subnets
	A predefined set of computers, including local subnet, default gateway, DNS servers, WINS servers, or DNS servers—or a list of such items.
Ports of endpoints (Represents the ports used by both sides of the connection. Used for TCP/UDP connections only; these are editable through netsh and read-only through the Monitoring node of the MMC snap-in.)	All Ports
	Specific ports (can be specified using a comma-separated list)

Table 27-21   **Filtering Conditions for Windows Firewall Connection Security Rules**

Condition	Possible Values
ICMP Type Code (For ICMPv4 and ICMPv6. This is editable through netsh, and read-only through the Monitoring node of the MMC snap-in.)	All ICMP Types Specific types of ICMP traffic
Interface type	All interface types Local area network Remote access Wireless
Action	Request for both inbound and outbound connections Require for inbound connections and request for outbound connections Require for both inbound and outbound connections No authentication (effectively disables security for the rule)
Authentication Method	Default Computer and User (Kerberos v5) Computer (Kerberos v5) User (Kerberos v5) Computer Certificate (with option to only accept Health certificates) Advanced (see Tables 27-18 and 27-19)
Tunnel endpoints	A specific IPv4 or IPv6 address A range of IPv4 or IPv6 addresses An entire IPv4 or IPv6 subnet A predefined set of computers, including local subnet, default gateway, DNS servers, WINS servers, or DNS servers IPv4 or IPv6 address of local and remote tunnel computers (closest computers to tunnel endpoints 1 and 2 respectively). Must be a single IPv4 or IPv6 address. The local and remote tunnel endpoints need to match in IP version. (In other words, you can't have one that is IPv4 and one that is IPv6.)
Authentication exemption (This isn't actually a property on a connection security rule—it's a connection security rule configured with these as endpoints and action of "no authentication." See Authentication Exemption in Table 27-22 for more information.)	A specific IPv4 or IPv6 address A range of IPv4 or IPv6 addresses An entire IPv4 or IPv6 subnet A predefined set of computers, including local subnet, default gateway, DNS servers, WINS servers, or DNS servers

> **Note**   You can configure connection rules on a per-profile basis.

Types of Connection Security Rules

Table 27-22 summarizes the types of connection rules you can create and the conditions that you can configure for each type of rule.

Table 27-22   Connection Security Rules and Their Configurable Conditions

Type	Description	Conditions
Isolation	Restricts connections to the computer based on authentication credentials such as membership in a domain or health status of the computer. You can use isolation rules to implement a server or domain isolation strategy on your network.	Actions Authentication method
Authentication exemption	Prevents the computer from authenticating connections from specified computers. This is typically used in conjunction with an isolation rule. For example, if you want to isolate all computers on your domain, but you know that a specific computer with a non-Windows operating system needs access, you can exempt this computer from the requirements by specifying its IPv4 or IPv6 address.	Exempt computers
Server-to-server	Enables the computer to authenticate connections with specified computers. You can use server-to-server rules to protect connections between critical servers on your network.	Endpoints Action Authentication method
Tunnel	Enables authenticated connections between gateway computers. You can use tunnel rules to protect a connection between two security gateways across the Internet.	Tunnel endpoints Authentication method
Custom	Enables creation of custom connection security rules. Use this type of rule when none of the default rule types can meet the protection needs of your network.	Endpoints Action Authentication method

Implementing IPsec Protection Strategies

Windows Vista's connection security rules greatly simplify implementing different kinds of IPsec protection strategies on your corporate network. These network protection strategies are of two basic types:

- Server and domain isolation strategies
- Network Access Protection

Server and Domain Isolation   Server and Domain Isolation are strategies that logically isolate server and domain resources to create secure logical networks within your physical network. These logical networks consist of computers that have common requirements for secure communication. They are used to limit access to server and domain resources to computers that are properly authenticated and authorized, and to prevent unauthorized (rogue) computers from inappropriately gaining access to these resources. The two types of isolation scenarios are:

- **Server Isolation**   In this scenario, selected servers or server applications have IPsec policy configured so that they will accept only authenticated and secured communications from other computers on the network. An example of a server isolation scenario would be configuring IPsec policy so that only users in the Finance Department can access the finance database, or only users in Human Resources can access HR servers. Server isolation thus provides protection to critical servers and network traffic between them.

- **Domain Isolation**   In this scenario, domain controllers and domain-member computers (both client computers and member servers) have IPsec policy configured so that they will accept only authenticated and secured communications from other domain-member computers on the network. Domain isolation protects traffic sent between domain members and prevents non-domain–joined computers from communicating with domain controllers or domain-member computers. Domain isolation thus prevents rogue computers from accessing domain resources or intercepting network traffic between domain computers.

Although you can use Windows 2000 or later to implement Server and Domain Isolation on Active Directory networks, IPsec in Windows Vista and Windows Server 2008 simplifies the task of implementing these strategies. For more information on how Server and Domain Isolation works and how to implement it in various scenarios, see *http://technet.microsoft.com/ en-us/network/bb545651.aspx* on Microsoft TechNet and the section titled "Additional Resources" at the end of this chapter.

Network Access Protection   Network Access Protection (NAP) is a strategy that helps protect network resources by forcing computers connecting to the network to comply with predefined computer health requirements. These health requirements can include policies such as ensuring that the connecting computers have the necessary software updates, the latest antivirus signatures, the necessary certificates, and so on. If a computer attempting to connect to the network does not comply with all health requirements, the NAP enforcement mechanism can either prevent the computer from establishing a connection to the network until it becomes compliant, or it can force compliance by downloading and installing the appropriate updates, signatures, and so on to the computer. NAP does not prevent malicious users or rogue computers from accessing domain resources, but it does help maintain your network's overall integrity by maintaining the health of computers on your network.

The NAP policy enforcement platform is built into the Windows Vista and Windows Server 2008 operating systems. A Network Access Protection Client is also included in Service Pack 3 for Windows XP. For more information on how NAP works and how to implement it in various scenarios, see *http://technet.microsoft.com/en-us/network/bb545879.aspx* on Microsoft TechNet and the section titled "Additional Resources" at the end of this chapter.

Understanding Windows Firewall Logging and Auditing

Windows Firewall in Windows XP and Windows Server 2003 log firewall activity in two locations:

- **%WinDir%\Pfirewall.log**   This is a flat text file that you can use for logging successful connections and dropped packets. By default, no information is written to this log unless you enable logging of passed or dropped packets. Information is written to this log file using the W3C Extended File format; you can analyze it using tools such as Logparser. For more information on Logparser and to download this tool, see *http://www.microsoft.com/technet/scriptcenter/tools/logparser/default.mspx*.

- **Security event log**   By default, the only events relating to Windows Firewall that are written to this log are policy-change events: starting or stopping the Windows Firewall service; creating or modifying a rule; changing the profile between public, private, or domain; processing Windows Firewall Group Policy settings; and several other actions.

The difficulty with separating packet logging events from policy events is twofold:

- Troubleshooting Windows Firewall connectivity issues is more difficult.

- Windows Firewall is not compliant with the Common Criteria.

The Common Criteria mandates that all security auditing be comprehensive in nature and contain all security-oriented events. Common Criteria also mandates that the system fail if auditing cannot be performed (for example, if the audit log becomes full), a condition known as CrashOnAuditFail. The legacy Pfirewall.log does not satisfy these two criteria, but the Windows Security Event Log is compliant with the Common Criteria. As a result, in Windows Vista all logging of both filtering and policy is done to the Security Event Log, which makes complying with Common Criteria requirements easier for enterprises in the government, healthcare, and financial industry sectors.

However, for administrators who still want to use the Pfirewall.log for logging passed and/or blocked traffic, Windows Vista still provides the Pfirewall.log, although it is now stored in a new location: %WinDir%\system32\LogFiles\Firewall\Pfirewall.log. The default size limit of this log file is 4,096 kilobytes (the same as in Windows XP), and by default the system logs neither successful connections nor dropped packets. To configure the Pfirewall.log in Windows XP, you use the Advanced tab of the Windows Firewall CPL properties in Control Panel. To configure Pfirewall.log in Windows Vista, you must instead use the Windows Firewall With Advanced Security snap-in (or its associated Group Policy user interface) as in the following steps:

1. Open the Windows Firewall With Advanced Security using an account that has administrator credentials on the computer. Right-click the root node and select Properties.

2. Choose a profile (Domain, Private, or Public), click Customize under Logging, and configure Pfirewall.log settings as desired.

> **Caution**   If you are using Group Policy to configure a new location for the Pfirewall.log, make sure that the Windows Firewall service account (this is LocalService by default) or (even better) the MPSSVC Service SID has at least Write permissions on the destination folder; otherwise, logging will fail.

You can also use the netsh command to display the Pfirewall.log logging settings for the domain Windows Firewall profile. Open a command prompt with administrator credentials and type **netsh advfirewall show domainprofile**. You can also use netsh to configure Pfirewall.log logging settings for the domain profile by using **netsh advfirewall set domainprofile**. For example, to enable logging of dropped packets, type **netsh advfirewall set domainprofile logging droppedconnections enable** at a command prompt. For more information, type **netsh advfirewall set ?** at a command prompt. The section titled "Common Management Tasks" later in this chapter includes more examples of how to use netsh to manage Windows Firewall.

The main location for logging Windows Firewall activity in Windows Vista is now the Windows Security event log. In addition to logging the firewall policy–change events that are logged in Windows XP (with some changes in event categories and event IDs)–Windows Vista can audit other global Windows Firewall activity, including:

■ IPsec filter-level policy changes, which are logged under the Policy Change event category

■ IPsec Main Mode and Quick Mode authentication events, which are logged under the Logon/Logoff event categories

■ IPsec driver events, which are logged under the System event category

Windows Vista can also log policy check events such as:

■ Connection creation events

■ Connection deletion events

■ Packet dropped events

These events are logged under the Object Access event category.

By default, these policy check events are not logged in the Security event log unless an administrator enables this auditing functionality because of the performance hit that the system can incur. To enable detailed auditing of Windows Firewall activity, you can use the Auditpol.exe from an elevated command prompt opened with administrative credentials. For example, to display the current audit settings for all categories and subcategories, type **auditpol /get /category:*** at a command prompt. To display all audit subcategories for which you can enable auditing, type **auditpol /list /subcategory:*** at a command prompt. To enable auditing of dropped packets to the Security log, you can enable the Filtering Platform Packet Drop subcategory under the Object Access category by typing **auditpol /set /subcategory:"Filtering Platform Packet Drop" /failure:enable** at a command prompt. For more information, type **auditpol /?** at a command prompt.

> **Note**   For information about using Group Policy to configure detailed security auditing for Windows Vista client and Windows Server 2008–based computers in a Window Server 2008, Windows Server 2003, or Windows 2000 domain, see Microsoft Knowledge Base article 921469 at *http://support.microsoft.com/kb/921469/*.

Managing Windows Firewall

Windows Vista has new and enhanced tools for managing Windows Firewall that make it easier for administrators to manage desktop firewall configuration across an enterprise. These tools include:

- The new Windows Firewall With Advanced Security snap-in for the MMC console
- The new Windows Firewall With Advanced Security node in Group Policy
- The new advfirewall context of the netsh command
- New COM APIs for programmatically managing Windows Firewall

> **Note**   The Windows Firewall tool in Control Panel is for use mainly by home users who need to enable/disable Windows Firewall or create exceptions to enable third-party applications on their computers to work.

How It Works: Windows Firewall Remote Management

The Windows Firewall service runs in a special process called SvcHost.exe (Service Host), which hosts two more built-in Windows Vista services. This instance of SvcHost.exe runs in the context of a LocalService account, which basically means two things:

- The LocalService account is yet another (built-in) user and has no special administrative rights or privileges.
- If this process tries to communicate over the network, it will show up as anonymous to the other side.

In addition, this specific SvcHost.exe instance runs in a service group called "LocalServiceNoNetwork" which, by means of Windows Service Hardening rules and privilege stripping, prohibits this process from sending or receiving any network traffic. These facts, together with the fact that the service has a write-restricted token, make it a super-tight service from a security point of view. If it cannot talk to the network, it cannot affect administrative settings, and it cannot write anywhere unless explicitly authorized to do so. These are all traits that you want to have on a firewall service, because the service controls your system's network and you want it to have the smallest attack vector possible. Now you need to support a configurable remote management feature for this service.

The attributes of this remote management feature are:

- The feature is off by default and the administrator can toggle it on and off at will.

- When the feature is turned off, the super-strict service restrictions mentioned previously must be in place. (The service cannot talk to the network.)

- When the feature is turned on, only administrators can remotely connect and manage the firewall settings. (For local configuration, administrators and network operators can view and manage the firewall's policy and authenticated users can only view it.)

- It supports RPC mutual authentication so that the remote management clients know they are really talking to the right computer and service.

- It keeps any breach that uses the remote management feature outside of the firewall service and available only for administrators.

It's pretty clear that satisfying the requirements of this feature can potentially undo many of the hardening efforts described in the first paragraph of this sidebar. The solution is to use a different service as a proxy. That other service should be able to authenticate on the network but should not be an omnipotent LocalSystem service—a NetworkService account is what we need. The PolicyAgent service was picked as the proxy service because it is auto-start by default and runs under a NetworkService account. Here is how it works:

1. The administrator enables the disabled-by-default built-in group of Windows Firewall rules called Windows Firewall Remote Management.

2. The PolicyAgent service detects this change and dynamically registers with the RPC subsystem. It exposes an RPC/TCP interface supporting mutual authentication with data encryption on the wire and tamper-proofing. Similarly, when the administrator disables this group of rules, the RPC interface closes.

3. A remote management client connects over RPC/TCP to the interface exposed by the PolicyAgent service. This is either a redirected Windows Firewall With Advanced Security MMC snap-in or a redirected advfirewall netsh extension.

4. The PolicyAgent service checks the authentication of the remote client and verifies that it is a member of the Administrators group.

5. For each management activity (an RPC interface call), the PolicyAgent impersonates the remote client and performs an identical local interface call to the Windows Firewall service.

This achieves the following benefits:

■   The Windows Firewall service can stay locked down and hardened even in the presence of a remote management feature.

■   A different access level is used for remote management (administrators only) versus local management. (Administrators and network operators can view and manage the firewall's policy and authenticated users can only view it.)

■   By impersonating the remote caller in the PolicyAgent service, auditing the user who made a policy change is preserved.

■   If the remote management proxy service (PolicyAgent) is somehow attacked and breached, it still cannot affect Windows Firewall settings because it does not have administrative privileges.

The key points to remember are:

■   To enable Windows Firewall remote management, all you have to do is enable the Windows Firewall group of rules called "Windows Firewall Remote Management."

■   The PolicyAgent service serves two purposes: legacy IPsec policy management and remote firewall management proxy.

■   Disabling the PolicyAgent service because you don't need legacy IPsec support also means that you lose the remote firewall management features.

Eran Yariv

Windows Firewall and IPsec Management Development Lead

Managing Windows Firewall Using the Windows Firewall With Advanced Security Snap-in

You can use the new Windows Firewall With Advanced Security snap-in to manage nearly all aspects of Windows Firewall on either the local computer or on a remote computer, including block/allow rules, connection security rules, and monitoring. (Some aspects of Windows Firewall can be managed only through netsh.) You can use this snap-in only for managing Windows Firewall on Windows Vista and Windows Server 2008 computers. You cannot use it to manage Windows Firewall on Windows XP or Windows Server 2003. To manage Windows Firewall on legacy Windows platforms, use either the Windows Firewall CPL (for local management) or the Computer Configuration\Policies\Administrative Templates\ Network\Network Connections\Windows Firewall policy settings in Group Policy (for remote management).

To use the Windows Firewall With Advanced Security snap-in to manage Windows Firewall on the local computer, follow these steps:

1. Click Start, click Control Panel, click System And Maintenance, and then click Administrative Tools.

2. Click Windows Firewall With Advanced Security.msc.

To use the snap-in to manage Windows Firewall on a remote computer, follow these steps:

1. Make sure that you are logged on to your administrative workstation using an account that is a member of the Administrators group on the remote computer. A domain user account that belongs to the Domain Admins group will provide these privileges.

2. Enable remote management of Window Firewall on the remote computer. You can do this in several ways:

    ❑ While logged on to the remote computer, use the Windows Firewall CPL on the remote computer to enable the Windows Firewall Remote Management rules. (This enables the Windows Firewall remote management rules only for the current firewall profile.)

    ❑ Use the Windows Firewall With Advanced Security snap-in on the remote computer to enable all rules for the active profile that belong to the Windows Firewall Remote Management rule group.

    ❑ Open a command prompt using administrator credentials and type **netsh advfirewall firewall set rule group="Windows Firewall Remote Management" enable=yes**. (You can use the netsh advfirewall set rule command only to enable or disable a rule group for all firewall profiles.)

    ❑ Use Group Policy to open the Windows Firewall Remote Management rule group on the remote computer. (See the discussion later in this section to learn how to do this.)

3. On the management workstation, click Start, type **mmc**, and then press Enter.

4. In the new MMC console that opens, click File and then click Add/Remove Snap-in.

5. Select the Windows Firewall With Advanced Security snap-in and click Add.

6. Select the Another Computer option in the Select Computer dialog box and click Browse to find the remote computer in Active Directory. When the remote computer name has been populated into the Another Computer field, click Finish and then click OK.

Figure 27-2 shows the general layout of the Windows Firewall With Advanced Security snap-in with its different sections and nodes.

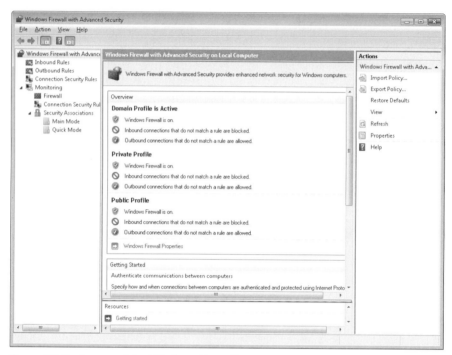

Figure 27-2   Layout of the Windows Firewall With Advanced Security snap-in.

Table 27-23 summarizes the management tasks that you can perform using the nodes in the left pane of the console.

Table 27-23   Management Tasks for Each Node in the Windows Firewall With Advanced Security Snap-in

Node	Tasks
Root node	Import/export Windows Firewall policy.
	Enable/disable Windows Firewall for the selected profile.
	Display or modify the default behavior for inbound or outbound connections that don't match a rule for the selected profile.
	Enable/disable Windows Firewall notifications for the selected profile.
	Enable/disable unicast respond to broadcast or multicast traffic for the selected profile.
	Configure Windows Firewall log settings for the selected profile.
	Configure IPsec defaults for key exchange, data protection, and authentication methods.
	Enable/disable exemption of ICMP traffic from IPsec.

Table 27-23   Management Tasks for Each Node in the Windows Firewall With Advanced Security Snap-in

Node	Tasks
Inbound Rules	Enable or disable an inbound rule.
	Create a new inbound rule or delete an existing rule.
	Display or edit properties of existing inbound rules.
	Display all inbound rules belonging to the same profile, rule group, or state.
	Export a list of inbound rules.
Outbound Rules	Enable or disable an outbound rule.
	Create a new outbound rule or delete an existing rule.
	Display or edit properties of existing outbound rules.
	Display all outbound rules belonging to the same profile, rule group, or state.
	Export a list of outbound rules.
Connection Security Rules	Enable or disable a connection security rule.
	Create a new connection security rule or delete an existing rule.
	Display or edit properties of existing connection security rules.
	Display authentication methods of existing connection security rules.
	Display all connection security rules belonging to the same profile or state.
	Export a list of connection security rules.
Monitoring	Display Windows Firewall's current profile state and settings.
Monitoring\Firewall	Display inbound/outbound rules that are currently applied and their properties.
Monitoring\Connection Security Rules	Display connection security rules that are currently active and their properties.
Monitoring\Security Associations	Export a list of active security associations (SAs).
Monitoring\Security Associations\Main Mode	Display Main Mode SAs that are currently active and their endpoints and settings.
Monitoring\Security Associations\Quick Mode	Display Quick Mode SAs that are currently active and their endpoints and settings.

Note   Note that the Monitoring\Firewall node displays rules that are currently applied, not rules that are enabled. It is possible to have an enabled local rule that isn't being applied, because Group Policy doesn't allow local rule merge.

> ### How It Works: Monitoring Windows Firewall
>
> In addition to the Monitoring node of the new Windows Firewall With Advanced Security snap-in, the IPsec Security Monitor snap-in remains available in Windows Vista for monitoring active IPsec policy and security associations (SAs). You can use both monitoring snap-ins to view the active SAs, but the new one (Windows Firewall With Advanced Security) displays more information. When using these tools, keep the following points in mind:
>
> ■ Although it's true that SAs show up in both places, you should generally use the tool that corresponds to policy creation: Windows Firewall With Advanced Security's Monitor node if you are using Windows Firewall With Advanced Security to create the policy, or IP Security Monitor if you are using IP Security Policies to create the policy. The policy from one snap-in will not show up in the monitor for the other snap-in.
>
> ■ You cannot apply Windows Firewall with Advanced Security policy to older Windows clients—it is for Windows Vista and later only.

Managing Windows Firewall Using Group Policy

The user interface for managing Windows Firewall using Group Policy is basically the same as the Windows Firewall With Advanced Security snap-in with the exception of the Monitoring node and its subnodes, which are available only from the snap-in when managing a single local or remote computer. Figure 27-3 shows a Group Policy Object (GPO) opened from a Windows Vista administrative workstation using the Group Policy Object Editor snap-in.

You can find the policy settings for the Windows Vista version of Windows Firewall in the following location:

Computer Configuration\Policies\Windows Settings\Security Settings\Windows Firewall With Advanced Security\Windows Firewall With Advanced Security

For more information on how to use Group Policy to manage desktop computers running Windows Vista, see Chapter 13, "Managing the Desktop Environment."

> **Note**   On Windows Vista RTM, you couldn't use Resultant Set of Policy (RSoP) to remotely report Windows Firewall policy settings that had been applied to a Windows Vista computer using Group Policy. Instead, you had to use the Windows Firewall With Advanced Security to view the resultant policy settings on a selected remote computer. With Windows Vista SP1, however, the Resultant Set of Policy report was improved, and is now able to show the Windows Firewall policy settings applied using Group Policy. Still, we recommend that you instead use the Windows Firewall With Advanced Security snap-in to view the resultant settings, because it offers more flexible and user-friendly views.

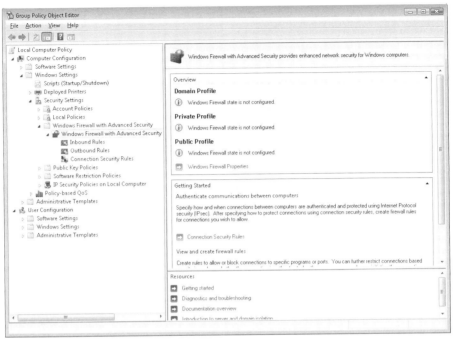

Figure 27-3   Windows Firewall policy settings displayed for a GPO using the Group Policy Object Editor.

Direct from the Source: Managing Windows Firewall and IPsec in Mixed Environments

Windows Vista introduces a lot of new and exciting functionality in Windows Firewall. However, policy created by the new management console, Windows Firewall With Advanced Security, is not understood by earlier versions of Windows.

Using WMI filtering to selectively apply policy to a Group Policy object (GPO) allows you to manage this mixed environment. Through Group Policy Management Console (GPMC), create two GPOs. Use a WMI query to target one of the GPOs to only computers running a version of Windows prior to Windows Vista. In this GPO, create a firewall policy using the Windows Firewall Administrative Template (located under Computer Configuration\Policies\Administrative Templates\Network\Network Connections\ Windows Firewall). Target the second GPO to Windows Vista and later computers. Configure the firewall policy for this GPO using the Windows Firewall with Advanced Security snap-in (located under Computer Configuration\Policies\Windows Settings\ Security Settings\Windows Firewall with Advanced Security).

For several reasons, we recommend that you take the split-GPO approach to firewall management even though Windows Vista understands the Windows Firewall Administrative Template policy. First, by using the Windows Firewall With Advanced Security snap-in for policy configuration instead, you can take advantage of the flexibility and granularity of the new functionality, allowing for rules that are scoped much more than they could be when you use the Windows Firewall Administrative Template. Additionally, Windows Firewall With Advanced Security ships with a number of rule groups that are already configured to provide features and experiences in Windows Vista with the network access they need. Trying to translate these rules into the Windows Firewall Administrative Template is in some cases not possible and in other cases would result in a rule that exposes much more attack surface than the Windows Vista equivalent rule. Finally, earlier versions of Windows Vista may be running different programs or updated versions of the programs for Windows Vista may have different networking requirements, so this split helps ensure that each computer gets only the rules it needs.

For IPsec management, you have a couple of options. If you are not using the new IPsec features in Windows Vista, such as new authentication types or cryptographic options, and would prefer to manage a single IPsec policy for all your client computers, regardless of operating system, create a single GPO for your clients and configure the policy using the IP Security Policies snap-in (located under Computer Configurations\Policies\Windows Settings\Security Settings). To take advantage of the new IPsec features, use the GPO that you created for Windows Vista computers as described previously and configure your IPsec policy using the connection security rules in the Windows Firewall with Advanced Security snap-in. With this approach, be sure to use settings for authentication, key exchange, and data protection that contain at least one suite that is compatible with IPsec in earlier versions of Windows.

For more information on WMI filtering through GPMC, see *http://technet2.microsoft.com/WindowsServer/en/library/6237b9b2-4a21-425e-8976-2065d28b31471033.mspx?mfr=true*.

Sarah Wahlert, Program Manager

Networking Core

Direct from the Source: Mixed Mode Policies Support

On Windows Vista SP1 and Windows Server 2008, Windows Firewall With Advanced Security includes new policy settings to support Suite B algorithms. The inclusion of new capabilities in the policy creates a management concern. How can administrators manage an environment or a network composed of a mixed set of Windows systems?

When this mixed set of systems consists of Windows XP or Windows Server 2003 together with Windows Vista, the recommendation has been either to manage all systems with Windows XP or Windows 2003 Server ADM policies, or to split the environment into two organizational units, one for Windows XP and Windows Server 2003 systems, and one for Windows Vista. Both of these approaches have disadvantages. The first approach has the disadvantage of not using the more advanced and more secure policy features found on Windows Vista systems. The second approach has the disadvantage of administrative overhead. Organizational units were intended to split an environment into business-oriented units such as finance department or production department or human resources department. Using the second approach will further split each of these groupings into two more groups to accommodate policy differences.

On Windows Vista and Windows Vista SP1, a third approach can remedy these disadvantages. It allows a mixed environment composed of Windows Vista and Windows Vista SP1 systems to receive policy constructed on a Windows Vista SP1 console using the features new to Windows Vista SP1. The earlier platform (Windows Vista) will simply ignore the portions it does not understand and implement the remaining policy objects as secure as in its original state. Hence new features will be used when the policy is applied to Windows Vista SP1 systems, but still the same policy will be applicable on lower Windows Vista systems without loss of security.

Specifically, for Windows Vista SP1, you can create a policy to contain suites (proposals) using Suite B algorithms on first and second authentication and on Main Mode and Quick Mode. When this policy is applied on a Windows Vista RTM system, the suites using Suite B algorithms will be simply ignored (or skipped) and the IKE/AuthIP negotiations will use the next available supported suites.

When you remotely manage a Windows Vista SP1 system containing Suite B algorithms from a Windows Vista system, the suites containing Suite B algorithms for first/second authentication and Main Mode and Quick Mode connection security will not be shown. A warning, however, will be given to the user notifying him that a portion of the set is not expressed because it is intended for newer systems versions. (The warning dialog box says "This Policy Contains Settings That Are Not Supported By This Version Of The Interface. These Settings Were Not Imported. All Other Policy Settings Were Successfully Imported.") When you import and export policies, these same messages can be displayed to the user, indicating that an upper-level policy was applied to a lower-level system, or an upper-level policy on an upper-level system was exported on a lower-level box, and hence policy portions were lost.

Gerardo Diaz Cuellar

Software Developer Engineer Technical Lead, Core Networking

Greg Page

Software Developer Engineer in Test, Core Networking

Managing Windows Firewall Using netsh

You can manage Windows Firewall from the command line using the new advfirewall context of the netsh command. To enter the advfirewall context, open a command prompt using administrative credentials and run the command netsh. Within netsh, run advfirewall to enter that context. When you are within this context, you can use any of the commands for that context (see Table 27-24) and for the available subcontexts (see Table 27-25).

> **Note**   The netsh firewall context is a legacy command and is not recommended for use in Windows Vista. Use the netsh advfirewall context instead.

Table 27-24   Commands Available in the netsh advfirewall Context

Command	Description
Import	Imports Windows Firewall policy from the specified file.
Export	Exports current Windows Firewall policy to the specified file.
Show	Displays global settings and the properties for the specified profile or for all profiles.
Set	Sets global or per-profile settings. Use set file to copy the console output to a file; use set machine to set the current computer on which to operate.
Dump	Creates a script that contains the current configuration of the firewall and can be used to restore altered configuration settings.
Reset	Restores the Windows Firewall configuration to its out-of-box policy.
Help or ?	Displays a list of available commands.

Table 27-25   Subcontexts Available in the netsh advfirewall Context

Subcontext	Description
Firewall	Lets you display and configure inbound and outbound firewall rules.
Consec	Lets you display and configure connection security rules.
Monitor	Lets you display or delete all matching security associations or dump their configuration.

> **Note**   To view the available commands for any subcontext, enter that subcontext and type **?** at the command prompt.

Managing Windows Firewall Using Scripts

You can also programmatically manage Windows Firewall using scripts. The new COM APIs for managing Windows Firewall in Windows Vista and Windows Server 2008 are described in the Windows SDK at *http://msdn2.microsoft.com/en-us/library/aa366453.aspx*. MSDN also has samples of how to use the new API to manage Windows Firewall using VBScripts; you can find these samples at *http://msdn2.microsoft.com/en-us/library/bb736292(VS.85).aspx*. Finally, the companion CD for this book also contains scripts that you can use to manage certain aspects of Windows Firewall; see the section titled "On the Companion CD" at the end of this chapter for more information.

Direct from the Source: How Do Windows Firewall Notifications Work?

Windows Firewall Notifications is not a security feature. It is a connectivity feature that helps users realize that the applications they are running are actually blocked from receiving inbound traffic. This feature is enabled by default in Windows Vista and disabled by default on Windows Server 2008. This feature can be toggled per firewall profile using the Windows Firewall Control Panel item, the Windows Firewall With Advanced Security MMC snap-in, the advfirewall netsh extension, or using scripts/programmatically through COM APIs (see the INetFwPolicy2 documentation).

The notifications mechanism works using the following logic:

1. An application either starts listening on a TCP socket or binds to a non-wildcard port on a UDP socket. Because UDP does not have the equivalent of a TCP listen operation, binding to a non-wildcard (specific) port number is used as a heuristic that the application is about to receive traffic on that port.

2. The TCP-listen or UDP-bind operation succeeds.

3. If the application is not interactive (does not have the interactive logon SID) or is a service (either has the Service logon SID or runs as LocalSystem), nothing happens. This is done because services and other noninteractive applications are usually not associated with an active console and displaying a notification in that case is futile.

4. If there's an active inbound firewall rule to allow this application or port, by means of any combination of rule conditions, the application will successfully receive traffic and no user notification is displayed.

5. Else if there's an active inbound firewall rule to block this application or port, by means of any combination of rule conditions, the application will not receive any traffic and no user notification is displayed. The application does not receive any error indication. It simply does not receive inbound traffic to its socket, as if the remote side did not transmit anything.

6. Else start the notification process as follows:

    a. A new local active inbound firewall rule is added to explicitly block this application for TCP and UDP traffic. This is done to make sure the notification is displayed only once per application. Further listen/bind attempts from this application will hit condition 4 listed previously and no further notifications will be displayed.

    b. The firewall service displays a notification dialog box to the user.

    c. If the user clicks the Keep Blocking button, the policy does not change and the dialog box is discarded.

> d. If the user clicks the Unblock button, the new firewall rule is modified from Block to Allow and the dialog box is discarded.
>
> *Eran Yariv*
>
> *Windows Firewall and IPsec Management Development Lead*

Common Management Tasks

The following common management tasks for administering Windows Firewall on Windows Vista computers are illustrated using Windows Firewall With Advanced Security UI (snap-in or Group Policy) and the netsh command. For information about troubleshooting connectivity problems that might be caused by a firewall, refer to Chapter 32, "Troubleshooting Network Issues."

Restore OOB Defaults

To restore the out-of-box default configuration of Windows Firewall, do the following:

■ **From the UI**   Right-click the root node and select Restore Defaults.

> **Caution**   Performing this action from Group Policy Object Editor will also delete all firewall rules and connection security rules that were previously created for the selected Group Policy Object.

■ **Using netsh**   Type **netsh advfirewall reset** at an elevated command prompt.

> **Caution**   Restoring the defaults on a Windows Vista client computer will prevent Windows Firewall on the computer from being remotely managed unless you reopen the Windows Firewall Remote Management rules.

To back up the current firewall configuration before restoring OOB settings, type **netsh advfir wall reset export filename=***path\filename* at an elevated command prompt.

Copy Configuration To Another Computer

In an unmanaged environment, you can copy the Windows Firewall configuration from one Windows Vista computer to other computers by exporting policy from the first computer and importing it into the others.

■ **From the UI**   Right-click the root node, select Export Policy, and specify a location for storing the Windows Firewall Policy (*.wfw) file. Copy the file to a network share or

USB key. On the target computers, right-click the root node, select Import Policy, and select the previously exported policy file.

■ **Using netsh**   Type **netsh advfirewall export** *path\filename* followed by **netsh advfirewall import** *path\filename*.

Enable/Disable a Rule Group

Enabling a rule group is equivalent to opening an exception in the Windows Firewall CPL. This may be necessary to enable some Windows Vista experiences to work properly or when third-party applications require additional firewall configuration to function.

■ **From the UI**   Right-click Inbound Rules and select Filter By Group to display all inbound rules for the rule group. Right-click each rule in the group that belongs to the active profile and then select Enable. (Multiple selection of rules is not supported.) Repeat for Outbound Rules if the rule group has outbound rules in it.

> **Note**   Enabling a rule group is easier using the Windows Firewall CPL—just open the corresponding exception. Note that doing this enables rules only in the group that belongs to the active profile.

■ **Using netsh**   Type **netsh advfirewall firewall set rule group="***name_of_rule_group***"** **enable=yes**.

> **Note**   Using netsh to enable a rule group enables rules within the group for all profiles, not just the active profile. Enabling a rule group using netsh also enables both inbound and outbound rules within the group.

To disable a rule group using netsh, use **enable=no** instead.

Create a New Firewall Rule

Third-party applications may require the configuration of additional firewall rules. The following shows two ways to block outbound traffic on TCP port 80:

■ **From the UI**   Right-click either Inbound Rules or Outbound Rules (depending on the type of rule you need to create) and select New Rule. Proceed through the New Inbound (or New Outbound) Rule Wizard to configure the rule conditions. The new rule is automatically enabled when you finish creating it. For example, to add an outbound rule to block traffic on port 80, select Port, select TCP, type **80**, and then select Block.

■ **Using netsh**   Type **netsh advfirewall firewall add rule name="allow80" protocol=TCP dir=out remoteport=80 action=block**.

> **Note**   For more help, type **netsh advfirewall firewall /?**

Create a New Connection Security Rule

You can use connection security rules to protect network traffic using IPsec.

- **From the UI**   Right-click Connection Security Rules and select New Rule. Proceed through the New Connection Security Rule Wizard to configure the IPsec settings for the rule. For example, to create a connection security rule for domain isolation using the default Computer (Kerberos v5) authentication method, select Isolation, select Require Authentication For Inbound Connections And Request Authentication For Outbound Connections, and then select Default.

- **Using netsh**   Type **netsh advfirewall consec add rule name="isolation" endpoint1=any endpoint2=any action=requireinrequestout**.

> **Note**   For more help, type **netsh advfirewall consec /?**

Turn Off Windows Firewall

Windows Firewall can run concurrently with other firewalls on the computer. Generally, if you install a third-party firewall on Windows Vista, this third-party firewall will use the APIs to automatically disable Windows Firewall. However, if necessary you can manually turn off Windows Firewall. For example, to disable Windows Firewall on a Windows Vista computer where the current network category is Private:

- **From the UI**   Right-click the root node, select Properties, select the tab for the active profile, and then change Firewall State from On to Off.

- **Using netsh**   Type **netsh advfirewall set privateprofile state off**.

  Here are two more useful netsh commands:

  ❑ To show the current state of all firewall profiles on the computer, type **netsh advfirewall show allprofiles state**.

  ❑ To turn off Windows Firewall completely on the computer, type **netsh advfirewall set allprofiles state off**.

> **Caution**   Do not try to disable Windows Firewall by stopping the Windows Firewall service (MspSvc); this service is also required for Windows Service Hardening to function properly.

Summary

The Windows Firewall in Windows Vista has been enhanced in several ways with more granular firewall rules, the ability to block both incoming and outgoing traffic, full support for IPv6, location-aware firewall profiles, network service hardening, and integrated IPsec protection. Using Group Policy, the netsh command, and scripts, administrators can easily manage the configuration of Windows Firewall on Windows Vista client computers across an enterprise.

Additional Resources

The following resources contain additional information and tools related to this chapter.

Related Information

- For information on Windows Firewall, see *http://technet.microsoft.com/en-us/network/bb545423.aspx*.

- For information about IPsec on Microsoft Windows platforms, see *http://technet.microsoft.com/en-us/network/bb531150.aspx*.

- "Step-by-Step Guide to Deploying Policies for Windows Firewall with Advanced Security" available at *http://go.microsoft.com/fwlink/?LinkID=102503*.

- "Windows Firewall with Advanced Security: Diagnostics and Troubleshooting" on Microsoft Technet at *http://technet2.microsoft.com/WindowsVista/en/library/9428d113-ade8-4dbe-ac05-6ef10a6dd7a51033.mspx?mfr=true*.

- Windows Firewall Event Log messages can be found on Microsoft TechNet at *http://technet2.microsoft.com/windowsserver2008/en/library/4e5fac24-08ee-4bd8-b23f-e21e61a3d5bf1033.mspx?mfr=true*.

- Windows Firewall APIs can be found on MSDN at *http://msdn2.microsoft.com/en-us/library/aa366459(VS.85).aspx*.

- KB 555914, "HOWTO: Adding a new rule for the Vista firewall using 'Netsh' command," at *http://support.microsoft.com/kb/555914*.

- KB 942957, "Security rules for Windows Firewall and for IPsec-based connections in Windows Vista and in Windows Server 2008," at *http://support.microsoft.com/kb/942957*.

- KB 929462, "Description of the relationship between Windows Firewall and Windows Security Center in Windows Vista," at *http://support.microsoft.com/kb/929462*.

- KB 938756, "A Windows Vista–based computer that is connected to a domain uses the public profile or the private profile for the Windows Firewall policy instead of the domain profile," at *http://support.microsoft.com/kb/938756*.

- KB 929455, "When you configure a custom location for the Windows Firewall log file in Windows Vista, information may not be written to the log file," at *http://support.microsoft.com/kb/929455*.

- KB 942965, "How the Windows Firewall exception settings in the Group Policy administrative template work together with the Windows Firewall Control Panel program in Windows Vista," at *http://support.microsoft.com/kb/942965*.

- KB 931207, "You cannot visit an Internet Information Services 7.0 Web site from a remote computer," at *http://support.microsoft.com/kb/931207*.

- KB 947045, "A Windows Vista–based or Windows Server 2008–based computer that has MADCAP installed cannot obtain a multicast address from the DHCP server," at *http://support.microsoft.com/kb/947045*.

- KB 947213, "The "netsh firewall" command together with the "profile=all" parameter does not configure the public profile on a Windows Vista–based computer," at *http://support.microsoft.com/kb/947213*.

- KB 922997, "Support WebCast: Improvements and New functionality in IPsec for Windows Vista," at *http://support.microsoft.com/kb/922997*.

- KB 947221, "Message Digest 5 (MD5) and the Data Encryption Standard (DES) have been removed from the default list of IPsec cryptographic algorithms in Windows Vista and in Windows Server 2008," at *http://support.microsoft.com/kb/947211*.

- KB 942963, "The "netsh advfirewall consec" command does not preserve the order of the authentication methods that are specified in a connection security rule on a Windows Vista–based computer," at *http://support.microsoft.com/kb/942963*.

- KB 944335, "The connection fails on a Windows Vista–based computer when you try to communicate with another computer through an IPsec tunnel-mode connection," at *http://support.microsoft.com/kb/944335*.

- KB 926168, "A certificate may not be enrolled, and you do not receive an error message in Windows Vista," at *http://support.microsoft.com/kb/926168*.

- KB 926182, "How to configure verification of additional fields in peer certificates during IKE negotiation for L2TP/IPsec tunnel connections in Windows Vista," at *http://support.microsoft.com/kb/926182*.

On the Companion CD

- EnableRemoteAdmin.vbs
- DisableRemoteAdmin.vbs
- TurnOnWindowsFirewall.vbs
- TurnOffWindowsFIrewall.vbs
- EnablePortException.vbs
- DisablePortException.vbs
- ResetFirewallToDefaults.vbs
- DisplayFirewallStatus.vbs
- ViewFireWallLogging.vbs

Chapter 28

Connecting Remote Users and Networks

Remote connectivity is an important aspect of enterprise networking, and Windows Vista supports several features for achieving it. Using the Connect To option on the Start menu, users can set up and dial a Virtual Private Network (VPN) connection to a corporate network, or a broadband or dial-up connection to the Internet. Windows Vista can also accept incoming connections over dial-up or VPN connections and thus act as a mini-RAS (remote access server) to other computers. Finally, Remote Desktop and Remote Desktop Connection allow users to remotely connect to their computers over any network connection and work as though they were interactively logged on to their computers. This chapter covers all these remote connectivity features and explains how they have been enhanced over previous Windows platforms.

Understanding Connection Types

Windows Vista supports both outgoing and incoming network connections. For outgoing connections, the Windows Vista computer acts as a client that connects to a remote computer, server, or network to access remote resources. For incoming connections, Windows Vista acts as a server to allow other computers to connect to the computer and access resources on it.

Outgoing Connection Types

Windows Vista supports a number of different types of outgoing (client-side) network connections:

- **LAN or high-speed Internet connection** A connection to an Ethernet local area network (LAN) or broadband router providing high-speed access to the Internet. LAN connections are computer-to-network connections that Windows Vista creates automatically when it detects the presence of an installed network interface card (NIC). Internet connections are computer-to-network connections that you can create and configure manually using the Connect To A Network Wizard to provide Internet access using a broadband Digital Subscriber Line (DSL) adapter or cable modem, an Integrated Services Digital Network (ISDN) modem, or an analog (dial-up) modem. Broadband Internet connections use Point-to-Point Protocol over Ethernet (PPPoE); dial-up Internet connections use Point-to-Point Protocol (PPP).

- **Wireless network connection** A connection to a wireless local area network (WLAN) through a wireless access point (AP) or wireless router. Wireless network connections are computer-to-network connections that you can create and configure manually using the Connect To A Network Wizard, provided that the computer has a wireless network adapter installed. Wireless network connections may be either secured or unsecured, depending on how the access point has been configured.

- **Wireless ad hoc connection** A connection to another computer that is enabled for wireless networking. Wireless ad hoc connections are temporary computer-to-computer connections that you can use to share files between users or share an Internet connection on one of the computers.

- **Wireless router or access point** A device used to network together wireless-enabled computers primarily for Small Office/Home Office (SOHO) environments so that users can share files and printers and connectivity to the Internet. Setting up this type of connection in Windows Vista using the Connect To A Network Wizard requires that the computer have a wireless network adapter installed or attached to the computer and the presence of an external wireless router or wireless access point device that can be configured.

- **Dial-up connection** A connection to a remote access server (RAS server) or modem pool at a remote location. Dial-up connections are computer-to-server or computer-to-network connections that you can create and configure manually using the Connect To A Network Wizard, provided that the computer has an analog or ISDN modem installed or connected to it. Dial-up connections either provide remote access to corporate networks or dial-up access to the Internet using the services of an Internet Service Provider (ISP).

- **Virtual Private Network connection** A connection to a remote workplace by tunneling over the Internet. VPN connections work by creating a secure tunnel that encapsulates and encrypts all traffic between the client computer and the remote corporate network. This tunnel creates a secure private link over a shared public infrastructure such as the Internet. After the user is connected, her experience on the client computer is similar to her computer being directly attached to the remote LAN (with performance limitations depending on the speed of the remote connection), with the exception of any restrictions imposed on remote connections by the network administrator. VPN connections are computer-to-server or computer-to-network connections that you can create and configure manually using the Connect To A Network Wizard and which can use either Internet connectivity or establish an existing broadband Internet connection or an existing analog or ISDN dial-up connection to obtain the Internet connectivity they require.

This chapter describes how to create and manage outgoing VPN and dial-up connections. For information about LAN and wireless connections in Windows Vista, see Chapter 26, "Configuring Windows Networking."

Incoming Connection Types

Windows Vista also supports the following types of incoming (server-side) network connections:

- **Incoming VPN connection**   A connection from a remote computer by tunneling over the Internet, either using a broadband Internet connection or a dial-up connection to an ISP

- **Incoming dial-up connection**   A connection from a remote computer using an analog or ISDN modem

For more information on how to create and configure incoming connections, see the section titled "Configuring Incoming Connections" later in this chapter.

Deprecated Connection Types

The following connection technologies supported in Windows XP have been deprecated in Windows Vista and are no longer available for VPN connections:

- X.25

- Microsoft Ethernet PVC

- Direct cable connection using a serial, parallel, USB, or IEEE 1394 cable

Note   Most types of network connections available in Windows Vista now support IPv6 out of the box and can be used to establish pure-IPv6 connectivity with remote servers or networks (provided they support incoming IPv6 connections). More information concerning IPv6 support for network connections in Windows Vista is provided throughout this chapter where appropriate.

Configuring Virtual Private Network Connections

Windows Vista supports both outgoing and incoming VPN connections. For outgoing connections, Windows Vista is the client and connects to a VPN server on a remote network, usually the corporate intranet. For incoming connections, Windows Vista acts as a server and allows a remote client computer to establish a VPN connection between the two computers. In enterprise environments, outgoing VPN connections are commonly used to allow mobile users to securely access resources on the corporate intranet from remote locations. Incoming VPN connections to client computers are rarely used in enterprise environments, so most of this discussion deals with outbound connections only. For information on how to create and configure an inbound connection on Windows Vista, see the section titled "Configuring Incoming Connections" later in this chapter.

Supported Tunneling Protocols

With the release of Service Pack 1, Windows Vista supports three tunneling protocols for creating secure VPN connections to remote corporate networks:

- **Point-to-Point Tunneling Protocol (PPTP)**   An open industry standard developed by Microsoft and others, PPTP provides tunneling over PPP frames (which themselves encapsulate other network protocols such as IP) and uses PPP authentication, compression, and encryption schemes. PPTP was first introduced in Windows NT 4.0 and is simpler to set up than L2TP but does not provide the same level of security as L2TP.

- **Layer Two Tunneling Protocol (L2TP)**   An industry-standard Internet tunneling protocol designed to run natively over IP networks and which encapsulates PPP frames like PPTP does. Security for L2TP VPN connections is provided by Internet Protocol security (IPsec), which provides the authentication, data integrity, and encryption needed to ensure that L2TP tunnels are protected. The combination of L2TP with IPsec for tunneling purposes is usually referred to as L2TP over IPsec or L2TP/IPsec.

- **Secure Socket Tunneling Protocol (SSTP)**   A new tunneling protocol added in Service Pack 1 that encapsulates PPP frames over HTTPS (HTTP over SSL) and facilitates VPN connectivity if the client is behind a firewall, NAT, or web proxy that allows outgoing TCP connection over port 443. The SSL layer provides data integrity and encryption while PPP provides user authentication. SSTP was introduced in Windows Vista Service Pack 1 and Windows Server 2008.

Note   For more information about deploying SSTP, see the section titled "Additional Resources" at the end of this chapter.

Enhancements to VPN Security in Windows Vista

VPN security using PPTP, L2TP/IPsec, and SSTP in Windows Vista has been enhanced by changes made to the cryptographic algorithms used for authentication, data integrity, and encryption.

Support for Advanced Encryption Standard

Support for Advanced Encryption Standard (AES) has been added to Windows Vista and Windows Server 2008. AES is a Federal Information Processing Standard (FIPS) encryption standard developed by the National Institute of Standards and Technology (NIST) that supports variable key lengths and that replaces Data Encryption Standard (DES) as the standard encryption algorithm for government and industry. For L2TP/IPsec-based VPN connections, the following AES encryption levels are supported:

- **Main Mode**   IPsec Main Mode supports AES 256- and 128-bit encryption using Elliptical Curve Diffie-Hellman (ECDH) with 384 and 256 bit respectively.

- **Quick Mode**   IPsec Quick Mode supports AES 128-bit and 3DES encryption when the encryption setting inside the Advanced Security Settings properties of the VPN connection is either Optional Encryption or Require Encryption. IPsec quick mode supports AES 256-bit and 3DES encryption when the encryption setting inside the Advanced Security Settings properties is Maximum Strength Encryption.

Note   Using AES is a requirement for many U.S. government agencies.

Weak Cryptography Removal from PPTP/L2TP

Support for weak or nonstandard cryptographic algorithms has been removed from Windows Vista. This initiative is based on a desire by Microsoft to move customers toward stronger crypto algorithms to increase VPN security, based on recommendations by the National Institute of Standards and Technology (NIST) and the Internet Engineering Task Force (IETF) as well as mandates toward stronger crypto algorithms from different industry standards bodies and regulators.

The following crypto algorithms are no longer supported on either Windows Vista or Windows Server 2008:

- 40- and 56-bit RC4 encryption, formerly used by the Microsoft Point-to-Point Encryption Protocol (MPPE) for PPTP-based VPN connections

- DES encryption, formerly used by IPsec policy within L2TP/IPsec-based VPN connections

- MD5 integrity checking, formerly used by IPsec policy within L2TP/IPsec-based VPN connections

The removal of support from the default configuration for 40- and 56-bit RC4 encryption means that PPTP-based VPN connections in Windows Vista now support only 128-bit RC4 for data encryption and integrity checking. This means the encryption strength remains the same as 128-bit RC4—that is, independent of the encryption settings (Optional Encryption, Require Encryption, or Maximum Strength Encryption) specified by the Advanced Security Settings properties of the VPN connections. This also means that if your existing VPN server does not support 128-bit encryption and supports only incoming PPTP-based VPN connections, Windows Vista clients will not be able to connect. If you are unable to upgrade your existing VPN servers to support 128-bit for PPTP, or if 128-bit encryption is unavailable to you because of export restrictions, you can enable weak crypto for PPTP by editing the following registry value:

HKLM\System\CurrentControlSet\Services\Rasman\Parameters\AllowPPTPWeakCrypto

The default value of this DWORD registry value is 0, and by changing it to 1, you can enable 40- and 56-bit RC4 encryption on the computer for both outgoing and incoming PPTP-based VPN connections. You must restart the computer for this registry change to take effect. As an alternative to restarting the computer, you can restart the Remote Access Connection Manager service by opening a command prompt and typing **net stop rasman** followed by **net start rasman**.

The removal of support for DES encryption and MD5 integrity checking for L2TP/IPsec-based VPN connections means that L2TP/IPsec-based VPN connections in Windows Vista now support the following data encryption and data integrity algorithms by default:

- 128-bit AES, 256-bit AES, and 3DES for data encryption using IPsec
- SHA1 for data integrity using IPsec

The removal of support for DES and MD5 from the default configuration means that L2TP/IPsec-based VPN connections in Windows Vista will not work if your existing VPN server supports only DES for data encryption and/or MD5 for data integrity checking. If you are unable to upgrade your existing VPN servers to support AES or 3DES for data encryption and/or SHA1 for integrity checking, or if these crypto algorithms are unavailable to you because of export restrictions, you can disable weak crypto for L2TP by editing the following registry value:

HKLM\System\CurrentControlSet\Services\Rasman\Parameters\AllowL2TPWeakCrypto

The default value of this DWORD registry value is 0, and by changing it to 1, you can enable DES encryption and MD5 integrity checking on the computer for both outgoing and incoming L2TP/IPsec-based VPN connections. You must restart the computer for this registry change to take effect. As an alternative to restarting the computer, you can restart the Remote Access Connection Manager service by opening a command prompt and typing **net stop rasman** followed by **net start rasman**.

> **Note**   Microsoft recommends that you upgrade your VPN server to support 128-bit RC4 for PPTP and/or AES and SHA1 for L2TP instead of disabling weak crypto support on your Windows Vista clients.

Table 28-1 summarizes the differences between Windows Vista and Windows XP with regard to crypto support for data integrity and encryption for VPN connections.

Table 28-1   Data Integrity and Encryption Support for VPN Connections in Windows Vista vs. Windows XP

Crypto Algorithm	Use	Windows Vista	Windows XP
40-bit RC4	Data encryption and integrity checking for PPTP		✓
56-bit RC4	Data encryption and integrity checking for PPTP		✓
128-bit RC4	Data encryption and integrity checking for PPTP	✓	✓
DES	Data encryption for L2TP/Ipsec		✓
3DES	Data encryption for L2TP/Ipsec	✓	✓
128-bit AES	Data encryption for L2TP/Ipsec	✓	
256-bit AES	Data encryption for L2TP/Ipsec	✓	
MD5	Integrity checking for L2TP/Ipsec		✓
SHA1	Integrity checking for L2TP/Ipsec	✓	✓

Supported Authentication Protocols

The following authentication protocols are supported for logon security for VPN connections in Windows Vista:

- **PAP**   Password Authentication Protocol. Uses plaintext (unencrypted) passwords.

- **CHAP**   Challenge Handshake Authentication Protocol. Uses one-way MD5 hashing with challenge-response authentication.

- **MS-CHAPv2**   Microsoft Challenge Handshake Authentication Protocol version 2. An extension by Microsoft of the CHAP authentication protocol that provides mutual authentication of Windows-based computers and stronger data encryption. MS-CHAPv2 is an enhancement of the earlier MS-CHAP protocol that provided only one-way authentication of the client by the server.

- **EAP**   Extensible Authentication Protocol. Extends PPP by adding support for additional authentication methods including using smart cards and certificates.

- **PEAP**   Protected Extensible Authentication Protocol or Protected EAP. Enhances the protection provided by EAP by using Transport Layer Security (TLS) to provide a secure channel for EAP negotiation. PEAP is also used in Windows Vista to support Network Access Protection (NAP) scenarios. For more information, see the section titled "Configuring Network Access Protection Settings" later in this chapter.

The following authentication protocols have been deprecated in Windows Vista for use by VPN connections:

- SPAP (Shiva Password Authentication Protocol)
- MS-CHAP
- EAP using MD5

Note that by default PAP and CHAP are not enabled as authentication protocols on new VPN connections you create using the Connect To A Network Wizard. This is because PAP and CHAP are not considered secure; use them only when connecting to ISPs whose network access devices support only these legacy authentication schemes. And although PPTP in Windows Vista no longer supports MD5 for data integrity checking using L2TP/IPsec-based VPN connections, support for MD5 usage in CHAP has been maintained because of the continuing popularity of this authentication protocol with many broadband- and dialup-based ISPs.

Table 28-2 summarizes the differences between Windows Vista and Windows XP with regard to user authentication protocols used for VPN connections.

> **Note**   In addition to the user authentication protocols listed in Table 28-2, L2TP/IPsec also supports machine-level authentication (using either preshared keys or machine certificates), and SSTP supports the client validating the server (using the certificate sent by server to the client during the SSL negotiation phase).

Table 28-2   Authentication Protocols Supported for VPN Connections in Windows Vista vs. Windows XP

Authentication Protocol	Windows Vista	Windows XP
PAP	✓	✓
SPAP		✓
CHAP	✓	✓
MS-CHAP		✓
MS-CHAPv2	✓	✓
EAP with MD5 challenge		✓
EAP with smart card	✓	✓
EAP with other certificate	✓	✓
PEAP	✓	

Direct from the Source: VPN Security Enhancements in Windows Vista

In Windows Vista, many extensions have been made regarding VPN security. First, all the weak crypto algorithms have been removed and new stronger crypto algorithms have been added to VPN tunnels. For PPTP, 40/56-bit RC4 encryption has been removed by default. This means PPTP now supports only 128-bit RC4 encryption by default. So if your VPN server or VPN client doesn't support 128-bit encryption, your calls may fail. You can still get 40/56-bit RC4 back by changing a registry key, but this is not recommended. It is better to upgrade your client or server to one that supports the more secure 128-bit RC4 encryption method.

For L2TP/IPsec, DES (for encryption) and MD5 (for integrity check) have been removed, but AES support has been added. This means that Windows Vista supports AES 128-bit, AES 256-bit, and 3DES for encryption, and SHA1 for integrity check. (AES is more CPU-efficient than 3DES.) So if your VPN server or VPN client doesn't support either DES or MD5, your connectivity may fail. You can still get DES and MD5 back by changing a registry key, but this is not recommended. It is better to upgrade your client or server to one that supports the more secure AES/3DES and SHA1 encryption methods.

Second, many new authentication algorithms have been added; EAP-MD5, SPAP, and MSCHAPv1 are now deprecated. Windows Vista supports (in increasing order of strength) PAP, CHAP, MSCHAPv2, EAP-MSCHAPv2, EAP-smartcard/certificate, PEAP-MSCHAPv2, and PEAP-smartcard/certificate. Using PAP or CHAP as an authentication algorithm over VPN tunnel is not recommended because it is weaker than other authentication algorithms. Arguably, it might be safe to use PAP/CHAP over a L2TP/IPsec VPN connection because IPsec provides a secure session before PPP authentication kicks in. But always remember this subtle security point: IPsec provides you with machine-level authentication, whereas PPP authentication provides you with user-level authentication, and both are important.

Finally, the L2TP/IPsec client in Windows Vista has added more verification of specific fields inside the server certificate used for IPsec negotiation to avoid the trusted man-in-the-middle (TMITM) attack. The L2TP/IPsec client checks for the SAN field in the server's X.509 certificate to verify that the server you are connecting to is the same as the server that was issued the certificate. It also checks for the EKU field to validate that the certificate issued to the server is for the purpose of server authentication. For legacy deployments, Windows Vista provides a registry key that if enabled will allow the VPN client to override the verification of the SAN and EKU fields of the server's certificate. However, it is recommended that you not override these checks. Instead, if your VPN server offering L2TP/IPsec connectivity has X.509 certificates issued to it that do not have the DNS name of the server in the SAN field, it is recommended that you reissue appropriately configured certificates to the server.

Samir Jain and Santosh Chandwai

Lead Program Managers for Windows Enterprise Networking

VPN Connection Negotiation Process

When a Windows Vista client tries to establish a connection with a remote VPN server, the tunneling protocol, authentication protocol, data encryption algorithm, and integrity-checking algorithm used depend on several factors:

- The enabled authentication protocols and crypto algorithms on the client side
- The remote access policy on the server side
- The available network transports (IPv4 and/or IPv6)

By default, if Type Of VPN is set to Automatic on the client side, the Windows Vista client attempts to establish a connection with the remote VPN server in the following order (provided that the DNS resolution of the VPN server name returns both IPv4 and IPv6 addresses—if only one type of address is returned, the steps that correspond to the other type of address are skipped):

1. PPTP using the IPv4 address of the VPN server. If this fails, the next type of connection is attempted.

2. L2TP/IPsec using the IPv4 address of the VPN server. If this fails, the next type of connection is attempted.

3. SSTP using the IPv4 address of the VPN server. If this fails, the next type of connection is attempted.

4. L2TP/IPsec using the IPv6 address of the VPN server. If this fails, the next type of connection is attempted.

5. SSTP using the IPv6 address of the VPN server.

> **Note**   Windows Vista supports L2TP/IPsec-based and SSTP-based VPN connections over both IPv4- and IPv6-based networks. PPTP-based VPN connections are supported only over IPv4-based networks, not over IPv6-based networks.

After a tunneling protocol has been selected for the connection, the authentication and crypto algorithms are then negotiated between the client and the server. For more information on configuring authentication and crypto algorithms on the client side, see the section titled "Configuring Connection Security Settings" later in this chapter.

> **Note**   You can reduce connection time by explicitly specifying the tunneling protocol you want your client to use (provided that the remote server also supports this protocol) instead of selecting the Automatic type of VPN on the Networking tab of the connection's properties. You can also specify the specific tunneling protocol used or which tunneling protocol to start with if the connections are created on the server side using Connection Manager Administration Kit (CMAK). For more information, see the section titled "Reducing Connection Time" later in this chapter.

Creating and Configuring VPN Connections

The new Connect To A Network Wizard in Windows Vista simplifies the task of creating VPN connections. The screens displayed when you use this wizard vary depending on the choices you make as you proceed through the wizard.

In addition to creating and configuring new connections on Windows Vista client computers, administrators can use the new version of the Connection Manager Administration Kit (CMAK) included with Windows Server 2008. CMAK is a set of tools that you can use to tailor the appearance and behavior of connections made using Connection Manager, the built-in remote access client dialer included in Windows Vista. Using CMAK, administrators can create and deploy custom connections for client computers to simplify the user experience of connecting to remote networks.

Note   You must use the new Windows Server 2008 version of CMAK to create and configure connections for Windows Vista clients. This is because the new CMAK includes multiple-locale support you can use to create Connection Manager profiles on a server of any locale for installation on a client of any other locale.

Creating a VPN Connection

To create a new VPN connection on a computer if you already have a broadband (PPPoE) or dial-up connection to the Internet, follow these steps:

1.   From the Start menu, select Connect To.

2.   In the Connect To A Network Wizard, click Set Up A Connection Or Network on the This Computer Is Connected To Network page.

3.   On the Choose A Connection Option page, select Connect To A Workplace and then click Next.

4.   If this is the first connection you have created on the computer, proceed to step 5. Otherwise, select Yes, I'll Choose An Existing Connection and then select one of the existing connections displayed on the Do You Want To Use A Connection That You Already Have page. For example, if you want to use an existing dial-up connection (analog or ISDN modem) to provide Internet access for your new VPN connection, select that connection and then click Dial when the Connect dialog box is displayed for that connection. After you've used your existing connection to connect to the Internet, you can continue setting up your new VPN connection.

5.   Click Use My Internet Connection (VPN).

6.   Specify the IPv4 or IPv6 address or fully qualified domain name of the remote VPN server you want to connect to. You can also give the connection a descriptive name to distinguish it from other connections on the computer. Typically, this will be the name of your remote network or remote VPN server.

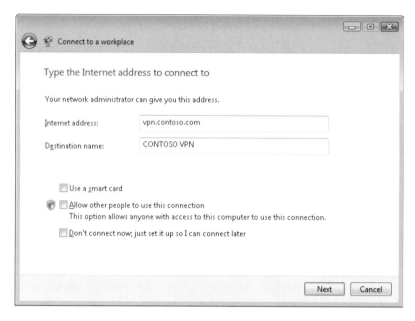

7. To use a smart card for authentication, select Use A Smart Card. You must have a smart card reader installed on the computer to use this option. If you select this option, proceed to step 10.

8. To allow other users of the computer to use the connection, select Allow Other People To Use This Connection. Selecting this option requires that you have local administrator credentials for the computer so that you can respond to the UAC prompt that appears. Selecting this option also configures your connection to be of the All Users type, rather than a Private connection, which can be used only by the user who created it. The All Users connection type is also used for Windows logon over your VPN connection.

9. To create a new connection that needs further configuration before you can use it, select Don't Connect Now Just Set It Up So I Can Connect Later.

10. Click Next and specify the credentials (user name, password, and optionally the domain) you will use to be authenticated by the remote VPN server. (This option is available only if you left the Use A Smart Card option cleared earlier in the wizard.)

11. If you chose to create a connection that needs further configuring before being used, click Create and then either click Close to create the connection or click Connect Now to initiate the connection.

 Note You can also start the Connect To A Network Wizard by right-clicking the network icon in the notification area and selecting Connect To A Network.

Initiating a Connection

To initiate a previously created connection, do one of the following:

- Start the Connect To A Network Wizard, select the connection, and then click Connect.

- Open the Network Connections folder, double-click the connection, and then click Connect.

Note You can also drag a connection to the desktop from either the Network Connections folder or the Connect To A Network Wizard to create a shortcut to your connection. You can then initiate your connection by double-clicking the shortcut and then clicking Connect.

Terminating a Connection

To disconnect an active connection, do one of the following:

- Start the Connect To A Network Wizard, select the connection, and then click Disconnect.

- Right-click the network icon in the notification area, select Disconnect From, and then select the connection.

Note Windows Vista supports Fast User Switching (FUS) on both domain-joined and workgroup computers. Active VPN connections of the all-users variety are not terminated when you switch your computer to another user.

Direct from the Source: Using a VPN Connection at Logon

To establish a RAS (VPN or Dial-Up) connection during logon, or to log on to a domain over a RAS connection, the user must have a connection for use by all users on the computer (called an All-User connection). To log on to a domain over a RAS connection, follow these steps:

1. On the Logon screen, click the Network Logon icon in the lower-right corner. This will display tiles representing each of the All-User connections that can be dialed during logon.

2. Click the tile representing the connection you want to dial. This will display the user interface for entering the connection credentials.

3. If the RAS connection requires a smartcard and you want to use user name/ password for logging on to Windows, select the Use Password For Logon To Windows check box below the RAS credential user interface. This will display the user interface for entering the user name and password that will be used for Winlogon.

4. Similarly, if the RAS connection requires user name/password and you want to use a smartcard for logging on to Windows, select the Use Smartcard For Logon To Windows check box below the RAS credential to display the smartcard user interface.

If both the RAS connection and logon to Windows require the same type of credentials, Windows will by default attempt to use the same credentials for establishing the RAS connection and for Winlogon. If the credentials required are different, you will establish a successful RAS connection, but logon to Windows will fail and the following error message will be displayed: "The network connection has been established successfully, but the logon to the local machine has failed using the credentials provided. Please click OK to retry logon to Windows." Clicking OK will give you the opportunity to enter the appropriate credentials for logging on to Windows.

5. If the RAS connection has been successfully established but the logon to Windows has failed, and you want to disconnect the RAS connection instead, click Disconnect Network Connection on the logon screen.

Santosh Chandwani

Lead Program Manager for Windows Enterprise Networking

Viewing Connection Details

You can view the state of connections on the computer by starting the Connect To A Network Wizard. A connection that has been established will be displayed as Connected (Figure 28-1).

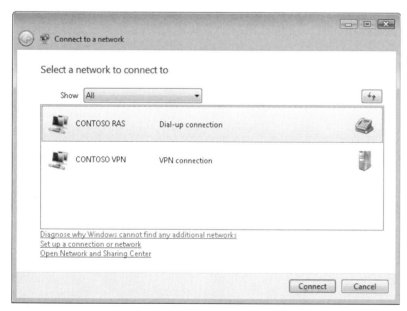

Figure 28-1 Using the Connect To A Network Wizard to view connection state.

You can display more details concerning connections (both active and inactive) by using the Network Connections folder and selecting Details from the Views menu. Using this method, you can view the connection status, device name, connectivity, network category, owner, type, and phone number of host address of the remote server (Figure 28-2).

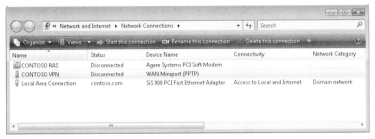

Figure 28-2   Using the Network Connections folder to view detailed information about connections.

> **Note**   You can view additional details of the status of a connection from the Network Connections folder by right-clicking the connection and then selecting Status.

Configuring a VPN Connection

To configure the settings of a connection that you have already created, open its Properties dialog box by doing one of the following:

- Start the Connect To A Network Wizard and then right-click the connection and select Properties.

- Click Start, click Network, click Network And Sharing Center, click Manage Network Connections under Tasks, and then right-click the connection and select Properties.

- At a command prompt or in the Start Search box, type **ncpa.cpl**, press Enter, and then right-click the connection and select Properties.

The properties sheet for configuring a VPN connection has five tabs, as shown in Figure 28-3.

Figure 28-3   Configuring the properties of a connection.

- **General**   Specify host name or IP address (IPv4 or IPv6) of the remote VPN server and whether to use another connection first to establish Internet connectivity before initiating the VPN connection.

- **Options**   Specify dialing options, redialing options, and PPP settings.

- **Security**   Specify authentication and data encryption settings.

- **Networking**   Specify the tunneling protocol(s) used (PPTP, L2TP/IPsec, SSTP, or Automatic), IP address settings (static or DHCP), and IPsec settings (for L2TP/IPsec-based connections only).

- **Sharing**   Enable Internet Connection Sharing for the connection and specify whether to dial another connection to establish Internet connectivity before initiating this connection.

For more information about configuring connection properties, use Help And Support. Some specific configuration options are discussed in the next section.

Configuring Connection Security Settings

The default authentication settings for a connection vary depending on the choices you make when you use the Connect To A Network Wizard to create the connection. For example, if you select the option to use a smart card, EAP will be used as the authentication protocol. If, however, you leave the smart card option cleared, MS-CHAPv2 will be used instead for authentication.

To configure the security settings for a connection, click the Security tab of the connection's Properties sheet, shown in Figure 28-4.

Figure 28-4   Configuring the security settings of a connection.

You have three basic ways to configure connection security on this tab:

- **Typical—Require Secured Password**   This is the resulting setting if you did not select the option to use a smart card when you created the connection. The resulting connection uses MS-CHAPv2 to authenticate the connection with the remote server. If you also select the option Automatically Use My Windows Logon Name And Password (And Domain If Any), the connection will attempt to use your Windows credentials to authenticate. If you do not select this additional option, the credentials you specified when you created the connection are used instead.

  If you also leave the Require Data Encryption (Disconnect If None) option selected (the default), the connection will disconnect during the negotiation process if the server declines to use encryption. If, however, you clear this option, the connection will support CHAP in addition to MS-CHAPv2 and will connect to the remote server even if no encryption is available on the server.

- **Typical—Use Smart Card**   This is the resulting setting if you selected the option to use a smart card when you created the connection. The resulting connection uses EAP to authenticate the connection with the remote server using the certificate stored on the smart card. The option to Automatically Use My Windows Logon Name And Password (And Domain If Any) is not available if you selected this option. If you also leave the Require Data Encryption (Disconnect If None) option selected (the default), the connection will disconnect during the negotiation process if the server declines to use encryption. If, however, you clear this option, the connection will connect to the remote server even if no encryption is available on the server.

■ **Advanced (Custom Settings)**   Choose this option to configure advanced security settings for data encryption and authentication as desired:

For example, you can specify that the connection should use the strongest encryption possible, use any level of encryption available, optionally use encryption if available, or never use encryption even if the server supports it. The default setting is Require Encryption (Disconnect If Server Declines). For logon security, you can choose any one of the following:

❑   EAP–Smart Card Or Other Certificate (Encryption Enabled)

❑   Protected EAP (PEAP) (Encryption Enabled)

❑   MS-CHAPv2

If you select the Use Extensible Authentication Protocol (EAP) option with Smart Card Or Other Certificate (Encryption Enabled) selected, you can click Properties to configure additional security settings for the connection:

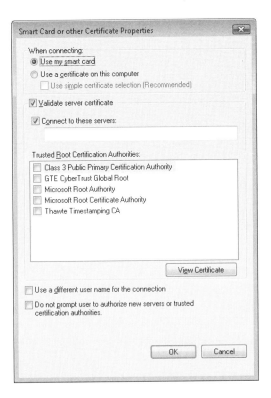

For example, if you are using certificates stored on the local computer rather than smart cards, you can select the Use A Certificate On This Computer option to enable certificates to be used for authenticating VPN connections. Selecting the Use Simple Certificate Selection (Recommended) option enables Windows Vista to determine which certificate on the computer should be used for VPN authentication.

Selecting the Valid Server Certificate option forces the client computer to verify that the certificate of the remote VPN server is valid (this option is selected by default). You should also specify the trusted root authorities you want the client computer to trust, and you can optionally specify the IP address or fully qualified domain name of your CA in the Connect To These Servers text box.

How It Works: Client-Side and Server-Side Encryption/ Authentication Settings

Understanding how to configure client- and server-side encryption and authentication settings for VPN connections is important—here's a quick guide.

Where Do You Select Encryption/Authentication Settings on the Client Side, and How Do These Settings Take Effect?

Open the properties of a VPN connection, click the Security tab, click Advanced, click Settings, and you'll see the data encryption settings in the top half of the properties sheet. It doesn't display your encryption algorithm, but it does display the action you want to take in each case. Why? Because the code is intelligent enough to select the encryption algorithms automatically. For example, in Windows Vista, PPTP always uses 128-bit RC4, whether in optional or require or maximum. And in Windows Vista, L2TP/IPsec will propose to the other side of the connection AES 128 and 3DES for optional or require mode and will propose AES 256 and 3DES in the case of maximum encryption. Based on what both sides of the connection propose, the common encryption algorithm with highest security is picked up.

Where Do You Select the Authentication Settings on the Server Side, and How Does This Work?

The authentication settings are configured inside the RRAS server (on the Security tab) and in the corresponding remote access policies (inside the RADIUS server). If the RADIUS server (the network policy server, or NPS) and the RRAS server reside on the same server, the authentication settings inside the RRAS server are disabled.

Where Do You Select the Encryption Settings on the Server Side, and How Does It Work?

The answer to this depends on which tunneling protocol you're using, specifically:

- **PPTP scenario** By default, when a Windows Server 2008 computer configured for RRAS-based VPN server starts, it accepts PPTP connections with only 128-bit MPPE encryption. When the client connects, the PPTP tunnel is established, and during the PPP authentication phase, RRAS will talk to the RADIUS server and get the encryption policy setting. Then during the PPP MPPE phase, RRAS ensures that the relevant encryption algorithm is negotiated.

- **L2TP IPsec scenario** By default, when a Windows Server 2008 computer configured for RRAS-based VPN server starts, it adds an IPsec policy to accept connections for all encryption algorithms (AES 256, AES 128, 3DES) because it doesn't know what the client is going to propose. But the server has one more policy setting that comes from the RADIUS server: the Encryption Type setting (which is No Encryption, Basic, Strong, or Strongest). When the client connects, an IPsec tunnel is established, and then IPSec gets latched onto one particular encryption algorithm. Then, during the PPP authentication phase, RRAS will talk to the RADIUS server and get the encryption policy setting. Then RRAS reads the encryption algorithm, which is negotiated at the IPsec level, and compares this against what the policy is saying. For example, if policy is saying Maximum and you have negotiated DES, your connection will fail. AES-128/3DES falls under the Basic and Strong encryption types, and AES-256/3DES falls under the Strongest encryption setting.

Samir Jain

Lead Program Manager for Enterprise Networking (RRAS)

Configuring Network Access Protection Settings

Network Access Protection (NAP) is a strategy that helps protect network resources by forcing computers connecting to the network to comply with predefined computer health requirements. These health requirements can include policies such as ensuring that the connecting computers have the necessary software updates, the latest antivirus signatures, the necessary certificates, and so on. If a computer attempting to connect to the network does not comply with all health requirements, the NAP enforcement mechanism can either prevent the computer from establishing a connection to the network until it becomes compliant, or it can force compliance by downloading and installing the appropriate updates, signatures, and so on to the computer. NAP does not prevent malicious users or rogue computers from accessing domain resources, but it does help maintain your network's overall integrity by maintaining the health of computers on your network. This NAP policy enforcement platform is built into the Windows Vista and Windows Server 2008 operating systems.

To enable NAP health policy enforcement for VPN connections on Windows Vista client computers, follow these steps:

1. Click Start, type **services.msc** in the Start Search box, press Enter, and then respond to the UAC prompt that appears.

2. In the Services console, double-click the Network Access Protection Agent service and then change the Startup type from Manual to Automatic.

3. Click Start, type **napclcfg.msc** in the Start Search box, press Enter, and then respond to the UAC prompt that appears.

4. Select Enforcement Clients in the console tree. In the details pane, right-click Remote Access Quarantine Enforcement Client and then select Enable:

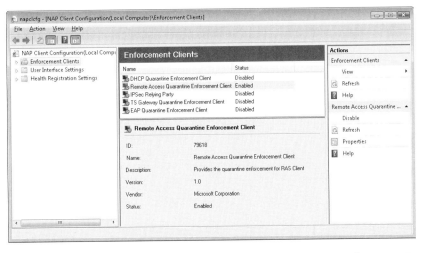

5. Restart the computer to apply the changes, open the properties of your VPN connection, and then click the Security tab (see Figure 28-4).

6. Select Advanced (Custom Settings) and then click Settings to open Advanced Security Settings.

7. Under Logon Security, select Use Extensible Authentication Protocol (EAP).

8. Select Protected EAP (PEAP) (encryption enabled) and then click Properties to open the Protected EAP Properties sheet.

9. Select the Enable Quarantine Checks option to enable support for NAP health policy enforcement:

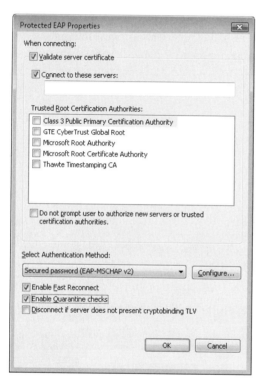

Note   You also must configure the server side of your NAP infrastructure using Windows Server 2008. For more information, see the white paper "Step-by-Step Guide: Demonstrate NAP VPN Enforcement in a Test Lab," which is available from the Microsoft Download Center at *http://www.microsoft.com/downloads/details.aspx?FamilyID=729bba00-55ad-4199-b441-378cc3d900a7&displaylang=en*. For more information on how NAP works and how to implement it in various scenarios, see *http://technet.microsoft.com/en-us/network/bb545879.aspx* on Microsoft TechNet.

Note the two additional settings at the bottom of the Advanced Security Settings dialog box. These settings are new in Windows Vista and configuring them does the following:

■ **Enable Fast Reconnect**   Enables an EAP authentication to occur very rapidly. (For PEAP, this means the inner authentication is skipped—it works after one successful authentication.)

■ **Disconnect If Server Does Not Present Cryptobinding TLV**   Reduces the risk of a man-in-the-middle attack where the tunnel and inner authentication originate on separate computers by ensuring that both the tunnel and the inner authentication originate on the same computer and not on separate computers.

> **Note**   These two new settings are useful for PEAP in general and not just for VPNs or for NAP.

Reducing Connection Time

You can reduce connection time by specifying the tunneling protocol you want your client to use (provided that the remote server also supports this protocol). To specify a tunneling protocol for a connection, follow these steps:

1. Open the properties of your VPN connection and then select the Networking tab.

2. Under Type Of VPN, change the setting from Automatic to either PPTP VPN, L2TP IPsec VPN, or SSTP as desired.

The default setting of Automatic means that Windows Vista negotiates the tunneling protocol to use based on the algorithm outlined earlier in this chapter in the section titled "VPN Connection Negotiation Process."

> **Note**   Using Fast User Switching (FUS) during a RAS/VPN session can affect your connectivity. For more information, see KB 289669 at *http://support.microsoft.com/kb/289669*.

How It Works: VPN Connections and IPv4/v6

First, a little background: After you establish VPN connectivity, you have two interfaces on your client computer. One is your Internet interface (Ethernet, Wireless, PPPoE, PPP over dialup, and so on); the other is your corporate or WAN interface (PPTP or L2TP VPN tunnel). This really means that you have two sets of IP addresses, and each of these can be IPv4 and/or IPv6.

How Do We Support Ipv4 and Ipv6 for VPN Connections?

In Windows Vista, we support SSTP and L2TP VPN tunnels over IPv6 (in other words, when your ISP connectivity is IPv6) and continue to support both SSTP/L2TP/PPTP VPN tunnels over IPv4. In all scenarios, IPv4 and/or IPv6 packets can be sent on top of a VPN tunnel. (Packets going to/from your corporate network can be IPv4/IPv6.)

■ If you are confused between over/on top of, here's my rule of thumb: Look at the connectivity between the VPN client and the VPN server (your ISP connectivity).

This determines how the tunnel packets flow over the Internet and indirectly determines which type of VPN tunnel to be used.

- Look at the connectivity between the VPN server and your corporate network (your corporate connectivity). This determines what flows on top of (or inside) the tunnel, and indirectly determines which network inside your corporate network you can access (IPv4 and/or IPv6).

How Can I Identify This While Configuring a VPN Connection?

Open the Properties sheet of your VPN connection and click the General tab. Here is where you specify the IP address (v4 or v6) or host name of the VPN server—the IP address you are going to use to connect to the VPN server or the IP address *over* which the VPN tunnel will be established. In other words, this determines your ISP connectivity. If you enter an IPv6 address here, L2TP and SSTP tunnels are supported. If you enter an IPv4 address, all PPTP, L2TP, and SSTP tunnels are supported. But if you enter a host name, the type of tunnel selection is deferred until you actually connect and a name lookup is performed. The DNS server could return to you both IPv4 as well as IPv6 addresses. In this scenario, IPv4 and IPv6 are tried in the order in which the addresses were returned by the DNS server inside the DNS response and depends upon the type of VPN tunnel type selection (PPTP, L2TP/IPsec, SSTP, or Automatic).

Switch to the Networking tab and look at This Connection Uses The Following Items. The protocols listed here include both IPv4 and IPv6, and this protocol will be the one that gets negotiated "on top of" (or "inside") the VPN tunnel. In other words, this determines your corporate connectivity—whether you will be sending IPv4 and/or IPv6 packets to the corporate network on top of the tunnel. You can typically get both IPv4 and IPv6 addresses from your corporate VPN server if your VPN server is configured accordingly. Depending on the name lookups, the appropriate address will be taken.

What Happens When I Select Automatic as My Type of VPN?

Automatic VPN tunnel logic is very simple:

- First try PPTP, and if that fails, try L2TP. If that fails, try SSTP.
- Let's say you have configured an IPv4 address as the destination VPN server. The logic remains same: first PPTP, then L2TP, and then SSTP.
- Let's say instead that you have configured an IPv6 address as the destination VPN server. Try L2TP. If that fails, try SSTP.
- Finally, let's say that you have configured host name as the destination VPN server. Now if your DNS server returns only IPv4 addresses (A records), go to step 1. If your DNS server returns only IPv6 addresses (AAAA records), go to step 2. If your DNS server returns both IPv4 and IPv6 addresses, the logic will be to go through each IP address returned and then go to either step 1 or 2 depending upon the IP address.

What Happens When I Select My Type of VPN Using Connection Manager Administration Kit (CMAK)?

CMAK (a tool for network administrators) on Windows Server 2008 also supports the following tunnel order strategies:

- PPTP only

- L2TP/IPSec only

- SSTP only

- PPTP first (PPTP followed by L2TP/IPSec followed by SSTP)

- L2TP first (L2TP/IPSec followed by PPTP followed by SSTP)

- SSTP first (SSTP followed by PPTP followed by L2TP/IPSec)

What Will Happen If I Connect a Windows Vista Client to a VPN Server That Doesn't Support Ipv6?

You won't be able to use the VPN server "over" IPv6 (you can only have IPv4 connectivity to ISP), which means your tunnel can be SSTP, L2TP, or PPTP. Then, "on top of" the VPN tunnel, the Windows Vista client will try to get an IPv4 as well as an IPv6 address from the VPN server, but it will get only an IPv4 address. Hence the connection will still go through. In other words, the connection fails only if you cannot get both IPv4 and IPv6 addresses on top of the VPN tunnel.

What Will Happen If I Connect A Windows Vista Client to a VPN Server That Doesn't Support SSTP?

The SSTP connection will fail (remove SSTP from the preceding tunnel order).

Samir Jain

Lead Program Manager for Enterprise Networking (RRAS)

Configuring Dial-Up Connections

Windows Vista supports both outgoing and incoming dial-up connections. For outgoing connections, Windows Vista is the client and connects to either a remote access server (RAS server) on a remote network (usually the corporate intranet) or a network access device (typically a modem bank) at an ISP. For incoming connections, Windows Vista acts as a mini-RAS server and allows a remote client computer to establish a dial-up connection between the two computers. Some enterprise environments still use RAS servers to provide mobile users with remote connectivity to the corporate network, but most enterprises now use VPN servers instead to save on long-distance telephone costs and the cost of maintaining multiple phone lines for RAS access. This section deals briefly with how to set up a dial-up connection to enable Windows Vista client computers to connect directly to a RAS server.

> **Note**   Incoming dial-up connections to client computers are rarely used in enterprise environments, so most of this discussion deals with outbound connections only. For information on how to create and configure an inbound connection on Windows Vista, see the section titled "Configuring Incoming Connections" later in this chapter.

Creating a Dial-Up Connection

To create a new dial-up connection to a server at your workplace, do the following:

1. On the Start menu, select Connect To.

2. On the Connect To A Network Wizard start page, click Set Up A Connection Or Network.

3. On the Choose A Connection Option page, select Connect To A Workplace and then click Next.

4. If this is the first connection you have created on the computer, proceed to step 5. Otherwise, select No, Create A New Connection and then click Next.

5. Click Dial Directly and specify a telephone number for the RAS server you want to connect to. (You can also give the connection a descriptive name to distinguish it from other connections on the computer. Typically, this will be the name of your remote network or RAS server.)

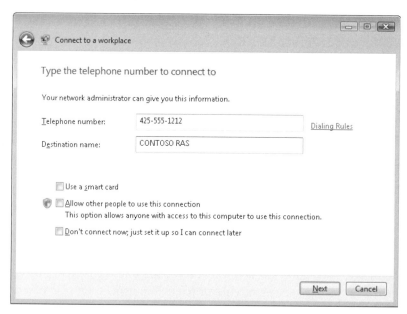

6. If dialing rules have not been configured for your computer, click Dialing Rules and then configure them as required.

7. To use a smart card for authentication, select Use A Smart Card. You must have a smart card reader installed on the computer to use this option. If you select this option, proceed to step 11.

8. To allow other users of the computer to use the connection, select Allow Other People To Use This Connection. Selecting this option requires that you have local administrator credentials for the computer so that you can respond to the UAC prompt that appears.

9. To create a new connection that needs further configuration before you can use it, select Don't Connect Now Just Set It Up So I Can Connect Later.

10. Click Next and specify the credentials (user name, password, and optionally the domain) you will use to be authenticated by the RAS server. (This option is available only if you left the option to Use A Smart Card cleared earlier in the wizard.)

11. If you chose to create a connection that needs further configuring before being used, click Create and then either click Close to create the connection or click Connect Now to initiate the connection.

Note Administrators can also use the new version of the Connection Manager Administration Kit (CMAK) included with Windows Server 2008 to tailor the appearance and behavior of connections made using Connection Manager, the built-in remote access client dialer included in Windows Vista. Using CMAK, administrators can create and deploy custom connections for client computers to simplify the user experience of connecting to remote networks. You must use the new Windows Server 2008 version of CMAK to create and configure connections for Windows Vista clients, because the new CMAK includes multiple-locale support that lets you create Connection Manager profiles on a server of any locale for installation on a client of any other locale.

Configuring a Dial-Up Connection

Configuring a dial-up connection is similar in many respects to configuring a VPN connection and supports the same authentication and data encryption features as VPN connections. See the section titled "Configuring a VPN Connection" earlier in this chapter for more information on VPN connection settings.

The same five tabs are displayed on the properties sheet for both dial-up and VPN connections, with the following changes for dial-up connections:

■ **General** Select and configure modem (analog or ISDN), specify phone number(s) for RAS server, and enable and configure dialing rules

■ **Options** An additional setting to prompt for phone number when connecting

■ **Security** Additional settings to optionally display a terminal window and run a connection script

■ **Networking** Same options as for VPN connections

■ **Sharing** Same options as for VPN connections

Note   If your Windows Vista computer has file sharing enabled on it, the File And Printer Sharing For Microsoft Networks option on the Networking tab is enabled on VPN connections but disabled on dial-up connections.

Advanced Connection Settings

Configure advanced connection settings for all connections on the computer by following these steps:

1. Open the Network Connections folder from Network And Sharing Center or by running Ncpa.cpl.

2. Press the Alt key to make the menu bar visible.

3. Select Advanced Settings under the Advanced menu option.

4. Rearrange the order of the network adapters, network bindings, and network providers on the computer as desired.

Configuring Incoming Connections

Windows Vista also supports incoming connections of both dial-up and VPN type. In this scenario, Windows Vista is acting as a mini-VPN or RAS server to other client computers on the network.

Creating an incoming connection on a Windows Vista computer requires administrator credentials on the computer and is supported only in workgroup environments. To create a new incoming connection, follow these steps:

1. Open the Network Connections folder from Network And Sharing Center or by running Ncpa.cpl.

2. Press the Alt key to make the menu bar visible.

3. Select New Incoming Connection under the File menu option.

4. Select the users you want to allow to connect to the computer. You can also click Add Someone to add additional users to the local user database on the computer.

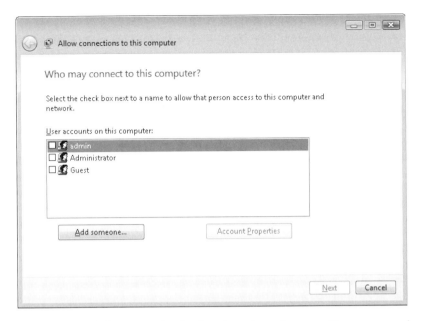

5. Click Next and then specify whether the selected users will connect to the computer through the Internet (using a VPN connection) or directly using a dial-up modem. For this scenario, we will assume that the VPN option has been selected.

6. Click Next and then specify which networking components to enable for the incoming connection. By default, IPv4 and File And Printer Sharing are enabled, and IPv6 is disabled.

7. Select Internet Protocol Version 4 (TCP/IPv4) and click Properties to configure the following:

    ❑ Whether or not the calling (connecting) computer can have access to your local area network using your computer as a gateway

    ❑ Whether the calling computer is assigned an IP address for its tunnel endpoint from a DHCP server on the network or is assigned an IP address from a range of addresses you specify

    ❑ Whether or not the calling computer can specify its own IP address for its tunnel endpoint

8. Click OK and then click Allow Access to enable the incoming connection.

9. The new incoming connection will be displayed in the Network Connections folder. (Incoming connections are not displayed in the Connect To A Network Wizard.)

10. To further configure an incoming connection, open the Network Connections folder, right-click the connection, and then select Properties. (For L2TP/IPSec- and SSTP-based VPN connection, you also need to install a machine certificate on the computer.) You

can also view and configure some properties of incoming connections from the command line by using the netsh command. For example, to show which users are allowed to connect to the computer, type **netsh ras show user** at a command prompt. For more help, type **netsh ras ?** at a command prompt.

> **Note**   You can create only one incoming connection on a Windows Vista computer per type of connection (PPTP, L2TP, SSTP, or dial-up), but you can configure the connection to support both VPN and dial-up connections.

Managing Connections Using Group Policy

In previous Windows platforms, you could use Group Policy to lock down or manage certain aspects of network connections on the computer. The Group Policy settings for doing this are located at:

User Configuration\Policies\Administrative Templates\Network\Network Connections

For example, by enabling the Prohibit Access To The Advanced Settings Item On The Advanced Menu policy setting, you could prevent users from opening Advanced Settings under the Advanced menu option in the Network Connections folder. If you also enable the Enable Windows 2000 Network Connections Settings For Administrators policy setting, even local administrators on the computer would not have access to Advanced Settings.

In Windows Vista, however, because of User Account Control (UAC) and how it is implemented, some of these Group Policy settings are no longer supported. Specifically:

- If a user is a local administrator on a Windows Vista computer, none of the restrictions from these Group Policy settings found under User Configuration\Policies\Administrative Templates\Network\Network Connections applies. Also, the Enable Windows 2000 Network Connections Settings For Administrators policy setting is no longer supported. This policy was used in legacy Windows platforms to enable Group Policy restrictions for Network Connections to apply to administrators and not just ordinary users.

- If a user is a standard user on a Windows Vista computer, most of the Group Policy settings found under User Configuration\Policies\Administrative Templates\Network\ Network Connections still apply. The exception is policies for actions that now require responding to a UAC prompt to perform them. An example of this is accessing Advanced Settings under the Advanced menu option in the Network Connections folder, which in Windows Vista requires administrative credentials to perform. As a result, the Prohibit Access To The Advanced Settings Item On The Advanced Menu policy setting in Windows Vista does not apply to standard users, because they cannot perform this action anyway without administrator credentials, and therefore this Group

Policy setting is superfluous. Another example is installing or removing network components for a connection, which requires responding to a UAC prompt. As a result, the Prohibit TCP/IP advanced configuration policy setting does not apply to standard users because this policy setting is superfluous for them—UAC prevents them from doing this anyway.

Table 28-3 summarizes support for Network Connection user policy settings in Windows Vista.

Table 28-3   Support for Group Policy User Settings for Network Connections for Standard Users in Windows Vista

Policy Setting	Supported in Windows Vista
Prohibit Adding And Removing Components For A LAN Or Remote Access Connection	
Prohibit Access To The Advanced Settings Item On The Advanced Menu	
Prohibit TCP/IP Advanced Configuration	
Prohibit Enabling/Disabling Components Of A LAN Connection	
Ability To Delete All User Remote Access Connections	
Prohibit Deletion Of Remote Access Connections	✓
Prohibit Access To The Remote Access Preferences Item On The Advanced Menu	✓
Enable Windows 2000 Network Connections Settings For Administrators	
Turn Off Notifications When A Connection Has Only Limited Or No Connectivity	
Prohibit Access To Properties Of Components Of A LAN Connection	
Ability To Enable/Disable A LAN Connection	
Prohibit Access To Properties Of A LAN Connection	✓
Prohibit Access To The New Connection Wizard	
Ability To Change Properties Of An All-User Remote Access Connection	✓
Prohibit Access To Properties Of Components Of A Remote Access Connection	
Prohibit Connecting And Disconnecting A Remote Access Connection	✓
Prohibit Changing Properties Of A Private Remote Access Connection	✓
Ability To Rename All User Remote Access Connections	
Ability To Rename LAN Connections Or Remote Access Connections Available To All Users	
Ability To Rename LAN Connections	
Prohibit Renaming Private Remote Access Connections	✓
Prohibit Viewing Of Status For An Active Connection	

Direct from the Source: Troubleshooting Connections

The error codes returned by Windows Vista's built-in remote access client have been improved to help you troubleshoot your connections. Table 28-4 describes some common error codes.

Table 28-4   Common Error Codes Returned by Windows Vista's Built-In Remote Access Client

Error Code	Cause	Resolution
806	GRE packets are getting dropped	Look for any firewall between VPN client and server and enable GRE (IP protocol 47) to pass through it.
812	Policy mismatch between client and server	Check the encryption and authentication settings between the client and server.
741, 742	Encryption type mismatch between client and server	Check the encryption settings between client and server.
807	VPN connection is disconnected after getting established	VPN server reaching capacity or latency has increased and your VPN server is no longer reachable. Troubleshoot server- or connectivity-related problems.

In Windows Vista, a failure to connect in a VPN connection will also provide a Diagnose option in addition to the error message describing the cause of failure. When you select the Diagnose option, Windows Vista attempts to diagnose the cause of failure in the VPN connection. Note that Windows Vista may not always be able to successfully diagnose the root cause of the problem, given the complexity of Internet architecture and that there is no access to the network infrastructure along the path between the VPN client and the VPN server.

In addition to PPP logging, which is still available in Windows Vista, netsh-based logging is also available, which can assist Microsoft support services in resolving your problem. To use netsh for diagnosing connection failures, perform the following steps from a command prompt. (Note that Administrator privileges are required to execute the following commands.)

1. Click Start, click All Programs, click Accessories, and then right-click Command Prompt to start an elevated command prompt. Select Run As Administrator and respond to the UAC prompt that appears.

2. Type the command **netsh ras set tracing * disable** in the elevated command prompt.

3. Delete all files (if any) in the %WinDir%\tracing folder.

4. Type the command **netsh ras set tracing * enable** in the elevated command prompt.

5. Reproduce the error condition (for example, launch the VPN connection and click Connect) and wait for failure to happen.

6. Type the command **netsh ras set tracing * disable** in the elevated command prompt.

7. Put all the files from the %WinDir%\tracing folder in a compressed (zip) file and send it to your Microsoft representative for analysis. This tracing will help Microsoft representatives to find a quicker resolution for your problem.

Samir Jain and Santosh Chandwani

Lead Program Managers for Windows Enterprise Networking

Using Remote Desktop

Remote Desktop is an extension of Terminal Services (TS) technology that provides users with the flexibility of working on their computers from anywhere, at any time. Remote Desktop has been enhanced and extended in Windows Vista and Windows Server 2008 to provide robust remote access capabilities for users in enterprise environments. Using Remote Desktop, users can run applications on a remote computer running Windows Vista from any other client running a supported Windows operating system. Additionally, Remote Desktop can allow administrators to remotely manage both desktop computers and servers as if they were interactively logged on at the local console of these computers.

Note   Remote Desktop is different from Remote Assistance, which is also based on TS technology. For more information about Remote Assistance, see Chapter 23, "Supporting Users Using Remote Assistance."

Understanding Remote Desktop

Remote Desktop consists of the following components:

- Remote Desktop Protocol (RDP)
- Remote Desktop client software—that is, Remote Desktop Connection (RDC)

Note   Windows Vista also includes a new feature called Windows Meeting Space that uses RDP but allows you to share your desktop or an application with multiple remote users and not just the single remote user that the Remote Desktop feature supports. For more information, see Chapter 18, "Managing Windows Meeting Space."

Remote Desktop Protocol

Remote Desktop Protocol (RDP) is a protocol that transmits keyboard input, mouse input, and display output information between a remote computer and either a Windows Terminal Server or a Windows computer that has Remote Desktop enabled (see Figure 28-5). The network connection between the computers can be any TCP/IP network connection, including LAN, WAN, VPN, or dial-up.

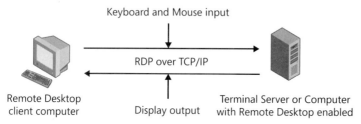

Figure 28-5   How Remote Desktop Protocol works.

In addition to transmitting keyboard and mouse input and display output between the two computers, RDP also enables the local computer (the computer running Remote Desktop client software) to access various resources on the remote computer (a Windows Terminal Server or a Windows computer with Remote Desktop enabled) by redirecting these resources to the local computer. These resources can include disks, printers, serial ports, smart cards, audio sources, and Plug and Play (PnP) devices. RDP also enables the computers to share a clipboard, allowing the interchange of data between applications running on the two computers.

The version of RDP included with Windows Vista Service Pack 1 and Windows Server 2008 is RDP 6.1. This new version of RDP updates the earlier RDP 5.1 used by Windows XP and Windows Server 2003, RDP 5.2 used by Windows Server 2003 Service Pack 1, and RDP 6.0 used by Windows Vista RTM.

RDP 6.1 provides the following new features and enhancements (note that as indicated in the following list, some of these new features require running Windows Server 2008 Terminal Servers on the back end of RDC sessions):

- **Plug and Play (PnP) device redirection for media players and digital cameras**   Users can now redirect supported Windows Portable Devices, such as certain media players and digital cameras that use the Media Transfer Protocol (MTP) or Picture Transfer Protocol (PTP). Plug and Play (PnP) device redirection over cascaded Remote Desktop connections is not supported, however.

- **Windows Embedded for Point of Service device redirection**   Users can now redirect Windows Embedded for Point of Service devices that use Microsoft Point of Service (POS) for .NET 1.1, a class library that provides .NET applications with an interface for communicating with POS peripheral devices from Windows Server 2008 Terminal Servers. You can download Microsoft POS for .NET 1.1 from the Microsoft Download

Center at *http://www.microsoft.com/downloads/details.aspx?FamilyID=6025b728-ec06-48f9-bc80-c38b2a27a242&displaylang=en*. It requires the .NET Framework Redistributable Package version 1.1 or higher.

- **Custom display ratios and resolutions**   Users can now customize Remote Desktop Connection to support monitors with resolution as high as 4096 × 2048 with display resolution ratios as large as 16:9 or 16:10. The previous version RDP 5.2 supports only a 4:3 display resolution ratio at a maximum resolution of 1600 × 1050.

- **Multiple monitor spanning**   Users can now span multiple monitors placed together to form a single, large desktop that can enhance productivity. Monitors must use the same resolution and can be spanned only side-by-side, not vertically. The maximum resolution across all spanned monitors cannot exceed 4096 × 2048. Repositioning of dialog boxes is not supported, including the Winlogon dialog box.

- **Desktop Experience**   By installing the Desktop Experience feature on a Windows Server 2008 Terminal Server, users on remote computers can now use Windows Vista features such as new desktop themes and Windows Media Player 11 within a Remote Desktop session.

- **Desktop Composition and Font Smoothing**   Lets you experience the full power of Windows Aero within a Remote Desktop session with a remote Windows Vista computer, including translucent windows, taskbar buttons with thumbnail-sized window previews, and open windows displayed as a 3D stack. (For more information about Aero, see Chapter 1, "Overview of Windows Vista Improvements.") Users can also now use ClearType font-smoothing technology within a Remote Desktop session to enhance readability on LCD monitors. RDP 6.1 also supports 32-bit color depth, which can be combined with ClearType or the Desktop Experience.

- **Display data prioritization**   Users can now customize Remote Desktop Connection to prioritize keyboard, mouse, and display traffic so that the Remote Desktop experience is not adversely affected when bandwidth-intensive tasks are being performed on the remote computer, such as copying large files or submitting large print jobs. For more information, see the section titled "Improving Remote Desktop Performance" later in this chapter.

- **Network Level Authentication Support**   Users can now configure Remote Desktop to enable a connection from only clients that support Network Level Authentication. With Network Level Authentication, the user/client and server can negotiate a secure channel for exchanging data prior to allocating resources for sessions.

- **Server authentication**   Enables you to verify that your Remote Desktop Connection client is connecting to the correct remote computer or server. This provides increased security and protection of confidential information by ensuring that you are connecting to the computer you intend to connect to.

- **TS Easy Print**   Provides a driverless solution for printer redirection over a Remote Desktop session by redirecting all printing-related work to the client computer without the need of installing matching printer drivers on your Terminal Server. Terminal Services Easy Print requires that your Terminal Server be running Windows Server 2008 and have the Terminal Services role installed.

- **TS RemoteApp**   Lets users access programs running on a Terminal Services and have them appear as if they were running on the user's local computer side by side with their local programs. Terminal Services RemoteApp requires that your terminal server be running Windows Server 2008 and have the Terminal Services role installed.

> **Note**   User Account Control (UAC) elevation prompts are also remoted from the host computer to the client computer during a Remote Desktop session.

Remote Desktop Connection

Also called Terminal Services Client, Remote Desktop Connection (RDC) is a client application that runs on the remote computer and enables the computer to establish a Remote Desktop session with either a Windows Terminal Server or a Windows computer that has Remote Desktop enabled. The RDC client is a Windows Vista component that is installed by default and can be accessed either from the Start menu or by running Mstsc.exe.

In typical usage, a user at a remote location must first connect to a private network before she can start a Remote Desktop session with a computer within the private network–typically by using a VPN connection to the target computer. When end-to-end network connectivity has been established between the user's computer and the host computer, the user can use the RDC client to open a Remote Desktop session that will provide an experience comparable to being interactively logged on at the local console of the host computer (depending on the available bandwidth of the network connection).

For more information on configuring and using the RDC client, see the section titled "Configuring and Deploying Remote Desktop Connection" later in this chapter.

> **Note**   Remote Desktop Connection version 6.1 (RDC 6.1) is included in Windows Vista Service Pack 1 and Windows Server 2008 and is also available for Windows XP by installing Service Pack 3 for Windows XP.

Terminal Services Web Access

Terminal Services Web Access (TS Web Access) is a role service in the Windows Server 2008 Terminal Services role that lets you make Terminal Services RemoteApp (TS RemoteApp) programs and a link to the terminal server desktop available to users from a web browser. Additionally, TS Web Access enables users to connect from a web browser to the remote desktop of any server or client computer where they have the appropriate access.

With TS Web Access, users can visit a website (either from the Internet or from an intranet) to access a list of available RemoteApp programs. When users start a RemoteApp program, a Terminal Services session is started on the Windows Server 2008–based Terminal Server that hosts the RemoteApp program.

For more information about TS Web Access, see *http://technet2.microsoft.com/ windowsserver2008/en/library/95258ce8-5ddd-42cb-9e95-cec19ef4f43d1033.mspx?mfr=true.*

> **Note**   Remote Desktop Web Connection, a web application that consists of an ActiveX control, sample web pages, and other files, enables users on client computers running earlier versions of Windows to create Remote Desktop connections using a web browser instead of using the RDC client. Remote Desktop Web Connection is no longer available for Windows Vista and has been replaced by TS Web Access.

Steps for Using Remote Desktop

To use the Remote Desktop feature to establish a Remote Desktop session with another computer, complete the following steps:

1. Enable Remote Desktop on the remote (host) computer.
2. Authorize users to access the host computer.
3. Configure Remote Desktop client software on the local (client) computer.
4. Establish network connectivity between the client and host computers.
5. Establish the Remote Desktop session from the client to the host.

The following sections describe each of these steps in detail.

Enabling Remote Desktop and Authorizing Users on a Single Computer

By default, Remote Desktop is not enabled on host computers running Windows Vista. To enable Remote Desktop on a single host computer, follow these steps:

1. Click Start, right-click Computer, and then click Properties.
2. Click the Remote Settings link to open the Remote tab of System Properties.
3. Choose either the second or third option under Remote Desktop.

Note   Enabling Remote Desktop on a computer generates a UAC prompt, because inbound rules must be enabled in Windows Firewall to allow the host computer to listen for incoming connection attempts from RDC clients over TCP port 3389. You can change the port that RDC uses by modifying the HKLM\System\CurrentControlSet\Control\TerminalServer\WinStations\RDP-Tcp registry value, but if you do this you must create and enable an inbound firewall rule on the host computer to allow it to listen for incoming RDP traffic. You also have to configure the RDP client to use the changed port. For more information about Windows Firewall, see Chapter 27, "Configuring Windows Firewall and IPsec."

The two options for enabling Remote Desktop are:

- **Allow Connections From Computers Running Any Version Of Remote Desktop (Less Secure)**   Choosing this option enables computers running a previous version of Windows to use a version of RDP earlier than 6.0 to connect to the host computer.

- **Allow Connections Only From Computers Running Remote Desktop With Network Level Authentication (More Secure)**   Choosing this option only allows RDP connections from client computers running either Windows Vista or Windows Server 2008. (Computers running Windows XP Service Pack 2 or Windows Server 2003 Service Pack 1 have version 6.0 of RDC installed can also connect when this option is selected.)

In previous versions of Windows, Remote Desktop authenticated users late in the connection sequence after the Remote Desktop session had started and Winlogon came up in the session. As a result, Remote Desktop sessions were susceptible to spoofing and man-in-the-middle attacks. With the new Network Level Authentication in RDP 6.0, however, the client and host computers negotiate a mutually authenticated, secure channel for exchanging data using the Security Service Provider Interface (SSPI). In an Active Directory environment, by default this mutual authentication is performed using the Kerberos v5 protocol and Transport Layer Security (TLS) 1.0.

If you try to establish a Remote Desktop session from a client computer running Windows Vista to a host computer running a version of Windows that supports only a version of RDP earlier than 6.0, the dialog box shown in Figure 28-6 will be displayed, warning that the identity of the host computer cannot be verified. When the client computer running Windows Vista connects to the host computer and establishes a Remote Desktop session, the absence of the lock icon indicates that Network Level Authentication has not been used to mutually authenticate the client and host computers.

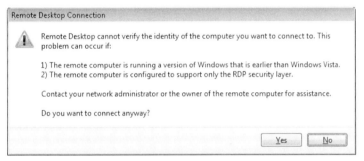

Figure 28-6 The identity of a host computer on which an earlier version of Remote Desktop has been enabled cannot be verified.

 Note The authentication response displayed while attempting to establish a Remote Desktop session depends on the configuration of the RDC client. For more information, see Table 28-5 later in this chapter.

When enabling Remote Desktop on a computer, you must also authorize which users will be allowed to remotely connect to that computer using Remote Desktop Connection. By default, only Administrators are authorized to remotely connect to the host computer. Authorize additional users by following these steps:

1. Click the Select Users button (shown in Figure 28-5) to open the Remote Desktop Users dialog box.

2. Click Add and then either specify or find user accounts in Active Directory (or on the local computer on standalone host computers) and add them to the list of Remote Desktop Users authorized to access the host computer using Remote Desktop. This adds the selected users to the Remote Desktop Users local group on the host computer.

Enabling Remote Desktop Using Group Policy

You can also use Group Policy to enable Remote Desktop on host computers. To enable Remote Desktop on all computers in a specified organizational unit (OU), open the Group Policy Object (GPO) linked to the OU using Group Policy Object Editor, enable the following policy setting, and add users to the Remote Desktop Users group:

Computer Configuration\Policies\Administrative Templates\Windows Components\Terminal Services\Terminal Server\Connections\Allow Users To Connect Remotely Using Terminal Services

Enabling Remote Desktop on computers using Group Policy also enables the Allow Connections From Computers Running Any Version Of Remote Desktop (Less Secure) option on the computers targeted by the GPO. To enable Remote Desktop using the Allow Connections Only From Computers Running Remote Desktop With Network Level Authentication (More Secure) option instead, you must enable the following policy setting in addition to the preceding one:

Computer Configuration\Policies\Administrative Templates\Windows Components\Terminal Services\Terminal Server\Security\Require User Authentication For Remote Connections By Using Network Level Authentication

> **Note**   By default, when the first policy setting is enabled but the second setting is not configured, local administrators on the targeted computers have the ability to change the Remote Desktop security level on their computers to Allow Connections Only From Computers Running Remote Desktop With Network Level Authentication (More Secure) if desired. When the second policy setting is enabled, the option Allow Connections From Computers Running Any Version Of Remote Desktop (Less Secure) on the Remote tab is unavailable and appears dimmed.

Configuring and Deploying Remote Desktop Connection

After you have enabled Remote Desktop on the host computer, you must configure the Remote Desktop Connection (RDC) client software on the client computer. You can configure RDC several ways:

- Click Start, click All Programs, click Accessories, and then click Remote Desktop Connection. This opens the Remote Desktop Connection user interface, shown in Figure 28-7.

- Type **mstsc** at a command prompt or in the Instant Search box to open the Remote Desktop Connection user interface, or type **mstsc** followed by various parameters to customize how the RDC client software will run. For help with Mstsc.exe parameters, type **mstsc /?** at a command prompt.

- Use Notepad to manually edit an *.rdp file previously saved from the Remote Desktop Connection user interface. For more information, read the section titled "Configuring Remote Desktop Connection Using Notepad" later in this chapter.

- Configure those Terminal Services Group Policy settings that apply to Remote Desktop.

Figure 28-7   The Remote Desktop Connection client user interface.

Table 28-5 summarizes the configuration options available on the different tabs of the Remote Desktop Connection client user interface.

Table 28-5   Configuration Options for Remote Desktop Connection Client

Tab	Setting	Notes
General	Local Settings: Computer	Specify the fully qualified name or IP address (can be IPv4 or IPv6) of the host computer.
	Local Settings: User Name	Specify the user account to be used to establish the Remote Desktop session. This is only displayed when credentials from previous Remote Desktop session have been saved.
	Local Settings: Always Ask For Credentials	Select this check box to require the user to always supply credentials. This is only displayed when credentials from previous Remote Desktop session have been saved.
	Connection Settings	Save the current configuration of RDC client as an *.rdp file or open a previously saved *.rdp file.

Table 28-5   **Configuration Options for Remote Desktop Connection Client**

Tab	Setting	Notes
Display	Remote Desktop Size	Change the size of your remote desktop.
	Colors	Specify color depth for your remote desktop.
	Display The Connection Bar When In Full-Screen Mode	Makes it easier to use Remote Desktop in full-screen mode without needing to remember keyboard shortcuts.
Local Resources	Remote Computer Sound	Redirect audio output on the host computer to the remote client.
	Keyboard	Specify how Windows key combinations such as Alt+Tab behave when used from within a Remote Desktop session.
	Local Devices And Resources: Printers	Print to network computers connected to the host computer from within the Remote Desktop session without having to install additional drivers.
	Local Devices And Resources: Clipboard	Share a clipboard between the client and host computers.
	Local Devices And Resources: More	Redirect additional devices local to the host computer to the remote client including serial ports, smart cards, disk drives, and supported PnP devices such as media players and digital cameras.
Programs	Start A Program	Specify a program that should automatically start when your Remote Desktop session is established.
Experience	Performance: Choose Your Connection Speed To Optimize performance	Specify the connection speed closest to actual available network bandwidth to obtain the optimal mix of functionality and performance for your Remote Desktop session.
	Reconnect If Connection Is Dropped	Specify that the RDC client should attempt to re-establish a connection with the remote host if the connection between them is unexpectedly terminated.
Advanced	Server Authentication: Authentication Options	Specify whether or not unauthenticated Remote Desktop sessions should be allowed; if they are allowed, specify whether or not a warning message should be displayed. For more information, see the sidebar titled "Remote Desktop Connection Server Authentication" following this table.
	Connect From Anywhere: Settings	Configure Terminal Services Gateway (TS Gateway) settings to allow RDC client to connect to remote computers behind corporate firewalls. For more information, see the sidebar titled "Understanding Terminal Services Gateway" later in this chapter.

In enterprise environments, administrators can also preconfigure RDC client configurations and save them as Remote Desktop files (*.rdp files). These *.rdp files can then be deployed to users as e-mail attachments or copied from a network share using a logon script.

Remote Desktop Connection Server Authentication

Remote Desktop Connection includes a Server Authentication setting that ensures that you are connecting to the remote computer or server you intend to connect to. To configure Server Authentication for a Remote Desktop Connection, open the Properties sheet of your connection, click the Advanced tab, and click Settings. Then select one of the following three options:

- **Connect And Don't Warn Me (Least Secure)**   Lets you connect even if Remote Desktop Connection can't verify the identity of the remote computer.

- **Warn Me (More Secure)**   Lets you choose whether or not to continue with the connection when Remote Desktop Connection can't verify the identity of the remote computer.

- **Do Not Connect (Most Secure)**   Prevents you from connecting to the remote computer when Remote Desktop Connection can't verify the remote computer's identity.

The default setting for Server Authentication is Warn Me.

Configuring Remote Desktop Connection from the Command Line

To use the RDC client from the command line or custom shortcut, type **mstsc** followed by the appropriate parameters. For example, to initiate a Remote Desktop session using a custom display resolution of 1680 × 1050, type **mstsc /w:1680 /h:1050** at a command prompt.

As a second example, to initiate a Remote Desktop session that spans across multiple monitors, type **mstsc /span** at a command prompt.

> **Note**   When both the */span* and */h: /w:* options are present, the */span* option takes precedence. In addition, when the */span* option is selected, the slider for adjusting remote desktop size is unavailable on the Display tab so that users cannot change their initial settings, which can cause confusion.

You can also type **mstsc /public** at a command prompt, which runs Remote Desktop in public mode. When an RDC client is running in public mode, it does not persist any private user data (such as user name, password, domain, and so on) either to disk or to the registry on the computer on which the client is running, nor does the client make use of any saved private data that may exist on the computer (a trusted sites list, the persistent bitmap cache, and so on). This means that the client essentially functions as if there were no registry or secondary storage present for storing private data. A client running in public mode still honors Group Policy settings, however.

Finally, the */console* switch used in previous versions of Mstsc.exe was removed in Service Pack 1 for Windows Vista and has been replaced with the new */admin* switch. For more information about this, see the following sidebar titled "Replacement of */console* by */admin.*"

> **Note**   For more help with Mstsc.exe parameters, type **mstsc /?** at a command prompt.

Replacement of */console* by */admin*

In Windows Server 2003, the */console* option for Mstsc.exe was used for several purposes. With the introduction of the */admin* option in Windows Vista SP1 and Windows Server 2008, the */console* option has now been deprecated. The following examples illustrate the */console* switch's significance in previous versions of Windows and why the scenario does not apply for Windows Vista SP1 and Windows Server 2008.

First, in earlier versions of Windows such as Windows XP and Windows Server 2003, the */console* option was used to connect to the session on the physical console (session 0), because some applications could not install and/or run in any session other than session 0. In Windows Vista and Windows Server 2008, the Windows components are re-architected, so that only services run in session 0 and applications do not need to run in session 0. Therefore, the administrator does not need the */console* option for this purpose.

Second, in earlier versions of Windows, the */console* option was also used for the purpose of reconnecting back and resuming work in the user session on the physical console. In Windows Vista and Windows Server 2008, this option is not required to get reconnected to the existing session on the physical console. (The blog post referenced at the end of this sidebar includes details on console behavior differences.)

Third, in Windows Server 2003, the */console* option was used for administering the Terminal Server remotely without consuming a CAL. In Windows Server 2008, */admin* option serves this purpose.

Thus you do not need the */console* option while connecting to Windows Vista or Windows Server 2008, and you can now use the */admin* switch to connect to the physical console of Windows Vista or Windows Server 2003.

For more information, see the following post on the Terminal Services Team Blog: *http://blogs.msdn.com/ts/archive/2007/12/17/changes-to-remote-administration-in-windows-server-2008.aspx.*

Mahesh Lotlikar, SDE II

Terminal Services team

Configuring Remote Desktop Connection Using Notepad

You can also configure a saved RDC client by opening its *.rdp file in Notepad and editing it. For example, to configure a saved RDC client to use a custom display resolution of 1680 × 1050, change the lines specifying screen resolution to read as follows:

```
desktopwidth:i:1680
desktopheight:i:1050
```

As a second example, to configure a saved RDC client to span a Remote Desktop session across multiple monitors, add or change the following line:

```
span:i:0
```

to

```
span:i:1
```

Configuring Remote Desktop Using Group Policy

You can also use Group Policy to manage some aspects of how Remote Desktop works. You can find the policy settings for managing Remote Desktop in two locations:

- Per-computer policy settings: Computer Configuration\Policies\Administrative Templates\Windows Components\Terminal Services

- Per-user policy settings: User Configuration\Policies\Administrative Templates\ Windows Components\Terminal Services

Table 28-6 lists Group Policy settings that affect Remote Desktop. Policies that are new to Windows Vista are marked with an asterisk (*). (Additional policy settings found in these locations apply only to Terminal Servers or only when a RDC client is used to connect to a Terminal Server.) If a computer and user policy setting are identical, the computer setting takes precedence if configured.

To use the Group Policy settings in this table, configure them in a GPO linked to an OU where the host computers (the computers that have Remote Desktop enabled) are located. For additional Group Policy settings that affect Remote Desktop, see the section titled "Enabling Remote Desktop Using Group Policy" earlier in this chapter.

Note   The folder layout of the Group Policy settings for Terminal Services—under Computer Configuration\Policies\Administrative Templates\Windows Components\Terminal Services and User Configuration\Policies\Administrative Templates\Windows Components\Terminal Services—has been reorganized in Windows Vista for ease of discoverability, but the registry keys are still the same. All policy settings common to both Windows Vista and Windows XP, even if located under different folders, will still be applied to all computers in the targeted OU.

Table 28-6 Group Policy Settings that Affect Remote Desktop

Folder	Policy Setting	Notes
Remote Desktop Connection Client	Do Not Allow Passwords To Be Saved	Prevents users from saving their credentials in the RDC client. Windows Vista saves the password using Credential Manager instead of saving it within the *.rdp file as in earlier versions of Windows.
Terminal Server\ Connections	Automatic Reconnection	Enables RDC clients to attempt to automatically reconnect when underlying network connectivity is lost.
	Allow Users To Connect Remotely Using Terminal Services	Enables Remote Desktop on the targeted computer.
	Deny Logoff Of An Administrator Logged In To The Console Session	Prevents an administrator on the client computer from bumping an administrator off of the host computer.
Device and Resource Redirection	Allow Audio Redirection	Enables redirection of audio sources.
	Do Not Allow Clipboard Redirection	Prevents sharing of a clipboard.
	Do Not Allow COM Port Redirection	Prevents redirection of serial port devices.
	Do Not Allow Drive Redirection	Prevents redirection of disk drive resources.
	Do Not Allow LPT Port Redirection	Prevents redirection of parallel port devices.
	*Do Not Allow Supported Plug And Play Device Redirection	Prevents redirection of supported PnP media players and digital cameras.
	Do Not Allow Smart Card Device Redirection	Prevents redirection of smart card readers.
Printer Redirection	Do Not Set Default Client Printer To Be Default Printer In A Session	Prevents users from redirecting print jobs from the remote computer to a printer attached to their local (client) computer.
	Do Not Allow Client Printer Redirection	Prevents the client default printer from automatically being set as the default printer for the Remote Desktop session.
Terminal Server\ Remote Session Environment	Limit Maximum Color Depth	Lets you specify the color depth to be used for Remote Desktop connections to the computer.
	Enforce Removal Of Remote Desktop Wallpaper	Prevents wallpaper from being displayed in the Remote Desktop session.

Table 28-6   **Group Policy Settings that Affect Remote Desktop**

Folder	Policy Setting	Notes
	Remove "Disconnect" Option From Shut Down Dialog	Removes the Disconnect button from the Start menu but doesn't prevent the remote user from disconnecting the session using other methods.
Terminal Server\ Security	Set Client Connection Encryption Level	Specifies the level of encryption used to protect RDP traffic between the client and host computers. The options available are High (128-bit), Low (56-bit), and Client Compatible (highest encryption level supported by the client). When this policy setting is Not Configured, the default encryption level used is Client Compatible.
	Always Prompt Client For Password Upon Connection	Requires remote users to always enter a password to establish a Remote Desktop session with the targeted computer.
	*Require Use Of Specific Security Layer For Remote (RDP) Connections	Specifies whether or not the client should attempt to authenticate the host computer during establishment of the Remote Desktop session. The options available are: ■ RDP, which means that no computer-level authentication is required. ■ SSL (TLS 1.0), which means that the client tries to use Kerberos or certificates to authenticate the host computer; if this fails, the session is not established. ■ Negotiate, which first attempts to authenticate the host using Kerberos or certificates; if this fails, the session is still established. When this policy setting is Not Configured, the default authentication method used is Negotiate.
	*Require User Authentication Using RDP 6.0 For Remote Connections	Requires client computers to be running Windows Vista or be running Windows XP Service Pack 2 with the downloadable RDC 6.0 client installed.
	*Server Authentication Certificate Template	Lets you specify a certificate template to be used for authenticating the host computer.
Terminal Server\Session Time Limits	Terminate Session When Time Limits Are Reached	Forcibly logs the remote user off of the Remote Desktop session when the session time limit has been reached.
	Set Time Limit For Disconnected Sessions	Forcibly logs the remote user off of the Remote Desktop session when the session time limit for disconnected sessions has been reached.

Table 28-6   Group Policy Settings that Affect Remote Desktop

Folder	Policy Setting	Notes
	Set Time Limit For Active But Idle Terminal Services Sessions	Specifies a time limit for no activity in Remote Desktop sessions. When the time limit is reached, the session is disconnected, but the remote user is not logged off. If, however, the Terminate Session When Time Limits Are Reached policy is enabled, the user is disconnected and then forcibly logged off.
	Set Time Limit For Active Terminal Services Sessions	Specifies a time limit for Remote Desktop sessions. When the time limit is reached, the session is disconnected, but the remote user is not logged off. If, however, the Terminate Session When Time Limits Are Reached policy is enabled, the user is disconnected and then forcibly logged off.

Understanding Terminal Services Gateway

Terminal Services Gateway (TS Gateway) is a new role service in the Terminal Services role for Windows Server 2008 that allows authorized users to remotely connect to Terminal Servers—and to computers on a corporate network that have Remote Desktop enabled on them—from any Internet-connected device. TS Gateway thus enables remote users to connect to the corporate network over the Internet using an encrypted connection and without needing to first configure VPN connections. TS Gateway works by using RDP over HTTPS to form a secure, encrypted connection between remote users on the Internet and Terminal Servers and desktop computers on the corporate network. Using this secure connection, users can remotely run their productivity applications when they are away from the corporate network.

Prior to Windows Server 2008, firewalls and network address translators (NATs) made it difficult for remote users to connect to Remote Desktop servers on private networks. For example, many enterprises block inbound traffic on TCP port 3389 (the port used by RDP) at the perimeter firewall for security reasons. TS Gateway, however, transmits RDP traffic instead to TCP port 443 by using an HTTP Transport Layer Security (TLS) tunnel. TS Gateway thus makes it easier for administrators to provide remote users with access to their desktop computers and to Terminal Services because no additional ports need to be opened on the perimeter firewall. TS Gateway also simplifies remote access for users by eliminating the need to configure VPN connections on their computers. Windows Vista and Windows Server 2008 include support for managing TS Gateway settings using Group Policy—the relevant settings are found at User Configuration\Policies\Administrative Templates\Windows Components\Terminal Services\TS Gateway.

Implementing TS Gateway requires deploying Windows Server 2008 on your corporate network. For more information on TS Gateway, see *http://technet2.microsoft.com/windowsserver2008/en/library/5b20b0e0-f621-4ccf-bf57-f4bac57cd0171033.mspx?mfr=true*.

Establishing a Remote Desktop Session

After the host computer has been configured to enable Remote Desktop for authorized users and the RDP client software has been configured and deployed on the client computer, the user can initiate establishment of a Remote Desktop session with the remote host computer by using one of the following methods:

- Double-click the desired *.rdp file (or a shortcut to this file) and (if required) click Yes. Then specify your credentials for connecting to the host computer (if required).

- Open a command prompt and type **mstsc** *"rdp_file"* where *"rdp_file"* is the name of the desired *.rdp file (path may be required) and (if required) click Yes. Then specify your credentials for connecting to the host computer, if required.

When a Remote Desktop session has been established, the client can end the session in two ways:

- **By disconnecting**   This ends the Remote Desktop experience on the client computer but leaves the session running on the host computer so that the client can reconnect later if desired. Any applications running in the session on the host continue to run until this session is terminated, either by the user on the client (who must reconnect and then log off) or by a user logging on interactively to the host.

- **By logging off**   This ends the Remote Desktop experience on the client computer and terminates the session on the host computer as well.

Note   You can also remotely shut down the host computer you are remotely connecting to, or you can put it into sleep mode. To do this from within a Remote Desktop session, click the taskbar, press Alt+F4, and then choose the option you want to select. You can also open a command prompt in your Remote Desktop session and type **shutdown -s -t 0** to immediately shut down the host computer or **shutdown -r -t 0** to immediately restart it. (Be sure to save any open files first.)

Improving Remote Desktop Performance

If available network bandwidth between a client computer and the remote host computer is limited, you can improve a Remote Desktop experience by reducing the color depth on the Display tab of the RDC client from its default 32-bit value. You can also selectively disable desktop experiences on the Experience tab to further improve Remote Desktop performance.

If you routinely transfer large files, submit large print jobs, or perform other bandwidth-intensive actions over a Remote Desktop connection, you may be able to improve the performance of a Remote Desktop experience by configuring display data prioritization on the host computer. Display data prioritization is designed to ensure that the screen performance aspect of a Remote Desktop experience is not adversely affected by such bandwidth-intensive actions. Display data prioritization works by automatically controlling virtual channel traffic between the client and host computer by giving display, keyboard, and mouse data higher priority than other forms of traffic.

The default setting for display data prioritization is to allocate 70 percent of available bandwidth for input (keyboard and mouse) and output (display) data. All other traffic, including use of a shared clipboard, file transfers, print jobs, and so on, is allocated by default only 30 percent of the available bandwidth of the network connection.

You can manually configure display data prioritization settings by editing the registry on the host computer, which can be either a Windows Vista computer that has Remote Desktop enabled or a Terminal Server running Windows Server 2008. The registry entries for display data prioritization are the following values, which are found under *HKLM\SYSTEM\Current-ControlSet\Services\TermDD*. (If these DWORD values are not present, you can create them.)

- **FlowControlDisable**   Set this value to 1 to disable all display data prioritization and handle all requests on a first-in-first-out (FIFO) basis. The default value of this setting is 0.

- **FlowControlDisplayBandwidth**   Specify a relative bandwidth priority for display and input data up to an allowed value of 255. The default value of this setting is 70.

- **FlowControlChannelBandwidth**   Specify a relative bandwidth priority for all other virtual channels up to an allowed value of 255. The default value of this setting is 30.

- **FlowControlChargePostCompression**   Determine if flow control will calculate bandwidth allocation based on pre-compression bytes (if the value is 0) or post-compression bytes (if the value is 1). The default value for this setting is 0.

By default, the ratio of *FlowControlDisplayBandwidth* to *FlowControlChannelBandwidth* is 70 to 30 or 70:30. This means that 70 percent of available bandwidth is reserved for display and input traffic, and the remaining 30 percent will be used for other types of traffic. If your Remote Desktop experience is being degraded during large file transfers and other bandwidth-intensive activity, you might change *FlowControlDisplayBandwidth* to 85 and *FlowControlChannelBandwidth* to 15, which allocates 85 percent of available bandwidth for display and input traffic while reserving only 15 percent for other traffic.

 Note   You must reboot your host computer for these registry changes to take effect.

Troubleshooting Remote Desktop

If you have trouble establishing a Remote Desktop session with the host computer, do the following:

- Verify that Remote Desktop has been enabled on the host computer.

- Verify that you are using credentials that have been authorized for remotely connecting to the host computer.

- Verify that you have the correct fully qualified name or IP address of the remote computer.

- Verify network connectivity with the remote computer by using the ping command.

If you are missing expected functionality during a Remote Desktop session, do the following:

- Check if the host computer is running a legacy version of Windows such as Windows XP Professional or Windows Server 2003.

- Verify that you have the latest version of Remote Desktop Connection client software installed on your computer.

- Verify that Group Policy is not locking down some aspect of Remote Desktop functionality that you expected to experience.

 Note   For additional troubleshooting guidance, read Chapter 32, "Troubleshooting Network Issues." When working through the troubleshooting processes in this chapter, keep in mind that RDP uses TCP port 3389.

Summary

Windows Vista includes several remote connectivity technologies, including Remote Desktop and Virtual Private Network connections. These technologies have been enhanced in many ways over their counterparts in previous versions of Windows to make them more reliable, more secure, and easier to use and manage.

Additional Resources

The following resources contain additional information and tools related to this chapter.

Related Information

- General information concerning Virtual Private Networking on Microsoft platforms is located on the Virtual Private Networks section of Microsoft TechNet at *http://technet.microsoft.com/en-us/network/bb545442.aspx.*

- Virtual Private Networking: Frequently Asked Questions at *http://www.microsoft.com/technet/network/vpn/vpnfaq.mspx.*

- The Routing and Remote Access Blog at *http://blogs.technet.com/rrasblog/* has some excellent information concerning Secure Socket Tunneling Protocol (SSTP), which was added in Windows Vista Service Pack 1.

- The Terminal Services Team Blog at *http://blogs.msdn.com/ts/* has some good information concerning the enhancements and changes made to Remote Desktop Protocol and Remote Desktop Connection (mstsc.exe) in Windows Vista Service Pack 1.

- The white paper "Step-by-Step Guide: Deploying SSTP Remote Access" at *http://download.microsoft.com/download/b/1/0/b106fc39-936c-4857-a6ea-3fb9d1f37063/Deploying%20SSTP%20Remote%20Access%20Step%20by%20Step%20Guide.doc.*

- Screencast: Deploying SSTP Remote Access available from *http://www.microsoft.com/downloads/details.aspx?FamilyID=fc4d7d3f-0376-45bf-9544-ec35329a2fc1&DisplayLang=en.*

- The Cable Guy article "IPv6 over Point-to-Point Protocol Links" at *http://www.microsoft.com/technet/community/columns/cableguy/cg1206.mspx.*

- KB 926179, "How to configure an L2TP/IPsec server behind a NAT-T device in Windows Vista and in Windows Server 2008" at *http://support.microsoft.com/kb/926179.*

- KB 926182, "How to configure verification of additional fields in peer certificates during IKE negotiation for L2TP/IPsec tunnel connections in Windows Vista," at *http://support.microsoft.com/kb/926182.*

- KB 289669, "Behavior of RAS Connections with the Fast User Switching Feature," at *http://support.microsoft.com/kb/289669.*

- KB 926170, "The MS-CHAP version 1 authentication protocol has been deprecated in Windows Vista," at *http://support.microsoft.com/kb/926170.*

- KB 922574, "The Microsoft Extensible Authentication Protocol-Message Digest 5 (EAP-MD5) implementation is being deprecated from versions of Windows," at *http://support.microsoft.com/kb/922574.*

- KB 947231, "After you create a VPN connection through a dial-up connection on a Windows Vista-based computer, VPN credentials are not cached," at *http://support.microsoft.com/kb/947231.*

- KB 923944, "List of Error Codes that you may receive when you try to make a dial-up connection or a VPN connection in Windows Vista," at *http://support.microsoft.com/kb/923944.*

- KB 929856, "You receive a '741' or a '742' error message when you try to establish a VPN connection by using L2TP/IPsec from a Windows client computer to a VPN server," at *http://support.microsoft.com/kb/929856.*

- KB 929857, "You receive error code 741 when you try to make a PPTP-based VPN connection on a computer that is running Windows Vista," at *http://support.microsoft.com/kb/929857.*

- KB 929853, "You cannot access network resources and domain name resolution is not successful when you establish a VPN connection to the corporate network from a Windows Vista–based computer," at *http://support.microsoft.com/kb/929853.*

- KB 930 085, "When you create a network connection that automatically calls another connection in Windows Vista, incorrect credentials appear when Windows Vista tests the connection," at *http://support.microsoft.com/kb/930085*.

- KB 929490, "Windows Vista–compatible third-party virtual private network (VPN) client schedules," at *http://support.microsoft.com/kb/929490*.

- KB 942429, "You cannot connect to a Cisco ASA Series VPN server by using an L2TP/IPsec-based VPN connection in Windows Vista," at *http://support.microsoft.com/kb/942429*.

- KB 945001, "When you use the Remote Desktop Connection feature to connect to a server from a Windows Vista–based client computer, Desktop Window Manager stops working on the server," at *http://support.microsoft.com/kb/945001*.

- KB 929709, "A Remote Desktop session disconnects even after you press a key when you receive the 'Idle timer expired' message in Windows Vista," at *http://support.microsoft.com/kb/929709*.

- KB 947224, "Error message when you try to connect to a computer that is running Windows XP or Windows Server 2003 through a RDP connection from a Windows Vista-based computer: 'the remote computer you want to connect to cannot recognize credentials'," at *http://support.microsoft.com/kb/947224*.

- KB 925876, "Remote Desktop Connection (Terminal Services Client 6.0)," at *http://support.microsoft.com/kb/925876*.

On the Companion CD

- ReportingDialUpAdapters.vbs

Chapter 29
Deploying IPv6

Windows Vista has a new Next Generation TCP/IP stack with enhanced support for Internet Protocol version 6 (IPv6). This chapter provides you with an understanding of why IPv6 is necessary and how it works. The chapter describes new IPv6 capabilities in Windows Vista and Windows Server 2008 and outlines how to migrate the IPv4 network infrastructure of your enterprise to IPv6 using IPv6 transition technologies such as Intra-Site Automatic Tunnel Addressing Protocol (ISATAP). Finally, the chapter describes how to configure and manage IPv6 settings in Windows Vista and how to troubleshoot IPv6 networking problems.

Understanding IPv6

The need for migrating enterprise networks from IPv4 to IPv6 is driven by a number of different technological, business, and social factors. The most important of these are:

- The exponential growth of the Internet is rapidly exhausting the existing IPv4 public address space. A temporary solution to this problem has been found in Network Address Translation (NAT), a technology that maps multiple private (intranet) addresses to a (usually) single, public (Internet) address. Unfortunately, using NAT-enabled routers can introduce additional problems such as breaking end-to-end connectivity and security for some network applications. In addition, the rapid proliferation of mobile IP devices is accelerating the depletion of the IPv4 public address space.

- The growing use of real-time communications (RTC) on the Internet, such as Voice Over Internet Protocol (VoIP) telephony, Instant Messaging (IM), and audio/video conferencing, exposes the limited support for Quality of Service (QoS) currently provided in IPv4. These new RTC technologies need improved QoS on IP networks to ensure reliable end-to-end communications. The design of IPv4 limits possible improvements.

- The growing threats faced by hosts on IPv4 networks connected to the Internet can be mitigated considerably by deploying Internet Protocol security (IPsec), both on private intranets and on tunneled connections across the public Internet. However, IPsec was designed as an afterthought to IPv4 and is complex and difficult to implement in many scenarios.

IPv6, developed by the Internet Engineering Task Force (IETF) to solve these problems, includes the following improvements and additions:

- IPv6 increases the theoretical address space of the Internet from 4.3×10^9 addresses (based on 32-bit IPv4 addresses) to 3.4×10^{38} possible addresses (based on 128-bit IPv6 addresses), which most experts agree should be more than sufficient for the foreseeable future.

- The IPv6 address space was designed to be hierarchical rather than flat in structure, which means that routing tables for IPv6 routers can be smaller and more efficient than for IPv4 routers.

- IPv6 has enhanced support for QoS that includes a Traffic Class field in the header to specify how traffic should be handled, and a new Flow Label field in the header that enables routers to identify packets that belong to a traffic flow and handle them appropriately.

- IPv6 now requires IPsec support for standards-based, end-to-end security across the Internet. The new QoS enhancements work even when IPv6 traffic is encrypted using IPsec.

Understanding how IPv6 works is essential if you plan to benefit from IPv6 by deploying it in your enterprise. The following sections provide an overview of key IPv6 concepts, features, and terminology.

Note   For more detailed information on IP concepts, features, and terminology, see the white paper titled "Introduction to IP Version 6" at *http://www.microsoft.com/downloads/details.aspx? FamilyID=CBC0B8A3-B6A4-4952-BBE6-D976624C257C&displaylang=en*. Another good reference for learning IPv6 is the book *Understanding IPv6, Second Edition*, by Joseph Davies (Microsoft Press, 2008). See *http://www.microsoft.com/MSPress/books/11607.aspx*.

Understanding IPv6 Terminology

The following terminology is used to define IPv6 concepts and describe IPv6 features:

- **Node**   An IPv6-enabled network device that includes both hosts and routers.
- **Host**   An IPv6-enabled network device that cannot forward IPv6 packets that are not explicitly addressed to itself. A host is an endpoint for IPv6 communications (either the source or destination) and drops all traffic not explicitly addressed to it.

- **Router**   An IPv6-enabled network device that can forward IPv6 packets that are not explicitly addressed to itself. IPv6 routers also typically advertise their presence to IPv6 hosts on their attached links.

- **Link**   One or more LAN (such as Ethernet) or WAN (such as PPP) network segments bounded by routers. Like interfaces, links may be either physical or logical.

- **Neighbors**   Nodes that are connected to the same physical or logical link.

- **Subnet**   One or more links having the same 64-bit IPv6 address prefix.

- **Interface**   A representation of a node's attachment to a link. This can be a physical interface (such as a network adapter) or a logical interface (such as a tunnel interface).

Note   An IPv6 address identifies an interface, not a node. A node is identified by having one or more unicast IPv6 addresses assigned to one of its interfaces.

Understanding IPv6 Addressing

IPv6 uses 128-bit (16 byte) addresses that are expressed in colon-hexadecimal form. For example, in the address 2001:DB8:3FA9:0000:0000:0000:00D3:9C5A, each block of 4-digit hexadecimal numbers represents a 16-bit digit binary number. The eight blocks of four-digit hexadecimal numbers thus equal 8 × 16 = 128 bits in total.

You can shorten hexadecimal-colon addresses by suppressing leading zeros for each block. Using this technique, the representation for the preceding address now becomes 2001:DB8:3FA9:0:0:0:D3:9C5A.

You can shorten hexadecimal-colon addresses even further by compressing contiguous 0 (hex) blocks as double colons ("::"). The address in our example thus shortens to 2001:DB8:3FA9::D3:9C5A. Note that only one double colon can be used per IPv6 address to ensure unambiguous representation.

Understanding IPv6 Prefixes

An IPv6 prefix indicates the portion of the address used for routing (a subnet or a set of subnets as a summarized route) or for identifying an address range. IPv6 prefixes are expressed in a similar fashion as the Classless Inter-Domain Routing (CIDR) notation used by IPv4. For example, 2001:DB8:3FA9::/48 might represent a route prefix in an IPv6 routing table.

In IPv4, CIDR notation can be used to represent individual unicast addresses in addition to routes and subnets. IPv6 prefixes, however, are used only to represent routes and address ranges, not unicast addresses. This is because unlike IPv4, IPv6 does not support variable length subnet identifiers, and the number of high-order bits used to identify a subnet in IPv6 is almost always 64. It is thus redundant to represent the address in our example as 2001:DB8:3FA9::D3:9C5A/64; the /64 portion of the representation is understood.

Understanding IPv6 Address Types

IPv6 supports three different address types:

- **Unicast**   Identifies a single interface within the scope of the address. (The scope of an IPv6 address is that portion of your network over which this address is unique.) IPv6 packets with unicast destination addresses are delivered to a single interface.

- **Multicast**   Identifies zero or more interfaces. IPv6 packets with multicast destination addresses are delivered to all interfaces listening on the address. (Generally speaking, multicasting works the same way in IPv6 as it does in IPv4.)

- **Anycast**   Identifies multiple interfaces. IPv6 packets with anycast destination addresses are delivered to the nearest interface (measured by routing distance) specified by the address. Currently, anycast addresses are assigned only to routers and can only represent destination addresses.

> **Note**   IPv6 address types do not include broadcast addresses as used by IPv4. In IPv6, all broadcast communications are performed using multicast addresses. See Table 29-2 for more information on multicast addresses.

Understanding Unicast Addresses

Unicast addresses are addresses that identify a single interface. IPv6 has several types of unicast addresses:

- **Global Unicast Address**   An address that is globally routable over the IPv6-enabled portion of the Internet. Therefore, the scope of a global address is the entire Internet, and global addresses in IPv6 correspond to public (non-RFC 1918) addresses used in IPv4. The address prefix currently used for global addresses as defined in RFC 3587 is 2000::/3, and a global address has the following structure:

  - ❏ The first 48 bits of the address are the global routing prefix specifying your organization's site. (The first three bits of this prefix must be 001 in binary notation.) These 48 bits represent the public topology portion of the address, which represents the collection of large and small Internet Service Providers (ISPs) on the IPv6 Internet, and which is controlled by these ISPs through assignment by the Internet Assigned Numbers Authority (IANA).

  - ❏ The next 16 bits are the subnet ID. Your organization can use this portion to specify up to 65,536 unique subnets for routing purposes inside your organization's site. These 16 bits represent the site topology portion of the address, which your organization has control over.

  - ❏ The final 64 bits are the interface ID and specify a unique interface within each subnet.

- **Link-Local Unicast Address**   An address that can be used by a node for communicating with neighboring nodes on the same link. Therefore, the scope of a link-local address is the local link on the network; link-local addresses are never forwarded beyond the local link by IPv6 routers. Because link-local addresses are assigned to interfaces using IPv6 address autoconfiguration, link-local addresses in IPv6 correspond to Automatic Private IP Addressing (APIPA) addresses used in IPv4 (which are assigned from the address range 169.254.0.0/16). The address prefix used for link-local addresses is FE80::/64, and a link-local address has the following structure:

    ❑ The first 64 bits of the address are always FE80:0:0:0 (which will be shown as FE80::).

    ❑ The last 64 bits are the interface ID and specify a unique interface on the local link.

  Link-local addresses can be reused—in other words, two interfaces on different links can have the same address. This makes link-local addresses ambiguous; an additional identifier called the zone ID (or scope ID) indicates to which link the address is either assigned or destined. In Windows Vista, the zone ID for a link-local address corresponds to the interface index for that interface. You can view a list of interface indexes on a computer by typing **netsh interface ipv6 show interface** at a command prompt. For more information on the zone ID, see the section titled "Displaying IPv6 Address Settings" later in this chapter.

- **Site-Local Unicast Address**   An address that is used by a node for communicating with other nodes on a private network having multiple subnets or links. The scope of a site-local address is the entire network at the site, which is typically a single geographical area, such as a building or campus. Since site-local addresses are not reachable except within an organization's intranet, site-local addresses in IPv6 correspond to private (RFC 1918) addresses used in IPv4. A site-local address has the following structure:

    ❑ The first 10 bits of the address are always FEC0::/10 or 1111 1110 11 (binary).

    ❑ The next 54 bits are the subnet ID. Your organization can use this portion to specify additional subnets for routing purposes inside your organization's site.

    ❑ The last 64 bits are the interface ID and specify a unique interface within each subnet.

  Note that RFC 3879 now deprecates the use of site-local addresses. The replacement for site-local addresses are unique local addresses. Existing IPv6 deployments may continue to use site-local addresses.

- **Unique Local Unicast Address**   Because a site-local address prefix can represent multiple sites within an organization, it is ambiguous and not well-suited for intraorganizational routing purposes. Therefore, RFC 4193 currently proposes a new type of address called a unique local unicast address. The scope of this address is global to all sites within the organization, and using this address type simplifies the configuration of an organization's internal IPv6 routing infrastructure. A unique local address has the following structure:

- ❑ The first seven bits of the address are always 1111 110 (binary) and the eighth bit is set to 1, indicating a unique local address. This means that the address prefix is always FD00::/8 for this type of address.

- ❑ The next 40 bits represent the global ID, a randomly generated value that identifies a specific site within your organization.

- ❑ The next 16 bits represent the subnet ID and can be used for further subdividing the internal network of your site for routing purposes.

- ❑ The last 64 bits are the interface ID and specify a unique interface within each subnet.

Identifying IPv6 Address Types

As Table 29-1 shows, you can quickly determine which type of IPv6 address you are dealing with by looking at the beginning part of the address—that is, the high-order bits of the address. Tables 29-2 and 29-3 also show examples of common IPv6 addresses that you can recognize directly from their colon-hexadecimal representation.

Table 29-1   Identifying IPv6 Address Types Using High-Order Bits and Address Prefix

Address Type	High-Order Bits	Address Prefix
Global unicast	001	2000::/3
Link-local unicast	1111 1110 10	FE80::/64
Site-local unicast	1111 1110 11	FEC0::/10
Unique local unicast	1111 1101	FD00::/8
Multicast	1111 1111	FF00::/8

Table 29-2   Identifying Common IPv6 Multicast Addresses

Function	Scope	Representation
All-nodes multicast	Interface-local	FF01::1
All-nodes multicast	Link-local	FF02::1
All-routers multicast	Interface-local	FF01::2
All-routers multicast	Link-local	FF02::2
All-routers multicast	Site-local	FF05::2

Table 29-3   Identifying Loopback and Unspecified IPv6 Addresses

Function	Representation
Unspecified address (no address)	::
Loopback address	::1

Note   For information on IPv6 address types used by different IPv6 transition technologies, see the section titled "Planning for IPv6 Migration" later in this chapter.

Understanding Interface Identifiers

For all the types of unicast IPv6 addresses described in the preceding sections, the last 64 bits of the address represent the interface ID and are used to specify a unique interface on a local link or subnet. In previous versions of Windows, the interface ID is uniquely determined as follows:

- For link-local addresses, such as a network adapter on an Ethernet segment, the interface ID is derived from either the unique 48-bit MAC-layer (Media Access Control) address of the interface or the unique EUI-64 (Extended Unique Identifier) address of the interface as defined by the Institute of Electrical and Electronics Engineers (IEEE).

- For global address prefixes, an EIU-64–based interface ID creates a public IPv6 address.

- For global address prefixes, a temporary random interface ID creates a temporary address. This approach is described in RFC 3041; you can use it to help provide anonymity for client-based usage of the IPv6 Internet.

In Windows Vista, however, the interface ID by default is randomly generated for all types of unicast IPv6 addresses assigned to LAN interfaces.

Note Windows Vista randomly generates the interface ID by default. You can also disable this behavior by typing **netsh int ipv6 set global randomizedidentifiers=disabled** at a command prompt.

Comparing IPv6 with IPv4

Table 29-4 compares and contrasts the IPv4 and IPv6 addressing schemes.

Table 29-4   IPv4 vs. IPv6 Addressing

Feature	IPv4	IPv6
Number of bits (bytes)	32 (4)	128 (16)
Expressed form	Dotted-decimal	Colon-hexadecimal
Variable-length subnets	Yes	No
Public addresses	Yes	Yes (global addresses)
Private addresses	Yes (RFC 1918 addresses)	Yes (unique local and site-local addresses)
Autoconfigured addresses for the local link	Yes (APIPA)	Yes (link-local addresses)
Support for address classes	Yes, but deprecated by CIDR	No
Broadcast addresses	Yes	Multicast used instead
Subnet mask	Required	Implicit /64 address prefix for addresses assigned to interfaces

> **Note**   For detailed specifications concerning IPv6 addressing, see RFC 4291 at
> *http://www.ietf.org/rfc/rfc4291.txt*. There are also other differences between IPv4 and IPv6,
> such as how the headers are structured for IPv4 versus IPv6 packets. For more information, see
> the white paper "Introduction to IP Version 6" at *http://www.microsoft.com/downloads/*
> *details.aspx?FamilyID=CBC0B8A3-B6A4-4952-BBE6-D976624C257C&displaylang=en*.

Understanding ICMPv6 Messages

Internet Control Message Protocol (ICMP) for IPv4 (ICMPv4) is used in IPv4 networks to allow nodes to send and respond to error messages and informational messages. For example, when a source node uses the ping command to send ICMP Echo Request messages (ICMP type 8 messages) to a destination node, the destination node can respond with ICMP Echo messages (ICMP type 0 messages) indicating its presence on the network.

On IPv6 networks, ICMP for IPv6 (ICMPv6) fulfills the same functions that ICMPv4 does on IPv4 networks—namely, to provide a mechanism for exchanging error messages and informational messages. ICMPv6 also provides information messages for the following:

- **Neighbor Discovery (ND)**   The process by which hosts and routers discover each other on the network so that they can communicate at the data-link layer. (Network Discovery serves the same purpose as ARP does in IPv4 networks.)

- **Multicast Listener Discovery (MLD)**   The process by which membership in multicast groups is determined and maintained.

> **Note**   For more information about Neighbor Discovery, see the section titled "Understanding
> Neighbor Discovery" later in this chapter. For more information about ICMPv6 message types
> and header formats, and about Multicast Listener Discovery, see the white paper "Introduction
> to IP Version 6" at *http://www.microsoft.com/downloads/details.aspx?FamilyID=CBC0B8A3-*
> *B6A4-4952-BBE6-D976624C257C&displaylang=en*.

Understanding Neighbor Discovery

Neighbor Discovery (ND) is the process by which nodes on an IPv6 network can communicate with each other by exchanging frames at the data-link layer. ND performs the following functions on an IPv6 network:

- Enables IPv6 nodes (IPv6 hosts and IPv6 routers) to resolve the link-layer address of a neighboring node (a node on the same physical or logical link)

- Enables IPv6 nodes to determine when the link-layer address of a neighboring node has changed

- Enables IPv6 nodes to determine whether neighboring nodes are still reachable

- Enables IPv6 routers to advertise their presence, on-link prefixes, and host configuration settings

- Enables IPv6 routers to redirect hosts to more optimal routers for a specific destination

- Enables IPv6 hosts to discover addresses, address prefixes, and other configuration settings

- Enables IPv6 hosts to discover routers attached to the local link

To understand how ND works, it helps to first compare it with the similar processes used in IPv4. In IPv4, you use three separate mechanisms to manage node-to-node communication:

- **Address Resolution Protocol (ARP)**   A data-link layer protocol that resolves IPv4 addresses assigned to interfaces to their corresponding MAC-layer addresses. This enables network adapters to receive frames addressed to them and send response frames to their source. For example, before a host can send a packet to a destination host whose IPv4 address is 172.16.25.3, the sending host first needs to use ARP to resolve this destination address (if the host is on the same LAN) or the IP address of the local gateway (if the host is on a different LAN) to its corresponding 48-bit MAC address (such as 00-13-20-08-A0-D1).

- **ICMPv4 Router Discovery**   These ICMPv4 messages enable routers to advertise their presence on IPv4 networks and enable hosts to discovery the presence of these routers. When Router Discovery is enabled on a router, the router periodically sends Router Advertisements to the all-hosts multicast address (224.0.0.1) to indicate to hosts on the network that the router is available. When Router Discovery is enabled on hosts, the hosts can send Router Solicitations to the all-routers multicast address (224.0.0.2) to obtain the address of the router and assign this address as the host's default gateway.

- **ICMPv4 Redirect**   Routers use these ICMPv4 messages to inform hosts of more optimal routers to use for specific destinations. ICMPv4 Redirect messages are needed because hosts typically cannot determine the best router on their subnet to send remote traffic for a given destination.

On IPv4 networks, these three mechanisms enable nodes on a network segment to communicate on a link. On IPv6 networks, these three mechanisms are replaced by the five ICMPv6 message types shown in Table 29-5.

Table 29-5   ICMPv6 Message Types Used for Neighbor Discovery

Message Type	ICMPv6 Type	Description
Router Solicitation	133	Sent by IPv6 hosts to the link-local scope all-routers multicast address (FF02::2) to discover IPv6 routers present on the local link.
Router Advertisement	134	Sent periodically by IPv6 routers to the link-local scope all-nodes multicast address (FF02::1), or sent to the unicast address of a host in response to receiving a Router Solicitation message from that host. (Windows Vista and later use multicast for optimization.) Router Advertisement messages provide hosts with the information needed to determine link prefixes, link MTU, whether or not to use DHCPv6 for address auto-configuration, and lifetime for autoconfigured addresses.
Neighbor Solicitation	135	Sent by IPv6 nodes to the solicited-node multicast address of a host to discover the link-layer address of an IPv6 node, or sent to the unicast address of the host to verify the reachability of the host.
Neighbor Advertisement	136	Sent by an IPv6 node to the unicast address of a host in response to receiving a Neighbor Solicitation message from the host, or sent to the link-local scope all-nodes multicast address (FF02::1) to inform neighboring nodes of changes to the host's link-layer addresses.
Redirect	137	Sent by an IPv6 router to the unicast address of a host to inform the host of a more optimal first-hop address for a specific destination.

Note   The solicited-node multicast address, which is used as the destination address for ICMPv4 Neighbor Solicitation messages (ICMPv6 type 135 messages) when address resolution is being performed, is a special type of multicast address composed of the prefix FF02::1:FF00:0/104 followed by the last 24 bits of the IPv6 address that is being resolved. IPv6 nodes listen on their solicited-node multicast addresses. The advantage of using this multicast address for address resolution in IPv6 is that typically only the targeted host is disturbed on the local link. By contrast, the ARP messages used in IPv4 for address resolution queries are sent to the MAC-layer broadcast address, which disturbs all hosts on the local segment.

Understanding Address Autoconfiguration

On IPv4 networks, addresses can be assigned to hosts in three ways:

■ Manually using static address assignment

■ Automatically using DHCP, if a DHCP server is present on the subnet (or a DHCP relay agent configured on the subnet)

■ Automatically using Automatic Private IP Addressing (APIPA), which randomly assigns the host an address from the range 169.254.0.0 to 169.254.255.255 with subnet mask 255.255.0.0

On IPv6 networks, static addresses are generally assigned only to routers and sometimes servers, but hardly ever to client computers. Instead, IPv6 addresses are almost always assigned automatically using a process called address autoconfiguration. Address autoconfiguration can work in three ways: stateless, stateful, or both. Stateless address autoconfiguration is based on the receipt of ICMPv6 Router Advertisement messages. Stateful address auto-configuration, on the other hand, uses DHCPv6 to obtain address information and other configuration settings from a DHCPv6 server.

Note   The DHCP Server service of Windows Server 2008 supports DHCPv6. The DHCP Server service of Windows Server 2003 does not support DHCPv6.

All IPv6 nodes (hosts and routers) automatically assign themselves link-local addresses (addresses having the address prefix FE80::/64); this is done for every interface (both physical and logical) on the node. (6to4 interfaces are an exception—they might not have link-local addresses automatically assigned.) These autoconfigured link-local addresses can be used only to reach neighboring nodes (nodes on the same link). When specifying one of these addresses as a destination address, you might need to specify the zone ID for the destination. In addition, link-local addresses are never registered in DNS servers.

Note   Manual assignment of IPv6 addresses is generally needed only for IPv6 routers and for some servers. You can configure a Windows Vista computer with multiple interfaces to be used as a router. For more information on configuring IPv6 routers, see the Cable Guy article titled "Manual Configuration for IPv6" at *http://technet.microsoft.com/en-us/library/bb878102.aspx*. For a description of the IPv6 routing table, see the Cable Guy article titled "Understanding the IPv6 Routing Table" at *http://technet.microsoft.com/en-us/library/bb878115.aspx*.

An autoconfigured IPv6 address can be in one or more of the states shown in Table 29-6.

Table 29-6   Possible States for an Autoconfigured IPv6 Address

State	Description
Tentative	The uniqueness of the address is still being verified using duplicate address detection.
Valid	The address is unique and can now send and receive unicast IPv6 traffic until the Valid Lifetime expires.
Preferred	The address can be used for unicast traffic until the Preferred Lifetime expires.
Deprecated	The address can still be used for unicast traffic during existing communication sessions, but its use is discouraged for new communication sessions.
Invalid	The Valid Lifetime for the address has expired and it can no longer be used for unicast traffic.

Note   The Valid and Preferred lifetime for stateless autoconfigured IPv6 addresses is included in the Router Solicitation message.

For detailed descriptions of how address autoconfiguration, address resolution, router discovery, redirect, duplicate address detection, and neighbor unreachability detection processes are performed, see the white paper "Introduction to IP Version 6" at *http://www.microsoft.com/ downloads/details.aspx?FamilyID=CBC0B8A3-B6A4-4952-BBE6-D976624C257C&displaylang=en.*

Note   To display the state for each autoconfigured IPv6 address on a Windows Vista computer, open a command prompt and type **netsh interface ipv6 show addresses** at a command prompt.

Understanding Name Resolution

The Domain Name System (DNS) is fundamental to how name resolution works on both IPv4 and IPv6 networks. On an IPv4 network, host (A) records are used by name servers (DNS servers) to resolve fully qualified domain names (FQDNs) like server1.contoso.com into their associated IP addresses in response to name lookups (name queries) from DNS clients. In addition, reverse lookups—in which IP addresses are resolved into FQDNs—are supported by using pointer (PTR) records in the in-addr.arpa domain.

Name resolution works fundamentally the same way with IPv6, with the following differences:

■ Host records for IPv6 hosts are AAAA ("quad-A") records, not A records.

■ The domain used for reverse lookups of IPv6 addresses is ip6.arpa, not in-addr.arpa.

Note   The enhancements to the Domain Name System that make IPv6 support possible are described in the draft standard RFC 3596 at *http://www.ietf.org/rfc/rfc3596.txt.*

Understanding Name Queries

Because Windows Vista's dual-layer TCP/IP stack means that both IPv4 and IPv6 are enabled by default, DNS name lookups by Windows Vista client computers can involve the use of both A and AAAA records. (This is true only if your name servers support IPv6, which is the case with the DNS Server role for Windows Server 2008 and Windows Server 2003.) By default, the DNS client component on Windows Vista uses the following procedure when performing a name lookup using a particular interface:

1. The client computer checks to see whether it has a non-link-local IPv6 address assigned to the interface. If it has no non-link-local addresses assigned, the client sends a single name lookup to the name server to query for A records and does not query for AAAA

records. If the only non-link-local address assigned to the interface is a Teredo address, the client again does not query for AAAA records. (The Teredo client in Windows Vista has been explicitly built not to automatically perform AAAA lookups or register with DNS to prevent overloading of DNS servers.)

2. If the client computer has a non-link-local address assigned to the interface, the client sends a name lookup to query for A records.

    ❏   If the client then receives a response to its query (not an error message), it follows with a second lookup to query for AAAA records.

    ❏   If the client receives no response or receives any error message (except for Name Not Found), it does not send a second lookup to query for AAAA records.

> **Note**   Because an interface on an IPv6 host typically has multiple IPv6 addresses, the process by which source and address selection works during a name query is more complex than when DNS names are resolved by IPv4 hosts. For a detailed description of how source and address selection works for IPv6 hosts, see the Cable Guy article titled "Source and Destination Address Selection for IPv6" at *http://technet.microsoft.com/en-us/library/bb877985.aspx*. For additional information on DNS and Windows Vista, see "Domain Name System Client Behavior in Windows Vista" at *http://technet.microsoft.com/en-us/library/bb727035.aspx*. For information about the different types of IPv6 addresses usually assigned to an interface, see the section titled "Configuring and Troubleshooting IPv6 in Windows Vista" later in this chapter.

> **Note**   Issues have arisen with poorly configured DNS name servers on the Internet. These issues, which are described in RFC 4074 (*http://www.ietf.org/rfc/rfc4074.txt*), do not cause problems on Windows Vista because Microsoft has altered the DNS client behavior specifically to compensate for them. However, administrators of DNS servers should make sure these issues are fixed, because they can cause problems with DNS name resolution for most IPv6 networking stacks, including stacks found in legacy Windows platforms such as Windows XP.

Understanding Name Registration

DNS servers running Windows Server 2003 can dynamically register both A and AAAA records for Windows Vista client computers. Dynamic registration of DNS records simplifies the job of maintaining name resolution on networks running the Active Directory directory service. When a Windows Vista client computer starts up on a network, the DNS Client service tries to register the following records for the client:

■   A records for all IPv4 addresses assigned to all interfaces configured with the address of a DNS server

■   AAAA records for all IPv6 addresses assigned to all interfaces configured with the address of a DNS server

■   PTR records for all IPv4 addresses assigned to all interfaces configured with the address of a DNS server

> **Note**   AAAA records are not registered for link-local IPv6 addresses that have been assigned to interfaces using address autoconfiguration.

PTR Records and IPv6

Windows Vista client computers do not try to register PTR records for IPv6 addresses assigned to interfaces on the computer. If you want to enable clients to perform reverse lookups for Windows Vista computers using IPv6, you must manually create a reverse lookup zone for the ip6.arpa domain on your DNS servers and then manually add PTR records to this zone. For detailed steps on how to do this, see "IPv6 for MicrosoftWindows: Frequently Asked Questions" at *http://www.microsoft.com/technet/ network/ipv6/ipv6faq.mspx*.

However, PTR records for reverse lookups using IPv6 are not often used, because the namespace for reverse queries is formed by using each hexadecimal digit in the colon-hexadecimal representation of an IPv6 address as a separate level in the reverse domain hierarchy. For example, the PTR record associated with the IPv6 address 2001:DB8::D3:00FF:FE28:9C5A, whose full representation is 2001:0DB8:0000:0000: 00D3:00FF:FE28:9C5A, would be expressed as A.5.C.9.8.2.E.F.F.F.0.0.3.D.0.0.0.0.0. 0.0.0.0.0.8.B.D.0.1.0.0.2.IP6.ARPA. The performance cost of resolving such a representation would generally be too high for most DNS server implementations.

By default, DNS servers running Windows Server 2003 do not listen for DNS traffic sent over IPv6. To enable these DNS servers to listen for IPv6 name registrations and name lookups, you must first configure the servers using the **dnscmd /config /EnableIPv6 1** command. By default, DNS servers running Windows Server 2008 listen for DNS traffic sent over IPv6. You must then configure each Windows Vista client computer with the unicast IPv6 addresses of your DNS servers using DHCPv6, the properties of the Internet Protocol Version 6 (TCP/ IPv6) component in the Network Connections folder, or the **netsh interface ipv6 add dns interface=NameOrIndex address=IPv6Address index=PreferenceLevel** command. (DHCP servers running Windows Server 2003 do not support stateful address assignment using DHCPv6.)

> **Note**   For more information on enabling Windows Server 2003 DNS server support for IPv6, see Chapter 9, "Windows Support for DNS" in the online book *TCP/IP Fundamentals for Microsoft Windows*, which you can download from *http://www.microsoft.com/downloads/ details.aspx?FamilyID=c76296fd-61c9-4079-a0bb-582bca4a846f &displaylang=en*. For further details on the DNS name query and registration behavior in Windows Vista, see the article titled "Domain Name System Client Behavior in Windows Vista" on Microsoft TechNet at *http://technet.microsoft.com/en-us/library/bb727035.aspx*.

IPv6 Enhancements in Windows Vista

The TCP/IP networking stack in the Windows XP and Windows Server 2003 platforms had a dual-stack architecture that used separate network and framing layers for IPv4 and IPv6 based on separate drivers: Tcpip.sys and Tcpip6.sys. Only the transport and framing layers for IPv4 were installed by default, and adding support for IPv6 involved installing an additional IPv6 protocol component through the Network Connections folder.

By contrast, in Windows Vista and Windows Server 2008, the TCP/IP stack has been completely redesigned and now uses a dual IP layer architecture in which both IPv4 and IPv6 share common transport and framing layers. In addition, IPv6 is installed and enabled by default in these new platforms to provide out-of-the-box support for new features such as the Windows Meeting Space application, which uses only IPv6. Finally, the dual IP layer architecture means that all of the performance enhancements of the Next Generation TCP/IP stack that apply to IPv4 also apply to IPv6. These performance enhancements include Compound TCP, Receive Window Auto-Tuning, and other enhancements that can dramatically improve performance in high-latency, high-delay, and high-loss networking environments.

> **Note**   For more information about the performance enhancements in the Next Generation TCP/IP stack, see Chapter 26, "Configuring Windows Networking."

Summary of IPv6 Enhancements in Windows Vista

The following list summarizes the changes to IPv6 support in Windows Vista compared with previous Windows platforms:

- **Dual IP layer architecture**   A new TCP/IP stack architecture that uses the same transport and framing layers for both IPv4 and IPv6.

- **Enabled by default**   Both IPv4 and IPv6 are installed and enabled by default, with the stack giving preference to IPv6 when appropriate without impairing the performance of IPv4 communications on the network. For example, if a DNS name query returns both an IPv4 and IPv6 address for a host, the client will try to use IPv6 first for communicating with the host. This preference also results in better network performance for IPv6-enabled applications.

- **User interface configuration support**   In addition to being able to configure IPv6 settings from the command line using the netsh interface ipv6 command context, you can also configure them in Windows Vista using the user interface. For more information, see the section titled "Configuring IPv6 in Windows Vista Using the User Interface" later in this chapter.

- **Full IPsec support**   IPv6 support in previous versions of Windows offered only limited support for IPsec protection of network traffic. In Windows Vista, however, IPsec support for IPv6 is the same as for IPv4, and you can configure IPsec connection security rules for IPv6 the same as for IPv4, using the Windows Firewall With Advanced Security console. For more information on configuring IPsec in Windows Vista, see Chapter 27, "Configuring Windows Firewall and IPsec."

■ **LLMNR support**   The implementation of IPv6 in Windows Vista supports Link-Local Multicast Name Resolution (LLMNR), a mechanism that enables IPv6 nodes on a single subnet to resolve each other's names in the absence of a DNS server. LLMNR works by having nodes send multicast DNS name queries instead of unicast queries. Windows Vista computers listen by default for multicast LLMNR traffic, which eliminates the need to perform local subnet name resolution using NetBIOS over TCP/IP when no DNS server is available. LLMNR is defined in RFC 4795.

■ **MLDv2 support**   The implementation of IPv6 in Windows Vista supports Multicast Listener Discovery (MLD) version 2 (MLDv2), a mechanism described in RFC 3810 that enables IPv6 hosts to register interest in source-specific multicast traffic with local multicast routers by specifying an include list (to indicate specific source addresses of interest) or an exclude list (to exclude unwanted source addresses).

■ **DHCPv6 support**   The DHCP Client service in Windows Vista supports Dynamic Host Configuration Protocol for IPv6 (DHCPv6) as defined in RFCs 3736 and 4361. This means that Windows Vista computers can perform both stateful and stateless DHCPv6 configuration on a native IPv6 network.

■ **IPV6CP support**   The built-in remote access client component in Windows Vista supports IPv6 Control Protocol (IPV6CP) (RFC 5072) to configure IPv6 nodes on a Point-to-Point Protocol (PPP) link. This means that native IPv6 traffic can be sent over PPP-based network connections such as dial-up connections or broadband PPP over Ethernet (PPPoE) connections to an Internet Service Provider (ISP). IPV6CP also supports Layer 2 Tunneling Protocol (L2TP), and for Windows Vista with Service Pack 1, Secure Socket Tunneling Protocol (SSTP)–based Virtual Private Network (VPN) connections. For more information on IPV6CP support in Windows Vista, see Chapter 28, "Connecting Remote Users and Networks."

■ **Random interface IDs**   By default, Windows Vista generates random interface IDs for nontemporary autoconfigured IPv6 addresses, including both public addresses (global addresses registered in DNS) and link-local addresses. For more information, see the section titled "Disabling Random Interface IDs" later in this chapter.

■ **Literal IPv6 addresses in URLs**   Windows Vista supports RFC 2732–compliant literal IPv6 addresses in URLs by using the new WinINet API support in Microsoft Internet Explorer 7.0. This can be a useful feature for troubleshooting Internet connectivity with IPv6-enabled Web servers.

■ **New Teredo Behavior**   The Teredo client in Windows Vista remains dormant (inactive) until it spins up (is activated by) an IPv6-enabled application that tries to use Teredo. In

Windows Vista, three things can bring up Teredo: an application trying to communicate using a Teredo address (the outbound instantiated scenario); a listening application that has the Edge Traversal rule enabled in Windows Firewall (any IPv6-enabled applications that need to use Teredo can easily do so by setting the Edge Traversal flag using the Windows Firewall APIs); and the *NotifyStableUnicastIpAddressTable* IP Helper API. For more information about Windows Firewall rules, see Chapter 27.

How It Works: Teredo Behavior in Windows Vista

Teredo is default-enabled but inactive in both workgroup and domain scenarios. Teredo becomes active in two main scenarios:

■ An application tries to communicate with a Teredo address (for example, by using a URL with a Teredo address in a Web browser). This is outbound-initiated traffic, and Teredo will go dormant again after 60 minutes of inactivity. The host firewall will allow only incoming Teredo traffic corresponding to the specific outbound request, ensuring that system security isn't compromised. This is really no different than how any outbound-initiated traffic works with the host firewall with IPv4. (In other words, all outbound traffic is allowed by default, and a state table allows responses that match the outgoing requests.)

■ An application or service is authorized to use Teredo with the advanced Windows Firewall Edge Traversal flag. If an application has the Edge Traversal option, it is allowed to receive any incoming traffic over Teredo from any source (such as unsolicited traffic). Windows Meeting Space and Remote Assistance automatically set this flag for themselves, but users can do it manually for other Windows Vista services if they prefer, such as with a web service.

Michael Surkan

Program Manager for TCP and IPv6

Configuring and Troubleshooting IPv6 in Windows Vista

Although IPv6 is designed to allow IPv6-enabled nodes such as Windows Vista computers to automatically configure their interfaces with link-local addresses, these autoconfigured addresses are not registered in DNS servers and can be used only for communicating with other nodes on the local link. Alternatively, by using a DHCPv6 server, you can automatically assign global, site-local, or unique local IPv6 addresses to IPv6-enabled interfaces of link-attached nodes. This is the preferred scenario for end-to-end IPv6 connectivity in enterprises that have a native IPv6-only network infrastructure.

However, you can also use two methods to configure IPv6 settings manually on Windows Vista computers:

- Using The new IPv6 graphical user interface
- Using The **netsh interface ipv6** command context

In addition, it is important to understand the different kinds of IPv6 addresses assigned to Windows Vista computers so that you can troubleshoot IPv6 connectivity when problems arise.

Displaying IPv6 Address Settings

To display the IPv4 and IPv6 address configuration of the local computer, open a command prompt window and type **ipconfig /all** at a command prompt. The following is an example of the information displayed by running this command on a domain-joined Windows Vista computer with a single LAN network adapter, no IPv6 routers on the attached subnet, and no other configured network connections:

```
Windows IP Configuration

    Host Name . . . . . . . . . . . . : KBERG-PC
    Primary Dns Suffix  . . . . . . . : contoso.com
    Node Type . . . . . . . . . . . . : Hybrid
    IP Routing Enabled. . . . . . . . : No
    WINS Proxy Enabled. . . . . . . . : No
    DNS Suffix Search List. . . . . . : contoso.com

Ethernet adapter Local Area Connection:

    Connection-specific DNS Suffix  . :
    Description . . . . . . . . . . . : Realtek RTL8139/810x Family Fast Ethernet NIC
    Physical Address. . . . . . . . . : 00-13-D4-C2-50-F5
    DHCP Enabled. . . . . . . . . . . : Yes
    Autoconfiguration Enabled . . . . : Yes
    Link-local IPv6 Address . . . . . : fe80::3530:6107:45a2:a92c%8(Preferred)
    IPv4 Address. . . . . . . . . . . : 172.16.11.13(Preferred)
    Subnet Mask . . . . . . . . . . . : 255.255.255.0
    Lease Obtained. . . . . . . . . . : Sunday, October 29, 2006 9:38:02 AM
    Lease Expires . . . . . . . . . . : Wednesday, November 08, 2006 12:38:00 PM
    Default Gateway . . . . . . . . . : 172.16.11.1
    DHCP Server . . . . . . . . . . . : 172.16.11.32
    DHCPv6 IAID . . . . . . . . . . . : 201331668
    DNS Servers . . . . . . . . . . . : 172.16.11.32
    NetBIOS over Tcpip. . . . . . . . : Enabled

Tunnel adapter Local Area Connection* 6:

    Connection-specific DNS Suffix  . :
    Description . . . . . . . . . . . : isatap.{1F1E1761-FF83-4866-AE6C-9FCEE1E49099}
    Physical Address. . . . . . . . . : 00-00-00-00-00-00-00-E0
    DHCP Enabled. . . . . . . . . . . : No
```

```
    Autoconfiguration Enabled . . . . : Yes
    Link-local IPv6 Address . . . . . : fe80::5efe:172.16.11.13%9(Preferred)
    Default Gateway . . . . . . . . . :
    DNS Servers . . . . . . . . . . . : 172.16.11.32
    NetBIOS over Tcpip. . . . . . . . : Disabled

Tunnel adapter Local Area Connection* 7:

    Connection-specific DNS Suffix  . :
    Description . . . . . . . . . . . : Teredo Tunneling Pseudo-Interface
    Physical Address. . . . . . . . . : 02-00-54-55-4E-01
    DHCP Enabled. . . . . . . . . . . : No
    Autoconfiguration Enabled . . . . : Yes
    IPv6 Address. . . . . . . . . . . : 2001:0:4136:e37c:4e8:3426:7c94:fffe(Preferred)
    Link-local IPv6 Address . . . . . : fe80::4e8:3426:53ef:f4f2%10(Preferred)
    Default Gateway . . . . . . . . . : ::
    NetBIOS over Tcpip. . . . . . . . : Disabled
```

The preceding command output displays three interfaces on this computer:

- Local Area Connection (the installed network adapter)
- Local Area Connection* 6 (a tunneling interface for ISATAP)
- Local Area Connection* 7 (a tunneling interface for Teredo)

The Local Area Connection interface is an Ethernet network adapter and has both an IPv4 address (172.16.11.13) assigned by DHCP and a link-local IPv6 address (fe80::3530:6107: 45a2:a92c) that has been automatically assigned using IPv6 address autoconfiguration. (You can recognize the link-local address by its address prefix, FE80::/64.)

The "%8" appended to this address is the zone ID (or scope ID) that indicates which connected portion of the network the computer resides on. This zone ID corresponds with the interface index for the Local Area Connection interface. To view a list of interface indexes on a computer, type **netsh interface ipv6 show interface** at a command prompt. For the preceding example computer, the output will be:

```
Idx  Met  MTU         State        Name
---  ---  -----       -----------  -------------------
  1   50  4294967295  connected    Loopback Pseudo-Interface 1
  9   25  1280        connected    Local Area Connection* 6
 10   10  1280        connected    Local Area Connection* 7
  8   20  1500        connected    Local Area Connection
```

The Idx column indicates the interface index. The zone ID might be needed when testing network connectivity with this computer from other computers using the ping and tracert commands. See the section titled "Troubleshooting IPv6 Connectivity" later in this chapter for more information.

The state of the link-local address assigned to the LAN connection is Preferred, which indicates a valid IPv6 address you can use to send and receive unicast IPv6 traffic.

The ISATAP tunneling interface has an autoconfigured link-local address of fe80::5efe:172.16.11.13. The format for an ISATAP address is:

- The first 64 bits are a unicast prefix that can be a link-local, global, site-local, or unique local unicast IPv6 address prefix. This example uses the link-local address prefix because no ISATAP router is present on the network. This means that the resulting ISATAP address can be used only for communicating with other ISATAP hosts on the IPv4 network, and this ISATAP address is not registered in DNS servers.

- The next 32 bits are either 0:5EFE or 200:5EFE in an ISATAP address. (RFC 4214 also allows 100:5EFE and 300:5EFE in this portion of an ISATAP address.)

- The final 32 bits consist of the 32-bit IPv4 address of the host in dotted-decimal form (172.16.11.13 in this example).

> **Note**   For more information on ISATAP addressing, see the white paper "IPv6 Transition Technologies" at *http://www.microsoft.com/downloads/details.aspx?FamilyID=afe56282-2903-40f3-a5ba-a87bf92c096d &displaylang=en* and the white paper "Intra-site Automatic Tunnel Addressing Protocol Deployment Guide" at *http://www.microsoft.com/downloads/details.aspx?FamilyID=0f3a8868-e337-43d1-b271-b8c8702344cd &displaylang=en.* See also the section titled "Understanding ISATAP" later in this chapter.

The Teredo tunneling pseudo-interface displays the IPv6 address of the Teredo client as 2001:0:4136:e37c:4e8:3426:53ef:f4f2. The format for a Teredo client address is:

- The first 32 bits are always the Teredo prefix, which is 2001::/32.

- The next 32 bits contain the public IPv4 address of the Teredo server that helped in the configuration of this Teredo address (here 4136:E37C hexadecimal, which converts to 65.54.227.124 in dotted-decimal format). By default, the Teredo client in Windows Vista and Windows Server 2008 automatically tries to determine the IPv4 addresses of Teredo servers by resolving the name teredo.ipv6.microsoft.com.

- The next 16 bits are reserved for various Teredo flags.

- The next 16 bits contain an obscured version of the external UDP port number that corresponds to all Teredo traffic for this Teredo client. (The external UDP port number is obscured XORing it with 0xFFFF, and in this example 0x3426 XOR 0xFFFF = 0xCBD9 or decimal 52185, meaning UDP port 52185.)

- The final 32 bits contain an obscured version of the external IPv4 address that corresponds to all Teredo traffic for this Teredo client. (The external IPv4 address is obscured, XORing it with 0xFFFF FFFF, and in this example is 0x7C94 FFFE XOR 0xFFFF FFFF = 0x836B 0001 or dotted-decimal 131.107.0.1.)

> **Note**   IANA has allocated the IPv6 address prefix 2001::/32 for Teredo as of January 2006.
> (See RFC 4830 at *http://www.rfc-editor.org/rfc/rfc4380.txt* for details.) Windows XP–based cli-
> ents originally used the 3FFE:831F::/32 Teredo prefix. Windows XP–based clients with the
> Microsoft Security Bulletin MS06-064 at *http://www.microsoft.com/technet/security/Bulletin/
> MS06-064.mspx* now use the 2001::/32 prefix.

Another way to display the IPv6 settings on a Windows Vista computer is to type the **netsh
interface ipv6 show address** command. The results for the computer in the preceding
example are:

```
Interface 1: Loopback Pseudo-Interface 1

Addr Type  DAD State    Valid Life Pref. Life Address
---------  -----------  ---------- ---------- -----------------------
Other      Preferred      infinite   infinite ::1

Interface 9: Local Area Connection* 6

Addr Type  DAD State    Valid Life Pref. Life Address
---------  -----------  ---------- ---------- -----------------------
Other      Preferred      infinite   infinite fe80::5efe:172.16.11.13%9

Interface 10: Local Area Connection* 7

Addr Type  DAD State    Valid Life Pref. Life Address
---------  -----------  ---------- ---------- -----------------------
Public     Preferred      infinite   infinite 2001:0:4136:e37c:1071:3426:31d2:bfce
Other      Preferred      infinite   infinite fe80::1071:3426:31d2:bfce%10

Interface 8: Local Area Connection

Addr Type  DAD State    Valid Life Pref. Life Address
---------  -----------  ---------- ---------- -----------------------
Other      Preferred      infinite   infinite fe80::3530:6107:45a2:a92c%8
```

> **Note**   An advantage of displaying IPv6 address settings using the netsh interface ipv6 show
> address command instead of ipconfig is that you can execute Netsh.exe commands remotely
> against a targeted computer by using the *–r* RemoteComputerName option.

For more information on how to use ipconfig, Netsh.exe, and other tools to display IPv6
configuration information, see the article "Using Windows Tools to Obtain IPv6 Configuration
Information" on Microsoft TechNet at *http://technet.microsoft.com/en-us/library/bb726952.aspx.*

Direct from the Source: Explanation of Teredo States

With netsh int teredo show state, you can see the current state of Teredo, which can be one of the following:

- **Offline state** In this state, something has failed and Teredo cannot be activated (cannot be in the Qualified state) to be used by applications. Teredo enters this state in three ways:

  - When the Administrator disables it via netsh int teredo set state disabled.

  - When Teredo detects that the computer is on a managed network (detects the presence of a domain controller on the network—see the section in this sidebar titled "Teredo in Enterprise Networks" for more information), it will go offline if its type is not set to "enterpriseclient".

  - When some internal mechanism has failed in Teredo, such as suddenly being unable to reach the Teredo server or being unable to resolve teredo.ipv6 .microsoft.com. In only this case, Teredo will attempt to move into the Dormant state using an exponential back-off time-out as follows: wait 5 seconds, try again; wait 10 seconds, try again; wait 20 seconds, try again; and continue until it tries every 15 minutes.

- **Dormant state** This is the state when Teredo is "enabled but not active." IPv6 traffic cannot flow over Teredo, but applications can trigger to activate Teredo. No edge traversal will occur in this state. No traffic is sent to the Teredo servers.

- **Probe state** This is the transition state from Dormant to Qualified. In this state, Teredo will try to establish communication with the Teredo server. If this succeeds, Teredo moves to the Qualified state. If this fails, Teredo will go to the Offline state.

- **Qualified state** In this state, IPv6 traffic can flow into and out of the system over Teredo and possibly traverse the edge firewall/NAT.

Teredo in Enterprise Networks

Whether a computer is domain-joined or in a workgroup doesn't matter to Teredo. Teredo looks only at the environment that the computer is in. If Teredo detects the presence of a domain controller, it will assume that the network is managed. In this case, Teredo will go offline and stay offline unless it was administratively set to "enterpriseclient" using the command netsh int teredo set state enterpriseclient. Hence, Teredo will go to the Offline state on a workgroup computer that is connected to a network with a domain controller. This is to avoid traversing the edge of a corporate network. Conversely, if you take a domain-joined laptop home, Teredo will detect that it is no longer in a managed network and will go to the Dormant state.

Note that if you disable Teredo via the DisabledComponents registry key, it will override all the Teredo netsh settings.

Kalven Wu, Software Design Engineer in Test

Windows Core Networking

Configuring IPv6 in Windows Vista Using the User Interface

To configure the IPv6 settings for a network connection in Windows Vista using the user interface, follow these steps:

1. Open the Network And Sharing Center in Control Panel.

2. Click Manage Network Connections and then double-click the connection you want to configure.

3. Click the Properties button and respond to the UAC prompt.

4. Select Internet Protocol Version 6 (TCP/IPv6) and click Properties to open the Internet Protocol Version 6 (TCP/IPv6) Properties sheet (see Figure 29-1).

5. Configure the IPv6 settings for the network connection as desired.

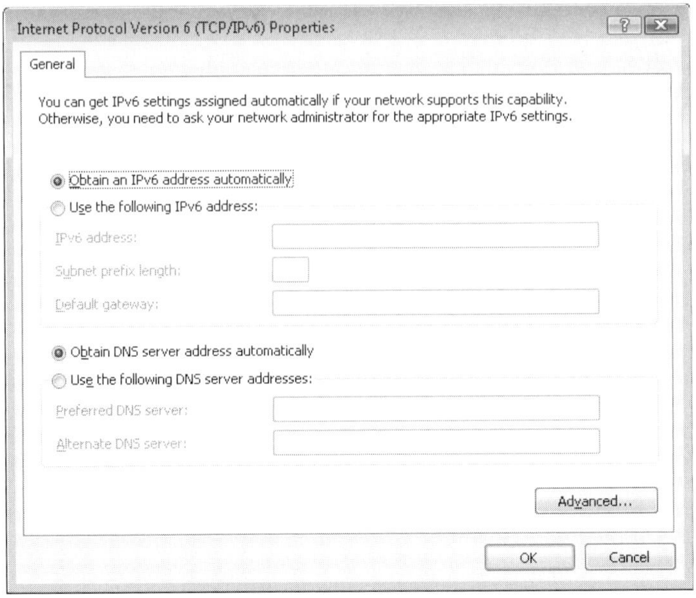

Figure 29-1   IPv6 properties of a network connection.

By default, the IPv6 settings for a network connection are configured as follows:

- **Obtain An IPv6 Address Automatically**   This specifies that the physical or logical interface associated with this connection uses stateful or stateless address auto-configuration to obtain its IPv6 address.

- **Obtain DNS Server Address Automatically**   This specifies that the physical or logical interface associated with this connection uses stateful address autoconfiguration (DHCPv6) to obtain the IPv6 addresses of preferred and alternate DNS servers.

By selecting Use The Following IPv6 Address, you can manually configure the IPv6 address settings for a network connection by specifying the following:

- **IPv6 Address**   Type the unicast IPv6 address you want to assign to the physical or logical interface associated with this connection in colon-hexadecimal form. If you need to assign additional unicast IPv6 addresses to the interface, click the Advanced button and then click the IP Settings tab.

- **Subnet Prefix Length**   Type the subnet prefix length for the IPv6 address you assigned to the physical or logical interface associated with this connection. For unicast IPv6 addresses, the subnet prefix length should almost always be specified as 64.

- **Default Gateway**   Type the unicast IPv6 address of the default gateway for the local IPv6 subnet in colon-hexadecimal form. If you need to specify additional default gateways, click the Advanced button and then click the IP Settings tab.

By selecting Use The Following DNS Server Addresses, you can manually specify IPv6 addresses for a preferred and an alternate DNS server to be used by your connection. If you need to specify additional alternate DNS servers, click the Advanced button and then click the DNS tab. The remaining settings on the DNS tab have similar functionality to those used for configuring IPv4 address settings.

 Note   The Advanced TCP/IP Settings dialog box does not have a WINS tab because IPv6 does not use NetBIOS for name resolution.

Configuring IPv6 in Windows Vista Using Netsh

To configure the IPv6 settings for a network connection in Windows Vista using the Netsh.exe command, open a command prompt window with local administrator credentials and type the appropriate Netsh.exe command from the netsh interface ipv6 context. Some examples of IPv6 configuration tasks that can be performed from this context include:

- To add the unicast IPv6 address 2001:DB8::8:800:20C4:0 to the interface named Local Area Connection as a persistent IPv6 address with infinite valid and preferred lifetimes, type the following command:

    netsh interface ipv6 add address "Local Area Connection" 2001:DB8::8:800:20C4:0

■ To configure a default gateway with unicast IPv6 address 2001:DB8:0:2F3B:2AA: FF:FE28:9C5A for the interface named Local Area Connection, add a default route with this address specified as a next-hop address by typing the following command:

netsh interface ipv6 add route ::/0 "Local Area Connection" 2001:DB8:0:2F3B:2AA:FF:FE28:9C5A

■ To configure a DNS server with unicast IPv6 address 2001:DB8:0:1::1 as the second (alternate) DNS server on the list of DNS servers for the interface named Local Area Connection, type the following command:

netsh interface ipv6 add dnsserver "Local Area Connection" 2001:DB8:0:1::1 index=2

For more information on using the netsh interface ipv6 context, type **netsh interface ipv6 /?** at a command prompt.

Other IPv6 Configuration Tasks

The following section describes some additional IPv6 configuration tasks that network administrators may need to know how to perform with Windows Vista computers.

Enabling or Disabling IPv6

You cannot uninstall IPv6 in Windows Vista, but you can disable IPv6 on a per-adapter basis. To do this, follow these steps:

1. Open the Network And Sharing Center in Control Panel.

2. Click Manage Network Connections and then double-click the connection you want to configure.

3. Clear the check box labeled Internet Protocol Version 6 (TCP/IPv6) and then click OK (see Figure 29-2).

Note that if you disable IPv6 on all your network connections using the user interface method as described in the preceding steps, IPv6 will still remain enabled on all tunnel interfaces and on the loopback interface.

As an alternative to using the user interface to disable IPv6 on a per-adapter basis, you can selectively disable certain features of IPv6 by creating and configuring the following DWORD registry value:

HKLM\SYSTEM\CurrentControlSet\Services\tcpip6\Parameters\DisabledComponents

Table 29-7 describes the flag values that control each IPv6 feature. By combining these flag values together into a bitmask, you can disable more than one feature at once. (By default, DisabledComponents has the value 0.)

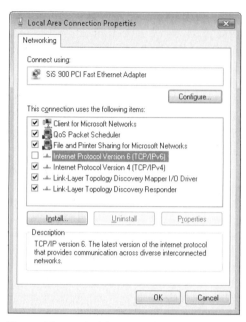

Figure 29-2 Disabling IPv6 for a network connection.

Table 29-7 Bitmask Values for Disabling IPv6 Features in Windows Vista

Flag Low-Order Bit	Result of Setting This Bit to a Value of 1
0	Disables all IPv6 tunnel interfaces, including ISATAP, 6to4, and Teredo tunnels
1	Disables all 6to4-based interfaces
2	Disables all ISATAP-based interfaces
3	Disables all Teredo-based interfaces
4	Disables IPv6 over all non-tunnel interfaces, including LAN and Point-to-Point Protocol (PPP) interfaces
5	Modifies the default prefix policy table* to prefer IPv4 over IPv6 when attempting connections

*For more information concerning the IPv6 prefix policy table, see the Cable Guy article "Source and Destination Address Selection" for IPv6 at *http://technet.microsoft.com/en-us/library/bb877985.aspx.*

For example, by setting the value of *DisabledComponents* to 0xFF, you can simultaneously disable IPv6 on all your network connections and tunnel interfaces. If you do this, IPv6 still remains enabled on the loopback interface, however.

> **Note** For some examples of common flag combinations that can be used to enable or disable different aspects of IPv6 functionality in Windows Vista, see the Cable Guy article "Configuring IPv6 with Windows Vista" at *http://technet.microsoft.com/en-us/library/bb878057.aspx.*

Depending on your scenario, there are other ways of effectively disabling IPv6 on Windows Vista computers, including:

■ **Disable the IP Helper service**   This service must be running for IPv6 transitional technologies such as ISATAP, Teredo, and 6to4 to function on the computer. This service provides automatic IPv6 connectivity over an IPv4 network, and if the service is stopped, the computer will have only IPv6 connectivity if it is connected to a native IPv6 network. Therefore, if your network is not native IPv6, disabling this service on Windows Vista computers effectively disables IPv6 on them. You can use Group Policy to disable this service on targeted Windows Vista computers.

■ **Use netsh to disable all IPv6 interfaces**   For example, the following commands will disable all IPv6 transition technologies (Teredo, 6to4, and ISATAP):

netsh interface teredo set state disabled

netsh interface ipv6 6to4 set state state=disabled undoonstop=disabled

netsh interface ipv6 isatap set state state=disabled

You can include these commands in a script and send them inside an SMS package to disable transition technologies on targeted computers.

■ **Configure Windows Firewall to block IPv6 traffic**   You could block incoming and outgoing IPv6 protocol 41 (for ISATAP and 6to4) and UDP 3544 (for Teredo) traffic using the Windows Firewall, and you can use Group Policy to push this out to targeted computers. Businesses that implement perimeter firewalls may want to do this as a best practice for safeguarding their networks.

Disabling Random Interface IDs

You can disable the default behavior of generating random interface IDs for nontemporary autoconfigured public addresses (global addresses registered in DNS) and link-local addresses by using the following command:

netsh interface ipv6 set global randomizeidentifiers=disabled

To re-enable the generating of random interface IDs, use the following command:

netsh interface ipv6 set global randomizeidentifiers=enabled

Note   Disabling random interface IDs causes link-local addresses to revert to using 48-bit MAC-layer (or 64-bit EUI) addresses for generating the interface ID portion of the address. In Windows, this happens immediately and does not require a reboot.

Resetting IPv6 Configuration

To remove all user-configured IPv6 settings and restore the IPv6 configuration of a computer to its default state, type the following command:

netsh interface ipv6 reset

You must reboot the computer for this command to take effect.

Displaying Teredo Client Status

To verify the current state of the Teredo client on your computer, open a command prompt window using local administrator credentials, and then type the following command:

netsh interface teredo show state

For a Windows Vista computer on which Teredo is currently inactive, the typical output for this command looks like this:

```
Teredo Parameters
-------------------------------------------
Type                      : default
Server Name               : teredo.ipv6.microsoft.com.
Client Refresh Interval   : 30 seconds
Client Port               : unspecified
State                     : dormant
Client Type               : teredo client
Network                   : managed
NAT                       : none (global connectivity)
```

Note   If your command output doesn't contain all of the preceding information, you probably started your command prompt session using standard credentials instead of administrator credentials.

If you now start an IPv6-enabled application that uses Teredo, such as Windows Meeting Space or Windows Remote Assistance, and then type the same Netsh command, the command output typically now looks like this:

```
Teredo Parameters
-------------------------------------------
Type                      : default
Server Name               : teredo.ipv6.microsoft.com.
Client Refresh Interval   : 30 seconds
Client Port               : unspecified
State                     : qualified
Client Type               : teredo client
Network                   : managed
NAT                       : restricted
```

Comparing these two command outputs shows that starting an application that uses Teredo changes the Teredo client state from Dormant (inactive) to Qualified (active).

> **Note**   The output of the netsh interface teredo show state command also tells you the type of NAT your computer is behind (if any). In the preceding example, the computer is behind a restricted NAT. Teredo works well behind restricted and cone NATs and can even work behind symmetric NATs, but communication between certain types of NATs doesn't work. If you plan to purchase a SOHO router for broadband Internet connectivity, the best choice is a router that supports 6to4. For more information on how Teredo works and on the different types of NATs, see "Teredo Overview" at *http://www.microsoft.com/technet/network/ipv6/teredo.mspx*.

Troubleshooting IPv6 Connectivity

The standard approach for troubleshooting TCP/IP network connectivity issues on IPv4 networks is to follow these steps:

1. Type **ipconfig /all** at a command prompt to verify the IPv4 configuration of the computer that is experiencing the problem.

2. If verifying the computer's IPv4 configuration doesn't resolve the issue, try using the ping command to test for network connectivity, beginning with the local computer and working outward until the cause of the problem is determined. Specifically, follow these steps in order listed:

    a. Ping the IPv4 loopback address 127.0.0.1 to verify that TCP/IP is installed and configured properly on the computer.

    b. Ping the IPv4 address of the local computer.

    c. Ping the IPv4 address of the default gateway.

    d. Ping the IPv4 address of an IPv4 host on a remote subnet.

Other TCP/IP troubleshooting steps you can use on IPv4 networks include:

- Use the **route print** command to verify the configuration of the local computer's routing table.

- Use **tracert** to verify that intermediate routers are configured properly.

- Use the **pathping** command to identify packet loss over multi-hop paths.

- Clear the ARP cache by typing **netsh interface ip delete arpcache** at a command prompt.

- Verify the computer's DNS configuration, clear the DNS client resolver cache, and verify DNS name resolution.

> **Note**   For more information on how to systematically troubleshoot IPv4 connectivity problems, read Chapter 32, "Troubleshooting Network Issues."

Troubleshooting IPv6 network connectivity issues requires many of the same tools you use when troubleshooting IPv4. However, you use some of these tools in a different way because of the nature of IPv6 addressing and the way IPv6 is implemented in Windows Vista. The differences include:

- You might need to specify a zone ID when attempting to verify IPv6 network connectivity with a target host using the ping command. The syntax for using ping with IPv6 is **ping IPv6Address%ZoneID,** where ZoneID is the zone ID (or scope ID) of the sending interface. For example, if the target host has the link-local unicast IPv6 address FE80::D3:00FF:FE28:9C5A, and the sending interface has a zone ID of 12, to verify IPv6 connectivity with this host you would type **ping FE80::D3:00FF:FE28:9C5A%12** at a command prompt. To determine the zone ID for an interface, you can either use the **ipconfig /all** command or type **netsh interface ipv6 show interface** at a command prompt. Note that since the zone ID is locally defined, a sending host and a receiving host on the same link may have different zone IDs. (Global and unique local unicast IPv6 addresses do not need a zone ID.)

- You should view and clear the neighbor cache on your computer before attempting to use ping to verify IPv6 network connectivity. The neighbor cache contains recently resolved link-layer IPv6 addresses; you can view it by typing **netsh interface ipv6 show neighbors** and flush it by typing **netsh interface ipv6 delete neighbors** at an elevated command prompt.

- You should also view and clear the destination cache on your computer before attempting to verify IPv6 network connectivity using ping. The destination cache contains next-hop IPv6 addresses for destinations. You can view the cache by typing **netsh interface ipv6 show destinationcache**; you can flush it by typing **netsh interface ipv6 delete destinationcache** at an elevated command prompt.

- You should use the **–d** option when attempting to trace the route to a remote IPv6 host using tracert, or the **–n** option when using pathping. These options prevent these commands from performing DNS reverse queries on every near-side router interface along the routing path. Using these options can help speed up the display of the routing path.

> **Note**   For more help on troubleshooting IPv6 network connectivity issues, see the Cable Guy article "Troubleshooting IPv6" at *http://technet.microsoft.com/en-us/library/bb878005.aspx*. See also Chapter 12, "Troubleshooting TCP/IP," in the online book *TCP/IP Fundamentals for Microsoft Windows*, which you can download from *http://www.microsoft.com/downloads/details.aspx?FamilyID=c76296fd-61c9-4079-a0bb-582bca4a846f&displaylang=en*.

> **Note**   Disabling IPv4 can also be a useful troubleshooting technique for developers who need to verify that their applications are IPv6-capable.

Planning for IPv6 Migration

Migrating your existing IPv4-based network infrastructure to IPv6 requires an understanding of different IPv6 transition technologies that you can use achieve your goal. Windows Vista and Windows Server 2008 support three transition technologies in particular:

- **ISATAP**   Stands for Intra-Site Automatic Tunnel Addressing Protocol, an address assignment and automatic tunneling technology defined in RFC 4214 that you can use to provide unicast IPv6 connectivity between IPv6/IPv4 hosts (hosts that support both IPv6 and IPv4) across an IPv4-based intranet (a private network whose infrastructure hardware, such as routers, only supports IPv4 and not IPv6).

- **6to4**   An address assignment and automatic tunneling technology defined in RFC 3056 that you can use to provide unicast IPv6 connectivity between IPv6/IPv4 hosts and sites across the IPv4-based public Internet. 6to4 enables you to assign global IPv6 addresses within your private network so that your hosts can reach locations on the IPv6 Internet without needing a direct connection to the IPv6 Internet or an IPv6 global address prefix obtained from an IPv6-supporting ISP. (Communication between a 6to4 site and a node on the IPv6 Internet requires the use of a 6to4 relay, however.)

- **Teredo**   An address assignment and automatic tunneling technology defined in RFC 4380 that you can use to provide unicast IPv6 connectivity between IPv6/IPv4 hosts across the IPv4 public Internet, even when the IPv6/IPv4 hosts are located behind zero or more NATs. Teredo provides similar functionality to 6to4 but without needing edge devices that support 6to4 tunneling.

> **Note**   For more information on IPv4/v6 transition technologies, see the white paper "IPv6 Transition Technologies" at *http://www.microsoft.com/downloads/details.aspx? FamilyID=afe56282-2903-40f3-a5ba-a87bf92c096d&DisplayLang=en*.

These three IPv6 transition technologies are supported by Windows Vista, Windows Server 2008, Windows XP Service Pack 2, and Windows Server 2003 Service Pack 1. Of the three, ISATAP is the primary transition technology that you should use for migrating an existing IPv4-based intranet to IPv6; it is discussed further in the following sections. Teredo is primarily useful in Small Office/Home Office (SOHO) networking environments, where NAT-enabled broadband routers provide Internet connectivity for users. (Think of Teredo as a transition technology of last resort, because as IPv6 connectivity becomes ubiquitous, the need for NAT traversal will decline until Teredo is no longer needed.)

How It Works: Blocking Teredo

Teredo is intended to be a consumer technology and has generally not been recommended for enterprises. This is because Teredo requires the edge device to allow all outbound UDP traffic. For example, because of security reasons, many enterprise administrators do not want client computers on the corporate network to be directly accessible from the Internet, and in that case turning off Teredo is a good idea.

If administrators want to disable Teredo on their client computers or simply prevent it from working, they can do so in one of three ways:

- Block all outbound UDP traffic by default. (This is the only reliable "external" method.)

- Block name resolution of the Teredo DNS host name, which by default on Windows Vista computers is teredo.ipv6.microsoft.com. (This method, however, leaves an easy workaround, because the user can hard-code IP addresses.)

- Use Group Policy or a script to create the following DWORD registry value, which turns off Teredo on targeted Windows Vista computers. (This registry setting is not exposed by default in Group Policy but can be pushed down using a custom ADMX file.)

  HKLM\SYSTEM\CurrentControlSet\Services\Tcpip6\Parameters\ DisabledComponents

  You can specify the following settings for this value:

  - ❏ **0x10** Setting this value will disable Teredo only on the computer.
  - ❏ **0x01** Setting this value will disable all tunnel interfaces on the computer.

If administrators want to support only native IPv6 in their networks, or if they don't want to support any IPv6 traffic until they deploy native IPv6, they can choose to turn off all tunneling technologies using the second choice in the preceding list.

Understanding ISATAP

By default, the IPv6 protocol in Windows Vista automatically configures a link-local unicast IPv6 address of the form FE80::5EFE:w.x.y.z (for private IPv4 addresses) or FE80::200:5EFE:w.x.y.z (for public IPv4 addresses). This address is a link-local ISATAP address, and it is assigned to the ISATAP tunneling interface. Using their link-local ISATAP addresses, two ISATAP hosts (such as Windows Vista computers) can communicate using IPv6 by tunneling across an IPv4-only network infrastructure (such as a network whose routers forward only IPv4 packets and not IPv6 packets).

Note   In Windows Vista with Service Pack 1, link-local ISATAP addresses are automatically configured only if the name "ISATAP" (the ISATAP router name) can be resolved. Otherwise, the ISATAP interface will be media-disconnected. However, if you administratively enable ISATAP by using netsh int isatap set state enabled, the link-local address will be configured regardless of whether the ISATAP router name can be resolved.

With the addition of one or more ISATAP routers (IPv6-enabled routers that advertise address prefixes, forward packets between ISATAP hosts and other ISATAP routers, and act as default routers for ISATAP hosts) a variety of transition topologies become possible, including:

- Connecting ISATAP hosts on an IPv4-only intranet to an IPv6-capable network
- Connecting multiple "islands" of ISATAP hosts through an IPv6-capable backbone

These configurations are possible because ISATAP routers advertise address prefixes that enable ISATAP hosts (such as Windows Vista computers) to autoconfigure global or unique local unicast IPv6 addresses.

Note   Without the presence of an ISATAP router, ISATAP hosts running Windows Vista RTM could only autoconfigure link-local unicast IPv6 addresses, which limited IPv6 communications to between hosts on the IPv4-only intranet. This was changed in Windows Vista SP1 so that without an ISATAP router, the interface will show media-disconnected. In other words, Windows Vista SP1 won't configure a link-local ISATAP address when no ISATAP router is configured.

Note   For more information on how ISATAP works, see the white paper "IPv6 Transition Technologies" at *http://www.microsoft.com/downloads/details.aspx?FamilyID=afe56282-2903-40f3-a5ba-a87bf92c096d &displaylang=en*.

Direct from the Source: ISATAP Interface Name

The ISATAP interface name is based on the DNS setting of the primary IPv4 interface of this ISATAP interface. For example, if the DNS suffix assigned to the primary IPv4 interface of this ISATAP interface is contoso.com, the ISATAP interface name will be isatap.contoso.com.

An alternate form of the ISATAP interface name is isatap.{GUID} where GUID is a globally unique identifier. However, this GUID form is used to name the ISATAP interface only if there is no DNS suffix setting on the primary IPv4 interface.

Xinyan Zan, Technical Lead

IPv6 Transition Technology

Migrating an Intranet to IPv6

Best practices for migrating existing IPv4-based network infrastructures to IPv6 are still evolving. Therefore, this section presents a general outline of how to migrate an intranet to IPv6 and provides references to more detailed information on the subject for interested readers.

The ultimate goal of IPv4 to IPv6 migration is to achieve an IPv6-only network infrastructure that has IPv6-only hosts. From a practical standpoint, however, the lesser goal of achieving a network infrastructure that supports both IPv6 and IPv4—and where hosts also support both IPv6 and IPv4 but use mainly IPv6—is a more reasonable goal to aim for. Achieving this goal is a lengthy process that involves seven main steps:

1. Upgrading your applications and services

2. Preparing your DNS infrastructure

3. Upgrading your hosts

4. Migrating from IPv4-only to ISATAP

5. Upgrading your routing infrastructure

6. Upgrading your DHCP infrastructure

7. Migrating from ISATAP to native IPv6

Step 1: Upgrading Your Applications and Services

To prepare your applications and services for migration, you will need to upgrade existing applications and services to support IPv6 in addition to IPv4. This may require upgrades from ISVs and third-party vendors or custom coding on your part. Although the ultimate goal is for all your applications and services to run native IPv6, a more appropriate target is to ensure that they work with both IPv4 and IPv6.

For further guidance, see the MSDN topic "IPv6 Guide for Windows Sockets Applications" at *http://msdn2.microsoft.com/en-us/library/ms738649.aspx*.

Step 2: Preparing Your DNS Infrastructure

You must prepare your DNS infrastructure to support the AAAA records used to resolve DNS names to IPv6 addresses. This might require upgrading your existing DNS servers. The DNS Server service of Windows Server 2008 and Windows Server 2003 supports dynamic registration of AAAA records for unicast IPv6 addresses (excluding link-local addresses).

For more information on configuring Windows Server 2003 DNS servers to support IPv6 hosts, see Chapter 9, "Windows Support for DNS," in the online book *TCP/IP Fundamentals for Microsoft Windows*, which can be found at *http://technet.microsoft.com/en-us/library/bb727009.aspx*.

Step 3: Upgrading Your Hosts

You may need to upgrade some of your hosts until all your hosts support both IPv6 and IPv4. Windows platforms from Windows XP Service Pack 2 onward support both IPv4 and IPv6, though full support for IPv6 functionality for built-in programs and services is only provided in Windows Vista and later.

Step 4: Migrating from IPv4-only to ISATAP

After you've prepared your applications, services, hosts, and DNS/DHCP infrastructure, you can begin deploying ISATAP routers to create islands of IPv6 connectivity within your IPv4-based intranet. You will need to add A records to the appropriate DNS zones so that your ISATAP hosts can determine the IPv4 addresses of your ISATAP routers.

You may decide to deploy zero or more ISATAP routers for inter-ISATAP subnet routing within your intranet, depending on the size of your intranet and the geographical distribution of its sites. You may decide to deploy redundant ISATAP routers to provide consistent availability of IPv6 address prefixes and other configuration settings for your ISATAP hosts. You will also likely deploy one or more ISATAP routers to provide IPv6 connectivity between your IPv4-based network infrastructure and the public IPv6 Internet as this evolves.

For more information on deploying ISATAP routers using different migration scenarios, see the white paper "Intra-site Automatic Tunnel Addressing Protocol Deployment Guide" at *http://www.microsoft.com/downloads/details.aspx?FamilyID=0f3a8868-e337-43d1-b271-b8c8702344cd &displaylang=en.*

Step 5: Upgrading Your Routing Infrastructure

After you have deployed ISATAP to enable IPv6 hosts to communicate over your IPv4 network infrastructure, you should begin upgrading your network infrastructure (including routers, gateways, and other access devices) to support IPv6. Rather than upgrading your infrastructure to support only IPv6, a more reasonable upgrade goal is dual IPv4/IPv6 support. In many cases, actual replacement of router hardware is not necessary. Because many modern hardware routers support both IPv4 and IPv6 routing, the task of upgrading of your routing infrastructure to support IPv6 becomes configuration, not replacement. As you enable IPv6 routing support for a subnet, also enable the DHCPv6 relay agent for the subnet.

Typically, you will begin upgrading your routing infrastructure early in your ISATAP deployment by upgrading the core routers on your network backbone to support IPv6. This will create islands of ISATAP hosts that connect to this backbone to communicate with other IPv6 hosts anywhere in your intranet.

Step 6: Upgrading Your DHCP Infrastructure

You can optionally upgrade your routing and DHCP infrastructure to support DHCPv6 for automatic assignment of global or unique local unicast IPv6 addresses or configuration settings for IPv4/IPv6 nodes on your network. By using DHCPv6, an IPv6 host can obtain subnet prefixes and other IPv6 configuration settings. A common use of DHCPv6 is to configure Windows Vista–based client computers with the IPv6 addresses of DNS servers on the network. (DNS servers are not configured through IPv6 router discovery.)

The DHCP Server service in Windows Server 2003 does not support stateful address autoconfiguration or the DHCPv6 protocol. The DHCP Server role in Windows Server 2008, however, supports both stateful and stateless IPv6 address autoconfiguration using DHCPv6. The DHCP Client service in Windows Vista and Windows Server 2008 supports address autoconfiguration using DHCPv6.

Just as with DHCP with IPv4, you also need to deploy and configure DHCPv6 relay agents for each subnet containing Windows Vista clients. Many hardware routers already support a DHCPv6 relay agent. You must configure relay agents with the IPv6 addresses of the DHCPv6 servers on your network. Relay agents can be configured but should not be enabled until you deploy IPv6 routing on your subnets.

When you are ready to enable DHCPv6 on subnets, configure your IPv6 routers to set the Managed Address Configuration and Other Stateful Configuration flags to the appropriate values for stateful or stateless DHCPv6 operation. For more information, see "The DHCPv6 Protocol" at *http://www.microsoft.com/technet/technetmag/issues/2007/03/CableGuy/default.aspx*.

Step 7: Migrating from ISATAP to Native IPv6

Finally, when all your network infrastructure devices support IPv6, you can begin to decommission your ISATAP routers, because you no longer need them. Whether you will also migrate your infrastructure and hosts to support only pure-IPv6 is a decision best left for the distant future.

Summary

This chapter described the features of IPv6 in Windows Vista, provided an overview of how IPv6 works, and outlined best practices for migrating an existing IPv4-only network to IPv6. An IPv6 migration requires careful planning and a thorough understanding of how IPv6 works, and Windows Vista, together with Windows Server 2008, provide the features and tools you need to migrate your network successfully.

Additional Resources

The following resources contain additional information and tools related to this chapter.

Related Information

- *Understanding IPv6, Second Edition* by Joseph Davies (Microsoft Press, 2008). See *http://www.microsoft.com/MSPress/books/11607.aspx*.

- The IPv6 home page on Microsoft TechNet at *http://technet.microsoft.com/en-us/network/bb530961.aspx*.

- The IPv6 blog of Sean Siler, IPv6 Program Manager, *http://blogs.technet.com/ipv6*.

- "IPv6 for Microsoft Windows: Frequently Asked Questions" at *http://www.microsoft.com/technet/network/ipv6/ipv6faq.mspx*.

- The white paper "Introduction to IP Version 6" at *http://www.microsoft.com/downloads/details.aspx?FamilyID=CBC0B8A3-B6A4-4952-BBE6-D976624C257C&displaylang=en*.

- The white paper "IPv6 Transition Technologies" at *http://www.microsoft.com/downloads/details.aspx?FamilyID=afe56282-2903-40f3-a5ba-a87bf92c096d &displaylang=en*.

- The white paper "Intra-site Automatic Tunnel Addressing Protocol Deployment" at *http://www.microsoft.com/downloads/details.aspx?FamilyID=0f3a8868-e337-43d1-b271-b8c8702344cd &displaylang=en*.

- The Cable Guy article "Changes to IPv6 in Windows Vista and Windows Server 'Longhorn'" at *http://technet.microsoft.com/en-us/library/bb878121.aspx*.

- The Cable Guy article "Performance Enhancements in the Next Generation TCP/IP Stack" at *http://technet.microsoft.com/en-us/library/bb878127.aspx*.

- The Cable Guy article "Understanding the IPv6 Routing Table" at *http://technet.microsoft.com/en-us/library/bb878115.aspx*.

- The Cable Guy article "Manual Configuration for IPv6" at *http://technet.microsoft.com/en-us/library/bb878102.aspx*.

- "Using Windows Tools to Obtain IPv6 Configuration Information" on Microsoft TechNet at *http://www.microsoft.com/technet/itsolutions/network/ipv6/ipv6config.mspx*.

- The Cable Guy article "Troubleshooting IPv6" at *http://technet.microsoft.com/en-us/library/bb878005.aspx*.

- The Cable Guy article "Source and Destination Address Selection for IPv6" found on Microsoft TechNet at *http://technet.microsoft.com/en-us/library/bb877985.aspx*.

- "Domain Name System Client Behavior in Windows Vista" on Microsoft TechNet at *http://technet.microsoft.com/en-us/library/bb727035.aspx*.

- KB 929852, "How to disable certain Internet Protocol version 6 (IPv6) components in Windows Vista," at *http://support.microsoft.com/kb/929852.*

- KB 932134, "An outdated network router may not function correctly when you use it together with new networking features in Windows Vista," at *http://support.microsoft.com/kb/932134.*

- KB 944007, "Unable to access shares via IPv6 address due to the ':' character," at *http://support.microsoft.com/kb/944007.*

- KB 934640, "In Windows, Event Viewer incorrectly displays IPv6 addresses in event descriptions," at *http://support.microsoft.com/kb/934640.*

- KB 946784, "How to obtain the IPv6 Ready Logo for Windows Vista and for Windows Server 2008 from IPv6 Forum," at *http://support.microsoft.com/kb/946784.*

- KB 929851, "The default dynamic port range for TCP/IP has changed in Windows Vista and in Windows Server 2008," at *http://support.microsoft.com/kb/929851.*

- Chapter 9, "Windows Support for DNS," and Chapter 12, "Troubleshooting TCP/IP," in the online book TCP/IP Fundamentals for Microsoft Windows, which you can download from *http://www.microsoft.com/downloads/details.aspx?FamilyID= c76296fd-61c9-4079-a0bb-582bca4a846f &displaylang=en.*

On the Companion CD

- DisableIPv6.vbs
- EnableIPv6.vbs
- viewIPv6Config.vbs
- viewIPv6Settings.vbs
- viewIPv6Stats.vbs

Part VI
Troubleshooting

Chapter 30
Configuring Startup and Troubleshooting Startup Issues

Diagnosing and correcting hardware and software problems that affect the startup process require different tools and techniques than troubleshooting problems that occur after the system has started, because the person troubleshooting the startup problem does not have access to the full suite of Windows Vista troubleshooting tools. Resolving startup issues requires a clear understanding of the startup process, the core operating system components, and the tools used to isolate and resolve problems.

This chapter covers changes to the Windows Vista startup process, how to configure startup settings, and how to troubleshoot problems that stop Windows Vista from starting and allowing a user to complete the interactive logon process successfully.

What's New with Windows Vista Startup

Several aspects of the Windows Vista startup process have changed when compared to Windows XP. Most significantly, Ntldr (the Windows XP component that displayed the boot menu and loaded the Windows XP kernel) has been replaced by the Windows Boot Manager and the Windows Boot Loader. The Boot.ini file (a file that contains entries describing the available boot options) has been replaced by the Boot Configuration Data (BCD) registry file. Ntdetect.com functionality has been merged into the kernel, and Windows Vista no longer supports hardware profiles. In fact, hardware profiles are no longer required: Windows Vista will automatically detect different hardware configurations without requiring administrators to explicitly configure profiles. Finally, the command-line recovery console has been replaced by the graphical Windows Recovery Environment, which simplifies troubleshooting. This chapter discusses these changes in more detail.

Boot Configuration Data

The BCD registry file replaces the Boot.ini files used in previous versions of Windows to track operating system locations, and it allows for a variety of new Windows Vista features, including the Startup Repair tool and the Multi-User Install shortcuts. The BCD is stored in a data file that uses the same format as the registry and is located on either the Extensible Firmware Interface (EFI) system partition (for computers that support EFI) or on the system volume. On BIOS-based operating systems, the BCD registry file is located at \Boot\Bcd on the active partition. On EFI-based operating systems, the BCD registry file is located in the \EFI\Microsoft\Boot\ folder on the EFI system partition.

The BCD registry file can contain the following types of information:

- Entries that describe Windows Boot Manager (\Bootmgr) settings
- Entries to start the Windows Boot Loader (\Windows\System32\WinLoad.exe), which can then load Windows Vista
- Entries to start Windows Resume Application (\Windows\System32\WinResume.exe), which can then restore Windows Vista from hibernation
- Entries to start Windows Memory Diagnostic (\Boot\MemTest.exe)
- Entries to start Ntldr to load previous versions of Windows
- Entries to load and execute a Volume Boot Record, which typically starts a non-Microsoft boot loader

Additionally, you can add more entries to load custom applications, such as recovery tools.

You can modify the BCD registry file in several different ways:

- **Startup And Recovery**   With the Startup And Recovery dialog box (available on the Advanced tab of the System Properties dialog box), you can select the default operating system to start if you have multiple operating systems installed on your computer. You can also change the time-out value. This dialog box has changed very little when compared to Windows XP; however, it now changes the BCD registry file instead of the Boot.ini file.

- **System Configuration utility (Msconfig.exe)**   Msconfig.exe is a troubleshooting tool that you can use to configure startup options. The Boot tab in Windows Vista provides similar functionality to the Boot.ini tab in Windows XP, such as starting in safe mode, enabling a boot log, or disabling the graphical user interface.

- **BCD Windows Management Instrumentation (WMI) provider**   The BCD WMI provider is a management interface that you can use to script utilities that modify BCD. This is the only programmatic interface available for BCD; you should always use this interface rather than attempting to access the BCD registry file directly. For more information, see "BCD Classes" at *http://msdn2.microsoft.com/en-us/library/aa362675.aspx.*

- **BCDEdit.exe**   BCDEdit.exe is a command-line utility that replaces Bootcfg.exe in Windows XP. BCDEdit can be run from within Windows Vista, from within System Recovery Tools, or even from within earlier versions of Windows (if the BCDEdit.exe file is available). BCDEdit provides more configuration options than the Startup And Recovery dialog box.

- **Non-Microsoft tools**   Third-party software vendors have released tools to simplify editing the BCD registry file, including:

  - ❏ VistaBootPRO, available at *http://www.vistabootpro.org/*

  - ❏ EasyBCD, available at *http://neosmart.net*

You cannot use Bootcfg.exe to modify BCD. However, Bootcfg.exe will remain in the operating system to support configuring older operating systems that might be installed on the same computer.

For EFI computers, BCDEdit also replaces NvrBoot. In previous versions of Windows, you could use NvrBoot to edit the EFI boot manager menu items.

How It Works: BCD Stores

Physically, a BCD store is a binary file in the registry hive format. A computer has a system BCD store that describes all installed Windows Vista operating systems and installed Windows boot applications. A computer can optionally have many nonsystem BCD stores. Figure 30-1 shows an example of how the BCD hierarchy is implemented in a typical BCD store.

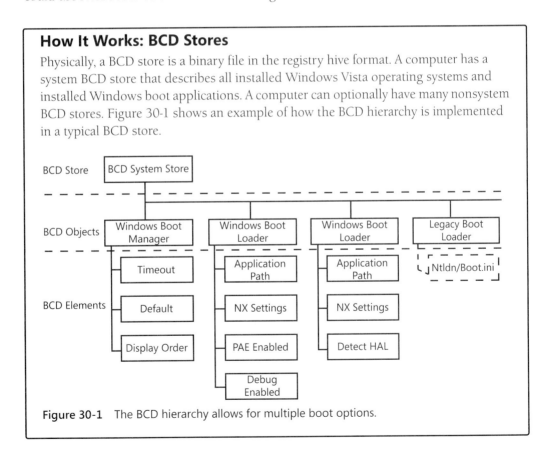

Figure 30-1   The BCD hierarchy allows for multiple boot options.

A BCD store normally has at least two (and optionally, many) BCD objects:

- **A Windows Boot Manager object**   This object contains BCD elements that pertain to the Windows boot manager, such as the entries to display in an operating system selection menu, boot tool selection menu, and time-out for the selection menus. The Windows boot manager object and its associated elements serve essentially the same purpose as the [boot loader] section of a Boot.ini file. A store can optionally have multiple instances of the Windows boot manager. However, only one of them can be represented by the Windows boot manager's well-known globally unique identifier (GUID). You can use the GUID's alias, {bootmgr}, to manipulate a store with BCDEdit.

- **At least one and optionally several Windows Boot Loader objects**   Stores contain one instance of this object for each version or configuration of Windows Vista or Windows Server 2008 that is installed on the system. These objects contain BCD elements that are used when loading Windows or during Windows initialization such as no-execute (NX) page protection policy, physical-address extensions (PAEs) policy, and kernel debugger settings. Each object and its associated elements serve essentially the same purpose as one of the lines in the [operating systems] section of Boot.ini. When a computer is booted into Windows Vista, the alias {current} represents the associated boot loader object. When manipulating a store with BCDEdit, the default boot loader object has the alias {default}.

- **An optional Windows {ntldr} object**   The {ntldr} object describes the location of Ntldr, which you can execute to boot earlier versions of Windows. This object is required only if the system includes versions of Windows that are earlier than Windows Vista. It is possible to have multiple instances of objects that describe Ntldr. However, as with the Windows boot manager, only one instance can be represented by the {ntldr} well-known GUID alias. You can use the GUID's alias, {ntldr}, to manipulate a store with BCDEdit.

- **Optional boot applications**   Stores can optionally have BCD objects that perform other boot-related operations. One example is the Windows Memory Tester, which runs memory diagnostics.

For detailed information about BCD, see "Boot Configuration Data in Windows Vista" at *http://www.microsoft.com/whdc/system/platform/firmware/bcd.mspx* and read "Boot Configuration Data Editor Frequently Asked Questions" at *http://technet2.microsoft.com/WindowsVista/en/library/85cd5efe-c349-427c-b035-c2719d4af7781033.mspx.*

System Recovery

Windows Vista replaces the Recovery Console troubleshooting tool with the new System Recovery tool (part of the Windows Recovery Environment). Typically, you will not launch the tool directly, but will instead launch the tool by starting from the Windows Vista DVD and then clicking Repair Your Computer (after configuring the language options). This loads a specialized version of Windows Pre-installation Environment (Windows PE) and then displays the System Recovery tool. For step-by-step instructions on how to load the System Recovery Tools, see the section titled "How to Start the System Recovery Tools" later in this chapter.

The System Recovery Tools provide access to the following tools:

- **Startup Repair**   The Startup Repair tool can solve many common startup problems automatically. Startup Repair performs an exhaustive analysis to diagnose your startup problems, including analyzing boot sectors, the boot manager, disk configuration, disk integrity, BCD registry file integrity, system file integrity, registry integrity, boot logs, and event logs. It will then attempt to solve the problem, which may involve repairing configuration files, solving simple disk problems, replacing missing system files, or running System Restore to return the computer to an earlier state. Because Startup Repair performs these tasks automatically, you can solve startup problems much faster than if you had to perform the analysis and repair manually.

- **System Restore**   Windows Vista automatically captures system state before installing new applications or drivers. You can later use the System Restore tool to return to this system if you experience problems. Because System Restore is available from the System Recovery Tools, you can use System Restore to repair problems that prevent Windows Vista from booting. Startup Repair can prompt you to initiate a System Restore, so you might never need to access this tool directly. For more information about System Restore, read Chapter 15, "Managing Disks and File Systems."

- **Complete PC Restore**   You use this tool to initiate a complete restore of the system hard disk. However, because any files saved since the last backup will be lost, you should use this only as a last resort. For information about backups and restores, see Chapter 15.

- **Windows Memory Diagnostics Tool**   The Windows Memory Diagnostics Tool performs an automated test of the reliability of your computer's memory. For more information, see Chapter 31, "Troubleshooting Hardware, Driver, and Disk Issues."

- **Command Prompt**   From the Command Prompt tool, you have access to many standard Windows Vista command-line tools. Some tools will not work properly, however, because Windows Vista is not currently running. For example, because the Windows Recovery Environment does not include networking capabilities, network tools will not function correctly. However, several tools in the Windows Recovery environment are useful:
    - ❑ BCDEdit.exe for making changes to the BCD registry file
    - ❑ Diskpart.exe for viewing and changing disk partitioning
    - ❑ Format.exe for formatting partitions

❑   Chkdsk.exe for finding and resolving some disk problems (note that Chkdsk cannot add events to the Event Log when started from System Recovery Tools)

❑   Notepad.exe for viewing log files or editing configuration files

❑   Bootsect.exe (available on the Windows Vista DVD in the \Boot\ folder) for updating the master boot code for hard disk partitions to switch between the Windows Vista boot manager and Ntldr, used by earlier versions of Windows

❑   Bootrec.exe for manually repairing disk problems if Startup Repair cannot fix them

Windows Boot Performance Diagnostics

Sometimes, Windows might start correctly but might take an unusually long time to do so. Such a problems can be difficult to troubleshoot, because there's no straightforward way to monitor processes while Windows is starting. To help administrators identify the source of startup performance problems, and to automatically fix some problems, Windows Vista includes Windows Boot Performance Diagnostics.

You can use the Group Policy settings to manage Windows Boot Performance Diagnostics in an Active Directory environment. In the Computer Configuration\Administrative Templates\System\Troubleshooting and Diagnostics\Windows Boot Performance Diagnostics node, edit the Configure Scenario Execution Level policy. When this policy is enabled, you can choose from the following two settings:

■   **Detection And Troubleshooting Only**   Windows Boot Performance Diagnostics will identify startup performance problems and will add an event to the Event Log, allowing administrators to detect the problem and manually troubleshoot it. Windows Boot Performance Diagnostics will not attempt to fix the problem, however.

■   **Detection, Troubleshooting, And Resolution**   Windows Boot Performance Diagnostics will identify startup performance problems and automatically take steps to attempt to alleviate the problems.

If you disable the setting, Windows Boot Performance Diagnostics will neither identify nor attempt to resolve startup performance problems. For Windows Boot Performance Diagnostics to function, the Diagnostic Policy Service must be running.

Settings for Windows Shutdown Performance Diagnostics, which function similarly to the Windows Boot Performance Diagnostics, are located in the Computer Configuration\Administrative Templates\System\Troubleshooting And Diagnostics\Windows Shutdown Performance Diagnostics node.

Understanding the Startup Process

To diagnose and correct a startup problem, you need to understand what occurs during startup. Figure 30-2 provides a high-level overview of the different paths startup can take.

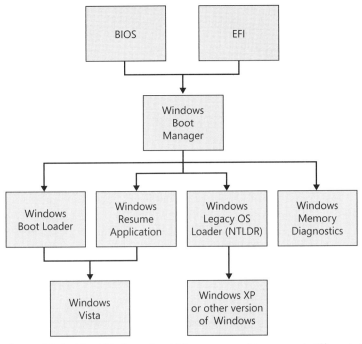

Figure 30-2   The Windows Boot Manager provides several different startup paths.

The normal startup sequence for Windows Vista is:

1. Power-on self test (POST) phase

2. Initial startup phase

3. Windows Boot Manager phase

4. Windows Boot Loader phase

5. Kernel loading phase

6. Logon phase

This sequence will vary if the computer is resuming from hibernation or if a non–Windows Vista option is selected during the Windows Boot Manager phase. The following sections describe the phases of a normal startup process in more detail.

Power-on Self Test Phase

As soon as you turn on a computer, its processor begins to carry out the programming instructions contained in the basic input/output system (BIOS) or Extensible Firmware Interface

(EFI). The BIOS and EFI, which are types of firmware, contain the processor-dependent code that starts the computer regardless of the operating system installed. The first set of startup instructions is the power-on self test (POST). The POST is responsible for the following system and diagnostic functions:

- Performs initial hardware checks, such as determining the amount of memory present
- Verifies that the devices needed to start an operating system, such as a hard disk, are present
- Retrieves system configuration settings from nonvolatile memory, which is located on the motherboard

The contents of the nonvolatile memory remain even after you shut down the computer. Examples of hardware settings stored in the nonvolatile memory include device boot order and Plug and Play information.

After the motherboard POST completes, add-on adapters that have their own firmware (for example, video and hard drive controllers) carry out internal diagnostic tests.

If startup fails before or during POST, your computer is experiencing a hardware failure. Generally, the BIOS or EFI displays an error message that indicates the nature of the problem. If video is not functioning correctly, the BIOS or EFI usually indicates the nature of the failure with a series of beeps.

To access and change system and peripheral firmware settings, consult the system documentation provided by the manufacturer. For more information, refer to your computer's documentation and see the section titled "How to Diagnose Hardware Problems" later in this chapter.

Initial Startup Phase

After the POST, computers must find and load the Windows Boot Manager. Older BIOS computers and newer EFI computers do this slightly differently, as the following sections describe.

Initial Startup Phase for BIOS computers

After the POST, the settings that are stored in the nonvolatile memory, such as boot order, determine the devices that the computer can use to start an operating system. In addition to floppy disks or hard disks attached to ATA, Serial ATA, and SCSI controllers, computers can typically start an operating system from other devices, such as:

- CDs or DVDs
- Network adapters
- USB flash drives
- Removable disks
- Secondary storage devices installed in docking stations for portable computers

It is possible to specify a custom boot order, such as "CDROM, Floppy, Hard Disk." When you specify "CDROM, Floppy, Hard Disk" as a boot order, the following events occur at startup:

1. The computer searches the CD-ROM for bootable media. If a bootable CD or DVD is present, the computer uses the media as the startup device. Otherwise, the computer searches the next device in the boot order. You cannot use a nonbootable CD or DVD to start your system. The presence of a nonbootable CD or DVD in the CD-ROM drive can add to the time the system requires to start. If you do not intend to start the computer from CD, remove all CDs from the CD-ROM drive before restarting.

2. The computer searches the floppy disk for bootable media. If a bootable floppy is present, the computer uses the floppy disk as the startup device and loads the first sector (sector 0, the floppy disk boot sector) into memory. Otherwise, the computer searches the next device in the boot order or displays an error message.

3. The computer uses the hard disk as the startup device. The computer typically uses the hard disk as the startup device only when the CD-ROM drive and the floppy disk drive are empty.

There are exceptions in which code on bootable media transfers control to the hard disk. For example, when you start your system by using the bootable Windows Vista DVD, Setup checks the hard disk for Windows installations. If one is found, you have the option of bypassing DVD startup by not responding to the Press Any Key To Boot From CD Or DVD prompt that appears. This prompt is actually displayed by the startup program located on the Windows Vista DVD, not by your computer's hardware.

If startup fails during the initial startup phase, you are experiencing a problem with the BIOS configuration, the disk subsystem, or the file system. The following error message is common during this phase. It indicates that none of the configured bootable media types was available.

```
Non-system disk or disk error
Replace and press any key when ready
```

If you have changed the disk configuration recently, verify that all cables are properly connected and jumpers are correctly configured. If booting from the hard disk, verify that all removable media have been removed. If booting from a CD or DVD, verify that the BIOS is configured to start from the CD or DVD and that the Windows Vista media is present. If the disk subsystem and BIOS are configured correctly, the problem may be related to the file system. For instructions on repairing the master boot record and the boot sector, see the section titled "How to Run Startup Repair" later in this chapter. For detailed information about troubleshooting problems with the file system, see Chapter 15. For more information about configuring the boot order, consult your computer's documentation.

If you boot from the hard disk, the computer reads the boot code instructions located on the master boot record (MBR). The MBR is the first sector of data on the startup hard disk. The MBR contains instructions (called boot code) and a table (called a partition table) that identify primary and extended partitions. The BIOS reads the MBR into memory and transfers control to the code in the MBR.

The computer then searches the partition table for the active partition, also known as a bootable partition. The first sector of the active partition contains boot code that enables the computer to do the following:

- Read the contents of the file system used.

- Locate and start a 16-bit stub program (Bootmgr) in the root directory of the boot volume. This stub program switches the processor into 32- or 64-bit protected mode and loads the 32- or 64-bit Windows Boot Manager, which is stored in the same bootmgr file. After the Windows Boot Manager loads, startup is identical for both BIOS and EFI computers.

> **Note**   The stub program is necessary because 32-bit and 64-bit computers first start in Real Mode. In Real Mode, the processor disables certain features to allow compatibility with software designed to run on 8-bit and 16-bit processors. The Windows Boot Manager is 32-bit or 64-bit, however, so the stub program sets up the BIOS computer to run the 32-bit or 64-bit software properly.

If an active partition does not exist or if boot sector information is missing or corrupt, a message similar to any of the following might appear:

- Invalid partition table

- Error loading operating system

- Missing operating system

If an active partition is successfully located, the code in the boot sector locates and starts Windows Boot Loader (WinLoad) and the BIOS transfers execution to it.

Initial Startup Phase for EFI Computers

Startup for EFI computers initially differs from startup for BIOS computers. EFI computers have a built-in boot manager that enables the computer's hardware to choose from multiple operating systems based on user input. When you install Windows Vista on an EFI computer, Windows Vista adds a single entry to the EFI boot manager with the title Windows Boot Manager. This entry points to the "\Efi\Microsoft\Boot\Bootmgfw.efi" 32-bit or 64-bit EFI executable program—the Windows Boot Manager. This is the same Windows Boot Manager that is eventually loaded on BIOS-based computers. Windows Vista configures the EFI boot manager to display the EFI startup menu for only two seconds and then load the Windows Boot Manager by default to minimize complexity and startup time.

If you install a different operating system or manually change the EFI boot manager settings, EFI might no longer load the Windows Boot Manager. To resolve this problem, use the Startup Repair tool, as described in the section titled "The Process of Troubleshooting Startup" later in this chapter. Alternatively, you might be able to update the EFI boot manager settings manually using your computer's built-in EFI tools. For more information about configuring EFI, consult your computer's documentation.

Windows Boot Manager Phase

The Windows Boot Manager is capable of natively reading supported file systems, and it uses that capability to parse the BCD registry file without fully loading the file system.

For computers that have a single operating system, Windows Boot Manager never displays a user interface. It does, however, wait for a few moments to allow the user to press a key to display the standard boot menu, as shown in Figure 30-3, or to press F8 to choose Advanced Boot Options, as shown in Figure 30-4. If the user does not press a key within a few seconds of POST completing, Windows Boot Manager starts the Windows Boot Loader, which in turn starts Windows Vista.

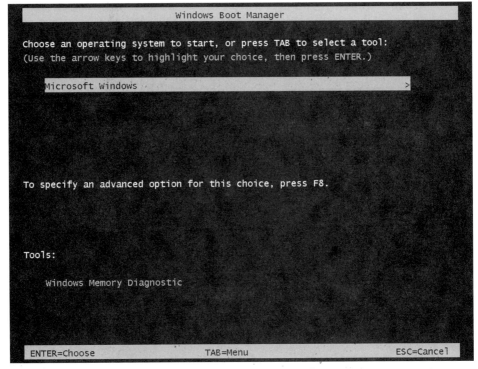

Figure 30-3   Windows Boot Manager enables you to choose from multiple operating systems or launch Windows Memory Diagnostics.

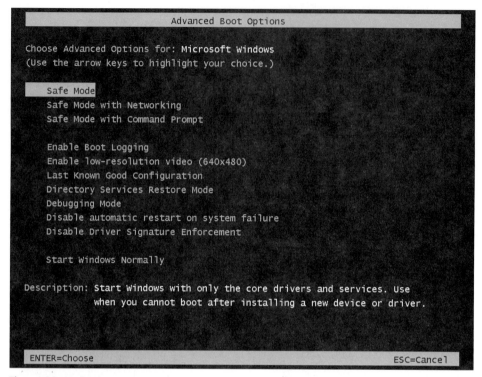

```
                          Advanced Boot Options

Choose Advanced Options for: Microsoft Windows
(Use the arrow keys to highlight your choice.)

     Safe Mode
     Safe Mode with Networking
     Safe Mode with Command Prompt

     Enable Boot Logging
     Enable low-resolution video (640x480)
     Last Known Good Configuration
     Directory Services Restore Mode
     Debugging Mode
     Disable automatic restart on system failure
     Disable Driver Signature Enforcement

     Start Windows Normally

Description: Start Windows with only the core drivers and services. Use
            when you cannot boot after installing a new device or driver.


 ENTER=Choose                                                ESC=Cancel
```

Figure 30-4 During startup, you can interrupt the default behavior of Windows Boot Manager to view the Advanced Boot Options.

For computers with multiple operating systems installed (such as both Windows Vista and Windows XP), Windows Boot Manager displays a menu of operating system choices at startup. Depending on what you choose, Windows Boot Manager will start a different process:

- If you choose Windows Vista, Windows Boot Manager starts the Windows Boot Loader to launch Windows Vista.

- If you choose Earlier Version Of Windows or another entry for Windows Server 2003, Windows XP Professional, Windows 2000, or Windows NT 4.0, Windows Boot Manager starts Ntldr, which then proceeds with the hardware-detection phase.

- If you select another operating system, control is passed to the boot sector for the other operating system.

- If you choose Windows Memory Diagnostic by pressing the Tab key, Windows Boot Manager launches the diagnostic tool without first starting Windows.

Windows Boot Loader Phase

The Windows Boot Manager starts the Windows Boot Loader phase when the user chooses to load Windows Vista. The Windows Boot Loader does the following:

1. Loads the operating system kernel, Ntoskrnl.exe, but does not yet run it.

2. Loads the hardware abstraction layer (HAL), Hal.dll. This will not be used until the kernel is run.

3. Loads the system registry hive (System32\Config\System) into memory.

4. Scans the HKEY_LOCAL_MACHINE\SYSTEM\Services key for device drivers and loads all drivers that are configured for the boot class into memory. The Windows Boot Loader does not, however, initiate the drivers. Drivers are not initiated until the kernel loading phase.

5. Enables paging.

6. Passes control to the operating system kernel, which starts the next phase.

Kernel Loading Phase

The Windows Boot Loader is responsible for loading the Windows kernel (Ntoskrnl.exe) and the hardware abstraction layer (HAL) into memory. Together, the kernel and the HAL initialize a group of software components that are called the Windows executive. The Windows executive processes the configuration information stored in the registry in HKLM\SYSTEM\CurrentControlSet and starts services and drivers.

The following sections provide more detail about the kernel loading phase.

Control Sets

The Windows Boot Loader reads control set information from the registry key HKEY_LOCAL_MACHINE\SYSTEM, which is stored in the file %SystemRoot%\system32\Config\System, so that the kernel can determine which device drivers need to be loaded during startup. Typically, several control sets exist, with the actual number depending on how often system configuration settings change.

The HKEY_LOCAL_MACHINE\SYSTEM subkeys used during startup are:

- \CurrentControlSet, a pointer to a ControlSet*xxx* subkey (where *xxx* represents a control set number, such as 001) designated in the \Select\Current value.

- \Select, which contains the following entries:

  - **Default**   Points to the control set number (for example, 001=ControlSet001) that the system has specified for use at the next startup. If no error or manual invocation of the LastKnownGood startup option occurs, this control set number is designated as the value of the Default, Current, and LastKnownGood entries (assuming that a user is able to log on successfully).

❑ **Current** Points to the last control set that was used to start the system.

❑ **Failed** Points to a control set that did not start Windows Vista successfully. This value is updated when the LastKnownGood option is used to start the system.

❑ **LastKnownGood** Points to the control set that was used during the last user session. When a user logs on, the LastKnownGood control set is updated with configuration information from the previous user session.

The Windows Boot Loader uses the control set identified by the \Select\Default value unless you choose the Last Known Good Configuration from the Advanced Boot Options menu.

The kernel creates the registry key HKEY_LOCAL_MACHINE\HARDWARE, which contains the hardware data collected at system startup. Windows Vista supports an extensive set of devices, with additional drivers not on the Windows Vista operating system DVD provided by hardware manufacturers. Drivers are kernel-mode components required by devices to function within an operating system. Services are components that support operating system and application functions and act as network servers. Services can run in a different context than user applications and typically do not offer many user-configurable options.

For example, the Print Spooler service does not require a user to be logged on to run and functions independently of the user who is logged on to the system. Drivers generally communicate directly with hardware devices, whereas services usually communicate with hardware through drivers. Windows Vista driver and service files are typically stored in the %SystemRoot%\System32 and %SystemRoot%\System32\Drivers folders and use .exe, .sys, or .dll filename extensions.

Drivers are also services. Therefore, during kernel initialization, the Windows Boot Loader and Ntoskrnl use the information stored in the HKEY_LOCAL_MACHINE\SYSTEM\CurrentControlSet\Services*Servicename* registry subkeys to determine both the drivers and services to load. In the *Servicename* subkeys, the entry Start specifies when to start the service. For example, the Windows Boot Loader loads all drivers for which Start is 0, such as device drivers for hard disk controllers. After execution is transferred to the kernel, the kernel loads drivers and services for which Start is 1.

Table 30-1 lists the values (in decimal) for the registry entry Start. Boot drivers (those for which Start is 0) and file system drivers are always loaded regardless of the value of Start because they are required to start Windows Vista.

Table 30-1   Values for the Start Registry Entry

Value	Start Type	Value Descriptions for Start Entries
0	Boot	Specifies a driver that is loaded (but not started) by the boot loader. If no errors occur, the driver is started during kernel initialization prior to any non-Boot drivers being loaded.
1	System	Specifies a driver that loads and starts during kernel initialization after drivers with a Start value of 0 have been started.
2	Auto load	Specifies a driver or service that is initialized at system startup by Session Manager (Smss.exe) or the Services Controller (Services.exe).
3	Load on demand	Specifies a driver or service that the SCM will start only on demand. These drivers have to be started manually by calling a Win32 SCM API such as the Services snap-in.
4	Disabled	Specifies a disabled (not started) driver or service.
5	Delayed start	A new start type that starts less-critical services shortly after startup to allow the operating system to be responsive to the user sooner.

Table 30-2 lists some of the values (in decimal) for the type registry entry.

Table 30-2   Type Registry Values

Value	Value Descriptions for Type Entries
1	Specifies a kernel device driver
2	Specifies a kernel mode file system driver (also a kernel device driver)
4	Specifies arguments passed to an adapter
8	Specifies a file system driver such as a file system recognizer driver
16	Specifies a service that obeys the service control protocol, runs within a process that hosts only one service, and can be started by the Services Controller
32	Specifies a service that runs in a process that hosts multiple services
256	Specifies a service that is allowed to display windows on the console and receive user input

Some drivers and services require that conditions, also known as *dependencies*, be met. You can find dependencies listed under the DependOnGroup and DependOnService entries in the HKEY_LOCAL_MACHINE\SYSTEM\CurrentControlSet\Services*Servicename* subkey for each service or driver. For more information about using dependencies to prevent or delay a driver or service from starting, see the section titled "How to Temporarily Disable a Service" later in this chapter. The Services subkey also contains information that affects how drivers and services are loaded. Table 30-3 lists some of these other entries.

Table 30-3   Other Registry Entries in the *Servicename* Subkeys

Entry	Description
DependOnGroup	At least one item from this group must start before this service is loaded.
DependOnService	Lists the specific services that must load before this service loads.
DisplayName	Describes the component.
ErrorControl	Controls whether a driver error requires the system to use the LastKnown-Good control set or to display a Stop message.
	If the value is 0x0 (Ignore, no error is reported), do not display a warning and proceed with startup.
	If the value is 0x1 (Normal, error reported), record the event to the System Event Log and display a warning message, but proceed with startup.
	If the value is 0x2 (Severe), record the event to the System Event Log, use the LastKnownGood settings, restart the system, and proceed with startup.
	If the value is 0x3 (Critical), record the event to the System Event Log, use the LastKnownGood settings, and restart the system. If the LastKnown-Good settings are already in use, display a Stop message.
Group	Designates the group that the driver or service belongs to. This allows related drivers or services to start together (for example, file system drivers). The registry entry List in the subkey HKEY_LOCAL_MACHINE\SYSTEM \ CurrentControlSet\Control\ServiceGroupOrder specifies the group startup order.
ImagePath	Identifies the path and filename of the driver or service if the ImagePath entry is present.
ObjectName	Specifies an object name. If the Type entry specifies a service, it represents the account name that the service uses to log on when it runs.
Tag	Designates the order in which a driver starts within a driver group.

Session Manager

After all entries that have Boot and Startup data types are processed, the kernel starts the Session Manager (Smss.exe), a user process that continues to run until the operating system is shut down. The Session Manager performs important initialization functions, such as:

- Creating system environment variables.

- Starting the kernel-mode portion of the Win32 subsystem (implemented by %SystemRoot%\system32\Win32k.sys), which causes Windows Vista to switch from text (used to display the Windows Boot Manager menu) to graphics mode (used to display the startup progress bar). Windows-based applications run in the Windows subsystem. This environment allows applications to access operating system functions, such as displaying information to the screen.

- Starting the user-mode portion of the Win32 subsystem (implemented by %System-Root%\system32\Csrss.exe). The applications that use the Windows subsystem are user mode processes; they do not have direct access to hardware or device drivers. Instead, they have to access Windows APIs to gain indirect access to hardware. This allows Windows to control direct hardware access, improving security and reliability. User-mode processes run at a lower priority than kernel-mode processes. When the operating system needs more memory, it can page to disk the memory used by user-mode processes.

- Starting the Logon Manager (%SystemRoot%\system32\Winlogon.exe).

- Creating additional virtual memory paging files.

- Performing delayed rename operations for files specified by the registry entry HKEY_LOCAL_MACHINE\SYSTEM\CurrentControlSet\Control\Session Manager\PendingFileRenameOperations. For example, you might be prompted to restart the computer after installing a new driver or application so that Windows Vista can replace files that are currently in use.

Session Manager searches the registry for service information contained in the following subkeys:

- HKEY_LOCAL_MACHINE\SYSTEM\CurrentControlSet\Control\Session Manager contains a list of commands to run before loading services. The Autochk.exe tool is specified by the value of the registry entry BootExecute and virtual memory (paging file) settings stored in the Memory Management subkey. Autochk, which is a version of the Chkdsk tool, runs at startup if the operating system detects a file system problem that requires repair before completing the startup process.

- HKEY_LOCAL_MACHINE\SYSTEM\CurrentControlSet\Control\Session Manager\SubSystems stores a list of available subsystems. For example, Csrss.exe contains the user-mode portion of the Windows subsystem.

If startup fails during the kernel loading phase after another operating system was installed on the computer, the cause of the problem is likely an incompatible boot loader. Boot loaders installed by older versions of Windows cannot be used to start Windows Vista. Use System Recovery to replace startup files with Windows Vista startup files.

Otherwise, if startup fails during the kernel loading phase, use boot logging to isolate the failing component. Then use safe mode to disable problematic components (if possible) or use System Recovery to replace problematic files. For more information, see the section titled "Startup Troubleshooting Before the Progress Bar Appears" later in this chapter. If you experience a Stop error during this phase, use the information provided by the Stop message to isolate the failing component. For more information about troubleshooting Stop errors, see Chapter 33, "Troubleshooting Stop Messages."

Logon Phase

The Windows subsystem starts Winlogon.exe, a system service that enables logging on and off. Winlogon.exe then does the following:

- Starts the Services subsystem (Services.exe), also known as the Service Control Manager (SCM). The Service Controller Manager initializes services that the registry entry Start designates as Autoload in the registry subkey HKEY_LOCAL_MACHINE\SYSTEM\ CurrentControlSet\Services*servicename*.

- Starts the Local Security Authority (LSA) process (Lsass.exe).

- Parses the Ctrl+Alt+Delete key combination at the Begin Logon prompt (if the computer is part of an Active Directory domain).

The logon user interface (LogonUI) component and the credential provider (which can be the standard credential provider or a third-party credential provider) collect the user name and password (or other credentials) and pass this information securely to the LSA for authentication. If the user supplied valid credentials, access is granted by using either the default Kerberos V 5 authentication protocol or NTLM.

Winlogon initializes security and authentication components while Plug and Play initializes auto-load services and drivers. After the user logs on, the control set referenced by the registry entry LastKnownGood (located in HKLM\SYSTEM\Select) is updated with the contents in the CurrentControlSet subkey. By default, Winlogon then launches Userinit.exe and the Windows Explorer shell. Userinit may then launch other processes, including:

- **Group Policy settings take effect**   Group Policy settings that apply to the user and computer take effect

- **Startup programs run**   When not overridden by Group Policy settings, Windows Vista starts logon scripts, startup programs, and services referenced in the following registry subkeys and file system folders:

    - ❑ HKEY_LOCAL_MACHINE\SOFTWARE\Microsoft\Windows\CurrentVersion \ Runonce

    - ❑ HKEY_LOCAL_MACHINE\SOFTWARE\Microsoft\Windows\CurrentVersion \ policies\Explorer\Run

    - ❑ HKEY_LOCAL_MACHINE\SOFTWARE\Microsoft\Windows\CurrentVersion\Run

    - ❑ HKEY_CURRENT_USER\Software\Microsoft\Windows NT\CurrentVersion\ Windows\Run

    - ❑ HKEY_CURRENT_USER\Software\Microsoft\Windows\CurrentVersion\Run

    - ❑ HKEY_CURRENT_USER\Software\Microsoft\Windows\CurrentVersion\RunOnce

    - ❑ *systemdrive*\Documents and Settings\All Users\Start Menu\Programs\Startup

    - ❑ *systemdrive*\Documents and Settings\username\Start Menu\Programs\Startup

Several applications might be configured to start by default after you install Windows Vista, including the Microsoft Windows Sidebar and Windows Defender. Computer manufacturers or IT departments might configure other startup applications.

Windows Vista startup is not complete until a user successfully logs on to the computer.

If startup fails during the logon phase, you have a problem with a service or application configured to start automatically. For troubleshooting information, see the section titled "How to Temporarily Disable Startup Applications and Processes" later in this chapter. If you experience a Stop error during this phase, use the information provided by the Stop message to isolate the failing component. For more information about troubleshooting Stop errors, see Chapter 33.

Important Startup Files

For Windows Vista to start, the system and boot partitions must contain the files listed in Table 30-4.

Table 30-4   Windows Vista Startup Files

Filename	Disk Location	Description
BootMgr	Root of the system partition	The Windows Boot Manager
WinLoad	%SystemRoot%\System32	The Windows Boot Loader
BCD	\Boot	A file that specifies the paths to operating system installations and other information required for Windows to start.
Ntoskrnl.exe	%SystemRoot%\System32	The core (also called the kernel) of the Windows Vista operating system. Code that runs as part of the kernel does so in privileged processor mode and has direct access to system data and hardware.
Hal.dll	%SystemRoot%\System32	The HAL dynamic-link library file. The HAL abstracts low-level hardware details from the operating system and provides a common programming interface to devices of the same type (such as video adapters).
Smss.exe	%SystemRoot%\System32	The Session Manager file. Session Manager is a user-mode process created by the kernel during startup. It handles critical startup tasks including creating page files and performing delayed file rename and delete operations.
Csrss.exe	%SystemRoot%\System32	The Win32 Subsystem file. The Win32 Subsystem is launched by Session Manager and is required by Windows Vista to function.
Winlogon.exe	%SystemRoot%\System32	The Logon Process file, which handles user logon requests and intercepts the Ctrl+Alt+Delete logon key sequence. The Logon Process is launched by Session Manager. This is a required component.

Table 30-4   Windows Vista Startup Files

Filename	Disk Location	Description
Services.exe	%SystemRoot%\System32	The Service Control Manager is responsible for starting and stopping services and is a required component of Windows Vista.
Lsass.exe	%SystemRoot%\System32	Local Security Authentication Server process is called by the Logon Process when authenticating users and is a required component.
System registry file	%SystemRoot%\System32\Config\System	The file that contains data used to create the registry key HKEY_LOCAL_MACHINE\SYSTEM. This key contains information that the operating system requires to start devices and system services.
Device drivers	%SystemRoot%\System32\Drivers	Driver files in this folder are for hardware devices, such as keyboard, mouse, and video.

In Table 30-4, the term %SystemRoot% is one of many *environment variables* used to associate string values, such as folder or file paths, to variables that Windows Vista applications and services use. For example, by using environment variables, scripts can run without modification on computers that have different configurations. To obtain a list of environment variables that you can use for troubleshooting, type **set** at the Windows command prompt.

How to Configure Startup Settings

Windows Vista enables administrators to configure startup settings using many of the same graphical tools that Windows XP provides. Command-line tools for configuring startup tools have been replaced with new tools, however, and you can no longer directly edit the startup configuration file (formerly the Boot.ini file). The following sections describe several different techniques for configuring startup settings.

How to Use the Startup And Recovery Dialog Box

The simplest way to edit the BCD registry file is to use the Startup And Recovery dialog box. To use the Startup And Recovery dialog box to change the default operating system, follow these steps:

1. Click Start, right-click Computer, and then click Properties.

2. Click Advanced System Settings.

3. In Startup And Recovery, click Settings.

4. Click the Default Operating System list and then click the operating system that you want to boot by default.

5. Click OK twice.

The default operating system will automatically load the next time you start the computer.

How to Use the System Configuration Tool

The System Configuration Tool offers more advanced control over startup settings, including some ability to configure the BCD registry file. This tool is specifically designed for troubleshooting, and you can use it to easily undo changes that you have made to the computer's configuration (even after restarting the computer). If you make changes with the System Configuration Tool, it will remind users logging on that settings have been temporarily changed—thus reducing the likelihood that settings will not be reset after the troubleshooting process has been completed.

Some common tasks for the System Configuration tool include:

- Temporarily disabling startup applications to isolate the cause of a post-logon problem.
- Temporarily disabling automatic services to isolate the cause of a pre- or post-logon problem.
- Permanently or temporarily configuring the BCD registry file.
- Configuring a normal, diagnostic, or selective startup for Windows Vista.

To use the System Configuration tool, click Start, type **Msconfig**, and then press Enter. The System Configuration tool provides five tabs:

- **General**   Use this tab to change the next startup mode. Normal Startup loads all device drivers and services. Diagnostic Startup is useful for troubleshooting startup problems, and it loads only basic devices and services. Use Selective Startup to specify whether you want to load system services or startup items.

- **Boot**   Use this tab to configure the BCD registry file and startup settings. You can remove startup operating system options, set the default operating system, configure advanced settings for an operating system (including number of processors, maximum memory, and debug settings), and configure Windows Vista for Safe Boot or to boot without a graphical interface.

- **Services**   Use this tab to change the startup settings for a service temporarily. This is an excellent way to determine whether an Automatic service is causing startup problems. After you disable a service, restart your computer and determine if the problem still exists. If the problem does still exist, you have eliminated one potential cause of the problem. You can then use this tab to re-enable the service, disable another service, and repeat the process. To disable services permanently, use the Services console.

- **Startup**   Lists applications that are configured to start automatically. This is the best way to disable applications temporarily during troubleshooting, because you can easily re-enable them later using the same tool. You should not use the System Configuration tool to permanently remove startup applications, however, because the System Configuration tool is designed to enable you to easily undo changes. Instead, you should manually remove the application or use Windows Defender.

- **Tool**   Provides links to other tools that you can start.

> **Note**   The Win.ini, System.ini, and Boot.ini tabs were removed from the System Configuration
> tool for Windows Vista because those files are no longer used.

Because the System Configuration tool is a graphical tool, it is primarily useful when
Windows Vista is booting successfully.

How to Use BCDEdit

The BCDEdit command-line tool provides you with almost unlimited control over the BCD
registry file and configuration settings.

> **Note**   If you have a computer with both Windows XP and Windows Vista installed and you
> want to modify the BCD registry file from Windows XP, you can run BCDEdit from Windows XP
> by launching it directly from the Windows Vista Windows\System32 folder. Although this
> might be useful in some multi-boot configurations, typically, you should run BCDEdit from the
> System Recovery command prompt if you cannot load Windows Vista.

You must use administrative credentials to run BCDEdit from within Windows Vista. To do
this, follow these steps:

1. Click Start, click All Programs, and then click Accessories.

2. Right-click Command Prompt and then click Run As Administrator.

3. Click Continue when prompted by User Account Control.

To view detailed information about using BCDEdit, run **BCDEdit /?** from a command
prompt. The following sections describe how to perform specific tasks with BCDEdit.

How to Interpret BCDEdit Output

You can view settings currently defined in your BCD registry file by using the bcdedit /enum
command. Optionally, you can follow the command with one of the following parameters
to change which entries are displayed:

- **Active**   The default setting that is displayed if you run bcdedit /enum without any
  additional parameters. Displays all entries in the boot manager display order.
- **Firmware**   Displays all firmware applications.
- **Bootapp**   Displays all boot environment applications.
- **Osloader**   Displays all operating system entries.
- **Resume**   Displays all resume from hibernation entries.
- **Inherit**   Displays all inherit entries.
- **All**   Displays all entries.

For example, to view the startup entry used to resume from hibernation, run the following command at an administrative command prompt:

```
bcdedit /enum resume
```

Similarly, to view all startup entries, use the following command:

```
bcdedit /enum all
```

How to Back Up and Restore Settings

Making changes to your BCD registry file can render your computer unbootable. Therefore, before making changes to your BCD registry file, you should make a backup copy, have a bootable Windows Vista DVD available, and be prepared to restore the original BCD registry file.

To make a backup of your current BCD registry, call the BCDEdit /export command, as shown here:

```
bcdedit /export backupbcd.bcd
```

Later, you can restore your original BCD registry file by calling the BCDEdit /import command, as shown here:

```
bcdedit /import backupbcd.bcd
```

> **Note**   The filename and extension you use are not significant.

If Windows Vista is unbootable, follow the instructions in the section titled "The Process of Troubleshooting Startup" later in this chapter.

How to Change the Default Operating System Entry

To view the current default operating system entry, run the following command and look for the *default* line:

```
bcdedit /enum {bootmgr}
```

```
Windows Boot Manager
--------------------
identifier              {bootmgr}
device                  partition=D:
description             Windows Boot Manager
locale                  en-US
inherit                 {globalsettings} default              {current}
resumeobject            {24a500f3-12ea-11db-a536-b7db70c06ac2}
displayorder            {ntldr}
                        {current}
                        {dff40777-015d-11db-865c-d47e9be63989}
toolsdisplayorder       {memdiag}
timeout                 30
```

To change the default operating system entry, first run the following command to view the existing entries and make note of the identifier for the entry that you want to be the default:

```
bcdedit /enum
```

Then run the following command to set a new default (where *<id>* is the identifier for the new entry:

```
bcdedit /default <id>
```

For example, to configure the Windows Boot Manager to start the previous version of Windows by default (which is identified as {ntldr}), run the following command:

```
bcdedit /default {ntldr}
```

To configure the currently running instance of Windows Vista as the default, run the following command:

```
bcdedit /default {current}
```

How to Change the Boot Menu Time-Out

The boot menu, by default, is displayed for 30 seconds if you have more than one boot menu entry. If you have only one boot menu entry, the menu is not displayed at all (though the boot manager does wait several seconds so that you can press a key to view the menu).

To change the time-out for the boot menu, use the bcdedit /timeout seconds command, as shown here:

```
bcdedit /timeout 15
```

How to Change the Order of Boot Manager Menu Items

To change the order of boot manager menu items, use the bcdedit /display command, and then list the menu item identifiers in the desired sequence, as shown in the following example:

```
bcdedit /display {current} {ntldr} {cbd971bf-b7b8-4885-951a-fa0344f5d71}
```

How to Create an Entry for Another Operating System

You can use BCDEdit to create an entry for an operating system other than Windows Vista. You may need to add boot entries to the BCD registry file if you want to be able to load different operating systems on a single computer. Although Windows Vista automatically creates boot entries for existing operating systems when installed, you might need to add a boot entry manually if you install another operating system after Windows Vista, or if you want to load an operating system from a newly attached hard disk.

By default, the BCD registry file contains an entry called {ntldr} that is configured to start an older version of Windows from your C:\ partition. If you have only one older operating system and Earlier Version Of Windows does not currently appear on the computer's boot menu, you can use this existing entry to start the older operating system. To do this, call BCDEdit /set to configure the boot volume. Then add the entry to the Windows Boot Manager operating system menu by calling the BCDEdit /displayorder command. The following code demonstrates how to do this:

```
REM Modify the following line to identify the other OS' partition
REM The following line could also be, "bcdedit /set {ntldr} device boot"
bcdedit /set {ntldr} device partition=C:

REM The following line makes the entry bootable by adding it to the menu
bcdedit /displayorder {ntldr} /addlast
```

You can verify that the new entry will appear on the boot menu by running the command bcdedit /enum ACTIVE and looking for the Windows Legacy OS Loader entry.

If you need to be able to choose from multiple legacy Windows operating systems, you should choose the {ntldr} entry from the boot menu. The Windows Boot Manager will then pass control to Ntldr, which will display a menu based on the Boot.ini file that you can use to choose from all Windows operating systems.

If you want to create an entry for a non-Microsoft operating system, you can either create an entry using the bcdedit /create command, or you can copy the existing {ntldr} entry and update it for the operating system. To base a new entry on {ntldr}, copy the entry, update the boot loader path, and then add it to the boot menu by following these commands:

```
bcdedit /copy {ntldr} /d "Other operating system (or other description)"

REM The previous command will display a new GUID that identifies the copy.
REM Use the GUID in the following command, and modify the partition identifier as needed.
bcdedit /set {NEW-GUID} device partition=C:
```

> **Note**   Don't retype the GUID by hand—you're likely to make a mistake. Instead, copy it to the clipboard. Click the command menu in the upper-left corner of the command prompt window, click Edit, and then click Mark. Select the GUID text (including the brackets) and then press Enter on your keyboard. To paste the GUID to the command prompt, click the command menu, click Edit, and then click Paste.

Now run the following command to identify the operating system's boot loader:

```
REM Replace the last parameter with the boot loader filename
bcdedit /set {NEW-GUID} path \boot-loader
```

If {ntldr} was not part of the boot menu when you copied it, you also need to run the following command to add the copied entry to the boot menu:

```
bcdedit /displayorder {NEW-GUID} /addlast
```

Additionally, you might need to configure the operating system's own boot loader.

How to Remove a Boot Entry

Typically, you do not need to remove entries from the BCD registry file. Instead, you should simply remove entries from the Windows Boot Manager menu. To remove an entry from the menu, first run bcdedit /enum and note the boot entry's identifier. Then run the following command, substituting the identifier:

```
bcdedit /displayorder {GUID} /remove
```

For example, to remove the entry to load the previous version of Windows from the boot menu, you would run:

```
bcdedit /displayorder {ntldr} /remove
```

You can later re-add the entry to the boot menu by calling the following command:

```
bcdedit /displayorder {GUID} /addlast
```

To permanently remove an entry from the BCD registry, run the following command:

```
bcdedit /delete {GUID} /remove
```

You should permanently remove an entry only if you have removed the operating system files from the computer.

How to View and Update Global Debugger Settings

To view debugger settings for startup entries, run the following command:

```
bcdedit /enum
```

For more information about viewing entries, see the section titled "How to Interpret BCDEdit Output" earlier in this chapter. To change debugger settings for a startup entry, run the following command:

```
bcdedit /dbgsettings DebugType [debugport:Port] [baudrate:Baud]
[channel:Channel] [targetname:TargetName]
```

Replace the parameters with your custom settings, as described in the following list:

- **DebugType**   Specifies the type of debugger. DebugType can be one of SERIAL, 1394, or USB. The remaining options depend on the debugger type selected.

- **Port**   For SERIAL debugging, specifies the serial port to use as the debugging port.

- **Baud**   For SERIAL debugging, specifies the baud rate to be used for debugging.

- **Channel**   For 1394 debugging, specifies the 1394 channel to be used for debugging.

- **TargetName**   For Universal Serial Bus (USB) debugging, specifies the USB target name to be used for debugging.

For example, the following command sets the global debugger settings to serial debugging over com1 at 115,200 baud:

```
bcdedit /dbgsettings serial debugport:1 baudrate:115200
```

The following command sets the global debugger settings to 1394 debugging using channel 23:

```
bcdedit /dbgsettings 1394 CHANNEL:32
```

The following command sets the global debugger settings to USB debugging using target name *debugging*:

```
bcdedit /dbgsettings USB targetname:debugging
```

How to Remove the Windows Vista Boot Loader

If you want to remove Windows Vista from a dual-boot environment that includes an earlier version of Windows, follow these steps:

> **Note**   You can follow these steps in the earlier version of Windows or in Windows Vista. If you follow these steps in Windows Vista, run the commands from a command prompt that has elevated user rights. To do this, click Start, click Accessories, right-click the command-prompt shortcut, and then click Run As Administrator.

1. Use Bootsect.exe to restore the Ntldr.exe program. To do this, type the following command, where D:\ is the drive containing the Windows Vista installation media:

   ```
   D:\Boot\Bootsect.exe –NT52 All
   ```

   After the computer restarts, it does not load the Windows Boot Manager program. Instead, Ntldr.exe loads and processes the Boot.ini to start an earlier version of Windows.

2. If Windows Vista is not installed on the active partition, you can now delete or remove the partition where Windows Vista is installed.

How to Configure a User Account to Automatically Log On

Requiring users to enter credentials when their computers start is an important part of Windows Vista security. If a user account automatically logs on, anyone who has physical access to the computer can restart it and access the user's files. Nonetheless, in scenarios where a computer is physically secure, automatic logon might be preferred. To configure a Windows Vista workgroup computer (you cannot perform these steps on a domain member) to automatically log on, follow these steps:

1.   Click Start, type **netplwiz**, and then press Enter.

2.   In the User Accounts dialog box, click the account you want to automatically log on to. Then, clear the Users Must Enter A User Name And Password To Use This Computer check box.

3.   Click OK.

4.   In the Automatically Log On dialog box, enter the user's password twice. Click OK.

The next time you restart the computer, it will automatically log on with the local user account you selected. Configuring automatic logon stores the user's password in the registry unencrypted, where someone might be able to retrieve it.

How to Disable the Windows Vista Startup Sound

By default, Windows Vista plays a sound as part of the startup process. This sound can be useful for troubleshooting startup problems, because it indicates if you have reached a specific startup phase. But if you prefer, you can disable the startup sound by following these steps:

1.   Click Start and then click Control Panel.

2.   In Control Panel, click Hardware And Sound.

3.   Click Change System Sounds.

4.   On the Sounds tab, clear the Play Windows Startup Sound check box. Click OK.

How to Speed Up the Startup Process

Although startup is a complex process, and the time required varies from computer to computer, you can often reduce the startup time. To optimize settings that might improve startup time, follow these steps:

1.   In the computer's BIOS settings, set the computer to boot first from the Windows boot drive. If you need to boot from removable media in the future, you will first need to change this setting.

2.   In the computer's BIOS settings, enable Fast Boot, if available, to disable time-consuming and often unnecessary hardware checks.

3. If you have more than one boot menu item, reduce the boot menu time-out value using the Boot tab of the Msconfig tool. Alternatively, you can use BCDEdit to reduce the time-out value, as described in the section titled "How to Change the Boot Menu Time-Out" earlier in this chapter.

4. Clear disk space if free disk space is below 15 percent, and then defragment the hard disk, as described in Chapter 15. Although defragmentation happens automatically by default, defragmentation is less effective if free disk space is low.

5. Disable unnecessary hardware using Device Manager, as described in Chapter 16, "Managing Devices and Services."

6. Use ReadyBoost, as described in Chapter 15, to cache some files used in the startup process to a USB flash drive.

7. Remove unnecessary startup applications.

8. For services (other than those included with Windows) that need to start automatically but do not need to start immediately, use the Services console to change the startup type to Automatic (Delayed Start). If services are set to start Automatically but are not required, change the startup type to Manual. For more information, refer to Chapter 16.

For detailed startup performance troubleshooting, examine the Applications And Services Logs\Microsoft\Windows\Diagnostics-Performance\Operational Event Log. Events with IDs from 100 to 199 provide startup performance detail in the event of long startup times. In particular, event ID 100 indicates the startup time in milliseconds. Other events identify applications or services that are causing a startup performance degradation.

The Process of Troubleshooting Startup

Startup problems can be divided into three distinct categories:

■ **Problems that occur before the progress bar appears**   These problems are typically caused by missing startup files (often as a result of installing a different operating system over Windows Vista), corrupted files, or hardware problems. For information about troubleshooting problems that occur after logon, read the next section, "Startup Troubleshooting Before the Progress Bar Appears."

■ **Problems that occur after the progress bar appears but before the logon prompt is displayed**   These problems are typically caused by faulty or misconfigured drivers and services. Hardware problems can also cause failure during this phase of startup. For information about troubleshooting problems that occur after the progress bar appears but before logon, read the section titled "Startup Troubleshooting After the Progress Bar Appears" later in this chapter.

■ **Problems that occur after logon**   These problems are typically caused by startup applications. For information about troubleshooting problems that occur after logon, read the section titled "Troubleshooting Startup Problems After Logon" later in this chapter.

Startup Troubleshooting Before the Progress Bar Appears

Troubleshooting startup problems is more challenging than troubleshooting problems that occur while Windows is running, because you cannot access the full suite of troubleshooting tools included with Windows. However, Windows Vista does provide several tools that you can use to identify the cause and resolve the problem if you cannot start the operating system. Most important, you can launch the System Recovery Tools by booting from the Windows Vista DVD, or if configured by the computer manufacturer, directly from the computer's hard disk. The System Recovery Tools include the Startup Repair tool, which can automatically fix many common startup problems.

Follow the process illustrated in Figure 30-5 to troubleshoot startup problems that occur before the progress bar appears. After each troubleshooting step, you should attempt to start the computer. If the computer starts successfully or if startup progresses far enough to display the progress bar, you can stop troubleshooting.

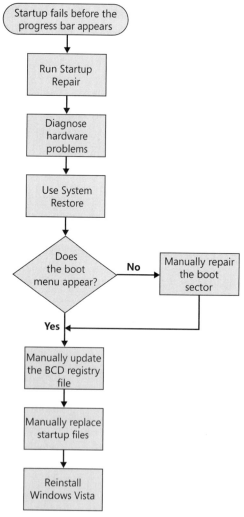

Figure 30-5   Follow this process to troubleshoot startup problems before logon.

The following sections describe each of these troubleshooting steps in more detail.

> **Note**   After you enable BitLocker, a lost encryption key can result in an unbootable computer. For information about BitLocker, see Chapter 15.

How to Run Startup Repair

To run Startup Repair, open the System Recovery Tools and then launch Startup Repair, as described in the following sections.

How to Start the System Recovery Tools   Windows Vista includes the System Recovery Tools, which are capable of fixing almost any startup problem related to boot sectors, master boot records, or the BCD registry file. The Startup Repair tool can fix most startup problems automatically, without requiring you to understand the details of how an operating system loads. The tool is so straightforward that you could easily talk end users through the troubleshooting process remotely.

To launch System Recovery Tools, follow these steps:

> **Note**   Some computers have the System Recovery Tools preinstalled by the computer manufacturer. On these computers, you can start the System Recovery Tools faster by pressing F8 before the Windows logo appears and then choosing Repair Your Computer from the Advanced Boot Options screen. These computers can also automatically detect startup failure (by noticing that the last startup failed) and launch Startup Repair.

1.   Insert the Windows Vista DVD in your computer.

2.   Restart your computer. When prompted to boot from the DVD, press any key. If you are not prompted to boot from the DVD, you may have to configure your computer's startup sequence. For more information, see the section titled "Initial Startup Phase" earlier in this chapter.

3.   Windows Vista setup loads.

4.   When prompted, select your regional preferences and keyboard layout and then click Next.

5.   Click Repair Your Computer to launch RecEnv.exe, as shown in Figure 30-6.

6.   System Recovery scans your hard disks for Windows Vista installations.

Figure 30-6   You can open System Recovery Tools by booting from the Windows Vista DVD.

7. If the standard Windows Vista drivers do not detect a hard disk because it requires drivers that were not included with Windows Vista, click Load Drivers to load the driver and then select an operating system to repair, as shown in Figure 30-7. Click Next.

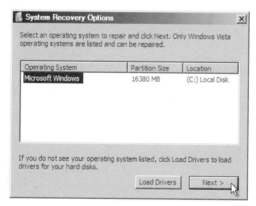

Figure 30-7   System Recovery attempts to find all Windows Vista installations.

8. If Windows failed to start during its last attempt, the Startup Repair tool will be launched automatically. Otherwise, the Choose A Recovery Tool page appears, as shown in Figure 30-8.

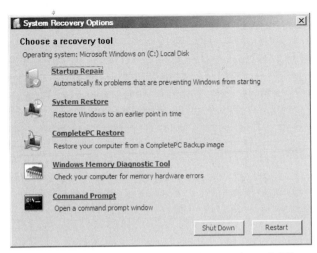

Figure 30-8   System Recovery provides a variety of different troubleshooting tools.

How to Run Startup Repair   The simplest way to solve startup problems is to load the System Recovery Tools, as described in the previous section, and then click Startup Repair and follow the prompts that appear. To run Startup Repair, follow these steps:

1. Load the System Recovery Tools, as described in the previous section.

2. Click Startup Repair and then follow the prompts that appear. The prompts may vary depending on the problem that Startup Repair identifies. You might be prompted to restore your computer using System Restore or to restart your computer and continue troubleshooting.

3. After the Startup Repair tool has completed diagnosis and repair, click Click Here For Diagnostic And Repair Details. As shown in Figure 30-9, at the bottom of the report, Startup Repair lists a root cause, if found, and any steps taken to repair the problem. Log files are stored at %WinDir%\System32\LogFiles\SRT\SRTTrail.txt.

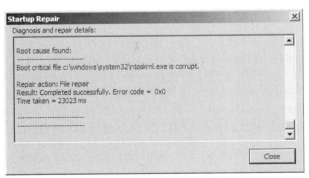

Figure 30-9   Startup Repair can fix many startup problems.

Allow Windows Vista to start normally. (Do not boot from the Windows Vista DVD.)

How to Use BootRec.exe

Startup Repair can automatically recover from most BCD problems. If you prefer to manually analyze and repair problems, you can use the command-line tool BootRec.exe by starting the System Recovery Tools and then clicking Command Prompt from the System Recovery Options dialog box.

BootRec.exe supports the following command-line parameters:

- **/FIXMBR** The /FIXMBR switch writes a Master Boot Record to the system partition.
- **/FIXBOOT** The /FIXBOOT switch writes a new boot sector onto the system partition.
- **/SCANOS** The /SCANOS switch scans all disks for Windows installation and displays entries currently not in the BCD Store.
- **/REBUILDBCD** The /REBUILDBCD switch scans all disks for Windows installations and provides a choice of which entries to add to the BCD Store.

Direct from the Source: Windows XP Recovery Console Equivalents

The Recovery Console has been deprecated in Windows Vista, so what happened to all those wonderful commands that were available in recovery console? Well, we were kind of hoping that you wouldn't need them anymore. But if you do, you'll be glad to know that most of them are available via the command line in the Windows Recovery Environment (WinRE). The recovery console commands listed in the following table are different or unavailable in WinRE.

Recovery Console Command	WinRE Equivalent(s)
BootCfg	BootRec /ScanOS
	BootRec /RebuildBcd
	bcdedit
FixBoot	BootRec /FixBoot
FixMBR	BootRec /FixMbr
Map	DiskPart
Logon	Not needed
LISTSVC	Not available
ENABLE	Not available
DISABLE	Not available
SYSTEMROOT	Not available

All the remaining commands have the same name in WinRE. You can work around the unavailable services-related commands (listsvc, enable, and disable) by using regedit to manually load the registry hive.

Parveen Patel, Developer

Windows Reliability

How to Diagnose Hardware Problems

If Startup Repair cannot solve the problem, or if you cannot start Windows Setup, you might have a hardware problem. Though most hardware-related problems will not stop Windows Vista from successfully starting, hardware-related problems may appear early in the startup process; symptoms include warning messages, startup failures, and Stop messages. The causes are typically improper device configuration, incorrect driver settings, or hardware malfunction and failure.

For detailed information about troubleshooting hardware problems, read Chapter 31.

How to Use System Restore

Windows Vista automatically captures system state before installing new applications or drivers. You can later use the System Restore tool to return to this system if you experience problems.

To launch System Restore from within Windows (including Safe Mode), click Start, click All Programs, click Accessories, click System Tools, and then click System Restore.

To launch System Restore when you cannot start Windows, follow these steps:

1. Start System Recovery Tools, as described in the section titled "How to Start the System Recovery Tools" earlier in this chapter.

2. Click System Restore. The System Restore Wizard appears.

After launching System Restore, follow these steps to restore Windows to an earlier state:

1. On the Restore System Files And Settings page, click Next.

2. On the Choose A Restore Point page, click a restore point. Typically, you should choose the most recent restore point when the computer functioned correctly. If the computer has not functioned correctly for more than five days, select the Show Restore Points Older Than 5 Days check box (as shown in Figure 30-10) and then select a restore point. Click Next.

3. On the Confirm Disks To Restore page, click Next.

4. On the Confirm Your Restore Point page, click Finish.

5. Click Yes to confirm the system restore. System Restore modifies system files and settings to return Windows Vista to the state it was in at the time the restore point was captured.

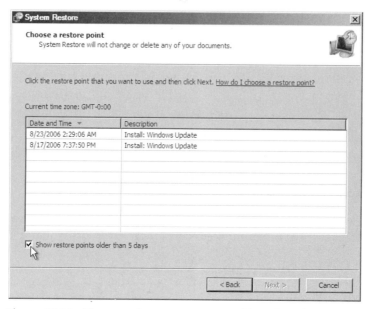

Figure 30-10   You can solve some startup problems by using System Restore.

6. When System Restore is done, click Restart. You should now attempt to start the computer and identify whether the problem was resolved.

7. When the computer restarts, Windows Vista will display a System Restore notification. Click Close.

How to Manually Repair the Boot Sector

Startup Repair is by far the quickest and easiest way to solve most startup problems. However, if you are familiar with troubleshooting startup problems and simply need to fix a boot sector problem after installing another operating system, you can run the following command from a command prompt (including the Command Prompt tool in the System Recovery Tools):

```
bootsect /NT60 ALL
```

Bootsect.exe is available from the \Boot\ folder of the Windows Vista DVD and can be run from within System Recovery or Windows XP.

After running Bootsect, you should be able to load Windows Vista, but you may not be able to load earlier versions of Windows that you have installed on the same computer. To load other operating systems, add entries to the BCD registry file, as described in the section titled "How to Create an Entry for Another Operating System" earlier in this chapter.

How to Manually Update the BCD Registry File

The simplest way to solve problems related to the BCD registry file is to run Startup Repair, as described earlier in this chapter. However, you can also use the System Recovery Tools to update the BCD registry file manually by following these steps:

1. Load the System Recovery Tools, as described in the previous section.

2. Click Command Prompt.

Use BCDEdit to update the BCD registry file.

For detailed information, read the section titled "How to Use BCDEdit" earlier in this chapter.

How to Manually Replace Files

If startup files are missing or become corrupted, Windows Vista may not be able to boot successfully. Often, Windows Vista will display an error message that shows the name of the missing file, as shown in Figure 30-11.

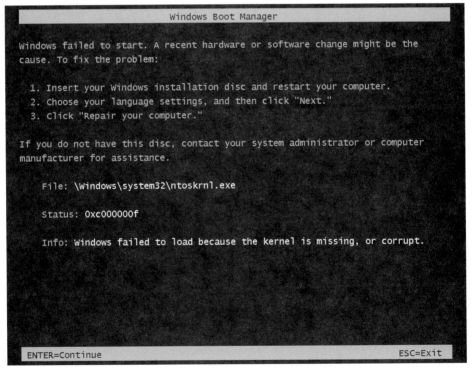

Figure 30-11   Windows Vista can display the names of missing startup files, which you can then manually replace.

Startup Repair can automatically replace missing system files, but may not detect corrupted files. However, you can manually replace files using the System Recovery Command-Line tool.

To replace files, follow these steps:

1. From another computer, copy the new files to removable media such as a CD-ROM or a USB flash drive. You cannot access Windows Vista system files from the Windows Vista DVD, because they are stored within a WIM file that is not accessible from within System Recovery.

2. Start System Recovery Tools as described in the section titled "How to Start the System Recovery Tools" earlier in this chapter.

3. After System Recovery Tools starts, click Command Prompt.

4. Your removable media will have a drive letter, just like a hard disk. System recovery Tools assigns hard disks letters starting with C, and then assigns letters to removable media. To identify the drive letter of your removable media, run the following commands:

```
C:\>diskpart
DISKPART> list volume
```

```
Volume ###  Ltr  Label        Fs     Type        Size     Status      Info
----------  ---  -----------  -----  ----------  -------  ----------  --------
Volume 0    C    Vista        NTFS   Partition    63 GB   Healthy
Volume 1    E    Windows XP   NTFS   Partition    91 GB   Healthy
Volume 2    D                 NTFS   Partition    69 GB   Healthy
Volume 3    I                        Removable     0 B    No Media
Volume 4    H                        Removable     0 B    No Media
Volume 5    F    LR1CFRE_EN_  UDF    Partition  2584 MB   Healthy
Volume 6    G    USBDRIVE     FAT32  Partition   991 MB   Healthy
```

5. Use the Copy command to transfer files from your removable media to the computer's hard disk.

How to Reinstall Windows

Infrequently, startup files and critical areas on the hard disk can become corrupted. If you are mainly concerned with salvaging readable data files and using the Backup And Restore Center to copy them to backup media or a network location, you can perform a parallel installation of Windows Vista. Although this may provide access to the file system, it will permanently damage your existing operating system and applications.

If you cannot start Windows Vista after following the troubleshooting steps in this guide, you can reinstall Windows Vista for the purpose of data recovery by following these steps:

1. Insert the Windows Vista DVD in your computer.

2. Restart your computer. When prompted to boot from the CD/DVD, press any key.

3. Windows Vista setup loads. When prompted, select your regional preferences and then click Next.

4. Click Install Now.

5. When prompted, enter your product key.

6. Select the I Accept The License Terms check box and then click Next.

7. Click Custom.

8. On the Where Do You Want to Install Windows page, select the partition containing your Windows Vista installation and then click Next.

9. When prompted, click OK.

Setup will install a new instance of Windows Vista and will move all files from your previous installation into the \Windows.Old folder (including the \Program Files, \Windows, and \Users folders). You now have two choices for returning the computer to its original state:

■ **Reformat the system partition**   If you have an automated deployment solution in place (as described in Part II of this book, "Deployment"), the quickest solution is to back up important files and redeploy Windows Vista. If you need to manually reinstall Windows Vista, you can follow this process:

1. Back up all important files by writing them to removable media, copying them to an external hard disk, or copying them to a shared folder on the network.

2. Reinstall Windows Vista. This time, choose to reformat the system partition.

3. Reinstall all applications and reconfigure all custom settings.

4. Restore important files.

■ **Continue working with the current system partition**   You can move important files to the proper locations within the new instance of Windows. Then, reinstall all applications and reconfigure any custom settings. Finally, you can delete the original Windows Vista instance by removing the \Windows.Old folder.

Startup Troubleshooting After the Progress Bar Appears

If your computer displays the graphical progress bar before failing, as shown in Figure 30-12, the Windows Vista kernel was successfully loaded. Most likely, the startup failure is caused by a faulty driver or service.

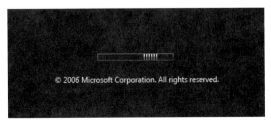

Figure 30-12   Displaying the progress bar indicates that Windows Vista has successfully loaded the kernel.

Use the process illustrated in Figure 30-13 to identify and disable the failing software component to allow Windows to start successfully. After Windows starts, you can perform further troubleshooting to resolve the problem with the component if necessary. If the startup problem occurs immediately after updating or installing a startup application, try troubleshooting the startup application. For information about troubleshooting startup applications, see the section titled "How to Temporarily Disable Startup Applications and Processes" later in this chapter.

The sections that follow describe each of these steps in more detail.

How to Run Startup Repair

Startup Repair can automatically fix many common startup problems, even if the problem occurs after the progress bar is displayed. Because Startup Repair is easy to use and has a very low likelihood of causing additional problems, it should be your first troubleshooting step. For detailed instructions, refer to the section titled "How to Run Startup Repair" in the "Startup Troubleshooting Before the Progress Bar Appears" section earlier in this chapter.

After running Startup Repair, attempt to start your computer normally and continue with the troubleshooting process only if Windows Vista fails to start.

How to Restore the Last Known Good Configuration

Last Known Good Configuration is usually used to enable the operating system to start if it fails after the progress bar is displayed. Using Last Known Good Configuration helps to correct instability or startup problems by reversing the most recent system, driver, and registry changes within a hardware profile. When you use this feature, you lose all configuration changes that were made since you last successfully started your computer.

Using the Last Known Good Configuration restores previous drivers and also restores registry settings for the subkey HKEY_LOCAL_MACHINE\SYSTEM\CurrentControlSet. Windows Vista does not update the LastKnownGood control set until you successfully start the operating system in normal mode and log on.

When you are troubleshooting, it is recommended that you use Last Known Good Configuration before you try other startup options, such as safe mode. However, if you decide to use safe mode first, logging on to the computer in safe mode does not update the Last Known Good control set. Therefore, Last Known Good Configuration remains an option if you cannot resolve your problem by using safe mode.

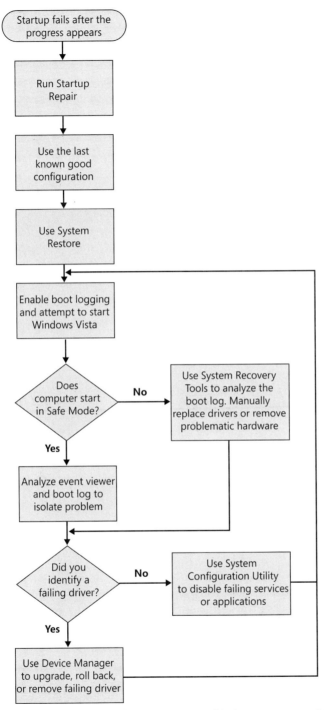

Figure 30-13   Follow this process to troubleshoot startup problems after the progress bar appears but before logon.

To access the Last Known Good Configuration startup option, follow these steps:

1. Remove all floppy disks, CDs, DVDs, and other bootable media from your computer and then restart your computer.

2. Press F8 at the operating system menu. If the operating system menu does not appear, press F8 repeatedly after the firmware POST process completes but before Windows Vista progress bar appears. The Advanced Boot Options menu appears.

3. On the Advanced Boot Options menu, select Last Known Good Configuration, as shown in Figure 30-14.

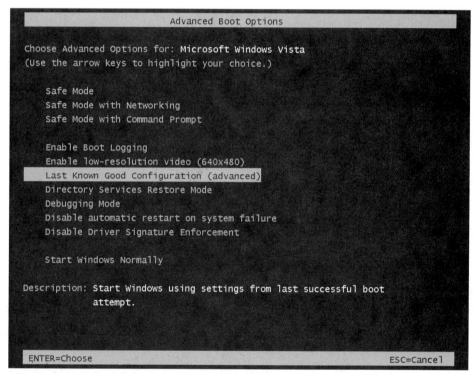

Figure 30-14   Use Last Known Good Configuration to restore some settings to their state the last time a user successfully logged on.

When Windows Vista starts, it reads status information from the file %WinDir%\Bootstat.dat. If Windows Vista detects that the last startup attempt was unsuccessful, it automatically displays the startup recovery menu, which provides startup options similar to the Advanced Boot Options menu, without requiring you to press F8.

> **Note**   If you suspect that changes made since you last successfully restarted the computer are causing problems, do not start Windows and log on normally—logging on overwrites the Last Known Good Configuration control set. Instead, restart the computer and use the Last Known Good Configuration. You can also log on in safe mode without overwriting the Last Known Good Configuration. For more information about control sets, see the section titled "Kernel Loading Phase" earlier in this chapter.

How to Use System Restore

If Last Known Good Configuration fails to resolve the problem, you can manually perform a system restore if Startup Repair did not initiate it. However, Startup Repair would typically have taken this step if it might have solved the problem. For information on how to use System Restore, see the section titled "How to Use System Restore" in the "Startup Troubleshooting Before the Progress Bar Appears" section earlier in this chapter.

How to Enable Boot Logging

Boot logging is useful for isolating the cause of a startup problem that occurs after the operating system menu appears. You can enable boot logging by following these steps:

1. Remove all floppy disks, CDs, DVDs, and other bootable media from your computer and then restart your computer.

2. Press F8 at the operating system menu. If the operating system menu does not appear, press F8 repeatedly after the firmware POST process completes but before Windows Vista progress bar appears. The Advanced Boot Options menu appears.

3. On the Advanced Boot Options menu, select Enable Boot Logging, as shown in Figure 30-15.

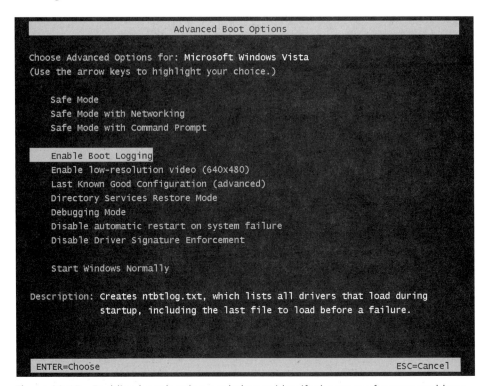

Figure 30-15   Enabling boot logging can help you identify the cause of startup problems.

Windows Vista starts and creates a log file at %WinDir%\Ntbtlog.txt. The log file starts with the time and version information and then lists every file that is successfully loaded, as shown here:

```
Service Pack 0, v.1 8 28 2006 17:59:07.489
Loaded driver \SystemRoot\system32\ntoskrnl.exe
Loaded driver \SystemRoot\system32\hal.dll
Loaded driver \SystemRoot\system32\kdcom.dll
Loaded driver \SystemRoot\system32\PSHED.dll
Loaded driver \SystemRoot\system32\BOOTVID.dll
Loaded driver \SystemRoot\system32\CLFS.SYS
Loaded driver \SystemRoot\system32\CI.dll
Loaded driver \SystemRoot\system32\drivers\wdf0100.sys
Loaded driver \SystemRoot\system32\drivers\WDFLDR.SYS
Did not load driver \SystemRoot\system32\drivers\serial.sys
Loaded driver \SystemRoot\system32\drivers\acpi.sys
```

The following sections will provide additional information about viewing and analyzing the boot log file.

How to Start in Safe Mode

Safe mode is a diagnostic environment that runs only a subset of the drivers and services that are configured to start in normal mode. Safe mode is useful when you install software or a device driver that causes instability or problems with starting in normal mode. Often, Windows can start in safe mode even if hardware failure prevents it from starting in normal mode. In most cases, safe mode allows you to start Windows Vista and then troubleshoot problems that prevent startup.

Logging on to the computer in safe mode does not update the LastKnownGood control set. Therefore, if you log on to your computer in safe mode and then decide you want to try Last Known Good Configuration, this option is still available to you.

In safe mode, Windows Vista uses the minimum set required to start the graphical user interface (GUI). The following registry subkeys list the drivers and services that start in safe mode:

- **Safe mode**   HKEY_LOCAL_MACHINE\SYSTEM\CurrentControlSet\Control\ SafeBoot\Minimal

- **Safe mode with networking**   HKEY_LOCAL_MACHINE\SYSTEM\CurrentControlSet\ Control\SafeBoot\Network

To access safe mode, follow these steps:

1. Remove all floppy disks and CDs from your computer and then restart your computer.

2. Press F8 at the operating system menu. If the operating system menu does not appear, press F8 repeatedly after the firmware POST process completes but before Windows Vista progress bar appears. The Advanced Boot Options menu appears.

4. Replace the driver file with a working version, using the Copy command at the command prompt. Start by replacing or deleting drivers that have been recently installed or updated. After replacing a driver, repeat this process until the system starts successfully in normal mode.

How to Roll Back Drivers

When you update a device driver, your computer might have problems that it did not have with the previous version. For example, installing an unsigned device driver might cause the device to malfunction or cause resource conflicts with other installed hardware. Installing faulty drivers might cause Stop errors that prevent the operating system from starting in normal mode. Typically, Stop message text displays the filename of the driver that causes the error.

Windows Vista provides a feature, Device Driver Roll Back, that might help you restore system stability by rolling back a driver update.

> **Note**   You can use System Information or the Sigverif tool to determine whether a driver on your computer is signed and to obtain other information about the driver, such as version, date, time, and manufacturer. This data, combined with information from the manufacturer's website, can help you decide whether to roll back or update a device driver.

To roll back a driver, follow these steps:

1. Click Start, right-click Computer, and then click Manage.

2. Under System Tools, click Device Manager.

3. Expand a category (Network Adapters, for example) and then double-click a device.

4. Click the Driver tab and then click Roll Back Driver. You are prompted to confirm that you want to overwrite the current driver. Click Yes to roll back the driver. The rollback process proceeds, or you are notified that an older driver is not available.

How to Temporarily Disable a Service

Many services automatically run at startup, but others are started only by users or by another process. When you troubleshoot startup issues that are related to system services, a useful technique is to simplify your computer configuration so that you can reduce system complexity and isolate operating system services. To decrease the number of variables, temporarily disable startup applications or services and re-enable them one at a time until you reproduce the problem. Always disable applications first, before attempting to disable system services.

The System Configuration Utility allows you to disable system services individually or several at a time. To disable a service by using the System Configuration Utility, follow these steps:

1. Click Start, type **msconfig**, and then press Enter.

2. Do one of the following:

   ❑ To disable services, on the General tab, click Selective Startup and then clear the Load System Services check box.

   ❑ To disable specific services, on the Services tab, click to clear the check boxes that correspond to the items you want to disable. You can also click Disable All to disable all items.

If you change any startup setting by using the System Configuration Utility, Windows Vista prompts you to return to normal operations the next time you log on. The System Configuration Utility prompt will appear each time you log on until you restore the original startup settings by clicking Normal Startup under Startup Selection on the General tab. To change a startup setting permanently, use the Services console, change a Group Policy setting, or uninstall the software that added the service.

Troubleshooting Startup Problems After Logon

If your computer fails immediately after a user logs on, use the process illustrated in Figure 30-16 to identify and disable the failing startup application to allow the user to log on successfully. If the problem occurs immediately after updating or installing an application, try uninstalling that application.

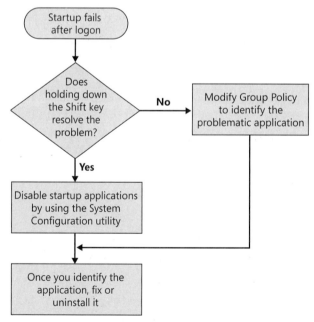

Figure 30-16   Follow this process to troubleshoot startup problems that occur after logon.

How to Temporarily Disable Startup Applications and Processes

If a problem occurs after installing new software, you can temporarily disable or uninstall the application to verify that the application is the source of the problem.

Problems with applications that run at startup can cause logon delays or even prevent you from completing Windows Vista startup in normal mode. The following subsections provide techniques for temporarily disabling startup applications.

How to Disable Startup Applications Using the Shift Key   One way you can simplify your configuration is to disable startup applications. By holding down the Shift key during the logon process, you can prevent the operating system from running startup programs or shortcuts in the following folders:

- %SystemDrive%\Users*Username*\AppData\Roaming\Microsoft\Windows\Start Menu\Programs\Startup

- %SystemDrive%\ProgramData\Microsoft\Windows\Start Menu\Programs\Startup

To disable the applications or shortcuts in the preceding folders, you must hold down the Shift key until the desktop icons appear. Holding down the Shift key is a better alternative than temporarily deleting or moving programs and shortcuts, because this procedure affects only the current user session.

To use the Shift key to disable applications and shortcuts in startup folders, log off the computer and then log on again. Immediately press and hold down the Shift key. Continue to hold down the Shift key until the desktop icons appear. If you can log on successfully, you have isolated the cause of the problem to your startup applications. Next, you should use the System Configuration Utility to temporarily disable applications one by one until you identify the cause of the problem. With the cause of the problem identified, you can fix the application or permanently remove it from your startup programs.

How to Disable Startup Programs Using the System Configuration Utility   System Configuration Utility allows you to disable startup applications individually or several at a time. To disable a startup program by using the System Configuration Utility, follow these steps:

1. Click Start, type **msconfig**, and then press Enter.

2. You can disable all or selective startup applications:

    ❑ To disable all startup applications, click the General tab, click Selective Startup, and then clear the Load Startup Items check box.

    ❑ To disable specific startup items, click the Startup tab, and then clear the check boxes that correspond to the items you want to disable temporarily. You can also click Disable All on the Startup tab to disable all items.

To change a startup setting permanently, you must move or delete startup shortcuts, change a Group Policy setting, or uninstall the application that added the startup application.

How to Disable Startup Applications Configured Using Group Policy or Logon Scripts

You can use the Group Policy snap-in to disable applications that run at startup. Local Group Policy can be applied to computers, in which case you would need to edit the Group Policy settings on the Windows Vista computer that you are troubleshooting. Group Policy objects are frequently applied within Active Directory domains, in which case you would need to connect to the domain to edit the appropriate policy. Before modifying domain Group Policy settings, you should follow the steps described later in this section to disconnect the computer you are troubleshooting from the network to determine if the problem is related to domain Group Policy settings.

To disable startup applications by using the Group Policy snap-in, follow these steps:

1. Click Start, type **gpedit.msc**, and then click OK.

2. Within either Computer Configuration (for computer-wide startup applications) or User Configuration (for user-specific startup applications), expand Administrative Templates, expand System, and then click Logon.

3. Double-click Run These Programs At User Logon, which is a Group Policy setting. Next, do one of the following:

    ❑ To disable all startup applications configured by that policy, click Disabled.

    ❑ To selectively disable individual programs that are listed in the computer-specific or user-specific policy, click Show. In the Show Contents dialog box, select a program to disable and then click Remove.

You can change additional Group Policy settings that might help you simplify your computer configuration when you are troubleshooting startup problems by enabling the Do Not Process The Run Once List policy. If you enable this Group Policy setting, the computer ignores the programs listed in the following RunOnce subkeys the next time a user logs on to the computer:

- HKEY_LOCAL_MACHINE\SOFTWARE\Microsoft\Windows\CurrentVersion\ RunOnce

- HKEY_CURRENT_USER\Software\Microsoft\Windows\CurrentVersion\RunOnce

Additionally, you can enable the Group Policy setting Do Not Process The Legacy Run List to disable the HKEY_LOCAL_MACHINE\SOFTWARE\Microsoft\Windows\CurrentVersion\ Run subkey that startup applications might use. The programs listed in this subkey are a customized list of programs that were configured by using the System Policy Editor for Windows NT 4.0 or earlier. If you enable this Group Policy setting, Windows ignores the programs listed in this subkey when you start your computer. If you disable or do not configure this Group Policy setting, Windows processes the customized run list that is contained in this registry subkey when you start the computer.

Group Policy changes do not always take effect immediately. You can use the Gpupdate (Gpupdate.exe) tool to refresh local Group Policy changes to computer and user policies. After you refresh the policy, you can use the Group Policy Result (Gpresult.exe) tool to verify that the updated settings are in effect.

Group Policy settings can be applied to locally or to an entire domain. To determine how settings are applied to a specific computer, use the Resultant Set Of Policy (Rsop.msc) tool. Then, edit those Group Policy objects to apply a change. For the purpose of isolating the source of the problem, you can prevent Group Policy, logon scripts, roaming user profiles, scheduled tasks, and network-related issues from affecting your troubleshooting by temporarily disabling the network adapter and then logging on by using a local computer account.

If local and domain Group Policy settings do not reveal the source of the startup problem, the application may be started by a logon script. Logon scripts are configured in the local or domain user properties. To view the logon script, open Computer Management and then view the user's properties. Then click the Profile tab. Make note of the path to the logon script and edit it in a tool such as Notepad to determine if any startup applications are configured. For more detailed information about Group Policy, read Chapter 13, "Managing the Desktop Environment."

How to Permanently Disable Startup Applications and Processes

You can permanently disable a startup application in several ways:

Uninstall the Application   If you find that recently installed software causes system instability or if error messages consistently point to a specific application, you can use Uninstall A Program under Programs in Control Panel to uninstall the software. If the application is required, you can install it in a lab environment and perform additional testing before reinstalling it on production computers.

Manually Remove the Entry   You can manually delete shortcuts from the Startup folder, remove startup entries from the registry, remove entries from Group Policy or logon scripts, or disable a service. For a list of registry subkeys that contain entries for service and startup programs, see the section titled "Logon Phase" earlier in this chapter.

Automatically Remove an Entry Using Windows Defender   Windows Defender simplifies the process of removing startup programs, and end users who don't have systems administration skills can use it.

To remove a startup program using Windows Defender, follow these steps:

1. Click Start.
2. Click All Programs.
3. Click Windows Defender.

4. In Windows Defender, click Tools.

5. Click Software Explorer.

6. Windows Defender displays startup programs. Select the program that you want to prevent from running and then click Disable, as shown in Figure 30-17.

Figure 30-17   You can use Windows Defender to disable startup programs.

7. When prompted, click Yes.

You can later re-enable the application by repeating this process and clicking the Enable button in Windows Defender.

Summary

Many critical aspects of Windows Vista startup are new and have not been used in other versions of Windows. These features include:

- Windows Boot Manager
- Windows Boot Loader
- The BCD registry file and the BCDEdit command line tool
- System Recovery Tools
- Startup Repair

However, if you are familiar with earlier versions of Windows, you will be comfortable trouble-shooting most problems that occur in the kernel loading phase of startup or later. Fortunately, you (or any user) can resolve many common startup problems simply by running the Startup Repair tool from the Windows Vista DVD.

Additional Resources

The following resources contain additional information and tools related to this chapter.

Related Information

- Chapter 15, "Managing Disks and File Systems," includes more information about startup problems related to disk configuration.
- Chapter 16, "Managing Devices and Services," includes information about configuring hardware and services.
- Chapter 31, "Troubleshooting Hardware, Driver, and Disk Issues," includes more information about hardware-related startup problems.
- Chapter 33, "Troubleshooting Stop Messages," includes more information about Stop errors that might occur during startup.
- "Boot Configuration Data in Windows Vista," which includes detailed information about the BCD registry file, is found at *http://www.microsoft.com/whdc/system/platform/firmware/bcd.mspx*.
- "BCD Classes," in MSDN, is found at *http://msdn2.microsoft.com/en-us/library/aa362675.aspx*.
- Article 92765 in the Microsoft Knowledge Base, "Terminating a SCSI Device," is found at *http://support.microsoft.com/?kbid=92765*.
- Article 154690 in the Microsoft Knowledge Base, "How to troubleshoot event ID 9, event ID 11, and event ID 15 error messages," is found at *http://support.microsoft.com/?kbid=154690*.
- Article 224826 in the Microsoft Knowledge Base, "Troubleshooting Text-Mode Setup Problems on ACPI Computers," is found at *http://support.microsoft.com/?kbid=224826*.

On the Companion CD

- BootConfig.vbs
- ListSystemDisk.vbs
- ListVolumeDirtySettings.vbs
- QueryServices.vbs

Chapter 31

Troubleshooting Hardware, Driver, and Disk Issues

This chapter describes how to use Windows Vista to troubleshoot common hardware problems. This chapter is not intended to be a comprehensive guide to troubleshooting hardware; instead, it focuses on using Windows Vista diagnostic and troubleshooting tools to solve hardware problems. First, this chapter describes improvements to Windows Vista that simplify the process of troubleshooting hardware problems. Then the chapter describes the process of using Windows Vista tools for troubleshooting hardware problems.

For hardware problems that prevent Windows Vista from starting, see Chapter 30, "Configuring Startup and Troubleshooting Startup Issues." For network problems, see Chapter 32, "Troubleshooting Network Issues." For problems that result in Stop errors (also known as blue screens), see Chapter 33, "Troubleshooting Stop Messages."

Windows Vista Improvements for Hardware and Driver Troubleshooting

Windows Vista includes several improvements and new features that will simplify how you troubleshoot hardware problems, allowing you to reduce client computer downtime. The following sections describe these improvements.

Windows Memory Diagnostics

Application failures, operating system faults, and Stop errors are often caused by failing memory. Failing memory chips return different data than the operating system originally stored. Failing memory can be difficult to identify: Problems can be intermittent and might occur only under very rare circumstances. For example, a memory chip might function perfectly when tested in a controlled environment but begin to fail when used within a hot computer. Failing memory can also cause secondary problems, such as corrupted files. Often, administrators take drastic steps to repair the problem, such as reinstalling applications or the operating system, only to have the failures persist.

Windows Vista includes Windows Memory Diagnostics to help administrators track down problems with unreliable memory. Previously, this technology was available only as a download and required installing the tool on a bootable floppy disk. In Windows Vista, if Windows Error Reporting (WER) or Microsoft Online Crash Analysis (MOCA) determine that failing memory might be the cause of an error, the software can prompt the user to perform memory diagnostics without requiring an additional download or separate boot disk. Additionally, you can run Windows Memory Diagnostics by choosing a special boot menu option or by loading the Startup Recovery Tools from the Windows Vista DVD.

If memory diagnostics identify a memory problem, Windows Vista can avoid using the affected portion of physical memory so that the operating system can start successfully and avoid application crashes. Upon startup, Windows Vista provides an easy-to-understand report detailing the problem and instructing the user on how to have the memory replaced. For detailed information, see the section titled "How to Use Windows Memory Diagnostics" later in this chapter.

Disk Failure Diagnostics

Disk reliability problems can vary in severity. Minor problems can cause seemingly random application failures. For example, if a user connects a new camera and the operating system fails to load the driver, disk corruption may be causing the problem. More severe problems can result in the total loss of data stored on the hard disk.

Windows Vista can eliminate much of the impact of a disk failure by detecting disk problems proactively, before total failure occurs. Hard disks often show warning signs before failure, but earlier Windows operating systems did not record the warning signs. Windows Vista listens for evidence that a hard disk is beginning to fail and warns the user or the support center of the problem. IT can then back up the data and replace the hard disk before the problem becomes an emergency. For administrators, Windows Vista acts as a guide through the process of backing up their data so that they can replace the drive without data loss.

Most new hard disks include Self-Monitoring Analysis and Reporting Technology (SMART) and Disk Self Tests (DSTs). SMART monitors the health of the disk using a set of degradable attributes, such as head-flying height and bad block reallocation count. DSTs actively check for failures by performing read, write, and servo tests.

Windows Vista queries for SMART status on an hourly basis and regularly schedules DSTs. If Windows Vista detects impending disk failure, Windows Vista can launch disk diagnostics to guide the user or IT professionals through the process of backing up the data and replacing the disk before total failure occurs. Windows Vista can also detect problems related to a dirty or scratched CD or DVD, and instruct the user to clean the media.

You can configure disk diagnostics using two Group Policy settings. Both are located in Computer Configuration\Policies\Administrative Templates\System\Troubleshooting And Diagnostics\Disk Diagnostic.

■ **Disk Diagnostic: Configure Execution Level**   Use this policy to enable or disable disk diagnostic warnings. Disabling this policy does not disable disk diagnostics; it simply blocks disk diagnostics from displaying a message to the user and taking any corrective action. If you have configured a monitoring infrastructure to collect disk diagnostic events recorded to the Event Log, and you prefer to manually respond to events, you can disable this policy.

■ **Disk Diagnostic: Configure Custom Alert Text**   Enable this property to define custom alert text (up to 512 characters) in the disk diagnostic message that appears when a disk reports a SMART fault.

For disk diagnostics to work, the Diagnostic Policy Service must be running. Note that disk diagnostics cannot detect all impending failures. Additionally, because SMART attribute definitions are vendor-specific, different vendor implementations can vary. SMART will not function if hard disks are attached to a hardware RAID controller.

> **Note**   Many hardware vendors use SMART failures as a warranty replacement indicator.

Self-Healing NTFS

Windows Vista now includes self-healing NTFS, which can detect and repair file system corruption while the operating system is running. In most cases, Windows Vista will repair file corruption without disrupting the user. Essentially, self-healing NTFS functions similarly to Chkdsk (described later in this chapter), but it works in the background, without locking an entire volume. Specifically, if Windows Vista detects corrupted metadata on the file system, it invokes NTFS's self-healing capabilities to rebuild the metadata. Some data may still be lost, but Windows Vista can limit the damage and repair the problem without taking the entire system offline for a lengthy check-and-repair cycle.

Self-healing NTFS is enabled by default and requires no management. Instead, it will serve to reduce the number of disk-related problems that require administrative intervention. If self-healing fails, the volume will be marked dirty, and Windows Vista will run Chkdsk on the next startup.

Reliability Monitor

Two of the biggest challenges of troubleshooting hardware problems are determining when the problem began occurring and what might have changed on the computer to introduce the problem. Windows Vista provides the Reliability Monitor snap-in (part of the Computer Management console) so that you can easily view application installations, driver installations, and significant failures over several weeks or months. Figure 31-1 shows Reliability Monitor.

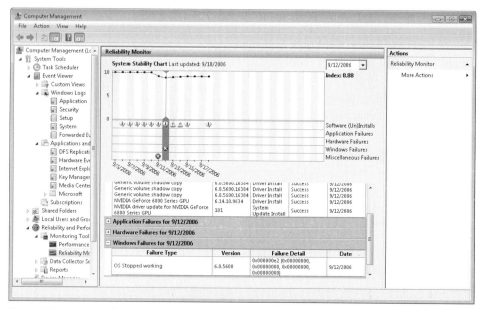

Figure 31-1   Reliability Monitor provides you with a history of changes and problems.

Reliability Monitor gives you a day-by-day analysis of application and driver installations, application failures, hardware failures, operating system failures, and other, uncategorized failures. Reliability Monitor is extremely valuable when troubleshooting hardware problems reported by end users because it allows you to quickly assess changes even if the user is not aware of them.

Reliability Monitor is discussed in more detail later in this chapter and in Chapter 22, "Maintaining Desktop Health."

Improved Driver Reliability

Windows Vista drivers should be more reliable in Windows Vista than they are in previous versions of Windows. Improved input/output (I/O) cancellation support has been built in to Windows Vista to enable drivers that might become blocked when attempting to perform I/O to gracefully recover. Windows Vista also has new Application Programming Interfaces (APIs) to allow applications to cancel I/O operations, such as opening a file.

To help developers create more stable drivers, Microsoft provides Driver Verifier. Developers can use the Driver Verifier to verify that their drivers remain responsive and to ensure that they correctly support I/O cancellation. Because driver hangs can affect multiple applications or the entire operating system, these improvements will have a significant impact on Windows Vista stability. This improvement requires no effort from administrators; you will simply benefit from a more reliable operating system.

Improved Error Reporting

Windows Vista will offer improved application reliability, and the new error reporting capabilities will allow applications to continue to become more reliable over time. In earlier versions of Windows, application hangs were very hard for developers to troubleshoot, because error reporting provided limited or no information about hangs. Windows Vista improves error reporting to give developers the information they need to permanently resolve the root cause of the problems, thus providing continuous improvements in reliability.

The Process of Troubleshooting Hardware Issues

Hardware problems can take several different forms:

- Hardware problems that prevent Windows from starting
- A newly installed hardware accessory that does not work as expected
- A hardware accessory that did work correctly, but now fails
- Unpredictable symptoms, such as failing applications and services, Stop errors, system resets, and accessories that behave unreliably

You should use a different process to troubleshoot each of these broad problem categories. The following sections discuss each of these suggested processes.

How to Troubleshoot Problems That Prevent Windows from Starting

Some hardware problems—especially those related to hard disks or core components such as the motherboard or processor—can prevent Windows from starting. For information about troubleshooting startup problems, see Chapter 30.

How to Troubleshoot Problems Installing New Hardware

Often, you might have difficulty installing a new hardware component, or an existing hardware component might suddenly fail. If you are having trouble installing a new hardware component, follow these steps:

1. If Windows will not start, see Chapter 30.
2. Install any updates available from Windows Update. For more information, see Chapter 24, "Managing Software Updates."

3. Download and install updated software and drivers for your hardware. Hardware manufacturers often release updated software for hardware components after they release the hardware. You can typically download software updates from the manufacturer's website.

4. Remove and reinstall any newly installed hardware by strictly following the manufacturer's instructions. You often need to install the software before connecting the hardware. See the following sections of this chapter for more information: "How to Diagnose Hardware Problems" and "How to Troubleshoot Driver Problems." For detailed information about troubleshooting USB devices, see the section titled "How to Troubleshoot USB Problems." For information about troubleshooting devices that connect using Bluetooth, see the section titled "How to Troubleshoot Bluetooth Problems."

5. Use the Event Viewer to find any related events that might provide useful information for diagnosing the problem. Typically, drivers will add events to the System Event Log. However, drivers could add events to any log. For information about using Event Viewer, see the section titled "How to Use Event Viewer" later in this chapter.

6. Install updated drivers for other hardware components, including BIOS and firmware updates for all hardware accessories and your computer. Updated drivers for other hardware components can sometimes solve incompatibility problems with new hardware.

7. If possible, move hardware to different connectors on your computer. For example, move internal cards to different slots, or connect USB devices to different USB ports. If this solves the problem, the original connector on your computer has failed or the device was not connected correctly.

8. Replace any cables used to connect the new hardware to your computer. If this solves the problem, the cable was faulty.

9. Connect the new hardware to a different computer. If the hardware fails on multiple computers, you might have faulty hardware.

10. Contact the failed hardware manufacturer for support. You might have a hardware or software failure; the hardware manufacturer can assist with additional troubleshooting.

How to Troubleshoot Problems with Existing Hardware

If a hardware component that previously worked suddenly fails, follow these troubleshooting steps:

1. If Windows will not start, see Chapter 30.

2. Open Problem Reports And Solutions and check to see if Windows Vista has registered the problem and if Microsoft has released a solution for the problem. For more information, see the section titled "How to Use Problem Reports And Solutions" later in this chapter. If the problem is not mentioned in Problem Reports And Solutions, or if no solution is available, continue with the following troubleshooting steps.

3. Use Reliability Monitor to determine how long the problem has been occurring and what related symptoms might be occurring. For more information, see the section titled "How to Use Reliability Monitor" later in this chapter. Then use Event Viewer to find any related events that might provide useful information for diagnosing the problem. For information about using Event Viewer, see the section titled "How to Use Event Viewer" later in this chapter.

4. Install any updates available from Windows Update. For more information, see Chapter 24.

5. Roll back any recently updated drivers, even if they are for other devices. Driver problems might cause incompatibilities with different devices. For more information, see the section titled "How to Roll Back Drivers" later in this chapter.

6. Download and install updated software and drivers for your hardware. Hardware manufacturers often release updated software for hardware components after they release the hardware. You can typically download software updates from the manufacturer's website.

7. Remove and reinstall any newly installed hardware. For more information, see the sections titled "How to Diagnose Hardware Problems" and "How to Troubleshoot Driver Problems" later in this chapter. For detailed information about troubleshooting USB devices, see the section titled "How to Troubleshoot USB Problems" later in this chapter.

8. Install updated drivers for other hardware components, including BIOS and firmware updates for all hardware accessories and your computer. Updated drivers for other hardware components can sometimes solve incompatibility problems with hardware.

9. Troubleshoot disk problems by using Chkdsk to identify and possibly fix disk-related problems. Disk problem can corrupt drivers, which might cause hardware to stop functioning. For more information, see the section titled "How to Troubleshoot Disk Problems" later in this chapter.

10. If possible, move hardware to different connectors on your computer. For example, move internal cards to different slots and connect USB devices to different USB ports. If this solves the problem, the original connector on your computer has failed or the device was not connected correctly.

11. Replace any cables used to connect the new hardware to your computer. If this solves the problem, the cable was faulty.

12. Connect problematic hardware to a different computer. If the hardware fails on multiple computers, you might have a hardware malfunction. Contact the hardware manufacturer for technical support.

13. Perform a System Restore to attempt to return the computer state when it was functioning correctly. To use System Restore, see the section titled "How to Use System Restore" later in this chapter.

14. Contact the hardware manufacturer for support. You might have a hardware or software failure, and the hardware manufacturer can assist with additional troubleshooting.

How to Troubleshoot Unpredictable Symptoms

Hardware, driver, and disk problems can cause unpredictable symptoms when Windows is running, including:

- Failing applications and services
- Stop errors
- System resets
- Accessories that behave unreliably

Many different types of problems can cause these symptoms. To identify the source of these problems and possibly fix the issue, follow these steps. After each step, determine if the problem continues.

1. If Windows will not start, see Chapter 30.

2. Open Problem Reports and Solutions and check to see if Windows Vista has registered the problem and if Microsoft has released a solution for the problem. For more information, see the section titled "How to Use Problem Reports And Solutions" later in this chapter. If the problem is not mentioned in Problem Reports And Solutions, or if there is no solution, continue with the following troubleshooting steps.

3. Use Reliability Monitor to determine how long the problem has been occurring and what other related symptoms might be occurring. For more information, read the section titled "How to Use Reliability Monitor" later in this chapter. Then use Event Viewer to find any related events that might provide useful information for diagnosing the problem. Typically, drivers will add events to the System Event Log. However, drivers could add events to any log. For information about using Event Viewer, see the section titled "How to Use Event Viewer" later in this chapter.

4. Install any updates available from Windows Update. For more information, see Chapter 24.

5. Install updated drivers available directly from the hardware manufacturer, including BIOS and firmware updates for all hardware accessories and your computer.

6. Roll back any recently updated drivers. For more information, see the section titled "How to Roll Back Drivers" later in this chapter.

7. Troubleshoot disk problems by using Chkdsk to identify and possibly fix disk-related problems. To resolve problems related to low free disk space, run the Disk Cleanup Wizard. For more information, see the section titled "How to Troubleshoot Disk Problems" later in this chapter.

8. Test your memory for problems by using Windows Memory Diagnostics. For more information, see the section titled "How to Use Windows Memory Diagnostics" later in this chapter.

9. Remove unnecessary hardware components one by one. If the problem disappears after removing a hardware component, you have identified the hardware component causing the problem. Continue troubleshooting that specific component by following the steps listed in the section titled "How to Troubleshoot Problems with Existing Hardware" earlier in this chapter.

10. Perform a System Restore to attempt to return the computer to a state when it was functioning correctly. To use System Restore, see the section titled "How to Use System Restore" later in this chapter.

11. Contact your computer manufacturer for support. You might have a hardware or software failure, and your computer manufacturer can assist with additional troubleshooting.

How to Diagnose Hardware Problems

Always remember to check basic issues first before attempting to remove and replace parts. Before installing new peripherals, refer to your motherboard and device manuals for helpful information, including safety precautions, firmware configuration, and expansion slot or memory slot locations. Some peripheral manufacturers recommend that you use a bus-mastering PCI slot and advise that installing their adapter in a secondary slot might cause it to function improperly.

 Note   Though all hardware might not be on the list, you can reduce the likelihood of incompatibilities by choosing hardware found on the Windows Tested Products List website at *http://testedproducts.windowsmarketplace.com*.

How to Use Device Manager to Identify Failed Devices

Windows Vista can detect hardware that is not working properly. View failed hardware by following these steps to use Device Manager:

1. Click Start, right-click Computer, and then click Manage.

2. Under System Tools, click Device Manager.

3. Device Manager displays all devices. Problem devices (including any devices Windows Vista was unable to successfully communicate with) are displayed with a warning sign. If no categories are expanded and no devices are visible, Windows Vista did not detect a problem with any device.

How to Check the Physical Setup of Your Computer

If you have recently opened the computer case, or the computer has been moved or shipped, connectors may have loosened. You should perform the following tasks to verify that connections are solid:

- **Confirm that the power cords for all devices are firmly plugged in and that the computer power supply meets hardware specifications**   Computer power supplies are available in different sizes and are typically rated between 200 and 400 watts. Installing too many devices into a computer with an inadequate amount of power can cause reliability problems or even damage the power supply. See the manufacturer's power specifications when installing new devices and verify that your computer can handle the increased electrical load.

- **Disconnect external accessories**   External accessories—such as those that connect using USB or IEEE 1394, PC cards, and ExpressCards—can malfunction and interfere with the startup process. You can either disconnect devices one by one and attempt to start the computer after disconnecting each device to identify the cause of the problem, or you can disconnect all devices, start the computer, and then reconnect devices one by one.

- **Verify that you correctly installed and firmly seated all internal adapters**   Peripherals such as keyboards and video cards often must be installed and functioning to complete the initial startup phase without generating error messages. Adapters might become loose if the computer is moved or bumped, or if the computer vibrates from moving parts such as hard disks.

- **Verify that you correctly attached cables**   Check that you have firmly seated all cable connectors by disconnecting and reconnecting cables. Search for damaged or worn cables and replace them as required. To ensure that contacts are solid, use a pencil eraser to clean dirty connectors.

- **Check the system temperature**   High temperatures inside a computer can cause unpredictable failures. Many computers will display internal temperatures for the processor, hard disk, graphics card, or other components if you start the firmware menu. Graphical, third-party tools also run within Windows for displaying temperature diagnostic information. If the temperature is high, verify that all fans are working properly and the vents are not blocked. Verify that the computer's case is completely assembled: Leaving panels open might seem like it would improve airflow, but it can actually misdirect air that should be cooling hot components. Verify that air can flow freely around the outside of the computer. Particularly with mobile PCs, verify that the computer is not resting on a soft surface that can prevent heat dissipation, such as a couch or carpet. Finally, reset processor and memory speeds to their default settings to verify that the computer has not been overclocked.

How to Check the Configuration of Your Hardware

If you have recently changed the hardware configuration of your computer, or you are configuring a new computer, you should check the configuration to identify the cause of a startup problem.

- **Verify that you correctly configured any jumpers or dual in-line package (DIP) switches** Jumpers and DIP switches close or open electric contacts on circuit boards. For hard disks, jumper settings are especially important because they can adversely affect the startup process if not correctly set. For example, configuring two master ATA disks that are installed on the same channel or assigning duplicate SCSI ID numbers to devices in the same SCSI chain might cause a Stop error or error messages about hard disk failure.

- **Configure BCD references correctly when a hard disk is added** Installing an additional hard disk or changing the disk configuration in a computer can prevent Windows Vista from starting. In this case, use the Startup Repair tool within System Recovery Tools to automatically resolve the problem. For more information, see Chapter 30.

- **Verify SCSI configuration** If your computer uses or starts from SCSI devices, and you suspect that these devices are causing startup problems, you need to check the items listed in Table 31-1.

Table 31-1   Checklist for Troubleshooting SCSI Devices

Item	Description
All devices are correctly terminated.	Verify that SCSI devices are correctly terminated. You must follow specific rules for termination to avoid problems with the computer not recognizing a SCSI device. Although these rules can vary slightly from one type of adapter to another, the basic principle is that you must terminate a SCSI chain at both ends.
All devices use unique SCSI ID numbers.	Verify that each device located on a particular SCSI chain has a unique identification number. Duplicate identification numbers can cause intermittent failures or even data corruption. For newer devices, you can use the SCSI Configures Auto Magically (SCAM) standard. The host adapter and all devices must support the SCAM standard. Otherwise you must set ID numbers manually.
The BIOS on the startup SCSI controller is enabled.	Verify that the SCSI BIOS is enabled for the primary SCSI controller and that the BIOS on secondary controllers is disabled. SCSI firmware contains programming instructions that allow the computer to communicate with SCSI disks before Windows Vista starts. Disabling this feature for all host adapters causes a startup failure. For information about disabling or enabling the BIOS, refer to the documentation provided with your SCSI controller.
You are using the correct cables.	Verify that the connecting cables are the correct type and length and are compliant with SCSI requirements. Different SCSI standards exist, each with specific cabling requirements. Consult the product documentation for more information.

Table 31-1   Checklist for Troubleshooting SCSI Devices

Item	Description
The firmware settings for the host SCSI adapter match device capabilities.	Verify that host adapter BIOS settings for each SCSI device are set correctly. (The BIOS for the SCSI adapter is separate from the computer motherboard firmware.) For each SCSI device, you can specify settings—such as Sync Negotiation, Maximum Transfer Rate, and Send Start Command—that can affect performance and compatibility. Certain SCSI devices might not function correctly if settings are set beyond the capabilities of the hardware. Consult the documentation for your SCSI adapter and device before changing default settings.
SCSI adapters are installed in a master PCI slot.	Verify that you installed the host adapter in the correct motherboard slot. The documentation for some PCI SCSI adapters recommends using busmaster PCI slots to avoid problems on 32-bit computers. Refer to the manufacturer's documentation for your motherboard or computer to locate these busmaster PCI slots. If your SCSI adapter is installed in a non-busmaster PCI slot, move it to a master slot to see if the change improves operation and stability.

Note   As a precaution, always shut down the computer and remove the power connector before troubleshooting hardware. Never attempt to install or remove internal devices if you are unfamiliar with hardware.

For more information about SCSI termination, see Microsoft Knowledge Base article 92765, "Terminating a SCSI Device," at *http://support.microsoft.com/?kbid=92765* and Microsoft Knowledge Base article 154690, "How to troubleshoot event ID 9, event ID 11, and event ID 15 error messages," at *http://support.microsoft.com/?kbid=154690*.

How to Verify That System Firmware and Peripheral Firmware Are Up to Date

You can sometimes trace instability and compatibility problems to outdated firmware. Whenever possible, use the latest firmware version. If Setup does not respond when you are installing the operating system, the cause might be the firmware for your DVD drive. Try upgrading the DVD firmware to the latest version.

How to Test Your Hardware by Running Diagnostic Tools

If the problem occurs after the POST routine finishes but before Windows Vista fully loads, run any diagnostic software that the manufacturer of the hardware adapter provides. This software typically includes self-test programs that allow you to quickly verify proper operation of a device and might help you to obtain additional information about the device, such as model number, hardware, and device firmware version.

Additionally, you can use Windows Vista to run a memory test on your computer. For detailed instructions, see the section titled "How to Use Windows Memory Diagnostics" later in this chapter.

How to Simplify Your Hardware Configuration

Hardware problems can occur when you have both newer and older devices installed on your computer. If you cannot resolve problems by using safe mode and other options such as rolling back drivers, temporarily disable or remove ISA devices that do not support Plug and Play. If you can start Windows Vista with these older devices removed, these devices are causing resource conflicts, and you need to manually reconfigure the resources assigned to them. For more information about rolling back drivers, see the section titled "How to Roll Back Drivers" later in this chapter.

While you are diagnosing startup problems related to hardware, it is recommended that you simplify your configuration. By simplifying your computer configuration, you might be able to start Windows Vista. You can then gradually increase the computer's hardware configuration complexity until you reproduce the problem, which allows you to diagnose and resolve the problem.

Avoid troubleshooting when you have several adapters and external peripherals installed. Starting with external and ISA devices, disable or remove hardware devices one at time until you are able to start your computer. Reinstall devices by following the manufacturer's instructions, verifying that each is functioning properly before checking the next device. For example, installing a PCI network adapter and a SCSI adapter at the same time can complicate troubleshooting, because either adapter might cause a problem.

ISA devices cause a large share of startup problems related to hardware because the PCI bus does not have a reliable method for determining ISA resource settings. Device conflicts might occur because of miscommunication between the two bus types. To avoid ISA and PCI conflicts, try temporarily removing ISA devices. After you install a new PCI device, you can use Device Manager to determine which system resources are available to ISA devices. Then reconfigure the ISA devices that do not support Plug and Play to eliminate any conflicts. If the problems continue after you reinstall ISA devices and you cannot resolve them with assistance from technical support, consider upgrading to newer hardware.

Simplifying your computer configuration also helps when problems prevent you from installing Windows Vista. For more information about simplifying your hardware configuration to resolve setup problems, see Microsoft Knowledge Base article 224826, "Troubleshooting Text-Mode Setup Problems on ACPI Computers," at *http://support.microsoft.com/?kbid=224826*.

How to Diagnose Disk-Related Problems

Disk-related problems typically occur before Windows Vista starts or shortly afterward. Refer to Table 31-2 for a list of symptoms, possible causes, and sources of information about disk-related startup problems.

Table 31-2   Diagnosing Disk-Related Startup Problems

Symptom, Message, or Problem	Possible Cause	For More Information

The POST routine displays messages similar to the following:
 	
`Hard disk error.`
`Hard disk absent/failed.`
	The system self-test routines halt because of improperly installed devices.	Verify that hardware is connected properly, as described earlier in this section.

The system displays MBR-related or boot sector-related messages similar to the following:
 	
`Missing operating system.`
`Insert a system diskette and`
`restart the system.`
	The MBR or partition boot sector is corrupt because of problems with hardware or viruses.	Run Startup Repair, as described in Chapter 30.

The system displays messages about the partition table similar to the following:
 	
`Invalid partition table.`
`A disk-read error occurred.`
	The partition table is invalid because of incorrect configuration of newly added disks.	Run Startup Repair, as described in Chapter 30. If Windows Vista still fails to start, use the System Recovery Command Prompt to configure your disks.

You cannot access Windows Vista after installing another operating system.	The Windows Vista boot sector is overwritten by another operating system's setup program.	Run Startup Repair, as described in Chapter 30.
System files are missing.	Required startup files are missing or damaged, or entries in the BCD registry file are pointing to the wrong partition.	Run Startup Repair, as described in Chapter 30.

The EFI boot manager or Windows Boot Manager displays messages similar to the following:
 	
`Couldn't find loader.`
`Please insert another disk.`
	System files are missing.	Run Startup Repair, as described in Chapter 30.

CMOS or NVRAM disk configuration settings are not retained.	The CMOS memory or NVRAM is faulty, data is corrupted, or the battery that retains these settings needs replacing.	Follow the manufacturer's instructions for replacing or recharging the system battery.

Infrequently, disk-related issues such as corrupted files, file system problems, or insufficient free space might cause Stop messages to appear. For more information about maintaining disks and troubleshooting disk-related problems, see Chapter 15, "Managing Disks and File Systems."

How to Use Built-In Diagnostics

Windows Vista includes several different tools to assist you in diagnosing the source of hardware problems. The following sections describe the most important tools.

How to Use Problem Reports And Solutions

With Problem Reports And Solutions, shown in Figure 31-2, you can track diagnostic results and errors.

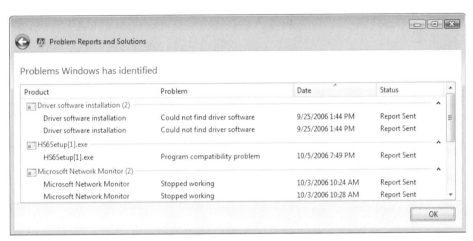

Figure 31-2   You can use Problem Reports And Solutions to track diagnostics results.

To open Problem Reports And Solutions, click Start, click All Programs, click Maintenance, and then click Problem Reports And Solutions. You can then click View Details to view information about any particular problem or result.

To determine if Microsoft has identified a solution to the problem, select the problem's check box and then click Check For Solutions. Problem Reports And Solutions will contact Microsoft servers, submit the error report, and look for a matching solution. Often, there may be no solution for your problem. However, submitting the error report can help Microsoft solve the problem in the future. Microsoft prioritizes problems based on their frequency, so submitting error reports increases the chances that the problem will be fixed.

How to Use Reliability Monitor

To view Reliability Monitor, follow these steps:

1. Click Start, right-click Computer, and then click Manage.

2. Expand Reliability And Performance, expand Monitoring Tools, and then click Reliability Monitor.

The System Stability Chart provides a day-by-day report of any problems or significant changes. To view events that occurred on a specific day, click the day in the System Stability Chart and then view the System Stability Report for detailed information. You can also click the drop-down list in the upper-right corner, and then click Select All to view a report that contains all events that Windows Vista has recorded. For more information, read Chapter 22.

How to Use Event Viewer

Event Viewer provides a central location for operating system and application event logging. On most computers, Event Viewer contains thousands of events generated by Windows, drivers, and applications. Most of these events can be safely ignored. However, when trouble-shooting problems, you should examine the Event Log to find events that might be related to your problem. It is entirely possible that no events will be related to your problem, however, because not all problems may initiate an event.

To open Event Viewer and view hardware-related events, follow these steps:

1. Click Start, right-click Computer, and then click Manage.

2. Under System Tools, expand Event Viewer.

3. Under Event Viewer, expand Windows Logs. Then click System.

4. In the Actions pane, click Filter Current Log.

5. In the Filter Current Log dialog box, select the Critical, Warning, and Error check boxes. Click OK.

Browse through the displayed events. Most of the events will not be related to your problem, but it is important to evaluate each event to determine any potential impact. In particular, pay close attention to events with a Source of ACPI or PlugPlayManager or another Source related to the hardware component that is experiencing problems. For more information, read Chapter 22.

How to Use Data Collector Sets

The Windows Vista Reliability And Performance snap-in includes Data Collector Sets and corresponding reports that perform detailed analysis of different aspects of a computer's configuration and performance.

To use Data Collector Sets and reports, follow these steps:

1. Click Start, right-click Computer, and then click Manage.

2. Expand Reliability And Performance, expand Data Collector Sets, and then click System.

3. In the middle pane, right-click the Data Collector Set you want to analyze and then click Start. For example, to analyze the computer's hardware, right-click System Diagnostics and then click Start. Windows Vista will begin collecting data.

4. Right-click the Data Collector Set and then click Latest Report. Windows Vista shows the report status while data is being collected (this might take several minutes). After enough data has been collected, it displays the report. Figure 31-3 shows a System Diagnostics report.

Figure 31-3   The System Diagnostics report includes detailed information about the computer, including possible sources of hardware problems.

Examine the report to determine if any of the causes might be related to the problem you are troubleshooting.

How to Use Windows Memory Diagnostics

Memory problems are one of the most common types of hardware problem. Memory problems can prevent Windows from starting and cause unpredictable Stop errors when Windows Vista has started. Because memory-related problems can cause intermittent failures, they can be difficult to identify.

> ## How It Works: Memory Failures
>
> Because of the massive number of memory chips hardware manufacturers produce, and the high standards customers have for reliability, memory testing is a highly refined science. Different memory tests are designed to detect specific types of common failures, including:
>
> - A bit may always return 1, even if set to 0. Similarly, a bit may always return 0, even if set to 1. This is known as a Stuck-At Fault (SAF).
>
> - The wrong bit is addressed when attempting to read or write a specific bit. This is known as an Address Decoder Fault (AF).
>
> - A section of memory may not allow values to change. This is known as a Transition Fault (TF).
>
> - A section of memory changes when being read. This is called a Read Disturb Fault (RDF).
>
> - One or more bits lose their contents after a period of time. This is known as a Retention Fault (RF) and can be one of the more challenging types of failures to detect.
>
> - A change to one bit affects another bit. This is known as a Coupling Fault (CF) if the faulty bit changes to the same value as the modified bit, an Inversion Coupling Fault (CFin) if the faulty bit changes to the opposite value as the modified bit, or an Idempotent Coupling Fault (CFid) if the faulty bit always becomes a certain value (1 or 0) after any transition in the modified bit. This behavior can also occur because of a short between two cells, known as a Bridging Fault (BF).
>
> Given these types of failures, it's clear that no single test could properly diagnose all the problems. For example, a test that wrote all 1s to memory and then verified that the memory returned all 1s would properly diagnose an SAF fault where memory was stuck at 0. However, it would fail to diagnose an SAF fault where memory was stuck at 1, and it would not be complex enough to find many bridging or coupling faults. Therefore, to properly diagnose all types of memory failures, Windows Memory Diagnostics provides several different types of tests.

Fortunately, Windows Vista includes Windows Memory Diagnostics, an offline diagnostic tool that automatically tests your computer's memory. Windows Memory Diagnostics tests your computer's memory by repeatedly writing values to memory and then reading those values from memory to verify that they have not changed. To identify the widest range of memory failures, Windows Memory Diagnostics includes three different testing levels:

- **Basic** Basic tests include:
  - ❑ MATS+
  - ❑ INVC
  - ❑ SCHCKR (This test enables the cache.)

- **Standard**   All basic tests, plus:
    - ❑ LRAND
    - ❑ Stride6 (This test enables the cache.)
    - ❑ CHCKR3
    - ❑ WMATS+
    - ❑ WINVC
- **Extended**   All standard tests, plus:
    - ❑ MATS+ (This test disables the cache.)
    - ❑ Stride38
    - ❑ WSCHCKR
    - ❑ WStride-6
    - ❑ CHKCKR4
    - ❑ WCHCKR3
    - ❑ ERAND
    - ❑ Stride6 (This test disables the cache.)
    - ❑ CHCKR8

Although the specifics of each of these tests are not important for administrators to understand, it is important to understand that memory testing is never perfect. Failures are often intermittent, and may occur only once every several days or weeks in regular usage. Automated tests such as those done by Windows Memory Diagnostics increase the likelihood that a failure can be detected; however, you can still have faulty memory while Windows Memory Diagnostics indicates that no problems were detected. To minimize this risk, run Extended tests and increase the number of repetitions. The more tests you run, the more confident you can be in the result.

After Windows Memory Diagnostic completes testing, the computer will automatically restart. Windows Vista will display a notification bubble with the test results, as shown in Figure 31-4, and you can view events in the System Event Log with the source Memory-DiagnosticsResults (event ID 1201).

Figure 31-4   Windows Memory Diagnostics displays a notification bubble after logon.

If you do identify a memory failure, it is typically not worthwhile to attempt to repair the memory. Instead, you should replace unreliable memory. If the computer has multiple memory cards and you are unsure which card is causing the problem, replace each card and then rerun Windows Memory Diagnostics until the computer is reliable.

If problems persist even after replacing the memory, the problem is caused by an outside source. For example, high temperatures (often found in mobile PCs) can cause memory to be unreliable. Although computer manufacturers typically choose memory specifically designed to withstand high temperatures, adding third-party memory that does not meet the same specifications can cause failure. Besides heat, other devices inside the computer can cause electrical interference. Finally, motherboard or processor problems may occasionally cause memory communication errors that resemble failing memory.

How Windows Vista Automatically Detects Memory Problems

When Windows Vista analyzes problem reports (as part of the Problem Reports And Solutions tool), it can determine that memory problems might be a source of the problem. If this happens, Problem Reports And Solutions prompts the user to run Windows Memory Diagnostics, as shown in Figure 31-5. From this page, users can click a link to either immediately restart Windows Vista and test for memory errors or to wait until the next time the computer is restarted.

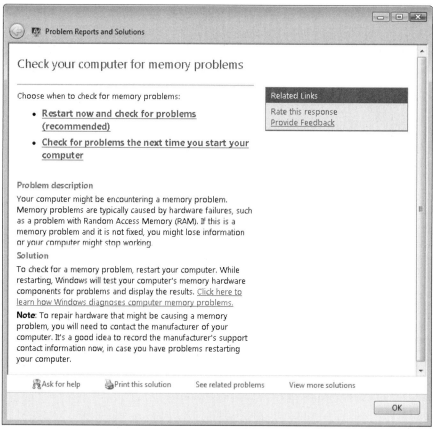

Figure 31-5   Problem Reports And Solutions can prompt you to schedule Windows Memory Diagnostics to run when you next restart your computer.

How to Schedule Windows Memory Diagnostics

If Windows Vista is running, you can schedule Windows Memory Diagnostics for the next startup by following these steps:

1. Click Start, type **mdsched.exe**, and then press Enter.

2. Choose to restart the computer and run the tool immediately or schedule the tool to run at the next restart, as shown in Figure 31-6.

Figure 31-6   You can schedule Windows Memory Diagnostics to run when you next restart your computer.

Windows Memory Diagnostic runs automatically after the computer restart.

How to Start Windows Memory Diagnostics When Windows Vista is Installed

If Windows Vista is already installed, you can start Windows Memory Diagnostics from the Windows Boot Manager menu. To do this, follow these steps:

1. Remove all floppy disks and CDs from your computer and then restart your computer.

2. If the Windows Boot Manager menu does not normally appear, press the space bar repeatedly as the computer starts up. If you are successful, the Windows Boot Manager menu will appear. If the Windows Vista progress bar appears, restart your computer and try again to interrupt the startup process by pressing the space bar.

3. On the Windows Boot Manager menu, press the Tab button on your keyboard to select Windows Memory Diagnostics, as shown in Figure 31-7, and then press Enter.

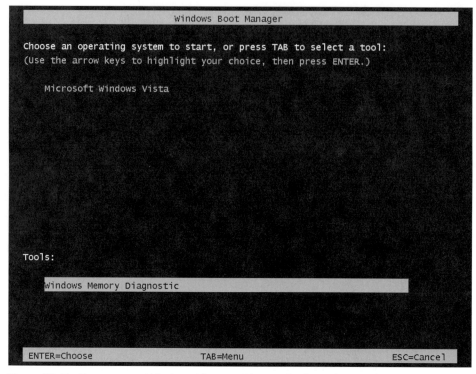

Figure 31-7   You can start Windows Memory Diagnostics from the Windows Boot Manager menu.

Windows Memory Diagnostics will start and automatically begin testing your computer's memory. For information on how to configure the automated tests, see the section titled "How to Configure Windows Memory Diagnostics" later in this chapter.

How to Start Windows Memory Diagnostics from the Windows Vista DVD

If Windows Vista is not installed, you can run Windows Memory Diagnostics from the Windows Vista DVD by following these steps:

> **Note**   Some computers have System Recovery Tools preinstalled by the computer manufacturer. On these computers, you can start System Recovery Tools faster by pressing F8 before the Windows logo appears and then choosing Repair Your Computer from the Advanced Boot Options screen.

1. Insert the Windows Vista DVD into your computer.

2. Restart your computer. When prompted to boot from the DVD, press any key. If you are not prompted to boot from the DVD, you may have to configure your computer's startup sequence. For more information, see the section titled "Initial Startup Phase" in Chapter 30.

3. Windows Vista setup loads. When prompted, select your regional preferences and then click Next.

4. Click Repair Your Computer.

5. Select your keyboard layout and then click Next.

6. System Recovery scans your hard disks for Windows Vista installations. If the standard Windows Vista drivers do not detect a hard disk because the drivers were not included with Windows Vista, click the Load Drivers button to load the driver. Select an operating system to repair, and then click Next.

7. The Choose A Recovery Tool page appears. Click Windows Memory Diagnostic Tool.

Windows Memory Diagnostics will start and automatically begin testing your computer's memory. For information on how to configure the automated tests, read the next section. For more information about System Recovery Tools, see Chapter 30.

How to Configure Windows Memory Diagnostics

As shown in Figure 31-8, you can configure different options for Windows Memory Diagnostics. You can use these options to configure more thorough (and more time-consuming) diagnostics.

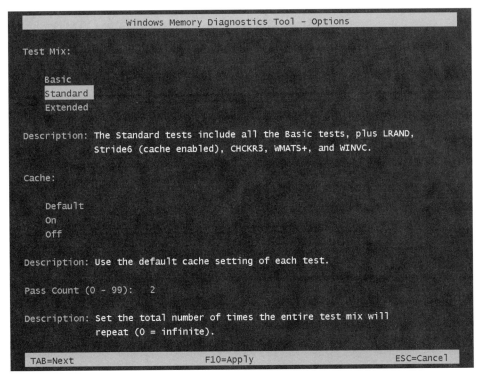

Figure 31-8   You can configure Windows Memory Diagnostics to use more thorough testing procedures.

To view Windows Memory Diagnostic options, start Windows Memory Diagnostics and then press F1. You can configure three different settings, which you select by pressing the Tab key:

- **Test Mix**   The default set of tests, Standard, provides efficient testing while catching most common types of memory failures. To reduce testing time (and the types of failures that might be caught), choose Basic. To increase the types of failures that might be caught (as well as testing time), choose Extended.

- **Cache**   Some tests use the cache, while others disable the cache. Tests are specifically designed to use or disable the cache to identify problems with different memory components. Therefore, you should typically leave this as the default setting.

- **Pass Count**   This defines the number of iterations. Increase this number to provide more thorough testing and to increase the likelihood that you will identify any existing problems. The higher the Pass Count, the more likely you are to find problems.

After you have configured settings, press F10 to apply your changes. Windows Memory Diagnostics will then restart the tests.

How to Troubleshoot Disk Problems

Disk problems can cause unpredictable behavior in Windows. First, disk problems can lead to corrupted files because important system files and drivers are stored on your hard disk. Second, disk problems can lead to corruption in the page file or temporary files. Third, low disk space can lead to failed attempts to allocate disk space for temporary files. Any of these types of problems can cause unpredictable behavior. As a result, one step in troubleshooting hardware problems should be to check for disk problems and free up available disk space. Additionally, if you have a hard disk with nonvolatile caching, you can disable that caching to determine if the cache is causing problems.

The following sections provide information about troubleshooting disk-related problems. For general information concerning disks, see Chapter 15.

How to Prepare for Disk Failures

You can take several steps to prepare yourself—and your computers—for troubleshooting disk problems before the problems occur. First, familiarize yourself with recovery and troubleshooting tools. Use of disk redundancy lessens the impact of hardware failures. Backups ensure minimized data loss when failures occur. Protect yourself from malicious attacks that use antivirus software. Finally, perform regular maintenance on your storage devices.

You should familiarize yourself with the System Recovery Tools and have a Windows Vista DVD available to start the tools if the hard disks are not available. For more information, see Chapter 30.

Run Chkdsk *-f -r* regularly to fix file system problems that may appear because of faulty hardware, power failures, or software errors. Schedule downtime to reboot the computer and allow Autochk to resolve problems on boot and system volumes. Regularly review the Chkdsk output and the Event Log to identify problems that Chkdsk cannot fix.

For desktop computers that store critical, constantly updated data, use hardware disk redundancy (known as RAID) to allow computers to continue to function if a hard disk fails. Keep replacement disks on hand.

At a minimum, back up critical files nightly. Redundancy does not eliminate the need for backups. Even redundant file systems can fail, and disk redundancy cannot protect against files that are corrupted by an application. You must restore corrupted files from an archival backup created before the corruption occurred.

Viruses are a significant source of disk and file system problems. Follow these guidelines to avoid infecting computers with viruses:

- Install a virus-detection program. Configure the virus-detection program to automatically retrieve updated virus signatures.

- Use Windows Update to ensure that operating system files stay up to date.

- Never run untrusted scripts or applications.

Although fragmentation will not cause a hard disk to fail, it will cause performance problems. To avoid performance problems, schedule the Defrag command-line tool to run regularly during off-peak hours. Store the output of the Defrag tool to a text file and review that text file regularly to ensure that defragmentation is performing as expected. To further minimize problems caused by fragmentation, ensure that all volumes have at least 15 percent free space available. For more information about using Defrag, see Chapter 15.

How to Use Chkdsk

Chkdsk (Chkdsk.exe) is a command-line tool that checks disk volumes for problems and attempts to repair any that it finds. For example, Chkdsk can repair problems related to bad sectors, lost clusters, cross-linked files, and directory errors. Disk errors are a common source of difficult-to-track problems, and Chkdsk should be one of the first tools you use when troubleshooting problems that do not appear to be the result of a recent system change. You must be logged on as an administrator or a member of the Administrators group to use Chkdsk.

Before running Chkdsk, be aware of the following:

- Chkdsk requires exclusive access to a volume while it is running. Chkdsk might display a prompt asking if you want to check the disk the next time you restart your computer.

■ Chkdsk might take a long time to run, depending on the number of files and folders, the size of the volume, disk performance, and available system resources (such as processor and memory).

■ Chkdsk might not accurately report information in read-only mode.

Chkdsk Examples

To correct disk errors from a command line, type:

```
chkdsk DriveLetter: /f /r
```

For example, to check drive C for errors, type:

```
chkdsk C: /f /r
```

If you need to run Chkdsk on a large D volume and you want Chkdsk to complete as quickly as possible, type:

```
chkdsk D: /f /c /i
```

Chkdsk Syntax

The command-line syntax for Chkdsk is:

```
chkdsk [volume[[path] filename]] [/f] [/v] [/r] [/x] [/i] [/c] [/b] [/l[:size]]
```

Table 31-3 lists all Chkdsk command-line parameters.

Table 31-3   Chkdsk Parameters

Parameter	Description
volume	Specifies the volume that you want Chkdsk to check. You can specify the volume by using any of the formats in the following examples:
	To run Chkdsk on the C volume, specify:
	c:
	To run Chkdsk on a mounted volume called **data** that is mounted on the C volume, specify:
	c:\data
	To run Chkdsk on a volume, you can specify the symbolic link name for a volume, such as:
	\\?\Volume{109d05a2-6914-11d7-a037-806e6f6e6963}\
	You can determine a symbolic link name for a volume by using the mountvol command.

Table 31-3   Chkdsk Parameters

Parameter	Description
path	FAT/FAT32 only. Specifies the location of a file or set of files within the folder structure of the volume.
filename	FAT/FAT32 only. Specifies the file or set of files to check for `<a ID="wPopUp" HREF="HELP=glossary.hlp TOPIC=gls_fragmentation">` fragmentation `</a>`. Wildcard characters (* and ?) are allowed.
/f	Fixes errors on the disk. The volume must be locked. If Chkdsk cannot lock the volume, Chkdsk offers to check it the next time the computer restarts.
/v	On FAT/FAT32: Displays the full path and name of every file on the disk. On NTFS: Displays additional information or cleanup messages, if any.
/r	Locates `<a ID="wPopUp" HREF="HELP=glossary.hlp TOPIC =glos_glo_cigj">` bad sectors `</a>` and recovers readable information (implies */f*). If Chkdsk cannot lock the volume, it offers to check it the next time the computer starts. Because NTFS also identifies and remaps bad sectors during the course of normal operations, it is usually not necessary to use the */r* parameter unless you suspect that a disk has bad sectors.
/x	Forces the volume to dismount first, if necessary. All opened handles to the volume are then invalid (implies */f*). This parameter does not work on the boot volume. You must restart the computer to dismount the boot volume.
/i	NTFS only. Performs a less-detailed check of index entries, reducing the amount of time needed to run Chkdsk.
/c	NTFS only. Skips the checking of cycles within the folder structure, reducing the amount of time needed to run Chkdsk.
/l:size	NTFS only. Changes the size of the log file to the specified number of kilobytes. Displays the current size if you do not enter a new size. If the system loses power, stops responding, or is restarted unexpectedly, NTFS runs a recovery procedure when Windows Vista restart. This procedure accesses information stored in this log file. The size of the log file depends on the size of the volume. In most conditions, you do not need to change the size of the log file. However, if the number of changes to the volume is so great that NTFS fills the log before all metadata is written to disk, then NTFS must force the metadata to disk and free the log space. When this condition occurs, you might notice that Windows Vista stops responding for five or more seconds. You can eliminate the performance impact of forcing the metadata to disk by increasing the size of the log file.
/b	NTFS only. Re-evaluates bad clusters on the volume. This is typically not necessary, but it might allow you to reclaim some lost disk space on a hard disk with a large number of bad clusters. However, these clusters might experience problems in the future, decreasing reliability.
/?	Displays this list of Chkdsk parameters.

How to Use the Graphical Chkdsk Interface

In addition to using the command-line version of Chkdsk, you can run Chkdsk from My Computer or Windows Explorer by following these steps:

1. Click Start and then click Computer.

2. Right-click the volume you want to check and then click Properties.

3. Click the Tools tab and then click Check Now.

4. Do one of the following:

    ❏   To run Chkdsk in read-only mode, clear all check boxes and then click Start.

    ❏   To repair errors without scanning the volume for bad sectors, select the Automatically Fix File System Errors check box and then click Start.

    ❏   To repair errors, locate bad sectors, and recover readable information, select both the Automatically Fix File System Errors and Scan For And Attempt Recovery Of Bad Sectors check boxes and then click Start.

Chkdsk will run immediately if the volume is not in use and then display the results in a dialog box. If the volume is in use, Chkdsk will request that you schedule a disk check for the next time the computer is restarted.

After running, Chkdsk adds the results to the Application Event Log with a source of Chkdsk, as shown in Figure 31-9. The Event Log entry will contain the entire Chkdsk output, including details about any changes made to the volume. To determine if a computer has had ongoing disk problems, search the Event Log for older Chkdsk entries.

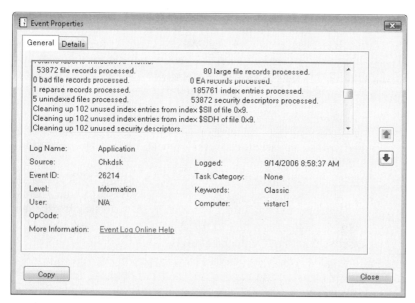

Figure 31-9   Chkdsk results are stored in the Application Event Log.

How to Determine if Chkdsk Is Scheduled to Run

Windows Vista might also configure Chkdsk to run automatically at startup if it detects problems with a volume. Volumes that Windows Vista determines need to be checked are considered "dirty." To determine if a volume is considered dirty, run the following command at a command prompt:

```
chkntfs volume:
```

For example, to determine if drive C is considered dirty, run the following:

```
chkntfs C:
```

You can also use the Chkntfs tool to prevent a dirty volume from being checked at startup, which is useful if you want to avoid the time-consuming Chkdsk process and will not be at the computer during startup to bypass Chkdsk. For more information, run the following at a command prompt:

```
Chkntfs /?
```

Chkdsk Process on NTFS Volumes

When you run Chkdsk on NTFS volumes, the Chkdsk process consists of three major stages and two optional stages. Chkdsk displays its progress for each stage with the following messages:

```
Windows is verifying files (stage 1 of 5)...
File verification completed.
CHKDSK is verifying indexes (stage 2 of 5)...
Index verification completed.
CHKDSK is verifying security descriptors (stage 3 of 5)...
Security descriptor verification completed.
CHKDSK is verifying file data (stage 4 of 5)...
File data verification completed.
CHKDSK is verifying free space (stage 5 of 5)...
Free space verification completed.
```

The following list describes each of the Chkdsk stages.

- **Stage 1: Chkdsk verifies each file record segment in the master file table**   During stage 1, Chkdsk examines each file record segment in the volume's master file table (MFT). A specific file record segment in the MFT uniquely identifies every file and directory on an NTFS volume. The percentage complete that Chkdsk displays during this phase is the percentage of the MFT that has been verified.

  The percentage complete indicator advances relatively smoothly throughout this phase, although some unevenness might occur. For example, file record segments that are not in use require less time to process than do those that are in use, and larger security descriptors take more time to process than do smaller ones. Overall the percentage complete is a fairly accurate representation of the actual time required for that phase.

■ **Stage 2: Chkdsk checks the directories in the volume**   During stage 2, Chkdsk examines each of the indexes (directories) on the volume for internal consistency and verifies that every file and directory represented by a file record segment in the MFT is referenced by at least one directory. Chkdsk also confirms that every file or subdirectory referenced in each directory actually exists as a valid file record segment in the MFT and checks for circular directory references. Chkdsk then confirms that the timestamps and the file size information associated with files are up-to-date in the directory listings for those files.

The percentage complete that Chkdsk displays during this phase is the percentage of the total number of files on the volume that are checked. For volumes with many thousands of files and folders, the time required to complete this stage can be significant.

The duration of stage 2 varies, because the amount of time required to process a directory is closely tied to the number of files or subdirectories listed in that directory. Because of this dependency, the percentage complete indicator might not advance smoothly during stage 2, though the indicator continues to advance even for large directories. Therefore, do not use the percentage complete as a reliable representation of the actual time remaining for this phase.

■ **Stage 3: Chkdsk verifies the security descriptors for each volume**   During stage 3, Chkdsk examines each of the security descriptors associated with each file and directory on the volume by verifying that each security descriptor structure is well formed and internally consistent. The percentage complete that Chkdsk displays during this phase is the percentage of the number of files and directories on the volume that are checked.

The percentage complete indicator advances relatively smoothly throughout this phase, although some unevenness might occur.

■ **Stage 4 (optional): Chkdsk verifies file data**   During stage 4, Chkdsk verifies all clusters in use. Chkdsk performs stages 4 and 5 if you specify the /r parameter when you run Chkdsk. The /r parameter confirms that the sectors in each cluster are usable. Specifying the /r parameter is usually not necessary, because NTFS identifies and remaps bad sectors during the course of normal operations, but you can use the /r parameter if you suspect the disk has bad sectors.

The percentage complete that Chkdsk displays during stage 4 is based on the percentage of used clusters that are checked. Used clusters typically take longer to check than unused clusters, so stage 4 lasts longer than stage 5 on a volume with equal numbers of used and unused clusters. For a volume with mostly unused clusters, stage 5 takes longer than stage 4.

■ **Stage 5 (optional): Chkdsk verifies free space**   During stage 5, Chkdsk verifies unused clusters. Chkdsk performs stage 5 only if you specify the /r parameter when you run Chkdsk. The percentage complete that Chkdsk displays during stage 5 is the percentage of unused clusters that are checked.

How to Use the Disk Cleanup Wizard

With Disk Cleanup (Cleanmgr.exe), you can delete unneeded files and compress infrequently accessed files. This tool is primarily useful for resolving problems that might be related to a shortage of disk space. Insufficient free disk space can cause many problems, ranging from Stop errors to file corruption. To increase free space, you can do the following:

- Move files to another volume or archive them to backup media.
- Compress files or disks to reduce the space required to store data.
- Delete unneeded files.

To run Disk Cleanup, follow these steps:

1. Click Start and then click Computer.

2. Right-click the drive you want to clean and then click Properties. On the General tab of the Properties dialog, click Disk Cleanup.

3. Click either My Files Only or Files From All Users On This Computer.

4. On the Disk Cleanup tab, select the files to delete and then click OK.

How to Disable Nonvolatile Caching

Windows Vista is the first Windows operating system to support caching hard disk data to nonvolatile cache on hard disks with the required cache. Windows Vista can use the cache to improve startup performance, improve the performance of frequently modified system data, and reduce utilization. In rare circumstances, the failing nonvolatile cache might cause problems. To eliminate the possibility that the nonvolatile cache is causing problems, you can disable different cache functionality using the following Group Policy settings (located in Computer Configuration\Policies\Administrative Templates\System\Disk NV Cache):

- **Turn Off Boot And Resume Optimizations**   Enable this policy to prevent Windows Vista from using the nonvolatile cache to speed startup times.

- **Turn Off Cache Power Mode**   Enable this policy to prevent Windows Vista from putting disks into a nonvolatile cache power-saving mode, which enables the hard disk to spin down while continuing to use the nonvolatile cache.

- **Turn Off Non Volatile Cache Feature**   Enable this policy to completely disable all use of the nonvolatile cache.

- **Turn Off Solid State Mode**   Enable this policy to prevent frequently written files such as the system metadata and registry from being stored in the nonvolatile cache.

How to Troubleshoot Driver Problems

Drivers are software components that Windows Vista uses to communicate with hardware accessories. Windows Vista typically has dozens of drivers active at any given point, allowing it to communicate with your graphics card, hard disks, sound card, USB devices, and other accessories. Without a driver, hardware cannot function properly. Additionally, you might have problems with hardware if a driver is outdated or unreliable.

The following sections describe how to work with drivers to solve hardware problems.

How to Find Updated Drivers

Microsoft or hardware vendors occasionally release updated drivers to improve hardware performance and reliability. Many updates are available directly from Windows Update. To find and download any updates available for a computer, follow these steps:

1. Click Start, click All Programs, and then click Windows Update.

2. If available, click Check For Updates.

3. If Windows Update displays any optional updates, click View Available Updates.

4. Windows Vista displays any driver updates if available, as shown in Figure 31-10. Select the update and then click Install.

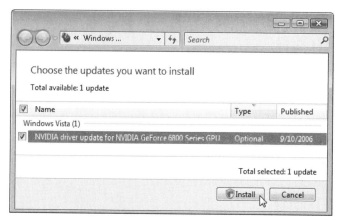

Figure 31-10 You can use Windows Update to install updated drivers.

5. Windows Update downloads any selected updates, creates a system restore point, and then installs the updates.

Additionally, hardware manufacturers might release updated drivers directly to users before they are available on Windows Update. Check manufacturer websites for updated drivers.

How to Roll Back Drivers

When you update a device driver, your computer might have problems that it did not have with the previous version. For example, installing an unsigned device driver might cause the device to malfunction or cause resource conflicts with other installed hardware. Installing faulty drivers might cause Stop errors that prevent the operating system from starting in normal mode. Typically, Stop message text displays the filename of the driver that causes the error.

Windows Vista provides a feature called Device Driver Roll Back that might help you restore system stability by rolling back a driver update.

Note   You can use System Information or the Sigverif tool to determine whether or not a driver on your computer is signed and to obtain other information about the driver, such as version, date, time, and manufacturer. This data, combined with information from the manufacturer's website, can help you decide whether to roll back or update a device driver.

To roll back a driver, follow these steps:

1.   Click Start, right-click Computer, and then click Manage.

2.   Under System Tools, click Device Manager.

3.   Expand a category (Network Adapters, for example) and then double-click a device.

4.   Click the Driver tab and then click Roll Back Driver.

5.   You are prompted to confirm that you want to overwrite the current driver. Click Yes to roll back the driver. The rollback process proceeds, or you are notified that an older driver is not available.

How to Use Driver Verifier

Windows Vista (and all versions of Windows since Windows 2000) includes the Driver Verifier (Verifier.exe). You can run either graphical or command-line versions of the Driver Verifier. To run a command-line version, open a command prompt and then type **Verifier.exe**. To run the graphical version, click Start, type **Verifier.exe**, and then press Enter.

Driver Verifier is useful for isolating a problematic driver that is causing a Windows Vista computer to intermittently fail, because you can use the tool to configure Windows Vista to actively test potentially problematic drivers. After driver verification has been configured for a driver, Windows Vista puts additional stress on the driver during normal operations by simulating conditions that include low memory and verification of input/output (I/O). Enabling driver verification for a problematic driver is highly likely to initiate a Stop error that identifies the driver.

To use Driver Verifier Manager to troubleshoot problems that might be related to a driver, enable driver verification for all drivers that might potentially be causing the problems. Restart the system and then wait. Driver verification happens in the background while the system performs normal tasks and might not yield immediate results. If a verified driver returns an inappropriate response, driver verifier will initiate a Stop error. If a Stop error has not occurred after several days, the verified drivers might not be the source of the problem you are troubleshooting. After you have completed the troubleshooting process, use Driver Verifier to delete the settings and disable driver verification.

> **Note**   Use Driver Verifier only on nonproduction systems to identify a problematic driver. Using Driver Verifier greatly increases the likelihood of a Stop error occurring and decreases system performance.

To verify unsigned drivers, follow these steps:

1. Click Start, type **Verifier**, and then press Enter.

2. Click Create Standard Settings and then click Next.

3. Click Automatically Select Unsigned Drivers and then click Next.

    As shown in Figure 31-11, Driver Verifier Manager finds unsigned drivers, enables verification of those drivers, and then displays the list of unsigned drivers.

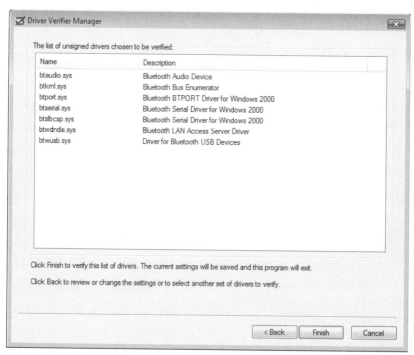

Figure 31-11   Driver Verifier Manager can help you identify problematic drivers.

4. Click Finish.

5. Click OK and then restart the computer.

To verify all drivers, follow these steps:

1. Click Start, type **Verifier**, and then press Enter.

2. Click Create Standard Settings and then click Next.

3. Click Automatically Select All Drivers Installed On This Computer and then click Finish.

4. Click OK and then restart the computer.

To disable driver verification, follow these steps:

1. Click Start, type **Verifier**, and then press Enter.

2. Click Delete Existing Settings and then click Finish.

3. Click Yes.

4. Click OK and then restart the computer.

How to Use the File Signature Verification

File Signature Verification (Sigverif.exe) detects signed files and allows you to:

■ View the certificates of signed files to verify that the file has not been tampered with after being certified.

■ Search for signed files.

■ Search for unsigned files.

 Note Unsigned or altered drivers cannot be installed on x64-based versions of Windows.

Driver signing is a multistage process in which device drivers are verified. For a driver to earn this certification, it must pass a series of compatibility tests administered by the Windows Hardware Quality Labs (WHQL). Because of stringent WHQL standards, using signed drivers typically results in a more stable system. When troubleshooting a problem that might be caused by a driver, you might choose to remove unsigned drivers to eliminate the possibility that the unsigned driver is causing the problem. Although most unsigned drivers will not cause problems, they have not been verified by Microsoft and therefore have a higher risk of causing problems than signed drivers. Microsoft digitally signs drivers that pass the WHQL tests, and Windows Vista performs signature detection for device categories such as:

■ Keyboards

■ Hard disk controllers

- Modems

- Mouse devices

- Multimedia devices

- Network adapters

- Printers

- Small computer system interface (SCSI) adapters

- Smart card readers

- Video adapters

A Microsoft Corporation digital signature indicates that a driver file is an original, unaltered system file that Microsoft has approved for use with Windows Vista. Windows Vista can warn or prevent users from installing unsigned drivers. If a driver is not digitally signed, the user receives a message that requests confirmation to continue. Microsoft digitally signs all drivers included with the Windows Vista operating system CDs. When you download updated drivers from a manufacturer's web page, always select drivers that are signed by Microsoft.

The following tools are useful for troubleshooting problems caused by unsigned files:

- File Signature Verification

- Device Manager

- Driver Verifier Manager

To identify unsigned drivers, follow these steps:

1. Click Start and then type **Sigverif**. Press Enter.

2. In the File Signature Verification window, click Start.

3. After several minutes, the Signature Verification Results page displays unsigned drivers. Unsigned drivers can be reliable, but they have not undergone the same testing required of signed drivers. If you are experiencing reliability problems, you should replace unsigned drivers with signed versions from Microsoft or the manufacturer.

4. Click Close to return to the File Signature Verification window.

5. Click Close again.

How to Use Device Manager to View and Change Resource Usage

Installing new hardware or updating drivers can create conflicts, causing devices to become inaccessible. You can use Device Manager to review resources used by these devices to manually identify conflicts. Typically, however, you should let Windows Vista automatically allocate resources. With modern hardware, there is almost never a valid reason to adjust resource usage manually, and you might cause more problems than you resolve.

To use Device Manager (Devmgmt.msc) to view or change system resource usage information, follow these steps:

1. Click Start, right-click Computer, and then click Manage.

2. Click Device Manager and then double-click a device.

3. Click the Resources tab to view the resources used by that device.

4. Click a resource and then clear the Use Automatic Settings check box.

5. Click Change Setting and then specify the resources assigned to the device.

For more information about managing devices, see Chapter 16, "Managing Devices and Services."

How to Use System Restore

System Restore regularly captures system settings so that you can restore them later if you experience a problem. Using System Restore to return your computer to an earlier state should be one of your last troubleshooting steps, however, because it might cause problems with recently installed applications and hardware.

You can run System Restore from within either the System Recovery tools or from within Windows Vista. To use System Restore from System Recovery tools (which is necessary only if Windows Vista will not start), see Chapter 30. To use System Restore from within Windows Vista, follow these steps:

1. Click Start, click All Programs, click Accessories, click System Tools, and then click System Restore. The System Restore Wizard appears.

2. If this is the first time you are running the System Restore Wizard, click Next to accept the default restore point. Then, skip to step 5.

3. If you have run System Restore previously and it did not solve the problem, click Choose A Different Restore Point and then click Next.

4. On the Choose A Restore Point page, select the most recent restore point when the computer was functioning correctly. Click Next.

5. On the Confirm Your Restore Point page, click Finish. When prompted, click Yes.

6. System Restore restarts your computer. When the restart has completed, System Restore displays a dialog box to confirm that the restoration was successful. Click Close.

If System Restore does not solve your problem, you can do one of two things:

■ **Undo the System Restore**   The problem might not be the result of changes to your computer at all, but rather a hardware failure. Therefore, using System Restore might not solve your problem. Because restoring the computer to an earlier state might remove important changes to your system configuration, you should undo any restorations that do not solve your problem. To undo a System Restore, simply rerun System Restore using the steps in this section and choose the default settings.

■ **Restore an earlier restore point**   Your problem may be caused by recent changes to your computer, but the negative changes occurred before the most recent System Restore. Therefore, restoring an earlier restore point might solve your problem. Repeat the steps in this section to restore to an earlier restore point.

How to Troubleshoot USB Problems

The most common way to connect external devices to a computer is USB. USB provides expandability without the complexity of connecting internal devices such as PCI cards. Connecting USB devices is so simple that most end users can connect and configure USB devices without help from the support center (provided that they have sufficient privileges). However, users do occasionally experience problems with USB devices. The following sections provide guidance for troubleshooting USB problems.

How to Solve USB Driver and Hardware Problems

If you do experience problems, following these steps might solve them:

1. Restart the computer. Some software might require the computer to be restarted before functioning properly. Additionally, restarting the computer forces Windows Vista to detect the USB hardware again.

2. Install updated driver software, if available. Check Windows Update and the hardware manufacturer's website for updates.

3. Uninstall the device's driver and software, disconnect the USB device, restart the computer, and then follow the manufacturer's instructions to reinstall the software. Many USB devices require a driver. Typically, the driver should be installed before connecting the USB device. If you are experiencing problems with a USB device, the most likely cause is a driver problem. For information on how to troubleshoot the driver problem, see the section titled "How to Troubleshoot Driver Problems" earlier in this chapter. External storage devices such as USB flash drives and external hard drives typically do not require a driver, because the required software is built into Windows.

4. Disconnect the USB device and reconnect it to a different USB port. This can cause Windows to detect the device as new and reinstall required drivers. Additionally, this will solve problems related to a specific USB port, such as a failed port or power limitations.

5. Replace the USB cable with a new cable or a different cable that you know works properly.

Understanding USB Limitations

If you installed the USB device's software correctly and you are using the most up-to-date version of the driver, you still might have problems because of USB's physical limitations. Limitations that can cause problems include:

- **Insufficient power**   Many USB devices receive power from the USB port. Connecting too many unpowered devices to a USB hub can result in a power shortage, which can cause a USB device to not respond properly. This is particularly common when using an unpowered external USB hub. To quickly determine if a problem is power-related, disconnect other USB devices and connect each USB device directly to the computer one by one. If devices work when connected separately but fail when connected simultaneously, the problem is probably power-related. Decrease the number of devices or add a powered USB hub.

- **Excessive length**   USB devices can be no more than 5 meters away from the USB hub they are connected to. Although USB devices will never ship with cables longer than 5 meters, some users connect USB extenders to allow longer distances. Depending on the quality of the cable and possible sources of interference, you might experience problems with shorter distances. To determine if length is the source of problems, remove any USB extenders and connect the USB device directly to the computer.

- **Too many devices**   USB can support up to a maximum of 127 devices connected to a single USB host controller, which is more than enough for the vast majority of client computer scenarios. You can have a maximum of seven layers of USB hubs connected to the computer's USB host controller, and no more than five external hubs.

- **Insufficient bandwidth**   Most USB devices are designed to work within USB bandwidth limitations. However, video cameras in particular might need more bandwidth than USB is capable of providing. If you receive a "Bandwidth Exceeded" message, first try disconnecting other USB devices. If the message continues to appear, attempt to reduce the bandwidth used by the device by lowering the resolution of the camera. For best results with a video camera, connect it to an IEEE 1394 (also known as Firewire or iLink) port.

Note   If you see the message, "Hi-speed USB device is plugged into non-hi-speed USB hub," the USB device is USB 2.0, but the USB port is an earlier version. The device will probably work, but it will work slowly. You can improve performance by adding a USB 2.0 port to the computer.

How to Identify USB Problems Using Performance Monitor

If you are concerned that you may have a USB bandwidth or performance problem, you can identify the problem by using the Performance snap-in:

1. If the problem you need to identify occurs when you are actively using a USB device, connect the USB device that you want to troubleshoot and turn it on. If the problem occurs when you first connect the USB device, do not connect the device until after you have begun logging.

2. Click Start, right-click Computer, and then click Manage.

3. Expand System Tools, Reliability And Performance, Monitoring Tools, and then click Performance Monitor.

4. On the Performance Monitor toolbar, click the green Add button.

5. In the Add Counters dialog box, in the Available Counters group, expand USB. If you are troubleshooting the failure of a USB device, add the following counters for the <All Instances> instance:

   ❑ Iso Packet Errors/Sec

   ❑ Transfer Errors/Sec

   If you are troubleshooting a USB performance problem, add the following counters for the <All Instances> instance:

   ❑ Bulk Bytes/Sec

   ❑ Avg. Bytes/Transfer

6. Click OK to add the counters to Performance Monitor.

Performance Monitor begins collecting data about your USB devices and connections. Attempt to reproduce the problem (for example, by copying a file to a USB hard disk or connecting a video camera). If you are troubleshooting performance problems, right-click the Performance Monitor display and click Clear immediately after you begin using the device to ensure the counters include only data created during your test. The longer you allow the test to run, the more accurate it will be. You should stop Performance Monitor before your test ends.

After reproducing the problem, pause Performance Monitor by clicking the Freeze Display button on the toolbar or by pressing Ctrl+F. Because you added performance counters for all instances, you probably have a large number of counters. To browse individual counters to identify the specific source of your problems, press Ctrl+H to enable highlighting.

Click the first counter in the list. After you select a counter, the graph related to that counter will be shown in bold. Examine the values for that particular counter. If the counter shows an error, make note of the USB controller and device causing the problem. Press the down arrow on your keyboard to select the next counter and continue analyzing USB performance values.

USB errors should not occur under normal circumstances; however, Windows Vista can automatically recover from many USB errors without affecting the user. After you identify the source of the USB problems, follow the steps in the section titled "How to Solve USB Driver and Hardware Problems" earlier in this chapter.

If you are troubleshooting USB performance problems, examine the Bulk Bytes/Sec counters to identify the instance that relates to the device you are using. Then select the counter and make note of the Average value. Theoretically, USB 2.0 can transfer a maximum of 60,000,000 bytes/sec. However, this theoretical maximum will never be realized. More realistically, you might be able to achieve half that value. USB storage devices are often much slower, and performance will vary depending on the performance of the device itself. USB hard disks typically average less than 10,000,000 bytes/sec but can peak over 20,000,000 bytes/sec. Performance of hard disks will also vary depending on the portion of the disk being written to or read from, the size of the files being accessed, and the disk fragmentation.

For more information on using Performance Monitor, see Chapter 22.

How to Examine USB Hubs

Connecting a USB device to a computer can include several different layers:

- A USB host controller, which is connected directly to your computer. USB host controllers are often built into the computer's motherboard, but you can add them by using an internal adapter or a PC card. If the name of the controller includes the word "Enhanced," the controller supports USB 2.0.

- A USB root hub, which is connected directly to the USB host controller. Typically, USB root hubs are built into the same device that contains the USB host controller—your computer's motherboard or an adapter card.

- Optionally, additional USB hubs that connect to the USB root hub to create additional USB ports. USB hubs can be external devices that you add, they can be an internal device within a computer, or they can be built into a docking station.

You can use Device Manager to examine the USB controllers and hubs in a computer, determine their power capabilities, and examine the power requirements of the connected devices. This can help you to identify the source of a USB problem. To examine USB devices, follow these steps:

1. Click Start, right-click Computer, and then click Manage.

2. In the Computer Management console, click Device Manager (under System Tools).

3. In the right pane, expand Universal Serial Bus Controllers.

4. Right-click an instance of USB Root Hub (there might be several) and then click Properties.

5. Click the Power tab, as shown in Figure 31-12. This tab displays the power capabilities of the hub and the power requirements of every connected device. To determine the requirements of any specific device, disconnect other devices and connect the devices one by one.

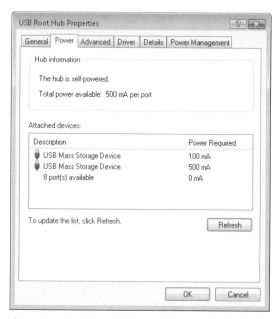

Figure 31-12   View USB root hub properties to determine power capabilities and requirements.

How to Troubleshoot Bluetooth Problems

Bluetooth is a wireless protocol for connecting accessories to computers. Bluetooth is commonly used to connect keyboards, mice, handheld devices, mobile phones, and GPS receivers.

Bluetooth is simple enough to configure that most users can connect Bluetooth devices without help from the support center. However, users may occasionally have problems initiating a Bluetooth connection. Other times, a connection that previously worked may stop working for no apparent reason.

If you cannot successfully connect a Bluetooth device, try these troubleshooting steps:

1. Verify that the device is turned on and that the batteries are charged.

2. Place the device within a few feet of your computer (but not too close to your Bluetooth adapter). Additionally, verify that the device is not near other devices that use radio frequencies, such as microwave ovens, cordless phones, remote controls, or 802.11 wireless networks.

3. Verify that the device has Bluetooth enabled and that it is configured as discoverable. For security reasons, many devices are not discoverable by default. For more information, refer to the instructions that came with the device.

4. Install any updates available from Windows Update. For more information, see Chapter 24.

5. Download and install updated software and drivers for your hardware. Hardware manufacturers often release updated software for hardware components after they release the hardware. You can typically download software updates from the manufacturer's website.

6. Verify that Windows is configured to accept incoming Bluetooth connections.

7. Verify that security is configured correctly. You might have configured a nondefault passkey for your device. By default, many devices use 0000 or 0001 as a passkey.

8. Remove and reinstall the Bluetooth device.

Troubleshooting Tools

The sections that follow describe free Microsoft tools that can be useful for advanced troubleshooting.

DiskView

DiskView shows how files are physically laid out on your disk and allows you to view where specific files are stored. To run DiskView, save the file to a folder that is allowed to run executable files, such as C:\Program Files\. Specifically, you cannot save it to a temporary files folder. Then, right-click the DiskView.exe and click Run As Administrator. Click the Volume list and select the volume you want to analyze. Then, click Refresh. DiskView will spend several minutes examining the contents of the disk.

As shown in Figure 31-13, the main window displays how files are laid out on a section of your disk. Below the main window is a map that shows your entire disk. The black overlay shows which portion of the disk is displayed in the main window.

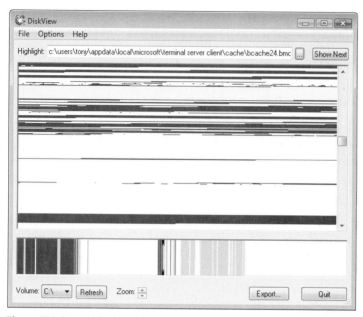

Figure 31-13   DiskView shows the physical layout of files on your disk.

Click any file in the main window to display the name of the file in the Highlight box. To view a specific file, click the "..." button and select the file. You can download DiskView from *http://technet.microsoft.com/en-us/sysinternals/bb896650.aspx.*

Handle

Handle allows you to determine which process has a file or folder open. Handle is useful any time you need to update or delete a file or folder, but access is denied because the object is in use.

To run Handle, save the file to a folder that is allowed to run executable files, such as C:\Program Files\. Specifically, you cannot save it to a temporary files folder. Then, open an administrative command prompt and select the folder containing the Handle executable.

To view all open handles, run Handle without any parameters. To view which process has a particular file or folder open, run Handle with a portion of the file's name. For example, if the sample music file Amanda.wma is locked, you can identify which process has it open by running the following command:

```
handle amanda
```

The following output demonstrates that Windows Media Player (wmplayer.exe) has the file locked:

```
Handle v3.3
Copyright (C) 1997-2007 Mark Russinovich
Sysinternals - www.sysinternals.com

wmplayer.exe        pid: 3236     2C0: C:\Users\Public\Music\Sample Music\Amanda.wma
```

Because the output lists the process name and process ID (PID) you can use Task Manager to kill the process, allowing you to access the locked file. You can download Handle from *http://technet.microsoft.com/en-us/sysinternals/bb896655.aspx.*

Process Monitor

Process Monitor is an extremely powerful troubleshooting tool that monitors file and registry accesses by an application. With Process Monitor, you can see exactly what an application is doing, allowing you to isolate the resources an application requires access to. If an application fails because a resource is unavailable or access is denied, Process Monitor can allow you to identify the resource. Often, you can use that information to resolve the problem.

To run Process Monitor, save the file to a folder that is allowed to run executable files, such as C:\Program Files\. Specifically, you cannot save it to a temporary files folder. Then, right-click the ProcMon.exe and click Run As Administrator.

When run, Process Monitor immediately begins capturing events. To stop or restart capturing events, press Ctrl+E or click Capture Events from the File menu.

To use process monitor, enable event capturing, and then run the application that you want to monitor. After you perform the task that you need to analyze, stop event capturing.

Process Monitor displays all disk and file accesses that occurred while capturing was enabled, as shown in Figure 31-14. To view events for just a specific process, right-click any event generated by the process and then click Include. Process Monitor will filter the displayed event so that only events generated by the selected process are visible. You can create more complex filters using the Filter menu.

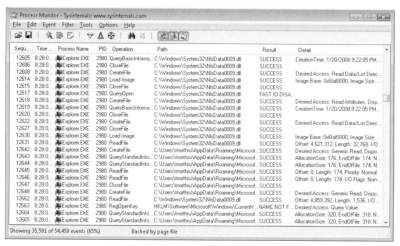

Figure 31-14   Process Monitor displays every file and registry access by an application.

When examining the captured events, pay close attention to events with a result other than Success. Although non-Success events are common and normal, they are more likely to indicate the cause of an error.

You can download Process Monitor from *http://www.microsoft.com/technet/sysinternals/ FileAndDisk/processmonitor.mspx.* For an example of how Process Monitor can be used, read "The Case of the Failed File Copy" at *http://blogs.technet.com/markrussinovich/archive/2007/ 10/01/2087460.aspx* and "The Case of the Missing AutoPlay" at *http://blogs.technet.com/ markrussinovich/archive/2008/01/02/2696753.aspx.*

Summary

Problems can arise when connecting hardware to a computer. Fortunately, Windows Vista provides many different tools for diagnosing the source of the problem. In many cases, Windows Vista also provides the tools required to resolve the problem by updating software or reconfiguring the hardware. If the cause of the problem is failed hardware, the device will need to be repaired or replaced before it can be used with Windows Vista.

Additional Resources

The following resources contain additional information and tools related to this chapter.

Related Information

- Chapter 15, "Managing Disks and File Systems," includes information about configuring disks and volumes.

- Chapter 16, "Managing Devices and Services," includes information about configuring hardware and drivers.

- Chapter 24, "Managing Software Updates," includes more information about updating device drivers.

- Chapter 30, "Configuring Startup and Troubleshooting Startup Issues," includes information about troubleshooting problems that prevent Windows from starting.

- Chapter 32, "Troubleshooting Network Issues," includes information about network connectivity problems.

- Chapter 33, "Troubleshooting Stop Messages," includes information concerning Stop errors.

On the Companion CD

- PerfPercentProcessorUsage.vbs

- PerfPercentPageFileInUse.vbs

- PerfDiskUtilization.vbs

- ListPlugAndPlayDrivers.vbs

- ListPlugAndPlayDevices.vbs

- ListIRQResources.vbs

Troubleshooting Network Issues

Users often rely on network connectivity to do their jobs, and network failures can dramatically affect an organization's productivity. When failures do occur, you need to quickly diagnose the problem. You will often need to escalate the troubleshooting to a network specialist. However, you can diagnose and resolve many common networking problems from a Windows Vista computer.

This chapter describes how to use important network troubleshooting tools and provides step-by-step instructions for troubleshooting common network problems.

Tools for Troubleshooting

The following common network problems are listed with the tools most likely to be useful in isolating, diagnosing, and resolving them. These tools are described in the appropriate sections in this chapter unless otherwise noted.

- **Some clients cannot connect to a server** Arp, Ipconfig, Nbtstat, Netstat, Network Monitor, Nslookup, PathPing, Portqry, Telnet Client, Windows Network Diagnostics

- **No clients can connect to a server** Ipconfig, Network Monitor, Portqry, Telnet Client, Windows Network Diagnostics

- **Clients cannot connect to shared resources** Ipconfig, Nbtstat, Net, Nslookup, Network Monitor, Portqry, Telnet Client, Windows Network Diagnostics

- **Clients cannot connect to the network** Ipconfig, Windows Network Diagnostics

- **Network performance is poor or unpredictable** Network Monitor, Performance Monitor, PathPing, Resource Monitor, Task Manager

Many factors affect network performance and reliability, including remote connections, hardware configuration (network adapters or the physical network connection), and device drivers. Quite often, network difficulties are related to protocol configuration errors. For example, using incorrect settings in TCP/IP-based networks can affect IP addressing, routing, and IP security.

Windows Vista provides a collection of useful troubleshooting tools with which you can monitor and test network performance. Table 32-1 lists the most important tools for trouble-shooting network problems.

Table 32-1   Network Troubleshooting Tools

Tool	Purpose	Permissions Required	Description
Arp	Displays and clears the ARP cache, which affects communications with hosts on the local network.	Users or Administrators, depending on the commands used	Operating system, command line
Ipconfig	Displays network configuration information about the local computer, requests new dynamically assigned IP addresses, manages the DNS client resolver cache, and registers new DNS records.	Users or Administrators, depending on the commands used	Operating system, command line
Nblookup	Tests WINS name resolution.	Users	Free download, command line
Nbtstat	Displays and clears NetBIOS names.	Users	Operating system, command line
Net	Displays information about shared resources and connects to shared resources.	Users	Operating system, command line
Netsh	Views and modifies network configuration settings.	Users or Administrators, depending on the commands used	Operating system, command line
Netstat	Displays detailed information about open connections.	Users	Operating system, command line
Network Monitor	Captures and displays network traffic sent to and from the local computer.	Administrators	Free download, GUI
Nslookup	Diagnoses DNS name-resolution problems.	Users	Operating system, command line
PathPing	Diagnoses network connectivity, routing, and performance problems.	Users	Operating system, command line

Table 32-1 Network Troubleshooting Tools

Tool	Purpose	Permissions Required	Description
Performance Monitor	Displays detailed information about hundreds of network performance counters.	Administrators	Operating system, GUI
Portqry	Identifies the availability of network services from a client that has the tool installed.	Users	Free download, command line
Resource Monitor	Displays information about network utilization.	Administrators	Operating system, GUI
Route	Displays and modifies the local computer's IP routing tables, which is primarily useful when multiple gateways are on the local network.	Users or Administrators, depending on the commands used	Operating system, command line
Task Manager	Quickly determines current network utilization, identifies processes that are using the network, and identifies processes that are consuming processor time.	Users or Administrators, depending on the commands used	Operating system, GUI
Telnet Client	Identifies the availability of network services from a client that does not have PortQry installed. This tool is an optional component and is not installed by default.	Users	Operating system, command-line
Test TCP	Tests TCP connectivity between two computers.	Users	Operating system, command-line
Windows Network Diagnostics	Automatically diagnoses some network problems and provides a user-friendly interface for resolving them.	Users	Operating system, GUI

Note In Windows Vista, troubleshooting IPv6 is identical to troubleshooting IPv4. Most of the same tools work, including Ping, PathPing, Nslookup, Ipconfig, Route, Netstat, Tracert, and Netsh. To use them, simply specify IPv6 addresses instead of IPv4 addresses. Unfortunately, Portqry does not currently support IPv6. However, you can use Telnet instead. Additionally, you cannot use the Route tool to add or delete IPv6 addresses. Instead, you should use the "netsh interface ipv6 add route" and "netsh interface ipv6 delete route" commands.

Arp

Arp (Arp.exe) is a useful command-line tool for diagnosing problems in connecting to systems on a local area network (LAN) where communications between computers do not travel through a router. Arp is also useful for diagnosing problems related to the client communicating with the default gateway. When a client contacts a server on the same subnet, it must address the frame with both the media access control (MAC) address and the IPv4 address. The MAC address is a 48-bit number that uniquely identifies a network adapter.

Arp is the name of a tool; it is also the acronym for the Address Resolution Protocol (ARP), which is used to find the MAC address corresponding to an IPv4 address. When a client communicates with a system on the same LAN, the ARP protocol broadcasts a message to all systems on the LAN, asking for a response from the system that has the requested IPv4 address. That system responds to the broadcast by sending its MAC address, and the ARP protocol stores the MAC address in the ARP cache.

> **Note**   IPv4 addresses are used to identify computers on different networks. However, computers communicating across a LAN use MAC addresses to identify each other. ARP lets a computer look up a MAC address based on an IPv4 address so that two computers on the same LAN can communicate.

Problems with ARP occur only occasionally. For example, if a system changes its network adapter, clients might store the incorrect MAC address in the ARP cache. You can also manually place MAC addresses into the ARP cache, but if a manually added MAC address is incorrect, communications sent to that IPv4 address will not succeed.

How to Identify a Problem with the ARP Cache

To identify an incorrect entry in the ARP cache, first determine the MAC addresses and IPv4 addresses of hosts or gateways on the LAN with which the computer cannot communicate (as shown in the ipconfig /all example in this section). View the ARP cache on the computer that is experiencing the problem. Compare the output with the correct IPv4 address and MAC address combinations. If an entry is incorrect, clear the ARP cache to resolve the problem.

To determine the MAC address of a computer, open a command prompt and run the following command. Then find the Physical Address line in the output for your network adapter:

```
ipconfig /all
```

```
Ethernet adapter Local Area Connection:

   Connection-specific DNS Suffix  . : contoso.com
   Description . . . . . . . . . . . : NVIDIA nForce Networking Controller
   Physical Address. . . . . . . . . : 00-13-D3-3B-50-8F
   DHCP Enabled. . . . . . . . . . . : Yes
```

After you use Ipconfig to determine the correct MAC address, you can view the ARP cache on the problematic computer to determine if the cached address is incorrect. To view the ARP cache, open a command prompt and run the following command:

```
arp –a
```

```
Interface: 192.168.1.132 --- 0xa
  Internet Address      Physical Address      Type
  192.168.1.1           00-11-95-bb-e2-c7     dynamic
  192.168.1.210         00-03-ff-cf-38-2f     dynamic
  192.168.1.241         00-13-02-1e-e6-59     dynamic
  192.168.1.255         ff-ff-ff-ff-ff-ff     static
  224.0.0.22            01-00-5e-00-00-16     static
```

How to Clear the ARP Cache

If you determine that one of the entries in the ARP cache is incorrect, resolve the problem by clearing the ARP cache. Clearing the ARP cache isn't harmful, even if all entries appear correct. Therefore, it's a safe step to take during troubleshooting.

To clear the ARP cache, open a command prompt and run the following command:

arp –d

Alternatively, you can clear the ARP cache by disabling and re-enabling a network adapter or by choosing the automated Repair option. For more information about the Arp tool, run **Arp -?** at a command prompt.

Event Viewer

The Network Diagnostics Framework records extremely detailed information in the System Event Log both when problems occur and when network connections are successful. Additionally, administrators can use Wireless Diagnostics tracing to capture and analyze diagnostic information by using graphical tools.

You can find network diagnostic information in two places in Event Viewer:

- **Windows Logs\System**   Look for events with a Source of Diagnostics-Network. These events detail troubleshooting options that were presented to the user (Event ID 4000) and the results of the user's choice (Event ID 5000). When troubleshooting wireless networks, events also include the name of the wireless network adapter and whether it is a native Windows Vista driver or a legacy driver; a list of visible wireless networks with the signal strength, channel, and protocol (such as 802.11b or 802.11g) for each; and the list of preferred wireless networks and each network's configuration settings. Event descriptions resemble the following:

```
The Network Diagnostics Framework has completed the repair phase of operation.
The following repair option or work-around was executed:
Helper Class Name: AddressAcquisition
Repair option: Reset the network adapter "Local Area Connection"
Resetting the adapter can sometimes resolve an intermittent problem.
RepairGuid: {07D37F7B-FA5E-4443-BDA7-AB107B29AFB9}
The repair option appears to have successfully fixed the diagnosed problem.
```

■ **Applications and Services Logs\Microsoft\Windows\Diagnostics-Networking\ Operational**   This event log details the inner workings of the Network Diagnostics Framework and will be useful primarily when escalating problems to Microsoft support.

Ipconfig

Ipconfig (Ipconfig.exe) is a useful command-line tool for troubleshooting problems with automatic configuration such as Dynamic Host Configuration Protocol (DHCP). You can use Ipconfig to display the current IP configuration, identify whether DHCP or Automatic Private IP Addressing (APIPA) is being used, and release and renew an automatic IP configuration.

To view detailed IP configuration information, open a command prompt and run the following command:

```
ipconfig /all
```

This command displays the current IP configuration and produces output similar to the following:

```
Windows IP Configuration

    Host Name . . . . . . . . . . . . : Vista1
    Primary Dns Suffix  . . . . . . . : hq.contoso.com
    Node Type . . . . . . . . . . . . : Hybrid
    IP Routing Enabled. . . . . . . . : No
    WINS Proxy Enabled. . . . . . . . : No
    DNS Suffix Search List. . . . . . : hq.contoso.com
                                        contoso.com

Ethernet adapter Local Area Connection:

    Connection-specific DNS Suffix  . : contoso.com
    Description . . . . . . . . . . . : NVIDIA nForce Networking Controller
    Physical Address. . . . . . . . . : 00-13-D3-3B-50-8F
    DHCP Enabled. . . . . . . . . . . : Yes
    Autoconfiguration Enabled . . . . : Yes
    Link-local IPv6 Address . . . . . : fe80::a54b:d9d7:1a10:c1eb%10(Preferred)
    IPv4 Address. . . . . . . . . . . : 192.168.1.132(Preferred)
    Subnet Mask . . . . . . . . . . . : 255.255.255.0
    Lease Obtained. . . . . . . . . . : Wednesday, September 27, 2006 2:08:58 PM
    Lease Expires . . . . . . . . . . : Friday, September 29, 2006 2:08:56 PM
    Default Gateway . . . . . . . . . : 192.168.1.1
    DHCP Server . . . . . . . . . . . : 192.168.1.1
    DHCPv6 IAID . . . . . . . . . . . : 234886099
    DNS Servers . . . . . . . . . . . : 192.168.1.210
    NetBIOS over Tcpip. . . . . . . . : Enabled
```

To determine whether or not DHCP addressing was successful, open a command prompt and run the following command:

```
ipconfig
```

```
Windows IP Configuration

Ethernet adapter Local Area Connection:

   Connection-specific DNS Suffix  . :
   Autoconfiguration IP Address. . . : 169.254.187.237
   Subnet Mask . . . . . . . . . . . : 255.255.0.0
   Default Gateway . . . . . . . . . :
```

If the IP address shown is in the range from 169.254.0.0 through 169.254.255.255, Windows used APIPA because the operating system was unable to retrieve an IP configuration from a DHCP server upon startup, and there was no alternate configuration. To confirm this, examine the Ipconfig output for the DHCP Enabled setting without a DHCP server address.

To release and renew a DHCP-assigned IPv4 address, open a command prompt with administrative credentials and run the following commands:

```
ipconfig /release
ipconfig /renew
```

Windows Vista will stop using the current IPv4 address and attempt to contact a DHCP server for a new IPv4 address. If a DHCP server is not available, Windows Vista will either use the alternate configuration or automatically assign an APIPA address in the range of 169.254.0.0 through 169.254.255.255.

To release and renew an automatically assigned IPv6 address, open a command prompt and run the following commands:

```
ipconfig /release6
ipconfig /renew6
```

IPsec Diagnostic Tool

The Microsoft IPsec Diagnostic Tool, available for download from *http://www.microsoft.com/ downloads/details.aspx?FamilyID=1d4c292c-7998-42e4-8786-789c7b457881 &displaylang=en*, helps troubleshoot any network problems—but it is particularly useful when IPsec is being used. Troubleshooting IPsec-related problems can be particularly difficult, because it is a challenge to determine whether a connectivity problem is caused by IPsec, a network or service outage, or a higher-level application failure. The IPsec Diagnostic Tool will automatically detect many common problems and can suggest ways to resolve the problems.

When you run the tool, you configure both a local IP address and a remote destination and choose between IPv4 and IPv6. The tool collects IPsec policy information on the system and parses the IPsec logs to deduce why a failure might have happened if the tool cannot connect to the remote host. Beyond IPsec, it collects data for VPN, NAP client, Windows Firewall, Group Policy updates, and Wireless and System events.

Nblookup

Windows Internet Naming Service (WINS) is a NetBIOS name-resolution protocol. WINS performs a function for NetBIOS names similar to the function that DNS performs for host names. For many years, WINS name resolution was the most common way for Windows computers to identify each other on networks. However, in Active Directory domain environments, DNS is used by default, and WINS is primarily used to support older clients and applications.

For environments that still rely on WINS servers, Nblookup is a valuable tool for diagnosing WINS name-resolution problems. Nblookup is not included with Windows Vista but is available as a free download from *http://support.microsoft.com/kb/830578*. After saving the Nblookup.exe to a computer, you can double-click the file to run it in interactive mode within a command prompt. Alternatively, command-line mode allows you to run it from any command prompt. The following examples demonstrate command-line mode.

To look up a NetBIOS name using the computer's configured WINS server, run the following command:

```
nblookup computer_name
```

To look up a NetBIOS name using a specific WINS server, add the */s server_ip* parameter, as the following example demonstrates:

```
nblookup /s server_ip computer_name
```

For example, to look up the name COMPUTER1 using the WINS server located at 192.168.1.222, you would run the following command:

```
nblookup /s 192.168.1.222 COMPUTER1
```

NetBIOS names actually identify services, not computers. If you want to attempt to resolve a NetBIOS name for a specific service, use the */x* parameter and specify the service's NetBIOS suffix. For example, the following command would look up domain controllers (which use a NetBIOS suffix of 1C) in a domain named DOMAIN:

```
nblookup /x 1C DOMAIN
```

Because WINS is not typically relied on for name resolution by Windows Vista in Active Directory environments, troubleshooting WINS name resolution is not discussed further in this chapter.

Nbtstat

Nbtstat (Nbtstat.exe) is a command-line tool for troubleshooting network basic input/output system (NetBIOS) name-resolution problems. NetBIOS is a session-layer protocol that formed the foundation of Microsoft network applications for several years. NetBIOS applications identify services on the network by using 16-character NetBIOS names. Each computer on a network might have several different NetBIOS names to identify NetBIOS services on that system.

Today, NetBIOS is implemented on TCP/IP networks by using NetBIOS over TCP/IP (NetBT). NetBT includes its own form of name resolution to resolve NetBIOS names to IP addresses. Names might be resolved by broadcast queries to the local network segment or by queries to a WINS server.

Unfortunately, NetBIOS name resolution is a common source of problems. You can use Nbtstat to reveal the NetBIOS names available on the local computer or remote computers. In troubleshooting scenarios, this helps you to verify that a NetBIOS service is available and its name is being correctly resolved.

To view the NetBIOS name cache, open a command prompt and run the following command:

```
nbtstat -c
```

```
Local Area Connection:
Node IpAddress: [192.168.1.132] Scope Id: []

              NetBIOS Remote Cache Name Table

        Name            Type      Host Address   Life [sec]
    ---------------------------------------------------------
        VISTA1      <00>  UNIQUE      192.168.1.196      602
        VISTA2      <00>  UNIQUE      192.168.1.200      585
```

To view the local NetBIOS service names, open a command prompt and run the following command:

```
nbtstat -n
```

```
Local Area Connection:
Node IpAddress: [192.168.1.132] Scope Id: []

              NetBIOS Local Name Table

        Name            Type      Status
    --------------------------------------------------
        VISTA1      <00>  UNIQUE    Registered
        HQ          <00>  GROUP     Registered
        HQ          <1E>  GROUP     Registered
        HQ          <1D>  UNIQUE    Registered
        .._MSBROWSE__.<01>  GROUP     Registered
```

To view the NetBIOS names on a remote system by using the computer name, open a command prompt and run the following command:

nbtstat –a computername

For example:

nbtstat –a vista1

```
Local Area Connection:
Node IpAddress: [192.168.1.132] Scope Id: []

        NetBIOS Remote Machine Name Table

    Name               Type         Status
    ---------------------------------------------
    VISTA1        <00>  UNIQUE       Registered
    VISTA1        <20>  UNIQUE       Registered
    MSHOME        <00>  GROUP        Registered
    MSHOME        <1E>  GROUP        Registered

    MAC Address = 00-15-C5-08-82-F3
```

Notice that the output is similar to the output when running nbtstat *–n* locally. However, this output also displays the remote computer's MAC address. To view the NetBIOS names on a remote system by using the IP address, open a command prompt and run the following command:

nbtstat –A IP_Address

Windows Vista prefers to use DNS host names instead of NetBIOS names. Therefore, if you have an Active Directory domain with a DNS server configured, you will rarely need to troubleshoot NetBIOS names. However, Windows Vista might still use NetBIOS names to communicate with computers on the local network and will use NetBIOS names if a host name cannot be resolved with DNS and you have configured a WINS server. To troubleshoot NetBIOS name resolution with WINS servers, use Nblookup, described earlier in this chapter.

Net

Net (Net.exe) is a command-line tool that is useful for changing network configuration settings, starting and stopping services, and viewing shared resources. Although other tools provide friendlier interfaces for much of the functionality provided by Net, Net is very useful for quickly determining the available shared resources on local or remote computers. When troubleshooting connections to resources, this tool is useful for verifying that shared resources are available and for verifying the names of those shared resources.

How to View Shared Folders on the Local Computer

Use the **net share** command to view shared resources located on the local computer. If the Server service is started, Net will return a list of shared resources names and locations. To view shared resources, open a command prompt and run the following command:

```
net share
```

```
Share name    Resource                              Remark

------------------------------------------------------------------------
C$            C:\                                   Default share
D$            D:\                                   Default share
E$            E:\                                   Default share
print$        C:\Windows\system32\spool\drivers
                                                    Printer Drivers
IPC$                                                Remote IPC
ADMIN$        C:\Windows                            Remote Admin
MyShare       C:\PortQryUI
HP DeskJet 930C932C935C
              LPT1:                     Spooled  HP DeskJet 930C/932C/935C
The command completed successfully.
```

How to View Shared Folders on Another Computer

Use the net view command to view shared resources located on another computer. To view shared folders on another computer, open a command prompt and run the following command:

```
net view computer
```

For example:

```
net view d820
```

```
Shared resources at d820

Share name   Type   Used as   Comment
------------------------------------------------------------------------
In Progress  Disk
Printer      Print            Microsoft Office Document Image Writer
publish      Disk
SharedDocs   Disk
Software     Disk
The command completed successfully.
```

You can identify *Computer* by using the computer name, host name, or IP address. If you receive an "Access is denied" error message when attempting to view shares on a remote computer, first establish a NetBIOS connection to the remote computer. For example, you could use "Net use" to establish a connection and then use "Net view," as the following example demonstrates:

```
net use \\vista1 /user:username
net view vista1
```

Netstat

For a network service to receive incoming communications, it must listen for communications on a specific TCP or UDP port. When troubleshooting network problems, you might want to view the ports on which your computer listens for incoming connections to verify that a service is properly configured and that the port number has not been changed from the default.

Netstat (Netstat.exe) is a useful command-line tool for identifying network services and the ports they listen on. Listing the ports a computer listens on is useful for verifying that a network service is using the expected port. It is common practice to change the port numbers that services listen on, and Netstat can quickly identify nonstandard listening ports.

To view open ports and active incoming connections, open a command prompt and run the following command:

```
netstat -a -n -o
```

Netstat will display a list of listening ports, as well as outgoing connections and the process IDs (PIDs) associated with each listener or connection. The following edited output from Netstat shows the listening ports on a Windows Vista computer that has Remote Desktop (which uses TCP port 3389) enabled:

```
Active Connections

  Proto  Local Address                    Foreign Address       State        PID
  TCP    0.0.0.0:135                      0.0.0.0:0             LISTENING    884
  TCP    0.0.0.0:3389                     0.0.0.0:0             LISTENING    1512
  TCP    0.0.0.0:49152                    0.0.0.0:0             LISTENING    592
  TCP    192.168.1.132:139                0.0.0.0:0             LISTENING    4
  TCP    192.168.1.132:3389               192.168.1.196:1732    ESTABLISHED  1512
  TCP    [::]:135                         [::]:0                LISTENING    884
  TCP    [::]:445                         [::]:0                LISTENING    4
  TCP    [::]:2869                        [::]:0                LISTENING    4
  TCP    [::]:3389                        [::]:0                LISTENING    1512
  UDP    [fe80::28db:d21:3f57:fe7b%11]:1900   *:*                            1360
  UDP    [fe80::28db:d21:3f57:fe7b%11]:49643  *:*                            1360
  UDP    [fe80::a54b:d9d7:1a10:c1eb%10]:1900  *:*                            1360
  UDP    [fe80::a54b:d9d7:1a10:c1eb%10]:49641 *:*                            1360
```

Notice that the line in bold is listening for incoming connections on TCP port 3389, which Remote Desktop uses. Because the Foreign Address column shows an IPv4 address, you can tell that a user is connected to the computer using Remote Desktop from a computer with the IP address of 192.168.1.196. If you notice that a computer is listening for incoming connections on unexpected ports, you can use the value in the PID column to identify the process. Tools such as the Processes tab in Task Manager can reveal which process is associated with a PID.

Note To identify processes by PID in Task Manager, select the Processes tab. On the View menu, click Select Columns. Select the PID (Process Identifier) check box and then click OK.

Alternatively, if you can open a command prompt with elevated privileges, you can use the –*b* parameter to resolve applications associated with active connections. The following example demonstrates that using the –*b* parameter shows the associated process in brackets before each connection:

```
netstat –a –n –o –b
```

```
Active Connections

   Proto  Local Address          Foreign Address        State        PID
   TCP    0.0.0.0:135            0.0.0.0:0              LISTENING    828
   RpcSs
  [svchost.exe]
   TCP    0.0.0.0:3389           0.0.0.0:0              LISTENING    1444
   Dnscache
  [svchost.exe]
   TCP    0.0.0.0:49152          0.0.0.0:0              LISTENING    508
  [wininit.exe]
   TCP    0.0.0.0:49153          0.0.0.0:0              LISTENING    972
   Eventlog
  [svchost.exe]
   TCP    0.0.0.0:49154          0.0.0.0:0              LISTENING    1236
   nsi
  [svchost.exe]
   TCP    0.0.0.0:49155          0.0.0.0:0              LISTENING    1076
   Schedule
  [svchost.exe]
   TCP    0.0.0.0:49156          0.0.0.0:0              LISTENING    564
  [lsass.exe]
   TCP    0.0.0.0:49157          0.0.0.0:0              LISTENING    552
  [services.exe]
   TCP    169.254.166.248:139    0.0.0.0:0              LISTENING    4
```

TCPView, a free download from Microsoft, provides similar functionality with a graphical interface. TCPView is described later in this chapter.

Network Monitor

Network Monitor 3, a free download from *http://www.microsoft.com*, is the most capable–and complicated–tool for analyzing network communications. Network Monitor is a protocol analyzer (commonly known as a *sniffer*) capable of capturing every byte transferred to and from a computer running Windows Vista. An experienced system administrator can use Network Monitor to troubleshoot a wide variety of problems, including:

- Network performance problems
- TCP connection problems
- IP protocol stack configuration problems
- Problems caused by network filtering
- Application-layer problems with text-based protocols, including Hypertext Transfer Protocol (HTTP), Post Office Protocol (POP), and Simple Mail Transfer Protocol (SMTP)

Network Monitor performs a significant amount of interpretation of captured information by separating the different protocols involved in network communications. Network Monitor can even interpret most common application-layer protocols. For example, when analyzing HTTP traffic, Network Monitor automatically identifies the packet containing the HTTP request and lists the request method, Uniform Resource Locator (URL), referrer, user agent, and other parameters included in the request. This information is extremely useful when troubleshooting compatibility problems with a specific browser.

To analyze network traffic by using Network Monitor, follow these steps:

1. Download and install Network Monitor 3.0 and then restart the computer to enable the Network Monitor driver for your network adapters.

2. Click Start, click All Programs, click Microsoft Network Monitor3, and then click Microsoft Network Monitor 3.0.

3. Select the Enable Conversations check box.

4. Click Create A New Capture Tab.

5. With the New Capture tab selected, click the Select Networks tab and select one or more network adapters.

6. Click the Play button to begin capturing communications.

7. Switch to the application from which you want to capture the network traffic and then perform the steps to generate the traffic. For example, if you want to capture a request to a web server, switch to Microsoft Internet Explorer and enter the web address. After you have generated the traffic you want to capture, return to Network Monitor.

8. On the Capture menu in Network Monitor, click Stop And View. Network Monitor displays the Capture window. The Capture window displays the frames that were captured.

9. Double-click a frame to view its contents.

Figure 32-1 shows a capture of a TCP connection and an HTTP request created by visiting a website with a browser. The center pane lists the captured packets. Frames 1 through 3 show the three-way TCP handshake. Notice that Frame 62 is a DNS query for go.microsoft.com. Frame 63 is the DNS response, providing the IP address to the web browser. Frames 64 through 66 show the three-way handshake that TCP uses to establish a connection to the web servers. Frame 67, which is selected, is the HTTP request from the web browser to the web server. As you can see from the Frame Details pane, the web browser is requesting /fwlink/ ?LinkId=69157 from the web server. Frame 68 is the response from the web server to the browser. The status code is 302, which indicates that the web server redirected the client to a different page.

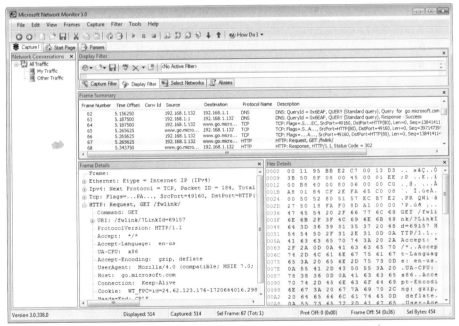

Figure 32-1   Use Network Monitor to capture and analyze traffic.

Nslookup

Nslookup (Nslookup.exe) is the primary tool for isolating DNS name-resolution problems when connected to the client experiencing the problems. Nslookup is a command-line tool capable of performing DNS lookups and reporting on the results. Other tools, such as PathPing, are capable of resolving host names to IP addresses and displaying the results, but only Nslookup displays the DNS server used to resolve the request. Additionally, Nslookup displays all the results returned by the DNS server and allows you to choose a specific DNS server rather than using the server automatically chosen by Windows Vista.

Nslookup is the correct tool to use when troubleshooting the following types of problems:

- Clients take several seconds to establish an initial connection.

- Some clients can establish a connection to a server, but other clients experience problems.

- The DNS server is configured correctly, but clients are resolving host names incorrectly.

> **Note**   The Hosts file, located in the %WinDir%\System32\Drivers\Etc folder, might contain static entries that override DNS lookups for most applications. Nslookup ignores this file, however. If applications resolve a host name differently than Nslookup, verify that the Hosts file does not contain an entry for the host name.

Verifying the Default DNS Server Resolves Correctly

To verify that a client is able to resolve a host name to the correct IP address, open a command prompt and type the command "nslookup *hostname*". Nslookup reports the server used to resolve the request and the response from the DNS server. If the client has been configured to use multiple DNS servers, this action might reveal that the client is not issuing requests to the primary DNS server.

To resolve a DNS host name to an IP address, open a command prompt and run the following command:

```
nslookup hostname
```

To resolve an IP address to a DNS host name by performing a reverse DNS lookup, open a command prompt and run the following command:

```
nslookup ipaddress
```

If the DNS server returns multiple IP addresses, Nslookup displays all addresses. Generally, applications use the first IP address returned by the DNS server. Some applications, including Internet Explorer, try each IP address returned by the DNS server until a response is received.

Verifying a Specific DNS Server Resolves Correctly

One of the most common sources of DNS resolution problems is the caching of an outdated DNS address. Particularly on the Internet, DNS servers might continue to return an outdated IP address several hours after a change has been made to the DNS server containing the record. If some clients are unable to correctly resolve an IP address, but other systems resolve it correctly, one or more DNS servers have probably cached the incorrect address. To identify the problematic DNS servers, use Nslookup to manually query each server.

To verify that a specific DNS server is able to resolve a host name to the correct IP address, open a command prompt and run the following command:

```
nslookup hostname server_name_or_address
```

Nslookup will query the specified server only, regardless of the DNS servers configured on the client. If a specific server returns an incorrect IP address, that server is the source of the problem. Generally, this problem will resolve itself after the incorrect entry expires in the DNS server's cache. However, you can also resolve the problem by manually clearing the DNS server's cache.

Direct from the Source: Looking Up Lists of DNS Records

If you need to frequently check if numerous DNS records correctly resolve on numerous DNS servers, consider using DNSLint with the *–ql* parameter instead of Nslookup. This command can test name resolution for specific DNS records across many DNS servers very quickly. DNSLint can also help troubleshoot some DNS issues related to Active Directory. DNSLint is a free download available from *http:// support.microsoft.com/kb/ 321045/*, and you can also find it on the companion CD for this Resource Kit.

Tim Rains, Program Manager

Windows Networking

Verifying Specific Types of Addresses

You can also use Nslookup to verify specific types of addresses, including MX (Mail eXchange) addresses used to identify the mail servers for a domain.

To identify the mail server for a domain, open a command prompt and run the following command:

```
nslookup "-set type=mx" domainname
```

For example, to use Nslookup to view all MX servers listed for the domain microsoft.com, using the client's default DNS servers, type the following command:

```
nslookup "-set type=mx" microsoft.com
```

Additionally, you can query a specific DNS server by listing the server name or IP address after the domain name in the following form:

```
nslookup "-set type=type" hostname server_name_or_address
```

Direct from the Source: Using TCP for DNS Lookups

When a DNS server returns a response to a DNS query, but the response contains more DNS records than can fit into a single UDP packet, the client may decide to send the query again, this time using TCP instead of UDP. With TCP, multiple packets can deliver all the DNS records in the response. You can use Nslookup to test and see if a DNS server can respond using either UDP or TCP. Use the following command to submit a UDP query to the DNS server:

```
nslookup microsoft.com
```

The following command uses TCP to query the DNS server:

```
nslookup "-set vc" microsoft.com
```

The "*–set vc*" parameter configures Nslookup to use a virtual circuit. This test can be especially useful when you are expecting a large number of DNS records in response to a query.

Tim Rains, Program Manager

Windows Networking

PathPing

Perhaps the most useful tool for isolating connectivity problems from the client, PathPing (PathPing.exe) can help diagnose problems with name resolution, network connectivity, routing, and network performance. For this reason, PathPing should be one of the first tools you use to troubleshoot network problems. PathPing is a command-line tool and is used with syntax similar to that of the Tracert and Ping tools.

Note   Ping's usefulness has become very limited in recent years, and it is no longer an effective tool for determining the state of network services. Ping often reports that it cannot reach an available server because a firewall, such as Windows Firewall, has been configured to drop Internet Control Message Protocol (ICMP) requests. If a host is still capable of responding to ICMP requests, Ping might report that the remote host is available even if critical services on the remote host have failed. To determine whether or not a remote host is responding, use the Portqry support tool instead of Ping.

To test connectivity to an endpoint, open a command prompt and run the following command:

```
pathping destination
```

The destination can be a host name, computer name, or IP address.

PathPing Output

PathPing displays its output in two sections. The first section is immediately displayed and shows a numbered list of all devices that responded between the source and the destination. The first device, numbered 0, is the host on which PathPing is running. PathPing will attempt to look up the name of each device, as shown here:

```
Tracing route to support.go.microsoft.contoso.com [10.46.196.103]over a maximum of
30 hops:  0  contoso-test [192.168.1.207]   1   10.211.240.1   2   10.128.191.245
3   10.128.191.73   4   10.125.39.213   5   gbr1-p70.cb1ma.ip.contoso.com [10.123.40.98]
6   tbr2-p013501.cb1ma.ip.contoso.com [10.122.11.201]
7   tbr2-p012101.cgcil.ip.contoso.com [10.122.10.106]
8   gbr4-p50.st6wa.ip.contoso.com [10.122.2.54]
9   gar1-p370.stwwa.ip.contoso.com [10.123.203.177]
10   10.127.70.6  11   10.46.33.225  12   10.46.36.210
13   10.46.155.17  14   10.46.129.51  15   10.46.196.103
```

To speed up the display of PathPing, use the *-d* command option to keep PathPing from attempting to resolve the name of each intermediate router address.

The second section of the PathPing output begins with the message "Computing statistics for *xxx* seconds." The amount of time for which PathPing computes statistics will vary from a few seconds to a few minutes, depending on the number of devices that PathPing found. During this time, PathPing is querying each of the devices and calculating performance statistics based on if—and how quickly—each device responds. This section will resemble the following:

```
Computing statistics for 375 seconds...              Source to Here
 This Node/LinkHop  RTT    Lost/Sent = Pct  Lost/Sent = Pct  Address   0
                                                      contoso-test [192.168.1.207]
                                    0/ 100 =  0%  |  1    50ms
      1/ 100 =  1%     1/ 100 =  1%  10.211.24.1
                                    0/ 100 =  0%  |  2    50ms
      0/ 100 =  0%     0/ 100 =  0%  10.128.19.245
                                    0/ 100 =  0%  |  3    50ms
      2/ 100 =  2%     2/ 100 =  2%  10.128.19.73
                                    0/ 100 =  0%  |  4    44ms
      0/ 100 =  0%     0/ 100 =  0%  10.12.39.213
                                    0/ 100 =  0%  |  5    46ms
      0/ 100 =  0%     0/ 100 =  0%  gbr1-p70.cb1ma.ip.contoso.com [10.12.40.98]
                                    0/ 100 =  0%  |  6    40ms
      2/ 100 =  2%     2/ 100 =  2%  tbr2-p013501.cb1ma.ip.contoso.com [10.12.11.201]
                                    0/ 100 =  0%  |  7    62ms
      1/ 100 =  1%     1/ 100 =  1%  tbr2-p012101.cgcil.ip.contoso.com [10.12.10.106]
                                    0/ 100 =  0%  |  8   107ms
      2/ 100 =  2%     2/ 100 =  2%  gbr4-p50.st6wa.ip.contoso.com [10.12.2.54]
                                    0/ 100 =  0%  |  9   111ms
      0/ 100 =  0%     0/ 100 =  0%  gar1-p370.stwwa.ip.contoso.com [10.12.203.177]
                                    0/ 100 =  0%  | 10   118ms
      0/ 100 =  0%     0/ 100 =  0%  10.12.70.6
```

```
                                    0/ 100 =   0%   | 11  ---
      100/ 100 =100%    100/ 100 =100%  10.46.33.225
                                    0/ 100 =   0%   | 12  ---
      100/ 100 =100%    100/ 100 =100%  10.46.36.210
                                    0/ 100 =   0%   | 13  123ms
        0/ 100 =   0%     0/ 100 =   0%  10.46.155.17
                                    0/ 100 =   0%   | 14  127ms
        0/ 100 =   0%     0/ 100 =   0%  10.46.129.51
                                    1/ 100 =   1%   | 15  125ms
        1/ 100 =   1%     0/ 100 =   0%  10.46.196.103 Trace complete.
```

Based on PathPing's output, you can often quickly identify the source of your connectivity problems as a name-resolution problem, a routing problem, a performance problem, or a possible connectivity issue. By using PathPing, you can also rule out active connectivity issues at the network layer or below.

Routing Loops

You can use PathPing to detect routing loops. Routing loops—a situation in which traffic is forwarded back to a router that has already forwarded a particular packet—are evident because the output from PathPing will show a set of routers repeated multiple times. For example, the following output indicates a routing loop between the routers at 10.128.191.245, 10.128.191.73, and 10.125.39.213:

```
Tracing route to support.go.microsoft.contoso.com [10.46.196.103]over a maximum of 30
hops:  0  contoso-
test [192.168.1.207]   1   10.211.240.1   2   10.128.191.245   3   10.128.191.73
4   10.125.39.213   5   10.128.191.245   6   10.128.191.73   7   10.125.39.213
8   10.128.191.245   9   10.128.191.73  10   10.125.39.213 (...continued...)
```

Routing loops are generally caused by router or routing protocol misconfiguration, and further troubleshooting must be performed on the network routing equipment.

Performance Problems

The RTT column of the performance section of the PathPing output might identify a performance problem. This column shows, in milliseconds, the two-way latency of communications with that particular device. Although all networks will show gradually increasing latency as the hop count increases, a large latency increase from one hop to the next identifies performance problems.

Performance problems might also be evident from a high percentage shown in the Lost/ Sent = Pct column. This column measures packet loss. Although packet loss in the single digits generally does not indicate a problem that would cause performance or connectivity problems, packet loss of greater than 30 percent generally indicates that the network node is experiencing problems.

Note If a network device shows packet loss of 100 percent, but packets are processed at later hops, the network device has been configured to not answer PathPing queries, which does not necessarily indicate a problem.

Possible Connectivity Issues

If the last item shown in the first section of PathPing output resembles the following example, PathPing was unable to communicate directly to the destination:

```
14      *      *      *
```

This might or might not indicate a possible connectivity problem, however. Although the device might be offline or unreachable, it is also likely that the destination—or a network node in the path to the destination—has been configured to drop the ICMP packets that PathPing uses to query devices. ICMP is disabled by default in many modern operating systems. Additionally, administrators often manually disable ICMP on other operating systems as a security measure to make it more difficult for malicious attackers to identify nodes on the network and to reduce the effects of some denial-of-service attacks.

Note Windows Firewall drops ICMP packets by default on public networks. Therefore, Windows XP Service Pack 2, Windows Server 2003, and Windows Vista computers on public networks will not respond to ICMP requests by default.

If PathPing is unable to reach the destination, you should attempt to communicate directly with the application by using Telnet, as described in the section titled "Telnet Client" later in this chapter.

No Connectivity Issues

If the PathPing output indicates that PathPing was able to communicate successfully with the destination, and the RTT time shown for the destination is less than 1000 milliseconds, there are probably no name-resolution or IP connectivity problems between the source and destination. However, PathPing will not show problems with a specific service or application. For example, PathPing might successfully communicate with a web server even if the web server services are stopped. For more information about troubleshooting application issues, see the section titled "How to Troubleshoot Application Connectivity Problems" later in this chapter.

Performance Monitor

You can use Performance Monitor, shown in Figure 32-2, to view thousands of real-time counters containing information about your computer or a remote computer. When troubleshooting network performance problems, you can use Performance Monitor to view current bandwidth utilization in a more detailed way than provided by Task Manager or Resource Monitor. Additionally, Performance Monitor provides access to counters measuring retries, errors, and much more.

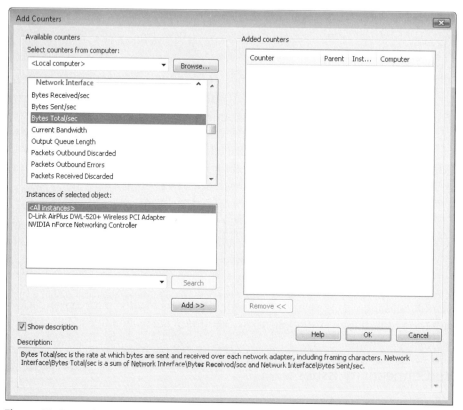

Figure 32-2   Performance Monitor provides real-time, detailed network statistics.

Performance Monitor provides access to the following categories, which contain counters that might be useful for troubleshooting network problems:

- **.NET CLR Networking**   Used to examine network statistics for specific .NET Framework applications. Use these counters if you are experiencing application-specific networking problems and the application is based on the .NET Framework.

- **BITS Net Utilization**   Provides statistics related to Background Intelligent Transfer Service (BITS), which is used to transfer files in the background. Windows Update, among other applications, uses BITS to transfer files. Use these counters if you think a network performance problem might be related to BITS transfers, or if BITS transfers do not perform as expected. For more information about BITS, see Chapter 26, "Configuring Windows Networking."

■ **Browser**   Provides statistics related to the Computer Browser service, which is used to browse network resources. Use these counters only if you are troubleshooting problems with browsing local networks, specifically for resources such as Windows XP or earlier versions of Windows. For more information about the Computer Browser service, see Chapter 26.

■ **ICMP and ICMPv6**   Provide ICMP statistics. ICMP is used by tools such as Ping, Tracert, and PathPing. Use these counters only if you are actively using IMCP to test network connectivity.

■ **IPsec AuthIPv4, IPsec AuthIPv6, IPsec Driver, IPsec IKEv4, and IPsec IKEv6**   Provide IPsec statistics. Use these counters if you are experiencing networking problems and IPsec is enabled in your environment.

■ **IPv4 and IPv6**   These categories provide Layer 3 networking information, such as fragmentation statistics. If you need to monitor total network utilization, you should use the Network Interface counters instead.

■ **NBT Connection**   Provides information about bytes sent and received for NetBIOS networking, such as file and printer sharing.

■ **Network Interface**   The most useful category for troubleshooting, this provides counters for all network traffic sent to and from a single network adapter. These counters are the most reliable way to measure total network utilization. Network Interface counters also provide information about errors.

■ **Redirector**   Provides statistics gathered from the Windows Vista redirector, which helps direct traffic to and from different networking components. Interpreting most of these counters requires a detailed understanding of the Windows Vista network stack. However, the Network Errors/sec counter can be useful for diagnosing network problems.

■ **Server**   Provides statistics related to sharing files and printers, including bandwidth used and the number of errors. Use these counters when troubleshooting file and printer sharing from the server.

■ **TCPv4 and TCPv6**   Provide information about TCP connections. Of particular interest for troubleshooting are the Connection Failures, Connections Active, and Connections Established counters.

■ **UDPv4 and UDPv6**   Provide information about UDP communications. Use these counters to determine whether a computer is sending or receiving UDP data, such as DNS requests. Monitor the Datagrams No Port/sec, and Datagrams Received Errors counters to determine if a computer is receiving unwanted UDP traffic.

To access Performance Monitor, follow these steps:

1. Click Start, right-click Computer, and then click Manage.

2. Expand System Tools, expand Reliability And Performance, and then expand Monitoring Tools. Click Performance Monitor.

3. Add counters to the real-time graph by clicking the green plus on the toolbar.

Ping

Ping is of limited usefulness today because most new computers drop Ping requests (which use ICMP). Therefore, you might Ping a computer that is connected to the network but not receive any response. Additionally, a computer might respond to Ping requests even if a firewall is dropping all other traffic—misleading you into thinking that you had connectivity.

However, Ping is still the best tool to easily monitor network connectivity on an ongoing basis. After using PathPing to identify network hosts that respond to ICMP requests, you can use Ping to constantly submit Ping requests and thereby easily determine whether or not you currently have connectivity to the host. If you are experiencing intermittent connectivity problems, a Ping loop will indicate whether or not your connection is active at any given time.

To start a Ping loop, run the following command:

```
ping -t hostname
```

Replies indicate that the packet was sent successfully, while Request Timed Out messages indicate that the computer did not receive a response from the remote host. The following example indicates how to monitor the connection to a host at the IP address 192.168.1.1:

```
ping -t 192.168.1.1
```

```
Pinging 192.168.1.1 with 32 bytes of data:

Reply from 192.168.1.1: bytes=32 time=1ms TTL=64
Reply from 192.168.1.1: bytes=32 time<1ms TTL=64
Reply from 192.168.1.1: bytes=32 time<1ms TTL=64
Reply from 192.168.1.1: bytes=32 time<1ms TTL=64
Request timed out.
Request timed out.
Request timed out.
Request timed out.
Request timed out.
Reply from 192.168.1.1: bytes=32 time<1ms TTL=64
Request timed out.
Request timed out.
Reply from 192.168.1.1: bytes=32 time<1ms TTL=64
```

Note that Ping loops provide only an approximate estimation of connectivity. Ping packets will occasionally be dropped even if connectivity is constant. Additionally, because Ping sends requests sooner if a reply is received than if the reply times out, you cannot use the ratio of replies to time-out errors as a useful indication of network uptime.

Direct from the Source: Finding Blackhole Routers

Ping can be useful to determine if upstream routers are blackhole routers, which drop datagrams larger than a specific size. For more information, see *http://support.microsoft.com/kb/314825*.

Tim Rains, Program Manager

Windows Networking

Portqry

Directly query critical services on the remote host to determine if it is available and accessible. You can use two troubleshooting tools to query services on a remote host: Portqry (Portqry.exe) and Telnet Client. Portqry is more flexible and simpler to use; however, because it is not included with Windows Vista and can be downloaded from Microsoft.com, it might not be installed on all systems. Use Telnet Client to query remote services only when Portqry is not available.

 Note   You can also find PortQry and PortQryUI on the companion CD of this resource kit.

Identifying the TCP Port for a Service

A single computer can host many network services. These services distinguish their traffic from each other by using port numbers. When testing connectivity to an application by using Telnet, you must provide Telnet with the port number the destination application is using.

 Note   Most services allow the administrator to specify a port number other than the default. If the service does not respond to the default port number, verify that the service has not been configured to use a different port number. You can run Netstat on the server to list listening ports. For more information, see the section titled "Netstat" earlier in this chapter.

For a list of common port numbers, see the section titled "How to Troubleshoot Network Connectivity Problems" later in this chapter.

Testing Service Connectivity

After you have identified the port number for the service, you can use Portqry to test connectivity to that service. To test connectivity to a service, open a command prompt and run the following command:

```
portqry -n destination -e portnumber
```

For example, to test HTTP connectivity to *www.microsoft.com*, type the following command at the command line:

```
portqry -n www.microsoft.com -e 80
```

This command produces output that is similar to the following:

```
Querying target system called:
 www.microsoft.com
Attempting to resolve name to IP address...
Name resolved to 10.209.68.190
TCP port 80 (http service): LISTENING
```

The destination might be a host name, computer name, or IP address. If the response includes LISTENING, the host responded on the specified port number. If the response includes NOT LISTENING or FILTERED, the service you are testing is not available.

> **Note**   NetCat is a great non-Microsoft tool for testing connectivity to specific ports or determining which ports a computer is listening for connections on. NetCat is an open-source tool freely available on the Internet.

Determining Available Remote Management Protocols

When troubleshooting a computer remotely, you might need to determine which remote management protocols are available. Portqry can test the default port numbers for common remote management protocols and identify which protocols are available.

To determine which management protocols are available on a remote host, open a command prompt and run the following command:

```
portqry -n destination -o 32,139,445,3389
```

This command queries the remote host to determine if Telnet Server, NetBIOS, CIFS, and the Remote Desktop are available.

Direct from the Source: Specifying the Source Port

The Portqry *–sp* option allows you to specify which source port you would like to use for the connectivity test. Use this parameter to specify the initial source port to use when you connect to the specified TCP and UDP ports on the destination computer. This functionality is useful to help you test firewall or router rules that filter ports based on their source ports.

Tim Rains, Program Manager

Windows Networking

The following Portqry output indicates that the remote system will respond to NetBIOS, CIFS, and Remote Desktop requests, but not to Telnet requests:

```
Querying target system called:
 192.168.1.200
Attempting to resolve IP address to a name...
IP address resolved to CONTOSO-SERVER
TCP port 32 (unknown service): NOT LISTENING
TCP port 139 (netbios-ssn service): LISTENING
TCP port 445 (microsoft-ds service): LISTENING
TCP port 3389 (unknown service): LISTENING
```

Direct from the Source: Why Portqry Is Great

The real advantage that Portqry has over the Telnet client and other such tools is the support for UDP-based services. The Telnet client can help test connectivity only on TCP ports. You can use Portqry to test TCP ports as well as UDP ports. The UDP ports that Portqry can test include Lightweight Directory Access Protocol (LDAP), Remote Procedure Calls (RPC), Domain Name System (DNS), NetBIOS Name, Service, Simple Network Management Protocol (SNMP), Internet Security and Acceleration Server (ISA), SQL Server 2000 Named Instances, Trivial File Transfer Protocol (TFTP), and Layer Two Tunneling Protocol (L2TP).

Tim Rains, Program Manager

Windows Networking

Reliability and Performance

If you have a recurring network problem, you can use tracing to capture and analyze detailed diagnostics information. Tracing provides extremely in-depth troubleshooting data, including extensive details about the system's state and events that occurred while tracing was active.

Although Event Viewer reveals enough information to troubleshoot most common problems, tracing provides sufficient information for even the most complex problems and can be useful to system administrators, driver developers, and hardware manufacturers.

To perform tracing, follow these steps:

1. Click Start, right-click Computer, and then click Manage.

2. Expand Reliability And Performance, Data Collector Sets, and System.

3. Under System, right-click LAN Diagnostics (to troubleshoot wired network problems) or Wireless Diagnostics (to troubleshoot wireless network problems) and then click Start.

   Starting diagnostics tracing causes Windows Vista to collect detailed information about network adapters, Group Policy settings, Windows Network Diagnostics, and overall operating system performance.

4. Now that you have started tracing, you should reproduce the networking problem. Then, stop tracing by right-clicking the data collector set you started and then clicking Stop.

5. Windows Vista takes a few seconds to generate a report after you stop tracing. Then, you can view the collected information in a report, as shown in Figure 32-3. To view the report, under Reliability And Performance, expand Reports and System. Then, expand either LAN Diagnostics or Wireless Diagnostics and click the appropriate report.

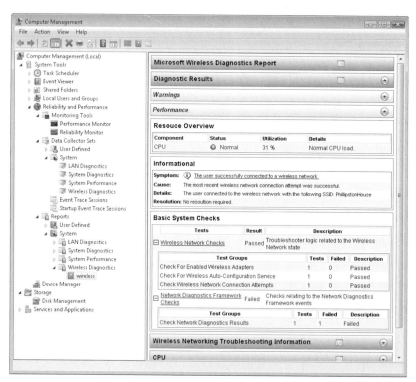

Figure 32-3 Tracing reports show detailed information gathered while tracing was enabled.

Depending on the type of report, it can include the following information:

- Current IP configuration (including data provided by IPConfig /all)
- A list of all connection attempts, and detailed information about each step of the connection process
- A detailed list of all Windows Network Diagnostics events
- Raw network tracing information
- Computer make and model
- Operating system version
- A list of all services, their current states, and their process IDs
- Network adapter driver information and networking system files and versions
- Group Policy network profiles that apply to your network connections
- Wireless configuration, including allowed and blocked wireless networks, wireless certificate information, and wireless profiles and their locations

Resource Monitor

Windows Vista provides Resource Monitor (also known as Reliability And Performance Monitor) so that you can view processor, disk, network, and memory utilization. Open Resource Monitor in one of two primary ways:

- Click Start, right-click Computer, and then click Manage. Under System Tools, click Reliability And Performance Monitor.
- Open Task Manager. Click the Performance tab and then click Resource Monitor.

In the context of troubleshooting network issues, the Network section is the most interesting section of the Resource Monitor. The network section displays bytes per minute that each process on your computer is using. With this information, you can identify a process that is transmitting large amounts of data and stop it if it should not be communicating on the network. To identify and terminate a process that is using the network, follow these steps:

1. Open Resource Monitor.
2. Expand the Network section. Click the Total column heading to sort the process list by bandwidth utilization.
3. The topmost process is sending and receiving the most data. Make note of the process name (in the Image column), the Process ID (PID), and the remote computer (in the Address column). If this is enough information to identify the process, you can close the application now.

4. If the process is Svchost.exe, you might not be able to identify the specific application generating the network traffic, because it is a Windows component (or it is using a Windows component for communications). If it is a different process, open Task Manager.

5. In Task Manager, click the Processes tab, click the View menu, and then click Select Columns.

6. In the Select Process Page Columns dialog box, select the PID check box. Click OK.

7. Click the PID column to sort by process ID. Click the process that corresponds to the PID you identified as generating the network traffic using the Resource Monitor. To kill the process, click End Process.

In most cases, an application that is sending or transmitting a large amount of data has a legitimate need for that data and you should not terminate it. However, in some cases, the process may be associated with malware. Verify that the computer has Windows Defender enabled and that Windows Defender is up to date.

Route

All IP-based networked devices, including computers, have *routing tables*. Routing tables describe the local network, remote networks, and gateways that you can use to forward traffic between networks. In networks with a single gateway, the routing table is very simple and indicates that local traffic should be sent directly to the local network, whereas traffic for any network other than the local network should be sent through the gateway.

However, some networks have multiple gateways. For example, you might have two gateways on a local area network: one that leads to the Internet and another that leads to a private network. In that case, the local computer's routing table must describe that specific networks are available through the internal gateway, and all other networks are available through the Internet gateway.

Note   A client computer is most often configured with multiple routes in remote access scenarios. Specifically, if a client is using a VPN connection, there might be separate routes for the networks accessible through the VPN connection, and all other traffic will be sent directly to the Internet.

Typically, Windows Vista computers will be automatically configured with the correct routing table. For example, network administrators will configure the DHCP server to assign a default gateway. When making a VPN connection, the VPN server will provide routing information that Windows Vista will use to update the routing tables. Therefore, you rarely need to use the Route command to view or update the routing table.

However, if you are having connectivity problems and you are connected to a remote network, or if your local network has multiple gateways, you can use Route to diagnose routing problems and even test different routing configurations. To view the local computer's IPv4 and IPv6 routing tables, open a command prompt and run the following command:

```
C:\Users\user1>route print
```

```
===========================================================================
Interface List
 11 ...00 80 c8 ac 0d 9e ...... D-Link AirPlus DWL-520+ Wireless PCI Adapter
  8 ...00 13 d3 3b 50 8f ...... NVIDIA nForce Networking Controller
  1 ........................... Software Loopback Interface 1
  9 ...02 00 54 55 4e 01 ...... Teredo Tunneling Pseudo-Interface
 12 ...00 00 00 00 00 00 00 e0  isatap.{B1A1A1DE-A1E5-4ED6-B597-7667C85F8999}
 13 ...00 00 00 00 00 00 00 e0  isatap.hsd1.nh.comcast.net.
===========================================================================

IPv4 Route Table
===========================================================================
Active Routes:
Network Destination        Netmask          Gateway       Interface  Metric
          0.0.0.0          0.0.0.0      192.168.1.1    192.168.1.132     20
        127.0.0.0        255.0.0.0         On-link        127.0.0.1    306
        127.0.0.1  255.255.255.255         On-link        127.0.0.1    306
  127.255.255.255  255.255.255.255         On-link        127.0.0.1    306
      169.254.0.0      255.255.0.0         On-link  169.254.166.248    286
  169.254.166.248  255.255.255.255         On-link  169.254.166.248    286
  169.254.255.255  255.255.255.255         On-link  169.254.166.248    286
      192.168.1.0    255.255.255.0         On-link    192.168.1.132    276
    192.168.1.132  255.255.255.255         On-link    192.168.1.132    276
    192.168.1.255  255.255.255.255         On-link    192.168.1.132    276
        224.0.0.0        240.0.0.0         On-link        127.0.0.1    306
        224.0.0.0        240.0.0.0         On-link    192.168.1.132    276
        224.0.0.0        240.0.0.0         On-link  169.254.166.248    286
  255.255.255.255  255.255.255.255         On-link        127.0.0.1    306
  255.255.255.255  255.255.255.255         On-link    192.168.1.132    276
  255.255.255.255  255.255.255.255         On-link  169.254.166.248    286
===========================================================================
Persistent Routes:
  None

IPv6 Route Table
===========================================================================
Active Routes:
 If Metric Network Destination      Gateway
  9     18 ::/0                      On-link
  1    306 ::1/128                   On-link
  9     18 2001::/32                 On-link
  9    266 2001:0:4136:e37a:14fc:39dc:3f57:fe7b/128
                                     On-link
  8    276 fe80::/64                 On-link
 11    286 fe80::/64                 On-link
  9    266 fe80::/64                 On-link
 12    296 fe80::5efe:169.254.166.248/128
                                     On-link
 13    281 fe80::5efe:192.168.1.132/128
```

```
                                     On-link
     9     266 fe80::14fc:39dc:3f57:fe7b/128
                                     On-link
     8     276 fe80::41e9:c80b:416d:717c/128
                                     On-link
    11     286 fe80::c038:ad1f:3cc6:a6f8/128
                                     On-link
     1     306 ff00::/8               On-link
     9     266 ff00::/8               On-link
     8     276 ff00::/8               On-link
    11     286 ff00::/8               On-link
===========================================================================
Persistent Routes:
  None
```

Fully interpreting the routing configuration requires a detailed understanding of IP networking; however, you can quickly identify default routes for traffic being sent to your default gateway by locating the Active Route with a Network Destination and Network Mask of 0.0.0.0 for IPv4 routes, and an Active Route with the prefix ::/0 for IPv6 routes. Other Active Routes with a Gateway assigned cause traffic for the specific Network Destination and Network Mask to be sent through that gateway, with a preference for the route with the lowest metric.

If you must manually update the IPv4 routing table (you should typically make changes to the network infrastructure that assigned the routes to the client), you can use the route add, route change, and route delete commands. For more information, type **route -?** at a command prompt.

To update the IPv6 routing table, you must use the netsh interface ipv6 add|set|delete route commands.

Task Manager

Task Manager (Taskmgr.exe) is a GUI tool that you can use to view or end a process or an unresponsive application. You can also use Task Manager to gather other information, such as CPU statistics. To start Task Manager, click Start, type **Taskmgr**, and then press Enter. Alternatively, you can right-click the taskbar and then click Task Manager.

The Windows Task Manager window contains six tabs: Applications, Processes, Services, Performance, Networking, and Users.

- The Applications and Processes tabs provide a list of applications or processes that are currently active on your system. These lists are valuable because active tasks do not always display a user interface, which can make it difficult to detect activity. Task Manager displays active processes and lets you end most items by clicking End Process. You cannot end some processes immediately; you might need to use the Services snap-in or Taskkill to end them. You can also customize Task Manager to increase or decrease the level of detail shown on the Processes tab.

■ The Services tab displays running services and their PID. If you determine that a specific PID is using network resources and you find the PID on this tab, you know that a service is causing the network utilization. To stop a service, right-click it and then click Stop Service, as shown in Figure 32-4.

Figure 32-4   Use the Services tab to identify services by PID and stop them.

■ The Performance tab graphically displays process and memory utilization. Viewing this tab quickly reveals the total utilization of all programs and services on the computer. The Performance tab also shows key performance counters, including the number of processes, the number of threads, and the total physical memory installed in the system.

■ The Networking tab shows the utilization of all network interfaces.

■ With the Users tab, you can disconnect and log off active users.

To view detailed information about processes, follow these steps:

1. Start Task Manager and then click the Processes tab.

2. Optionally, click Show Processes From All Users and respond to the User Account Control (UAC) prompt that appears.

3. On the View menu, click Select Columns.

4. Select or clear the columns that you want to add to, or remove from, the Processes tab.

5. Click OK to return to Task Manager.

To identify the cause of high processor utilization, follow these steps:

1. Start Task Manager and then click the Performance tab.

2. Click the View menu and then select Show Kernel Times if it is not already selected.

3. Examine the CPU Usage History graph. If the graph shows values close to 100 percent, one process or multiple processes are consuming the bulk of the computer's processing capability. The red line shows the percentage of the processor consumed by the kernel, which includes drivers. If the bulk of the processing time is consumed by the kernel, verify that you are using signed drivers and have the latest version of all drivers installed. If the kernel is not responsible for the majority of the processor usage, continue following these steps to identify the process.

4. Click the Processes tab.

5. Click the CPU column heading twice to sort the processes by processor utilization with the highest utilization at the top of the list.

The process or processes consuming the processor will show high CPU utilization values. When the processor is not being used heavily, the System Idle Process shows high CPU utilization.

To find the PID of an application, follow these steps:

1. Start Task Manager and verify that the Process ID (PID) column is displayed on the Processes tab. If it is not displayed, open the View menu, click Select Columns, and then select PID. Click OK.

2. Click the Applications tab.

3. Right-click the application and then click Go To Process.

Task Manager will display the Processes tab. The process associated with the application will be highlighted. The PID is shown in the PID column.

To stop a process, follow these steps:

1. Start Task Manager and then click the Processes tab.

2. Right-click the process you want to stop and then click End Process.

Task Manager will attempt to end the process. If Task Manager fails, use Taskkill.

To identify the network utilization, start Task Manager and then click the Networking tab. Task Manager shows the utilization of each network adapter. The percentage of utilization is measured in relation to the reported Link Speed of the adapter. In most cases, network adapters are not capable of 100-percent utilization; peak utilization is approximately 60 percent to 70 percent.

TCPView

TCPView, shown in Figure 32-5, monitors both incoming and outgoing connections, as well as listening applications, in real time. You can use TCPView to identify exactly which servers a client connects to, including the port numbers, or identify the clients connecting to a server.

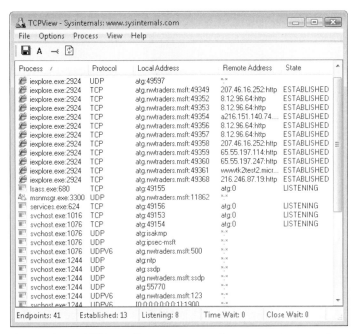

Figure 32-5 TCPView allows you to monitor network connections in real time.

To download TCPView, visit *http://technet.microsoft.com/en-us/sysinternals/bb897437.aspx*. You do not need to install TCPView; simply copy the executable file to a folder that allows applications to be run (such as C:\Program Files\) and then double-click Tcpview.exe. TCPView also includes Tcpvcon.exe, a command-line tool that provides similar functionality.

Telnet Client

Although it is not primarily a troubleshooting tool, Telnet Client is extremely useful for determining if TCP-based network services are reachable from a client. Most commonly used network services are TCP-based, including web services, mail services, and file transfer services. Telnet Client is not useful for troubleshooting UDP-based network services such as DNS and many streaming media communications.

Telnet Client is not installed by default in Windows Vista. To install it, run the following command from a command prompt with administrative privileges:

```
start /w pkgmgr /iu:"TelnetClient"
```

Alternatively, you can install it by following these steps:

1. Click Start and then click Control Panel.

2. Click Programs.

3. Click Turn Windows Features On Or Off.

4. In the Windows Features dialog box, select the Telnet Client check box. Click OK.

Telnet Client is useful only for determining if a service is reachable, and it will not provide information that you can use for troubleshooting name resolution, network performance, or network connectivity problems. Use Telnet Client only after you have used Ping to eliminate the possibility of name resolution problems. For more information about Ping, see the section titled "Ping" earlier in this chapter.

Testing Service Connectivity

After you have identified the port number for the service, you can use Telnet Client to test connectivity to that service. To test connectivity to a service, open a command prompt and run the following command:

```
telnet destination portnumber
```

For example, to test HTTP connectivity to *www.microsoft.com*, type the following command at the command line:

```
telnet www.microsoft.com 80
```

The destination might be a host name, computer name, or IP address. The response you receive will indicate whether or not a connection was established. If you receive the message "Could not open connection to the host," the host did not respond to the request for a connection on the port number you specified, and the service you are testing is unreachable.

If you receive any other response, including all text disappearing from the command window, the connection was successfully established. This eliminates the possibility that the problem you are troubleshooting is caused by a connectivity issue between the client and the server. Depending on the service you are testing, Telnet Client can be automatically disconnected, or the session might remain open. Either circumstance indicates a successful connection. If the Telnet Client session remains open, you should disconnect Telnet Client to close the connection.

To disconnect Telnet Client, follow these steps:

1. Press Ctrl+].

2. When the Microsoft Telnet> prompt appears, type:

```
quit
```

Test TCP

With Test TCP (Ttcp), you can both initiate TCP connections and listen for TCP connections. You can also use the Ttcp tool for UDP traffic. With Ttcp, you can configure a computer to listen on a specific TCP or UDP port without having to install the application or service on the computer. This allows you to test network connectivity for specific traffic before the services are in place.

Test TCP (Ttcp.exe) is a tool that you can use to listen for and send TCP segment data or UDP messages between two nodes. Ttcp.exe is provided with Windows Server 2003 in the Valueadd\Msft\Net\Tools folder of the Windows Server 2003 product CD-ROM.

> **Note**   Ttcp can also be found on the companion CD of this Resource Kit.

Test TCP differs from Port Query in the following ways:

- With Test TCP, you can configure a computer to listen on a specific TCP or UDP port without having to install the application or service on the computer. This allows you to test network connectivity for specific traffic before the services are in place. For example, you could use Test TCP to test for domain replication traffic to a computer before you make the computer a domain controller.

- Test TCP also supports Internet Protocol version 6 (IPv6) traffic.

The basic syntax for Ttcp.exe on the listening node (the receiver) is:

```
To listen on a TCP port:
ttcp -r -pPort

To listen on a UDP port:
ttcp -r -pPort -u
```

After starting Test TCP in receive mode, the tool will wait indefinitely for a transmission before returning you to the command prompt. The first time you use Test TCP to listen from a Windows Vista computer, you might be prompted to create a Windows Firewall exception. You must create the exception for Test TCP to work. If you choose to unblock the application, Windows Firewall will allow all traffic for that computer on the specified port in the future. Therefore, you will not need to create a new exception for that network type, even if you listen on a different port. In Windows Firewall, the exception is named Protocol Independent Perf Test Command.

The basic syntax for Ttcp.exe on the sending node (the transmitter) is:

```
REM Send on a TCP port:
ttcp -t -pPort hostname

REM Send on a UDP port:
ttcp -t -pPort -u hostname
```

If the two computers are able to communicate, the transmitting computer will display output such as the following:

```
ttcp-t: Vista1 -> 192.168.1.132
ttcp-t: local 192.168.1.196 -> remote 192.168.1.132
ttcp-t: buflen=8192, nbuf=2048, align=16384/+0, port=81  tcp  -> Vista1
ttcp-t: done sending, nbuf = -1
ttcp-t: 16777216 bytes in 1423 real milliseconds = 11513 KB/sec
ttcp-t: 2048 I/O calls, msec/call = 0, calls/sec = 1439, bytes/call = 8192
```

Meanwhile, the receiving computer will display output similar to the following:

```
ttcp-r: local 192.168.1.132 <- remote 192.168.1.196
ttcp-r: buflen=8192, nbuf=2048, align=16384/+0, port=81  tcp
ttcp-r: 16777216 bytes in 1416 real milliseconds = 11570 KB/sec
ttcp-r: 3492 I/O calls, msec/call = 0, calls/sec = 2466, bytes/call = 4804
```

You can use Test TCP to connect to any computer listening for incoming TCP connections, even if that computer is not running Test TCP. However, to accurately test UDP connectivity, Test TCP must be running on both the receiver and transmitter. For example, to attempt a connection to *www.microsoft.com* on TCP port 80, you would run the following command:

```
ttcp -t -p80 www.microsoft.com
```

```
ttcp-t: local 192.168.1.196 -> remote 10.46.20.60
ttcp-t: buflen=8192, nbuf=2048, align=16384/+0, port=80  tcp  -> www.microsoft.com
send(to) failed: 10053
ttcp-t: done sending, nbuf = 2037
ttcp-t: 81920 bytes in 16488 real milliseconds = 4 KB/sec
ttcp-t: 11 I/O calls, msec/call = 1498, calls/sec = 0, bytes/call = 7447
```

In this example, the TCP connection was successful, even though the output includes the line "send(to) failed." If the connection was unsuccessful, the output would have included the phrase "connection refused." Alternatively, some servers will simply not respond to invalid communications, which will cause the Test TCP transmitter to hang while it awaits a response from the server. To cancel Test TCP, press Ctrl+C.

Each instance of Test TCP can listen on or send to only a single port. However, you can run it in multiple command prompts to listen or send on multiple ports. For additional command-line options, type **Ttcp** at the command prompt.

Windows Network Diagnostics

Troubleshooting network problems is complicated, especially for end users. Many users discover network problems when they attempt to visit a web page with Internet Explorer. If the web page is not available, Internet Explorer returns the message "Internet Explorer cannot display the webpage." The problem could be any one of the following, however:

- The user mistyped the address of the web page.

- The web server is not available.

- The user's Internet connection is not available.

- The user's local area network is not available.

- The user's network adapter is misconfigured.

- The user's network adapter has failed.

The cause of the problem is important for the end user to understand. For example, if the web server is not available, the user does not need to take any action—the user should simply wait for the web server to become available. If the Internet connection has failed, the user might need to call her ISP to troubleshoot the problem. If the user's network adapter has failed, he should attempt to reset it, and contact his computer manufacturer's technical support for additional assistance.

Windows Network Diagnostics and the underlying Network Diagnostics Framework assist users in diagnosing and, when possible, resolving network connectivity issues. When Windows Vista detects network problems, it will prompt the user to diagnose them. For example, Internet Explorer displays a link to launch Windows Network Diagnostics if a web server is unavailable, and the Network And Sharing Center will display a diagnostic link if a network is unavailable.

Applications might prompt users to open Windows Network Diagnostics in response to connectivity problems. To launch Windows Network Diagnostics manually, open Internet Explorer, click the Tools menu, and then click Diagnose Connection Problems. Alternatively, in Network And Sharing Center, click Diagnose And Repair. Unlike many of the tools described in this chapter, Windows Network Diagnostics is designed to be useful without a deep understanding of network technologies.

For more information about Windows Network Diagnostics, see Chapter 26.

The Process of Troubleshooting Network Problems

To most users, the term *connectivity problems* describes a wide range of problems, including a failed network connection, an application that cannot connect because of firewall filtering, and serious performance problems. Therefore, the first step in troubleshooting connectivity problems is to identify the scope of the connectivity problem.

To identify the source of a connectivity problem, follow these steps and answer the questions until you are directed to a different section:

1. Open the Network And Sharing Center by clicking Start, clicking Network, and then clicking Network And Sharing Center. If a red X is displayed over a network link, as shown in Figure 32-6, click the link to start Windows Network Diagnostics and follow the prompts that appear. Windows Network Diagnostics can solve more than 360 different network problems. If Windows Network Diagnostics does not identify or resolve the problem, please choose to send the information to Microsoft to help improve Windows Network Diagnostics. Then, continue following these steps.

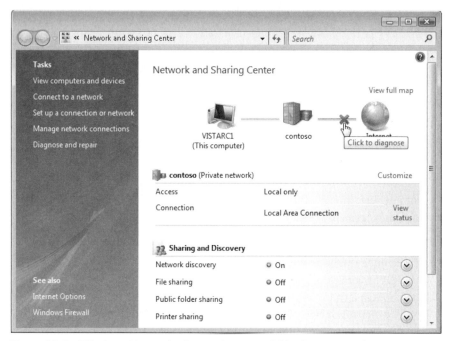

Figure 32-6 Windows Network Diagnostics can quickly diagnose or fix many common problems.

2. Are you attempting to connect to a wireless network, but your connection attempt is rejected? If so, see the section titled "How to Troubleshoot Wireless Networks" later in this chapter.

3. Are you attempting to connect to a remote network using a virtual private network (VPN) connection, but your connection attempt is rejected? If so, see Chapter 28, "Connecting Remote Users and Networks."

4. Can you occasionally access the network resource, but it is unreliable or slow? If so, see the section titled "How to Troubleshoot Performance Problems and Intermittent Connectivity Issues" later in this chapter.

5. Can you access other network resources using different applications, such as e-mail or different websites? If not, you have a network connectivity problem or a name-resolution problem. If you can contact servers using the IP address instead of the host name, see the section titled "How to Troubleshoot Name-Resolution Problems" later in this chapter. If servers are not accessible when you specify an IP address, or if you do not know an IP address, see the next section, "How to Troubleshoot Network Connectivity Problems."

6. Are you trying to join a domain or attempting to log on to your computer using a domain account but are receiving an error message that the domain controller is unavailable? If so, see the section titled "How to Troubleshoot Joining or Logging on to a Domain" later in this chapter.

7. Open a command prompt and run the command "Nslookup *servername*." If Nslookup does not display an answer similar to the following, you have a name-resolution problem. See the section titled "How to Troubleshoot Name Resolution Problems" later in this chapter.

```
C:\>nslookup contoso.com


Non-authoritative answer:
Name:    contoso.com
Addresses:  10.46.232.182, 10.46.130.117
```

8. Are you trying to connect to a shared folder? If so, see the section titled "How to Troubleshoot File and Printer Sharing" later in this chapter.

9. If other network applications work, and name resolution succeeds, you might have a firewall problem. See the section titled "How to Troubleshoot Application Connectivity Problems" later in this chapter.

How to Troubleshoot Network Connectivity Problems

If you have a network connectivity problem, you will be unable to reach any network resource that would normally be accessible using the failed network. For example, if your Internet connection has failed, you will be unable to access Internet resources, but you might still be able to access resources on your LAN. If your LAN fails, however, nothing will be accessible. Most network connectivity problems result from one of the following issues:

■ Failed network adapter

■ Failed network hardware

■ Failed network connection

■ Faulty network cables

■ Misconfigured network hardware

■ Misconfigured network adapter

> **Note**   Often, people jump to the conclusion that the network has failed when only a single network resource has failed. For example, a failed DNS server will stop your computer from resolving host names, which would prevent the computer from finding resources on the network by name. Similarly, if the only network resource a user accesses is her e-mail server and that server has failed, the failure might appear to be a total loss of connectivity to that user. To avoid spending time troubleshooting the wrong problem, the processes in this chapter always start by isolating the cause of the problem.

After you isolate the failed component, you can work to resolve that specific problem, or you can escalate the problem to the correct support team. For example, if you determine that the network adapter has failed, you will need to contact the hardware manufacturer for a replacement part. If you determine that the Internet connection has failed, you will need to contact your ISP. To isolate the cause of a network connectivity problem, follow these steps:

1. Open the Network And Sharing Center by clicking Start, clicking Network, and then clicking Network And Sharing Center. If a red X is displayed over a network link, click the link to start Windows Network Diagnostics and follow the prompts that appear. Windows Network Diagnostics can solve many common configuration problems. If Windows Network Diagnostics does not identify or resolve the problem, continue following these steps.

2. Open a command prompt on the computer experiencing the problems. Run the command ipconfig /all. Examine the output:

   ❑ If no network adapters are listed, the computer either lacks a network adapter, or (more likely) it does not have a valid driver installed. Refer to Chapter 31, "Troubleshooting Hardware, Driver, and Disk Issues."

   ❑ If all network adapters show a Media State of Media Disconnected, the computer is not physically connected to a network. If you are using a wireless network, see the section titled "How to Troubleshoot Wireless Networks" later in this chapter. If you are using a wired network, disconnect and reconnect both ends of the network cable. If the problem continues, replace the network cable. Attempt to connect a different computer to the same network cable; if the new computer can connect successfully, the original computer has a failed network adapter. If neither computer can connect successfully, the problem is with the network wiring, the network switch, or the network hub. Replace the network hardware as necessary.

   ❑ If the network adapter has an IPv4 address in the range of 169.254.0.1 through 169.254.255.254, the computer has an Automatic Private IP Addressing (APIPA) address. This indicates that the computer is configured to use a DHCP server, but no DHCP server was available. With administrative credentials, run the following commands at a command prompt:

   ```
   ipconfig /release
   ipconfig /renew
   ipconfig /all
   ```

If the network adapter still has an APIPA address, the DHCP server is offline. Bring a DHCP server online and then restart the computer. If the network does not use a DHCP server, configure a static or alternate IPv4 address provided by your network administration team or your ISP. For information about configuring static IP addresses, see Chapter 26. For more information about Ipconfig, read the section titled "Ipconfig" earlier in this chapter.

❑ If all network adapters show DHCP Enabled: No in the display of the ipconfig /all command, the network adapter might be misconfigured. If DHCP is disabled, the computer has a static IPv4 address, which is an unusual configuration for client computers. Update the network adapter IPv4 configuration to Obtain An IP Address Automatically and Obtain DNS Server Address Automatically, as shown in Figure 32-7. Then configure the Alternate Configuration tab of the IP Properties dialog box with your current, static IP configuration. For information about configuring IP addresses, see Chapter 26.

Figure 32-7   Enable DCHP for most client computers.

For most networks, set client configuration to Obtain An IP Address Automatically.

3. Having arrived at this step, you know that your computer has a valid, DHCP-assigned IPv4 address and can communicate on the local network. Therefore, any connectivity problems are caused by failed or misconfigured network hardware. Although you cannot solve the problem from a Windows Vista client, you can still diagnose the problem. View the output from the ipconfig command and identify the IPv4 address of your default gateway. Verify that the IPv4 address of the default gateway is on the same subnet as the network adapter's IP address. If they are not on the same subnet, the default gateway address is incorrect—the default gateway must be on the same subnet as the client computer's IPv4 address.

> **Note**   To determine if an IPv4 address is on the same subnet as your computer's IPv4
> address, first look at your subnet mask. If your subnet mask is 255.255.255.0, compare the
> first three sets of numbers (called *octets*) in the IPv4 addresses (for example, 192.168.1 or
> 10.25.2). If they match exactly, the two IPv4 addresses are on the same subnet. If your
> subnet mask is 255.255.0.0, compare the first two octets. If your subnet mask is 255.0.0.0,
> compare only the first octet (the first grouping of numbers before the period in the IP
> address). If any of the numbers in the subnet mask are between 0 and 255, you will need
> to use binary math and the AND operation to determine if they are on the same subnet.

4. Attempt to Ping the default gateway using the following command:

   ```
   ping default_gateway_ip_address
   ```

   For example, given the following Ipconfig output:

   ```
   Ethernet adapter Local Area Connection:

       Connection-specific DNS Suffix  . : hsd1.nh.contoso.com.
       Link-local IPv6 Address . . . . . : fe80::1ccc:d0f4:3959:7d74%10
       IPv4 Address. . . . . . . . . . . : 192.168.1.132
       Subnet Mask . . . . . . . . . . . : 255.255.255.0
       Default Gateway . . . . . . . . . : 192.168.1.1
   ```

   you would run the following command:

   ```
   ping 192.168.1.1
   ```

   If the Ping results show "Request timed out", your computer either has the incorrect IP
   address configured for your default gateway or your default gateway is offline or is blocking
   ICMP requests. If the Ping results show "Reply from ...", your default gateway is correctly
   configured, and the problem is occurring elsewhere on the network.

> **Note**   Ping is not a reliable tool for determining whether computers or network
> equipment are available on the network. Today, to reduce security risks, many adminis-
> trators configure devices not to respond to Ping requests. However, Ping is still the most
> reliable tool for testing routers, and most administrators configure routers to respond to
> Ping requests from the local network. It's a good idea to ping your network equipment
> when everything is working properly just to know whether or not it responds under
> normal conditions.

5. Use the Tracert command to test if you can communicate with devices outside of your
   LAN. You can reference any server on a remote network; however, this example uses the
   host *www.microsoft.com*:

   ```
   C:\>tracert www.microsoft.com
   ```

```
Tracing route to www.microsoft.com [10.46.19.30]
over a maximum of 30 hops:
  0  Vista1.hsd1.nh.contoso.com. [192.168.1.132]
  1  192.168.1.1
  2  c-3-0-ubr01.winchendon.ma.boston.contoso.com [10.165.8.1]
  3  ge-3-37-ur01.winchendon.ma.boston.contoso.com [10.87.148.129]
  4  ge-1-1-ur01.gardner.ma.boston.contoso.com [10.87.144.225]
  5  10g-9-1-ur01.sterling.ma.boston.contoso.com [10.87.144.217]
```

The 0 line is your client computer. The 1 line is the default gateway. Lines 2 and above are routers outside your local area network.

- ❏ If you see the message "Unable to resolve target system name," your DNS server is unreachable because the DNS server is offline, your client computer is misconfigured, or the network has failed. If your DNS server is on your local area network (as displayed by the ipconfig /all command), and you can still Ping your router, the DNS server has failed or is misconfigured; see the section titled "How to Troubleshoot Name-Resolution Problems" later in this chapter. If your DNS server is on a different network, the problem could be either a network infrastructure problem or a name-resolution problem. Repeat this step, but use Ping to contact your DNS server IP address (as displayed by the ipconfig /all command). Then, follow the steps outlined in "How to Troubleshoot Name-Resolution Problems" to further isolate the issue.

- ❏ If nothing responds after line 1, your default gateway cannot communicate with external networks. Try restarting the default gateway. If the default gateway is connected directly to the Internet, the Internet connection or the device that connects you to the Internet (such as a cable or DSL modem) might have failed. Contact your ISP for additional troubleshooting.

- ❏ If the same gateway appears multiple times in the Tracert route, the network is experiencing a routing loop. Routing loops can cause performance problems or cause communications to fail entirely. Networks typically fix routing loops automatically; however, you should contact your network support team to make sure they are aware of the problem. The following Tracert output demonstrates a routing loop, because nodes 5, 6, and 7 repeat:

```
C:\>tracert www.contoso.com
```

```
Tracing route to www.contoso.com [10.73.186.238]
over a maximum of 30 hops:
  0  d820.hsd1.nh.contoso.com. [192.168.1.196]
  1  192.168.1.1
  2  c-3-0-ubr01.winchendon.ma.boston.contoso.com [10.165.8.1]
  3  ge-3-37-ur01.winchendon.ma.boston.contoso.com [10.87.148.129]
  4  ge-1-1-ur01.gardner.ma.boston.contoso.com [10.87.144.225]
  5  10g-9-1-ur01.sterling.ma.boston.contoso.com [10.87.144.217]
  6  te-9-2-ur01.marlboro.ma.boston.contoso.com [10.87.144.77]
```

```
 7  10g-8-1-ur01.natick.ma.boston.contoso.com [10.87.144.197]
 8  10g-9-1-ur01.sterling.ma.boston.contoso.com [10.87.144.217]
 9  te-9-2-ur01.marlboro.ma.boston.contoso.com [10.87.144.77]
10  10g-8-1-ur01.natick.ma.boston.contoso.com [10.87.144.197]
11  10g-9-1-ur01.sterling.ma.boston.contoso.com [10.87.144.217]
12  te-9-2-ur01.marlboro.ma.boston.contoso.com [10.87.144.77]
13  10g-8-1-ur01.natick.ma.boston.contoso.com [10.87.144.197]
```

❑ If any routers on line 2 or above respond (it doesn't matter if the final host responds), the client computer and the default gateway are configured correctly. The problem exists with the network infrastructure, or your Internet connection may have failed. Follow the troubleshooting steps described in the section titled "How to Troubleshoot Application Connectivity Problems" or contact network support to troubleshoot the problem.

To double-check your results, repeat these steps from another client computer on the same network. If the second client computer exhibits the same symptoms, you can be confident that part of the network infrastructure has failed. If the second client can successfully communicate on the network, compare the Ipconfig /all output from the two computers. If the Default Gateway or DNS Server addresses differ, try configuring the problematic computer with the other computer's settings. If this does not resolve the problem, the problem is unique to the problematic computer and may indicate a hardware or driver problem (see Chapter 31).

How to Troubleshoot Application Connectivity Problems

Sometimes, you might be able to access the network with some applications but not others. For example, you might be able to download your e-mail, but not be able to access web servers. Or, you might be able to view pages on a remote web server, but not be able to connect to the computer with Remote Desktop.

Several issues might cause these symptoms (in rough order of likelihood):

■ The remote service is not running. For example, Remote Desktop might not be enabled on the remote computer.

■ The remote server has a firewall configured that is blocking that application's communications from your client computer.

■ A firewall between the client and server computer is blocking that application's communications.

■ Windows Firewall on the local computer might be configured to block the application's traffic.

■ The remote service has been configured to use a nondefault port number. For example, web servers typically use TCP port 80, but some administrators might configure TCP port 81 or a different port.

To troubleshoot an application connectivity problem, follow these steps:

1. Before you begin troubleshooting application connectivity, first verify that you do not have a name-resolution problem. To do this, open a command prompt and run the command Nslookup *servername*. If Nslookup does not display an answer similar to the following example, you have a name-resolution problem. See the section titled "How to Troubleshoot Name-Resolution Problems" later in this chapter.

    ```
    C:\>nslookup contoso.com
    ```

    ```
    Non-authoritative answer:
    Name:    contoso.com
    Addresses:  10.46.232.182, 10.46.130.117
    ```

2. Identify the port number used by the application. Table 32-2 lists port numbers for common applications. If you are not sure which port numbers your application uses, consult the application's manual or contact the technical support team. Alternatively, you can use a protocol analyzer such as Network Monitor to examine network traffic to determine the port numbers used.

Table 32-2   Default Port Assignments for Common Services and Tasks

Service Name or Task	UDP	TCP
Web servers, HTTP, and IIS		80
HTTP-Secure Sockets Layer (SSL)		443
DNS client-to-server lookup (varies)	53	53
DHCP client		67
File and printer sharing	137	139, 445
FTP-control		21
FTP-data		20
Internet Relay Chat (IRC)		6667
Outlook (see for ports)		
IMAP		143
IMAP (SSL)		993
LDAP		389
LDAP (SSL)		636
MTA – X.400 over TCP/IP		102
POP3		110
POP3 (SSL)		995
Remote Procedure Calls (RPC) endpoint mapper		135
SMTP		25
NNTP		119
NNTP (SSL)		563

Table 32-2   Default Port Assignments for Common Services and Tasks

Service Name or Task	UDP	TCP
POP3		110
POP3 (SSL)		995
SNMP	161	
SNMP Trap	162	
SQL Server		1433
Telnet		23
Terminal Server and Remote Desktop		3389
PPTP (See Chapter 28.).		1723
Joining an Active Directory domain (See the section titled "How to Troubleshoot Joining or Logging on to a Domain" later in this chapter.)		

After identifying the port number, the first step in troubleshooting the application connectivity problem is to determine whether or not communications are successful using that port. If it is a TCP port, you can use either Portqry, Ttcp, or Telnet. Of those three tools, Telnet is the least flexible, but it is the only tool included with Windows Vista (but not installed by default). For more information about Telnet, including how to install it, see the "Telnet Client" section under "Tools for Troubleshooting" earlier in this chapter.

To test a TCP port with Telnet, run the following command:

Telnet *hostname_or_address TCP_port*

For example, to determine if you can connect to the web server at *www.microsoft.com* (which uses port 80), you would run the following command:

Telnet www.microsoft.com 80

If the command prompt clears or if you receive text from the remote service, you have successfully established a connection. Close the command prompt to cancel Telnet. This indicates that you can connect to the server; therefore, the server application is listening for incoming connections and no firewall is blocking your traffic. Instead of troubleshooting the problem as a connectivity issue, you should consider application-level issues, including:

- **Authentication issues**   View the server's Security Event Log or the application's log to determine if it is rejecting your client connections because of invalid credentials.

- **Failed service**   Restart the server. Test whether or not other client computers can connect to the server.

- **Invalid client software**   Verify that the client software running on your computer is the correct version and is configured properly.

If Telnet displays "Could not open connection to the host," this indicates an application connectivity issue, such as a misconfigured firewall. Follow these steps to continue trouble-shooting the problem:

1. If possible, verify that the server is online. If the server is online, attempt to connect to a different service running on the same server. For example, if you are attempting to connect to a web server and you know that the server has file sharing enabled, attempt to connect to a shared folder. If you can connect to a different service, the problem is almost certainly a firewall configuration problem on the server.

2. Attempt to connect from different client computers on the same and different subnets. If you can connect from a client computer on the same subnet, you might have an application configuration problem on the client computer. If you can connect from a client computer on a different subnet but not from the same subnet, a firewall on the network or on the server might be filtering traffic from your client network.

3. If possible, connect a client computer to the same subnet as the server. If you can connect from the same subnet but not from different subnets, a router-based firewall is blocking traffic. If you cannot connect from the same subnet, the server has a firewall running that is blocking traffic. Alternatively, the server application might not be running or might be configured to use a different port.

4. Log on to the server and use Telnet to attempt to connect to the server application port. If you can connect to the server from the server but not from other computers, the server definitely has firewall software configured. Add an exception for the application. If you cannot connect to the server application from the server, the application is not listening for connections or is configured to listen for incoming connections on a different port. Refer to the application documentation for information on how to start and configure the application. If the server is running Windows, you can use Netstat to identify on which ports the server is listening for incoming connections. For more information, read the section titled "Netstat" in the "Tools for Troubleshooting" section earlier in this chapter.

Sometimes, specific applications might require additional troubleshooting steps:

- For more information about troubleshooting sharing and collaboration, see Chapter 17, "Managing Sharing."

- For more information about troubleshooting Windows Meeting Space, see Chapter 18, "Managing Windows Meeting Space."

- For more information about troubleshooting printing, see Chapter 19, "Managing Printing."

- For more information about troubleshooting web and e-mail access, see Chapter 21, "Managing Internet Explorer."

How to Troubleshoot Name-Resolution Problems

Computers use numeric IP addresses (such as 192.168.10.233 or 2001:db8::1) to identify each other on networks. However, IP addresses are difficult for people to remember, so we use more friendly host names (such as *www.contoso.com*). *Name resolution* is the process of converting a host name to an IP address, and DNS is by far the most common name-resolution technique.

Many apparent connectivity problems are actually name-resolution problems. If any of these problems occur, the client will be unable to contact a server using its host name:

- DNS servers have failed.

- The network connecting the client to the DNS server has failed.

- A host name is missing from the DNS database.

- A host name is associated with an incorrect IP address. Often, this happens because a host has recently changed IP addresses, and the DNS database has not been updated.

- The client does not have DNS servers configured or is configured with the incorrect DNS server IP addresses.

To diagnose a name-resolution problem, follow these steps:

1. Open the Network And Sharing Center by clicking Start, clicking Network, and then clicking Network And Sharing Center. If a red X is displayed over a network link, click the link to start Windows Network Diagnostics and follow the prompts that appear. Windows Network Diagnostics can solve many common configuration problems. If Windows Network Diagnostics does not identify or resolve the problem, continue following these steps.

2. Verify that you can connect to other computers using IP addresses. If you cannot connect to servers by using their IP address, the source of your problems is network connectivity, rather than name resolution. See the section titled "How to Troubleshoot Network Connectivity Problems" earlier in this chapter. If you can connect to servers by using their IP address but not by using their host names, continue following these steps.

Note   When your network is working properly, look up the IP addresses of several different computers, including computers on your subnet, other subnets on your intranet, and computers on the public Internet. Test the IP addresses to verify that they respond to Ping requests. Keep this list available so that you can use the IP addresses to test for network connectivity without relying on name resolution.

3. Open a command prompt and use Nslookup to look up the host name you are attempting to contact, as the following example shows:

```
Nslookup www.microsoft.com
```

Examine the output:

❑ If Nslookup displays addresses or aliases for the host name, name resolution was successful. Most likely, the server you are trying to reach is offline, you have a connectivity problem preventing you from reaching the server, the application you are using is misconfigured, or the DNS server database is incorrect. See the sections titled "How to Troubleshoot Network Connectivity Problems" and "How to Troubleshoot Application Connectivity Problems" earlier in this chapter. If you believe the DNS server database is incorrect, contact your DNS server administrator.

❑ If Nslookup displays only "DNS request timed out," the DNS server is not responding. First, repeat the test several times to determine whether it is an intermittent problem. Then, use the Ipconfig command to verify that the client computer has the correct DNS servers configured. If necessary, update the client computer's DNS server configuration. If the DNS server IP addresses are correct, the DNS servers or the network they are connected to is offline. Contact the server or network administrator for additional assistance.

❑ If Nslookup displays the message "Default servers are not available," the computer does not have a DNS server configured. Update the client network configuration with DNS server IP addresses or configure the computer to acquire an address automatically.

4. If you can connect to the server from a different client computer, run **ipconfig /all** from a command prompt to determine which DNS servers the client computer is configured to use. If the IP addresses are different, consider changing the problematic client computer to use those IP addresses.

How to Verify Connectivity to a DNS Server

Although DNS traffic can use either TCP port 53 or UDP port 53, UDP is almost always used because it is more efficient for short communications. Because Telnet always uses TCP, it is not useful for testing UDP DNS connectivity. Instead, you can install and use the PortQry tool, as described earlier in this chapter.

To test for connectivity to DNS traffic, install PortQry, and then run the following command:

```
portqry -n DNS_server_name_or_IP_address -p UDP -e 53
```

If PortQry can connect to the specified DNS server, it will respond with "LISTENING." If PortQry cannot connect, it will respond with "LISTENING OR FILTERED." After displaying "LISTENING OR FILTERED," PortQry will attempt to issue a DNS request to the remote computer and then display whether or not the server responded to the request.

If you prefer graphical tools, you can use the PortQueryUI tool to query for UDP port 53, as shown in Figure 32-8.

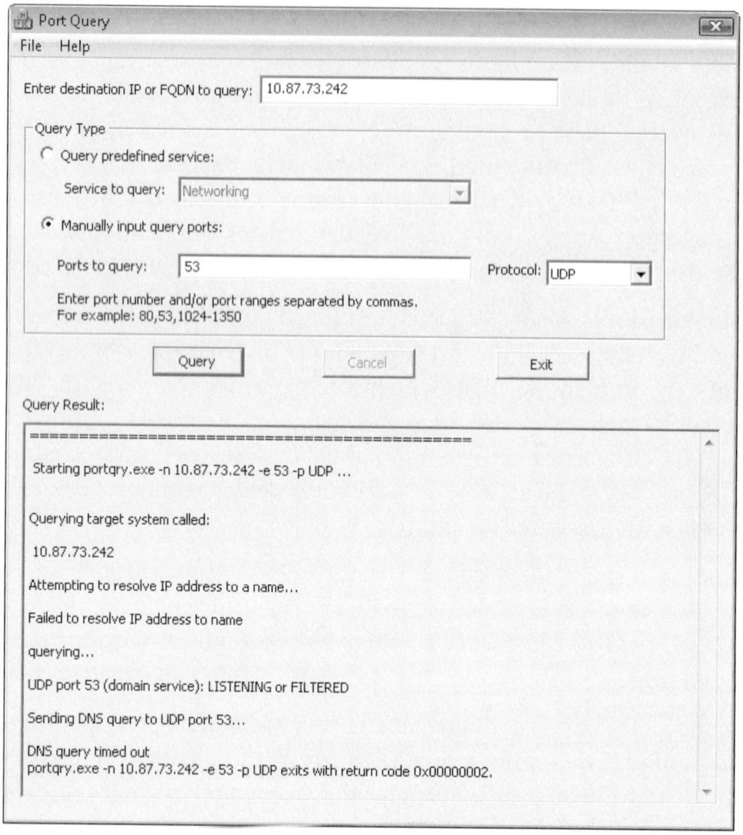

Figure 32-8   PortQryUI provides a graphical interface that you can use to test DNS connectivity.

How to Use the Hosts File

You can use the Hosts file as another name-resolution method. You might do this if you know that your DNS server is unavailable or the database is out of date, you need to access a server, and you know the server's IP address. It's also useful when you've recently installed a new server and you want to contact it using a host name before the DNS database is updated. Although you can typically contact servers using their IP addresses, websites often need to be reached using the correct host name, and IP addresses might not work.

Your Hosts file is located at %WinDir%\system32\drivers\etc\Hosts. It is a text file, and you can edit it using Notepad. To open the Hosts file, run Notepad using administrative permissions. Then, open the Notepad %WinDir%\system32\drivers\etc\hosts file (it does not have a file extension). To add an entry to the Hosts file to enable name resolution without using DNS, add lines to the bottom of the Hosts file, as demonstrated here for IPv4 and IPv6 addresses:

```
192.168.1.10 www.microsoft.com
10.15.33.25 www.contoso.com
2001:db8::1   www.microsoft.com
```

After updating the Hosts file, you can contact servers by using the host name. When an entry is in the Hosts file, Windows Vista will use the associated IP address without contacting a DNS server. In fact, the only application that bypasses the Hosts file is Nslookup, which always contacts DNS servers directly. Remember to remove entries from the Hosts file after you are done using them; otherwise, you might have name-resolution problems later if the server's IP address changes.

How to Troubleshoot Performance Problems and Intermittent Connectivity Issues

Often, network problems don't result in total loss of connectivity. Network problems can be file transfers that take longer than they should for your network bandwidth, jumpy streaming audio and video, or extremely unresponsive network applications.

To troubleshoot network performance problems, you must first identify the source of the problem. Several different components can cause performance problems:

- **The local computer**   Your local computer might have an application that is using all of the processor's time, thus slowing down everything on your computer, including networking. Alternatively, failing hardware or problematic drivers can cause performance problems or intermittent failures. To solve these problems, you can stop or reduce the impact of problematic applications, replace hardware, or upgrade drivers.

- **The network infrastructure**   Overutilized routers cause increased latency and dropped packets, both of which can cause performance problems and intermittent failures. Routing problems, such as routing loops, can cause traffic to be routed through an unnecessarily long path, increasing network latency. Sometimes, such as when you are using a satellite link, latency and the performance problems caused by latency are unavoidable. Although solving network infrastructure problems is outside the scope of this book, you can identify the source of the problem so that you can intelligently escalate the problem to the correct support team. For information about how Windows Vista adapts to provide the best possible performance over different types of links, see Chapter 26.

- **The server**   If the server is overutilized, all network communication to that server will suffer performance problems. Solving server performance problems is outside of the scope of this book. However, when you have identified the source of the problem, you can escalate it to the correct support team.

To identify the source of a network performance problem, follow these steps. After each step, test your network performance to determine whether or not the problem still exists.

1. Launch Task Manager by right-clicking the taskbar, clicking Task Manager, and then clicking the Performance tab. If processor utilization is near 100 percent, that might cause the perceived network performance problem. Click the Processes tab, find the process that is using the processor time, and close it.

2. In Task Manager, click the Networking tab. This tab shows a chart for each network adapter installed in the computer. If network utilization is near the practical capacity of the network link, that is the cause of your performance problem. For wired Ethernet networks (such as 10 Mbps, 100 Mbps, or 1000 Mbps links), utilization cannot typically exceed about 60 to 70 percent of the link speed. For wireless networks, utilization cannot exceed about 50 percent of the link speed. However, wireless utilization often peaks at much lower than 50 percent of the link speed, so even 15 or 20 percent utilization may indicate that your performance problems are caused by insufficient bandwidth on the wireless network. To identify the source of the bandwidth, click the Performance tab in Task Manager and then click the Resource Monitor button. In Resource Monitor, expand the Network section, as shown in Figure 32-9. Identify the process that is creating the most bandwidth, the process ID (PID), and the destination server. You can then return to Task Manager to identify the specific process creating the network bandwidth. Stop the process to determine if it is the cause of your performance problems.

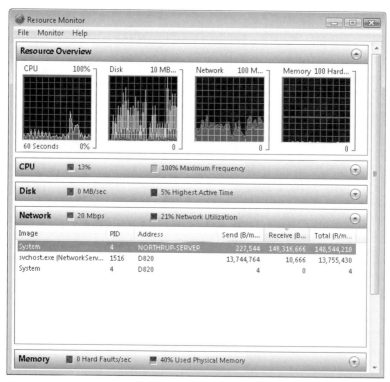

Figure 32-9   Use Resource Monitor to help identify the source of network bandwidth.

Note   The network utilization displayed in Task Manager and Resource Monitor only accounts for traffic sent to or from your computer. If another computer on your network is using bandwidth, that bandwidth won't be available to you—but neither Task Manager nor Resource Monitor can show you bandwidth used by other hosts.

3. If possible, use the same application to connect to a different server. If the performance problem occurs when connecting to different servers, the problem is probably local host– or network-related. The following steps will help you further isolate the problem. If the problem occurs only when connecting to a single server, the problem might be related to the server's performance or performance problems with the network the server is attached to. Contact the server administrator for assistance.

4. If possible, run the same application from a different computer on the same network. If both computers experience the same problem, the problem is probably related to network performance. The following steps will help you further isolate that problem. If other computers on the same network do not experience the same problem, it is probably related to your local computer. First, apply any updates and restart the computer. Then, install any network adapter driver updates. If problems persist, replace network cables and replace the network adapter. For more information, see Chapter 31.

At this point in the troubleshooting process, you have identified the network infrastructure as the most likely source of your problem. Open a command prompt and then run the PathPing tool, using your server's host name. PathPing will identify the route between your computer and the server and then spend several minutes calculating the latency of each router and network link in the path.

Ideally, each network link will add only a few milliseconds of latency (displayed in the RTT column) onto the time measured for the prior link. If latency increases more than 100 milliseconds for a single link and stays at that level for following links, that link may be the cause of your performance problems. If the link is a satellite or intercontinental link, that latency is to be expected and probably cannot be improved.

If, however, the link is your Internet connection or another network that is part of your intranet, your performance problems may be caused by overutilized network infrastructure. For example, if several computers are backing up their disk content to a folder on the network, a link can become overutilized, which can cause performance problems. Similarly, if several users are transferring large files across your Internet connection, other applications (especially real-time video or audio streaming, such as Voice over IP [VoIP]), may suffer. Contact network support for assistance. You might also be able to use Quality of Service (QoS) to prioritize time-sensitive traffic over file transfers. For more information about QoS, see Chapter 26.

Note If you are an administrator on a small or home network, you can quickly determine if other computers on the network are causing Internet performance problems by connecting your computer directly to your Internet connection and disconnecting all other computers. If the problems disappear, another computer on your network is causing the problem.

If the same gateway appears multiple times in the PathPing route, the network is experiencing a routing loop. Routing loops can cause performance problems or cause communications to fail entirely. Networks that use routing protocols typically fix routing loops automatically; however, you should contact your network support team to make sure they are aware of the problem. The following PathPing output demonstrates a routing loop, because nodes 5, 6, and 7 repeat:

```
C:\>pathping www.contoso.com
```

```
Tracing route to www.contoso.com [10.73.186.238]
over a maximum of 30 hops:
  0  d820.hsd1.nh.contoso.com. [192.168.1.196]
  1  192.168.1.1
  2  c-3-0-ubr01.winchendon.ma.boston.contoso.com [10.165.8.1]
  3  ge-3-37-ur01.winchendon.ma.boston.contoso.com [10.87.148.129]
  4  ge-1-1-ur01.gardner.ma.boston.contoso.com [10.87.144.225]
  5  10g-9-1-ur01.sterling.ma.boston.contoso.com [10.87.144.217]
  6  te-9-2-ur01.marlboro.ma.boston.contoso.com [10.87.144.77]
  7  10g-8-1-ur01.natick.ma.boston.contoso.com [10.87.144.197]
  8  10g-9-1-ur01.sterling.ma.boston.contoso.com [10.87.144.217]
  9  te-9-2-ur01.marlboro.ma.boston.contoso.com [10.87.144.77]
 10  10g-8-1-ur01.natick.ma.boston.contoso.com [10.87.144.197]
 11  10g-9-1-ur01.sterling.ma.boston.contoso.com [10.87.144.217]
 12  te-9-2-ur01.marlboro.ma.boston.contoso.com [10.87.144.77]
 13  10g-8-1-ur01.natick.ma.boston.contoso.com [10.87.144.197]
```

How to Troubleshoot Joining or Logging on to a Domain

Administrators often encounter problems when joining a Windows Vista computer to an Active Directory domain. Additionally, users might receive error messages about domain controllers being unavailable when trying to log on to their computer with a domain account.

The first step in troubleshooting domain join problems is to click the Details button in the Computer Name/Domain Changes dialog box to view the error information. For example, the error shown in Figure 32-10 indicates that the DNS server does not have a DNS entry for the domain controller. If you want to view this error information after closing the Computer Name/Domain Changes dialog box, open the %WinDir%\debug\dcdiag.txt log file.

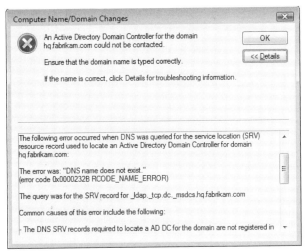

Figure 32-10   In most cases, Windows Vista will reveal the source of the problem in the detailed error message.

How to Analyze the NetSetup.Log file

If the Computer Name/Domain Changes dialog box does not reveal the source of the problem, view the %WinDir%\debug\netsetup.log file. This log details the process of joining a domain, as well as the details of any problems encountered. For best results, compare a log file generated on a computer that successfully joined your domain to a computer that failed to join the domain. For example, the following entry indicates that the computer successfully located the hq.contoso.com domain controller (note the return value of 0x0):

```
----------------------------------------------------------------
NetpValidateName: checking to see if 'HQ.CONTOSO.COM' is valid as type 3 name
NetpCheckDomainNameIsValid [ Exists ] for 'HQ.CONTOSO.COM' returned 0x0
NetpValidateName: name 'HQ.CONTOSO.COM' is valid for type 3
----------------------------------------------------------------
```

And the following entry indicates that the computer failed to locate the hq.fabrikam.com domain controller (note the return value of 0x54b):

```
----------------------------------------------------------------
NetpValidateName: checking to see if 'hq.fabrikam.com' is valid as type 3 name
NetpCheckDomainNameIsValid for hq.fabrikam.com returned 0x54b, last error is 0x3e5
NetpCheckDomainNameIsValid [ Exists ] for 'hq.fabrikam.com' returned 0x54b
----------------------------------------------------------------
```

If you see this type of name resolution failure during an unattended setup but you are able to manually join a domain, verify that clients are receiving a valid DHCP configuration. Specifically, verify that the DNS server addresses are correct and that the identified DNS servers contain SRV resource records for your domain controllers in the format _ldap._tcp.dc._msdcs.*DNSDomainName*.

If you see an error resembling the following, it indicates that the computer was previously joined to a domain using the same computer name but a different account. This might fail, because the administrative user account does not have permission to modify the existing account. To work around the problem, change the computer name, have the computer account deleted from the domain, or use the original user account to join the computer to the domain.

```
NetpManageMachineAccountWithSid: NetUserAdd on '\\hq.contoso.com' for
'43L2251A2-55$' failed: 0x8b0
04/06 06:36:20 SamOpenUser on 3386585 failed with 0xc0000022
```

If you see an error resembling the following, it indicates that the client could not establish a Server Message Block (SMB) session to the domain controller to manage the client computer account. One possible cause of this issue is missing Windows Internet Naming Service (WINS) registrations for a domain controller.

```
NetUseAdd to \\ntdev-dc-02.ntdev.corp.microsoft.com\IPC$ returned 53
```

To reproduce this problem (and test whether or not you have fixed it), open a command prompt and run the following command:

```
net use \\<server from above>\ipc$ /u:<account used for join> <password>
```

To determine if the edition of Windows Vista supports joining a domain, search for the keyword *NetpDomainJoinLicensingCheck* (most recent entries are at the bottom of the log file). If the *ulLicenseValue* is anything other than 1, it indicates that the edition of Windows cannot join a domain. To join a domain, a computer must be running Windows Vista Business, Windows Vista Enterprise, or Windows Vista Ultimate. The following shows a log file entry for a computer running a supported version of Windows (as indicated by *ulLicenseValue=1*):

```
NetpDomainJoinLicensingCheck: ulLicenseValue=1, Status: 0x0
```

How to Verify Requirements for Joining a Domain

To join or log on to a domain successfully, you must meet several different requirements. When troubleshooting a problem joining a domain, verify each of these requirements:

- **The client computer must be able to resolve the IP address for a domain controller**   In most enterprise networks, client computers receive an IP address assignment from a DHCP server, and the DHCP server provides addresses for Active Directory–enabled DNS servers that can resolve the domain controller IP address. If another DNS server is configured, you should update the client computer's IP configuration to use an Active Directory–enabled DNS server. If this is not possible, you can add two records to your existing DNS server that resolve to a domain controller's IP address:
  - ❑ The _ldap._tcp.dc._msdcs.*DNSDomainName* SRV resource record, which identifies the name of the domain controller that hosts the Active Directory

domain. *DNSDomainName* is the DNS name of the Active Directory domain the computer is attempting to join.

❑ A corresponding address (A) resource record that identifies the IP address for the domain controller listed in the _ldap._tcp.dc._msdcs.*DNSDomainName* SRV resource record.

■ **The client computer must be able to exchange traffic with the domain controller on several different TCP and UDP ports**   These ports include:

❑ TCP port 135 for Remote Procedure Call (RPC) traffic

❑ TCP port 389 and UDP port 389 for LDAP traffic

❑ TCP port 636 for LDAP over Secure Sockets Layer (SSL) traffic

❑ TCP port 3268 for LDAP Global Catalog (GC) traffic

❑ TCP port 3269 for LDAP GC SSL traffic

❑ TCP port 53 and UDP port 53 for DNS traffic

❑ TCP port 88 and UDP port 88 for Kerberos traffic

❑ TCP port 445 for Server Message Block (SMB) (also known as Common Internet File System [CIFS]) traffic

Note   For information about determining if specific ports are available, see the section titled "How to Troubleshoot Application Connectivity Problems" earlier in this chapter. The easiest way to test for all of these ports at one time is to use Portqueryui.exe and the "Domains and Trusts" predefined service.

■ **The administrator must have privileges to add a computer to a domain**   Administrators who add a computer to a domain must have the Add Workstations To Domain user right.

■ **The computer must be running Windows Vista Business, Windows Vista Enterprise, or Windows Vista Ultimate**   Windows Vista Starter, Home, and Home Premium cannot join a domain.

How to Troubleshoot Network Discovery

With Network Discovery, users can browse shared network resources from the Network window. On private networks, this is convenient because users can connect to resources without knowing the names of other computers on the network. On public networks, however, Network Discovery is a security concern, because it will announce the presence of the computer on the public network, and users might use it to connect to a potentially malicious computer.

For these reasons, Network Discovery is enabled on private networks but disabled on public networks by default. When connected to an Active Directory domain, Network Discovery is controlled by Group Policy settings but is disabled by default. Therefore, if the Network window does not display shared resources on the local network, it is almost certainly because Network Discovery is disabled. To remedy this, follow these steps (all of which require administrator privileges and can increase your computer's exposure to security attacks):

1. Verify that the Function Discovery Provider Host service is running.

2. Verify that Windows Firewall has exceptions enabled for Network Discovery.

3. Change the type of network from public to private. Alternatively, you can manually enable Network Discovery by opening the Network And Sharing Center window and enabling network discovery.

For more information about Network Discovery, see Chapter 26.

How to Troubleshoot File and Printer Sharing

Several different factors can cause problems with connecting to shared files and printers (which use the same communications protocols):

- Windows Firewall or another software firewall is blocking traffic at the client or server.

- A network firewall between the client and server is blocking traffic.

- The client is providing invalid credentials, and the server is rejecting the client's connection attempt.

- Name-resolution problems prevent the client from obtaining the server's IP address.

First, start troubleshooting from the client computer. If the server is a Windows Vista computer and you have administrator access to it, you can also troubleshoot from the server.

 Note   Installing Windows Vista Service Pack 1 expands the capabilities of Windows Network Diagnostics to also troubleshoot common file sharing problems.

How to Troubleshoot File and Printer Sharing from the Client Computer

Follow these steps to troubleshoot problems connecting to shared files and printers:

1. If you can connect to the shared folder but receive an Access Is Denied message when attempting to open the folder, your user account has permission to access the share, but lacks NTFS permissions for the folder. Contact the server administrator to grant the necessary NTFS file permissions. If the server is a Windows Vista computer, see the

section titled "How to Troubleshoot File and Printer Sharing from the Server Computer" later in this chapter.

2. Verify that you can resolve the server's name correctly. At a command prompt, type **ping** *hostname*. If Ping displays an IP address, as shown here, you can resolve the server's name correctly. It does not matter whether the server replies to the pings or not. If this step fails, it indicates a name-resolution problem. Contact your Active Directory or DNS administrator.

```
ping server
```

```
 Pinging server [10.1.42.22] with 32 bytes of data:
```

3. Attempt to connect using the server's IP address, as identified in the previous step, rather than the server's host name. For example, instead of connecting to *server*\printer, you might connect to \\10.1.42.22\printer.

4. From a command prompt, attempt to establish a connection to a server using the net use *ip_address* command. If it succeeds, you have sufficient network connectivity, but your user account lacks privileges to connect to the folder or printer share. Have the server administrator grant your account the necessary share permissions. Share permissions are separate from NTFS file permissions.

5. Use Telnet or PortQry to test whether or not your computer can connect to TCP port 445 of the remote computer. If you cannot connect using TCP port 445, test TCP port 139. For instructions on how to test for connectivity using a specific port, see the section titled "How to Troubleshoot Application Connectivity Problems" earlier in this chapter. If you cannot connect using either TCP port 139 or TCP port 445, verify that File And Printer Sharing is enabled on the server. Then, verify that the server has a firewall exception for TCP ports 139 and 445, or an exception in Windows Firewall is enabled for File And Printer Sharing. For more information about configuring Windows Firewall, see Chapter 27, "Configuring Windows Firewall and IPsec."

6. Attempt to connect to the server using an account with administrative credentials on the server. If you can connect with a different account, your normal account lacks sufficient credentials. Have the server administrator grant your account the necessary privileges. Depending on the server configuration, you might be able to identify authentication problems by viewing the Security Event Log. However, logon failure auditing must be enabled on the server for the events to be available.

If you are still unable to connect, continue troubleshooting from the server. If you do not have access to the server, contact the server administrator for assistance.

How to Troubleshoot File and Printer Sharing from the Server Computer

To troubleshoot file and printer sharing from a Windows Vista computer that is sharing the folder or printer, follow these steps:

> **Note**   These steps assume that the computer is a member of an Active Directory domain. Troubleshooting steps for standalone computers differ.

1. Verify that the folder or printer is shared. Right-click the object and then click Sharing. If it does not indicate that the object is already shared, share the object and then attempt to connect from the client.

2. If you are sharing a folder and it is not already shared, right-click the folder and click Share. In the File Sharing Wizard, click Change Sharing Permissions. If the File Sharing Wizard does not appear, the Server service is not running. Continue with the next step. Otherwise, verify that the user account attempting to connect to the share appears on the list, or that the user account is a member of a group that appears on the list. If the account is not on the list, add it to the list. Click Share and then click Done.

3. Verify that the Server service is running. The Server service should be started and set to start automatically for file and printer sharing to work. For more information about configuring services, see Chapter 16, "Managing Devices and Services."

4. Verify that users have the necessary permission to access the resources. Right-click the object and then click Properties. In the Properties dialog box, click the Security tab. Verify that the user account attempting to connect to the share appears on the list, or that the user account is a member of a group that appears on the list. If the account is not on the list, add it to the list.

5. Check the Windows Firewall exceptions to verify that it is configured properly by following these steps:

   a. Click Start and then click Control Panel.

   b. Click Security and then click Windows Firewall.

   c. In the Windows Firewall dialog box, note the Network Location. Click Change Settings.

   d. In the Windows Firewall Settings dialog box, click the Exceptions tab. Verify that the File And Printer Sharing check box is selected.

   e. If the File And Printer Sharing exception is enabled, it applies only for the current network profile. For example, if Windows Firewall indicated your Network Location was Domain Network, you might not have the File And Printer Sharing exception enabled when connected to private or public networks. Additionally, Windows Firewall will, by default, allow file and printer sharing traffic from the local network only when connected to a private or public network. For more information about configuring Windows Firewall, see Chapter 27.

How to Troubleshoot Wireless Networks

Wireless networks are now very common. However, users often have problems connecting to wireless networks, because these networks are more complex than wired networks. To troubleshoot problems connecting to a wireless network, follow these steps. For information about configuring a wireless network connection, see Chapter 26.

> **Note** This section focuses only on configuring a Windows Vista wireless client; it does not discuss how to configure a wireless network infrastructure.

1. Verify that the wireless network adapter is installed and has an active driver. Click Start, right-click Network, and then click Properties. Click Manage Network Connections. If your wireless network connection does not appear as shown in Figure 32-11, your network adapter or driver is not installed. See Chapter 31 for more information.

Figure 32-11 Network Connections will display the adapter if your wireless network adapter and driver are properly installed.

2. If a wireless network adapter is installed, right-click it in Network Connections and then click Diagnose. Follow the prompts that appear. Windows Vista might be able to diagnose the problem.

Direct from the Source: Network Diagnostics

Network diagnostics is capable of diagnosing more than 180 different issues related to wireless networking. To get the most from network diagnostics for wireless networks, ensure that you are using Native Wi-Fi drivers instead of Legacy Wi-Fi drivers. To determine which type of driver(s) is installed on a system, run the following command at a command prompt:

```
netsh wlan show drivers
```

> In the resulting output, look for the line labeled "Type." It should be either Legacy Wi-Fi Driver or Native Wi-Fi Driver. If a legacy driver is installed, contact the manufacturer of the wireless network adapter to see if a Native Wi-Fi driver for the adapter is available.
>
> *Tim Rains, Program Manager*
>
> *Windows Networking*

3. Open Event Viewer and view the System Event Log. Filter events to view only those events with a Source of Diagnostics-Network. Examine recent events and analyze the information provided by the Network Diagnostics Framework for the possible source of the problem.

4. Verify that wireless networking is enabled on your computer. To save power, most portable computers have the ability to disable the wireless network radio. Often, this is controlled by a physical switch on the computer. Other times, you must press a special, computer-specific key combination (such as Fn+F2) to enable or disable the radio. If the wireless radio is disabled, the network adapter will appear in Network Connections but it will not be able to view any wireless networks.

5. If the wireless network adapter shows Not Connected, attempt to connect to a wireless network. Within Network Connections, right-click the Network Adapter and then click Connect. In the Connect To A Network dialog box, click a wireless network and then click Connect.

6. If the wireless network is security-enabled and you are prompted for the passcode but cannot connect (or the wireless adapter indefinitely shows a status of Identifying or Connected With Limited Access), verify that you typed the passcode correctly. Disconnect from the network and reconnect using the correct passcode.

7. If you are still unable to connect to a wireless network, perform a wireless network trace and examine the details of the report for a possible cause of the problem, as described in the section titled "Reliability and Performance" earlier in this chapter.

If the wireless network adapter shows the name of a wireless network (rather than Not Connected), you are currently connected to a wireless network. This does not, however, necessarily assign you an IP address configuration, grant you access to other computers on the network, or grant you access to the Internet. First, disable and re-enable the network adapter by right-clicking it, clicking Disable, right-clicking it again, and then clicking Enable. Then, reconnect to your wireless network. If problems persist, move the computer closer to the wireless access point to determine if the problem is related to signal strength. Wireless networks have limited range, and different computers can have different types of antenna and therefore different ranges. If the problem is not related to the wireless connection itself, read the section titled "How to Troubleshoot Network Connectivity Problems" earlier in this chapter.

How to Troubleshoot Firewall Problems

Many attacks are initiated across network connections. To reduce the impact of those attacks, Windows Firewall by default blocks unrequested, unapproved incoming traffic and unapproved outgoing traffic. Although Windows Firewall will not typically cause application problems, it has the potential to block legitimate traffic if not properly configured. When troubleshooting application connectivity issues, you will often need to examine and possibly modify the client or server's Windows Firewall configuration.

Misconfiguring Windows Firewall can cause several different types of connectivity problems. On a Windows Vista computer that is acting as the client, Windows Firewall might block outgoing communications for the application (though blocking outgoing communications is not enabled by default). On a Windows Vista computer that is acting as the server (for example, a computer that is sharing a folder), Windows Firewall misconfiguration might cause any of the following problems:

- Windows Firewall blocks all incoming traffic for the application.

- Windows Firewall allows incoming traffic for the local area network but blocks incoming traffic for other networks.

- Windows Firewall allows incoming traffic when connected to a Domain network but blocks incoming traffic when connected to a Public or Private network.

The symptoms of client- or server-side firewall misconfiguration are the same: application communication fails. To make troubleshooting more complex, network firewalls can cause the same symptoms. Answer the following questions to help identify the source of the problem:

1. Can you connect to the server from other clients on the same network? If the answer is yes, you have a server-side firewall configuration problem that is probably related to the configured scope of a firewall exception. See Chapter 27 for information about adjusting the scope of an exception. If adjusting the scope of the firewall exception does not solve the problem, it is probably caused by a network firewall, and you should contact your network administrators for further assistance.

2. Can you connect to the server when the client is connected to one type of network location (such as a home network or a domain network), but not when it is connected to a different type of network location? If the answer is yes, you have a client-side firewall configuration problem that is probably caused by having an exception configured for only one network location type. See Chapter 27 for information about how to add exceptions for different network location types.

3. Can other clients on the same network connect to the server using the same application? If the answer is yes, you have a client-side firewall configuration problem that is probably caused by having a rule that blocks outgoing traffic for the application. See Chapter 27 for information about how to adjust outgoing firewall rules.

4.   Can the client connect to other servers using the same application? If the answer is yes, you have a server-side firewall configuration problem, and the server needs a firewall exception added. See Chapter 27 for information about how to add a firewall exception. If adding an exception does not solve the problem, it is probably caused by a network firewall, and you should contact your network administrators for further assistance.

Summary

Windows Vista can automatically diagnose many common network problems. Other problems are more complicated and require you as an administrator to perform additional trouble-shooting to isolate the source of the problem. When you have isolated the source of the problem, you may be able to fix the problem yourself. If the problem is related to a failed network circuit or another factor outside of your control, isolating the problem allows you to escalate the issue to the correct support team and allow the support team to resolve the problem as quickly as possible.

Additional Resources

The following resources contain additional information and tools related to this chapter.

Related Information

- Chapter 16, "Managing Devices and Services," includes information about configuring services to start automatically.

- Chapter 17, "Managing Sharing," includes information about configuring and trouble-shooting sharing and collaboration.

- Chapter 18, "Managing Windows Meeting Space," includes information about configuring and troubleshooting Windows Meeting Space.

- Chapter 19, "Managing Printing," includes information about configuring and trouble-shooting shared printers.

- Chapter 21, "Managing Internet Explorer," includes information about configuring and troubleshooting Internet Explorer and Windows Mail.

- Chapter 26, "Configuring Windows Networking," includes information about configuring network settings.

- Chapter 27, "Configuring Windows Firewall and IPsec," includes information about configuring Windows Firewall.

- Chapter 28, "Connecting Remote Users and Networks," includes information about virtual private networks.

- Chapter 31, "Troubleshooting Hardware, Driver, and Disk Issues," includes information about troubleshooting hardware- and driver-related network adapter problems.

On the Companion CD

- PortQry
- PortQryUI
- DNSLint
- TTCP
- DetectNetworkAdapterConnection.vbs
- DetermineDCSiteInfo.vbs
- DisplayLocalTime.vbs
- DisplayNetworkConfiguration.vbs
- PingMachines.vbs
- A link to where you can download the latest version of the whitepaper "Network Diagnostics Technologies in Windows Vista"

Chapter 33
Troubleshooting Stop Messages

When Windows Vista detects an unexpected problem from which it cannot recover, a Stop error occurs. A Stop error serves to protect the integrity of the system by immediately stopping all processing. Although it is theoretically possible for Windows Vista to continue functioning when it detects that a core component has experienced a serious problem, the integrity of the system would be questionable, which could lead to security violations, system corruption, and invalid transaction processing.

When a Stop error occurs, Windows Vista displays a Stop message, sometimes referred to as a *blue screen*, which is a text-mode error message that reports information about the condition. A basic understanding of Stop errors and their underlying causes improves your ability to locate and understand technical information or perform diagnostic procedures requested of you by technical support personnel.

Note Windows Vista Service Pack 1 includes many updates that resolve problems that previously caused Stop errors. Therefore, ensure that Service Pack 1 is installed to help minimize the number of Stop errors in your organization.

Stop Message Overview

Stop errors occur only when a problem cannot be handled by using the higher-level error-handling mechanisms in Windows Vista. Normally, when an error occurs in an application, the application interprets the error message and provides detailed information to the system administrator. However, Stop errors are handled by the kernel, and Windows Vista is only able to display basic information about the error, write the contents of memory to the disk (if memory dumps are enabled), and halt the system. This basic information, known as a *Stop message*, is described in more detail in the section titled "Stop Messages" later in this chapter.

As a result of the minimal information provided in a Stop message, and the fact that the operating system stops all processing, Stop errors can be difficult to troubleshoot. Fortunately, they tend to occur very rarely. When they do occur, they are almost always caused by driver problems, hardware problems, or file inconsistencies.

Identifying the Stop Error

Many different types of Stop errors occur. Each has its own possible causes and requires a unique troubleshooting process. Therefore, the first step in troubleshooting a Stop error is to identify the Stop error. You need the following information about the Stop error to begin troubleshooting:

- **Stop error number**   This number uniquely identifies the Stop error.
- **Stop error parameters**   These parameters provide additional information about the Stop error. Their meaning is specific to the Stop error number.
- **Driver information**   When available, the driver information identifies the most likely source of the problem. Not all Stop errors are caused by drivers, however.

This information is often displayed as part of the Stop message. If possible, write it down to use as a reference during the troubleshooting process. If the operating system restarts before you can write down the information, you can often retrieve the information from the System Log in Event Viewer.

If you are unable to gather the Stop error number from the Stop message and the System Log, you can retrieve it from a memory dump file. By default, Windows Vista is configured to create a memory dump whenever a Stop error occurs. If no memory dump file was created, configure the system to create a memory dump file. Then, if the Stop error reoccurs, you will be able to extract the necessary information from the memory dump file.

Finding Troubleshooting Information

Each Stop error requires a different troubleshooting technique. Therefore, after you identify the Stop error and gather the associated information, use the following sources for troubleshooting information specific to that Stop error:

- **"Common Stop Messages" later in this chapter**   The section in this chapter titled "Common Stop Messages" is intended as a reference for troubleshooting Stop errors; however, it does not include every possible Stop error. If the Stop error number you are troubleshooting is not listed in "Common Stop Messages," refer to the Debugging Tools For Windows Help.

- **Microsoft Debugging Tools For Windows Help**   Install Microsoft Debugging Tools For Windows and consult Help for that tool. This Help contains the definitive list of Stop messages, including many not covered in this chapter, and explains how to troubleshoot a wide variety of Stop errors. To install Debugging Tools For Windows, visit *http://www.microsoft.com/whdc/devtools/debugging/*.

- **Microsoft Knowledge Base**   The Microsoft Knowledge Base includes timely articles about a limited subset of Stop errors. Stop error information in the Microsoft Knowledge Base is often specific to a particular driver or hardware component and generally includes step-by-step instructions for resolving the problem.

- **Microsoft Help and Support**   For related information, see Microsoft Help and Support at *http://support.microsoft.com*.

- **Microsoft Product Support Services**   If you cannot isolate the cause of the Stop error, obtain assistance from trained Microsoft Product Support Services personnel. You might need to furnish specific information and perform certain procedures to help technical support investigate your problem. For more information about Microsoft product support, visit *http://www.microsoft.com/services/microsoftservices/ srv_enterprise.mspx*.

Stop Messages

Stop messages report information about Stop errors. The intention of the Stop message is to assist the system administrator in isolating and eventually resolving the problem that caused the Stop error. Stop messages provide a great deal of useful information to administrators who understand how to interpret the information in the Stop message. In addition to other information, the Stop message includes the Stop error number, or bugcheck code, that you can use to find or reference troubleshooting information about the specific Stop error in the section titled "Common Stop Messages" later in this chapter.

When examining a Stop message, you need to have a basic understanding of the problem so that you can plan a course of action. Always review the Stop message and record as much information about the problem as possible before searching through technical sources. Stop messages use a full-screen character mode format, as shown in Figure 33-1.

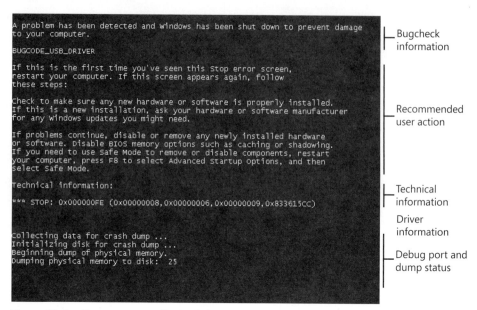

A problem has been detected and windows has been shut down to prevent damage
to your computer.

BUGCODE_USB_DRIVER

If this is the first time you've seen this stop error screen,
restart your computer. If this screen appears again, follow
these steps:

Check to make sure any new hardware or software is properly installed.
If this is a new installation, ask your hardware or software manufacturer
for any windows updates you might need.

If problems continue, disable or remove any newly installed hardware
or software. Disable BIOS memory options such as caching or shadowing.
If you need to use Safe Mode to remove or disable components, restart
your computer, press F8 to select Advanced Startup Options, and then
select Safe Mode.

Technical information:

*** STOP: 0x000000FE (0x00000008,0x00000006,0x00000009,0x833615CC)

Collecting data for crash dump ...
Initializing disk for crash dump ...
Beginning dump of physical memory.
Dumping physical memory to disk: 25

— Bugcheck information

— Recommended user action

— Technical information

Driver information

— Debug port and dump status

Figure 33-1   Stop messages display information to help you troubleshoot the Stop error.

As shown in Figure 33-1, a Stop message screen has several major sections, which display the following information:

- Bugcheck information
- Recommended user action
- Technical information
- Driver information (if available)
- Debug port and dump status information

Note   If the video display drivers have stopped functioning, the kernel might not be able to fully display the entire Stop message. In such a case, only the first line may be visible, or the screen may be black. Wait several minutes to allow the memory dump file to be created and then use standard troubleshooting techniques described in this chapter.

Bugcheck Information

The Bugcheck information section lists the Stop error descriptive name. Descriptive names are directly related to the Stop error number listed in the Technical information section.

Recommended User Action

The Recommended user action section informs the user that a problem has occurred and that Windows was shut down. It also provides the symbolic name of the Stop error. In Figure 33-1, the symbolic name is BUGCODE_USB_DRIVER. It also attempts to describe the problem and lists suggestions for recovery. In some cases, restarting the computer might be sufficient, because the problem is not likely to recur. But if the Stop error persists after you restart the operating system, you must determine the root cause to return the operating system to an operable state. This process might involve undoing recent changes, replacing hardware, or updating drivers to eliminate the source of the problem.

Technical Information

The Technical information section lists the Stop error number, also known as the bugcheck code, followed by up to four Stop error–specific codes (displayed as hexadecimal numbers enclosed in parentheses), which identify related parameters. Stop error codes contain a 0x prefix, which indicates that the number is in hexadecimal format. For example, in Figure 33-1, the Stop error hexadecimal code is 0x000000FE (often written as 0xFE).

Driver Information

The Driver information section identifies the driver associated with the Stop error. If a file is specified by name, you can use safe mode to verify that the driver is signed or has a date stamp that coincides with other drivers. If necessary, you can replace the file manually (in Startup Repair or in safe mode), or use Roll Back Driver to revert to a previous version. For more information about Startup Repair and safe mode, see Chapter 30, "Configuring Startup and Troubleshooting Startup Issues." For more information about troubleshooting drivers, see Chapter 31, "Troubleshooting Hardware, Driver, and Disk Issues." Figure 33-1 does not display a driver name.

Debug Port and Dump Status Information

The Debug port and dump status information section lists COM port parameters that a kernel debugger uses, if enabled. If you have enabled memory dump file saves, this section also indicates whether one was successfully written. As a dump file is being written to the disk, the percentage shown after *Dumping physical memory to disk* is incremented to 100. A value of 100 indicates that the memory dump was successfully saved.

For more information about installing and using kernel debuggers, see the section titled "Using Symbol Files and Debuggers" later in this chapter.

Types of Stop Errors

A hardware or software problem can cause a Stop error, which causes a Stop message to appear. Stop messages typically fit into one of the following categories:

- **Stop errors caused by faulty software**   A Stop error can occur when a driver, service, or system component running in Kernel mode introduces an exception. For example, a driver attempts to perform an operation above its assigned interrupt request level (IRQL) or tries to write to an invalid memory address. A Stop message might seem to appear randomly, but through careful observation, you might be able to associate the problem with a specific activity. Verify that all installed software (especially drivers) in question is fully Windows Vista–compatible and that you are running the latest versions. Windows Vista compatibility is especially important for applications that might install drivers.

- **Stop errors caused by hardware issues**   This problem occurs as an unplanned event resulting from defective, malfunctioning, or incorrectly configured hardware. If you suspect a Stop error is caused by hardware, first install the latest drivers for that hardware. Failing hardware can cause Stop errors regardless of the stability of the driver, however. For more information about how to troubleshoot hardware issues, read Chapter 31.

- **Executive initialization Stop errors**   Executive initialization Stop errors occur only during the relatively short Windows executive initialization sequence. Typically, these Stop errors are caused by corrupted system files or faulty hardware. To resolve them, run Startup Repair as described in Chapter 30. If problems persist, verify that all hardware components have the latest firmware and then continue troubleshooting as described in Chapter 31.

- **Installation Stop errors that occur during setup**   For new installations, installation Stop errors typically occur because of incompatible hardware, defective hardware, or outdated firmware. During an operating system upgrade, Stop errors can occur when incompatible applications and drivers exist on the system. Update the computer's firmware to the version recommended by the computer manufacturer before installing Windows Vista. Consult your system documentation for information about checking and upgrading your computer's firmware.

Memory Dump Files

When a Stop error occurs, Windows Vista displays information that can help you analyze the root cause of the problem. Windows Vista writes the information to the paging file (Pagefile.sys) on the %SystemDrive% root by default. When you restart the computer in normal or safe mode after a Stop error occurs, Windows Vista uses the paging file information to create a memory dump file in the %SystemRoot% folder. Analyzing dump files can provide more information about the root cause of a problem and lets you perform offline analysis by running analysis tools on another computer.

You can configure your system to generate three types of dump file:

- **Small memory dump files**   Sometimes referred to as "minidump" files, these dump files contain the least amount of information but are very small in size. Small memory dump files can be written to disk quickly, which minimizes downtime by allowing the operating system to restart sooner. Windows Vista stores small memory dump files (unlike kernel and complete memory dump files) in the %SystemRoot%\Minidump folder, instead of using the %SystemRoot%\Memory.dmp filename.

- **Kernel memory dump files**   These dump files record the contents of kernel memory. Kernel memory dump files require a larger paging file on the boot device than small memory dump files and take longer to create when a failure has occurred. However, they record significantly more information and are more useful when you need to perform in-depth analysis. When you choose to create a kernel memory dump file, Windows Vista also creates a small memory dump file.

■ **Complete memory dump files**   These dump files record the entire contents of physical memory when the Stop error occurred. A complete memory dump file's size will be slightly larger than the amount of physical memory installed at the time of the error. When you choose to create a complete memory dump file, Windows Vista also creates a small memory dump file.

By default, Windows Vista is configured to create kernel memory dump files. By default, small memory dump files are saved in the %SystemRoot%\Minidump folder, and kernel and complete memory dump files are saved to a file named %SystemRoot%\Memory.dmp. To change the type of dump file Windows Vista creates or to change their location, follow these steps:

1. Click Start, right-click Computer, and then click Properties.

2. Click Advanced System Settings.

3. In the System Properties dialog box, click the Advanced tab. Under Startup And Recovery, click Settings.

4. Use the drop-down Write Debugging Information list and then select the debugging type.

5. If desired, change the path shown in the Dump File box. Figure 33-2 shows the Startup And Recovery dialog box.

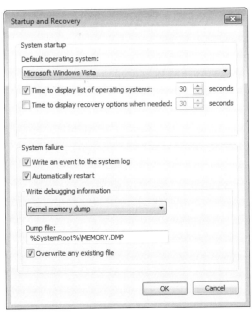

Figure 33-2   Use the Startup And Recovery dialog box to change dump types and locations.

6. Click OK twice and then restart the operating system if prompted.

The sections that follow describe the different types of dump file in more detail.

Configuring Small Memory Dump Files

Small memory dump files contain the least amount of information, but they also consume the least amount of disk space. By default, Windows Vista stores small memory dump files in the %SystemRoot%\Minidump folder.

Windows Vista always creates a small memory dump file when a Stop error occurs, even when you choose the kernel dump file or complete memory dump file options. Small memory dump files can be used by both Problem Reports And Solutions and debuggers. These tools read the contents of a small memory dump file to help diagnose problems that cause Stop errors. For more information, see the sections titled "Using Problem Reports And Solutions" and "Using Memory Dump Files to Analyze Stop Errors" later in this chapter.

A small memory dump file records the smallest set of information that might identify the cause of the system stopping unexpectedly. For example, the small memory dump includes the following information:

- **Stop error information**   Includes the error number and additional parameters that describe the Stop error.

- **A list of drivers running on the system**   Identifies the modules in memory when the Stop error occurred. This device driver information includes the filename, date, version, size, and manufacturer.

- **Processor context information for the process that stopped**   Includes the processor and hardware state, performance counters, multiprocessor packet information, deferred procedure call information, and interrupts.

- **Kernel context information for the process that stopped**   Includes offset of the directory table and the page frame number database, which describes the state of every physical page in memory.

- **Kernel context information for the thread that stopped**   Identifies registers and interrupt request levels and includes pointers to operating system data structures.

- **Kernel-mode call stack information for the thread that stopped**   Consists of a series of memory locations and includes a pointer to the initial location. Developers might be able to use this information to track the source of the error. If this information is greater than 16 kilobytes (KB), only the topmost 16 KB is included.

A small memory dump file requires a paging file of at least 2 megabytes (MB) on the boot volume. The operating system saves each dump file with a unique filename every time a Stop error occurs. The filename includes the date the Stop error occurred. For example, Mini011007-02.dmp is the second small memory dump generated on January 10, 2007.

Small memory dump files are useful when space is limited or when you are using a slow connection to send information to technical support personnel. Because of the limited amount of information that can be included, these dump files do not include errors that were not directly caused by the thread that was running when the problem occurred.

Configuring Kernel Memory Dump Files

By default, Windows Vista systems create kernel memory dump files. The kernel memory dump file is an intermediate-size dump file that records only kernel memory and can occupy several MB of disk space. A kernel memory dump takes longer to create than a small dump file, and thus increases the downtime associated with a system failure. On most systems, the increase in downtime is minimal.

Kernel memory dumps contain additional information that might assist troubleshooting. When a Stop error occurs, Windows Vista saves a kernel memory dump file to a file named %SystemRoot%\Memory.dmp and creates a small memory dump file in the %SystemRoot%\Minidump folder.

A kernel memory dump file records only kernel memory information, which expedites the dump file creation process. The kernel memory dump file does not include unallocated memory or any memory allocated to user-mode programs. It includes only memory allocated to the Executive, kernel, hardware abstraction layer (HAL), and file system cache, in addition to nonpaged pool memory allocated to kernel-mode drivers and other kernel-mode routines.

The size of the kernel memory dump file will vary, but it is always less than the size of the system memory. When Windows Vista creates the dump file, it first writes the information to the paging file. Therefore, the paging file might grow to the size of the physical memory. Later, the dump file information is extracted from the paging file to the actual memory dump file. To ensure that you have sufficient free space, verify that the system drive would have free space greater than the size of physical memory if the paging file were extended to the size of physical memory. Although you cannot exactly predict the size of a kernel memory dump file, a good rule of thumb is that roughly 50 MB to 800 MB, or one-third the size of physical memory, must be available on the boot volume for the paging file.

For most purposes, a kernel memory dump file is sufficient for troubleshooting Stop errors. It contains more information than a small memory dump file and is smaller than a complete memory dump file. It omits those portions of memory that are unlikely to have been involved in the problem. However, some problems do require a complete memory dump file for troubleshooting.

Note   By default, a new kernel memory dump file overwrites an existing one. To change the default setting, clear the Overwrite Any Existing File check box. You can also rename or move an existing dump file prior to troubleshooting.

Configuring Complete Memory Dump Files

A complete memory dump file, sometimes referred to as a "full" dump file, contains everything that was in physical memory when the Stop error occurred. This includes all of the information included in a kernel memory dump file, plus user-mode memory. Therefore, you can examine complete memory dump files to find the contents of memory contained within applications, although this is rarely necessary or feasible when troubleshooting application problems.

If you choose to use complete memory dump files, you must have available space on the *systemdrive* partition large enough to hold the contents of the physical RAM. Additionally, you must have a paging file equal to the size of your physical RAM.

When a Stop error occurs, the operating system saves a complete memory dump file to a file named %SystemRoot%\Memory.dmp and creates a small memory dump file in the %SystemRoot%\Minidump folder. A Microsoft technical support engineer might ask you to change this setting to facilitate data uploads over slow connections. Depending on the speed of your Internet connection, uploading the data might not be practical, and you might be asked to provide the memory dump file on removable media.

 Note   By default, new complete memory dump files overwrite existing files. To change this, clear the Overwrite Any Existing File check box. You can also choose to archive or move a dump file prior to troubleshooting.

How to Manually Initiate a Stop Error and Create a Dump File

To be absolutely certain that a dump file will be created when a Stop error occurs, you can manually initiate a Stop error by creating a registry value and pressing a special sequence of characters. After Windows Vista restarts, you can verify that the dump file was correctly created.

To initiate a crash dump manually, follow these steps:

1. Click Start and type **Regedit**. On the Start menu, right-click Regedit and click Run As Administrator. Respond to the UAC prompt that appears.

2. In the registry editor, navigate to HKEY_LOCAL_MACHINE\SYSTEM\Current-ControlSet\Services\i8042prt\Parameters.

3. On the Edit menu, click New | DWORD (32-bit) Value and then add the following registry value:

   ❑ Value Name: CrashOnCtrlScroll

   ❑ Value: 1

4. Close the registry editor and then restart the computer.

5. Log on to Windows Vista. While holding down the right Ctrl key, press the Scroll Lock key twice to initiate a Stop error.

You cannot manually initiate a Stop error on a virtual machine that has virtual machine extensions installed.

Using Memory Dump Files to Analyze Stop Errors

Memory dump files record detailed information about the state of your operating system when the Stop error occurred. You can analyze memory dump files manually by using debugging tools or by using automated processes provided by Microsoft. The information you obtain can help you understand more about the root cause of the problem.

You can use Problem Reports And Solutions to upload your memory dump file information to Microsoft. You can also use the following debugging tools to analyze your memory dump files manually:

■ Microsoft Kernel Debugger (Kd.exe)

■ Microsoft WinDbg Debugger (WinDbg.exe)

You can view information about the Stop error in the System Log after a Stop error occurs. For example, the following information event (with a source of Bugcheck and an Event ID of 1001) indicates a 0xFE Stop error occurred:

```
The computer has rebooted from a bugcheck.  The bugcheck was: 0x000000fe (0x00000008,
0x00000006, 0x00000001, 0x87b1e000). A dump was saved in: C:\windows\MEMORY.DMP.
```

Using Problem Reports And Solutions

When enabled, the Windows Error Reporting Service monitors your operating system for faults related to operating system components and applications. By using the Windows Error Reporting Service, you can obtain more information about the problem or condition that caused the Stop error.

When a Stop error occurs, Windows Vista displays a Stop message and writes diagnostic information to the memory dump file. For reporting purposes, the operating system also saves a small memory dump file. The next time you start your system and log on to Windows Vista as an Administrator, Problem Reports And Solutions gathers information about the problem and performs the following actions:

1. Windows Vista displays the Windows Has Recovered From An Unexpected Shutdown dialog box, as shown in Figure 33-3. To view the Stop error code, operating system information, and dump file locations, click View Problem Details. Click Check For Solution to submit the minidump file information and possibly several other temporary files to Microsoft.

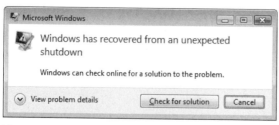

Figure 33-3   Windows Vista prompts you to check for a solution after recovering from a Stop error.

2. You might be prompted to collect additional information for future errors. If prompted, click Enable Collection, as shown in Figure 33-4.

Figure 33-4   Windows Vista might prompt you to collect additional information for future error reports.

3. You might also be prompted to enable diagnostics. If prompted, click Turn On Diagnostics, as shown in Figure 33-5.

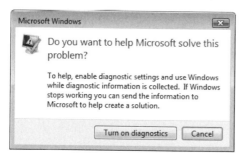

Figure 33-5   Windows Vista might prompt you to enable diagnostics to gather more trouble-shooting information.

4. If prompted to send additional details, click View Details to review the additional information being sent. Then, click Send Information.

5. If prompted to automatically send more information about future problems, choose Yes or No.

6. When a possible solution is available, Problems Reports And Solutions displays an icon in the system tray with a notification message, as shown in Figure 33-6.

Figure 33-6 Problem Reports And Solutions can automatically notify you when a solution is available.

7. Click the icon in the system tray to view the solution. Alternatively, you can manually open Problem Reports And Solutions by clicking Start, pointing to All Programs, pointing to Maintenance, and then clicking Problem Reports And Solutions. When you have reviewed the solution, as shown in Figure 33-7, click OK.

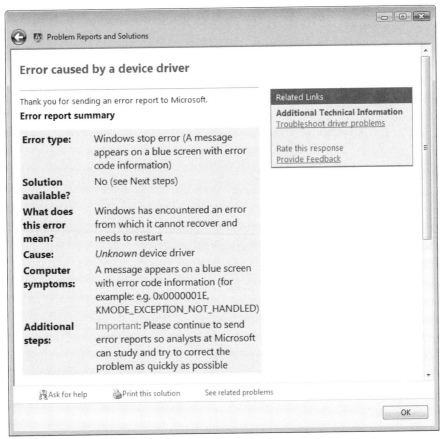

Figure 33-7 Problem Reports And Solutions provides a summary of a Stop error.

If Problem Reports And Solutions does not identify the source of an error, you might be able to determine that a specific driver caused the error by using a debugger, as described in the next section.

Using Symbol Files and Debuggers

You can also analyze memory dump files by using a kernel debugger. Kernel debuggers are primarily intended to be used by developers for in-depth analysis of application behavior. However, kernel debuggers are also useful tools for administrators troubleshooting Stop errors. In particular, kernel debuggers can be used to analyze memory dump files after a Stop error has occurred.

A debugger is a program that users with the Debug Programs user right (by default, only the Administrators group) can use to step through software instructions, examine data, and check for certain conditions. The following two examples of kernel debuggers are installed by installing Debugging Tools For Windows.

- **Kernel Debugger** Kernel Debugger (Kd.exe) is a command-line debugging tool that you can use to analyze a memory dump file written to disk when a Stop message occurs. Kernel Debugger requires that you install symbol files on your system.

- **WinDbg Debugger** WinDbg Debugger (WinDbg.exe) provides functionality similar to Kernel Debugger, but it uses a GUI interface.

Both tools allow users with the Debug Programs user right to analyze the contents of a memory dump file and debug kernel-mode and user-mode programs and drivers. Kernel Debugger and WinDbg Debugger are just a few of the many tools included in the Debugging Tools For Windows installation. For more information about these and other debugging tools included with Debugging Tools For Windows, see Help in Debugging Tools For Windows.

To use WinDbg to analyze a crash dump, first install the debugging tools available at *http://www.microsoft.com/whdc/devtools/debugging/default.mspx*.

To gather the most information from a memory dump file, provide the debugger access to symbol files. The debugger uses symbol files to match memory addresses to human-friendly module and function names. The simplest way to provide the debugger access to symbol files is to configure the debugger to access the Microsoft Internet-connected symbol server.

To configure the debugger to use the Microsoft symbol server, follow these steps:

1. Click Start, point to All Programs, point to Debugging Tools For Windows, right-click WinDbg, and then click Run As Administrator.

2. On the File menu, click Symbol File Path.

3. In the Symbol path box, type

   SRV*localpath***http://msdl.microsoft.com/download/symbols**

where *localpath* is a path on the hard disk that the debugger will use to store the downloaded symbol files. The debugger will automatically create *localpath* when you analyze a dump file.

For example, to store the symbol files in C:\Websymbols, set the symbol file path to "SRV*c:\websymbols*http://msdl.microsoft.com/download/symbols."

4. Click OK.

Debuggers do not require access to symbol files to extract the Stop error number and parameters from a memory dump file. Often, the debugger can also identify the source of the Stop error without access to symbols.

Note   You can also download symbol files for offline use from *http://www.microsoft.com/ whdc/devtools/debugging/ default.mspx.*

To analyze a memory dump file, follow these steps:

1. Click Start, point to All Programs, point to Debugging Tools For Windows, right-click WinDbg, and then click Run As Administrator.

2. On the File menu, click Open Crash Dump.

3. Type the location of the memory dump file and then click Open. By default, this location is %SystemRoot%\memory.dmp.

4. In the Save Workspace Information dialog box, click No.

5. Select the Command window.

   As shown in Figure 33-8, the Bugcheck line tells you the Stop error number. The Probably Caused By line indicates the file that was being processed at the time of the Stop error.

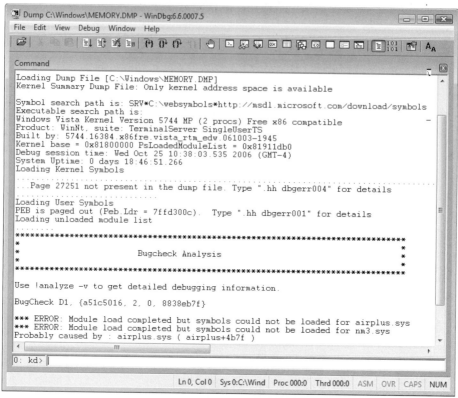

Figure 33-8 WinDbg displays the Stop error code and the driver that caused the Stop error.

The Command window displays feedback from the debugger and allows you to issue additional commands. When a crash dump is opened, the Command window automatically displays the output of the !analyze command. In many cases, this default information is sufficient to isolate the cause of the Stop error.

If the default analysis does not provide all the information you need for troubleshooting, run the following command in the Command window:

```
!analyze -v
```

This command will display the *stack*, which contains a list of method calls preceding the Stop error. This might give clues to the source of a Stop error. For example, the following stack trace output, created by calling !analyze –v, correctly indicates that the Stop error was related to the removal of a USB device:

```
STACK_TEXT:
WARNING: Frame IP not in any known module. Following frames may be wrong.
ba4ffb2c ba26c6ff 89467df0 68627375 70646f52 0x8924ed33
ba4ffb5c ba273661 88ffade8 8924eae0 89394e48 usbhub!USBH_PdoRemoveDevice+0x41
ba4ffb7c ba26c952 88ffaea0 89394e48 00000002 usbhub!USBH_PdoPnP+0x5b
ba4ffba0 ba26a1d8 01ffaea0 89394e48 ba4ffbd4 usbhub!USBH_PdoDispatch+0x5a
```

```
ba4ffbb0 804eef95 88ffade8 89394e48 88eac2e0 usbhub!USBH_HubDispatch+0x48
ba4ffbc0 ba3f2db4 88eac228 88eac2e0 00000000 nt!IopfCallDriver+0x31
ba4ffbd4 ba3f4980 88eac228 89394e48 89394e48 USBSTOR!USBSTOR_FdoRemoveDevice+0xac
ba4ffbec b9eed58c 88eac228 89394e48 89394f48 USBSTOR!USBSTOR_Pnp+0x4e
```

Being Prepared for Stop Errors

Some useful software- and hardware-related techniques can help you prepare for Stop errors when they occur. Stop messages do not always pinpoint the root of the problem, but they do provide important clues that you or a trained support technician can use to identify and troubleshoot the cause.

Prevent System Restarts After a Stop Error

When a Stop error occurs, Windows Vista displays a Stop message related to the problem, followed by one of these events:

- Windows Vista becomes unresponsive.

- Windows Vista automatically restarts.

By default, Windows Vista automatically restarts after a Stop error occurs, unless the system becomes unresponsive. If Windows Vista restarts your system immediately after a Stop error occurs, you might not have enough time to record Stop message information that can help you analyze the cause of a problem. Additionally, you might miss the opportunity to change startup options or start the operating system in safe mode.

Disabling the default restart behavior allows you to record Stop message text, information that can help you analyze the root cause of a problem if memory dump files are not accessible. To disable the Automatically Restart option, follow these steps:

1. Click Start, right-click Computer, and then click Properties.

2. Click Advanced System Settings.

3. In the System Properties dialog box, click the Advanced tab. Then, under Startup And Recovery, click Settings.

4. In the System Failure box, clear the Automatically Restart check box.

If you cannot start your computer in normal mode, you can perform the preceding steps in safe mode.

Record and Save Stop Message Information

With the automatic restart behavior disabled, you must restart your computer manually after a Stop message appears. Stop messages provide diagnostic information, such as Stop error numbers and driver names, which you can use to resolve the problem. However, this information disappears from the screen when you restart your computer. Generally, you can retrieve this information after the system is restarted by examining the memory dump file, as described in the section titled "Using Memory Dump Files to Analyze Stop Errors" earlier in this chapter. In some situations, Stop error information is not successfully logged, and therefore it is important to record the information displayed in the Stop message for future reference. Before restarting the system, take the following actions to ensure that you have saved important information, which you can reference when using the resources listed in this chapter.

To record and save Stop message information, follow these steps:

1. Record data that is displayed in the Technical information and Driver information sections of the Stop message for later reference. These sections are described in the section titled "Stop Messages" earlier in this chapter.

2. Record and evaluate suggestions in the Recommended User Action section. Stop messages typically provide troubleshooting tips relevant to the error.

3. Check the Debug Port and Dump File Status sections to verify that Windows Vista successfully created a memory dump file.

4. If a memory dump file does exist, copy the file to removable media, another disk volume, or a network location for safekeeping. You can use Startup Repair to copy the dump file if you are not able to start Windows Vista in normal mode or safe mode.

Analyzing memory dump files can assist you with identifying root causes by providing you with detailed information about the system state when the Stop error occurred. By following the preceding steps, you can save important information that you can refer to when using the resources listed in the section titled "Stop Messages" earlier in this chapter. For more information about creating and analyzing memory dump files, see the section titled "Memory Dump Files" earlier in this chapter.

Check Software Disk Space Requirements

Verify that adequate free space exists on your disk volumes for virtual memory paging files and application data files. Insufficient free space might cause Stop errors and other symptoms, including disk corruption. To determine the amount allocated to paging files, see the section titled "Memory Dump Files" earlier in this chapter.

You can move, delete, or compress unused files manually or by using Disk Cleanup to increase free space on disk volumes.

To run Disk Cleanup, click Start, type **Cleanmgr**, and then press Enter. Follow the prompts to increase free disk space on your system drive. Note that Disk Cleanup provides you with the option to delete memory dump files. For more information about managing disks, see Chapter 15, "Managing Disks and File Systems."

Install a Kernel Debugger and Symbol Files

You can use a kernel debugger to gather more information about the problem. For more information about installing and using debugging tools, see the section titled "Using Memory Dump Files to Analyze Stop Errors" earlier in this chapter.

Common Stop Messages

The following Stop error descriptions can help you to troubleshoot problems that cause Stop errors. The "Stop Message Checklist" at the end of this chapter also provides suggestions useful for resolving all types of Stop errors. If errors persist after you have followed the recommendations given, request assistance from your hardware manufacturer or a Microsoft support engineer.

Stop 0xA or IRQL_NOT_LESS_OR_EQUAL

The Stop 0xA message indicates that a kernel-mode process or driver attempted to access a memory location to which it did not have permission, or at a kernel IRQL that was too high. A kernel-mode process can access only other processes that have an IRQL lower than or equal to its own. This Stop message is typically the result of faulty or incompatible hardware or software.

Interpreting the Message

This Stop message has four parameters:

1. Memory address that was improperly referenced

2. IRQL that was required to access the memory

3. Type of access (0x00 = read operation, 0x01 = write operation)

4. Address of the instruction that attempted to reference memory specified in parameter 1

If the last parameter is within the address range of a device driver used on your system, you can determine which device driver was running when the memory access occurred. You can typically determine the driver name by reading the line that begins with

```
**Address 0xZZZZZZZZ has base at <address>- <driver name>
```

If the third parameter is the same as the first parameter, a special condition exists in which a system worker routine–carried out by a worker thread to handle background tasks known as work items–returned at a higher IRQL. In that case, some of the four parameters take on new meanings:

1. Address of the worker routine

2. Kernel IRQL

3. Address of the worker routine

4. Address of the work item

Resolving the Problem

The following suggestions are specific to Stop 0xA errors. For additional troubleshooting suggestions that apply to all Stop errors, see "Stop Message Checklist" later in this chapter.

- To resolve an error caused by a faulty device driver, system service, or BIOS, follow these steps:

  1. Restart your computer.

  2. Press F8 at the character-based menu that displays the operating system choices.

  3. Select the Last Known Good Configuration option from the Windows Advanced Options menu. This option is most effective when only one driver or service is added at a time.

- To resolve an error caused by an incompatible device driver, system service, virus scanner, or backup tool, follow these steps:

  1. Check the System Log in Event Viewer for error messages that might identify the device or driver that caused the error.

  2. Try disabling memory caching of the BIOS.

  3. Run the hardware diagnostics supplied by the system manufacturer, especially the memory scanner. For details on these procedures, see the owner's manual for your computer.

  4. Make sure the latest Service Pack is installed.

  5. If your system has small computer system interface (SCSI) adapters, contact the adapter manufacturer to obtain updated Windows drivers. Try disabling sync negotiation in the SCSI BIOS, checking the cabling and the SCSI IDs of each device, and confirming proper termination.

  6. For integrated device electronics (IDE) devices, define the onboard IDE port as Primary only. Also, check each IDE device for the proper master/subordinate/ standalone setting. Try removing all IDE devices except for hard disks.

- If you encounter a Stop 0xA message while upgrading to Windows Vista, the problem might be due to an incompatible driver, system service, virus scanner, or backup. To avoid problems while upgrading, simplify your hardware configuration and remove all third-party device drivers and system services (including virus scanners) prior to running setup. After you have successfully installed Windows Vista, contact the hardware manufacturer to obtain compatible updates. For more information about simplifying your system for troubleshooting purposes, see Chapter 31.

- If the Stop error occurs when resuming from hibernation or suspend, read Microsoft Knowledge Base articles 941492 and 945577.

- If the Stop error occurs when starting a mobile computer that has the lid closed, refer to Microsoft Knowledge Base article 941507.

For more information about Stop 0xA messages, see the Microsoft Knowledge Base at *http://support.microsoft.com/*. Search using the keywords *vista*, *0x0000000A*, and *0xA*.

Stop 0x1E or KMODE_EXCEPTION_NOT_HANDLED

The Stop 0x1E message indicates that the Windows Vista kernel detected an illegal or unknown processor instruction. The problems that cause Stop 0x1E messages share similarities with those that generate Stop 0xA errors in that they can be due to invalid memory and access violations. This default Windows Vista error handler typically intercepts these problems if error-handling routines are not present in the code itself.

Interpreting the Message

This Stop message has four parameters:

1. Exception code that was not handled

2. Address at which the exception occurred

3. Parameter 0 of the exception

4. Parameter 1 of the exception

The first parameter identifies the exception generated. Common exception codes include:

- **0x80000002: STATUS_DATATYPE_MISALIGNMENT**   An unaligned data reference was encountered. The trap frame supplies additional information.

- **0x80000003: STATUS_BREAKPOINT**   A breakpoint or ASSERT was encountered when no kernel debugger was attached to the system.

- **0xC0000005: STATUS_ACCESS_VIOLATION**   A memory access violation occurred. Parameter 4 of the Stop error (which is Parameter 1 of the exception) is the address that the driver attempted to access.

- **0xC0000044: STATUS_QUOTA_EXCEEDED**   The text Insufficient Quota Exists To Complete The Operation indicates a pool memory leak. A quota allocation attempt necessary for the system to continue operating normally was unsuccessful because of a program or driver memory leak.

The second parameter identifies the address of the module in which the error occurred. Frequently, the address points to an individual driver or faulty hardware named on the third parameter of the Stop message. Make a note of this address and the link date of the driver or image that contains it.

The last two Stop message parameters vary, depending on the exception that has occurred. If the error code has no parameters, the last two parameters of the Stop message are listed as 0x00.

Resolving the Problem

The following suggestions are specific to Stop 0x1E errors. For additional troubleshooting suggestions that apply to all Stop errors, see "Stop Message Checklist" later in this chapter.

- Stop 0x1E messages typically occur after you install faulty drivers or system services, or they can indicate hardware problems, such as memory and IRQ conflicts. If a Stop message lists a driver by name, disable it, remove it, or roll it back to correct the problem. If disabling or removing applications and drivers resolves the issue, contact the hardware manufacturer about a possible update. Using updated software is especially important for multimedia applications, antivirus scanners, and CD mastering tools.

- If the Stop message mentions the file Win32k.sys, the source of the error might be a third-party remote control program. If such software is installed, you might be able to disable it by starting the system in safe mode. If not, use Startup Repair to manually delete the system service file that is causing the problem. For more information about safe mode and Startup Repair, see Chapter 30.

- Problems can result from system firmware incompatibilities. You can resolve many Advanced Configuration and Power Interface (ACPI) issues by updating to the latest firmware.

- Other possible causes include insufficient disk space while installing applications or performing certain functions that require more memory. You can free up space by deleting unneeded files. Use Disk Cleanup to increase available disk space. For more information about Disk Cleanup, see Chapter 31.

- The problem might be due to a memory leak caused by an application or service that is not releasing memory correctly. Poolmon (Poolmon.exe) helps you to isolate the components that are causing kernel memory leaks. For more information about troubleshooting memory leaks, see Microsoft Knowledge Base articles 177415, "How to Use Poolmon to Troubleshoot Kernel Mode Memory Leaks," at *http://support.microsoft.com/ kb/177415* and 298102, "Finding Pool Tags Used by Third Party Files Without Using the Debugger," at *http://support.microsoft.com/kb/298102*.

To find additional articles, search using keywords *vista, poolmon, pool tag, pooltag,* and *memory leak*. For more information about Stop 0x1E messages, see the Microsoft Knowledge Base at *http://support.microsoft.com/*. Search using keywords *vista* and *0x1E*.

Direct from the Source: Understanding Kernel Stack Overflows

Kernel stack overflows are a common error in many cases reported to us by customers. These are caused by drivers taking up too much space on the kernel stack. This results in a kernel stack overflow, which will then crash the system with one of the following bugchecks:

- STOP 0x7F: UNEXPECTED_KERNEL_MODE_TRAP with Parameter 1 set to EXCEPTION_DOUBLE_FAULT, which is caused by running off the end of a kernel stack.

- STOP 0x1E: KMODE_EXCEPTION_NOT_HANDLED, 0x7E: SYSTEM_THREAD_EXCEPTION_NOT_HANDLED, or 0x8E: KERNEL_MODE_EXCEPTION_NOT_HANDLED, with an exception code of STATUS_ACCESS_VIOLATION, which indicates a memory access violation.

- STOP 0x2B: PANIC_STACK_SWITCH, which usually occurs when a kernel-mode driver uses too much stack space.

Each thread in the system is allocated with a kernel mode stack. Code running on any kernel-mode thread (whether it is a system thread or a thread created by a driver) uses that thread's kernel-mode stack unless the code is a deferred procedure call (DPC), in which case it uses the processor's DPC stack on certain platforms.

The stack grows negatively. This means that the beginning (bottom) of the stack has a higher address than the end (top) of the stack. For example, let's say the beginning of your stack is 0x80f1000, and this is where your stack pointer (ESP) is pointing. If you push a DWORD value onto the stack, its address would be 0x80f0ffc. The next DWORD value would be stored at 0x80f0ff8 and so on up to the limit (top) of the allocated stack. The top of the stack is bordered by a guard-page to detect overruns.

The size of the kernel-mode stack varies among different hardware platforms. For example, on 32-bit platforms, the kernel-mode stack is 12KB, and on 64-bit platforms, the kernel-mode stack is 24KB. The stack sizes are hard limits that are imposed by the system, and all drivers need to use space conservatively so that they can coexist. When we reach the top of the stack, one more push instruction is going to cause an exception, which in turn can lead to a Stop error. This could be either a simple push instruction or something along the lines of a call instruction that also pushes the return address onto the stack.

For a more detailed description and a troubleshooting example, read *http://blogs.msdn.com/ntdebugging/archive/2008/02/01/kernel-stack-overflows.aspx*.

Omer Amin, Escalation Engineer

Microsoft Global Escalation Services Team

Stop 0x24 or NTFS_FILE_SYSTEM

The Stop 0x24 message indicates that a problem occurred within Ntfs.sys, the driver file that allows the system to read and write to NTFS file system drives. A similar Stop message, 0x23, exists for the file allocation table (FAT16 or FAT32) file systems.

Interpreting the Message

This Stop message has four parameters:

1. Source file and line number

2. A non-zero value that contains the address of the exception record (optional)

3. A non-zero value that contains the address of the context record (optional)

4. A non-zero value that contains the address where the original exception occurred (optional)

Parameters for this Stop message are useful only to Microsoft technical support with access to Windows Vista source code. Stop messages resulting from file system issues have the source file and the line number within the source file that generated the error encoded in their first parameter. The first four hexadecimal digits (also known as the high 16 bits) after the 0x identify the source file number, and the last four hexadecimal digits (the low 16 bits) identify the source line in the file where the stop occurred.

Resolving the Problem

The following suggestions are specific to Stop 0x24 errors. For additional troubleshooting suggestions that apply to all Stop errors, see "Stop Message Checklist" later in this chapter.

- Malfunctioning SCSI and Advanced Technology Attachment (ATA) hardware or drivers can also adversely affect the system's ability to read and write to disk, causing errors. If using SCSI hard disks, check for cabling and termination problems between the SCSI controller and the disks. Periodically check Event Viewer for error messages related to SCSI or FASTFAT in the System Log or any messages in the Applications And Services Logs\Microsoft\Windows\DiskDiagnostic\Operational log. For more information about troubleshooting SCSI adapters and disks, see Chapter 31.

- Verify that the tools you use to continually monitor your system—such as virus scanners, backup programs, or disk defragmenters—are compatible with Windows Vista. Some disks and adapters come packaged with diagnostic software that you can use to run hardware tests. For more information, see the documentation for your computer, hard disk, or controller.

- Check your hard disk for problems. For more information, see Chapter 31.

- Nonpaged pool memory might be depleted, which can cause the system to stop. You can resolve this situation by adding more RAM, which increases the quantity of nonpaged pool memory available to the kernel.

For more information about Stop 0x24 messages, see the Microsoft Knowledge Base at *http://support.microsoft.com/*. Search using keywords *vista*, *0x00000024*, and *0x24*.

Stop 0x2E or DATA_BUS_ERROR

The Stop 0x2E message indicates a system memory parity error. The cause is typically failed or defective RAM (including motherboard, Level 2 cache, or video memory), incompatible or mismatched memory hardware, or a device driver attempting to access an address in the 0x8*xxxxxxx* range that does not exist (meaning that it does not map to a physical address). A Stop 0x2E message can also indicate hard disk damage caused by viruses or other problems.

Interpreting the Message

This Stop message has four parameters:

1. Virtual address that caused the fault
2. Physical address that caused the fault
3. Processor status register
4. Faulting instruction register

Resolving the Problem

The following suggestions are specific to Stop 0x2E errors. For additional troubleshooting suggestions that apply to all Stop errors, see "Stop Message Checklist" later in this chapter.

- Stop 0x2E is typically the result of defective, malfunctioning, or failed memory hardware, such as memory modules, Level 2 (L2) SRAM cache, or video adapter RAM. If you added new hardware recently, remove the hardware and replace it to determine whether it is causing or contributing to the problem. Run Windows Memory Diagnostics as described in Chapter 31 to determine if the component has failed.

- Stop 0x2E messages can also occur after you install faulty drivers or system services. If a filename is given, you need to disable, remove, or roll back that driver. Disable the service or application and confirm that this resolves the error. If so, contact the hardware manufacturer about a possible update. Using updated software is especially important for backup programs, multimedia applications, antivirus scanners, and CD mastering tools.

- Hard disk corruption can also cause this Stop message. For more information about checking hard disk integrity, see Chapter 31.

■ The problem might also be due to cracks, scratched traces, or defective components on the motherboard. If all else fails, take the system motherboard to a repair facility for diagnostic testing.

For more information about Stop 0x2E messages, see the Microsoft Knowledge Base at *http://support.microsoft.com/*. Search using keywords *vista*, *0x0000002E*, and *0x2E*.

Stop 0x3F or NO_MORE_SYSTEM_PTES

The Stop 0x3F message indicates one or more of the following problems:

■ The system Page Table Entries (PTEs) are depleted or fragmented because the system is performing a large number of input/output (I/O) actions.

■ A faulty device driver is not managing memory properly.

■ An application, such as a backup program, is improperly allocating large amounts of kernel memory.

Interpreting the Message

Depending on the configuration of your system, the value of the first parameter might vary. Possible values for the first parameter and the information returned are:

■ 0x0A – PTE type: 0x00 = system expansion, 0x01 = nonpaged pool expansion

■ 0x0B – Requested size

■ 0x0C – Total free system PTEs

■ 0x0D – Total system PTEs

Resolving the Problem

The following suggestions are specific to Stop 3F errors. For additional troubleshooting suggestions that apply to all Stop errors, see "Stop Message Checklist" later in this chapter.

■ Stop 0x3F messages can occur after you install faulty drivers or system services. If a file-name is given, you need to disable, remove, or roll back that driver. Disable the service or application and confirm that this resolves the error. If so, contact the hardware manufacturer about a possible update. Using updated software is especially important for backup programs, multimedia applications, antivirus scanners, and CD mastering tools.

■ The system might not actually be out of PTEs, but a contiguous memory block of sufficient size may not be available to satisfy a driver or application request. Check for the availability of updated driver or application files and consult the hardware or program documentation for minimum system requirements.

A related Stop message, 0xD8: DRIVER_USED_EXCESSIVE_PTES, is described later in this chapter.

For more information about Stop 0x3F messages, see the Microsoft Knowledge Base at *http://support.microsoft.com/*. Search using keywords *vista*, *0x0000003F*, and *0x3F*.

Stop 0x50 or PAGE_FAULT_IN_NONPAGED_AREA

The Stop 0x50 message indicates that requested data was not in memory. The system generates an exception error when using a reference to an invalid system memory address. Defective memory (including main memory, L2 RAM cache, and video RAM) or incompatible software (including remote control and antivirus software) might cause Stop 0x50 messages.

Interpreting the Message

This Stop message has four parameters:

1. Memory address that caused the fault

2. Type of access (0x00 = read operation, 0x01 = write operation)

3. If not zero, the instruction address that referenced the address in parameter 0x01

4. This parameter is reserved (set aside for future use)

Resolving the Problem

The following suggestions are specific to Stop 0x50 errors. For additional troubleshooting suggestions that apply to all Stop errors, see "Stop Message Checklist" later in this chapter.

■ If you added new hardware recently, remove and replace the hardware to determine whether it is causing or contributing to the problem. Run Windows Memory Diagnostics as described in Chapter 31 to determine if the component has failed.

■ Stop 0x50 messages can also occur after you install faulty drivers or system services. If the filename is listed, you need to disable, remove, or roll back that driver. If not, disable the recently installed service or application to determine whether this resolves the error. If this does not resolve the problem, contact the hardware manufacturer for updates. Using updated drivers and software is especially important for network interface cards, video adapters, backup programs, multimedia applications, antivirus scanners, and CD mastering tools. If an updated driver is not available, attempt to use a driver from a similar device in the same family. For example, if printing to a Model 1100C printer causes Stop 0x50 errors, using a printer driver meant for a Model 1100A or Model 1000 might temporarily resolve the problem.

■ Check your hard disk for problems. For more information, see Chapter 31.

For more information about Stop 0x50 messages, see the Microsoft Knowledge Base at *http://support.microsoft.com/*. Search using keywords *vista*, *0x00000050*, and *0x50*. Specifically, refer to Microsoft Knowledge Base article 938239.

Stop 0x77 or KERNEL_STACK_INPAGE_ERROR

The Stop 0x77 message indicates that a page of kernel data requested from the paging (virtual memory) file could not be found or read into memory. This Stop message can also indicate disk hardware failure, disk data corruption, or possible virus infection.

Interpreting the Message

This Stop message has four parameters. The following set of definitions applies only if the first and third parameters are both zero:

1. This value is 0x00 (zero)

2. Value found in the stack

3. This value is 0x00 (zero)

4. Address of signature on kernel stack

Otherwise, the following definitions apply:

1. Status code

2. I/O status code

3. Page file number

4. Offset into page file

Frequently, you can determine the cause of this error from the second parameter, the I/O status code. Some common status codes include:

- 0xC000009A, or STATUS_INSUFFICIENT_RESOURCES, indicates a lack of nonpaged pool resources.

- 0xC000009C, or STATUS_DEVICE_DATA_ERROR, generally indicates bad blocks (sectors) on the hard disk.

- 0xC000009D, or STATUS_DEVICE_NOT_CONNECTED, indicates defective or loose data or power cables, a problem with SCSI termination, or improper controller or hard disk configuration.

- 0xC000016A, or STATUS_DISK_OPERATION_FAILED, also indicates bad blocks (sectors) on the hard disk.

- 0xC0000185, or STATUS_IO_DEVICE_ERROR, indicates improper termination, defective storage controller hardware, defective disk cabling, or two devices attempting to use the same system resources.

Resolving the Problem

The following suggestions are specific to Stop 0x77 errors. For additional troubleshooting suggestions that apply to all Stop errors, see "Stop Message Checklist" later in this chapter.

■ Stop 0x77 messages can be caused by bad sectors in the virtual memory paging file or a disk controller error. In extremely rare cases, depleted nonpaged pool resources can cause this error. If the first and third parameters are zero, the stack signature in the kernel stack is missing, which is an error typically caused by defective hardware. If the I/O status is 0xC0000185 and the paging file is on a SCSI disk, check for cabling and termination issues. An I/O status code of 0xC000009C or 0xC000016A indicates that the requested data could not be found. You can try to correct this by restarting the computer. Additionally, use Chkdsk to check the disk for problems. For more information about Chkdsk, see Chapter 31.

■ Another cause of Stop 0x77 messages is defective, malfunctioning, or failed memory hardware, such as memory modules, Level 2 (L2) SRAM cache, or video adapter RAM. If you added new hardware recently, remove and replace the hardware to determine whether it is causing or contributing to the problem. Run Windows Memory Diagnostics as described in Chapter 31 to determine if the component has failed.

■ The problem might also be due to cracks, scratched traces, or defective components on the motherboard. If all else fails, take the system motherboard to a repair facility for diagnostic testing.

■ Problems that cause Stop 0x77 messages can also cause Stop 0x7A messages. For more information about Stop 0x7A messages, see the following section, "Stop 0x7A or KERNEL_DATA_INPAGE_ERROR."

For more information about Stop 0x77 messages, see the Microsoft Knowledge Base at *http://support.microsoft.com/*. Search using keywords *vista*, *0x00000077*, and *0x77*.

Stop 0x7A or KERNEL_DATA_INPAGE_ERROR

The Stop 0x7A message indicates that a page of kernel data was not found in the paging (virtual memory) file and could not be read into memory. This might be due to incompatible disk or controller drivers, firmware, or hardware.

Interpreting the Message

This Stop message has four parameters:

1. Lock type value (0x01, 0x02, 0x03, or page table entry [PTE] address)

2. I/O status code

3. If lock type is 0x01, this parameter represents the current process; if lock type is 0x03, this parameter represents the virtual address

4. The virtual address that could not be read into memory

Frequently, the cause of this error can be determined from the second parameter, the I/O status code. Some common status codes are:

- 0xC000009A, or STATUS_INSUFFICIENT_RESOURCES, indicates a lack of nonpaged pool resources.

- 0xC000009C, or STATUS_DEVICE_DATA_ERROR, indicates bad blocks (sectors) on the hard disk.

- 0xC000009D, or STATUS_DEVICE_NOT_CONNECTED, indicates defective or loose data or power cables, a problem with SCSI termination, or improper controller or disk configuration.

- 0xC000016A, or STATUS_DISK_OPERATION_FAILED, indicates bad blocks (sectors) on the hard disk.

- 0xC0000185, or STATUS_IO_DEVICE_ERROR, indicates improper termination, defective storage controller hardware, defective disk cabling, or two devices attempting to use the same resources.

Resolving the Problem

The following suggestions are specific to Stop 0x7A errors. For additional troubleshooting suggestions that apply to all Stop errors, see "Stop Message Checklist" later in this chapter.

- Stop 0x7A can be caused by bad sectors in the virtual memory paging file, disk controller error, virus infection, or memory hardware problems. In extremely rare cases, depleted nonpaged pool resources can cause this error. If the first and third parameters are zero, the stack signature in the kernel stack is missing, an error typically caused by defective hardware. If the I/O status is 0xC0000185 and the paging file is on a SCSI disk, check for cabling and termination issues. An I/O status code of 0xC000009C or 0xC000016A indicates that the requested data could not be found. You can try to correct this by restarting the computer. If a problem with disk integrity exists, Autochk—a program that attempts to mark bad disk sectors as defective so that they are not used in the future— starts automatically. If Autochk fails to run, you can manually perform the integrity check yourself by following the instructions to run Chkdsk provided in the section titled "Stop 0x24 or NTFS_FILE_SYSTEM" earlier in this chapter. For more information about Chkdsk, see Chapter 31.

- Another cause of Stop 0x7A messages is defective, malfunctioning, or failed memory hardware, such as memory modules, Level 2 (L2) SRAM cache, or video adapter RAM. If you added new hardware recently, remove and replace the hardware to determine if it is causing or contributing to the problem. Run Windows Memory Diagnostics as described in Chapter 31 to determine whether the component has failed.

- Check the hardware manufacturer's website for updates to disk adapter firmware or drivers that improve compatibility. Verify that your disks and controller support the same set of advanced features, such as higher transfer rates. If necessary, select a slower transfer rate if an update is not yet available. Consult your hardware or device documentation for more information.

■   The problem might also be due to cracks, scratched traces, or defective components on the motherboard. If all else fails, take the system motherboard to a repair facility for diagnostic testing.

■   Problems that cause Stop 0x7A messages can also cause Stop 0x77 messages. For more information about Stop 0x77 messages, see the section titled "Stop 0x77 or KERNEL_STACK_INPAGE_ERROR" earlier in this chapter.

For more information about Stop 0x7A messages, see the Microsoft Knowledge Base at *http://support.microsoft.com/*. Search using keywords *vista*, *0x0000007A*, and *0x7A*.

Stop 0x7B or INACCESSIBLE_BOOT_DEVICE

The Stop 0x7B message indicates that Windows Vista has lost access to the system partition or boot volume during the startup process. Installing incorrect device drivers when installing or upgrading storage adapter hardware typically causes Stop 0x7B errors. Stop 0x7B errors could also indicate possible virus infection.

Interpreting the Message

This Stop message has four parameters:

1. The address of a Unicode string data structure representing the Advanced Reduced Instruction Set Computing (RISC) Computing (ARC) specification name of the device at which you attempted startup

2. Pointer to ARC name string in memory

3. This value is 0x00 (zero)

4. This value is 0x00 (zero)

The first parameter typically contains two separate pieces of data. For example, if the parameter is 0x00800020, 0x0020 is the actual length of the Unicode string and 0x0080 is the maximum ARC name string length. The next parameter contains the address of the buffer. This address is in system space, so the high-order bit is set.

If the file system is unable to mount the boot device or simply does not recognize the data on the boot device as a file system structure, the following parameter definition applies:

1. The address of the device object that could not be mounted

2. Error code value or 0x00 (zero)

3. This value is 0x00 (zero)

4. This value is 0x00 (zero)

The value of the first parameter determines if the parameter is a pointer to an ARC name string (ARC names are a generic method of identifying devices within the ARC environment) or a device object, because a Unicode string never has an odd number of bytes, and a device object always has a Type code of 0003.

The second parameter is very important, because it can indicate whether the Stop 0x7B message was caused by file system issues or problems with storage hardware and drivers. Values of 0xC000034 or 0xC000000E typically indicate:

- Disks or storage controllers that are failing, defective, or improperly configured.
- Storage-related drivers or programs (tape management software, for example) that are not fully compatible with Windows Vista.

Resolving the Problem

The following suggestions are specific to Stop 0x7B errors. For additional troubleshooting suggestions that apply to all Stop errors, see "Stop Message Checklist" later in this chapter.

- During I/O system initialization, the controller or driver for the startup device (typically the hard disk) might have failed to initialize the necessary hardware. File system initialization might have failed because of disk or controller failure, or because the file system did not recognize the data on the boot device.
- Repartitioning disks, adding new disks, or upgrading to a new disk controller might cause the information in the Windows Boot Manager or Boot Configuration Data (BCD) file to become outdated. If this Stop message occurs after you install new disks to your system, edit the BCD file or adjust the Boot Manager parameters to allow the system to start. If the error occurs after upgrading the disk controller, verify that the new hardware is functioning and correctly configured. For more information about Windows Boot Manager, the BCD file, and automatically correcting configuration problems, see Chapter 30.
- Verify that the system firmware and disk controller BIOS settings are correct and that the storage device was properly installed. If you are unsure, consult your computer's documentation about restoring default firmware settings or configuring your system to auto-detect settings. If the error occurs during Windows Vista setup, the problem might be due to unsupported disk controller hardware. In some cases, drivers for new hardware are not in the Windows Vista Driver.cab library, and you need to provide additional drivers to complete the Windows Vista setup successfully. If this is the case, follow the hardware manufacturer's instructions when installing drivers. Periodically check for driver and firmware updates.
- Hard disk corruption can also cause this Stop message. For more information about checking hard disk integrity, see the instructions provided in the section titled "Stop 0x24 or NTFS_FILE_SYSTEM" earlier in this chapter.

- Problems that cause 0x7B errors might also cause Stop 0xED errors. For more information about Stop 0xED messages, see the section titled "Stop 0xED or UNMOUNTABLE_BOOT_DEVICE" later in this chapter.

For more information about Stop 0x7B messages, see the Microsoft Knowledge Base at *http://support.microsoft.com/*. Search using keywords *vista, 0x0000007B, 0x7B,* and *Txtsetup.oem.* Specifically, refer to Microsoft Knowledge Base article 935806.

Stop 0x7F or UNEXPECTED_KERNEL_MODE_TRAP

The Stop 0x7F message indicates that one of three types of problem occurred in kernel mode:

- A condition that the kernel is not allowed to have or intercept (also known as a *bound trap*)
- Software problems
- Hardware failures

Interpreting the Message

This Stop message has four parameters:

1. Processor exception code
2. This value is 0x00 (zero)
3. This value is 0x00 (zero)
4. This value is 0x00 (zero)

The first parameter is the most important and can have several different values, indicating different causes of this error. You can find all conditions that cause a Stop 0x7F in any x86 microprocessor reference manual, because they are specific to the x86 platform. Some of the most common exception codes are:

- 0x00, or a divide-by-zero error, occurs when a divide (DIV) instruction is run and the divisor is 0. Memory corruption, other hardware failures, or software problems can cause this message.
- 0x04, or Overflow, occurs when the processor carries out a call to an interrupt handler when the overflow (OF) flag is set.
- 0x05, or Bounds Check Fault, indicates that the processor, while carrying out a BOUND instruction, found that the operand exceeded the specified limits. BOUND instructions are used to ensure that a signed array index is within a certain range.
- 0x06, or Invalid Opcode, is generated when the processor attempts to run an invalid instruction. This typically occurs when the instruction pointer is corrupted as a result of a hardware memory problem and is pointing to a wrong location.

■ 0x08, or Double Fault, indicates an exception while trying to call the handler for a prior exception. Normally, two exceptions can be handled serially, but certain exceptions (almost always caused by hardware problems) cause the processor to signal a double fault.

Less common codes include:

■ **0x01** A system-debugger call

■ **0x03** A debugger breakpoint

■ **0x0A** A corrupted Task State Segment

■ **0x0B** An access to a memory segment that was not present

■ **0x0C** An access to memory beyond the limits of a stack

■ **0x0D** An exception not covered by some other exception; a protection fault that pertains to access violations for applications

Resolving the Problem

The following suggestions are specific to Stop 0x7F errors. For additional troubleshooting suggestions that apply to all Stop errors, see "Stop Message Checklist" later in this chapter.

■ Stop 0x7F messages are typically the result of defective, malfunctioning, or failed memory hardware. If you added new hardware recently, remove and replace the hardware to determine whether it is causing or contributing to the problem. Run Windows Memory Diagnostics as described in Chapter 31 to determine if the component has failed.

■ Running the CPU beyond the rated specification, known as *overclocking*, can cause Stop 0x7F or other error messages because of heat buildup. When diagnosing problems on overclocked systems, first restore all clock and bus speed settings to the manufacturer recommended values to determine if this resolves the issues.

■ The problem might also be due to cracks, scratched traces, or defective components on the motherboard. If all else fails, take the system motherboard to a repair facility for diagnostic testing.

■ Stop 0x7F messages can occur after you install incompatible applications, drivers, or system services. Contact the software manufacturer about possible Windows Vista–specific updates. Using updated software is especially important for backup programs, multimedia applications, antivirus scanners, and CD mastering tools.

For more information about Stop 0x7F messages, see the Microsoft Knowledge Base at *http://support.microsoft.com/*. Search using keywords *vista*, *0x0000007F*, and *0x7F*.

Stop 0x9F or DRIVER_POWER_STATE_FAILURE

The Stop 0x9F message indicates that a driver is in an inconsistent or invalid power state.

Interpreting the Message

Table 33-1 describes the information provided by Stop 0x9F messages. The value of the first parameter indicates the type of violation (see the Description column) and determines the meaning of the next three parameters.

Table 33-1   Parameter Listing for Stop Message 0x9F

Parameter 1	Parameter 2	Parameter 3	Parameter 4	Description
0x01	Pointer to the device object	Reserved	Reserved	The device object being freed still has an incomplete power request pending.
0x02	Pointer to the target device object	Pointer to the device object	Reserved	The device object completed the I/O request packet for the system power state request but failed to call PoStartNextPowerIrp.
0x03	Pointer to the target device object	Pointer to the device object	The I/O request packet	The device driver did not properly set the I/O request packets pending or complete the I/O request packet.
0x00000100	Pointer to the nonpaged device object	Pointer to the target device object	Pointer to the device object to notify	The device objects in the devnode were inconsistent in their use of DO_POWER_PAGABLE.
0x00000101	Child device object	Child device object	Parent device object	A parent device object has detected that a child device has not set the DO_POWER_PAGABLE bit.

This Stop error typically occurs during events that involve power state transitions, such as shutting down, suspending, or resuming from sleep.

Resolving the Problem

The following suggestions are specific to Stop 0x9F errors. For additional troubleshooting suggestions that apply to all Stop errors, see "Stop Message Checklist" later in this chapter.

- Stop 0x9F messages can occur after you install faulty applications or drivers or system services. If a file is listed by name and you can associate it with an application, uninstall the application. For drivers, disable, remove, or roll back that driver to determine if this resolves the error. If it does, contact the hardware manufacturer for a possible update. Using updated software is especially important for backup programs, multimedia applications, antivirus scanners, and CD mastering tools.

- Stop 0x9F messages can occur when you perform one of the following operations on a Windows Vista–based computer:

  - Connect to a shared printer on the network, and then run the "Common Scenario Stress with IO" test in Driver Test Manager (DTM).

  - Print to a shared printer on the network.

  - Perform a power management operation. For example, put the computer to sleep or into hibernation. Or wake the computer from sleep or from hibernation.

For more information about Stop 0x9F messages, see the Microsoft Knowledge Base at *http://support.microsoft.com/*. Search using keywords *vista*, *0x0000009F*, and *0x9F*. Specifically, refer to Microsoft Knowledge Base articles 937322, 941858, 937322, 937500, and 931671.

Stop 0xBE or ATTEMPTED_WRITE_TO_READONLY_MEMORY

The Stop 0xBE message indicates that a driver attempted to write to read-only memory.

Interpreting the Message

This Stop message has four parameters:

1. Virtual address of attempted write

2. PTE contents

3. Reserved

4. Reserved

Resolving the Problem

A Stop 0xBE message might occur after you install a faulty device driver, system service, or firmware. If a Stop message lists a driver by name, disable, remove, or roll back the driver to correct the problem. If disabling or removing drivers resolves the issues, contact the manufacturer about a possible update. Using updated software is especially important for multimedia applications, antivirus scanners, DVD playback, and CD mastering tools.

For more information about Stop 0xBE messages, see the Microsoft Knowledge Base at *http://support.microsoft.com/*. Search using keywords *vista*, *0x000000BE*, and *0xBE*.

Stop 0xC2 or BAD_POOL_CALLER

The Stop 0xC2 message indicates that a kernel-mode process or driver incorrectly attempted to perform memory operations in the following ways:

- By allocating a memory pool size of zero bytes

- By allocating a memory pool that does not exist

- By attempting to free a memory pool that is already free
- By allocating or freeing a memory pool at an IRQL that was too high

This Stop message is typically the result of a faulty driver or software.

Interpreting the Message

Table 33-2 describes the information provided by Stop 0xC2 messages. The value of the first parameter indicates the type of violation (see the Description column) and determines the meaning of the next three parameters.

Table 33-2 Parameter Listing for Stop Message 0xC2

Parameter 1	Parameter 2	Parameter 3	Parameter 4	Description
0x00	This value is always 0	The pool type being allocated	The pool tag being used	The caller is requesting a zero-byte pool allocation
0x01, 0x02, or 0x04	Pointer to pool header	First part of pool header contents	This value is always zero	Pool header has been corrupted
0x06	Reserved	Pointer to pool header	Pool header contents	Attempt to free a memory pool that was already freed
0x07	Reserved	Pointer to pool header	This value is always zero	Attempt to free a memory pool that was already freed
0x08	Current IRQL	Pool type	Size of allocation	Attempt to allocate pool at invalid IRQL
0x09	Current IRQL	Pool type	Address of pool	Attempt to free pool at invalid IRQL
0x40	Starting address	Start of system address space	This value is always zero	Attempt to free usermode address to kernel pool
0x41	Starting address	Physical page frame	Highest physical page frame	Attempt to free a nonallocated nonpaged pool address
0x42 or 0x43	Address being freed	This value is always zero	This value is always zero	Attempt to free a virtual address that was never in any pool

Table 33-2   Parameter Listing for Stop Message 0xC2

Parameter 1	Parameter 2	Parameter 3	Parameter 4	Description
0x50	Starting address	Start offset in pages from beginning of paged pool	Size in bytes of paged pool	Attempt to free a nonallocated paged pool address
0x99	Address being freed	This value is always zero	This value is always zero	Attempt to free pool with invalid address or corruption in pool header
0x9A	Pool type	Size of allocation in bytes	Allocation's pool tag	Attempt to allocate must succeed

Resolving the Problem

The following suggestions are specific to Stop 0xC2 errors. For additional troubleshooting suggestions that apply to all Stop errors, see "Stop Message Checklist" later in this chapter.

- A Stop 0xC2 message might occur after you install a faulty device driver, system service, or firmware. If a Stop message lists a driver by name, disable, remove, or roll back the driver to correct the problem. If disabling or removing drivers resolves the issues, contact the manufacturer about a possible update. Using updated software is especially important for multimedia applications, antivirus scanners, DVD playback, and CD mastering tools.

- A Stop 0xC2 message might also be due to failing or defective hardware. If a Stop message points to a category of devices (such as disk controllers, for example), try removing or replacing the hardware to determine if it is causing the problem. For more information, see Chapter 31.

- If you encounter a Stop 0xC2 message while upgrading to Windows Vista, the problem might be due to an incompatible driver, system service, virus scanner, or backup. To avoid problems while upgrading, simplify your hardware configuration and remove all third-party device drivers and system services (including virus scanners) prior to running setup. After you have successfully installed Windows Vista, contact the hardware manufacturer to obtain compatible updates.

For more information about Stop 0xC2 messages, see the Microsoft Knowledge Base at *http://support.microsoft.com/*. Search using keywords *vista*, *0x000000C2*, and *0xC2*.

Stop 0xCE or DRIVER_UNLOADED_WITHOUT_CANCELLING_PENDING_OPERATIONS

This Stop message indicates that a driver failed to cancel pending operations before exiting.

Interpreting the Message

This Stop message has four parameters:

1. Memory address referenced
2. Type of access (0x00 = read operation, 0x01 = write operation)
3. If non-zero, the address of the instruction that referenced the incorrect memory location
4. Reserved

Resolving the Problem

Stop 0xCE messages can occur after you install faulty drivers or system services. If a driver is listed by name, disable, remove, or roll back that driver to confirm that this resolves the error. If so, contact the manufacturer about a possible update. Using updated software is especially important for backup programs, multimedia applications, antivirus scanners, DVD playback, and CD mastering tools.

For more information about Stop 0xCE messages, see the Microsoft Knowledge Base at *http://support.microsoft.com/*. Search using keywords *vista*, *0x000000CE*, and *0xCE*.

Stop 0xD1 or DRIVER_IRQL_NOT_LESS_OR_EQUAL

The Stop 0xD1 message indicates that the system attempted to access pageable memory using a kernel process IRQL that was too high. Drivers that have used improper addresses typically cause this error.

Interpreting the Message

This Stop message has four parameters:

1. Memory referenced
2. IRQL at time of reference
3. Type of access (0x00 = read operation, 0x01 = write operation)
4. Address that referenced memory

Resolving the Problem

Stop 0xD1 messages can occur after you install faulty drivers or system services. If a driver is listed by name, disable, remove, or roll back that driver to confirm that this resolves the error. If so, contact the manufacturer about a possible update. Using updated software is especially important for backup programs, multimedia applications, antivirus scanners, DVD playback, and CD mastering tools.

For more information about Stop 0xD1 messages, see the Microsoft Knowledge Base at *http://support.microsoft.com/*. Search using keywords *vista*, *0x000000D1*, and *0xD1*.

Stop 0xD8 or DRIVER_USED_EXCESSIVE_PTES

The Stop 0xD8 message typically occurs if your computer runs out of page table entries (PTEs) because of a driver that requests large amounts of kernel memory.

Interpreting the Message

Depending on the configuration of your system, the number of parameters returned might vary. The four possible values are:

1. If this parameter has a non-null value, it contains the name of the driver that caused the Stop error.

2. If the first parameter has a non-null value, this parameter contains the number of PTEs used by the driver that is causing the error.

3. This parameter represents the total free system PTEs.

4. This parameter represents the total system PTEs.

Resolving the Problem

For suggestions about resolving problems related to inadequate PTEs, see "0x3F or NO_MORE_SYSTEM_PTES" earlier in this chapter.

For more information about Stop 0xD8 messages, see the Microsoft Knowledge Base at *http://support.microsoft.com/*. Search using keywords *vista*, *0x000000D8*, and *0xD8*.

Stop 0xEA or THREAD_STUCK_IN_DEVICE_DRIVER

A device driver problem is causing the system to pause indefinitely. Typically, this problem is caused by a display driver waiting for the video hardware to enter an idle state. This might indicate a hardware problem with the video adapter or a faulty video driver.

Interpreting the Message

This Stop message has four parameters:

1. Pointer to the thread object that is caught in an infinite loop
2. Pointer to a DEFERRED_WATCHDOG object, useful when using a kernel debugger to find out more information about this problem
3. Pointer to graphics device interface (GDI)–supplied context
4. Additional debugging information

Resolving the Problem

Stop 0xD1 messages can occur after you install faulty drivers (especially video drivers) or system services. If a driver is listed by name, disable, remove, or roll back that driver to confirm that this resolves the error. If so, contact the manufacturer about a possible update. Using updated software is especially important for backup programs, multimedia applications, antivirus scanners, DVD playback, and CD mastering tools.

For more information about Stop 0xEA messages, see the Microsoft Knowledge Base at *http://support.microsoft.com/*. Search using keywords *vista*, *0x000000EA*, and *0xEA*.

Stop 0xED or UNMOUNTABLE_BOOT_VOLUME

The kernel-mode I/O subsystem attempted to mount the boot volume and failed. This error might also occur during an upgrade to Windows Vista on systems that use higher-throughput ATA disks or controllers with incorrect cabling. In some cases, your system might appear to work normally after you restart.

Interpreting the Message

This Stop message has two parameters:

1. Device object of the boot volume
2. Status code from the filesystem on why it failed to mount the volume

Resolving the Problem

The following suggestions are specific to Stop 0xED errors. For additional troubleshooting suggestions that apply to all Stop errors, see "Stop Message Checklist" later in this chapter.

- If you are using higher-throughput ATA disks and controllers, those capable of data transfer rates above 33.3 megabytes per second, replace the standard 40-pin cable with an 80-pin cable. Using an 80-pin cable is optional for transfer rates up to and including

33.3 megabytes per second, but is mandatory for higher transfer rates. The additional grounded pins are required to avoid data loss.

■ Some firmware allows you to force higher transfer rates even when you are using the incorrect cable type. Your firmware might issue a warning but allow the startup process to proceed. Restore the default firmware setting for ATA cable detection.

■ Problems that cause 0xED errors might also cause Stop 0x7B errors. For more information about 0x7B Stop messages, see the section titled "Stop 0x7B or INACCESSIBLE_BOOT_DEVICE" earlier in this chapter.

For more information about Stop 0xED messages, see the Microsoft Knowledge Base at *http://support.microsoft.com/*. Search using keywords vista, *0x000000ED*, and *0xED*.

Stop 0xFE or BUGCODE_USB_DRIVER

The Stop 0xFE message occurs if the kernel detects an error in a USB driver.

Interpreting the Message

This Stop message has four parameters. Parameter 1 indicates the type of violation, whereas parameters 2 through 4 provide more information specific to that error type. Typically, only the first parameter is useful to system administrators, though parameters 2 through 4 might be useful to Microsoft developers who will be able to extract that information from the memory dump.

Parameter 1 can have a value of 0x1 to 0x5, as described here:

1. An internal error has occurred in the USB stack.

2. The USB client driver has submitted a USB request block (URB) that is still attached to another IRP that is pending in the bus driver.

3. The USB miniport driver has generated a Stop error. This usually happens in response to a catastrophic hardware failure.

4. The caller has submitted an I/O request packet (IRP) that is already pending in the USB bus driver.

5. A hardware failure has occurred because of a bad physical address found in a hardware data structure. This is not due to a driver bug.

Resolving the Problem

The following suggestions are specific to Stop 0xFE errors. For additional troubleshooting suggestions that apply to all Stop errors, see "Stop Message Checklist" later in this chapter.

To resolve this problem, follow these procedures:

- Verify that Service Pack 1 or the Cumulative update rollup for USB core components in Windows Vista is installed. For more information, read Microsoft Knowledge Base article 941822.

- Check the computer or motherboard manufacturer's website for updated system firmware.

- Upgrade the firmware and drivers of all USB devices attached to the computer.

- Verify that all hardware is compatible with Windows Vista.

- Remove USB devices and external hubs one by one and determine whether or not the Stop error reoccurs. If the Stop error does not reoccur when a specific device is not attached, that device might be malfunctioning, or it might not be compatible with Windows Vista. Contact the device manufacturer for additional support.

- If problems persists, you might have a computer hardware failure. Contact your computer manufacturer for additional assistance.

For more information about Stop 0xFE messages, see the Microsoft Knowledge Base at *http://support.microsoft.com/*. Search using keywords *vista*, *0x000000FE*, and *0xFE*. Specifically, refer to Microsoft Knowledge Base article 934374.

Stop 0xC000021A or STATUS_SYSTEM_PROCESS_TERMINATED

The Stop 0xC000021A message occurs when Windows Vista switches into kernel mode and a user-mode subsystem, such as Winlogon or the Client Server Runtime Subsystem (CSRSS), is compromised and security can no longer be guaranteed. Because Windows Vista cannot run without Winlogon or CSRSS, this is one of the few situations in which the failure of a user-mode service can cause the system to stop responding. You cannot use the kernel debugger in this situation because the error occurred in a user-mode process.

A Stop 0xC000021A message can also occur when the computer is restarted after a system administrator has modified permissions in such a way that the System account no longer has adequate permissions to access system files and folders.

Interpreting the Message

This Stop message has three parameters:

1. Status code

2. This value is 0x00 (zero)

3. This value is 0x00 (zero)

Resolving the Problem

The following suggestions are specific to Stop 0x21A errors. For additional troubleshooting suggestions that apply to all Stop errors, see "Stop Message Checklist" later in this chapter.

- Stop 0xC000021A messages occur in a user-mode process. The most common causes are third-party applications. If the error occurs after you install a new or updated device driver, system service, or third-party application, you need to remove, disable, or roll back the driver, or uninstall the new software. Contact the software manufacturer about a possible update.

- System file mismatch caused by partially restoring the system from backup media might cause this error. (Some backup programs do not restore files that they determine are in use.) Always use backup software that is Windows Vista–compatible.

For more information about Stop 0xC000021A messages, see the Microsoft Knowledge Base at *http://support.microsoft.com/*. Search using keywords *vista* and *0xC000021A*.

Stop 0xC0000221 or STATUS_IMAGE_CHECKSUM_MISMATCH

This Stop message indicates driver, system file, or disk corruption problems (such as a damaged paging file). Faulty memory hardware can also cause this Stop message to appear.

Interpreting the Message

This Stop message typically displays the name of the damaged file as follows:

```
STOP: 0xC0000221 STATUS_IMAGE_CHECKSUM_MISMATCH <path>\<file name>
- or -
Unable to load device driver <driver_name>
```

Resolving the Problem

The following suggestions are specific to Stop 0xC0000221 errors. For additional troubleshooting suggestions that apply to all Stop errors, see "Stop Message Checklist" later in this chapter.

- You can use Driver Rollback or System Restore from safe mode to restore a previous driver. You can also use Windows Vista recovery features such as the Last Known Good Configuration startup option, Backup, or Automated System Recovery to restore a previous working configuration. For more information, see Chapter 30. After restoring from backup media, you might need to reapply service packs or hotfixes, depending on when the backups were made.

- If the Stop message names the specific file, try replacing it manually with a fresh copy from another Windows Vista computer using safe mode or Startup Repair. For more information, see Chapter 31.

- Stop message 0xC000026C, caused by similar conditions, provides the name of the system file. You can also use the preceding suggestions to resolve this error.

For more information about Stop 0xC0000221 messages, see the Microsoft Knowledge Base at *http://support.microsoft.com/*. Search using keywords *vista* and *0xC0000221*.

Hardware Malfunction Messages

Stop messages also take the form of hardware malfunction messages. Like all Stop messages, they are displayed in non-windowed text mode. These Stop messages occur after the processor detects a hardware malfunction; the first one or two lines of the message contain a description. The error description typically points to a hardware problem, as shown in this example.

```
Hardware malfunction.
Call your hardware vendor for support.
```

Prior to proceeding with the recommendation provided by the message, it is best to contact the manufacturer for technical support. Record the information displayed after the first two lines of the message, which might prove useful to the support technician.

Under certain circumstances, driver problems can generate Stop messages that appear to be related to a hardware malfunction. For example, if a driver writes to the wrong I/O port, the device at the destination port might respond by generating a hardware malfunction message. Errors of this kind, which are typically detected and debugged in advance of public release, underscore the need to periodically check for updated drivers.

Stop Message Checklist

Stop messages provide diagnostic information, such as Stop codes and driver names, that you can use to resolve the problem. However, this information disappears when you restart your computer. Therefore, for future reference, it is important to record the information displayed. When a Stop message appears, follow these steps before restarting the system:

1. Record data found in the Bugcheck information and Driver information sections for later reference.

2. Record and evaluate suggestions found in the Recommended User Action section. Stop messages typically provide troubleshooting tips relevant to the error.

3. Check the Stop message Debug Port And Dump Status section to verify that Windows Vista successfully dumped memory contents to the paging file. Then proceed with your troubleshooting efforts.

4. After you resolve the problem or can at least start the computer, you can copy the memory dump file to another location, such as removable media, for further evaluation. Analyzing memory dump files can assist you with identifying root causes by providing you with detailed information about the system state when the Stop message occurred.

For more information about creating and analyzing memory dump files, see the section titled "Memory Dump Files" earlier in this chapter.

By following the preceding steps, you can save important information that you can refer to when using the resources listed in the section titled "Stop Message Overview" earlier in this chapter. Stop messages do not always point to the root of the problem, but they do provide important clues that you or a trained support technician can use to identify and troubleshoot a problem.

Check Your Software

The following are useful software-related techniques that you can use to recover from problems that cause Stop messages.

Check Software Disk Space Requirements

Verify that adequate free space exists on your disk volumes for virtual memory paging files and application data files. Insufficient free space might cause Stop messages and other symptoms, including disk corruption. Always check the minimum system requirements recommended by the software publisher before installing an application. To determine the amount allocated to paging files, see the section titled "Memory Dump Files" earlier in this chapter. You can move, delete, or compress unused files manually or by using Disk Cleanup (Cleanmgr.exe) to increase free space on disk volumes.

Use the Last Known Good Configuration

If a Stop message occurs immediately after you install new software or drivers, use the Last Known Good Configuration startup option to undo the registry and driver changes. To use this option, restart your computer and then press F8 when prompted to activate the Windows Advanced Options menu. Last Known Good Configuration is one of the available options. For more information about Windows Vista startup and recovery options, see Chapter 30.

Use Disaster Recovery Features

Disaster recovery features such as System Restore and Driver Rollback can undo recent changes. For more information about recovery options, see Chapter 30.

Restart the System in Safe Mode

Safe mode is a diagnostic environment that loads a minimum set of drivers and system services, increasing your chances of successfully starting the operating system. After Windows Vista has started, you can enable or disable drivers and make the necessary changes to restore stability. To enter safe mode, restart your computer and then press F8 when prompted to activate the Windows Advanced Options menu. Safe mode is one of the available options. For more information about startup and recovery options, see Chapter 30.

Use Startup Repair

You can use Startup Repair to perform advanced operations, such as replacing corrupted files. You can also disable a service by renaming the file specified in a Stop message. For more information about using Startup Repair to recover from startup problems, see Chapter 30.

Check Event Viewer Logs

Check the Event Viewer System and Application logs for warnings or error message patterns that point to an application or service. Record this information and refer to it when searching for more information or when contacting technical support.

Check Application and Driver Compatibility

Categories of software known to cause Stop messages if they are not fully compatible with Windows Vista (such as those meant for previous versions of Windows) include backup, remote control, multimedia, CD mastering, Internet firewall, and antivirus tools. If temporarily disabling a driver or uninstalling software resolves the problem, contact the manufacturer for information about an update or workaround. You need to disable a service that is causing Stop errors or other problems rather than stop or pause it. A stopped or paused service runs after you restart the computer. For more information about disabling services for diagnostic or troubleshooting purposes, see Chapter 30.

Install Compatible Antivirus Tools

Virus infection can cause problems such as Stop errors (for example, Stop 0x7B) and data loss. Before running antivirus software, verify that you are using updated virus signature files. Signature files provide information that allows the antivirus scanning software to identify viruses. Using current signature files increases the chances of detecting the most recent viruses. Verify that your virus scanner product checks the master boot record (MBR) and the boot sector. For more information about MBR and boot sector viruses, see Chapter 31.

Check for and Install Service Pack Updates

Microsoft periodically releases service packs containing updated system files, security enhancements, and other improvements that can resolve problems. You can use Windows Update to check for and install the latest versions as they become available. To check the service pack revision installed on your system, click Start, right-click Computer, and then click Properties. For more information about Windows Update, see Chapter 24, "Managing Software Updates."

Report Your Errors

You can find out more information about the conditions that caused the Stop message by using Problem Reports And Solutions. For more information about options for analyzing memory dump files, see the section titled "Using Memory Dump Files to Analyze Stop Errors" earlier in this chapter.

Install Operating System and Driver Updates

Occasionally, Microsoft and third parties release software updates to fix known problems. For more information about software updates, read Chapter 24.

Check Information Sources

You might find information about a workaround or solution to the problem. Information sources include the Microsoft Knowledge Base and manufacturer's technical support web pages.

Install and Use a Kernel Debugger

You can use a kernel debugger to gather more information about the problem. The Debugging Tools Help file contains instructions and examples that can help you find additional information about the Stop error affecting you. For more information about installing and using debugging tools, see the sections titled "Stop Message Overview" and "Using Memory Dump Files to Analyze Stop Errors" earlier in this chapter.

Check Your Hardware

You can use the following hardware-related techniques to recover from problems that cause Stop messages.

Restore a Previous Configuration

If a Stop message appears immediately after you add new hardware, see if removing or replacing the part and restoring a previous configuration resolves the problem. You can use recovery features such as Last Known Good Configuration, Driver Rollback, and System Restore to restore the system to the previous configuration or to remove a specific driver. For more information about startup and recovery options, see Chapter 30.

Check for Nondefault Firmware Settings

Some computers have firmware that you can use to change hardware settings such as power management parameters, video configuration, memory timing, and memory shadowing. Do not alter these settings unless you have a specific requirement to do so. If you are experiencing hardware problems, verify that firmware values are set to default values. To restore default firmware values, follow the instructions provided by the computer or motherboard manufacturer.

Check for Nondefault Hardware Clock Speeds

Verify that hardware is running at the correct speed. Do not set clock speeds for components such as the processor, video adapter, or memory above the rated specification (overclocking). This can cause random errors that are difficult to diagnose. If you are experiencing problems with overclocked hardware, restore default clock speed and CPU voltage settings according to the instructions provided by the hardware manufacturer.

Check for Hardware-Related Updates

Check the manufacturer's website to see if updated firmware is available for your system or individual peripherals.

Check by Running Hardware Diagnostic Tools

Run hardware diagnostic software to verify that your hardware is not defective. These tools are typically built into or bundled with your hardware.

Check ATA Disk and Controller Settings

If your system uses Advanced Technology Attachment (ATA) storage devices such as hard disks, determine if the firmware setting Primary IDE Only is available. If the setting is available, enable it if the second ATA channel is unused. Verify that primary and secondary device jumper settings are set correctly. Storage devices (including CD and DVD-ROM drives) use their own firmware, so check the manufacturer's website periodically for updates. Verify that you are using a cable that is compatible with your device—certain ATA standards require you to use a different cable type.

Check for SCSI Disk and Controller Settings

If your system uses a SCSI adapter, check for updates to device drivers and adapter firmware. Try disabling advanced SCSI firmware options, such as sync negotiation for low-bandwidth devices (tape drives and CD-ROM drives). Verify that you are using cables that meet the SCSI adapter's requirements for termination and maximum cable length. Check SCSI ID settings and termination to ensure that they are correct for all devices. For more information, see Chapter 31.

Check for Proper Hardware Installation and Connections

Verify that internal expansion boards and external devices are firmly seated and properly installed, and that connecting cables are properly fastened. If necessary, clean adapter card electrical contacts using supplies available at electronics stores. For more information about troubleshooting hardware, see Chapter 31.

Check Memory Compatibility

If a Stop message appears immediately after you add new memory, verify that the new part is compatible with your system. Do not rely solely on physical characteristics (such as chip count or module dimensions) when purchasing new or replacement memory. Always adhere to the manufacturer's specifications when purchasing memory modules. For example, you can fit a memory module rated for 66-megahertz (MHz) or 100-MHz operation (PC66 or PC100 RAM, respectively) into a system using a 133-Mhz memory bus speed, and it might initially appear to work. However, using the slower memory results in system instability. To test memory, use Windows Memory Diagnostics as described in Chapter 31.

Check by Temporarily Removing Devices

Installing a new device can sometimes cause resource conflicts with existing devices. You might recover from this problem by temporarily removing devices not needed to start the operating system. For example, temporarily removing a CD-ROM or audio adapter might allow you to start Windows Vista. You can then examine the device and operating system settings separately to determine what changes you need to make. For more information about simplifying your hardware configuration for troubleshooting purposes, see Chapter 30.

Check by Replacing a Device

If you are unable to obtain diagnostic software for the problem device, install a replacement to verify that this action resolves the problem. If the problem disappears, the original hardware might be defective or incorrectly configured.

Check Information Sources

You might be able to find information about a workaround or solution to the problem. Information sources include the Microsoft Knowledge Base and manufacturer's technical support web pages.

Contact Technical Support

As a last resort, Microsoft technical support can assist you with troubleshooting. For more information about Microsoft technical support options, see the Support link on the Microsoft website at *http://www.microsoft.com*.

Summary

Stop errors can be frustrating to troubleshoot. However, by following the procedures outlined in this chapter, you can identify the source of Stop errors and begin working to resolve them. Most of the time, Stop errors are caused by drivers or faulty hardware. Where Stop errors are caused by drivers, you need to work with the hardware manufacturer to develop an improved driver. If a Stop error is caused by faulty hardware, you should repair or replace the hardware.

Additional Resources

The following resources contain additional information and tools related to this chapter.

Related Information

- Chapter 15, "Managing Disks and File Systems," includes information about configuring disks.
- Chapter 16, "Managing Devices and Services," includes information about configuring services to start automatically.
- Chapter 30, "Configuring Startup and Troubleshooting Startup Issues," includes information about using safe mode and Startup Repair.
- Chapter 31, "Troubleshooting Hardware, Driver, and Disk Issues," includes information about troubleshooting hardware- and driver-related network adapter problems.
- The Microsoft Global Escalation Services team blog at *http://blogs.msdn.com/ntdebugging/* includes useful articles about troubleshooting stop errors and other complex problems.
- Windows Driver Kit (WDK) includes information about Stop errors not listed here. To download the WDK, visit *http://www.microsoft.com/whdc/DevTools/WDK/WDKpkg.mspx.*

On the Companion CD

- DetectMiniDump.vbs
- DisplayDumpConfig.vbs
- DisplayDumpLocation.vbs
- DisplayErrorLogInfo.vbs
- ConfigureCrashSettings.vbs
- Download the latest version of the Windows Debugging Tools and Symbols
- A link to where you can download the latest versions of the Windows Debugging Tools and Symbols

Appendix A
System Files Reference

When you install Windows Vista, the Setup program creates folders on your system drive into which it places files that the system requires. Knowing the names and locations of essential system files can help you understand and troubleshoot your Windows Vista installation.

System Files

The files listed in Table A-1 are core components of the Windows Vista operating system.

Table A-1   Windows Vista Core System Files

File Name	Disk Location	Description
Ntoskrnl.exe	%SystemRoot%\System32	The core (also called the kernel) of the Windows Vista operating system. Code that runs as part of the kernel does so in privileged processor mode and has direct access to system data and hardware.
Hal.dll	%SystemRoot%\System32	The *HAL* dynamic-link library *file*. The HAL abstracts low-level hardware details from the operating system and provides a common programming interface to devices of the same type (such as video adapters).
Smss.exe	%SystemRoot%\System32	The Session Manager file. Session Manager is a user-mode process created by the kernel during startup that handles critical startup tasks including creating page files and performing delayed file rename and delete operations.

Table A-1   Windows Vista Core System Files

File Name	Disk Location	Description
Csrss.exe	%SystemRoot%\System32	The Win32 Subsystem file. The Win32 Subsystem is launched by Session Manager, and is required by Windows Vista to function.
Winlogon.exe	%SystemRoot%\System32	The Logon Process file, which handles user logon requests and intercepts the Ctrl+Alt+Del logon key sequence. The Logon Process is launched by Session Manager. This is a required component of Windows Vista.
Services.exe	%SystemRoot%\System32	The Service Control Manager is responsible for starting and stopping services and is a required component of Windows Vista.
Lsass.exe	%SystemRoot%\System32	Local Security Authentication Server process is called by the Logon Process when authenticating users and is a required component of Windows Vista.
System registry file	%SystemRoot%\System32\Config\System	The file that contains data used to create the registry key HKEY_LOCAL_MACHINE\SYSTEM. This key contains information that the operating system requires to start devices and system services.
Device driver packages	%SystemRoot%\System32\Driver Store	Driver package files in this folder are used for hardware devices such as keyboard, mouse, and video.
Pagefile.sys	Root of a disk	The Windows Vista paging file, which Windows Vista uses to store virtual memory.

Startup Files

For Windows Vista to start, the system and boot partitions must contain the files listed in Table A-2.

Table A-2   Windows Vista Startup Files

File Name	Disk Location	Description
BootMgr	Root of the system partition	The Windows Boot Manager.
WinLoad	%SystemRoot%\System32	The Windows Boot Loader.
BCD	\Boot	A file that specifies the paths to operating system installations and other information required for Windows Vista to start.
Ntoskrnl.exe	%SystemRoot%\System32	The core (also called the kernel) of the Windows Vista operating system. Code that runs as part of the kernel does so in privileged processor mode and has direct access to system data and hardware.

Table A-2   **Windows Vista Startup Files**

File Name	Disk Location	Description
Hal.dll	%SystemRoot%\System32	The *HAL* dynamic-link library *file*. The HAL abstracts low-level hardware details from the operating system and provides a common programming interface to devices of the same type (such as video adapters).
Smss.exe	%SystemRoot%\System32	The Session Manager file. Session Manager is a user-mode process created by the kernel during startup that handles critical startup tasks including creating page files and performing delayed file rename and delete operations.
Csrss.exe	%SystemRoot%\System32	The Win32 Subsystem file. The Win32 Subsystem is launched by Session Manager and is required by Windows Vista to function.
Winlogon.exe	%SystemRoot%\System32	The Logon Process file, which handles user logon requests and intercepts the Ctrl+Alt+Del logon key sequence. The Logon Process is launched by Session Manager. This is a required component of Windows Vista.
Services.exe	%SystemRoot%\System32	The Service Control Manager is responsible for starting and stopping services and is a required component of Windows Vista.
Lsass.exe	%SystemRoot%\System32	Local Security Authentication Server process is called by the Logon Process when authenticating users and is a required component of Windows Vista.
System registry file	%System-Root%\System32\Config \System	The file that contains data used to create the registry key HKEY_LOCAL_MACHINE\SYSTEM. This key contains information that the operating system requires to start devices and system services.
Device driver packages	%SystemRoot%\System32\ Driver Store	Driver package files in this folder are used for hardware devices such as keyboard, mouse, and video.

Important Folders

Windows Vista uses the following folders:

- **\$Recycle.Bin**   Hidden by default, this folder contains files that have been deleted. You should never need to directly interact with this folder. Instead, use the Recycle Bin object on the desktop and in Explorer to recover or permanently delete files.

- **\Boot**   On BIOS-based computers, this folder contains the BCD registry file, BCD log files, the Windows Memory Diagnostics file (Memtest.exe), and many subfolders containing regional versions of Windows Boot Manager (Bootmgr.exe.mui) and Windows Memory Diagnostics (Memtest.exe.mui). The \Boot\Fonts\ folder contains several

TrueType fonts used during startup. On EFI-based operating systems, the BCD registry file is located in the \EFI\Microsoft\Boot\ folder on the EFI system partition.

- **\Documents and Settings**   This junction point simply links to the \Users folder for backward compatibility with applications developed prior to Windows Vista. In Windows XP and earlier versions of Windows, the \Documents and Settings folder was used to store user profiles.

- **\Program Files**   The standard location for installing application executable files. To help prevent standard users from installing new applications, standard users can read files in this folder but cannot write files to the folder.

- **\ProgramData**   The standard location for applications to store non-user-specific data, such as shared settings that all users should be able to update.

- **\System Volume Information**   A system folder that stores information about the disk volume. You should never need to directly access this folder.

- **\Users**   The folder used to store user files and documents. This folder contains a sub-folder (the user profile) for each user on the computer. Additionally, the \Users\Public folder contains documents and settings available to all users of the computer.

- **\Windows**   This folder contains Windows system files, including drivers, log files, the registry, and more. Read the next section for more information about the contents of this folder.

Windows Folders

The %SystemRoot% folder, located at \Windows, contains many subfolders:

- **<language-region>**   Contains regional versions of some Windows tools. This folder is named using the *language-region* format. For example, the \Windows\en-US folder contains United States English-language version of Windows tools.

- **Addins**   ActiveX controls (.ocx) files.

- **AppPatch**   Application compatibility files.

- **Assembly**   Assembly files used for Microsoft .NET Framework–based applications.

- **Boot**   Copies of files located in the \Boot folder.

- **Branding**   Used by computer manufacturers that want to insert custom branding into the operating system.

- **CSC**   Offline files that are used during client-side caching.

- **Cursors**   Cursor and icon files.

- **Debug**   Log files.

- **DigitalLocker**   Contains the Digital Locker Assistant, which facilitates downloading and purchasing software.

- **Downloaded Program Files**   Downloaded program files.

- **e-home**   Contains Windows Media Center files.

- **Fonts**   All font files.

- **Globalization**   Contains globalization files, but might be empty, depending on the computer configuration.

- **Help**   Help files.

- **IME**   Language files.

- **inf**   Contains driver files.

- **L2Schemas**   Contains networking profiles.

- **LiveKernelReports**   A system folder used to store nonfatal error reports generated during the failure of a kernel mode application or driver.

- **Logs**   Contains some Windows log files.

- **Media**   Sound and music files (for example, WAV and MIDI files) used by the operating system.

- **Microsoft.NET**   Contains files related to the .NET Framework, including XML-based configuration files.

- **Minidump**   Contains small memory dump files created after stop errors.

- **ModemLogs**   Contains modem log files.

- **MSAgent**   Microsoft Agent files. (Microsoft Agent is a set of programmable software services that support the presentation of interactive animated characters within the Microsoft Windows interface.)

- **nap**   Contains files related to Network Access Protection (NAP).

- **Offline Web Pages**   Downloaded web pages for offline reading.

- **Panther**   Files related to Windows setup.

- **Performance**   Files related to Windows System Assessment (WinSAT).

- **PLA**   Performance logs and alerts information.

- **PolicyDefinitions**   .admx files for extending Group Policy.

- **Prefetch**   Data files related to enhancing the speed at which applications start.

- **Provisioning**   XML schema files related to authentication.

- **Registration**   COM+ files, which are enhancements to the Microsoft Component Object Model (COM).

- **rescache**   Resource cache folder.

- **Resources**   User interface files.

- **SchCache**   Schema cache folder.

- **Schemas**   XML schema files.

- **Security**   Log files, templates for snap-ins, and security database files.

- **ServiceProfiles**   Virtualized profile data for different classifications of services.

- **Servicing**   Installable Windows components.

- **Setup**   Dynamic Update storage location.

- **ShellNew**   Used to store document templates. This folder is available to provide backward compatibility with earlier versions of Windows.

- **SoftwareDistribution**   Microsoft Update files.

- **Speech**   Speech synthesis files.

- **System**   Backward-compatibility files related to the System folder (for example, applications that look for a System folder).

- **system32**   Core operating system files. (For more information, see the section titled "System32 Folder" later in this appendix.)

- **Tapi**   Telephony Application Programming Interface (API) folders. This folder contains the Tsec.ini file, which includes the list of users who are telephony administrators.

- **Tasks**   Scheduled Task files.

- **Temp**   Temporary files.

- **Tracing**   Stores Remote Access Services tracing files. For more information about these files, see *http://support.microsoft.com/kb/816110*.

- **twain_32**   Imaging files (for scanners).

- **Web**   Printer and wallpaper files.

- **Windows Mobile**   Files for connecting to Windows Mobile devices.

- **WinSxS**   Side by Side (shared components).

System32 Folder

The system32 folder and its subfolders contain the core operating system files for your Windows Vista installation:

- **### (three numeric digits)**   Localization (language) files for a specific language, corresponding to the number assigned to this folder.

- **<language-region>**   Contains regional versions of some Windows tools. This folder is named using the *language-region* format. For example, the \Windows\System32\en-US folder contains United States English-language version of Windows tools.

- **AdvancedInstallers**   DLL files used by application installation programs.

- **Boot**   Copies of files located in the \Boot folder.

- **Branding**   Used by computer manufacturers that want to insert custom branding into the operating system.

- **CatRoot**   Catalog files and signature files.

- **CatRoot2**   Catalog files and signature files.

- **CodeIntegrity**   Files used to verify the integrity of system files.

- **Com**   Component Object Model (COM) objects.

- **Config**   Registry files and event logs.

- **Drivers**   Installed drivers.

- **DriverStore**   Windows File Protection backup files.

- **GroupPolicyUsers**   Stores the user-specific local Group Policy cache for Multiple Local Group Policy Objects (MLGPOs).

- **Ias**   Internet Authentication Service files.

- **Icsxml**   Universal Plug and Play files.

- **Ime**   Language files.

- **Inetsrv**   Internet Information Services files.

- **Licensing**   Files related to Windows licensing.

- **LogFiles**   Log files for Windows components.

- **Microsoft**   Cryptography files.

- **Migration**   Files used for computer-to-computer migration.

- **MigWiz**   Files used for computer-to-computer migration.

- **MsDtc**   Microsoft Distributed Transaction Coordinator files.

- **Mui**   Multiuser interface files.

- **NDF**   Event Log trace files.

- **NetworkList**   Icons for different types of networks.

- **Oobe**   Windows Welcome files.

- **Printing_Admin_Scripts**   Scripts for managing printers.

- **Ras**   Remote access server encryption files.

- **RemInst**   Boot-manager files.

- **Restore**   Data files or System Restore–related files.

- **Setup**   Optional component-manager files.

- **Slmgr**   Settings for Windows Product Activation.

- **SLUI**   Files related to Windows Product Activation.

- **Speech**   Speech synthesis files.

- **Spool**   Print spooling files.

- **Sysprep**   Sysprep files, which are used for automating Windows deployment.

- **Tasks**   Scheduled Task files.

- **Usmt**   User State Migration tool.

- **Wbem**   Web-based Enterprise Management data files. Windows Management Instrumentation (WMI) is the Microsoft implementation of WBEM.

- **WCN**   Information about configuring wireless networks with Windows Connect Now.

- **WDI**   Windows diagnostic information.

- **WFP**   Windows File Protection files.

- **Winevt**   Windows trace logs.

- **Winrm**   Configuration settings for Windows Remote Management.

- **XPSViewer**   Files for viewing XML Paper Specification (XPS) documents.

Additional Resources

The following resource contains additional information and tools related to this chapter.

Related Information

- Chapter 30, "Configuring Startup and Troubleshooting Startup Issues," includes information about troubleshooting startup.

Appendix B
User Rights Reference

User rights fall into two general categories: logon rights and privileges. Logon rights control who is authorized to log on to a computer and how he or she can log on. Privileges control access to system-wide resources on a computer and can override the permissions that are set on particular objects.

Logon Rights

Logon rights control how security principals are allowed access to the computer—whether from the keyboard or through a network connection, or whether as a service or as a batch job. For each logon method, there exists a pair of logon rights—one to allow logging on to the computer and another to deny logging on to the computer. Use a deny logon right as you would use a deny permission—to exclude a subset of a group that has been assigned an allow logon right. For example, suppose that Alice wants all users except the members of the domain Marketing group to be able to log on locally at her computer's keyboard. With this in mind, Alice creates a local group, which she names LocalLogonDenied. Then she configures her computer as follows:

1. She assigns the Log On Locally user right to the Users group.

2. She assigns the Deny Local Logon user right to the LocalLogonDenied group.

3. She makes the Marketing domain group a member of the LocalLogonDenied group.

Deny rights take precedence over allow rights, so members of the Marketing group are denied the right to log on locally even though they are also members of the Users group, which is allowed to log on locally.

Caution   The rule to keep in mind is "Allow a set, and then deny a subset." Reversing the order can be disastrous. For example, Alice might want to allow no one but herself to log on locally. If she allowed herself the right to log on locally and denied the Users group the right to log on locally, she would be unpleasantly surprised to find that she had locked herself out of the computer. Alice, after all, is a member of the Users group, so the deny right she assigned to the Users group would take precedence over the allow right she assigned to herself.

Table B-1 describes logon rights. The display names for logon rights are followed by the string constant (in parentheses). Many command-line tools refer to rights by string constant rather than by display name. The default settings are taken from the Windows Vista local computer policy.

Table B-1   Logon Rights

Right	Description
Access This Computer From The Network (*SeNetworkLogonRight*)	Allows a user to connect to the computer from the network.
	Default setting: Everyone, Administrators, Users, and Backup Operators.
Allow Log On Through Terminal Services (*SeRemoteInteractiveLogonRight*)	Allows a user to log on to the computer by using a Remote Desktop connection.
	Default setting: Administrators and Remote Desktop Users.
Log On As A Batch Job (*SeBatchLogonRight*)	Determines whether or not users can log on through a batch-queue facility such as the Task Scheduler service. When an administrator uses the Add Scheduled Task Wizard to schedule a task to run under a particular user name and password, that user is automatically assigned the Log On As A Batch Job user right. When the scheduled time arrives, the Task Scheduler service logs the user on as a batch job instead of as an interactive user, and the task runs in the user's security context.
	Default setting: Administrators, Backup Operators.
Allow Log On Locally (*SeInteractiveLogonRight*)	Allows a user to start an interactive session on the computer. Users who do not have this right can start a Remote Desktop session on the computer if they have the Allow Logon Through Terminal Services right.
	Default setting: Administrators, Users, Guest, and Backup Operators.
Log On As A Service (*SeServiceLogonRight*)	Allows a security principal to log on as a service. Services can be configured to run under the Local System, Local Service, or Network Service accounts, which have a built-in right to log on as a service. Any service that runs under a separate user account must be assigned the right.
	Default setting: Not assigned.
Deny Access To This Computer From The Network (*SeDenyNetworkLogonRight*)	Prohibits a user from connecting to the computer from the network.
	Default setting: Guest.
Deny Log On Locally (*SeDenyInteractiveLogonRight*)	Prohibits a user from logging on directly at the keyboard.
	Default setting: Guest.

Table B-1 **Logon Rights**

Right	Description
Deny Log On As A Batch Job (*SeDenyBatchLogonRight*)	Prohibits a user from logging on by using a batch-queue facility. Default setting: Not assigned.
Deny Log On As A Service (*SeDenyServiceLogonRight*)	Prohibits a user from logging on as a service. Default setting: Not assigned.
Deny Log On Through Terminal Services (*SeDenyRemoteInteractiveLogonRight*)	Prohibits a user from logging on to the computer using a Remote Desktop connection. Default setting: Not assigned.

Privileges

To ease the task of security administration, it is recommended that you assign privileges primarily to groups rather than to individual user accounts. When you assign privileges to a group, the privileges are assigned automatically to each user who is added to the group. This is easier than assigning privileges to individual user accounts as each account is created.

Table B-2 describes the privileges that can be assigned. The display name for each privilege is followed by the corresponding string constant (in parentheses). Many command-line tools refer to privileges by string constant rather than by display name. The default settings are taken from the Windows Vista Local Computer policy.

Table B-2 **Privileges**

Privilege	Description
Access Credential Manager As A Trusted Caller (*SeTrustedCredManAccesPrivilege*)	New with Windows Vista, this right is used to back up and restore Credential Manager. Only the Winlogon process needs this right; users should never need to use this privilege directly. Default setting: Not assigned.
Act As Part Of The Operating System (*SeTcbPrivilege*)	Allows a process to assume the identity of any user and thus gain access to the resources that the user is authorized to access. Typically, only low-level authentication services require this privilege. Potential access is not limited to what is associated with the user by default; the calling process might request that arbitrary additional privileges be added to the access token. The calling process might also build an access token that does not provide a primary identity for tracking events in the audit log. When a service requires this privilege, configure the service to log on using the Local System account, which has the privilege inherently. Do not create a separate account and assign the privilege to it. Default setting: Not assigned.

Table B-2   **Privileges**

Privilege	Description
Add Workstations To Domain (*SeMachineAccountPrivilege*)	Allows the user to add a computer to a specific domain. For the privilege to take effect, it must be assigned to the user as part of the Default Domain Controllers Policy for the domain. A user who has this privilege can add up to 10 workstations to the domain. Users can also join a computer to a domain if they have Create Computer Objects permission for an organizational unit or for the Computers container in Active Directory. Users who have this permission can add an unlimited number of computers to the domain regardless of whether they have been assigned the Add Workstations To A Domain privilege. Default setting: Not assigned.
Adjust Memory Quotas For A Process (*SeIncreaseQuotaPrivilege*)	Allows a process that has access to a second process to increase the processor quota assigned to the second process. This privilege is useful for system tuning, but it can be abused: In the wrong hands, it could be used to launch a denial-of-service attack. Default setting: Administrators, Local Service, and Network Service.
Back Up Files And Directories (*SeBackupPrivilege*)	Allows the user to circumvent file and directory permissions to back up the system. The privilege is selected only when an application attempts access by using the NTFS backup application programming interface (API). Otherwise, normal file and directory permissions apply. See also "Restore Files And Directories" in this table. Default setting: Administrators and Backup Operators.
Bypass Traverse Checking (*SeChangeNotifyPrivilege*)	Allows the user to pass through folders to which the user otherwise has no access while navigating an object path in the NTFS file system or in the registry. This privilege does not allow the user to list the contents of a folder; it allows the user only to traverse its directories. Default setting: Administrators, Backup Operators, Local Service, Network Service, Power Users (if upgraded from Windows XP), Users, and Everyone.
Change The System Time (*SeSystemTimePrivilege*)	Allows the user to adjust the time on the computer's internal clock. This privilege is limited to administrators because system time must be accurate for Active Directory domain authentication to work properly. This privilege is not required to change the time zone or other display characteristics of the system time. Default setting: Administrators and Local Service.

Table B-2   Privileges

Privilege	Description
Change The Time Zone (*SeTimeZone-Privilege*)	New with Windows Vista, this right allows the user to adjust the time zone on the computer's internal clock. Standard users can do this to provide the correct time when traveling.
	Default setting: Administrators, Users, and Local Service.
Create A Pagefile (*SeCreatePagefilePrivilege*)	Allows the user to create and change the size of a pagefile. This is done by specifying a paging file size for a particular drive in the Performance Options box on the Advanced tab of System Properties.
	Default setting: Administrators.
Create A Token Object (*SeCreateTokenPrivilege*)	Allows a process to create an access token by calling *NtCreateToken()* or other token-creating APIs. When a process requires this privilege, use the Local System (or System) account, which has the privilege inherently. Do not create a separate user account and assign the privilege to it.
	Default setting: Not assigned.
Create Global Objects (*SeCreateGlobal-Privilege*)	Determines whether or not users can create global objects that are available to all sessions. Users can still create objects that are specific to their own sessions if they do not have this user right. Users who can create global objects could affect processes that run under other users' sessions, which could lead to application failure or data corruption.
	Default setting: Administrators, Local Service, Network Service, Service.
Create Permanent Shared Objects (*SeCreatePermanentPrivilege*)	Determines whether or not users can create directory objects in the object manager. Users who have this capability can create permanent shared objects, including devices, semaphores, and mutexes. This user right is useful to kernel-mode components that extend the object namespace; they have this user right inherently. Therefore, it is typically not necessary to specifically assign this user right to any users.
	Default setting: Not assigned.
Create Symbolic Links (*SeCreate-SymbolicLinkPrivilege*)	New with Windows Vista, this right allows users to create symbolic links.
	Default setting: Administrators.
Debug Programs (*SeDebugPrivilege*)	Allows the user to attach a debugger to any process. This privilege provides access to sensitive and critical operating system components.
	Default setting: Administrators.

Table B-2 Privileges

Privilege	Description
Enable Computer And User Accounts To Be Trusted For Delegation (*SeEnableDelegationPrivilege*)	Allows the user to change the Trusted For Delegation setting on a user or computer object in Active Directory. The user or computer that is granted this privilege must also have write access to the account control flags on the object. Delegation of authentication is a capability that is used by multitier client/server applications. It allows a front-end service to use the credentials of a client in authenticating to a back-end service. For this to be possible, both client and server must be running under accounts that are trusted for delegation. Misuse of this privilege or the Trusted For Delegation settings can make the network vulnerable to sophisticated attacks that use Trojan horse programs, which impersonate incoming clients and use their credentials to gain access to network resources. Default setting: Not assigned to anyone on member servers and workstations because it has no meaning in those contexts.
Force Shutdown From A Remote System (*SeRemoteShutdownPrivilege*)	Allows a user to shut down a computer from a remote location on the network. See also "Shut Down The System" in this table. Default setting: Administrators.
Generate Security Audits (*SeAuditPrivilege*)	Allows a process to generate audit records in the security log. The security log can be used to trace unauthorized system access. See also "Manage Auditing And Security Log" in this table. Default setting: Local Service and Network Service.
Impersonate A Client After Authentication (*SeImpersonatePrivilege*)	Allows programs that run on behalf of a user to impersonate that user. This right is typically used only by services. Default setting: Administrators, Service, Local Service, Network Service.
Increase A Process Working Set (*SeIncreaseWorkingSetPrivilege*)	Allows a user to increase the working set of a process. This privilege gets checked for explicit quota set requests and is (typically) required inside of *CreateProcessAsUser*, which may set the process quotas. Default setting: Users.
Increase Scheduling Priority (*SeIncreaseBasePriorityPrivilege*)	Allows a user to increase the base priority class of a process. (Increasing relative priority within a priority class is not a privileged operation.) This privilege is not required by administrative tools supplied with the operating system but might be required by software development tools. Default setting: Administrators.

Table B-2   Privileges

Privilege	Description
Load And Unload Device Drivers (*SeLoadDriverPrivilege*)	Allows a user to install and remove drivers for Plug and Play devices. This privilege is not required if a signed driver for the new hardware already exists in the Driver.cab file on the computer. Do not assign this privilege to any user or group other than Administrators. Device drivers run as trusted (highly privileged) code. A user who has the Load And Unload Device Drivers privilege could unintentionally install malicious code masquerading as a device driver. It is assumed that administrators will exercise greater care and install only drivers with verified digital signatures. You must have this privilege and also be a member of either Administrators or Power Users to install a new driver for a local printer or manage a local printer by setting defaults for options such as duplex printing. Default setting: Administrators.
Lock Pages In Memory (*SeLockMemoryPrivilege*)	Allows a process to keep data in physical memory, which prevents the system from paging the data to virtual memory on disk. Assigning this privilege can result in significant degradation of system performance. Default setting: Not assigned.
Manage Auditing And Security Log (*SeSecurityPrivilege*)	Allows a user to specify object access auditing options for individual resources such as files, Active Directory objects, and registry keys. Object access auditing is not performed unless you enable it by using Audit Policy (under Security Settings, Local Policies). A user who has this privilege can also view and clear the security log from Event Viewer. Default setting: Administrators.
Modify An Object Label (*SeRelabel-Privilege*)	Allows a subject to modify the integrity level of a resource object that has higher integrity level than the subject does. This is a very powerful privilege; you should assign it only to Administrators. Default setting: Not assigned.
Modify Firmware Environment Values (*SeSystemEnvironmentPrivilege*)	Allows modification of system environment variables either by a process through an API or by a user through System Properties. Default setting: Administrators.
Perform Volume Maintenance Tasks (*SeManageVolumePrivilege*)	Allows a nonadministrative or remote user to manage volumes or disks. The operating system checks for the privilege in a user's access token when a process running in the user's security context calls *SetFileValidData()*. Default setting: Administrators.

Table B-2   Privileges

Privilege	Description
Profile Single Process (*SeProfileSingleProcessPrivilege*)	Allows a user to sample the performance of an application process. Ordinarily, you do not need this privilege to use the Performance Monitor snap-in. However, you do need the privilege if a tool is configured to collect data by using Windows Management Instrumentation (WMI). Default setting: Administrators and Power Users (if upgraded from Windows XP).
Profile System Performance (*SeSystemProfilePrivilege*)	Allows a user to sample the performance of system processes. This privilege is required by the Performance snap-in only if it is configured to collect data by using WMI. Ordinarily, you do not need this privilege to use the Performance Monitor snap-in. However, you do need the privilege if a tool is configured to collect data by using WMI. Default setting: Administrators.
Remove Computer From Docking Station (*SeUndockPrivilege*)	Allows the user of a portable computer to undock the computer by clicking Eject PC on the Start menu. Default setting: Administrators, Power Users (if upgraded from Windows XP), and Users.
Replace A Process Level Token (*SeAssignPrimaryTokenPrivilege*)	Allows a parent process to replace the access token associated with a child process. Default setting: Local Service and Network Service.
Restore Files And Directories (*SeRestorePrivilege*)	Allows a user to circumvent file and directory permissions when restoring backed-up files and directories and to set any valid security principal as the owner of an object. See also "Back Up Files And Directories" in this table. Default setting: Administrators and Backup Operators.
Shut Down The System (*SeShutdownPrivilege*)	Allows a user to shut down the local computer. See also "Force Shutdown From A Remote System" in this table. Default setting: Administrators, Backup Operators, Power Users (if upgraded from Windows XP), and Users.
Synchronize Directory Service Data (*SeSyncAgentPrivilege*)	New with Windows Server 2003, this right allows a process to read all objects and properties in the directory, regardless of the protection on the objects and properties. This privilege is required to use Lightweight Directory Access Protocol (LDAP) directory synchronization (Dirsync) services. Default setting: Not assigned. The privilege is relevant only on domain controllers.

Table B-2 Privileges

Privilege	Description
Take Ownership Of Files Or Other Objects (*SeTakeOwnershipPrivilege*)	Allows a user to take ownership of any securable object in the system, including Active Directory objects, NTFS files and folders, printers, registry keys, services, processes, and threads.
	Default setting: Administrators.

Additional Resources

The following resource contains additional information and tools related to this chapter.

Related Information

- Chapter 30, "Configuring Startup and Troubleshooting Startup Issues," includes information about troubleshooting startup.

Appendix C

Accessibility

Windows Vista includes new and enhanced accessibility features to make it easier for users to see, hear, and use their computers. The accessibility settings and programs in Windows Vista are particularly helpful to people with visual difficulties, hearing loss, pain in their hands or arms, or reasoning and cognitive issues.

- **Visual difficulties** Includes poor lighting conditions, individuals who have low vision, or individuals who are blind.

- **Dexterity difficulties** Includes pain in the hands, arms, or wrists; or difficulty using a keyboard, mouse, other pointing device, or pen.

- **Hearing difficulties** Includes environments with high background noise and individuals who are hard of hearing or deaf.

- **Cognitive issues** Includes difficulty concentrating and focusing on tasks, difficulty remembering things, and learning disabilities such as dyslexia.

Ease of Access Center

The new Ease of Access Center (Figure C-1) provides a convenient, central location where the user can quickly adjust accessibility settings and manage assistive technology (AT) programs. The Ease of Access Center replaces the Accessibility Wizard and the Utilities Manager found in previous versions of Microsoft Windows.

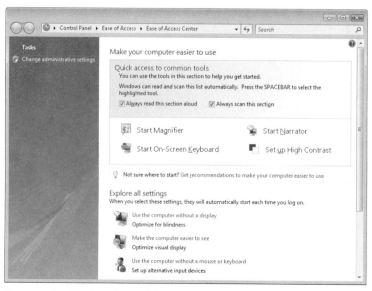

Figure C-1   The new Ease of Access Center.

With the Ease of Access Center, the user can enable and configure the following accessibility settings:

- **Start Narrator**   A text-to-speech program that reads on-screen text aloud and describes some events (such as error messages) that happen while you're using the computer.

- **Start Magnifier**   Enlarges a portion of the screen where the user is working. You can choose magnification levels from 2 to 16 times the original, as well as whether to track the mouse, the keyboard, or text editing.

- **Start On-Screen Keyboard**   A visual, on-screen keyboard with all the standard keys. You can use this instead of a physical keyboard. On-Screen Keyboard also lets you type using an alternative input device.

- **High Contrast**   High Contrast heightens the color contrast of some text and images on your computer screen, making those items more distinct and easier to identify.

- **Make The Focus Rectangle Thicker**   Thickens the rectangle around the currently selected item in a dialog box.

- **Turn On Sticky Keys**   Instead of having to press multiple keys at once (such as pressing the Ctrl, Alt, and Del keys simultaneously to log on to Windows), you can press one key at a time when Sticky Keys is turned on.

- **Turn On Toggle Keys**   Causes Windows to play an alert when Caps Lock, Num Lock, or Scroll Lock are pressed.

- **Turn On Filter Keys**   Causes Windows to ignore keystrokes that occur in rapid succession or keystrokes caused by unintentionally holding down keys for several seconds.

- **Underline Keyboard Shortcuts And Access Keys**   Makes using the keyboard to access controls in dialog boxes easier.

- **Change The Color And Size Of Mouse Pointers**   Makes the mouse pointer larger or a different color.

- **Activate A Window By Hovering Over It With A Mouse**   Lets the user select and activate a window by pointing at it instead of clicking it.

- **Turn On Mouse Keys**   Lets users move the mouse pointer using the arrow keys on the keyboard or on the numeric keypad.

- **Turn On Audio Description**   Causes Windows use videos to describe what is happening on the computer.

- **Turn Off All Unnecessary Animations (Where Possible)**   Turns off animation, such as fading effects when windows are closed.

- **Remove Background Images (Where Available)**   Turns off all unimportant, overlapping background content and all background images.

- **Turn On Or Off High Contrast When Left Alt+Left Shift+Print Screen Is Pressed**   Sets the screen to display using a high-contrast color scheme.

- **How Long Should Windows Notification Dialog Boxes Stay Open?**   Specifies the time Windows notification dialog boxes are displayed before disappearing.

- **Turn On Visual Notifications For Sounds (Sound Sentry)**   Replaces system sounds with visual cues such as a flashing caption bar, flashing window, or flashing desktop.

- **Turn On Text Captions For Spoken Dialog (When Available)**   Displays text captions in place of sounds to indicate that activity is happening on your computer.

Additional Accessibility Features

Additional accessibility features not managed by the Ease of Access Center include:

- **Keyboard Shortcuts**   Allows the user to control actions that programs perform using the keyboard instead of the mouse.

- **Windows Speech Recognition**   Allows the user to interact with the computer using voice as an input device.

Table C-1 maps Windows Vista accessibility features with the types of challenges they can help to address.

Table C-1   Windows Vista Accessibility Features

Accessibility Feature	Visual Difficulties	Dexterity Problems	Hearing Difficulties	Cognitive Issues
Start Narrator	✓			✓
Start Magnifier	✓			
Make The Focus Rectangle Thicker	✓			✓
Turn On Sticky Keys		✓		✓
Turn On Toggle Keys		✓		✓
Turn On Filter Keys		✓		✓
Underline Keyboard Shortcuts And Access Keys	✓	✓		
Change The Color And Size Of Mouse Pointers	✓	✓		✓
Activate A Window By Hovering Over It With A Mouse		✓		
Turn On Mouse Keys		✓		✓
Turn On Audio Description	✓			
Turn Off All Unnecessary Animations (Where Possible)	✓			✓
Remove Background Images (Where Available)	✓			✓
Turn On Or Off High Contrast When Left Alt+Left Shift+Print Screen Is Pressed	✓			
How Long Should Windows Notification Dialog Boxes Stay Open?	✓	✓		✓
Turn On Visual Notifications For Sounds (Sound Sentry)			✓	
Turn On Text Captions For Spoken Dialog (When Available)			✓	
Use On-Screen Keyboard		✓		
Keyboard Shortcuts		✓		
Windows Speech Recognition		✓		

Using the Ease of Access Center

To open the Ease of Access Center, do one of the following:

- Click Start, click Control Panel, click Ease Of Access, and then click Ease Of Access Center.
- Press the Windows logo key+U.

In addition, you can enable the following subset of Ease of Access features directly from the logon screen by clicking the Ease Of Access icon at the lower left of the logon screen:

- Narrator
- Magnifier
- High Contrast
- On-Screen Keyboard
- Sticky Keys
- Filter Keys

The Ease of Access Center includes:

- **Quick Access**   Start Magnifier, Narrator, On-Screen Keyboard, and High Contrast.
- **Recommended Settings**   Based on answers to questions about performing routine tasks, such as if you have difficulty seeing faces or text on TV, hearing conversations, or using a pen or pencil, Windows Vista provides a personalized recommendation of the accessibility settings and programs that are likely to improve your ability to see, hear, and use your computer.
- **Explore available settings by category**   The Ease of Access Center also lets you explore settings options by categories, including making the computer easier to see, using the computer without a display, changing mouse or keyboard settings or using the computer without a mouse or keyboard, using alternatives for sounds, and making it easier to focus on tasks.

> **Note**   When you enable accessibility features by using Quick Access To Common Tools, the features are available only during the current logon session; when you log off, the enabled features are disabled. To enable accessibility features and have them persist across logon sessions, use either Get Recommendations To Make Your Computer Easier To Use or Explore All Settings.

Using Magnifier

Magnifier enlarges a portion of the computer screen in a separate window to make it easier to see. By default, Magnifier enlarges the screen by a factor of 2, but you can configure Magnifier (Figure C-2) to enlarge up to 16 times compared to only 9 times available in previous versions of Microsoft Windows. You can also invert colors in the Magnifier window to increase screen legibility.

Magnifier can track any or all of the following user actions:

- Mouse pointer
- Keyboard focus
- Text editing

New features of Magnifier in Windows Vista include:

- By default, the tool starts minimized.
- It can be docked to the left, right, top, or bottom of the screen.
- It can also be undocked as a floating window that you can drag around.

Figure C-2   Configuring Magnifier.

Using Narrator

Narrator is a text-to-speech program that reads the contents of the active window, menu options, or text that the user has typed. New features of Narrator in Windows Vista include:

■ The tool has a more pleasant, natural-sounding voice called Microsoft Anna, which replaces the Microsoft Sam voice used in previous versions of Microsoft Windows.

■ The tool can read Narrator menus without leaving the active window.

■ The user can move around the desktop with the number keys using virtual focus, and Narrator will read aloud any contents that each desktop window or object contains.

■ The user can use bookmarks to find commonly used programs.

In addition, Narrator is compatible with any Speech Application Programming Interface (SAPI)–compliant voice.

Figure C-3   Configuring Narrator.

Using the On-Screen Keyboard

The On-Screen Keyboard (Figure C-4) displays a visual keyboard with which the user can type without relying on a physical keyboard. The functionality of the On-Screen Keyboard in Windows Vista is similar to its functionality in previous versions of Microsoft Windows, with the exception that the appearance of the keyboard has been enhanced to make it easier to see and work with.

Figure C-4   The On-Screen Keyboard.

Ease of Access Keyboard Shortcuts

As shown in Table C-2, you can enable some accessibility features by using keyboard shortcuts.

Table C-2   Keyboard Shortcuts for Ease of Access Features

Press This Key	To Do This
Right Shift for eight seconds	Turn Filter Keys on and off
Left Alt+Left Shift+Print Screen (or Prtscrn)	Turn High Contrast on or off
Left Alt+Left Shift+Num Lock	Turn Mouse Keys on or off
Shift five times	Turn Sticky Keys on or off
Num Lock for five seconds	Turn Toggle Keys on or off
Windows logo key+U	Open the Ease of Access Center

Note   You can find additional keyboard shortcuts for Windows Vista at *http://www.microsoft.com/enable/products/keyboard.aspx.*

Windows Speech Recognition

Windows Speech Recognition is a new feature in Windows Vista that lets the user interact with the computer using his or her voice. Windows Speech Recognition was designed for the individual who wants to use the mouse and keyboard less while still maintaining and even increasing overall productivity. In addition, Windows Speech Recognition can provide benefits to individuals with physical disabilities by allowing them to interact with their computers without the need of a keyboard or mouse.

Windows Speech Recognition supports the following languages:

- English (United States)
- English (United Kingdom)
- German (Germany)

- French (France)
- Spanish (Spain)
- Japanese
- Traditional Chinese
- Simplified Chinese

For more information about Windows Speech Recognition, see the white paper titled "Windows Vista Speech Recognition Step-by-Step Guide," available from the Microsoft Download Center at *http://www.microsoft.com/downloads/details.aspx?FamilyID=311f4be8-9983-4ab0-9685-f1bfec1e7d62&DisplayLang=en*.

Assistive Technology Products

Individuals with physical and cognitive difficulties can use third-party assistive technology (AT) products to use computers more easily and effectively. Many AT products, including multiple screen readers, will be available on Windows Vista. Be sure to check with your AT manufacturer before upgrading if you have concerns. Assistive technology products include:

- Alternative input devices
- Speech and voice recognition software
- Screen readers
- Screen magnifiers and screen enlargers
- On-screen keyboards
- Other types of hardware and software

At the time of writing this Resource Kit, more than 300 AT products were compatible with Windows. To learn whether or not a specific AT product is compatible with Windows Vista, go to *http://www.microsoft.com/enable/at/*.

Microsoft Accessibility Resource Centers

Microsoft has also developed a network of Microsoft Accessibility Resource Centers where users can learn more about technology solutions that meet their needs, including how to effectively use the accessibility features found in Windows Vista.

For more information and to locate a Microsoft Accessibility Resource Center near you, go to *http://www.microsoft.com/enable/centers/*.

Additional Resources

The following resources contain additional information and tools related to this chapter.

Related Information

- "Windows Vista Speech Recognition Step-by-Step Guide" at *http://www.microsoft.com/downloads/details.aspx?FamilyID=311f4be8-9983-4ab0-9685-f1bfec1e7d62&DisplayLang=en.*

- "Assistive Technology Products for Windows Vista" at *http://www.microsoft.com/enable/at/vista/.*

- "Windows Vista Accessibility Tutorials" at *http://www.microsoft.com/enable/training/windowsvista/.*

- Go to *http://www.microsoft.com/enable/at/* for a list of assistive technology products compatible with Windows Vista.

- Go to *http://www.microsoft.com/enable/centers/* to find a Microsoft Accessibility Resource Center near you.

Glossary

- **802.1X**   A standard that defines port-based, network access control used to provide authenticated network access for Ethernet networks. This standard uses the physical characteristics of the switched LAN infrastructure to authenticate devices attached to a LAN port.

- **802.11**   An industry standard for a shared, wireless local area network (WLAN) that defines the physical layer and media access control (MAC) sublayer for wireless communications.

- **ABE**   *See Access-Based Enumeration.*

- **Access-Based Enumeration (ABE)**   A new feature in Windows Vista that allows users to see only those files and folders within a network share that the user actually has permissions to access. When using ABE, an administrator can, for example, share C:\Budgets and assign ACLs as before, but ordinary users who browse the BUDGETS share will only see the Public.doc file. The Secret.doc file will not be visible to them—they won't even know of its existence. ABE thus increases the security of shared data and also helps protect its privacy.

- **activation**   The process of registering an instance of Windows with Microsoft to confirm the legitimacy of the product key and license.

- **Address Resolution Protocol (ARP)**   A Layer 2 protocol that TCP/IP clients, such as Windows Vista, use to resolve local IP addresses to Machine Access Control (MAC) addresses. Windows Vista also includes a tool named Arp to display and clear the ARP cache.

- **Address Space Layout Randomization (ASLR)**   A Windows Vista feature that randomly assigns executable images (.dll and .exe files) included as part of the operating system to one of 256 possible locations in memory. This makes it harder for exploit code to locate these images and therefore take advantage of functionality inside the executables by using a buffer overrun attack.

- **Admin Approval Mode**   A Windows Vista feature that prompts administrators to confirm actions that require more than Standard privileges.

- **admin broker**   A component of Internet Explorer Protected Mode that allows Internet Explorer to install ActiveX controls.

- **ADML template file**   One of a set of Windows Vista files used to add custom registry-based Group Policy settings. ADML files provide language-specific translations of Group Policy setting names and descriptions.

- **ADMX template file**   One of a set of Windows Vista files used to add custom registry-based Group Policy settings. ADMX files specify the registry location and possible values. Optionally, ADMX files can include descriptions for a single language, or translations can be stored in ADML template files.

- **answer file**   An XML-based file that contains settings to use during a Windows Vista installation.

- **ARP**   *See Address Resolution Protocol.*

- **ASLR**   *See Address Space Layout Randomization.*

- **Authorization Manager (AzMan)**   An MMC user interface that administrators can use to configure Role-Based Access Control (RBAC) settings for supported applications.

- **AzMan**   *See Authorization Manager.*

- **Background Intelligent Transfer Service (BITS)**   A file-transfer service designed to transfer files across the Internet using only idle network bandwidth. Unlike standard HTTP, FTP, or shared-folders file transfers, BITS does not use all available bandwidth, so you can use BITS to download large files without impacting other network applications. BITS transfers are also very reliable and can continue when users change network connections or restart their computers. BITS is used to transfer data between the Software Update Services or Windows Update server to the Automatic Updates client.

- **bench deployment**   A deployment process in which a technician deploys and configures a computer in a lab environment before physically moving it to the user's desk.

- **BitLocker Drive Encryption**   A Windows Vista feature capable of encrypting the entire system volume, thus protecting the computer in the event of attacks that bypass the operating system security.

- **BITS**   *See Background Intelligent Transfer Service.*

- **blue screen**   *See Stop error.*

- **Bluetooth**   A short-range radio technology for device networking that is most commonly used by mobile phones and handheld devices, such as PDAs/Pocket PCs.

- **boot image**   An operating system image that is directly bootable without being installed. For example, Windows PE can be run from a boot image.

- **buffer overflow**   An attack that submits larger or longer values than an application or application programming interface (API) is designed to process.

- **build**   In the context of Microsoft Deployment, the association of source files from the distribution share with a configuration.

- **catalog**   The system index together with the property cache.

- **catalog file**   A binary file that contains the state of all settings and packages in a Windows Vista image.

- **central store**   In the context of Group Policy, a location for storing administrative templates for use throughout an organization. Only Windows Vista and later versions of Windows support using a central store.

- **channel** In Meeting Space, the basis for communication between participants in a meeting. There are three kinds of Meeting Space channels: metadata, file, and streaming. The term *channel* can also refer to an application-specific event log.

- **Clear key** Key stored in the clear on the disk volume. This key is used to freely access the VMK and, in turn, the FVEK in the event that BitLocker protection is disabled but disk volume remains encrypted.

- **Client-Side Cache (CSC)** A Microsoft internal term referring to Offline Files.

- **cloud** In peer-to-peer networks, a grouping of computers that uses addresses of a specific scope. A scope is an area of the network over which the address is unique.

- **CNG** *See Crypto Next Generation services.*

- **Code Integrity** A Windows Vista feature that detects changes to system files and drivers.

- **compatibility layer** A component of Internet Explorer Protected Mode that redirects requests for protected resources (such as the user's Documents folder) to safe locations (such as the temporary Internet files folder).

- **component** A part of the Windows Vista operating system that specifies the files, resources, and settings for a specific Windows Vista feature or part of a Windows Vista feature.

- **component store** A portion of an operating system image that stores one or more operating system components or language packs.

- **configuration pass** A phase of Windows Vista installation. Different parts of the Windows Vista operating system are installed and configured in different configuration passes. You can specify Windows Vista unattended installation settings to be applied in one or more configuration passes.

- **configuration set** A file and folder structure containing files that control the preinstallation process and define customizations for the Windows Vista installation.

- **confirmation identifier** A digitally signed value returned by a Microsoft clearinghouse to activate a system.

- **core application** An application that is common to most computers in your organization, such as a virus scanner or a management agent.

- **Crypto Next Generation (CNG) services** An internal Windows Vista infrastructure that provides greater flexibility for application developers using encryption.

- **Cryptographic Service Provider (CSP)** An infrastructure that developers can use to create applications that use cryptographic functions such as encryption, hashes, and digital signatures.

- **CSC** *See Client-Side Cache.*

- **CSP** *See Cryptographic Service Provider.*

- **data store**   In deployment, the location in which the User State Migration Tool (USMT) stores user state between the time it is read from the original computer and deployed to the target computer.

- **defense-in-depth**   A proven technique of layered protection that reduces the exposure of vulnerabilities. For example, you might design a network with three layers of packet filtering: a packet-filtering router, a hardware firewall, and software firewalls on each of the hosts (such as Internet Connection Firewall). If an attacker manages to bypass one or two of the layers of protection, the hosts are still protected.

- **Deploying Phase**   In deployment, this is the phase in which computers are actually set up and configured. Additionally, the deployment team verifies that deployed computers are stable and usable.

- **deployment point**   A subset of a distribution share, the deployment point specifies which source files and builds to distribute and how to distribute them.

- **Desktop Window Manager (DWM)**   A component of Windows Vista that performs desktop composition to enable visual effects such as glass window frames, 3D window transition animations, Windows Flip and Windows Flip3D, and high-resolution support.

- **destination computer**   The computer on which you install Windows Vista during deployment. You can either run Windows Setup on the destination computer or copy a master installation onto a destination computer.

- **Developing Phase**   In deployment, the period during which the team builds and unit-tests the solution.

- **directory junction**   A technique for redirecting requests for a specific folder to a different location. Directory junctions are used to provide backward compatibility for folder locations used in earlier versions of Windows.

- **discoverable**   A state in which a Bluetooth-enabled device sends out radio signals to advertise its location to other devices and computers.

- **distribution share**   A folder that contains the source files for Microsoft Windows products that you install. It may also contain additional device drivers and application files. This folder can be created manually or by using Windows SIM. In BDD 2007, the distribution share contains operating system, device driver, application, and other source files that you configure by creating builds and distribute through deployment points.

- **DLL**   *See Dynamic Link Library.*

- **DWM**   *See Desktop Window Manager.*

- **Dynamic Link Library (DLL)**   A file containing executable code that programs can run. Multiple programs can reference a single DLL, and a single program might use many different DLLs.

- **end user**   The person in the organization who ultimately receives the computer.

- **envisioning phase**   The phase in a BDD 2007 deployment in which management creates teams, performs an assessment of existing systems and applications, defines business goals, creates a vision statement, defines scope, creates user profiles, develops a solution concept, creates risk-assessment documents, writes a project structure, and approves milestones.

- **escalated Remote Assistance (RA)**   *See solicited Remote Assistance.*

- **expert**   In a Remote Assistance scenario, the user who provides help.

- **feature team**   In the context of BDD, a cross-organizational team that focuses on solving a particular problem, such as security.

- **feature team guide**   In the context of BDD, a document that addresses the tasks required of a specific feature team.

- **file sharing**   The process of making files or folders available to other users.

- **folder redirection**   A technique for configuring computers to access user profile data from an alternate location. Folder redirection is commonly used to store user documents and data files on a shared folder.

- **forced guest**   *See ForceGuest.*

- **ForceGuest**   A common term for one of the network access models used by Windows XP that requires all network users to be treated as guests. With Windows Vista, however, forced guest is no longer a supported setting; toggling this setting on is not recommended.

- **Full Volume Encryption Key (FVEK)**   The algorithm-specific key used to encrypt (and optionally, diffuse) data on disk sectors. Currently, this key can vary from 128 bits through 512 bits. The default encryption algorithm used on disk volumes is AES 128 bit with Diffuser.

- **FVEK**   *See Full Volume Encryption Key.*

- **Gadgets**   Mini-applications that can do almost anything including show news updates, display a picture slideshow, or show weather reports.

- **GPT**   *See GUID Partition Table.*

- **GUID Partition Table (GPT)**   A new disk-partitioning technology that offers several advantages over MBR, including support for larger partitions and up to 128 partitions on a single disk.

- **HAL**   *See Hardware Abstraction Layer.*

- **Hardware Abstraction Layer (HAL)**   A component of Windows operating systems that simplifies how Windows accesses hardware by providing a single interface that behaves identically across different platforms.

- **helper**   *See expert.*

- **high-volume deployment**   A deployment project that involves a large number of computers.

- **hybrid image**   An imaging strategy that combines thick and thin images. In a hybrid image, you configure the disk image to install applications on first run, giving the illusion of a thick image but installing the applications from a network source. Hybrid images have most of the advantages of thin images. However, they aren't as complex to develop and do not require a software distribution infrastructure. They do require longer installation times, however, which can raise initial deployment costs.

- **ICMP**   *See Internet Control Message Protocol.*

- **IFilter**   A component of the Windows search engine that is used to convert documents in different formats into plain text so that they can be indexed. IFilters are also responsible for extracting a number of format-dependent properties such as Subject, Author, Locale, and so on. Microsoft provides IFilters for many common document formats by default, while third-party vendors such as Adobe provide their own IFilters for indexing other forms of content.

- **IID**   *See Installation Identifier.*

- **image-based setup**   A setup process based on applying a disk image of an operating system to the computer.

- **in place sharing**   *See in profile sharing.*

- **in profile sharing**   Sharing a file or folder from within your user profile.

- **Installation Identifier (IID)**   A code generated by combining a system's hardware ID (created by scanning the system hardware) and the product ID (derived from the Windows installation). This code is transmitted to a Microsoft activation clearinghouse during system activation.

- **installation image**   An operating system image that can be installed on a computer. Unlike boot images, installation images cannot be booted directly from the image and must be deployed to a computer before running.

- **IntelliMirror**   A set of change and configuration management features based on Active Directory that enables management of user and computer data and settings, including security data. IntelliMirror also provides limited ability to deploy software to Windows 2000 and later workstations or servers.

- **Internet Control Message Protocol (ICMP)**   A Layer 3 protocol that IP applications use to test connectivity and communicate routing changes. ICMP is most commonly used by the Ping tool.

- **Ipconfig**   A command-line tool that displays the current network configuration.

- **Kernel Mode**   A processing mode provided by x86-based processors that provides processes with unrestricted access to memory and other system resources. In Windows Vista, only system components and trusted drivers should run in Kernel Mode.

- **Key Management Service (KMS)** An infrastructure that simplifies tracking product keys in enterprise environments.

- **KMS** *See Key Management Service.*

- **knownfolders** Windows Vista user profile folders that can be redirected with Folder Redirection.

- **legacy mode** A Windows Deployment Services (Windows DS) mode that uses OSChooser and RIPREP (sector-based) images. This mode is compatible with RIS. Moving from RIS-only functionality to legacy mode happens when you install the Windows DS update on a server that's running RIS.

- **Lite Touch Installation (LTI)** A deployment option in BDD that deploys client computers with little human interaction. An alternative deployment option, ZTI, deploys client computers with zero human interaction, but requires more preparation and engineering time beforehand. Therefore, LTI is more appropriate for environments that will be deploying fewer computers.

- **local sharing** The process of making files and folders available to other users on the same computer.

- **local user profile** The default approach for storing user profiles in Windows Vista in which the user profile is stored on the computer's hard disk.

- **LTI** *See Lite Touch Installation.*

- **MAK** *See Multiple Activation Key.*

- **malware** A term that describes a broad range of malicious software including viruses, worms, Trojan horses, spyware, and adware.

- **Mandatory Integrity Control (MIC)** A model in which lower-integrity processes cannot access higher-integrity processes. The primary integrity levels are Low, Medium, High, and System. Windows Vista assigns processes an integrity level in their access token. Securable objects, such as files and registry keys, have a new mandatory access control entry (ACE) in the System Access Control List (ACL).

- **mandatory label** An Access Control Entry used by Mandatory Integrity Control (MIC).

- **mandatory user profile** A user profile that cannot be modified by the user. Mandatory user profiles are useful for ensuring consistent desktop environments.

- **Master Boot Record (MBR)** The most common disk partition system, MBR is supported by every version of Windows. Gradually, MBR is being replaced by GPT.

- **master computer** A fully assembled computer containing a master installation of Windows Vista.

- **master image** A collection of files and folders (sometimes compressed into one file) captured from a master installation. This image contains the base operating system, as well as additional configurations and files.

- **master index**   A single index formed by combining shadow indexes together by using a process called the master merge.

- **master installation**   A Windows Vista installation on a master computer to be captured as a master image. You create the master installation by using automation to ensure a consistent and repeatable configuration each time.

- **master merge**   The process of combining index fragments (shadow indexes) together into a single content index called the master index.

- **MBR**   *See Master Boot Record.*

- **MBSA**   *See Microsoft Baseline Security Analyzer.*

- **MBSACLI**   *See Microsoft Baseline Security Analyzer Command Line Interface.*

- **MIC**   *See Mandatory Integrity Control.*

- **Microsoft Baseline Security Analyzer (MBSA)**   A free tool available for download from Microsoft.com that administrators can use to scan computers for security vulnerabilities and missing security updates.

- **Microsoft Baseline Security Analyzer Command Line Interface (MBSACLI)**   A command-line interface for MBSA, which administrators can use to scan computers for security vulnerabilities and missing security updates from scripts.

- **mixed mode**   A Windows Deployment Services (Windows DS) mode that supports both OSChooser and Windows PE for boot environments and RIPREP and ImageX imaging. Moving from legacy mode to mix mode happens when you configure Windows DS and add .wim image files to it.

- **Multiple Activation Key (MAK)**   Limited-use product keys that can be used to activate Windows on multiple computers.

- **name resolution**   The process of converting a host name to an IP address.

- **NAP**   *See Network Access Protection.*

- **native mode**   A Windows Deployment Services (Windows DS) mode that supports only the Windows PE boot environment and ImageX image files. The final move to native mode occurs after you've converted all legacy images to the .wim image file format and disabled the OSChooser functionality.

- **Nbtstat**   A command-line tool used to display NetBIOS networking information, including cached NetBIOS computer names.

- **Net**   A command-line tool used to perform a variety of networking tasks including starting and stopping services, sharing resources, and connecting to shared resources.

- **Netstat**   A command-line tool used to display networking statistics.

- **Network Access Protection (NAP)**   A feature supported by Windows Vista and Windows Server Code Name Longhorn that uses network authentication to validate the identity and integrity of client computers before they are allowed to connect to the network.

- **Network Monitor**   A graphical tool that administrators can use to capture and analyze network communications.

- **network sharing**   The process of making a folder available across the network.

- **New Computer scenario**   In BDD, a deployment scenario that deploys the operating system and applications to a computer that has not been previously configured and therefore contains no user data.

- **nondestructive imaging**   A deployment technique supported by ImageX and Windows Vista Setup in which an operating system image is deployed without destroying the existing data.

- **novice**   In a Remote Assistance scenario, the user seeking assistance.

- **Nslookup**   A command-line tool used to test DNS name resolution.

- **offer Remote Assistance (RA)**   *See unsolicited Remote Assistance.*

- **Office Genuine Advantage (OGA)**   An initiative that tracks the product keys from licensed versions of Microsoft Office programs to ensure that they are not reused on other computers. Users who validate their copies of Microsoft Office products gain access to add-ins and updates to those products.

- **offline**   When preparing an image for deployment, the operating system is not started, and changes or updates are made directly to the image.

- **Offline Files**   A feature in recent versions of Windows that locally stores a copy of a file located on a shared folder. Windows can then access the local copy of the file if the user needs it while disconnected from the network. Windows includes technology for synchronizing Offline Files that have been modified and resolving synchronization conflicts.

- **OGA**   *See Office Genuine Advantage.*

- **online**   When preparing an image for deployment, the operating system is started and changes or updates are made while Windows is running.

- **opt-in**   An online process by which a user chooses to receive information (such as e-mail newsletters) or software, often by checking a check box on a Web page or software installation screen. Internet Explorer 7 makes it easy to use common sites with important controls, but lets users opt in to use the advanced features that might be exposed by more obscure ActiveX® controls. This Internet Explorer 7 feature is called ActiveX Opt-In.

- **Original Equipment Manufacturer (OEM)**   The organization that designs and manufactures computer hardware.

- **P2P**   *See Peer-to-Peer.*

- **package**   A group of files that Microsoft provides to modify Windows Vista features. Package types include service packs, security updates, language packs, and hotfixes.

- **panning hand**   A specialized cursor that enables dragging a page.

- **PatchGuard**   Microsoft's kernel patch protection technology for 64-bit versions of Windows Vista that is designed to prevent unauthorized and unsupported access to the kernel. It prohibits all software from performing unsupported patches.

- **PathPing**   A command-line tool used to test connectivity to an endpoint. PathPing collects connectivity statistics for every gateway between the client and the tested end-point and displays latency and availability statistics for every node.

- **PCR**   *See Platform Configuration Register.*

- **Peer Name Resolution Protocol (PNRP)**   A mechanism for distributed, serverless name resolution of peers in a P2P network.

- **Peer-to-Peer (P2P)**   A method for communicating directly between client computers without involving a separate server. In Windows Vista, P2P refers to a set of networking and collaboration technologies that are used by Windows Meeting Space and other applications.

- **pen flicks**   A Tablet PC pen technique that enables users to call menu commands by moving the pen in a special way.

- **People Near Me**   A subnet-level system that enables users who are signed onto this service to automatically publish their availability onto the local subnet and discover other users using the Web Services Discovery (WS-Discovery) protocol. Once users are published using People Near Me, they can be invited to start activities, such as Windows Meeting Space.

- **Personal Identification Number (PIN)**   This is an administrator-specified secret value that must be entered each time the computer starts (or resumes from hibernation). The PIN can have 4 to 20 digits and internally is stored as a 256-bit hash of the entered Uni-code characters. This value is never displayed back to the user in any form or for any reason. The PIN is used to provide another factor of protection in conjunction with TPM authentication.

- **phishing**   A form of Internet fraud that aims to steal valuable information such as credit cards, social security numbers, user IDs, and passwords. A fake Web site is created that is similar to that of a legitimate organization, typically a financial institution such as a bank or insurance company. An e-mail is sent requesting that the recipient access the fake Web site (usually a replica of a trusted site) and enter their personal details, including security access codes. The page looks genuine because it is easy to fake a valid Web site. Any HTML page on the Web can be modified to suit a phishing scheme.

- **PIN**   *See Personal Identification Number.*

- **Ping**   A command-line tool used to test connectivity to an endpoint.

- **Planning Phase**   A phase in a BDD 2007 deployment in which the deployment team lays the groundwork for the deployment.

- **Platform Configuration Register (PCR)**   A register of a TPM. This register is sufficiently large to contain a hash (currently only SHA-1). A register can normally only be "extended," which means that its content is a running hash of all values that are loaded to it. To learn when these registers are reset, refer to the TCG specification document.

- **PNRP**   *See Peer Name Resolution Protocol.*

- **Point-to-Point Tunneling Protocol (PPTP)**   A networking technology that supports multi-protocol virtual private networks (VPNs). This enables remote users to securely access corporate or other networks across the Internet, to dial into an Internet service provider (ISP), or to connect directly to the Internet. PPTP tunnels, or encapsulates, Internet Protocol (IP) or Internetwork Packet Exchange (IPX) banter traffic inside IP packets. This means that users can remotely run applications that depend on particular network protocols. PPTP is described in RFC 2637.

- **Portqry**   A command-line tool that tests connectivity to a network service by attempting to establish a TCP connection to an endpoint.

- **PPTP**   *See Point-to-Point Tunneling Protocol.*

- **Preboot Execution Environment (PXE)**   A DHCP-based remote boot technology used to boot or install an operating system on a client computer from a remote server. A Windows Deployment Services (Windows DS) Server is an example of a PXE Server.

- **Print Management**   A Windows Vista MMC snap-in that administrators can use to manage printers, print servers, and print jobs across an enterprise.

- **Printer Migrator**   A Windows Vista tool for backing up printer configurations on print servers so that the configuration can be moved between print servers or consolidated from multiple servers onto a single server. A command-line version (Printbrm.exe) is also available.

- **product key**   A code used to validate installation media, such as CDs, during installation. Product keys, also known as CD keys, do not prove licensing for a product, but they do discourage casual copying of software. All Windows product keys use five groups of five characters, with the format XXXXX-XXXXX-XXXXX-XXXXX-XXXXX.

- **protocol handler**   A component of the Windows search engine that is used to communicate with and enumerate the contents of stores such as the file system, Messaging Application Program Interface (MAPI) e-mail database, and the client-side cache (CSC) or offline files database.

- **proximity**   A measurement of the network latency between two computers. For Windows Media Sharing to work, the network latency between two computers must be 7 milliseconds (msec) or less.

- **punycode**   The self-proclaimed "bootstring encoding" of Unicode strings into the limited character set supported by the Domain Name System (DNS), as defined in RFC 3492. The encoding is used as part of IDNA, which is a system enabling the use of internationalized domain names in all languages that are supported by Unicode where the burden of translation lies entirely with the user application (such as a Web browser).

- **PXE**   *See Preboot Execution Environment.*

- **RAC**   *See Reliability Analysis Component.*

- **Reliability Analysis Component (RAC)**   A Windows Vista component that gathers and processes reliability data.

- **Replace Computer scenario**   In BDD, a deployment scenario that involves giving a new computer to an existing user. In this scenario, the user receives a new computer, and the user's data is migrated to the replacement computer to minimize impact on the user.

- **requested execution level manifest**   An application marking that indicates the privileges required by the application. Windows Vista uses the requested execution level manifest, among other factors, to determine whether to provide a UAC prompt to the user to elevate privileges when the application is run.

- **roaming user profile**   An alternative approach for storing user profiles that involves storing them on a shared folder on the network. Roaming user profiles provide simplified backup and enable users to use the same profile on different computers.

- **SAM**   *See Software Asset Management.*

- **same computer sharing**   *See local sharing.*

- **screen scraping**   A technique for automating applications by simulating keystrokes, as if a human were sitting at the keyboard. Screen scraping is the least reliable automation technique and should be used only when no other automation option is available.

- **Server Message Block (SMB)**   A network protocol used for file and printer sharing.

- **Server Performance Advisor (SPA)**   A report that provides a summary of logged performance data.

- **shadow indexes**   Temporary indexes creating during the indexing process that are later combined into a single index called the master index.

- **sharing**   The process of making files, folders, printers, or other resources available to other users.

- **shatter attacks**   Attacks in which a process attempts to use Windows messages to elevate privileges by injecting code into another process.

- **Simple Service Discovery Protocol (SSDP)**   This protocol forms the basis of the discovery protocol used by Universal Plug and Play (UPnP) and is used by PNRP.

- **single instance storage**   A technique for storing multiple Windows Vista operating system images efficiently and in a single location. The deployment engineer configuring a computer has the option to select one of the images for deployment from the client computer.

- **Sleep**   A new power state that combines the quick resume time of Standby with the data protection benefits of Hibernate.

- **slipstreaming**   The process of integrating a service pack into operating system setup files so that new computers immediately have the service pack installed.

- **SMB**   *See Server Message Block.*

- **SME**   *See subject matter experts.*

- **SMS**   *See Systems Management Server.*

- **sniffer**   A tool, such as Network Monitor, that collects network communications. Sniffers are also known as protocol analyzers.

- **Software Asset Management (SAM)**   An initiative promoted by Microsoft as a way to maintain accurate inventories of installed and licensed software. This practice helps organizations maintain legally licensed versions of all the software they need.

- **solicited Remote Assistance (RA)**   Remote Assistance requests initiated by the novice (the user seeking help).

- **SPA**   *See Server Performance Advisor.*

- **SSDP**   *See Simple Service Discovery Protocol.*

- **Stabilizing Phase**   In deployment, the phase that addresses the testing of a solution that is feature complete. This phase typically occurs when pilots are conducted, with an emphasis on real-world testing and with the goal of identifying, prioritizing, and fixing bugs.

- **stack**   A list of memory locations that identify the calling methods of return locations. Windows uses the stack to remember the location to return to when a called method has finished running.

- **start address**   A URL that points to the starting location for indexed content. When indexing is performed, each configured starting address is enumerated by a protocol handler to find the content to be indexed.

- **startup key**   Key stored on a USB flash drive that must be inserted every time the computer starts. The startup key is used to provide another factor of protection in conjunction with TPM authentication.

- **Stop error**   An error that Windows Vista raises when a Kernel Mode process has been compromised or has experienced an unhandled exception.

- **subject matter experts (SMEs)**   People who are skilled in a particular topic. During deployment, you should use SMEs to help in the planning, development, and stabilizing processes. SMEs are users who are most familiar (not necessarily experts) with the applications and data to migrate, and they're usually stakeholders in seeing that the process is properly performed.

- **subscriptions**   The ability to collect copies of events from multiple remote computers and store them locally.

- **supplemental application**   An application installed on select few computers in your environment, such as specialized applications used by individual groups. Supplemental applications are in contrast to core applications, which are installed on most computers.

- **Sync Center**   A Windows Vista tool that provides a user interface for managing content synchronization activities, including redirected folders and other folders marked for offline use.

- **Systems Management Server (SMS)**   A Microsoft computer management infrastructure used to improve administrative efficiency and help distribute and manage software.

- **task sequence**   A sequence of tasks to run on a destination computer to install Windows Vista and applications and then configure the destination computer. In BDD 2007, the task sequence is part of a build, and the component responsible for executing the task sequence is the Task Sequencer.

- **Task Sequencer**   The BDD 2007 component that runs the task sequence when installing a build.

- **TCP receive window size**   The number of bytes that a TCP/IP host can transmit without receiving a response back from the remote computer. The TCP receive window size can have a significant impact on performance. If the size is too large and the network is unreliable, a great deal of data might need to be retransmitted if data is lost. If the size is too small, utilization will be unnecessarily low while the sending computer waits for confirmations from the receiving computer.

- **technician computer**   The computer on which you install BDD 2007 or Windows SIM. This computer is typically in a lab environment, separated from the production network. In BDD 2007, this computer is usually called the build server.

- **Telnet**   A protocol and tool for remotely managing computers using a text-based interface similar to a command prompt.

- **Test TCP**   A network troubleshooting tool for testing TCP connectivity between two computers.

- **thick image**   An operating system installation image that contains core, and possibly supplemental, applications. Thick images simplify deployment by installation applications alongside the operating system. However, because they are more specialized, you typically require more thick images than thin images.

- **thin image**   An operating system installation image that contains few if any core applications. Thin images have the advantage of being applicable to a larger number of computers in your organization than a thick image, which is more specialized.

- **TPM**   *See Trusted Platform Module.*

- **Trusted Platform Module (TPM)**   The Trusted Platform Module is a hardware device defined by the Trusted Computing Group (TCG). A TPM provides a hardware-based root of trust and can be leveraged to provide a variety of cryptographic services. Version 1.2 TPMs with TCG-compliant BIOS upgrades allow BitLocker to provide drive encryption as well as integrity checking of early boot components, which helps prevent tampering and provides a transparent startup experience.

- **UIPI**   *See User Interface Privilege Isolation.*

- **Unattend.xml**   The generic name for the Windows Vista answer file. Unattend.xml replaces all of the answer files in earlier versions of Windows, including Unattend.txt, Winbom.ini, and others.

- **unhandled exception**   An error that is not processed by an application. When a User Mode process has an unhandled exception, the process is closed and Windows Vista can present the user with an opportunity to send an error notification to Microsoft. When a Kernel Mode process has an unhandled exception, a Stop error occurs.

- **unsolicited Remote Assistance (RA)**   Remote Assistance requests initiated by the expert (the user offering help).

- **Upgrade Computer scenario**   In BDD, a deployment scenario that deploys a new version of Windows to an existing computer that has an earlier version of Windows installed. The Upgrade Computer scenario preserves user data.

- **user**   *See novice.*

- **user broker**   A component of Internet Explorer protected mode that provides a set of functions that lets the user save files to areas outside of low-integrity areas.

- **User Interface Privilege Isolation (UIPI)**   A feature that blocks lower-integrity processes from accessing higher-integrity processes. This helps protect against shatter attacks.

- **User Mode**   A processing mode provided by x86-based processors that provides only limited access to memory and other system resources. Processes that run in User Mode can access memory allocated to the process, but must be elevated to Kernel Mode by calling system APIs before the process can access protected resources.

- **user profile**   The set of user documents and settings that makes up a user's desktop environment.

- **user profile namespace**   The hierarchy of folders within a user's profile folder.

- **user state**   The data files and settings associated with a user profile.

- **user state migration**   The process of transferring user files and settings from one computer to another computer or from an older version of Windows to a newer version of Windows installed on the same computer hardware.

- **VMK**   *See Volume Master Key.*

- **volume license**   A license, purchased from Microsoft or another software vendor, to use multiple copies of an operating system or program.

- **Volume Master Key (VMK)**   The key used to encrypt the FVEK.

- **WAU**   *See Windows Anytime Upgrade.*

- **WCS**   *See Windows Color System.*

- **Web Services for Devices (WSD)**   A new type of network connectivity supported by Windows Vista. WSD enables users to have a Plug and Play experience similar to that of USB devices, except over the network instead of for locally connected devices.

- **WER**   *See Windows Error Reporting.*

- **WGA**   *See Windows Genuine Advantage.*

- **.wim**   A file name extension that identifies Windows image files created by ImageX.

- **Windows Anytime Upgrade (WAU)**   An upgrade service, primarily intended for home users, to allow upgrades from one edition of Windows Vista to a more advanced edition. WAU is available in Windows Vista Business as a way to upgrade to Windows Vista Ultimate (also a business-compatible product). This feature can be disabled by administrators. For more information about WAU, see *http://technet.microsoft.com/en-us/windowsvista/bb892849.aspx.*

- **Windows Color System (WCS)**   A component of Windows Vista that works together with the Windows Vista print subsystem to provide a richer color printing experience that supports wide-gamut printers (inkjet printers that use more than four ink colors) for lifelike printing of color photos and graphic-rich documents.

- **Windows Defender**   A feature of Windows Vista that provides protection from spyware and other potentially unwanted software.

- **Windows Easy Transfer**   The Windows Vista feature that replaces the Windows XP Files And Settings Transfer Wizard. This tool leads the user through a series of pages to determine how much data to migrate and which migration method (disc or removable media, direct cable connection, or network) to use.

- **Windows Error Reporting (WER)**   The client component for the overall Watson Feedback Platform (WFP), which allows Microsoft to collect reports about failure events that occur on a user's system, analyze the data contained in those reports, and respond back to the user in a meaningful and actionable manner. WER is the technology that reports user-mode hangs, user-mode faults, and Kernel-Mode faults to the back-end servers at Microsoft or to an internal error-reporting server.

- **Windows Genuine Advantage (WGA)**   A Microsoft initiative to ensure that users of copied Windows operating systems become aware of their counterfeit versions. By recording the product key and a signature from the computer's basic input/output system (BIOS), Microsoft can effectively determine when retail versions of Windows have been copied and when volume-activated versions of Windows have been excessively distributed.

- **Windows Imaging**   A single compressed file containing a collection of files and folders that duplicate a Windows installation on a disk volume.

- **Windows Media Sharing**   A feature of Windows Vista that lets users share the media files on their computers so that other users on the network can play or view them. This includes music files, video files, images, and playlists that are normally stored in the Music, Pictures, and Video folders within the user's profile. When Media Sharing is enabled, other users can play or view your files but cannot add, modify, or delete files in these folders. Windows Media Sharing is disabled by default and can be enabled in the Network and Sharing Center and in Windows Media Player for private or domain networks.

- **Windows Product Activation (WPA)**   A way to ensure that customers are using genuine Windows operating systems purchased from Microsoft resellers. This tool, which began with Microsoft Windows XP, defeated casual copying of Windows XP by ensuring that other systems had not recently been activated with the same product key.

- **Windows Server Update Services (WSUS)**   A free server tool available for download from Microsoft.com that administrators can use to manage which updates are distributed to Windows computers on their internal network.

- **Windows System Assessment Tool (WinSAT)**   A command-line tool included with Windows Vista for assessing the features, capabilities, and attributes of computer hardware.

- **WinSAT**   *See Windows System Assessment Tool.*

- **WPA**   *See Windows Product Activation.*

- **WSD**   *See Web Services for Devices.*

- **WSUS**   *See Windows Server Update Services.*

- **XML Paper Specification (XPS)**   A set of conventions for using XML to describe the content and appearance of paginated documents.

- **XPS**   *See XML Paper Specification.*

- **Zero Touch Installation (ZTI)**   A BDD deployment option that fully automates the deployment of client computers. During a ZTI installation, the Windows operating system and all applications are automatically deployed the first time a computer is connected to the network and turned on.

- **ZTI**   *See Zero Touch Installation.*

Index

About the Authors

Mitch Tulloch

Mitch Tulloch, lead author for the *Microsoft Windows Vista Resource Kit*, is a widely recognized expert on Windows administration, networking, and security and has been repeatedly awarded Most Valuable Professional (MVP) status by Microsoft for his outstanding contributions in supporting users who deploy Microsoft platforms, products, and solutions. Mitch has written or contributed to almost two dozen books on computing and networking topics including the *Microsoft Encyclopedia of Networking*, the *Microsoft Encyclopedia of Security, Introducing Windows Server 2008*, and the *Microsoft Office Communications Server 2007 Resource Kit*, all from Microsoft Press.

Mitch has published over three hundred articles on WindowsNetworking.com, WindowsDevCenter.com, ITworld.com, and other IT pro Web sites. Mitch has also written feature articles for leading industry magazines including BizTech Magazine and NetworkWorld, and his articles have been widely syndicated on sites ranging from TechTarget.com to CNN.com. Mitch has also developed and taught graduate-level courses in Information Security Management (ISM) for the Masters of Business Administration (MBA) program of Jones International University (JIU).

Prior to starting his own business in 1998, Mitch worked as a Microsoft Certified Trainer (MCT) for Productivity Point International. Mitch currently resides in Winnipeg, Canada. For more information about Mitch, visit his Web site at http://www.mtit.com.

Tony Northrup

Tony Northrup (MVP, MCSE, MCTS, CISSP) is a Windows consultant and author living in Phillipston, Massachusetts. Tony started programming before Windows 1.0 was released, but has focused on Windows administration and development for the last 15 years. He has written more than a dozen books covering Windows networking, security, and development. Among other titles, Tony is coauthor of the *Microsoft Windows Server 2003 Resource Kit* (Microsoft Press, 2005).

When he's not consulting or writing, Tony enjoys cycling, hiking, and nature photography. Tony lives with his cat, Sam, and his dog, Sandi. You can learn more about Tony by visiting his technical blog at http://www.vistaclues.com or his personal Web site at http://www.northrup.org.

Jerry Honeycutt

Jerry Honeycutt empowers people to work more productively by helping them deploy and use popular technologies, including the Microsoft Windows and Microsoft Office suite product families. He reaches out to the community through his frequent writings, talks, and consulting practice.

Jerry is intimately involved in Microsoft's desktop-deployment initiatives. He was the documentation lead for Microsoft Deployment and frequently writes white papers and articles for Microsoft about desktop deployment.

Jerry owns and operates Deployment Forum at http://www.deploymentforum.com/. This Web site is a member-driven community for IT professionals who deploy the Windows operating system.

Jerry has written more than 30 books. His most recent titles include the *Microsoft Windows Desktop Deployment Resource Kit* (Microsoft Press, 2004) and *Microsoft Windows XP Registry Guide* (Microsoft Press, 2002), which is part of the *Microsoft Windows Server 2003 Resource Kit*. See Jerry's Web site at www.honeycutt.com or send mail to jerry@honeycutt.com.

Ed Wilson

Ed Wilson is a senior consultant at Microsoft Corporation and a scripting expert. He is a Microsoft Certified Trainer who delivers immensely popular workshops world-wide on VBScript, WMI, and Windows PowerShell. He's written more than one dozen books with four on scripting, including *Microsoft VBScript Step by Step* (Microsoft Press, 2006), *Microsoft Windows PowerShell Step by Step* (Microsoft Press, 2007), and *Microsoft Windows Scripting with WMI: Self-Paced Learning Guide* (Microsoft Press, 2005). Ed holds more than 20 industry certifications, including the MCSE and CISSP.

Ralph Ramos

Ralph Ramos (MCSE) is a full-time systems engineer in Cincinnati, Ohio. He specializes in deployment of the Microsoft Windows product family and various scripting technologies. He is a columnist for the Microsoft TechNet Desktop Deployment Portal (*http://www.microsoft.com/technet/desktopdeployment/default.mspx*) and was a technical reviewer for the *Microsoft Windows XP Registry Guide* (Microsoft Press, 2002) and the *Microsoft Windows Desktop Deployment Resource Kit* (Microsoft Press, 2004).

System Requirements

The system requirements for the scripts, tools, and other resources on the companion CD-ROM for this Resource Kit vary depending on the item being used or installed:

- The admin scripts written in VBScript can be run from an elevated command prompt on a computer running Windows Vista with Service Pack 1 or Windows Server 2008. These scripts do not require any installation and can be copied directly from the subfolders on the companion CD to a folder on your computer. The total disk space required for these scripts is less than 1 megabyte (MB).

- The admin scripts written in Windows PowerShell can be run from an elevated command prompt on an administrative workstation running Windows Vista with Service Pack 1 or later or from a server running Windows Server 2008. These scripts do not require any installation and can simply be copied directly from the subfolders on the companion CD to a folder on your computer. The total disk space required for these scripts is less than 1 MB. In order to run these scripts, however, you must first install Windows PowerShell on your computer.

    - To install Windows PowerShell on a computer running Windows Vista, download the Windows PowerShell 1.0 Installation Package for Windows Vista from the Microsoft Download Center.

    - To install Windows PowerShell on a computer running Windows Server 2008, use the Add Features Wizard in Server Manager or on the Initial Configuration Tasks screen.

- For the system requirements for running other scripts, tools, and resources found on the companion CD, refer to the Readme.txt file in the root of the CD or see the chapters where these items are mentioned. For example, some of the scripts and other items discussed in the chapters of Part II, "Deployment," require that Microsoft Deployment Toolkit be installed on your computer. To view the sample chapters and eBook samplers from Microsoft Press, you will need Adobe Acrobat Reader or some other PDF reader.

To utilize the contents of the companion CD, you can use a computer running Microsoft Windows Server 2008, Windows Vista, Windows Server 2003, or Windows XP. The computer must meet the following minimum requirements:

- 1 GHz 32-bit (x86) or 64-bit (x64) processor (depending on the minimum requirements of the operating system)

- 1 gigabyte (GB) of system memory (depending on the minimum requirements of the operating system)

- A hard disk partition with at least 700 MB of available space

- A monitor capable of at least 800 × 600 display resolution
- A keyboard
- A mouse or other pointing device
- An optical drive capable of reading CD-ROMs

The computer must also have the following software installed:

- A Web browser such as Internet Explorer version 6 or later
- An application that can display PDF files, such as Adobe Acrobat Reader, which can be downloaded at *http://www.adobe.com/reader*

What do you think of this book?

We want to hear from you!

Do you have a few minutes to participate in a brief online survey?

Microsoft is interested in hearing your feedback so we can continually improve our books and learning resources for you.

To participate in our survey, please visit:

www.microsoft.com/learning/booksurvey/

...and enter this book's ISBN-10 or ISBN-13 number (located above barcode on back cover*). As a thank-you to survey participants in the United States and Canada, each month we'll randomly select five respondents to win one of five $100 gift certificates from a leading online merchant. At the conclusion of the survey, you can enter the drawing by providing your e-mail address, which will be used for prize notification only.

Thanks in advance for your input. Your opinion counts!

*Where to find the ISBN on back cover

ISBN-13: 000-0-0000-0000-0
ISBN-10: 0-0000-0000-0

Example only. Each book has unique ISBN.

Microsoft®
Press